ENCYCLOPEDIA *of* AFRICAN~AMERICAN CULTURE *and* HISTORY

Editorial Board

second edition

THE BLACK EXPERIENCE IN THE AMERICAS

ENCYCLOPEDIA *of* AFRICAN~AMERICAN CULTURE *and* HISTORY

published in association with
THE SCHOMBURG CENTER FOR RESEARCH IN BLACK CULTURE

COLIN A. PALMER
Editor in Chief

VOLUME 5 Q-Z

MACMILLAN REFERENCE USA
An imprint of Thomson Gale, a part of The Thomson Corporation

Detroit • New York • San Francisco • San Diego • New Haven, Conn. • Waterville, Maine • London • Munich

Encyclopedia of African-American Culture and History, Second Edition

Colin A. Palmer, Editor in Chief

For more information, contact
Macmillan Reference USA
An imprint of Thomson Gale
27500 Drake Rd.
Farmington, Hills, MI 48331-3535
Or you can visit our Internet site at
http://www.gale.com

LIBRARY OF CONGRESS CATALOGING-IN-PUBLICATION DATA

Encyclopedia of African-American culture and history : the Black experience in the Americas / Colin A. Palmer, editor in chief.— 2nd ed.
p. cm.
Includes bibliographical references and index.
ISBN 0-02-865816-7 (set hardcover : alk. paper) —
ISBN 0-02-865817-5 (v. 1) — ISBN 0-02-865818-3 (v. 2) —
ISBN 0-02-865819-1 (v. 3) — ISBN 0-02-865820-5 (v. 4) —
ISBN 0-02-865821-3 (v. 5) — ISBN 0-02-865822-1 (v. 6)
1. African Americans—Encyclopedias. 2. African Americans—History—Encyclopedias. 3. Blacks—America—Encyclopedias. 4. Blacks—America—History—Encyclopedias. I. Palmer, Colin A., 1942-

E185.E54 2005
973'.0496073'003—dc22 2005013029

This title is also available as an e-book.
ISBN 0-02-866071-4

Contact your Thomson Gale representative for ordering information.

Printed in the United States of America
10 9 8 7 6 5 4 3 2

Editorial and Production Staff

PROJECT EDITORS
Christine Slovey
Jeffrey Lehman

CONTRIBUTING EDITORS
Shawn Corridor
Kristin Hart
Alan Hedblad
Jenai Mynatt

EDITORIAL TECHNICAL SUPPORT
Mark Springer

MANUSCRIPT EDITORS
Sheryl A. Ciccarelli
Judith Culligan
Andrew Cunningham
Peter Jaskowiak
Michael J. O'Neal

ADDITIONAL EDITORIAL SUPPORT
Jennifer Albers
Mark Drouillard
Anjanelle Klisz
Jaime E. Noce
Nicole Watkins

PROOFREADERS
Judith A. Clinebell
Amanda Quick

INDEXER
Laurie Andriot

PRODUCT DESIGN
Kate Scheible
Tracey Rowens

IMAGING
Dean Dauphinais
Leitha Etheridge-Sims
Lezlie Light
Christine O'Bryan

GRAPHIC ART
GGS Information Services
XNR Productions

RIGHTS ACQUISITION AND MANAGEMENT
Margaret Chamberlain-Gaston
Ronald Montgomery
Susan Rudolph

COMPOSITION
Evi Seoud
Mary Beth Trimper

COMPOSITOR
Datapage Technologies International, Inc.

MANUFACTURING
Wendy Blurton

DIRECTOR, NEW PRODUCT DEVELOPMENT
Hélène Potter

PUBLISHER
Frank Menchaca

Contents

Quarles, Benjamin

January 28, 1904
November 16, 1996

The historian Benjamin Quarles was born in Boston, Massachusetts. The son of a subway porter, Benjamin Quarles entered college at the age of twenty-three and received degrees from Shaw University (B.A., 1931) in North Carolina, and the University of Wisconsin (M.A., 1933; Ph.D., 1940). He taught at Shaw, served as dean at Dillard University in New Orleans, and chaired the history department at Morgan State University in Baltimore.

Quarles began his scholarly career at a time when racist assumptions hampered research and writing on African-American history. White historians questioned whether blacks could write history objectively, and they believed that African-American history lacked sufficient primary sources for serious research and writing. Quarles proved both notions were false. Building on the pioneering research of Carter G. Woodson (1875–1950) and other black historians of the previous generation, Quarles confirmed the existence of a rich documentary record of African-American life and culture. His early writings demonstrated both his careful research and his ability to present a balanced historical narrative. His essays in the *Mississippi Valley Historical Review* in 1945 and 1959 were the first from a black historian to appear in a major historical journal.

Quarles's first scholarly article, "The Breach Between Douglass and Garrison," appeared in the *Journal of Negro History* in 1938 and revealed his interest in race relations. Many of his subsequent studies explored the way in which blacks and whites have helped shape each other's identity on individual and collective levels. In *Lincoln and the Negro* (1962) and *Allies for Freedom: Blacks and John Brown* (1974), Quarles investigated the relationship between blacks and two notable whites in American history. He focused on the eighteenth and nineteenth centuries, particularly the collective contribution of African Americans in two dramatic events, in *The Negro in the Civil War* (1953) and *The Negro in the American Revolution* (1961). In *Black Abolitionists* (1969), he highlighted the participation of blacks in the nation's most important social reform movement.

Quarles shared with his contemporary John Hope Franklin (b. 1915) an optimistic appraisal of racial progress in American history. He brought his scholarship to the classroom through two textbooks, *The Negro in the Making of America* (1964) and *The Negro American: A*

Documentary History (1967, written with Leslie H. Fishel Jr.), and he has advanced African-American history as a contributing editor of *Phylon* and as associate editor of the *Journal of Negro History*. On February 6, 1997, Morgan State University honored his legacy with a special event called the Memorial Convocation Celebrating the Life and Legacy of Benjamin Quarles.

See also Franklin, John Hope; Historians/Historiography

Bibliography

McFeely, William F. "Introduction." In *The Negro in the Civil War,* by Benjamin Quarles. New York: Da Capo, 1989, pp. 3–6.

Meier, August. "Introduction: Benjamin Quarles and the Historiography of Black America." In *Black Mosaic: Essays in Afro-American History and Historiography,* by Benjamin Quarles. Amherst: University of Massachusetts Press, 1989, pp. 3–21.

MICHAEL F. HEMBREE (1996)

Queen Latifah (Owens, Dana Elaine)

March 18, 1970

Born in East Orange, New Jersey, singer and actress Queen Latifah may be the most influential female MC to date. She chose her name—an Arabic word meaning "sensitive and delicate"—at age eight. As a teenager, she beatboxed as part of the female group Ladies Fresh. In 1988 she released "Wrath of my Madness," a song touting her strength and ability as an able MC. Her first album, *All Hail the Queen,* was released in 1989. Her second single, "Ladies First," received national attention for its assertive, woman-centered verses, and her Afrocentric image-filled video exposed her to MTV's wide range of viewers. In 1991 she released *Nature of a Sista* and left Tommy Boy Records to join Motown.

In 1993 Queen Latifah found her greatest success to date with *Black Reign* and won a Grammy for Best Rap Solo for "U.N.I.T.Y." The album, dedicated to her late brother, murdered during a car-jacking, achieved gold status and helped secure her acting career. In the same year, she began her role as the straightforward yet humorous "Kadijah" on the FOX network sitcom *Living Single.* In 1997 she received the Entertainer of the Year Soul Train Lady of Soul award. In 1998 she costarred in the movies *Sphere* with Dustin Hoffman and Samuel Jackson, *Living Out Loud,* and *The Bone Collector* with Denzel Washington. She also released her fourth album, *Order in the Court.* In 1999—with the prompting of Rosie O'Donnell—she began hosting her own talk show. She also released her autobiography, *Ladies First: Revelations of a Strong Woman.*

Queen Latifah was nominated for a Golden Globe award and an Academy Award in 2003 for her role in the film *Chicago.* She has won or has been nominated for many other awards for her roles in *Chicago* and another blockbuster, *Bringing Down the House,* later starring in the films *Taxi* (2004) and *Beauty Shop* (2005). Latifah was honored as the Harvard Foundation's Artist of the Year in 2003.

See also Music in the United States; Rap

Bibliography

Latifah, Queen, with Karen Hunter. *Ladies First: Revelations of a Strong Woman.* New York: Morrow, 1999.

Rose, Tricia. *Black Noise: Rap Music and Black Culture in Contemporary America.* Middletown, Conn.: Wesleyan University Press, 1994.

RACHEL ZELLARS (2001)
Updated by publisher 2005

Querino, Manuel

July 28, 1851
February 14, 1923

Manuel Raimundo Querino was a teacher, an artist, an abolitionist, a labor activist, and a historian. He was the first Afro-Brazilian to offer his perspective on Brazilian history and the first Brazilian to publish a detailed analysis of Afro-Brazilian contributions to Brazilian history, culture, and development. During a period of national redefinition, Querino boldly wrote, "In truth, it was the black who developed Brazil" (Querino, 1978).

During the second half of the nineteenth century, Brazil was characterized by its system of slavery and its status as a Portuguese empire. Unlike most blacks at the time, Querino was born free. Born in Santo Amaro, Bahia, Querino was sent to live in the state capital, Salvador, after a cholera epidemic claimed the lives of his parents. There he learned to read and write. At the age of seventeen, he joined the army and fought against Paraguay in the War of the Triple Alliance (1864–1870). He returned to Salvador in 1871 and became heavily involved in several political activities, including working as an advocate for the laboring classes. In 1875 he organized the Bahian Workers Society League and published articles in labor newspapers protesting low wages and political corruption. In 1878 he joined the Republican Club of Bahia and became an avid supporter of republicanism. He also fought for the abolition of slavery, calling for complete freedom for all slaves. He was a member of the Bahian Liberation Society, but he believed that total liberation for blacks in Brazil could only be achieved through education.

At the age of thirty, Querino attended the Academia de Belas Artes in Salvador, Bahia, where he studied architecture and design. He later became a teacher of design at the Liceu de Artes e Ofícios and the Colégio dos Orfãos de São Joaquim. He was eventually hired as a designer for the provincial directory of public works. The year 1888 marked the end of slavery as a legal institution in Brazil, and 1889 marked the creation of the Republic of the United States of Brazil. During this time, Querino was elected to the city council, and in 1896 he became an official of the Secretariat of Agriculture. He later became a founder of the Geographical and Historical Institute of Bahia.

During the early twentieth century, Brazil was redefining itself, and this included changing its reputation abroad. Most pressing was the question of race. The new Brazilian government began a campaign for "whitening" its population through the encouragement of European migration. Querino challenged this campaign by writing about the significant role Afro-Brazilians played in Brazil's history. Querino felt that the government resources that were being used to attract Europeans to Brazil could better be used to educate former slaves. Historians writing during this time emphasized Portuguese contributions to Brazilian development with little mention of the history of Afro-Brazilians. Querino dedicated himself to balancing this disproportionate emphasis. He challenged Brazilians, both black and white, to acknowledge the substantial involvement Afro-Brazilians had in the modernization of Brazil.

Querino's professional history, political activities, and ideological views resulted in a series of published works about Afro-Brazilians. In 1909 Querino published *Artistas Bahianas* and *As artes da Bahia,* both on Bahian culture and art. Several collections of Querino's essays were published after his death in 1923. *A arte culinaria na Bahia* was published in 1951, *Costumes Africanos no Brasil* in 1938, and *A raça Africana* in 1955. Querino also wrote on other subjects including Capoeira. Most noted by historians is *O colono prêto como fator da civilização Brasileira,* later translated into English as *The African Contribution to Brazilian Civilization.* In this essay, Querino argues that Africans came to Brazil not just as slaves but as skilled colonists whose abilities enabled the Portuguese to survive in unfamiliar and hostile territory. He writes of the relationship between blacks and whites during colonization as the beginning of a history of interdependence in which black labor sustained the economic and cultural growth of the new republic. To Querino, there would be no Brazil without its black citizens.

Querino wrote that, "History and all its justice has to respect and praise the valuable services which the black has given to this nation for more than three centuries" (Querino, 1978). While he wrote of the horrors of slavery and the continual resistance of slaves, he was the first historian to portray slaves as colonists and collaborators with Portuguese colonizers. As a result of this work, the lives, culture, and thoughts of Afro-Brazilians became a field of academic study and a celebrated element of Brazilian history. Yet, in spite of his many accomplishments, Querino died in poverty.

See also Emancipation in Latin America and the Caribbean; Historians/Historiography

▪▪ *Bibliography*

Burns, E. Bradford. "Bibliographical Essay: Manuel Querino's Interpretation of the African Contribution to Brazil." *Journal of Negro History* 59, no. 1 (January 1974): 78–86.

Querino, Manuel Raimundo. *O Colono Prêto como Fator da Civilização Brasileira.* Salvador, Brazil: Imprensa Oficial do Estado, 1918. Translated into English by E. Bradford Burns as *The African Contribution to Brazilian Civilization.* Tempe: Arizona State University, Center for Latin American Studies, 1978.

Querino, Manuel Raimundo. *A raça Africana e os seus costumes.* Salvador, Brazil: Livraria Progresso Editôra, 1955.

JILLEAN MCCOMMONS (2005)

Race, Scientific Theories of

Although physical differences among peoples had been recognized by the ancients, those differences were invariably interpreted as local, not global. It was not until the late seventeenth century that European scholars began seeing physical variation in terms of continents, in other words, contrasting "the African" with "the European." This was doubtless connected to the political economy of the age, involving the slave trade and long sea voyages; when long voyages were taken over land, the peoples could be seen to intergrade into one another. By the early nineteenth century, race and subspecies had been roughly synonymized, and became the framework for any scientific study of the human species. Scientific racism and the marshaling of empirical data to support theories of racial inferiority/superiority intensified during the early 1800s after the expansion of knowledge within the biological sciences enhanced the professional status of science in Europe and America. By the late eighteenth century, however, Enlightenment philosophers had already laid a foundation for later typologists with a series of natural history treatises that classified "races" according to environmental and geographic conditions.

David Hume's *Of National Characters* (1748) and Baron Montesquieu's *Spirit of Laws* (1748) both explained how local climatic factors had produced the human "varieties" that Europeans encountered during imperialist voyages. The influential classification system of Johann Friedrich Blumenbach, with its five continental types—Caucasian, Mongolian, Ethiopian, American, and Malayan—would, at century's end, provide an important typological framework for empiricists who increasingly assigned race significance as a static, natural entity.

Scientific theories of race in Europe and America during the first half of the nineteenth century were directly linked to speculations on the role of evolution in the development of plant and animal diversity. Monogenists asserted that all human races could be traced to the traditional biblical story of Adam and Eve, but that a process of "degeneration" left each distinct type at various stages of mental, moral, and physical development. Polygenists, on the other hand, maintained that God created an Adam and Eve for each racial group and that immutable biological differences among races belonging to individual species resulted from these separate acts of creation.

Polygenism was popular in the South because it seemed to provide a scientific rationalization for the practice of slavery in the United States and imperialist expansionism abroad. One northern adherent was Louis Agassiz, a Harvard naturalist, whose lectures during the 1840s reinforced societal fears about the alleged deleterious evolutionary effects of miscegenation, or race mixing, between blacks and whites. Abolitionists, on the other hand, tended to gravitate to monogenism, which emphasized the genealogical unity of all peoples.

Samuel George Morton, in *Crania Americana* (1839), measured the skull volume of representatives of different races and assembled a scale of development that demonstrated the superiority of Europeans. Josiah C. Nott and George R. Gliddon, two indefatigable champions of polygenism, built on Morton's work. Their most famous publication, *Types of Mankind* (1854), declared that zoological investigations proved that races constituted "permanent" types, and ranked them in a predictable fashion.

The intellectual revolution brought on by Charles Darwin's *Origin of Species* (1859) had little effect upon scientific racism. By the early nineteenth century, pre-Darwinian scholars were making associations between non-Europeans and the apes, although not acknowledging actual biological connections between the human species and the ape species. Cuvier's famous dissection of the "Hottentot Venus" (a southern African Khoe woman called Sarah Baartman, displayed in Europe in the early 1800s alive and after her death, and ultimately repatriated to South Africa in 2002) emphasized her apelike qualities, although Cuvier was no evolutionist. The first generation of post-Darwinian biologists, such as Thomas Huxley in England and Ernst Haeckel in Germany, were faced with the absence of fossil materials connecting the human species to the apes. Their response was to link Europeans to the apes through the nonwhite races, capitalizing on the preexisting creationist imagery.

Among racial typologists, the cephalic index developed by Anders Retzius (a measure of skull shape), and the facial angle developed by Petrus Camper (a measure of the profile), supplied important statistical dimensions for craniometric studies into the twentieth century. They commonly were invoked to reinforce the animality of non-Europeans. Many physical anthropologists inferred as well that high mortality rates among late nineteenth-century black Americans forecast imminent "extinction," and that mental and physical distinctions (rather than the economic and political disfranchisement that characterized the experience of blacks in post-Reconstruction America) explained the high disease rates.

Darwin's work also became a catalyst of hereditary and genetic explanations of racial distinctions in the late nineteenth and early twentieth centuries, when eugenicists launched aggressive campaigns for human action to transform the evolutionary process with social policies designed to promote good "breeding" among the better "stocks." Charles B. Davenport pioneered the study of human genetics in the United States at the Eugenics Record Office in Cold Spring Harbor, Long Island, New York. The American Eugenics Society was founded in the 1920s as a mainstream scientific organization to promote the sterilization of "feebleminded" people and to restrict the immigration of poor Italians and Jews, entering America in large numbers and living in urban slums. Davenport's friend, a New York lawyer named Madison Grant, articulated these arguments in his 1916 best seller, *The Passing of the Great Race*, which was lauded in the journal *Science* and admired by politicians as diverse as Theodore Roosevelt and Adolf Hitler.

During the first half of the twentieth century, significant challenges to biological and genetic characterizations of race stressed the importance of environmental and cultural factors in human behavior. Franz Boas and other reform-minded anthropologists criticized earlier scientific research and pointed to overlapping physical variation, while social scientists, such as W. E. B. Du Bois, and reformers, such as Anna Julia Cooper, provided stark analyses of the persistent socioeconomic conditions that maintained racial disparities in health, education, and general economic status. By the mid-twentieth century, a coalition of cultural and physical anthropologists, empirical sociologists, and geneticists would also advance the biological data from population genetics that affirmed overlapping genetic variation to undermine static portraits of race and intelligence depicted in many IQ studies.

The most powerful statement rejecting the biological model of race was articulated in the UNESCO Statement on Race in 1950, drafted principally by the anthropologist Ashley Montagu, and subsequently revised following a rightwing backlash. The "new physical anthropology" articulated by Sherwood Washburn in the 1950s would focus on local populations rather than on artificial aggregates, on adaptation rather than on classification, on evolutionary dynamics rather than on static typologies, and on the diverse ways of being human rather than on the parochial ranking of human groups.

There was, however, an inevitable reaction against these new scientific sensibilities. Physical anthropologist Carleton Coon's *The Origin of Races* (1962) was widely brandished against the civil rights movement by segregationists for its assertion that blacks had evolved 200,000 years after whites. Psychologist Arthur Jensen (1969) asserted that intelligence was a largely innate property, gauged accurately by IQ tests, and that the average differences between black and white populations in America were caused by innate differences in intellectual capacity. This was reiterated a generation later by psychologist Richard Herrnstein and political theorist Charles Murray in their 1994 best seller, *The Bell Curve.*

During the public uproar over *The Bell Curve*, it emerged that a New York–based foundation, the Pioneer Fund, had been clandestinely funding scientific racism for decades. One of its largest beneficiaries, and later its president, was Canadian psychologist J. Philippe Rushton, whose theory is that evolution has produced a racial spectrum with law-abiding, intelligent, and undersexualized Asians at one end, and their African antitheses at the other. The interesting historical note is that in this scheme Europeans fall in the middle, having apparently been leapfrogged by Asians.

The lesson to be drawn is that in a society in which science confers legitimacy upon ideas, there is always strong pressure to package political ideologies in the science of the day. This is no less true in the modern United States than it was in Soviet Russia or Nazi Germany. The American eugenics movement achieved two notable successes: the Johnson Immigration Bill (restricting immigration in 1924) and the Supreme Court's decision in *Buck v. Bell* (1926, allowing states to sterilize citizens against their will, on the basis of poor genes). Even after the eugenics movement had begun to fade in the United States, the Tuskegee Study on the Effects of Untreated Syphilis in the Negro Male (1932–1972) showed that American science is indeed susceptible to popular prejudices about the unequal value of human lives. It need hardly be pointed out that where political inequality is pervasive, it is expedient to explain the inequality as an outgrowth of natural differences, rather than as the historical products of human agency and human evil.

See also Identity and Race in the United States; Social Psychology, Psychologists, and Race

Bibliography

Aptheker, Herbert, ed. *Against Racism: Unpublished Essays, Papers, Addresses, 1887–1961.* Edited by Herbert Aptheker. Amherst: University of Massachusetts Press, 1985.

Banton, Michael. *Racial Theories.* New York and Cambridge, UK: Cambridge University Press, 1987; 2d ed., 1998.

Fish, Jefferson, ed. *Race and Intelligence: Separating Science from Myth.* Mahwah, N.J.: Erlbaum, 2002.

Herrnstein, Richard, and Charles Murray. *The Bell Curve: Intelligence and Class Structure in American Life.* New York: Free Press, 1994.

Gould, Stephen Jay. *The Mismeasure of Man.* New York: Norton, 1981; rev. and expanded ed., 1996.

Jackson, John P. *Science for Segregation: Race, Law, and the Case Against Brown v. Board of Education.* New York: New York University Press, 2005.

Jensen, Arthur. "How much can we boost IQ and scholastic achievement?" *Harvard Educational Review* 39 (1969) 1–123.

Kevles, Daniel J. *In the Name of Eugenics: Genetics and the Uses of Human Heredity.* Berkeley: University of California Press, 1985.

Marks, Jonathan. *Human Biodiversity: Genes, Race, And History.* New York: de Gruyter, 1995.

Montagu, Ashley. *Statement on Race: An Extended Discussion in Plain Language of the UNESCO Statement by Experts on Race Problems.* New York: Schuman, 1951.

Nott, Josiah C., and Geo R. Gliddon. *Types of Mankind: Or, Ethnological Researches Based Upon the Ancient Monuments, Paintings, Sculptures, and Crania of Races, and Upon Their Natural, Geographical, Philological and Biblical History.* Philadelphia: Lippincott, Grambo, 1854.

Omi, Michael, and Howard Winant. *Racial Formation in the United States: From the 1960s to the 1980s.* New York and London: Routledge and Kegan Paul, 1986.

Rushton, J. Philippe. *Race, Evolution, and Behavior: A Life-History Approach.* New Brunswick, N.J.: Transaction, 1995.

Tucker, William H. *The Funding of Scientific Racism: Wickliffe Draper and the Pioneer Fund.* Urbana: University of Illinois Press, 2002.

Washburn, S. L. "The Study of Race." *American Anthropologist* 65 (1963): 521–531.

GERARD FERGESON (1996)
JONATHAN MARKS (2005)

Race and Education in Brazil

At the end of the twentieth century, Brazilian universities, both public and private, began to implement affirmative action and quota programs to promote the more equitable inclusion of Afro-Brazilians in higher education. For the country with the largest population of African descent outside of Nigeria, this development was a stunning turnaround from a century in which, despite glaring racial inequalities, much of the public and in many cases even the state proclaimed that Brazil was a racial democracy—a racially mixed paradise free from intolerance and discrimination. What is all the more notable is that these new policies do not respond to a perceived social need to compensate for errors in the past. Instead, these policies are based on a growing perception that racial inequality is an ongoing facet of Brazilian society, reproduced by cultural values, economic factors, and the functioning of public and private institutions. The relationship between

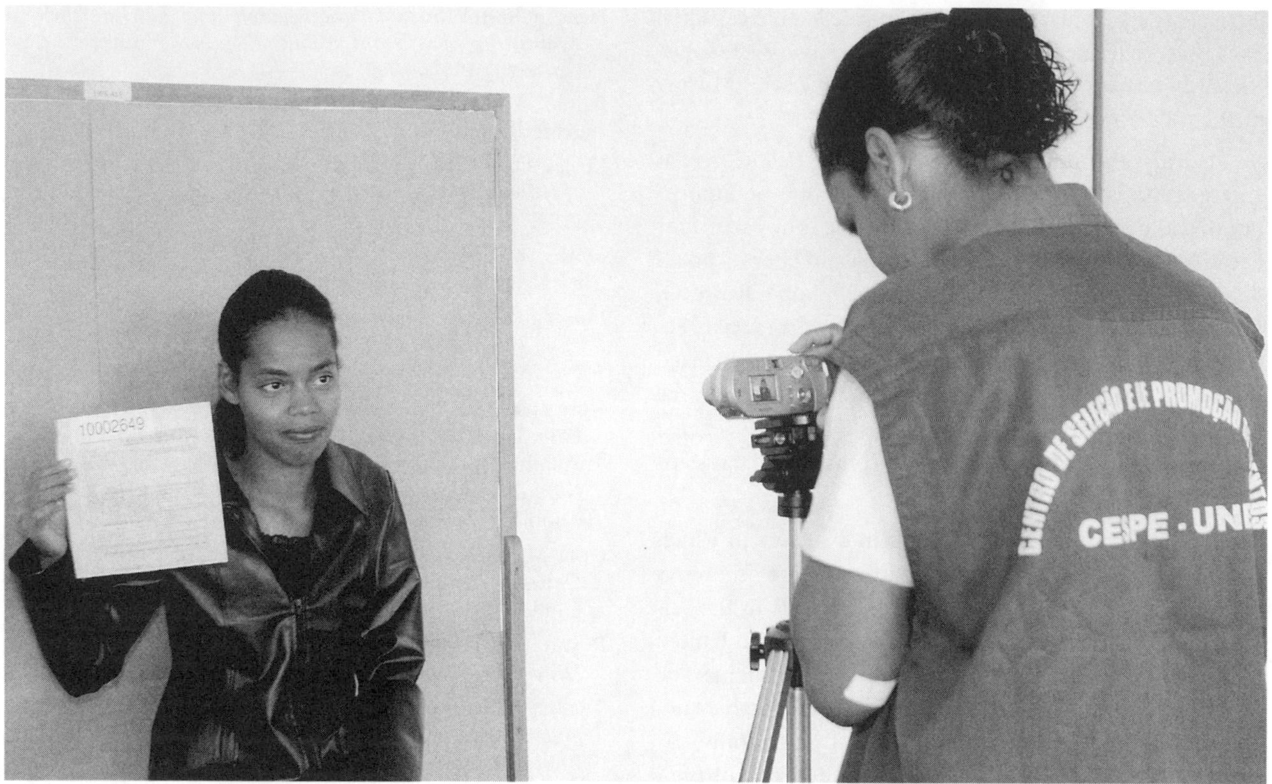

Student Gilmara Braga is photographed as a candidate for the University of Brasilia's black quota program, 2004. *The university was the first in Brazil to introduce quotas to promote the more equitable inclusion of Afro-Brazilians in higher education.* © JAMIL BITTAR/REUTERS/CORBIS

race and education is central to this emerging national debate on discrimination and its remedies in Brazil, and analysis of the history of race and education sheds light on the mechanisms that have sustained and reproduced racial inequality in this society so central to the African diaspora.

Historian Evelyn Brooks Higginbotham (1992) offers a way of thinking about the role of race in American society that helps understand the relationship between race and education in Brazil. Higginbotham suggests that race functions as a "metanarrative"—that once race enters as a factor into a society, cultural values, social policies, and political discourse are all shaped by race (p. 252). Until 1888 Brazil was the largest slave-holding society in the Americas, receiving nearly half of all the slaves brought from Africa. As in other slave-holding societies, Brazilian masters contrived to withhold literacy from their slaves, and across the country, until the end of slavery, local legislation was repeatedly passed to prevent the education of slave children. But the institution of slavery influenced Brazilian society in a number of indirect ways as well. It propelled Brazilian elites to remain closely identified with Europe both through economic ties and through cultural and social values. These ties were so intense that from the colonial period through the end of the nineteenth century, these elites endeavored to educate their sons and daughters in Europe. While Brazil's monarchs established law, medical, engineering, and military academies at the beginning of the nineteenth century, the first full university was not founded until 1922.

Through the nineteenth century, education at all levels remained almost exclusively the province of those who could provide for themselves, so only a few Brazilian cities offered even limited public instruction. Catholic institutions provided much of the education available until the twentieth century, both for Brazil's small, predominantly white elite and for a small number of free blacks, mulattoes and lower-class whites who received instruction in religious charities. Those few free people of color who received a full elementary education or all or part of a secondary education—almost always at the hands of religious institutions—became a part of a small educated semi-elite and occupied such positions as teachers, clerks, or accountants. Others received a vocational apprenticeship and worked in vocational trades. Until the turn of the twentieth century, Brazilian education mirrored the social hierarchies framed by the slave regime. In the absence of a large, lower-class free white population, the large immigrant waves of the turn of the twentieth century also created some interstitial opportunities for those few free people of color who were able to attain an education, even if only at the primary level.

The rise of public education in Brazil in the first decades of the twentieth century had everything to do with racial thought. It emerged from the racial thinking of elite, typically white Brazilians who envisioned transforming a nation they increasingly perceived as backward. These Brazilians, drawn from the ranks of doctors, social scientists, and other educated professionals, were modernists and progressives who envisioned remaking Brazil through vigorous action by the state. For these self-styled "educational pioneers," education could be the means of effecting a particular type of social transformation. They began to revise a long-held view adopted from international intellectual currents of the late nineteenth century that held that black and racially mixed peoples were racially inferior. Instead, they promoted a view gaining international currency that rejected scientific racism and instead viewed what they called "degeneracy" as a condition associated with race but tied to environment.

This public education combined vocational training to support industrialization, a nationalist curriculum designed to "Brazilianize" the population, and a host of psychological, anthropological, sociological, medical, and hygienic measures intended to build a future "Brazilian race" freed from perceived degeneracy (Dávila, 2003). These measures were inspired by eugenics—a movement within the human sciences that envisioned "improving racial stock" either by preventing the reproduction of perceived degenerates, as occurred in involuntary sterilization programs in the United States and Nazi Germany, or by seeking to increase the "robustness" of individuals with the hope this would be transmitted to their progeny. The educational model created by this movement was a paradoxical experience. On the one hand, this logic served to make education increasingly available to all Brazilians, and disproportionately extended opportunities to those of African descent who had been so systematically excluded in the past. It came with varying degrees of health care, assistance with meals, and dental service. On the other hand, this educational model relied on testing and tracking students based on their perceived potential—a standard that was applied through a reading of health, hygiene, and psychological adaptation to learning. This mentality carried over to the curriculum, which emphasized Afro-Brazilian passivity in the face of slavery and reproduced pejorative stereotypes. One of the leading high-school history texts of the mid-century, for instance, listed Afro-Brazilian contributions to Brazilian society as: "Superstition, love for music and dance, a certain 'creole negligence,' heroic resignation in the face of misery, a fatalistic and lighthearted attitude in regards to work" (Serrano, p. 164).

The results of this model, developed and implemented between the world wars, was a form of de facto racial segregation. This segregation was based on the classification of students of color as medically, psychologically, and sociologically problematic. At the same time, the number of teachers of color declined as the profile of new teachers changed. Whereas some Afro-Brazilians gained teaching positions in the nineteenth and early twentieth centuries based on their education, new standards of professionalization and the entrance of affluent white women into the workforce diminished the space for Afro-Brazilians to gain the training that would net them teaching jobs. The outcome of decades of institution building in public education in the first half of the twentieth century in Brazil was a network of school systems that reached increasing numbers of Brazilians, including Brazilians of color. Paradoxically, it was an educational system that reproduced prevailing beliefs about the cultural and social inferiority of Brazilians of color and did so within an environment that conceded or withheld opportunities based on socially constructed conceptions of merit. Perversely, as educators increasingly relied on social-scientific and medical measures to define students, it became easier to imagine that race was not an explicit factor shaping educational opportunity. In other words, the sublimated role of race in public education, as in other facets of Brazilian society, made it easier to assert that race was not a factor in Brazilian social inequality—that Brazil was, indeed, a racial democracy.

During the second half of the twentieth century, education in Brazil underwent another transformation that again held considerable significance for the nation's race relations. Increasingly, affluent and predominantly white parents withdrew their children from public schools and used their purchasing power to secure private education. The upper- and middle-class disengagement from public primary and secondary schools stigmatized these educational spaces, which became synonymous with the education of the poor and nonwhites. Under these conditions, support for public education waned and resources were drained. In yet another paradox, the decline of public education involved a decline in teacher wages, which propelled affluent women out of the profession and reopened its doors to teachers of color, though under increasingly precarious and less prestigious conditions.

This Brazilian experience with regard to race and education is paralleled by that of other societies in the Americas. National identity myths celebrate race mixture in societies as diverse as Mexico, Colombia, Venezuela, Puerto Rico, and Cuba. This belief in a national ethos of race mixture softening social lines belies a long and lingering history of exclusion and inequality. Yet, in Brazil, a movement for racial equality that organized in the opposition to that country's military dictatorship (1964–1985) gained ground in both local and national government during the process of redemocratization, which it used to advocate for compensatory action by the state as well as to promote racial solidarity among Afro-Brazilians, movements that have begun to redraw the relationship between race and education.

See also Education in the Caribbean; Education in the United States; Emancipation in Latin America and the Caribbean; Identity and Race in the United States; Race, Scientific Theories of

Bibliography

Dávila, Jerry. *Diploma of Whiteness: Race and Social Policy in Brazil, 1917–1945.* Durham, N.C.: Duke University Press, 2003.

Higginbotham, Evelyn Brooks. "African-American Women's History and the Metalanguage of Race." *Signs: Journal of Women in Culture and Society* 17, no. 2 (winter, 1992): 251–274.

Serrano, Jonathas. *Epítome de história do Brasil*, 3d ed. Rio de Janeiro, Brazil: F. Briguet & Cia., 1941.

JERRY DÁVILA (2005)

RACE AND SCIENCE

Throughout American history, scientific thinkers have offered varied explanations for the visible, or phenotypic, differences between the peoples of the world, commonly referred to as races or racial groups. Although the concept of race did not originate as a scientific idea—its use is most likely traced back to descriptions of the breeding of domestic animals—science has often been turned to for biological justifications of racial types, as well as a scientific vocabulary for describing beliefs about the relationship between race and physical, social, and intellectual traits. At various times in American history racial science has sought to justify slavery, define the capacity for citizenship of nonwhites, and make claims about the intellectual and physical inferiority of African Americans and other groups.

Racial science is not solely an American phenomenon. After all, scientific racism's intellectual pedigree can be traced to European thinkers such as the Swedish botanist Carolus Linnaeus and other Enlightenment-era scientists including the Frenchmen Louis LeClerc (the Comte de Buffon) and the German Johann Blumenbach. In the *Systema Naturae* (1735), Linnaeus, the founder of modern scientific taxonomy, divided the human species into four groups: *Americanus, Asiaticus, Africanus,* and *Europeaeus,* to which he assigned physical, social, and behavioral characteristics. In his taxonomy, for example, *Africanus* were described derisively as "black, phlegmatic . . . nose flat; lips tumid; women without shame . . . crafty, indolent, negligent . . . governed by caprice," whereas *Europeaeus* were described sympathetically as "white, sanguine, muscular . . . eyes blue, gentle . . . inventive . . . governed by laws."

Since the early days of the Republic, American racial scientists have proffered their views, developing uniquely American perspectives on race and science. Just ten years after he asserted that "all men are created equal" in the Declaration of Independence, Thomas Jefferson, third president of the United States and one of its early racial scientists, wrote in *Notes on the State of Virginia* that the difference between the races "is fixed in nature" and hypothesized that blacks were "originally a distinct race."

The nineteenth century was especially fertile for racial scientists as America debated the future of racial slavery. Americans such as Samuel Morton, a Philadelphia physician, and Josiah Nott, a Mobile, Alabama, physician, contributed to the early development of racial science, their theories offering a variety of explanations for the nature of white racial superiority. Morton, founder of the American School of Anthropology, popularized the theory of polygeny, the idea that a hierarchy of human races had separate creations. Morton was also known for a body of work that linked cranial capacity to race and intelligence, which suggested Africans had the lowest cranial capacity and hence the lowest intelligence. These studies were the empirical foundation of polygeny and focused the attention of racial scientists on the relationship between race and intelligence, an emphasis that continues today. Toward the end of the twentieth century, evolutionary biologist Steven Jay Gould discovered that Morton, hailed in his time as "the objectivist of his age," based his conclusions on racial difference on fundamentally flawed data. Gould concluded that Morton's a priori beliefs about race influenced his methods and conclusions.

In the twentieth century, explanations for difference shifted from linking race to measurable human traits such as skin color and cranial capacity to linking racial characteristics directly to genetics, a shift that was driven in large part by the emergence of the fields of eugenics and genetics. Eugenics correlated certain negative and deviant social behaviors with particular ethnic and racial populations and claimed these behaviors to be hereditary and genetic. Eugenic teaching on heredity suggested that race and racial differences in social and intellectual traits were unalterable through education, change in environment or climate, or the eradication of racism itself. For example, the eugenicist Charles Davenport's *Race Crossing in Jamaica* sought to prove the genetic basis for mental differences between whites and blacks, while eugenicists Paul Popenoe and Roswell Hill Johnson, in their influential textbook *Applied Eugenics,* sought to justify segregation by arguing that African-American physical, emotional, and mental inferiority prevented blacks from becoming part of modern civilization.

Response to the speculations of racial scientists played an important part in the development of antiracist thought. In the late 1820s abolitionist and political essayist David Walker challenged the underpinnings of Jefferson's racial science in *An Appeal to the Coloured Citizens of the World.* In the early part of the twentieth century Kelly Miller, dean at Howard University, and W. E. B. Du Bois, founder of the NAACP and editor of *The Crisis,* were among those who offered stinging critiques of racial science. In the 1920s Du Bois even debated the notorious eugenicist Lothrop Stoddard on this subject. The work of many anthropologists and biologists during the first half of the twentieth century also rebutted racial scientific thought. For example, the work of anthropologist Franz Boas, who dedicated his career to antiracism, showed that skull shape varied within human populations and that cranium size even varied within an individual's lifetime. In a later study of American immigrants, Boas also discovered that changes in environment could influence skull shape and size. These studies helped to illustrate the dynamic nature of human populations and also discredited notions of cranial differences between racial groups.

The intellectual and theoretical discussions about race, science, and medicine have had, since the days of slavery, real and sometimes horrific consequences for African Americans. In the nineteenth-century American South, slaves were sometimes used against their will in the course of scientific and medical experimentation. Less than a year into his presidency, Thomas Jefferson used two hundred slaves to test whether Edward Jenner's cowpox vaccine protected against smallpox. The vaccinations were successful and contributed to the acceptance of cowpox vaccination in Virginia and across the United States. Georgia physician Thomas Hamilton used a slave to carry out a brutal experiment testing remedies for heatstroke. The goal of his experiment was to find ways to help slaves withstand work during hot days. Finally, Alabama surgeon J. Marion Sims, considered to be a pioneer of gynecological medicine, used slave women to perfect a procedure to repair vesicovaginal fistulas. His test subjects underwent repeated operations without anesthesia until the procedure was perfected.

The belief by many racial scientists in the biological inferiority of African Americans, and the association of such diseases as tuberculosis and syphilis with African Americans, led to predictions that the race would eventually die out. The consequences of being viewed by the scientific and medical establishments as either constitutionally weaker or more vulnerable to a variety of ailments led to both stigmatization and poor medical treatment, and also a subsequent distrust by many African Americans of the medical and scientific community. Syphilis rates among African Americans were, for example, often ascribed to biological factors or the inherent moral inferiority of blacks rather than to social conditions or the nature of *Treponema pallidum,* the pathogen that causes syphilis.

The most notorious example of the intersection between race, science, and medicine is the Tuskegee study, conducted in Macon County, Alabama, by the U.S. Public Health Service from 1932 to 1972. The study examined the effects of late-stage untreated syphilis on 399 generally poor and illiterate African-American men who were recruited into the study with incentives that included burial costs and free medical care. When the study was exposed in 1972, it was discovered that study participants were never told the nature of their condition, that there was no formal protocol for the experiments, and that the men were not offered treatment for their condition, even after penicillin was found to be effective in the 1940s. The Tuskegee study is an unfortunate reminder of the damage theories of racial inferiority can wreak—damage to the individuals and their families who suffered as study subjects, damage to the integrity of the scientific and medical communities, and damage to the trust that is necessary between patient and doctors, or in this case, between the African-American community and the medical establishment. In the 1970s the moral outrage at the treatment of the Tuskegee study participants triggered the development of government-mandated protections for human subjects in scientific and medical research.

In the second half of the twentieth century, natural and social scientists, including anthropologist Ashley Montagu, psychologist Kenneth Clark, and biologist Richard Lewontin, challenged scientific notions of race. For example, Lewontin's studies in the 1970s showed that more genetic diversity exists within named racial groups than between them. In the early twenty-first century, the results of the Human Genome Project confirmed the belief that human genetic diversity and human differences cannot be accounted for by the concept of race. Yet, despite the data and the rebukes, science continues to be used to buttress and rationalize America's view of race and American racism.

See also Du Bois, W. E. B.; Tuskegee Syphilis Experiment; Walker, David

Bibliography

Gould, Stephen Jay. *The Mismeasure of Man.* New York: Norton, 1996.

Jones, James. *Bad Blood: The Tuskegee Syphilis Experiment.* New York: Free Press, 1993.

Savitt, Todd L. *Medicine and Slavery: The Diseases and Health Care of Blacks in Antebellum Virginia.* Chicago: University of Illinois Press, 1978.

Smedley, Agnes. *Race in North America: Origin and Evolution of a Worldview.* Boulder, Colo.: Westview Press, 1999.

Walker, David. *An Appeal to the Coloured Citizens of the World.* New York: Hill and Wang, 1965.

MICHAEL YUDELL (2005)

Racial Democracy in Brazil

The term *racial democracy* refers to a certain pattern of race relations in Brazil. Specifically, it suggests that Brazilian race relations have developed in a tolerant and conflict-free manner, in contrast to the presumed hostile form of race relations that evolved in the United States. The concept of racial democracy had at one point received such widespread acceptance that it was regarded as an essential component of Brazilian national identity. Brazilians distinguished themselves as unique for having achieved a level of racial tolerance that few other societies had attained.

The origin of the term racial democracy remains unclear. António Sérgio Guimarães, a professor at the University of São Paulo, suggests that its usage goes back to the 1940s, when the Brazilian anthropologist Arthur Ramos and the French sociologist Roger Bastide employed the term to link this pattern of race relations to Brazil's postwar democracy, which began to emerge at the end of the dictatorship of Getúlio Vargas (1937–1945). However, the concept is more generally associated with the work of Gilberto Freyre (1900–1987), who proposed the idea in the 1930s in a daring departure from the scientific racist thinking that had prevailed within Brazilian intellectual circles since the beginning of the twentieth century. Freyre stood the scientific racist thinking of the day on its head by arguing that Brazil's pervasive mixing of the races was not a factor in Brazil's failure to develop, but instead was testament to the achievements of a Brazilian civilization that had encouraged a pattern of tolerant race relations that was unique in the world. Freyre urged Brazilians to take pride in this, as well as in the displays of Afro-Brazilian culture that were prevalent throughout Brazil.

International factors contributed to the widespread acceptance of the notion of racial democracy, including the events surrounding the defeat of Nazism in Europe. Revelations of the racial horrors perpetrated by the Nazi regime stimulated the search for situations where, contrary to the European experience, race relations seemed to have evolved in a benign way. Brazil appeared to provide such a situation of racial tolerance. This was the motivation behind a United Nations Economic and Social Council (UNESCO) initiative in the 1950s to commission systematic studies of Brazilian race relations. However, UNESCO-sponsored research in Northern Brazil, led by anthropologist Charles Wagley, found patterns of discrimination that were attributed to the class position of Afro-Brazilians. UNESCO researchers in the South, in São Paulo specifically, led by Roger Bastide and Florestan Fernandes, unearthed systematic patterns of racial discrimination that called into question the validity of the notion of racial democracy.

While the notion of racial democracy assumed importance in both scholarly analysis and popular discussions for several decades, its credibility has since declined as the result of criticism from both black activists and from within academic circles. The activist critics emerged as early as the 1920s and 1930s when a black press developed in the City of São Paulo with the aim of calling attention to practices of racial discrimination. In addition, a protest movement known as the Black Brazilian Front (1931–1937) emerged and raised challenges to the ideal of a conflict-free pattern of Brazilian race relations. Subsequently, in the 1940s, Abdias Nascimento (b. 1914) founder of the Black Experimental Theatre, continued to provide organized expressions that ran contrary to the idea of racial democracy. In more recent times, the Black Unified Movement, created in 1978, has served as one of the principal activist vehicles for contesting the idea of racial democracy. In addition, a number of Black nongovernmental organizations have worked to bring to light racial issues that have been ignored in public discourse because of the widespread belief that a presumed racial democracy made such issues immaterial in the Brazilian context.

Alongside the activists' challenge to the idea of racial democracy, there has emerged a body of literature that has reinforced the findings uncovered by Bastide and Fernandes in the 1950s. Included in this literature are works by Carlos Hasenbalg, António Sérgio Guimarães, Nelson do Vale Silva, Lilia Monitz Schwarcz, and the scholars associated with the Centro de Estudos Afro-Asiáticos of the Cándido Mendes University in Rio de Janeiro. North American scholars also have made a contribution to the rethinking of the notion of racial democracy. Among them are Michael Hanchard, Kim Butler, Edward Telles, Melissa Nobles, George Reid Andrews, Anthony Marx, Robin Sheriff, and Anani Dzidzienyo (of Ghana).

One strong indication of the abandonment of the idea of racial democracy is the set of laws and policies implemented to address the issue of racial discrimination in Brazil. One of these is Brazil's antidiscrimination law of 1989, known as the Caó Law, which defines racial discrimination as a felony crime and which imposes stiff prison penalties on those found guilty of discrimination. Also, a number of public universities have implemented policies of affirmative action in student admissions on the grounds of redressing the low numbers of Afro-Brazilians in higher education.

Despite the erosion of adherence to the notion of racial democracy, it still occasions disputes about the genuine nature of Brazilian race relations. Social scientists such as Peter Fry and Livio Sansone have argued that Brazilian race relations, even acknowledging patterns of racial discrimination, still do not reach the level of hostility seen in the United States.

See also Black Press in Brazil; Movimento Negro Unificado; Nascimento, Abdias

Bibliography

Andrews, George Reid. "Brazilian Racial Democracy: An American Counterpoint, 1900–1990." *Journal of Contemporary History* 31, no. 3 (1996): 483–507.

Bastide, Roger, and Florestan Fernandes. *Brancos E Negros Em São Paulo,* 3d ed. São Paulo, Brazil: Companhia Editrora Nacional, 1970.

Butler Kim D. *Freedoms Given, Freedoms Won: Afro-Brazilians in Post-Abolition São Paulo and Salvador.* New Brunswick, N.J.: Rutgers University Press, 1998.

Fry, Peter. "Politics, Nationality, and the Meanings of 'Race' in Brazil." *Daedalus* 129, no. 2 (2000): 83–118.

Guimarães, António Sérgio Alfredo. "Democracia Racial." 2003. Available at <www.fflch.usp.br/sociologia/asag>.

Hanshard, Michael. *Orpheus and Power: The Movimento Negro of Rio de Janeiro and São Paulo, Brazil.* Princeton, N.J.: Princeton University Press, 1994.

Hasenbalg, Carlos. "Race and Socio-Economic Inequalities in Brazil." In *Race, Power, and Class in Brazil,* edited by Pierre-Michel Fontaine. Los Angeles: Center for Afro-American Studies, University of California, 1985.

Marx, Anthony. *Making Race and Nation: A Comparison of the United States, South Africa, and Brazil.* Cambridge, UK: Cambridge University Press, 1998.

Nascimento, Abdias do. *O Negro Revoltado.* Rio de Janeiro, Brazil: GRD, 1968.

Nobles, Melissa. *Shades of Citizenship: Race and the Census in Modern Politics.* Stanford, Calif.: Stanford University Press, 2000.

Sansone, Livio. *Blackness Without Ethnicity: Constructing Race in Brazil.* New York: Palgrave Macmillan, 2003.

Schwarcz, Lilia Moritz. *O Espetáculo das Raças: Cientistas, Instituições, e a Questão Racial no Brasil.* São Paulo, Brazil: Companhias das Letras, 1993.

Sheriff, Robin. *Dreaming Inequality: Color, Race, and Racism In Urban Brazil.* New Brunswick, N.J.: Rutgers University Press, 2001.

Skidomore, Thomas. *Black Into White: Race and Nationality in Brazilian Thought.* Durham: Duke University Press, 1993.

Telles, Edward E. *Race in Another America: The Significance of Skin Color in Brazil.* Princeton, N.J.: Princeton University Press, 2004.

Wagley, Charles, ed. *Race and Class in Rural Brazil.* Paris: UNESCO, 1952.

MICHAEL MITCHELL (2005)

Radio

African-American radio can be divided into three general periods of historical development: blackface radio (1920–1941), black-appeal radio (1942–1969), and black-controlled radio (1970 to the present). Blackface radio was characterized by the appropriation of African-American music and humor by white entertainers, who performed their secondhand imitations for a predominantly white listening audience. During this period, black people were essentially outside of the commercial broadcasting loop; they were marginal as both radio entertainers and consumers. In the era of black-appeal radio, African Americans entered into the industry as entertainers and consumers, but the ownership and management of the stations targeting the black radio market remained mostly in the hands of white businessmen. This situation constrained the development of independent black radio operations, while the radio industry in general prospered from it. During the most recent period, African Americans have striven to own and operate their own radio stations, both commercial and public. In addition, they have established black-controlled radio networks and trade organizations.

However, the percentage of African-American-owned stations still lags far behind the percentage of black listeners.

The appropriation of black song, dance, and humor by white entertainers who blackened their faces with charcoal goes back to the early days of slavery. The resulting radical stereotypes were embedded in the blackface minstrel tradition, which dominated American popular entertainment in the antebellum period, and remained resilient enough in the postbellum years to reappear in film and radio in the early decades of the twentieth century. Popular black music styles like blues and jazz were first performed on the radio by such white performers as Sophie Tucker, the first singer to popularize W. C. Handy's "Saint Louis Blues," and Paul Whiteman, the so-called king of jazz in the 1920s. A parallel trend developed with respect to black humor with the emergence of *Amos 'n' Andy* (starring Freeman Gosden and Charles Correll) as radio's most popular comedy series.

Indeed, *Amos 'n' Andy* was radio's first mass phenomenon: a supershow that attracted 53 percent of the national audience, or 40 million listeners, during its peak years on the NBC network in the early 1930s. In addition, the series provoked the black community's first national radio controversy. Robert Abbot, editor of the *Chicago Defender,* defended Gosden and Correll's caricatures of black urban life as inoffensive and even humane. Robert Vann, editor of the *Pittsburgh Courier,* countered by criticizing the series as racist in its portrayal of African Americans. He also launched a petition campaign to have the program taken off the air that amassed 740,000 signatures—but to no avail, for the Federal Radio Commission ignored it. Meanwhile, *Amos 'n' Andy* dominated black comedy on radio throughout its heyday as the "national pastime" in the 1930s. In addition to Gosden and Correll, the other major blackface radio entertainers of the era included George Mack and Charles Moran, known as the Two Black Crows on the CBS network, as well as Marlin Hunt, who created and portrayed the radio maid Beulah on the series of the same name.

During the period when blackface comedy performed by whites dominated the portrayal of African Americans over the airways, its audience was mostly white; fewer than one in ten black households owned a radio receiver. There were black entertainers and actors who managed to get hired by the radio industry in the pre–World War II era, and for the most part they were restricted to playing stereotyped roles. The renowned black comedian Bert Williams was the first important black performer to be linked to commercial broadcasting, in the 1920s; he was featured on a New York station doing the same routines he popularized while performing in blackface on the Broadway stage. During the Great Depression, as if to add insult to injury, a number of black actors and actresses who auditioned for radio parts were told that they needed to be coached in the art of black dialect by white coaches if they wanted the jobs. This perverse chain of events happened to at least three African-American performers: Lillian Randolph (*Lulu and Leander Show*), Johnny Lee (*Slick and Slim Show*), and Wonderful Smith (*Red Skelton Show*). The most famous black comic to appear regularly on network radio in the 1930s was Eddie Anderson, who played the role of the butler and chauffeur Rochester on the *Jack Benny Show.* Anderson was often criticized in the black press for playing a stereotypical "faithful servant" role, even as he was being praised for his economic success and celebrity.

After blackface comedy, the African-American dance music called jazz was the next most popular expression of black culture broadcast over the airways in the 1920s and 1930s. As was the case with humor, the major radio jazz bands were made up of white musicians, and were directed by white bandleaders such as Paul Whiteman, B. A. Rolfe, and Ben Bernie. The first black musicians to be broadcast with some regularity on network radio were New York bandleaders Duke Ellington and Noble Sissle. A number of influential white radio producers such as Frank and Ann Hummert, the king and queen of network soap operas, began to routinely include black doctors, teachers, and soldiers in their scripts. In addition, the federal government produced its own radio series, entitled *Freedom's People,* to dramatize the participation of African Americans in past wars, and it recruited Paul Robeson as a national and then international radio spokesman for the U.S. war effort. But at the end of the war, the government withdrew from the domestic broadcasting sphere, allowing the logic of the marketplace to reassert itself. Then with the advent of the new television networks, and their subsequent domination of the national broadcasting market, radio was forced to turn to local markets in order to survive as a commercial enterprise. Inadvertently, this led to the discovery of a "new Negro market" in regions where African Americans' numbers could no longer be ignored by broadcasters. This was especially the case in large urban centers, where nine out of ten black families owned radios by the late 1940s. The result of this convergence of economic necessity and a mushrooming listening audience was the emergence of black-appeal radio stations and the rise of the African-American disc jockey—two interrelated developments that transformed the landscape of commercial radio in the postwar era.

A few black DJs were playing records over the airways in the 1930s; they worked through a brokerage system that charged them an hourly fee for airtime. The disc jockeys, in turn, solicited advertising aimed at the local black community and broadcast it in conjunction with recorded "race" music. Jack L. Cooper pioneered this approach in Chicago on his radio show *The All Negro Hour,* which first aired on WSBC in 1929. At first, he developed a live variety show with local black talent, but within two years he had switched to recorded music in order to cut costs. He played jazz discs, hosted a popular "missing persons" show, pitched ads, made community-service announcements, and also developed a series of weekend religious programs. This format was successful enough to make him into a millionaire; by the end of the 1930s, he had a stable of African-American DJs working for him on a series of black-appeal programs broadcast on two stations. In the 1940s Cooper was challenged as Chicago's premier black disc jockey by Al Benson, who also built up a small radio empire on local outlets with his own style of black-appeal programming. Cooper targeted the middle-class African-American audience; he played the popular big-band jazz recordings of the day and prided himself in speaking proper English over the air. Benson played the down-home blues of the era and spoke in the vernacular of the new ghetto populace, most of whom were working-class southern migrants. A new era of black radio was at hand.

By the end of the 1940s there was a growing number of aspiring DJs in urban black communities ready to take advantage of the new "Negro-appeal" formats springing up on stations throughout the country. In Memphis, Nat D. Williams was responsible for broadcasting the first African-American radio show there, on WDIA in 1948; he also created the station's new black-appeal format and launched the careers of numerous first-generation African-American DJs over WDIA's airways. Two of the most important were Maurice "Hot Rod" Hulbert, who moved on to become the dean of black disc jockeys in Baltimore, on WBEE; and Martha Jean "the Queen" Stienburg, who later became the most popular black DJ in Detroit, on WCHB. In 1950, WERD, in Atlanta, became the first African-American-owned radio station in the country when it was purchased by J. B. Blayton, Jr. He appointed his son as station manager and then hired Jack "the Rapper" Gibson as program director. Other black-appeal stations that came into prominence during the early 1950s included WEDR in Birmingham, Alabama; WOOK in Washington, D.C.; WCIN in Cincinnati; WABQ in Cleveland; KXLW in St. Louis; and KCKA in Kansas City, which became the second African-American-owned radio outlet in the nation in 1952. By 1956 more than four hundred radio stations in the United States were broadcasting black-appeal programming. Each of these operations showcased its own homegrown African-American disc jockeys, who were the centerpiece of the on-air sound.

The powerful presence and influence of the African-American DJs on the airways in urban America in the 1950s stemmed from two sources. On the one hand, they were the supreme arbiters of black musical tastes; they could make or break a new record release, depending on how much they played and promoted it. On the other hand, the black disc jockeys were also the new electronic griots of the black oral tradition, posturing as social rappers and cultural rebels. As such, they collectively constituted a social grapevine that was integral not just to the promotion of rhythm and blues but also to the empowerment of the growing civil rights movement in the South. Such black-appeal radio stations as WERD in Atlanta and WDIA in Memphis, as well as Al Benson's shows in Chicago, played a vital role in informing people about the early civil rights struggles. In a speech to black broadcasters late in his life, civil rights leader the Rev. Dr. Martin Luther King, Jr., paid special tribute to disc jockeys Tall Paul White (WEDR, Birmingham), Purvis Spann (WVON, Chicago), and Georgie Woods (WHAT, Philadelphia) for their important contributions to the civil rights efforts in their respective cities.

During the 1950s African-American radio DJs also had a profound effect on commercial radio in general. Some stations—such as WLAC in Nashville, a high-powered AM outlet heard at night throughout the South—devoted a hefty amount of their evening schedules to rhythm-and-blues records. In addition, the white disc jockeys at WLAC (John R., Gene Noble, Hoss Allen, and Wolfman Jack) adopted the on-air styles, and even dialect, of the black DJs. Many of their listeners, both black and white, thought that WLAC's disc jockeys were African Americans. This was also the case on WJMR in New Orleans, where the white DJs who hosted the popular *Poppa Stoppa Show* were actually trained to speak in black dialect by the creator of the show, an African-American college professor named Vernon Winslow. Other white DJs who became popular by emulating the broadcast styles of their black counterparts included Dewey Phillips in Memphis; Zenas "Daddy" Sears in Atlanta; Phil Mckernan in Oakland, California; George "Hound Dog" Lorenz in Buffalo, New York; and Allen Freed in Cleveland. Freed moved on to become New York City's most famous rock-and-roll disc jockey before his fall from grace as the result of payola scandals in the early 1960s.

Payola, the exchange of money for record airplay, was a common practice throughout the radio industry. It was an easy way for disc jockeys to supplement the low wages they were paid by their employers. Hence, many well-known black DJs were adversely affected by the payola exposés. Some lost their jobs when their names were linked to the ongoing investigations, and an unfortunate few were even the targets of income-tax-evasion indictments. The industry's solution to the payola problem was the creation of the "top forty" radio format, which in effect gave management complete control over the playlists of records to be aired on their stations. Formerly, the playlists had been determined by the individual DJs. This change led to the demise of both the white rock-and-roll disc jockeys and the black "personality" DJs associated with rhythm and blues, and then "soul" music. Black-appeal stations were centralized even further by the emergence of five soul radio chains in the 1960s, all of which were white-owned and -managed. By the end of the decade, these corporations controlled a total of twenty stations in key urban markets with large African-American populations, including New York, Chicago, Memphis, and Washington, D.C. The chain operations not only established standardized top-forty soul formats at their respective outlets, thus limiting the independence of the black DJs they employed, but they also eliminated most of the local African-American news and public-affairs offerings on the stations.

In spite of the trend toward top-forty soul formats, a number of black personality DJs managed to survive and even prosper in the 1960s. The most important were Sid McCoy (WGES, WCFL), Purvis Spann (WVON), and Herb Kent (WVON) in Chicago; LeBaron Taylor and Georgie Woods (both WDAS) in Philadelphia; Eddie O'Jay in Cleveland (WABQ) and Buffalo (WUFO); Skipper Lee Frazier (KCOH) in Houston; the Magnificent Montegue (KGFJ) in Los Angeles; and Sly Stone (KSOL) in San Francisco. LeBaron Taylor and Sly Stone went on to successful careers in the music industry—Taylor as a CBS record executive and Stone as a pioneering pop musician. The Magnificent Montegue's familiar invocation, "Burn, baby, burn," used to introduce the "hot" records he featured on his show, inadvertently became the unofficial battle cry of the 1967 Watts rebellion. The new mood of black militancy sweeping the nation also found its way into the ranks of the African-American DJs, especially among the younger generation just entering the radio industry. Two of the more influential members of this "new breed," as they came to be known, were Del Shields (WLIB) in New York and Roland Young (KSAN, KMPX) in San Francisco. Both men independently pioneered innovative black music formats, mixing together jazz, soul, and salsa recordings.

The 1970s ushered in the current era of black-owned and -controlled radio operations, both stations and networks. In 1970, of the more than 300 black-formatted stations, only sixteen were owned by African Americans. During the next decade, the number of black-owned stations rose to 88, while the number of formatted stations surpassed 450. Some of the more prominent African Americans who became radio station owners during this era included entertainers James Brown and Stevie Wonder, Chicago publisher John Johnson, and New York City politician Percy Sutton. In particular, Sutton's Harlem-based Inner City Broadcasting (WLIB-AM, WBLS-FM) has been the national trendsetter in a black-owned and -operated radio from the early 1970s to the present. In 1977 African-American broadcasters organized their own trade organization, the National Association of Black-Owned Broadcasters. By 1990 there were 206 black-owned radio stations—138 AM and 68 FM—in the country.

It was also during the 1970s that two successful black radio networks were launched: the Mutual Black Network, founded in 1972, which became the Sheridan Broadcasting Network in 1979; and the National Black Network, started in 1973. Both of these operations provide news, talk shows, public affairs, and cultural features to their affiliate stations throughout the nation. In the 1980s the Sheridan network had more than one hundred affiliates and 6.2 million weekly listeners; in addition to news and public affairs, it offered a wide range of sports programming, including live broadcasts of black college football and basketball games. The National network averaged close to one hundred affiliates and four million weekly listeners in the 1980s; its most popular programs, in addition to its news reports, were journalist Roy Woods's *One Man's Opinion* and Bob Law's *Night Talk.* In 1991 Sheridan Broadcasting Corporation purchased National Black Network to form the American Urban Radio Network (AURN). As of 2005 AURN is the only African-American-owned network radio company in the United States, broadcasting three hundred weekly news, entertainment, sports, and information programs to more than 475 radio stations that reach some twenty-five million listeners nationwide.

Two major formats have dominated black-owned commercial radio in the 1970s and 1980s—"talk" and "urban contemporary." Talk radio formats emerged on African-American AM stations in the early 1970s; in essence they featured news, public affairs, and live listener call-in shows. By this time, the FM stations dominated the broadcasting of recorded music because of their superior reproduction of high-fidelity and stereo signals. The AM stations were left with talk by default. Inner City Broadcasting initiated the move toward talk radio formats among African-American stations when it turned WLIG-

AM, which it purchased in New York City in 1972, into "your total news and information station" that same year. The logic of the commercial radio market encouraged many of the other black AM operations, such as WOL-AM in Washington, D.C., to follow suit. Likewise, Inner City Broadcasting also pioneered the urban contemporary format on WBLS-FM during this same period. Much of the credit for the new format is given to Frankie Crocker, who was the station's program director at the time. To build up WBLS's ratings in the most competitive radio market in the country, Crocker scuttled the station's established jazz programming in favor of a crossover format featuring black music currently on the pop charts along with popular white artists with a black sound. The idea was to appeal to an upscale black and white audience. The formula worked to perfection; WBLS became the top station in the New York market, and scores of other stations around the country switched to the new urban contemporary format. One example was WHUR-FM, owned by Howard University in Washington, D.C. The station's original jazz and black-community-affairs format was sacked in favor of the urban contemporary approach in the mid-1970s. The new format allowed WHUR to become one of the top-rated stations in the Washington market. In the process, it gave birth to an innovative new nighttime urban contemporary style called "quiet storm," after the Smokey Robinson song of the same name. The architect of this novel format was Melvin Lindsey, a former Howard student and WHUR intern. In 1980 WOL-AM in Washington, D.C., was purchased by Catherine and Dewey Hughes. Catherine Hughes later bought out her now ex-husband's interest, and WOL-AM was the start of Radio One, Inc., the seventh-largest radio broadcasting company (as of 2003) to target African-American and urban listeners. Radio One owns and/or operates sixty-nine radio stations in twenty-two urban markets.

The 1970s and 1980s also marked the entrance of African Americans into the public broadcasting sphere. By 1990 thirty-two public FM stations were owned and operated by black colleges around the country, and another twelve were controlled by black community boards of directors. These stations are not subject to the pervasive ratings pressures of commercial radio, giving them more leeway in programming news, public affairs, talk, and unusual cultural features. Many of these stations—such as WCLK-FM, owned by Clarke College in Atlanta; WSHA-FM, owned by Shaw College in Raleigh, North Carolina; and WVAS-FM, from Alabama State University in Montgomery—have adopted the jazz formats abandoned by African-American-owned commercial FM stations. Others, such as WPFW-FM in Washington, D.C. (the number one black public radio outlet in the country), have developed a more ambitious "world rhythms" format embracing the many musics of the African diaspora. In general, the growth of black public radio has expanded the variety and diversity of African-American programming found on the airways, while also increasing the numbers of African Americans working in radio.

However, since the passage of the 1996 Telecommunications Act, independent black radio stations have struggled to survive. The Telecom Act has allowed conglomerates in a single market to have radio holdings that receive up to 40 percent of the market's advertising revenue and has eliminated the forty-station nationwide ownership limit; broadcasters may purchase up to eight radio stations in large markets and five in small markets. This has led to a consolidation in which conglomerates, with greater financial resources, have benefited while black-owned stations with less capital have gone up for sale. According to the U.S. Department of Commerce, from 1995 to 1996 the number of black-owned FM stations dropped from 86 to 64 and AM radio stations from 109 to 101; in 1997 there were 169 minority-owned broadcasters but by 2001 the number was 149. The largest black-controlled radio broadcaster (and seventh-largest in the country), Radio One, owns 69 radio stations; in contrast, Clear Channel, the largest U.S. radio broadcaster, owned 1,200 stations as of 2003—76 of which targeted black and urban audiences. Single-station owners are going the way of the dodo, but various entrepreneurs are acquiring their own, albeit small, clusters of stations to maintain a presence within the industry by offering grassroots community appeal and diversity of programming—and marketing that programming to more than the African-American market in order to survive and grow.

See also Jazz; Minstrels/Minstrelsy; Rhythm and Blues; Robeson, Paul; Walker, George; Williams, Bert

Bibliography

Baraka, Rhonda. "American Urban Radio Networks." *Billboard* (October 13, 2001): 25.

Barlow, William. *Voice Over: The Making of Black Radio.* Philadelphia, Pa: Temple University Press, 1999.

Dates, Jannette, and William Barlow, eds. *Split Image: African Americans in the Mass Media.* Washington, D.C.: Howard University Press, 1989.

Dawkins, Walter. "Battle for the Airwaves!" *Black Enterprise* (May 2003): 64–70.

Downing, John. "Ethnic Minority Radio in the USA." *Howard Journal of Communication* 1, no. 4 (1989): 135–148.

Edmerson, Estelle. "A Descriptive Study of the American Negro in U.S. Professional Radio, 1922–1953." M.A. thesis, University of California at Los Angeles, 1954.

Ferretti, Frank. "The White Captivity of Black Radio." *Columbia Journalism Review* (summer 1970): 35–39.

George, Marsha Washington. *Black Radio. . .Winner Takes All.* Philadelphia, Pa: Xlibris Corp., 2002.

Jones, Charisse. "Owning the Airwaves." *Essence* (October 1998): 112–120.

Tyson, Timothy B. *Radio Free Dixie: Robert F. Williams and the Roots of Black Power.* Chapel Hill: University of North Carolina Press, 1999.

Ward, Brian. *Radio and the Struggle for Civil Rights in the South.* Gainesville: University Press of Florida, 2004.

Williams, Gilbert A. *Legendary Pioneers of Black Radio.* Westport, Conn.: Praeger Publishers, 1998.

WILLIAM BARLOW (1996)
CHRISTINE TOMASSINI (2005)

Ragtime

Ragtime was the first music of African-American origin to play a significant role in American popular culture. It had both vocal and instrumental forms, flourished from the mid-1890s until the late 1910s, and had important exponents among both black and white composers.

In the public mind during the late nineteenth century, syncopated rhythm was a major element of black music. Such rhythms were used to caricature black music and were widely heard in minstrel shows that toured the nation, bringing an incipient ragtime to the public consciousness.

The term "rag" was used before the full term "ragtime." Black newspapers in Kansas from 1891 to 1893 refer to "rags" as social dance events. Anecdotes place ragtime music in Chicago during the 1893 World's Fair, though the first documented use of the term "rag" in a musical sense appears in the black *Leavenworth Herald* of December 8, 1894. Possibly the first music publication to refer to "rag" as a style is Ernest Hogan's song "All Coons Look Alike to Me" (copyright August 3, 1896), which includes a syncopated "Choice Chorus, with Negro 'Rag,' Accompaniment." The full term "rag time" (later "rag-time" and "ragtime") may be found first in the *Brooklyn Eagle* of September 6, 1896, in a report of pianist Ben Harney playing "what may be called rag time airs."

Vocal Ragtime

Most early ragtime songs were known as "coon songs," "coon" being a then–widely used, contemptuous term for blacks. These songs typically had lyrics in stereotypical black dialect and played upon such negative themes as

Cover of sheet music for **Under the Bamboo Tree,** *with music and lyrics by Bob Cole, J. Rosamond Johnson, and James Weldon Johnson, 1902.* MANUSCRIPTS, ARCHIVES AND RARE BOOKS DIVISION, SCHOMBURG CENTER FOR RESEARCH IN BLACK CULTURE, THE NEW YORK PUBLIC LIBRARY, ASTOR, LENOX AND TILDEN FOUNDATIONS

black men being shiftless, lazy, thieving, gambling, and violent and of black women being mercenary and sexually promiscuous. A typical song lyric would be "I don't like no cheap man / Dat spends his money on de 'stallment plan." (Bert Williams and George Walker, 1897). Adding to the songs' negative impressions were sheet music covers that usually portrayed African Americans in grotesquely exaggerated caricatures. With the relatively insensitive ethnic climate of the time, there was little protest from the black community, and black artists—including such sophisticated individuals as composer Will Marion Cook and poet-lyricist Paul Laurence Dunbar—contributed to the genre.

Not all early ragtime songs were abusive, even though they retained racial stereotypes. Among those whose popularity outlived the ragtime years was Joseph E. Howard and Ida Emerson's "Hello! Ma Baby" (1899), which celebrates courtship over the telephone. "Bob" Cole and J. Rosamond Johnson, black artists who were sensitive to the stigma of demeaning lyrics, wrote their enormously suc-

Sheet music covers of ragtime compositions by Scott Joplin and Tom Turpin. PHOTOGRAPHS AND PRINTS DIVISION, SCHOMBURG CENTER FOR RESEARCH IN BLACK CULTURE, THE NEW YORK PUBLIC LIBRARY, ASTOR, LENOX AND TILDEN FOUNDATIONS

cessful "Under the Bamboo Tree" (1902) to demonstrate that a racial song could express tasteful and universally appreciated sentiments.

Around 1905, the ragtime song began to lose its overtly racial quality, and the category came to include any popular song of a strongly rhythmic character. Typical examples were "Some of These Days" (1910) and "Waiting for the Robert E. Lee" (1913). Irving Berlin's hit song "Alexander's Ragtime Band" (1911), which was regarded by many as the high point of ragtime, retains only slight racial suggestions in its lyrics, and these are not derogatory.

Instrumental Ragtime and Dance

Ragtime developed both as a solo-piano vehicle and as an ensemble style for virtually all instrumental groupings. Ensemble ragtime was played by marching and concert bands; by dance orchestras; and in such diverse combinations as xylophone-marimba duos and trios, piano-violin duos, and mandolin-banjo groupings. Solo-piano ragtime was heard on the vaudeville stage, in saloons and brothels, in the home parlor, and on the mechanical player piano.

Ragtime was closely associated with dance. In the early days, the two-step was most common, along with such variants as the slow-drag. The cakewalk remained popular throughout the ragtime years but was a specialty dance reserved mostly for exhibitions and contests. In the 1910s many new dances joined the ragtime category, including the one-step; the fox-trot; the turkey trot; the grizzly bear; and such waltz variants as the Boston, the hesitation, and the half-and-half. The tango and the maxixe, though Latin-American rather than ragtime dances, were performed to syncopated music and became part of the ragtime scene in the mid-1910s.

Piano Ragtime

Ragtime was published primarily for the piano and contributed significantly to the development of American popular music and jazz piano. Piano ragtime, like the ragtime song, flourished as published sheet music, but it also existed as an improvised art, giving it a direct link to early jazz. However, since improvised ragtime was not preserved on sound recordings, there exists little detailed knowledge of it.

The defining elements of ragtime were established by 1896 with the printed piano parts in ragtime music publications. Of primary importance was the syncopation, for it was from this uneven, ragged, rhythmic effect that the term "ragtime" was derived. As applied to piano music, syncopation typically appeared as a right-hand pattern played against an even, metric bass. Around 1906 a new pattern known as secondary ragtime gained acceptance. This is not true syncopation, but the shifting accents within a three-note pattern create a polyrhythmic effect that was successfully integrated with the other ragtime gestures. After 1911, dotted rhythms made inroads into ragtime, further diluting the distinctiveness of the early ragtime syncopations.

The form into which ragtime was cast, though not a defining element, was consistent. The form followed that of the march and consisted of a succession of sixteen-measure thematic sections, each section being evenly divided into four phrases. Typically the two opening thematic sections were in the tonic key and were followed by one or two sections (known as the "trio") in the subdominant key. (As an example of the key relationships, if the tonic key were C, the subdominant key would be F.) Diagrammatically, with each section depicted with an uppercase letter, the form with repeats might appear as AA BB A CC or AA BB CC DD. To these patterns might be added four-measure introductions to A and to C and interludes between repeats of C or between C and D. Though these patterns were typical, they were not invariable; many rags used different numbers of sections and different key relationships.

Blues, another style that emerged from the African-American community, had some influence on the rags of a few composers, particularly in the use of so-called blue notes. What in later years was to become known as the classic twelve-bar blues form made its earliest appearances in piano rags. The first known example was in "One O' Them Things?" (James Chapman and Leroy Smith, 1904), in which a twelve-bar blues replaces the usual sixteen-bar A section. Both the form and the term appear in a New Orleans ragtime publication of 1908, A. Maggio's "I Got the Blues." The first blues to achieve popularity was W. C. Handy's "Memphis Blues" (1912), which combines twelve-bar blues and sixteen-bar ragtime sections and was subtitled "A Southern Rag." Throughout the rest of the ragtime era, the term "blues" was applied indiscriminately to many rags.

Though instrumental ragtime lacked the precise verbal communication of ragtime song lyrics, early published rags still conveyed a racial connotation with cover pictures that caricatured blacks, frequently in an offensive manner. As with the songs, piano ragtime's gradual acceptance as American music rather than as an exclusively racial expression was accompanied by the reduction of offensive racial depictions.

The Composers and Performers

The first ragtime performer to acquire fame was vaudeville pianist, singer, and composer Ben Harney, who appeared in New York in 1896 with "plantation negro imitations." Though he was known as "the first white man to play ragtime," his racial origins remain uncertain.

The publication of piano ragtime began in 1897 with "Mississippi Rag," by white bandmaster William Krell. Several months later, Tom Turpin, with his "Harlem Rag," became the first black composer to have a piano rag published. Turpin, a St. Louis saloon keeper, was an important figure in the development of ragtime in that city and reportedly had composed this piece as early as 1892. The most prominent ragtime success of 1897 was Kerry Mills's "At a Georgia Campmeeting," known in both song and instrumental versions and recorded by the Sousa Band, among others.

Scott Joplin, composer of "The Maple Leaf Rag." FISK UNIVERSITY LIBRARY. REPRODUCED BY PERMISSION.

Piano ragtime quickly caught on, and from 1897 to 1899 more than 150 piano rags were published, the most important and influential being Scott Joplin's "Maple Leaf Rag" (1899). Joplin was a composer with serious aspirations, and his frequent publisher John Stark adopted the term "classic ragtime" to describe the music of Joplin and others he published. These included black Missourians James Scott, Arthur Marshall, Louis Chauvin, and Artie Matthews, and such white composers as J. Russel Robinson, Paul Pratt, and Joseph Lamb. Though virtually all classic rags are superior examples of the genre, the term did not embrace any single style. Nor were classic rags the best known. More popular were the easier and more accessible rags of such composers as Ted Snyder, Charles Johnson, Percy Wenrich, and George Botsford.

New York City, with its flourishing entertainment centers and music publishing industry (Tin Pan Alley), naturally attracted many ragtimers. Because of the competition and high musical standards in the city, some of the more adept ragtime pianists developed a virtuosic style known as "stride." Among the leaders of this style were

Eubie Blake, James P. Johnson, and Luckey Roberts. These musicians—along with such figures as Joe Jordan, Will Marion Cook, Bob Cole, and J. Rosamond Johnson—also became involved in black musical theater, which made extensive use of ragtime.

Bandleader James Reese Europe disliked the term "ragtime" but became one of the most influential musicians on the late ragtime scene in New York. In 1910 he formed the Clef Club, an organization that functioned both as a union and booking agency for New York's black musicians. As music director for the popular white dance team of Irene and Vernon Castle, beginning in 1914, Europe created a demand both for black music and for black dance-band musicians.

Many who were admired during the ragtime years left little or no record of their music. Among these were "One-Leg" Willie Joseph, Abba Labba (Richard McLean), and "Jack the Bear" (John Wilson). "Jelly Roll" Morton was active from the early ragtime years but did most of his publishing and recording in the 1920s and 1930s. Tony Jackson was widely praised as a performer and composer but is remembered today primarily for his song "Pretty Baby." Though black women were active as performers and composers, they are now mostly forgotten because they did not record and few published. Thus, the history of ragtime is slanted in favor of those who left a documented record.

Reaction to Ragtime

Within the context of the genteel parlor music of the 1890s, ragtime was shockingly new. Nothing like it had ever been heard. For some, ragtime became America's statement of musical independence from Europe; it was hailed as a new expression, reflecting the nation's exuberance and restlessness. American youth, regardless of race, embraced the music as its own.

Inevitably, opposition to ragtime emerged. One sector of opposition was generational—the ever-present syndrome of the older generations rejecting the music of the younger. There was also opposition from musical elitists, those who objected to a musical form that lacked a proper pedigree and feared it would drive out "good music." Some denied that ragtime was at all innovative; they argued that the ragtime rhythms had been used by the European "old masters" and in various European folk music. Then there were the blatant racists, who rejected the idea that an American music could have black origins and denied that African Americans were capable of creating anything original. Most of all, they feared that white youth was being "infected" by this developing black music.

Certain parts of African-American society also objected to ragtime. Church groups, noting that ragtime was played in saloons and brothels and used for dancing, concluded that the music contributed to sinfulness. Blacks striving for middle-class respectability were also wary of ragtime because of its lower-class associations. *The Negro Music Journal* (1902–1903), which encouraged blacks to cultivate tastes for classical music, denounced ragtime and denied that it was an African-American expression.

Despite such opposition, ragtime thrived and evolved. During the mid- to late 1910s jazz emerged as an offshoot of ragtime. At first there was little distinction between the two, but by the end of World War I (1914–18) jazz had replaced ragtime as the most important vernacular music in America.

See also Blues, The; Jazz; Joplin, Scott; Minstrels/Minstrelsy; Music in the United States

Bibliography

Badger, Reid. *A Life in Ragtime: A Biography of James Reese Europe.* New York: Oxford University Press, 1995.

Berlin, Edward A. *Ragtime: A Musical and Cultural History.* Berkeley: University of California Press, 1980.

Berlin, Edward A. *Reflections and Research on Ragtime.* Brooklyn, N.Y.: Institute for Studies in American Music, 1987.

Berlin, Edward A. *King of Ragtime: Scott Joplin and His Era.* New York: Oxford University Press, 1994.

Blesh, Rudi, and Harriet Janis. *They All Played Ragtime.* 4th ed. New York: Oak Publications, 1971.

Hasse, John Edward, ed. *Ragtime: Its History, Composers, and Music.* New York: Schirmer Books, 1985.

Jasen, David A. *Recorded Ragtime, 1897–1958.* Hamden, Conn.: Archon Books, 1973.

Jasen, David A., and Gene Jones. *That American Rag: The Story of Ragtime from Coast to Coast.* New York: Schirmer Books, 2000.

Jasen, David A., and Trebor Tichenor. *Rags and Ragtime.* New York: Seabury Press, 1978.

Ping-Robbins, Nancy R. *Scott Joplin: A Guide to Research.* New York and London: Garland Publishing, 1998.

Riis, Thomas L. *Just before Jazz: Black Musical Theater in New York, 1890–1915.* Washington, D.C.: Smithsonian Institution Press, 1989.

Waldo, Terry. *This Is Ragtime.* New York: Hawthorn Books, 1976.

EDWARD A. BERLIN (1996)
Updated bibliography

Jesse Jackson during his 1984 presidential campaign. *Jackson founded the Rainbow Coalition in 1984. Two years later, the organization merged with PUSH (People United to Serve Humanity), which Jackson had founded in the early 1970s.* UPI/CORBIS-BETTMANN. REPRODUCED BY PERMISSION.

Rainbow/PUSH Coalition

The Rainbow/PUSH Coalition is the result of the merger of two organizations founded by the Rev. Jesse Jackson Sr.: Operation PUSH, founded in 1971, and the National Rainbow Coalition, founded in 1984. The two organizations merged in September 1996 in order to maximize financial, staff, and leadership resources.

Operation PUSH

The idea for the Rainbow/PUSH Coalition lies originally with another program—Operation Breadbasket. Founded by the Southern Christian Leadership Conference (SCLC) in 1962, Operation Breadbasket worked to improve the economic status of African Americans by boycotting businesses that did not employ or buy products made by blacks. In 1966 Jackson became the director of the Chicago campaign; besides using economic boycotts, Jackson also advocated support for African-American banks as a route to economic opportunity. Both boycotts and economic empowerment would become familiar issues within the Rainbow/PUSH Coalition. Jackson was appointed the National Director of Operation Breadbasket in 1967, but the program was losing momentum by 1971 when Jackson left the SCLC to found Operation PUSH (People United to Save Humanity, later changed to People United to Serve Humanity) in Chicago. The mission of the self-help group, which Jackson served as president of operations, was to obtain economic power to enhance the living conditions of working and poor African Americans through the use of corporate economic boycotts as a way to obtain more jobs and business opportunities. Among the corporate targets were Coca-Cola, Burger King, Kentucky Fried

Chicken, Adolph Coors, Montgomery Ward, and Nike. Besides economic opportunities, Jackson was also interested in social issues such as housing, welfare, politics, education, and youth affairs.

In 1985, with $6 million in government funding from the National Institute of Education of the Department of Health, Education, and Welfare, Jackson turned his attention to problems in public education through an affiliate group called PUSH for Excellence (PUSH-EXCEL) with its emphasis on upgrading the quality of education nationwide, urging teens to stay in school, and building self-esteem among the young. During Jackson's presidential bids in 1984 and 1988, Operation PUSH also sponsored numerous voter registration drives. However, the group came under scrutiny with allegations of fiscal mismanagement that led to federal audits and civil claims.

The Rainbow Coalition

During his address at the 1984 Democratic Convention, which was held in San Francisco, Jackson used a rainbow as a metaphor for the nation and its ethnic and racial diversity—"red, yellow, brown, black, and white. . . . The white, the Hispanic, the black, the Arab, the Jew, the woman, the Native American, the small farmer, the businessperson, the environmentalist, the peace activist, the young, the old, the lesbian, the gay, and the disabled make up the American quilt." The Rainbow Coalition was founded as a national social justice organization based in Washington, D.C., that was devoted to political empowerment, education, and changing public policy. The coalition allowed for third-party views in a two-party political system and lobbied for a more active role for African Americans and others marginalized by society. The Rainbow Coalition also lobbied for more of the national budget going toward domestic programs and health care and for a focus on international peace building. However, Jackson's public stance of defiance through various presidential administrations has been thought to hinder his ability to be an effective political insider.

Rainbow/PUSH Coalition

The merged Rainbow/PUSH Coalition, with its national headquarters located in Chicago, is a multiracial, multi-issue membership organization whose stated mission is "uniting people of diverse ethnic, religious, economic, and political backgrounds to make America's promise of 'liberty and justice for all' a reality." The Rainbow/PUSH Coalition has a broad range of issues and goals, including voter registration and civic education; political empowerment; assisting in the election of local, state, and federal officials; election law reform; mediating labor disputes; challenging broadcast station licenses to ensure equal employment opportunities in the media; including more minorities in all areas of the entertainment industry; fairness in the media, sports, and criminal justice system; jobs and economic empowerment; employee rights and livable wages; educational access; fair and decent housing; negotiating with major corporations to obtain minority-owned franchises and other business opportunities; affirmative action and equal rights; a voice in trade and foreign policy; gender equality; and environmental justice. Jackson regards the current stage in the struggle for equality as economic empowerment and access to capital, industry, and technology.

Among the Rainbow/PUSH Coalition's programs is the International Trade Bureau, which has been in existence for over thirty years and is intended to bring parity within the business community for minority and women-owned businesses by strengthening business contacts and opportunities. It provides technical assistance through workshops, training, presentations, and business counseling. The Wall Street Project, which began in 1998, is aimed at increasing minority involvement in business and investment in inner cities through hiring and promoting more minorities, naming more minorities to corporate boards, and awarding more contracts to minority businesses. In 1999 a financial ministry called 1,000 Churches Connected was begun to bring the message of economic responsibility to families. The program connects twenty religious organizations in the top fifty minority markets to use the pulpit, Sunday school classes, and church-sponsored seminars to teach financial stewardship, equal economic opportunity, and shared economic security. The Push for Life HIV & AIDS Initiative began in March 2000 to prevent disease and create healthy African-American and Latino communities. According to the RPC's Web site, African Americans account for 52 percent and Hispanics account for 18 percent of total HIV infections. The initiative has developed a political platform to assist the HIV/AIDS community in the eradication of HIV through increased funding and creation of a public awareness campaign regarding education, prevention, care, and treatment. Another goal is to create an international adoption program intended to link African-American churches with orphanages in South Africa. The RPC also maintains a Prison Outpost Project that provides information and programs to prisoners and to the larger community as well as offering worship and other spiritual services.

At the Rainbow/PUSH Coalition's 2002 annual convention, Jackson announced that his successor would be the Rev. James Meeks, the pastor of Chicago's Salem Baptist Church, who began working with the RPC's leadership in the mid-1990s. However, Jackson said he had no timetable to step down from the organization but merely wanted to plan for the long-term success and leadership of the coalition.

See also Civil Rights Movement, U.S.; Jackson, Jesse

Bibliography

Asante, Molefi, and Ama Mazama, eds. *Encyclopedia of Black Studies.* Thousand Oaks, Calif.: Sage Reference, 2005.

Ayers-Williams, Roz. "The New Rights Agenda." *Black Enterprise* (August 1997): 85.

Ballard, Scotty. "Civil Rights Groups: Why They're Essential Today." *Jet* (January 31, 2005): 4.

Collins, Sheila D. *From Melting Pot to Rainbow Coalition: The Future of Race in American Politics.* New York: Monthly Review Press, 1986.

Huse, Ernest R. *Jesse Jackson and the Politics of Charisma: The Rise and Fall of the PUSH/Excel Program.* Boulder, Colo: Westview Press, 1988.

Jaynes, Gerald, editor. *Encyclopedia of African American Society.* Thousand Oaks, Calif.: Sage Reference, 2005.

Rainbow/PUSH Coalition. "Push for Life HIV & AIDS Initiative." Available from <http://www.rainbowpush.org>.

CHRISTINE TOMASSINI (2005)

Raines, Franklin D.

January 14, 1949

One of seven children, public official and investment banker Franklin D. Raines grew up in Seattle, Washington. His working-class family had been a recipient of Aid to Families with Dependent Children, or welfare. He received his B.A. degree from Harvard College in 1971 and his J.D. degree from Harvard University Law School in 1976. He also attended Magdalen College at Oxford University as a Rhodes Scholar.

From 1977 to 1979 Raines was an associate director for economics and government with the Office of Management and Budget (OMB) and assistant director of the White House Domestic Policy Staff, handling such issues as welfare reform, food stamps, and social security. He then was a general partner with the international investment banking firm, Lazard Freres & Company from 1979 to 1991.

From 1991 to 1996 Raines was vice chair of the Federal National Mortgage Association, better known as Fannie Mae, which provides financial assistance for lower-income Americans who are in the market for a home. It is also the world's largest nonbank financial service and the largest financier of home mortgages in the country. Raines then joined President Bill Clinton's cabinet from April 1996 to May 1998, where he was director of the Office of Management and Budget—the first director in a generation to balance the federal budget. He resigned to join the private sector and became chair and chief executive officer of the Washington, D.C.–based Fannie Mae Corporation on January 1, 1999, becoming the first African American CEO of a major *Fortune* 500 company.

Raines's memberships have included the board of directors of Pfizer Inc., America Online, Inc., the Boeing Company, and chair of the Visiting Committee of the Harvard Kennedy School of Government. He has served also as president of the Board of Overseers of Harvard.

In 2004 Raines resigned his executive office at Fannie Mae following a ruling by the Securities and Exchange Commission that the corporation had been using improper accounting procedures.

See also Politics in the United States

Bibliography

"Fannie Mae CEO, Franklin Raines, Retires." *Jet* 107, no. 3 (January 17, 2005): 34–35.

Farmer, Paula. "The First African American to Head a Fortune 500 Company, Franklin D. Raines Takes Over Fannie Mae." Available from <http://www.black-collegian.com/issues/1999-08/fdraines.shtml>.

RAYMOND WINBUSH (2001)
Updated by publisher 2005

Rainey, Ma

April 26, 1886
December 22, 1939

One of the most beloved blues and vaudeville singers of the first three decades in the twentieth century, Gertrude Pridgett "Ma" Rainey, the "Mother of the Blues," was born Gertrude Pridgett in Columbus, Georgia. Rainey was the second of five children born to Thomas and Ella Pridgett. She performed in a local show, "A Bunch of Blackberries," at fourteen and married a tent showman, Will Rainey, when she was eighteen. They performed together for several years as a comedy song-and-dance act, billed as the "Assassinators of the Blues," with the Rabbit Foot Minstrels.

Supposedly, Rainey coined the term "blues" after she began singing the mournful songs that she had heard sung by a young woman along the tent show's route. Rainey left her husband after twelve years but continued to follow the TOBA (Theater Owners Booking Association) circuit as a solo act because she was so popular with country folk, white and black. She sang with jug bands as well as small jazz bands, which included at times Tommy Ladnier, Joe Smith, and Coleman Hawkins. She was a seasoned performer who sang about the worries and tribulations of country folk in the traditional style of the rural South. Her subject matter was earthy, her renditions were often comedic, yet she did not resort to trivia.

Rainey's first recording, "Moonshine Blues," was produced by Paramount Records in 1923. She recorded a total of ninety-three songs, which included traditional country and folk blues, vaudeville songs, and popular songs. Rainey wrote many of her songs, addressing topics as diverse as homosexuality, prostitution, jail, and the impact of the boll weevil on cotton crops. Although she was overshadowed by her younger counterpart, Bessie Smith (1894?–1937), Rainey had a loyal following until her last days on the tent show circuit in the 1930s. She handled her business affairs well and retired to her native city of Columbus, Georgia, where she opened her own theater. She died there on December 22, 1939.

See also Blues, The; Blueswomen of the 1920s and 1930s; Smith, Bessie

Bibliography

Harrison, Daphne Duval. *Black Pearls: Blues Queens of the 1920s.* New Brunswick, N.J.: Rutgers University Press, 1988.

Lieb, Sandra R.. *Mother of the Blues: A Study of Ma Rainey.* Amherst: University of Massachusetts Press, 1981.

DAPHNE DUVAL HARRISON (1996)

RANDOLPH, ASA PHILIP

APRIL 15, 1889
MAY 16, 1979

The labor and civil rights leader A. Philip Randolph was the younger son of James William Randolph, a minister in the African Methodist Episcopal Church. He was born in Crescent City, Florida, and raised in Jacksonville. In 1911, after graduating from the Cookman Institute in Jacksonville, the twenty-two-year-old Randolph migrated to New York City and settled in Harlem, then in an early stage of its development as the "Negro capital of the world." While working at odd jobs to support himself, he attended the City College of New York (CCNY, adjoining Harlem), where he took courses in history, philosophy, economics, and political science. During his enrollment at CCNY, he also became active in the Socialist Party, whose leader, Eugene Debs, was one of his political heroes.

THE HARLEM RADICALS

Between 1914 and the early 1920s, Randolph belonged to a group of young African-American militants in New York, called the Harlem radicals, who regarded themselves as the New Negro political avant-garde in American life. Some of them, including Randolph, combined race radicalism with socialism. Others, such as Marcus Garvey, who arrived in Harlem in 1916, emphasized a black nationalism that was oriented toward Africa—they were averse to movements that advocated social reform or racial integration within the mainstream of American society. But all Harlem radicals defied the established African-American leadership, even though it included so distinguished a member as W. E. B. Du Bois.

To race radicalism and socialism, Randolph soon added an interest in trade unionism, which was to form a basic part of his approach to the struggle for black progress. In 1917, he and his closest socialist comrade in Harlem, Chandler Owen, founded and began coediting *The Messenger,* a monthly journal that carried the subtitle "The Only Radical Magazine Published by Negroes." *The Messenger* campaigned against lynching in the South; opposed America's participation in World War I; counseled African Americans to resist the military draft; proposed an economic solution to the "Negro problem"; and urged blacks to ally themselves with the socialist and trade-union movements. For its irreverent editorial stands, *The Messenger* came under the close surveillance of the federal government. In 1918 Postmaster General Albert Burleson revoked the magazine's second-class mailing privileges, and in 1919 a Justice Department report ordered by Attorney General A. Mitchell Palmer described *The Messenger* as "by long odds the most able and most dangerous of the Negro publications."

In 1917 Randolph also helped organize the Socialist Party's first black political club in New York, located in Harlem's Twenty-first Assembly District. In 1920, the party recognized his growing importance as a spokesperson by naming him its candidate for New York State comptroller, one of the highest positions for which a black socialist had run. He lost the election but polled an impressive 202,361 votes, about a thousand fewer than Eu-

Civil rights activist and labor leader A. Philip Randolph (center) speaking to President Lyndon B. Johnson. *Johnson awarded Randolph the Presidential Medal of Freedom, the nation's highest civilian honor, in 1964.* AP/WIDE WORLD PHOTOS

gene Debs polled in New York State that year as the Socialist Party's candidate for president.

In the early 1920s, Randolph began dissolving his formal ties to the party when it became clear to him that the black masses were not as responsive to the socialist message as he had hoped. This was partly because of their traditional distrust for ideologies they deemed to be un-American; partly because black nationalism was, emotionally and psychologically, more appealing to them; and partly because the Socialist Party failed to address the special problems of black exclusion from the trade-union movement. But despite his retirement from formal party activities, Randolph continued to consider himself a democratic socialist.

Brotherhood of Sleeping Car Porters

In 1925 a delegation of Pullman porters approached him with a request that he organize their work force into a legitimate labor union, independent of employer participation and influence. Randolph undertook the task—a decision that launched his career as a national leader in the fields of labor and civil rights. But establishing the Brotherhood of Sleeping Car Porters was a far more difficult task than he had anticipated. The Pullman Company had crushed a number of earlier efforts to organize its porters, and for the next twelve years it remained contemptuous of Randolph's. Not until 1937, after Congress had passed enabling labor legislation, did the Pullman executives recognize the Brotherhood of Sleeping Car Porters as a certified bargaining agent.

This victory gained the brotherhood full membership in the American Federation of Labor (AFL). It also gave Randolph—as the brotherhood's chief delegate to annual AFL conventions—an opportunity to answer intellectuals in Harlem who criticized him for urging blacks to ally themselves with the trade-union movement. The black intelligentsia generally regarded the AFL as a racist institution, most of whose craft unions barred nonwhite membership. How, then (his critics argued), could Randolph call on blacks to invest their economic aspirations in organized labor? Randolph maintained that trade unionism was the main engine of economic advancement for the working class, the class to which a majority of the black population belonged. He believed that achieving the political rights for which all blacks were struggling would be meaningless without comparable economic gains.

Throughout his tenure as a delegate to the annual conventions of organized labor (in 1955 he became a vice president of the merged American Federation of Labor-Congress of Industrial Organizations—the AFL-CIO), Randolph campaigned relentlessly against unions that excluded black workers. When he retired as a vice president in 1968, the AFL-CIO had become the most integrated public institution in American life, although pockets of resistance remained. Randolph was not the sole instrument of that revolution, but he was its opening wedge, and much of the change was due to his unyielding agitation.

A. Philip Randolph

"As to the compositions of our movement. Our policy is that it be all-Negro, and pro-Negro but not anti-white, or anti-Semitic or anti-labor or anti-Catholic. The reason for this policy is that all oppressed people must assume the responsibility and take the initiative to free themselves."

KEYNOTE ADDRESS TO THE POLICY CONFERENCE OF THE MARCH ON WASHINGTON MOVEMENT, MEETING IN DETROIT, MICHIGAN, SEPTEMBER 26, 1942. REPRINTED IN JOHN BRACEY, AUGUST MEIER, AND ELLIOTT RUDWICK, EDS. *BLACK NATIONALISM IN AMERICA*. INDIANAPOLIS: BOBBS-MERILL, 1970, P. 391.

Civil Rights Leadership

The brotherhood's victory in 1937 also inaugurated Randolph's career as a national civil rights leader; he emerged from the struggle with Pullman as one of the more respected figures in black America. In 1937 the recently formed National Negro Congress (NNC), recognizing Randolph's potential as a mass leader, invited him to be its president. Randolph saw the NNC as a potential mass movement, and he accepted. But he resigned the NNC's presidency in 1940, when he discovered that much of the organization had come under communist control. He was a resolute anticommunist for the rest of his life. He wrote to a colleague in 1959, "They [communists] are not only undemocratic but anti-democratic. They are opposed to our concept of the dignity of the human personality, the heritage of the Judeo-Christian philosophy, and hence they represent a totalitarian system in which civil liberties cannot live."

Randolph's withdrawal from the NNC freed him to organize, early in 1941, the March on Washington Movement, based on the Gandhian method of nonviolent direct action. It achieved its first major victory in June 1941. Faced with Randolph's threat to lead a massive invasion of the nation's capital, President Franklin D. Roosevelt issued an executive order banning the exclusion of blacks from employment in defense plants—the federal government's earliest commitment to the policy of fair employment. That breakthrough brought Randolph to the forefront of black mass leadership, making him "the towering civil rights figure of the period," according to James Farmer, one of his younger admirers. The March on Washington Movement disintegrated by the end of the 1940s, but by then Randolph had secured another historic executive order—this one from President Harry S. Truman, in 1948, outlawing segregation in the armed services. Scholars were to see his movement as one of the most remarkable in American history. Aspects of its influence went into the formation of Farmer's Congress of Racial Equality (CORE; 1942) and Rev. Dr. Martin Luther King's Southern Christian Leadership Conference (1957), both of which helped lead the great nonviolent protest movement of the 1960s.

Randolph was the elder statesman of that movement, a unifying center of the civil rights coalition that composed it. His collaboration with its various leaders culminated in the 1963 March on Washington, the largest demonstration for racial redress in the nation's history. Randolph had conceived that event, and it is appropriate that he should have called it a March for Jobs and Freedom; it represented his two-pronged approach, political and economic, to the black struggle.

After 1963, Randolph the architect of black mass pressure on the federal government faded gradually from the scene. In 1964 President Lyndon B. Johnson awarded him the Presidential Medal of Freedom, the nation's highest civilian honor. He spent the remaining years of his active life chiefly as a vice president of the AFL-CIO. He died in 1979, at the age of ninety.

See also Brotherhood of Sleeping Car Porters; Congress of Racial Equality (CORE); Du Bois, W. E. B.; Garvey,

Marcus; Labor and Labor Unions; *Messenger, The*; National Negro Congress; New Negro; Southern Christian Leadership Conference (SCLC)

Bibliography

Anderson, Jarvis. *A. Philip Randolph: A Biographical Portrait.* New York: Harcourt Brace Jovanovich, 1973.

Brazeal, Brailsford R. *The Brotherhood of Sleeping Car Porters: Its Origin and Development.* New York: Harcourt and Brothers, 1946.

Miller, Calvin Craig. *A. Philip Randolph and the African American Labor Movement.* Greensboro, N.C.: Morgan Reynolds, 2005.

Patterson, Lillie. *A. Philip Randolph: Messenger for the Masses.* New York: Facts on File, 1996.

Pfeffer, Paula F. *A. Philip Randolph: Pioneer of the Civil Rights Movement.* Baton Rouge: Louisiana State University Press, 1990.

JERVIS ANDERSON (1996)
Updated bibliography

Rangel, Charles Bernard

June 11, 1930

Politician Charles Rangel was born and raised in Harlem. His parents separated when he was a small child, and he lived with his mother and grandfather. He dropped out of high school in his junior year and worked at odd jobs until 1948, when he enlisted in the army. He was deployed to South Korea, where he was stationed for four years and served in the Korean War, earning a Bronze Star Medal of Valor and a Purple Heart.

After the war Rangel returned to high school in New York and received his diploma in 1953. He then entered the New York University School of Commerce, earning a B.S. in 1957. He went on to St. John's University Law School, where he obtained his J.D. in 1960. After law school he worked as an attorney and provided legal assistance to civil rights activists. In 1961 he was appointed an assistant United States attorney in the Southern District of New York. He resigned from this position after one year and worked as legal counsel to the New York City Housing and Redevelopment Board, as legal assistant to Judge James L. Watson, as an associate counsel to the speaker of the New York State Assembly, and as general counsel to the National Advisory Commission on Selective Service. In the winter of 1963–1964 Rangel and his friend Percy Sutton founded the John F. Kennedy Democratic Club in Harlem, later renamed the Rev. Martin Luther King Jr. Democratic Club.

Rangel began his career in politics in 1966, when he was elected to represent central Harlem in the New York State Assembly. He served two two-year terms as a leading liberal in the legislature, supporting the legalization of abortion, opposing stiffer penalties on prostitution, and endorsing antiwar protests.

Rangel moved into national politics in 1970, when he narrowly defeated the longtime incumbent congressman Adam Clayton Powell Jr., who had represented Harlem since 1945. Once in office Rangel immediately established as his top priority the elimination of the drug trade. He called for the elimination of foreign aid to Turkey for its cultivation of opium poppies and opposed New York City Mayor John V. Lindsay's plan to issue maintenance doses of heroin to addicts.

In the 1970s Rangel took a leading position as a congressional dove. He consistently voted to reduce the military budget, opposed the development of the B-1 bomber and nuclear aircraft carriers, and vigorously criticized the war in Southeast Asia. Rangel's liberalism extended to domestic issues as well. He voted for busing to desegregate schools, federal assistance for abortions, the creation of a consumer protection agency, and the implementation of automobile pollution controls.

Rangel gained national exposure in 1974 as a member of the House Judiciary Committee during the impeachment hearings for President Nixon. That year he was also elected chair of the Congressional Black Caucus, a position he held through 1975. In 1975 Rangel became the first African American appointed to the House Ways and Means Committee. He obtained the chairmanship of the influential health subcommittee of the Ways and Means Committee in 1979. In 1980 he became a member of the Democratic Steering and Policy Committee, and in 1983 he was made a deputy whip by Speaker of the House Tip O'Neill and appointed chair of the Select Committee on Narcotics.

Through the 1980s Rangel served as the chief congressional gadfly on drug issues and repeatedly chastised the Reagan and Bush administrations for their "turtlelike speed" in addressing the narcotics crisis. In 1989, as chair of the House Narcotics Task Force, Rangel led a congressional delegation to the Caribbean and Mexico to help coordinate the international crackdown on drugs. In later years he served as a leading voice against the movement to legalize narcotics. In 1994 Rangel was challenged in the Democratic primary by Adam Clayton Powell IV, the son of the man he had unseated, but he emerged victorious.

Called "Mr. Harlem," Rangel has been elected to serve seventeen consecutive terms in Congress through 2005.

He is the ranking member of the House Committee on Ways and Means, chair of the board of the Democratic Congressional Campaign Committee, and dean of the New York State Congressional Delegation. Rangel is also credited as the principal architect of the five billion dollar Federal Empowerment Zone project to revitalize the nation's urban areas.

See also Congressional Black Caucus; Politics in the United States

Bibliography

Clay, William L. *Just Permanent Interests: Black Americans in Congress, 1870–1991.* New York: Amistad Press, 1992.

Ragsdale, Bruce, and Joel D. Treese. *Black Americans in Congress, 1870–1989.* Washington, D.C.: U.S. Government Printing Office, 1990.

THADDEUS RUSSELL (1996)
Updated by publisher 2005

Run-D.M.C. *From left, Run (Joseph Simmons), Jam Master Jay (Jason Mizell), and DMC (Darryl McDaniels) combined to form one of the pioneering rap groups of the early 1980s.*

Rap

Rap is an African-American term that describes a stylized way of speaking. Salient features of a rap include metaphor, braggadocio, repetition, formulaic expressions, double entendre, mimicry, rhyme, and "signifyin'" (i.e., indirect references and allusions). Folklorists credit the introduction of the term to the masses by the 1960s black nationalist H. "Rap" Brown, whose praise name "rap" suggested his mastery of a "hip" way of speaking, aptly called rappin'. Although Brown is lauded for the name of this genre, the roots of rap can be traced from southern black oral forms such as toasts, blues, game songs (e.g., "hambone") to northern urban street jive—all of which make use of the aforementioned features.

While rap's antecedents developed in the rural South during the eighteenth and nineteenth centuries, its northern counterpart, jive, emerged in urban communities as the prototype of rap around the early part of the twentieth century. Dan Burley, a scholar of jive, observed that jive initially circulated among black Chicagoans around 1921. The primary context of its development was in secular environs remote from home and religious centers, such as street corners, taverns, and parks, known among black urbanites as "the streets." Jive can be defined as a metaphorical style of communicating via the use of words and phrases from American mainstream English but reinterpreted from an African-American perspective. For example, in rap lingo, man becomes "cat," woman becomes "chick," and house becomes "crib." The art of jive resided in its ability to remain witty and original, hence its constant fluctuation in vocabulary over the years.

From the 1920s to the 1950s jive proliferated on all levels in the urban milieu—from the church to the street corner; but it was also incorporated in the literary works of noted black writers of the time, such as Langston Hughes. Alongside its use by writers, jive became the parlance of jazz musicians. "Jam" (having a good time), "bad" (good), and "axe" (instrument) are some jive words commonplace in the jazz vernacular. By the late 1940s and 1950s this urban style of speaking was introduced over radio airwaves by two Chicago disc jockeys, Holmes "Daddy-O" Daylie and Al Benson, who utilized jive in rhyme over music. Even the boastful poetry of former heavyweight champion boxer Muhammad Ali as well as comedian Rudy Ray Moore, known for popularizing audio recordings of toasts like "Dolemite" and "The Signifying Monkey," moved jive further into the American mainstream.

By the 1960s jive was redefined and given a newer meaning by black nationalist H. "Rap" Brown, who laced his political speeches with signifyin', rhyme, and metaphor. Although Brown's stylized speech inaugurated the shift from jive to rap, it soon gained popular acceptance among young urban admirers as rappin'. It was not, however, until the late 1960s that Brown's speaking style was set to musical accompaniment by such political poets as the Watts Prophets of Los Angeles, the Last Poets of Harlem, Nikki Giovanni, and singer-pianist-poet Gil Scott-Heron, who recited rhyming couplets over an African percussion accompaniment.

In the late 1960s and the 1970s rappin' to music emerged as two distinct song styles: the soul rap and the funk-style rap. The soul rap, a rappin' monologue celebrating the feats and woes of love, was popularized by Isaac Hayes and further developed by Barry White and Millie Jackson. The funk-style rap, introduced by George Clinton and his group Parliament, consisted of rappin' monologues on topics about partying. Unlike the music of the political poets, the love and funk-style raps were not in rhyme but rather loosely chanted over a repetitive instrumental accompaniment. These artists nonetheless laid the foundation for a type of musical poetry begun primarily by African-American youth of the Bronx called rap music: a musical form that makes use of rhyme, rhythmic speech, and street vernacular, recited or loosely chanted over a musical soundtrack.

There are certain factors that gave rise to rap music. With the overcommercialization of popular dance forms such as 1970s disco, geopolitics in the Bronx, and ongoing club gang violence particular to New York City, black and Latino youth left the indoor scene and returned to neighborhood city parks, where they created outdoor discotheques, featuring a disc jockey (DJ) and an emcee (MC). These circumstances are instrumental to the development of rap music, which is marked by four distinct phases: the mobile DJ (c. 1972–1978); the rhyming MC and the emergence of the rap music genre (1976–1978); the early commercial years of rap music (1979–1985); and the explosion of rap in the musical mainstream (1986–present).

During the first phase, an itinerant DJ, the mobile DJ, provided music performed in neighborhood city parks. Mobile DJs were evaluated by the type of music they played as well as by the size of their sound systems. Similar to radio jockeys, mobile DJs occasionally spoke to their audiences in raps while simultaneously dovetailing one record after the other, a feat facilitated by two turntables. They were well known in their own boroughs and were supported by local followers. Popular jockeys included Pete "DJ" Jones of the Bronx and Grandmaster Flowers and Maboya of Brooklyn. The most innovative of mobile DJs, whose mixing technique immensely influenced the future sound direction and production of rap music, was Jamaican-born Clive Campbell, known as Kool "DJ" Herc. He tailored his disc-jockeying style after the dub music jockeys of Jamaica, such as Osbourne "King Tubby" Ruddock, by mixing collages of musical fragments, referred to

Rap star Snoop Dogg. *Among the best known of the G-Funk or "gangsta rap" artists, Snoop Dogg made his solo debut in 1993 with his* Doggy Style *album for Death Row Records, which sold 800,000 copies in its first week of release and helped to popularize the gangsta sub-style.* SCOTT GRIES/GETTY IMAGES

as "break-beats" or "beats" from various recordings in order to create an entire new soundtrack.

Herc's contemporaries included Grandmaster Flash, Grand Wizard Theodore, and Afrika Bambaataa. Flash extended the Jamaican DJ-ing style with a mixing technique called backspinning (rotating one record counterclockwise to the desired beat, then rotating the second record counterclockwise to the same location, thus creating an echo effect) and "phasing" (repeating a word or phrase in a rhythmic fashion on one turntable during or in between another recording). Grand Wizard Theodore popularized another mixing technique called "scratching" (moving a record back and forth in a rhythmic manner while the tone arm's needle remains in the groove of the record, producing a scratching sound). Bambaataa, on the other hand, perfected Herc's style of mixing by incorporating diverse beats ranging from soul, funk, and disco to commercial jingle and television themes. But, more importantly, he is credited with starting a nonviolent organization called the Zulu Nation—a youth organization composed of local inner-city break-dancers, graffiti artists, DJs, and

MCs—which laid the foundation for a youth arts mass movement that came to be known as hip-hop. Hip-hop not only encompassed street art forms, it also denoted an attitude rendered in the form of dress, gestures, and language associated with street culture.

The second phase of rap music began around the mid-1970s. Since mixing records had become an art in itself, some DJs felt the need for an MC. For example, with the hiring of MCs Clark Kent and Coke La Rock, Kool "DJ" Herc became the Herculords. At many of his performances, Bambaataa was also accompanied by three MCs, Cowboy (not to be mistaken with Cowboy of the Furious Five), Mr. Biggs, and Queen Kenya. Other noted MCs during this phase were DJ Hollywood, Sweet G, Busy Bee, Kurtis Blow, Grandmaster Caz, and Lovebug Starski (the latter credited with the term "hip-hop"). MCs talked intermittently, using phrases like "Get up," and "Jam to the beat," and recited rhyming couplets to motivate the audience to dance while the DJ mixed records. However, it was Grandmaster Flash's MCs, the Furious Five (Melle Mel, Cowboy, Raheim, Kid Creole, Mr. Ness), who set the precedent for rappin' in rhythm to music through a concept called "trading phrases"—the exchange of rhyming couplets or phrases between MCs in a percussive, witty fashion, and in synchrony with the DJ's music—as best illustrated by their hit "Freedom" (1980).

During rap's third phase, the early commercial years from 1979 to 1985, independent record companies like Winley, Enjoy, and Sugar Hill Records initially recorded rap music. Of the three, Sugar Hill Records, cofounded by Sylvia and Joe Robinson, succeeded in becoming the first international rap record company, producing such artists and groups as Sequence, Spoonie G., Lady B., Grandmaster Flash and the Furious Five, and Sugarhill Gang (best known for recording the first commercial rap song "Rapper's Delight"). By 1982 Afrika Bambaataa pioneered the "electro-funk" concept with rap—the fusing of "techno-pop" or synthesized computerized sounds with funk as heard in "Planet Rock" recorded by his group, Soul Sonic Force. Bambaataa's electro-funk concept ushered in more experimental ventures with rap through the art of sampling, the digital reproduction of prerecorded sounds—musical or vocal—in whole or fragmentary units anywhere throughout an entire soundtrack.

Bambaataa's musical innovation also provided the transition from the early commercial sound of rap, known as the "old school," to the "new school" rap. The former refers to earlier innovators and performers of rap music—for example, Kool Moe Dee, Melle Mel, Fat Boys, and Whodini.

The "new school" performers are basically protégés of the pioneers, who comprise those of the fourth phase. In the fourth phase (1986 to the present), rap music gained access to the musical mainstream. Prior to the mid-1980s, this genre received minimal radio airplay outside urban areas. Contributing to its ascension into the mainstream is Run-D.M.C. and their fusion of rap music with rock as popularized by "Rock Box" (1984), the first rap song aired on the syndicated rock video station MTV, followed by the trio's rendition of Aerosmith's "Walk This Way" (1986). Also contributing to Run-D.M.C.'s success was the vision of its then management, Rush Productions, founded by Russell Simmons, rap's first "b-boy" mogul. Simmons and his business partner, Rick Rubin, cofounded Def Jam Records. Their initial roster of artists consisted of LL Cool J, the Beastie Boys, and Public Enemy.

During the mid-1980s, rap's musical production shifted from manual mixing (hands-on-the-turntable) by DJs to digitally produced tracks facilitated by drum machines, samplers, and computers. Among groups who worked with production units was black nationalist act Public Enemy. The Bomb Squad, masterminded by Hank Shocklee, produced Public Enemy's musical tracks, most notably with sampled sounds from James Brown's music and 1970s funk to black nationalists' speech excerpts. Furthermore, the use of sampling, funk-style drum rhythms with heavy bass drum (kick), a boisterous-aggressive vocal style of delivery, and/or moderate to excessive application of expletives and rhymes contributed to rap music's hard edge, a street-style aesthetic called "keepin' it real."

Other factors that contributed to the broadened appeal of rap in the mainstream during the mid-1980s included the distribution of independent rap music recordings by major record labels and the rise of female MCs (e.g., Roxanne Shanté, Salt N Pepa, MC Lyte, Queen Latifah), and the diversified sound of rap: social conscious rap (e.g., Poor Righteous Teachers, X-Clan); party rap (e.g., Kid 'N' Play, De La Soul, Big Daddy Kane, Biz Markie, DJ Jazz Jeff and the Fresh Prince); a cross between party and hardcore (e.g., Eric B & Rakim, Schoolly D, Heavy D, EPMD).

Because of the entertainment industry's use of rap to advertise fashion and other products, rap artists forayed into acting from television to the silver screen. Some of these early film classics are *Wild Style* (1983), *Breakin'* and *Breakin' 2* (1984), and *Krush Groove* (1985).

The late 1980s and the early 1990s marked more stylistic shifts in rap. For example, rap fused with other styles like rhythm and blues, dubbed "new jack swing," as well as jazz, as evident with such acts as A Tribe Called Quest, Gang Starr, Digable Planets, and Us3. Also, this shift expanded to include artists from California, who introduced a heavy bass sound of rap with a laid-back feel.

Rap singer Missy Elliott. MATTHEW PEYTON/GETTY IMAGES

Commercially dubbed G-funk or "gangsta rap," the West Coast sound is driven by funk music and lyrical themes about harsh life in the ghetto, gangbanging, and police repression. Pioneers of the West Coast rap scene include Toddy Tee, Ice-T, and NWA, formed by Eazy-E along with Dr. Dre, Ice Cube, MC Ren, and DJ Yella. However, it is Dr. Dre who is credited with establishing a West Coast signature sound identified by the sampled sounds of Parliament and the Funkadelics. In 1992 Dr. Dre left NWA and joined forces with ex-college football player and bodyguard Marion "Suge" Knight to form Death Row Records. Both Knight, known for his shrewd yet brutal tactics, and Dr. Dre, respected for his music production skills, made Death Row a major force of the gangsta rap substyle. Death Row recording artists included Dr. Dre (*Chronic,* 1992), Snoop Doggy Dogg, alternately known as Snoop Dogg (*Doggystyle,* 1993), and Tupac Shakur or 2Pac (*All Eyez on Me,* 1996). The latter was considered one of the label's most visionary and prolific artists who also had a blossoming but short-lived acting career owing to his murder in 1996. Other West Coast artists who emerged on the scene are Digital Underground, MC Hammer, Paris, Too $hort of Oakland, and Sir-Mix-A-Lot of Seattle.

Gangsta rap was further exploited by the Geto Boys of Houston and the sexually explicit lyrics of 2 Live Crew of Miami, whose first album, *As Nasty as They Wanna Be,* became rap's first censorship court case sensation.

By 1994 rap music embraced an MC from Brooklyn, Biggie Smalls or the Notorious B.I.G. of the Bad Boy Entertainment label. Sean "Puffy" Combs, also known as "Puff Daddy" or "P. Diddy," founded Bad Boy in 1994 at a time when Death Row was at its commercial peak. Although Smalls employed graphic lyrics, he also created radio-friendly rhymes about urban romance, complemented by Combs's soul-pop musical productions with heavy bass. Among these songs were "Big Poppa" and "One More Chance" from *Ready to Die* (1994) and "Hypnotize" and "Mo Money Mo Problems" from *Life After Death* (1997), released posthumously. Small's success was joined by other East Coast MCs: Jay-Z, Junior M.A.F.I.A. with Lil' Kim, Nas, Terror Squad, Wu-Tang Clan, the Fugees, and Busta Rhymes, to name a few. Despite commercial success, East and West coast rappers eventually succumbed to unhealthy rivalry resulting in the unsolved murders of 2Pac and Biggie Smalls nearly six months apart. Nonetheless, rap artists managed to ameliorate coastal rivalries by promoting themes of unity via music projects.

While gangsta rap undoubtedly impacted rap's landscape, a "dirtier" sound emerged from Atlanta and New Orleans, commonly referred to as "the Dirty South." Sometimes called "crunk," the Dirty South style is distinguished by its voluminous bass, sung refrains, and singsongy execution with a noticeable southern drawl. A pioneer of "The Dirty South" is Master P of New Orleans, who is not only an MC but also a successful entrepreneur and founder of No Limit Records. Similar to Russell Simmons, Sean Combs, and Jay-Z, who own record labels and clothing lines (e.g., Phat Farm/Def Jam Rec., Sean John/Bad Boy Ent., Roca Wear/Roc-a-Fella Rec, respectively), Master P has ventured into filmmaking and sports management. Artists affiliated with his label are Tru, consisting of his brothers Silkk the Shocker and C-Murder, his son Lil Romeo, and the production team Beats by the Pound. What distinguishes a New Orleans hip-hop sound from other southern rap styles are ticking snare drum beats and a booming bass style called "bounce." Other prominent rap acts of New Orleans include Juvenile and members of The Hot Boys (Lil' Wyne, B.G., and Turk) with producer Mannie Fresh of Cash Money Records.

Atlanta established its place in rap during the early 1990s with acts like Da Brat (of Chicago), Kriss Kross, rap/rhythm-and-blues trio TLC, and the nation-conscious group Arrested Development. However, its "Dirty South" concept, masterminded by Rico Wade and the production crew Organized Noize, laid the foundation for its unique sound. Atlanta-based acts (collectively known as ATLiens) like OutKast, the Goodie MOb, and Ludacris have moved successfully into the twenty-first century, joined by producer Lil Jon and his affiliates.

While the 1990s witnessed a proliferation of artists from various areas—Nelly and the St. Lunatics of St. Louis, Three 6 Mafia of Memphis, Bone-Thugs-N-Harmony of Cleveland, Missy Elliott and Timbaland of Portsmouth—rap expanded its roster to include nonblack acts. Once existing in the shadows of black artists, white rap acts—the Beastie Boys, Third Bass, and House of Pain—crossed over into wider acceptance in the 1990s. Following his bitter departure from Death Row Records, Dr. Dre launched his own label, Aftermath. Within two years, he added Eminem, a white MC from Detroit, whose successful debut album, *The Slim Shady LP* (1999), and sophomore follow-up, *The Marshal Mathers LP* (2000), became the first all-rap album to be nominated by the Grammy Awards under the "Best Album of the Year" category.

Rap music flourishes in the mainstream via television, film, commercials, and fashion, thus making it a vital component of youth culture, nationally and internationally. Because rap artists bring to their performances all that hip-hop embodies from street fashions, attitude, gesture, and language, hip-hop is used interchangeably with rap and as a marketing term to denote rap music. Although rap music continues to be exploited in the mainstream by the entertainment industry and is subjected to much criticism by the media, other arenas such as underground venues—local clubs and neighborhood hangouts—remain as vital sites for rap's creative sustenance.

See also Hip-Hop; Music in the United States; Run-D.M.C.

Bibliography

Forman, Murray. *The 'Hood Comes First: Race, Space, and Place in Rap and Hip-Hop*. Midddletown, Conn.: Wesleyan University Press, 2002.

Keyes, Cheryl L. *Rap Music and Street Consciousness*. Urbana: University of Illinois Press, 2002.

Krims, Adam. *Rap Music and the Poetics of Identity*. New York: Cambridge University Press, 2000.

Mitchell, Tony, ed. *Global Noise: Rap and Hip-Hop Outside the USA*. Middletown, Conn.: Wesleyan University Press, 2001.

Pinn, Anthony B, ed. *Noise and Spirit: The Religious and Spiritual Sensibilities of Rap Music*. New York: New York University, 2003.

Pough, Gwendolyn D. *Check It While I Wreck It: Black Womanhood, Hip-Hop Culture, and the Public Sphere*. Boston: Northeastern University Press, 2004.

Schloss, Joseph G. *Making Beats: The Art of Sampled-Based Hip-Hop*. Middletown, Conn.: Wesleyan University Press, 2004.

Toop, David. *Rap Attack #3. African Rap to Global Hip Hop*. 1984. Reprint, London: Serpent's Tail, 2000.

CHERYL L. KEYES (1996)
Updated by author 2005

Rapier, James Thomas

November 13, 1837
May 31, 1883

The son of a prosperous free barber in Florence, Alabama, congressman, farmer, and teacher James Rapier received much of his early formal education in Nashville, Tennessee, where his grandmother lived. Deciding that he needed further education, in 1856 Rapier traveled to Buxton, Canada West (now Ontario), a utopian community of African Americans where his father owned property, and began studying again. His proficiency made his tutors encourage him to go on for further study at a teacher's training school in Toronto. He stayed in the city for three years.

As the Civil War raged in the United States, Rapier felt a desire to return and aid in the reconstruction process. After returning to Tennessee in 1863 and participating in several black conventions in Nashville, he became disillusioned when the 1865–1866 Tennessee constitution denied suffrage to African Americans. Borrowing money to purchase some cotton land, he moved to Seven Mile Island in the Tennessee River in Alabama.

Rapier quickly rose in local and state estimation as an intelligent, educated, and reasonable African-American Republican. Despite heated debate about the role of African Americans in the Alabama Republican Party, he participated in party conventions and was one of the ninety-six delegates to draft the Alabama constitution. While he was part of a moderate group that favored less strict disfranchisement provisions and more strict equality statutes, the gains of Rapier and other black delegates were few. They defeated proposals to legalize segregation, but they were also unable to explicitly make discrimination illegal.

As a result of his visible campaigning, Rapier became a target of racist hate across the state. After Rapier and several associates were accused of burning a girl's school, they were hunted by a lynch mob. Rapier escaped, leaving behind his plantation and his belongings; three other men were hanged without legal proceedings. Shortly thereafter he was completely exonerated by a local magistrate.

Despite the amount of hostile opposition to blacks participating in the electoral process, Rapier, an eloquent orator, won a seat in Congress in 1872 by a plurality of almost 3,200 votes, including significant support from whites. He made several speeches during his first term on the need for Reconstruction to go further in guaranteeing civil rights, a federally controlled universal education system, and land redistribution to freedmen.

While the 1874 election initially ended with a Democratic victor, Rapier successfully challenged the result and was seated for his second consecutive term. Again, he spoke militantly about civil rights and segregation. In 1876, after gerrymandering by the Alabama legislature, only one predominantly black district remained in Alabama. Both Rapier and Congressman Jeremiah Haralson decided to run for the seat. When Haralson failed to secure the Republican nomination in 1875, he pledged to run as an independent candidate. The two black candidates split the vote and a white Democrat was elected.

Retiring from politics, Rapier settled down to run his farm. Appointed to the lucrative patronage post of Collector of Internal Revenue for the Second Alabama District (1877–1883), Rapier continued to have influence in Republican circles although he was never again a candidate for office. As a result of his lack of faith in Alabama's government, he became an ardent emigrationist, urging African Americans to move to Kansas or to the West to escape racism and discrimination. His health began to decline, and he died of tuberculosis in Alabama in 1883.

See also Canada, Blacks in; Politics in the United States

Bibliography

Christopher, Maurine. *Black Americans in Congress.* New York: Crowell, 1976.

Foner, Eric. *Freedom's Lawmakers: A Directory of Black Officeholders during Reconstruction.* New York: Oxford University Press, 1993.

McFarlin, Annjennette Sophie. *Black Congressional Reconstruction Orators and their Orations, 1869–1879.* Metuchen, N.J.: Scarecrow Press, 1976, pp. 257–279.

Schweninger, Loren. *James T. Rapier and Reconstruction.* Chicago: University of Chicago Press, 1978.

ALANA J. ERICKSON (1996)

Rastafarianism

On November 2, 1930, Ras Tafari Makonnen (1892–1975) was crowned emperor of Ethiopia, an event that received wide international attention. Makonnen assumed as his imperial name and titles Haile Selassie I, King of Kings, Lord of Lords, Conquering Lion of the Tribe of Judah, Elect of God, and Light of the World. In what was one of the first countries to adopt Christianity, the Makonnens had long before claimed descent from the biblical Judaic king, Solomon, and Candace, the queen of Sheba. The story of Candace's visit to the famous king, of his seduction and her return home with his child Menelik, of Menelik's visit to his father and his rescue of the ark of the covenant, which he brought to Ethiopia for safekeeping, is set out in the ancient text, *Kebra Nagast.*

In Jamaica, a few followers of Marcus Garvey (1887–1940) interpreted Ras Tafari's coronation as the fulfillment of two prophecies, one by Garvey that the redemption of black people was at hand, and the other by the Old Testament prophet Isaiah that the messiah would bear the title King of Kings, Lord of Lords, Conquering Lion of the Tribe of Judah. The person generally credited with being the first to go public with this insight was Leonard Howell (Lee, 1999), but others followed—including Joseph Hibbert, Archibald Dunkley, and Robert Hinds. They all took to the street corners of the capital, Kingston, with the message: Black people have a king; their king is black; he is the messiah, the son sent by God to set free his captive people.

The message found fertile ground among the thousands of migrants fleeing rural poverty. By August 1, 1934, it had taken definite shape: followers of Howell staged a march demanding to be repatriated to Africa. The date marked the one hundredth anniversary of the end of slavery in Jamaica.

Background

The emergence of the Rastafari needs to be understood in the context of a society with a long history of deep racial divisions based on a brutally prosecuted enslavement of Africans by the British, an equally long history of some of the fiercest resistance seen in the Americas, and the culture-building imperative of the Africans centered around a new religious cosmology.

Captured in 1655 from the Spanish, Jamaica became one of Britain's most lucrative sugar-producing colonies based on African slave labor. Until the abolition of the slave trade in 1807, the steady influx of Africans guaranteed huge fortunes for the planter class, even as it kept memories of "Guinea" alive among the black population.

There evolved on each estate a social structure in which the divisions between those who exploited labor and those whose labor was exploited were racialized. The whites, notwithstanding differences between planters, professionals, and artisans, soon came to regard themselves as members of the ruling elite by virtue of their race. The blacks, notwithstanding differences among themselves between the newcomers, or "salt-water Negroes," and those born in Jamaica, or Creoles, soon came to regard themselves as members of an oppressed class by virtue of their race—the field slaves. And wedged in between these two groups was a new group, the people of mixed racial origins, who attended to the personal needs of the whites in the great house—the house slaves, who regarded themselves as better than the field slaves. An ideology based on skin color emerged: white was associated with power, beauty, enlightenment, virtue, privilege, and wealth; black was aligned with poverty, ignorance, ugliness, vice, and evil. These divisions, formed as early as the seventeenth century, were still current in the twentieth century, inducing theories of cultural pluralism based on an ethnicity of color (Smith 1965).

Slavery met stiff, multiform resistance, ranging from suicide to poison, from sabotage to go-slows, from *marronage* to uprising. By the turn of the eighteenth century, the Maroons had become a viable community able to defend their freedom.

Two extensive revolts occurred, the first in 1760 engulfing two-thirds of the country. The second revolt, from 1831 to 1832, was led by Samuel Sharpe and is regarded as hastening the abolition of slavery in 1834. Their widespread nature was a function of the solidarity brought about by the emergence of a new religion called Myal, which played the same role in Jamaica as vodou was to play a few decades later among the Haitian slaves. Belief in a supreme deity, possession by spiritual powers, and blood sacrifice were central to Myal, one of whose other characteristics was its ability to absorb new influences. When, following the American Revolution of 1776, several American planters and their Christian slaves fled to Jamaica and began proselytizing, Myalists incorporated such powerful Christian figures as Jesus, John the Baptist, the Holy Spirit, and Isaiah, along with a new instrument, the Bible. The Bible gave them a different vision of themselves. They identified themselves in its mention of Ethiopia (in, for example, *Psalms* 68:31 and 87:4), appropriating its myths of exile, exodus, and redemption as their own. Myal thus grew into the Native Baptist movement, and later in the 1860s into Revival. Jamaican followers of Marcus Garvey were steeped in the Revival cosmology, according to which the children of Israel would soon be delivered into the "promised land." That deliverance, they believed, began with the crowning of the Lion of Judah.

Selassie Addresses the United Nations

On October 6, 1963, Haile Selassie addressed the United Nations with praise, criticism, and deep sincerity. He proclaimed, "It is the sacred duty of this Organization to ensure that the dream of equality is finally realized for all men to whom it is still denied, to guarantee that exploitation is not reincarnated in other forms in places whence it has already been banished."

Selassie was instrumental in founding the United Nations, viewing it as an institution that would provide the best hope for the peaceful survival of humankind, replace inhumane self-interest with tolerance and goodwill, and protect the small and weak against those with the most power. He hoped that this institution would devise *peaceful* methods and procedures to resolve conflicts between nations. Selassie, however, was not a pacifist and acknowledged the use of force as often being necessary to prevent injustice and human suffering. He praised the United Nations for being an effective defense against violations of human rights and for daring to take action in Palestine, Korea, Suez, and Congo. The guaranteeing of basic human freedoms, he noted in the address, require the courage to speak and act—and if necessary, suffer and die—for truth and justice.

Beards and Dreadlocks

Rastafari tenets have been a function of its interaction and response to society. Initially, the main focus of its new prophets was preaching allegiance to the "King of Kings," a black man, and the reincarnation of the messiah. This often brought Rastafarians into confrontation with the colonial state, especially in the tense years leading up to World War II, when disloyalty to the British Crown was a serious offense. In the postwar years, when Jamaicans began to migrate to the United Kingdom, repatriation, an idea present from the beginning, came to the fore. Its difference from Garvey's back-to-Africa movement lay in the

Rastafari belief that repatriation was to be a divine act instead of a movement executed by humans. By then a clear identity had been established in the beards worn by the men and the uniforms embroidered in the colors of the Ethiopian flag—red, gold, and green. In addition, a younger generation had joined the movement. Their impatience and aggression led to a series of reforms that further transformed the outlook of the entire Rastafari movement.

First, the younger generation instituted a clear break with Revival, out of which the early founders had come, by denouncing all forms of possession and eliminating certain ritual practices, such as the use of candles to signal the presence of the powers. Younger Rastafari also introduced several far-reaching innovations: the ritualization of "Reasoning," and with it the elevation of ganja *(cannabis)* smoking to sacramental status; the ritual dance known as the *nyabinghi* (pronounced *nai-ya-bing-gi*, with a hard *g;* meaning "death to white and black oppressors"); the wearing of dreadlocks; the ritualization of the patriarchy; the use of dread talk; and a naturalistic style of living.

The Reasoning ritual brought Rastafari into a circle of discussion in which national and international events were interpreted within the framework of the Bible and the words of Haile Selassie. Insights were thereby gained, and thoughts and attitudes were shaped. Facilitating the process was the ritual partaking of the "chalice," or ganja-stuffed chillum pipe. The use of ganja, a banned substance, drew the attention of the police, out of whose repressive actions the young Rastafari developed the notion of "Babylon," the powerful captor of the children of Israel, whose downfall was already prophesied. They enacted this in the *nyabinghi* on the occasions of Haile Selassie's coronation; the Ethiopian Christmas (January 7); the birthday of Marcus Garvey, who was revered for his role as John the Baptist announcing the coming of the messiah (August 17); and, since 1966, Selassie's visit to Jamaica (April 21).

Out of the Reasoning also came the dreadlocks, a hairstyle that identified the Rastafari with Kenyan freedom fighters known as the Mau-Mau. Dreadlocks inspired dread and signaled their rejection of a society in which the characteristics of African phenotype—color, nose, lips, hair—were not only denigrated but subject to chemical as well as physical attempts to suppress them. Dreadlocks symbolized a radical acceptance of the racial self and thereby became a practical criticism of white racism.

Dread Talk

Another important innovation was dread talk: homonyms, inversions, and other wordplay elevated to the level of philosophy. The central word is *I*, the singular first-person pronoun. The power of *I* transforms the objectified and possessive self (you, me, yours, mine) into a singular subject of unity or *I*nity—*I an' I*; breathes new life into others—*I*ncient, *I*lalu, for*I*ver, *I*ly (holy), *I*ses (praises); and uncovers new meaning—the *I* (eye) of sight and of position ('igh). Other words are restored to their true meaning hidden by the English captors: *over*stand, *down*pressor.

Such innovations, which quickly became institutionalized throughout the movement, were accompanied by a radicalization of patriarchal relations. Women were subject to the Levite strictures of the Old Testament concerning menstrual flow and relegated to the periphery of Reasoning circles, while their domestic subordination found expression in the generic word "daughter," or *I*aata. Their status as queens and empresses within the movement derived from their spouses, their kings.

Reggae and Internationalization

During the 1960s and 1970s, Rastafari embraced the youths alienated by the unfulfilled hopes of national independence in 1962. Rastafari gave them its philosophy of an integrated black self and a vision of an end to the historic injustice done to the children of Africa. The movement received in return their creative energy and passion. The young people became the new missionaries, and their medium was reggae music. They spread both music and vision around the world. Since the 1970s Rastafari groups may be found throughout the rest of the Caribbean, including Cuba, Brazil, and in other countries of Latin America, West Africa, South Africa, Europe, North America, New Zealand, and Japan.

The global spread of the movement has not come about without the development of differences in beliefs, particularly those concerning the divinity or merely prophetic character of Haile Selassie. But such divergence is nothing new, since throughout Rastafari history variations in beliefs and practices have been marked. The Bobo, a Rastafari group that worships on the Sabbath, believe in a divine trinity: Haile Selassie the Father; their founder, Immanuel, the Son; and Marcus Garvey the Holy Spirit. The Twelve Tribes of Israel, on the other hand, believe in Jesus Christ, "who has revealed himself in the personality of His Imperial Majesty, Emperor Haile Selassie *I*." The Nyabinghi, who believe only in Jah, the almighty, regard such differences as an example of what Jesus (which they pronounce *Jess-us*) meant when he said that "in my father's house are many mansions." The fact, then, that Italian Rastafari believe that Haile Selassie is God, while some Africans do not, regarding him instead as a great man, or that those in New Zealand do not uphold repatriation to Africa, does not attenuate the power of Rastafari identity, which is constructed on the basis of a menu of beliefs and practices characterized by a radical opposition to all forms of oppression.

The women's movement of the 1970s and 1980s also had an impact on the Rastafari. Recognition is now given to the matriarchs in the Nyabinghi mansion, who may speak on behalf of the house and participate in the ritual Reasoning. This change has been effected by an internal struggle by Rastafari women.

Livity

A common thread running through all the movement's various groups is the naturalistic style of living called *livity*. Livity refers to a life in harmony with nature as created by God and in avoidance of manmade intrusions into that order. Thus, Rastafari favor a diet of fresh fruits, vegetables, legumes, and nuts, and avoid processed and packaged foods and bottled juices. A salt taboo is part of the livity, as are such ritual observances as the wearing of dreadlocks and the maintenance of good, principled relations with one another. As a way of living, livity is intended as a practical criticism of the hubris of Western, Babylonian civilization, which puts humans above God.

Future

Founded in the 1930s, Rastafari has taken its current shape from developments of the 1950s, which saw the emergence of dreadlocks. Rastafari continues its growth in the twenty-first century in response to the opportunities offered by the communications revolution and other aspects of globalization.

See also Garvey, Marcus; Myal; Revivalism

Bibliography

Chevannes, Barry. *Rastafari: Roots and Ideology*. Syracuse, N.Y.: Syracuse University Press, 1994.

Chevannes, Barry, ed. *Rastafari and Other African-Caribbean Worldviews*. New Brunswick, N.J.: Rutgers University Press, 1998.

Hausman, Gerald, ed. *The Kebra Nagast: The Lost Bible of Rastafarian Wisdom and Faith from Ethiopia and Jamaica*. New York: St. Martin's Press, 1997.

Lee, Hélène. *Le premier rasta*. Paris: Flammarion, 1999. Translated by Lily Davis and Hélène Lee as *The First Rasta: Leonard Howell and the Rise of Rastafarianism*. Chicago: Lawrence Hill, 2003.

Smith, Michael G. *The Plural Society in the British West Indies*. Berkeley: University of California Press, 1965.

BARRY CHEVANNES (2005)

Rebouças, André

January 13, 1838
May 9, 1898

André Rebouças, a pivotal figure in Brazil's abolitionist movement and a scientist committed to the project of modernity during the last decades of the Brazilian empire, was born in Cachoeira, Bahia, in 1838. A child during the decline of Bahia's sugar slave society, a witness to the final decree that abolished slavery in 1888, and a self-imposed exile after the fall of the Brazilian monarchy, Rebouças lived during a transitional era that he himself recognized in his autobiography. Rebouças was born into an educated, middle-class mulatto family, which had ascended socially owing to the support of white patrons. This family background informed his subjectivity. Many of his biographers have described him as a self-made man and a staunch antitraditionalist, albeit a monarchist, in the oligarchic political culture of the late nineteenth century.

In 1846 Rebouças and his family moved to Rio de Janeiro, an event that transformed his educational, professional, and political development. The capital city and cultural center of the Brazilian empire, Rio de Janeiro had, since the transfer of the Portuguese court to Brazil in 1808, a botanical garden, an imperial library and museum, and a variety of technical schools and universities. Rebouças studied engineering in military school and in the nearby city of Petrópolis, where he met Emperor Dom Pedro II, whom he greatly admired and with whom he developed a long-lasting friendship. Devoted to the project of modernity, as was the enlightened Dom Pedro II, Rebouças studied engineering in France and in England, but was denied further study abroad due to his skin color, and returned to a Brazil that had expansionist ideals. The outbreak of the Paraguayan War in 1864 saw the conscription of many free blacks and mulattoes, as well as slaves who were promised their freedom once the war ended. Rebouças was a military engineer during the war and with his brother directed the infrastructure of several forts around the Brazil-Paraguay border. This experience resulted in a book on the Paraguayan War authored by Rebouças.

On his return, Rebouças coordinated a variety of public works related to water management and distribution in the states of Rio de Janeiro, Pernambuco, Bahia, and Maranhão. Being a hygienist, Rebouças was highly committed to the reformation of urban infrastructure, and his multiple accomplishments in this area resulted in the naming of the "Rebouças Tunnel" in Rio de Janeiro. In addition to his dedication to urban planning, he was a student of agricultural systems. He wrote several works on post-abolition land tenure and agriculture, and elaborated a legislative project that was intended to facilitate the transition from slavery to free labor. He believed education was the key instrument for the integration of freedpeople into society, and advocated the transformation of ex-slaves into yeoman farmers. During this period, he was a professor at Rio de Janeiro's Polytechnic School, where he founded an abolitionist center and published several abolitionist articles.

As the abolitionist movement gained momentum in the 1870s and 1880s, Rebouças became a close friend of the renowned abolitionists Joaquim Nabuco and Alfredo Taunay. In his memoirs, Nabuco dedicates pages to Rebouças, whom he described as an engineer, mathematician, astronomer, botanist, geologist, industrialist, moralist, hygienist, and philanthropist. Rebouças's political orientations were as diverse as his professional development; he traveled through a political spectrum of "isms," from Yankeeism to Jacobinism to purist individualism. In the 1870s he was a great admirer of U.S. post-Emancipation society, and particularly what he saw as the success of the reconstruction and modernization of the U.S. South. However, his travel experience to the United States in 1873 is likely to have changed this perception; he was relegated to inferior hotels, denied service in restaurants, and not allowed to attend a performance at the Grand Opera House in New York City. Rebouças believed Brazil would follow a different path, transforming into a multiracial and equal society after abolition.

The Golden Law abolished slavery a year before the monarchy was deposed by a military coup d'état in 1889. Rebouças followed the imperial family into exile, thinking the monarchy would be restored, but this dream, as well as his return to Brazil, was never realized. While in exile, Rebouças traveled to France, West Africa, and Madeira. In Africa, he returned to his activities as a reformer and engineer, but disillusionment with increasing racism and inequality, as well as the deterioration of his financial situation, changed his outlook of the future. At the age of sixty he committed suicide in Madeira; patriotic histories suggest that he "slipped" off a cliff.

See also Emancipation in Latin America and the Caribbean; Gama, Luiz

Bibliography

De Carvalho, Maria Alice Rezende. *O quinto século: André Rebouças e a construção do Brasil.* Rio de Janeiro, Brazil: Editora Revan, 1998.

Dos Santos, José Rufino, ed. *Negro brasileiro negro.* Revista do Patrimonio Historico e Artistico Nacional, Num 25 (1997).

Dos Santos, Sydney M. G. *André Rebouças e seu tempo.* Rio de Janeiro, Brazil: Ed. Vozes, 1985.

Spitzer, Leo. *Lives in Between: Assimilation and Marginality in Austria, Brazil, and West Africa, 1780–1945.* New York: Cambridge University Press, 1989.

PATRICIA ACERBI (2005)

Rebouças, Antônio Pereira

August 10, 1798
March 28, 1880

Antônio Pereira Rebouças, a free-born Brazilian mulatto, rose to be a prominent lawyer, jurist, and member of Parliament. He was born in the province of Bahia, the legitimate son of a Portuguese tailor and a mulatta ex-slave. With only an elementary formal education, he taught himself Greek, Latin, and French, and he read voraciously. A man of unflagging energy, Rebouças worked as a legal clerk and eventually learned so much law that his employer recommended he be allowed to take the bar exam, which he easily passed.

When Brazil's political fate lay in the balance in 1822–1823, with the Portuguese army in the coastal city of Salvador hoping to reassert colonial rule over the country, Rebouças astutely sided with the slave-owning planter elite who were plotting independence, and not with Portuguese officials, some of whom hinted that freedom might be offered to those slaves who supported them. Rebouças was named member and secretary of the planter-led insurgent council, and, when the Portuguese were finally driven out, he was rewarded with the prestigious Imperial Order of the Southern Cross and named secretary, similar to a chief-of-staff position, to the president of the neighboring province of Sergipe, who directly represented the newly enthroned Brazilian emperor.

Prominent local politicians, however, were quick to protest the appointment of a mulatto to this post, and they invented the story that Rebouças fomented unrest among slaves and free people of color, an allegation that, although easily disproven in the ensuing investigation, cost him his job. He went on to serve in both the provincial and national legislatures and became a sought-after lawyer at the national capital, where his legal opinions carried much weight. His library, with books in many languages, was one of the largest in the city, containing not only legal texts but many plays and novels.

In his legal writings and parliamentary speeches, Rebouças displayed a deep commitment to the principle that individual rights enshrined in the Brazilian Constitution should be enjoyed by all citizens equally, regardless of their color. He turned his back, however, on efforts to assert the collective rights of blacks and opposed all revolutions. When, in 1837, radicals in Salvador expressed their grievances by declaring the independence of the province, he once again joined the white planters of the interior who opposed the insurgents, even though free blacks and mulattoes of the city made up the bulk of the revolting forces. Over a thousand of them were killed after the defeat of the movement, but there is no record that Rebouças regretted his choice or saw the black and mulatto victims of repression as his fellows.

Indeed, Rebouças argued that among the rights of the individual was the right to own property and not have it confiscated by the government, even if such property included slaves. He did, however, urge that the law recognize the right of slaves to purchase their own freedom and thus become citizens who would be the equal of any white before the law. Like others of his class, regardless of their color, he owned several slaves of his own. As Brazilian elite opinion in the late 1840s shifted away from a liberal philosophy and toward a more conservative and hierarchical view of society, Rebouças found himself marginalized and even forgotten. As an old man he reported to his son that over the course of his lifetime he had often suffered racial discrimination but had kept his peace rather than acknowledge the slight.

See also Emancipation in Latin America and the Caribbean; Politics and Politicians in Latin America

Bibliography

Grinberg, Keila. *O fiador dos brasileiros: Cidadania, escravidão e direito civil no tempo de Antônio Pereira Rebouças*. Rio de Janeiro, Brazil: Civilização Brasileira, 2002.

Kraay, Hendrik. "'As Terrifying as Unexpected': The Bahian Sabinada, 1837–1838." *Hispanic American Historical Review* 72, no. 4 (1992): 501–527.

Spitzer, Leo. *Lives in Between: Assimilation and Marginality in Austria, Brazil, West Africa, 1780-1945*. Cambridge, UK: Cambridge University Press, 1989.

RICHARD GRAHAM (2005)

Recording Industry

In the development of sound recording, primarily an enterprise of European Americans, the cultural input of African Americans was initially relegated to the margins. Even "coon" songs, a staple of early commercial recordings dating from minstrelsy, were almost invariably sung by whites until World War I. Notable exceptions included Bert Williams (1867–1922), the great black vaudevillian, and George Washington Johnson (c. 1850–c. 1910), perhaps the first black recording artist, whose hits "The Whistling Coon" and "The Laughing Song" brought him fame and fortune.

The "blues" craze that swept the country in the 1910s was driven by a number of African-American composers, including W. C. Handy (the Father of the Blues) and Arthur Seals, as well as a number of white blues writers. As with coon songs, however, most of these blues compositions were recorded by whites singing in "Negro dialect."

In 1914 the American Society of Composers, Authors, and Publishers (ASCAP) was founded to protect the rights of songwriters. Membership in the society was generally skewed toward writers of pop tunes and semiserious works. Of the society's 170 charter members, only six were black: Harry Burleigh, Will Marion Cook, J. Rosamond Johnson, James Weldon Johnson, Cecil Mack, and Will Tyers. Although other "literate" black writers and composers, such as W. C. Handy and Duke Ellington, were able to gain entrance to ASCAP, the vast majority of "untutored" black artists were excluded from the society and thereby denied the full benefits of copyright protection.

With the advent of recorded jazz in the late 1910s, patterns of racial exclusion skewed public perceptions of African-American music even more. In 1917, when the Victor label decided to take a chance on "jass," the band they chose to record was the all-white Original Dixieland Jazz Band. Though they were heavily influenced by the King Oliver Creole Jazz Band (which included the trumpeter Louis Armstrong), the Oliver ensemble itself did not record until 1923. The first ensemble of color to receive a recording contract was James Reese Europe's Syncopated Society Orchestra, signed by Victor in 1914 to supervise a series of dance records for the white dance team of Vernon and Irene Castle.

An African-American market for African-American records was not "discovered" until 1920, and even then quite by accident. The enterprising black producer and songwriter Perry Bradford convinced the Okeh record company to let him record a black contralto named Mamie Smith. Her recording of Bradford's "Crazy Blues" sold 7,500 copies a week, mostly to black buyers. Ralph Peer, the Okeh recording director who assisted at the sessions, dubbed these records "race records," which remained the designation for black music, by black artists, for a black audience until 1949. Smith's overwhelming success ushered in an era of classic blues recordings by African-American women such as Ida Cox, Chippie Hill, Sarah Martin, Clara Smith, Trixie Smith, Victoria Spivey, Sippie Wallace, and the most famous of all, Bessie Smith, the "Empress of the Blues."

The initial success of the "race market" encouraged the formation of a handful of black-owned independent labels. W. C. Handy and his publishing partner, Harry Pace, started Black Swan Records in 1921. Mayo "Ink" Williams, head of Paramount's race series, founded the Black Patti label in 1927. However, such labels were soon bought up by the major companies or forced out of the industry. With the onset of the Great Depression, the race market was slowly taken over by Okeh, Columbia, and Paramount, and not a single black-owned label survived the 1920s intact.

As the record companies began to test the limits of the race market, they discovered that there was also a considerable demand for country blues, particularly among southern blacks. In 1924, the same year they acquired the Black Swan catalog, Paramount released Papa Charlie Jackson's "Papa's Lawdy Lawdy Blues." This record was followed by releases by Arthur "Blind" Blake and, perhaps the most popular country blues singer of the decade, Blind Lemon Jefferson. Throughout the 1920s and early 1930s, a number of companies, including Okeh, Columbia, and Victor, engaged in extensive "field" recordings. As a result, dozens of country blues artists—among them Furry Lewis, Blind Willie McTell, Mississippi John Hurt, Son House, Charlie Patton, Huddie "Leadbelly" Ledbetter, and Robert Johnson—were brought to wider public attention. The country blues artist who dominated the 1930s was Big Bill Broonzy.

In mainstream music, it was the era of big band jazz. Again, patterns of racial segregation obscured the origins of the music. A number of African-American bands managed to achieve major success, however. Among the best known, Duke Ellington's band became famous through their live broadcasts from the Cotton Club in Harlem, New York. William James "Count" Basie, playing at the Reno Club in Kansas City, injected jazz with a heavy dose of the blues. Both the Ellington and Basie bands recorded for major labels and were among the few African-American ensembles that could be heard on radio.

In the 1940s, tension between radio and music publishers signaled a new era in black popular music. The National Association of Broadcasters (NAB), representing some six hundred radio stations, formed their own performing rights organization, Broadcast Music Incorporated (BMI), in 1939, and they proceeded shortly thereafter to boycott all ASCAP music. The Broadway-Hollywood monopoly on popular music, and its considerable influence in shaping public taste, was challenged publicly for the first time, creating a cultural space for rhythm-and-blues (R&B) artists like Arthur "Big Boy" Crudup, Roy Brown, Ivory Joe Hunter, Fats Domino, and Wynonie Harris.

The success of these artists in the late 1940s speaks to what the critic Nelson George has referred to as "an aesthetic schism between high-brow, more assimilated black styles and working-class, grassroots sounds" (1988, p. 10). Until this time, the most notable African-American acts were the more pop-sounding artists like Nat "King" Cole ("For Sentimental Reasons"), Ella Fitzgerald ("My Happiness"), the Mills Brothers ("Across the Valley from the Alamo"), and the Ink Spots ("The Gypsy"). All of these artists recorded for major labels, which failed to appreciate the appeal of rhythm and blues (R&B) in working-class black communities.

With a much smaller horn section and more pronounced rhythm, Louis Jordan and His Tympani Five, something of a transitional act, anticipated the decline of the big bands and helped to define the instrumentation for the R&B combos that followed. Jordan's material was composed and arranged, but selections like "Saturday Night Fishfry," "Honey Chile," and "Ain't Nobody Here but Us Chickens" evoked blues images not found in most black pop of the day. While Jordan was said to have "jumped the blues," other R&B stars screeched, honked, and shouted. "Suddenly it was as if a great deal of the Euro-American humanist facade Afro-American music had taken on had been washed away by the war" (Jones, 1963, p. 171). The raucous styles of such artists as Wynonie Harris ("Good Rockin' Tonight"), John Lee Hooker ("Boogie Chillen"), saxophonist Big Jay McNeely ("Deacon's Hop"), and pianist Amos Milburn ("Chicken Shack Boogie") all deviated significantly from the sound of mainstream black pop.

Since this music did not readily lend itself to the production styles of the major labels, they decided to ignore the relatively smaller R&B market. This situation made it possible for a large number of independent labels to enter the business. It is estimated that by 1949 over four hundred new labels came into existence. Most important among these were Atlantic in New York City; Savoy in Newark; King in Cincinnati; Chess in Chicago; Peacock in Houston; and Modern, Imperial, and Specialty in Los Angeles. White-owned, except for Don Robey's Peacock label, most of these labels specialized in R&B.

This music found a ready home among independent deejays (or disc jockeys) who often experimented with "specialty" music as an antidote to the trivial popular fare of network radio. Early R&B hits that were popular among both black and white audiences included Fats Domino's "The Fat Man," Jackie Brenston's "Rocket 88," Lloyd Price's "Lawdy Miss Clawdy," and Joe Turner's "Chains of Love," "Sweet Sixteen," and "Honey Hush." All were recorded for independent labels. Pioneer black deejays such as "Jockey" Jack Gibson in Atlanta, "Professor Bop" in Shreveport, and "Sugar Daddy" in Birmingham paved the way for white R&B deejays such as Alan Freed, the self-appointed "Father of Rock and Roll."

With its roots in the Deep South, the music that became rock and roll issued from just about every region in the country. Most of its formative influences, as well as virtually all of its early innovators, were African American: B. B. King ("The Thrill Is Gone"), Muddy Waters ("Got My Mojo Working"), Bo Diddley ("Bo Diddley"), Fats Domino ("Ain't That a Shame," "I'm in Love Again," and "Blueberry Hill"), Ray Charles ("I Got a Woman"), Clyde McPhatter ("A Lover's Question"), Sam Cooke ("You Send Me"), Ruth Brown ("Mama, He Treats Your Daughter Mean"), Laverne Baker ("Tweedle Dee," "Jim Dandy"), Little Richard ("Tutti-Frutti," "Long Tall Sally," "Rip It Up"), Chuck Berry ("Maybellene," "Sweet Sixteen," "School Days," "Johnny B. Goode"), the Orioles ("Crying in the Chapel"), the Crows ("Gee"), the Chords ("Sh-Boom"), and the Penguins ("Earth Angel"). Even with the new name, there was no mistaking where this music came from. As late as 1956, Billboard referred to the music as "a popularized form of rhythm & blues."

Several dozen "rock and roll" songs were successfully "covered" by white artists in the early years of rock and roll, but the vintage rock and roll years were generally good for black musicians. African-American artists made such significant inroads into the pop market that, for a time, Billboard's pop charts and R&B charts were virtually indistinguishable. At the end of the decade the "payola" scandal, which involved offering deejays cash, gifts, or other inducements to air a record, threatened to halt their progress. Deejays became the main target of government hearings that were largely orchestrated by ASCAP with support from the major record companies. The deejays were considered largely responsible for the crossover of black music into the pop market.

Chubby Checker ushered in the 1960s with "The Twist," which remains the only record to reach number one on the pop charts twice, first in 1960 and then again in 1962. It was still listed as the best-selling single of all time well into the 1970s. The twist craze was so powerful that major R&B artists and labels felt compelled to jump on the bandwagon. In 1962 alone, Sam Cooke recorded "Twistin' the Night Away," Gary U.S. Bonds released "Dear Lady Twist" and "Twist, Twist Senora," and the Isley Brothers followed their classic "Shout" with "Twist and Shout." Atlantic Records reissued an album of old Ray Charles material as *Do the Twist with Ray Charles.* Relative unknowns Little Eva and Dee Dee Sharp had hits with two twist spin-offs, "The Loco-Motion" and "Mashed Potato Time," respectively.

During this period, R&B producers emerged as artists in their own right. "Uptown rhythm & blues," to use Charlie Gillett's term, was established in Lieber and Stoller's pioneering work with the Drifters ("There Goes My Baby," "This Magic Moment," "Save the Last Dance for Me") in 1959 to 1960 (Gillett, 1970, p. 220). Luther Dixon's work with the Shirelles ("Will You Still Love Me Tomorrow?," "Dedicated to the One I Love," "Soldier Boy"), Phil Spector's with the Crystals ("He's a Rebel," "Da Doo Ron Ron," "Then He Kissed Me") and the Ronnettes ("Be My Baby"), and Berry Gordy's with Martha and the Vandellas ("Heat Wave," "Quicksand," "Dancing in the Street"), the Marvelettes ("Please Mr. Postman"), and the Supremes ("Where Did Our Love Go?" "Baby Love," "Stop! In the Name of Love," "You Can't Hurry Love") developed the style further and rekindled the spirit of early rock and roll. In the hands of these producers, black female vocal harmony groups, known collectively as "girl groups," became a recognized trend in rock and roll for the first time.

During this period, Berry Gordy started the most significant black-owned record label ever—Motown. Until its sale to MCA (and ultimate incorporation into the Universal Music Group), Motown was the centerpiece of the largest black-owned corporation in the United States. As a businessman, Gordy addressed all aspects of career development for African-American artists such as Marvin Gaye, the Temptations, the Four Tops, and Stevie Wonder, in addition to the women mentioned above. As a producer, he had an uncanny ability to incorporate white audience tastes without abandoning a black sound.

As the early civil rights movement gave way to the more radical demand for black power, Motown's hegemony over black pop was challenged by a resurgence of closer-to-the-roots, hard-driving R&B from the Deep South. Chiefly responsible for the popularization of "southern soul" was a short-lived but highly successful collaboration between Atlantic Records and a number of southern studios, most notably Stax in Memphis and Fame in Muscle Shoals (Guaralnick, 1986). From 1965 on, artists like Otis Redding ("I've Been Loving You Too Long"), Wilson Pickett ("Land of 1000 Dances"), Sam and Dave ("Soul Man"), Arthur Conley ("Sweet Soul Music"), and Percy Sledge ("When a Man Loves a Woman") echoed the spirit of the new militancy with raw, basic recordings easily distinguished from the cleaner, brighter Motown sound.

Stax was originally a white-owned company; its "Memphis sound" was created by the house band, Booker T. and the MGs, and was the product of cross-racial teamwork. Initially the credits on all Stax recordings read simply "produced by the Stax staff." In the late 1960s, leadership was increasingly taken over by black vice president Al Bell, often under controversial circumstances. Motown was not only black-owned, but virtually all of its creative personnel—artists, writers, producers, and session musicians—were black as well. It was clearly a haven for black talent. Paradoxically, Motown is remembered as being "totally committed to reaching white audiences," while Stax recordings, by contrast, were "consistently aimed at R&B fans first, the pop market second" (George, 1988, p. 86).

The two artists who best expressed the spirit of the era were James Brown and Aretha Franklin. In the 1950s, James Brown's music was intended for, and in many ways confined to, the black community. When he "crossed over," he did so on his own terms. His string of uncompromising Top Ten hits ("Papa's Got a Brand New Bag," "I Got You," "Cold Sweat") made few concessions to mainstream sensibilities. His 1968 hit single "Say It Loud—I'm Black and I'm Proud" became an anthem in the struggle for black liberation. Signed to Atlantic records in 1967, Aretha Franklin earned the title "Lady Soul" with her recording of Otis Redding's song "Respect." The vocal and emotional range of her Atlantic releases ("Baby, I Love You," "Natural Woman," "Chain of Fools," "Think," and "Young, Gifted and Black," to name a few) uniquely expressed all the passion and forcefulness of the era.

Two black-led mixed bands in the late 1960s incorporated "psychedelic" sounds into their music—Sly and the Family Stone ("Dance to the Music," "Everyday People," "Hot Fun in the Summertime," "Thank You Falettinme Be Mice Elf Agin," "Family Affair") and the Jimi Hendrix Experience ("Purple Haze," "All Along the Watchtower"). Chemical indulgence guided the careers of both. Sly married the funk and rock cultures in a way that no other artist, black or white, had been able to do. Hendrix explored the electronic wizardry of his instrument and recording studio to a greater extent than any other African-American musician. At his Electric Ladyland studios, he also logged some eight hundred hours of tape with musicians like Miles Davis, John McLaughlin, and other avant-garde jazz notables. None of these tapes was released during Hendrix's lifetime, and he never attracted a black audience to the music with which he was identified.

In the early 1970s a breakthrough of sorts for African-American songwriters was provided by so-called blaxploitation films. Popular movies like *Shaft*, *Superfly*, and *Troubleman* were scored by Isaac Hayes, Curtis Mayfield, and Marvin Gaye, respectively.

Reflecting the "quieter" mood of the early 1970s was the "soft soul" sound pioneered by Kenny Gamble and Leon Huff and producer-arranger Thom Bell, in league with Sigma Sound Studios in Philadelphia. Working with Jerry Butler, the Intruders, and the Delphonics, Gamble and Huff parlayed a $700 bank loan into thirty million-selling singles in a five-year period. The Philadelphia enterprise hit its stride in 1971 with the formation of Philadelphia International Records (PIR) and a distribution deal with CBS. Harold Melvin and the Blue Notes ("If You Don't Know Me By Now") and the O'Jays ("Back Stabbers," "Love Train") on PIR, the Stylistics ("You Make Me Feel Brand New") on Avco, and the Spinners ("Could It Be I'm Falling in Love") on Atlantic set the standard in black pop for the next few years. Southern soul yielded the velvety smooth Al Green ("Let's Stay Together," "I'm Still in Love with You"). Other artists, such as the Chicago-based Chi-Lites ("Oh Girl") and the ever-changing Isley Brothers ("That Lady") also followed suit. Soft soul was one of the formative influences on the trend that would dominate the rest of the decade—disco.

Disco began as deejay-created medleys of existing (mostly African-American) dance records in black, Latino, and gay nightclubs. As it evolved into its own musical genre, its sources of inspiration came, to some extent, from self-contained funk bands such as Kool and the Gang ("Funky Stuff," "Jungle Boogie"), the Ohio Players ("Skin Tight," "Fire"), and Earth, Wind, and Fire ("Shining Star"), but more clearly from "soft soul" and the controlled energy of what came to be known as Eurodisco.

Most of the early disco releases in the United States were by black artists. Among those that made the rare crossover from clubs to radio were "Soul Makossa," an obscure French import by Manu Dibango, "Rock the Boat" by the Hues Corporation, and George McRae's "Rock Your Baby." The first disco hit to reach the charts as disco was Gloria Gaynor's "Never Can Say Good-bye" in 1974, and the following year Donna Summer's "Love to Love You Baby" moved disco closer to the surface. And by 1975 Van McCoy and the Soul City Orchestra had established the hustle as the most important new dance craze since the twist.

With the exception of deejay Frankie Crocker on WBLS in New York, disco was systematically excluded from radio. The music received its primary exposure in clubs, popularized only by the creative genius of the disco deejays. Initially shunned by the record companies, the club deejays had to make the rounds to each label individually in order to get records. Organizing themselves into "record pools," disco deejays quickly developed an alternative to the airplay marketing structure of the industry.

Disco's fanatical following turned out to be not only an underground party culture but also a significant record-buying public. By the mid-1970s, the pop charts were bursting with disco acts like the Silver Convention ("Fly, Robin, Fly," "Get Up and Boogie"), Hot Chocolate ("You Sexy Thing"), Wild Cherry ("Play That Funky Music"), K.C. and the Sunshine Band ("Shake Your Booty"), Rhythm Heritage ("Theme from S.W.A.T."), Sylvers ("Boogie Fever"), Johnny Taylor ("Disco Lady"), Maxine Nightingale ("Right Back Where We Started From"), the Emotions ("Best of My Love"), Thelma Houston ("Don't Leave Me This Way"), Rose Royce ("Car Wash"), Brick ("Dazz"), Hot ("Angel in Your Arms"), Taste of Honey ("Boogie Oogie Oogie"), Peter Brown ("Dance with Me"), Yvonne Elliman ("If I Can't Have You"), Chic ("Dance, Dance, Dance"), Heatwave ("The Groove Line"), and, of course, Donna Summer. Most of these acts were black.

The full commercial potential of disco was realized when WKTU, an obscure soft rock station in New York, converted to an all-disco format in 1978 and, within months, became the most listened-to station in the country. By 1979 there were some two hundred disco stations broadcasting in almost every major market. Disco records captured eight of the fourteen pop Grammy Awards in 1979. Syndicated television programs like "Disco Magic" and "Dance Fever" brought the dance craze to the heartland. Some thirty-six million adults thrilled to the musical mixes of eight thousand professional deejays who serviced a portion of the estimated twenty thousand disco clubs. The phenomenon spawned a subindustry whose annual revenues ranged from $4 billion to $8 billion.

Because of disco's roots, the inevitable backlash had racial overtones. Slogans like "death to disco" and "disco sucks" were as much racial epithets as they were statements of musical preference. In the early 1980s, rock radio reasserted its primacy (and its racism) with a vengeance. Black-oriented radio was forced to move in the direction of a new format—urban contemporary (UC). UC was multicultural in its original conception: black artists in the soul, funk, and jazz categories—such as Stevie Wonder, Donna Summer, Rick James, Third World, Funkadelic, Quincy Jones, and George Benson— remained central to a station's playlist, and white acts who fit the format— like David Bowie or Hall and Oates—were added. Paradoxically, UC may well have proven to be a net loss for black artists. While UC provided greater access for white musicians on what had been black-oriented stations, black performers did not gain any reciprocal access to rock radio.

More blatant acts of racial exclusion were occurring in video. In 1983 *People* magazine reported that "on MTV's current roster of some 800 acts, 16 are black" (Bricker, 1983, p. 31). MTV's rejection of five Rick James videos at a time when his album *Street Songs* had sold almost four million copies was rivaled only by their initial reluctance to air even Michael Jackson's "Beat It" and "Billy Jean" videos. New music video outlets formed in reaction to MTV's restrictive programming policies. Black Entertainment Television (BET) and the long-standing Soul Train provided the primary video exposure for black talent in the early 1980s. Ironically, *Yo! MTV Raps* subsequently became one of MTV's most popular offerings.

This restricted access for African-American artists occurred during the first recession in the music business since the late 1940s. Recovery, beginning in 1983, was signaled by the multiplatinum, worldwide success of Michael Jackson's *Thriller,* with international sales of some forty million units, making it the largest-selling record of all time. *Thriller* began a trend toward blockbuster LPs featuring a limited number of superstar artists as the solution to the industry's economic woes. Interestingly, quite a few of these superstars—including Michael Jackson, Prince, Lionel Richie, Tina Turner, and others—were African Americans.

The phenomenal pop successes of these artists immediately catapulted them into an upper-level industry infrastructure fully owned and operated by whites. In this rarified atmosphere, they were confronted with considerable pressure to sever their ties with the attorneys, managers, booking agents, and promoters who may have been responsible for building their careers in the first place. "Aside from Sammy Davis Jr., Nancy Wilson, and Stephanie Mills," said Nelson George, citing a 1984 *Ebony* story, there were "no other black household names with black management. . . . Michael Jackson, Lionel Richie, Prince, Luther Vandross, the Pointer Sisters, Earth, Wind and Fire, Ray Parker Jr., and Donna Summer all relied on white figures for guidance" (1988, p. 177). These artists were further distinguished from less successful black artists in that they were now marketed directly to the mainstream audience, a practice that has since proven successful even with the debut releases of artists like Whitney Houston and Mariah Carey.

A number of cross-racial, pop-oriented duets—including Stevie Wonder and Paul McCartney ("Ebony and Ivory"), Michael Jackson and Paul McCartney ("The Girl Is Mine," "Say Say Say"), Diana Ross and Julio Iglesias ("All of You"), James Ingram and Kenny Rogers ("What

About Me?"), Dionne Warwick and Friends ("That's What Friends Are For"), Patti LaBelle and Michael McDonald ("On My Own"), Aretha Franklin and George Michael ("I Knew You Were Waiting for Me"), and James Ingram and Linda Ronstadt ("Somewhere Out There")—brought a new dimension to the term "crossover." Michael Jackson's and Lionel Richie's "We Are The World" (1985)—the ultimate crossover recording—initiated the phenomenon of "charity rock."

It remained for rap to take African-American music back to the streets. Rap, one cultural element in the larger hip-hop subculture, began in the South Bronx at about the same time as disco, but, given its place of origin, the movement developed in almost complete isolation for more than five years. In the late 1970s, hip-hop was "discovered" in turn by the music business, the print media, and the film industry. Through films like the low-budget *Wild Style* (1982) and the blockbuster *Flashdance* (1983), followed by *Breakin'* (1984) and *Beat Street* (1984), hip-hop was brought to the attention of a mass audience.

In the mid-1980s, early hip-hop culture heroes like Afrika Bambaataa, Kool Herc, and Grandmaster Flash passed the baton to a second generation of artists such as Whodini, the Force MDs, the Fat Boys, and Run-D.M.C., who recorded the first gold rap album, *Run-D.M.C.*, in 1984. This was a new wrinkle for rap, which had always been based on 12-inch singles. In the relative absence of radio play, even on black radio, rap artists such as Run-D.M.C., UTFO, L.L. Cool J, Whodini, Heavy D. & the Boyz, Salt-n-Pepa, and the Fat Boys made significant inroads into the album and cassette market. Eight of Billboard's top thirty black albums for the week of November 28, 1987, were rap albums.

Beginning as a street movement, rap was initially produced by independent labels, some of which (the notorious Sugar Hill, which has since faded from the scene, and Russell Simmons's Def Jam) were black-owned, all of which were independently distributed. In signing Curtis Blow, Mercury was the only major label to take a chance on rap before it was a proven commodity. Mainstream success, however, demanded the kind of national distribution provided by the major labels. In the mid-1980s, Columbia Records concluded a custom label deal with Def Jam, Jive Records entered into distribution arrangements with both RCA and Arista, Cold Chillin' Records signed a distribution deal with Warner (who also bought a piece of Tommy Boy), Delicious Vinyl entered into a national distribution deal with Island, and Priority contracted with Capitol for national distribution (Garofalo, 1990, pp. 116–117).

Roundly criticized for violence, sexism, and bigotry in the late 1980s, rap endeavored to clean up its image while becoming the main target in the controversy over censorship. Following the lead of Nelson George, a number of rap groups—including Stetsasonic, Boogie Down Productions, and Public Enemy, among others—initiated the Stop the Violence Movement, aimed specifically at black-on-black crime. West Coast rappers followed with "We're All in the Same Gang." Artists such as Queen Latifah and Salt-n-Pepa offered a female—if not a feminist—corrective to abusive sexual rantings. Highly politicized rappers like Public Enemy and NWA remained controversial, even as they sold millions of records to black as well as white teenagers.

During this period, rap gained a measure of mainstream acceptability, as the National Academy of Recording Arts and Sciences added a rap category to the Grammys in 1988 and, immediately following, Billboard unceremoniously inaugurated a rap chart. This momentum soon propelled rap to the upper reaches of the pop market; pop rapper/dancer (M.C.) Hammer's *Please Hammer Don't Hurt 'Em* remained at pop number one for twenty-one weeks, achieving sales of over ten million units. It also propelled rappers into leading roles in other media, including television (Will Smith, Queen Latifah) and film (Ice-T, Ice Cube, Tupac Shakur).

Having achieved a certain level of respectability, rap could not outrun its legacy of controversy. In the 1992 election year, presidential candidate Bill Clinton traded barbs over the Rodney King affair with Sister Souljah, who more than held her own as she graced the cover of *Newsweek*. Ice-T's "Cop Killer" was denounced by public figures ranging from George Bush Sr., Dan Quayle, and Mario Cuomo to Charleton Heston, Beverly Sills, and Oliver North, while sixty congressmen complained to Time Warner, the parent company for Ice-T's label, who then dropped the rapper. Later, Snoop Doggy Dogg, Tupac Shakur, and Flavor Flav made headlines for allegedly crossing the line into violence in real life.

By this time the well-worn path from citizen outrage to government hearings had been taken up by African-American activists, as Dr. C. DeLores Tucker, chairwoman of the National Political Congress of Black Women enlisted the support of Dionne Warwick for a round of Senate hearings scheduled by Senator Carol Moseley-Braun. After 1994, government hearings on rap began to subside, only to pick up again two years later when the violence associated with gangsta rap climaxed with the shooting deaths of Tupac Shakur and then the Notorious B.I.G. (Biggie Smalls).

With the focus on sensationalized rap murders, it was easy to lose sight of the fact that African-American aesthetics, performance styles, and production techniques had

Record producers Jimmy Jam and Terry Lewis. FLYTE TYME PRODUCTIONS. REPRODUCED BY PERMISSION.

contributed significantly to the development of popular music styles ranging from rage rock and teen pop to electronic dance music and R&B. Again, the work of talented African-American producers was clearly in evidence. Beginning in the 1980s, producers such as Quincy Jones, Nile Rogers, Narada Michael Walden, and the team of Jimmy Jam and Terry Lewis paved the way for a next generation that included: Teddy Riley, who invented New Jack Swing; Sean "Puffy" Combs, who established the signature sounds of Jodeci and Mary J. Blige; and Antonio "L.A." Reid and Kenneth "Babyface" Edmunds, who founded LaFace Records.

By the mid-1990s, African-American artists had contributed significantly to a number of trends that peppered the pop landscape: the blockbuster dance-pop of artists like Mariah Carey, who debuted with five number-one pop hits in a row; the growth of hip-hop–flavored R&B vocal groups like Color Me Badd ("All for Love"), Boyz II Men ("End of the Road"), and Jodeci ("Lately"); the sexualized R&B stylings of R. Kelly ("Bump and Grind"); the social engagement of rap groups ranging from Arrested Development ("People Everyday") to the Fugees ("Killing Me Softly"); and the turn toward real life violence that cost the lives of Tupac Shakur (*All Eyez on Me*) and the Notorious B.I.G. (*Ready to Die*).

By this time, hip-hop had expanded geographically beyond the East Coast–West Coast axis of the late 1980s, creating new vocabularies of place and space. In addition to Miami (2 Live Crew), Houston (Geto Boys), Seattle (Sir Mix-A-Lot), and San Francisco (Too Short), hip-hop had established bases in the Midwest and what Tony Green (1999) referred to as "The Dirty South." New Orleans boasted Master P's No Limit Army (Silkk The Shocker, C-Murder, Mo B. Dick, Mia X) and the Cash Money label (Juvenile, B.G., Turk, Lil' Wayne, and Big Tymers), as well as Mystikal on Jive Records. La Face (OutKast, Goodie Mob) was headquartered in Atlanta, as was So So Def (Jermaine Dupri, Lil' Bow Wow, Da Brat). And in 2000, Def Jam opened an Atlanta subsidiary with Scarface as its president and Ludacris as its flagship artist. Timbaland and Magoo represented Virginia Beach, along with Missy "Misdemeanor" Elliott; while Bone Thugs-N-Harmony was in Cleveland and, later, Eminem came out of Detroit.

There was also a next generation of labels in rap's historical strongholds. Dr. Dre had launched Aftermath in Los Angeles. In addition to Bad Boy (Puff Daddy, Notorious B.I.G., MASE, Lil' Kim, Black Rob, Faith Evans), New York added two other significant new rap labels as well—Roc-A-Fella (Jay Z, Beanie Sigel, Cam'ron, M.O.P., Kayne West) and Ruff Ryders (DMX, Eve).

Clearly, rap could no longer be dismissed as a wild street culture; it was a major corporate enterprise, with the most successful artists often playing the multiple roles of performer, writer, producer, and label head. By 1997, Sean "Puffy" Coombs presided over a Bad Boy Entertainment empire that grossed $200 million and employed three hundred people. Master P built a diversified business that included No Limit Records, No Limit Films, No Limit Sports Enterprises, a No Limit clothing line (Soldier Gear), and a multimillion dollar deal with the shoe company Converse, Inc.

The major labels were only too happy to distribute these successful independent rap labels. Bad Boy and La Face were distributed by Arista. Aftermath, Ruff Ryders, Roc-A-Fella, and Cash Money were linked to Interscope and Def Jam, both of which were part of Universal. Still, a number of social practices prompted the major labels to keep rap at arms length: the constant political pressure from conservative watchdog organizations; rap's propensity to sample copyrighted works without permission; and the tendency of hip-hop artists to operate as extended social groups, posses, or crews (e.g., the Bad Boy Family, the No Limit Army, Tha Dogg Pound, Wu Tang Clan). These practices made it more difficult for the industry to track such details as chart position, market share, and royalty rates. This collective ethos led to the routine appearance

Producer Russell Simmons, holding a microphone, is joined by (from left) Antonio "L.A." Reid, Jay Z, and Tony Austin, New York City, 2005. *Simmons, whose efforts and vision as rap producer and artists' manager helped propel rap music onto the national scene in the 1980s, holds a press conference to announce the launch of Russell Simmons Music Group (RSMG), a joint label venture with Def Jam Music Group.* SCOTT GRIES/GETTY IMAGES

of rap artists on each other's recordings, often across label affiliations and to a number of successful ensemble tours at the end of the decade, including No Way Out (Puffy and the Bad Boy Family, Jay-Z, Foxy Brown, Busta Rhymes, Usher); Hard Knock Life (Jay-Z, DMX, Method Man and Redman, DJ Clue); Ruff Ryders/Cash Money (DMX, Juvenile as co-headliners, and both labels' other artists as support); and Up in Smoke (Snoop Dogg, Dr. Dre, Eminem, Ice Cube, MC Ren).

If the Up In Smoke tour rekindled a focus on Los Angeles (and Eminem), New York had become the center for hard-core rap, from verbal jousts like the ones between Jay-Z and Nas and DMX and Ja Rule, to the more menacing real-life violence that hovered around 50 Cent. In a more dispersed rap world, New York itself had become significantly more decentralized. In its run-down of the fifty most influential hip-hop players, *Rolling Stone* went so far as to identify the particular borough or "hood" that each New York artist "represented"—Beastie Boys (Manhattan), Busta Rhymes (Brooklyn), KRS-One (The Bronx), Mase (Harlem), and Wu Tang Clan (Staten Island). Not mentioned by *Rolling Stone* were Jay Z from Brooklyn, DMX from Yonkers, and 50 Cent from Hollis, Queens.

Although the most publicized rap of the era was drenched in testosterone, it is important to note that there were other tendencies as well. OutKast *(Stankonia)* epitomized the Dirty South with less reliance on aggression, more sophisticated lyrics, and more intricate arrangements. Shaggy *(Hot Shot)* was the antithesis of the New York gangsta: polite, well-mannered, and completely nonthreatening. In 2002 Nelly *(Country Grammar)* ascended to the number one slot on the year-end pop charts with a laid back Southern drawl, tongue-twister rhymes, and infectious pop hooks.

If there were any doubts as to the popularity of rap and hip-hop-influenced R&B, they were more than laid to rest on October 11, 2003, when *Billboard* reported a first in the magazine's fifty-year history: all of the Top Ten singles in the country were by black artists—nine rappers and the singer Beyoncé, who was at number one with "Baby

Boy." As the strongest measure of popularity across audience demographics, this phenomenon suggested that, in cultural terms, hip-hop had imposed a new paradigm supplanting rock as the major youth cultural force.

See also Blues, The; Hip-Hop; Music in the United States; Rap; Rhythm and Blues

Bibliography

Bricker, Rebecca. "Take One." *People* 4 (April 1983): 31.

Forman, Murray. *The 'Hood Comes First: Race, Space, and Place in Rap and Hip-Hop.* Middletown, Conn.: Wesleyan University Press, 2002.

Garofalo, Reebee. "Crossing Over, 1939-1992." In *Split Image: African Americans in the Mass Media,* 2d ed., edited by Jannette L. Dates and William Barlow. Washington, D.C.: Howard University Press, 1990.

Garofalo, Reebee. *Rockin' Out: Popular Music in the USA,* 3d ed. Upper Saddle River, N.J.: Pearson/Prentice Hall, 2005.

George, Nelson. *The Death of Rhythm & Blues.* New York: Pantheon, 1988.

Gillett, Charlie. *The Sound of the City.* New York: Dutton, 1970.

Green, Tony. "The Dirty South." In *The VIBE History of Hip Hop,* edited by Alan Light. New York: Three Rivers Press, 1999.

Guaralnick, Peter. *Sweet Soul Music: Rhythm and Blues and the Southern Dream of Freedom.* New York: Harper, 1986.

Jones, LeRoi (Amiri Baraka). *Blues People: Negro Music in White America.* New York, 1963. Reprint, Westport, Conn.: Greenwood, 1980.

Negus, Keith. *Music Genres and Corporate Cultures.* New York: Routledge, 1999.

Ramsey, Guthrie P. *Race Music: Black Cultures from Bebop to Hip-Hop.* Los Angeles: University of California Press, 2003.

Southern, Eileen. *The Music of Black Americans: A History.* New York: Norton, 1971.

REEBEE GAROFALO (2005)

Redding, Jay Saunders

October 13, 1906
March 2, 1988

Born and raised in a middle-class family in Wilmington, Delaware, writer J. Saunders Redding attended Lincoln University in Pennsylvania for one year before transferring to Brown University, where he received his Ph.B. (bachelor of philosophy) in 1928 and his M.A. in 1932; afterward, he studied at Columbia University for one year on a graduate fellowship. Redding began his career teaching English at a series of colleges and universities: Morehouse College in Atlanta (1928–1931), Louisville Municipal College (1934–1936), and Southern University in Baton Rouge, Louisiana, where he was chair of the English department (1936–1938).

After Redding's publication of *To Make a Poet Black* (1939), a critical study unique in its time for its examination of African-American literature from the perspective of a black scholar, the Rockefeller Foundation awarded Redding a fellowship to write *No Day of Triumph* (1942), an exploration of the condition of African Americans in the South. The partly autobiographical book was a critical success and established Redding's reputation as an acute observer of social realities who spoke eloquently both to black and white Americans about the struggles and the achievements of African Americans. In 1943 Redding returned to teaching, this time as a professor at the Hampton Institute in Virginia, where he remained until 1966, and subsequently at George Washington University (1968–1970) and at Cornell University (1970–1975; as professor emeritus, 1975–1988). He also served as an official of the National Endowment for the Humanities (1966–1970) and as a State Department–sponsored lecturer at colleges and universities in India (1952), Africa (1962), and South America (1977).

During his career, Redding wrote ten books, among them an influential psychological study of race relations, *On Being Negro in America* (1951), a novel, *Stranger and Alone* (1950), and several sociohistorical studies, including *They Came in Chains: Americans from Africa* (1950), *An American in India* (1954), and *The Negro* (1967). He coedited two anthologies, *Reading for Writing* (1952), with Ivan E. Taylor, and *Cavalcade: Negro American Writing from 1760 to the Present* (1971), with Arthur P. Davis. Redding's many articles and book reviews have appeared in anthologies and in such periodicals as *The Atlantic Monthly, The Saturday Review, The Nation, The North American Review,* and *American Heritage.* While denying neither the specificity of his perspective nor his abiding interest in the experience and culture of African Americans, Redding continually stressed in his works the necessity for full integration of African Americans into the larger community.

Redding received many awards and honorary degrees for his work, including two Guggenheim fellowships (1944–1945 and 1959–1960), a citation from the National Urban League (1950), a Ford Foundation fellowship (1964–1965), and honorary degrees from Brown University (1963), Virginia State College (1963), Hobart College

(1964), the University of Portland (1970), Wittenberg University (1977), Dickinson College, and the University of Delaware. Redding died in Ithaca, New York, at the age of seventy-one.

See also Intellectual Life; Literary Criticism, U.S.

Bibliography

Davis, Arthur P. *From the Dark Tower: Afro-American Writers, 1900–1960.* Washington, D.C.: Howard University Press, 1974.

Metzger, Linda, ed. *Black Writers: A Selection of Sketches from Contemporary Authors.* Detroit, Mich.: Gale, 1989.

Thompson, Thelma Barnaby. "J. Saunders Redding." In *Dictionary of Literary Biography.* Vol. 76, *Afro-American Writers, 1940–1955.* Detroit, Mich.: Gale, 1988.

Wagner, Jean. *Black Poets of the United States: From Paul Lawrence Dunbar to Langston Hughes.* Translated by Kenneth Douglas. Urbana: University of Illinois Press, 1973.

STEVEN J. LESLIE (1996)
ALEXIS WALKER (1996)

Redding, Otis

September 9, 1941
December 10, 1967

The soul singer and composer Otis Redding was one of the most powerful and original singer-songwriters of the 1960s. He was the mainstay of Stax Records, the Memphis label that became internationally successful releasing gritty southern soul records. Born in Dawson, Georgia, Redding grew up in Macon, 100 miles to the north. He began playing drums in school and was paid six dollars an hour on Sundays to accompany gospel groups appearing on the local radio station, WIBB. Redding stayed in school until the tenth grade (1957), but he quit to help support his family, working variously at a gas station, as a well-digger, and occasionally as a musician. As a singer, he began to win local talent contests with his spontaneous and tough vocal style. He traveled to Los Angeles in mid-1960, where he recorded four songs, and returned to Macon in 1961, where he cut "Shout Bamalama" for the Confederate label, a minor hit that received airplay on area radio stations.

Redding's break came in 1963, when he sang his song "These Arms of Mine" at a Stax recording session of Johnny Jenkins and the Pinetoppers, a group for whom he was guest vocalist and chauffeur. When the record made it into the Rhythm-and-Blues Top Twenty in 1964, Redding's career was launched. Over the next five years, his popularity grew steadily through fiery live performances, hit singles such as "I've Been Loving You Too Long," "Try a Little Tenderness," and "I Can't Turn You Loose," and critically acclaimed LPs such as *Otis Blue, The Soul Album,* and *The Great Otis Redding Sings Soul Ballads.* Like Aretha Franklin (b. 1942), who immortalized his song "Respect", Redding was able to capitalize on the liberal climate of the 1960s, crossing over to white listeners on both sides of the Atlantic. His performances in England in early 1967 so enthralled audiences that he was subsequently named Best Male Vocalist in a poll sponsored by the music publication *Melody Maker,* an accolade won by Elvis Presley the previous eight years. Later in 1967, nestled between rock acts, he captivated an audience of 55,000 at the Monterey Pop Festival in California, one of the milestones of the hippie era.

Redding's death in a plane crash near Madison, Wisconsin, on December 10, 1967, came at the peak of his career and left fans wondering what might have been. His song "(Sittin' on) The Dock of the Bay," recorded three days before his death, revealed a different, introspective musical direction. It became his biggest record, heading the pop charts for four weeks and becoming a posthumous signature song.

See also Franklin, Aretha; Music in the United States; Rhythm and Blues

Bibliography

Brown, Geoff. *Otis Redding: Try a Little Tenderness.* Edinburgh, Scotland: Mojo Books, 2001.

Freeman, Scott. *Otis! The Otis Redding Story.* New York: St. Martin's, 2001.

Guralnick, Peter. "Otis Redding" and "Stax Goes to Europe/ The Big O Comes Home: Triumph and Tragedy." In *Sweet Soul Music: Rhythm and Blues and the Southern Dream of Freedom.* New York: Harper & Row, 1986.

BUD KLIMENT (1996)
Updated bibliography

Red Summer

"Red Summer" was the term coined in 1919 by NAACP investigator James Weldon Johnson to describe the summer and early fall of that year, when twenty-five race riots and other racially based incidents erupted across the United States—the largest in Charleston, South Carolina;

Washington, D.C.; Chicago; Knoxville, Tennessee; Omaha, Nebraska; and Elaine, Arkansas. Although the riots had different immediate causes, they had many common roots.

Tensions between blacks and whites were high in the aftermath of World War I. Overly rapid demobilization and the end of price controls led to inflation and unemployment. Whites in the North were angered and frightened by the presence of blacks who had migrated during the war, and white Southerners were aroused by blacks' new self-confidence and willingness to challenge the racial status quo. Black soldiers came home from Europe, where they had been treated as equals by the French (one black unit was decorated for bravery), expecting gratitude and employment opportunity. They received neither. There were seventy-six lynchings in a month and a half, a dozen of them of black veterans still in uniform. Racial tensions were augmented by the postwar anti-Bolshevik "red scare." Whites feared radicalism and reacted hysterically to rumors of subversion. Attempts at social change, particularly in the racial status quo, were stigmatized as "radical" and "subversive."

The riots themselves were generally white-instigated affairs, generated by real or fictitious black challenges to white authority. However, unlike most earlier racial disturbances, blacks often actively resisted white violence, and shot and beat white attackers. Radical black leaders such as A. Philip Randolph gave speeches and wrote articles proclaiming blacks' right to commit violence in self-defense.

Red Summer, though brief, convinced many African Americans that their participation in a war for democracy did not mean that white domination in America was going to disappear. The events pushed many blacks into militant action. Some blacks responded by redoubling their commitment to civil rights protest. Others supported black nationalist leaders, notably Marcus Garvey.

See also Johnson, James Weldon; Riots and Popular Protests

Bibliography

Tuttle, William M., Jr. *Race Riot: Chicago in the Red Summer of 1919.* New York: Atheneum, 1970.

ALANA J. ERICKSON (1996)

Reed, Ishmael

February 22, 1938

The author Ishmael Reed was born in Chattanooga, Tennessee, but was raised and educated in Buffalo, New York. In high school he discovered the writings of Nathanael West, whose black comedy influenced his own distinctive expressionistic style. Later, while at the University of Buffalo (1956–1960), he discovered the works of William Butler Yeats and William Blake, who taught him the importance of creating personal mythological systems. In 1962 he moved to New York City to become a writer. While living on the Lower East Side he encountered a group of young black writers, including Calvin Hernton, David Henderson, and Askia Muhammad Toure, from the Umbra Workshop, who convinced him of the importance of black literature. His first novel, *Free-Lance Pallbearers* (1967), a parody of Ralph Ellison's *Invisible Man,* is a savage satire of the United States during the Vietnam War years, personified by the president, Harry Sam, who literally eats American children.

In 1967 Reed moved to Berkeley, California, where he cofounded and published *The Yardbird Reader* (1972–1976), which reflected his new multiethnic spirit, engendered by his move to the multicultural West Coast. His second novel, *Yellow Back Radio Broke-Down* (1969), a surreal western, introduces the theme of the repressive forces of Western culture embattled against the life-affirming forces of black culture, which have survived the Middle Passage from Africa to the New World. In this novel Reed presents voodoo religion as a source of authentic black folk culture and values. In his next novel, *Mumbo Jumbo* (1972), he initiated his countermythology. He argues that there is a conspiracy at the core of the Western tradition: Its mythology preaches the glory of the West at the expense of all other cultures. It therefore became imperative, for Reed, to revise this mythology in order to expose the lies of the Western tradition and affirm the virtues of African civilizations, including Egypt. In his later creative works, his countermythology, which he usually calls Neo-HooDooism, he has drawn on many non-European cultures, including Haitian, black American, and Native American. In 1976 Reed cofounded the Before Columbus Foundation, devoted to the dissemination of multicultural literature. *Flight to Canada* (1976), his fifth novel, is a modern slave narrative, in which he defines freedom as the ability to tell one's own story instead of allowing it to be appropriated by alien and hostile cultures. With *Reckless Eyeballing* (1986), Reed continues his exploration of freedom in the explosive area of sexual politics, where he argues against white feminist hegemony. In 1993 he published his ninth novel, *Japanese by Spring*, which parodies black neoconservatism and multiethnic abuse of power by the powerful, whether they are white, black, or yellow.

Even though Reed is known primarily as a novelist, he has produced a number of books of poetry and essays. He also has had several plays produced, including *Mother Hubbard* (1981) and *Savage Wilds* (1989). Among his poetry collections are *Conjure* (1972), *Chattanooga* (1974), *A Secretary to the Spirits* (1978), and *New and Collected Poems* (1988). Mostly in free verse, these poems are experimental, humorous, and satiric. In his poetry, as in his fiction, he creates a countermythology, drawing on many non-European cultures for its symbolism. Reed's books of essays include *Shrovetide in Old New Orleans* (1978), *God Made Alaska for the Indians* (1982), *Writin' Is Fightin': Thirty-Seven Years of Boxing on Paper* (1988), *Airing Dirty Laundry* (1993), *The Reed Reader* (2000), *Another Day at the Front: Dispatches from the Race War* (2002), and *Blues City: A Walk in Oakland* (2003). In his essays he tries to refute false and pernicious myths about black people. In recent years he has focused more on black men than on African Americans in general, arguing that they are in a particularly precarious position in American society: that, indeed, they are everybody's scapegoat for the evils of civilization. Reed's impassioned polemics in defense of black men have catapulted him into the center of many heated debates with both black and white feminists. Since all of Reed's works spring from the same individual vision, both his poems and essays help the reader clarify the more significant novels.

Reed is a major innovative writer who relentlessly uses comedy and satire to show the myopia, egotism, and brutality of eurocentric culture. Yet he does not let black culture off scot-free: he criticizes individual blacks when they do not live up to the ideals of freedom and creativity that he finds inherent in the African-American tradition. His critique of the West is often more subtle and penetrating than that of many scholars, and it is always much more amusing.

See also Black Arts Movement; Caribbean/North American Writers (Contemporary); Literature of the United States

Bibliography

Boyer, Jay. *Ishmael Reed.* Boise, Idaho: Boise State University, 1993.

Byerman, Keith E. *Fingering the Jagged Grain: Tradition and Form in Recent Black Fiction.* Athens: University of Georgia Press, 1985.

Fox, Robert Elliot. *Conscientious Sorcerers: The Black Postmodernist Fiction of LeRoi Jones/Amiri Baraka, Ishmael Reed, and Samuel R. Delany.* Westport, Conn.: Greenwood, 1987.

Martin, Reginald. *Ishmael Reed and the New Black Aesthetic Critics.* New York: St. Martin's, 1988.

McGee, Patrick. *Ishmael Reed and the Ends of Race.* New York: St. Martin's, 1997.

WILLIAM J. HARRIS (1996)
Updated bibliography

Reggae

Reggae is a late twentieth-century black musical phenomenon that draws deeply from Afro-Jamaican religious, dance, and musical practices while positing a distinctive series of meanings and representations about slavery, colonialism, history, and Africa. These meanings have been largely influenced by the theology, cultural practices, and language of Rastafari. In the late 1960s Larry Marshall's *Nanny Goat* with its organ shuffle was one of the signals of the birth of a new musical sound. This sound was crafted in the studios of producers such as Coxsone Dodd and Arthur "Duke" Reid. The musicians who comprised the various studio bands along with the singers who experimented with musical forms lived in districts of Jones Town, Trench Town, or Denham Town, located in the western end of Jamaica's capital city and populated by thousands of migrants bringing religious and other cultural traditions from rural Jamaica. These musicians were inspired by two musical currents: indigenous ska and African-American rhythm and blues.

Ska was an early 1960s urban musical synthesis that transformed twentieth-century Jamaican popular musical culture. It replaced mento, a musical form that was born of the cultural encounter between African musical traditions and the melodies of European instruments. This encounter produced instruments such as the rhumba scraper. Many claim that the first popular indigenous Jamaican music record was the Folkes Brothers' *Oh Carolina.* With the *nyabinghi*-style repeater drumming of Count Ossie holding the entire spine of the track together, the song became an exemplar of the different ingredients that eventually merged to create reggae. When Derrick Morgan sang "Forward March" in honor of Jamaican independence, he did so to the hard driving, horn blowing, and rhythm section of the studio band. Ska was big band music influenced by jazz and swing. But ska sped up the second

Reggae musician, songwriter, and singer Bob Marley performs in Stockholm, Sweden, 1978. *Rising from an early life of austere poverty in his native Jamaica, the charismatic Marley helped to bring reggae music to international popularity. His 1974 hit song "No Woman No Cry" was entered into the Grammy Hall of Fame in 2005.* HULTON ARCHIVE/GETTY IMAGES

beat while slowing down the fourth, so that the music seemed off beat with loose skips to it that would then be reconciled in the male dances of the "legs" and "splits." The ska musical pantheon of horn, drum, bass, and piano players includes Tommy Cook, Roland Alphonso, Dizzy Moore, Rico Rodriguez, Lloyd Knibbs, Lloyd Brevett, Jackie Mitoo, and perhaps the most accomplished of them all, Don Drummond. This group eventually came together as the Skatalites, and their musical skills remain a rich archive of Jamaican music.

There is no popular Jamaican music without the dance steps. For Jamaican popular music the dance steps were often created in the dances in which the ubiquitous sound system provided thousands of watts. With names in the 1970s such as Black Harmony, Black Scorpio, Black Roots, Gemini, Jack Ruby, and perhaps the most dynamic of them all, King Tubby's Hi Fi, the sound system dances became sites in which audience, dancers, and music were integrated into a tight fit. When the audience members are primarily urban dwellers alienated from official society, then the relationship between the music, musicians, and audience often becomes a practice of counter-signification. This is clearly illustrated by the morphing of ska into the musical form of rock steady. In the transition the music slowed down, the loose skip was transformed into a tighter bass, and the fast-paced ska dance movements became languid movements of the shoulders and hands operating in different time to the pelvic motions. The combined effect of the dance and music was a sense of dread, of bodies about to explode: The figure that best represented this was the "rude bwoy." The rude bwoy was unemployed, had lost faith in the dream of political independence, and chafed under the postcolonial dispensation of class and color. Their behavior was a direct confrontation with the conceptions of working-class black respectability and official ideas about how the new Jamaican citizen should comport himself. The era of the rude bwoys produced singers and groups such as The Wailers, Heptones, Ethiopians, Jimmy Cliff, Alton Ellis, Delroy Wilson, and Ken Boothe, as well as producer Prince Buster. Two songs were exemplars of this period: Prince Buster's "Judge Dread" and The Wailers' appeal to the rude bwoys to "Simmer Down." The immediate roots of reggae are therefore to be found in the urban popular Jamaican culture of the dispossessed that developed in the island's postindependence period.

In reggae the drum and bass become pronounced. The singer is given scope, the horns surround the bridge segments of the music, and the dancer skips and moves with feet that are now free from the chains of racial slavery while the body moves in memory of the Middle Passage. There are many streams of reggae, but one of the most popular streams is sometimes called *roots rock reggae.* This music relies heavily upon the message it delivers. From Marley's *Trench Town Rock* to the Abyssinians' classic *Satta Massagana* to Gregory Isaacs's *Roughneck,* reggae music operates in the languages of black struggle and redemption. This is the music of groups and singers with names such as Burning Spear, Black Uhuru, and Culture. The emergence of reggae also saw the development of creative producers who were musical techno-innovators creating new sounds within the general "riddim" structure of the music. Here Lee "Scratch" Perry's Black Ark Studio was the most important site. Roots reggae's musical vocabulary explores the New World black experience through the themes of exile, redemption, and imagery of Africa and slavery. These themes are shaped by Rastafari and therefore are often expressed in the language of black prophecy. As reggae became internationally popular, it carried with it the freight of Rastafari. In the contemporary period, reggae has remained the preferred musical idiom of what is sometimes called "conscious" or "culture" music as distinct from dance hall.

If the internal Jamaican migration eventually led to reggae as a musical and cultural practice, then external migration allowed the music to develop another distinct genre. Here the story is about the passage from Millie Small's "My Boy Lollipop" to the drum and bass (sometimes called jungle music) of artists like LTJ Bukem. Jamaican music arrived in the United Kingdom on board the *Empire Windrush* in 1948 as part of the cultural makeup of the newly arrived West Indians. Initially it was the cloak of home comfort, something in which the new arrivals could wrap themselves in the strange gray land of the former colonial power.

However, as these new communities put down roots and second-generation West Indians began searching for an identity that located them in the United Kingdom—while retaining the connections to the Caribbean—the music changed, and black British identity became a locus for a radical transformation and representation of the self. The first wave of this change occurred in the 1970s with the development of "lovers rock," ostensibly as the antithesis to the more bass-heavy Rasta-influenced roots and culture forms that dominated the reggae scene in the 1970s. In lovers rock the baselines were unmistakably reggae but with an added emphasis on melodic composition and lyrics that dealt almost exclusively with matters of the heart. This reflected a mainstream pop music influence as well as that of soul music. Powered by labels such as Lovers Rock, Arawak, Santic, and Hawkeye and featuring artists such as Janet Kay and Carroll Thompson, lovers rock enjoyed some mainstream success before petering out in the 1980s when the fun pop sensibilities that it embraced were rejected for a harder, bass heavy sound.

This is not to say that Rastafari and roots reggae became lost in translation. More traditional forms were being produced by the likes of Steel Pulse and the dub poet Linton Kewsi Johnson, bubbling under the more commercially accessible lovers rock and satisfying the desire for musical content that directly expressed the problems faced by young blacks. Police brutality, employment difficulties, and other social inequalities were all covered, maintaining the social commentary/criticism that had long been part of reggae, as well as keeping open and vibrant the direct link to Jamaica. In the 1980s, when the conservative political ideology of Thatcherism took hold and young black men in particular found it increasingly difficult to obtain jobs, lovers rock began to lose its appeal and was eventually replaced by "drum and bass." This musical form developed out of the network of sound systems modeled on the sound systems of Jamaica, complete with selectors and box boys. The best known of these was Soul II Soul. Drum and bass practitioners like Goldie, LTJ, and Roni Size started life as mixers on sound systems across the country in such places as Bristol before branching out into music production. With its elongated basslines and irregular, fast-paced drum patterns voiced by the MCs, drum and bass quickly became the voice of disaffected young blacks.

Though its style was more reminiscent of the dancehall style that dominates sound systems in twenty-first-century Jamaica, the influences did not stop there. Hiphop shares some similarities in production techniques. More recently, jazz sensibilities that allowed improvisation have shaped a new musical style dubbed "intelligent drum and bass." A key individual in this move is LTJ Bukem and his Good Looking/Looking Good record label. A good example of this new form is the title track of Bukem's 2000

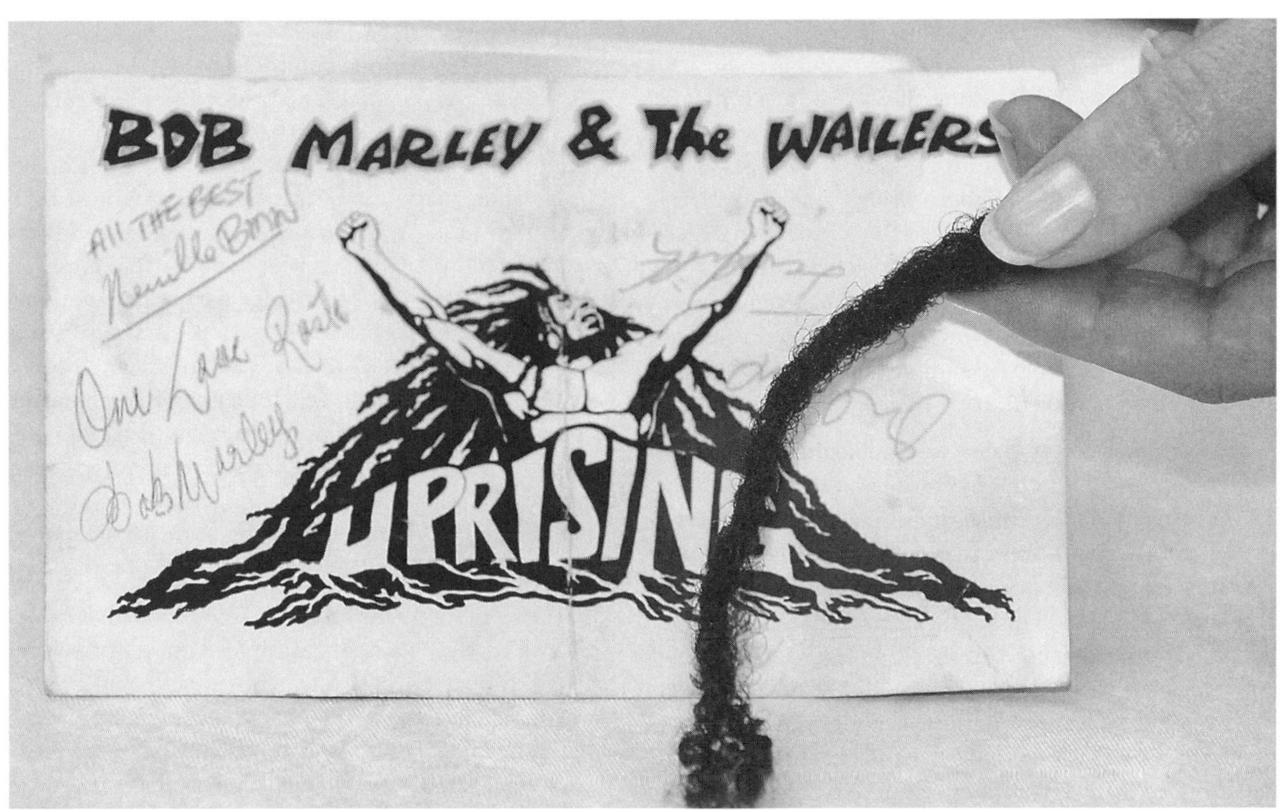

A dreadlock from reggae legend Bob Marley is displayed in front of a signed promotional postcard for auction at Christie's in London. *As indicated by the illustration on the postcard, reggae art speaks the language of black struggle and redemption.* SCOTT BARBOUR/GETTY IMAGES

release, "Journey Inwards," in which the shimmering sounds of a keyboard caress and envelop the rhythm created by an upright bass.

But reggae has not only followed a Jamaican diaspora. It has become one of the most popular international musical forms, with artists deploying its rhythmical syntax in Africa, Europe, and beyond. The CD *Reggae Over Africa* (2000), with tracks of Japanese reggae and major tracks by the South African artist Lucky Dube, illustrates this.

In the end reggae remains a form of black cultural production in which its practitioners speak to conditions of oppression and experiences of Africa and peoples of African descent. Its lyrical and musical power resides in its messages and sounds of redemption.

See also Dancehall; Marley, Bob; Rastafarianism; Reggae Aesthetics

Bibliography

Bradley Lloyd. *Bass Culture.* London: Viking, 2000.

Bradley, Lloyd, *Reggae: The Story of Jamaican Music.* London: BBC, 2002.

Hebdige Dick. *Cut 'n' Mix.* London: Methuen, 1987.

Thompson Dave. *Reggae and Caribbean Music.* San Francisco: Backbeat, 2002.

ANTHONY BOGUES (2005)
MACHEL BOGUES (2005)

Reggae Aesthetics

Through the concept of reggae aesthetics, as outlined in his work, *Natural Mysticism: Towards a New Reggae Aesthetic* (1999), Kwame Dawes offers a framework for reading Caribbean literature written since the late 1960s. Dawes is certain that "contained in reggae music are principles of beauty that can help to define the arts that emerge from the world that has shaped reggae" (p. 29). Grounding his exploration of the evolution of Caribbean literature in the region's history of enslavement and colonialism, Dawes speaks to the social and political milieu that provides the context within which literature and the reggae aesthetic must be analyzed. Colonial society, defined by European/British cultural hegemony, perpetuated a system by which the elites oppressed the working class and denied them access to their own history and culture, while elevating the history and culture of the colonizer. Such a system encouraged the working class, descendants of enslaved Africans, to look upon their African past with disdain but to glorify the culture of Europeans/whites. This ensured that emergent Caribbean writing grappled with issues of identity and "almost inevitably wrote in dialogue with the standard Western texts that they learned in school" (p. 46). Furthermore, Caribbean literature was often steeped in a Europe-centered aesthetic and reflected the "peculiarly schizophrenic attitude" of a Caribbean native straddling both worlds (p. 16).

Later works began to defy the rudiments of a Europe-centered aesthetic both stylistically and thematically. Dawes argues that this transition from a literature that reflected an uncertain and insecure Caribbean identity to one that was more self-assured and African-centered was facilitated by the dawn of reggae music. Though the 1950s and 1960s saw the emergence of Wilson Harris and Kamau Brathwaite, who began to usher in a solid "Caribbean literary aesthetic," it was not until reggae surfaced in the late 1960s that Jamaica and the wider Caribbean finally got "an artistic form that has a distinctively postcolonial aesthetic" (p. 17). "Exploring literary connections with reggae," Dawes argues, is critical to the project of understanding Caribbean literature written since the late 1960s. Dawes maintains that reggae provided the vehicle through which Caribbean writing moved from a colonial to a postcolonial posture. He encourages critics of Caribbean writing to use reggae as an analytical tool, maintaining that reggae has given impetus to a paradigm shift in the Caribbean literary world. Reggae, according to Dawes, through its "language," "themes," "form," and "overarching ideology," offers a model for the expression of a confident and multifaceted Caribbean identity (p. 94). This model, he contends, has impacted and is evident in the writing of authors such as Lorna Goodison and Robert Lee (p. 242).

Dawes argues that reggae is able to provide this model because it is "grounded in the history of working-class black Jamaican ideologies that have carried across the centuries from Africa through the complicated cauldron of Caribbean society" (p. 96). The relationship between reggae and black working-class Jamaican ideologies emanates from reggae's "inextricable connection with Rastafarian discourse" (p. 99). Rasta's focus on "history and race" is important to the reggae aesthetic, as Rasta beckons to Jamaicans to remember their African roots and their history. Rasta's firm rejection of a European-centered aesthetic is crucial to reggae. There is no doubt that Rastafarianism "abolished the white world or at least cast it into the outer darkness" (p. 65) and that the most famous ambassador of both Rasta and reggae, Bob Marley, was unflinching in his "embrace of African culture" (p. 54). In addition, Rastafari's subversion of colonial sensibilities through language has resulted in the creation of a Rastafarian lexicon, which provides insight into the Rastafarian critique of European cultural hegemony. The wholesale adoption of this lexicon into reggae lyrics demands that reggae and Rasta be considered in tandem, and supports Dawes's assertion that "Rastafarian ideology provided a clear and appealing cosmology for the reggae artist" (p. 100). Rasta gives reggae an ideological base, which gives Caribbean writers a postcolonial scaffold upon which they can freely hang the themes they seek to probe. The example of reggae, Dawes maintains, has given contemporary Caribbean writers a template, enabling them to depart from the Europe-centered standards that define the traditional Anglophone canon.

The reggae aesthetic boasts an accommodative framework, which allows authors to explore not only issues of race and history but also issues of sexuality and gender. In a conservative society like Jamaica, where a pervasive Protestant ethic serves to dichotomize sexuality and piety, Dawes argues that early writing has reflected the repression that characterizes such a society. Reggae, through its unapologetic treatment of sexuality, sexual pleasure, courtship, and love, has initiated a dialogue about such issues that rivals the closed space of the Protestant ethic. Dawes admits that his analysis of exactly how the reggae aesthetic allows literature to handle issues of misogyny (which is also present in reggae) and sexuality is partial, and that future works that will build on the groundbreaking scholarship of Carolyn Cooper will be well served by the reggae aesthetic.

Dawes presents reggae as a uniquely Jamaican phenomenon that is applicable to the wider Caribbean and beyond. As seen by Dawes, reggae is both local and global, and its proven international appeal demonstrates that "it is possible for a particular genre of music, emerging from a small locale, to have an international impact" (p. 31). It is precisely reggae's ability to adapt to different environments and circumstances while maintaining its uniqueness that provides the "most telling argument for the existence of a reggae aesthetic" (p. 103). Importantly, Dawes is not arguing that the reggae aesthetic is the only prism through which all contemporary Caribbean literature should be read. Instead, he contends that the aesthetic is one of the lenses through which contemporary Caribbean writing should be analyzed.

Dawes urges critics of Caribbean writing to acknowledge a link between reggae music and Caribbean writing of the last three decades. Through an analysis of the components of reggae, that is, lyrics, form, and performance, Dawes shows reggae's entrenchment in an uninhibited and unique Caribbean culture. This, he argues, has influenced how authors perceive of Caribbean identity, as well as the topics they examine in their works. Reggae has aided Caribbean writers in their departure from the limits of a colonial discourse.

See also Caribbean/North American Writers (Contemporary); Literature of the English-Speaking Caribbean; Rastafarianism; Reggae

Bibliography

Cooper, Carolyn. *Noises in the Blood: Orality, Gender, and the Vulgar Body of Jamaican Popular Culture.* London: Macmillan Caribbean, 1993.

Cooper, Carolyn. *Sound Clash: Jamaican Dancehall Culture at Large.* New York: Palgrave Macmillan, 2004.

Dawes, Kwame. *Natural Mysticism: Towards a New Reggae Aesthetic.* Leeds, England: Peepal Tree Press, 1999.

MONIQUE BEDASSE-SAMUDA (2005)

Religion

Carter G. Woodson, founder of the Association for the Study of Negro Life and History, wrote in 1939: "A definitive history of the Negro Church . . . would leave practically no phase of the history of the Negro in America untouched." Understanding African-American religion—or more accurately, the religious history of peoples of African descent in North America—is crucial for any rounded view of the African-American experience. Religion is often inseparable from culture, as was the case in traditional Africa, and encompasses more than institutional expressions. B. B. King once said that he felt closest to God when he was singing the blues, and African-American art, dance, and literature incorporate and reflect symbols, values, and themes. This essay will focus primarily on some of the principal issues, institutional and intellectual developments, and periods in the study of African-American religious history and culture.

A guiding principle for understanding this topic is that African-American religion is not simply an extension or form of Euro-American Christianity. Early historical work on African-American religion, such as that of Carter G. Woodson on "the Negro Church," focused almost exclusively on the institutional history of Protestantism. Yet to view African-American religious history as merely another chapter in the expansion of European Christianity would be to ignore the special circumstances of the religious pilgrimage of African Americans and gloss over the impact of other religious traditions.

A second guiding principle is that African-American religion is an evolving phenomenon that has taken shape over three centuries of slavery and that has continued to develop since the late nineteenth century. Today African-American religion takes on a variety of expressions, institutional and intellectual, creative and mundane, yet always acknowledging the past, while addressing the present and envisioning the future.

A final guiding principle is the fact that African-American religion is not monolithic. The differences within African-American religious culture are as important as the similarities. The religious outlook of someone of African descent in the Low Country of Carolina and Georgia about 1710, before the impact of the Great Awakening, might understandably be different from that of someone subject to the religious instruction of a white Presbyterian clergyman active in organized plantation missions after 1829. The religious profiles of a member of the Mother Bethel African Methodist Church in Philadelphia in 1880, a communicant of St. Cyprian's Roman Catholic Church in Chicago in 1924, of Zion Baptist Church in rural Mississippi in 1954, and of the Pentecostal C. H. Mason Temple in Memphis today will have significant differences. Generalizations about African-American religion must account for changes over time, including changing demographics and geographic variables.

Indeed, regional geography is an important qualifying factor in understanding the uniqueness of the African-American religious experience in the United States. *Vaudou* in Haiti, the Trinidadian cult of *Shango*, the practices of *Santería* in Cuba, and the *Candomblé* rituals found in Brazil exemplify a high degree of syncretism, or perhaps better what James Noel calls "creolization," between West African traditions and Euro-Christian, principally Roman Catholic, culture. In contrast, Africans who were brought or born into the predominantly British environment of North America were more likely to adapt or remodel their religious beliefs and practices in terms of the prevailing regional religious culture—low church Protestant Evangelicalism. Except for the Sea Islands of the Georgia coast, and a few other places where African slaves were isolated from the dominant white society, the children and grandchildren of those who survived the ordeal of the Middle Passage created a new syncretic religious worldview in America.

Slave Religion

Most Africans who were brought into the colonies of British North America originated from the coast and interior of West and West Central Africa. Approximately 60 percent of the slaves imported into the territory later known as the United States arrived between 1720 and 1780. Legal United States involvement in the international slave trade ended in 1808. Unlike what occurred in much of the Americas, the growth of the slave population in the United States, particularly in the American South, was by natural increase. The end of the slave trade did little to retard the increase of this population. In fact, in 1825 the United States had approximately 36 percent (1,750,000) of the slaves in the Americas, despite the dramatic increase in the arrival of new imports. For many of these individuals, knowledge of Africa was acquired indirectly and was only one of many cultural influences. Therefore, an understanding of the formative influences on the religious experience of African-American slaves, while recognizing the importance of the African cultural base, must take into account the New World cultural experience.

Traditional African languages had no single word for religion—religion was synonymous with a way of life. The importation of Africans into the Americas marked a transference of African ways of perceiving and responding to the spirit world, but just how strongly African influences or Africanisms survived is subject to debate. Proponents of the retention of African beliefs and practices, such as Melville Herskovits, Lawrence Levine, Sterling Stuckey, and Albert J. Raboteau point to spirit possession, musical forms, dance patterns such as the "ring shout," mounded-grave decorations, conjuring practices, and the identification of African divinities with specific saints in Roman Catholic folk piety as evidence of the survival of African traditional religion in the New World. The slaves' preference for the baptismal ritual of total immersion ("river baptisms") is often cited as an especially strong link with the West African river cults.

Other scholars, such as the early Herskovitz, E. Franklin Frazier, W. E. B. Du Bois, and Robert E. Park, have taken the view that traditional African beliefs and practices gradually weakened and in some cases died as the result of the complex interplay of forced acculturation, voluntary adaptation, and assimilation. The terrors of the Middle Passage called into question the omnipotence of the African gods and the ability of the ancestors to come to the aid of the distressed. Dealers in slaves intentionally broke up families and kinship groups and sought to create cultural anomie and linguistic confusion among the new arrivals. Slave buyers shunned the purchase of individuals who had operated as religious specialists in Africa and waged a destructive campaign against all religious practices, including the use of ritual drums that might serve as the focal point for the reconstruction of traditional African social groups on the plantations.

A third group of scholars navigate the complex issue of African influences by interpreting African-American religion as a modern phenomenon that emerges from the encounter of African slaves with European slave traders and slave holders. Charles Long, a historian of religion and the preeminent proponent of this view, maintains that African-American religion is black people's collective awareness of their own autonomy and experience of a divine other, not just a version of Christianity or any other faith tradition. This communal experience is also not confined to institutions. It is a way of being, a perspective on life that allows African Americans to liberate themselves from the oppression of Euro-Americans and to seek new and authentic expressions of human consciousness and community that take into account their value and origins. What is specifically African in African-American religion, then, is a religious consciousness that emerged out of the encounter of African slaves with Europeans.

The Christianity of Europeans is the faith tradition with which African Americans are most associated. African slaves in the Americas did not receive intensive indoctrination in Christianity for several generations. Europeans at first doubted that Africans had souls worth saving, and owners of slaves in the English colonies initially opposed the introduction of Christianity, not only because of lingering doubts about the religious capacity of the African but also because of fears that offering baptism to Africans implied spiritual equality and might spark resistance. European missionaries, such as those of the Society for the Propagation of the Gospel, who sponsored preaching among Africans in the Carolinas, persisted, and over time converts were made. The conflict between proponents of chattel slavery and the church diminished after the mid-1600s, when new laws partially relieved owners' anxieties by stating that baptism did not alter the civil estate of a slave. By 1706 at least six colonies had legislation stipulating that baptism did not make any change in the slave's status "as to his bondage, or freedom."

In the New World environment, Africans adapted and transformed European language and religious beliefs and in the process created a new African-American identity. The southern-born children and grandchildren of the Africans who participated in the transatlantic passage had to find religious meaning and seek religious expression within the predominantly white Protestant evangelical environment. The outburst of religious revivals in the 1740s and again in the early 1800s helped dismantle the colonial establishment of Anglicanism in the South and Congregationalism in New England and proved attractive to many African Americans, slave and free. Black converts and lower-class whites shared in the evangelical emphasis on conviction of sin, individual salvation, ecstatic worship, and the recompense of heaven.

An African-American Christian population of significant size and, in some places, of surprising independence developed during and after the American Revolution. Most black Christians belonged to mixed congregations where the egalitarian legacy of the Great Revival lingered on, despite inroads made by white racism among evangelicals. Independent African-American preachers, such as the Rev. Andrew Bryan of the First African Church of Savannah, established in 1788, planted numerous congregations, mostly Baptist, until a frightened white South curbed the religious freedom of blacks in the wake of the Denmark Vesey insurrection of 1822 and that led by Nat Turner in 1831. No reliable figures exist for the number of African Americans who became Christians during the era of the pioneer black preachers, but it is important to acknowledge that this experience of relative religious independence and a shared evangelical ethos provided a benchmark by which blacks could judge later efforts to use Christianity as a means of social control.

Although growing numbers of blacks, slave and free, had embraced Christianity by the beginning of the nineteenth century, the camp meetings and other mechanisms used by the evangelical preachers were limited in scope. In some places, such as among the Gullah peoples of the Sea Island district of South Carolina, and in Louisiana, where Roman Catholicism and West Indian-derived practices of voodoo intermixed, religious syncretism or creolization was so strong as to violate mainstream Christian sensibilities. Even in parts of the South, where free blacks and whites experienced common fellowship in local churches, little effort was made to reach the plantation slave.

Although many slave owners were made uneasy by some of the radically egalitarian implications of Christianity, many became convinced that Christianity, properly catechized, could make slaves more docile. In 1829, the Reverend William Capers appealed to plantation owners in South Carolina to allow him to go to their slaves. Supporters of the plantation missions were motivated by the biblical mandate to share the gospel, but they also wanted to rid the slaves of their "heathen" ways, and, as Capers argued, improve plantation efficiency on the premise that a Christian slave would be more obedient.

Nat Turner's insurrection in 1831 cast doubt on Capers's assertion, but gradually many in the white South were won over to the notion that "lessons on salvation and lessons on duty" were compatible and that the South had a divine mandate to convert and civilize the "children of Ham"—as Africans were often called because of the proslavery interpretation of the story told in Genesis 9. When abolitionists chastised southerners for the sin of slavery, the apologists of "the peculiar institution" pointed to plantation missions as evidence of their fulfillment of the Christian duty to civilize and convert and of the legitimacy of their custodial rule over "the darker race."

Just how strongly, if at all, African-American slaves internalized the religious model placed before them by whites is a difficult question. Was the Christian slave successfully indoctrinated with the notion that piety and obedience were inseparable? Or did Christianity, as expressed in the secret or "hush arbor" meetings of slaves, in their prayers and in their songs (spirituals), offer a basis from which both individual psychological independence and organized resistance could spring forth? Frederick Douglass reported that he observed fellow slaves who scoffed at the religious pretensions of whites; personally he found hypocrisy at the root of slaveholding Christianity, which he termed "bad, corrupt, and wicked." But he thought of the Christianity of Christ as impartial and "good, pure, and holy." If we are to judge by the testimony of ex-slaves, many of whom eagerly sought to read the Bible for themselves once freedom came, they had successfully appropriated Christianity in order to give meaning to their lives and cope with systematic efforts to deny their humanity. Estimates are that one in seven of the adult slaves belonged to an organized church, primarily Baptist or Methodist, by the time of the Civil War, and many more had been exposed to the influence of Christianity.

The religious outlook of the African-American slave was a complex and highly creative adaptation of European Christianity and African traditional religion to everyday needs. A few rejected Christianity altogether and retained Islam or their traditional African religion, or became persistent skeptics. Many slaves originally sought the protection and power of the conjurer, but after a period of religious instruction and Christian baptism, many came to the conclusion that conjuration was the work of the devil. Although masters attempted to enforce discipline through the use of Christianity, the slaves heard the sermons preached in the plantation chapels with a critical ear, sorted out the wheat from the chaff, and constructed a religious story in which they were the chosen of God. Although they might have, as the spirituals reflect, trouble and sorrow in this world, they could hope for the joys of heaven where "de' bottom rail become de' top rail."

Labeled as "otherworldly" and "compensatory," this use of Christianity has been judged dysfunctional by those who emphasize the need for radical political and social transformation. Discussed in the manner of Gary Marx and others, the "opiate-versus-inspiration debate," as it is sometimes referred to, forces our view of the religious culture of the African-American slave into opposing and limiting channels. By recognizing the multiple dimensions of the sacred cosmos operative in the slave quarters and "hush-arbors," we come close to understanding what the African-American slaves meant when they spoke of their beliefs in God as helping them to "keep on keeping on." They testified that they had a "home in glory land" and that no earthly master could close them out of God's house. As historian John Boles wrote, "There was a fateful ambiguity at the heart of the slave response to Christianity, and the fervent rebel, and the passive, long-suffering servant were equally authentic expressions of black religion." Once they had been "killed dead" in the spirit and were reborn, African-American Christian slaves became participants in another community than that which numbered them with cattle and cotton. This suggests Charles Long's view that African-American religion is black people's awareness of their own autonomy and experience of a divine other independent of whites.

Christianity in the Antebellum North

By focusing too exclusively on the South, we run the risk of missing important facets of the antebellum African-American religious experience. There were individual African-American Christians of note in the North, such as Lemuel Haynes, the first African American officially ordained to the Christian ministry and who served as pastor of white congregations in New England; Phillis Wheatley, who wrote religious verse read in both America and Europe; and Jupiter Hammon, a slave on Long Island, New York, who counseled Christian endurance in the hope of heaven. Though few in number until after 1800, independent black churches were organized in the North. Separated from the bulk of the country's black population, African-American Christians in the North kept the plight of their sisters and brothers in chains in their prayers; supported causes such as temperance and education, so as not to provide the apologists for slavery with an argument that freedom would ruin the slave; served as Underground Railroad stations; and assisted in the cause of abolition. They organized voluntary associations to support educational endeavors and to care for widows and orphans, and they served as the focal points of black life in the northern city, where prejudice and discrimination were prevalent.

The northern religious landscape took on more definition with the formation of the first black denominations. Following the pattern of white Christians in the post-Revolutionary era, black Christians organized into denominations. Sometimes the struggle for denominational independence was a particularly dramatic one, as was the case with black Methodists in the Philadelphia area led by Richard Allen. A former slave and convert to Christianity, Allen was convinced that the plain and simple gospel as preached by the spiritual heirs of John Wesley, the English founder of Methodism, was best suited to the unlettered black. However, white authorities resisted when Allen and other Philadelphia black Methodists in the 1790s sought greater control over their own religious affairs by establishing their own church. Armed with a decision from the Supreme Court of Pennsylvania in 1816, to the effect that Allen and his coadjutors had a legal right to the church property and self-governance, the African Methodist Episcopal (AME) denomination was organized in 1816. About six years later, black Methodists in New York City likewise achieved denominational independence under the banner of the African Methodist Episcopal Zion Church. As suggested by the label "Methodist," both groups replicated much of white Methodist ritual, doctrine, and polity while seeking to liberate themselves from the prejudicial control of white Methodists.

By the Civil War, the AME church had about twenty thousand members and had planted new missions as far west as California. Urged on by the zealous efforts of Daniel Alexander Payne, the AME church established its first institution of higher education, Wilberforce College (now Wilberforce University) and theological school, Payne Seminary, at Xenia, Ohio. The AME Zion denomination numbered about five thousand and would not expand significantly beyond the Northeast until after the Civil War, when the denomination's representatives worked aggressively among the freedmen. Eventually the denomination transferred most of its central operations to North Carolina, where it established a church newspaper and publishing house, and at Livingstone College in Salisbury.

The earliest separate black Baptist congregations appeared in northern cities in the early 1800s. Blacks customarily worshiped with white Baptists, but the "Negro Pew" was tolerated and eventually blacks sought to organize their own congregations. In 1805, Thomas Paul became the first pastor of the First African (or Joy Street) Baptist Church of Boston, and in 1808 he assisted in the organization of Abyssinian Baptist Church in New York City. Independent black Baptist congregations eventually emerged in most northern cities, but the traditional Baptist emphasis on local autonomy retarded the development of regional associations until the formation of the Providence Association in 1834 and the Union Association in 1836, both in Ohio, and the Wood River Association in 1839 in southwestern Illinois.

Sparked by interest in developing missions in Africa, black Baptists gradually moved toward more national organizations. The American Baptist Missionary Convention became the first such cooperative arrangement in 1840. In the decades after the Civil War, black Baptists debated whether or not to continue partnerships with northern white Baptists in foreign missions and the publication of religious literature. The nationalist or independent spirit finally triumphed in the formation of the first truly national black organization, the National Baptist Convention, U.S.A. Inc., in 1895. The cooperationists formed the Lott Carey Foreign Mission Convention in 1897.

Because of Baptist disunity during most of the nineteenth century, the African Methodist story tends to assume center stage in accounts of the institutional history of African-American religion. Better organized than the Baptists—and fortunate to have denominational historians such as Bishop Daniel A. Payne and Bishop Benjamin Tucker Tanner—the northern-based African Methodists dominate the documentary record. But statistics of denominational membership published by the U.S. Census Bureau reveal that black Baptists outnumbered black Methodists as the century drew to a close. This was largely due to expansion in the South after Emancipation when the ex-slaves, though heavily recruited by agents of the northern-based denominations, black and white, elected to form new congregations in which they could hear preachers familiar with the religious style found in the antebellum plantation congregations.

Civil War to World War II

When slaves deserted their masters during the Civil War or became contraband as Union troops advanced on Southern soil, a new religious landscape began to emerge. Eager to read the Bible on their own and worship without white oversight, the freed slaves were convinced that their emancipation was tantamount to the deliverance of the Children of Israel from the pharaoh of Egypt. African-American Christians seized the moment and left the denominations of their former masters in large numbers. The Colored Methodist Episcopal Church was organized in 1870 at Jackson, Tennessee, and was comprised principally of former members of the Methodist Episcopal Church, South, who did not desire to join the northern-based African Methodists. As if by spontaneous combustion, black Baptist congregations appeared in great numbers throughout the South. These Baptist churches and their Methodist counterparts in the small towns and rural areas represented the core religious culture of African Americans in the South between the Civil War and World War I. Heavily influenced by the folk practices of the "invisible institution" and often criticized for its demonstrative religious style—with emphasis on dramatic conversion experiences, emotional preaching and "testifying"—southern African-American religion developed its own internal dynamic. African-American churches in the North, with their educated ministers and more formal worship styles, developed differently. On the eve of World War I, therefore, two African-American religious cultures existed: one northern and urban, the other mostly southern and rural.

Despite the cultural differences between the northern and southern black religion, most observers agreed that the church was central to African-American life as the twentieth century dawned. "The Negro Church," Booker T. Washington wrote in 1909, "was the first institution to develop out of the life of the Negro masses and still retains the strongest hold upon them." "The Negro church of today," W. E. B. Du Bois had written six years earlier, "is the social center of Negro life in the United States, and the most characteristic expression of the African character." An institution so central to African Americans could not escape internal discussion of the prevailing social and political issues raised in the larger society.

One of the most important issues concerned the role that women should play in male-dominated institutions such as the church, where the pulpit had been traditionally defined as "men's space" and the pew as "women's place." The AME Zion church authorized the ordination of women in the 1890s, the AME church in 1948, and the CME church in 1954. Appealing to the principle of congregational autonomy, the major black Baptist conventions avoided legislating policy on the ordination of women. Conservative attitudes at the congregational level, where gender bias among the male clergy is strong, has proved to be an obstacle to many women who have sought ordination. The Church of God in Christ, the largest black Pentecostal body, prohibits the ordination of women.

Historically, women have been in the majority in the mainline black denominations, yet men have dominated the leadership. Women serve as "mothers of the church," are active in missionary societies, educational efforts, and a wide variety of charitable causes, and serve local congregations in numerous capacities, such as teachers, stewardesses, and deaconesses. Yet men hold denominational offices and monopolize the clergy rosters to a greater degree than in the more liberal white Protestant churches. Women who wish to exercise the gift of the spirit have had to operate as independent evangelists, such as Jarena Lee did after an originally futile appeal to Richard Allen and

A Southern baptism. *A group of African Americans line up along a river's edge in Aiken, South Carolina, preparing to be baptized.* RARE BOOKS AND SPECIAL COLLECTIONS DIVISION, THE LIBRARY OF CONGRESS. REPRODUCED BY PERMISSION.

the African Methodists in the early 1800s. Sojourner Truth, Harriet Tubman, and Rebecca Cox Jackson (who eventually joined the Shakers) possessed spiritual gifts that the established black denominations did not formally recognize. Amanda Berry Smith left the AME Church in order to exercise her ministry more freely, joined the Holiness Movement, and thereby served as a precursor for the many women who found the freedom to develop their own ministries within the orbit of the burgeoning Pentecostal and Holiness movement, which flourished in the "sanctified" storefronts of the urban North. For example, Elder Lucy Smith (1874–1952) founded All Nations Pentecostal Church in Chicago and conducted a multidimensional ministry that dealt with the material as well as the spiritual needs of her members.

African-American women such as Maria W. Stewart, Frances Ellen Watkins Harper, and Ida Wells-Barnett channeled their gifts for ministry into social justice causes outside of the male-dominated churches. Stewart and especially Watkins Harper became well known in their time as champions of abolition, temperance, the civil rights of African Americans and women, and the education of African-American children. In the late nineteenth century, Wells-Barnett championed these causes, and also became well known for her anti-lynching campaign. Although working independently of established black churches, these women nevertheless remained affiliated with them, particularly African Methodism. Watkins Harper, whom Carla Peterson calls a "poet-preacher," published her poetry, stories, and essays in the major papers of the AME church throughout her long career.

The majority of reform- and ministerially-minded black women, however, formed auxiliary organizations in churches that maintained and supported the financial and spiritual health of these institutions. For example, the Women's Parent Mite Missionary Society of the AME Church, founded in 1874, supported new churches in the western United States and in South Africa. Sarah Elizabeth Miller Tanner, an active member of this group whose son was active in AME missions in South Africa, and whose husband was Bishop Benjamin Tucker Tanner, witnessed to the efforts of these churchwomen in an 1896 article in the *A. M. E. Church Review*. Black Baptist women also founded organizations that served as the "backbone" of their churches and communities. Baptist women led by Nannie Helen Burroughs formed the Women's Convention of the National Baptist Convention in 1900, and operated the National School for Girls in Washington.

Many of these church women—AME, Baptist, and otherwise—were also active in the club movement, which stressed self-help, charitable, and civic work, and served as a focal point for women's independent identity. Beset by racism in the larger society and confronted by patriarchal attitudes within their denominations, African-American churchwomen had to confront multiple challenges. They played an especially important role in bridging the gap between church work as traditionally defined and secular reform activity. The demands upon them intensified with the outbreak of World War I.

The centrality of women in the local congregation became all the more apparent because of external social forces in the flight from field to factory once the call for labor went out from the North. After 1910, in the early years of the Great Migration, males, particularly young males, went north lured by the promise of better jobs. Women and the young were left to carry on congregational life. Urbanization proved to be no panacea. Indeed, in poor urban areas, church adherence was increasingly the sphere of women and children. This is especially true of the independent churches, known as "storefronts." In an extensive study done in the 1980s, researchers found that in 2,150 black churches, of various denominations, women outnumbered men by a factor of 2.5 to 1. Some observers have spoken of the "feminization of the black church" because of the relative absence of males, especially young males, in urban congregations.

The urbanization of African-American religion also precipitated an institutional crisis in the existing black churches. In 1910 nearly 90 percent of the nation's black population lived in the South, mostly in rural regions and small towns. Since the end of the Civil War, the church had assumed a dominant position in the life of southern blacks, whose institutional development in other areas was restricted by racial apartheid. By default, then, the churches served multiple purposes worship, education, recreation, and socialization. Northern black leaders, as well as some Southern leaders (e.g., Booker T. Washington) pointed to such problems as overchurching, undereducated ministers, pastors with multiple charges, congregations too small to maintain programs and property, and too little emphasis on the social and political problems of the day. Carter G. Woodson referred to rural churches as "mystic shrines" while writing approvingly of northern urban churches as progressive centers of "social uplift." This debate over the mission of the black church was heightened by the Great Migration because it placed new demands upon existing denominational and local church resources and programs.

The population shift put severe strains upon existing denominational structures. Home missionary boards lacked adequate resources to cope with the need in the North, and congregations in the South were left depleted and deserted. Competition among the three major black Methodist bodies prevented a cooperative effort in addressing the needs of the migrants. The National Baptist Convention, U.S.A., Inc., underwent a contentious division in 1915, which resulted in the formation of a rival body, the National Baptist Convention of America Unincorporated, later named National Baptist Convention of America in 1916. The internecine war continued for years, draining away critically needed resources. The secretary of the Home Mission Board of the National Baptist Convention, U.S.A., Inc., reported in 1921: "We have quite a number of destitute fields both North and South and in many cases no opportunity for religious worship."

The regional shift in America's black population portended difficulties because as World War I began the black denominations were heavily weighted to the South. In 1916 the U.S. Census of Religious Bodies credited the National Baptists with 2,939,579 members, 89 percent of whom were in the South. The AME Church had 548,355 members and was 81.2 percent southern. The AME Zion Church was 84.6 percent southern with a total membership of 257,169. The CME Church, composed principally of the descendants of ex-slaves, was 95.5 percent southern and 245,749 members strong. None of the Pentecostal or Holiness bodies, which became so important in the urban North after the Great Migration, receive recognition in the 1916 religious census.

In addition to placing strains upon ecclesiastical structures inherited from the nineteenth century and oriented primarily toward the small town and rural church, urbanization offered African Americans new religious options. Baptist and Methodist preachers now had to compete with the agents of the Pentecostal and Holiness churches. These churches put great emphasis on an intense personal experience of the Holy Spirit. The Church of God in Christ, led by Charles Harrison Mason, held its first Pentecostal general assembly in 1907. Having started as a rural church in Mississippi, the denomination grew to become a fixture in the northern city. Ill at ease in the more formal worship services of the established northern churches, many migrants organized prayer bands, started house churches, or moved into the storefronts where speaking in tongues (sometimes referred to as the practice of glossolalia) received the blessing of the Pentecostals. The Church of Christ (Holiness), U.S.A., under the leadership of Elder C. P. Jones, likewise expanded as a result of the burgeoning black populations of urban industrial America. Other Holiness and Pentecostal churches were founded by denominationally independent religious entrepreneurs who recognized that the migrants from the South desired something that the northern black middle-class churches did not offer.

Many of the migrants wanted religious environments that reminded them of their churches back home, where they were known by and part of an extended family. The ecstatic worship services and musical styles favored by the Pentecostal and Holiness preachers caught the attention of these ex-southerners. When hard times befell them in the North, migrants sought out spiritual havens in the urban wilderness. Holiness and Pentecostal churches multiplied everywhere, and existing Baptist and Methodist churches split or sponsored daughter congregations as the migrant population swelled. On occasion, northern black Christians criticized their "brothers and sisters" from the South for falling short of northern cultural expectations and the existing class norms. In turn, migrants shunned some northern black churches, where the elaborate and elegant services made them feel out of place. Some fell away from organized religion all together. Others responded to their crisis of faith in the city by transplanting churches from the South led by the pastors who had followed them northward.

The tension between the two cultural streams that came together after the beginning of World War I is illustrated by the reluctance of the older African-American congregations in Chicago to accept gospel music. Gospel music was popularized by Thomas Dorsey, the "father of gospel music," who joined Pilgrim Baptist Church in Chicago in 1921. Unlike the purveyors of commercialized gospel today, early gospel music was church centered. Yet as Mahalia Jackson, the best-known singer of gospel, learned while growing up in New Orleans, the musical distance between the honky-tonk and a Holiness revival with its beating and tambourine shaking is not that great. Dorsey, building on the work of predecessors such as Charles Albert Tindley, was the principal force behind the introduction of blueslike gospel songs into the northern black churches. About 1930, observers of the Chicago scene reported that "Negro churches, particularly the storefront congregations, the Sanctified groups and the shouting Baptists, were swaying and jumping as never before. Mighty rhythms rocked the churches. A wave of fresh rapture came over the people." Jackson earned worldwide acclamation for her solo renditions of gospel classics, and the pioneering touring groups such as the Dixie Hummingbirds and the Five Blind Boys of Mississippi helped make gospel so popular that today it is rare to find a black church, of whatever denomination or class composition, that closes its doors to the gospel sound.

Religious diversity, even dissonance, resonated from the large, densely crowded, black urban centers after World War I. After examining data from the 1926 Federal Census of Religious Bodies, Miles Mark Fisher exclaimed: "Almost in every center, particularly urban, is some unorthodox religious group which makes a definite appeal to Negroes." The Jamaican-born black nationalist Marcus Garvey discouraged talk of founding a new church, but he and his Universal Negro Improvement Association (1918–1927) had many followers who sought collective redemption in the back-to-Africa ideology. There were also some supporters, such as George Alexander McGuire, the founder of the African Orthodox Church, who did initiate Garveyite-inspired demonstrations. The UNIA collapsed after the deportation of its "Black Moses" in 1927, but other charismatic personalities came forward offering often exotic visions of heaven on earth. Father Divine set up a series of Peace Missions during the Great Depression, offering his devotees the unusual mix of "God" in the flesh and a refuge from society's problems. Scores of religious entrepreneurs opened shop in the black ghettos, where they competed with the mainline denominations. Frequently referred to as cults and sects, the groups led by these new messiahs often died when their founders did, but some managed to survive under different leadership, as, for example, the one led by Daddy Grace (the United House of Prayer for All People). Representatives of the mainline churches frequently decried the proliferation of these alternative groups, arguing, as the Baptist Miles Mark Fisher did, that the principal message of the cults and sects was "Let us prey," not "Let us pray."

The appearance on urban street corners of black adherents of Islam and Judaism added to the perception that African-American religion was undergoing a radical reorientation in the interwar period at the expense of the historic black denominations. The first black Jewish group recognized by the federal religious census was founded in 1896 by William S. Crowdy, a Santa Fe Railroad cook, in Lawrence, Kansas. African Americans wearing the yarmulke and speaking Yiddish came to the attention of a wider public in the 1920s. Located primarily in the boroughs of New York City, these teachers of black Hebraism appropriated and adapted the rituals and teachings of Orthodox Judaism. Though never large in number, the followers of Rabbi Arnold Ford and other proponents of Black Judaism generated a great deal of interest among the curious and the skeptical.

Islam was not entirely unheard of among African Americans before the mysterious figure of Wallace D. Fard appeared in the "Paradise Valley" of Detroit in 1930 to wake up the sleeping "Lost-Found Nation of Islam." There is increasing evidence that a small but not insignificant number of enslaved Africans brought knowledge of the Qur'an and Islamic law to North America. But modern Islam among African Americans begins with the career of

Noble Drew Ali, a native of North Carolina and founder of Moorish Science in Newark, New Jersey, about 1913. However, the man who most popularized Islam for African Americans was the one-time disciple of Wallace Fard, Elijah Muhammad, who capitalized on the interest of urbanized blacks in the religiously exotic. Himself a migrant from Georgia, Muhammad (formerly Elijah Poole) assumed leadership of the Nation of Islam after Fard's disappearance in 1934, and moved its headquarters to Chicago. The Nation's version of Islam did not fare well under the scrutiny of orthodox scholars of the Qur'an, and eventually the sect broke into rival factions. Nevertheless, it has had a significant impact upon many African Americans, chiefly the young and angry like Malcolm X who believed that traditional black Christianity was a "pie-in-the-sky" religion.

Attention to the new religious options that appeared in black urban America during the period between World War I and World War II should not be at the expense of the story of the mainline black churches. Stimulated by the crisis brought about by the influx of thousands from the South, the established churches struggled with a redefinition of mission during these decades. Richard R. Wright, Jr., examined the record of black church involvement within the public sphere in 1907 and concluded that only a few churches had "attacked the problems of real city Negroes." His own work in Chicago's Institutional Church and Social Settlement, founded by Reverdy Ransom, and later at Chicago's Trinity Mission and Culture Center, which Wright organized in 1905, convinced Wright that black churches needed a more compelling definition of urban mission than presently at hand. Prior to World War I outreach primarily involved mission and charity work with the intent of recruiting new members. As Wright and Ransom discovered for themselves, pastors who addressed contemporary social problems born of urban and industrial growth were deemed too radical by denominational officials.

Most black preachers, urban and rural, still thought of sin and salvation in individualistic terms. The black denominations lagged behind their white counterparts in adopting the theological message of the social gospel movement with its focus upon the problems of urban America. Beginning with the era of the Great Migration, however, many more black churches incorporated programs into their understanding of "church work" that went beyond the traditional emphasis on praying and preaching. They assisted with needs in housing, employment, education, recreation, and health care. The instrumentalist use of the church to better the community is today so widely accepted that black clergy or congregations who show no interest in everyday problems have little appeal or credibility among African Americans.

Although black denominations were spared the bitter internecine battles that erupted in the 1920s between the white fundamentalists and modernists over such issues as the interpretation of the Creation story in Genesis, their efforts to merge have failed. Concerned about institutional inefficiency and lost opportunities to influence the larger society and motivated by the ideal that Christ's church be one, representatives of the three principal branches of black Methodism began meetings in 1915 to discuss the possibility of merger. But leaders of the CME church (formerly the Colored Methodist Episcopal church and since 1954 the Christian Methodist Episcopal Church), balked at union because of fears of being dominated by the two larger northern black Methodist bodies: the AME and the AME Zion churches. Division among black Methodists was widened by the segregation of 315,000 in the Central Jurisdiction, a nongeographical entity, of the predominantly white United Methodist Church in 1939 after the merger of the northern and southern branches of Methodism (the segregated structure was abolished in the 1960s). Black Baptists likewise have been unable to heal the divisions within their ranks. The National Baptist Convention, U.S.A., Inc., remains the largest of all black church connections, claiming about 7.5 million members and 30,000 local churches in the late 1980s.

The contemporary black Baptist story is still best told in terms of the local congregation. Ministerial alliances at the local level have fostered interdenominational cooperation where there has been sufficient need for common action. In many congregations, the minister is still the dominant personality. Critics have argued that the domineering role played by the pastor in black congregations has retarded the development of lay leadership. The preeminence of the black minister in African-American religious culture has historical roots. Because of the class and caste attitudes of whites in the South, the ministry remained one of the few professions accessible to blacks. Even in the North, where political boundaries were defined by patterns of residential segregation and black political participation was restricted, black ministers were called upon to speak for their community before local authorities. Participation in electoral and protest politics has engaged the energies of many contemporary black clergy, but they have had to divide their time between their civic roles and their pastoral roles.

Civil Rights Era to the Present

The internal life of African-American churches probably escaped the attention of most of white America until the Rev. Dr. Martin Luther King, Jr., began to catch the eye and ear of the news media. Rooted deep in the black Baptist tradition, King was schooled in the preaching tradition of the black church of the South. While doing advanced theological training in the North, he became proficient in the major currents of thought among liberal, socially aware Protestants. This made it possible for him to appeal to the conscience of white America during the civil rights struggle and to enlist the aid of allies from the more liberal white denominations. Yet the grassroots participation of thousands of black churchgoers who marched and sang and prayed transformed King's protest of racial segregation in Montgomery, Alabama, into a mass movement. From the vantage point of these people of faith, a civil rights march was as much a religious crusade as a social movement. While the cause of civil rights united black religious leaders across denominational lines and cemented alliances with progressive forces in the predominantly white Protestant, Catholic, and Jewish communities, there were disharmonious chords. The Rev. Joseph H. Jackson, who served as president of the National Baptist Convention from 1953 to 1982, resisted the attempt of King and others to move the largest Protestant denomination in the world into activist or protest politics. As a result, King, with the Rev. Ralph David Abernathy, Gardner C. Taylor, and others, formed the Progressive National Baptist Convention in 1961 under the motto: "Unity, service, fellowship, peace."

One of the most important influences on King's thought and activism was Howard Thurman, an African-American churchman of major stature in his own right. A theologian, mystic, professor, and founder of the first interracial church in the United States, Thurman knew King informally through his father. Like many others in the civil rights movement, though, King was compelled by Thurman's *Jesus and the Disinherited*, a small but powerful book that Thurman wrote in the late 1940s in the wake of his meeting with Mohandas K. Gandhi.

The civil rights movement, of course, was not confined to institutional church circles. Nor are its religious dimensions fully measured by focusing, for example, on the Southern Christian Leadership Conference (SCLC) led by King. Organizations with a more secular orientation, such as the Student Nonviolent Coordinating Committee (SNCC), also had crucial roles to play. But even the members of SNCC were animated by a vision of the grassroots black church, especially in the South, an institution that propelled the crusade that eventually broke down the barriers of legalized segregation. While a form of religious sectarianism among many African Americans has led to withdrawal and isolation from the public sphere, orthodox or mainline black churches have for the most part been instrumental in bringing America closer to Dr. King's dream of the "beloved community."

A dramatic scenario for the re-envisioning of America unfolded in the decade of the 1960s, when the call for Black Power was heard. Originating among young radicals, many of whom were estranged from the traditional black church, the largely secular Black Power movement quickly drew a theological response. It came first from individuals such as James Cone, who were situated in academic environments, but it eventually engaged the thinking of denominational representatives. Their statements revealed both agreement with the diagnosis of the wrongs of American society as portrayed by advocates of Black Power, but also some uneasiness regarding the means necessary to achieve a just society. King had taught that nonviolence was ethically essential given the witness of the New Testament. During the civil rights crusade, local churches served as training grounds in nonviolent resistance. In contrast, the more strident advocates of Black Power carried weapons and, rhetorically at least, endorsed their use in conflicts with the police and others in authority. Steeped in the traditional Christian doctrine that the use of violence is a betrayal of the ethics of Jesus, most black Christians remained skeptical of the means the militants justified.

Nevertheless, the Black Power advocates made a lasting impact on black churches. By raising cultural awareness, black nationalists—as Garvey had done in the 1920s and earlier back-to-Africa proponents such as Bishop Henry M. Turner of the AME church did in the 1880s—stimulated interest in and debate over the essential question of "how black is black religion?" Black Muslims also played a significant role in this challenge to black Christian churches. African-American clergy in the predominantly white Protestant groups organized caucuses in which they examined their historic and contemporary relationship with their host denominations. This analysis led to demands for representation in the higher echelons of institutional life, for more black clergy, and for the incorporation of distinctively African-American religious styles in worship. Black Roman Catholics also experienced a renaissance of pride in "blackness," variously defined. Representations of a Black Jesus appeared in Roman Catholic sanctuaries, and the refrains of gospel music could be heard during Mass sung in English following the reforms of Vatican II (1963–1965). In other religious traditions such as the Presbyterian, Episcopal, and Lutheran, African Americans also pressed for a greater appreciation of the rich African and African-American religious heritage.

Womanism is one of the most important intellectual and activist traditions of the black Christian churches to emerge from the civil rights, black theology, and women's movements of the 1960s, 1970s, and 1980s. In the late

1980s Jacquelyn Grant, Katie Geneva Cannon, Delores Williams, and Cheryl Townsend Gilkes, some of the major figures of this black feminist movement, confronted the paternalism of the black churches, the racism of white feminist theologians, and the sexism, racism, and classism of American society at large. Recognizing their roots in the struggles of generations of black women, and taking their name from an expression in Alice Walker's *In Search of Our Mother's Gardens*, they identify themselves as thinkers, teachers, activists, and preachers with a commitment to the well being of African-American women, men, and children. These pioneering women have initiated a powerful and growing movement in seminaries and divinity schools throughout the United States. By training both male and female ministers to think more holistically, they have made an impact—however modest—on both black and white denominations.

One of the most prominent and successful ministers in this tradition is the Reverend Vashti Murphy McKenzie. A graduate of Howard University's divinity school and a member of a prominent black Baltimore family, McKenzie is the first black woman preacher to speak at the democratic national convention. She is one of a few female ministers to lead a large AME congregation, and more important, one of the few black women to be appointed to the office of bishop in the AME church. McKenzie is also a much sought-after speaker.

For all of the gains of womanists such as McKenzie, Grant, Cannon, and others—including being part of the leadership of mainline African-American churches, sitting on the faculty of major seminaries and divinity schools, heading venerable professional organizations such as the Society for the Study of Black Religion, and sitting on the boards of powerful educational organizations such as the Association of Theological Schools and the Fund for Theological Education, African-American women still fight for recognition in black churches. Obtaining such recognition means getting congregants to revise their sense of a male, preacher-centered culture.

At the core of the complex religious pilgrimage of peoples of African descent in America is the importance of the local congregation of believers who celebrate together the rites of passage of its members from baptism to Christian burial. Most black churches, however, emphasize preaching over the sacraments, in contrast to liturgical traditions such as Roman Catholicism and Lutheranism. The spoken word, whether in sermon or song, is at the core of black worship, and the male preacher remains the embodiment of the word. Indeed, the roster of celebrated black preachers is long. The Rev. C. L. Franklin of Detroit is but one example. Called "the most imitated soul preacher in history" by the Rev. Jesse Jackson, Franklin shepherded more than ten thousand members of Detroit's New Bethel Baptist Church at the height of his popularity. He carried the sermon to an art form, was heard on the radio by a large audience, and sold millions of records.

In spite of their paternalism, black churches historically have served as the centers of African-American life and identity. Benjamin Mays, the distinguished educator in Atlanta and mentor of Martin Luther King, Jr., wrote of the church of his youth in rural South Carolina: "Old Mount Zion was an important institution in my community. Negroes had nowhere to go but to church. They went there to worship, to hear the choir sing, to listen to the preacher, and to hear and see the people shout. The young people went to Mount Zion to socialize, or simply to stand around and talk. It was a place of worship and a social center as well. There was no other place to go."

The black mainline denominations so central to the lives of persons like Benjamin Mays experienced a renewal in the 1970s, 1980s, and 1990s that was largely spawned by a growing black middle class. Churches such as Trinity United Church of Christ in Chicago under Jeremiah Wright reinterpreted the ongoing issues of civil justice and economic empowerment in terms appropriate to an African-American laity with college and graduate degrees, middle-class aspirations, and professional careers. This educated and upwardly mobile laity, also known as buppies, demanded an equally educated and professionalized ministry with graduate degrees from prestigious institutions such as the University of Chicago Divinity School. By the same token, this prosperous laity itself brought resources of its own to these churches. As Cheryl Gilkes and Beverly Hall point out, such churches, many of them large complexes or megachurches, have health and wellness programs, day care and fitness centers, job training, and men's, women's, and youth's programs staffed by qualified professionals from among the laity.

The nondenominational Word of Faith Movement, which exploded in the 1980s, and continues to thrive into the twenty-first century, also draws adherents from the black middle class. This movement, however, appeals to a larger cross section of African Americans, and preaches a theology of prosperity. According to its adherents, God wants his people to be prosperous, even wealthy. But in order for one to obtain material prosperity, one must have unwavering faith in God's promises and follow God's commands. While not exclusively an African-American phenomenon, blacks nevertheless constitute a large part of the leadership and the membership of these Word churches. Fred Price of South Central Los Angeles is one of the most prominent black ministers in this movement.

Milmon Harrison notes that blacks are attracted to this movement because it foregrounds the material well-being that has always been a part of black religious traditions.

In spite of their differences, the Word of Faith churches and revitalized mainline churches share a common criticism. Critics contend that neither the revitalized mainline black denominations nor the Word of Faith churches are concerned about poor blacks. Both groups succumb to the lure of middle-class America and leave the poorest of the poor behind. Such critics often credit the Nation of Islam with being able to reach into the ranks of the youthful street gangs and to make converts among African Americans in the country's prisons. While there is some truth to their criticisms, they overlook the various street ministries sponsored by mainline black churches or independent evangelical preachers and the extensive community services such as "meals on wheels" programs, Head Start schools, and recreational facilities, found in most places where black churches are active.

The work that black churches do to meet the needs of African Americans often entails a kind of grassroots ecumenism. In his study of a group of small congregations in northern California, theologian and pastor James Noel noted that "it is quite common for members of a particular Marin City congregation to have members of their immediate or extended family represented in . . . other Marin City congregations. Consequently, when it comes to things like pastoral care, and even more self-conscious corporate efforts such as economic development, Marin City pastors [of different denominations] have been involved in 'an ecumenical team ministry' directed toward the community." This kind of collaborative effort and pooling of resources across denominational lines has always characterized black religious institutional life, and is even carried on in the academy, where, as Cheryl Gilkes rightly observes, African-American seminarians in field education placements regularly work across denominations. In professional organizations, African Americans of different denominations and faiths also collaborate with their Hispanic, Asian, and Euro-American colleagues. Examples of the latter are exemplified in anthologies such as *Inheriting Our Mothers' Gardens*, edited by Katie Cannon, Ada María Isasi-Díaz, Kwok Pui-Lan, and Letty Russell, and *The Ties That Bind*, edited by Anthony Pinn and Benjamin Valentin.

Formal expressions of ecumenism on the order of Euro-Christian institutions, however, have been minimal. The major black denominations have indeed been involved in ecumenical agencies such as the National Council of Churches. But there exists no national organization made up exclusively of representatives of the black denominations that could work for a reduction in competition and redundancy at the local level, as well as speak more authoritatively on matters of public concern. The partially successful attempts at African-American ecumenism include: the Fraternal Council of Negro Churches (1934–early 1950s); the Black Power–oriented National Conference of Black Churchmen (1967–1973); the Congress of National Black Churches (1978–present). One of the most successful formal ecumenical efforts by the black church is the Interdenominational Theological Center, a consortium of six primarily black denominations at the Atlanta University Center.

However successful these ecumenical efforts might be, whether formal or informal, they do not diminish the fact that the needs and issues facing most black churches are often overwhelming. HIV/AIDS, troubles facing black youth, especially black males, women and welfare reform, and the like outstrip the resources of these institutions, and often exacerbate the churches' own inability to address the sexuality and gender issues at the core of many of these social ills. Recently, financial assistance has come from the conservative wing of the federal government. Only time will tell whether this kind of support will fuel the biblical conservatism dogging these churches and testing their fifty-year-old identity as grassroots civil-rights organizations. Robert Franklin, Kelly Brown Douglas, and Cornel West bring these matters to the fore and offer fresh assessments and challenges.

During the 1950s, when the crusade to break down the walls of prejudice and discrimination crested, some observers wondered what the fate of the black churches would be if racial assimilation replaced racial apartheid. Since the historic African-American denominations had originated in protest to the exclusionary policies prevalent among white Christians, so the argument went, the rationale for separate black religious institutions weakened as the predominantly white denominations became more egalitarian. That African-American religious institutions continue to expand some four decades after Martin Luther King Jr. trumpeted the call for a new day in the relationship between black and white America should signal that African-American religion has been more than a simple reaction to the religious experiences and practices of Americans of European descent. It stands as an enduring witness to the multicultural texture of the entire American experience.

See also African Methodist Episcopal Church; African Methodist Episcopal Zion Church; African Orthodox Church; African Union Methodism; Baptists; Black Power Movement; Candomblé; Catholicism in the

Americas; Christian Denominations, Independent; Christian Methodist Episcopal Church; Du Bois, W. E. B.; Frazier, Edward Franklin; Gospel Music; Gullah; Islam; Judaism; Nation of Islam; National Baptist Convention, U.S.A.; National Black Evangelical Association; Protestantism in the Americas; Santería; Tanner, Benjamin Tucker; Voodoo

Bibliography

Andrews, William L., ed. *Sisters of the Spirit: Three Black Women's Autobiographies of the Nineteenth Century*. Bloomington: Indiana University Press, 1986.

Angell, Stephen Ward, and Anthony B. Pinn, eds. *Social Protest Thought in the African Methodist Episcopal Church, 1862–1939*. Knoxville: University of Tennessee Press, 2000.

Austin, Allen D. *African Muslims in Antebellum America: A Sourcebook*. New York: Routledge, 1984.

Baer, Hans A., and Merrill Singer. *African American Religion in the Twentieth Century: Varieties of Protest and Accommodation*. Knoxville: University of Tennessee Press 1992.

Baraka, Imamu Amiri (Leroi Jones). *Blues People: Negro Music in White America*. New York: William Morrow, 1963; rev. ed., 1999.

Billingsley, Andrew. *Mighty Like a River: The Black Church and Social Reform*. New York: Oxford University Press, 1999.

Blassingame, John, ed. *Slave Testimony: Two Centuries of Letters, Speeches, Interviews, and Autobiographies*. Baton Rouge: Louisiana State University Press, 1977.

Boles, John B., ed. *Masters and Slaves in the House of the Lord: Race and Religion in the American South, 1740–1870*. Lexington: University Press of Kentucky, 1988.

Burkett, Randall. *Black Redemption: Garveyism as a Religious Movement*. Metuchen, N.J.: Scarecrow Press, 1978.

Burkett, Randall, and Richard Newman, eds. *Black Apostles: Afro-American Clergy Confront the Twentieth Century*. Boston: G. K. Hall, 1978.

Burnham, Kenneth E. *God Comes to America: Father Divine and the Peace Mission Movement*. Boston: Lambeth Press, 1979.

Cannon, Katie Geneva. *Black Womanist Ethics*. Atlanta: Scholars Press, 1988.

Cone, James. *For My People: Black Theology and the Black Church*. Maryknoll, N.Y.: Orbis Books, 1984.

Cone, James. *God of the Oppressed*. New York: Seabury Press, 1975; rev. ed., Maryknoll, N.Y.: Orbis Books, 1997.

Davis, Cyprian. *The History of Black Catholics in the United States*. New York: Crossroads, 1990.

Dodson, Jualynne. "Nineteenth-Century A.M.E. Preaching Women: Cutting Edge of Women's Inclusion in Church Polity." In *Women in New Worlds: Historical Perspectives on the Wesleyan Tradition*, Vol. 1, edited by Hilah Thomas and Rosemary Skinner Keller, pp. 276–289. Nashville, Tenn.: Abingdon Press, 1981.

Douglass, Kelly Brown. *Sexuality and the Black Church: A Womanist Perspective*. Maryknoll, N.Y.: Orbis Books, 1999.

Du Bois, William Edward Burghardt. *The Souls of Black Folk: Essays and Sketches*. Chicago: A.C. Mcclurg, 1903.

Epstein, Dena J. *Sinful Tunes and Spirituals: Black Folk Music to the Civil War*. Urbana: University of Illinois Press, 1977.

Faryna, Stan, Brad Stetson, and Joseph Conti, eds. *Black and Right: The Bold New Voice of Black Conservatives in America*. Westport, Conn.: Praeger, 1997.

Fluker, Walter Earl, and Catherine Tumber, eds. *A Strange Freedom: The Best of Howard Thurman on Religious Experience and Public Life*. Boston: Beacon Press, 1998.

Franklin, Robert Michael. *Another Day's Journey: Black Churches Confronting the American Crisis*. Minneapolis: Fortress Press, 1997.

Frazier, E. Franklin, and C. Eric Lincoln. *The Negro Church in America: The Black Church Since Frazier*. New York: Schocken Books, 1974.

Fulap, Timothy, and Albert J. Raboteau, eds. *African American Religion: Interpretive Essays in History and Culture*. New York: Routledge, 1996.

George, Carol V. R. *Segregated Sabbaths: Richard Allen and the Emergence of Independent Black Churches, 1760–1840*. New York: Oxford University Press, 1973.

Gilkes, Cheryl Townsend. "Plenty Good Room: Adaptation in a Changing Black Church." *The Annals of the American Academy of Political and Social Science* 558 (July 1998): 101–121.

Gilkes, Cheryl Townsend. *If It Wasn't for the Women: Black Women's Experience and Womanist Culture in Church and Community*. Maryknoll, N.Y.: Orbis Books, 2001.

Gomez, Michael Angelo. *Exchanging Our Country Marks: The Transformation Of African Identities in the Colonial and Antebellum South*. Chapel Hill: University of North Carolina Press, 1998.

Grant, Jacquelyn. *White Women's Christ and Black Women's Jesus: Feminist Christology and Womanist Response*. Atlanta: Scholars Press 1989.

Harris, Michael W. *The Rise of Gospel Blues: The Music of Thomas Andrew Dorsey in the Urban Church*. New York: Oxford University Press, 1992.

Harrison, Milmon F. *Righteous Riches: The Word of Faith Movement in Contemporary African American Religion*. New York: Oxford University Press, 2005.

Herskovits, Melville J. *The Myth of the Negro Past*. New York: Harper and Brothers, 1941.

Higginbotham, Evelyn Brooks. *Righteous Discontent: The Women's Movement in the Black Baptist Church, 1880–1920*. Cambridge, Mass.: Harvard University Press, 1993.

Hurston, Zora Neale. *The Sanctified Church*. New York: Marlow and Company, 1981.

Jackson, Joseph H. *A Story of Christian Activism: The History of the National Baptist Convention, U.S.A., Inc.* Nashville, Tenn.: Townsend Press, 1980.

Levine, Lawrence W. *Black Culture and Black Consciousness: Afro-American Folk Thought from Slavery to Freedom*. New York: Oxford University Press, 1977.

Lincoln, C. Eric, and Lawrence H. Mamiya. *The Black Church in the African American Experience*. Durham: Duke University Press, 1990.

Long, Charles H. *Significations: Signs, Symbols, and Images in the Interpretation of Religion*. Philadelphia: Fortress Press, 1986.

Martin, Sandy D. *Black Baptists and African Missions: The Origins of a Movement 1880–1915.* Macon, Ga.: Mercer University Press, 1989.

Mays, Benjamin Elijah, and Joseph William Nicholson. *The Negro's Church.* New York: Institute of Social and Religious Research, 1933.

Murphy, Larry G. *Down by the Riverside: Readings in African American Religion.* New York: New York University Press, 2000.

Murphy, Larry G., J. Gordon Melton, and Gary L. Ward, eds. *Encyclopedia of African American Religions.* New York: Garland, 1993.

Noel, James Anthony. "Search for Zion: A Social-Historical Study of African American Religious Life and Church Culture in Marin City, California, from the Migration Period to the Present, 1942–1996." Ph.D. diss., Graduate Theological Union, Berkeley, Calif.,1999.

Noel, James Anthony. "African-American Religions." In *The Encyclopedia of Religion,* 2d ed. Detroit, Mich.: Macmillan Reference, 2005.

Paris, Peter J. *The Social Teachings of the Black Churches.* Philadelphia: Fortress, 1985.

Paris, Peter J. *Black Religious Leaders: Conflict in Unity.* Louisville, Ky: Westminster/John Knox Press, 1991.

Peterson, Carla L. *"Doers of the Word": African-American Women Speakers and Writers in the North (1830–1880).* New Brunswick, N.J.: Rutgers University Press, 1995.

Pinn, Anthony B., and Benjamin Valentin, eds. *The Ties That Bind: African American and Hispanic American/Latino/A Theology in Dialogue.* New York: Continuum, 2001.

Raboteau, Albert. *Slave Religion: The "Invisible Institution" in the Antebellum South.* New York: Oxford University Press, 1978.

Reichley, A. James. *Faith in Politics.* Washington, D.C.: Brookings Institute, 2002.

Richardson, Harry V. *Dark Salvation: The Story of Methodism as It Developed Among Blacks in America.* Garden City, N.Y.: Anchor, 1976.

Ross, Rosetta E. *Witnessing and Testifying: Black Women, Religion, and Civil Rights.* Minneapolis: Fortress Press, 2003.

Russell, Letty M., Kwok Pui-Lan, Ada María Isasi-Díaz, and Katie Geneva Cannon, eds. *Inheriting Our Mothers' Gardens: Feminist Theology in Third World Perspective.* Philadelphia: Westminster Press, 1988.

Sernett, Milton. *Black Religion and American Evangelicalism: White Protestants, Plantation Missions and the Flowering of Negro Christianity, 1787–1865.* Metuchen, N.J.: Scarecrow Press, 1975.

Sernett, Milton, ed. *Afro-American Religious History: A Documentary Witness.* Durham: Duke University Press, 1985.

Smith, Edward D. *Climbing Jacob's Ladder: The Rise of the Black Churches in Eastern American Cities, 1740–1877.* Washington, D.C.: Smithsonian Institution Press, 1988.

Sobel, Mechal. *Trabelin' On: The Slave Journey to an Afro-Baptist Faith.* Westport, Conn.: Greenwood Press, 1979.

Spencer, Jon Michael. *Protest and Praise: Sacred Music of Black Religion.* Minneapolis: Fortress, 1990.

Stuckey, Sterling. *Slave Culture: Nationalist Theory and the Foundations of Black America.* New York: Oxford University Press, 1987.

Stuckey, Sterling. *Going Through the Storm: The Influence of African American Art in History.* New York: Oxford University Press, 1993.

Thurman, Howard. *With Head and Heart: The Autobiography of Howard Thurman.* New York: Harcourt Brace Jovanovich, 1979.

Townes, Emilie M. "Because God Gave Her a Vision: The Religious Impulse of Ida B. Wells-Barnett." In *Spirituality And Social Responsibility: Vocational Vision Of Women in the United Methodist Tradition,* edited by Rosemary Skinner Keller, pp. 139–164. Nashville: Abingdon Press, 1993.

Warrick, Susan E., ed. *Women in the Wesleyan and United Methodist Traditions: A Bibliography.* Madison, N.J.: General Commission on Archives and History, United Methodist Church, 1991, 2003.

Washington, James M. *Frustrated Fellowship: The Black Baptist Quest for Social Power.* Macon, Ga.: Mercer University Press, 1986.

Washington, James M., ed. *A Testament of Hope: The Essential Writings of Martin Luther King, Jr.* San Francisco: Harper San Francisco, 1986.

West, Cornel. *Prophesy Deliverance!: An Afro-American Revolutionary Christianity.* Philadelphia: Westminster Press, 1982.

West, Cornel. *Democracy Matters: Winning the Fight Against Imperialism.* New York: Penguin Books, 2004.

Williams, Ethel L., and Clifton F. Brown. *Afro-American Religious Studies: A Comprehensive Bibliography with Locations in American Libraries,* 2nd ed. Metuchen, N.J.: Scarecrow Press, 1979.

Williams, Melvin D. *Community in a Black Pentecostal Church: An Anthropological Study.* Pittsburgh: University of Pittsburgh Press, 1974.

Wilmore, Gayraud. *Black Religion and Black Radicalism: An Interpretation of the Religious History of Afro-American People.* Maryknoll, N.Y.: Orbis Books, 1983.

Woodson, Carter G. *The History of the Negro Church,* 3rd ed. Washington, D.C.: Associated Publishers, 1972.

MILTON C. SERNETT (1996)
MARCIA C. ROBINSON (2005)

Remond, Charles Lenox

1810
December 22, 1873

The abolitionist Charles Lenox Remond was born in Salem, Massachusetts, in 1810, the eldest son of John and Nancy Remond. John Remond, a hairdresser and successful merchant originally from Curaçao, was a prominent figure in Salem's black community and led the campaign to desegregate the city's public schools. Charles Remond received his education from a private tutor and attended integrated schools in Salem.

Remond adopted his parents' antislavery commitment as his own. He participated in the early life of the American Anti-Slavery Society (AASS). He embraced the Garrisonian principles of nonresistance and moral suasion, and he acquired the reputation as an eloquent and persuasive antislavery speaker. In 1838 he became the first full-time black lecturer hired by the Massachusetts Anti-Slavery Society. Over the following two years, he traveled through New England delivering antislavery lectures and organizing a network of local antislavery societies.

Remond drew on his lecturing and organizational experience during an eighteen-month tour of the British Isles. He represented the AASS at the World's Anti-Slavery Convention in London in 1840. When the convention refused to seat women delegates, he created a sensation by chastising the assembly for their exclusionary policy and by withdrawing from the proceedings.

Remond continued his antislavery lecturing when he returned to the United States in December 1841. He worked with Frederick Douglass (1818–1895) on the lecture circuit and participated in the widely publicized "One-Hundred Conventions" antislavery tour of midwestern states. Although an advocate of moral suasion, Remond revealed an interest in political antislavery as president of the Essex County Anti-Slavery Society in the late 1840s.

In the wake of federal laws and legal decisions restricting black citizenship, Remond became increasingly pessimistic about the prospects for racial progress. In the late 1850s he judged the antislavery movement a failure. He abandoned nonresistance, defended slave revolts, and predicted a violent resolution to the question of southern slavery. In the 1850s Remond advocated more aggressive tactics in the struggle for equal rights, but he remained committed to racial integration. He continued to oppose expressions of black separatism and criticized those who advocated racially exclusive schools, churches, and reform organizations.

During the Civil War, Remond recruited black soldiers for the Fifty-fourth and Fifty-fifth Massachusetts regiments. He spoke out on Reconstruction issues and urged AASS to extend its commitment to racial justice beyond slave emancipation. Remond attended the 1867 meeting of the American Equal Rights Association, but he apparently retired from public life shortly thereafter. He suffered from ill health most of his life. The deaths of his first wife—Amy Williams, in 1856—and his second wife—Elizabeth Magee, in 1872—further aggravated his condition. Remond spent his last years working as a clerk in the Boston Customs House and died in 1873.

See also Abolition; Remond, Sarah Parker; Slavery

Bibliography

Usrey, Miriam L. "Charles Lenox Remond: Garrison's Ebony Echo at the World's Anti-Slavery Convention. 1840." *Essex Institute Historical Collections* 106 (1970): 112–125.

Ward, William Edward. "Charles Lenox Remond: Black Abolitionist, 1838–1873." Ph.D. diss., Clark University, Worcester, Mass., 1977.

MICHAEL F. HEMBREE (1996)

Remond, Sarah Parker

June 6, 1826
December 13, 1884

Born in Salem, Massachusetts, one of eight children, abolitionist Sarah Remond was the daughter of John Remond, a black immigrant from Curaçao, and Nancy Lenox Remond, daughter of African-American Revolutionary War veteran Cornelius Lenox. The family was noted for its abolitionist activities. In 1832 Remond's mother helped found the Salem Anti-Slavery Society, and her sister Caroline became an active member. In 1835 her father became a life member of the Massachusetts Anti-Slavery Society, and three years later, her brother, Charles Lenox Remond, began lecturing for the society. In 1835 Sarah Remond completed grade school, but she was denied admission to the local high school on racial grounds, so the family moved to Newport, Rhode Island, returning to Salem after her graduation in 1841. In July 1842 Remond joined her brother as an antislavery lecturer and began protesting segregation in churches, theaters, and other public places. In a well-publicized incident in 1853 at Boston's Howard Athenaeum, she refused to vacate a seat in the "whites-only" gallery during an opera. Arrested and thrown down the stairs, she subsequently won $500 in damages in a civil suit. In 1856 she was appointed a lecturing agent of the American Anti-Slavery Society, and she and her brother covered the Northeast and Midwest. Antislavery leaders hailed her dignified bearing and eloquent speech.

In 1859 Sarah Remond and her brother left for England to further the cause of abolition. Denied a visa to France by the American delegation in London, who claimed that because of her color she was not an American citizen, she toured Great Britain and Ireland. Bitter about the lack of educational opportunity in America, she welcomed the chance to study in Europe. She may have attended the Bedford College for Ladies in the years 1859 to 1861.

Remond stayed in England through the Civil War, urging the British to support the blockade of the Confederacy and raising money for freed slaves. In 1866 she returned to the United States. She attended the New York Constitutional Convention, where she lobbied unsuccessfully for universal suffrage. In 1867 she went back to Europe and settled in Italy, where she spent the rest of her life. She is believed to have studied medicine at the Santa Maria Nuova Hospital in Florence. Remond received her diploma for "Professional Medical Practice" in 1868, married Lorenzo Pintor in 1877, and died in Rome seven years later.

See also Abolition; Remond, Charles Lenox; Slavery

Bibliography

Bogin, Ruth. "Sarah Parker Remond: Black Abolitionist from Salem." In *Black Women in American History from Colonial Times through the Nineteenth Century,* vol. 1, edited by Darlene Clark Hine. Brooklyn, N.Y.: Carlson, 1990.

KIM ROBBINS (1996)

Renaissance Big Five (Harlem Rens)

The premier African-American professional basketball team of the 1930s, the Harlem Renaissance (nicknamed the Rens) was founded by Robert L. Douglas (1884–1979) in 1922, and named for their home court, the Renaissance Casino Ballroom in Harlem, New York. The original team consisted of former Negro League baseball player Clarence (Pat) Jenkins, Bill Yancey, John Holt, James (Pappy) Ricks, and Eyre Saith. Later Charles "Tarzan" Cooper and "Wee" Willie Smith joined the team. The Rens were noted for their flashy, quick passing attack, and players seldom dribbled. While the 6'4" Cooper and 6'5" Smith were inside shooters, most of the players relied on outside shots.

In the early 1930s the Renaissance Casino closed, and the Rens were forced to play all their games on the road as the visiting team. The team bought a $10,000 custom-made bus for travel for the long rides. More importantly, the Rens had just seven players, and members of the team were thus forced to play games virtually without breaks. Still, the Rens reached the peak of their strength during these years. In 1931 the Rens beat their archrivals, the Harlem Globetrotters, in the World Championship Tournament in Chicago. From 1932 to 1934 the team won 473 games out of the 491 it played, including 88 straight in 1934. In 1933 the Rens played a series of games with the original (Boston) Celtics, a champion white team, in Cleveland and Kansas City. The Rens won seven of eight contests. In 1939 the Rens achieved a record of 112–7 and were one of eleven teams invited to the World Tournament in Chicago. They were unbeatable in the tournament and defeated the Oshkosh All-Stars, champions of the National Basketball League (ancestor of the National Basketball Association), to take the world title. The Rens ended their existence in 1944 when professional basketball integrated. Their record was reportedly an estimated 2,300 victories against 500 losses. In 1963 the Harlem Renaissance was inducted into the Naismith Memorial Basketball Hall of Fame in Springfield, Massachusetts.

See also Basketball; Sports

Bibliography

Dickey, Glenn. *The History of Professional Basketball since 1896.* New York: Stein and Day, 1982.

GREG ROBINSON (1996)

Reparations

In May 1969, a man interrupted the Sunday service at the Riverside Church in New York City. Reading from a "Black Manifesto," the late African-American civil rights activist James Forman (1928–2005) made several demands. Among them was a call for reparations from whites to African Americans for historical and ongoing repression. In the first phase of the program, white churches and synagogues would be called upon to pay $500 million to be distributed to black community groups and institutions.

The most recent surge of attention to the cause of reparations for African Americans was actually prompted by the actions of a hostile source. In the spring of 2001, David Horowitz, a former 1960s radical activist who underwent a conversion to neoconservatism, placed an advertisement in a number of college newspapers throughout the United States, listing ten arguments why reparations for African Americans for slavery is a bad idea. The advertisement stimulated more attention than the reparations question had received since the early part of the twentieth century. Subsequently, conferences and symposia have been held on the subject at a wide range of college campuses, including a national teleconference in 2003 held jointly by Duke University, Spelman College, and Harvard University.

Horowitz's attack on reparations was directed exclusively at the case for reparations based upon slavery. He had nothing to say, at the time, about a rationale for reparations based upon the harms of the century-long Jim Crow era that followed slavery and Reconstruction. In fact, Boris Bittker, in his book *The Case for Black Reparations* (1973), argues that the basis for compensation should be anchored exclusively on the costs imposed upon black Americans by the Jim Crow system of American apartheid.

The demand for reparations is hardly a new phenomenon. Even before the Civil War, various groups advocated the redistribution of wealth or property to African Americans, particularly the land that they worked as enslaved laborers. In 1854, the abolitionist Sojourner Truth (1797–1983) warned whites that they "owed the colored race a big debt, and if they paid it all back, they wouldn't have anything left for seed." Although its motives were racist, the nineteenth-century American Colonization Society called for government support of their program to provide free transportation and land in Liberia for any blacks willing to settle there. The champion of the African emigration in the late nineteenth century, Bishop Henry McNeal Turner of the African Methodist Episcopal Church, believed that the government should be financially responsible for the "repatriation" effort.

"Forty Acres and a Mule" became the historic rallying cry for reparations immediately after the Civil War. On January 16, 1865, General William T. Sherman issued Special Field Orders, No. 15, which declared that "not more than forty acres of tillable ground" would be "reserved" for families of four from "[the] islands from Charleston, south, the abandoned rice fields along the rivers from thirty miles back from the sea, and the country bordering the St. John's River, Florida" for "the settlement of the negroes now made free by the acts of war and the Proclamation of the President."

Both the first Freedmen's Bureau Act and the Homestead Act of the late 1860s also contained land allocation provisions of at least forty acres per black family as well. However, opposition to and obstruction of Radical Reconstruction from President Andrew Johnson prevented the massive racial land redistribution from taking place. Such a distribution would have given the ex-slaves a strong economic foundation in the postbellum period. Indeed, by the end of 1865, Johnson had already had blacks removed from the lands they had settled along the South Carolina and Georgia coasts under Sherman's orders, and the property was restored to the white former slave owners.

In 1890, the white Alabaman Walter Vaughan, a lifelong southern Democrat and editor of an Omaha, Nebraska, newspaper, crafted a reparations bill. The bill was introduced in Congress by William Connell, a white Nebraska Republican, who had close connections to Vaughan; the bill would grant government pensions to blacks in partial recompense for the suffering of slavery. African Americans Callie House and Isaiah Dickerson formed the National Ex-Slave Mutual Relief, Bounty, and Pension Association to promote the passage of legislation of this type. House's conviction on mail fraud charges in October 1917 (which were similar to the charges brought against Marcus Garvey in 1922) signaled the end of serious efforts to achieve Congressional approval of pensions for ex-slaves.

Demands for compensation came from other areas as well. In 1892, in the British colony of Natal (part of present-day South Africa), a white missionary named Joseph Booth created an "African Christian Union," whose goal was uplifting Africans. Booth foresaw the formation of a Christian nation of Africans. In order to fund its activities, the organization requested that the United States pay one hundred pounds sterling for every African American who volunteered to emigrate.

Proposals for reparations on behalf of African Americans have surfaced continuously throughout the twentieth century from a wide range of voices. In a somewhat obscure 1913 book, *Prophetic Liberator of the Coloured Race of the United States of America: Command to His People,* Arthur Anderson proposed the creation of a black state in the South. In 1928 the Communist Party of the United States argued that African Americans, especially in the South, were a distinct people and had a national identity. As such, the party argued, blacks were entitled to a homeland and had the right to carve out an independent African-American polity in the "Black belt" states of the South.

Demands for reparations have frequently combined ideological radicalism with black nationalism. In 1934, the Chicago-based National Movement for the Establishment of a 49th State advanced its own agenda for redistribution, calling for a new state to be created in the American South. Through the creation of a new polity, blacks would "have the opportunity to work out their own destiny, unbridled and unhampered by artificial barriers." This state would provide an "opportunity for the nation to reduce its debt to the Negro for past exploitation."

A more recent manifestation of this perspective has been advanced by the members of the Republic of New Africa (RNA) who have sought territory in the U.S. South for a separate black nation, encompassing the states of Louisiana, Mississippi, Alabama, Georgia, and South Carolina. Although little support remains for the RNA, Imari

Obadele (Richard Henry), one of the leaders of the organization, continued to advocate reparations as recently as 1993.

In 1955 black activist "Queen Mother" Audley Moore (1898–1997), a former Garveyite and Communist, began her campaign to press for reparations, especially in the pamphlet "Why Reparations? Money for Negroes." Moore believed that there was an effective one-hundred-year statute of limitations for an oppressed group to press legal claims against former captors. At one point in 1962, she even met with President John F. Kennedy to air her views. On the one hundredth anniversary of the Emancipation Proclamation, Moore formed the Reparations Committee for the Descendants of American Slaves. The primary demand of $500 million was to be partial compensation for historic wrongs. Her organization did file a suit in at least one court in California.

While Moore's calls for reparations seemed to go unheeded, the subject of reparations was a major component of black nationalist rhetoric during the 1950s and 1960s. In the 1950s, the Nation of Islam called for the establishment of a separate black state. In 1962, its leader Elijah Muhammad asserted that "former slave masters are obligated to provide" choice land for the descendants of slaves to create an African-American nation. In addition, under the Nation of Islam's plan, the United States would support and maintain the population of the proposed black state for at least twenty to twenty-five years until it had reached some level of economic and political autonomy.

In a 1966 platform, the Black Panther Party called for economic restitution from the white community. Citing the promises of "forty acres and a mule" and the example of German aid to Jews after the Holocaust, the Panthers desired monetary payments that would be distributed to "our many communities." Other groups also made calls for reparations. One group located in Harlem, the "Provisional Government of the African-American Captive Nation," advocated the creation of a state, supported and aided by the American government, in all areas south of the Mason-Dixon Line where African Americans constituted a majority—a policy similar to that promoted by the RNA.

The most vocal of all those urging reparations during the 1960s was James Forman, best known as the executive secretary of the Student Nonviolent Coordinating Committee (SNCC) from 1961 until 1966. Forman also led the Black Economic Development Conference (BEDC), which was the organization that had assembled the "Black Manifesto." While some response came from the white community, it never approached the demands made by the BEDC. Reparations money received by the BEDC reputedly was used to create Black Star Publications, which distributed black militant writings by Forman and others. One organization that received its start from funds generated in responses to the manifesto was the Black Economic Research Center (BERC). Originally started by donations from the National Council of Churches, the BERC began publishing the *Review of Black Political Economy,* a journal now published under the auspices of the National Economic Association, the professional organization of black economists. In the early issues of the *Review*, Robert S. Browne, the director of the BERC, advocated substantial reparations to correct disparities in wealth between blacks and whites. Struck by data from a survey that showed that blacks only held two percent of the nation's wealth, Browne felt that reparations would be an appropriate remedy.

The economist David Swinton, formerly a colleague of Browne's at the BERC and now president of Benedict College in South Carolina, argued in 1991 that the "gap between black and white America never changes because of the impact of slavery and Jim Crow on the accumulation of wealth—both financial material, and in terms of human capital." Swinton endorsed reparations of a magnitude that would have a present-day value of anywhere from $1 trillion to $5 trillion to begin to make a transition to a more economically powerful African-American community. Another group in Maryland, the Black Reparations Commission, placed the recommended payment as high as $4 trillion.

During the 1980s, many black activists insisted that at least some discussion of reparations was required. The Detroit City Council passed a resolution in the late 1980s encouraging some compensation for slavery, and a Massachusetts state senator introduced a reparations bill into the state senate in 1989. Arguing in 1992 that the nation owes a singular debt to African Americans above and beyond normal affirmative action programs, the sociologist Paul Starr called for the establishment of a privately funded National Endowment for Black America, which would foster the economic growth of the black community. The neoconservative journalist Charles Krauthammer actually endorsed a limited reparations program as a substitute for affirmative action.

A body of activists and organizations known as the National Coalition of Blacks for Reparations in America (NCOBRA) began to agitate for reparations in 1989. From the early 1990s, led by Johnita Scott Obadele, Kalonji Olusegun, and Adjoa Aiyetoro, NCOBRA has supported congressional legislation (proposed annually by Congressman John Conyers of Michigan) to explore the question of reparations. However, that legislation has never been reported out of committee to the floor of Congress.

Today, the primary reparations activity involves a growing array of court cases, particularly those brought by the attorney Deadria Farmer-Paellmann against several U.S. corporations—including insurance companies such as Aetna who provided policies for slave owners to protect them from losses of their enslaved human property, and railroad companies such as CSX that used enslaved blacks to lay their railway tracks. The attorney Jerry Leaphart has been developing a case—as has a team of lawyers and scholars led by Charles J. Ogletree of Harvard Law School—to be brought forward against the U.S. government or individual states.

A major difficulty with court cases brought against corporations is their capacity to argue that while their activities might have been immoral during slavery times, they were not illegal. Cases against the government or the state face two problems: (1) the barrier of sovereign immunity, and (2) the nature of implementation of a compensation program if the litigants were to prevail. Arguably, the most effective means of executing reparations would be via legislation, because successful legislation would require significant political support across the population. However, a 2000 survey conducted by the political scientists Michael Dawson and Rovana Popoff shows that ninety percent of white Americans opposed compensation for African Americans for slavery; a majority even opposed a formal apology. Therefore, the task of building national political support for reparations that would translate into legislation is obviously a challenging one.

Logistical issues of concern to advocates of reparations include the following: How should a program of reparations be funded? Should existing assets be transferred from nonblacks to blacks? Should the government undertake additional borrowing to effect such a transfer? Should reparations be distributed to blacks as individuals, to families, to community-based organizations, or to all three? Would eligibility for receipt require genealogical evidence to establish that recipients are descendants of enslaved Africans? How would the distribution ensure that there is a long-term closure of the gap between blacks and whites rather than a renewed transfer of funds back to nonblacks via black consumption expenditure?

There have been historical precedents for both formal apologies and economic reparations by nation-states to various groups. Japanese-Americans subjected to incarceration in American concentration camps during World War II have received an official national apology and payment of $20,000 per victim. Various Native American nations have received settlements in court for prior seizure of their lands and discrimination. Since World War II, the German government has paid about $50 billion to Holocaust survivors and their near relatives. In 1988, Daimler-Benz, the German industrial giant, agreed to pay the equivalent of almost $12 million to victims of Nazi forced-labor polices and to their families. President Bill Clinton apologized to Hawaiians in 1993 for American involvement in the overthrow of the Hawaiian sovereign at the turn of the twentieth century. And in 2003 the envoy to the United States from Benin apologized to African Americans for Benin's involvement in the slave trade. But neither apology nor compensation has ever been awarded to African Americans for slavery, Jim Crow, or ongoing discrimination.

See also Black Panther Party for Self-Defense; Garvey, Marcus; Jim Crow; Moore, Audley "Queen Mother"; Nation of Islam; Slavery; Student Nonviolent Coordinating Committee (SNCC); Truth, Sojourner; Turner, Henry McNeal

Bibliography

America, Richard F. *Paying the Social Debt: What White America Owes Black America*. Westport, Conn.: Praeger, 1993.

America, Richard F., ed. *The Wealth of Races: The Present Value of Benefits from Past Injustices*. New York: Greenwood, 1990.

Benton-Lewis Dorothy. *Black Reparations NOW!* Rockville, Md.: Black Reparations Press, 1978.

Berry, Mary F. "Reparations for Freedmen, 1890–1916: Fraudulent Practices or Justice Deferred?" *Journal of Negro History* 57, no. 3 (July 1972): 219–230.

Bittker, Boris I. *The Case for Black Reparations*. New York: Vintage, 1973. Reprint, Boston, Mass.: Beacon Press, 2003.

Browne, Robert S. "The Economic Basis for Reparations to Black America" *Review of Black Political Economy* 21, no. 3 (1993): 99–110.

Carson, Clayborne. *In Struggle: SNCC and the Black Awakening in the 1960s*. Cambridge Mass.: Harvard University Press, 1981. Reprint, 1995.

Corbett, J. Angelo. *Race, Racism, and Reparations*. Ithaca, N.Y.: Cornell University Press, 2003.

Darity, William, Jr., and Dania Frank. "The Economics of Reparations." *American Economic Review* 93, no. 2 (May 2003) 326–329.

Dawson, Michael and Rovana Popoff. "Reparations: Justice and Greed in Black and White." *DuBois Review* 1, no. 1 (March 2004): 47–91.

Forman, James. *The Making of Black Revolutionaries*. New York: Macmillan, 1972. Reprint, Seattle: University of Washington Press, 1997.

Horowitz, David. *Uncivil Wars: The Controversy over Reparations for Slavery*. San Francisco, Calif.: Encounter Books, 2002.

Thompson, Janna. *Taking Responsibility for the Past: Reparation and Historical Justice*. Malden, Mass.: Blackwell, 2002.

Winbush, Raymond A., ed. *Should America Pay? Slavery and the Raging Debate on Reparations.* New York: Amistad, 2003.

WILLIAM A. DARITY JR. (1996)
Updated by author 2005

Representations of Blackness

This entry consists of two distinct articles with differing geographic domains.

Representations of Blackness in Latin America and the Caribbean
Jean Muteba Rahier

Representations of Blackness in the United States
Joseph Boskin

Representations of Blackness in Latin America and the Caribbean

For a great part of the twentieth century, largely through the work of American anthropologist Melville Herskovits and his followers, the African diaspora was conceived in terms of isolated and scattered communities of descendants of enslaved Africans in the Americas. Herskovits's model consisted of defining the research project of African-Americanist anthropology, and of African diaspora studies more generally, exclusively in terms of cultural continuity: the cultures of the African diaspora in the Americas were nothing but, in final analysis, transplanted African cultures (Herskovits, 1938, 1941, 1966). The emphasis of his work on the study and discovery of "africanisms," "African retentions," and "cultural reinterpretations" that would have allowed Africa to survive in the Americas is well known (Rahier, 1999a, pp. xiii–xxvi; Gershenhorn, 2004; Price, 2003).

In the 1990s, other conceptualizations of the African diaspora emerged in the work of various scholars, among which one of the most visible was Paul Gilroy's *Black Atlantic* (1993): the Atlantic Ocean was transformed from being a site of unidirectional traveling of African cultures from Africa to the Americas (the Middle Passage) into the more complicated scene of multidirectional circulations of black cultures among a great variety of locations in the Americas, Europe, and Africa. This multidirectional traveling, Gilroy asserted, had in fact characterized the very formation of the African diaspora since its inception in forms such as the return of slaves from Brazil to Benin; the migration of Afro-Caribbeans to Central America; the founding of Liberia; the diasporic writings of African-American intellectuals; and other transnational exchanges (see also Kelley, 1999).

More recently, Percy Hintzen (2003) has theorized the African diaspora in terms that contradict the common understanding of diasporic identity as a subjectivity produced out of a collective phenomenon of displacement and dispersal from a real or imagined homeland. He criticizes the arguments that claim a universality of diasporic subjectivity and a fixity of diasporic identity. Such a common understanding of diasporic identity, he asserts, ignores the integral way in which identity is embedded in national and local, social, cultural, and political geographies. Specifically, he writes, diasporic identity emerges out of historical, social, and cultural conjunctures when constructed discourses of national belonging deny claims of citizenship on racial, cultural, religious, linguistic, or other communal grounds.

Diasporic identity emerges from situations in which representations and practices of cultural citizenship and belonging to national citizenship are actually denied. It is constructed out of memories of movement across local and national boundaries even while inculcating ideas of belonging across different localities. Rather than being based on claims of common origin and on a commonality of culture inherited from an originary "homeland," diasporic identity is a response to nationally-based notions of peoplehood from which diasporic subjects are excluded. It creates solidarities across fragmented geographies. Its manifestations can be multivalent, polysemous, ambiguous, and contradictory. It is a floating signifier of cultural citizenship that facilitates mobility across space, time, and social position. "Someone is West Indian or Black, or Jamaican, or African American, for example, not with reference to originary myths that are fixed in Africa, but in response to the social, political, and cultural geography of location, to her/his social and economic positionality, and to social and institutional context" (Hintzen, 2003, p. 1). Transnationally, blackness—as opposed to whiteness—is ultimately what ties together the different populations of the African diaspora, since whiteness and its association to uncontaminated origin in Europe have conferred a "natural," "ineluctable," and "deserved advantage" over those who are not white and who have been constructed and represented as being "naturally" inferior.

Representations and the Racial Ordering of People

Representations constitute, in part, the world in which we live. As Michel Foucault explained, discursive formations, modes of thought, or modes of representation are used by people for conceptualizing the world, their existence, and the existence of "others." Dominant groups produce and reproduce—differently in different times and in different geographic contexts—representations of themselves and of "others" that justify or naturalize their position at the apex of racial/spatial orders and the socioeconomic and political subjugation of the negatively depicted or racialized "others." Throughout Latin America and the Spanish-speaking Caribbean, the colonial period has been characterized by a more or less important (depending on the specific locations) mode of production based on the enslavement of Africans; blackness has been associated with notions of savagery, backwardness, cultural deprivation, hypersexuality, and other negative qualities. An important aspect of the dominated black populations' struggles for justice has consisted in—more or less overtly—challenging, manipulating, combating, negating, and sometimes inverting representations of themselves that are reproduced in the dominant discourse of their national society or of the society in which they live. In effect, as Stuart Hall puts it, racism should be seen as a "structure of knowledge and representations," with a symbolic and narrative energy and work that aim to secure "us" over here and the "others" over there, down there, fixing each in its "appointed species place" (Hall, 1992, p. 16).

Mestizaje and *Mulataje* in Latin American Ideologies of National Identity

Mestizaje, *mulataje*, and other notions of "race" and cultural mixings have played a central role in "official" and dominant imaginations of Latin American national identities from the end of the nineteenth century to the beginning of the twenty-first. These ideologies of national identities have usually downplayed the importance of contemporary racism by proclaiming the myth of "racial democracy" (*En nuestro país no hay racismo porque todos nosotros tenemos un poco de cada sangre en nuestras venas*; "In our country there is no racism because we all have a mixture of different bloods running in our veins"). At the same time, these ideologies have marginalized and marked as "others" the individuals and communities that do not fit—phenotypically and culturally—the prototypical imagined, national, and hybridized (modern) identities.

A long tradition of scholarship on nationalism has emphasized the "homogenizing processes" of the ideologies of national identity from the end of the eighteenth through the first half of the twentieth centuries. According to Benedict Anderson (1983/1991), for example, "national cultures" helped to accommodate and resolve differences by ideologically constructing a singular "national identity." Too often, scholars writing on nationalism have failed to recognize a contingent phenomenon of nationalism that elides a superficial reading and that contradicts its homogenizing ambition: the creation of one or various "others" within and without the limits of the "national space." Indeed, to secure unity and to make their own history, the dominating powers have always worked best with practices that differentiate and classify.

An archaeology of such Latin American ideologies of national identity shows that despite their self-proclaimed antiracism and apparent promotion of integration and harmonious homogeneity, they constitute little more than narratives of white supremacy that always come with an attendant concept of whitening (*blanqueamiento* or *branqueamento*). Early Latin American foundational texts about *mestizaje*, written by "white" and white-mestizo or *Ladino* intellectuals, clearly demonstrate that the discussions of race and cultural mixings have been grounded on racist premises and theories that were popular in nineteenth-century Europe and North America. These texts were usually inspired by Spencerian positivism, unilineal evolutionism, polygenism, eugenics, and social Darwinism. Their arguments were based on an understanding of society as a social organism, which functioned similarly to biological organisms. Latin American (white, white-mestizo, and Ladino) intellectuals, who were convinced of the superiority of the so-called white race vis à vis blacks and "reds," deployed organistic notions and ideas of diseases and infection to support their claim to the inferiority and dysfunctionality of black and indigenous populations in their societies.

Many Latin American intellectuals of the late nineteenth and early twentieth centuries shared the idea that race mixing between "superior" and "inferior" races was unnatural. Lourdes Martínez-Echazábal has summarized the Latin American racialized discourses on identity, development and progress, and nationalisms. She argues that the period between the 1850s and 1920 was marked by an opposition between two "pseudo-polarities." These were:

> . . .on one hand, the deterministic discourse of naturally "inferior" races accursed by the biblical judgement against Ham and grounded primarily in evolutionary theory and the "scientific" principles of social Darwinism and, on the other, a visionary faith in the political and social viability of increasingly hybridized populations. Advo-

> cates of the former equated miscegenation with barbarism and degeneration; adherents of the latter prescribed cross-racial breeding as the antidote to barbarism and the means to creating modern Latin American nation-states. Closer examination of these supposedly antithetical positions, however, reveals them to be differently nuanced variations of essentially the same ideology, one philosophically and politically grounded in European liberalism and positivism, whose role it was to "improve" the human race through "better breeding" and to support and encourage Western racial and cultural supremacy. (Martínez-Echazábal, 1998, p. 30)

In the early twentieth century, many intellectuals felt the need to proclaim both uniquely Latin American identities in contradistinction to European and North American identities, and the respectability of original "Latin American cultures." This was the golden age of indigenism. Accordingly, in many Latin American nation-states, the idea of *mestizaje* became the "trope for the nation." *Mestizaje* was seen as the source of all possibilities yet to come, and a new image of the "inferior races" eventually emerged. The racial and cultural mixing of "inferior" with "superior" races would provide Latin American nations with what would become their characteristic strength, superior even to the "actual strength" of the white race. This would become a fifth race, the "cosmic race," as José Vasconcelos called it (1961).

This briefly summarized ideological history took, of course, different shapes in different national contexts at different times. *Mestizaje* and *mulataje* are polysemic, they mean different things, at different times, in different places (Rahier, 2003). Although it was first coined for the study of the U.S. racial order, Michael Omi's and Howard Winant's notion of "racial formation" (i.e., "racially structured social formations") captures well the idea of race as a polysemic signifier in Latin American national contexts:

> We define *racial formation* as the sociohistorical process by which racial categories are created, inhabited, transformed, and destroyed. . . .racial formation is a process of historically situated *projects* in which human bodies and social structures are represented and organized. . . . [We] think of racial formation processes as occurring through a linkage between structure and representation. Racial *projects* do the ideological "work" of making these links. *A racial project is simultaneously an interpretation, representation, or explanation of racial dynamics, and an effort to reorganize and redistribute resources along particular racial lines.* Racial projects connect what race *means* in a particular discursive practice and the ways in which both social structures and everyday experiences are racially *organized*, based upon that meaning. (Omi and Winant, 1994, pp. 55–56)

The ideology of white supremacy at work in all Latin American racial formations behind the cover of "all-inclusive *mestizaje*" is undergirded by "signifying practices that essentialize and naturalize human identities" (Winant, 2001, p. 317). The racialization of these identities is produced out of understandings of hierarchical biological difference. It is against this ideology of white supremacy that Latin American indigenous and black movements have been struggling—more successfully in the last two decades of the late twentieth century and the first decade of the twenty-first century, perhaps—by voicing their opposition to "official *mestizaje*" (see, among others, Whitten, 2003; Sheriff, 2003; Beck and Mijeski, 2000).

Representations of Blackness

In Ecuador, as in other Latin American contexts, white and white-mestizo urban and national elites have imagined or invented the national identity around the notion of *mestizaje* (race mixing). These elites have reproduced an "Ecuadorian ideology" of national identity that proclaims the mestizo (mixed race individual who has both European [Spanish] and indigenous ancestry) as the prototype of modern Ecuadorian citizenship. This ideology is based on a belief in the indigenous population's inferiority, and on an unconditional—although sometimes contradictory—admiration and identification with occidental civilization (see, among others, Whitten, 1981; Stutzman, 1981; Silva, 1995).

Despite this hegemonic attempt at racial and ethnic homogenization, the Ecuadorian ideology of national identity results in a racist map of national territory: urban centers (mostly Quito, Guayaquil, and Cuenca) are associated with modernity, while rural areas are viewed as places of racial inferiority, violence, backwardness, savagery, and cultural deprivation. These areas, mostly inhabited by nonwhites or nonwhite-mestizos, have been viewed by the elites as representing major challenges to the full national development toward the ideals of modernity. As Norman Whitten explained in a discussion with Jean Muteba Rahier in early 1997, *mestizaje*, for Ecuador, does not mean that the white Indianizes himself or herself but that, on the contrary, the Indian whitens himself "racially" and culturally: the official imagination of Ecuadorian national identity is "an ideology of *blanqueamiento* within the globalizing framework of *mestizaje*."

In this official imagination of Ecuadorianness, there is logically no place for blacks: they must remain peripheral. Afro-Ecuadorians—who represent between 5 and 10 percent of the national population—constitute the ultimate "other," some sort of a historical accident, a noise in the ideological system of nationality, a pollution in the Ecuadorian genetic pool. The best example of "noncitizenship," "they are not part of *mestizaje*," unlike indigenous peoples (Muratorio, 1994). In the logic of the national "racial"/spatial order, the two "traditional" regions of blackness (both developed during the colonial period), the province of Esmeraldas and the Chota-Mira Valley, are looked down upon by whites and white-mestizos.

The ideological outsiderness of blacks in the biology of national identity is denoted in the representations of black peoples' bodies and their stereotypical hypersexuality, in the representations of black men in urban settings as being physically powerful athletes and dangerous social predators, and in the representations of black women as being nothing more worthy than being either domestic servants or prostitutes. The situation of blacks in Ecuador is of course not unique. Comparable representations can be found in other Latin American national contexts. A series of caricatural drawings called *Negritos de Navidad* circulated on the internet during the Christmas season of 2003. The drawings originated in Peru, and were viewed in Mexico, Ecuador, and, apparently, throughout Latin America. They clearly represent the racializing stereotypes of black males' hypersexuality that participate in the naturalization of racist socioeconomic and political orders. These images have been circulating in Latin American countries and beyond and contribute to the equating of black bodies with savagery. The fact that such drawings continue to be passed around as simple jokes is illustrative of ingrained antiblack racism, and denotes the normalized structural violence that blacks in Latin America have to face on a daily basis.

In Latin America, few national contexts allowed for the development of a black middle class. Brazil is probably the Latin American country where the emergence of a black middle class (according to local standards), in the urban areas of Rio de Janeiro and São Paulo, has perhaps been the most "visible." As a consequence of this process, representations of blacks as respectable professionals are making their appearance, particularly in the black-owned popular magazine *Raça (Brasil)*.

In Puerto Rico and in the Dominican Republic, blackness continues to be associated with undesirable qualities, and few choose to self-identify as Afro–Puerto Ricans or Afro-Dominicans, while many prefer to call themselves mestizos or even Taínos or Indios in order to justify the brown color of their skin with something other than references to African origins. In the Dominican Republic, *antihaitianismo* brings many to consider blackness, above and beyond its association with savagery and backwardness, as a sign of non-Dominicanness (see Howard, 2001; Sagás, 2000). Even in Haiti and Jamaica, blackness has been associated with negative qualities (see Labelle, 1978; Ulysse, 1999).

Conclusion

Representations of blackness in Latin America and the Caribbean have served the reproduction of ideologies of domination and of socioeconomic and political orders more or less overtly grounded on white supremacy. These representations have had as their objective to naturalize the subjugation of black populations at the same time that they eventually celebrated race-mixing, *mestizaje*, and *mulataje* and their attendant processes of "whitening." That is because such representations have played such a central ideological role that they have been one of the principal targets of antiracist movements throughout the region.

See also Identity and Race in the United States; Media and Identity in the Caribbean; Representations of Blackness in the United States

Bibliography

Anderson, Benedict. *Imagined Communities: Reflections on the Origin and Spread of Nationalism.* London: Verso, 1983; rev. ed., 1991.

Beck, Scott, and Kenneth Mijeski. "Indigena Self-Identity in Ecuador and the Rejection of Mestizaje." *Latin American Research Review* 35, no. 1 (2000): 119–137.

Gershenhorn, Jerry. *Melville J. Herskovits and the Racial Politics of Knowledge.* Lincoln, University of Nebraska Press, 2004.

Gilroy, Paul. *The Black Atlantic: Modernity and Double Consciousness.* Cambridge, Mass.: Harvard University Press, 1993.

Hall, Stuart. "Race, Culture, and Communications: Looking Backward and Forward at Cultural Studies." *Rethinking Marxism* 5, no. 1 (1992): 10–18.

Herskovits, Melville. "Les noirs du nouveau monde: Sujet de recherches Africanistes." *Journal de la Société des Africanistes* 8 (1938): 65–82.

Herskovits, Melville. *The Myth of the Negro Past.* London and New York: Harper, 1941.

Herskovits, Melville. *The New World Negro: Selected Papers in Afroamerican Studies.* Edited by Frances S. Herskovits. Bloomington: Indiana University Press, 1996.

Hintzen, Percy C. *Diaspora, Globalization, and the Politics of Identity.* Poitiers, France: National Center of Scientific Research, 2003.

Howard, David. *Coloring the Nation: Race and Ethnicity in the Dominican Republic.* Boulder, Colo.: Lynne Rienner, 2001.

Kelley, Robin. "The Nation and Beyond—Ways of Writing Transnational History—'But a Local Phase of a World Problem': Black History's Global Vision, 1883–1950." *The Journal of American History* 86, no. 3 (1999): 1045–1078.

Labelle, Micheline. *Idéologie de couleur et classes sociales en Haïti.* Montreal: Presses de l'Université de Montréal, 1978; 2d ed., 1997.

Martínez-Echazábal, Lourdes. "*Mestizaje* and the Discourse of National/Cultural Identity in Latin America, 1845–1959." *Latin American Perspectives* 25 (May 3, 1998): 21–42.

Miller, Marylin Grace. *Rise and Fall of the Cosmic Race: The Cult of Mestizaje in Latin America.* Austin: University of Texas Press, 2004.

Muratorio, Blanca. "Nación, identidad, y etnicidad: Imágenes de los Indios Ecuatorianos y sus imagineros a fines del siglo XIX." In *Imágenes e imagineros: Representaciones de los indígenas ecuatorianos, siglos XIX y XX.* Quito, Ecuador: FLACSO-Sede Ecuador, 1994.

Omi, Michael, and Howard Winant. *Racial Formation in the United States: From the 1960s to the 1990s*, 2d ed. New York: Routledge. 1994.

Price, Richard, and Sally Price. *The Root of Roots: Or, How Afro-American Anthropology Got its Start.* Chicago: Prickly Paradigm Press, 2003.

Rahier, Jean Muteba, ed. *Representations of Blackness and the Performance of Identities.* Westport, Conn.: Bergin & Garvey, 1999a.

Rahier, Jean Muteba. "Mami, ¿qué será lo que quiere el negro?: Representaciones racistas en la revista Vistazo, 1957–1991." In *Ecuador racista: Imágenes e identidades*, edited by Emma Cervone and Fredy Rivera. Quito, Ecuador: FLACSO-Sede Ecuador, 1999b.

Rahier, Jean Muteba. "*Mestizaje, Mulataje, Mestiçagem* in Latin American Ideologies of National Identities." *Journal of Latin American Anthropology* 8, no. 1 (2003): 40–50.

Sagás, Ernesto. *Race and Politics in the Dominican Republic.* Gainesville: University Press of Florida, 2000.

Sheriff, Robin. "Embracing Race: Deconstructing *Mestiçagem* in Rio de Janeiro." *Journal of Latin American Anthropology* 8, no. 1 (2003): 86–115.

Silva, Erika. *Los mitos de la ecuatorianidad: Ensayo sobre la identidad nacional.* Quito, Ecuador: Abya-Yala, 1995.

Stutzman, Ronald "El Mestizaje: An All-Inclusive Ideology of Exclusion." In *Cultural Transformations and Ethnicity in Modern Ecuador*, edited by Norman Whitten. Urbana, University of Illinois Press, 1981.

Ulysse, Gina "Uptown Ladies and Downtown Women: Female Representations of Class and Color in Jamaica." In *Representations of Blackness and the Performance of Identities*, edited by Jean Muteba Rahier. Westport, Conn.: Bergin & Garvey, 1999.

Vasconcelos, José. *La raza cosmica: Misión de la raza iberoamericana.* Madrid: Aguilar, 1961.

Whitten, Norman, ed. *Cultural Transformations and Ethnicity in Modern Ecuador.* Urbana: University of Illinois Press, 1981.

Whitten, Norman. "Symbolic Inversion, the Topology of '*el mestizaje*,' and the Spaces of '*las razas*' in Ecuador." *Jounal of Latin American Anthropology* 8, no. 1 (2003): 52–85.

Winant, Howard. *The World is a Ghetto: Race and Democracy Since World War II.* New York: Basic Books, 2001.

JEAN MUTEBA RAHIER (2005)

Representations of Blackness in the United States

Stereotypes are the cultural prisms, shaped over time and reinforced through repetition, that predetermine thought and experience. Although based on a semblance of historical reality, once implanted in popular lore, such images penetrate the deepest senses and profoundly affect behavioral actions. Philosopher Walter Lippmann in *Public Opinion* (1922, pp. 89–90) believed that in the twentieth century, stereotypes are "the subtlest and most pervasive of all influences" because people imagine most things before experiencing them.

The collective aspect of stereotyping is self-confirming and provides a continuing sense of reality, "a kernel of truth," as historian H. R. Trevor-Roper observed in *The Crisis of the Seventeenth Century* (1965, pp. 190–191), a study of the witchcraft frenzy in sixteenth- and seventeenth-century Europe. "Once established, the stereotype creates, as it were, its own folklore, which becomes in itself a centralizing force." As a result, stereotypes pervade personal fantasies and become cultural commodities; they are dislodged only after a series of protracted assaults.

Racist Ideology

In the history of race relations in the United States, stereotypes preceded and accompanied the origins and legalization of slavery. Equipped with stereotypes, whites fastened the dogma of inferiority on Africans and African Americans. With the termination of slavery, stereotypes were then extensively employed to legitimate segregationist policies. Throughout the course of American history, such ingrained stereotypes have subverted black identity and seriously undermined the formation of a biracial society based on egalitarian practices.

The Child and the Savage

The early images of the African American revolved around a conception of primitivism. The English defined this condition as being "uncivilized," a view that posited the indi-

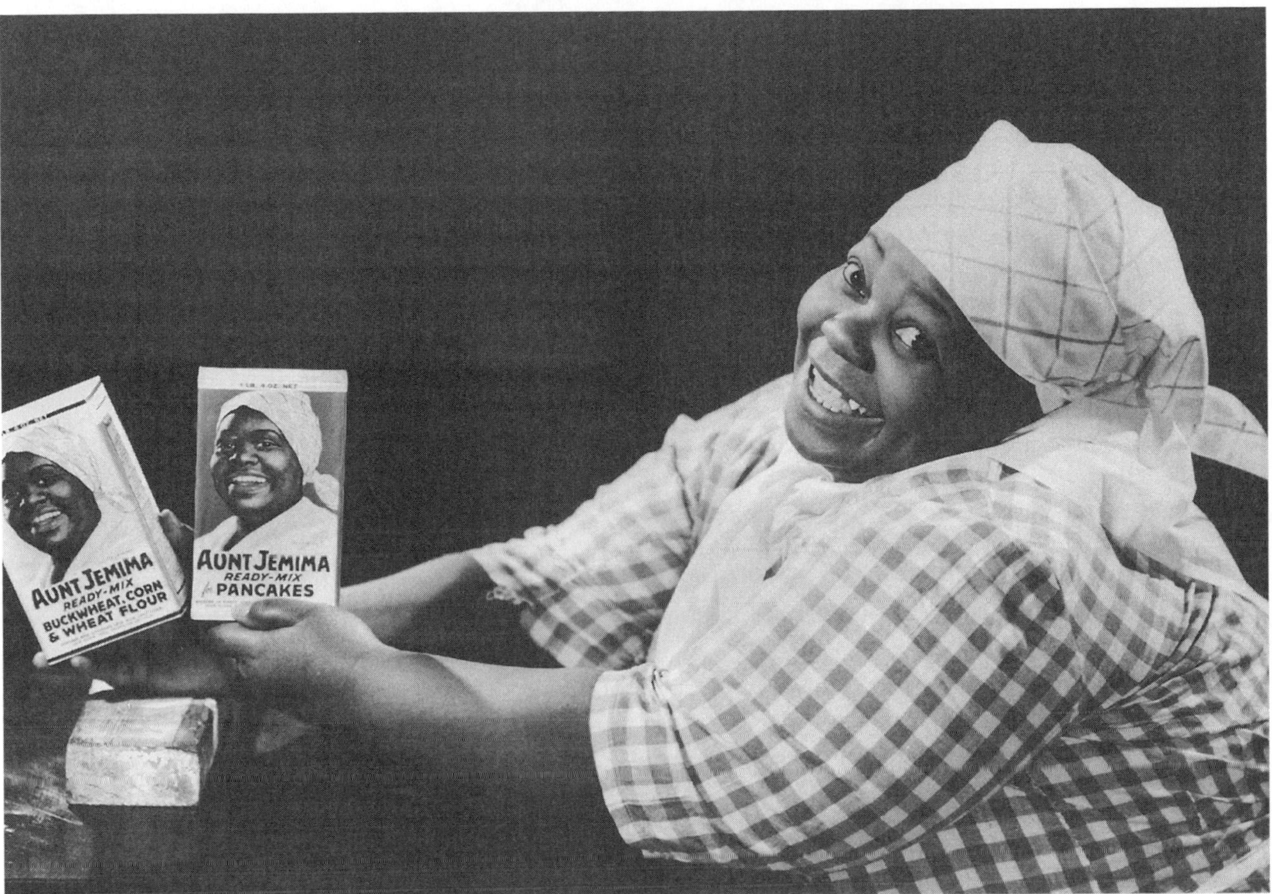

"Aunt Jemima." *In response to the civil rights movement, the image of Aunt Jemima, derived from the "Mammy" figure, changed during the last decades of the twentieth century, with stereotypical elements being progressively removed.* CORBIS. REPRODUCED BY PERMISSION.

vidual as "child" and "savage." Intriguingly, many of the stock traits ascribed to American blacks existed in other slave cultures. "The white slaves of antiquity and the Middle Ages," noted David B. Davis in *The Problem of Slavery in Western Culture* (1966), "were often described in terms that fit the later stereotype of the Negro. Throughout history it has been said that slaves, though occasionally as loyal and faithful as good dogs, were for the most part lazy, irresponsible, cunning, rebellious, untrustworthy, and sexually promiscuous."

Thus, on the one hand, American blacks were seen as savages, inherently brutish and vigorously sexual. Males in particular were cast as being physically well endowed. Examples of this were found in southern newspapers in the decades following the Civil War; their spurious accounts of black assaults on white women resulted in numerous lynchings. The definitive example of this stereotype is undoubtedly director D. W. Griffith's (1875–1948) early film classic *Birth of a Nation* (1915), which depicted black men as intellectually crude, sexually predatory, and physically volatile.

However, on the whole, the nonthreatening side of the stereotype dominated the popular culture, perhaps because of a fear of encouraging black sexuality or retaliation. Traits of nonaggression, servility, loyalty, docility, and comicality were heavily accentuated. Images fixated on male amiability and female nurturing that became labeled, respectively, as Sambo and Mammy. There were other related images that permeated the culture. In literature and film, women were often delineated as the child "pickaninny," the tragic mulatto, the innocent or ingenue, the hot mama, and the exotically promiscuous. Males were toms, coons, dandies, and bucks who possessed natural rhythm, had flashy dress habits, craved watermelon and chicken, shot dice, and resorted to petty theft.

There were additional factors that led to Mammy and Sambo, not the least of which was Southerners' phobic need for security. Slave rebellions and retaliations, numerous instances of sabotage, acts of miscegenation, and the suspicion that no black person (and especially no black male) could be completely trusted led whites to yearn for a worker beyond question. For these reasons, Mammy was portrayed, as was her male counterpart, as invariably cheerful, backward, and harmless.

Mammy

As with all stereotypes, these figures held a partial truth. That certain black women achieved relatively high status on the plantation and in other white households is unquestionable. Women were highly skilled workers who supervised a variety of domestic operations, counseled and caressed people of all ages in white homes as well as in their own homes, and played a predominant role in the black community. The portrait of the black woman as loyal without bounds, caring solely for her white charges, cheerfully administering all duties regardless of personal circumstances, and fulfilling her own wants by being a slave and worker was a creation arising out of white requirements. The stereotype was intended to legitimize her enslavement and serve as a role model for all black women.

A Mammy prototype appeared extensively in diaries, novels, speeches, anecdotes, lithographs, and advertising throughout the South in the nineteenth century. She was invariably portrayed as large-girthed, apron-wrapped, shining-faced, and bandannaed; her face was wreathed in a smile, her wisdom often delivered in comical dialect. It was a portrait that eventually became widely recognized in the 1890s in advertising as Aunt Jemima, a popular brand of pancake batter. At various times Mammy was depicted as being tough and domineering, soft and judicious, or slow-witted and comical, but she was always the household worker and nurturer, the one person on whom all could depend when needed. White males in particular were unabashed about their "Mammy" and publicly extolled her.

Southern women were no less effusive in their praise of Mammy, although their relationship was more complex. The request of one aging mistress in the antebellum period that her favorite servant—who had been relegated to sleeping on the floor near her mistress—be interred alongside her was unusual but not unheard of. In 1923, at the prodding of the United Daughters of the Confederacy, a bill was submitted to Congress authorizing "the erection in the city of Washington of a monument to the memory of the faithful colored mammies of the South." Strong protests from African-American newspapers and organizations ended the only attempt to place a statue to "Black Mammy" in the nation's capital.

Nonetheless, the durable Mammy stereotype extended well into the twentieth century in all levels of print, from folklore to novels. Novelist William Faulkner (1897–1962), for example, depicted several literary Mammies. In *The Sound and the Fury* (1929), the character Dilsey is an interesting literary variation on the Mammy theme. In *Go Down, Moses* (1940), Faulkner poignantly dedicated the novel to his family's servant, whose energies touched many generations: "To Mammy CAROLINE BARR / Mississippi (1840–1940) / Who was born in slavery and gave to my family a fidelity without stint or calculation of recompense and to my childhood an immeasurable devotion and love." But novelist Margaret Mitchell's (1900–1949) "Mammy" in *Gone with the Wind* (1936), the book that became one of the most popular novels and films of the twentieth century, was the archetypal portrait. The Mammy, as portrayed by Mitchell and others, was a composite of the different types of women that had worked on the plantation: firm, compassionate, smart, morally exemplary, and privy to the inner workings of the family. Her language was ungrammatical and provincial, and, as was often the case with the black male as well, her name always lacked family designation. She answered to the call of Jasmine, Aida, Dilsey, Sapphire, Beulah, Hester, Gossip, Stella, Aunt Dinah, and Aunt Petunia.

Mammy was feted in popular songs and ballads. The new immigrants from Eastern Europe, like the older ethnic groups, astutely recognized her iconical status and wrote lyrically about this ideal American servant. In the popular 1919 song "Swanee," written by George Gershwin and Irving Caesar, there is a longing homage to the figure. But by far the most famous stage and film scene spotlighting the form was rendered by Al Jolson (1886–1950), one of the most prominent of the blackface performers. It came at the end of *The Jazz Singer* (1927), the first major film to include sound. On one knee, his clasped hands in white gloves, eyes rolled upward, Jolson sang to his imaginary servant: "Oh, Oh, Oh, Mammy, My little Mammy / The sun shines East, the sun shines West / I know where the sun shines best. . . . Mammy, Mammy / I'd walk a million miles for one of your smiles / My Mammy." (While Jolson's song is directed at his white mother, the stereotypes of the black Mammy dominate the song's imagery.)

Nowhere was the Mammy stereotype more durable than in film and on radio and television. A number of distinguished actresses, among them Hattie McDaniel (1895–1952), Ethel Waters (c. 1896–1977), and Louise Beavers (1902–1962), fashioned careers playing numerous incarnations and variations of the jolly house servant. The first television series to feature a black female actress, *Beulah* (1950–1953), had a housemaid as the central character.

Sambo

That black men presented a sunny and entertaining stance was a constant observation made by whites. Yet it is appar-

***Scene from* Amos 'n' Andy.** Amos 'n' Andy *was originally conceived for radio by Freeman Gosden and Charles Correll, the two white actors who portrayed the black characters in the show. When the program was aired on television, the series had an all-black cast, but lasted only two seasons amid protests about racial stereotypes.* CORBIS-BETTMANN. REPRODUCED BY PERMISSION.

ent that Sambo was a form of resistance, a type of disguise used to survive the systems of slavery and segregation by deflecting physical and mental assault. It was also a particular form of retaliatory humor. A nineteenth-century slave song expressed the strategy: "I fooled Ole Master seven years / Fooled the overseer three / Hand me down my banjo / and I'll tickle your bel-lee."

The roots of the name "Sambo" were both African and Latino—from the Hausa fashioning of a spirit or the second son, and "Zambo," meaning a type of monkey—but the English "Sam" had an important role in transposing it into popular lingo. From the mid-nineteenth century to the early decades of the twentieth century, Sambo became the nickname for the black male along with other designations that found popular expression: Tambo, Rastus, John, Pompey, George, Uncle Tom, Nigger, and Boy. In popular songs he was called Old Black Joe and Uncle Ned; in advertising there was Uncle Ben's Rice and Ben the Pullman Porter; in literature some of the most widely read literary characters were Uncle Remus and Little Black Sambo; and in radio and films he was Amos 'n' Andy, Rochester, and Stepin Fetchit.

The essential features of Sambo consisted of two principal parts. On one hand, he was childish and comical, employed outlandish gestures, and wore tattered clothes. Irresponsibility was a cardinal characteristic and buffoonery an inherent trait. On the flip side, he was the natural slave and servant who displayed the qualities of patience, humility, nonbelligerence, and faithfulness. Here responsibility was expected and intelligence rewarded, though both virtues were carefully monitored by whites.

These two separate sides eventually were translated into theatrical forms. The child became the "plantation darky" called Jim Crow; the servant became the urban mulatto known as Zip Coon or Jim Dandy. There were variations on the Sambo theme, but all varieties involved individuals who fit the stereotypes of being lazy, shiftless, and natural entertainers. On the plantation, the dancing and singing slave was a common sight. Musical abilities were often an important selling point at slave auctions, and masters pressured slaves to perform in order to increase production, undercut hostility, and enliven everyday life. For their part, slaves resorted to music and dance as a release from sunup to sundown labor, a means of communication, and a retention of African folkways.

Early forms of Jim Crow made their way into dramatic theater in the latter half of the eighteenth century, but it was in the minstrels of the 1830s and 1840s that the figure emerged fully developed. It occurred when the popular white performer Thomas D. Rice (1808–1860) applied blackface; dressed in outlandish costume, he caroused around the stage, singing and dancing in a black idiom: "Wheel about, turn about / Do jis do / An' every time I wheel about / I jump Jim Crow."

The heyday of white minstrelsy lasted for more than fifty years, from the 1830s to the 1880s, and was one of the prevailing forms of theater, reaching into many of the remotest geographical corners of the United States and beyond. Almost every white community (and many black communities) boasted a minstrel troupe that performed in blackface and comical dialect. As a neighborhood production, the minstrel continued into the 1960s, reaching millions of persons who had scant knowledge of African-American culture. By distorting black language and emphasizing comicality, the show perpetuated the image of the black male as a natural buffoon.

The plantation black was given heightened profile in the late-nineteenth-century stories of Joel Chandler Harris (1848–1908), one of the first writers to use the folktale as a literary medium. Harris's Uncle Remus tales, which first appeared in *Uncle Remus: His Songs and Sayings* (1881), were popular with children and adults for decades and were later adapted to radio and film. By the latter decades of the nineteenth century, Sambo existed in every nook and cranny of popular culture. In journals, weeklies, newspapers, magazines, novels, short stories, children's stories, humor books, comic pamphlets, and burlesque essays there was a Sambo figure speaking in malapropisms and mispronouncing words. His graphic expressions were even more ubiquitous. On the covers of sheet music, Currier & Ives prints, posters, calendars, book illustrations, dime novels, postage stamps, playing cards, stereoscopic slides, children's toys and games, postcards, cartoons, and comic strips there was a saucer eyed, thick-lipped, round-faced, kinky-haired, grinningly toothed figure clad in plantation clothing or foppishly attired in formal dress. Sambos also filled the material culture as ceramic figurines on dining-room tables, lawn jockeys, whiskey pourers, men's canes, placemats, wooden coins, salt shakers, and countless bric-a-brac.

From its earliest years, the electronic media made extensive use of the stereotype. Film companies inserted Sambo characters—some of whom were white men in blackface—who savored watermelon and chicken, shot dice, wielded razors, and fearfully escaped from ghostly spirits in animated cartoons and feature movies. On radio, the long-running serial program *Amos 'n' Andy* (1928–1960) was performed by two white men in simulated blackface. And the most widely recognized servant on radio was Rochester on the *Jack Benny Show,* which ran from 1932 through 1958.

Termination and Replacement

Constant pressure from the African-American community, combined with powerful external events such as World War II (1939–45), gradually transformed the harshest aspects of the stereotypes. Their eventual elimination, however, was the consequence of the demands of the civil rights and black nationalist movements of the 1950s, 1960s, and 1970s. For instance, in response to the civil rights movement, some of the more offensive qualities of the Aunt Jemima image on the pancake-batter package were modified by its manufacturer; in the 1960s, the bandanna was changed to a headband, and since 1990 she has been depicted without any head covering.

The rise to prominence of black legislators, writers, intellectuals, filmmakers, performers, and comedians in the latter decades of the century consigned Mammy and Sambo to the historical dustbin. In the 1980s and 1990s, such films as *Malcolm X* (1992) by Spike Lee (1957–) and *Boyz in the Hood* (1991) by John Singleton (1968–), as well as the extraordinarily popular television sitcom *The Cosby Show* (1984–1992), brought to national attention the complex levels of black history and community life. Whatever traces of the stereotype that may have remained at the turn of the twenty-first century were expunged from the public consciousness with the emergence of a new generation of comedians, among them Richard Pryor (1940–), Eddie Murphy (1961–), Chris Rock (1965–), and the Wayans brothers, whose seminal routines fused retaliation with self-mockery.

If the Mammy and Sambo stereotypes have faded, however, new negative images of African Americans in the mass media have replaced them. In the latter decades of the twentieth century, urban blacks were often stereotypically identified with city crime, gang violence, welfare, and the firebombing and looting accompanying urban uprisings. Such extreme emphasis on the negative aspects of blacks continued to impede the democratic dialogue vital for a biracial society.

See also Identity and Race in the United States; Jim Crow; Media and Identity in the Caribbean; Minstrels/Minstrelsy; Representations of Blackness in Latin America and the Caribbean

Bibliography

Allport, Gordon. *The Nature of Prejudice.* New York: Addison Wesley Publishing Company, 1954.

Bogle, Donald. *Toms, Coons, Mulattoes, Mammies, and Bucks.* New York: Continuum International Publishing Group, 1973. Rev. ed. New York: Continuum, 1989.

Boskin, Joseph. *Sambo: The Rise & Demise of an American Jester.* New York: Oxford University Press, 1986.

Cripps, Thomas F. *Slow Fade to Black: The Negro in American Films.* New York: Oxford University Press, 1977.

Entman, Robert M., and Andrew Rojecki. *The Black Image in the White Mind: Media and Race in America.* Chicago: University of Chicago Press, 2000.

Jordan, Winthrop D. *White over Black: American Attitudes toward the Negro, 1550–1812.* Chapel Hill: University of North Carolina Press, 1968.

Levine, Lawrence W. *Black Culture and Black Consciousness: Afro-American Folk Thought from Slavery to Freedom.* New York: Oxford University Press, 1977.

Mills, Charles W. *Blackness Visible: Essays on Philosophy and Race.* Ithaca, N.Y.: Cornell University Press, 1998.

Riggs, Marlon. *Ethnic Notions: Black Images in the White Mind* (documentary film). California Newsreel, 1987.

Smith, Jessie Carney, ed. *Images of Blacks in American Culture.* New York: Greenwood Press, 1988.

Toll, Robert C. *Blacking Up: The Minstrel Show in Nineteenth Century America.* New York: Oxford University Press, 1974.

JOSEPH BOSKIN (1996)
Updated by author 2005

Republican Party

See Political Ideologies; Politics in the United States

Republic of New Africa

In 1967 Milton Henry, an African-American attorney and former acquaintance of Malcolm X, and his brother, Richard Henry, founded the Malcolm X Society, an organization based in Detroit whose purpose was to encourage the establishment of an autonomous black nation within the United States. By 1968 the brothers had adopted new names—Milton became Brother Gaidi Obadele and Richard renamed himself Imari Abubakari Obadele—and issued a call to black nationalists for the creation of an independent black republic in the Deep South.

In March 1968 the Obadeles, along with black militant activist Robert F. Williams, convened several hundred nationalists in Detroit, where a declaration of independence was adopted and the Republic of New Africa (RNA) was established. The delegates called for the creation of an independent, communitarian black nation stretching across "the subjugated territory" of Louisiana, Mississippi, Alabama, Georgia, and South Carolina. The republic's economy would be organized according to the guidelines of *ujamaa*, the Tanzanian model of cooperative economics and community self-sufficiency, but political rights and freedom of the press would be limited, unions discouraged, military service made compulsory, and men allowed multiple wives.

Soon several "consulates" were established across the country, officials were chosen, and members declared their allegiance to the "provisional government." In its manifestos, largely written by Imari Obadele, the RNA called on the U.S. government to grant $400 billion in reparations for slavery and racist oppression and to cede the five "homeland" states to the Republic. In anticipation of the government's rejection of the proposal, the RNA's leaders developed a contingency plan of armed resistance in the South and guerrilla sabotage in the North.

Detroit police conducted a violent raid on the RNA's one-year anniversary conference, held in 1969 at the New Bethel Baptist Church. One police officer was killed and four RNA members were wounded after hundreds of rounds of ammunition were fired into the church. Three RNA members were tried and acquitted of murder charges. One of the accused, Chaka Fuller, was stabbed to death several months later by an undiscovered assailant.

In 1971 the RNA purchased twenty acres of land in Hinds County, Mississippi, to be used as the capital, El Malik, but the original owner of the land, an African-American farmer, reneged on the agreement. Soon thereafter local police conducted a raid on the RNA headquarters in Jackson, Mississippi, during which a white police officer was killed. Eleven RNA members, including Imari Obadele, president of the provisional government, were arrested and convicted on charges of murder, assault, and sedition. Ten of the "RNA-11" served sentences ranging from two to ten years. Hekima Ana was convicted of firing the shot that killed the officer and was sentenced to life in prison.

In 1971 five RNA members were accused of robbing a bank in Manhattan. Three of the five were caught at the scene, and a fourth was killed. The fifth, a twenty-four-year-old schoolteacher, Patrick Critton, who was the lookout, escaped. He later hijacked a plane to Havana. In 2004 a police detective in Canada investigating the old case found Critton in Mount Vernon, New York. Critton was arrested and convicted.

Three RNA members who were driving through New Mexico on route to Mississippi to assist the besieged headquarters murdered a police officer when he stopped their car. The three, Michael Finney, Charles Hill, and Ralph Goodwin, then hijacked a commercial airplane and ordered it flown to Cuba. Finney and Hill continue to live in Cuba (Goodwin died there in 1973).

Imari Obadele was released from prison in 1973, but shortly thereafter he and six others were convicted on federal conspiracy charges and incarcerated in a federal pris on in Illinois. While serving his seven-year sentence, Obadele filed a civil suit against the Federal Bureau of Investigation (FBI) in 1977, which resulted in the release of government documents confirming that the RNA had been targeted for subversion by COINTELPRO, the FBI's antiradical program.

Formed at the height of the Black Power movement, the RNA attracted a significant number of sympathizers in both radical and liberal political circles. Communist Party leader Angela Davis organized support campaigns for the group, and prominent Democratic politicians such as Julian Bond, John Conyers, and George Crockett provided legal assistance on various occasions. At the grassroots level, the diffusion of RNA offices in cities throughout the United States attested to the group's position as one of the most popular and influential black nationalist organizations.

Imari Obadele was released from prison in 1980 and went on to pursue an academic career. He received a Ph.D. in political science from Temple University in 1985 and through the late 1980s taught at several colleges, including Beaver College in Pennsylvania and the College of Wooster in Ohio. Obadele has also published numerous books and articles on the RNA and black separatism in which he continues to advocate reparations, the acquisition of land, and the establishment of an independent, socialist republic where a distinctive and autonomous black culture could flourish. His works include *War in America: The Malcolm X Doctrine* (1968), *Revolution and Nation-Building: Strategy for Building the Black Nation in America* (1970), and *America the Nation-State: The Politics of the United States from a State-Building Perspective* (1988).

After the imprisonment of most of its leaders the RNA declined in prominence but remained committed to its original principles. In the mid-1980s the group moved its headquarters from Detroit to Washington, D.C., and claimed a membership of between five thousand and ten thousand. The RNA, which considers all African Americans to be citizens of the Republic, periodically holds elections on street corners in black neighborhoods to elect officials for the provisional government.

See also Malcolm X; Revolutionary Action Movement; Williams, Robert Franklin

Bibliography

Hough, Robert. "Unusual Suspect: Thirty Years After He Robbed a Bank and Hijacked a Plane to Cuba, Patrick Critton Was Finally Busted." *Toronto Life* 38, no. 3 (March 2003): 54.

Lumumba, Chokwe. "Short History of the U.S. War on the Republic of New Africa." *Black Scholar* 12 (January–February 1981): 72–81.

Milloy, Courtland. "State of a Nation." *Washington Post*, March 30, 1986, p. B3.

Obadele, Imari. *Free the Land! The True Story of the Trials of the RNA-11 in Mississippi and the Continuing Struggle to Establish an Independent Black Nation in Five States of the Deep South.* Washington, D.C.: House of Songhay, 1984.

Van Deburg, William L. *New Day in Babylon: The Black Power Movement and American Culture, 1965–1975.* Chicago: University of Chicago Press, 1992.

THADDEUS RUSSELL (1996)
Updated by publisher 2005

Revels, Hiram Rhoades

September 1, 1822
January 16, 1901

Politician Hiram Rhoades Revels was the first black man to sit in the U.S. Senate, where he completed the unexpired term of Jefferson Davis. Revels was born in Fayetteville, North Carolina. His parents, who were free blacks, sent him to an elementary school run by a black woman. Moving north, Revels studied at several seminaries in Indiana and Ohio. He then became a minister in the African Methodist Episcopal Church (AME) and pastored congregations in Indiana, Illinois, Ohio, Missouri, and Maryland. In 1854 Revels left the AME Church after the congregation where he was pastor in St. Louis was divided by squabbling. He joined the ministry of the Presbyterian Church and was posted to Baltimore, where he worked until the outbreak of the Civil War.

Once hostilities commenced, Revels helped organize the first black regiments in Maryland and Missouri. Leaving the Presbyterian Church, he went south; reunited with the AME Church, Revels became active in Republican politics, serving on the city council of Natchez, Mississippi, briefly as a state senator, and in 1870–1871 replacing Jefferson Davis in the U.S. Senate.

Compared to other AME ministers who entered Reconstruction politics, Revels was rather lackluster. During his tenure in the Senate, Revels delivered a few speeches, but none of the legislation he introduced was passed. After his term expired, he returned to Mississippi, left the AME Church, and became a minister in the Methodist Episcopal Church (North). After he left the Senate, Revels served as president of Alcorn University, Mississippi State College for Negroes.

See also African Methodist Episcopal Church; Politics in the United States; Presbyterians

Bibliography

Walker, Clarence E. *A Rock in a Weary Land: The African Methodist Episcopal Church during the Civil War and Reconstruction.* Baton Rouge: Louisiana State University Press, 1982.

Wharton, Vernon Lane. *The Negro in Mississippi, 1865–1890.* Westport, Conn: Greenwood Press, 1984.

CLARENCE E. WALKER (1996)

Revivalism

Revivalism, the term derived from the Great Revival of 1860–1861, is a religious movement in Jamaica that is a syncretism of the Christian faith and African rituals and beliefs. It can be traced to the Myal movement, which first came to European notice during the Tacky Rebellion of 1760. Myal enabled enslaved Africans to unite and protect themselves against what was perceived as European sorcery. With the arrival of the enslaved Baptist preachers George Leile, Moses Baker, and George Lewis in 1776 and their creation of the class-leader system in which their most talented converts were appointed leaders over new converts, Myal reinterpreted and refashioned the symbols and teachings of Christianity.

On the coming of the great religious revival to Jamaica in 1860, Myal split into two variants, Zion and Pukumina (also known as Pocomania). Zion, the first to become public, retained a closer resemblance to Christianity, making greater use of the Bible and Christian symbols. Pukumina, emerging in the early months of 1861, was closer to traditional African religions. Unlike Revivalists, who refused to respect hostile spirits, followers of Pukumina believed that all spirits, including the malevolent ones, can possess and consequently deserve respect.

The Revival religion today attaches great importance to a pantheon of spirits that has at the apex God, the Creator. There are good and bad spirits, and Revivalists worship only the good ones, although they acknowledge the bad ones called *fallen angels*, chief of which is Satan. The use of the red flag, a pair of scissors, or a Bible is designed to expel evil spirits. Spirits are believed to possess individuals and can injure, protect, assist, and induce revelations in the faithful. Revivalists bring about possession by vigorous dancing and singing.

Important among ritual paraphernalia are water, stones, and herbs. The most important religious services of Jamaican Revivalists are: divine worship, baptismal rites, tables, death rites, dedication of a new church building, and installation of new officers. Divine worship services, held weekly, feature drumming, singing, handclapping, praying, Bible reading, preaching, spirit possession, testimonials, and healing. A table is a combined religious service and feast.

One of the main features of the Revival religion is ritual healing. Healing applies not only to physical and mental illness but also to social ills, including failed love affairs and litigation in law courts. Divination, which can be part of the healing process, is important in Revivalism and is often a characteristic of a good Revival leader.

The moral code of Revivalism is based on that found in the Christian Bible. Taboos among the Revivalists include the eating of pork, using profanity, and going to cemeteries at prohibited times.

Revivalism has had a revolutionary role in major rebellions, including the Tacky and Sam Sharpe Rebellions. Charismatic leadership is an important aspect of the Revival complex. The Great Rebellion of 1831–1832, also known as the Baptist War, arguably one of the main factors that led to the abolition of slavery on August 1, 1834, was led by Sam Sharpe, a Baptist deacon and Native Baptist leader (Native Baptist referred to the more Christianized form of Myal).

Revivalism as a form of cultural resistance has helped to shape and reinforce the values of the Jamaican peasantry. In the early twentieth century Revival leader Alexander Bedward combined religion with black nationalist sentiments by urging his followers to rise above their oppression and cast down their oppressors, considered at this time to be the white Jamaican ruling class.

Revivalism has played a role in the emergence and development of Rastafarianism. Barry Chevannes, a leading authority on the Revival and Rastafarian faiths, argues that Rastafari can be regarded as the fulfillment of Revivalism as it retains many of the attributes of Revivalism, although it isolates blackness as divine rather than sinful. Chevannes has observed that the Rastafari faith retained many Revival rituals, including similar hymns, dancing, and drumming. Certain Revival taboos are also preserved, including refraining from the use of salt in foods.

See also Myal; Rastafarianism; Religion

Bibliography

Chevannes, Barry. *Rastafari: Roots and Ideology*. Syracuse, N.Y.: Syracuse University Press, 1994.

Schuler, Monica. "Myalism and the African Religious Tradition in Jamaica." In *Africa and the Caribbean: The Legacies of a Link,* edited by M. E. Crahan and F. W. Knight. Baltimore, Md.: Johns Hopkins University Press, 1979.

Simpson, George Eaton. "Jamaican Revivalist Cults." *Social and Economic Studies* 5, no. 4 (December 1956): 321–442.

NICOLE PLUMMER (2005)

Revolta da Chibata

On November 23, 1910, the black navy sailor João Cândido led a revolt of 2,379 men, who took charge of three modern navy ships in the Bay of Guanabara, Rio de Janeiro, in the midst of the festivities for the inauguration of President Hermes da Fonseca. The incident, known as the Revolta da Chibata (revolt against corporal punishment) was not so much against the new president as it was an indictment of the horrific working conditions and the outdated practice of corporal punishment (*chibata*) applied in the navy, particularly as a disciplinary measure for the rank and file. The rebellion escalated as the protesters shot the commanding officer Batista das Neves and threatened to bomb the capital. Even though the revolting sailors did not list race as a motivating factor for their actions, race played a significant part in the revolt. While navy officers came mostly from white aristocratic Brazilian families, the rank and file comprised Afro-Brazilians or poor whites who were often treated as slaves.

Although the republic had outlawed corporal punishment in November 1889, it continued as a matter of course as a suitable practice to ensure proper behavior within the armed forces. Moreover, racial and class prejudice pervaded the officer corps, members of whom frequently abused corporal punishment and maintained unhealthy conditions for the sailors while they often lived and worked in splendor. Although sailors were routinely whipped, the violent flogging of the Bahian sailor Marcelino Rodrigues Meneses, on November 16, 1910, was the final incident that led the sailors to take action.

On the evening of November 22, 1910, a group of enlisted sailors led by João Cândido (on the ship *Minas Gerais*), Ricardo Freitas and Francisco Dias Martins (on the *Bahia*), Gregorio Nascimento (on board the *São Paulo*), and an organized committee on land decided to strike. The sailors succeeded in gaining command of all three vessels, although not without a fight that led to the death of several men who resisted, including officers. On behalf of the sailors, Cândido negotiated with the national government to surrender and turn over the vessels in exchange for a general pardon for the sailors, the abolition of corporal punishment, improvement in living conditions, and better salaries for the enlisted men. The next day, on November 23, 1910, Brazil's National Congress approved general amnesty for the revolutionaries and promised to meet the sailors' demands.

Unfortunately, rather than honor the amnesty, the Brazilian state sent a strong message to the population that challenges to the national order would not be tolerated. Many of the participants were jailed, executed, or exiled to labor camps in the Amazon region. João Cândido received an eighteen-month prison term and was eventually dismissed from the navy. He died in poverty and has never been given his rightful place in Brazilian social history. Nonetheless, the revolt marked an important moment in the social history of Brazil.

Bibliography

Da Silva, Marcos. *Contra a chibata.* São Paulo: Brasileinse, 1982.

Filho, Mario. *1910: A revolta dos marinheiros.* Rio de Janeiro: Globo, 1982.

Lopes, Moaicir C. *O almirante negro.* Rio de Janeiro: Quartet, 2000.

Morel, Edgar. *A revolta da chibata,* 4th ed. São Paulo: Graal, 1986.

DARIÉN DAVIS (2005)

Revolutionary Action Movement

The Revolutionary Action Movement (RAM) was one of the earliest expressions of revolutionary black nationalism. It was founded in 1963 by Robert Franklin Williams, former head of a local National Association for the Advancement of Colored People (NAACP) branch in North Carolina who gained national attention for advocating black self-defense and was in exile in Cuba, then China, while serving as RAM's president. RAM was a Marxist-Leninist organization that believed that violence was the only way fundamentally to alter the structure of American society and "free black people from colonial and imperialist bondage." Based in Philadelphia and New York, RAM claimed several hundred members, including teachers, students, clerks, and businesspeople, all of whom were passionately dedicated to the struggle of which they were a part.

RAM's goal was to build a liberation army by educating and mobilizing young African Americans. Through grassroots organizing, it sought to maintain a base in the black community. The organization published a bimonthly magazine, *Black America*, and distributed a free weekly titled *RAM Speaks*. RAM also sent out field organizers to form local groups, organize street meetings, and hold African and African-American history classes. RAM worked with more traditional civil rights groups, but its members were critical of their piecemeal reform agenda. On one occasion, RAM joined the NAACP in demonstrations over discrimination on a school construction site. However, RAM was less interested in integrating the job site than in educating people on the pitfalls of reform struggles and the necessity of revolutionary organization.

Despite its small size and relative obscurity, RAM's militant posture and commitment to grassroots organizing made it a target of Federal Bureau of Investigation (FBI) infiltration. By 1965, as part of a larger program to undermine radical black organizations, undercover FBI agents had penetrated RAM's structure. On June 21, 1967, New York City and Philadelphia police rounded up seventeen RAM members, including Maxwell Sanford, field chair of RAM, in predawn raids and seized about 130 weapons. Fifteen members were charged with criminal conspiracy, but they were never brought to trial and charges were eventually dropped. The other two, Herman Ferguson, an assistant principal at a New York City school, and Arthur Harris, unemployed at the time, were convicted of conspiracy to assassinate Roy Wilkins of the NAACP and Whitney Young of the National Urban League and sentenced to three and a half to seven years in prison. After failed attempts at appeals, Harris fled to Sweden, where he remains today, and Ferguson went to Guyana, where he lived for nineteen years. Upon returning to the United States in 1989, Ferguson was immediately taken into custody, but he was released on parole in 1993.

In another raid, in September 1967, seven RAM members in Philadelphia were charged with conspiring to assassinate local and national leaders, blow up city hall, and foment a riot, during which time they planned to poison the city's police force. Charges against RAM members consisted of conspiracy and intent based on fiery speeches or militant rhetoric rather than acts committed. The testimony of informers was the primary evidence used to convict RAM members, who vehemently denied the allegations and claimed that local police and FBI agents had instituted a frame-up to discredit them.

The FBI infiltration and raids on RAM were devastating. With most of the leadership either in prison, under surveillance, or in hiding, few were left to sustain the organization's activities. In 1968 RAM collapsed. Some ex-RAM members helped form the Republic of New Africa, which was intended to be a provisional government of a separate black state within the United States. Despite the short-lived existence of RAM, it was an important example of the changing nature of the black political movement of the 1960s: the disillusionment with conventional politics and the desire to effect social and political change by more radical means.

See also Political Ideologies; Republic of New Africa; Williams, Robert Franklin

Bibliography

Bracey, John H., Jr., August Meier, and Elliot Rudwick, eds. *Black Nationalism in America*. Indianapolis: Bobbs-Merrill, 1970.

Brisbane, Robert. *Black Activism: Racial Revolution in the U.S., 1954–70*. Valley Forge, Pa.: Judson, 1974.

NANCY YOUSEF (1996)
PREMILLA NADASEN (1996)

Rhythm and Blues

The term *rhythm and blues* was a product of the post-World War II music industry's effort to find a new word to replace the category that had been known for several decades as "race records." First used by *Billboard* magazine in 1949, *rhythm and blues* was intended to describe blues and dance music produced by black musicians for black listeners, so that rhythm and blues—often abbreviated R&B—was more a marketing category than a well-defined musical style. In effect, R&B reflected the confluence of jazz, blues, gospel, and vocal-harmony group music that took place in cities such as New York, Detroit, Chicago, Memphis, Philadelphia, and New Orleans after World War II. In the 1950s, successful marketing efforts that targeted white listeners made rhythm and blues, and the related category of rock and roll, the most popular music not only in the United States but in the rest of the world as well. Although much rhythm-and-blues music was produced by small, white-owned record labels such as Savoy, Atlantic, and Chess—in the 1960s Motown would be an exception—and was aimed at a multiracial market, rhythm and blues has always drawn its core influences from African-American culture.

The Roots of Rhythm and Blues: Jazz

The most obvious ancestor of rhythm and blues was jazz, which in the 1920s and 1930s was black America's popular music, produced mostly to accompany dancing. In the 1940s many big bands featured "honking" tenor saxophonists who played in a bluesy, at times histrionic style that drove dancers to ever more frenzied steps and tempos. Lionel Hampton's (1909–2002) "Flyin' Home" (1943), with its famous solo by Illinois Jacquet (1922–2004), was the model for such performances. Many tenor saxophonists followed Jacquet's model, including Bill Doggett (1916–1996), Arnett Cobb (1918–1989), Ike Quebec (1918–1963), Hal "Cornbread" Singer (1919–), and Willis "Gatortail" Jackson (1928–1987). Important recordings in this style include "Juice Head Baby" (1944)

R&B trio Destiny's Child performing at the "Concert Celebrating America's Youth," part of the 2001 inaugural festivities in Washington, D.C. AP/WIDE WORLD PHOTOS. REPRODUCED BY PERMISSION.

and "Deacon's Hop" (1948) by Big Jay McNeely (1929–) and "The Hucklebuck" (1949) by Paul Williams (1915–2002).

Another jazz influence on rhythm and blues was the jump bands that were popular starting in the mid-1940s. These midsized ensembles, named for their buoyant tempos, combined the extroverted solo style of the honking tenors with the relentless momentum of shuffle and boogie-woogie rhythms of pianists Albert Ammons (1907–1949), Meade "Lux" Lewis (1905–1964), and Pete Johnson (1904–1967), whose "Roll 'Em Pete" (1938) with vocalist Big Joe Turner (1911–1985) was one of the first great rhythm-and-blues performances. Tiny Bradshaw (1905–1958), Slim Gaillard (1916–1991), and Johnny Otis (1921–1984), the latter a white musician whose bands were largely black, all led jump ensembles. The greatest of the jump band leaders was saxophonist and vocalist Louis Jordan (1908–1975). His biggest hits, including "Is You Is or Is You Ain't My Baby?" (1944), "Let the Good Times Roll" (1945), "Caldonia" (1945),"Choo Choo Ch'Boogie" (1946), and "Saturday Night Fish Fry" (1940), were novelty numbers suffused with earthy humor. Jordan was a masterful saxophonist in the jazz tradition, yet most of his records were carefully composed, and his rejection of jazz improvisation became a major characteristic of rhythm and blues.

In the late 1950s and 1960s, the relationship between jazz and rhythm and blues was sometimes reversed, with musicians—especially the pianist Horace Silver (1928–), who recorded "Opus de Funk" in 1953—drawing inspiration from rhythm and blues. In the 1960s, Jimmy Smith (1920–2005), Cannonball Adderley (1928–1975), David "Fathead" Newman (1933–), Eddie Harris (1934–1996), King Curtis (1934–1971), Stanley Turrentine (1934–2000), and Ramsey Lewis (1935–) all performed in the bluesy, funky style known as *soul jazz.* Herbie Hancock (1940–), a groundbreaking avant-garde jazz pianist in the 1960s, went on to experiment with funk music in the 1970s and rap in the 1980s.

Vocal Groups

The vocal harmonizing groups of the 1940s helped develop the heavily rhythmic backing of passionate vocals that characterize rhythm and blues. Some of these groups were called *doo-wop* groups, after the wordless, nonsense-syllable accompaniments they often sang. The Ink Spots, formed in 1934, were among the earliest important rhythm-and-blues vocal groups, although the group's smooth approach on songs such as "If I Didn't Care" (1939), "To Each his Own" (1946), and "The Gypsy" (1946) was less influential in the development of rhythm and blues than the more heavily rhythmic performances of the Mills Brothers, who had hits with "Paper Doll" (1942) and "You Always Hurt the One You Love" (1944).

After World War II, dozens of important vocal groups, starting with the "bird groups," drew heavily from the gospel tradition and dominated black popular music. Groups such as the Ravens ("Ol' Man River," 1946), the Orioles ("Crying in the Chapel," 1953), the Platters ("Only You," 1955; "The Great Pretender," 1956), the Dominoes ("Sixty Minute Man," 1951), and the Clovers ("Fool, Fool, Fool," 1951; "Good Lovin'," 1953; and "Love Potion Number Nine," 1959), and the 5 Satins ("In the Still of the Night," 1956) used simple arrangements and minimal instrumental accompaniment to highlight their passionate, gospel-style vocals. The Penguins ("Earth Angel," 1954) were notable for their juxtaposition of high falsetto with deep bass voices. The Coasters had a more raucous and humorous style than other doo-wop groups, evidenced on "Riot in Cell Block No. 9" (1954) and "Charlie Brown" (1959). The Drifters were hugely popular throughout the 1950s and early 1960s ("Money Honey," 1953; "Save the Last Dance for Me," 1960; "Up on the Roof," 1962; "On Broadway," 1963; and "Under the Boardwalk," 1964).

In the 1950s and 1960s impromptu, street-corner doo-wop–style singing was an essential part of African-American urban life. Solo rhythm-and-blues singers who drew on gospel, vocal harmony, and doo-wop traditions were among the most popular recording artists of the era. An early member of the Drifters, Clyde McPhatter (1933–1972), topped the R&B and pop charts with "Without Love" (1956), "Long Lonely Nights" (1957), and "A Lover's Question" (1958). Jackie Wilson (1934–1984), another falsetto tenor and Drifters alumnus, had a huge following for his "To Be Loved" (1958), "Lonely Teardrops" (1958), and "Higher and Higher" (1959). Ben E. King (1938–) also worked with the Drifters before recording "Spanish Harlem" (1960) and "Stand by Me" (1960). Frankie Lymon (1942–1968) and the Teenagers achieved great popularity with songs such as "Why Do Fools Fall in Love?" (1956), "The ABCs of Love" (1956), and "I'm Not a Juvenile Delinquent" (1956). A doo-wop group that came to prominence relatively late was Little Anthony Gourdine (1940–) and the Imperials, whose "Tears on My Pillow" was a hit record in 1958.

Gospel music was a direct influence on many important R&B singers. Sam Cooke (1935–1964) sang gospel with the Soul Stirrers starting in 1950 and eventually recorded such secular songs as "You Send Me" (1957), "Chain Gang" (1960), and "Another Saturday Night" (1963). Solomon Burke (1936–), who recorded "Just Out of Reach" (1960) and "Got to Get You off My Mind" (1965), also sang in a gospel-influenced R&B style. The vocals and even the themes of Curtis Mayfield (1942–1999) and the Impressions' "I'm So Proud" (1964) and "People Get Ready" (1965) both have strong connections to black sacred music. Al Green (1946–), a child gospel sensation later known for soul recordings such as "Let's Stay Together" (1972) and "Take Me to the River" (1973), returned to the church in the late 1970s and has since concentrated on gospel music.

Blues

The urban blues styles of the late 1940s and early 1950s, with loud, amplified guitars, anguished vocals, and churning rhythms, are also direct descendants of rhythm and blues. Perhaps the best examples of this influence are Muddy Waters (1915–1983), Howlin' Wolf (1910–1976), and B. B. King (1925–), all of whom were prominent on the rhythm-and-blues charts in the 1950s. Bo Diddley (1928–; "Who Do You Love," 1955; "Bo Diddley," 1955; "I'm a Man," 1955) and Screamin' Jay Hawkins (1929–2000), who had a 1956 hit with "I Put a Spell on You," represent a less pure blues style that was nonetheless equally influential in creating rhythm and blues. Big Joe Turner (1911–1985), whose "Roll 'Em Pete" with pianist Pete Johnson is considered one of the founding songs of rhythm and blues, was known in the 1950s for his shouting renditions of "Chains of Love" (1951) and "Shake, Rattle and Roll" (1954), both of which are considered classic examples of a time when rock and roll was virtually synonymous with rhythm and blues. Another early rhythm-and-blues figure was Arthur "Big Boy" Crudup (1905–1974), a guitarist and singer who was popular throughout the 1940s but was best known for writing "That's All Right" (1946), which became a hit for Elvis Presley (1935–1977) in 1954.

Along with the Chicago blues style, a different kind of blues, at once more derived from jazz and country music but with the same reliance on electric instruments, exerted a strong influence on early rhythm and blues. T-Bone Walker (1910–1975), a singer and guitarist who successfully negotiated the boundary between blues and jazz on "Stormy Monday" (1945), had several hit rhythm and blues–influenced records in the early 1950s, including "Strolling with Bones" (1950) and "Street Walkin' Woman" (1951). Wynonie Harris (1915–1969), a blues shouter with a strong Louis Jordan influence, recorded

"Good Rocking Tonight" (1948) and had several hits in the mid-1940s. A mellower approach was represented by Roy Brown (1925–1981), Amos Milburn (1926–1980), and Lowell Fulson (1921–1999), whose "Every Day I Have the Blues" (1950) later became B. B. King's signature tune.

An even more restrained, elegant blues vocal style, used by the "Sepia Sinatras," also gained a large following among rhythm-and-blues audiences in the 1940s and 1950s. Nat "King" Cole (1919–1965) started out as a jazz pianist but achieved his greatest acclaim as a singer, starting in 1950 with "Mona Lisa." Other singers in this genre included Cecil Gant (1915–1951) and Charles Brown (1922–1999).

Ray Charles (1930–2004) is often grouped with blues singers, but his synthesis of many early rhythm-and-blues influences, in particular the melding of sacred and secular black music traditions, is unique. Starting in the mid-1950s, he combined a smooth, almost country singing style on ballads with infectious gospel inflection and solid jazz rhythms on both slow and up-tempo numbers, including "I Got a Woman" (1955), "Drown in My Tears" (1955), "What'd I Say?" (1959), "Georgia on My Mind" (1960), and "Hit the Road, Jack" (1961).

Female blues singers often landed on the rhythm-and-blues charts in the 1950s. Ruth Brown (1928–), who worked with Lucky Millinder (1900–1966) and Blanche Calloway (1902–1978) in the late 1940s, sang in a jump blues style on "Teardrops from My Eyes" (1950), "Mama He Treats Your Daughter Mean" (1952), and "Wild Wild Young Men" (1954). LaVern Baker (1928–1997), a niece of the blues singer Memphis Minnie (Lizzie Douglas, 1897–1973), recorded "Jim Dandy" (1956) and "I Cried a Tear" (1958), both of which were hits on the R&B chart. Etta James (1938–), who sang blues for Chess Records, recorded "Something's Got a Hold on Me" in 1962, a song that made her reputation in a rhythm-and-blues vein. Dinah Washington (1924–1963) had considerable success as a jazz singer before entering the rhythm-and-blues market with such records as "Baby Get Lost" (1949). Washington later crossed over into the pop field with the ballad "What a Difference a Day Makes" (1959).

New Orleans rhythm and blues almost constitutes its own genre, no doubt because of the city's unique confluence of African-American and Creole cultures. Fats Domino (1928–), whose first hit was "The Fat Man" (1949), became an archetypal crossover success, whose gently rocking voice and piano-playing on "Ain't That a Shame" (1955), "Blueberry Hill" (1956), "I'm Walkin'" (1957), "I Hear You Knockin'" (1958), and "I'm Ready" (1959) appealed to a large white audience. Other important New Orleans rhythm-and-blues musicians include Dave Bartholomew (1920–), Huey "Piano" Smith (1934–), Allen Toussaint (1938–), Irma Thomas (1941–), the Meters, and the Neville Brothers.

Rock and Roll

In the early 1950s, rock and roll—originally a euphemism for sex—was virtually synonymous with rhythm and blues. By the mid-1950s, as more and more white teenagers began to listen to rhythm and blues, the scope of the term *rock and roll* expanded and was primarily applied to white musicians such as Elvis Presley (1935–1977), Buddy Holly (1936–1959), Roy Orbison (1936–1988), or Bill Haley (1925–1981), whose music copied aspects of rhythm-and-blues styles but was aimed at white audiences. However, black musicians remained crucial to the development of rock and roll even after the term was being applied mostly to white musicians. Chuck Berry (1926–), whose country-influenced, bluesy tunes were extraordinarily successful with white audiences, exemplified the adolescent themes, rebellious sound and look, and aggressive guitar-playing of early rock and roll. His "Maybellene" (1955), "Johnny B. Goode" (1958), and "Sweet Little Sixteen" (1958) became rock standards almost immediately. This was also true of Little Richard (1932–), whose "Tutti Frutti" (1955), "Long Tall Sally" (1956), and "Good Golly Miss Molly" (1958) brought to early rock and roll a frenetic, updated version of New Orleans piano styles.

Chuck Berry and Little Richard were enormously influential in England. In fact, the biggest rock groups of the 1960s, including the Beatles and the Rolling Stones, rebelled against the bland, staid sounds of white pop rockers like Pat Boone (1934–) and Paul Anka (1941–) and began their careers by performing mostly cover versions of black rock-and-roll songs. Other rhythm-and-blues musicians who played an important role in the development of rock and roll include Junior Parker (1927–1971), who recorded "Mystery Train" (1953), "Next Time You See Me" (1957), and "Sweet Home Chicago" (1958), as well as Ike Turner (1931–), Jackie Brenston (1930–1979), Willie Mae "Big Mama" Thornton (1926–1984; "Hound Dog," 1953), the Isley Brothers ("Shout," 1959; "Twist and Shout," 1962), and Chubby Checker (1941–; "The Twist," 1960). During the late 1960s, relatively few black musicians remained involved in rock and roll, notable exceptions being Richie Havens (1941–) and Jimi Hendrix (1942–1970), who had performed as an accompanist with Little Richard, the Isley Brothers, and Ike and Tina Turner (1939–) before leading a popular rock ensemble.

Marvin Gaye (1939–1984), winner of two Grammy Awards for his song "Sexual Healing." AP/WIDE WORLD PHOTOS. REPRODUCED BY PERMISSION.

Soul

By 1964 black popular music had acquired a new name: *soul music.* There is no clear chronological or stylistic division between rhythm and blues and soul music, but there are some important differences. Soul music displayed a more pronounced gospel influence, whether in up-tempo, unrestrained shouting or in slower, more plaintive styles. Furthermore, soul's general rejection of extended instrumental soloing marked the continuing retreat of jazz as the popular music of the black middle class. Finally, even though most soul music consisted of solo singing with vocal backgrounds, the influence of carefully arranged close harmonies also waned.

It is no coincidence that soul flourished alongside the black pride movement. The music was made almost exclusively by blacks, at first almost exclusively for blacks, and was part of a rising black middle-class culture that celebrated black values and black styles in hair and clothing. In addition, soul's secular stance allowed the music to directly confront political issues central to African-American culture in the 1960s. James Brown (1933–), who had been a successful recording artist throughout the 1950s and achieved great popularity in the 1960s with live performances and recordings of songs such as "I Got You" (1965) and "I Feel Good" (1965), forever linked soul music and the Black Power movement with "Say It Loud, I'm Black and Proud" (1968).

Two record companies, Atlantic and Motown, dominated the soul-style rhythm-and-blues markets starting in the late 1950s and defined two major approaches. Atlantic and its Stax subsidiary often concentrated on funky instrumentals. Wilson Pickett (1941–) sang with a thrilling gospel feeling on songs such as "In the Midnight Hour" (1965) and "Mustang Sally" (1966). Otis Redding's (1941–1967) brief career included "These Arms of Mine" (1962), "I've Been Loving You Too Long" (1965), "Try a Little Tenderness" (1966), and "Sittin' on the Dock of the Bay" (1967). Ballad singer Percy Sledge (1941–) recorded "When a Man Loves a Woman" (1966) for Stax. Sam and Dave specialized in energetic, shouting vocals on hits such as "Hold On, I'm Coming" (1966), "Soul Man" (1967), and "I Thank You" (1968). Booker T. Jones (1944–) and the MG's personified the Memphis rhythm-and-blues sound on their instrumental hits for the Stax label, including "Green Onions" (1962) and "Hip Hug-Her" (1967). Aretha Franklin (1942–) reached her prime at Atlantic in the mid-1960s, when her white producer, Jerry Wexler (1917–), encouraged her to return to her gospel roots. She responded by creating perhaps the defining performances of the soul genre. Her majestic, emotional voice made songs such as "I Never Loved a Man the Way I Love You" (1967), "Respect" (1967), "Chain of Fools" (1967), and "Think" (1968) bona fide soul masterpieces.

If Stax and Atlantic musicians cultivated a funky, gritty sound, the founder of Motown, Berry Gordy Jr. (1929–), encouraged a sweeter sound, one that came to represent the classic soul sound even more than Atlantic or Stax. Those efforts produced dozens of hits during Motown's peak years in the 1960s by figures such as Marvin Gaye (1939–1984), Stevie Wonder (1950–), Mary Wells (1943–1992), and Gladys Knight (1944–). Important vocal groups included Smokey Robinson (1940–) and the Miracles, the Jackson Five featuring Michael Jackson (1958–), the Four Tops, the Temptations, and the Supremes with Diana Ross (1944–).

Atlantic and Motown were by no means the only producers of soul music. Aside from James Brown, perhaps the most important, independent soul musicians of the 1960s were Tina Turner and her husband, Ike Turner, who had led his own groups and backed the blues guitarist Elmore James (1918–1963) in the early 1950s. The duo had a string of influential hits in the 1960s, including "A Fool in Love" (1960), "It's Gonna Work Out Fine" (1961), and "River Deep, Mountain High" (1966).

In the 1970s, soul-style vocal groups remained popular, although the high lead vocals of the early vocal-harmony groups were backed with sleek, electrified rhythms. These groups included the Chi-Lites, the Stylistics, Harold Melvin (1941–1997) and the Bluenotes, the O'Jays, the Spinners, and Earth, Wind, and Fire. Solo singers in the soul idiom in the 1970s included Roberta Flack (1939–), Barry White (1944–2003), Al Green (1946–), and Teddy Pendergrass (1950–), all of whom created slow, emotional ballads and love songs. In the 1980s and 1990s, Whitney Houston (1963–) and Luther Vandross (1951–2005) have continued the tradition of the gospel-influenced singing style that characterizes soul.

Funk

In the mid-to-late 1960s a new style known as *funk*, derived from the black vernacular term for anything with a coarse, earthy smell, began to dominate the rhythm-and-blues charts. James Brown, who had been so influential in the 1950s and early 1960s in pioneering soul music, once again broke new ground, this time with stripped-down, forceful rhythms and simple, melodic riffs on "Papa's Got a Brand New Bag" (1965). This style was picked up by Sly Stone (1944–) on "Dance to the Music" (1968), "Everyday People" (1968), "Hot Fun in the Summertime" (1969), and by George Clinton's (1941–) work with his groups Parliament and Funkadelic in the 1970s. Other R&B musicians who adopted the funk style included Isaac Hayes (1942–), who recorded the soundtrack for the movie *Shaft* in 1971, and Curtis Mayfield (1942–1999), who recorded "Super Fly" in 1972. Disco music by 1970s figures such as Donna Summer (1948–), Gloria Gaynor (1949–), Kool and the Gang, and Rick James (1948–2004) drew directly on funk's interpretation of rhythm and blues.

Although the category of rhythm and blues, created by white music-industry executives to describe a range of musical styles, has undergone dramatic transformations, the term continues to express the essential characteristics of African-American popular music. In the 1980s and 1990s, musicians such as Prince (1958–), Lenny Kravitz (1964–), and Living Color took inspiration from Little Richard, James Brown, and Jimi Hendrix, while groups of younger musicians, such as the group Boyz II Men, updated the close-harmony vocal ensemble sound of the 1940s and 1950s. Black popular music—including funk, rock, rap, and pop-gospel ballads—continued to freely borrow and mix jazz, blues, and gospel, validating rhythm and blues as the common ground of modern African-American popular music.

In 1988 the Rhythm & Blues Foundation was founded in New York as a nonprofit service organization dedicated to the historical and cultural preservation of R&B music. It also provides financial support, medical assistance, and educational outreach programs to support the artists of the 1940s to the 1970s. The foundation's Pioneer Awards Program has recognized more than 150 artists—both individuals and groups—whose contributions have been instrumental in the development of R&B. Past recipients include such legends as Etta James, Ray Charles, Aretha Franklin, The Staple Singers, Cissy Houston (1932–), Martha Reeves (1941–) & the Vandellas, James Brown, Little Richard, Sam Cooke, Gladys Knight and the Pips, The Isley Brothers, Marvin Gaye, Al Green, Jackie Wilson, and Dionne Warwick (1940–).

With that range of variety in the past, how does one decide who is an R&B singer in the twenty-first century? Do the late Aaliyah (1979–2001) and the mono-monikered singers Ashanti, Beyoncé, Brandy, Monica, Mya, and Tweet conform to R&B standards? And what of such male counterparts as Babyface, D'Angelo, Maxwell, and Usher? R. Kelly and Keith Sweat? Are Natalie Cole, Anita Baker, and Jill Scott soul divas? Do Alicia Keys and Cassandra Wilson belong in the jazz category? Where does one put the adventurous vocal stylings of Mary J. Blige, Macy Gray, Lauryn Hill, and Erykah Badu? Perhaps, with R&B, one just knows it when one hears it.

See also Blues, The; Gospel Music; Jazz; Music

Bibliography

Broven, John. *Rhythm and Blues in New Orleans.* Gretna, La.: Pelican, 1978.

Deffaa, Chip. *Blue Rhythms: Six Lives in Rhythm and Blues.* Urbana: University of Illinois Press, 1996.

George, Nelson. *The Death of Rhythm & Blues.* New York: Pantheon, 1988.

Gillet, Charlie. *The Sound of the City: The Rise of Rock and Roll,* 2d rev. ed. New York: Pantheon, 1996.

Gonzalez, Fernando. *Disco-File: The Discographical Catalog of American Rock & Roll and Rhythm & Blues Vocal Harmony Groups—Race, Rhythm & Blues, Rock & Roll, Soul, 1902–1976,* 2d ed. Flushing, N.Y.: Gonzalez, 1977.

Gregory, Hugh. *The Real Rhythm and Blues.* London: Blandford, 1998.

Guralnick, Peter. *Sweet Soul Music: Rhythm and Blues and the Southern Dream of Freedom.* New York: Harper, 1986. Reprint, Boston: Little, Brown, 1999.

Haralambos, Michael. *Right On: From Blues to Soul in Black America.* New York: Da Capo, 1974.

Hildebrand, Lee. *Stars of Soul and Rhythm & Blues: Top Recording Artists and Showstopping Performers, from Memphis and Motown to Now.* New York: Billboard, 1994.

Rosalsky, Mitch. *Encyclopedia of Rhythm and Blues and Doo-Wop Vocal Groups.* Lanham, Md.: Scarecrow, 2000.

Shaw, Arnold. *Honkers and Shouters: The Golden Years of Rhythm and Blues.* New York: Macmillan, 1978.

Ward, Brian. *Just My Soul Responding: Rhythm and Blues, Black Consciousness, and Race Relations.* Berkeley: University of California Press, 1998.

Werner, Craig. *A Change Is Gonna Come: Music, Race, and the Soul of America.* New York: Plume, 1999.

White, Adam, and Fred Bronson. *The Billboard Book of Number One Rhythm & Blues Hits.* New York: Billboard, 1993.

PETER EISENSTADT (1996)
JONATHAN GILL (1996)
CHRISTINE TOMASSINI (2005)

Rice, Condoleezza

November 14, 1954

Condoleezza Rice was born in Birmingham, Alabama, the only child of Rev. John W. Rice Jr., a pastor at the Westminster Presbyterian Church, and his wife, Angelena Ray Rice, who taught science and music at an all-black high school in the segregated city. Her parents named her after a musical term, *con dolcezza,* which means to play with sweetness, and the young girl, nicknamed Condi, began piano lessons at the age of three. Besides music, Rice became an accomplished ice skater and a sports fan, particularly of football, an interest she shared with her father.

Rice grew up in the black middle-class neighborhood of Titusville, where her parents encouraged education and achievement. Her family left Birmingham for Tuscaloosa when Rice was eleven and her father became the dean of Stillman College. Two years later, he became an administrator at the University of Denver, and Condoleezza was enrolled at her first integrated school, a private academy from which she graduated at fifteen; she enrolled as a freshman at the University of Denver in 1970. After realizing she would not become a first-tier concert pianist, Rice switched her focus to political science, influenced by the lectures of former Central European diplomat Josef Korbel (the father of the first female secretary of state, Madeleine Albright), who sparked Rice's interest in Soviet and East-Central Europe studies.

Rice received a B.A. in political science from the University of Denver in 1974, a master of arts from the University of Notre Dame in 1975, and her Ph.D. from the Graduate School of International Studies at the University of Denver in 1981, where her doctoral thesis was on the ties between the Soviet and Czech militaries. Rice's father had become a registered Republican in 1952 when Democrats in Alabama would not register African Americans to vote. Rice herself registered as a Democrat in 1976 in order to cast her first presidential vote for fellow southerner Jimmy Carter. Disappointed with Carter's weak response to the 1979 Soviet invasion of Afghanistan, Rice voted for Ronald Reagan in 1980 and changed her registration to Republican in 1982.

Rice joined the faculty of Stanford University in 1981 as a political science professor. While at Stanford, Rice received the 1984 Walter J. Gores Award for Excellence in Teaching and the 1993 School of Humanities and Sciences Dean's Award for Distinguished Teaching. She published *Uncertain Allegiance: The Soviet Union and the Czechoslovak Army: 1948–1983* (1984); *The Gorbachev Era,* coedited with Alexander Dallin (1986); and coauthored with Philip Zelikow *Germany Unified and Europe Transformed: A Study in Statecraft* (1995). Rice was also a founding board member for the Center for a New Generation, an educational support fund for schools in East Palo Alto and East Menlo Park, California, which offers at-risk children tutoring, music lessons, and college preparation courses. In 1993, she became Stanford's youngest, first female, and first African-American provost.

Rice stepped down in 1999 and in 2000 became a foreign policy adviser for then–Texas governor George W. Bush, who was in the midst of his presidential campaign. In 1986, while an International Affairs Fellow of the Council of Foreign Relations, Rice had served under his father, President George H. W. Bush, as a special assistant to the director of the Joint Chiefs of Staff. From 1989 to March 1991, she was the director and then senior director of Soviet and East European Affairs in the National Security Council. President George W. Bush named Rice as assistant to the president for national security affairs, more commonly referred to as the national security adviser, and she was confirmed on December 22, 2001, becoming the first woman to hold this position. Considered an expert on international security policy and the military, Rice followed Colin Powell as the sixty-sixth U.S. Secretary of State, confirmed by the Senate on January 26, 2005. She is the first African-American woman to hold that position.

Rice is a Fellow of the American Academy of Arts and Sciences and has been awarded a number of honorary doctorates, including those from Morehouse College (1991), the University of Alabama (1994), the University of Notre Dame (1995), the National Defense University (2002), the Mississippi College School of Law (2003), the University of Louisville (2004), and Michigan State University (2004).

See also Politics in the United States

Bibliography

Balz, Dan. "The Republicans Showcase Rising Star Rice." *Washington Post* (August 1, 2000): A11.

Hawkins, B. Denise. "Condoleezza Rice's Secret Weapon." *Today's Christian* (September–October 2002): 18.

LaFranchi, Howard. "The Rise of Rice and a New 'Realism.'" *Christian Science Monitor* (March 17, 2005).

Mufson, Steven. "For Rice, a Daunting Challenge Ahead." *Washington Post* (December 18, 2000): A1.

Russakoff, Dale. "Lessons of Might and Right." *Washington Post Magazine* (September 9, 2001): W23.

U.S. Department of State. "Biography: Condoleezza Rice." (January 26, 2005). Available from <http://www.state.gov>.

CHRISTINE TOMASSINI (2005)

Rier, Carl P.

January 23, 1863
April 14, 1917

Carl P. Rier, who eventually became a Baptist minister, was born in Paramaribo to Jannie Rier and Elizabeth Helena Daalen, who were converts to the Moravian Brotherhood. After limited secondary schooling at the Van Meerten School, he followed in his father's footsteps, working as a carpenter from 1878 to 1888. Then despite bitter opposition from his father, he moved to Demerara, in British Guiana, to work as a plantation supervisor, and he remained abroad for several years. It was during this period that he first joined a local church affiliated with the newly formed American National Baptist Convention, the largest association of black Baptists in the United States. In 1890 Rier returned to Paramaribo and joined the Free Gospel Church (*Vrije Evangelisatie*), a Moravian sect that had been started by Moses Salomo Bromet in 1889. Rier assisted Bromet in his work, and it was in this church that he married Louisa Elisabeth Dunfries on January 25, 1893. They were to have eight children, four boys and four girls.

Around 1898 Rier left the Free Gospel Church, in part because he was not allowed to preach in Sranan (or Sranang, a creole language spoken in Suriname) which he hoped would help him to reach the lower classes. Cornelius Blijd, the first Surinamer to attain the rank of deacon in the Moravian Brotherhood, was among several others who also departed Bromet's church at that juncture. Rier led this group in founding the Suriname Baptist Congregation (*Surinaamsche Baptist Gemeente*) in 1898, but the others soon departed. His financial condition improved at this time through an inheritance left to him upon the death of his father. (While his father had earlier disinherited him because of opposition to Rier's new religious persuasion, in the end he left his son a conciliatory will.) The additional resources enabled Rier to remodel his house and open part of it as the church meeting hall in February 1899. By 1900 the congregation had twenty members and ran a Sunday school, but it then dissolved over an internal dispute concerning finances. Rier then joined a church in Paramaribo associated with the National Baptist Convention. In 1903 he passed the examinations in the theological seminary of that congregation and was sent to the United States to be formally ordained as a minister. His Baptist congregation in Paramaribo never flourished, however, mainly because of difficulties experienced while he was away. For example, there was dissension over finances, and no one else was willing to continue preaching in Sranan. Nevertheless, for the final thirteen years of his life he was to continue to use the church as a platform for the advocacy of social concerns in the black community. His congregation, which at its high point may have just exceeded one hundred, had dwindled to low double digits by the end of his life. In 1908 he sent his eldest son, John P. Rier, to the United States to be educated to become a Baptist minister; but the latter chose to remain there to pursue his career, rather than to return to work with his father as the elder Rier had hoped. Rier's wife, Louisa, died suddenly in 1909. His second marriage, to Sophie Elisa Meeren on August 16, 1911, produced no children. Sophie died on March 7, 1917; Rier soon followed on April 14. He was buried in Lina's Rust Cemetery in Paramaribo. In his will he left his church sufficient funds to purchase a building on Zwartenhovenbrughstraat.

Rier was, by all accounts, a fiery orator, and he preached and wrote Bible passages and church songs in Sranan, some his own compositions. Some of his brief, didactic writings were used in the public schools as well as those of the Moravians. Harking back to emancipation from slavery, a persistent theme throughout his career, was the theme of social and spiritual emancipation for the black population. Sounding at times like his North American contemporary Booker T. Washington, whose example he liked to cite, and like Washington, addressing both blacks and a wider audience, Rier emphasized the work ethic in his teachings. One of his main proposals centered on the need for black Surinamers to engage in agriculture, which both the history of the colony and urbanization had conditioned them to avoid. Unlike Washington, however, Rier emphasized connection with Africa, usually preferring the term "Ethiopia[n]." He was a precursor of later full-blown black nationalists.

See also Baptists; Moravian Church

■ ■ *Bibliography*

Abbenhuis, Fr. M. F.. "Carel Paulus Rier 1863–1917." In *Emancipatie: 1863–1963.* Paramaribo: Surinaamse historische Kring, Lionarons, 1964. Translation from the Dutch available at Moorland-Spingarn Research Center, Howard University, Washington, D.C.

Neus, N. C. J. "25th Commemoration of the Surinaamsche Baptist Gemeente; Biography of the late Rev. C.P. Rier, Founder and Pastor of the Surinaamsche Baptist Gemeente." Unpublished biographical sketch delivered as a speech by Neus in Paramaribo in 1924. Translation from the Dutch available from Rier Collection, Moorland-Spingarn Research Center, Howard University, Washington, D.C.

Yoder, Hilda van Neck. "Surinam's Cultural Memory: of Crown and Knife." *CLA Journal* 24 (1980): 173–183.

ALLISON BLAKELY (2005)

Riggs, Marlon

February 3, 1957
April 5, 1994

Filmmaker Marlon Troy Riggs was born in Fort Worth, Texas. After a childhood spent in Texas, Augusta, Georgia, and Germany, where his father was in the U.S. Army, Riggs received his bachelor's degree from Harvard University in 1978. After a short stint as an assistant with a television station in Texas, he entered the Graduate School of Journalism at the University of California at Berkeley, where in 1981 he received a master's degree in journalism with a concentration in documentary filmmaking. The next year, he began work as a filmmaker. In 1986 Riggs wrote, produced, and directed *Ethnic Notions,* a study of different stereotypes of African Americans. The film won an Emmy Award in 1988. In 1987 Riggs was hired as a professor by the University of California at Berkeley, and he held the post of professor of arts and sciences until his death.

In 1988 Riggs began work on *Tongues Untied,* a documentary about gay black men, and in 1989 he received a grant from the National Endowment for the Arts (NEA) for the film. Shortly after beginning the project, Riggs learned he was HIV-positive. He claimed the diagnosis helped personalize the film. The finished work, a mélange of documentary film, poetry, and Riggs's personal reminiscences, was released in 1989. In 1991 *Tongues Untied* became the center of a national controversy after it was scheduled to be shown on the public television series *P.O.V.* Its frank discussions of black homosexuality horrified such conservative critics as Senator Jesse Helms, who attacked the NEA for its sponsorship of Riggs's work. In

> *Marlon Riggs*
>
> "In this great gay Mecca, I was an invisible man, still. . . ."
>
> *TONGUES UNTIED*, 1991

1992 conservative Republican presidential candidate Pat Buchanan used a section of the work in a campaign commercial. Riggs, in turn, complained that Buchanan and others distorted his work through selective presentation.

Riggs continued to produce works about the gay black male experience, including the short film *Anthem* (1990) and *Non, Je Ne Regrette Rien/No Regret* (1991), a study of black men in the AIDS epidemic. He also produced films with nongay themes. In 1989 Riggs wrote and produced *Color Adjustment,* a documentary about images of African Americans in television sitcoms. The work won him a Peabody Award the same year. His last project was *Black Is . . . Black Isn't,* an unfinished documentary about African-American intellectuals. While Riggs championed black culture and the fight against racism, he remained critical of black homophobia and silence on AIDS. Riggs died of AIDS at his home in Oakland, California, in 1994.

See also Documentary Film; Film in the United States

■ ■ *Bibliography*

Guthmann, Edward. "Marlon Riggs—A Voice Stilled." *San Francisco Chronicle,* April 6, 1994, p. E1.

GREG ROBINSON (1996)

Ringgold, Faith

October 8, 1930

Born in Harlem, painter and sculptor Faith Ringgold was one of three children of Andrew Louis Jones Sr. and Willi Posey Jones, a fashion designer. She was married to Robert Earl Wallace, a pianist, from 1950 to 1956 and had two daughters in 1952: writer Michele Wallace (author of the 1970s feminist classic *Black Macho and the Myth of the Superwoman*) and Barbara, a linguist. Ringgold graduated from City College, New York, in 1955, and taught art in New York public schools until 1973. In 1959 she received a master's degree, also from City College. She began spending summers in Provincetown, Massachusetts, in 1957, took her first trip to Europe in 1961, and married Burdette Ringgold in 1962.

Ringgold's work and life exemplify her interests in civil rights and feminism. Some of her early paintings, such as *The Flag Is Bleeding* (1967), are large with stylized figures; others are abstract, like *Flag for the Moon, Die Nigger* (1969). Her radical use of potent national symbols, such as the flag and, later, postage stamps and maps, fiercely counterpointed American values with their ingrained racism. To achieve greater recognition for blacks and women in the mainstream art world, Ringgold participated in demonstrations at the Whitney Museum (1968, 1970) and at the Museum of Modern Art (1968). She was a cofounder in 1971 of Where We At, a group of black women artists. The following year she created a mural at the Women's House of Detention in New York that used only images of women.

The women's movement and Ringgold's close relationship with her mother influenced her to begin using fabrics, traditionally a women's medium, to express her art. She began to make masks and dolls—soft sculptures. Her mother made the dolls' clothes. They portray, among others, Rev. Dr. Martin Luther King Jr., the murdered children of Atlanta (the Atlanta child murder cases of 1979–1982), and various people in the community. Some of Ringgold's paintings were bordered in tankas, cloth frames made by her mother. Ringgold and her mother also collaborated on the production of Sew Real doll kits in 1979.

Ringgold then began working in the medium that brought her acclaim, story quilts. The first, *Who's Afraid of Aunt Jemima?* (1983), is a visual narrative of a woman restaurateur in painting, text, and patchwork. The quilts' stories vividly raise the issues of racism and feminism. As the stories became more complex, Ringgold began to create multiple quilts to encompass them. Each consists of a large painted panel bordered by printed patches pieced together, with text at the bottom or in the body of the quilt. The quilt series include *The Bitter Nest* (1988), *Woman on the Bridge* (1988), and *The French Connection* (1991). Ringgold used one of her quilts as the basis for her first children's book, *Tar Beach,* which was a Caldecott Honor Book and received the Coretta Scott King Award in 1992. Ringgold has authored a dozen more books for children. The original quilt was acquired by the Guggenheim Museum.

Ringgold's numerous awards include a grant from the National Endowment for the Arts (1989), Warner Communications' Wonder Woman (1983), and the National Coalition of 100 Black Women's Candace Award (1986). She holds honorary degrees from Moore College of Art, the College of Wooster, Ohio, the City College of New York, as well as from thirteen other colleges or universities. A twenty-five-year retrospective of her work traveled from 1990 to 1993. Beginning in 1984 Ringgold taught at the University of California at San Diego, spending half of each year there, before retiring in 2002. Ringgold began the Anyone Can Fly Foundation in an effort to broaden the canon of the art establishment to include artists from the African diaspora and to introduce their works to both children and adults. To this end, the foundation offers grants to scholars and educators whose work will invigorate publishing and teaching about African-American artists. A series of paintings, titled *Faith's Garden Party #1, 2, and 3,* documents the launch of the foundation.

Ringgold's designs from *Street Story Quilt* (1985) were selected by Judith Lieber for a limited edition of jeweled evening bags. She designed a mosaic mural for the 125th Street subway station in Manhattan. A painted quilt adorns the atrium of Hostos Community College in the Bronx. Numerous private collections and institutions hold her quilts and paintings. Her works have been acquired by the High Museum in Atlanta, the Metropolitan Museum of Art and the Museum of Modern Art in New York, and the Newark Museum in New Jersey, among others.

Ringgold's lengthy and prolific career shows no sign of slowing down as she plans new creations and administers the Anyone Can Fly Foundation.

See also Art; Painting and Sculpture

Bibliography

Faith Ringgold Web site. Available from <http://www.faithringgold.com>.

Farrington, Lisa E. *Faith Ringgold.* San Francisco, Calif.: Pomegranate, 2004.

Flomenhaft, Eleanor. *Faith Ringgold: A 25 Year Survey.* Hempstead, N.Y.: Fine Arts Museum of Long Island, 1990.

Moore, Sylvia. *Yesterday and Tomorrow: California Women Artists.* New York: Midmarch Arts Press, 1989.

Ringgold, Faith. *We Flew over the Bridge: The Memoirs of Faith Ringgold.* Boston: Little, Brown, 1995.

BETTY KAPLAN GUBERT (1996)
Updated by author 2005

Riots and Popular Protests

The categorization of the regional histories of riots and popular protest throughout the African diaspora requires a broad understanding of the term *race riot*. On the one hand, the term applies to the mass opposition embodied by violent protest among peoples of African descent challenging the socioeconomic oppression, violence, apartheid, and poverty that they faced throughout the Americas, in Europe, and in colonial Africa. However, the term *race riot* is also applied to the racialized attacks carried out by whites against black communities or individuals in retribution for their perceived transgressions, or to dissuade any future transgressions.

The nature of racially motivated popular protest is related to the very definition of race in a region (in this case, North America, Africa, Europe, and Latin America) and how race is related to political, social, and economic power. Popular protests involving people of color are much more likely to be defined racially in those parts of the African diaspora where the racial difference between black and white populations was once defined and defended by legal categorization, such as in the United States under segregation, in South Africa under apartheid, or in Great Britain when nonwhites immigrated in and threatened white job security and the Commonwealth Immigration Act was passed.

Whereas popular protest throughout Latin America has at times reflected the racial hierarchy that places whites at the top and nonwhites at the bottom, these incidents have often been described as "class violence." This is not to argue that race is unimportant to socioeconomic divisions in Latin American. The overwhelming reliance on forced labor—first indigenous, then African—to support plantation economies throughout the colonial period in both the Spanish and Portuguese colonies left a legacy of poor people of color in many modern Latin American states. However, the lack of *de jure* segregation between whites and blacks following abolition in much of Latin America has led to very different models of race relations and patterns of violence than have been seen in the United States.

The United States

The history of the United States is permeated by hundreds of race riots—there were thirty-three race riots during the Reconstruction era, and twenty-six in the year 1919 alone. During this history, the nature of racially motivated rioting and popular protest changed radically. For nearly a century following the era of abolition, the term *race riot* generally implied white populations violently attacking black individuals or communities. Starting in the 1930s and 1940s, however, the term began to identify African-American uprisings against social hardships, legal inequity, and police mistreatment. This shift in the racial makeup of the rioter was not unique to the United States.

ANTEBELLUM AND RECONSTRUCTION ERAS. In the nineteenth century there were numerous urban race riots in the United States; African-American populations faced violent attacks in Memphis, New Orleans, Cincinnati, and Wilmington, North Carolina. The destruction peaked with the New York Draft Riots in July 1863. Following the Emancipation Proclamation in January 1863, the Democratic Party warned white immigrant populations (largely Irish and German) that Emancipation would draw free blacks from the South into Northern cities, and thus into competitions for jobs. The passage of the new draft laws in March 1863 heightened racial tension in the city. All white men of fighting age were to be entered into a draft lottery, though men who could hire a substitute or pay the government an exception fee could avoid enlisting in the Civil War. Black men, not granted citizenship, were exempted from the draft. Early in the morning on the Monday following the first conscription lottery, held Saturday, July 11, New York erupted into a bloody riot that lasted for five days. During the first hours of the uprising the mobs exclusively targeted military and government buildings, but later that day the tide shifted toward a violent attack on African-Americans, their community, and the whites perceived as supporters of blacks. Before the riot ended, scores of people were killed, eleven black men were lynched, and millions of dollars worth of property had been destroyed. In the years following the riots, blacks fled the city, and the black population dwindled to a forty-year low.

THE WORLD WARS. During the first decade of the twentieth century, white attacks on black communities, which had previously occurred mostly in the South, shifted to urban centers in the North. Mobs attacked blacks in New York City in August 1900 and burned black homes in Springfield, Illinois, in 1908. However, a new surge of racial attacks took place after World War I, as whites struggled to take back the gains African Americans had made during the war. A backlash against the Great Migration, a period of mass movement of blacks from the South to the North, motivated scores of riots. This culminated in the Red Summer of 1919, during which cities across both the North and South exploded into race riots. The worst

Protest Parade, New York City, July 28, 1917. *Marchers, including James Weldon Johnson and W. E. B. Du Bois, parade up Fifth Avenue in response to a race riot in East St. Louis.* PHOTOGRAPHS AND PRINTS DIVISION, SCHOMBURG CENTER FOR RESEARCH IN BLACK CULTURE, THE NEW YORK PUBLIC LIBRARY, ASTOR, LENOX AND TILDEN FOUNDATIONS.

of the violence took place in Chicago, Washington, D.C., and Elaine, Arkansas. Each violent incident was initiated by whites, but increasingly there was shock in the popular press at black willingness to fight back. When the Chicago Riot ended, there were fifteen whites killed along with twenty-three blacks, and in Washington, D.C., four whites and only two blacks were killed. This change was generally attributed to black involvement in the war, but it marked an important turning point in racial violence.

The Harlem Riot of 1935 marked a second critical shift in racialized violence in the United States. On March 19, 1935, a sixteen-year-old African-American boy was caught stealing a penknife from a white-owned store in Harlem. The owner called the police, but by the time they arrived a crowd of African-Americans had formed and called for the boy's release. The owner convinced the police to release the boy out the back door to avoid trouble. Rumors quickly spread among the black community that the boy had been killed, and the crowd of picketers turned unruly. Violence and looting followed, but the crowds spared several black-owned businesses (and some with signs in the window that claimed black ownership). In the end, there were 125 arrests, 100 injuries, and three people killed—all were black. This marked the first racially motivated riot started by blacks in a northern city, and it was the first time that white-owned businesses were targeted, or at least the first time that black-owned business were consciously spared. The Harlem and Detroit riots of 1943 followed this model—they started as black protests—and they also followed the model that blacks paid the price, through arrests and attacks at the hands of police and white mobs.

CIVIL RIGHTS ERA AND BEYOND. A series of riots swept inner-city America during the 1960s, affecting Harlem, Boston, Chicago, Newark, Watts, Rochester, Cleveland, Cincinnati, and Detroit, to name only a few. By one count, over 300 "important" racial disturbances impacted more than 250 cites, causing more than 300 deaths, 8,000 injuries, and destroying property valued in the hundreds of millions. While the civil rights movement fought legal, or *de jure*, segregation in the South, issues of police brutality, crime, and poverty had been overlooked. As the Kerner Commission reported in 1968, in trying to explain three

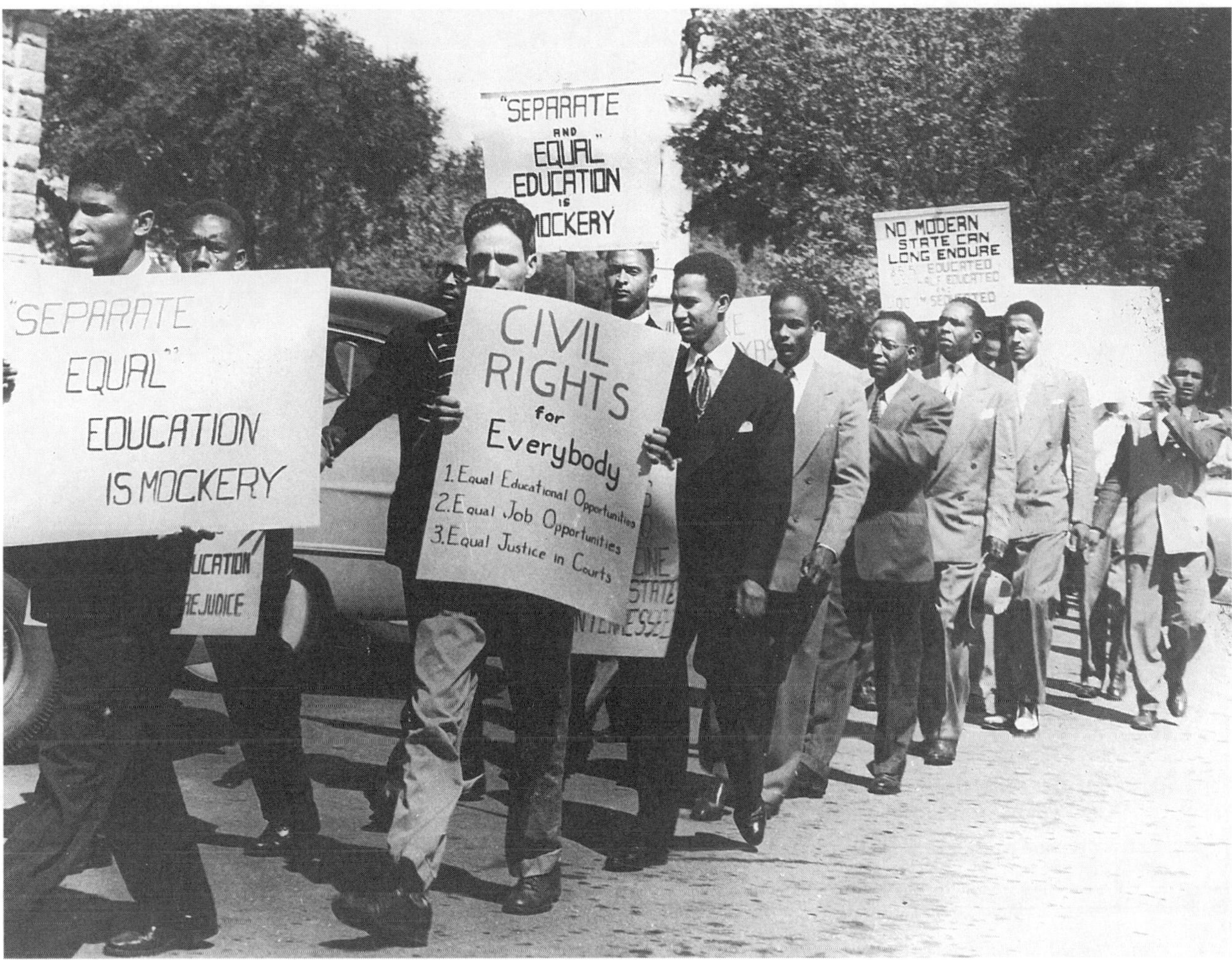

Civil rights march, Texas, 1949. *Students march to the state capitol in Austin, holding signs demanding civil rights and equal opportunity.* THE LIBRARY OF CONGRESS.

years of racialized violence, "our nation is moving toward two societies, one black, one white separate and unequal."

Black men and women eventually used violence to address these issues, and violence continues to serve in this role into the twenty-first century. In 1980 and 1989 crowds in Miami erupted into violence, first when four white police officers were acquitted after the beating death of a black man, and then when a black man on a motorcycle was killed by a Hispanic policeman. In Los Angeles in 1992, fifty-two people were killed and thousands were wounded following the acquittal of the police officers accused of beating Rodney King, the African-American motorist who was stopped for speeding and whose brutal beating at the hands of Los Angeles police was recorded on videotape by a witness. And in 2001, the African-American community in Cincinnati burst into violence following the killing of an African-American man by the police.

South Africa

The intersection of black and white in South Africa came about as a result of European colonization beginning in the seventeenth century, rather than the importation of enslaved Africans to support the institution of plantation slavery, as was generally the case throughout the Americas. Following the British victory over the white Afrikaners in 1902, the British Parliament established the Union of South Africa in 1910. Segregation and discrimination against nonwhites had already been practiced throughout South Africa for decades, but it was only in 1948, following the election of the all-white National Party (NP), that racial division was written into law with the implementation of apartheid ("separateness" in Afrikaans). Two years later, in 1950, the Group Areas Act was passed. This law called for separate areas for each of the four racial groups (blacks, whites, coloreds, and Asians), and in 1952 strict "pass laws," which controlled black movement in white

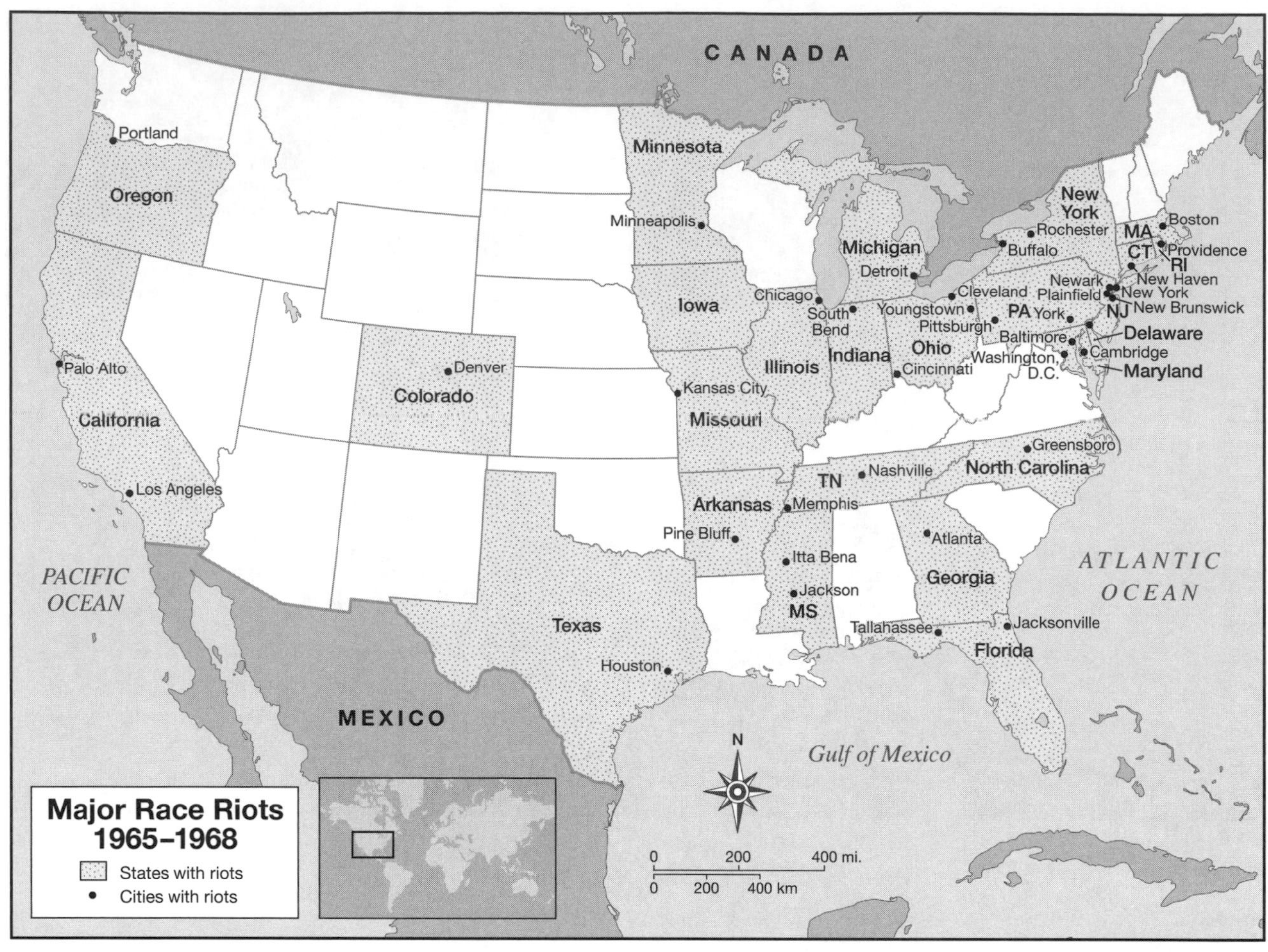

Map of the United States showing the locations of major race riots, 1965–1968. *By the mid-1960s, young blacks became increasingly impatient with the slow progress of civil rights and disillusioned with the concept of nonviolent protests that were often met with brutal and violent opposition from authorities as well as from spectators. Two admired black leaders, Malcolm X (1965) and Martin Luther King (1968) were assassinated during these years, fueling "black power" movements and a desire to meet violence with violence.* MAP BY XNR PRODUCTIONS. THE GALE GROUP.

areas, were implemented. Black men who remained in urban areas for more than seventy-two hours were subject to arrest and imprisonment.

The African National Congress (ANC), founded in 1912 as the South African Native National Congress and renamed in 1923, originally defended black voting rights, but it became one of the primary opposition groups to the apartheid regime. It started under black leadership but was open to white and Asian membership. In 1952 the ANC launched the Defiance of Unjust Laws Campaign, and following months of nonviolent protest and thousands of arrests, rioting erupted in several cities, leading to numerous deaths and extensive property damage. Then, in 1956, police killed three black women following protests that involved thousands of black women who opposed the extension of the pass laws, which for the first time would apply to black women as well as men.

After breaking with the ANC in 1958, Robert Mangaliso Sobukwe (1924–1978) founded the Pan-African Congress (PAC) the following year. Shunning the multiracial membership of the ANC, the PAC would only accept blacks into its membership. In 1960 the PAC called for a mass demonstration in which people would gather without passes and offer themselves to the police for arrest. Tens of thousands of people gathered at various locations, including a crowd of more than five thousand in the town of Sharpeville, the site of the Sharpeville Massacre on March 21, 1960. White police fired on the demonstration, killing sixty-nine and wounding at least 180, though some reports put that number as high at three hundred. This attack led to strikes, demonstrations, and protest marches, as well at riots across the nation. Both the ANC and the PAC were outlawed and forced underground, and an international outcry led to the United Nations's first sanction vote against South Africa.

Finally, on June 16, 1976, thousands of black students protested in Soweto against new legislation that required that some high school subjects no longer be taught in English, but exclusively in Afrikaans, a language associated with oppression. The violence spread to neighboring townships, and eventually upwards of 575 people were killed, the majority in Soweto.

Although it would be years before the NP and the ANC reached an agreement that would end apartheid in South Africa, popular protests such as those mentioned here were essential parts of the organized resistance that led to the downfall of apartheid on November 13, 1993.

Britain

In the years following World War I, with the return of both black and white British veterans, tensions grew around the small black immigrant communities in Liverpool, Cardiff, and London. In 1919, Britain experienced several race riots between white and black workers. At the core of these events were tensions among white workers who perceived this new immigrant population as a threat to their well-being. The victims of the violence were people of Caribbean descent, Ethiopians, Somalis, and Egyptians.

In the years following World War II, England experienced a large-scale growth among its immigrant West Indian population. In 1951 Britain's nonwhite population (including both West Indians of African descent and South Asians) was estimated at 74,000; in 1959 it was 336,000, and when the Commonwealth Immigration Act was implemented in 1962 to slow this immigration through a series of quotas on arriving immigrants, the nonwhite population had reached 500,000 people.

Although West Indians were welcomed by the British industrialists and by the government as workers in the years following 1948, working-class whites quickly began to view this population as a threat to their job security. Black settlement in England led to an increased white backlash, and white membership in racist and fascist organizations grew in response to the growing Afro-British population. West Indians faced inadequate housing, unemployment, discrimination, and violent attacks.

NOTTING HILL AND NOTTINGHAM RIOTS OF 1958. At the end of the summer of 1958, Britain faced a period of unprecedented racial violence. Initially, the town of Nottingham experienced a weekend of riots following a bar fight on August 23, touched off by white outrage over a white woman talking to a black man. Following the incident, more than 1,000 whites attacked the black community with rocks and sticks. While some blacks retaliated against their attackers, most fled to their homes. Although the bulk of the violence was controlled by the end of the weekend, racial violence flared up over the following two weekends.

Then, in West London one week later, on Saturday, August 30, a mob of white men attacked the white Swedish wife of a black West Indian, irate over the couple's alleged racial betrayal. After throwing stones, glass, and sticks at her and striking her across the back with an iron rod, the mob allowed the police to escort her home. This event was the catalyst to a week of nightly clashes between whites and West Indians in the areas of Notting Hill and Notting Dale. Mobs of white men, sometimes numbering in the hundreds, attacked blacks, broke the windows of stores that sold to blacks, and fought with the police. Most blacks stayed indoors during the riots, but some fought back with knives and razors, and the police arrested both white and black rioters.

TOXTETH AND BRIXTON RIOTS OF 1981. By the 1980s the nature of race riots in Britain underwent an important shift (one can argue that these changes began a decade earlier, given the Notting Hill Carnival Riots of 1976, which ignited among poor Afro-British over arbitrary police arrests). Following the patterns of rioting in the United States in the 1960s, most British riots stopped representing white rage against black settlement in Britain, and instead reflected black hostility towards racially discriminatory patterns of employment, housing, and especially community policing. Rather than attacks by white mobs on black communities, most of the riots that took place in Britain in the 1980s followed the pattern of black outrage at the social injustice carried out in the inner cities where they lived.

In July 1981, in Toxteth, an inner-city area of Liverpool, fierce battles between police and members of the community—largely, but not entirely, young Afro-British men—broke out over the police arrest and handling of a young black man. The police applied the "sus" laws, which allowed them to stop and search anyone who was "suspicious." These laws were overwhelmingly applied to detain young Afro-British men. A fracas broke out between police and an angry crowd who witnessed police handling the man, and three officers were injured. Over the following weekend, this violence erupted into a riot involving Molotov cocktails (thrown by rioters) and tear gas (by the police). In the following week 470 police were injured, 500 people were arrested, and more than seventy buildings were destroyed.

Similar tensions over the "sus" laws and police procedure were brewing in Brixton, South London. On Monday, April 13, 1981, a police patrol stopped to assist a black youth who had been stabbed in the back. They called for an ambulance and were in the process of bandaging the man up in the back of their car when they were attacked by a crowd of black youths who assumed that the police were responsible for the young man's injury. An ambulance arrived, and the youth was taken to the hospital. When police reinforcements arrived the incident concluded, though the immediate increase in police patrols in the area heightened tensions in the community. For the next three days there was violent rioting against the police by inner-city youths, both white and black. There was also significant looting of stores in the area. Only two people were injured (both police), and 282 people were arrested (mostly black). Twenty-eight buildings were burned while scores of businesses reported losses to looters.

"GREAT BRITISH RIOTS" OF 1985. The tension between police and predominantly black youths continued to simmer, and it exploded again in the summer and fall of 1985, with the worst violence occurring in London and Birmingham. Though each uprising resulted from a separate incident, the violence of 1985 was the result of the same social conditions that previously sparked the uprisings of 1981. In each case, the spark was produced by the tension between the police and the black youth whom they hoped to control.

In September 1985, three different race riots broke out following altercations between police and black citizens. In Birmingham, on September 9, a parking ticket led to an altercation between the police and a black driver. When the police arrested the man, a crowd of angry onlookers protested and a fight ensued; eleven officers were injured and two people were arrested. In Brixton, on September 28, while attempting to arrest a black man for the possession of a firearm, the police shot and permanently paralyzed the mother of their suspect. On October 5, at the Broadwater Farm Estate (a majority black public housing development in the predominantly white Tottenham district of London), the arrest of a black driver led to the death of another black mother. The police had implemented a heavy stop-and-search procedure around the housing project. After arresting a twenty-three-year-old black man with an improperly licensed car, they arrested him for auto theft and, following an altercation, for assaulting a police officer. They then went to his home to follow up, and while they were searching the property his mother collapsed and died. The man was eventually cleared of all charges and collected monetary damages from the police.

In each case, community backlash led to rioting; firebombing; the destruction of homes, stores, and vehicles; massive arrests (black and white); and the widespread injury of police officers and civilians alike—one police officer was stabbed to death in the Broadwater Farm Estate Riots. Indirectly, these patterns of violence impacted police policy; in the period following these uprisings there was an increased commitment to the recruitment and training of black officers, attempts to improve police and community relations, and the repeal of the infamous "sus" laws that allowed police to stop and search "suspicious individuals" without cause.

Brazil

Obviously, not all popular urban uprisings are race riots; labor, class, and gender have been at the center of many popular protests. That said, it is easier to define a race riot as such when the divide between blacks and whites in a society is easily defined and absolute. However, since the abolition of slavery in 1888 in Brazil, there has been a conscious effort to deny racial division, racial hierarchy, and racism in general. Thus, even if a popular protest involves or impacts large numbers of Afro-Brazilians, it is generally not called a race riot.

Before the abolition of slavery, Brazil was the site of numerous slave rebellions. In 1835 in Salvador, the capital of Bahia in northeastern Brazil, a group of enslaved Africans—Muslims who had attained literacy through their religion—organized an uprising in that city. When it was put down by the ruling elite, whites took violent revenge against the African community overall, enslaved and freemen alike, following a violent pattern of revenge replicated in the days following slave rebellions throughout the African diaspora.

Salvador, the former capital of the Brazilian colony, was the site of many episodes of violent protest in the early nineteenth century. Bahia was near the center of the plantation sugar economy, and the overwhelming majority of its population consisted of Brazilian-born blacks and Africans. In the years following Brazilian independence, Brazil claimed its independence as a royalist empire in 1822 under the crown rule of Dom Pedro I, and there were violent struggles between geographic regions and among the various ruling classes throughout the nation. Although wealthy Brazilians had spearheaded the war against the Portuguese elite who had retained political and economic power during the colonial period, once independence was achieved, wealthy Brazilians recognized the Portuguese as essential business partners. More important to this study is the fact that these movements were actually fought by populations on the fringe of political power: soldiers, freed slaves, urban poor, landless peasants, and, in some cases, slaves. Underlying the broad antiroyalist revolutionary movements were street riots and looting in which predominantly Afro-Brazilian mobs targeted the white Portuguese ruling class. Following Brazilian independence in 1822, Salvador experienced anti-Portuguese uprisings in 1823, 1824, and 1831. These were not explicitly racially motivated attacks, but following centuries of violent oppression under slavery, Europeans (as opposed to Brazilian-born whites) were suddenly politically vulnerable, and African and Afro-Brazilian resentment suddenly took form in acts of organized violence.

In Rio de Janeiro—which was made Brazil's capital in 1763, reflecting the economic shift from the sugar industry in the Northeast to coffee in the South—popular revolts took place in 1880 and 1904. Although neither is defined as a race riot, race played a central role in each. The *Vintem* Riot of 1880 was an uprising against a tax on public transportation (a *vintem* was the coin of smallest value in Brazil at the time) in the city of Rio de Janeiro. Rio had grown rapidly in the second half of the nineteenth century, quadrupling in size between 1822 and 1888 to a population of 500,000. This tax affected Rio's poor, predominantly Afro-Brazilian free-blacks and slaves, as well as growing Portuguese and Italian immigrant populations. On the first day of the tax, a group of approximately four thousand protesters at first only demanded that passengers not pay the tax, but later in the day they became violent. They tore up tracks, overturned tram cars, beat up drivers, and built barricades from pavestones and tram tracks. The police and army were called in, and that night peace returned to Rio. Three men had been killed; all were European immigrants. In 1904 the Brazilian administration set out to modernize Rio, in part through a forced vaccination plan against smallpox. The political opposition opposed mandatory vaccinations, and in November 1904 crowds took to the streets for a week of on-and-off rioting. The police reports describe the central role of Rio's underclass, specifically pointing out prostitutes, pimps, drunks, and professional troublemakers. Although neither uprising fits within the traditional rhetoric of the race riot, the role of race among the rioters, and the fact that the overall attempt to "modernize" the city was part of the general attempt to "whiten" Brazil and its capital, cannot be overlooked.

There was a popular movement in Rio de Janeiro that was clearly divided along race lines. During the four-day Revolt of the Lash in November 1910, more than 2,500 Brazilian sailors in Rio (85 percent of whom were Afro-Brazilian) rose up against the use of corporal punishment by white officers in the Brazilian navy. They took over four modern dreadnought battleships and held the city hostage for four days until the national congress met their demands. In this case, the racial division was identifiable because of the segregation practiced in the Brazilian navy. Even though these Afro-Brazilian sailors couched their demands in the language of slavery and race, Brazilian historians have traditionally placed this revolt in a context of class, not race.

See also Black Power Movement; Civil Rights Movement, U.S.; Identity and Race in the United States

Bibliography

Graham, Sandra Lauderdale. "The Vintem Riot and Political Culture: Rio de Janeiro, 1880." In *Riots in the Cities: Popular Politics and the Urban Poor in Latin America, 1765–1910,* edited by Silvia M. Arrom and Servando Ortoll. Wilmington, Del.: Scholarly Resources, 1996.

Harris, Leslie M. *In the Shadow of Slavery: African Americans in New York City, 1626–1863.* Chicago: University of Chicago Press, 2004.

Keith, M. *Race, Riots, and Policing: Lore and Disorder in a Multi-Racist Society.* London: UCL Press, 1993.

Kerner Commission. *The Kerner Report: The 1968 Report of the National Advisory Commission on Civil Disorders.* New York: Dutton, 1968. Reprint, New York: Pantheon, 1988.

Mazrui, Ali Alamin. *Africa Since 1935.* London: Heinemann, 1993.

Morgan, Zachary R. "The Revolt of the Lash, 1910." In *Naval Mutinies of the Twentieth Century: An International Perspective,* edited by Christopher M. Bell and Bruce A. Elleman. London: Frank Cass, 2003.

Needell, Jeffrey D. "The *Revolta Contra Vacina* of 1904: The Revolt Against 'Modernization' in *Belle-Epoque* Rio de Janeiro." In *Riots in the Cities: Popular Politics and the Urban Poor in Latin America, 1765–1910,* edited by Silvia M. Arrom and Servando Ortoll. Wilmington, Del.: Scholarly Resources, 1996.

Pilkington, Edward. *Beyond the Mother Country: West Indians and the Notting Hill White Riots.* London: Tauris, 1988.

Reis, João José. *Slave Rebellion in Brazil: The Muslim Uprising of 1835 in Bahia,* translated by Arthur Brakel. Baltimore, Md.: Johns Hopkins University Press, 1993.

Shapiro, Herbert. *White Violence and Black Response: From Reconstruction to Montgomery.* Amherst: University of Massachusetts Press, 1988.

Waters, Chris. "'Dark Strangers in Our Midst': Discourses of Race and Nation in Britain, 1947–1963." *Journal of British Studies* 36, no. 2 (1997): 207–238.

ZACHARY R. MORGAN (2005)

Risquet, Jorge

May 6, 1930

With the exception of Fidel Castro, his brother Raúl Castro, and Che Guevara, no Cuban has played a more prominent role in African affairs than Jorge Risquet Valdés, a man of intelligence, wit, and unswerving commitment to the Cuban Revolution. Born in Havana, Risquet is the descendant of an African slave, her white master, a Chinese indentured servant, and a Spanish immigrant. His parents were tobacco workers who were sympathetic to the Cuban Communist Party. While they could not afford to send their children to secondary school, they did give them a political education.

Jorge Risquet joined the party's youth organization in 1943 and two years later, at age fifteen, he was elected to its executive committee. A self-taught intellectual with a passion for reading, he was not yet twenty when he became the editor of the organization's newspaper. Over the next decade he endured the lot of a committed communist activist: detentions, torture, underground life. He joined Castro's guerrillas in the Sierra Maestra in mid-1958, and, after Castro's victory, he held senior positions in the army and the party.

In July 1965, Castro summoned Risquet. A column of 120 Cubans had secretly left Cuba to join the Congolese insurgents in Congo Leopoldville (now the Democratic Republic of the Congo) who were battling an army of mercenaries that the U.S. Central Intelligence Agency (CIA) had organized to prop up that country's pro-American regime. A second column of 250 Cubans was preparing to leave for Congo Brazzaville (now the Republic of the Congo) at the request of that country's left-leaning government, which felt threatened by Washington's intervention in the neighboring country. The Cubans believed that Central Africa was ripe for revolution, and that the two Congos would be the seedbed from which revolution would spread. Che Guevara headed the column in Congo Leopoldville; Castro wanted Risquet to lead the other.

For sixteen months Risquet's column remained in Congo Brazzaville. The Cubans saved the host government from a military uprising without bloodshed, instead using bluster and diplomacy. They carried out the country's first vaccination campaign against polio, and they provided critical assistance to the Popular Movement for the Liberation of Angola (MPLA), which was fighting for independence from Portugal. It was during this period that the first Cubans entered Angola (from Congo Brazzaville) to assist the MPLA, forging a bond that would blossom a decade later.

After returning to Cuba in January 1967, Risquet served as secretary of labor and held other senior positions until, in November 1975, he went to Angola. He left in a hurry, for civil war had broken out the previous spring in the Portuguese colony, which was slated for independence on November 11, 1975. The MPLA was struggling against two movements supported by the United States and South Africa. On October 14, to prevent an imminent MPLA victory, South African troops invaded Angola from neighboring Namibia (a de facto South African colony) and raced toward Luanda, the MPLA's stronghold, smashing all resistance. In an effort to stop the South Africans, Castro decided to send troops to Angola on November 4, and he sent Risquet as his personal representative. By late March 1976, the Cubans had forced the South Africans back into Namibia. Risquet remained in Angola until 1979.

Throughout the next decade, Cuba was a major protagonist in Africa. Tens of thousands of Cuban soldiers and technical advisers were in Angola, Ethiopia, and other African countries; Cuban instructors trained Namibian and South African rebels; and, through it all, Risquet was Castro's point man for Africa. As general Ulises Rosales del Toro, chief of staff of the Cuban armed forces, told a Soviet general in September 1984, "in my country whenever we discuss strategy, even military strategy, about Angola, Risquet has to be present, because for many years he has been at the center of all matters relating to Angola" (Rosales del Toro, 1984).

Risquet, a member of the Communist Party's political bureau, led the Cuban delegation during the 1988 negotiations on Namibian independence between Cuba, South Africa, Angola, and the United States. Meanwhile, the Soviet Union was rushing toward implosion. Havana compensated for the growing irrelevance of the Soviet Union in southern Africa with an unprecedented, and successful, military effort on the battlefield (against the South Africans in southern Angola) and with superb diplomatic skill. "Reading the Cubans is yet another art form," Risquet's U.S. counterpart, Assistant Secretary of State Chester Crocker, cabled Secretary of State George Shultz in August 1988. "They are prepared for both war and peace. . . . We witness considerable tactical finesse and genuinely creative moves at the table" (Crocker, 1988). The following December, South Africa acceded to Namibian independence. Cuban troops and Cuban diplomats had played an indispensable role in forcing Pretoria to accept a settlement it had bitterly resisted.

In July 1991, Nelson Mandela visited Havana and wrote the epitaph to the story of Cuba's aid to Africa during the Cold War. "We come here with a sense of the great debt that is owed the people of Cuba," he said. "What other country can point to a record of greater selflessness than Cuba had displayed in its relations to Africa?" (Mandela, 1991).

Risquet began working as a senior adviser for Raúl Castro in 1991. He is also a writer, telling the story of what he and his countrymen and women sought to accomplish in Africa. No other Cuban has written about this important chapter in global history with such verve, insight, and authority.

See also Political Ideologies; Politics

Bibliography

Crocker, Chester. Communication to Secretary of State George Shultz. Brazzaville, Republic of the Congo, August 25, 1988. Washington, D.C.: National Security Archive.

García Eloseguis, Francisco. *Cien días después del Granma.* Havana, Cuba: Editorial del Ciencias Sociales, 2002.

Gleijeses, Piero. "Truth or Credibility: Castro, Carter, and the Invasions of Shaba." *International History Review* 18, no. 1 (1996): 70–103.

Gleijeses, Piero. *Conflicting Missions: Havana, Washington, and Africa, 1959–1976.* Chapel Hill: University of North Carolina Press, 2002.

León Rojas, Gloria. *El Pavel Cubano: Jorge Risquet, del solar a la Sierra.* Havana, Cuba: Editorial de Ciencias Sociales, 2004.

Mandela, Nelson. "Cuito Cuanavale marca el viraje en la lucha para librar al continente y a nuestro pueblo del azote del apartheid." *Granma* (July 27, 1991): 3–4.

Risquet Valdés, Jorge. *El Segundo frente del Che en el Congo: Historia del batallón Patricio Lumumba.* Havana, Cuba: Casa Editora Abril, 2000.

Risquet Valdés, Jorge. "Angola: El camino hacia la victoria." *Temas* 37–38 (April 2004): 159–167.

Risquet Valdés, Jorge. "Las profundas raíces del internacionalismo de los cubans." *Tricontinental* 158 (2004): 103–114.

Rosales del Toro, Ulises. Conversación del general de división Ulises Rosales del Toro con el general de ejèrcito Varennikov V. I. Moscow, September 5, 1984. Havana, Cuba: Archives of the Central Committee of the Cuban Communist Party.

PIERO GLEIJESES (2005)

Roach, Max

January 10, 1924

The jazz drummer and bandleader Maxwell Lemuel "Max" Roach was born in Elizabeth City, North Carolina, and raised in Brooklyn, New York. He studied music as a child with his mother, a gospel singer, and received piano lessons from his aunt. He also received music lessons in public school, and by the age of ten he was playing drums in church bands. He performed in Coney Island sideshows, such as the Darktown Follies, while in high school. During this time he also began frequenting Minton's Playhouse in Harlem, where he met some of the leading jazz musicians of the day. In 1941 Roach graduated with honors from Brooklyn's Boys' High School. Soon after, he started performing regularly with the saxophonist Charlie Parker at Clark Monroe's Uptown House in Harlem, and by the next year he had a strong enough reputation to fill in for Sonny Greer for several nights with Duke Ellington's orchestra.

In 1943 and 1944 Roach recorded and performed with the saxophonist Coleman Hawkins at Kelly's Stable as a replacement for Kenny Clarke ("Woody'n' You," 1944; "Bu-Dee-Daht," 1944). In 1944 he also joined the trumpeter Dizzy Gillespie's quintet at the Onyx Club, becoming a member of the first bebop band to open on 52nd Street, which had become the central location for New York jazz nightclubs. The next year Roach began working with Charlie Parker, an association that would last more than five years. On Roach's first important recording with Parker, the uptempo "Ko-Ko" (1945), Roach had already left swing drumming behind for a bebop style, keeping time on the cymbal and reserving the drums themselves for accents.

Together with Kenny Clarke, Roach redefined the rhythmical and structural architecture of jazz drumming, while also creating a new solo role for modern jazz drum performance. Initially influenced by the imaginative "melodic" solo style of Sid Catlett, the driving intensity of Chick Webb, and the fluid swing and finesse of Jo Jones, Roach distilled their stylistic characteristics through Clarke's polyrhythmic innovations. By the end of the 1940s, Roach was recognized as one of the leading drummers in jazz. He performed on Miles Davis's "Birth of the Cool" recordings (1949) and on Bud Powell's "Un Poco Loco" (1951). In the early 1950s he continued his prolific career while pursuing studies in composition and tympani at the Manhattan School of Music. From 1954 to 1956 he co-led the Clifford Brown-Max Roach Quintet, which pioneered the hard-driving style known as hard hop (*Study in Brown,* 1955; *At Basin Street,* 1956).

In the 1960s Roach began to combine his music with his politics, with a particular emphasis on racial oppression in both the United States and South Africa. His 1960 recording of *We Insist: Freedom Now Suite* used free-form musical structures, including an emotionally charged interplay between the drummer and his then-wife, the vocalist Abbey Lincoln, to explore the theme of racial oppression in America. That work also used West African drumming and Afro-Cuban percussion to draw parallels between slavery in the United States, segregation, and apartheid in South Africa.

In the 1960s Roach began to move away from appearing solely in strict jazz contexts. He began performing solo drum compositions as independent pieces, an effort dating back to his "Drum Conversation" of 1953. He also recorded original works for vocal choruses and pianoless quartets. In the 1960s Roach taught at the Lenox School of Jazz, and in 1972 he assumed a faculty position at the University of Massachusetts, Amherst. Among Roach's most significant work from the 1970s are duet recordings he made with some of the leading figures from the post-bebop avant-garde, including Archie Shepp, Anthony Braxton, Abdullah Ibrahim, and Cecil Taylor. In the 1980s, Roach's astoundingly protean career included performances and recordings with a jazz quartet, the percussion ensemble M'Boom, the Uptown String Quartet (with his daughter Maxine on viola), rap and hip-hop musicians and dancers. In 1980 Roach recorded an interactive drum solo with a tape recording of the Reverend Dr. Martin Luther King Jr.'s 1963 "I Have A Dream" speech (*Chattahoochee Red*), and in 1989 he recorded duets with Dizzy Gillespie. Roach, who wrote music as early as 1946 ("Coppin' The Bop"), has in recent years dedicated more and more of his time to composition. His *Shepardsets,* a work for the theater, received an Obie Award in 1985, and he has also composed for film and television, and for symphony orchestra.

Throughout the 1990s, Roach was involved with a number of collaborations and creative efforts. He recorded the two-CD set, *To the Max!*, in 1992 and performed with the Atlanta Symphony Orchestra. Attentive to new musical ideas, Roach viewed rap as a creative improvisational form and collaborated with MTV's rap-music host Fab Freddie Five in recording the program *From Bebop to Hip-hop*. In 1998, Roach performed with his So What Brass Quintet, which was comprised of five brass instruments and drums, and with dancers in choreographer Donald Byrd's production "Jazz Train."

Roach, who has lived in New York all of his life, is recognized not only as one of the most important drummers in the history of jazz, but as one of the leading African-American cultural figures of the twentieth century, with a decades-long commitment to fighting racial injustice. In addition to the several honorary doctorates he has received throughout his career, in 1988 Roach became the first jazz musician to receive a MacArthur Foundation Fellowship.

See also Gillespie, Dizzy; Jazz; Lincoln, Abbey; Parker, Charlie

Bibliography

Brown, Anthony. "The Development of Modern Jazz Drumset Artistry." *Black Perspective in Music* 18, nos. 1, 2 (1990): 39–58.

Roach, Max. "What Jazz Means to Me." *Black Scholar* 3, no. 2 (1972): 3.

Weinstein, Norman C. *A Night in Tunisia: Imaginings of Africa in Jazz.* Metuchen, N.J.: Scarecrow Press, 1992, pp. 118–126.

Whitehead, Kevin. "Max Roach: Drum Architect." *Down Beat* 52, no. 10 (1985): 16.

ANTHONY BROWN (1996)
Updated by publisher 2005

Robeson, Eslanda

December 15, 1895
December 13, 1965

The anthropologist and activist Eslanda Cardozo Goode Robeson was born on December 15, 1895, in Washington, D.C. Her father, John Goode, was a clerk in the War Department. Her mother, Eslanda Cardozo, was the daughter of Francis Lewis Cardozo, a prominent pastor and Reconstruction-era politician.

When Eslanda Goode was six, her father died from alcoholism. Her mother moved the family to New York City, where her children could attend nonsegregated schools. Eslanda Goode graduated from Columbia University in 1917 with a bachelor of science degree in chemistry and took a job as a histological chemist at New York's Presbyterian Hospital, the first African American employed there in a staff position. It was there, in 1920, that she met Paul Robeson, who was recovering from a football injury. They were married a year later, and from then on Eslanda Robeson pursued her career as an anthropologist and journalist while managing her husband's singing and acting commitments. She combined both careers in 1930, when she published *Paul Robeson, Negro.*

In the 1920s and 1930s, Eslanda Robeson accompanied her husband on most of his travels. At the same time she studied anthropology at the University of London and at the London School of Economics (1936–1937). She received a Ph.D. in anthropology from the Hartford Seminary Foundation in 1945. She also traveled and worked on her own. A trip through Africa in 1936 resulted in a book, *African Journey* (1945), and led to her commitment to African anticolonialism. She was active on the Council on African Affairs, and in a 1946 address before the United Nations Trusteeship Council urged self-determination for all African people.

The combination of her political activities, a visit to China in 1949 and her public support of its government, and her vocal enthusiasm for the Soviet Union led her to be called before Senator Joseph McCarthy's Subcommittee of the Senate Committee on Government Operations in 1953. From 1958 through 1963 she and her husband lived in self-imposed exile in the Soviet Union. Eslanda Robeson died of cancer in New York City on December 13, 1965.

See also Anthropology and Anthropologists; Council on African Affairs; Robeson, Paul

Bibliography

Dorinson, Joseph, ed. *Paul Robeson: Essays on His Life and Legacy.* Jefferson, North Carolina: McFarland, 2002.

Duberman, Martin Bauml. *Paul Robeson.* New York, 1988.

Logon, Rayford W., and Michael R. Winston, eds. *Dictionary of American Negro Biography.* New York: Norton, 1982.

SIRAJ AHMED (1996)
Updated bibliography

Robeson, Paul

April 9, 1898
January 23, 1976

Actor, singer, and political activist Paul Robeson was born in Princeton, New Jersey, where his father, William Drew Robeson, was the minister of a local Presbyterian church, and his mother, Maria Louisa Bustill, was a schoolteacher. His childhood was happy but marred by two defining events. His mother died when he was six, after she was accidentally set on fire at home; and his father lost his church following a fierce dispute among his congregation. After working at menial jobs in Princeton, his father moved first to Westfield and then to Somerville, both in New Jersey, where he again led churches affiliated with the African Methodist Episcopal Zion denomination.

An uncommonly brilliant student and athlete, Paul Robeson entered Rutgers College (later Rutgers University) in New Brunswick in 1916. Although he was the only black student there, he became immensely popular. He was elected to Phi Beta Kappa as a junior and selected twice (1917 and 1918) as an All-American football player by the famed journalist Walter Camp. After graduating in 1919, he moved to Harlem, and in 1920 entered the law school of Columbia University in New York. To support himself he played professional football on weekends, then turned to acting after winning a role in *Simon the Cyrenian* at the Harlem YMCA in 1921.

Graduating from law school in 1923, he was admitted to the bar and served briefly in a law firm. Then, chafing at restrictions on him as a black, and urged on by his wife, Eslanda Cardoza Goode (a fellow student, in chemistry, at Columbia), he left the law for the stage. He enjoyed immediate success, particularly with the Greenwich Village–based Provincetown Players in Eugene O'Neill's *The Emperor Jones* (1923) and *All God's Chillun Got Wings* (1925). In 1925, with his longtime accompanist Lawrence Brown, he launched his celebrated career as an interpreter of African-American spirituals and of folk songs from around the world with a concert of the former in New York. He then traveled to Europe and Great Britain (where in 1922 he had been well-received as an individual and as an actor in the play *Voodoo*). Critics hailed his acting in the 1925 London production of *The Emperor Jones.*

In the 1928 London production of Jerome Kern and Oscar Hammerstein II's musical *Show Boat,* his stirring rendition of "Ol' Man River" took his popularity to new heights. Although he triumphed again when *Show Boat* opened in New York in 1930, Great Britain was the scene of many of his greatest achievements. In the following years he starred there in a number of plays, including *Othello* (1930), *The Hairy Ape* (1931), and *Stevedore* (1933). Robeson also had prominent roles in almost a dozen films, such as *Sanders of the River* (1935), *Show Boat* (1936), *King Solomon's Mines* (1935), and *Proud Valley* (1941). In most of these efforts, his depictions of a black man contrasted starkly with the images of subservience, ignorance, criminality, or low comedy usually seen on the Hollywood screen.

Handsome and blessed with a commanding physique and a voice of unusual resonance and charm, Robeson might have capitalized on his stage and screen success and ignored politics altogether. However, his resentment of racism and his attraction to radical socialism, especially after an outstanding welcome in the Soviet Union in 1934, set him on a leftward course. A frequent visitor to the USSR thereafter, Robeson learned to speak Russian (and eventually almost two dozen other languages, in which he recorded many songs). His son, Paul Jr. attended school there for several years. Robeson became a dependable supporter of progressive causes, including the rights of oppressed Jews and of antifascist forces in Spain. In London, he befriended several students and other intellectuals, such as Kwame Nkrumah, George Padmore, and Jomo Kenyatta, who would later be prominent in the anticolonialist movements in Africa.

Paul Robeson as Othello, with Uta Hagen as Desdemona, in a 1943 Theatre Guild production of the Shakespeare play. PHOTOGRAPHS AND PRINTS DIVISION, SCHOMBURG CENTER FOR RESEARCH IN BLACK CULTURE, THE NEW YORK PUBLIC LIBRARY, ASTOR, LENOX AND TILDEN FOUNDATIONS.

Resettling in the United States in 1939, Robeson joined enthusiastically in the war effort and maintained his stellar position as an entertainer—although racism, including that on Broadway and in Hollywood, still disturbed him. In 1943 his critically acclaimed portrayal of Othello, in the first Broadway production of Shakespeare's play with an otherwise white cast, created a sensation. He was awarded the NAACP's Spingarn Medal in 1945. He fared less well after the war, when the cold war intensified. In 1946 he vowed to a special committee of the California State Legislature that he had never been a member of the Communist Party. However, when accusations continued, he resolutely refused to cooperate with the authorities. Despite his protests, he was identified as a communist by the House Committee on Un-American Activities. Such opposition hampered his career as a recording artist and actor.

In 1949, in a major controversy, he told a gathering in Paris that it was "unthinkable" to him that African Americans would go to war against the Soviet Union, whose fair treatment of blacks was a rebuke to racist American laws and conventions. Later that year the announcement of his participation in a musical festival sponsored by liberals and leftists in Peekskill, New York, led to rioting in the town that left scores of attendees injured. The next year, the State Department impounded his passport. With Robeson refusing to sign an oath disavowing communism, his singing and acting career in effect came to an end. He was widely ostracized by whites and blacks, except those among the far left.

In 1958 the Supreme Court declared the oath and other government rules unconstitutional. That year, Robeson published *Here I Stand,* which combined autobiography with a considered statement of his political concerns and other beliefs. He sang at Carnegie Hall in what was billed as a farewell concert, and also performed in California. Leaving the United States, he was welcomed as a hero in the Soviet Union, which had awarded him the Stalin Peace Prize in 1952, but he fell ill there. Complaining of chronic exhaustion and other ailments, he entered a series of hospitals in the Soviet Union, Europe, and Britain.

In 1963, when he and his wife returned to the United States and a home in Harlem, he announced his formal retirement. In 1965 Eslanda Robeson died. With a further deterioration in health, including a nervous breakdown, Robeson moved to Philadelphia to live with his sister. A seventy-fifth birthday celebration at Carnegie Hall in 1973 found Robeson (whose illness kept him away) saluted, in a more liberal age, by prominent blacks, liberals, and socialists as one of the towering figures of the twentieth century. In a message to the gathering, Robeson described himself as "dedicated as ever to the worldwide cause of humanity for freedom, peace, and brotherhood." He died in Philadelphia in 1976.

See also Folk Music; Musical Theater; Spingarn Medal; Spirituals

■ ■ *Bibliography*

Duberman, Martin B. *Paul Robeson.* New York: Knopf, 1988.

Robeson, Paul. *Here I Stand.* Boston: Beacon Press, 1971.

Robeson, Paul, Jr. *The Undiscovered Paul Robeson: An Artist's Journey, 1898–1939.* New York: Wiley, 2001.

Stewart, Jeffrey C. *Paul Robeson: Artist and Citizen,* New Brunswick, N.J.: Rutgers University Press, 1998.

ARNOLD RAMPERSAD (1996)
Updated bibliography

Robinson, A. N. R.

December 16, 1926

Arthur Napoleon Raymond Robinson was born in Calder Hall, Tobago, to James Andrew and Isabella Muir Robinson. He grew up in Castara, a rural fishing village, and attended the Castara Methodist Primary School, where his father, a strict disciplinarian, was headmaster. As a child, Robinson played cricket and football and ran track, but he never made the school or village team in these sports. Instead, he excelled academically.

In 1938 Robinson won a Bowles Scholarship, which allowed him to attend Bishop's High School in Scarborough, Tobago, where he continued to excel academically. In 1944 he narrowly missed winning an Island Scholarship to a university, so he accepted a teaching position at Bishop's High School. After six months he left this post to become a second-class clerk in the Department of Public Works. This did not suit his ambitions, however, and he enrolled in the University of London's external program in Tobago. He graduated in 1951 with a Bachelor of Laws degree and was called to the bar of the Inner Temple. That same year, he entered St. John's College, Oxford, where he studied philosophy, politics, and economics.

While at Oxford, Robinson was a member of the Oxford Union Society, and he won a number of prizes for his debating skills. He also established a friendship with a fellow debater, Robert K. Woetzel, and he took an interest in Woeztel's thesis on international law concerning the Nuremberg Trials. On the invitation of Woetzel, Robinson joined the Oxford Political Study Circle. He joined other student organizations and later became the president of the West Indian Students Society and secretary of the study circle. Among the other Caribbean students he met at Oxford was Tom Adams, who became prime minister of Barbados. Robinson also established close relationships with several fellow countrymen, including Eldon Warner, Max Ifill, and Doddridge Alleyne. Some of these individuals would later become his political allies. Robinson also participated in discussions on the foundation of the West Indies Federation, which was established in 1958 but lasted only four years.

Robinson returned to Trinidad and Tobago in 1955 to practice law. Initially, Robinson's interest was in local politics, and he joined a group called the Scarborough Political Circle, a spin-off from his Oxford study circle. His interest in developing better social, political, and economic conditions seems to have focused at first on the place of Tobagonians within the twin-island colony of Trinidad and Tobago, but he soon linked this interest to the international arena. His first acquaintance with Eric Williams was at the Scarborough Political Circle, probably in 1955. This meeting would eventually lead Robinson to an active engagement in politics. He later attended a discussion group with John Donaldson, Elton Richardson, and W. J. Alexander at the Chancellor Street residence of Dr. Williams in Port of Spain. The group agreed to form a political party, with Williams as leader. Williams was to be introduced to the electorate through public lectures and other social events throughout the country. The principal venue was Woodford Square—renamed the "University of Woodford Square" by Williams. Robinson worked on the constitution of the party, and he thus became a founding member of the People's National Movement (PNM). After the establishment of the party, he served as its treasurer and deputy leader, and a large section of the citizenry saw him as heir apparent to Eric Williams.

As the PNM's spokesman for Tobago, Robinson was a candidate for Parliament in the 1956 general election. He was defeated, however, by A. P. T. "Fargo" James, a very popular "grassroots" politician. Robinson, fairly well known but new to politics, was portrayed by James as too "proud, too social, and too stuck up" to lead Tobagonians. In 1958, however, Robinson won the Tobago seat in the federal Parliament. He then had to deal with the disappointment of the withdrawal of Jamaica and Trinidad and Tobago from the West Indies Federation, which he had nurtured since his Oxford days. The federation completely collapsed the following year. However, Robinson won the Tobago seat in the House of Representatives in the election of 1961, which followed the granting of full self-government. He was appointed the minister of finance in the ruling PNM government of the newly independent state of Trinidad and Tobago in 1962.

Robinson inherited the daunting task of developing a financial system for the newly independent state. Unfortunately, his Finance Act of 1966 set off plans within the PNM to marginalize him because the act went against the interests of certain importers and businesspeople. The act sought to reform the tax system, particularly with regard to the export of foreign exchange earned in Trinidad and Tobago. The new tariff structure was a deliberate attempt to change a colonial economy to one suited to independence. Consequently, higher duties were imposed on imported goods in order to protect the local manufacturers. The politics surrounding the Finance Act is explained in his book, *The Mechanics of Independence: Patterns of Political and Economic Transformation in Trinidad and Tobago* (1971).

Robinson felt that the PNM failed to lead the country into real political and economic independence through sound economic structures and policies. He was also impatient with the failure of the party's leadership to insist on integrity in government, and he felt that the government had not changed much from its colonial predecessor. The result of the PNM's policies was an increase in government corruption, manifested in a system of patronage in the appointment of key personnel to head state enterprises. As a result, popular support for the PNM weakened.

By mid-1969, amid economic and social stresses, the dissatisfaction of students and laborers, and the activities of the Black Power movement, the PNM government was viewed by many as unresponsive and impotent. Increasingly critical of the government's handling of a Black Power–induced crisis, Robinson resigned from the PNM on April 13, 1970. He was accused of wanting to overthrow the government and of being involved in the Black Power movement, leading Williams to declare a state of emergency. Having resigned from the PNM, Robinson became the spokesman for reform.

Robinson's quest for political empowerment for all continued when he formed the Action Committee of Dedicated Citizens (ACDC). The group gradually evolved into a political party and struck an alliance with the traditional opposition party, the Democratic Labour Party (DLP). The merger between the two groups broke down after the DLP became a spent force in 1971. The ACDC evolved into the Democratic Action Congress (DAC), which was viewed principally as a Tobago party, since Robinson had returned there to live. In 1976 Tobagonians rejected the PNM and elected DAC members Robinson and Dr. Winston Murray as their representatives. For the next four years, Robinson engaged in a political struggle with Williams for internal self-government for Tobago, which was finally realized in 1980. Robinson then resigned his seat in the House of Representatives to contest the first Tobago House of Assembly (THA) elections. He was successful and became the assembly's first chair. The island, which had launched his political career twenty-two years earlier, now had his full attention. It was in Tobago that Robinson again developed a political base from which he would compete with, and eventually triumph over, the PNM.

Meanwhile, Robinson sought to build a multicultural and multiracial political party that was truly representative of the people of Trinidad and Tobago. He therefore joined with the leaders of the other main opposition parties to form the National Alliance for Reconstruction (NAR). Robinson's popularity made him the unquestioned leader of the NAR, which defeated the PNM in the 1986 elections, winning thirty-three seats to the PNM's three, and Robinson became the prime minister of Trinidad and Tobago. Yet, in spite of the fact that he successfully restructured the economic foundations of the state, placing it on a path of growth, he lost the general elections of 1991 to Patrick Manning and the PNM. The principal reason for this loss was not the painful economic adjustments he instituted, but the issue of race, as the NAR government was viewed as a marriage of convenience rather than an alliance of genuine unity between the African and East Indian groups. Before leaving office in 1991, Robinson became the victim of an attempted coup led by Imam Yasin Abu Bakr, a black Muslim leader. Robinson was held hostage for six days, along with other members of the government, but he called for the armed forces to defy the insurgents and "attack with full force." He was finally released by the insurgents who, respecting his bravery, carried him triumphantly out of the parliamentary building. While losing the 1991 elections decisively, Robinson won his seat in Tobago and remained in Parliament.

Contrary to popular opinion, Robinson's defeat did not lead to his political demise, for the 1995 general elections brought him back into national prominence. In this election, the United National Congress (UNC) and the PNM were tied, with seventeen seats each. It was left to Robinson, with the two Tobago DAC seats, to decide which party he would support to form the new government. By supporting the UNC, Robinson made history by creating the first "Indian" government of Trinidad and Tobago, and he selected Basdeo Panday as prime minister.

Robinson was appointed president of Trinidad and Tobago in 1997, and he served in that post until March 2003. He has since retired from politics, but he is still viewed as the country's most well-known, statesmanlike, enigmatic, and misunderstood figure. He has certainly had the longest, and one of the most memorable, political careers in Trinidad and Tobago.

See also Black Power Movement; James, A. P. T.; International Relations of the Anglophone Caribbean; Manning, Patrick; Peoples National Movement; Williams, Eric; Woodford Square

Bibliography

Kublalsingh, Hayden H. "The Political Life of Arthur Napoleon Raymond Robinson, 1956–1986: A Historical Perspective." UC 300 Project, April 22, 1991. West Indian Library, University of the West Indies, St. Augustine, Trinidad.

Pantin, Raoul. *Black Power Day: The 1970 February Revolution.* Trinidad and Tobago: Hatuey Productions, 1990.

Robinson, A. N. R. *The Mechanics of Independence: Patterns of Political and Economic Transformation in Trinidad and Tobago.* Cambridge, Mass.: MIT Press, 1971.

Robinson, A. N. R. *Caribbean Man: Speeches from a Political Career*. Edited and introduced by Gregory Shaw. Trinidad and Tobago: Inprint Publications, 1986.

Ryan, Selwyn D. *Race and Nationalism in Trinidad and Tobago: A Study of Decolonization in a Multiracial Society*. Toronto, Ontario: University of Toronto Press, 1972.

Ryan, Selwyn D. *The Politics of Succession: A Study of Parties and Politics in Trinidad and Tobago*. St. Augustine, Trinidad and Tobago: University of the West Indies, 1978.

Ryan, Selwyn D. *The Confused Electorate: A Study of Political Attitudes and Opinions in Trinidad and Tobago*. St. Augustine, Trinidad and Tobago: Institute of Social and Economic Research, University of the West Indies, 1979.

Ryan, Selwyn D. *The Disillusioned Electorate: The Politics of Succession in Trinidad and Tobago*. Port of Spain, Trinidad and Tobago: Inprint Caribbean, 1989.

Sampson, Ingrid Damian. "A History of the Foreign Policy of Trinidad and Tobago, 1962–1986: A Question of Diplomacy of a Small State." UC 300 Project, April 22, 1991. West Indian Library, University of the West Indies, St. Augustine, Trinidad.

SELWYN H. H. CARRINGTON (2005)
FIONA ANN TAYLOR (2005)

Robinson, Bill "Bojangles"

May 25, 1878
November 25, 1949

Bill "Bojangles" Robinson, perhaps the most famous of all African-American tap dancers, demonstrated an exacting yet light footwork that was said to have brought tap "up on its toes" from the flat-footed shuffling style prevalent in the previous era. Born Luther Robinson in Richmond, Virginia, he was orphaned when both his parents, Maria and Maxwell Robinson, died in 1885; he and his brothers were subsequently reared by his grandmother, Bedilia Robinson.

Robinson gained his nickname, "Bojangles"—possibly from the slang term *jangle*, meaning "to quarrel or fight"—while still in Richmond. It was also in Richmond that Robinson is said to have coined the phrase "everything's copasetic," meaning "fine, better than all right." He ran away to Washington, D.C., earning nickels and dimes by dancing and singing, and then got his first professional job in 1892, performing in the "pickaninny" chorus (in vaudeville, a chorus of young African-American children performing as backup for the featured performer) in Mayme Remington's *The South Before the War*. When Robinson arrived in New York City around 1900, he challenged the tap dancer Harry Swinton, the star dancer in *Old Kentucky*, to a buck-dancing contest, and won.

From 1902 to 1914, Robinson teamed up with George W. Cooper. Bound by the "two-colored" rule in vaudeville, which restricted blacks to performing in pairs, Cooper and Robinson performed as a duo on the Keith and Orpheum circuits. They did not, however, wear the blackface makeup performers customarily used. Robinson, who carried a gold-plated revolver, was a gambler with a quick temper. He was involved in a series of off-stage scrapes, and it was allegedly his arrest for assault in 1914 that finally put an end to the partnership with Cooper.

After the split, Robinson convinced his manager, Marty Forkins, to promote him as a soloist. Forkins managed to book him at the Marigold Gardens Theater in Chicago by promising its star and producer, Gertrude Hoffman, Robinson's services as a dance instructor. In this way Robinson launched his solo career, and he eventually became one of the first black performers to headline at New York's prestigious Palace Theatre.

Hailed as "the Dark Cloud of Joy" on the Orpheum circuit, Robinson performed in vaudeville from 1914 to 1927. Onstage, Robinson's open face, flashing eyes, infectious smile, easygoing patter, and air of surprise at what his feet were doing made him irresistible to audiences. His tapping was delicate, articulate, and intelligible. He usually wore a hat cocked to one side, and often exited with a Chaplinesque waddle, or with another signature step, a kind of syncopated "camel walk" (which would later be called the "moonwalk" when it was used by pop star Michael Jackson). Robinson always danced in split-clog shoes, in which the wooden sole was attached from the toe to the ball of the foot and the rest was left loose, allowing for greater flexibility and tonality. Dancing upright and swinging to clean six-bar phrases, followed by a two-bar break, Robinson set new standards of performance, despite the fact that he invented few new steps.

In 1922 Robinson married Fannie Clay, who became his business manager and secretary. (The marriage was his second: in 1907, he had married Lena Chase, from whom he was divorced in 1922.) After twenty-one years he divorced Fannie and married a young dancer, Elaine Plaines.

Broadway fame came with an all-black revue, *Blackbirds of 1928*, in which he sang "Doin' the New Low Down" while dancing up and down a flight of five steps. Success was immediate: Robinson's performance was acclaimed by the major New York newspapers, and he was heralded by several as the greatest of all tap dancers. The dance Robinson performed in *Blackbirds* developed into his signature "stair dance"; notable for the clarity of Robinson's taps and for its unusual tonalities—each step yielded a different pitch—Robinson's appealing showmanship made it seem effortless. *Brown Buddies* (1930) was kept alive by Robinson's performance, as were *Blackbirds of 1933, The Hot Mikado* (1939), *All in Fun* (1940), and *Memphis Bound* (1945). Largely in recognition of his Broadway success, Robinson was named an honorary "Mayor of Harlem" by Mayor Fiorello LaGuardia. In 1939 he celebrated his sixty-first birthday by tapping down Broadway, one block for each year.

Robinson turned to Hollywood, a venue largely closed to blacks, in the 1930s. His films included *Dixiana* (1930), which had a predominantly white cast, and *Harlem Is Heaven* (1933), with an all-black cast. Robinson also appeared in the films *Hooray for Love* (1935), *In Old Kentucky* (1935), *The Big Broadcast of 1937* (1936), *One Mile from Heaven* (1937), *Road Demon* (1938), *Up the River* (1938), *By an Old Southern River* (1941), and *Let's Shuffle* (1941); in a newsreel about the 1939 World's Fair in Chicago, *It's Swing Ho! Come to the Fair;* and in a short, *Broadway Brevities* (1934). But of all his many stage and film performances, those that brought him the most fame were his appearances with the child star Shirley Temple, in *The Littlest Colonel* (1935), *The Littlest Rebel* (1935), *Just Around the Corner* (1938), and *Rebecca of Sunnybrook Farm* (1938). In 1943, the all-black film *Stormy Weather*, with Robinson, Cab Calloway, Lena Horne, and Katherine Dunham's dance troupe, met with some success.

A founding member of the Negro Actors Guild of America, Robinson performed in thousands of benefits over the course of his career, and he made generous contributions to charities and individuals. However, Robinson's career had peaked in the late 1930s, and when he died in 1949 he was in debt. According to contemporary accounts, nearly a hundred thousand people turned out to watch his funeral procession; the numbers testify to the esteem in which he was still held by his community and by the audiences who loved him. The founding of the Copasetics Club in the year that Robinson died ensured that his brilliance as a performer would not be forgotten.

See also Musical Theater; Tap Dance

Bibliography

Fletcher, Tom. *100 Years of the Negro in Show Business.* New York: Burdge, 1954. Reprint, New York: Da Capo, 1984.

Haskins, Jim, and N. R. Mitgang. *Mr. Bojangles: The Biography of Bill Robinson.* New York: William Morrow, 1988.

Stearns, Marshall, and Jean Stearns. *Jazz Dance: The Story of American Vernacular Dance.* New York: Macmillan, 1968. Reprint, New York: Da Capo, 1994.

Vered, Karen Orr. "White and Black in Black and White: Management of Race and Sexuality in the Coupling of Child Star Shirley Temple and Bill Robinson." *Velvet Light Trap* (Spring 1997): 52.

CONSTANCE VALIS HILL (1996)
Updated bibliography

Robinson, Jackie

January 31, 1919
October 24, 1972

Baseball player, civil rights leader, and businessman Jack Roosevelt "Jackie" Robinson was born in Georgia, the youngest of five children of sharecropper farmers Jerry and Mallie Robinson. He was raised in Pasadena, California, where the Robinson family confronted the West Coast variety of American racism. White neighbors tried to drive the family out of their home; segregation reigned in public and private facilities. Robinson became an outstanding athlete at Pasadena Junior College before transferring to the University of California at Los Angeles in 1940, where he won renown as the "Jim Thorpe of his race," the nation's finest all-around athlete. Robinson was an All-American football player, leading scorer in basketball, and record-setting broad jumper, in addition to his baseball exploits.

Drafted into the army in the spring of 1942, Robinson embarked on a stormy military career. Denied access to Officer Candidate School, Robinson protested to heavyweight champion Joe Louis, who intervened with officials in Washington on Robinson's behalf. Once commissioned, Robinson fought for improved conditions for blacks at Camp Riley, Kansas, leading to his transfer to Fort Hood, Texas. At Fort Hood Robinson was court-martialed and acquitted for refusing to move to the back of a bus. Robinson's army career demonstrated the proud, combative personality that would characterize his postwar life.

After his discharge from the army in 1944, Robinson signed to play with the Kansas City Monarchs of the Negro American League. After several months of discontent in the Jim Crow league, Robinson was approached by Branch Rickey of the Brooklyn Dodgers, who offered him the opportunity to become the first black player in major league baseball since the 1890s. Robinson gladly accepted the opportunity and responsibility of this pioneering role in "baseball's great experiment."

In 1946 Robinson joined the Montreal Royals of the International League, the top farm club in the Dodger system. Following a spectacular debut in which he stroked

Jackie Robinson stealing home, 1949. © CORBIS-BETTMANN

four hits, including a three-run home run, Robinson proceeded to lead the league with a .349 batting average. An immediate fan favorite, Robinson enabled the Royals to set new attendance records while winning the International League and Little World Series championships. Robinson's imminent promotion to the Dodgers in 1947 triggered an unsuccessful petition drive on the part of southern players to keep him off the team. In the early months of the season, beanballs, death threats, and rumors of a strike by opposing players swirled around Robinson. Through it all Robinson paraded his excellence. An electrifying fielder and base runner as well as an outstanding hitter, Robinson's assault on baseball's color line captured the imagination of both black and white Americans. He batted .297 and won the Rookie of the Year Award (since renamed the Jackie Robinson Award in his honor) en route to leading the Dodgers to the pennant.

Over the next decade Robinson emerged as one of the most dominant players and foremost gate attractions in the history of the major leagues. In 1949 he batted .342 and won the National League Most Valuable Player Award. During his ten years with the Dodgers the team won six pennants and one World Championship. By his retirement in 1956 Robinson had compiled a .311 lifetime batting average. He was elected to the Baseball Hall of Fame on the first ballot in 1961.

But Robinson's significance transcended his achievements on the baseball diamond. He became a leading symbol and spokesperson for the postwar integration crusade, both within baseball and in broader society. During his early years in Montreal and Brooklyn, Robinson adhered to his promise to Branch Rickey to "turn the other cheek" and avoid controversies. After establishing himself in the major leagues, however, Robinson's more combative and outspoken personality reasserted itself. Robinson repeatedly pressed for baseball to desegregate more rapidly and to remove discriminatory barriers in Florida training camps and cities like St. Louis and Cincinnati. He also demanded opportunities for black players to become coaches, managers, and front-office personnel. Baseball officials and many sportswriters branded Robinson an ingrate as controversies marked his career.

Upon retirement Robinson remained in the public eye. He continued to voice his opinions as speaker, newspaper columnist, and fund-raiser for the NAACP. A believer in "black capitalism" through which blacks could become producers, manufacturers, developers and creators of businesses, providers of jobs, Robinson engaged in many successful business ventures in the black community. He became an executive in the Chock full o'Nuts restaurant chain and later helped develop Harlem's Freedom National Bank and the Jackie Robinson Construction Company. Robinson also became active in Republican Party politics, supporting Richard Nixon in 1960 and working closely with New York governor Nelson Rockefeller, who appointed him Special Assistant for Community Affairs in 1966. These activities brought criticism from young black militants in the late 1960s. Ironically, at this same time Robinson had also parted ways with the NAACP, criticizing its failure to include "younger, more progressive voices."

By the late 1960s Robinson had become bitterly disillusioned with both baseball and American society. He refused to attend baseball events to protest the failure to hire blacks in nonplaying capacities. In his 1972 autobiography, *I Never Had It Made,* he attacked the nation's waning commitment to racial equality. Later that year the commemoration of his major league debut led him to lift his boycott of baseball games. "I'd like to live to see a black manager," he told a nationwide television audience at the World Series on October 15, 1972. Nine days later he died of a heart attack. In 1997 major league baseball commemorated the fiftieth anniversary of Robinson's breaking of the baseball color line by retiring his number 42 from every team.

See also Baseball; Civil Rights Movement, U.S.; Jim Crow

Bibliography

Rampersad, Arnold. *Jackie Robinson: A Life*. New York: Knopf, 1997.

Robinson, Jackie, with Alfred Duckett. *I Never Had It Made.* New York: G. P. Putnam's Sons, 1972.

Rowan, Carl. *Wait Till Next Year.* New York: Random House, 1960.

Tygiel, Jules. *Baseball's Great Experiment: Jackie Robinson and His Legacy*. New York: Oxford University Press, 1983.

JULES TYGIEL (1996)
Updated bibliography

Robinson, Jo Ann Gibson

April 17, 1912
August 29, 1992

Teacher and civil rights leader Jo Ann Gibson Robinson was at the forefront of the movement to desegregate public transportation and a leader of the 1955 Montgomery bus boycott in Alabama, in which over fifty thousand African Americans participated. Born in Culloden, Georgia, the youngest of twelve children, Gibson attended Macon public schools before entering Fort Valley State College. She taught in Macon schools for five years, then went to Atlanta University, where she received a master's degree in English in 1948. One year later, Robinson accepted a position as a member of the English department at Alabama State College in Montgomery.

Shortly after moving to Montgomery, Robinson joined the Women's Political Council (WPC), an organization of mostly middle-class black women. The WPC was founded in 1946 by Mary Fair Burks, an English professor at Alabama State, to increase the black community's involvement in civic affairs by promoting voter registration and teaching high school students about politics and government. In 1950 Robinson became president of the WPC, and under her leadership the organization grew to over two hundred members and began to challenge the demeaning form of segregation on the city's buses. The WPC lobbied the city in the early 1950s to revise its seating policy so black passengers would not have to give up their seats for whites or stand over an empty seat reserved for a white rider. In May 1954 Robinson wrote a letter to Montgomery's Mayor W. A. Gayle threatening a boycott unless reforms were forthcoming.

After Claudette Colvin, a young black teenager, was arrested in March 1955 for violating a segregation law, Robinson and other black leaders negotiated with the city commissioner about changing the city's seating policy. The meetings yielded very little, and Robinson supported launching a boycott, but other black leaders opposed the idea. When Rosa Parks, secretary of a local chapter of the National Association for the Advancement of Colored People (NAACP), was arrested on December 1, 1955, for refusing to give up her seat for a white man on the bus, members of the WPC were prepared for a boycott. After speaking with Parks and E. D. Nixon, former chair of the NAACP in Alabama, they made a flier calling for a boycott the following Monday. Putting her job on the line, Robinson mimeographed fifty thousand copies late one night at Alabama State and, with help from two of her students, distributed them within forty-eight hours of Parks's arrest. The WPC also planned a mass meeting at the Dexter Avenue Baptist Church for the afternoon of the boycott, at which time it was decided to continue the boycott indefinitely. It was primarily because of the previous five years of political groundwork laid by women in the WPC, under the direction of Robinson, that the black community in Montgomery was prepared to endure a boycott that lasted over a year.

Although men were the most visible leaders of the Montgomery Improvement Association (MIA), the organization created to coordinate the boycott, women played important roles. Robinson, in particular, was an influential political strategist and an indispensable contributor to the movement. She wielded political power on the executive board of the MIA; served as an important negotiator with the city; produced the MIA newsletter, which not only provided support and encouragement for boycotters but kept people around the country informed about the progress of the protest; and volunteered time in the car pool to help the thousands of ordinary participants get to work on time. In December 1956 a court order desegregating public transportation ended the boycott. Although the importance of the WPC began to diminish, it nevertheless continued to exist for several years.

Robinson left Alabama State College in 1960 after several teachers had been fired for their participation in the boycott. She taught for one year at Grambling State College in Grambling, Louisiana, then moved to Los Angeles, where she taught English in the public schools until 1976, when she retired. After retiring, Robinson remained active in a host of civic and social groups, giving one day a week of free service to the city of Los Angeles and serving in the League of Women Voters, the Alpha Gamma Omega chapter of the Alpha Kappa Alpha Sorority, the Angel City chapter of the Links, the Black Women's Alliance, the Founders Church of Religious Science, and Women on Target. In 1987 Robinson published her memoir about the boycott, *The Montgomery Bus Boycott and the Women Who Started It,* which won the publication prize by the Southern Association for Women's Historians. Through her historical work, Robinson helped restore women to their proper place in the Montgomery boycott, and through her political commitment, she helped launch one of the most important civil rights struggles in the Jim Crow South. Robinson died in 1992 at age eighty.

See also Civil Rights Movement, U.S.; Montgomery Improvement Association; Montgomery, Ala., Bus Boycott

Bibliography

Burks, Mary Fair. "Trailblazers: Women in the Montgomery Bus Boycott." In *Women in the Civil Rights Movement: Trailblazers and Torchbearers, 1941–65*, edited by Vicki L. Crawford, Jacqueline Anne Rouse, and Barbara Woods. Brooklyn, N.Y.: Carlson, 1990.

Hine, Darlene Clark, ed. *Black Women in America: An Historical Encyclopedia*. Brooklyn, N.Y: Carlson, 1993.

King, Martin Luther, Jr. *Stride Toward Freedom*. New York: Harper, 1958.

Robinson, Jo Ann. *The Montgomery Bus Boycott and the Women Who Started It: The Memoir of Jo Ann Robinson*. Knoxville: University of Tennessee Press, 1987.

PREMILLA NADASEN (1996)
Updated by publisher 2005

Robinson, Sugar Ray

May 3, 1921
April 12, 1989

Boxer "Sugar Ray" Robinson was born Walker Smith Jr. in Detroit to Marie and Walker Smith. He moved with his mother in 1933 to Harlem, where he attended DeWitt Clinton High School. Representing the Salem Athletic Club, he began boxing, using the identification card of a Ray Robinson. He won the New York Golden Gloves in 1939 and 1940 and turned professional late in 1940. A reporter described his technique as "sweet as sugar." Robinson won his first forty fights (twenty-six knockouts) until Jake LaMotta beat him on a decision in 1943. He served as a private during World War II, mainly boxing in exhibitions on tour with his idol, Joe Louis. Robinson demanded fair treatment for blacks in the military, refusing to appear at one show until blacks were allowed into the audience and getting into a fight with a military policeman who had threatened Louis for using a phone in a whites-only area.

Robinson won the vacant welterweight (147 pounds) championship on December 20, 1946, in a fifteen-round decision over Tommy Bell. In Robinson's first defense, Jimmy Doyle suffered fatal brain injuries in an eighth-round knockout. When asked if he had intended to get Doyle into trouble, Robinson responded, "Mister, it's my business to get him in trouble." He moved up to the middleweight division (160 pounds), besting champion Jake LaMotta in the 1951 "St. Valentine's Day Massacre," which got its name from the punishment LaMotta took until the fight was stopped in the thirteenth round. Robinson lost the title on a decision five months later to Randy Turpin in London, making his record 128–1–2. Two months later he regained the title from Turpin with a dramatic tenth-round knockout in New York as he bled heavily from a cut above the left eye. In 1952 he fought Joey Maxim for the light heavyweight championship at Yankee Stadium. He was far ahead on points, but he collapsed after the thirteenth round in 100-degree heat.

Robinson retired from the ring and worked for two years as a tap dancer. He returned to boxing in 1955 and in his seventh bout regained the middleweight crown with a second-round knockout of Bobo Olson on December 9, 1955. He lost the title on January 2, 1956, to Gene Fullmer, regaining it in a rematch four months later, knocking Fullmer unconscious in the fifth. Carmen Basilio dethroned Robinson on September 23 but lost the rematch on March 25, 1958, by decision. Robinson held the middleweight title until Paul Pender defeated him on January 22, 1960. Robinson lost the rematch and two other title bouts, and he retired in 1965. He held the middleweight championship a record five times.

Robinson was renowned for his flashy living. He owned a nightclub, Sugar Ray's, and other Harlem properties, and on tours he took a large entourage, including a valet and barber. He appeared in television and films. Once he was well established, he acted as his own manager and was regarded as a tough negotiator. An Internal Revenue Service tax dispute led to a ruling that allowed income averaging. However, Robinson went through $4 million so fast he had to continue boxing well past his prime. In 1969 he moved to Los Angeles, where he established the Sugar Ray Robinson Youth Foundation for inner-city youth. He lived there with his second wife, Millie Bruce, until he died of Alzheimer's disease and diabetes. Robinson had a record of 174–19–6, with 109 knockouts and two no-decisions. Renowned for his superb footwork, hand speed, and leverage, he was so powerful that he could knock out an opponent when moving backwards. He was elected to the Boxing Hall of Fame in 1967.

See also Boxing; Sports

Bibliography

Nathan, David A. "Sugar Ray Robinson, the Sweet Science, and the Politics of Meaning," *Journal of Sport History* 26 (spring 1999): 163–174.

Obituary. *New York Times,* April 13, 1989, I, 1-1.

Robinson, Sugar Ray, and Dave Anderson. *Sugar Ray.* New York: Viking, 1969.

STEVEN A. RIESS (1996)
Updated bibliography

Rodney, Walter

March 23, 1942
June 13, 1980

Walter Rodney, whose father was a tailor and whose mother was a homemaker, was born in Georgetown, Guyana. He won a government scholarship that enabled him to enter Queen's College, then the leading secondary educational institution in the colony. There he did well scholastically, edited the school's newspaper, and took an active part in the debating society. The 1940s and the early 1950s, which saw the emergence of the People's Progressive Party (PPP), Guyana's first mass-based political party, was a period of intense political activity oriented specifically toward the attainment of political independence. Rodney's own political awakening and the beginning of his lifelong adherence to Marxist theory and praxis occurred in the 1950s, when as a youngster he distributed PPP manifestos. He learned while doing so that it was imprudent to enter yards with long driveways, because those who lived in the houses there were of a higher social class and lighter pigmentation than he, and therefore unlikely to be sympathetic to the nationalist aspirations of the PPP.

After winning an open scholarship in 1960 to study at the University College of the West Indies, later called the University of the West Indies (UWI), Rodney majored in history and graduated with first-class honors in 1963. While at the UWI, his intellectual and political sensibilities were further sharpened when he noted that West Indian history was deemphasized, which to him meant seeing reality through European eyes with no connection between history and politics. Upon graduation, Rodney continued the study of history in England and was awarded a Ph.D. in 1966 by the University of London. His doctoral thesis, "A History of the Upper Guinea Coast, 1545–1800," involved research in fascist Portugal, where he became aware of the contradiction of imperialist racism that privileged an educated black like himself while exploiting and repressing uneducated blacks.

In England Rodney also continued to be exposed to a brand of scholarship that divorced history from politics and politics from scholarship, as well as to the trials of racism. Undaunted, he took the opportunity to hone his public-speaking skills by addressing audiences at London's famous Hyde Park, where soap box orators who exercised the right of free speech found willing audiences for whatever topic interested them.

Leaving England in 1966, Rodney accepted an appointment as lecturer in African history at University College in Tanzania, but left to accept a teaching appointment in January 1968 at the Jamaica campus of the UWI, where he launched and taught a course in African history. Consistent with his view that scholarship should not be divorced from politics and that the most meaningful education comes from an understanding of the condition of the people, Rodney took his pedagogy to the "dungles," or the most dispossessed parts of Kingston. This led him, perhaps inevitably, to a sustained critique of the government of Jamaica, whose policies, he maintained, perpetuated the dispossession of black Jamaicans. However, after attending a Conference of Black Writers held at McGill University in Montreal, Canada, in October 1968, Rodney was declared persona non grata by the Jamaican government and banned from reentering the island.

Rodney's exclusion from Jamaica led to various protest demonstrations and confrontations by students and others with the police. Another significant result of the ban was the publication of his 1969 book, *The Groundings with My Brothers.* This book provided Rodney with the opportunity to address issues of major concern to African intellectuals in the diaspora and enabled him to fuse scholarship and reality through the eyes of a person of African descent. Rodney thus addressed the Jamaican situation that had led to his exclusion by challenging what he referred to as the myth of a harmonious Jamaican society that was being perpetuated by the same people who had named Marcus Garvey a national hero, while at the same time using the full force of the law to repress darker-skinned Jamaicans. He warned that black youths were becoming "aware of the possibilities of unleashing armed struggle in their own interests" (Rodney, 1969, p. 15).

Turning his attention to Black Power, Rodney continued to revert to history to explain the oppression of peoples of color by whites. However, fully cognizant of the differences between the experience of the colonized in the United States and those in the West Indies, some of whose territories, like Guyana and Trinidad, had large East Indian populations, Rodney noted that the *Black* in Black Power in the Caribbean must include all colonized individuals who were not of European descent and whose forebears earlier on had been forced to work on the plantations in the West Indies. Black Power, he continued, must involve efforts by these individuals to control their own "destinies." Moreover, he argued, the major and first responsibility of the nonwhite intellectual in the diaspora was the struggle over ideas and, as a "guerrilla intellectual," participation in the struggle for the transformation of his own orbit.

After his exclusion from Jamaica, Rodney taught in Tanzania from 1968 to 1974 before returning to Guyana to accept a position as professor of history at the University of Guyana (UG). In Tanzania he concluded that he had contributed as much as he could, and that as a non-Tanzanian, his participation in the political culture of that country would be marginal and thus restricted to the university. He could more easily master the nuances of Caribbean culture than those of Tanzania, which were so critical to political activity. However, following the blocking of the UG appointment by the repressive government of President Forbes Burnham, Rodney remained permanently in the country of his birth, where he became a founding member of a political party, the Working People's Alliance. A dynamic speaker with a penchant for breaking down complex ideas into everyday language, Rodney set about mobilizing the Guyanese masses against the regime of Burnham by educating and raising the consciousness of the thousands who attended his lectures in the heart of Georgetown, the capital, all the while using his knowledge of history as his main weapon.

Since some of Rodney's rhetoric was uncompromising and directed at Burnham personally, some felt that Guyana had reached a point where the country was too small for the two antagonists. Thus, in addition to various retaliatory acts by the government, in July 1979, along with seven others, Rodney was arrested and charged, but later acquitted, with arson in connection with the burning of two government offices. At a mass rally on June 6, 1980, Rodney used humor not merely to ridicule Burnham and his government but to criticize the constitution, which arrogated a tremendous amount of power to Burnham as president for life, which Rodney felt was incompatible with democratic socialism. Interspersing his speech with historical references, and much to the amusement of his listeners, Rodney dealt with the serious issue of oppression and death meted out to so-called enemies of the state, referring to Burnham as "King Kong," revealing that some individuals had decided that a certain public convenience should be renamed "Burnham's Palace."

On June 13, 1980, Walter Rodney was killed instantly when a walkie-talkie in his possession, allegedly given to him by an electronics expert in the Guyana Defense Force, exploded. Before his death Rodney had revised a manuscript, which he had submitted for publication to the Johns Hopkins University Press. In that manuscript, published posthumously as *A History of the Guyanese Working People, 1881–1905,* Rodney continued to emphasize the class nature of Guyanese history, whether he was analyzing the political economy of slavery in general, the capricious labor withdrawal by the Creoles (the former slaves), the role of the planter-controlled legislature in perpetuating the peculiar institution, or Creole opposition to immigration policies that resulted in the introduction of indentured laborers from India to plantation life in the colony. Thus, he remained faithful to the significance of social class and its race/color dimensions, which he had first observed in the 1950s during the struggle for political independence, in his treatment of a particular moment in Guyanese history.

See also Anti-Colonial Movements; Black Power; Burnham, Forbes; Historians and Historiography; Political Ideologies

Bibliography

Alpers, Edward. "The Weapon of History in the Struggle for African Liberation: The Work of Walter Rodney." In *Walter Rodney, Revolutionary and Scholar: A Tribute,* edited by Edward Alpers and Pierre-Michel Fontaine. Los Angeles: Center for Afro-American Studies and African Studies Center, University of California, 1982.

Dodson, Howard, and Robert Hill. *Walter Rodney Speaks: The Making of an African Intellectual.* Trenton, N.J.: Africa World Press, 1990.

Lewis, Rupert Charles. *Walter Rodney's Intellectual and Political Thought.* Kingston, Jamaica: The Press, University of the West Indies; Detroit, Mich.: Wayne State University Press, 1998.

Rodney, Walter. *The Groundings with My Brothers.* London: Bogle L'Ouverture, 1969.

Rodney, Walter. *A History of the Guyanese Working People, 1881–1905.* Baltimore, Md., and London: Johns Hopkins University Press, 1981.

MAURICE ST. PIERRE (2005)

Rolle, Esther

November 8, 1920
November 18, 1998

Actress Esther Rolle was born in Pompano Beach, California, probably in 1920, the tenth of eighteen children of parents of Bahamian descent. After her family relocated to Florida, she finished Booker T. Washington High School in Miami, and attended Spelman College in Atlanta for one year before moving to New York City. There, while trying to break into theater, Rolle supported herself by working at a pocketbook factory. She was taking drama classes at George Washington Carver School in Harlem when she obtained a scholarship to study acting at New York's innovative New School for Social Research.

During this time, Rolle was introduced to African dance master Asadata Dafora and became a member of his dance troupe, Shogola Oloba. After many years with the troupe, she became its director in 1960. During her dancing career Rolle continued to pursue her interest in theater, and in 1962 she made her professional acting debut as Felicity in Jean Genet's *The Blacks.* Rolle worked in theater throughout the early 1960s, appearing in such productions as *Blues for Mr. Charlie* (1964), *Amen Corner* (1965), and Douglas Turner Ward's *Day of Absence* (1965). She made her film debut as Sister Sarah in 1964's *Nothing But a Man,* and in 1967 she became an original member of the Negro Ensemble Company.

Rolle continued to work steadily in the theater through the early 1970s. She was performing in Melvin Van Peebles's *Don't Play Us Cheap* (1972) when a casting director asked her to audition for the role of the maid on *Maude,* a Norman Lear television show being spun off from *All in the Family.* Rolle won the role and, that same year, with the understanding that her character, Florida Evans, would not be a typical maid, she proceeded to turn the limited role into a popular character. In 1974 the characters of Florida Evans and her husband were spun off into a new television series, *Good Times.*

Good Times depicted a lower-middle-class family living in a tenement on the South Side of Chicago as they struggled to survive economically in the face of layoffs and unemployment. Originally the show was praised for addressing the economic difficulties faced by many inner-city blacks. However, Rolle and costar John Amos constantly struggled with producers over the role of the oldest son, played by Jimmie Walker, who was portrayed as a fast-talking, womanizing buffoon, and who increasingly became the central figure of the show. Rolle left the show in 1977 over these and other disputes, but returned in 1978. *Good Times* was canceled in 1979.

Rolle continued to act in other roles on television and in the theater through the late 1970s and 1980s. She won an Emmy for her performance as a housekeeper in the 1978 television movie *Summer of My German Soldier* and she was nominated for an Emmy for her role in a 1979 television adaptation of Maya Angelou's *I Know Why the Caged Bird Sings.* During the 1980s she appeared on such television shows as *Flamingo Road* (1982) and *The Love Boat* (1983, 1985). In 1989 she played a housekeeper in *The Member of the Wedding* at the Roundabout Theater, a role she had originated in Philadelphia four years earlier. Rolle played the matriarch in an American Playhouse remake of *A Raisin in the Sun* (1989) with Danny Glover as the errant son. That same year, she also played the maid, Idella, in the Academy Award–winning film *Driving Miss Daisy.*

In 1987 Rolle was inducted into the NAACP Hall of Fame, and in 1990 she became the first woman to win the NAACP chair's Civil Rights Leadership Award. For her achievements in film and television, Rolle was inducted into the Black Filmmakers Hall of Fame in 1991. Rolle appeared in John Singleton's *Rosewood* (1995) and Maya Angelou's *Down in the Delta* (1998). Rolle died on November 18, 1998, of complications from diabetes.

See also Drama; Television

Bibliography

Bogle, Donald. *Blacks in American Films and Television.* New York: Garland, 1988.

Helbing, Terry. "Esther Rolle: Invitation to the Wedding." *Theater Week,* April 3–9, 1989, pp. 13–16.

KENYA DILDAY (1996)
Updated by publisher 2005

ROMAINE-LA-PROPHÉTESSE

c. 1760
?

Details on the life of Romaine-la-Prophétesse (Romaine Rivière), a late eighteenth-century insurgent leader during the early stages of the Haitian Revolution, are sparse. The most reliable contemporary source describes him as a "free black," although most scholarly accounts generally, and perhaps uncritically, identify him as a *griffe,* which in the French plantation colony of Saint Domingue (1697–1804) designated someone who was three-fourths black and one-fourth white. Either way, good reasons exist to believe that Romaine was born in the Kingdom of Kongo; these include the nature of his military and religious leadership, which each suggest strong Kongolese influences. It is more certain that at the time of the Haitian Revolution's outbreak in 1791, he was a landowner who was married with two children.

Romaine rose to prominence as an insurgent leader in the southern part of the colony around the same time that slave uprisings in Bois Caiman, led by Boukman Dutty and Cecile Fatiman, and in Plaine-du-Nord sparked the widespread rebellion that mushroomed into history's only successful national slave revolt. By September 1791 Romaine had established a base camp in the mountains near Leogane in the rural hamlet of Trou-Coffy. There he occupied a Catholic shrine, administered the sacraments, and inspired his troops to raids of legendary violence on plantations, which he led on horseback with his trademark "magic" rooster tied to his horse's saddle. Calling himself "the godson of the Virgin Mary," he would say mass in the Trou-Coffy shrine beneath an inverted cross with a saber in his hand. At the height of these syncretic communal rituals, Roman the Prophetess (as his name translates literally from the French) would find written messages from the Virgin Mary in the tabernacle, which would instruct him to liberate slaves and declare to them that the king had set them free. Slaves who remained loyal to their white masters were, like their masters, usually slaughtered by Romaine's troops.

Romaine's military activity ranged from Jacmel to Leogane, covering an impressive expanse of mountains and plains. His troops took part, for instance, in the massive November 1791 assault on Jacmel, in which a total of thirteen thousand slaves (up to four thousand of whom could have been under Romaine's direct command) conquered the city. But his greatest conquest was the port city of Leogane, which he ruled for several months. At least one successful act of nautical piracy had allowed Romaine's forces to attack this city in October 1791 from both sea and land. The conquest of Leogane also relied on an informal alliance that Romaine had made with the city's mulatto elite; they would later come to regret this alliance, however, because of Romaine's increasing religious and royalist fanaticism (one source indicates that his ultimate objective was to rule the entire island of Saint-Domingue as its king). Firmly in control of the city by later that year, on New Year's Eve 1791 Romaine summoned all the white and mulatto residents and prisoners to a meeting, where he made them sign a treaty that recognized him as the "commander of all assembled citizens" in Leogane.

By early 1792 it was apparent that Napoleon's regime had a full-scale revolution on its hands in its most lucrative colony. To quell the revolt in the south of Saint Domingue, Civil Commissioner Saint-Léger was dispatched with a large battalion to retake Leogane and to disband Romaine's highly troublesome band of rebel Maroons. Bringing an end to the protracted guerilla struggle, Saint-Léger's forces finally defeated Romaine's in March 1792. One perhaps legendary contemporary account of the attempted capture of Romaine has survived: Disarmed and surrounded, the Virgin's godson threw his wife into his would-be captors' arms and vanished into thin air, much as the prototypical Dominguean Maroon rebel, Makandal, is said to have done when he turned into a fly to escape his execution.

Romaine-la-Prophétesse is commonly referred to as a Vodou priest, although this title is perhaps anachronistic, because he rose to prominence at precisely the time when Vodou was just emerging as a religion. Other issues pertaining to his identity are likewise shrouded in mystery. Why, for instance, did he choose to refer to himself at one and the same time as the Virgin Mary's godson and as a prophetess? Extant letters written or dictated by Romaine and addressed to a French abbot of Les Amis des Noirs in Paris indicate that he was literate and thus deliberately chose a feminine title for himself. Whatever his true identity, it is clear that Romaine-la-Prophétesse had as great an impact as any of the more celebrated religiously inspired Maroon raiders during the early phase of the Haitian Revolution.

See also Haitian Revolution

Bibliography

Fick, Carolyn E.. *The Making of Haiti: The Saint-Domingue Revolution from Below.* Knoxville: The University of Tennessee Press, 1990.

Rey, Terry. "The Virgin Mary and Revolution in Saint-Domingue: The Charisma of Romaine-la-Prophétesse." *Journal of Historical Sociology* 11, no. 3 (1998): 341–369.

TERRY REY (2005)

Roman Catholicism

See Catholicism in the Americas

Roosevelt's Black Cabinet

Disaffected by Republican Party politics in the decades following the Civil War, victimized by racism, and ravaged by the Great Depression, African Americans transferred their allegiance to Franklin D. Roosevelt and the Democratic Party during the New Deal when they perceived that his efforts to improve conditions for all citizens included them as well. While Roosevelt did not propose specific civil rights legislation during his administrations, he did move to repeal particularly egregious racial restrictions within the federal government bureaucracy, many of which had been initiated by his Democratic predecessor, Woodrow Wilson. Moreover, the First Lady, Eleanor Roosevelt, remained a vocal and active champion of racial equality. As a consequence of Mrs. Roosevelt's lobbying, of the concerns and interest of former Chicago NAACP president Harold Ickes, a key figure in the Roosevelt administration, and, most important, of concentrated efforts to secure political appointments for blacks, Roosevelt was made aware of the plight of black Americans. In response, African Americans came to view the Democratic Party as a haven.

Two seminal events in 1933 helped to set the stage for the appointment of a number of blacks to second-level positions within the administration. The first was the Second Amenia Conference, hosted by Joel Spingarn, the chairman of the board of the NAACP. The second was the Julius Rosenwald Fund meeting to discuss the economic status of blacks. Out of both of these meetings grew a determination to seek and secure appointments of racial advisers in the administration in order to ensure that blacks would not be excluded from New Deal programs. An Interracial Interdepartmental Group (IIG), supported by the Rosenwald Fund, was set up to promote black appointees. Working closely with Ickes and Eleanor Roosevelt, the IIG helped to secure the appointment of at least one black adviser in all but five of some two dozen New Deal agencies by 1937. This network of officeholders became known as the "Black Cabinet."

Appointees included people such as Robert Weaver, later appointed by Lyndon B. Johnson to serve as the secretary of Housing and Urban Development; Mary McLeod Bethune, director of Negro affairs, National Youth Organization; Henry Hunt and Charles Hall, who, along with Weaver, were original members of the IIG; Joseph H. B. Evans, Farm Security Administration; Lawrence A. Axley, Department of Labor; Edgar G. Brown, Civilian Conservation Corps; N. Robinson, Agriculture; and Alfred E. Smith, Works Project Administration. Bethune convened the members of this unofficial Black Cabinet in 1935. Thereafter, they met regularly (although unofficially), remaining in constant touch with one another and creating a network whose purpose and goal was to promote the interests of black Americans. With greater direct access to power than they had ever had before, they lobbied actively throughout the administration. Although their achievements were limited, they did realize some success. The Black Cabinet helped to ensure that by 1935 approximately 30 percent of all black Americans participated in New Deal relief programs.

See also Bethune, Mary McLeod; Great Depression and the New Deal; Politics in the United States; Weaver, Robert Clifton

Bibliography

Louchheim, Katie, ed. *The Making of the New Deal: The Insiders Speak*. Cambridge, Mass.: Harvard University Press, 1983.

Sitkoff, Harvard. *A New Deal for Blacks*. New York: Oxford University Press, 1978.

CHRISTINE A. LUNARDINI (1996)

Ross, Diana

March 26, 1944

Born in a low-income housing project in Detroit, Diana Ross developed an interest in music at an early age, when she sang with her parents in a church choir. In high school she studied dress design, illustration, and cosmetology, spending her free time singing on Detroit street corners with her friends Mary Wilson and Florence Ballard. Betty McGlowan was soon added to the group, and the quartet became known as the Primettes. They came to the attention of Motown Records founder Berry Gordy, who used them as background singers for Mary Wells, Marvin Gaye, and the Shirelles. The group was renamed the Supremes, and from the mid-1960s to 1970 they were one of the most popular groups in pop music, with a string of influential hits. In 1970, however, Ross, who had always sought to dominate what was nominally a balanced trio, left to pursue a solo career.

After leaving the Supremes, Ross's popularity continued ("Ain't No Mountain High Enough," 1970), and she also began a career as a film actress. She was nominated for an Academy Award for her performance as Billie Holiday in *Lady Sings the Blues* (1972), and starred in *Mahagony* (1975), which yielded the hit ballad "Do You Know Where You're Going To?" the next year. By the mid-1970s Ross was also considered a top disco diva, recording "Love Hangover" (1976) and "Upside Down" (1980). During this time she also had a starring role in the musical film *The Wiz* (1978).

Ross reached the top of the pop charts again in 1981 with "Endless Love," a duet with Lionel Ritchie. Since then she has recorded less frequently (*Muscles,* 1982; *Eaten Alive,* 1985; and *Workin' Overtime,* 1989; *The Force Behind the Power,* 1991; *Every Day Is a New Day,* 1999). Ross, who was married from 1971 to 1975 to Robert Silberstine, was remarried in 1985 to the Norwegian shipping tycoon and mountaineer Arne Naess. They have two sons and live in Norway and Connecticut.

Ross has had nineteen number-one recordings on the pop charts—the most to date for a solo performer—and continues to perform sporadically in concert and on television. In the 1990s she produced and appeared in the made-for-television movies *Out of Darkness* (1994) and *Double Platinum* (1999). In 2000 the Supremes attempted a reunion tour, but Mary Wilson declined to join and the tour, surrounded by controversy and with low ticket sales, was canceled.

See also Music in the United States; Supremes, The

Bibliography

Brown, Geoff. *Diana Ross.* New York: St. Martin's Press, 1983.

George, Nelson. *Where Did Our Love Go? The Rise and Fall of the Motown Sound.* New York: St. Martin's Press, 1985.

Hirshey, Gerry. *Nowhere to Run: The Story of Soul Music.* New York: Penguin, 1984.

Ross, Diana. *Upside Down: Wrong Turns, Right Turns, and the Road Ahead.* New York: Regan Books, 2005.

KAREN BENNETT HARMON (1996)
Updated by publisher 2005

ROWAN, CARL T.

AUGUST 11, 1925
SEPTEMBER 23, 2000

Born in Ravenscroft, Tennessee, the son of a lumber worker, journalist and governmental official Carl Thomas Rowan grew up in poverty. After graduating from local schools in 1942, he saved enough money to attend Tennessee State University. While at Tennessee State, Rowan was drafted and was selected for a special program to train African-American officers in the then segregated U.S. Navy. In 1945, after completing his military service, Rowan registered at Oberlin College in Ohio; he graduated in 1947. Determined to become a journalist, he moved to Minneapolis and received an M.A. from the University of Minnesota in 1948.

That same year Rowan was hired as a copywriter by the white-owned *Minneapolis Tribune* and was made a reporter in 1950, becoming one of the first African-American reporters for a large urban daily newspaper. The next year Rowan toured the southern states, reporting on racial discrimination. His articles (which were collected in the book *South of Freedom* in 1952) won him national attention. Rowan continued as a reporter for the *Tribune* for ten years and won several journalism awards for his coverage of such issues as the U.S. Supreme Court's *Brown v. Board of Education* school desegregation case in 1954, the Bandung Conference of Nonaligned Nations in Indonesia in 1955, and the 1960 civil war in the former Belgian Congo. In 1956 Rowan made a second trip to the South and was one of the first national journalists to cover the Montgomery bus boycott. He recounted his journey in *Go South to Sorrow* (1957). During the late 1950s he wrote two other books: *The Pitiful and the Proud* (1956), a report on society and culture in India, and *Wait Till Next Year* (1960), a biography of baseball star Jackie Robinson.

In 1961 Rowan was appointed deputy assistant secretary of state by President John F. Kennedy. He spent two years in the position, directing the drafting of position papers. Rowan also assisted Vice President Lyndon B. Johnson, accompanying him on a tour of the Middle East, India, and Vietnam. In 1962 he was assigned to the U.S. delegation to the United Nations. In January 1963 Kennedy appointed Rowan U.S. ambassador to Finland. Rowan was one of the first African Americans ever assigned as ambassador to a largely white country.

In December 1963 President Lyndon B. Johnson named Rowan to head the United States Information Agency (USIA), replacing Edward R. Murrow. As USIA director, Rowan held by far the highest executive branch position occupied by an African American up to that time. He also attended cabinet meetings and served as a political adviser. Rowan remained at the agency for a little more than a year before resigning because of friction with Johnson over Vietnam and other policies.

In 1965 Rowan was hired as a columnist and lecturer by the Field Newspaper Syndicate, becoming the first African American with a nationally syndicated column. During the next three decades Rowan remained one of the most visible and respected journalists in the United States. In addition to his newspaper column, Rowan served as a syndicated radio commentator on the daily program *The Rowan Report,* as a regular panelist/commentator on the syndicated television show *Agronsky & Company* (1976–1988), and as a frequent panelist on *Meet the Press.* During the 1970s he wrote *Just Between Us Blacks* (1974), a book of essays on racial topics, and *Race War in Rhodesia*

(1978). In 1987 he was named annual president of the prestigious journalists' group, the Gridiron Club. In 1991 Rowan published *Breaking Barriers: A Memoir.* The following year, he founded the Project Excellence program, a million-dollar college scholarship fund. In recognition of his educational efforts, in 1993 the Lynch Annex Elementary School in Detroit was renamed the Carl T. Rowan Community School in his honor.

Rowan was a committed integrationist and mainstream liberal who attacked both conservatives and black nationalists. He and his writings remained controversial. In 1988 Rowan, long a champion of gun control legislation, drew national headlines after he shot and wounded a white man who had broken into his Washington, D.C., home. He was threatened with arrest on charges of possessing an illegal handgun, but the charges were later dropped. Rowan claimed he was the victim of a politically motivated prosecution led by Mayor Marion Barry, whose administration he had attacked in his column.

In 1986 Rowan wrote and produced *Thurgood Marshall: The Man* (1986), two television documentary programs on Marshall's career. In 1987 he began collaborating on Marshall's memoirs, but the project was abandoned when Marshall refused to discuss his Supreme Court cases. Rowan then wrote a biography, *Dream Makers, Dream Breakers: The World of Justice Thurgood Marshall,* which was published in 1993.

Though plagued by health problems, which ultimately required the amputation of one leg, Rowan continued to write his column and to speak out on racial issues. In 1995 he denounced the Million Man March as racist. In 1996 he published *The Coming Race War in America,* in which he warned of the potential for violence if white prejudice and denial of equal opportunity were not addressed.

Rowan died of natural causes at the age of seventy-five.

See also Barry, Marion; *Brown v. Board of Education of Topeka, Kansas*; Journalism; Robinson, Jackie

Bibliography

Rowan, Carl T. *Breaking Barriers: A Memoir.* Boston: Little, Brown, 1991.

GREG ROBINSON (1996)
Updated by publisher 2005

Rudolph, Wilma

June 23, 1940
November 12, 1994

Olympic athlete Wilma Glodean Rudolph, the twentieth of twenty-two children, was born in Bethlehem, Tennessee, and raised in Clarksville. As a child she suffered from scarlet fever and pneumonia and was stricken with polio, which left her without the use of her left leg. She wore a leg brace until the age of nine, when she was able to regain the strength in her legs. By age twelve Rudolph was the fastest runner in her school. She entered Cobb Elementary School in 1947 and then attended Burt High School in Clarksville, where she played basketball and ran track.

Rudolph met Edward Temple, the track coach at Tennessee State University, while she was at Burt. After her sophomore year Temple invited Rudolph to a summer training camp and began to cultivate her running abilities. In 1956, at age sixteen, she participated in the Olympics in Melbourne, Australia, where her team won the bronze medal in the 4 x 100-meter relay race. Two years later, Rudolph entered Tennessee State to run track and study elementary education and psychology. She was determined to return to the Rome Olympics in 1960. She trained and ran with the Tigerbelles, the Tennessee State University team, which was one of the premier teams in the country. In 1960 Rudolph became the first woman to receive three gold medals, which she won for the 100-meter race, the 200-meter race, and the 4 x 100-meter relay. She instantly became a celebrity, drawing large crowds wherever she went. The French press called her "*la Gazelle.*" Rudolph retired from amateur running at the height of her career, in 1962.

Rudolph graduated from Tennessee State in 1963 and accepted a job as teacher and track coach at Cobb Elementary School. Although she lived in many places and held a number of different jobs, she invariably dedicated herself to youth programs and education. She worked as the director of a community center in Evansville, Indiana, with the Job Corps program in Boston and St. Louis, with the Watts Community Action Committee in California, and as a teacher at a high school in Detroit. In 1981 she started the Wilma Rudolph Foundation, a nonprofit organization that nurtures young athletes.

Wilma Rudolph received many awards and distinctions. She was chosen in 1960 as the United Press Athlete of the Year, and the next year the Associated Press designated her Woman Athlete of the Year. She was inducted in 1973 into the Black Sports Hall of Fame, seven years later into the Women's Sports Hall of Fame, and in 1983 into the U.S. Olympic Hall of Fame. In 1993 she became the only woman to be awarded the National Sports Award. In addition, her 1977 autobiography, *Wilma: The Story of Wilma Rudolph,* was made into a television movie. Rudolph's achievements as a runner gave a boost to women's track in the United States and heightened awareness about racial and sexual barriers within sports. In addition, Rudolph served as a role model and inspiration to thousands of African-American and female athletes, as well as people trying to overcome physical disabilities.

See also Olympians; Sports

Bibliography

Biracree, Tom. *Wilma Rudolph.* New York: Chelsea House, 1988.

Jacobs, Linda. *Wilma Rudolph: Run for Glory.* St. Paul, Minn: EMC Corp., 1975.

Rudolph, Wilma. *Wilma.* New York: New American Library, 1977.

PREMILLA NADASEN (1996)

Ruggles, David

March 15, 1810
December 26, 1849

Abolitionist and journalist David Ruggles was born of free parents in Connecticut and educated at a Sabbath School for the Poor in Norwich. Ruggles moved to New York City at the age of seventeen; in 1829 he opened a grocery, with goods of "excellent quality," but no "spiritous liquors." Ruggles began his antislavery work with a letter to the Marquis de Lafayette in 1830, seeking the revolutionary hero's endorsement of immediate abolition. In 1833 he sharpened his speaking skills as a traveling agent for the *Emancipator,* the New York antislavery newspaper. In his speeches he attacked colonization and spoke of antislavery experiences in New York, of the Conventions of Colored Peoples, and of the recently established Phoenix Society.

With Henry Highland Garnet, Ruggles organized the Garrison Literary and Benevolent Association and was an officer in the New York City Temperance Union. He opened the first known African-American bookshop in New York City, which was located at 67 Lispenard Street, in 1834; it served the abolitionist and black communities until destroyed by a mob in 1835.

In 1834 Ruggles published his first pamphlet, the anticolonization satire *Extinguisher, Extinguished . . . or David M. Reese, M.D. "Used Up."* This pamphlet and the later *An Antidote for a Furious Combination . . .* (1838) attacked the procolonizationist arguments of the Methodist cleric David Reese. Ruggles expanded his abolitionist arguments in the 1835 feminist appeal *The Abrogation of the Seventh Commandment by the American Churches.* The pamphlet, published on Ruggles's own press (another African-American first), stood proslavery arguments and fearful fantasies on their heads and called for northern feminists to shun or ostracize the southern wives of slaveholders. In 1835 he penned numerous articles in William L. Garrison's *Emancipator.*

In 1835 Ruggles founded and headed the New York Vigilance Committee, which protected free blacks from kidnapping. He was a daring conductor on the Underground Railroad, harboring Frederick Douglass and one thousand other blacks before transferring them north to safety.

A fearless activist and fundraiser, Ruggles also went to the homes of whites where he believed black servants were unlawfully held. He served writs against slave-catchers and directly confronted them in the street. In the frequent columns he wrote for the *Colored American,* he exposed racism on railroads. In 1839 he published a *Slaveholders Directory,* which identified the names and addresses of politicians, lawyers, and police in New York who "lend themselves to kidnapping."

Between 1838 and 1841 Ruggles published five issues of the *Mirror of Liberty,* the first African-American magazine. Circulated widely throughout the East, the Midwest, and even the South, the *Mirror of Liberty* chronicled the activities of the Vigilance Committee, gave accounts of kidnappings and related court cases, and printed antislavery speeches and notices from black organizations. Despite its irregular appearances, the magazine was a significant achievement.

Burdened by a fractious and costly dispute with Samuel Cornish, accused of mishandling funds, having been jailed for his activities, and suffering from near blindness, Ruggles moved to Northampton, Massachusetts, in 1842. There Lydia Maria Child and the Northampton Association of Education and Industry gave him succor in the 1840s while he continued his activities on the Underground Railroad. In Northampton, Ruggles overcame his poor health and built a prosperous practice as a doctor of hydropathy, using water in the treatment of various diseases. He attended a huge variety of patients, from the wife of a southern slave owner to William Lloyd Garrison to Sojourner Truth. He died in 1849 from a severe intestinal illness.

See also Abolition; Underground Railroad

Bibliography

Porter, Dorothy B. "David Ruggles, an Apostle of Human Rights." *Journal of Negro History* 28 (1943): 23–50.

Porter, Dorothy B. "David Ruggles." In *Dictionary of American Negro Biography.* New York: Norton, 1982.

GRAHAM RUSSELL HODGES (1996)

Runaway Slaves

This entry consists of two distinct articles with differing geographic domains.

Runaway Slaves in Latin America and the Caribbean
Richard Price

Runaway Slaves in the United States
Freddie Parker

Runaway Slaves in Latin America and the Caribbean

Throughout the colonial Americas, runaway slaves were called "Maroons." The English word *Maroon* comes from Spanish *cimarrón,* itself based on a Taíno Indian root. *Cimarrón* originally referred to domestic cattle that had taken to the hills in Hispaniola, and soon after to American Indian slaves who had escaped from the Spaniards. By the end of the 1530s the word was being used primarily to refer to Afro-American runaways and already had strong connotations of "fierceness," of being "wild" and "unbroken," of being indomitable.

In 1502 the man who would become the first Afro-American Maroon arrived on the first ship carrying enslaved Africans to the New World. In the 1970s one of the last surviving runaway slaves in the hemisphere was still alive in Cuba. For more than four centuries, the communities formed by Maroons dotted the fringes of plantation America from Brazil to Florida, from Peru to Texas. Usually called *palenques* in the Spanish colonies and *mocambos* or *quilombos* in Brazil, they ranged from tiny bands that survived less than a year to powerful states encompassing thousands of members and lasting for generations or even centuries. Today their descendants still form semi-independent enclaves in several parts of the hemisphere—for example, in Jamaica, Brazil, Colombia, Belize, Suriname, and French Guiana—remaining fiercely proud of their Maroon origins and, in some cases at least, faithful to unique cultural traditions that were forged during the earliest days of Afro-American history.

Drawing of a runaway slave, 1672. *The English referred to escaped slaves as "maroons." Free from white dominance, these refugees established communities in remote areas of the Caribbean and Latin America.* HULTON ARCHIVE/GETTY IMAGES

During the past several decades anthropological fieldwork has underlined the strength of historical consciousness among the descendants of these rebel slaves and the dynamism and originality of their cultural institutions. Meanwhile, historical scholarship on Maroons has flourished, as new research has done much to dispel the myth of the docile slave. Marronage represented a major form of slave resistance, whether accomplished by lone individuals, by small groups, or in great collective rebellions. Throughout the Americas Maroon communities stood out as a heroic challenge to white authority, as living proof of the existence of a slave consciousness that refused to be limited by the whites' conception or manipulation of it. It is no accident that in much of the Caribbean and Latin America today, the historical Maroon—often mythologized into a larger-than-life figure—has become a touchstone of identity for the region's writers, artists, and intel-

Map depicting the locations of revolts and fugitive slave communities in the Caribbean and parts of North and South America, sixteenth century. *In 1502, the first African slaves were brought to Cuba from West Africa. By the middle of that century, the entire Caribbean and most of Central and South America were settled by the Spanish with the support of large African and Indian slave populations. Many slaves revolted and formed what came to be known as* maroon *communities, often in hostile and unproductive regions such as swamps, mountains, and jungles, where they could defend themselves more easily.* MAP BY XNR PRODUCTIONS. THE GALE GROUP.

lectuals, the ultimate symbol of resistance and the fight for freedom.

More generally, Maroons and their communities can be seen to hold a special significance for the study of Afro-American societies. For while they were, from one perspective, the antithesis of all that slavery stood for; they were also a widespread and embarrassingly visible part of this system. Just as the very nature of plantation slavery implied violence and resistance, the wilderness setting of early New World plantations made marronage and the existence of organized Maroon communities a ubiquitous reality. And in Haiti Maroons played a signal role as catalysts in the Haitian Revolution that created the first nation in the Americas where all citizens were free (for the scholarly debates on this issue, see Manigat [1977]).

The meaning of marronage differed for enslaved people in different social positions, varying with their perception of themselves and their situation, which was influenced by such diverse factors as their country of birth, the period of time they had been in the New World, their task assignment as slaves, their family responsibilities, and the particular treatment they were receiving from overseers or masters, as well as more general considerations such as the proportion of blacks to whites in the region, the proportion of freedmen in the population, and the opportunities for manumission. Many African runaways, particularly men, escaped during their first hours or days in the Americas. Enslaved Africans who had already spent some time in the New World seem to have been less prone to flight. But enslaved Africans or Creole slaves who were particularly acculturated, who had learned the ways of the plantation best, seem to have been highly represented among runaways, often escaping to urban areas where they could pass as free because of their independent skills and ability to speak the colonial language.

Planters generally tolerated *petit marronage*—truancy with temporary goals such as visiting a friend or lover on a neighboring plantation. But in most slaveholding colonies, the most brutal punishments—amputation of a leg, castration, suspension from a meathook through the ribs, slow roasting to death—were reserved for long-term, recidivist Maroons, and in many cases these were quickly written into law. Marronage on the grand scale (*grand marronage*), with individual fugitives banding together to create communities, struck directly at the foundations of the plantation system, presenting military and economic threats that often taxed the colonists to their very limits. Maroon communities, whether hidden near the fringes of the plantations or deep in the forest or swamps, periodically raided plantations for firearms, tools, and women, often permitting families that had formed during slavery to be reunited in freedom.

To be viable, Maroon communities had to be inaccessible, and villages were typically located in remote, inhospitable areas. In Jamaica some of the most famous Maroon groups lived in the intricately accidented "cockpit country," where deep canyons and limestone sinkholes abound but water and good soil are scarce; in Suriname and Brazil, seemingly impenetrable jungles provided Maroons with a safe haven. Throughout the hemisphere Maroons developed extraordinary skills in guerrilla warfare. To the bewilderment of their colonial enemies, whose rigid and conventional tactics were learned on the open battlefields

March thro' a Swamp or, Marsh in Terra Firma, ***by John Gabriel Steadman.*** *Steadman's drawings, engraved for publication by William Blake and others, accompanied his* Narrative, of a Five Years' Expedition, against the Revolted Negroes of Surinam, in Guiana, on the wild coast of South America, from the year 1772 to 1777. *Pictured are colonial troops and slaves searching for maroon villages.*

of Europe, these highly adaptable and mobile warriors took maximum advantage of local environments, striking and withdrawing with great rapidity, making extensive use of ambushes to catch their adversaries in crossfire, fighting only when and where they chose, depending on reliable intelligence networks among non-Maroons (both slaves and white settlers), and often communicating by drums and horns.

In many cases the beleaguered colonists were eventually forced to sue their former slaves for peace. In Brazil, Colombia, Cuba, Ecuador, Hispaniola, Jamaica, Mexico, Panama, Peru, Suriname, and Venezuela, for example, whites reluctantly offered treaties granting Maroon communities their freedom, recognizing their territorial integrity, and making some provision for meeting their economic needs, in return for an end to hostilities toward the plantations and an agreement to return future runaways. Of course, many Maroon societies were crushed by massive force of arms, and even when treaties were proposed they were sometimes refused or quickly violated. Nevertheless, new Maroon communities seemed to appear almost as quickly as the old ones were exterminated, and they remained, from a colonial perspective, the "chronic plague" and "gangrene" of many plantation societies right up to final emancipation.

African Origins, New World Creativity

The initial Maroons in any New World colony hailed from a wide range of societies in West and Central Africa—at the outset, they shared neither language nor other major aspects of culture. Their collective task, once off in the forests or mountains or swamplands, was nothing less than to create new communities and institutions, largely via a process of inter African cultural syncretism or blending. Those scholars, mainly anthropologists, who have examined contemporary Maroon life most closely seem to agree that such societies are often uncannily "African" in feeling but at the same time largely devoid of directly transplanted systems. However "African" in character, no Maroon social, political, religious, or aesthetic *system* can be reliably traced to a specific African ethnic provenience—they reveal rather their syncretistic composition, forged in the early meeting of peoples of diverse African, European, and Amerindian origins in the dynamic setting of the New World.

The political system of the great seventeenth-century Brazilian Maroon kingdom of Palmares, for example, which historian R. K. Kent (1965) has characterized as an "African" state, did not (he tells us) derive from a *particular* Central African model but from several. In the development of the kinship system of the Ndyuka Maroons of Suriname, argues anthropologist André Köbben (1996), their West African heritage undoubtedly played a part and the influence of the matrilineal Akan tribes is unmistakable, but so is that of patrilineal tribes, and there are significant differences between the Akan and Ndyuka matrilineal systems. Historical and anthropological research has revealed that the magnificent woodcarving of the Suriname Maroons, long considered "an African art in the Americas" on the basis of formal resemblances, is in fact a fundamentally new, Afro-American art for which it would be pointless, argues Jean Hurault (1970), to seek the origin through direct transmission of any particular African style. And detailed investigations—both in museums and in the field—of a range of cultural phenomena among the Saramaka Maroons of Suriname have confirmed the dynamic, creative processes that continue to animate these societies.

Maroon cultures do possess direct and sometimes spectacular continuities from particular African peoples, from military techniques for defense to recipes for warding off sorcery. These are, however, of the same type as those that can be found, if with lesser frequency, in Afro-American communities throughout the hemisphere. In stressing these isolated African "retentions," there is a danger of neglecting cultural continuities of a more significant kind. Roger Bastide (1972, pp. 128–151) divided Afro-American religions into those he considered "preserved" or "canned," like Brazilian Candomblé, and those that he considered "alive," like Haitian vodou. The former, he argued, manifest a kind of "defense mechanism" or "cultural fossilization," a fear that any small change may bring on the end, while the latter are more secure of their future and freer to adapt to the changing needs of their adherents. And indeed, tenacious fidelity to "African" *forms* seems, in many cases, to indicate a culture finally having lost meaningful touch with the vital African past. Certainly, one of the most striking features of West and Central African cultural systems is their internal dynamism, their ability to grow and change. The cultural uniqueness of the more developed Maroon societies (e.g., those in Suriname) rests firmly on their fidelity to "African" cultural principles at these deeper levels—whether aesthetic, political, religious, or domestic—rather than on the frequency of their isolated "retentions." With a rare freedom to extrapolate ideas from a variety of African societies and adapt them to changing circumstances, Maroon groups included (and continue to include today) what are in many respects *at once* the most meaningfully African *and* the most truly "alive" and culturally dynamic of all Afro-American cultures.

Famous Runaway Communities

Some of the best known Maroon societies are Palmares in Brazil, Palenque de San Basilio in Colombia, the Maroons of Esmeraldas in Ecuador, San Lorenzo de los Negros in Mexico, the Maroons of Jamaica, and the Saramaka, Ndyuka, and other Maroons of Suriname.

Because Palmares, in northeastern Brazil, was finally crushed by a massive colonial army in 1695 after a century of success and growth, actual knowledge of its internal affairs remains limited, based as it is on soldiers' reports, the testimony of a captive under torture, official documents, modern archaeological work, and the like. But as a modern symbol of black (and anticolonial) heroism, Palmares continues to evoke strong emotions throughout Brazil, as do the names of its great leaders, first Ganga Zumba and, later, Zumbi. (For a compilation of historical scholarship, including work in archaeology and anthropology, see Reis and Santos Gomes [1996].)

Palenque de San Basilio, near the Atlantic coast of Colombia, boasts a history stretching back to the seventeenth century. In recent years historians, anthropologists, and linguists—working in collaboration with palenqueros—have uncovered a great deal about continuities and changes in the life of these early Colombian freedom fighters. (For an illustrated introduction to this community, see de Friedemann and Cross [1979].)

In Esmeraldas, on the Pacific coast of Ecuador, Maroon history began in the early sixteenth century, when Spanish ships carrying slaves from Panama to Guayaquil and Lima were wrecked amid strong currents and shifting sandbars. A number of slave survivors sought freedom in the unconquered interior, where they allied with indigenous peoples. In the 1580s, having beaten back military expeditions sent to capture them, several Maroon bands tried to make peace in Quito. All were guaranteed continued autonomy in exchange for safe passage of further shipwreck victims and promises not to ally with English and later Dutch pirates. A 1599 portrait of one such Maroon leader, Don Francisco de Arobe, and his two sons was commissioned in Quito and sent to Philip III of Spain to commemorate these negotiations. (For more on this story, see Lane [2002].)

San Lorenzo de los Negros, in Veracruz, is probably the best known of the seventeenth-century Maroon towns in Mexico. Under their leader Yanga, the Maroons attempted to make peace as early as 1608, but it was not until 1630, after years of intermittent warfare, that the Viceroy and the crown finally agreed to establish the town of free Maroons. (For a summary of Maroon communities in Mexico, see Pereira [1994].)

The Jamaica Maroons, who continue to live in two main groups centered in Accompong (in the hills above Montego Bay) and in Moore Town (deep in the Blue Mountains), maintain strong traditions about their days as freedom fighters, when the former group was led by Cudjoe and the latter by the redoubtable woman warrior Nanny. Two centuries of scholarship, some written by Maroons themselves, offers diverse windows on the ways these men and women managed to survive and build a vibrant culture within the confines of a relatively small island. (A useful entree to Jamaica Maroon literature is provided in Agorsah [1994].)

The Suriname Maroons now constitute the most fully documented case of how former slaves built new societies and cultures, under conditions of extreme deprivation, in the Americas—and how they developed and maintained semi-independent societies that persist into the present. From their late seventeenth-century origins and the details of their wars and treaty making to their current struggles with multinational mining and timber companies, much is now known about these peoples' achievements, in large part because of the extensive recent collaboration by Saramaka and Ndyuka Maroons with anthropologists. Today, Suriname Maroons—who number some 120,000 people—live in the interior of the country in and around the capital Paramaribo, and in neighboring French Guiana. (The relevant bibliography on Suriname Maroons numbers in the thousands of references; useful points of entry are Price and Price [1999] and Thoden van Velzen and van Wetering [2004].) Because of their numerical importance as well as the unusually rich scholarship devoted to them, Suriname Maroons merit expanded discussion here.

Suriname (formerly known also as Dutch Guiana) is in northeastern South America and gained its independence in 1975. Suriname's Maroons (formerly known also as "Bush Negroes") have long been the hemisphere's largest Maroon population, representing one extreme in the range of cultural adaptations that Afro-Americans have made in the New World. Between the mid-seventeenth and late eighteenth centuries, the ancestors of the present-day Maroons escaped, in many cases soon after their arrival from Africa, from the coastal plantations on which they were enslaved and fled into the forested interior, where they regrouped into small bands. Their hardships in forging an existence in a new and inhospitable environment were compounded by the persistent and massive efforts of the colonial government to eliminate this threat to the plantation colony.

The Dutch colonists reserved special punishments for recaptured slaves—hamstringing, amputation of limbs, and a variety of deaths by torture. The organized pursuit of Maroons and expeditions to destroy their settlements date at least from the 1670s, but these rarely met with success, for the Maroons had established and protected their settlements with great ingenuity and had become expert at all aspects of guerrilla warfare. By the middle of the eighteenth century, when, in the words of a prominent planter, "the colony had become the theater of a perpetual war," (Nassy, 1788, p. 87) the colonists finally sued the Maroons for peace. In 1760 and 1762 peace treaties were successfully concluded with the two largest Maroon peoples, the Ndyukas and the Saramakas, and in 1767 with the much smaller Matawai, guaranteeing Maroons their freedom and territory (even though slavery persisted for another hundred years on the coast) in return for nonaggression and an agreement not to harbor posttreaty escaped slaves. New slave revolts and the large-scale war of subsequent decades, for which an army of mercenaries was imported from Europe, eventually led to the formation of the Aluku (Boni), as well as the smaller Paramaka and Kwinti groups.

Map depicting the locations of revolts and fugitive slave communities in the Americas and the Caribbean, seventeenth century. MAP BY XNR PRODUCTIONS. THE GALE GROUP.

Today, there are six politically distinct Maroon peoples in Suriname and neighboring French Guiana; the Ndyuka and Saramaka each have a population of about fifty thousand, the Aluku (Boni) and Paramaka are each closer to six thousand, the Matawai are some four thousand, and the Kwinti number fewer than five hundred. Their traditional territories are deep in the forests of the country, although today large numbers of Maroons live outside of these areas, mainly in Paramaribo and the coastal towns of French Guiana. Although formed under broadly similar historical and ecological conditions, these societies display significant variation in everything from language, diet, and dress to patterns of marriage, residence, and migratory wage labor. From a cultural point of view, the greatest differences are between the Maroons of central Suriname (Saramaka, Matawai, and Kwinti) on the one hand, and those of eastern Suriname and western French Guiana (Ndyuka, Aluku, and Paramaka) on the other.

Since the colonial government of Suriname signed treaties with the Ndyuka, Saramaka, and Matawai in the 1760s and later recognized the Aluku, Paramaka, and Kwinti, a loose framework of indirect rule has obtained. Except for the Kwinti, each group has a paramount chief (who from an internal perspective might better be described as a "king"), as well as a series of headmen and other village-based officials. Traditionally, the role of these people in political and social control has been exercised in a context replete with oracles, spirit possession, and other forms of divination. Until the mid-twentieth century almost all Maroons lived by a combination of, on the one hand, forest horticulture, hunting, and fishing, and on the other, men doing wage labor on the coast to buy and bring back Western-manufactured goods. But rapid change began in the 1960s, as the widespread use of outboard motors and the development of air service to the interior encouraged increased traffic of people and goods between Maroon villages and the coast. At the same time the construction, by Alcoa and the Suriname government, of a giant hydroelectric project brought a dramatic migration toward the coast, with some six thousand people forced to abandon their homes as an artificial lake gradually flooded almost half of Saramaka territory. Meanwhile in French Guiana, beginning in the 1970s, the Aluku were subjected to intense pressures for "*francisation,*" which caused wrenching economic, cultural, and political transformations. Suriname's independence in 1975 changed life for most Maroons less than for the coastal population, but a civil war (1986–1992), which pitted the national army of Suriname against the "Jungle Commandos" (largely made up of Ndyukas but with a significant number of Saramakas as well), annihilated the Ndyuka villages along the Cottica River and sent some ten thousand Maroons fleeing to French Guiana. Today, continuing battles over the control of the valuable gold mining and timber rights in the interior affect every aspect of contemporary Maroon life in Suriname, with the national government claiming sovereignty over the territories the Maroons' ancestors died for. Many outside observers now fear the government has embarked on a policy of ethnocide toward the Maroons.

The Suriname Maroons, whose ancestors came from a wide variety of West and Central African societies, created new, vibrant Afro-American cultures in the rainforest, drawing primarily on their diverse African backgrounds but with lesser contributions as well from Amerindians (primarily subsistence techniques) and Europeans. Their enormously rich religious systems, their unique Creole languages, and their vibrant artistic and performance achievements are remarkably African in feeling yet unlike those of any particular culture or society in Africa. In building creatively upon their collective past, the early Maroons synthesized African cultural principles and adapted, played with, and reshaped cultural forms into ones that were new, yet still organically related to that past. The culture of the Suriname Maroons, forged in an inhospitable rainforest by people under constant threat of annihilation, stands as enduring testimony to African-American resilience and creativity and to the exuberance of the Maroon imagination working itself out within the rich, broad framework of African cultural ideas.

Current Issues

Since the fieldwork of pioneer Afro-Americanists Melville and Frances Herskovits in Suriname in the 1920s (see their 1934 book and the Prices' 2003 pamphlet), Maroons have moved to the center of scholarly debates, ranging from the origins of Creole languages and the "accuracy" of oral history to the nature of the African heritage in the Americas and the very definition of Afro-American anthropology. Indeed, David Scott argues that the Saramaka Maroons have by now become "a sort of anthropological metonym . . . providing the exemplary arena in which to argue out certain anthropological claims about a discursive domain called Afro-America" (1991, p. 269). Much of the most recent anthropological research has focused on Maroon historiography—how Maroons themselves conceptualize and transmit knowledge about the past—and has privileged the voices of individual Maroon historians. Eric Hobsbawm, commenting on this work in the more general context of the social sciences, notes that "Maroon societies raise fundamental questions. How do casual collections of fugitives of widely different origins, possessing nothing in common but the experience of transportation in slave ships and of plantation slavery, come to form structured communities? How, one might say more generally, are societies founded from scratch? What exactly did or could such refugee communities . . . derive from the old continent?" (1990, p. 46). Questions such as these are sure to keep students of Maroon societies engaged in active research for many years to come.

See also Maroon Societies in the Caribbean; Nanny of the Maroons; Palenque San Basilio; Palmares; Runaway Slaves in the United States

Bibliography

Agorsah, E. Kofi, ed. *Maroon Heritage: Archaeological, Ethnographic and Historical Perspectives.* Kingston, Jamaica: Canoe Press, 1994.

Bastide, Roger. *African Civilizations in the New World.* New York: Harper & Row, 1972.

de Friedemann, Nina S., and Richard Cross. *Ma ngombe: Guerreros y ganaderos en Palenque.* Bogotá: Carlos Valencia Editores, 1979.

Herskovits, Melville J., and Frances S. Herskovits. *Rebel Destiny: Among the Bush Negroes of Dutch Guiana.* New York: McGraw-Hill, 1934.

Heuman, Gad, ed. *Out of the House of Bondage: Runaways, Resistance and Marronage in Africa and the New World.* London: Frank Cass, 1986.

Hobsbawm, Eric J. "Escaped Slaves of the Forest." *New York Review of Books* (December 6, 1990): 46–48.

Hurault, Jean. *Africains de Guyane: la vie matérielle et l?art des Noirs Réfugiés de Guyane.* The Hague: Mouton, 1970.

Kent, R. K. "Palmares: An African State in Brazil." *Journal of African History* 6 (1965): 161–175.

Köbben, A. J. F. "Unity and Disunity: Cottica Djuka Society as a Kinship System." In *Maroon Societies: Rebel Slave Communities in the Americas,* 3rd ed., edited by Richard Price, pp. 320–369. Baltimore: Johns Hopkins University Press, 1996.

Lane, Kris. *Quito 1599: City and Colony in Transition.* Albuquerque: University of New Mexico Press, 2002.

Manigat, Leslie F. "The Relationship Between Marronage and Slave Revolts and Revolution in St. Domingue-Haiti." In *Comparative Perspectives on Slavery in New World Plantation Societies,* edited by Vera Rubin and Arthur Tuden, pp. 420–473. New York: New York Academy of Sciences, 1977.

Nassy, David de Ishak Cohen et al. *Essai historique sur la colonie de Surinam . . . Le tout redige sur des pieces authentiques y Jointes, & mis en ordre par Ies regens & representans de ladite Nation Juive Portugaise,* Paramaribo, 1788

Pereira, Joe. "Maroon Heritage in Mexico." In *Maroon Heritage: Archaeological, Ethnographic and Historical Perspectives,* edited by E. Kofi Agorsah, pp. 94–107. Kingston, Jamaica: Canoe Press, 1994.

Price, Richard. *Alabi's World.* Baltimore, Md.: Johns Hopkins University Press, 1990.

Price, Richard. *First-Time: The Historical Vision of an African American People,* 2nd ed. Chicago: University of Chicago Press, 2002.

Price, Richard, ed. *Maroon Societies: Rebel Slave Communities in the Americas,* 3rd ed. Baltimore, Md.: Johns Hopkins University Press, 1996.

Price, Richard, ed. Special issue: "Maroons in the Americas: Heroic Pasts, Ambiguous Presents, Uncertain Futures." *Cultural Survival Quarterly* 25, no. 4 (2001).

Price, Richard and Sally. *The Root of Roots: Or, How Afro-American Anthropology Got Its Start.* Chicago: Prickly Paradigm Press/University of Chicago Press, 2003.

Price, Sally and Richard. *Maroon Arts: Cultural Vitality in the African Diaspora.* Boston: Beacon Press, 1999.

Reis, Joao J., and Flávio dos Santos Gomes, eds. *Liberdade por um fio: Historia dos quilombos no Brasil.* São Paulo: Companhia das Letras, 1996.

Scott, David. "That Event, This Memory: Notes on the Anthropology of African Diasporas in the New World." *Diaspora* 1, no. 3 (1991): 261–284.

Stedman, John Gabriel. *Narrative of a Five Years Expedition Against the Revolted Negroes of Surinam.* (Newly transcribed from the original 1790 manuscript, edited, and with an introduction and notes, by Richard and Sally Price.) Baltimore, Md.: Johns Hopkins University Press, 1988.

Thoden van Velzen, H. U. E., and W. van Wetering. *In the Shadow of the Oracle: Religion as Politics in a Suriname Maroon Society.* Long Grove, Ill: Waveland Press, 2004.

RICHARD PRICE (2005)

Runaway Slaves in the United States

On June 27, 1838, Betty—a slave belonging to Micajah Ricks of Nash County, North Carolina—ran away with her two children, Burrel and Gray, aged seven and five. Betty had violated one of her owner's rules because, a few days before she fled, Ricks had burned the letter *M* on the left side of her face. Humiliated by this, Betty tried to hide the brand by covering her head and face with a piece of cloth and a "fly bonnet." The branding of Betty's face was the spark that forced her to strike a personal blow against the institution of slavery in North Carolina. Ricks presumed that Betty and her children would "attempt to pass as free."

Betty's flight for some measure of psychological and physical freedom was an act played out by thousands of slaves in North Carolina and throughout the South during slavery. From slavery's inception until its end, black slaves employed several methods to resist the dehumanization and horrors the institution presented. Slaves committed acts of day-to-day resistance, dozens of revolts occurred, and they ran away from their masters, often placing great distance between themselves and enslavement. Virginia, the first British colony in North America, was plagued with the problem of slave flight. As other American colonies were established, including Maryland, the Carolinas, New York, New Jersey, Pennsylvania, and even the New England colonies, wherever slavery existed, there is evidence of slave flight.

Slave owners throughout America were confronted with the problems that runaways presented in their quest to be free. Fugitive slaves lurked about farms and plantations, sometimes robbing owners, stealing food, and generally doing what was necessary to survive in a hostile environment where they were the targets of slave catchers and citizens seeking rewards for capturing runaways. Runaway slaves sometimes committed felonies, including bur-

$200 Reward.

RANAWAY from the subscriber, on the night of Thursday, the 30th of Sepember.

FIVE NEGRO SLAVES,

To-wit: one Negro man, his wife, and three children.

The man is a black negro, full height, very erect, his face a little thin. He is about forty years of age, and calls himself *Washington Reed*, and is known by the name of Washington. He is probably well dressed, possibly takes with him an ivory headed cane, and is of good address. Several of his teeth are gone.

Mary, his wife, is about thirty years of age, a bright mulatto woman, and quite stout and strong.

The oldest of the children is a boy, of the name of FIELDING, twelve years of age, a dark mulatto, with heavy eyelids. He probably wore a new cloth cap.

MATILDA, the second child, is a girl, six years of age, rather a dark mulatto, but a bright and smart looking child.

MALCOLM, the youngest, is a boy, four years old, a lighter mulatto than the last, and about equally as bright. He probably also wore a cloth cap. If examined, he will be found to have a swelling at the navel.

Washington and Mary have lived at or near St. Louis, with the subscriber, for about 15 years.

It is supposed that they are making their way to Chicago, and that a white man accompanies them, that they will travel chiefly at night, and most probably in a covered wagon.

A reward of $150 will be paid for their apprehension, so that I can get them, if taken within one hundred miles of St. Louis, and $200 if taken beyond that, and secured so that I can get them, and other reasonable additional charges, if delivered to the subscriber, or to THOMAS ALLEN, Esq., at St. Louis, Mo. The above negroes, for the last few years, have been in possession of Thomas Allen, Esq., of St. Louis.

WM. RUSSELL.

ST. LOUIS, Oct. 1, 1847.

Poster advertising reward for runaway slaves, St. Louis, 1847. THE LIBRARY OF CONGRESS

glary, arson, and murder. As troublesome as these actions were, simply put, runaway slaves represented a huge economic loss to their owners. During the 1820s, more than two thousand runaway slaves, valued at more than one million dollars, lived in the Great Dismal Swamp in Virginia and North Carolina.

Because of this enormous loss in revenue and the expenses that owners accrued in attempting to capture runaway slaves, along with the acts of violence and theft committed by runaways, slaveholders and nonslaveholders petitioned legislative bodies across America to enact laws to prevent and control the problem of slave flight. The colony of Virginia enacted runaway slave legislation soon after slavery was legally established in the early 1660s. Virginia passed a law that required that slaves have in their possession a "pass" or "ticket" when they were allowed to leave the farm or plantation. The pass contained the slave's name, destination, order of business, and the owner's signature. Slave owners were held responsible and subject to a fine for slaves who were off the plantation without a pass. The Virginia legislature also established a reward system for citizens who apprehended runaway slaves. In addition to the reward, owners were required to pay a fee based on the distance (in miles) the runaway was apprehended from the owner's property.

The reward system provided an incentive to would-be apprehenders to be vigilant in the quest to return slaves to the rightful owner. Most subscribers began their runaway notices with the reward amount offered. In 1741, following Virginia's and South Carolina's lead, North Carolina established a reward system based on proximity from the owner's residence. If a slave were captured in the

Map depicting the locations of revolts and fugitive slave communities in the Americas and the Caribbean, eighteenth century. *As more African slaves were brought to the Americas during the 1700s, the number of maroon communities continued to grow. Among the best known in North America were largely inaccessible camps in the Florida everglades and in the bayous of Louisiana.* MAP BY XNR PRODUCTIONS. THE GALE GROUP.

owner's county, five dollars plus any expenses accrued to the apprehender were due. A minimum of ten dollars and expenses were due if the slave was brought back from another county, and if the slave ventured into the Great Dismal Swamp, twenty-five dollars in addition to expenses were due.

Runaway slaves were often harbored by whites and free blacks throughout slaveholding America. To confront this problem, legislative bodies passed laws that imposed fines, jail terms, and public whippings on those who concealed and harbored fugitives. Some owners warned in their notices for runaways that "all persons are forewarned from harboring" or "whoever harbors him will be prosecuted with the utmost rigour" of the law. The extent to which politicians and the citizenry, as a whole, fought to secure runaway legislation is evident in the North Carolina

Revised Slave Code of 1741. Of the dozens of laws passed that year, thirty-seven percent were devoted to some aspect of the runaway problem in North Carolina. Virginia, North Carolina, and South Carolina enacted "outlawry" legislation. Such laws mandated that owners who wished to have their runaway slave designated an outlaw go before two justices of the peace and draw up a proclamation stating that citizens could kill the outlawed slave without judicial reprisal. If the slave were killed, the owner would be compensated with at least two-thirds the slave's value. Such legislation proved effective in reducing slave flight.

Runaway slaves proved to be such a problem that southern representatives attending the Constitutional Convention in 1787 fought for federal legislation securing the rights of slave owners. Representative Pierce Butler of South Carolina led the effort to ensure that the new federal government would recognize that flight from a slave to a free state did not guarantee freedom. Thus, Article IV, Section 2, Clause 3 of the Constitution states that: "No Person held to Service or Labour in one State, under the Laws thereof, escaping into another, shall, in Consequence of any Law or Regulation therein, be discharged from such Service or Labour, but shall be delivered up on Claim of the Party to whom such Service or Labour may be due."

Later, Congress passed the 1793 Fugitive Slave Act, which allowed owners to claim their property in the North. Judges and magistrates were empowered to provide a certificate to the slave's owner upon proof of ownership. A fine of $500 was imposed on individuals who harbored or impeded the arrest of runaway slaves. Over the years, the law was highly ineffective and usually not enforced. As a result, slave owners fought to secure stronger legislation year after year, and were finally successful in 1850. The 1850 Fugitive Slave Act was far more stringent, and unlike the 1793 law, it was usually enforced, as evidenced by the thousands of slaves who were returned to the South during the 1850s.

Advertisements placed in hundreds of newspapers across America provide material for the study of runaway slaves. Thousands of slave owners across the South used the press to advertise for their absconded property. Runaway notices appeared in Virginia newspapers very early and continued during the Civil War. More than any other source, these advertisements provide vivid descriptions of who slaves were. The advertisements included the absconded slave's name, gender, age, height, weight, attire, and possible destination, along with a description of the runaway's personality, offers of rewards, and other information owners believed would lead to the return of their valuable property.

An analysis of the notices in all of the slaveholding states reveals that, on average, men constituted 78 to 82 percent of the runaway population. Female slaves composed the remaining 18 to 22 percent. Though female slaves desired freedom as well as men, familial ties kept them bound to the farms and plantations to a greater degree than men. Women were encouraged to have children at a young age, and as primary caregivers, running away with children obviously proved more difficult. Deborah White (1985) has shown that owners provided incentives to female slaves to reproduce would-be laborers for their owners. Despite the risks, some female slaves fled with their children, and there are hundreds of instances where they ran while pregnant.

Typical runaways, both male and female, were in their mid- to late twenties. By the time slaves reached their mid-twenties, they had usually been owned by more than one person. Many of these slaves had a spouse and children on each farm or plantation where they had been enslaved. They became familiar with the different parts of the state in which they lived, and in some instances different parts of the South, as many were shipped from other states. African-born slaves often ran away after being in the United States for only a short time. In order to secure their return, slave owners placed signs around the county and advertised in local newspapers, which described the slave's inability to speak English or fluency in other languages. Owners also sometimes described African-born slaves as having "filed teeth" and ethnic "markings" on the face and arms.

Notices for runaway slaves throughout the South and even the northern states provided rich detail about the slave's physical makeup. Specifically, advertisements described the slave's complexion (or whether a slave was a mulatto), along with height, weight, cuts, bruises, oral health, scars that may have resulted from floggings, and other aspects of the slave's anatomy. Slave owners also described the clothing that slaves wore when they fled and any clothing taken by them. Vivid descriptions about clothing were provided to alert would-be captors that the slave could present himself or herself in a variety of ways. Notices also pointed out that runaways would likely sell any additional clothing. The following advertisement, typical of colonial-era runaway notices, appeared in the *Virginia Gazette* on September 12, 1771.

> PRINCE GEORGE, August 27, 1771. RUN away from the Subscriber, on Tuesday the 6th Instant, a NEGRO FELLOW, named FRANK, twenty seven Years of Age, five Feet five or six Inches high, of a yellow Complexion, has a Scar in his right Cheek, and the Sinews in one of his Hams seem to be drawn up in Knots. He has run away several Times, and always passed for a Freeman.

> As he may possibly try to get out of the Country, I hereby forewarn all Masters of Vessels from carrying out the said Slave, at their Peril. I imagine he is sculking about Indian Town on Pamunkey among the Indians, as in one of his former Trips he got himself a Wife amongst them. Whoever brings the said Slave to me shall be handsomely rewarded. DAVID SCOTT.

In an effort to place distance between themselves and their masters, one would expect slaves to have fled by horseback. However, flight by horseback or horse and buggy occurred infrequently because it drew attention to runaways; additionally, horses required feeding and rest. Some slaves fled by boat, but boat travel was slow and exposed the runaway. Slaves often found freedom by boarding vessels leaving southern ports bound for the North. Boarding outbound vessels became such a problem that states enacted legislation to prevent ship captains from harboring, employing, or conveying runaways to the North. It was a capital offense in Virginia, North Carolina, and South Carolina for ship captains to carry slaves to the North. Slave owners warned captains in their notices by writing that: "Masters of vessels and others are cautioned at their peril" not to take runaway slaves out of the state. In 1837 Governor Edward B. Dudley of North Carolina offered a $1,000 reward for the return of his slave who had been taken to Boston by a "master of vessel." Dudley pledged $500 for the slave and $500 for the capture of the captain who carried his slave to Boston.

Overwhelmingly, slaves resorted to "foot flight." This mode of escape was safest because it allowed runaways to hide in the woods and swamps free of any encumbrances. Typical of the notices for such runaway slaves is the following advertisement for Quash, who fled from his Wilmington, North Carolina, owner on January 7, 1805.

> Ten Dollars Reward. RAN Away from the subscriber on the 7th inst. A Negro man named QUASH; he is about Twenty-five years old, five feet ten or eleven inches high. The above reward will be given to any person who will deliver him to the Subscriber. Masters of vessels are forewarned from employing or carrying him away. Wilmington, Jan. 22. Thomas Robeson

In the United States, as in Jamaica, Brazil, Cuba, and other slave-owning societies, slaves who fled from farms and plantations formed Maroon societies. These runaway communities provided a sanctuary for thousands of slaves. They could be found deep in the woods, in the mountains, and in the swamps throughout the southern part of the United States. Some slaves lived in these communities for weeks, months, and even years. Slaves used Maroon societies as a launching pad to take livestock, chickens, and vegetables from neighboring farms and plantations. The Great Dismal Swamp—known as the site of the largest Maroon society in North America—was located in southeastern Virginia and northeastern North Carolina. Before its drainage in the 1780s and 1790s, the swamp covered 2,200 square miles, encompassing Norfolk and Nansemond counties in Virginia, and Currituck, Camden, Pasquotank, and Gates counties in North Carolina. The Great Dismal Swamp provided refuge for thousands of runaway slaves for more than two hundred years.

Whites in Virginia and North Carolina were aware of the black presence and how dangerous it was to venture near or into the Great Dismal Swamp. The swamp was nearly impenetrable, and slave catchers in Virginia and North Carolina received substantially higher rewards when they returned runaways from the Great Dismal Swamp. A recollection of a contemporary of the era indicated that if a runaway slave made it to the swamp, "unless he was betrayed, it would be a matter of impossibility to catch him" (Arnold, p. 6). Writing in 1817, Samuel H. Perkins, a Yale College graduate hired to tutor the children of a prominent citizen in Hyde County, North Carolina, wrote that: "Traveling here without pistols is considered very dangerous owing to the great number of runaway Negroes. They conceal themselves in the woods & swamps by day and frequently plunder by night." Perkins further exclaimed that the Dismal Swamp was "inhabited almost exclusively by run away Negroes, bears, wild cats & wild cattle" (McLean, p. 56). Stories of the Great Dismal Swamp encouraged the poet Henry Wadsworth Longfellow to pen a poem titled "The Slave in the Dismal Swamp" (1842). Harriet Beecher Stowe, author of *Uncle Tom's Cabin* (1851–1852), wrote a novel about the swamp titled *Dred: A Tale of the Great Dismal Swamp* (1856).

The driving forces behind slave flight were many. Overwhelmingly, the desire to find loved ones from whom slaves had been separated was a primary motive for running away. Husbands and wives were separated from their children and other loved ones through the domestic slave trade that lasted through the Civil War. In their private correspondence and advertisements for fugitives, slave owners revealed where they believed slaves were headed. In many cases, fugitives were destined for other farms and plantations in the state where they lived. Slaves would run away from their new owner back to the area where they had lived and raised families. In some cases, slaves risked their lives to find family members in other states. During the 1820s and 1830s, slave owners moved to the virgin soils of Mississippi, Alabama, Louisiana, and Texas, often

Map depicting the locations of revolts and fugitive slave communities in the Americas and the Caribbean, nineteenth century. *With the abolition of slavery in Brazil in 1888, the institution of slavery was formally prohibited throughout the western hemisphere. Nevertheless, many maroon communities in isolated, inaccessible areas continued to exist into the twentieth century.* MAP BY XNR PRODUCTIONS. THE GALE GROUP.

taking their slaves with them. This flight by whites to the Deep South and Southwest resulted in the breaking up of many slave families. Thousands of slaves reportedly lurked about the farms and plantations of former owners to reunite with family members. This action by slaves is testimony to the desire to maintain an intact family unit, despite the constant strain that the family was under on a daily basis.

Slaves ran when they thought their owner would sell them to another owner, within or out of the state in which they lived. The fear of the unknown undoubtedly served as a catalyst for flight. Other slaves fled after being whipped or in fear of such punishment. And there were always slaves who simply sought total freedom from the environs of slavery. Heading north to a free state or to Canada, many of these slaves would obtain free papers and write passes for themselves and their loved ones. Slave flight to the North occurred from colonial times through the end of the Civil War. Though flight was an individual and occasionally a group effort, there is some evidence that an organized system of aid to runaways developed in the mid-1700s and continued through the end of slavery.

It was the advent of the Underground Railroad in the 1830s that compelled larger numbers of slaves to flee to freedom. It is estimated that as many as fifty thousand slaves ran away from southern plantations and farms between the late 1820s and 1865. The Underground Railroad was not a formal organization, but a loosely structured series of connections that helped slaves reach freedom in the North. Thousands of Americans, black and white, were involved in the intricate network of stations that dotted the South to North corridors to freedom. Both land and water routes were used by slaves traveling to freedom in the North. Individuals who assisted runaway slaves in the Underground Railroad were known as *agents*. Persons who physically aided slaves from station to station were known as *conductors*. Harriet Tubman, who assisted at least three hundred slaves to freedom was one of the best-known conductors of the Underground Railroad.

In 1827 the *Freedom's Journal* became the first abolitionist newspaper in the United States. It was founded in New York City by two black journalists, Samuel Cornish and John B. Russwurn. In 1830 free blacks in Philadelphia established the National Negro Convention Movement. William Lloyd Garrison founded *The Liberator* in 1831 and the American Anti-Slavery Society in 1833. Many readers of these publications and members of these organizations were involved in Underground Railroad activity through the end of the Civil War

Whether slaves ran away to find loved ones from whom they had been separated, to escape a flogging, out of fear of being sold, or to find permanent freedom in the North, flight by slaves is a testimony to the human quest to be free from the oppression of enslavement. Slaves usually fled alone, at night, to face wild animals, snakes, and weather so cold that it sometimes caused frostbite. Running away was not a frivolous act, but slaves were able to achieve some measure of physical and psychological freedom by "stealing themselves."

See also Runaway Slaves in Latin America and the Caribbean; Slave Codes; Slave Narratives; Slave Trade; Slavery

Bibliography

Aptheker, Herbert. "Maroons within the Present Limits of the United States." *Journal of Negro History* 24 (1939): 167–184.

Arnold, Robert. *The Dismal Swamp and Lake Drummond: Early Recollections, With Vivid Portrayals of Amusing Scenes.* Norfolk: Evening Telegram Print, 1888.

Blockson, Charles L. *The Underground Railroad: Dramatic Firsthand Accounts of Daring Escapes to Freedom.* New York: Prentice Hall, 1987.

Franklin, John Hope, and Loren Schweninger. *Runaway Slaves: Rebels on the Plantation.* New York: Oxford University Press, 1999.

Hodges, Graham Russell, and Alan Edward Brown, eds. *"Pretends to Be Free": Runaway Slave Advertisements from Colonial and Revolutionary New York and New Jersey.* New York: Garland, 1994.

Johnson, Michael P. "Runaway Slaves and the Slave Communities in South Carolina, 1799–1830." *William and Mary Quarterly* 38 (July 1981): 1–39.

McLean, Robert, ed. "A Yankee Tutor in the Old South" *North Carolina Historical Review* XLVII (January 1970).

Morgan, Philip. "Colonial South Carolina Runaways: Their Significance for Slave Culture." *Slavery and Abolition* 6 (December 1985): 57–78.

Parker, Freddie L. *Running for Freedom: Slave Runaways in North Carolina, 1775–1840.* New York: Garland, 1993.

Parker, Freddie L., ed. *Stealing a Little Freedom: Advertisements for Slave Runaways in North Carolina, 1791–1840.* New York: Garland, 1994.

Price, Richard, ed. *Maroon Societies: Rebel Slave Communities in the Americas*, 3d ed. Baltimore, Md.: Johns Hopkins University Press, 1996.

Prude, Jonathan. "To Look upon the 'Lower Sort': Runaway Ads and the Appearance of Unfree Laborers in America, 1750–1800." *Journal of American History* 78, no. 1 (1991): 124–159.

Still, William. *The Underground Railroad: A Record of Facts, Authentic Narratives, Letters, etc.* Philadelphia: Porter & Coates, 1872.

Windley, Latham A., comp. *Runaway Slave Advertisements: A Documentary History from the 1730s to 1790,* 4 vols. Westport, Conn.: Greenwood, 1983.

White, Deborah Gray. *Ar'n't I A Woman? Female Slaves in the Plantation South.* New York: W. W. Norton & Company, 1985.

FREDDIE PARKER (2005)

Run-D.M.C.

Flaunting untied Adidas sneakers, pricey Kangol hats, sweatsuits, and thick-rope gold chains, Run-D.M.C.'s ostentatious image and electric guitar-ridden sound captivated America's white youth culture in the 1980s. Joseph "Run" Simmons (b. November 14, 1964) and Darryl "DMC" McDaniels (b. May 31, 1964) began rapping together and convinced Jason "Jam Master Jay" Mizell (b.

January 21, 1965) to join them as their deejay. Thanks to the fusion of hard-core rock and rap in songs like "Rock Box," Run-D.M.C.'s self-titled debut album struck a chord with white male, suburban rock fans, and the album sold over 500,000 copies to merit gold status. Their punchy, simple rhyme style and sparse tracks also appealed to rap and rock audiences.

In 1985 the group starred in the classic hip-hop film *Krush Groove* and released the platinum-selling *King of Rock*. A year later, the group released *Raising Hell*, whose phenomenal success was propelled by the group's duet with the rock band Aerosmith on "Walk This Way" and MTV's heavy rotation of the crossover video. The album sold over three million copies. The year 1988 saw the release of *Tougher Than Leather*, and while the album was platinum-selling, it was a commercial disappointment.

Audiences were gravitating away from hip-hop toward the more violent gangsta rap genre by the dawn of the 1990s, and the disappointing sales for Run-D.M.C.'s album of the year, *Back From Hell*, indicated that trend. *Down with the King* found a hit single and went gold in 1993. However, the group largely disappeared from sight for the remainder of the decade, although Run-D.M.C. planned a comeback in 2001 with their album *Crown Royal*.

Crown Royal turned out to be Run-D.M.C.'s final release. The band retired in 2002.

See also Hip-Hop; Rap

Bibliography

George, Nelson. *Hip-Hop America*. New York: Viking, 1998.

McDaniels, Darryl, with Bruce Haring. *King of Rock: Respect, Responsibility, and My Life with Run-DMC*. New York: St. Martin's, 2001.

Rose, Tricia. *Black Noise: Rap Music and Black Culture in Contemporary America*. Hanover, N.H.: University Press of New England, 1994.

Simmons, Joseph "Reverend Run." *It's Like That: A Spiritual Memoir*. New York: St. Martin's, 2001.

RACHEL ZELLARS (2001)
Updated by publisher 2005

Russwurm, John Brown

October 1, 1799
June 9, 1851

Abolitionist and Liberian government official John Brown Russwurm was born in Jamaica of an unknown slave mother and a white American merchant father, John Russwurm. After eight years as a free black in Jamaica, young John Brown, as he was then known, was sent by his father to Quebec for formal schooling. His father brought the child to Portland, Maine, in 1812 when he married Susan Blanchard, who insisted that John Russwurm acknowledge his son's paternity by name. After the death of John Russwurm Sr. in 1815, John Brown Russwurm stayed with Blanchard until he entered Hebron Academy in Hebron, Maine. Later he attended and graduated (in 1826) from Bowdoin College, becoming one of the first black university graduates in the United States. In his graduation speech, Russwurm praised the Republic of Haiti and encouraged American blacks to consider settling there.

Russwurm moved to New York City in 1827 and helped found *Freedom's Journal*, the first black newspaper. The paper employed itinerant abolitionist blacks to publicize the antislavery cause and gain subscribers across the country and in Europe. *Freedom's Journal* demanded an end to southern slavery and equal rights for blacks in the North. After Samuel Cornish resigned as coeditor on September 14, 1827, to return to the Presbyterian ministry, Russwurm continued to publish the paper until February 1829. Despairing of any hope for an African-American future in the United States, he resigned to take a post in Liberia, scandalizing black New York. Generally condemned by his contemporaries, Russwurm in fact anticipated the Pan-Africanism of Alexander Crummell, Henry Highland Garnet, and Edward Blyden twenty years later.

Arriving in Monrovia, Liberia, in November 1829, Russwurm quickly gained prominence. He edited the *Liberia Herald* from 1830 to 1835, when he resigned in protest over the American Colonization Society's attempts to control the newspaper. At the same time he was superintendent of education for Monrovia. Despite his differences with the colonization society, Russwurm served as its agent, recruiting American blacks to migrate to Africa. He became fluent in several African languages.

In 1836 Russwurm became the first black governor of the Maryland sections of Liberia. He was an able administrator and successfully established relations with nearby African nations, encouraged arriving African Americans, and worked diplomatically with whites. His administration supported agriculture and trade, and in 1843 completed a census of the colony. Throughout the 1840s, Russwurm negotiated for absorption of the Maryland colony into Liberia. He died, a distinguished leader, on June 9, 1851, five years before that union became a reality. A monument was erected to his memory near his burial place in Harper, Cape Palmas, Liberia. Russwurm Island, off Cape Palmas, is named for him. His shift in favor of colonization offended many in 1829, but he is now remembered as a significant and successful Pan-Africanist.

See also Abolition; Cornish, Samuel E.; Pan-Africanism

Bibliography

Brewer, William M. "John Brown Russwurm." *Journal of Negro History* (1928): 413–422.

Shick, Tom W. *Behold the Promised Land: A History of Afro-American Settler Society in Nineteenth Century Liberia.* Baltimore: Johns Hopkins University Press, 1980, pp. 20–23.

Smith, James Wesley. *Sojourners in Search of Freedom: The Settlement of Liberia by Black Americans.* Lanham, Md.: University Press of America, 1987.

GRAHAM RUSSELL HODGES (1996)

Rustin, Bayard

March 17, 1910
August 24, 1987

Bayard Rustin was a civil rights leader, pacifist, political organizer, and controversial public figure. He was born in West Chester, Pennsylvania, in 1910, the youngest of nine children. He accumulated a colorful personal history, beginning with his youthful discovery that the woman he had assumed was his older sister was actually his mother. Reared by his mother and grandparents, who were local caterers, he grew up in the relatively privileged setting of a large mansion in town. Like the rest of his family, Rustin became a Quaker, maintaining an enduring commitment to personal pacifism as a way of life. Tall, thin, usually bushy-haired, and with an acquired West Indian accent, Rustin was noticed wherever he appeared.

He attended college at West Chester State College, then moved to Harlem during the 1930s, where he cultivated a bohemian lifestyle, attending classes at City College, singing with jazz groups and at night clubs, and gaining a reputation as a chef. His most notable activity, however, was aligning with the Communist Party through the Young Communist League, a decision based on the party's position on race issues. In 1941, when asked by the party to abandon his program to gain young black recruits in favor of a singular emphasis on the European war effort, Rustin quit the party.

His public personality and organizing skills subsequently brought him to the attention of A. Philip Randolph, who recruited him to help develop his plans for a massive March on Washington to secure equal access to defense jobs. The two men, despite brief skirmishes, remained lifelong friends. When President Franklin D. Roosevelt capitulated to Randolph's threat to hold the march—though Rustin believed that Randolph should not have canceled the march—Randolph arranged for Rustin to meet with A. J. Muste, the head of the radical pacifist Fellowship of Reconciliation (FOR). Muste came to regard the younger man almost as a son, naming him in 1941 as a field staff member for FOR, while Rustin also continued as a youth organizer for the March on Washington movement.

Now possessed of a reputation as an activist in the politics of race, Rustin was able to offer advice to the members of the FOR cell who became the nucleus for a new nonviolent action organization, the Congress of Racial Equality (CORE). Until 1955 Rustin remained a vital figure in the FOR/CORE alliance, holding a variety of offices within both groups, conducting weekend and summer institutes on nonviolent direct action in race relations, and serving as a conduit to the March on Washington movement for ideas and techniques on nonviolence. In 1947 he worked closely with Randolph again in a movement opposing universal military training and a segregated military, and he once again believed Randolph wrong in abandoning his strategies when met with a presidential executive order intended to correct the injustice. They argued briefly and publicly, then reconciled. Rustin is sometimes credited with persuading Randolph to accept nonviolence as a strategy.

Rustin's dual commitment to nonviolence and racial equality cost him dearly. In the summer of 1942, refusing to sit in the black section of a bus going from Louisville, Kentucky, to Nashville, Tennessee, he was beaten and arrested. The following year, unwilling to accept either the validity of the draft or conscientious-objector status—though his Quaker affiliation made that option possible—he was jailed as a draft resister and spent twenty-eight months in prison. Following his release, in 1947, he proposed that a racially integrated group of sixteen FOR/CORE activists undertake a bus trip through the Upper South to test a recent Supreme Court decision on interstate travel.

Termed the Journey of Reconciliation, the trip was essentially peaceful, although participants encountered violence outside Chapel Hill, North Carolina, where Rustin and three others were charged with violating the segregation laws. In a sham trial, Rustin and the others were convicted and sentenced to thirty days hard labor on a chain gang. His continuing visible role in racial policies brought him additional arrests and beatings.

After his release from the chain gang, Rustin traveled to India, where he was received by Mohandas K. Gandhi's sons. He had earlier blended strands of Gandhian nonviolence into his conception of pacifism. When the bus boycott developed in Montgomery, Alabama, Rustin appeared on the scene to offer support, advice, and information on nonviolence. Martin Luther King Jr., the leader of the boycott, accepted his help. But when word leaked of Rustin's former ties to the Communist Party and his 1953 conviction on a morals charge—allegedly for homosexual activity—he was rushed out of town. The gossip led to Rustin's resignation from both CORE and FOR in 1955, although he continued the pacifist struggle in the War Resisters League.

A 1952 visit to countries in North and West Africa convinced him of the need to assist Africans in their independence struggle. And he continued to be an active, though less visible, force in the effort to achieve racial justice, invited by King to assist in the creation of the Southern Christian Leadership Conference and to serve as a publicist for the group. Conservative members, however, eventually sought his ouster, and from 1960 until 1963 Rustin had little contact with King.

In 1963, as Randolph renewed his plans for a massive March on Washington, he proposed Rustin as the coordinator for the national event. Though initially opposed by some major civil rights leaders and under surveillance by the FBI, Rustin successfully managed the complex planning for the event and avoided violence. He was named executive director of the A. Philip Randolph Institute in 1964, while continuing to lead protests against militarism and segregation.

After the mid-1960s, Rustin's calls for blacks to work within the political system and his close ties with Jewish groups and labor unions made him the target of attacks by younger radicals, while his support for American investment and educational efforts in South Africa during the 1970s and 1980s outraged opponents of the Apartheid regime. Toward the end of his life, he also became increasingly open about his homosexuality and spoke out in favor of equal rights for gays and lesbians. Following his death, the Bayard Rustin High School for the Humanities in New York City was named in his honor.

See also Civil Rights Movement, U.S.; Congress of Racial Equality (CORE); King, Martin Luther, Jr.; Montgomery, Ala., Bus Boycott; Randolph, Asa Philip; Southern Christian Leadership Conference (SCLC)

Bibliography

Anderson, Jervis. *Bayard Rustin: The Troubles I've Seen.* New York: HarperCollins, 1996.

Levine, Daniel. *Bayard Rustin and the Civil Rights Movement.* New Brunswick, N.J.: Rutgers University Press, 2000.

Rustin, Bayard. *Down the Line: The Collected Writings of Bayard Rustin.* Chicago: Quadrangle Books, 1971.

Rustin, Bayard. "On the Economic Condition of Blacks." *Crisis* (March 1985): 24–29, 32.

CAROL V. R. GEORGE (1996)
Updated bibliography

Saar, Alison

1956

The visual artist Alison Saar was raised in Los Angeles during the 1960s and early 1970s. She attended Scripps College in Claremont, California, where she majored in studio art and art history. After graduating from Scripps in 1978, she earned an M.F.A. from Otis Art Institute in Los Angeles. Since her 1981 thesis show at Otis, Saar has been creating sculptures, installations, and other mixed-media works that have been widely shown, extensively collected, and justly praised. Her artwork is characterized by its range of influences and the use of recycled materials.

Saar's mother, the artist Betye Saar, has been a major influence. In particular, her mother's interests in mysticism, ritual, and the occult, as well as African and black diasporic artistic practices, have been central to the direction of Saar's art. In addition her father, Richard Saar, in his work as a conservator, brought her into contact with arts and artifacts from all over the globe, including Chinese frescoes, Egyptian mummies, and pre-Columbian and African art. In fact, it was an apprenticeship with her father that led to her sculpting—she learned to carve in order to restore art. At Scripps College, Alison Saar studied African, Haitian, and Afro-Cuban art with the art historian Samella Lewis, and she wrote her undergraduate thesis on African-American folk art. In addition, her interest in African influences on the art of the black diaspora parallels the work of the art historian Robert Farris Thompson, and she acknowledges his research as a source of inspiration.

Since the creation of her first mixed-media sculpture in 1981, Saar has consistently grappled visually with black diasporic history and culture. Her first sculpture, *Si j'étais blanc* (If I Were White), takes as its theme a Josephine Baker song about inequality. This carved figurative sculpture depicts a young black boy seated in a bright red chair. Suggesting the horror of Baker's lament, the artist portrays the boy with an open chest filled with shards of glass. Drawing from black diasporic practices, this filled cavity evokes figurative Kongo *minkisi* (sing. *nkisi*), traditional sacred objects from the Congo-Angola region used to effect change. Similarly, the boy's legs are made of cement and embedded with fragments of blue and white tile. Glass and tile have both been found at Kongo-inspired gravesites and yards in the United States, and both materials are also "found objects," typical of the materials used by the black folk artists Saar admires.

While conducting research for her undergraduate thesis, Saar came to admire the way informally trained art-

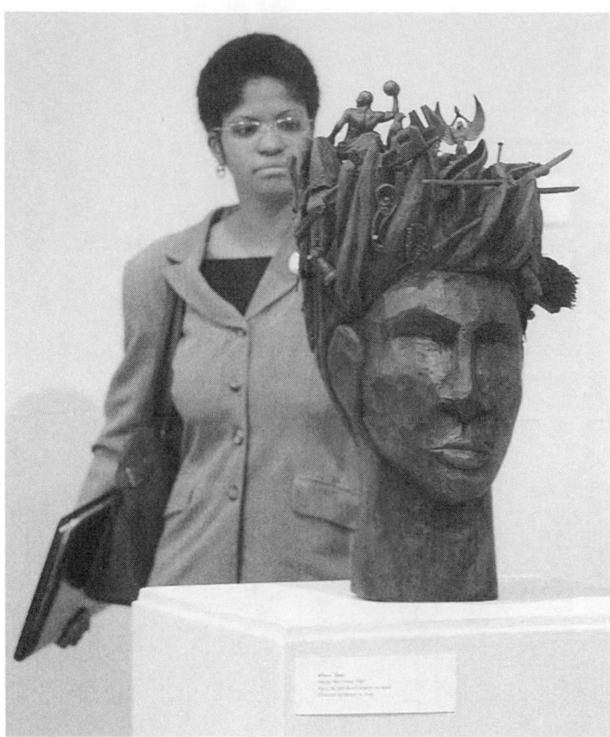

***A visitor at the Chicago Cultural Center examines Alison Saar's sculpture* Nappy Red Head.** *Saar's piece features among other things a fish, flower, locomotive, scrub brush, angel, pocket knife, butterfly, skull and crossbones, comb, wheel, plane, key, bus, football player, and alligator, all nestled in the wild hair.* TIM BOYLE/GETTY IMAGES

ists often work with abandoned materials. This admiration is evident in her art. Working with found materials such as old floor beams, pressed ceiling tin, rusty nails, iron skillets, linoleum sheeting, and broken glass, Saar recycles and reuses discarded objects for their evocative power and energy. By using previously used objects to explore vital themes of ritual, myth, magic, mystery, and healing, Alison Saar creates artwork powerfully infused with themes of the black diaspora.

Saar has received numerous awards, including grants from the National Endowment for the Arts and the Guggenheim Foundation. Her work has also been collected by major art museums, including The Metropolitan Museum of Art, The Studio Museum in Harlem, The Whitney Museum of American Art, The Walker Art Center, and The High Museum in Atlanta, Georgia.

See also Art in the United States, Contemporary; Painting and Sculpture

Bibliography

Collins, Lisa Gail. *The Art of History: African American Women Artists Engage the Past.* New Brunswick, NJ: Rutgers University Press, 2002.

Shepherd, Elizabeth, ed. *Secrets, Dialogues, Revelations: the Art of Betye and Alison Saar.* Los Angeles: Wight Art Gallery, University of California, 1990.

LISA GAIL COLLINS (2005)

Saar, Betye Irene

July 30, 1926

The artist Betye Brown (later Saar) was born in Los Angeles and moved to Pasadena, California, at age six, following the death of her father. While her mother worked as a seamstress and receptionist to support her family, Brown attended public school in Pasadena and then enrolled at Pasadena City College. She earned a B.A. in design from the University of California at Los Angeles in 1949 and married the artist Richard Saar (pronounced "Say-er") shortly thereafter.

During the early part of her career, Saar worked as a costume designer in theater and film in Los Angeles. In the late 1950s and early 1960s, she resumed formal art training at California State University in Long Beach, at the University of Southern California, and at California State University in Northridge. In graduate school, Saar mastered the techniques of graphics, printmaking, and design, but after seeing a Joseph Cornell exhibition at the Pasadena Art Museum in 1967 she turned to what would become her signature work: three-dimensional assemblage boxes. Saar's encounter with Cornell's surrealist boxes led her away from her early, two-dimensional work in prints to her first landmark piece, "Black Girl's Window" (mixed media, 1969). Here Saar used Cornell-inspired elements like a segmented window and a surrealist combination of objects to explore issues of personal identity. The piece presents a black girl, possibly Saar, pressing her face and hands against a glass pane, surrounded by images of the occult.

During the late 1960s and 1970s, Saar's boxes reflected her political engagement with the civil rights movement by satirizing persistent derogatory images of African Americans. In "The Liberation of Aunt Jemima" (1972), Saar appropriated the racist stereotype of Aunt Jemima by transforming her from a passive black female into a militant revolutionary. Her later work took on a more personal, autobiographical dimension, exploring her own mixed heritage—she is of Native American, Irish, and African descent—and her spiritual beliefs. The death of her Aunt Hattie in particular pushed her work inward and inspired such nostalgic collages as "Keep for Old Memoirs" (1976), made from old family photographs and personal remnants such as gloves and handkerchiefs.

In 1974 Saar traveled to Haiti and Mexico on a National Endowment for the Arts grant, then to Nigeria for the second World Black and African Festival of Arts and Culture (1977). These trips, together with Saar's visits to the Egyptian, Oceanic, and African collections at the Field Museum of Natural History in Chicago, resulted in a series of altarpieces (1975–1977) combining personal emblems with totems from African, Caribbean, and Asian cultures. "Dambella" (1975) contains obvious references to Haitian Vodou, with its ritualistic animal parts and snakeskin, whereas "Spiritcatcher" (1976–1977), with its spiral structure and found objects, recalls Simon Rodia's Watts Towers in Los Angeles, which Saar had visited as a child.

In the 1980s and 1990s, Saar continued to create assemblage boxes and collages while also experimenting with room-sized installations. As always, she worked in materials culled and recycled from foreign markets, thrift shops, or her own personal history; she intended these "found treasures" to stir emotion and personal or collective memories in the viewer. Her "Mojotech" installation at the Massachusetts Institute of Technology (1988) explored the relationship between technology and magic, creating hybrid altars out of high-tech elements like computer-system circuit boards as well as traditional religious objects.

Saar's work has been shown at numerous solo exhibitions, including the Studio Museum in Harlem in New York (1980); the Museum of Contemporary Art, Los Angeles (1984); and the Pennsylvania Academy of the Arts, Philadelphia (1987). Since 1983, she has been awarded several commissions to create installations for public sites in Los Angeles, New Jersey, and Miami. Saar won a John Simon Guggenheim Memorial Foundation Award in 1991, and she was one of the two artists chosen to represent the United States in the 1994 São Paulo Biennial in Brazil.

See also Art in the United States, Contemporary

Bibliography

Albright-Knox Art Gallery. *The Appropriate Object.* Buffalo, N.Y.: Albright-Knox Art Gallery, 1989.

Carpenter, Jane H., with Betye Saar. *Betye Saar.* San Francisco: Pomegranate, 2003.

Dallow, Jessica. "Reclaiming Histories: Betye and Alison Saar, Feminism, and the Representation of Black Womanhood." *Feminist Studies* 30, no. 1 (Spring 2004): 74.

Studio Museum in Harlem. *Rituals: Betye Saar.* New York: Studio Museum in Harlem, 1980.

TAMARA L. FELTON (1996)
Updated bibliography

Saddler, Joseph

See Grandmaster Flash (Saddler, Joseph)

Salem, Peter

c. 1750
August 16, 1816

American Revolutionary War soldier Peter Salem was born a slave in Framingham, Massachusetts. He was originally owned by New England historian Jeremy Belknap and took his last name from Belknap's previous residence, Salem, Massachusetts. Salem was subsequently sold to Maj. Lawson Buckminster.

At the outbreak of the War for Independence, Salem's owners temporarily released him so that he could serve with the Continental army. He enlisted in Cpt. Thomas Drury's company in Col. John Nixon's Fifth Massachusetts Regiment and served at the Battle of Bunker Hill on June 17, 1775. A number of participants in the battle identified Salem as the soldier who fired the shot that killed British major John Pitcairn at Bunker Hill. In 1787 Belknap recorded in his diary that a person present at the battle informed him that "A negro man . . . took aim at Major Pitcairn, as he was rallying the dispersed British troops and shot him thro' the head." Samuel Swett, whose chronicle of the battle was published in 1818, specifically identifies Salem as Pitcairn's killer: "Among the foremost of the leaders was the gallant Maj. Pitcairn, who exultingly cried 'the day is ours,' when Salem, a black soldier, and a number of others, shot him through and he fell." Since no conclusive evidence exists and other black soldiers were present at the battle, historians differ on whether these accounts are accurate and actually refer to Salem, but they generally agree that he was at least present at the Battle of Bunker Hill.

Shortly after the battle Salem was nearly discharged from the army because of Gen. George Washington's decree that no more slaves were to be recruited for the militia. But Salem's owners granted him full freedom so that he could continue fighting, and he served at Saratoga and Stony Point.

The legend of Salem's exploits at Bunker Hill was given popular currency by John Trumbull's 1786 painting *The Battle of Bunker's Hill,* which depicts a black soldier, commonly thought to be Salem, standing with musket in hand while Pitcairn lies mortally wounded.

After the war Salem built a cabin in Leicester, Massachusetts, and wove cane for a living. He died in a poorhouse in Framingham in 1816. As a soldier of the American Revolution, Salem was paid respects at his death by the citizens of Framingham. They erected a monument to his memory, with the inscription: "Peter Salem / A Soldier of the Revolution / Concord / Bunker Hill / Saratoga / Died, August 16th, 1816."

A U.S. postage stamp bearing a reproduction of Trumbull's painting was issued in 1968.

See also Free Blacks, 1619–1860; Military Experience, African-American

Bibliography

Kaplan, Sidney. *The Black Presence in the Era of the American Revolution, 1770–1800.* Greenwich, Conn.: New York Graphic Society, 1973.

Quarles, Benjamin. *The Negro in the American Revolution.* Chapel Hill: University of North Carolina Press, 1961.

THADDEUS RUSSELL (1996)

SAMBA

The first known printed reference to *samba* music in Brazil dates to 1838. That reference, found in Pernambuco in northeastern Brazil, does not mention peoples of African descent. The next known reference, found in 1844 in nearby Bahia, describes black slaves playing *samba,* but does not indicate whether those slaves were born in Africa or Brazil.

In the seventeenth century, the Portuguese used the word *calundú* to describe dances and ceremonies that preceded spirit possession and divination. Beginning at the end of the eighteenth century in Brazil and Portugal, the term *lundu* referred to a dance performed by free men and women of mixed racial background. Until the middle of the nineteenth century, Brazilian and Portuguese sources also used the word *batuque* to refer to celebrations and entertainment among slaves.

Descriptions of *batuques* and *lundus* coincide on many points: dancers, singers, and observers are arranged in circles; observers participate through palm clapping and singing refrains; couples dance in the middle of a larger circle; and there is a frequent use of *umbigada,* the movement through which dancers select partners by touching navels. *Lundus* were also frequently described as including stringed instruments, and they served as inspiration for a genre of *cançonetas,* or ditties, sold as sheet music for piano and voice beginning in the middle of the nineteenth century. In 1944 the author and musical scholar Mário de Andrade declared that *lundu* was the first Afro-Brazilian cultural form accepted in elite circles, even if ridicule often accompanied that acceptance.

The word *samba* began to appear regularly in newspapers and literature during the second half of the nineteenth century. The word's roots are most likely Bantu, but more specific details are difficult to trace. The most accepted version suggests that the word comes from the Quimbundo (Angola) word *semba,* which probably included the pelvic thrusts of *umbigada.* Other scholars also cite Amerindian origins.

Current knowledge of post-1860s *samba* is based primarily on research and sources from Bahia and Pernambuco, with Bahia having received the most attention from scholars. Late nineteenth-century references describe a *samba* quite similar to the one performed today in the Recôncavo (the hinterland beyond the bay around Salvador, Bahia). Recôncavo *samba* relies heavily on small, rapid steps (the famous *miudinho*), is accompanied by *violas* (guitarlike instruments with varying numbers of strings) and *pandeiros* (similar to tambourines), and includes a vocal passage known as *chula.*

Rio de Janeiro

The first references to *samba* in Rio de Janeiro appear at the end of the nineteenth century. They often mention black immigrants from Bahia, who migrated around the time of abolition, in 1888. As Roberto Moura (1995) and others have shown, a number of those immigrants established themselves in the area surrounding Rio de Janeiro's ports, where they built community networks, developed economic support systems, and maintained traditional religious and cultural practices, including *samba.* Some of the principal figures of early *carioca samba* (*carioca* refers to people or things from Rio de Janeiro) frequented the port scene. Among them were Donga (Ernesto dos Santos, 1889–1974), João da Baiana (João Machado Guedes, 1887–1974), Sinhô (José Barbosa de Silva, 1888–1930), and Pixinguinha (Alfredo Viana Filho, 1897–1973). The first two were sons of immigrants from Bahia; the last two were sons of *cariocas*.

The mothers of Donga and João da Baiana—Tia Amélia and Tia Perciliana de Santo Amaro, respectively—were initiates of João Alabá's Afro-Brazilian religious (Candomblé) community. Alabá's Nagô (Yoruba) community was one of the most important in early twentieth-century Rio de Janeiro. Ciata, one of the most famous *tias* (female Afro-Brazilian community and spiritual leaders, often from Bahia), hosted gatherings that often combined musical improvisation and African-influenced worship. An important biography of Pixinguinha by Sérgio Cabral does not mention the Afro-Brazilian religion Candomblé, but, according to Mário de Andrade, the famous musician frequented spiritual gatherings and developed substantial knowledge about Candomblé. It was most likely Pixinguinha who, in 1926, provided Andrade with the information about *macumba* (a generic term used to refer to numerous African-derived religious practices and music forms) that would form the basis of the chapter "Macumba" in Andrade's modernist masterpiece, *Macunaíma* (1928). It is also possible that the scar-faced Pixinguinha inspired a character in the same chapter, a drum player described by Andrade as the "the pock-marked son of Ogum [the Afro-Brazilian god of War]" (p. 57).

Pixinguinha was not the only important musician with links to Afro-Brazilian religions. For example, Sinhô was linked to the spiritual leader Henrique Assumano Mina do Brasil, also known as the Prince of Alufás (an *alufá* is an Islamic-Brazilian cleric). According to one researcher, "the first performance of [Sinhô's] music took place in Assumano's residence. Sinhô believed that his own popularity was due to Assumano's spiritual influence" (cited in Alencar, 1981, p. 42). References to Afro-Brazilian religion are also found in the titles and genres of numerous early twentieth-century compositions, including Sinhô's "Ai Ué Dendê," "Bofé Pamim Dge," "Ojaré," and "Oju Burucu," as well as Pixinguinha's "Que querê" (with Donga and João da Baiana, 1932); "Xou, curinga" (with João da Baiana, 1932); "Yaô africano" (with Gastão Viana, 1938); "Uma festa de Nanã" (with Gastão Viana, 1941); and "Benguelê" (with Gastão Viana, 1946); and Donga's "Sai, Exu" (with Pixinguinha's brother, Otávio "China" Viana); and "Macumba de Iansã" and "Macumba de Oxóssi" (with Zé Espinguela).

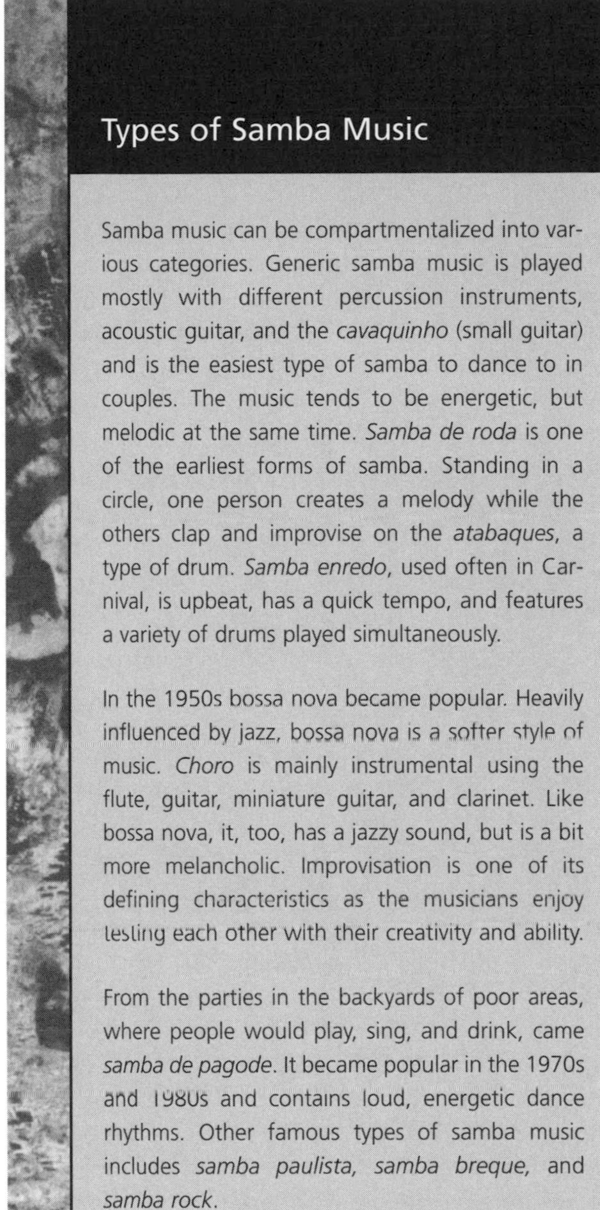

Types of Samba Music

Samba music can be compartmentalized into various categories. Generic samba music is played mostly with different percussion instruments, acoustic guitar, and the *cavaquinho* (small guitar) and is the easiest type of samba to dance to in couples. The music tends to be energetic, but melodic at the same time. *Samba de roda* is one of the earliest forms of samba. Standing in a circle, one person creates a melody while the others clap and improvise on the *atabaques*, a type of drum. *Samba enredo*, used often in Carnival, is upbeat, has a quick tempo, and features a variety of drums played simultaneously.

In the 1950s bossa nova became popular. Heavily influenced by jazz, bossa nova is a softer style of music. *Choro* is mainly instrumental using the flute, guitar, miniature guitar, and clarinet. Like bossa nova, it, too, has a jazzy sound, but is a bit more melancholic. Improvisation is one of its defining characteristics as the musicians enjoy testing each other with their creativity and ability.

From the parties in the backyards of poor areas, where people would play, sing, and drink, came *samba de pagode*. It became popular in the 1970s and 1980s and contains loud, energetic dance rhythms. Other famous types of samba music includes *samba paulista, samba breque*, and *samba rock*.

"Pelo Telefone" and the Oito Batutas

The first song labeled as a *samba* to achieve success in Rio de Janeiro was "Pelo telefone," released during Carnival in 1917 by Donga and Mauro de Almeida (1882–1956). (The song is often called the "first recorded *samba*," even though, since the 1960s, researchers have noted the existence of *samba* recordings from the early 1910s.) In his meticulous study of "Pelo telefone," Flávio Silva shows that the song's release was strategically orchestrated by Donga, who sought to transform into "popular music" what had up until that point belonged to a select group, organized by the Bahian *tias* around Praça Onze (like the port area, a geographical landmark of early *samba*). Donga incorporated traditional motifs previously played only independently and asked Almeida (a white journalist) to write the lyrics. He then registered the work at the Nation-

A group of samba *dancers perform during Carnival in Rio de Janeiro.* © ABRIL/CORBIS

al Library (citing himself and Almeida as authors), had the song arranged for a band (at the time, the principal means for publicizing music), and then recorded the song. In some respects, Donga's efforts resulted in a resounding success, turning *samba* into the music of the moment and paving the way for the genre's future consecration. But even this success failed to alter Donga's economic situation. His claims of authorship of "Pelo telefone" were contested by Tia Ciata and other important figures of Afro-Brazilian music in Rio, such as Sinhô and Hilário Jovino. In 1933 the writer Vagalume declared that "Pelo telefone" was the creation of musicians at Tia Ciata's gatherings, and had simply been adapted and registered by Donga and Mauro de Almeida.

It is difficult to gauge whether the population of Rio de Janeiro thought of "Pelo telefone" as an Afro-Brazilian musical production. Aside from Donga's presumed authorship and the fact that the song was called a *samba*, there is little about the song that is specifically African-Brazilian. Despite the official *samba* label, the song was often referred to as either a *tango* or a *modinha*. In fact, there were no racist reactions against "Pelo telefone," as there would be a short time later against the musical group Os Oito Batutas, another enterprise organized largely by Donga.

With four whites and four blacks—Donga, Pixinguinha, Pixinguinha's brother China (Otávio Viana, 1890–1927), and Nélson Alves (1895–1960)—the Oito Batutas were created in 1919 and began playing in the lobby at the Palais cinema in downtown Rio de Janeiro. The Palais was frequented by rich *cariocas* with cosmopolitan pretensions (the French-named theater showed mainly North American films). Despite playing music that Europhile elites often dismissed as "national" or "rural" and wearing clothes associated with poor folk from Brazil's interior, the Batutas still appealed to would-be cosmopolitans. However, not all the elites approved of the Batuta's appearance, and various journalists publicly criticized the group, often including racist attacks in their criticism. Negative reactions were exacerbated in 1922 when the millionaire Arnaldo Guinle financed a trip to Paris for the Batutas, even though the group's success in Parisian cafés and clubs delighted numerous Brazilians, including those elites who had followed the band since its days at the Palais. Interestingly, the group's repertoire did not highlight *samba*, although the genre was represented. Further, there exists no record that the group played "Pelo telefone" a single time.

While the Oito Batutas were becoming famous in Brazil and abroad, the career of Sinhô— the most prolific and original individual composer of the 1920s—took off. Sinhô enjoyed success in the streets, especially during Carnival and the *Festa da Penha*, the then widely-popular religious celebration held on Sundays in October. His success also came through the sale of sheet music for voice and piano and in the *teatro da revista*, the musical theater, which enjoyed its apogee during the 1920s. (The radio would not become the most important vehicle for music until the 1930s.) With compositions like "Jura!," "Gosto que me enrosco," and "A favela vai abaixo," Sinhô consolidated the principal characteristics of *samba*'s first period of popularity more than any other artist.

The 1930s

The death of Sinhô in 1930, and the success of musicians from the Estácio de Sá neighborhood, such as Bide (Alcebíades Barcellos, 1902–1975), Brancura (Sílvio Fernandes, 1908–1935), Nílton Bastos (1899–1931), and above all Ismael Silva (1905–1978), signaled important transformations in Rio de Janeiro *samba*. These composers belonged to the Carnival group Deixa Falar, which, according to most accounts, was the first group to parade during Carnival while singing *sambas* and using instruments that would become the basis for modern *samba* school drum-lines: the *surdo* (bass drum played with a felt-headed wooden stick with Iberian origins); *tamborim* (also Iberian, a small tambourine with no jingles, played with a single or double stick); and *cuíca* (friction drum, originally from sub-Saharan Africa).

It was also at the beginning of the 1930s that these instruments began to find their way into the recording studios. A historic landmark often cited is the *samba* "Na Pavuna," a Carnival success from 1930 recorded by the Bando de Tangarás (a group of middle-class white musicians) with the accompaniment of the rhythmists Canuto and Puruca (*ritmistas,* as those who played the *surdo, cuíca,* and *tamborim* came to be known), who were both black and lived in the *morro* (hillside shantytown) Salgueiro.

From a rhythmic perspective, the Estácio group's principal contribution was the repeated use of an accompaniment pattern two times longer than those previously used in recordings and sheet music for *carioca samba.* That new pattern resembled more clearly the rhythmic characteristics of African music noted by ethnomusicologists such as Nketia, A. M. Jones, G. Kubik, and S. Arom than did the *samba* forms that preceded it.

The Estácio composers also introduced *malandragem* (guile and street-hustling associated with zoot-suited *malandros*) into *samba* lyrics, which became a staple of popular culture in Rio de Janeiro during the first half of the 1930s. The *malandro* of the 1930s notoriously avoided work and familial obligations and survived through shady means, like gambling and pimping. An activity often associated with *malandragem* was the *pernada* or *batucada,* a type of *capoeira* practiced to *samba* rhythms, in which one fighter attempts to knock down an opponent with a single strike. The most feared and respected *malandros*—known as *bambas*—reportedly dressed in white suits as a sign of confidence that they would never fall.

Malandragem became an important theme in Brazilian social thought, consecrated in the literary critic Antonio Candido's influential essay "Dialectic of Malandroism" (1995) and anthropologist Roberto DaMatta's equally famous text, *Carnivals, Rogues, and Heroes* (1991). Neither work explicitly discusses 1930s *malandros* from Rio, instead focusing on earlier figures, like Pedro Malasartes (a rural character in popular stories, discussed by DaMatta), and Leonardo, from the classic nineteenth-century novel *Memórias de um Sargento de Milícias.*

Samba Schools and the Post-1930s Era

The 1930s were also marked by an association between *samba* and Rio's *morros*—then, as now, inhabited predominantly by the poorest groups, who were mostly black. Many observers saw *samba* as the "melodious soul of the *morro*" and the *morro* as the *malandro*'s domain. By extension, *samba* was often seen as the *malandro*'s melody. *Samba* created by the Deixa Falar group spread through the shantytowns, influencing composers such as Cartola (1908–1980) and Paulo da Portela (1901–1949), and Carnival groups, which came to be known as *samba* "schools" (e.g., *Estação Primeira* from the *morro* Mangueira, and *Acadêmicos* from Salgueiro). In 1933 the mayor's office of Rio de Janeiro designated financial support for the Carnival clubs for the first time. The following year, *samba* schools united to form the first umbrella organization to protect and defend the schools' interests.

Estácio samba also influenced professional composers not linked to the *samba* schools, including middle-class whites like Noel Rosa (1910–1937, perhaps the most celebrated *samba* composer of the twentieth century) and Ary Barroso (1903–1964, author of the classic "Aquarela do Brasil"), as well as black composers from humble origins, such as Ataulfo Alves (1909–1969) and Geraldo Pereira (1918–1955).

The process through which *samba* schools secured the dominant position that they now hold in Rio's famous Carnival celebration was a slow one. Only at the end of the 1950s did the parade come to be held on the thoroughfare Avenida Rio Branco, and it was not until 1962 that spectators had to purchase tickets to witness the festivities. The year 1968 saw the release of a record that included *sambas-enredo,* the songs played by each school during their turn in the Carnival parade. The initiative was repeated in following years, and the annual recording is now one of the perennial best sellers in Brazil's enormous music market. Construction of the Sambodrome (*Sambódromo*), a massive runway surrounded by concrete bleachers, began in 1983 and was first put to use for Carnival parades a year later.

The trajectory of Rio's *samba* schools has generated much controversy, both inside and outside the academy, about supposed "commercialization," "domestication," and "whitening." Critics of *samba* and Carnival transformations include Maria Isaura Pereira de Queiroz (1999), Nei Lopes (1981), and Alison Raphael (1980). These critics often point to the increased presence and decision-making power, especially after 1960, of middle-class and university-educated white outsiders within the schools. This includes *carnavalescos* (professional choreographers charged with conceptualizing and unifying the visual and theatric aspects of the school's parade) and *bicheiros* (illegal-numbers kings who sustained many schools economically, often through money laundering, in the process gaining social prestige as patrons of national culture). Other authors, such as Maria Laura Cavalcanti (1994), Hermano Vianna (1995), and Samuel Araújo (1992), have pointed to the fact that, since the schools' earliest existence, their representatives appear to have adopted growth strategies based in social, political, and ethnic alliances. These scholars also argue that independent of any judgment about those strategies, a large percentage of Rio's African-derived population continues to see the schools as an expression of their identity and of their *joie de vivre.*

The most important *samba* composers from the 1960s and 1970s include Paulinho da Viola (b. 1942), associated with the *samba* school Portela, and Martinho da Vila (b. 1938), part of Unidos de Vila Isabel. Paulinho da Viola is perhaps the most respected living *samba* musician, known for honoring traditional styles and predecessors, such as Cartola and Nelson Cavaquinho (1910–1986). Martinho da Vila reinvigorated the increasingly commercial language of 1970s *samba,* producing hits like "Casa de bamba" and "Canta, canta minha gente."

The 1980s witnessed the success of underutilized *samba* styles like *partido alto* (improvisation-based group song organized around short refrains) and *pagode* (a variety of styles played most often in informal settings, such as familial gatherings). Both genres were popularized through groups like Fundo de Quintal, composers like Jovelina Pérola Negra (1944–1998), and performers like Beth Carvalho (b. 1946). *Pagode* was also used as a label for 1990s commercial *samba* groups famous for their romantic style and timbre and vocal elements typical of North American soul music. At the turn of the millennium, the most popular composer and performer was Zeca Pagodinho, a holdover from the days of Fundo de Quintal but also versed in more traditional *samba* forms.

It is also worth mentioning the development in Bahia during the 1980s of *samba-reggae,* a genre closely related to Afro-Brazilian Carnival groups from Salvador. In this context, the vindication and valorization of black identity and affiliation with Africa, through song lyrics and composers' political discourse, is more evident than ever was the case in *carioca samba.* Samba from Rio de Janeiro was always associated ideologically with a more inclusive and nationalist posture, leaving room, for example, for the famous praise of racial mixing made by anthropologists like Gilberto Freyre (Vianna, 1995) and Darcy Ribeiro, who was responsible for pushing through legislation for construction of the Sambodrome.

See also Carnival in Brazil and the Caribbean; Music in Latin America

Bibliography

Alencar, Edigar de. *Nosso Sinhô do samba.* Rio de Janeiro, Brazil: Funarte, 1981.

Andrade, Mário de. *Macunaíma: O herói sem nenhum caráter* (1928). Paris: ALLCA, Brasília, Brazil: CNPq, 1998.

Andrade, Mário de. "Cândido Inácio da Silva e o lundu." In *Revista Brasileira de Música,* X. Rio de Janeiro, Brazil: Instituto Nacional de Música da Universidade do Rio de Janeiro, 1944.

Araújo, Samuel. "Acoustic Labor in the Timing of Everyday Life: A Critical Contribution to the History of Samba in Rio de Janeiro." Ph.D. diss., University of Illinois–Urbana, 1992.

Barbosa, Orestes. *Samba: Sua história, seus poetas, seus músicos, e seus cantores* (1933). Rio de Janeiro, Brazil: Funarte, 1978.

Cabral, Sérgio. *Pixinguinha: Vida e obra.* Rio de Janeiro, Brazil: Edição Funarte, 1978; 2d ed., Lumiar, 1997.

Candido, Antonio. "Dialectic of Malandroism." In *On Literature and Society,* edited and translated by Howard S. Becker. Princeton, N.J.: Princeton University Press, 1995.

Cavalcanti, Maria Laura Viveiros de Castro. *Carnaval carioca: Dos bastidores ao desfile.* Rio de Janeiro, Brazil: UFRJ, 1994.

DaMatta, Roberto. *Carnivals, Rogues, and Heroes: An Interpretation of the Brazilian Dilemma.* Translated by John Drury. Notre Dame, Ind.: University of Notre Dame Press. 1991.

Donga, Pixinguinha, and João da Baiana. *As vozes desassombradas do museu.* Rio de Janeiro, Brazil: MIS, 1970.

Lopes, Nei. *O samba na realidade.* Rio de Janeiro, Brazil: Codecri, 1981.

Lopes, Nei. *O Negro no Rio de Janeiro e sua tradição musical.* Rio de Janeiro, Brazil: Pallas, 1992.

Marcondes, Marco Antônio, ed. *Enciclopédia da música brasileira: Erudita, Folclórica, popular.* São Paulo, Brazil: Art, 1977.

Moura, Roberto. *Tia Ciata e a pequena África no Rio de Janeiro* (1983). Rio de Janeiro, Brazil: Secretaria de Cultura, 1995.

Mukuna, Kazadi Wa. *Contribuição Bantu na música popular brasileira* (1978). São Paulo, Brazil: Terceira Margem, 2000.

Raphael, Alison. "Samba and Social Control: Popular Culture and Racial Democracy in Rio de Janeiro." Ph.D. diss., Columbia University, New York, 1980.

Sandroni, Carlos. *Feitiço decente: Transformações do samba no Rio de Janeiro, 1917–1933.* Rio de Janeiro, Brazil: UFRJ/Zahar, 2001.

Silva, Flávio. *Origines de la samba urbaine à Rio de Janeiro.* Paris: EPHE, 1975.

Siqueira, Batista. *Origem do termo "samba."* São Paulo, Brazil: UBDC, 1978.

Tinhorão, José Ramos. *Os sons dos negros no Brasil.* São Paulo, Brazil: Art, 1988.

Vagalume (Francisco Guimarães). *Na roda do samba* (1933). Rio de Janeiro, Brazil: Funarte, 1978.

Vianna, Hermano. *The Mystery of Samba: Popular Music and National Identity in Brazil,* translated by John Charles Chasteen. Chapel Hill: University of North Carolina Press. 1999.

Waddey, Ralph. "*Samba e Viola* and *Viola de Samba*." *Latin American Music Review* 1/2 (Fall/Winter 1980): 196–212; and 2/2 (Fall/Winter 1981): 252–279.

CARLOS SANDRONI (2005)

Sanchez, Sonia

September 19, 1934

The poet Sonia Sanchez was born Wilsonia Benita Driver, the daughter of Wilson L. and Lena Jones Driver, in Birmingham, Alabama. During her childhood in the South and in Harlem, she was outraged by the way American society systematically mistreated black people. This sense of racial injustice transformed her from a shy, stuttering girl into one of the most vocal writer-activists in contemporary literature. In the early 1960s she began publishing poems under her married name, Sonia Sanchez, which she continued to use professionally after she and her husband divorced. Although best known for her verse, which urges black unity and action and reflects the cadences of African-American speech and music, she is also an accomplished dramatist, essayist, and editor, as well as an enduring proponent of black studies.

Sanchez studied at Hunter College in New York (B.A., 1955) and at New York University and has taught at many institutions, including Rutgers, the University of Pittsburgh, and Amherst College. She worked during the civil rights movement as a supporter of the Congress of Racial Equality, but in 1972 she joined the Nation of Islam because she thought that it was doing more to instill cultural pride and morality in young people. In a 1983 interview, Sanchez said that her political and cultural affiliations, harassment by the FBI, and her insistence that black writers be included in curricula explained why she did not gain a permanent academic position until 1978, when she became a professor at Temple University. Sanchez later held the chair of the English department and directed the women's studies program at Temple.

In *Homecoming* (1969), her first collection of poetry, Sanchez addressed racial oppression using angry voices derived from street talk. She soon became sought after for her passionate, confrontational readings. Although her use of profanity was shocking to some, she has never regretted her artistic approach: "There is vulgar stuff out there. One has got to talk about it in order for it not to be."

While the plight of African Americans in a white society is her major subject, Sanchez has also critiqued struggles within the black community. *Sister Son/ji*, a play produced off-Broadway in 1972, is about a militant young woman fighting the sexism of the black revolutionary movement. Sanchez herself left the Nation of Islam in 1975 because the organization would not change the subservient role it assigned to women.

Books by Sanchez include poetry collections, such as *We a BaddDDD People* (1970), *A Blues Book for Blue Black Magical Women* (1973), *homegirls & handgrenades* (1984), *Like the Singing Coming Off the Drums: Love Poems* (1998), and *Shake Loose My Skin: New and Selected Poems* (1999); juvenile fiction, including *A Sound Investment and Other Stories* (1979); plays, such as *Uh, Huh: But How Do It Free Us?* (1975), and *Malcolm Man/Don't Live Here No More* (1979); as well as numerous contributions to journals, recordings, and anthologies as a poet, essayist, and editor. *Does Your House Have Lions?* chronicles her brother's struggle with AIDS and was nominated for both the 1997 NAACP Image Award and the National Book Critics Circle Award. *Wounded in the House of a Friend* (1995) confronts topics such as rape and drug abuse in a mixture of poetry and prose.

Sanchez has received major awards from PEN (1969), the National Institute of Arts and Letters (1970), and the National Endowment for the Arts (1978–1979). Other honors include the Lucretia Mott Award (1984), the Smith College Tribute to Black Women Award (1982), doctorates from Wilberforce University (1972) and Temple University (1998), and the American Book Award from the Before Columbus Foundation (1985).

See also Nation of Islam; Poetry, U.S.

Bibliography

Barksdale, Richard, and Keneth Kinnamon, eds. *Black Writers of America: A Comprehensive Anthology.* New York: Macmillan, 1972.

Joyce, Joyce Ann. *Ijala: Sonia Sanchez and the African Poetic Tradition.* Chicago: Third World Press, 1996.

Kelly, Susan. "Discipline and Craft: An Interview with Sonia Sanchez." *African American Review* 34, no. 4 (winter 2000).

Salaam, Kalamu ya. "Sonia Sanchez." In *Dictionary of Literary Biography: Afro-American Poets Since 1955,* edited by Trudier Harris and Thadious M. Davis. Detroit, Mich.: Gale Research, 1985.

Tate, Claudia, ed. *Black Women Writers at Work.* New York: Continuum, 1983.

DEKKER DARE (1996)
Updated by author 2005

Sangster, Donald

October 26, 1911
April 11, 1967

Donald Burns Sangster, the second prime minister of independent Jamaica, was born in Mountainside, St. Elizabeth, Jamaica. He was educated at Munro College and was admitted to the Jamaican Bar in 1937 as a solicitor of the Supreme Court. He began his political career in 1933 when he was elected to the Parochial Board of St. Elizabeth, which functioned as the local governing council. He was elected vice chairman of the board in 1941 and chairman in 1949.

Sangster's foray into national politics began in 1944—a momentous year in Jamaican history, for it was the year of the first general elections under universal adult suffrage. The two major political parties, the Jamaica Labour Party (JLP) and the People's National Party (PNP), dominated this contest, which the JLP, under the leadership of Alexander Bustamante (1884–1997), won handily. Sangster, who ran as an independent candidate, was defeated.

This reversal was only a temporary setback, however. In 1949 Sangster joined the JLP and won the South St. Elizabeth seat, as the JLP scored another political victory at the polls. After this, Sangster's political fortunes grew—he was appointed minister of social welfare and labour, and he became deputy party leader. Sangster owed this success to Bustamante, the popular prime minister, labor leader, and party chief, who had handpicked him for these posts.

Because of Bustamante's legendary penchant for exercising unchallenged authority, it is arguable that he would have wanted a loyalist for these positions, someone who would not challenge his authority or show overweening political ambition. Sangster's uncomplaining eighteen-year wait to become prime minister only confirmed that he was indeed a loyal, hardworking, and self-effacing team player.

These qualities were much in evidence in succeeding years, as Sangster assumed additional duties. On the international scene he represented Jamaica at Commonwealth Parliamentary Conferences in the 1950s. Furthermore, as prospects for the creation of the West Indies Federation (WIF) increased, Sangster headed the bipartisan Jamaican delegation to regional economic conferences on the federation. At home, he became finance minister and leader of the House of Representatives in 1953.

This period also saw a brief reversal of fortunes for Sangster and the JLP, as each met political defeat in the 1955 elections that brought the PNP to power. For Sangster, however, the year was not without its compensations. First, despite losing his seat in the St. Elizabeth constituency, he won a vacant seat in a by-election that was held in the North-East Clarendon constituency, thereby retaining a seat in the House of Representatives. Second, the *Daily Gleaner,* the island's influential newspaper, named him "Political Man of the Year" for his 1955 electoral win, and for being the brainchild behind "Jamaica 300," a year-long festival that marked three hundred years of artistic and cultural achievements by the Jamaican people. The *Gleaner*'s accolade therefore called attention to unnoticed aspects of Sangster's personality—his cultural nationalism, his defense of sovereignty for colonized peoples, and his concern for racial democracy.

Still, Sangster was no black militant. Nor was he a foe of the West. At a time when many in Jamaica, and elsewhere in the colonial world, were espousing black nationalist and anti-imperialist sentiments, Sangster subscribed to the multiracial nationalism typical of the brown middle class to which he belonged. He complemented this moderate cultural nationalism with democratic commitments, a pro-Western stance, and an outlook that favored Caribbean regionalism.

But Sangster's regional outlook did not make him an advocate of Jamaica's continued membership in the West Indies Federation, the regional organization that was founded in 1958. Thus, when Bustamante broke with the bipartisan approach on the issue in 1960, calling instead for Jamaica's withdrawal from the federation, Sangster did not oppose him. To settle the issue, the PNP administration, which backed Jamaican membership, held a referendum in September 1961. In a stunning decision that would ultimately doom the regional body, the Jamaican electorate sided with the JLP and voted to remove the island from the federation. The JLP followed up this victory with another win at the polls in the April 1962 general elections. Sangster was reappointed minister of finance and leader of the House. He became deputy prime minister after Jamaica's independence on August 6, 1962.

Sangster's major achievements as a political leader occurred in the immediate years after independence. Most notably, as Bustamante's deputy, he guided the fledgling nation into the turbulent postwar world. As an architect of Jamaica's foreign policy, Sangster affirmed the country's alliance with the United States and secured the island's membership in the United Nations, the International Monetary Fund, and the World Bank.

Sangster also established a reputation as a statesman and parliamentarian in the Caribbean and in the British Commonwealth of Nations. He was the lead spokesman at the Caribbean Heads of Government Conferences in the early 1960s, and he advocated for more influence for the less-developed countries in the Commonwealth.

The Rhodesian prime minister Ian Smith's Unilateral Declaration of Independence in 1965 gave Sangster the opportunity to lead by example. Smith's declaration threatened the breakup of the Commonwealth, as Britain rebuffed the members' call for military intervention. Sangster helped avert a walkout of African and other delegates when his compromise resolution was accepted. According to press reports, this achievement earned him the sobriquet "Mr. Commonwealth."

At home, Sangster had little to show that could match these achievements. This was partly due to serving in Bustamante's shadow. Indeed, Sangster's intermittent role as acting prime minister (due to Bustamante's poor health) since 1964 prevented him from putting his own imprimatur on power. When Bustamante did retire in January 1967, Sangster finally won power in his own right by defeating the PNP in the February 1967 general elections. His victory was short-lived, however. A month later, the international statesman and parliamentarian who had smoothed Jamaica's entry onto the world stage and established the island's reputation as a stable and well-governed nation, suffered a cerebral hemorrhage. He was flown to Montreal, Canada, for treatment but soon slipped into a coma. Sangster was knighted on his deathbed and passed away on April 11, after serving less than two months as prime minister.

See also Bustamante, Alexander; International Relations of the Anglophone Caribbean; Jamaica Labour Party; People's National Party

Bibliography

Daily Gleaner, 13 April, 1967.

Eaton, George E. *Alexander Bustamante and Modern Jamaica.* Kingston: Kingston Publishers, 1975.

Gray, Obika. *Radicalism and Social Change in Jamaica, 1960–1972.* Knoxville: University of Tennessee Press, 1991.

Gray, Obika. *Demeaned but Empowered: The Social Power of the Urban Poor in Jamaica.* Kingston, Jamaica: University of the West Indies Press, 2004.

The Sunday Gleaner, 30 December, 1962.

The Sunday Gleaner, 25 December, 1955.

OBIKA GRAY (2005)

San Lorenzo de los Negros

After the fall of the Mexica (Aztec) Empire in 1521, Spanish colonists brought increasing numbers of enslaved Africans into Mexico. These slaves immediately began escaping. As most of Mesoamerica remained unconquered in the 1520s, *cimarrones* (Maroons, or escaped slaves) sometimes fled to native communities. The chronicler Antonio Herrera later wrote that, as early as 1523, "many negro slaves fled to the [unconquered] Zapotecs and they [the slaves] went about rebelling throughout the country" (Palmer, 1976, p. 122). However, due to language and cultural barriers, and because Africans had sometimes joined the Spanish Conquest as black conquistadors, *cimarrones* were not always welcome in native towns, and many formed their own settlements. Maroon communities sprang up wherever Europeans brought African slaves to the Americas, from Florida to Brazil. Between the 1520s and 1650, a quarter of a million Africans were imported to colonial Mexico, making it (after Brazil) the second most important destination for slaves in the Americas during this period. Mexico was thus a center of Maroon activity, and Spanish officials in the colony considered *cimarrones* to be a major problem, with the solution being the complete destruction of Maroon communities.

The most extensive and violent confrontations between Spaniards and *cimarrones* took place near the Gulf Coast port of Veracruz, in the Orizaba region, between 1606 and 1619. In each of the first three years of this period, Viceroy Don Luis de Velasco ordered—in vain—that the region be cleared of *cimarrones* because, he claimed, for decades they had been liberating other slaves, destroying Spanish property, and "assaulting and killing the Indians and the Spaniards along the highways" (Palmer, 1976, p. 126). An attempt to use a Franciscan as a spy failed in 1609 when the friar was expelled from the main Maroon community (named Yanga, after its leader or king, but subsequently renamed San Lorenzo de los Negros).

Meanwhile, Spaniards prepared to destroy the village with a military force of 450 men led by Pedro González de Herrera. Before the attack, Herrera received a letter from King Yanga (or Ñanga), an elderly African, reputedly from the royal family of the Bram nation in West Africa, who had survived as an escapee in Mexico for three decades. He eloquently denounced Spanish colonialism and the treatment of black slaves, arguing that he and his followers were justified in seeking refuge from "the cruelty and treachery of the Spaniards who, without any right, had become owners of their freedom" (Palmer, 1976, p. 129).

Yanga defied the Spaniards to defeat him, although his villagers were fewer in number than Herrera's soldiers, and half of them were more accustomed to tending crops and cattle than to fighting.

In the ensuing battle the Spaniards overran the settlement, but most of the *cimarrones* fled and—led by Yanga and his general, Francisco Angola—fought the colonists to a stalemate. Under the ensuing peace agreement, the *cimarrones* offered to return all slaves who had escaped after September 1608 and to respect Spanish property and life. In return, their community was formally recognized as the *pueblo* of San Lorenzo de los Negros. Yanga was officially made governor, and he ruled the town along with a *cabildo* (town council) of his peers. San Lorenzo's residents also paid tribute, built a church (there had been a chapel in the earlier Maroon village), received a Spanish priest, and pledged to defend the colony from its enemies. This agreement reflected the degree to which the *cimarrones* had adopted aspects of Spanish culture, as well as their concern to preserve their own freedom. What had begun in the 1580s as a roving band of men had become by the 1610s a fully developed community of families, and they wanted to preserve this way of life more than they wanted to destroy colonial rule or the institution of slavery.

Violence by and against *cimarrones* continued in the region of San Lorenzo, as it did in much of Mexico. But the town survived and grew, a symbol of how enslaved Africans in the Americas could not only seize their freedom, but, with audacity and tenacity, win formal recognition as free colonists. The symbolism of this victory became blurred during the seventeenth century, as mixed-race people of indigenous, Spanish, and African descent moved into San Lorenzo. By 1700 the community was indistinguishable from other villages and small towns in the region. Nevertheless, San Lorenzo's origins were not forgotten. Its residents continued to call the village Yanga, as that was its popular name by 1821, the year of Mexican independence, when its population was almost 800. In the nineteenth century its history was promoted by the Afro-Mexican politician and historian Vicente Riva Palacio (1832–1896). Today Governor (or King) Yanga is viewed as a Mexican nationalist hero, and the town, now officially called Yanga, has a prominent statue of its founder, holds an annual Festival of the First Free People of the Americas, and is recognized as a heritage site by the Mexican government.

See also Runaway Slaves in Latin America and the Caribbean

Bibliography

Carroll, Patrick J. *Blacks in Colonial Veracruz: Race, Ethnicity, and Regional Development*, 2d ed. Austin: University of Texas Press, 2001.

Palmer, Colin. *Slaves of the White God: Blacks in Mexico, 1570–1650*. Cambridge, Mass.: Harvard University Press, 1976.

Price, Richard, ed. *Maroon Societies: Rebel Slave Communities in the Americas*, 3d ed. Baltimore, Md.: Johns Hopkins University Press, 1996.

Sánchez de Anda, Guillermo. *Yanga: Un guerrero negro*. Mexico City: Circulo, 1998.

Vincent, Theodore G. *The Legacy of Vicente Guerrero, Mexico's First Black Indian President*. Gainesville: University Press of Florida, 2001.

MATTHEW RESTALL (2005)

San Martín de Porras

November/December 1579
November 3, 1639

In 1962 Pope John XXIII canonized Martín de Porras Velásquez, thereby making an illegitimate son of a Spanish noble and a free African from colonial Peru into a saint of a new Catholic era. As the patron of racial justice, San Martín de Porras inspired progressive and disenfranchised Catholics who embraced his image as a symbol of a reformed church dedicated to social justice in the twentieth century. However, Martín de Porras asserted spiritual authority through humble service to simultaneously challenge and reinforce the colonial order of a slavery society. Exemplifying the complicated hegemonic location of a free man of color considered holy in his time, he accepted the curse of "*mulato* dog," an epithet normally directed to slaves, out of his deep humility to God and, perhaps, as a strategy to further his good works.

Born to a free woman of African descent, Martín de Porras was maintained by, and later publicly recognized by, his Spanish noble father. The pious youth was raised near the public slave market and indigenous fishing communities in the plebeian neighborhood of San Lázaro in Lima, the Spanish viceregal capital of Peru. Apprenticed first to an apothecary and then to a surgeon, he learned to cure common ailments, extract teeth, set bones, and lance boils. Trained as a healer and able to read and write, Martín chose to enter the Dominican monastery of Nuestra Señora del Rosario in 1594. As a *mulato* (a child of a Spanish-African union in colonial Latin America) and an illegitimate son, the aspirant could not obtain the positions of friar or priest. He therefore agreed to serve as a simple "donated" brother. At age twenty-nine he swore obedience, poverty, and chastity to the order and became Brother (Hermano) Martín de Porras. For the rest of his life, he was entrusted with the order's dispensary and served as an assistant nurse whose main duties included washing, feeding, and comforting the ill.

With medicinal plants from the monastery's gardens, as well as clothing and food from its stores, Martín de Porras attended to the poor of Lima, including Africans, Indians, and Spaniards. His gentle attentions included herbal baths, regular prayer, and bloodletting. Like other devout men and women of the seventeenth century, he engaged in self-flagellation, wore a hair shirt, fasted regularly (always refusing meat), and slept on a stone pillow. In the testimony supplied for his posthumous case for sainthood, both elite persons and commoners claimed that Brother Martín had the gift of prophecy, could transport himself from one place to another, and levitated during prayer. In 1660, and again from 1679 to 1685, Lima's populace recounted that Brother Martín de Porras performed humble miracles such as inviting a rat, a cat, and a dog to eat from the same bowl and affecting a quick cure on an injured, lowly slave. Welcomed throughout the city, Brother Martín provided counsel to Lima's archbishops and solicited funds to sustain his charitable acts only to succumb to an epidemic in 1639. After a lengthy funeral procession, the Dominicans buried the illegitimate *mulato* in their exclusive crypt, where his uncorrupted body would be exhumed in 1664 to begin the process of making him a black saint of the Americas.

See also Catholicism in the Americas

Bibliography

Busto Duthurburu, José Antonio del. *San Martín de Porras (Martín de Porras Velásquez).* 2d ed. Lima, Peru: Pontificia Universidad Católica del Perú, Fondo Editorial. 2001.

Cussen, Celia Langdeau. "Fray Martín de Porres and the Religious Imagination of Creole Lima." Ph.D. diss., University of Pennsylvania, 1996.

Iwasaki Cauti, Fernando. "Fray Martín de Porras: Santo, ensalmador y sacamuelas." *Colonial Latin American Review* 3, nos. 1–2 (1994): 159–184.

Tardieu, J. P. "Genio y semblanza del santo varón limeño de origen africano (Fray Martín de Porras)." *Hispania Sacra* 45 (1993): 555–574.

RACHEL SARAH O'TOOLE (2005)

SANTERÍA

Santería, or "saint worship," is a religion that has its roots in both the spiritual practices of the Yoruba people of western Africa and in Roman Catholicism. The Yoruba people believed in the supreme God Olodumare and in lesser deities known as *orishas.* As slaves brought to work on sugar plantations in Cuba, they were baptized and catechized in the Roman Catholic Church in accordance with the Slave Code of 1789. The synthesis of these two religious practices occurred as slaves began to recognize Catholic saints as spiritual beings similar to their *orishas.* Eventually each *orisha* was matched with a Catholic saint and came to be known by both the African and Christian name (for instance, Orula and St. Francis of Assisi describe the same being). Under Spanish rule, the followers of this religion, santeros, continued to honor their spiritual ancestors and sought power through them. They communicated to the *orishas* through the ashe, the blood and power, of animal sacrifice and other offerings, such as food or clothing; today, community service is also a method of communication. The *orishas,* in turn, spoke to santeros through divination, performed by *babalawos,* who could read the future in sea- or coconut shells or in cards immersed in clear water.

Santería became a presence in the United States largely as a result of the exodus of Cubans after the revolution of 1959. There is little public display of the religion. Botanicas, which sell candles, beads, oils, herbs, plants, and plaster statues of Catholic saints, are found in Latino sections of New York, Miami, and Los Angeles. The number of followers is not easily determined. In southern Florida, which has had a large Caribbean immigration, roughly seventy thousand people practice Santería.

The Society for the Prevention of Cruelty to Animals has protested the ritual slaughter of animals by adherents to Santería on several occasions. One 1980 raid on an apartment in the Bronx where Santería was reportedly being practiced yielded three goats and eighteen chickens. A larger case arose when Ernesto Pichardo opened a public church for Santería followers—the first in the United States—in Hialeah, Florida, in 1987. After a two-year struggle, the town passed an ordinance banning animal sacrifice. Pichardo and others claimed such rulings to be hypocritical in a society where meat is slain daily for consumption, especially since in Santería the animal sacrificed is often eaten afterward. In June 1993 the Supreme Court removed the ban on religious animal sacrifices as discrimination against religious practice.

See also Catholicism in the Americas; Orisha; Yoruba Religion and Culture in the Americas

Bibliography

Gonzalez-Wippler, Migene. *Santería, the Religion: A Legacy of Faith, Rites, and Magic.* New York: Harmony, 1989.

Murphy, Joseph M. *Santería: An African Religion in America.* Boston: Beacon Press, 1988.

WALTER FRIEDMAN (1996)
GRISSEL BORDONI-SEIJO (1996)

Santería Aesthetics

Santería aesthetics is a Yoruba-American artistic expression rooted in the history of enslaved Africans' desire to preserve their religion and culture during their enslavement in the Americas. Art is seminal to the cultural identity of all African peoples and, in particular, the Yoruba of southwestern Nigeria, for whom the arts are intricately connected to their religion. Yoruba artistic preeminence in the visual arts is legendary, dating back to the first millennium. In *Flash of the Spirit,* African art historian Robert Farris Thompson (1983) stated, "Yoruba assess everything aesthetically." Thompson's observation applies to the Yoruba diaspora as well. Everywhere in the Americas where the Yoruba presence is found there is evidence that art and aesthetics play a dominant role in daily life. According to Yoruba religious belief, Olodumare, the supreme being, sent down lesser deities known as *orishas* to begin life on earth. One of the first *orishas* sent by Olodumare was Obatalá, who was given charge of creativity.

The transatlantic slave trade brought about the dispersal of Yoruba religion and culture in the Americas, particularly in Cuba, Brazil, Haiti, and Trinidad, where the first wave of the Yoruba diaspora landed. With the abolition of slavery in the nineteenth century, peoples of African descent were able to move freely, resulting in a second wave of Yoruba culture dispersing to other parts of the Caribbean and Central and North America. A third wave spread the religion and culture in the mid-twentieth century as large numbers of Cubans migrated to the United States and other parts of Latin America in the aftermath of the Cuban Revolution of 1959. Finally, the Mariel exodus of 1980 provided a fourth wave of Cuban exiles. Santería practitioners in the last two waves have made significant contributions to religion and culture throughout America. In *The Yoruba of Southwestern Nigeria,* William Bascom (1969), a pioneer scholar of African and African-American culture, writes that "no African group has had greater influence on New World culture than the Yoruba."

The term *Santería* is one of many used to describe a Yoruba-American religion that is based on the traditional religion of the Yoruba known as *Ifa* or *Esin Abalaye* in Nigeria, and on Roman Catholicism. In Cuba it is known as Santería, Lucumí, or Regla de Ocha. It is known as Santería in the Dominican Republic, Panama, the United States, and other parts of the world as a result of the Cuban migration. In Trinidad and Tobago, as well as in other Windward Caribbean islands, it is known as Shango, while in Brazil it is known as Candomblé. Literally translated, *Santería* means "the way of the saints," an apt, albeit mistaken, characterization for what might appear to the uninitiated to be a Roman Catholic cult dedicated to the worship of Christian saints. Another mistaken characterization of the religion is that it is a syncretic faith. Many scholars arrived at this conclusion because of a now defunct practice of requiring Santería devotees to be baptized in the Roman Catholic Church prior to initiation, the presence of statues and polychrome pictures of Roman Catholic saints on home altars, the celebration of the feast days of these saints, and the reference to devotees as *santeros.*

The commingling of the two religions in the Yoruba diaspora began as a subterfuge by enslaved Yoruba who were forced to accept Roman Catholicism. To avoid persecution, the Yoruba and their descendents camouflaged their *orishas* with the images, color symbolism, and iconography of Catholic saints. Essentially, they overtly accepted Roman Catholicism, misleading their enslavers into believing that they had become Christian converts while they covertly continued to practice their religion. This subterfuge also made it possible for them to develop and preserve a Yoruba-American aesthetic from one generation to another through oral tradition, music, literature, dance, folklore, and the visual arts. As religious persecution abated and tolerance increased throughout the Americas in the twentieth century, a number of *santeros* started abandoning vestiges of Roman Catholicism. Also, by the end of the twentieth century many devotees began to view the term *Santería* as pejorative and preferred to refer to their religion as Yoruba religion, Afro-Cuban Orisha worship, Orisha worship, or Lucumí. In spite of semantics, the term *Santería* still has currency with many devotees who refuse to remove the Catholic saints from their altars because of personal allegiances. Santería aesthetics therefore comprises a complex mythology, a pantheon of deities, color symbolism, rituals, and ceremonies that *santeros* employ in the veneration of the *orishas.* This aesthetic also gained currency with modern and contemporary artists beginning in the twentieth century.

A Santería Religious Altar in Cuba. *Santería, literally translated "the way of the saints," is based on the traditional religion of the Yoruba in Nigeria. The resolve of the Yoruba to maintain an intimate relationship with their orishas (gods) in a sacred space led to the phenomenon of home altars like the one pictured here.* © ROBERT VAN DER HILST/CORBIS. REPRODUCED BY PERMISSION.

Traditional Yoruba aesthetics in the Americas experienced a serious setback as their art-making traditions became severely curtailed during slavery. Although limited, the making or displaying of religious objects did not become extinct. To avoid punishment, however, the display of such objects, like the religion itself, became secretive. Cuban anthropologist Fernando Ortiz amassed a large and impressive collection of dolls that were used in Lucumí devotional practices in the late nineteenth and early twentieth century. His collection is now in the permanent collection of Casa de Africa in Havana, Cuba.

The Yoruba had also distinguished themselves with an impressive legacy in the architectural arts. However, the practice of building palaces, public shrines, altars, and temples with religious and/or political significance was eclipsed in the "New" World. Nevertheless, the resolve of the Yoruba to maintain an intimate relationship with their *orishas* in a sacred space—an important tenet in the religion—led to the phenomenon of home altars called *tronos,* or thrones.

Santería Aesthetics in Modern Art

European avant-garde artists' search for new influences to invigorate their work at the beginning of the twentieth century lead them to investigate the aesthetic properties of African art. Whereas most modern artists were influenced by the formal elements of African art, artists of the African diaspora sought to explore deeper cultural and spiritual meaning in these objects. In his 1925 essay "The Legacy of the Ancestral Arts," Alain Locke (1992), the principal aesthetician of the Harlem Renaissance, urged African-American artists to look to African art for inspiration. Locke believed that the arts could serve as a vehicle to reverse negative stereotypical images of the "Negro" in an era when racism was at its peak. He wrote, "any vital artistic expression of the Negro theme and subject in art must break thorough the stereotypes to a new style, a distinctive fresh technique, and some sort of characteristic idiom." While Locke was advocating for a cutting-edge Afrocentric aesthetic, so too were the African and Caribbean artists and intellectuals of the *Négritude* movement. The Cuban artist Wifredo Lam, who was part of the *Négritude* movement, was the first to introduce a secular Santería aesthetic in the visual arts when he presented the *orishas* in his paintings as subject matter, albeit camouflaged. Although African-American artists in the United States, at the insistence of Locke, did include African images in their work, in the early years these images appeared more like

African icons. This would change, however, by mid- to late century.

Santeria Aesthetics in Contemporary Art

The aftermath of the civil rights movement in the latter part of the twentieth century shaped the postmodern era with concerns for pluralism, multiculturalism, appropriation, and hybridization, resulting in the mainstream art world becoming more sensitive to the art and culture of the peoples of African descent. During this period new genre art forms were introduced that accommodated Santería aesthetic concerns rather well. Concurrently, the Pan-Africanist movement had politicized artists of African descent with concerns for rediscovering and preserving African legacies. They were determined to produce what Locke called a "racial art" that positively depicted their communities. The intersection of a new climate interested in multiculturalism in the art world, new genre art forms, and Afrocentricity in the arts created a fertile ground in which a secular Santería aesthetic would grow. The result has been a Yoruba aesthetic renaissance. Santería *tronos,* rituals, and ritual objects have been transformed into contemporary art as installations, performance art, concept art, and body art, while the *orishas* have become the subject matter for paintings, drawings, collages, and assemblages. These works are now being exhibited in prestigious galleries and museums worldwide, sometimes with the assistance of *santeros* as collaborators and/or consultants. Locke's call for "a new style, a distinctive fresh technique, and some sort of characteristic idiom" has been realized. At the beginning of the twenty-first century, Santería aesthetics continues to thrive in both sacred and secular art.

See also Healing and the Arts in Afro-Caribbean Cultures; Orisha; Santería; Yoruba Religion and Culture in the Americas

Bibliography

Abiodun, Rowland, Henry J. Drewal, and John Pemberton III. *Yoruba: Nine Centuries of African Art and Thought.* New York: Harry N. Abrams, 1989.

Bascom, William. *The Yoruba of Southwestern Nigeria.* New York: Holt, Rinehart, and Winston, 1969.

Eyo, Ekpo, and Frank Willett. *Treasures of Ancient Nigeria.* New York: Knopf, Detroit Institute of Arts, 1980.

Jacob, Mary Jane. *Ana Mendieta: The "Silueta" Series.* New York: Galerie Lelong, 1991.

Lawal, Babatunde. "From Africa to the Americas, Art in Yoruba Religion." In *Santería Aesthetics in Contemporary Latin American Art,* edited by Arturo Lindsay. Washington, D.C.: Smithsonian Institution Press, 1996.

Lindsay, Arturo. "Orishas: Living Gods in Contemporary Latino Art." In *Santería Aesthetics in Contemporary Latin American Art,* edited by Arturo Lindsay. Washington, D.C.: Smithsonian Institution Press, 1996.

Locke, Alain. "The Legacy of the Ancestral Arts." In *The New Negro: Voices of the Harlem Renaissance,* edited by Alain Locke. New York: Harper, 1925. Reprint, New York: Simon and Schuster, 1992.

Ramos, Miguel (Willie). "Afro-Cuban Orisha Worship." In *Santería Aesthetics in Contemporary Latin American Art,* edited by Arturo Lindsay. Washington, D.C.: Smithsonian Institution Press, 1996.

Sims, Lowery Stokes. "Syncretism and Syntax in the Art of Wifredo Lam." In *Crosscurrents of Modernism: Four Latin American Pioneers,* edited by Valerie Fletcher. Washington, D.C.: Smithsonian Institution Press, 1992.

Sims, Lowery Stokes. "Wifredo Lam: From Spain Back to Cuba." In *Wifredo Lam and His Contemporaries, 1938–1952.* New York: Studio Museum in Harlem; Harry N. Abrams, 1992.

Sims, Lowery Stokes. *Wifredo Lam and the International Avant-Garde, 1923–1982.* Austin: University of Texas Press, 2002.

Thompson, Robert Farris. *Flash of the Spirit.* New York: Random House, 1983.

ARTURO LINDSAY (2005)

Santos-Febres, Mayra

1966

The Puerto Rican writer Mayra Santos-Febres has published two novels, two collections of short stories, two collections of poems, and various articles of literary criticism. In her work she deals with themes of female sexuality, the erotic, gender fluidity, desire, and power. Representations of female sexuality in women's fiction is not new in Puerto Rican women's writing, nor in that of the wider Caribbean, but Santos-Febres's work marks a new modality of erotic openness. She often focuses on the powers of seduction, often in the context of a dystopic contemporary Puerto Rico, while the nostalgia that is part of so much Puerto Rican prose is absent in her writing. Puerto Rico's urbanized and industrialized metropolitan areas provide the setting for much of this work, and the denizens of these areas are the key players.

She has published several collections of poetry in Spanish. Her prose work in English translation includes *Urban Oracles* (1997), *Sirena Selena* (2000), and *Any Wednesday I'm Yours* (2005). The stories in *Urban Oracles* deal with the powers and transformations of the female body, though this theme is treated in a unique way by Santos-Febres, at least compared with most literature by black authors. In "Broken Strand," for example, the beauty of black womanhood is restored through a protagonist who visualizes herself becoming the pinnacle of beauty through the ministrations of a beautician. The story's tone is celebratory, representing nappy hair not as a problem, but as yet another element of black women's beauty. Similarly, in "Marina's Fragrance," a woman protagonist has a particular gift: when she thinks about an aroma, it becomes manifest in the world. Magical and dreamlike, the narrative places women in a position of power. Another story features a gardener who must prepare dead prostitutes for burial after a cataclysmic storm. Yet in performing this task, rubbing oils into the bodies of these women becomes a ritual of love and respect.

Sirena Selena, an iconoclastic first novel, features an underage transvestite who seeks success and money among the rich and powerful in the nighttime world of the Dominican Republic and San Juan. Much is made of transformations of the body as ways to attain the male gaze, the socially accepted dominance of the male through the act of looking at the female. This novel was, and remains, controversial because it questions gender categories in a way that had never been done before in Puerto Rico. The closest anyone had previously come to destabilizing these categories was Luis Rafael Sánchez, in some of the stories in *En cuerpo de camisa* (1966), but even there, the specifics of what, where, and how were not as openly portrayed as they are in Santos-Febres's novel. As in her shorter fiction, there is here a celebration of the erotic, of the body, and of sexual expression in all its forms.

Santos-Febres's second novel, *Any Wednesday I'm Yours*, features a would-be novelist who loses his job at a newspaper and takes a job working nights in a motel. Educated and sophisticated, he discovers ties between a narcotics kingpin and a corrupt labor lawyer who is supposedly engaged in contract negotiations for electrical workers. The power outages common in Puerto Rico turn out to be due to sabotage engineered by this lawyer and the druglord, who meet in the motel where the protagonist works. This is one of the novel's mysteries; another is the identity of a mysterious and sensual woman who makes love with the protagonist every Wednesday (hence the novel's title). Her purloined manuscript contains the necessary clue to solving the novel's crimes, which is the impetus for the protagonist to overcome his difficulties with writing.

The novel also features a secondary character whose identity is Haitian and Dominican. He is trying to make enough money working in the motel and delivering cocaine to Miami to be able to install electricity in his mother's home back in Haiti. There is also a rich episode featuring Santería rituals, complete with the names of African gods and Yoruba prayers, a ritual attended by representatives of all social classes, including professionals.

A promising and talented young writer with a bright future ahead, Santos-Febres represents the newest generation of self-consciously diasporic Puerto Rican authors who embrace rather than bemoan that identity.

See also Women Writers of the Caribbean

Bibliography

DeCosta-Willis, Miriam, ed. *Daughters of the Diaspora: Afra-Hispanic Writers.* Kingston, Jamaica: Ian Randle, 2003.

Villafane, Camille-Marie. "La reconceptualización del CUERPO en la narrativa de Mayra Montero y Mayra Santos-Febres." Ph.D. diss., Arizona State University, Tempe, 2001.

DIANA L. VÉLEZ (2005)

Savage, Augusta

February 29, 1892
March 26, 1962

The seventh of fourteen children, portrait sculptor and educator Augusta Christine Fells was born in Green Cove Springs, Florida, to Cornelia and Edward Fells. Fells, a Methodist minister, initially punished his young daughter for making figurines in the local red clay, then came to accept her talent. Augusta attended public schools and the state normal school in Tallahassee (now Florida A&M) briefly. At sixteen she married John T. Moore, who died within a few years of the birth of their only child. In the mid-1910s she married James Savage, a laborer and carpenter; the two divorced in the early 1920s. In 1915 Savage moved to West Palm Beach, where one of her clay pieces won twenty-five dollars at a county fair. Public support encouraged Savage to move north in the Great Migration to New York, where she arrived in 1921 with just $4.60 and a letter of recommendation from the superintendent of the county fair to sculptor Solon Borglum, director of the School of American Sculpture.

Through Borglum's influence Savage was admitted to the tuition-free college Cooper Union ahead of 142 women on the waiting list. She completed the four-year program in three years, specializing in portraiture. In the early 1920s she sculpted realistic busts of W. E. B. Du Bois,

Frederick Douglass, W. C. Handy, and Marcus Garvey. In 1923 she married Robert L. Poston, a Garveyite journalist who died five months later. The same year, Savage was one of a hundred American women who received a $500 scholarship from the French government for summer study at the palace of Fontainebleau. However, when the American committee of seven white men discovered her racial identity, they withdrew the offer. One committee member, Hermon A. MacNeil, gave her private instruction instead. Two years later Countess Irene Di Robilant of the Italian-American Society gave Savage a scholarship for study at the Royal Academy of Fine Arts in Rome, but Savage was unable to raise money for expenses abroad as she struggled to support her parents while working at a laundry.

In 1926 Savage exhibited her work in three locations—at the New York Public Library, at the Frederick Douglass High School in Baltimore, and at the sesquicentennial exhibition in Philadelphia. The following year she studied privately with sculptor Onorio Ruotolo, former dean of the Leonardo da Vinci Art School. She also worked with sculptor Antonio Salemme and taught soap sculpture classes to children at Procter & Gamble.

In 1928, recognition from the Harmon Foundation, which exhibited her *Evening and Head of a Negro,* brought Savage sales. Eugene Kinckle Jones, executive secretary of the National Urban League, was so impressed with his purchase of a baby's bust Savage had sculpted that he asked the Carnegie Corporation to sponsor her training. Through Carnegie Savage began study with sculptor Victor Salvatore, who urged her to continue her studies in France.

In the fall of 1929 Savage went to Paris with funds from both Carnegie and the Julius Rosenwald Fund. There she studied privately with Felix Benneteau and created realistic portrait busts in plaster and clay. The most notable works Savage created abroad are of black female nudes, such as *Amazon* (a female warrior holding a spear) and *Mourning Victory* (a standing nude who gazes at a decapitated head on the ground), and works that celebrate her African heritage, such as *The Call* (in response to Alain Locke's call for racially representative art) and *Divinité nègre* (a female figurine with four faces, arms, and legs). In 1930 *La dépêche africaine,* a French journal, ran a cover story on Savage, and three of her figurative works were exhibited at the Salon d'Automne. Savage also sent works to the United States for display; the Harmon Foundation exhibited *Gamin* in 1930 and *Bust* and *The Chase* (in palm wood) in 1931. In 1931 Savage won a gold medal for a piece at the Colonial Exposition and exhibited two female nudes (*Nu* in bronze, and *Martiniquaise* in plaster) at the Société des Artistes Français.

After her return to New York Savage exhibited three works (*Gamin, Envy,* and *Woman of Martinique*) at the American Art–Anderson Galleries in 1932. That same year she opened the Savage School of Arts and Crafts. Some of her students, who included Jacob Lawrence, Norman Lewis, William Artis, and Ernest Crichlow, participated in Vanguard, a group Savage founded in 1933 to discuss art and progressive causes. She disbanded the group the following year when membership became communist-controlled.

In 1934 Argent Galleries and the Architectural League exhibited Savage's work, and she became the first African American elected to the National Association of Women Painters and Sculptors. Two years later Savage supervised artists in the WPA's Federal Art Projects and organized classes and exhibitions at the Uptown Art Laboratory. In 1937 she became the first director of the Harlem Community Art Center. After receiving a commission from the New York World's Fair Board of Design, she left that position in 1938 to sculpt a sixteen-foot plaster harp, the strings of which were the folds of choir robes on singing black youths. Named after James Weldon Johnson's poem/song (also called the Negro National Anthem), *Lift Every Voice and Sing* was exhibited at the New York World's Fair of 1939 but was bulldozed afterward. (Savage could not afford to have it cast in bronze.)

In June 1939 Savage opened the Salon of Contemporary Art, the first gallery devoted to the exhibition and sale of works by African-American artists. It folded within a few months for lack of funds. The same year, she exhibited fifteen works in a solo show at Argent Galleries; among them were *Green Apples, Sisters in the Rain, Creation, Envy, Martyr, The Cat,* and a bust of James Weldon Johnson. She also exhibited at the American Negro Exposition and at Perrin Hall in Chicago in 1940.

Around 1945 Savage retired to Saugerties, New York, where she taught children in nearby summer camps, occasionally sold her work, and wrote children's stories and murder mysteries. She died of cancer in New York City.

See also Art in the United States, Contemporary; Harlem Renaissance; Painting and Sculpture

Bibliography

Bearden, Romare, and Harry Henderson. *A History of African-American Artists: From 1792 to the Present.* New York: Pantheon, 1993.

Bibby, Deirdre. *Augusta Savage and the Art Schools of Harlem.* New York: Schomburg Center for Research in Black Culture, 1988.

The Savoy Ballroom, c. 1950s. *Harlem's famed Lenox Avenue dance palace opened in 1926 and became a top nightspot for bands during the Swing Era.* PHOTOGRAPH BY AUSTIN HANSEN. USED BY PERMISSION OF JOYCE HANSEN AND THE SCHOMBURG CENTER.

Poston, T. R. "Augusta Savage." *Metropolitan Magazine* (January 1935): 28–31, 55, 66–67.

THERESA LEININGER-MILLER (1996)

Savoy Ballroom

Dubbed the "Home of Happy Feet," the Savoy Ballroom was Harlem's first and greatest swing era dance palace; for more than three decades it was the premiere showcase for the greatest of the swing big bands and dancers.

At the time of the Savoy's opening—on March 12, 1926, at 596 Lenox Avenue, between 140th and 141st streets—Harlem boasted no dance halls to match the opulence of the Roseland and Arcadia ballrooms in midtown Manhattan. Instead, there were primarily cramped, rundown, and often illegal clubs. The Savoy featured two mirrored flights of marble stairs, leading from street level up to a chandeliered lobby, and to the orange-and-blue room itself, which measured 200 by 500 feet and could hold up to 7,000 people. There were two bandstands, a disappearing stage under multicolored spotlights, and a vast dance floor, which was worn down and replaced every three years. Despite the elegance of the setting, the ballroom attracted a working-class audience who paid low-priced entrance fees for an evening of swing dancing. However, none of the Harlem ballrooms that opened after the Savoy ever approached the Savoy's opulence.

Every black big band of note, and many white ones as well, eventually performed at the Savoy. Opening night featured Fletcher Henderson's Orchestra, and in the late 1920s Duke Ellington, King Oliver, and Louis Armstrong brought their orchestras to the Savoy. In 1932, Kansas City swing made its New York debut at the Savoy, as Bennie

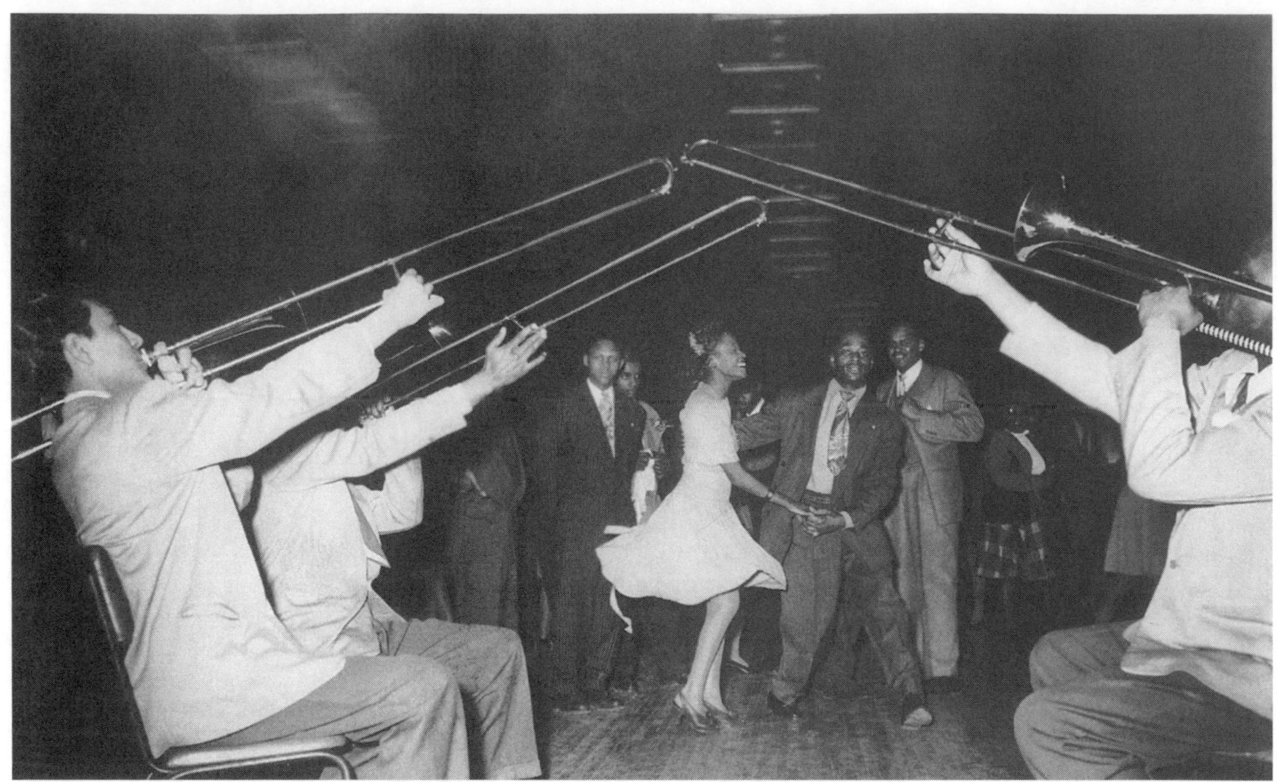

Dancers and musicians at the Savoy Ballroom, swinging to the ballroom's anthem, "Stompin' at the Savoy." CORBIS/BETTMANN. REPRODUCED BY PERMISSION.

Moten brought a band that included the pianist Count Basie, the trumpeter Oran "Hot Lips" Page, and the saxophonist Ben Webster. Although Al Cooper's Savoy Sultans served as the house band, Chick Webb's orchestra, featuring the vocalist Ella Fitzgerald, became identified with the Savoy during its 1932 to 1939 stay. An arranger and saxophonist with Webb, Edgar Sampson, composed the ballroom's anthem, "Stompin' at the Savoy," in 1934.

Often more than one band was booked into the Savoy for an evening. As the bands alternated tunes and sets, a " battle of the bands," in which the two ensembles would vie for the acclamation of the audience, would ensue. Among the most memorable confrontations was Chick Webb's 1938 victory over an orchestra led by Count Basie.

In the 1940s the Savoy encountered competition from the Golden Gate, the Apollo, the Alhambra, the Rockland Palace, and the Audubon Ballroom. Nonetheless, in the early years of the decade, Coleman Hawkins, Erskine Hawkins, Benny Carter, and Louis Armstrong all led big bands there. In 1942, Jay McShann's appearance at the Savoy and on radio broadcasts from the ballroom introduced the saxophonist Charlie Parker to a wider audience. In the summer of 1943 the temporary closing of the Savoy was a precipitating factor in the Harlem riots that August. More than 250 bands eventually performed at the Savoy, including those of Earl "Fatha" Hines, Don Redman, Jimmie Lunceford, Teddy Hill, and Andy Kirk. Unlike the Cotton Club and Connie's Inn, which enforced a strict whites-only clientele, the Savoy welcomed both black and white patrons and performers.

The dancing at the Savoy was as remarkable as the music. The ballroom was the center for the development of Lindyhopping, the energetic and acrobatic style of swing dancing that made a dramatic break with the previous conventions of popular dance in the 1930s. In the 1920s and 1930s dancers such as Leon James, Leroy Jones, Shirley "Snowball" Jordan, "Killer Joe" Piro, and couples such as George "Shorty" Snowden and "Big Bea" (and Sketch Jones and "Little Bea") created and perfected patterns such as "The Itch" and "The Big Apple." The extraordinary inventiveness and agility of the Savoy dancers was credited not only to a cross-fertilization with the bands on the stage but also to the unwritten rule against Savoy dancers copying each others' steps. In the mid-1930s a new generation of Lindyhoppers, including Frankie Manning, Norma Miller, Al Minns, Joe Daniels, Russell Williams, and Pepsi Bethel, favored leaping "air steps," such as the "Hip to Hip," "Side Flip," "Over the Back,"

"Over the Head," and "the Scratch," which came to dominate the older, more earthbound "floor steps."

During its thirty-two-year existence, the Savoy represented a remarkably successful example of an interracial cultural meeting place, an embodiment of the wide-scale acceptance of black urban culture by whites during the 1930s and 1940s. But unlike the earlier settings of the Harlem Renaissance, the Savoy's music and dance were presented without racial exoticism. The Savoy flourished as long as white audiences saw Harlem as an attractive and safe spot for nightlife. Unfortunately, the heyday of the Savoy lasted only until the postwar economic decline of Harlem. Also, with the rise of bebop and rock and roll, big-band jazz ceased to be America's dominant form of popular music, and the owners of the Savoy found it harder to continue to book new big bands each week. The Savoy's doors closed in the late 1950s, and the building was torn down in 1958 to make way for a housing project.

See also Apollo Theater; Cotton Club; Harlem, New York; Harlem Renaissance; Jazz

Bibliography

Charters, Samuel Barclay, and Leonard Kunstadt. *Jazz: A History of the New York Scene* (1962). New York: Da Capo, 1984.

Engelbrecht, Barbara. "Swinging at the Savoy." *Dance Research Journal* 15, no. 2 (spring 1983): 3–10.

Stearns, Marshall, and Jean Stearns. *Jazz Dance: The Story of American Vernacular Dance* (1964). New York: Schirmer Books, 1979.

JONATHAN GILL (1996)

Scholes, Theophilus

c. 1854
c. 1937

Theophilus E. Samuel Scholes was a black Jamaican physician, Christian minister, author, and missionary to Africa. Espousing a strong anti-imperialist and antiracist line of argument, Scholes promoted the idea of absolute political and social equality between Europeans and Africans. He was convinced that the reclamation of ancient African history was the foundation on which continental and diasporic Africans could build toward a future in which they would once again occupy the upper echelons of world civilization. Despite his primary focus on colonized Africans, however, Scholes also demonstrated significant concern for the plight of Indians, Chinese, and aboriginal peoples resulting from European imperial policies. An acknowledged voice within educated black circles in England, Jamaica, and New York, Scholes authored several works, including *Sugar and the West Indies* (1897), *The British Empire and Alliances* (1899), *Chamberlain and Chamberlainism* (under the pseudonym Bartholomew Smith, 1903), and his two-volume opus *Glimpses of the Ages*, published in 1905 and 1908. In these texts he embarked on a detailed analysis and critique of European (and in particular, British) imperial policies, and the race-based ideology, science, and political economy that sustained them. Though Scholes was highly critical of colonialism and imperialism, he did not advocate its abolishment. Instead, he sought for a more modern arrangement in which a network of nations would work together with mutual respect and in total equality.

Scholes was born in Stewart Town in the northwestern Jamaican parish of Trelawny, and he studied at schools there before leaving Jamaica in 1873. He spent the next several years travelling to South America, Central America, parts of North America, and the Sandwich Islands. He then moved to Great Britain, where he studied theology at the Grattan-Guinness Missionary College in London in 1879. Subsequently, he studied medicine in Edinburgh, earning a licentiate from the Royal College of Physicians and Surgeons in 1884. After sojourning briefly in the United States and Jamaica, Scholes ventured to Africa in 1886 as the pioneer missionary and physician of the newly formed Missionary Society of the Western Churches, eventually spending a total of seven years there. Within this seven-year period, he journeyed to Belgium where he took another medical degree (at the University of Brussels). He returned to Africa in 1894 to supervise an industrial school run by the Alfred Jones Institute at New Calabar in Nigeria.

Scholes was elected a member of the African Society in 1903 in England, and, after 1911, also became a member of the New York–based Negro Society for Historical Research. Influenced by European nationalists such as Giuseppe Mazzini, Lajos Kossuth, and Giuseppe de Garibaldi, as well as by black Caribbean radicals such as Edward Blyden, Scholes himself exerted some influence on thinkers such as Robert Love, John Edward Bruce, Ras Makonnen, and Jomo Kenyatta. His reception among black intellectuals of the nineteenth and early twentieth centuries, his early championing of the rights of the colonized majority, and his assault on European racism and imperialism helped establish a discursive anticolonial tradition within the Anglophone black Atlantic.

See also Intellectual Life; Missionary Movements

Bibliography

Geiss, Imanuel. *The Pan-African Movement,* translated by Anne Keep. London: Methuen, 1974.

Scholes, Theophilus E. Samuel. *Glimpses of the Ages; or, the "Superior" and "Inferior" Races, So-Called, Discussed in the Light of Science and History,* vols. 1 and 2. London: John Long, 1905 and 1908.

WIGMOORE WASHINGTON ADOLPHUS FRANCIS (2005)

Schomburg, Arthur

January 24, 1874
June 10, 1938

Bibliophile Arthur Alfonso Schomburg was born in San Juan, Puerto Rico, to a German merchant and an unmarried black laundress who was a native of Saint Thomas, Virgin Islands. He received some formal education but was largely self-taught. He emigrated to the United States in 1891, moving to New York City. Schomburg worked in a law office, was active in the "Porto [sic] Rican Revolutionary Party," and began his lifelong quest to amass a collection of African-American books and other materials in order to demonstrate the existence and significance of black history. In 1906 he went to work at Bankers Trust Company, where he eventually became head of the mail room, staying with the company for twenty-three years.

With his broad knowledge and passion for African-American history, Schomburg became a leading spirit in the Harlem Renaissance and an inspiration to a generation of historians. He was an active Prince Hall Mason, he cofounded with John Edward Bruce in 1911 the Negro Society for Historical Research, and in 1922 he became president of the soon-to-be moribund American Negro Academy. Schomburg wrote numerous pamphlets and bibliographical studies. His best-known essay is "The Negro Digs Up His Past" in Alain Locke's *The New Negro* (1925), a call to the important task of careful scholarly research into African and African-American history.

In 1925 the New York Public Library established a special Negro Division at the 135th Street Branch. The next year the Carnegie Corporation purchased for $10,000 Schomburg's vast and unequalled collection of books, manuscripts, and art works and donated it to the library. Schomburg, who was a librarian at Fisk University from 1930 to 1932, became curator of his own collection with another Carnegie grant, which he received in 1932. His

Arthur Alfonso Schomburg. *A self-taught historian, the bibliophile Schomburg amassed an unparalleled collection of books and materials on black history and culture. These works are preserved in one of the world's largest repositories of such materials—Harlem's Schomburg Center for Research in Black Culture.* PHOTOGRAPHS AND PRINTS DIVISION, SCHOMBURG CENTER FOR RESEARCH IN BLACK CULTURE, THE NEW YORK PUBLIC LIBRARY, ASTOR, LENOX AND TILDEN FOUNDATIONS.

Arthur A. Schomburg

"We need the historian and philosopher to give us with trenchant pen, the story of our forefathers, and let our soul and body, with phosphorescent light, brighten the chasm that separates us. We should cling to them just as blood is thicker than water."

RACIAL INTEGRITY: A PLEA FOR THE ESTABLISHMENT OF A CHAIR OF NEGRO HISTORY IN OUR SCHOOLS, COLLEGES, ETC. PUBLISHED IN 1913 IN NANCY CUNARD'S WORK, *NEGRO.*

collection forms the core of the present Schomburg Center for Research in Black Culture, the largest collection of materials by and about people of African descent.

An Arthur Schomburg Award for Excellence in African Studies is awarded each year.

See also Harlem Renaissance; Locke, Alain Leroy

Bibliography

Knight, Robert. "Arthur 'Afroborinqueno' Schomburg." Available from *Civil Rights Journal,* <http://www.escape.com/~rknight/schombrg.html>.

Sinnette, Elinor Des Verney. *Arthur Alfonso Schomburg: Black Bibliophile and Collector.* Detroit: Wayne State University Press, 1989.

RICHARD NEWMAN (1996)
Updated bibliography

Schuyler, George S.

February 25, 1895
August 31, 1977

The journalist George Samuel Schuyler, often considered a political gadfly because of his move from young radical socialist to arch-conservative later in life, was born in Providence, Rhode Island, in 1895. Raised in Syracuse, New York, he attended school until he was seventeen, when he dropped out to enter the U.S. Army. He spent seven years in the service and saw action as a first lieutenant in France during World War I.

After leaving the service, Schuyler was active in the labor movement, sometimes moving between Syracuse and New York City. He finally settled in New York as the Harlem Renaissance began. Although never a star of the Renaissance, he served as its goad. It was Schuyler's essay, "The Negro-Art Hokum," for example, that spurred Langston Hughes's now classic 1926 response, "The Negro Artist and the Racial Mountain." Both essays appeared in the *Nation.* In 1923 Schuyler joined A. Philip Randolph's *Messenger* as a columnist and assistant editor, and he later became its managing editor. The publication was considered so fiery that several southern members of Congress brought it under House investigation.

Schuyler moved on to do publicity for the NAACP, whose publication *The Crisis,* under the editorship of W. E. B. Du Bois, had opposed the radicalism of Randolph, Schuyler, and others. Schuyler's first book, *Racial Intermarriage in the United States,* was published in 1929.

In 1931 Schuyler published two novels—*Black No More* and *Slaves Today: A Story of Liberia.* The first is a scathing satire in which black people are able to ingest a certain chemical that causes them to vanish from Harlem and reappear elsewhere as whites. *Slaves Today* describes the slavelike labor conditions in Liberia. A third novel, *Black Empire,* assembled from fiction serialized from 1936 through mid-1937 in the *Pittsburgh Courier,* a black weekly newspaper, was posthumously published in book form in 1991. The novel tells of a black elite, headed by a fascist-like black genius, that revenges wrongs done by whites in the United States, gathers an army and air force, and heads to Africa, where the genius of black scientists carves out a black empire that defeats all incursions by European whites. Schuyler wrote this work under the pen name of Samuel I. Brooks. (He also used Brooks and other pseudonyms until 1939 while publishing fiction in the *Courier.*)

From 1927 to 1933, Schuyler published nine essays in H. L. Mencken's *American Mercury.* Eugene Gordon, a black communist of the period, wrote in 1934 in Nancy Cunard's *Negro* that Schuyler was "an opportunist of the most odious sort," which indicates that to some he had already distanced himself from socialism. Shortly thereafter, Schuyler began a forty-year sojourn with the *Courier.* While he published furiously, he noted that his primary interest was in "having enough money to live on properly." He supplemented his sixty-dollar weekly *Courier* salary by publishing in several white-owned journals, including the *Nation, Plain Talk,* and *Common Ground.*

During his prime, Schuyler was considered to be one of the best journalists working. His satire was called Rabelaisian, and he frequently played devil's advocate. He and his wife, Josephine, had a daughter, Philippa, in 1931. A prodigy who had grown to become a noted concert pianist, she was killed in 1967, at age thirty-five, in a helicopter crash while on tour in Vietnam. Schuyler died in 1977.

See also *Crisis, The*; Du Bois, W. E. B.; Journalism; Randolph, Asa Philip

Bibliography

Peplow, Michael W., *George S. Schuyler,* New York: Twayne, 1980.

Schuyler, George S. *Black and Conservative: The Autobiography of George S. Schuyler.* New Rochelle, N.Y.: Arlington House, 1966.

JOHN A. WILLIAMS (1996)

Science

As a race, people of African origin have been the object of scientific scrutiny and analysis in America since the colonial period. The practice of science—and the perspectives of its practitioners—were shaped to a large extent by prevailing social and theological notions of racial hierarchy. Science operated on the assumption that "the Negro race" was inferior; it helped define race and was subsequently abused in the promotion of racism in America.

Racial Concepts

Models of racial classification had roots in the work of the eighteenth-century Swedish naturalist Carl Linnaeus. Linnaeus's framework was adopted by nineteenth-century naturalists and broadened by Georges Cuvier, Charles Lyell, Charles Darwin, and others to include analysis of hair, skull, and facial features. Lyell and Darwin thought of the "Negro" as an intermediate step on the ladder of evolution, somewhere between monkey and Caucasian. Cuvier held that blacks were "the most degraded of human races, whose form approaches that of the beast." Louis Agassiz, the Swiss-born American naturalist and professor at Harvard University, considered the Negro almost a separate species. It was difficult, he said, in observing "their black faces with their thick lips and grimacing teeth . . . to repress the feeling that they are not of the same blood as us."

The racially charged views of these and other scientists became part of the legacy passed on to succeeding generations. Nineteenth-century America, for example, saw the rise of craniometry (measurement of the brain) and anthropometry (the taking of anatomical measurements in general) as methods of exploring and comparing the physical, mental, and moral condition of the races. This work was carried out, during the Civil War and afterward, largely by white physicians in the service of governmental bodies such as the U.S. Sanitary Commission, a predecessor of the U.S. Public Health Service.

Physicians played a vital role in developing a science-based analysis of black people. The condition of African Americans (often referred to as "the other race") was a common topic of discussion in professional journals, at conferences, and in articles on health topics for popular newspapers and magazines during the nineteenth century. White physicians portrayed African Americans as constitutionally weak—more prone to disease than whites, with a higher mortality rate, and exhibiting signs that pointed toward eventual extinction. Data and statistics, generally void of appropriate context, were used to buttress this thesis. The low rate of suicide among blacks, for example, was interpreted as a reflection of limited intellectual capacity—an indication that blacks lived only for the moment and, unlike whites, lacked the conceptual skills necessary to plan and shape the future.

Nineteenth-century black physicians remained more or less silent about the racial dogmas advanced by their white counterparts for several reasons. First, since white organizations generally refused to admit them to membership, black physicians were kept busy developing alternative forums—their own professional societies, discussion groups, journals—to provide opportunities for shared learning and experience. The National Medical Association, the black counterpart of the American Medical Association, was founded in 1895 through the efforts of prominent physicians such as Miles Vandahurst Lynk and Robert Fulton Boyd. Second, black physicians recognized that generating racial or political controversy risked a backlash that could undermine efforts to place their own professional role and community on a solid foundation. And third, some black professionals accepted the truth of racial stereotypes and distanced themselves from the perceived taint of their race by thinking of themselves as unique, as somehow different from the "typical" African American.

Eugenics and Other Movements

In the early twentieth century, activities pursued under the guise of science continued to point to the alleged inferiority of African Americans. The eugenics movement is a good example. While it had always been present in some form (in spirit if not in name), eugenics assumed formal standing as a science with the rediscovery of botanist Gregor Mendel's seminal paper on genetics in 1900 and the establishment in 1910 of the Eugenics Record Office at Cold Spring Harbor, Long Island, New York. Defined as the science of improving the hereditary qualities of particular races or breeds, eugenics found devotees among geneticists and reputable practitioners in other branches of the biological sciences. It captured the public imagination, bringing issues of racial inferiority into focus not only in the realm of natural science, but in the social arena as well. Eugenics, with its growing stock of data on what were termed "weak races," fed into regressive social policies, such as the anti-immigration movement and programs of coercive sterilization aimed at "purifying" the nation's population stocks. Its ideas permeated American society, promoting racial fear among whites and self-antipathy among some blacks. Although eugenics slipped out of the mainstream of American science in the 1930s following its adoption by the Germans as a social-engineering tool, its assumptions remained firmly embedded in the American social fabric.

The racial thrust underlying the work of the craniometrists, anthropometrists, physician-scientists, and eugenicists persisted past the middle of the twentieth century—in spite of the rise of the civil rights movement. In some respects, it persists down to the present day. Examples are numerous. From 1932 to 1972, the U.S. Public Health Service carried out the Tuskegee Study of Untreated Syphilis in the Negro Male (popularly known as the Tuskegee Syphilis Experiment). This project gathered together four hundred African-American "guinea pigs"; misled them about the nature of their illness by reinforcing the subjects' belief that they were suffering from vague ailments related to "bad blood"; and withheld treatment from them in order to observe the progress of the disease. One rationale underlying the project was the need to assess racial differences in the impact of the disease. Then there was the segregation of blood in the armed services during World War II. Still later, during the 1960s and 1970s, Arthur Jensen, Richard Herrnstein, and William Shockley applied IQ and other data in studies of racial differences. These scientists drew broad conclusions, for example, about the genetic inferiority—and, in particular, the inherently lower intelligence—of blacks as compared to whites. Since the 1980s, some work in sociobiology and genetic engineering has attempted to identify genes with behavioral traits. In 1992 the National Institutes of Health awarded funds for a conference on heredity and criminal behavior but later withdrew support to placate critics who felt that linking genetics and crime in this way could add renewed authority to theories that blacks (represented disproportionately in U.S. crime statistics) were biologically inferior.

African Americans in Science

Science may have been used and abused in racially motivated ways, but this has not stopped African Americans from being drawn to careers in the field. The history of blacks in American science is as old as the history of science in America. In colonial America, free blacks were known for their inventive, scientific, and technical skills. The first to achieve a national reputation in science was Benjamin Banneker (1731–1806), known in the latter part of the eighteenth century as a mathematician, astronomer, and compiler and publisher of almanacs. In 1791 Banneker served as part of a team of surveyors and engineers who contributed to planning the city of Washington, D.C. Other free blacks, including Thomas L. Jennings (1791–1859) and Norbert Rillieux (1806–1894), developed and patented technical devices in the years leading up to the Civil War. Some slaves were known for their inventive abilities, but their legal status prevented them from holding patents and from receiving widespread public recognition of their achievement.

After the Civil War, the number of blacks undertaking scientific work increased slowly. The establishment of black institutions of higher learning—necessary because white institutions did not routinely admit African-American students—provided an essential start. Nevertheless, black colleges and universities tended to focus on curricula in theology, education, medicine, and other fields that were more practical (or technical) than scientific, geared primarily toward creating a niche or foothold for African-American professionals in the social and economic mainstream. Science, in the sense of an activity devoted to pure or basic research, did not fit readily into this framework. As a result, African Americans wanting specialized science education or training were obliged to seek out programs at white institutions. It was a difficult proposition that only a few tackled successfully before the end of the nineteenth century. One of the earliest was Edward Alexander Bouchet (1852–1918), who earned a Ph.D. in physics from Yale University in 1876. Bouchet was said to have been the first African American to earn a Ph.D. from an American university. His subsequent career did not, however, include research in the sciences. He became a high-school science teacher at the Institute for Colored Youth in Philadelphia. Because of his race, professional opportunities in science were essentially closed to him. Bouchet's was nonetheless an important accomplishment, a counterexample to the widespread mythology about the mental inferiority of blacks.

The number of blacks entering scientific fields increased markedly after the turn of the twentieth century. Among these were Charles Henry Turner, zoologist; George Washington Carver, agricultural botanist; Ernest Everett Just, embryologist; St. Elmo Brady, chemist; Elmer Samuel Imes, physicist; William Augustus Hinton, bacteriologist; and Julian Herman Lewis, pathologist. Percy Lavon Julian, a chemist, and Charles Richard Drew, a surgeon and pioneer of the blood-banking system, followed a couple of decades later. This cohort represents the first group of black scientists to receive graduate degrees from major white universities, pursue science at the research level, and publish in leading scientific journals.

World War II brought African-American scientists, as a distinct group, to public attention for the first time. Prior to this, they had worked primarily as teachers at black colleges and universities, and had not—with the notable exception, perhaps, of Ernest Just—exerted their influence widely or made their presence felt in the larger scientific community. As part of the war mobilization effort at the Los Alamos National Laboratory in New Mexico and in the various branches of the Manhattan Project attached to laboratories at the University of Chicago, Columbia University, and other universities, some white scientists witnessed for the first time a sizable number of black physicists and chemists entering their world. African Americans who worked on the atom bomb project included Edwin Roberts Russell, Benjamin Franklin Scott, J. Ernest Wilkins Jr., Jasper Brown Jeffries, George Warren Reed Jr., Moddie Daniel Taylor, and the brothers Lawrence Howland Knox and William Jacob Knox Jr. At a postwar conference in 1946, one eminent white scientist, Arthur Holly Compton, remarked on how the bomb project had brought races and religions together for a common purpose.

After the war, even though a few white universities began to open up faculty appointments and graduate fellowships to blacks, racial discrimination continued to operate at many levels within the professional world of science. It was common for major associations, including the American Association for the Advancement of Science, to hold conventions in cities where segregation was both customary and legally enforced, and where hotels serving as convention sites denied accommodation to anyone of African-American origin. Blacks often relied on their own scientific associations, such as the National Institute of Science (founded in 1942) and Beta Kappa Chi Scientific Society (incorporated in 1929), to share ideas and foster collegial ties. Furthermore, most science education for African Americans—certainly at the undergraduate level—continued to take place within the confines of historically black colleges and universities.

Following passage of the 1964 U.S. Civil Rights Bill, new educational opportunities gradually opened up for blacks, and scientific careers—in both academia and industry—became more of a tangible, realistic goal. Rosters of noteworthy scientists from the 1960s to the 1990s mention a number of African Americans, including Harold Amos, bacteriologist; Shirley Ann Jackson, physicist; Edward William Hawthorne, physiologist; Marie Maynard Daly, biochemist; and Ronald Erwin McNair, astronautical physicist. Scientific organizations, learned societies, and educational institutions grew more inclusive during this period. David Harold Blackwell, a mathematician, was elected to the National Academy of Sciences in 1965. The physicist Walter Eugene Massey became the first African-American president of the American Association for the Advancement of Science in 1988 and the first African-American director of the National Science Foundation in 1990.

President George H. W. Bush's Goals 2000 initiative, in which he pledged to make America's students "first in math and science," gave the scientific renaissance of the 1970s and the mid-1980s a boost in 1989. In the ensuing years, African Americans gained greater access to all levels of education in the sciences, increased the percentage of degrees in the sciences they earned relative to their population in the general society, and entered science-related fields in academia and the professions in unprecedented numbers. However, disparities still remain in precollege, undergraduate, and graduate science education and contribute to persistent racial inequalities in the American workforce in the first decade of the twenty-first century. Although African Americans represented around 12 percent of the total U.S. population in 2004, they constituted less than 3 percent of American scientists.

Science in the Twenty-First Century

The postindustrial revolution gained momentum in the early 1990s and prompted dramatic social, economic, and cultural changes in the United States and the international community. The economy in twenty-first-century America, for instance, no longer relies primarily on manufacturing but rather on information. Computers are the engines that drive the information age, and, though underrepresented in the field, black scientists have made basic contributions to advance digital technologies in the global society. For instance, Mark Dean (b. 1957), a Stanford Ph.D. and vice president of IBM and widely considered to be the architect of the modern personal computer, led the design team that created the first one-gigahertz computer processor. Thus, not only was he central to making computers accessible to the common person, he helped to make them faster and much more efficient, too. In addition, Philip Emeagwali (b. 1954), the Nigerian-born Internet and supercomputer pioneer, made scientific breakthroughs that helped to make the world a much smaller place, opening the door to modes of communication that many now take for granted, such as e-mail and text messages.

See also Banneker, Benjamin; Carver, George Washington; Inventors and Inventions; Race and Science; Race, Scientific Theories of

Bibliography

Bolner, Myrtle S., and Gayle A Poirier. *The Research Process: Books and Beyond.* Dubuque, Ia.: Kendall/Hunt, 2003.

Branson, Herman. "The Negro and Scientific Research." *Negro History Bulletin* 15 (April 1952): 131–136, 151.

Drew, Charles Richard. "Negro Scholars in Scientific Research." *Journal of Negro History* 35 (April 1950): 135–149.

Haber, Louis. *Black Pioneers of Science and Invention.* New York: Harcourt, Brace, & World, 1970.

Hudson, Wade. *Book of Black Heroes: Scientists, Healers, and Inventors.* East Orange, N.J.: Just Us Books, 2003.

Klein, Aaron E. *The Hidden Contributors: Black Scientists and Inventors in America.* Garden City, N.Y.: Doubleday, 1971.

Manning, Kenneth R. "The Complexion of Science." *Technology Review* 94 (November/December 1991): 60–69.

Manning, Kenneth R. "Race, Science, and Identity." In *Lure and Loathing: Essays on Race, Identity, and the Ambivalence of Assimilation,* edited by Gerald Early. New York: A. Lane/Penguin, 1993.

"Minorities in Science: The Pipeline Problem." *Science* 258 (1992): 1175–1237.

National Science Foundation. *Employed Science and Engineering Doctorate Holders, by Race/Ethnicity and Field of Doctorate, 2001.* Washington, D.C.: Authors, 2004. Available from <http://www.nsf.gov/sbe/srs/wmpd/figh 2.htm>.

Pearson, Willie, Jr. *Black Scientists, White Society, and Colorless Science: A Study of Universalism in American Science.* Millwood, N.Y.: Associated Faculty Press, 1985.

Sullivan, Otha Richard. *African American Inventors.* New York: Wiley, 1998.

Sullivan, Otha Richard. *African American Women Scientists and Inventors.* New York: Wiley, 2002.

Warren, Wini. *Black Women Scientists in the United States.* Bloomington: Indiana University Press, 2000.

Wright, Clarence. "The Negro in the Natural Sciences." In *Negro Year Book: A Review of Events Affecting Negro Life, 1941–1946,* edited by Jessie P. Guzman. Tuskegee, Ala.: Dept. of Records and Research, Tuskegee Institute, 1947.

KENNETH R. MANNING (1996)
GARRETT ALBERT DUNCAN (2005)

SCLC

See Southern Christian Leadership Conference (SCLC)

Scott, Emmett J.

February 13, 1873
December 12, 1957

The author and administrator Emmett Scott was born in Houston, Texas, and briefly attended Wiley College in Marshall, Texas, before beginning to work as a journalist at the *Houston Post* in 1881. (He was awarded an honorary M.A. from Wiley College in 1901.) In 1894 he founded and edited his own weekly African-American newspaper, the *Houston Freeman.* Because his views were generally in close agreement with those of Booker T. Washington, Washington asked Scott to become his personal secretary. From this position, which Scott held until Washington's death in 1915, he was elected secretary of the Tuskegee Institute in 1912. Scott was widely recognized as a leader in what later became known as the Tuskegee Machine, the group of people close to Booker T. Washington who wielded great influence over African-American presses, churches, and schools in order to promote Washington's views.

After Washington's death, Scott became special assistant to the U.S. secretary of war in charge of Negro affairs at the start of World War I. At a time when race relations in the military were an issue of debate, Scott became the liaison between black soldiers and the War Department. From 1919 until 1939, Scott held positions as secretary, treasurer, or business manager at Howard University, in Washington, D.C. There he helped create procedures for electing the first alumni trustees. In the business community, Scott became the principal organizer of the National Negro Business League. Like Washington, Scott believed that African Americans who achieved business success and property ownership would be given political and civil rights. His views are set forth in such works as *Tuskegee and Its People* (1910), *The American Negro in the World War* (1919), and a biography of his mentor, *Booker T. Washington, Builder of a Civilization* (1916).

See also Washington, Booker T.

Bibliography

Emmett Jay Scott papers, Morris A. Soper Library of Morgan State University, Baltimore, Md.

Logan, Rayford, ed. *Dictionary of American Negro Biography.* New York: W. W. Norton, 1982.

Low, W. Augustus, ed. *Encyclopedia of Black America.* New York: McGraw-Hill, 1981.

SASHA THOMAS (1996)

Scott, Hazel

June 11, 1920
October 2, 1981

The pianist and singer Hazel Dorothy Scott was born in Port of Spain, Trinidad, to Alma Long Scott, a musician, and Thomas Scott, a college professor. In 1924 her father obtained a teaching position in the United States, and the family moved to New York City.

Scott began playing the piano at age two and made her performance debut at age three in Trinidad. At the initiative of her mother, she began formal musical training when the family moved to New York; she made her U.S. debut as a five-year-old at New York's Town Hall. Three years later, Scott auditioned for a scholarship at Juilliard School of Music. Although it was decided that she was too young to enter the school, Professor Paul Wagner, who presided over the audition, was so impressed with her rendition of Rachmaninoff's Prelude in C-Sharp Minor that he offered to take her on as a private student.

Scott's father died in 1934, and her mother took a job as a saxophonist in Lil Hardin Armstrong's all-female band. A few months later, Scott's mother decided to organize her own band—Alma Long Scott's All-Woman Orchestra—with Hazel playing both piano and trumpet. In 1936, at age sixteen, Scott played with the Count Basie Orchestra at the Roseland Ballroom and on a radio program broadcast on the Mutual Broadcasting System. By age eighteen, already a veteran of the road, Scott appeared on Broadway in the musical *Sing Out the News.* She then became a film actress in the 1940s and played herself in such films as *Something to Shout About* (1943), *Broadway Rhythm* (1944), and *Rhapsody in Blue* (1945). In 1945, in a high-profile marriage, Scott married New York Representative Adam Clayton Powell Jr. Although the marriage quickly faltered, beginning with a separation of several years and finally ending in divorce in 1956, the couple produced one child, Adam Clayton Powell III, in 1946.

In 1950 Scott hosted a summer television program, *Hazel Scott,* on which she performed show tunes and café favorites, becoming the first black woman to host her own television program. However, as a political activist who had refused to appear before segregated audiences and was a vocal critic of McCarthyism, she was listed in the notorious *Red Channels,* a publication of names of entertainers who were thought to be involved in Communist Party activity. On September 14, 1950, Scott testified before the House Un-American Activities Committee in defense of her right to appear at rallies and events for political causes. Her show was canceled shortly thereafter.

In 1961 Scott moved to Europe after remarrying, but when her marriage ended in divorce five years later, she returned to the United States. Upon her return, she made guest appearances on such television shows as *Julia* and *The Bold Ones.* Scott continued to perform in New York–area clubs until a few months before her death from cancer in 1981.

See also Basie, William James "Count"; Jazz; Music in the United States

Bibliography

Bogle, Donald. *Blacks in American Films and Television.* New York: Garland, 1988.

Hine, Darlene Clark, ed. *Black Women in America,* 2d ed. New York: Oxford University Press, 2005.

KENYA DILDAY (1996)
Updated bibliography

Scott, James Sylvester

February 12, 1885
August 30, 1938

The ragtime composer James Scott was born in Neosho, Missouri. As a child, he taught himself to play piano. After his family moved to Carthage, Missouri, around the turn of the twentieth century, Scott worked as a shoeshine boy. He also began to play music professionally, often performing on piano and steam calliope at local fairs and amusement parks. From 1902 to 1914 he worked as a window washer and picture framer, as well as a clerk and song plugger at Dumar's Music Store. It was during this time that he also began composing and publishing ragtime songs. Among his earliest successes were "A Summer Breeze" (1903) and "The Fascinator" (1903). In 1906 he visited Scott Joplin (1868–1917) in St. Louis, and though the two never worked together, Joplin did introduce Scott to John Stark, who became Scott's publisher and gave titles to most of Scott's compositions.

In his prime Scott was considered one of the "big three" of ragtime (along with Scott Joplin and the white composer Joseph Lamb). Scott's compositions, with their manic leaps, buoyant rhythms and rich, moody tonalities, helped define the classic ragtime sound. His most important ragtime compositions from this time include "Frog Legs Rag" (1906), "Great Scott Rag" (1909), "The Ragtime Betty" (1909), "Sunburst Rag" (1909), "Grace and Beauty" (1909), and "Hilarity Rag" (1910). Although Scott made no piano rolls, there is evidence to suggest that, in addition to writing many of the classics of ragtime, he was a fine pianist as well.

In 1914 Scott moved to Kansas City, Kansas, where he taught, arranged, and worked as piano accompanist at the Paramount, Eblon, and Lincoln Theaters. He continued to compose as well, publishing "Climax Rag" (1914), "Evergreen Rag" (1915), "Prosperity Rag" (1916), "Paramount Rag" (1916), "Peace and Plenty Rag" (1919), and "Modesty Rag" (1920). He also wrote waltzes, including "Suffragette" (1914) and "Springtime of Love" (1919).

In the 1920s and 1930s, Scott led a band in Kansas City, but he never regained his previous success and popularity. During his last years Scott lived in relative anonymity. The rise of jazz eclipsed the popularity of ragtime, and the introduction of sound into movies prevented him from earning a living as an accompanist to silent films. Scott suffered from dropsy and died of kidney failure in 1938. His grave in Kansas City was unmarked until 1981, when a resurgence of interest in his music, and of ragtime in general, led to the establishment of a fund to purchase a headstone for the grave.

See also Jazz; Joplin, Scott; Ragtime

Bibliography

DeVeaux, Scott, and William H. Kenney. *The Music of James Scott.* Washington, D.C.: Smithsonian Institution Press, 1992.

Haase, John Edward, ed. *Ragtime: Its History, Composers, and Music.* New York: Schirmer Books, 1985.

JONATHAN GILL (1996)

Scott-Heron, Gil

April 1, 1949

Composer and writer Gil Scott-Heron spent his childhood in Jackson, Tennessee, until the age of thirteen, when he moved to New York City. He attended Lincoln University in Pennsylvania because two men he greatly admired, Langston Hughes and African leader Kwame Nkrumah, had gone to Lincoln. After his freshman year he took a leave of absence to write a novel, *The Vulture,* and a book of poetry, *Small Talk at 125th and Lenox,* both published in 1970. He returned to Lincoln to complete his sophomore year and then applied to the graduate program at Johns Hopkins University. In 1972 he received an M.A. and published a second novel, *The Nigger Factory.*

Although he published a second book of poetry, *So Far, So Good,* in 1988, Scott-Heron has concentrated on composing, performing, and recording music. From 1974 on, he was accompanied by the Midnight Band, led by Brian Jackson. With Jackson, a pianist, generally concentrating on musical arrangements and Scott-Heron collaborating on lyrics, the group has produced nearly twenty recordings, including *Winter in America, Sun City, From South Africa to South Carolina,* and his last album, in 1994, *Spirits.* Combining Latin, blues, and jazz rhythms with a distinct vocal style, Scott-Heron uses music to interpret the political and social experience of black people throughout the world.

In 2001 Scott-Heron was sentenced to from one to three years in prison for failing to enter a drug rehabilitation program after pleading guilty to cocaine possession in 2000.

See also Music in the United States

Bibliography

"*BBB* Interviews Gil Scott-Heron." *Black Books Bulletin* 6, no. 3 (1979): 36–41.

Chatman, Priscilla. "Gil Scott-Heron and His Music." *Black Stars* 5, no. 2 (1975): 14–18.

Salaam, Kalamu ya. "Where He's Coming From: Gil Scott-Heron." *Black Collegian* 35 (1980): 182–190.

GENETTE MCLAURIN (1996)
Updated by publisher 2005

Scottsboro Case

On April 9, 1931, an Alabama judge sentenced eight black teenagers to death: Haywood Patterson, Olen Montgomery, Clarence Norris, Willie Roberson, Andrew Wright, Ozie Powell, Eugene Williams, and Charley Weems. After perfunctory trials in the mountain town of Scottsboro, all-white juries convicted the youths of raping two white women (Victoria Price and Ruby Bates) aboard a freight train as it moved across northern Alabama on March 25. The case of the ninth defendant—thirteen-year-old Leroy Wright—ended in a mistrial after a majority of the jury refused to accept the prosecution's recommendation for life imprisonment because of his extreme youth.

The repercussions of the Scottsboro case were felt throughout the 1930s; by the end of the decade, it had become one of the great civil rights cases of the twentieth century.

After the quick conviction and draconian verdict, the Communist Party's legal affiliate, the International Labor Defense (ILD), took over the case from the National Association for the Advancement of Colored People. Using both propaganda and aggressive legal action, the ILD succeeded in obtaining a new trial for the eight defendants. In a landmark case, *Powell v. Alabama* (1932), the U.S. Supreme Court ruled that defendants in capital cases had to receive more than a pro forma defense. (One Scottsboro attorney had been drunk at the original trial; the other was elderly and incompetent.)

The April 1933 retrial of Haywood Patterson was moved to Decatur, Alabama. Defense attorney Samuel Leibowitz introduced extensive evidence that the two women had concocted the charge of rape in order to avoid prosecution for prostitution and vagrancy. The highlight of the trial came when Ruby Bates—who had disappeared in 1932—dramatically renounced her earlier accusations and testified on behalf of Patterson and the other Scottsboro defendants.

But the jurors—reflecting the belief of the local white community that Bates was bribed by communist agitators ("Jew money from New York" in the words of one prosecutor)—ignored her testimony. They were particularly incensed by the willingness of Alabama's African-American population to join the defense in attacking the state's all-white jury system. (In pretrial hearings before Judge James E. Horton Jr., ten members of Decatur's black community defied Klan cross burnings and threats to insist that they were qualified to serve as jurors but had never been called.) The jury convicted Patterson and mandated the judge to order the death penalty.

To the surprise of almost everyone, Judge Horton—convinced that Patterson and the other defendants were innocent—set aside the verdict, pointing out that the evidence "overwhelmingly preponderated" in favor of the Scottsboro defendants. He ordered a new trial and announced that the nine defendants would never be convicted in his court. In the next election, however, voters defeated Horton and elected a judge more amenable to the prosecution's case to preside over the trial of Patterson and Clarence Norris.

Many in Alabama had come to see the Scottsboro Case as a test of white Southerners' resolve against the forces of "communism" and "racial amalgamation." The guilt or innocence of the defendants thus seemed irrelevant.

The trials that followed were travesties of justice. Horton's replacement, Judge William Washington Callahan, barred critical defense evidence, bullied and belittled defense attorneys and witnesses, and effectively acted as co-prosecutor. In the fall of 1933 all-white juries convicted both Patterson and Clarence Norris.

ILD attorneys once again successfully appealed to the Supreme Court, this time on the grounds that African Americans had been systematically excluded from Alabama juries. In *Norris v. Alabama* (1935), the Court accepted the defense argument, overturned the Norris and Patterson verdicts, and returned the case to Alabama for retrial. The decision, though not ending all-white juries, marked another step in the Supreme Court's willingness to chip away at the legal system of the South.

In 1936 oversight of the case passed from the Communist Party to a coalition of mainline civil rights organizations. This shift gave Alabama officials—by now embarrassed over the continuing judicial rebukes—an opportunity to compromise. The state dropped the charges against the four youngest defendants, and the other five received prison sentences from twenty years to life with the understanding that once publicity in the case had subsided, they would be quietly released. Despite the intense lobbying of national civil rights leaders (and the secret intervention of President Franklin Roosevelt), Alabama officials blocked their release. It was 1950 before the last of the Scottsboro defendants, Andrew Wright, received his parole.

For a generation of African Americans who came of age in the 1930s, the Scottsboro Case was a vivid reminder of white legal oppression, and it helped further their resolve to mobilize against Jim Crow.

See also Criminal Justice System

Bibliography

Carter, Dan T. *Scottsboro: A Tragedy of the American South*, 2d ed. Baton Rouge: Louisiana State University Press, 1976.

Kinshasa, Kwando Mbiassi. *The Man From Scottsboro: Clarence Norris and the Infamous 1931 Alabama Rape Trial, In His Own Words.* Jefferson, N.C.: McFarland, 1997.

Norris, Clarence, and Sybil Washington. *The Last of the Scottsboro Boys: An Autobiography.* New York: Putnam, 1979.

Patterson, Haywood, and Earl Conrade. *Scottsboro Boy.* New York: Doubleday, 1950.

DAN T. CARTER (1996)
Updated bibliography

SEACOLE, MARY

1805
MAY 14, 1881

Mary Grant Seacole's autobiography, *The Wonderful Adventures of Mrs. Seacole in Many Lands,* was published in England in 1857. Although the book provides some details of her personal life, the text is primarily concerned with detailing Seacole's "roving inclination." Seacole was born in Kingston, Jamaica, to a free black Creole woman and a white Scotsman. As a young woman, she trained under her mother, an eminent "doctress," and she went on to minister to many members of Britain's military force stationed in Kingston, as well as to local people. In addition to her medical skills, which would continue to expand, she was also an entrepreneur, running a series of business ventures in Jamaica, Panama, England, and the Crimea. Although widowed after a brief marriage, she chose to pursue her goal "to be useful" rather than retire from life and society.

In 1850, Seacole's "roving inclination" persuaded her to follow her brother to Panama, where she planned to help him run his hotel and store. Her autobiography describes her unwavering refusal to let the difficulty of travel deter or dissuade her resolve. In 1854, this perseverance sustained her when she volunteered her services to the War Department in England at the outbreak of the Crimean War. She was rebuffed at every turn, due to what she called the "infection of American racism" upon officials at War Department, British aid agencies, and Florence Nightingale's organization serving in the Crimea. Undeterred, Seacole decided to go to the Crimea anyway, with the intent of opening up a small hotel and hospital. When Seacole returned to England she was destitute. After the failure of a few business ventures, she eventually wrote her memoirs.

Seacole's autobiography is significant for a number of reasons. Her zest for life and adventure are evident through the narrative. Although successful in the womanly arts of nurturance, Seacole consistently portrays herself as a strong and capable woman, willing and able to assert her independence with fortitude and humor. The narrative is strewn with her shrewd observations of various peoples, classes, and nationalities, especially as they pertain to race. Although as a brown, or "yaller," woman, Seacole expresses the sharpest scorn for Americans and others who dislike blacks for no reason other than skin color, she also admonishes lazy blacks and Indians. She also asserts that, due to the enterprising blood of her Scotsman father, she is unlike the usual lazy Creoles. One of the most striking features of the narrative, in addition to the author's strong voice, is Seacole's decision to tell her story in the way she wanted. Unlike other travel narratives, and narratives of the Crimean War, Seacole does not adhere to a strict chronological or diary-style arrangement. Instead, Seacole's narrative is a glorious mélange of letters, narrative description, adventure tale, medical treatise, and social commentary.

See also Women Writers of the Caribbean

Bibliography

Baggett, Paul. "Caught between Homes: Mary Seacole and the Question of Cultural Identity." *MaComère* 3 (2000): 45–56.

Hawthorne, Evelyn J. "Self-Writing, Literary Traditions, and Post-Emancipation Identity: The Case of Mary Seacole." *Biography* 23, no. 2 (2000): 309–331.

Paravisini-Gebert, Lizabeth. "Mrs. Seacole's *Wonderful Adventures in Many Lands* and the Consciousness of Transit." In *Black Victorians/Black Victoriana,* edited by Gretchen Holbrook Gerzina. New Brunswick, N.J.: Rutgers University Press, 2003.

Seacole, Mary. *The Wonderful Adventures of Mrs Seacole in Many Lands,* edited by Ziggi Alexander and Audrey Dewjee. Bristol, UK: Falling Wall Press, 1984.

NICOLE N. ALJOE (2005)

Seale, Bobby

October 22, 1936

Activist Robert George "Bobby" Seale was born to George and Thelma Seale in Dallas, Texas. Before he had reached the age of ten, his family moved to California, where his father continued in his profession as a building carpenter. At the age of eighteen, Bobby Seale was accepted into the U.S. Air Force and sent to Amarillo, Texas, for training as an aircraft sheet-metal mechanic. After training for six months, he graduated as an honor student from the Technical School Class of Air Force Training. He was then sent to Ellsworth Air Force Base in Rapid City, South Dakota, where he served for three and a half years and was discharged as a corporal. He attended Merrit College in Oakland, California, after his discharge.

When he enrolled in college in 1961, Seale intended to study engineering. He joined the Afro-American Association, an organization formed by young militant African Americans in Oakland to explore the various problems confronting the black community. Influenced by the association's regular book discussion sessions, Seale became interested in the works of Mao Zedong and Kwame Nkrumah, and he also began to read W. E. B. Du Bois and Booker T. Washington. His awareness of and involvement in the Afro-American Association were shaped by a fellow student, Huey Newton, whose articulation of the social problems victimizing the black community attracted his interest.

With Newton, Seale formed the Soul Students Advisory Council, which was concerned with ending the drafting of black men into the service to fight in the Vietnam War. Fired by nationalist zeal, especially after he heard Malcolm X speak, Seale invited three friends, Kenny, Isaac, and Ernie, to create the Revolutionary Action Movement to organize African Americans on the West Coast for black liberation. In October 1966, he and Huey Newton formed the Black Panther Party in Oakland. The party's objectives were reflected in its ten-point platform and program, which emphasized freedom, full employment, and equality of opportunity for African Americans. It called for an end to white racism and police brutality against black people. Although the FBI under J. Edgar Hoover's directorship declared Seale's party to be the greatest threat to the internal security of the United States, the party's programs for the poor won it broad support from the community as well as praise from civic groups. The Black Panthers also recognized the need for political participation by African Americans. To this end, it frequently organized voter registration drives. In 1968 he was one of the Chicago Eight, a group of antiwar activists put on trial for inciting a riot outside the Democratic National Convention in Chicago. He was sentenced to four years in jail, during which time he was indicted and tried for ordering the murder of a suspected Black Panther government informer. The trial ended in a hung jury.

Three years after the formation of the party, Seale shifted his philosophical and ideological stance from race to class struggle, stressing the unity of the people and arguing that the Panthers would not "fight racism with more racism." In 1973 he ran for mayor of Oakland, forcing a runoff with John Reading, the incumbent, who defeated him. In 1974 he resigned as the chairman of the Black Panther Party, perhaps in an effort to work within the mainstream political system. Since the late 1980s, Seale has been involved in an organization called Youth Employment Strategies, which he founded, and in encouraging black youth to enroll in doctoral programs. Based in Philadelphia, he describes himself as "the old cripple-footed revolutionary humanist," sells books and videos from his Web site, and shares barbecue recipes from his book, *Barbeque'n with Bobby Seale.*

See also Black Panther Party for Self-Defense; Newton, Huey P.

Bibliography

Foner, Philip, ed. *The Black Panthers Speak.* New York: Lippincott, 1976. Reprint. New York: Da Capo, 1995.

Pinckney, Alphonso. *Red, Black, and Green: Black Nationalism in the United States.* New York, 1976.

Seale, Bobby. *Seize the Time.* New York: Random House, 1970.

Seale, Bobby. *A Lonely Rage: The Autobiography of Bobby Seale.* New York: Times Books, 1978.

LEVI A. NWACHUKU (1996)

Shabazz, Betty

May 28, 1936

June 23, 1997

Betty Shabazz, the widow of Malcolm X who subsequently built a career of her own as an educator and activist, was born Betty Sanders in Detroit, Michigan, and was adopted by the Malloy's, a neighborhood family. After attending Tuskegee Institute, she moved to New York and transferred to Jersey City State College, where she received a B.A. degree. Sanders then began training at the Brooklyn State Hospital School of Nursing, where she received her R.N. in 1958. During this period she joined the Nation of Islam and changed her name to Betty X (she became Betty Shabazz in 1964). She also met the charismatic leader Malcolm X, with whom she struck up a friendship. The couple married in 1958.

During the following seven years, as Malcolm X grew into a national figure, Shabazz rarely saw him, although they remained on good terms. Shabazz gave birth to their six daughters during this period. In 1965 Shabazz and four of the girls were listening to Malcolm X speak at New York's Audubon Ballroom as he was assassinated. Following the death of her husband, Shabazz cut her ties with the Nation of Islam and became an orthodox Muslim.

Following her husband's death, Shabazz earned a Ph.D. in educational administration from the University of Massachusetts. She worked for two decades as director of public relations for Medgar Evers College in New York. During these years she also served as the guardian of Malcolm X's legacy. In 1995 Shabazz began a weekly radio program on New York's WLIB. Two years later, she was badly burned in a fire set by her twelve-year-old grandson Malcolm to protest his mother's absence. Despite many community blood donations, she died three weeks later.

See also Malcolm X

Bibliography

Brown, Jamie Foster, ed. *Betty Shabazz: A Sisterfriends' Tribute in Words and Pictures.* New York: Simon and Schuster, 1998.

Rickford, Russell John. *Betty Shabazz: A Remarkable Story of Survival and Faith Before and After Malcolm X.* Naperville, Ill.: Sourcebooks, 2003.

GREG ROBINSON (2001)
Updated by publisher 2005

Shakur, Assata (Chesimard, Joanne Deborah Bryon)

July 16, 1947

Born in Queens, New York, Joanne Deborah Bryon, a nationalist and activist, spent her early childhood alternately with her grandparents in Wilmington, North Carolina, and with her mother in New York. She dropped out of high school at seventeen but returned to college during her early twenties, attending Manhattan Community College and City College of New York. She was married for a year while in school and continued to use her married name. She became a student activist and participated in rent strikes, antiwar demonstrations, and sit-ins, protesting racial injustices. As a reflection of her new political consciousness and her commitment to her African heritage, she changed her name to Assata ("she who struggles") Shakur ("the thankful"). The assassination of the Rev. Dr. Martin Luther King Jr. in 1968 precipitated Assata Shakur's embrace of the militant Black Power movement and her rejection of nonviolence.

Assata Shakur moved to Oakland, California, where she joined the Black Panther Party (BPP) in Oakland and helped organize community education programs, demonstrations, and political rallies. When she returned to New York, she became a key member of the BPP's Harlem chapter. She helped organize and staff the Free Breakfast Program for community children, oversaw the planning of a free clinic, and coordinated member health care, first aid, and community outreach.

Assata Shakur, as well as many other members of the Harlem chapter, believed that politically motivated armed actions were a viable tactic in the struggle for black liberation. It is unclear what specific actions she participated in, but she became a prime target of the Federal Bureau of Investigation's (FBI) Counterintelligence Program (COINTELPRO). Partially because of this surveillance and harassment, Assata Shakur went into hiding and became a member of the Black Liberation Army (BLA), a clandestine nationwide network largely composed of former BPP members who had gone underground to escape criminal charges or police and FBI repression and who believed that structural change could be precipitated by armed struggle.

While underground, Assata Shakur was placed on the FBI's Most Wanted List and indicted for three bank robberies (April 5, 1971, August 23, 1971, and September 1, 1972), the kidnapping and murder of two drug dealers (December 28, 1972, and January 2, 1973), and the attempted murder of policemen on January 23, 1973. On May 2, 1973, Assata Shakur and two other BLA members were stopped on the New Jersey Turnpike by New Jersey state troopers. After the officers discovered guns in their cars, a confrontation ensued, and Assata Shakur was shot, one state trooper suffered minor injuries, and another, Werner Forrester, was killed. Assata Shakur's companions escaped. Accounts of this incident conflict, and it is unclear if Assata Shakur discharged any weapon that night. She was hospitalized and charged with Forrester's murder.

During the next four years Assata Shakur was held in detention. The trials for the indictments brought while she was underground either ended in acquittal or were dropped because of lack of evidence. During her imprisonment she was confined to a men's prison, placed in solitary confinement for a year, given inadequate medical attention, and faced physical abuse. While in prison she became pregnant by Kamau, her codefendant during her New York bank robbery trial, and gave birth to a girl in 1974. Assata Shakur's imprisonment and what many of her supporters believed was a false arrest brought international attention to her plight as a political prisoner.

In March 1977 Assata Shakur was convicted of murdering state trooper Werner Forrester, although medical experts testified that her injuries would have rendered her incapable of firing the fatal shot. She was imprisoned at the maximum security prison for women in Alderson, West Virginia, then moved to New Jersey's Clinton Correctional Facility for Women. Two years after her conviction, she escaped from prison and was given political asylum in Cuba. The circumstances behind the escape are unknown.

In 1987 Assata Shakur's autobiography, which chronicles her life and ideological development, was published. Although many of her activities in Cuba have been shrouded in secrecy, Assata Shakur continued to be a vocal activist in the 1980s and 1990s, speaking out on global justice issues and the prison industrial complex. In 1998 the U.S. Congress passed a resolution to demand Shakur's extradition from Cuba, spurring Shakur's supporters to create the "Hands of Assata" campaign.

See also Black Panther Party for Self-Defense; King, Martin Luther, Jr.

Bibliography

Perkins, Margo V. *Autobiography as Activism: Three Black Women of the Sixties.* Jackson: University Press of Mississippi, 2000.

Shakur, Assata. *Assata: An Autobiography.* Westport, Conn.: Lawrence Hill & Co., 1987.

Van DeBurg, William. *New Day in Babylon: The Black Power Movement and American Culture.* Chicago: University of Chicago Press, 1992.

ROBYN C. SPENCER (1996)
Updated by author 2005

Shange, Ntozake

October 18, 1948

Playwright, poet, novelist, and performer Ntozake Shange was born Paulette Williams in Trenton, New Jersey. She took the Zulu name Ntozake ("she who comes with her own things") Shange ("she who walks like a lion") in 1971. Shange grew up in an upper-middle-class family that was very involved in political and cultural activities. She earned degrees in American studies from Barnard (1970) and the University of Southern California (1973). She has one daughter.

Shange's writing is marked by unique spelling and punctuation, partly to establish a recognizable style, like that of a musician, but also as a reaction against Western culture. Much of her work is in the form of a "choreopoem," blending music, drama, and dance. Her work is brutally honest, reflective, and intense. She writes for those whose voices have often been ignored, especially African-American women.

Her best-known work is the landmark play *for colored girls who have considered suicide / when the rainbow is enuf* (1976). Despite many harrowing scenes the work is essentially optimistic, showing the "infinite beauty" of black women. The play's conception took place over many years; it opened on Broadway in September 1976 and played there for almost two years before going on a national and international tour.

Shange is a highly prolific author whose other published plays include *a photograph: lovers in motion, boogie woogie landscapes,* and *spell #7,* which were collected in *Three Pieces* (1981). Many other plays have not been published as yet, including *Three Views of Mt. Fuji* (1987) and a powerful adaptation of Bertolt Brecht's *Mother Courage.* (1980).

Her volumes of poetry include *Nappy Edges* (1978), *A Daughter's Geography* (1983), *From Okra to Greens* (1984), *Ridin' the Moon in Texas: Word Paintings* (1987), and *The Love Space Demands: A Continuing Saga* (1991).

Ntozake Shange. AP/WIDE WORLD PHOTOS. REPRODUCED BY PERMISSION

She has also written three novels, *Sassafrass, Cypress & Indigo* (1982), *Betsey Brown* (1985), and *Liliane: Resurrection of the Daughter* (1994). Many of these works have been adapted into theatrical form. Her prose is collected in *See No Evil: Prefaces, Essays and Accounts, 1976–1983* (1984).

In recent years Shange has continued to experiment with forms. She has written a cookbook, *If I Can Cook / You Know God Can* (1998), combining recipes with historical, literary, and cultural discussion. She has also collaborated with the photographic group Kamoinge Workshop on *The Sweet Breath of Life: A Poetic Narrative of the African-American Family* (2004), which alternates poems and photos. Increasingly, Shange has turned her attention to works for young adults. These include *Whitewash* (1997), Muhammad Ali, the Man Who Could Float like a Butterfly and Sting like a Bee (2002), and *Daddy Says* (2003), a novel about the two daughters of African-American rodeo stars.

Shange has received many awards, including the Obie and the Outer Critics Circle awards, and she won the

Heavyweight Poetry champion of the World title, awarded at the Taos Poetry Circus poetry event, from 1991 to 1993. She remains one of the most vital, influential figures in contemporary American literature.

See also Drama; Poetry, U.S.

Bibliography

Brown-Guillory, Elizabeth. *Their Place on the Stage: Black Women Playwrights in America.* New York: Praeger, 1990.

Lester, Neal A. *Ntozake Shange: A Critical Study of the Plays.* New York: Garland, 1995.

Richards, Sandra L. "Ntozake Shange." In *African American Writers,* edited by Valerie Smith, pp. 379–393. New York: Scribner's, 1991.

LOUIS J. PARASCANDOLA (1996)
Updated by author 2005

Sharpe, Samuel

c. 1801
May 23, 1832

Samuel Sharpe, a Jamaican National Hero, is best known as the chief organizer of the 1831–32 Emancipation War that hastened the passing of the British Abolition Act in 1833. In keeping with a historiographical trend that gives little visibility to the individual enslaved, biographical details on Sharpe are sketchy. Historians generally agree, however, that he was born around 1801, his parents having arrived in Jamaica from Africa between 1787 and 1801. Sharpe himself was a Creole (that is, born in Jamaica). He was named after the lawyer Samuel Sharpe, Esquire, his enslaver. He had a brother, William (who accompanied him when he decided to give himself up in 1832), and a nephew who worked at a printer's shop in Montego Bay. His mother survived him, but his father died years earlier. He was married, but (not unusually) his wife, whose father was among the rebels, lived on another property. According to a letter in the *Jamaica Advocate* in 1896, he had a daughter who married a Mr. Gaynor; and Mrs. Gaynor and her daughter, Mrs. Scott, were living in Montego Bay in 1896.

In 1831 Sharpe was working in a nonfield capacity at Cooper's Hill on the outskirts of Montego Bay in the western parish of St. James. He was, therefore, among that group of enslaved that historians characterize as the "slave elite." Converted to Christianity, he became a deacon in the First Baptist Church in Montego Bay, now the Burchell Memorial Baptist Church. He encouraged enslaved people to strike for wages after the Christmas holidays of 1831 and to resort to armed resistance if their demands were not met. When word came that the whites were planning to break the strike, arson and violence erupted. The ensuing rebellion was, according to a petition to the Jamaica House of Assembly in 1832, one "unparalleled in the history of the colony, whether for depth of design or the extent of misery and ruin which it has entailed on the inhabitants." Not only did Sharpe plan and fight in the war, but he organized subleaders on every plantation or cluster of plantations—revolutionary cells—more effectively to fight the war. The British suppressed the rebellion brutally, killing about 1,000 enslaved rebels during the war or after, through judicial decree.

On April 19, 1832, Sharpe was tried and sentenced to hanging for his role in the war. The testimonies of nine enslaved people who gave evidence against him (and that appear in the records of the Jamaica House of Assembly) confirmed the objectives and strategies of Sharpe's war as well as his deep involvement. James Stirling testified that "[Sharpe] gave me an Oath not to work after X'mas." Edward Barrett confirmed: "Sharpe said we must sit down, we free and we must not work again unless we get half pay"; and Edward Hill reiterated the freedom mission of the rebels: "Sharpe told we all we going to get free; he sent Edward Ramsay to Thomas Reid at Mahoney to swear all the people [to an oath on the Bible]."

At the end of Sharpe's trial, the following sentence, signed by John Coates and others, was handed down:

> . . .That the said Negro man slave named Samuel Sharpe be taken from hence to the place from whence he came and from thence to the place of Execution at such time and place as shall be appointed by His Excellency the Governor and there to be hanged by the neck until he be dead.

According to the historical accounts, Sharpe, age thirty-one, dressed in a white suit, walked in a dignified manner to the gallows on May 23, 1832. After a short speech, he prayed, then declared: "I now bid you farewell! That is all I have to say." Sixteen pounds ten shillings, Sharpe's estimated value, was eventually paid as compensation to his enslaver.

See also Anti-Colonial Movements; Emancipation in Latin America and the Caribbean; Maroon Wars; Protestantism in the Americas

Bibliography

Colonial Office (C.O.) 137/185. Public Records Office, London.

Craton, Michael. *Testing the Chains*. Ithaca, N.Y.: Cornell University Press, 1982.

Jamaica Archives. Spanish Town, St. Catherine. *Jamaica House of Assembly Votes*, 1832.

Reid, C. S. *Samuel Sharpe: From Slave to National Hero*. Kingston, Jamaica: Bustamante Institute for Public and International Affairs, 1988.

VERENE A. SHEPHERD (2005)

Sharpton, Al

October 3, 1954

Born in Brooklyn, New York, political activist Alfred Charles Sharpton Jr. began preaching as a Pentecostal minister at age four and soon began touring the preaching circuit as the "wonder boy preacher." In 1964, the year his father died, Sharpton was ordained as a minister and preached at the New York World's Fair and on tour with gospel singer Mahalia Jackson. In the late 1960s he was attracted to Congressman Adam Clayton Powell Jr., who became his political mentor. In 1969 he was appointed youth director of the Rev. Jesse Jackson's Operation Breadbasket, where he arranged boycotts and led demonstrations to force employers to hire blacks.

In 1971 Sharpton formed the National Youth Movement, an outgrowth of his Operation Breadbasket activities. The next year he was the youngest delegate to attend the National Black Political Convention in Gary, Indiana. In 1973 he met soul singer James Brown and became involved in promoting him. During the next eight years Sharpton split his time among managing Brown's singing tours, trying to manage the growth and boycott activity of the National Youth Movement, and making political connections in New York's African-American community. In 1978 he ran unsuccessfully for the New York State Senate.

During the early 1980s Sharpton became a leading community activist and led marches for black political and economic empowerment. He first became widely known in 1987, when he led protests after the murder of blacks in Howard Beach, New York, and served as an "adviser" to Tawana Brawley, whose claim that she had been raped by white police sparked a major controversy. Sharpton was discredited by the discovery that Brawley had invented her story and by accusations that he had acted as an informant for the Federal Bureau of Investigation. Sharpton was also indicted on charges of financial improprieties in the National Youth Movement. (In 1990 he was acquitted on the fraud charges, and in 1993 he pleaded guilty to a misdemeanor charge of failing to file a 1986 federal tax return.) He regained the spotlight when he led marches in Bensonhurst, New York, after the 1989 murder of a young African American, Yusef Hawkins.

During the early 1990s Sharpton, still a controversial figure, continued his protest activity on behalf of African Americans and other causes. In January 1991 he was stabbed in the chest just minutes before he was to lead a protest march in Brooklyn, but he quickly recovered. He also turned to mainstream electoral politics. In 1992 he ran in the Democratic primary for the U.S. Senate from New York. While he finished third in a bitter four-way race, he earned praise for his refusal to attack opponents personally. In 1993 he served a well-publicized forty-five-day jail sentence that grew out of a 1988 protest march. In 1994 he ran for the state's other U.S. Senate seat. While badly beaten by the popular incumbent, Sharpton realized his own goal by attracting 25 percent of the primary vote.

In 1997, on the strength of a heavy black vote, Sharpton finished second in the Democratic primary race for mayor of New York City and narrowly missed qualifying for a runoff with the leading candidate, Ruth Messinger. However, Sharpton's efforts to moderate his image and reach out beyond blacks were set back in the 1990s. In 1996 he was blamed for inciting a gunman to burn down a Harlem store operated by a Jewish immigrant, where Sharpton had led an angry protest campaign. In 1998 he was drawn back into the Tawana Brawley controversy when Officer Steven Pagones won a judgment for libel against Sharpton and his partners, who had accused him of participation in the alleged rape.

Sharpton campaigned for nomination as the Democratic Party's candidate for president of the United States in 2004, later actively supporting eventual nominee John Kerry.

See also Brown, James; Jackson, Mahalia; Jackson, Jesse Louis; Politics in the United States

Bibliography

Klein, Michael. *The Man Behind the Soundbite: The Real Story of Reverend Al Sharpton*. New York: Castillo International, 1991.

Sharpton, Al, and Anthony Walton. *Go and Tell Pharoah: The Autobiography of Al Sharpton*. New York: Doubleday, 1996.

Sharpton, Al, and Karen Hunter. *Al on America*. New York: Kensington Books, 2002.

GREG ROBINSON (1996)
Updated by publisher 2005

Shearer, Hugh

May 18, 1923
July 5, 2004

Hugh Lawson Shearer's political life spanned the first fifty years of Jamaica's modern political system. Throughout his career, he respected electoral democracy, defended workers' rights, practiced bipartisanship, and supported convergence between Jamaica's two leading political parties, the People's National Party (PNP) and the Jamaica Labour Party (JLP). Shearer played a decisive role in consolidating Jamaica's party and parliamentary systems in their formative years since 1944, and eventually became prime minister of Jamaica.

Shearer started his public life in the Bustamante Industrial Trade Union (BITU) in 1941 at the age of eighteen, when the union was two years old. It has remained Jamaica's largest trade union. He made his political debut in the 1947 local government elections, the first local elections under universal adult suffrage. Shearer won a seat as a councilor for the Jamaica Labour Party. This improved his status as a young leader of the BITU. As early as 1947 Shearer was regarded as Alexander Bustamante's protégé and the heir apparent of the BITU. Bustamante was leader of both the BITU and the JLP.

Shearer's rise in the BITU went more smoothly than his rise in representational politics. He lost his first general election contest in 1949 to Ken Hill (PNP), himself a labor organizer. However, Shearer was successful in 1955. The JLP lost that election and Shearer became a great asset to Bustamante when the JLP went into the opposition.

From 1955 to 1958 Shearer made many proposals in the legislature to provide severance pay for workers with long service who were dismissed or retrenched, and for holidays with pay for domestic workers. He put workers' rights above politics by supporting much of the PNP's labor legislation. This included legislation establishing the Pensions Authority, the Sugar Workers Pension Fund, amendments to the Holidays with Pay Law, and the Trades Disputes (Arbitration and Enquiry) Law.

In these years in opposition, Shearer became one of the frontline members of the JLP in the Jamaican legislature. He was quick to point to those PNP policies that supported the emerging private-sector market and those favoring labor, as evidence of the convergence between the two parties. The JLP represented a combination of free enterprise and labor rights, and the PNP, a socialist party, favored a larger role for state planning and advocacy of labor.

Shearer and a younger generation of JLP leaders also provided thoughtful advice to the aging Bustamante and represented a new guard of more professional JLP parliamentarians. Despite this, Shearer lost his seat in the 1959 elections. This loss reduced the party's labor representation in the legislature. It signaled a shift to more business and professional middle-class leaders in the party.

Shearer was able to concentrate more on trade union matters. In 1959 he became Island Supervisor of the BITU. In these early days a unique political friendship developed between himself and Michael Manley, later Jamaica's prime minister. As Manley's biographer Darrell Levi said, "Shearer and Manley have shared a friendship which has survived sometimes bitter union and political struggles" (1989, p. 16).

Shearer was appointed senator when the JLP won the general elections in 1962. He became a minister in Jamaica's first government at independence. He was minister of External Affairs. Speaking at the United Nations in 1963, he proposed that 1968 be designated International Year of Human Rights, and this was so done.

Shearer was elected again to the Jamaican parliament in 1967. After the retirement of Bustamante and the sudden death of Prime Minister Donald Sangster in that year, Bustamante steered the succession for the prime ministership in favor of Shearer in order to preserve the labor wing of the party from encroachment by the business wing.

Shearer became Jamaica's third prime minister, serving from 1967 to 1972. He was forty-three years old and the youngest prime minister in the British Commonwealth. During this period, Jamaica achieved its highest continuous rate of growth and reached maturity as a manufacturing economy. He explained that Jamaica's success should be based on "hard work, not faith, hope and foreign charity" (Neita, 2004).

Despite some economic success, the gap between rich and poor widened and the government was attacked for this during the Rodney Black Power riots of 1968. The Shearer government alleged that it could possibly be overthrown and overreacted by limiting rights to march and censoring radical literature.

Shearer's government was voted out in 1972, and he resigned as JLP leader in 1974. But in the ideologically polarized period of the 1970s, Shearer remained the one major figure in the JLP that Michael Manley, prime minister from 1972 to 1980, could reach out to for bipartisan understanding.

Shearer returned to government as deputy prime minister and minister of Foreign Affairs and Trade in the 1980s. While Prime Minister Edward Seaga concentrated on Jamaica-U.S. relations and finance and investments, Shearer kept the administration committed to Jamaica's third-world policy through the United Nations; the Non-Aligned Movement; the Group of 77; the African, Caribbean, and Pacific organization; and the Caribbean Community, a foreign policy championed by Michael Manley but more militantly so.

The JLP lost the elections of 1989, and Shearer lost his parliamentary seat in 1993. He then retired from representational politics. However, one of his greatest achievements has been to detribalize the workers movement through his efforts in the 1990s in building the Joint Confederation of Trade Unions (JCTU), an association of Jamaica's leading trade unions. Shearer remained president of the JCTU until his death in 2004. He passed away as the elder statesman of Jamaica's labor movement and was widely commended for his conciliatory leadership style. Shearer was awarded the Order of the Nation, Jamaica's second highest honor, in 2002.

See also Jamaica Labour Party; People's National Party

Bibliography

Ashley, Paul. "Jamaica's Foreign Policy in Transition." In *The Caribbean in World Politics: Cross Currents and Cleavages*, edited by Jorge Heine and Leslie Manigat. New York and London: Homes and Meier, 1988.

Eaton, George. *Alexander Bustamante and Modern Jamaica.* Kingston, Jamaica: LMH, 1995.

Levi, Darrell. *Michael Manley: The Making of a Leader.* Kingston, Jamaica: Heinemann Caribbean, 1989.

Neita, Hartley. "Remembering Hugh Lawson Shearer, 1923–2004: Shearer the Prime Minister." *Jamaica Gleaner* (July 7, 2004).

ROBERT MAXWELL BUDDAN (2005)

Sherlock, Philip

February 5, 1902
December 4, 2000

Philip Manderson Sherlock was a historian, civil leader, and vice chancellor of the University of the West Indies. A characteristic of his remarkable public career was that each job seemed to have prepared him for the next. Born in Jamaica, he was a young teacher in a small private secondary school (Calabar High School) from 1919 to 1927. He then went on to become the youthful headmaster of a small private rural secondary school, and then the headmaster of large, long-established urban secondary school (Wolmers Boys School). Subsequently, he became a civil servant, taking the post of secretary of the Institute of Jamaica (1939–1944). This was followed by a short stint as an education officer with a nongovernmental social welfare organization. After serving as a member of the Irvine Committee, which set up the University College of the West Indies in 1944, he was appointed director of the university's Department of Extra-Mural Studies from 1947 to 1960. Sherlock was by then known as a writer of short history books for schools, as a folklorist, as a minor poet, and as a quiet legislator in Jamaica's Legislative Council. A higher university position followed when he was made principal of the Trinidad and Tobago campus of the University College of the West Indies from 1960 to 1963. This was followed by his assumption of the top job of vice chancellor of the autonomous University of the West Indies, a position he held until 1969. Sherlock then established a regional grouping of Caribbean universities, which he directed from 1969 to 1979.

Sherlock's most notable achievement as a young man of twenty-five years was to gain a first class honors degree in English as an external student of the University of London. This underlined his talent, discipline, and energy. Nevertheless, his color (he was nearly white in appearance) probably assisted him in achieving a high public salience in official circles as head of the institute, then the island's premier cultural institution.

Sherlock himself consistently rejected the conservative social, racial, and political values of race-conscious Jamaica, and developed a liberal viewpoint. He was not carried away by political radicalism, however, but committed to cultural nationalism. Influenced positively by Garveyism in his younger days, Sherlock became a patriotic promoter of cultural activism, in the process acquiring an understanding and acceptance of the African-rooted culture of the black masses.

Assessments of Sherlock as a university administrator were also positive. In the early days of the university, the Extra-Mural Department under his leadership committed itself to the cultural development of the West Indies, with a view to self-government and even a federation of the territories. As vice chancellor he presided over an expansion of the university and dealt with government challenges to its autonomy. As a historian, Sherlock's first significant work (coauthored with John Parry) was *A Short History of the West Indies* (1956). Its importance is that it was a part of an effort by West Indian historians in the 1950s and 1960s to create a corpus of historical works to liberate West Indian history from the hands of British imperial historians and to give it a truly West Indian focus.

Sherlock's greatest service to the region as a historian was to have been a persistent popularizer of its history.

From his earliest short books for children, such as *Caribbean Citizen* (1957), to his postretirement tourist guidebooks on Jamaica, Sherlock cultivated a simple narrative style, avoiding all the major controversies about slavery or emancipation and delivering as his main message his conviction that, despite the fragmented island histories, they were in the process of building unified multiracial communities and federal associations across the region. He believed in the need to use history as a tool in multiracial democratic nation building. He turned to West Indian literature, folklore, song, and the environment, not just to official historical documents, to weave his stories about West Indian history. He was preeminently a historian and a storyteller, and he was without equal as a radio broadcaster in the 1960s. His talks in Trinidad in the 1960s and later in Jamaica were anecdotal, insightful, and lucid, and still highly readable in typescript.

Yet Sherlock is not recognized as a major historian, mostly because he did not write an outstanding book of his own until near his death. At the age of ninety-six, Sherlock (with a junior coauthor) produced what was his only radical work, *The Story of the Jamaican People* (1998). In this work he placed African culture and the experiences of the black masses—identified unequivocally as African—in the center of his interpretation of Jamaica's historical development. It is this revisionist book, written to stimulate patriotism, that in the long run will mark his own individual contribution to West Indian historiography.

See also Historians and Historiography; University of the West Indies

Bibliography

Baugh, Edward. "Caribbean Man: The Life and Times of Philip Sherlock" (interview). *Jamaica Journal* 16, no. 3 (1983): 22–30.

Sherlock, Philip. *Norman Manley*. London: Macmillan, 1980.

Sherlock, Philip, and Hazel Bennett. *The Story of the Jamaican People*. Kingston, Jamaica: Ian Randle, 1998.

CARL C. CAMPBELL (2005)

Shrine of the Black Madonna

See Pan-African Orthodox Church (The Shrine of the Black Madonna)

Shuttlesworth, Fred L.

March 18, 1922

The minister and civil rights leader Fred Lee Shuttlesworth was born in Mugler, Alabama. He received a B.A. from Selma University in Alabama and a B.S. from Alabama State Teachers College. He became pastor of several Baptist churches, including the First Baptist Church in Birmingham, Alabama, and the Revelation Baptist Church in Cincinnati, Ohio. He involved himself with civil rights causes, including participating in an unsuccessful attempt in 1955 to secure positions for African Americans on the local police force. When the National Association for the Advancement of Colored People (NAACP) was banned in Alabama, he joined the Alabama Christian Movement for Human Rights (ACMHR) and was elected its first president. As head of both the ACMHR and the integration movement in Birmingham, Shuttlesworth focused his attention on ending discrimination in public transportation. Although his home was destroyed by dynamite, he succeeded in overturning Birmingham's segregation law in 1961.

A believer in the Reverend Dr. Martin Luther King Jr.'s philosophy of nonviolent direct action, Shuttlesworth helped organize the Southern Christian Leadership Conference (SCLC) and in 1957 he became secretary of the organization. During the spring of 1960, he aided student civil rights sit-ins in Birmingham and was arrested for his participation. In the spring of 1963, he led a major antisegregation campaign in Birmingham, which influenced passage of the 1964 Civil Rights Act. Also in 1963, Shuttlesworth received the Rosa Parks Award from SCLC. Remaining a key adviser to King in the 1960s, he was also active in the Congress of Racial Equality (CORE) and the NAACP. In 2003, Shuttlesworth served a term as interim president of the SCLC.

See also Civil Rights Movement, U.S.; Congress of Racial Equality (CORE); King, Martin Luther, Jr.; National Association for the Advancement of Colored People (NAACP); Southern Christian Leadership Conference

Bibliography

Manis, Andrew Michael. *A Fire You Can't Put Out: The Civil Rights Life of Birmingham's Reverend Fred Shuttlesworth*. Tuscaloosa: University of Alabama Press, 1999.

Ploski, Harry A. *The Negro Almanac.* New York: Bellwether, 1982.

White, Marjorie L., comp. *A Walk to Freedom: The Reverend Fred Shuttlesworth and the Alabama Christian Movement for Human Rights, 1956-1964.* Birmingham Historical Society, 1998.

NEIL GOLDSTEIN (1996)
Updated by publisher 2005

Sickle-Cell Disease

Sickle-cell disease is a genetically acquired disorder of the red blood cells. A person who inherits the sickle-cell gene from both parents is born with the disease; a person inheriting the gene from only one parent is a sickle-cell carrier. Sickling disorders in the United States are concentrated in areas where there are large groups of African Americans, such as the Northeast, Midwest, and rural South. Sickle-cell disease (a term preferred to the older "sickle-cell anemia") can also be found among the populations of West Africa, the Caribbean, Guyana, Panama, Brazil, Italy, Greece, and India. Eight percent of African Americans are heterozygous for the sickling gene or trait. These carriers may become ill at high altitudes, and some unexpected deaths have occurred to soldiers during extreme maneuvers. The gene for sickle-cell hemoglobin was first introduced to the Americas through the slave trade. Carriers of the disease have some immunity to the fatal form of malaria, something that proved useful to African slaves in swampy tidal regions, as in the Chesapeake and South Carolina.

The sickle cell, so called because of its bent shape, was not named until 1910, when J. B. Herrick described the blood cells of an anemic patient. In 1949 Linus Pauling discovered the chemical abnormality that causes red blood cells to become misshapen and also found the link between the sickle cell and malaria. Although the attention given the disease has increased substantially since World War II, misinformation about the illness persists and often causes discrimination against sickle-cell carriers in the insurance industry and the job market. In the 1970s the prevalence and consequences of sickle-cell disease became widely publicized in both the African-American and mainstream media.

Several organizations have been established for education and research about the disease, including the National Association for Sickle-Cell Disease, founded in 1971 in Los Angeles. Numerous hospitals have centers for the study of sickle-cell disease, including the Columbia University Comprehensive Sickle-Cell Center at Harlem Hospital in New York City, founded in 1972, and the Center for Sickle-Cell Disease at Howard University, founded by Ronald B. Scott in 1972. These organizations have undertaken extensive fund-raising campaigns for research and treatment of the illness. Government funding for research has risen since the early 1970s. Attempts to cut federal research support in the 1980s drew vehement opposition from many black organizations. In 1993 thirty-eight states and the District of Columbia required testing of newborns for sickle-cell traits, and the number now is over forty. Support organizations include the Sickle Cell Disease Association of America, the American Sickle Cell Association, The National Heart, Lung, and Blood Institute, the Sickle Cell Information Center, and the Joint Center for Sickle Cell and Thalassemic Disorders.

In persons with sickle-cell disease, deoxygenated hemoglobin S causes the red blood cells in the body to assume the sickle shape. These cells cannot carry oxygen as normal red blood cells do, and they lodge in small blood vessels, causing ischemia (oxygen deficiency) and necrosis. This blockage of vessels is called vaso-occlusive crisis and gives rise to intense pain.

Symptoms of sickle-cell disease usually appear after six months of age when the last of the fetal hemoglobin, which increases oxygen supply in the blood, leaves the infant's body. Untreated, a patient may develop circulatory collapse. Such a patient is given large amounts of intravenous fluids to support circulation and prevent shock. Older patients may have pain in the larger bones, chest, back, joints, and abdomen and can develop hemorrhages into the eye and brain.

Treatment for sickle-cell patients commonly calls for pain medication ranging from oral analgesics to injectable narcotics for pain management. Intravenous fluids are prescribed to prevent dehydration and flood the vasculature with the intention of floating the sickling cells from occluded vessels. Antibiotics are ordered for infections, and prophylactic penicillin is suggested for infants to prevent infections. Blood transfusions are not routinely recommended for short-term crises but may be indicated during prolonged episodes and when lung and central nervous system involvement is evident.

Experimental treatment for sickle-cell patients includes the use of hydroxyurea, which can increase the level of fetal hemoglobin circulating in the body. Bone-marrow transplants have been performed on some children. This remains a risky procedure, however, carrying a 5 to 10 percent mortality rate. Though no cure exists, methods of treating chronic sickle-cell patients have improved in the past twenty years. Conservative treatment methods offer a prudent course of disease management. People with sickle-cell disease, once expected to live only to their forties, now live longer and healthier lives.

Bibliography

Edelstein, Stuart J. *The Sickled Cell: From Myth to Molecules.* Cambridge, Mass.: Harvard University Press, 1986.

Hill, Shirley A. *Managing Sickle Cell Disease in Low-Income Families.* Philadelphia. Pa.: Temple University Press, 2003.

Kiple, Kenneth F., and Virginia Himmelsteib King. *Another Dimension to the Black Diaspora: Diet, Disease, and Racism.* New York: Cambridge University Press, 1981.

Oski, Frank A. *Principles and Practice of Pediatrics,* 2d ed. Philadelphia, Pa.: Lippincott, 1994.

JANE M. DELUCA (1996)
Updated by publisher 2005

Simmons, Russell

October 4, 1957

Russell Simmons was born in the Hollis section of Queens, New York. Although his family was middle class, the entrepreneur, nicknamed "Rush" because of the frenetic pace of his life, joined a gang and briefly sold drugs before enrolling at the Harlem branch of New York's City College to study sociology. However, in 1978, Simmons began promoting concerts and worked with his friend, Curtis Walker, who rapped under the name Kurtis Blow. Simmons became Blow's manager and cowrote Blow's 1979 single, "Christmas Rappin'."

Simmons founded his own management company, Rush Artist Management, in 1982 and also became the manager for younger brother Joseph's group, Run-DMC. Simmons then cofounded the hip-hop/rap music label Def Jam Recordings in 1984 with producer Rick Rubin. The label's first release was the LL Cool J single, "I Need a Beat," and Def Jam also signed such artists as the Beastie Boys, Slick Rick, and Public Enemy. In 1985, Simmons turned the story of the label's founding into the film *Krush Groove,* with Blair Underwood starring as the Simmons character Russell Walker. (Rubin played himself while Simmons took a cameo role.)

After Rubin left in 1988 to form the Def American label, Simmons continued to expand his business, founding Rush Communications in 1990, which includes his management company, the movie production company Def Pictures, and other ventures. Simmons also produced the films *Tougher Than Leather* (1988), *The Nutty Professor* (1996), and *How to Be a Player* (1997); two HBO series, *Russell Simmons' Def Comedy Jam* (1991) and *Russell Simmons' Def Poetry Jam* (2001); and *Russell Simmons' Def Poetry Jam on Broadway,* for which he received a 2003 Tony Award. In 1999, Simmons sold his remaining share in Def Jam to Universal Music for a reported one hundred million dollars but remained as nominal chair; Def Jam later merged with Island Records. However, in 2005, Simmons became the head of the Russell Simmons Music Group, a joint venture with Island Def Jam Music Group.

Simmons also founded Phat Fashions in 1992, which includes the urban clothing lines Phat Farm, Baby Phat, and Phat Farm Kids, although he sold a majority stake in the company in 2004. Simmons is also the founder of the nonprofit Hip-Hop Summit Action Network (HSAN), which holds forums in various cities to encourage community development issues, voter registration, and political action; and the Rush Philanthropic Arts Foundation, which provides arts funding and education to inner-city youth. Simmons married model-designer Kimora Lee in 1998; they have two daughters. His autobiography, *Life and Def: Sex, Drugs, Money + God,* was published by Crown Publishing in 2001.

See also Entrepreneurs and Entrepreneurship; L. L. Cool J (Smith, James Todd); Recording Industry; Run-D.M.C.

Bibliography

Falsani, Cathleen. "'We get what we give . . . it's a karma thing.'" Published in *Chicago Sun-Times* (April 3, 2005). Available from <http://www.suntimes.com>.

Reingold, Jennifer. "Rush Hour." Published in *Fast Company* (November 2003). Available from <http://www.fastcompany.com>.

Rose, Charlie. "Russell Simmons, Unplugged." Published in *CBSNews.com* (February 11, 2004). Available from <http://www.cbsnews.com>.

Stark, Jeff. "Brilliant Careers: Russell Simmons." Published in *Salon.com* (July 6, 1999). Available from <http://www.salon.com>.

CHRISTINE TOMASSINI (2005)

Simmons, Ruth J.

July 3, 1945

Educator and college president Ruth Jean Simmons was born in Grapevine, Texas, one of twelve children born to

Isaac Stubblefield, a farmer and factory worker, and Fannie Stubblefield, a homemaker. After graduating from Dillard University with a B.A. degree in 1967, she studied for a year in France on a Fulbright grant. She returned to earn a master's degree (1970) and doctorate in Romance languages (1973) from Radcliffe College, now part of Harvard University.

From 1970 to 1990 Simmons held a number of positions at such colleges as Radcliffe and the University of New Orleans. She then became assistant dean, then associate dean, first at the University of Southern California at Los Angeles, then at Princeton University. From 1990 to 1992 she was provost at Spelman College and then returned to Princeton, where she was vice provost in 1992.

Although she was a candidate for many college president vacancies, Simmons was the unanimous choice among 350 candidates on the Smith College list. In 1995 she was appointed the ninth president of Smith, and when she was inaugurated on September 30, she became the first African-American woman president of a top-ranked college or university in the United States. Her tasks were to lead the institution into the twenty-first century, serve as a scholarly role model for students, develop the faculty, engage in financial planning, and become involved in all aspects of leadership of Smith. Soon after her tenure began, applications for admission poured into the college.

In 2001 Simmons left Smith to become the eighteenth president of Brown University, and the first black woman to preside over an Ivy League college. Highly regarded in academic circles and elsewhere as a capable, vibrant, and dedicated leader, she also holds a seat on the boards of several major U.S. corporations, including Pfizer, Texas Instruments, and investment firm Goldman Sachs.

See also Education

Bibliography

Kantrowitz, Barbara. "Ruth Simmons: President, Brown University." *Newsweek* (December 31, 2001): 76.

O'Reilly, David. "A Conversation with Ruth Simmons." *Philadelphia Inquirer,* March 2, 1995.

Simmons, Ruth J. "My Mother's Daughter: Lessons I Learned in Civility and Authenticity." *Texas Journal of Ideas, History and Culture* (fall/winter 1998).

JESSIE CARNEY SMITH (2001)
Updated by publisher 2005

Simone, Nina (Waymon, Eunice Kathleen)

February 21, 1933
April 21, 2003

Born in Tryon, North Carolina, singer Nina Simone was encouraged to study piano and organ starting at age three by her mother, an ordained black Methodist minister. She was soon able to play hymns on the organ by ear, and at age six she became the regular pianist at her family's church. She studied privately, as well as at Asheville (N.C.) High School, to become a classical pianist. She also studied at the Curtis Institute of Music in Philadelphia (1950–1953) and the Juilliard School in New York (1954–1956). Simone's career as a vocalist, which spanned nearly four decades and more than forty albums, came almost by accident: During a 1954 nightclub engagement in Atlantic City, New Jersey, she was informed that in addition to playing piano she would have to sing. She adopted the stage name Nina Simone for this occasion, which marked the beginning of her career as a jazz singer.

From the very start, Simone chafed under the restrictions of the label "jazz singer," and indeed, her mature style integrated classical piano techniques with a repertory drawn from sources as varied as the blues and folk music, as in *Jazz as Played* (1958). Early in her career she also began addressing racial problems in the United States. In 1963, angered by the death of Medgar Evers and the bombing of an African-American church in Birmingham, Alabama, she composed her first civil rights anthem, "Mississippi Goddam," and during the next decade much of her work was explicitly dedicated to the civil rights movement, sung in her forceful and clear alto voice. In 1963 she composed "Four Women" with Langston Hughes. Her other popular songs from this time include "Young, Gifted, and Black," "Old Jim Crow," and "Don't Let Me Be Misunderstood." In the 1970s Simone continued to perform internationally and recorded the album *Baltimore* in 1978. Starting in the late 1970s she divided her time between Los Angeles and Switzerland. In more recent years she lived in Paris, but she continued to appear regularly in New York. In 1987 she released *Let It Be Me.* Her autobiography, *I Put a Spell on You,* was published in 1991. In 2003 Nina Simone died in France after a long illness.

See also Jazz Singers

Bibliography

Grieske, Tony. "Jazz Legend, Civil Rights Voice Nina Simone Dies." *Hollywood Reporter,* April 22, 2003, p. 6.

Powell, Allison, with Nina Simone. "The American Soul of Nina Simone." *Interview* 27, no. 1 (January 1997): 76-80.

Simone, Nina. *I Put a Spell on You.* New York: Pantheon Books, 1991.

Sischy, Ingrid, with Elton John. "Nina Simone: Remembering a Fiery Trailblazer of Song and Freedom." *Interview* 33, no. 7 (August 2003): 108.

ROSITA M. SANDS (1996)
Updated by publisher 2005

Simpson, Lorna

August 13, 1960

Born in Brooklyn, New York, photographer Lorna Simpson enrolled as an undergraduate at the School of Visual Arts in New York City to study painting. She soon turned to documentary photography and received a B.F.A. in photography from the school in 1982. In 1985 Simpson earned an M.F.A. degree in visual arts from the University of California at San Diego (UCSD), where she also studied and taught film and became involved in performance art. Her first large-scale series of photographs, *Gestures and Reenactments* (1985), launched her ongoing project of rethinking the relationships among photographic images, textual description, and the representation of African Americans, particularly women.

Simpson's work reflects an awareness of the ways in which photography has been traditionally used by the social sciences and the media to classify, study, objectify, and ultimately control black men and women. In large multipaneled or sequential works such as *You're Fine* (1988), *Stereo Styles* (1988), and *Guarded Conditions* (1989), Simpson typically presents a black Everywoman with her back turned to the viewer or her face deliberately obscured by cropping; the viewer is thus effectively denied access to the woman's identity and inner psychological state. Instead, Simpson provides clues as to subjective meaning in the accompanying captions, which usually refer to issues of gender and racial oppression. In contrast to the neutral, carefully controlled tone of her photographs, Simpson's captions can be emotionally charged, thereby creating an interpretive tension between word and image. In *You're Fine* Simpson presents an anonymous black woman lying on her side in a simple white shift, her back turned away from the viewer in a pose that recalls the reclining pose of the nineteenth-century female nude. The ominous text comments on the invasive and objectifying qualities of public surveillance.

Social commentary also informs Simpson's *Stereo Styles,* which consists of ten Polaroid prints in two tiers; each print shows the back of the same black woman's head done in a different hairstyle. Simpson here comments on the popular idea expressed in cosmetics advertisements that hairstyles can communicate personality traits. Since 1988 Simpson has abstracted the female body even further and combined its parts with such symbolic objects as African masks, black hair, and articles of women's clothing (*Flipside,* 1991; *1978–1988,* 1990; *Bio,* 1992).

In 1991 Simpson created *Five Rooms* with composer Alva Rogers, a site-specific, multimedia installation for the 1991 Spoleto Festival U.S. exhibition in Charleston, South Carolina, which presented a narrative of black slavery in America. She created another installation, *Standing in the Water,* for the Whitney Museum of American Art in New York City in 1994. Simpson's work has been shown in more than ninety major exhibitions throughout the United States and Europe; sites of solo exhibits include the Museum of Modern Art (1990) and the Museum of Contemporary Art, Chicago (1992–1993), both of which have also acquired her work. Simpson was the first African-American woman ever chosen to exhibit in the Venice Biennale (1990).

See also Art in the United States, Contemporary; Photography, U.S.

Bibliography

Willis, Deborah. *Lorna Simpson: Untitled 54.* San Francisco: The Friends of Photography, 1992.

Wright, Beryl J. *Lorna Simpson: For the Sake of the Viewer.* Chicago: Museum of Contemporary Art, 1992.

DEIRDRE A. SCOTT (1996)

Simpson, O. J.

July 9, 1947

The football player and actor Orenthal James "O. J." Simpson was born in San Francisco, where he starred in football, baseball, and track at Galileo High School. In 1965 Simpson enrolled at City College of San Francisco, where he set several junior-college football rushing records in his two seasons. In 1967 the highly recruited halfback transferred to the University of Southern California

(USC), where he emerged as a national star, displaying tremendous speed and open-field running abilities. In two seasons he carried the ball 649 times for 3,295 yards and 34 touchdowns, led USC to a national championship in 1967, and won the Heisman Memorial Trophy in 1968.

Simpson was selected first overall by the American Football League's Buffalo Bills in the 1969 professional football draft. While he failed to live up to expectations in his first three years with Buffalo, in 1972 he rushed for 1,251 yards and established himself as one of the National Football League's best running backs. The following season, Simpson rushed for 2,003 yards, becoming the first player to rush for more than 2,000 yards in one season. He rushed for more than 1,000 yards in each of his next four seasons with Buffalo, and in 1976 he set a single-game rushing record with 273 yards against the Detroit Lions. After that year, Simpson's statistics declined, and following the 1977 season he was traded to the San Francisco Forty-Niners, where he spent the final two years of his football career. Simpson retired in 1979 with a professional rushing record of 2,404 carries for 11,236 yards and 61 touchdowns. He was inducted into the NFL Hall of Fame in 1985.

Following his retirement from football, Simpson lived in Los Angeles and capitalized on his good looks and polished public persona by launching a successful career in television, film, and advertising. He appeared in several made-for-television and feature films, including *Roots* (1977) and three *Naked Gun* films (1988, 1991, 1993). He also served as a network sports commentator, and he was featured in commercials.

Simpson became the center of a sensational murder case when his former wife, Nicole Brown, and a male friend of hers were stabbed to death in Los Angeles on June 12, 1994. Suspicion focused on Simpson, who led the police on a nationally televised car chase before surrendering at his home in a Los Angeles suburb. He was subsequently indicted and pleaded not guilty to both counts of murder. In the avalanche of publicity surrounding the case, some disquieting information about Simpson was revealed, including a pattern of wife abuse that included a little-publicized 1989 conviction for spousal battery. Information also surfaced later about possible police misconduct in the investigation of the case. After a lengthy pretrial hearing, a protracted jury selection process, and an eight-month trial, he was acquitted of all charges on October 3, 1995. During the trial, he published a best-selling book, *I Want to Tell You*. In 1997 the victims' families won a multimillion-dollar settlement in a wrongful death suit against Simpson. By this time, however, most of Simpson's considerable assets had been depleted by legal and tax bills and he was living largely off of a retirement trust from his football career, so little of the money was paid. The case continued in the news when Nicole Brown's parents sued unsuccessfully for custody of the couple's two children.

The O. J. Simpson case, in the eyes of many observers, riveted Americans because of its complex stew of social class, economic status, celebrity status, issues of gender and domestic violence, and, particularly, race. Among the twelve jurors that found Simpson not guilty at his criminal trial, eight were African American; the civil-trial jury that ruled against Simpson, however, was largely white. Further, a 1996 CNN/*USA Today*/Gallup poll found that while only 20 percent of white Americans believed that the criminal trial jury's acquittal was the correct verdict, 62 percent of African Americans believed that it was the correct verdict. This split suggested deep racial divisions in perceptions of the U.S. criminal justice system. Indeed, an element of the trial that benefited Simpson was his defense attorneys' ability to prove that one of the lead investigators on the case, Mark Fuhrman, had routinely used racial slurs (introducing the phrase "the N-word" to the lexicon), despite his denials that he had done so.

Many scholars and analysts have examined the Simpson case through the lens of what is called "critical race theory," a view that sees racism as endemic in American society, as simply part of the American landscape. The result, according to these theorists, is disparate treatment of blacks and whites by police and in the courts. The viewpoint was summarized by Mari Matsuda in 1995: "When notions of right and wrong, justice and injustice, are examined not from an abstract position but from the position of groups who have suffered through history . . . [we discover] a new epistemological source for critical scholars: the actual experience, history, culture, and intellectual tradition of people of color in America. Looking to the bottom for ideas about law will tap a valuable source previously overlooked by legal philosophers" (pp. 63–64). In the viewpoint of analysts of the critical race school, Simpson was found not guilty—despite the strong possibility that he may have committed the crime—because the jury sympathized with a strong, handsome black man, married to a white woman, and rejected a "white" legal system that routinely suppresses the African-American community. Many opponents of this view believe that the evidence overwhelmingly pointed to Simpson's guilt, but that racial divides have created a situation in which murder could go unpunished because of race-based perceptions of bias in the legal system.

See also Criminal Justice System; Football

■ ■ *Bibliography*

Ashe, Arthur R., Jr. *A Hard Road to Glory: A History of the African-American Athlete Since 1946.* New York: Amistad, 1988.

Hamilton, William. "O. J. Simpson Surrenders After Freeway Drama." *Washington Post* (June 18, 1994): A1.

Matsuda, Mari "Looking to the Bottom: Critical Legal Studies and Reparations." In *Critical Race Theory: The Key Writings that Formed the Movement,* edited by Kimberlé Crenshaw. New York: New Press, 1995.

Morrison, Toni, and Claudia Brodsky Lacour, eds. *Birth of a Nation'hood: Gaze, Script, and Spectacle in the O. J. Simpson Case.* New York: Pantheon, 1997.

Porter, David L., ed. *Biographical Dictionary of American Sports: Football.* Westport, Conn.: Greenwood, 1988.

THADDEUS RUSSELL (1996)
MICHAEL O'NEAL (2005)

Simpson Miller, Portia

December 2, 1945

Born in Woodhall, St. Catherine Parish, Jamaica, Portia Lucretia F. Simpson joined the People's National Party (PNP), beginning an active career in Jamaican politics when she became PNP Parish Councilor for Rose Town and Trench Town in 1974. By 1978, Simpson had become one of the vice presidents of the PNP.

Simpson married business executive Errald Miller and changed to her name to Simpson Miller. By the early 1980s she was gaining notice in the PNP, working on a number of influential party committees. In 1983 Simpson Miller became the PNP's spokesperson on women's issues, pension and social security, and consumer affairs, serving in this capacity for six years until she became a member of Parliament representing South-West St. Andrew in 1989.

As Simpson Miller performed her governmental duties, she did not hide her growing desire to rise within the party ranks. She announced her intention to become Jamaica's first female prime minister and seized an opportunity in 1992 to challenge the PNP's Percival James "P.J." Patterson, who as deputy prime minister had taken over after Prime Minister Michael Manley stepped down for health reasons. Though she did not defeat Patterson, Simpson Miller served as acting prime minister over the next several years whenever Patterson was out of the country.

Simpson Miller held office as Minister of Labour and Welfare from her arrival in Parliament in 1989 to 2000. (During these years, her duties and title varied: Minister of Labour and Welfare; Minister of Labour, Welfare, and Sports; Minister of Labour, Social Security, and Sports.) Hers was an enormous responsibility in a time of mounting turmoil in Jamaica. Not only was there constant friction between the country's two political parties, but unemployment, crime, and violence in the parishes around Kingston, the island's capital, increased. Simpson Miller, however, persevered, initiating programs for the homeless, promoting women's rights, and gaining better funding for sports teams and events. She remained in these posts until early 2000, while earning a bachelor's degree in Public Administration from the Union Institute in Miami, Florida, in 1997.

Simpson Miller was named Minister of Tourism and Sports in 2000. The following year she faced a special challenge in her new role when violence erupted in Kingston. With tourism as Jamaica's top source of income, the economy could not withstand a sharp decline. Simpson Miller rose to the occasion by luring travel agents and travel writers to the island for weekend conferences; promoting the country's own Caribbean jewel, the Sandals Resorts chain; and offering a number of incentives to travelers and businesses.

In 2002 Simpson Miller was named Minister of Local Government, Community Development, and Sports and over the next few years she helped bring both public awareness and respect to the island's athletes, who brought home five medals from the 2004 Olympic Games in Athens, Greece. Simpson Miller also improved funding for sports facilities and programs, including greater participation in the Special Olympics and Para Olympics, and captured part of the Cricket World Cup's 2007 tournament action—including the opening ceremony, several first-round matches, and a semifinal—all to be held on Jamaican soil.

Simpson Miller was handed another opportunity to reach her ultimate goal when Patterson announced he would not seek another term as prime minister and would likely retire before the next general elections in 2007. She wasted no time announcing her candidacy, proclaiming she was the perfect candidateto replace Patterson. Simpson Miller told the *Jamaica Observer* that she embodied the best traits of all of the island's previous prime ministers, including "the political savvy and passionate love for the poor and oppressed of Alexander Bustamante; the penchant for hard work of Donald Sangster; the quiet dignity and sincerity of Hugh Shearer; . . .the vision and toughness of Edward Seaga; the charisma and astuteness of Michael Manley; and the shrewdness as well as humility of P. J. Patterson."

By 2005 Simpson Miller had become one of the most popular female politicians in Jamaica, known affectionately as "Sister P." She maintained her commitment to the betterment of her people and continued to participate in programs such as the Eleanor Roosevelt Caucus of Women Political Leaders, the Women in Leadership Conference at Harvard University (1997), and the Fourth World Summit on Women (2000). Simpson Miller was named one of the United Nations' women of "Great Esteem," and she received an honorary doctorate of Humane Letters from the Union Institute in 2001.

See also Patterson, Percival James "P. J."; People's National Party

Bibliography

"Jamaica May Have Its First Woman Prime Minister in Portia Simpson Miller." *Caribbean Times,* January 7, 2005.

"No New Dawn: Jamaica." *The Economist* 322, no. 7751 (March 21, 1992): 48.

Smith, Lloyd B. "Come to Mama, Says Sister P." *Jamaica Observer,* July 5, 2005.

NELSON RHODES (2005)

SINGLETON, BENJAMIN "PAP"

c. 1809
1892

Little is known about the life of migrationist Benjamin "Pap" Singleton before the 1870s. He was born and raised a slave in Nashville but escaped to Canada as a young adult, stayed there briefly, and then settled in Detroit, where he worked as a scavenger and ran a boarding house that was often used by fugitive slaves.

After the end of the Civil War, Singleton returned to the Nashville area, worked as a carpenter and coffin maker, and began what he saw as his mission to deliver black people from the former slave states. During the late 1860s and 1870s, many of the coffins Singleton made were for victims of the racist violence prevalent during Reconstruction. He later cited this as the reason for his urgent desire to see former slaves leave what he considered the irredeemable South. Throughout his career Singleton considered himself a messianic leader created by God to lead his people to an all-black promised land on earth.

In the late 1860s Singleton, along with W. A. Sizemore and Columbus Johnson, urged black Tennesseans to acquire land in rural parts of the state and establish independent farms. Faced with white landowners who refused to sell to African Americans at affordable prices, Singleton and his allies looked to westward migration as the only hope for freedom. They conducted a scouting tour of Kansas, returned to Nashville, and touted the western state as the best location for African-American settlement. Several black families from Nashville took up Singleton's call and moved to Kansas in the early 1870s.

In 1874 Singleton and Johnson issued fliers throughout the Nashville area urging African Americans to emigrate to Kansas. From 1877 to 1879 Singleton and his associates settled hundreds of black families in Kansas colonies. In 1879, when the largely spontaneous mass migration to Kansas by former slaves from Mississippi, Louisiana, and Texas began, the "exodusters" filled Singleton's colonies and overwhelmed his movement.

In 1880, while living in one of his own colonies, Singleton was vaulted to fame when he was called to testify before a Senate committee investigating the exodus. Countering charges made by Democratic committee members that the entire migration was merely a plot by Republicans to win political control in western states, Singleton exclaimed, "I am the whole cause of the migration. Nobody but me. I am the Moses of the colored exodus!" In fact, the mass settlement of approximately twenty thousand former slaves in Kansas lacked any one leader or central organization and originated in states Singleton had not attempted to organize. It is likely, however, that Singleton's work in bringing the first families to Kansas may have partly inspired the 1879 exodus.

In 1881 Singleton led a short-lived movement in Topeka to establish a racially integrated, cooperative economy. The organization Singleton founded to achieve this purpose, the United Colored Links, attempted to form a coalition with the white Greenback Party but folded in less than a year.

In 1883 Singleton moved his focus to international migration and selected Cyprus as the next destination of the black exodus. His new organization for settlement in Cyprus, the Chief League, failed to accomplish its original goal, and in 1885 Singleton reorganized it into the Trans-Atlantic Society. Reflecting Singleton's turn toward a more pronounced black nationalism, the Trans-Atlantic Society declared its commitment to returning former slaves to Africa in order to establish "a separate national existence." There are no records of the Trans-Atlantic Society after 1887, when Singleton fell into obscurity. He died in St. Louis in 1892 after a long spell of ill health.

See also Black Towns; Migration

Bibliography

Bontemps, Arna, and Jack Conroy. *Anyplace but Here* (1945). New York: Hill and Wang, 1966.

Painter, Nell Irvin. *Exodusters: Black Migration to Kansas After Reconstruction.* New York: Knopf, 1977.

THADDEUS RUSSELL (1996)

Singleton, John

January 6, 1968

Born in South Central Los Angeles, John Daniel Singleton began his interest in film as a director, writer, producer, and actor when he enrolled in Pasadena City College in 1986. Shortly after, he began studies at the University of Southern California in Los Angeles. While studying film at USC he won three writing awards from the university and was signed by the Creative Artists Agency. He made his debut with the 1991 Columbia Picture *Boyz N the Hood,* whose widespread acclaim at the Cannes Film Festival that year popularized the film nationally. The film garnered Oscar nominations for Best Original Screenplay and Best Director, making Singleton the first African American and the youngest person to be nominated for the latter honor. Singleton's next two efforts were *Poetic Justice* (1993), which was nominated for an Academy Award for Best Original Song, and *Higher Learning* (1995). He received critical acclaim with his next film, the 1997 Warner Bros. release *Rosewood,* the historically based tale of an African-American town destroyed by a lynch mob. Singleton's next feature, *Shaft,* debuted in June 2000, meeting with mixed reactions from critics and initial popularity with audiences.

In addition to his own movies, Singleton has developed other projects through his production company, New Deal Productions. His awards include the 1991 Los Angeles Film Critics Association Award and the New York Film Critics Circle Best New Director Award for *Boyz N the Hood.* In 1992 he won the MTV Movie Award for Best New Filmmaker for *Boyz N the Hood,* as well.

Singleton continues to direct movies, including *2 Fast 2 Furious* in 2003 and *Luke Cage,* due to be released in 2005. He has been nominated for numerous awards, including three Black Reel awards. In 2003 Singleton was awarded a star on the Walk of Fame in Hollywood.

See also Film in the United States, Contemporary; Filmmakers, Los Angeles School of

Bibliography

Bart, Peter. "Way to 'Hustle,' John." *Variety,* Jan 31, 2005, 4-6.

Gleiberman, Owen. "Man Child: John Singleton makes an incisive return to the hood with Baby Boy." *Entertainment Weekly,* July 13, 2001, 56.

McCarthy, Todd. "Action's in high gear for '2 Fast' joyride." *Variety,* June 9, 2003, 25-26.

Schanzer, Karl and Thomas Lee Wright. *American Screenwriters.* New York: Avon Books, 1993.

"Singleton, John." Internet Movie Database. Available from <http://www.imdb.com>.

RACHEL ZELLARS (1996)
Updated by publisher 2005

Sisters of the Holy Family

Sisters of the Holy Family, one of the earliest religious orders of black women in America, was founded in 1842 by Henriette Delille in New Orleans, Louisiana. Delille was an educated free woman of African descent who had worked with Sister Ste. Marthe Fontier and Marie Jeanne Aliquot, two Catholic women from France who went to New Orleans in the 1820s to serve the black community. Their efforts to form an integrated religious community were unsuccessful because of state segregation laws. In the late 1820s Delille and Juliette Gaudin, a Cuban-born woman of African descent, continued their service to the black community by teaching religion to slaves. Delille and Gaudin tried to form a community of black nuns but confronted entrenched racism among Catholics and widespread discrimination. In the late 1820s the Ursuline Sisters refused to allow them to become a black branch. When they tried to found an independent order, they faced institutional barriers for recognition under civil law and had to challenge prevalent notions about the inability of black women to become nuns. In 1842, with the support of Abbé Rousselon, the pastor of St. Augustine parish, the diocese finally allowed them to begin a new order in St. Augustine's Church. Only in 1872 did they gain the right to wear the habit publicly, and not until 1949 were they officially recognized by the Vatican as an independent religious congregation.

Although the Holy Family Sisters was a small order—there were only six members in 1960—they provided many important services for the African-American community. They encouraged slave couples to have their unions blessed in the church and discouraged concubinage between white men and women of color in Louisiana. They nursed the ill during a yellow fever epidemic in 1853. After the Civil War and Reconstruction they supervised an asylum for African-American girls and organized a home for orphaned African-American boys in 1896. In 1920 the boys' home was converted into a home for the aged. Their most important work, however, was in the field of education. They opened schools in Texas and Belize in addition to six schools in New Orleans. The schools served both the middle class and the poor. By 1970 the sisters were also offering day care services. The Sisters of the Holy Family continue to provide crucial social services and religious and academic training for the African-American community into the early 2000s.

See also Catholicism in the Americas

Bibliography

Davis, Cyprian. *The History of Black Catholics in the United States.* New York: Crossroad, 1990.

Detiege, Sister Audrey Marie. *Henriette Delille: Free Woman of Color.* New Orleans, La.: Sisters of the Holy Family, 1976.

Deggs, Mary Bernard. *No Cross, No Crown: Black Nuns in Nineteenth-Century New Orleans.* Bloomington: Indiana University Press, 2001.

Hart, Sister Mary Francis. *Violets in the King's Garden: A History of the Sisters of the Holy Family of New Orleans.* New Orleans, La., 1976.

PREMILLA NADASEN (1996)
Updated by publisher 2005

Skin Color

Color symbolism has been a potent force in various cultures throughout the world. It has figured prominently in religion, literature, art, and a wide range of human relationships. The emotional or connotative significance of color has translated into attitudes toward the various shades of pigmentation evident in the world's population. While white-dominated Western culture has long exhibited a preference for light or pale-skinned peoples, such a preference has by no means been absent among societies in Asia, the Middle East, and even Africa. Various theories, based on sociological, anthropological, and psychological analyses, as well as historical experience, have been advanced to explain the existence of pigmentocracies that reward peoples of light complexion and penalize those of dark skin color. For many of these theories, the point of reference has been the significance of skin color in defining the status of African Americans, both within the larger white-dominated society and the black community.

In the centuries following the initial contact between sub-Saharan Africans and Europeans, differences in skin color helped shape the relations between the two peoples and also significantly influenced intraracial behavior and attitudes. In time, visible complexional differences, as well as their causes and implications, spawned a vast literature and a host of popular conceptions drawn from a hodgepodge of observations, scripture, pseudoscientific pronouncements, and self-congratulatory speculation. For northern Europeans, especially the English, the most striking characteristic of Africans initially was their "blackness." Conditioned to associate black with baseness and white with purity, Europeans ultimately invented the idea of race based on their perception of differences in skin color, culture, and other elements between themselves and Africans. The ideology of race that gradually emerged classified whites as superior and blacks as inferior. Although the skin color of Africans may not explain their enslavement by Europeans, it did serve as a convenient rationale for a system of bondage.

By the time black slavery had been firmly established in the British colonies of North America, whites had transformed the Africans' color from a matter of intense curiosity into a serious social issue, one complicated by the offspring of black/white and black/Indian unions, who were neither black nor white. The progeny of the black/white unions, commonly called mulattoes, appeared early and multiplied at varying rates throughout the colonial era and the early history of the new republic. Denounced in colonial statutes as an "abominable mixture and spurious issue," mulattoes of numerous shades of dark and light complexion came to occupy an anomalous position in a white-dominated society inclined to associate whites with freedom and blacks with slavery.

In the slave South, the status of mulattoes, quadroons, octoroons, and other "mixed-blood" people varied from section to section. The upper South, which contained the majority of the mulatto population, early embraced the "one-drop rule," whereby anyone with any known Negro ancestor, regardless of how fair his or her complexion, was classified as black. But even in the upper South, such a code neither entirely eliminated the privileges accorded mulattoes nor destroyed the belief that mulattoes were superior to blacks. Travelers' accounts and various other sources clearly indicate that whites exhibited a promulatto bias, especially in employing light-skinned slaves as house servants rather than field hands. Although a majority of the mulattoes in the upper South were slaves, the many free families of color in the region were also characterized by fair complexions. Although the white ancestry of mixed-blood slaves was of varied social origins, well-to-do white fathers of fair-complexioned mulatto children sometimes granted them freedom and provided them with education, property, and opportunities unavailable to other blacks. Through this and other means, especially the purchase of freedom, there came into existence throughout the South free mulatto families whose members tended to marry other light-skinned individuals.

During most of the pre–Civil War era, the lower South, where mulattoes were less numerous, refused to adhere rigidly to the "one-drop rule." In certain lower southern cities, especially along the Gulf and Atlantic coasts, there developed a color-caste system similar to one in the Caribbean, in which mixed-blood people occupied a middle tier between free whites and enslaved blacks. Color assumed symbolic significance in these cities. In no other city did the reputation for colorphobia and snobbery equal that of the free-mulatto elite of Charleston, South Carolina, a reputation that persisted well into the twentieth century. Viewed with favor and leniency by the white establishment, Charleston's slaveholding mulatto elite, intricately related to one another by blood and marriage, was sometimes so fair in complexion that it was impossible to discern any African ancestry. Nothing underscored the color consciousness of this mulatto elite more dramatically than the long-lived Brown Fellowship Society, which was organized in 1790 and limited to light-skinned "free brown men." This prompted the later formation of the Society of Free Dark Men, made up of descendants of Charleston's privileged blacks.

The significance of color was only slightly less evident in New Orleans, where three-quarters of the slaves were dark-skinned and about the same proportion of the *gens de couleur libres* was fair complexioned. The presence of Creoles of color—those claiming French or Spanish as well as African ancestry—in New Orleans; Pensacola, Florida; Mobile, Alabama; and other Gulf Coast cities involved an interplay of color and ethnocultural distinctions that created a more complex situation than that existing in Charleston. New Orleans's reputation as a "modern Golgotha" owed much to its alleged sexual permissiveness across the color line. Often cited by critics were the "quadroon balls" involving white men and mulatto women and especially the institution of formalized mistress-keeping known as *plaçage,* in which white males established liaisons with fair-complexioned mulatto girls, who became their "second wives" and the mothers of their "second families." Though less formalized than *plaçage,* the "shadow family" was a phenomenon that existed throughout the South. Both practices contributed to the lightening of the skin color of mixed-blood people, who usually chose fair-skinned mates, further expanding the light-complexioned black population.

By 1850, when the United States census began distinguishing between blacks and mulattoes, a more complex and specific sliding scale of color was already well-established in common usage (and would be refined even further in the future), especially by African Americans. So pervasive was color consciousness that the word *color* became virtually synonymous with race. For example, petitions and resolutions issued by gatherings of northern free blacks often spoke of equal rights "without distinction of color." Skin color also figured significantly in antebellum "mulatto fiction." Novels and stories about light-skinned blacks, especially works produced by antislavery advocates, described with great specificity the complexion of their almost-white characters, who were also usually of extraordinary intelligence, talent, and grace. For such writers, the presence of the "tragic mulattoes" stood as indisputable evidence of the immorality of slaveholding white Southerners, which was considered all the more gross because they often enslaved their own blood kin—"the white children of slavery."

One by-product of the siege mentality that gripped the white South in the wake of the abolitionist crusade was the hardening of the opposition to miscegenation and the acceptance of the "one-drop rule" throughout the region as the means of distinguishing between whites and blacks—no matter how fair the complexion of the latter. The results were momentous. Sizable numbers of light-skinned free blacks migrated out of the South, while free mulattoes who had once identified with the white elite and had stood aloof from dark-skinned blacks, free as well as slave, gradually shifted their allegiance. The Civil War and Emancipation, followed by Reconstruction, accelerated the engagement of light-complexioned mulattoes with the black masses in matters of public concern. In fact, light-complexioned blacks occupied a disproportionately large share of leadership positions in the post–Civil War South. Despite the blending of peoples of widely different skin color in the public life of black America and the existence of the "one-drop rule," color differences among African Americans continued to have meaning for both whites and blacks. Even though whites embraced a two-category (black/white) system of race relations, preached race purity, subscribed to contradictory theories about the "hybrid" nature of mulattoes, and subjected African Americans of all hues to legal and extralegal discrimination, they nonetheless accorded preferential treatment to light-complexioned blacks, especially in employment. At the same time, skin color in the Negro world exercised an influence that was as pervasive as it was mischievous.

Color, according to one observer, "appeared mysteriously in everything" in the black community at the beginning of the twentieth century. An elaborate sliding scale of color among blacks existed and figured in varying degrees in considerations regarding prestige, status, selection of marriage partners, education, church affiliation—virtually every aspect of social life. An accumulation of distortions and unfounded allegations, perpetrated in particular by color-conscious "mulatto baiters," could easily lead to the conclusion that complexion alone determined one's place in the class structure in the African-American community—a conclusion that obscures the fact that the majority of fair-skinned blacks constituted what has been referred to as "nameless mulatto nobodies." Nevertheless, color gradation among African Americans was often an indicator of a range of interrelated variables such as opportunity, education, acculturation, and even wealth. Such variables focused on the minuscule light-skinned aristocracy of color that did, in fact, occupy the highest stratum of the black class structure from the nineteenth century until well into the twentieth century.

Viewing themselves as cultural brokers, these aristocrats of color spoke to blacks and for blacks to whites. The alleged colorphobia of this elite became the target of bitter criticism that was aired in black newspapers and magazines. Such criticism became increasingly shrill in the early twentieth century with the triumph of Jim Crow on the grounds that the "white fever" among certain light-skinned blacks disrupted racial solidarity at the moment it was most needed. The concern over color gradations even surfaced in the late nineteenth-century debate among blacks over the proper terminology to be applied to people of African descent. Arguing that whites and blacks had "mixed so thoroughly" that there were few "full-blooded Negroes left" in the United States, some advocated *Afro-American* or *colored* as more accurate terms. Others who preferred to be called Negroes claimed that all other terms were merely subterfuges invoked by fair-complexioned hybrids intent upon distancing themselves from people of darker hue.

Of all the charges leveled against the fair-complexioned upper class, none circulated more widely or persisted longer than those related to "blue veinism," a reference to skin fair enough to reveal one's blue veins. Rumors abounded, from the late nineteenth to the mid-twentieth centuries, that a blue-vein society or club consisting exclusively of fair-skinned blacks had been or was being established in one city or another. Churches that attracted such people were likely to be known as blue vein, or B.V., churches. Opposition to the dominant position occupied by the light-complexioned elite promoted a succession of well-publicized struggles, involving especially the control of schools, churches, and various other organizations. The controversy that erupted in the 1906 convention of the National Association of Colored Women focused on the light complexion of Josephine Wilson Bruce, the wife of the former senator from Mississippi, who was a candidate for president of the organization. Dark-skinned delegates defeated Bruce because they desired a president who was visibly "altogether a Negro" rather than one whose complexion would allow whites to link her ability to her "white blood." Shocked to discover the existence of color lines within black society, white reporters believed that they had witnessed a "new phase of color discrimination."

Obviously such whites were unacquainted with the verbal assaults leveled against the fair-complexioned black aristocrats, called "accidental puny colored exquisites," that appeared regularly in African-American newspapers, magazines, and even novels throughout the opening decades of the twentieth century. Voicing a common sentiment among dark-complexioned blacks, Nannie H. Burroughs declared in 1904 that "many Negroes have colorphobia as bad as the white folks have Negrophobia." Among other African Americans who denounced the color consciousness of blacks as a serious impediment to racial progress were three well-known clergymen: Henry Highland Garnet, Alexander Crummell, and Francis J. Grimké. Critics intent upon combating the white notion that mulattoes were intellectually superior to blacks pointed to the achievements of poet Paul Laurence Dunbar, scholar Kelly Miller, and other dark-skinned individuals. But no African American waged a more relentless battle against those blacks who allegedly placed a premium on their light skin color, hair quality, and other European features than John E. Bruce, a prominent journalist who wrote under the pen name Bruce Grit. From 1877 until his death in 1924, he delighted in referring to mixed-blood blacks as "the illegitimate progeny of vicious white men of the South." The linking of a light skin with bastardy lent support to the exclusiveness practiced by at least some dark-complexioned families who, boasting of "pure African blood," forbade their offspring to associate in any romantic way with persons of light skin.

It scarcely seems surprising that some fair-skinned mulattoes keenly experienced the uncertainties and ambiguities of the "marginal man" described by Everett V. Stonequist in 1937. Proscribed by the white-imposed "one-drop rule," light mulattoes also confronted contradictory perceptions and expectations in the black community. In expressing this sense of marginality, the young, fair-complexioned Charles W. Chesnutt, who became a famous novelist, confided in his journal: "I am neither fish nor fowl, neither 'nigger,' white, nor 'buckrah.' Too 'stuck up' for the colored folks, and of course, not recognized by the whites." Cyrus Field Adams, a well-known black editor who was regularly accused of trying to "pass" for white, stoutly denied the charge, declaring that he had spent most of his life "trying to pass for colored." Light-skinned individuals coped with the problems of marginality in various ways, from black identity and assuming leadership roles in movements combating antiblack discrimination, to disappearing from the black world and assuming a white identity. The phenomenon of passing for white assumed an extraordinarily fair complexion and physical features identified with whites. Passing could be either permanent or temporary, yet both involved risks and sacrifices.

Even though critics of the African-American preoccupation with the color scale may well have exaggerated the extent to which a light skin shaped one's self-image, behavior, and attitude, especially toward those of darker complexion, the historical evidence clearly suggests that the color preferences of blacks mirrored those of whites. "The whites," a black observer noted in 1901, "regulate all our tastes." As a result, concoctions claiming to change the skin color of African Americans from dark to light or almost-white found a lucrative market in the black community and constituted a staple source of advertising revenue for the black press. From the late nineteenth century on, such products—along with those guaranteed to "de-kink" hair—appeared in profusion under such labels as Dr. Read's Magic Face Bleach, Imperial Whitener, Black Skin Remover, Mme. Turner's Mystic Face Bleach, Dr. Fred Palmer's Skin Whitener, Shure White, and numerous others. Of all such mail-order preparations, none surpassed Black-No-More for extravagant claims. Produced in Chillicothe, Ohio, by Dr. James H. Herlihy, a self-proclaimed famous chemist, Black-No-More promised to solve the nation's race problem by turning blacks white. "Colored people," one advertisement asserted, "your salvation is at hand. The Negro need no longer be different in color from the white man." This "greatest discovery of the age" guaranteed to transform "the blackest skin into the purest white without pain, inconvenience or danger." Complaints that Black-No-More and several similar concoctions made fraudulent claims and did, in fact, cause severe pain and skin damage prompted the U.S. Post Office to bar them from the mails in 1905. But the crackdown by the post office by no means halted the sale of skin lighteners, which continued in the ensuing decades to proliferate, although they made slightly more guarded claims. As late as the 1960s, skin-bleaching preparations, including Dr. Fred Palmer's Skin Whitener, still found ready markets among African Americans. By 1920, however, those concerned about the implications of the widespread popularity of skin bleaches became more strident in their criticism of people who used them. African-American cosmetic specialists were more forthright in warning about the dangers of "strong" bleaches and the inappropriateness of applying white powder to dark complexions. One such specialist assured black women in 1917 that a light skin was "no prettier than a dark one" and that the beauty of any skin, light or dark, was found in "the clarity and evenness of color." The wording of skin-lightener advertisements increasingly referred to skin tone rather than skin color.

This shift occurred within the context of two important developments: the accelerated engagement of light- and dark-skinned blacks in the public arena; and the "browning" of black America. The former was especially evident in the emergence of the "New Negro" associated with the cultural phenomenon known as the Harlem Renaissance in the 1920s, in which the mulatto elite led the way in articulating and popularizing the nation's black heritage and in condemning blacks' obsession with skin-color gradations. At the same time, the majority of Negro Americans had become neither visibly white nor black; rather the skin color of most consisted of various shades of brown. Although the mixing of blacks and whites declined in the decades after Reconstruction, the widespread mixing of light- and dark-skinned blacks generally had the effect of lightening the complexion of African Americans. Social scientists began to refer to "brown," rather than "black," America. By 1957, *Ebony* could report that "the old definition of 'the true Negro,' one with black skin, woolly hair, a flat nose and thick lips, no longer obtains."

Notwithstanding the emergence of "brown America," the impact of the Harlem Renaissance, and repeated claims that "blue vein societies" and color snobbery were rapidly disappearing, the color question remained an emotion-laden issue among African Americans. In the 1920s and later, black writers commented on the irony involved in the African-American concern with skin color, noting that while whites drew a single color line between themselves and people with "one drop" of Negro blood, blacks who condemned such a practice drew multiple color lines among themselves. The wide variety of complexional shades among African Americans ultimately gave rise to a skin-color lexicon in which minutely defined classifications ranged from peaches-and-cream and high yellow to brown and blue-black. For some African Americans, embarrassed by the obvious color consciousness present in the black community and troubled by its implications, the less said about "the nasty business of color," the better. Yet, as a black journalist noted early in the twentieth century: "The question of tints is one of the racial follies that die hard."

Among those who refused to remain silent regarding the issue was Marcus Garvey, a flamboyant native of Jamaica whose Harlem-based back-to-Africa movement used the emotive power of blackness to win wide appeal among the urban black masses during the 1920s. Whatever else Garvey may have accomplished, his bellicose discussions of skin color served to keep alive and exacerbate the "question of tints." Deeply distrustful of light-complexioned blacks, he preached race pride and purity, castigated mulattoes, especially those involved in the National Association for the Advancement of Colored People and the National Urban League, and stood the prevailing eschatology of color on its head by equating black with good and white with evil. His newspaper, *The Negro World,* refused to accept advertisements for skin lighteners and hair straighteners. Garvey's emphasis on skin color figured prominently in the controversy that developed between him and W. E. B. Du Bois of the NAACP. Du Bois responded to Garvey's description of him as a "hater of dark people" and "a white man Negro" by describing the Jamaican as a fat, black, and ugly charlatan who "aroused more bitter color enmity inside the race" than ever previously existed. Du Bois denied that a black/mulatto schism had ever possessed "any substantial footing" in the United States and maintained that by the 1920s such a schism had been rejected by "every thinking Negro." Clearly, Garvey had struck a nerve, and Du Bois responded with assertions that, at best, obscured the influence of color gradations among African Americans.

If color consciousness among African Americans received less notice in the popular media in the decades following Garvey's imprisonment and deportation in the mid-1920s, the topic increasingly attracted the attention of scientists and social scientists. By the mid-twentieth century, scientific inquiry regarding human skin pigmentation had evolved into the field of pigment-cell biology. Much of the research in this field focused on the pigment melanin, a term derived from the Greek word for "black." Although scientists generally agree that human skin color is based predominantly on melanin and have discovered much about its origins and pathology, questions about the evolution and distribution of skin pigmentation in the world's population, as an authority noted in 1991, are likely to remain "an ongoing conundrum for a long time." Perhaps even more pertinent to African Americans than biological investigations of pigmentation were the findings of social scientists, both black and white, whose works shed light on the role of skin color in determining everything from status, self-image, and personality development to educational and employment opportunities, the selection of marriage partners, and wealth in the black community. While the results of tests and surveys designed to measure the influence of color gradations upon virtually every aspect of African-American life were by no means identical, they did agree that blacks, to an extraordinary degree, had accepted the skin-color preferences of the dominant white society and that a light skin in all social strata of the Negro community had definite advantages. But Gunnar Myrdal's classic study, *An American Dilemma,* published in 1944, noted that as the black community became increasingly "race conscious," it was no longer considered proper for African Americans to reveal their color preferences publicly. Ten years later, *Ebony* admitted that some fair-complexioned blacks were still "cashing in on color" but that most African Americans of all complexional shades were embracing a common cause and identity.

Such an embrace became even closer as the civil rights movement gained momentum and the "black is beautiful" slogan achieved popularity in the 1950s and 1960s. Rejecting skin bleaches and hair straighteners, young blacks of all skin colors donned dashikis and Afro hairstyles and insisted upon being called "black Americans" or "Afro-Americans," often over the objections of their elders. Although *Ebony* continued to accept advertisements for bleaches, its editorials nonetheless reflected the change in color preference by noting that the "old black magic that made Sheba Queen" was again "sending red corpuscles racing up and down male veins." For a time, dark skin was in vogue and many fair-complexioned blacks found themselves on the defensive. Their skin color meant that they had to work harder at proving loyalty to their African heritage and to the larger black community. Some even complained of discrimination and ostracism by dark-skinned persons. Studies conducted during the 1970s suggested that the "black is beautiful" movement was without effect: One demonstrated that black children exhibited a clear preference for "light brown" skin color over that of either "black" or a "very light shade"; another suggested that a light skin retarded rather than facilitated upward mobility in the black class structure; still another indicated that blacks no longer preferred those whose complexions were lighter than their own as mates.

Even while "black is beautiful" was in vogue and African Americans were encouraged to "be proud of the Negro Look," old methods of lightening dark skin continued to flourish and new ones gained in popularity. Skin bleaches, both for the face and entire body, appeared in various forms—liquid, powder, and cream—and constituted a fourteen million dollar business in 1968. In adjusting to the times, some bleaching products referred to themselves as skin toners. All the while, techniques of lightening skin color other than the use of bleaches had made their appearance. The 1940s and 1950s witnessed the introduction of various new methods of lightening skin, ranging from depigmentation processes to the use of monobenzyl ether of hydroquinone. Later, dermatologists and plastic surgeons developed procedures for lightening dark skin and converting "broad features into aquiline ones." The most widely used dermatological procedures were chemical peel and dermabrasion, which proved to be painful, risky, and expensive. Tinted contact lenses, however, made possible a change of eye color without risk or pain.

Sociological studies of the color question as related to blacks clearly suggested that in the early 1990s skin color remained one of the mechanisms that determined "who gets what" in black America. Light-skinned blacks still enjoyed a more advantageous economic position and higher standing in the black community. One well-known study in 1990 concluded that there was "little evidence that the association between skin color and socioeconomic status [had] changed during the 30-year period from 1950 to 1980." Despite pressure on blacks "to keep quiet" about their color prejudices, antagonism resulting from such prejudices occasionally erupted into public controversies. For example, some cases arising under affirmative action involved charges of intraracial color discrimination. When the fair-complexioned, green-eyed Vanessa Williams, an African American, was chosen Miss America in 1983, some blacks angrily complained that she was "half white" and not "in essence black." Later claims that Michael Jackson, an African-American superstar in the entertainment world, had altered both his skin color and facial features occasioned much comment, including allegations that he was attempting to "get away from his race." In June 1994 a controversy over skin color erupted in response to the portrait of African-American athlete O. J. Simpson that appeared on the cover of *Time* magazine following his arrest on suspicion of murdering his former wife and her friend. That *Time* substantially darkened Simpson's complexion in transforming a mug shot into a "photo-illustration" prompted charges that the magazine had darkened Simpson's face to make him look more sinister and guilty.

Beginning in the 1980s, the significance of skin color preference among African Americans has been explored at length on television talk shows and in films, novels, social science studies, and even autobiographies. African Americans may still consider the issue a bit of dirty linen, but they are less reluctant to discuss it publicly. By candidly confronting the color consciousness and prejudices of African Americans, films such as Kathe Sandler's television documentary "A Question of Color" (1992), as well as scholarly treatises and other works, contributed to a greater understanding of a phenomenon that has persistently helped to shape the experiences, attitudes, and life chances of African Americans.

See also Abolition; Free Blacks, 1619–1860; Race, Scientific Theories of; Universal Negro Improvement Association

Bibliography

Berzon, Judith R. *Neither Black nor White: The Mulatto Character in American Fiction.* New York: New York University Press, 1978.

Davis, Floyd James. *Who Is Black? One Nation's Definition.* University Park: Pennsylvania State University Press, 1991.

Dominguez, Virginia R. *White by Definition: Social Classification in Creole Louisiana.* New Brunswick, N.J.: Rutgers University Press, 1986.

Embree, Edwin E. *Brown America: The Story of a New Race.* New York: Viking, 1931.

Evans, William M. "From the Land of Canaan to the Land of Guinea: The Strange Odyssey of the Sons of Ham." *American Historical Review* 85 (February 1980): 15–43.

Gatewood, Willard B. *Aristocrats of Color: The Black Elite, 1880–1920.* Bloomington: Indiana University Press, 1990.

Gergen, Kenneth J. "The Significance of Skin Color in Human Relations." *Daedalus* 96 (September 1967): 390–406.

Hirsch, Arnold, and Joseph Logsdon, eds. *Creole New Orleans: Race and Americanization.* Baton Rouge: Louisiana State University Press, 1992.

Hughes, Michael, and Bradley R. Hertel. "The Significance of Color Remains: A Study of Life Chances, Mate Selection, and Ethnic Consciousness among Black Americans." *Social Forces* 69 (June 1990): 1105–1119.

Jordan, Winthrop D. *White over Black: American Attitudes toward the Negro, 1550–1812.* Chapel Hill: University of North Carolina Press, 1968.

Mencke, John G. *Mulattoes and Race Mixture: American Attitudes and Images.* Ann Arbor, Mich.: UMI Research Press, 1979.

Reuter, Edward B. *The Mulatto in the United States.* New York: Negro Universities Press, 1969.

Robins, Ashley H. *Biological Perspectives on Human Pigmentation.* Cambridge, U.K.: Cambridge University Press, 1991.

Russell, Kathy, Midge Wilson, and Ronald Hall. *The Color Complex: The Politics of Skin Color among African Americans.* New York: Harcourt Brace Jovanovich, 1992.

Sweet, Frank W. "Essays on the Color Line and the One-Drop Rule." Published on Backintyme.com (March 1, 2005). Available from <http://backintyme.com/Essay050301.htm>.

Toplin, Robert Brent. "Between Black and White: Attitudes toward Southern Mulattoes, 1830–1861." *Journal of Southern History* (May 1979): 185–200.

Williamson, Joel. *New People, Miscegenation, and Mulattoes in the United States.* New York: Free Press, 1980.

WILLARD B. GATEWOOD (1996)
Updated by publisher 2005

Slave Codes

During the fifteenth century, as Portuguese explorers and traders moved down the Atlantic coast of sub-Saharan Africa, the Atlantic slave trade was legally justified by the papacy of the Roman Catholic Church as an extension of the Spanish Reconquest: a means to convert Muslim and other non-Christian Africans to Christianity. During the first two centuries of the Atlantic slave trade (c. 1440–1640), the Portuguese crown enjoyed and profited from the monopoly of trade in sub-Saharan Africa sanctioned by the pope.

Iberian law was deeply influenced by Islamic slave law, which was derived from the Qur'an. It was quite complex and contained provisions for humane treatment of slaves. It recognized several distinct, named forms of slavery, including the status of the partially free and their right to own part of their time as well as their production during their free time. Muslims were not to be enslaved. Slaves were usually non-Muslim captives taken in clearly defined, just wars. It gave positive encouragement to manumission.

During the thirteenth century, Toledo, Spain, was a major center for translations of works from Arabic and Hebrew into Latin. These Latin translations were often presented as original works. Although historians have long attributed the slave law of the Siete Partidas of King Alfonso X to Roman and sometimes to Visigothic law, these attributions need to be questioned. In Visigothic law, the distinction between slave and "free" dependents was unclear. Roman law did not define a "just" war, nor did it touch upon the relationship between masters and slaves or the care or treatment to which slaves were entitled. Roman law gave the master the right to free the slave, but it neither encouraged nor discouraged this process. Roman law focused on defining the slave as a form of property and clearly stated that all the property of the slave belonged at all times and circumstances to the master. This element of Roman slave law can be found in the Siete Partidas, but it is contradicted by other provisions in the same law.

The relevance of the Siete Partidas to Iberian slave law in the Americas has been exaggerated. It dealt with domestic slavery and was grounded in feudal principles. It referred to slaves as "serfs" *(siervos)* and never used the word "slave" *(esclavo)*. It stated that human beings were naturally free and servitude was contrary to nature. It gave masters full power over their *siervos*, but they were not allowed to starve them. In addition, they could not wound or kill them without a judge's order unless a slave was caught in sexual relations with the master's wife or daughter, in which case the master had the right to kill him. Slaves who were starved or gravely injured by masters had the right to complain to a judge, who could force them to be sold to another master. Neither Jews nor Moors could own Christian *siervos*. There were no provisions preventing the separation of families of *siervos*. The best explanation is that children born in the house of the masters *(señores)* were automatically free. An echo of this assumption can be found in several manumission documents from Spanish Louisiana that explained that a slave was being formally freed for having been born in the master's house. But the silence in Iberian law about protection of the family resulted in the highest level of slave family breakup in the Spanish American colonies, higher than in French and even in British colonies.

The crowns of Spain and Portugal were merged between 1580 and 1640, and African slavery began to develop in Brazil after this merger. The Siete Partidas of King Alfonso X was in theory relevant to both Portuguese and Spanish America. The Portuguese Manueline Ordinances of 1521 had little relevance to Portuguese America. They required the baptism of all black slaves and contained some very specific marketing regulations applying to finders of lost birds, slaves, and other property, but they were silent about treatment of slaves by masters. Portuguese wealth derived overwhelmingly from taxation of international trade and the creation of far-flung trading posts throughout the world. The bureaucratic and religious reach of the Portuguese empire was therefore weak. In early colonial Brazil, Portuguese settlements remained largely on the coast until the discovery of gold and diamonds in the interior at the very end of the seventeenth century. Laws protective of slaves, including the slave family, were promulgated in Bahia, Brazil, in 1720. They were contained in a large, general code called Constituições do Arcebispado da Bahia de 1720, which emerged from a meeting of priests. It provided that a master could not prevent his slaves from marrying and could not separate the members of slave families. These protective measures arose out of conditions in Brazil, where slaves were frequently married in the church.

In early Spanish America from the earliest years of colonization, the bureaucratic and legal arm of the metropolis reached far into the interior, where mining of precious metals was the major source of wealth. Nevertheless, there were very few laws or legal cases in Spanish America demonstrating royal concern with the protection of black slaves. Spanish law in the Americas focused on protection of Indians, not blacks. Indian slavery was outlawed, and slave law focused almost entirely on the policing rather than the protection of black slaves and on minimizing their contacts with and influence upon Indians. The Spanish slave code of 1789 containing protective regulations for slaves was copied to a great extent from the French Code Noir but without its clauses protecting the slave family. The 1789 Spanish code was successfully and formally abrogated by enraged colonists throughout the Spanish empire shortly after it was promulgated, and its protective provisions continued to be suppressed in the Spanish empire throughout the nineteenth century.

Misinformation has been widely spread by historians who deny the severity of slavery and racism in Latin America. In medieval Iberia, Slavic peoples rather than blacks were viewed as natural slaves. Indeed the word for slave, *esclavo,* means "Slav." But in Spanish and Portuguese America, slavery quickly became associated with blacks, and antiblack racism became and remains very powerful. Aside from varying legal traditions, the intensity and forms of racism throughout the Americas varied over time and place depending on a number of important factors. White blood in the subaltern population carried much more weight in French, Spanish, and Portuguese America than it did in the British mainland colonies that later became part of the United States. In Spanish and Portuguese America, corporatism was the foundation of law. It made legal and social distinctions based on comparative amounts of white blood within the population and the number of generations individuals were removed from slavery.

Thus, Iberian law made important distinctions among nonwhites, a very efficient mechanism of social control in societies where the Spanish and Portuguese were usually a small minority. Except in strategic colonies and at times and places where blacks and mixed bloods were especially needed for police and military reasons, the enforcement of legal protection of slaves and encouragement of manumission by colonial authorities were spotty. During the Latin American wars for independence, many mixed-blood and black slaves were manumitted by both sides in return for military service. Thus, colonial administrators in Ibero-American colonies used free black and mixed-blood layers within the subaltern population to control the slaves. Unlike Ibero-America, British America tended to lump all peoples with any degree of African ancestry together. Some scholars from the United States, impressed by these formal contrasts with racism in their own country, have at times unjustifiably accepted Spanish, Portuguese, and elite Latin American myths of mild slavery and benign race relations in Latin America. But throughout the Americas, restrictions on manumissions and racially exclusive attitudes increased over time.

British colonizers in the Americas lacked a tradition of slave law upon which to build. British law was based on common law rather than legal codes. British slave law was established over time through precedents set by case law. Early preoccupations were the distinction between slavery and indentured servitude and whether slaves who converted to Christianity must be freed. Once slaves were defined as property, what kind of property were they? Were they real estate attached to the land, or were they chattel to be mortgaged, inherited, and/or sold separately from the land, a process that undermined primogeniture? Could slaves brought to England, where slavery did not exist, be forced to return to America with their masters and returned to slavery against their wills?

French slave law was again different. Slavery did not exist in France, and the influence of Roman slave codes was not great. The Code Noir was first promulgated in 1685 for the French West Indies after a careful study of the conditions existing in these colonies. This code was eminently practical. It focused upon how to control the slaves through police measures, established the obligations of masters to feed and clothe their slaves, and restricted the master's right to punish the slave. These protective measures did not stem from humanitarian concerns. They were aimed at controlling mistreatment and exasperation of slaves to avoid theft, running away, and revolts. The original Code Noir encouraged manumission of slaves and gave full rights of French citizenship to all slaves manumitted in French colonies. It provided that masters, regardless of race, had to free and marry their slave concubines and free the children born of these unions or they would be confiscated for the benefit of charity. The first version of the Code Noir was promulgated when effective occupation was the basic principle determining which European power would possess a particular Caribbean colony. It was intended to increase the population considered French.

The Code Noir was modified for Louisiana in 1724. It was reissued several times and changed by royal decree for French colonies throughout the eighteenth century. Manumission became increasingly restricted over time. Nonwhites were increasingly discriminated against and could not, in theory, inherit property from whites, a provision that was totally ignored in Louisiana, as well as in the

French West Indies. Mixed-blood elites arose in both Louisiana and in the French Caribbean, creating three-tiered societies in which the colored elite played a major role in the economy and culture. The free colored elite in Saint Domingue/Haiti initiated the Haitian Revolution, attempting to use the slaves for their own military purposes. But the slaves revolted against both the white and colored elites, destroyed slavery, and declared the second independent nation in the Americas. One of the greatest achievements of the French Revolution, inspired and enforced by the slave revolt in Saint Domingue/Haiti, was the unanimous vote in the French General Assembly in 1794 outlawing slavery in all French colonies and giving full rights of French citizenship to the former slaves. This legislation was annulled by the Napoleonic reaction in France. Fear of slave revolts inspired by the Haitian Revolution became a major factor in sharply restricting manumission of slaves and increasing racial discrimination during the nineteenth century in the United States and in Cuba as their slave plantation systems reached their highest levels of wealth, power, and influence.

Criticism of the widely held myth of benevolent slavery and mild race relations in Latin America is growing. This myth arose as a justification for slavery in Latin America. It has been widely disseminated by mainly white historians in the United States, as well as by a few scholars in Latin America. This myth makes it hard to combat antiblack racism in Latin America because its very existence is denied. It is now being forcefully rejected by the Afro-Latino population throughout America, including in the United States.

See also Black Codes

Bibliography

Finkleman, Paul, ed. *Slavery and the Law.* Madison, Wis.: Madison House, 1996.

Hall, Gwendolyn Midlo. *Social Control in Slave Plantation Societies: A Comparison of St. Domingue and Cuba.* Baltimore, Md.: Johns Hopkins University Press, 1971. Reprint, Baton Rouge: Louisiana State University Press, 1996.

King, P. D. *Law and Society in the Visigothic Kingdom.* Cambridge, UK: Cambridge University Press, 1972.

Lang, James. *Portuguese Brazil: The King's Plantation.* New York: Academic Press, 1979.

Ordenações Manuelinas (Manueline Ordinances). Complete text in Portuguese available from <http://www.uc.pt/ihti/proj/manuelinas>.

Pottonaiis, Dandrea de. *Las Siete Partidas.* Vol. 2, *Partida Quarta.* Salamanca, Spain: 1555.

Watson, Alan. *Roman Slave Law.* Baltimore, Md.: Johns Hopkins University Press, 1987.

Willis, John Ralph, ed. *Slaves and Slavery in Muslim Africa: Islam and Ideology of Enslavement.* London and Totowa, N.J.: F. Cass, 1985.

GWENDOLYN MIDLO HALL (2005)

Slave Narratives

The autobiographical narratives of former slaves compose one of the most extensive and influential traditions in African-American literature and culture. The best-known slave narratives were authored by fugitives from slavery who used their personal histories to illustrate the horrors of America's "peculiar institution." But a large number of former slaves who either purchased their freedom or endured their bondage until emancipation also recounted their experiences under slavery. Most of the major authors of African-American literature before 1900, including Frederick Douglass, William Wells Brown, Harriet Jacobs, and Booker T. Washington, launched their writing careers via the slave narrative.

During the formative era of African-American autobiography, from 1760 to the end of the Civil War (1861–65) in the United States, approximately seventy narratives of fugitive or former slaves were published as discrete entities, some in formats as brief as the broadside, others in bulky, sometimes multivolume texts. Slave narratives dominated the literary landscape of antebellum black America, far outnumbering the autobiographies of free people of color, not to mention the handful of novels published by American blacks during this time. After slavery was abolished in North America, ex-slaves continued to produce narratives of their bondage and freedom in substantial numbers. From 1865 to 1930, during which time at least fifty former slaves wrote or dictated book-length accounts of their lives, the ex-slave narrative remained the preponderant subgenre of African-American autobiography. During the Great Depression of the 1930s, the Federal Writers' Project gathered oral personal histories and testimony about slavery from 2,500 former slaves in 17 states, generating roughly 10,000 pages of interviews that were eventually published in a "composite autobiography" of 18 volumes. One of the slave narratives' most reliable historians has estimated that a grand total of all contributions to this genre, including separately published texts, materials that appeared in periodicals, and oral histories and interviews, numbers approximately 6,000.

The earliest slave narratives have strong affinities with popular white American accounts of Indian captivity and Christian conversion in the New World. But with the rise of the antislavery movement in the early nineteenth century came a new demand for slave narratives that would highlight the harsh realities of slavery itself. White abolitionists were convinced that the eyewitness testimony of former slaves against slavery would touch the hearts and change the minds of many in the northern population of the United States who were either ignorant of or indifferent to the plight of African Americans in the South. In the late 1830s and early 1840s, the first of this new brand of outspoken slave narratives with strong antislavery messages found their way into print. These set the mold for what would become by mid-century a standardized form of autobiography and abolitionist propaganda.

Typically, the antebellum slave narrative carries a black message inside a white envelope. Prefatory (and sometimes appended) matter by whites attests to the reliability and good character of the narrator and calls attention to what the narrative will reveal about the moral abominations of slavery. The former slave's contribution to the text centers on his or her rite of passage from slavery in the South to freedom in the North. Usually the antebellum slave narrator portrays slavery as a condition of extreme physical, intellectual, emotional, and spiritual deprivation, a kind of hell on earth. Precipitating the narrator's decision to escape is some sort of personal crisis, such as the sale of a loved one or a dark night of the soul in which hope contends with despair for the spirit of the slave. Impelled by faith in God and a commitment to liberty and human dignity comparable (the slave narrative often stresses) to that of America's founding fathers, the slave undertakes an arduous quest for freedom that climaxes in his or her arrival in the North. In many antebellum narratives, the attainment of freedom is signaled not simply by reaching the free states but by renaming oneself and dedicating one's future to antislavery activism.

Advertised in the abolitionist press and sold at antislavery meetings throughout the English-speaking world, a significant number of antebellum slave narratives went through multiple editions and sold in the tens of thousands. This popularity was not solely attributable to the publicity the narratives received from the antislavery movement. Readers could see that, as one reviewer put it, "the slave who endeavours to recover his freedom is associating with himself no small part of the romance of the time." To the noted transcendentalist clergyman Theodore Parker, slave narratives qualified as America's only indigenous literary form, for "all the original romance of Americans is in them, not in the white man's novel." The most widely read and hotly debated American novel of the nineteenth century, Harriet Beecher Stowe's *Uncle Tom's Cabin* (1852), was profoundly influenced by its author's reading of a number of slave narratives, to which she owed many graphic incidents and the models for some of her most memorable characters.

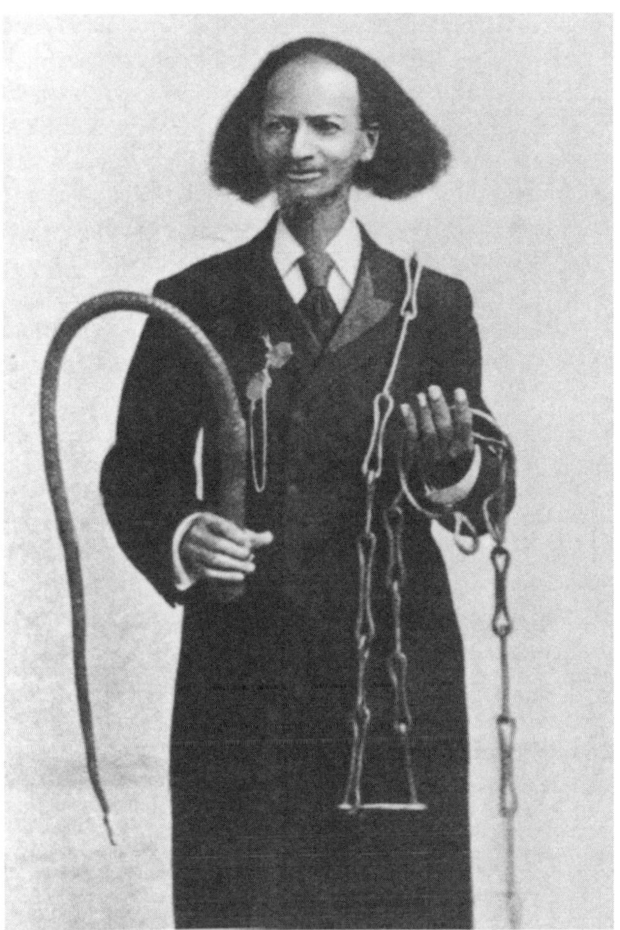

***Postcard of Dr. Thomas L. Johnson, author of* Twenty-eight Years a Slave: or, The Story of My Life in Three Continents.** GENERAL RESEARCH AND REFERENCE DIVISION, SCHOMBURG CENTER FOR RESEARCH IN BLACK CULTURE, THE NEW YORK PUBLIC LIBRARY, ASTOR, LENOX AND TILDEN FOUNDATIONS.

In 1845 the slave narrative reached its epitome with the publication of the *Narrative of the Life of Frederick Douglass, an American Slave, Written by Himself.* Selling more than thirty thousand copies in the first five years of its existence, Douglass's *Narrative* became an international best-seller, its contemporary readership far outstripping that of such classic white autobiographies as Henry David Thoreau's *Walden* (1854). The abolitionist leader William Lloyd Garrison introduced Douglass's *Narrative* by stressing how representative Douglass's experience of slavery was. But Garrison could not help but note the extraordinary individuality of the black author's manner of rendering that experience. It is Douglass's style of self-presentation, through which he re-created the slave as an evolving self bound for mental as well as physical freedom, that makes his autobiography so important. After Douglass's *Narrative,* the presence of the subtitle *Written by Himself* on a slave narrative bore increasing political and literary significance as an indicator of a narrator's self-determination independent of external expectations and conventions. In the late 1840s well-known fugitive slaves such as William Wells Brown, Henry W. Bibb, and James W. C. Pennington reinforced the rhetorical self-consciousness of the slave narrative by incorporating into their stories trickster motifs from African-American folk culture, extensive literary and biblical allusion, and a picaresque perspective on the meaning of the slave's flight from bondage to freedom.

As the slave narrative evolved in the crisis years of the 1850s and early 1860s, it addressed the problem of slavery with unprecedented candor, unmasking as never before the moral and social complexities of the American caste and class system in the North as well as the South. In *My Bondage and My Freedom* (1855), Douglass revealed that his search for freedom had not reached its fulfillment among the abolitionists, although this had been the implication of his *Narrative*'s conclusion. Having discovered in Garrison and his cohorts some of the same paternalistic attitudes that had characterized his former masters in the South, Douglass could see in 1855 that the struggle for full liberation would be much more difficult and uncertain than he had previously imagined. Harriet Jacobs, the first African-American female slave to author her own narrative, also challenged conventional ideas about slavery and freedom in her strikingly original *Incidents in the Life of a Slave Girl* (1861). Jacobs's autobiography shows how sexual exploitation made slavery especially oppressive for black women. But in demonstrating how she fought back and ultimately gained both her own freedom and that of her two children, Jacobs proved the inadequacy of the image of victim that had been pervasively applied to female slaves in the male-authored slave narratives.

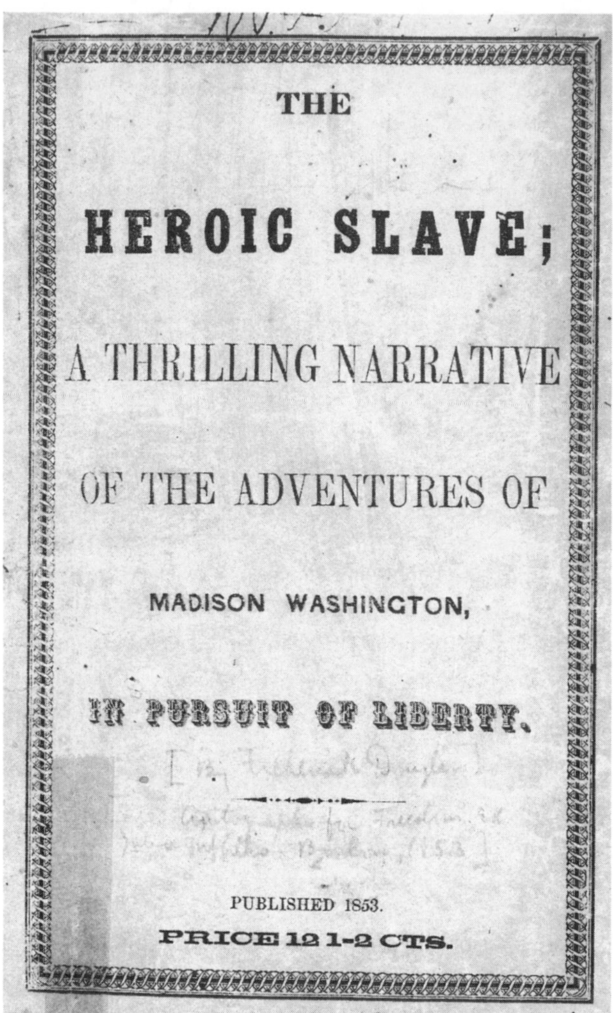
THE HEROIC SLAVE; A THRILLING NARRATIVE OF THE ADVENTURES OF MADISON WASHINGTON, IN PURSUIT OF LIBERTY.

PUBLISHED 1853.

PRICE 12 1-2 CTS.

Cover of **The Heroic Slave.** *Frederick Douglass's novella is based on a successful slave mutiny led by Madison Washington in 1841.* MANUSCRIPTS, ARCHIVES AND RARE BOOKS DIVISION, SCHOMBURG CENTER FOR RESEARCH IN BLACK CULTURE, THE NEW YORK PUBLIC LIBRARY, ASTOR, LENOX AND TILDEN FOUNDATIONS.

In most post-Emancipation slave narratives, slavery is depicted as a kind of crucible in which the resilience, industry, and ingenuity of the slave was tested and ultimately validated. Thus the slave narrative argued that readiness of the freedman and freedwoman for full participation in the post–Civil War social and economic order. The best-selling of the late nineteenth- and early twentieth-century slave narratives was Booker T. Washington's *Up from Slavery* (1901), a classic American success story. Because *Up from Slavery* extolled black progress and interracial cooperation since Emancipation, it won a much greater hearing from whites than was accorded those former slaves whose autobiographies detailed the legacy of injustices burdening blacks in the postwar South. Washington could not dictate the agenda of the slave narrative indefinitely, however. Modern black autobiographies, such as Richard Wright's *Black Boy* (1945), and twentieth-century African-American novels, such as Ernest J. Gaines's *The Autobiography of Miss Jane Pittman* (1971) and Toni Morrison's *Beloved* (1989), display unmistakable formal and thematic allegiances to the antebellum slave narrative, particularly in their determination to probe the origins of psychological as well as social oppression and in their searching critique of the meaning of freedom for twentieth-century blacks and whites alike.

NARRATIVE

OF

SOJOURNER TRUTH;

A Bondswoman of Olden Time,

EMANCIPATED BY THE NEW YORK LEGISLATURE IN THE EARLY PART OF THE PRESENT CENTURY;

WITH A HISTORY OF HER

Labors and Correspondence,

DRAWN FROM HER

"BOOK OF LIFE."

BOSTON:
PUBLISHED FOR THE AUTHOR.
1875.

Narrative of Sojourner Truth. *The title page from an 1875 edition of Sojourner Truth's* Narrative, *which was told to and written by Olive Gilbert and first published by Truth in 1850.* MANUSCRIPTS, ARCHIVES AND RARE BOOKS DIVISION, SCHOMBURG CENTER FOR RESEARCH IN BLACK CULTURE, THE NEW YORK PUBLIC LIBRARY, ASTOR, LENOX AND TILDEN FOUNDATIONS.

See also Autobiography, U.S.; Bibb, Henry Walton; Brown, William Wells; Douglass, Frederick; Jacobs, Harriet Ann; Pennington, James W. C.; Washington, Booker T.; Wright, Richard

Bibliography

Andrews, William L. *To Tell a Free Story: The First Century of Afro-American Autobiography, 1760–1865.* Urbana: University of Illinois Press, 1986.

Bland, Sterling Lecater Jr. *Voices of the Fugitives.* Westport, Conn.: Greenwood, 2000.

Davis, Charles T., and Henry Louis Gates Jr., eds. *The Slave's Narrative.* New York: Oxford University Press, 1985.

Foster, Frances Smith. *Witnessing Slavery: The Development of Ante-bellum Slave Narratives.* Westport, Conn.: Greenwood Press, 1979.

Jackson, Blyden. *A History of Afro-American Literature.* Vol. 1, *The Long Beginning, 1746–1895.* Baton Rouge: Louisiana State University Press, 1989.

Sekora, John, and Darwin T. Turner, eds. *The Art of Slave Narrative.* Macomb: Western Illinois University, 1982.

Starling, Marion Wilson. *The Slave Narrative: Its Place in American History.* Washington, D.C.: Howard University Press, 1988.

WILLIAM L. ANDREWS (1996)
Updated bibliography

Slave Narratives of the Caribbean and Latin America

Research by historians and literary scholars has discovered that a significant number of narratives by Caribbean and Latin American slaves have survived to the present day—albeit not quite as many as the extant slave narratives from the United States. Generally defined as the written testimony of enslaved black human beings, these stories of slave lives manifest a vital yet complex presence within the narratives of the global slave era. Although the majority of these documents exist in the colonial archive—and as such are entangled with the politics of domination, these narratives provide an important resource for understanding the experience of slavery and its aftermath throughout the African diaspora. Attention to the varied yet global institutional nature of New World slavery—and, more specifically, the slave narrative—is a crucial component in mapping the literary history of the African diaspora.

Although there are some similarities among all slave cultures, there are also very important cultural distinctions. For example, slaves in the Caribbean and Latin America were more likely than their U.S. counterparts to live on large plantations with fifty or more slaves; the white settler population was much smaller than that in the United States; more U.S. slaves in the nineteenth century were native-born than were Caribbean slaves (ninety percent in United States, versus less than seventy-five percent in Jamaica); and finally, due to their larger numbers, slaves in the Caribbean and Latin America were more likely to retain elements of their African cultural heritage than those in the United States.

These distinctions among slave cultures are also reflected within the slave narrative form. In addition to separately published narratives (which predominate in the United States), stories about the lives of slaves in the Caribbean and Latin America were more frequently incorporated or embedded within other texts, such as travel narratives, diaries, letters, and abolitionist newspapers, as well as church documents, spiritual conversion narratives, legal records, and other forms. Caribbean and Latin American slave narratives share a number of formal and structural characteristics, in addition to offering specific descriptions and details of Caribbean slavery. Like most slave narratives, they not only provided documentary, historical, and persuasive evidence for European readers but also a means to satisfy curiosity about Africans and their descendants.

One of the most striking features of slave narratives produced in the Caribbean and Latin America is that an overwhelming majority of them were narrated to an editor or transcriber. Consequently, these narratives must be viewed as composite texts in which both the narrator and transcriber/editor work together to create meaning. Although the narratives are mediatory in nature, it is important not to view these narratives as "corrupted and inferior forms," but rather to read them as Creole texts emblematic of the dialectical relationships of power in the slave system. Numerous scholars have pointed out the polyvocal nature of the documents such as manumission papers and letters frequently appended to U.S. slave narratives. In the case of the Caribbean and Latin American texts, this polyvocality also exists within the body of the narrative as well. As a result, rather than placing an emphasis on the notion of voice as a historical fact, these narratives make clear the manner in which voice also operates as a discursive act.

For a number of critics, one of the primary problems of dictated narratives is the concern that the voice of the editor/transcriber, rather than the slave, controls the narrative. Others contend that due to the mediated nature of these narratives, there can be no "authentic" subject or author behind these words. However, critical work on the genre of *testimonio,* or dictated narratives, from Latin America and those of Native Americans has made it clear that assumptions of an all-encompassing editorial power are unsupportable. Dictated narratives are written dialogues, in which both the voice of the narrator and the voice of the transcriber work together to create the text. Although the editor or transcriber might have the final word in arranging and ordering the final narrative, the oral storytelling of the narrator is a vital component of the eventual written product. The narrative could therefore not exist without the participation of the narrator.

The multiplicity signaled by the polyvocality of the Creole testimony of Caribbean slaves illuminates the complexity of the slave narrative form. Far from a rigid or unchanging genre, it incorporates numerous rhetorical and narrative strategies that develop out of each narrative's particular cultural context. Plantation slavery was an incredibly complex and varied system of power relationships. It is vital to embrace this complexity by attending to the various ways in which slaves communicated their stories. Although the Caribbean narratives are not always easily accessed, it is necessary to engage with them because they have so much to say. To ignore them is to silence once again the voices of Caribbean slaves.

See also Slave Narratives; Slave Religions; Slave Trade

Bibliography

Caribbean and Latin American Slave Narratives

De Verteuil, Anthony, ed. *Seven Slaves and Slavery: Trinidad 1777–1838.* Port of Spain, Trinidad and Tobago: Scrip-J Printers, 1992.

A Dreadful Account of a Negro Who for Killing the Overseer of a Plantation in Jamaica Was Placed in an Iron Cage Where He Was Left to Expire (1834).

The History of Mary Prince, a West Indian Slave, Related by Herself. Transcribed by Susanna Strickland and edited by Thomas Pringle, 1831.

Lee, Hannah Farnham Sawyer. *Memoir of Pierre Toussaint.* Boston: Crosby, Nicols, & Company, 1854.

"Letter from W. A. Gilbert, a Runaway Slave from the Danish West Indies to the Danish King (1847)." In *Slave Society in the Danish West Indies,* edited by B. W. Higman, pp. 137–138. Baltimore, Md.: Johns Hopkins University Press, 1992.

Manzano, Juan Francisco. *Autobiography of a Cuban Slave.* Transcribed and translated into English by Robert Madden, 1830s–1850s.

Moore, Samuel. *Biography of Mahommah Gardo Baquaqua.* Detroit, Mich.: Geo. E. Pomeroy & Co., Tribune Office, 1854.

Montejo, Esteban. *Autobiography of a Runaway Slave.* Transcribed by Miguel Barnet, 1963. Translated by Nick Hill, 1999.

A Narrative of Events since the first of August, 1834 by James Williams, an Apprenticed Labourer in Jamaica. Transcribed by Dr. Palmer, 1836.

Narratives of Sibell and Ashy, two Barbadian Slaves. Transcribed by John Ford, 1799. (Bodleian MS. Eng. Misc. b.4, fols. 50–51.)

Negro Slavery Described by a Negro: Being the Narrative of Ashton Warner, a Native of St. Vincent. Transcribed and edited by Susanna Strickland, 1831.

Embedded Narratives

Archibald Monteith: Native Helper & Assistant in the Jamaica Mission at New Carmel (1853). Moravian conversion narrative, edited by Geissler and Kummer.

The History of Abon Becr Sadika. In Robert Madden, *A Twelvemonths Residence in the West Indies.* Philadelphia: Carey, Lea, and Blanchard, 1835.

Memoir of the Life of the Negro-Assistant Salome Cuthbert (1831). Moravian conversion narrative.

The Narrative of Joanna, a Female Slave, a Tale of the West Indies (1824). Excised from John Gabriel Stedman, *A Narrative of an Expedition against the Revolted Negroes of Surinam* (1796).

NICOLE N. ALJOE (2005)

SLAVE RELIGIONS

When captive Africans reached the various shores of the Americas via the transatlantic slave trade, they brought their cultures with them. In addition to artistry, familial patterns, agriculture, and cuisine, they also carried beliefs about worlds seen and unseen, permeating all other aspects of life. Scholars acknowledge that enslaved Africans in the Americas were cultural carriers. But there is debate over the ways in which African cultures changed in the Americas because of contact with European and Native American cultures, enslavement, and separation from Africa. What follows embraces the premise that cultures are dynamic in nature and change over time and in connection with other cultures. However, the context of slavery is critical to understanding how African cultures, and specifically African religions, changed in the Americas.

At least three forms of religious activity were undertaken by enslaved Africans and their descendants. The first involved beliefs and practices that were clearly African but that also underwent some alteration in the American setting. Whereas the assumptions that such activity was more prevalent with native-born Africans than their offspring and that the intensity of such practices lessened with the passing of time are both reasonable, they are not necessarily verified by the historical record. The second form of religious activity concerns Christianity, and here there was a wide-ranging response to Christian teachings on the part of the enslaved. A third form of activity in fact brings together the first two, so that some slaves sought to practice some form of Christianity while maintaining their belief in African deities and rituals. At times Christianity and African religions melded, while at other times they were kept separate. Precisely how religion was pursued was not unrelated to powerful, slaveholding interests. However, the evidence is clear that the enslaved were perfectly capable of feigning certain beliefs in the presence of slaveholders, while practicing a very different set of convictions in private.

RESURGENT AFRICAN RELIGIONS

There are many examples of African religions operating throughout the Americas for as long as there was slavery. For example, Islam arrived early by way of captive Africans

RULES
For the Society of
NEGROES. 1693.

WE the Miſerable Children of *Adam*, and of *Noah*, thankfully Admiring and Accepting the Free-Grace of GOD, that Offers to Save us from our Miſeries, by the Lord Jeſus Chriſt, freely Reſolve, with His Help, to become the Servants of that Glorious LORD.

And that we may be Aſſiſted in the Service of our *Heavenly Maſter*, we now Join together in a SOCIETY, wherein the fallowing RULES are to be obſerved.

I. It ſhall be our Endeavour, to Meet in the *Evening* after the *Sabbath*; and *Pray* together by Turns, one to Begin, and another to Conclude the Meeting; And between the two *Prayers*, a *Pſalm* ſhall be Sung, and a *Sermon* Repeated.

II. Our coming to the Meeting, ſhall never be without the *Leave* of ſuch as have Power over us: And we will be Careful, that our Meeting may Begin and Conclude between the Hours of *Seven* and *Nine*; and that we may not be *unſeaſonably Abſent* from the Families whereto we pertain.

III. As we will, with the Help of God, at all Times avoid all *Wicked Company*, ſo we will Receive none into our Meeting, but ſuch as have ſenſibly *Reformed* their Lives from all manner of Wickedneſs. And therefore, None ſhall be Admitted, without the Knowledge and Conſent of the *Miniſter* of God in this Place; unto whom we will alſo carry every Perſon, that ſeeks for *Admiſſion* among us; to be by Him Examined, Inſtructed and Exhorted.

IV. We will, as often as may be, Obtain ſome Wiſe and Good Man, of the *Engliſh* in the Neighbourhood, and eſpecially the Officers of the Church, to look in upon us, and by their Preſence and Counſil, do what they think fitting for us.

V. If any of our Number, fall into the Sin of *Drunkenneß*, or *Swearing*, or *Curſing*, or *Lying*, or *Stealing*, or notorious *Diſobedience* or *Unfaithfulneß* unto their Maſters, we will *Admoniſh* him of his Miſcarriage, and Forbid his coming to the Meeting, for at leaſt *one Fortnight*; And except he then come with great Signs and Hopes of his *Repentance*, we will utterly Exclude him, with Blotting his *Name* out of our Liſt.

VI. If any of our Society Defile himſelf with *Fornication*, we will give him our *Admonition*; and ſo, debar him from the Meeting, at leaſt *half a Year*: Nor ſhall he Return to it, ever any more, without Exemplary Teſtimonies of his becoming a *New Creature*.

VII. We will, as we have Opportunity, ſet our ſelves to do all the Good we can, to the other *Negro-Servants* in the Town; And if any of them ſhould, at unfit Hours, be *Abroad*, much more, if any of them ſhould *Run away* from their Maſters, we will afford them *no Shelter*: But we will do what in us lies, that they may be diſcovered, and puniſhed. And if any *of us*, are found Faulty, in this Matter, they ſhall be no longer *of us*.

VIII. None of our Society ſhall be *Abſent* from our Meeting, without giving a *Reaſon* of the Abſence; And if it be found, that any have pretended unto their *Owners*, that they came unto the *Meeting*, when they were otherwiſe and elſewhere Employ'd, we will faithfully *Inform* their Owners, and alſo do what we can to Reclaim ſuch Perſon from all ſuch Evil Courſes for the Future.

IX. It ſhall be expected from every one in the Society, that he learn the *Catechiſm*; And therefore, it ſhall be one of our uſual Exerciſes, for one of us, to ask the *Queſtions*, and for all the reſt in their Order, to ſay the *Anſwers* in the *Catechiſm*; Either, The *New-Engliſh* Catechiſm, or the *Aſſemblies* Catechiſm, or the Catechiſm in the *Negro Chriſtianized*.

Rules for the Society of Negroes, 1693. *Broadside written by the Reverend Cotton Mather, a Boston clergyman, outlining ten primary rules of good Christian conduct for both free and enslaved blacks.* PHOTOGRAPHS AND PRINTS DIVISION, SCHOMBURG CENTER FOR RESEARCH IN BLACK CULTURE, THE NEW YORK PUBLIC LIBRARY, ASTOR, LENOX AND TILDEN FOUNDATIONS.

and was practiced in various parts of the Americas through much of the nineteenth century. As early as 1503 Hispaniola's governor, Nicolás de Ovando, complained that African *ladinos* (persons who had acquired facility in either Spanish or Portuguese) were colluding with the Taíno population and fleeing to the mountains to establish Maroon, or runaway, communities. Two decades later these same *ladinos* would be accused of leading an insurrection on the island, the first recorded revolt of Africans in the Americas. The *ladinos,* in turn, were composed largely of Senegambians, some of whom were Muslims. Senegambians would continue to lead revolts in Hispaniola through the middle of the sixteenth century.

Muslims arrived all over the Americas, although they were never in the numerical majority and usually in the very decided minority. In what became the United States, a number of Muslims achieved some notoriety. For example, Ayuba bin Sulayman, or Job Ben Solomon, arrived in Maryland in 1732 but was able to return to West Africa the following year. Another Muslim who received perhaps the greatest amount of attention because of both his Arabic literacy and his possible conversion to Christianity was Umar bin Said, or Omar ben Said (c. 1765–1864), who came to be known as Prince Moro or Moreau. Initially brought to Charleston, he would wind up in North Carolina. Lamine Kaba, renamed "Old Paul" in America, was held in captivity in at least three southern states. His participation in a Bible-dissemination strategy was a major factor in his manumission and repatriation to Liberia in 1835 after nearly forty years of enslavement. Abd ar-Rahman, known as Prince, arrived in New Orleans in 1788, but like Ayuba bin Sulayman was able to return to West Africa in 1829.

It appears that African Muslims were more numerous along coastal Georgia, where Salih Bilali (known as Tom) lived on St. Simons Island. Initially captured around 1790, he eventually came to St. Simons, where he died in the 1850s. His coreligionist Bilali (d. 1859) lived on nearby Sapelo Island. They were both drivers on their respective plantations.

There were also small but significant Muslim communities in the Caribbean. In Jamaica, for example, Muhammad Kaba (b. 1756) and Abu Bakr (b. 1790) were both well-educated and literate individuals who provided leadership for their fellow believers. In Trinidad was an even larger group of Muslims led by Muhammad Bath, who arrived on the island around 1804. Like Abd ar-Rahman in the United States, these Muslims would repeatedly petition the British for safe passage back to West Africa, some successfully.

Brazil probably had the largest number of African Muslims. Muslim groups had different experiences in the Americas, owing to the particular West African area of origin and to specific political developments relating to Islam in those areas, in combination with their relative concentration and treatment in differing American locales. Consistent with the behavior of Muslims in sixteenth-century Hispaniola, but in contrast to their colleagues in North America and the Caribbean, Muslims in Brazil were continuously involved in multiple insurrections. In particular, the northeastern province of Bahia was a hotbed of discontent. The Hausa, Muslims from what is now northern Nigeria, had been implicated in revolts there as early as 1807; a series of subsequent smaller revolts culminated in what has been called the *malê* revolt of 1835 in Salvador, in the province of Bahia. The revolt involved some five hundred Africans, enslaved and free, led by the "Nagôs," or Yoruba from what is now southwestern Nigeria. Brutally repressed with over seventy killed, the *malê* revolt revealed the importance of Islam, as well as an impressive level of Arabic literacy among the participants, who wore distinctive clothing, maintained their own religious schools, and observed Islamic rituals such as fasting during Ramadan.

The discussion of Islam reveals that much of what is known about African religions comes from the critical roles they played in resistance to slavery. Thus, consideration of vodou in Haiti, Martinique, Louisiana, and Mississippi during slavery is very much connected with revolution in the former. *Voodoo, vodou,* or *vodun* are terms that derive from Dahomean words for "good" and "gods" (as is the term *loas*). The Bight of Benin, a leading source of captives for Haiti and other French-claimed territories, exported such groups as the Fon (contemporary Benin) and Ewe (concentrated in present-day Togo and southeastern Ghana). There are many exceptional features of Fon-Ewe cultures, but the numerous and unique gods of the Fon-Ewe further distinguish the region, and include Mawu-Lisa (high god), Aziri (a riverain goddess), Gu (god of iron, warfare), Papa Legba (god of the crossroads, keeper of the gate, a trickster), and Damballah or Li Grand Zombi (serpent god of the sky). Mawu-Lisa, for example, is a composite of female and male characteristics, representing the Fon-Ewe ideal. These beliefs would become central to practices in such places as Haiti, Brazil, and Louisiana.

Vodou was practiced by François Makandal, probably the most famous of the Maroon leaders of Saint Domingue (Haiti). His background is curious, as he was supposedly raised a Muslim in West Africa and was literate in Arabic. Captured at the age of twelve, he was a full-blown Vodou priest by the time he appeared in Saint Domingue. An eloquent man with extensive knowledge of both the medicinal and injurious properties of plants and herbs, he attracted a following of undetermined size and developed a conspiracy to destroy slavery on the island. Carelessness led to his arrest in early 1758 before the revolt could begin, and after a brief but sensational escape, he was recaptured and burned at the stake. Makandal's career, however, set the stage for events forty years later, when the forces of *marronage* combined with those on the plantation to effect sweeping change. One of the leaders of the 1791 conspiracy was Boukman Dutty, a Vodou priest. Women played important roles as well, and their ranks included Cécile Fatiman, a Vodou high priestess, or *mambo.* In the dense forest of Bois-Caïman, she and Boukman officiated at a solemn Vodou ceremony for the conspirators that signaled the start of the Haitian Revolution.

Two traditions would develop within vodou. The Rada tradition refers to practices from certain parts of what is now Benin and is called the "cool" side of vodou, as it is concerned with producing harmony and peace. In contrast there is the Petro-Lemba tradition, the "hot" side of vodou, which focuses on healing and the destruction of evil. Petro-Lemba is heavily influenced by rites and beliefs from West Central Africa, specifically what was northern Kongo.

African religion also provided the organizing principles for slave revolts in the Anglophone Caribbean. In Antigua, for example, a 1736 conspiracy engulfing the whole of the island was led by Court (or Tackey), an Akan speaker from the Gold Coast (contemporary Ghana and eastern Ivory Coast). Women were prominent among the Akan, who believed that ancestresses came from the sky or earth to found the first Akan towns in the forests. Matrilineal for the most part, Akan clans each claimed descent from a common mother. Each clan had a male and a female head, and women played critical roles as advisors and heads of the matriclans. The Akan espoused belief in the earth mother Asase Yaa, who together with the high god Onyame (or Onyankopon) created the world. In keeping with most African theologies, the Akan high gods were remote, but the next order of deity, the *abosom* (who numbered in the hundreds), were accessible. Akan speakers were either a part of the expansionist Asante empire (established around 1680 and ruled by the *Asantehene,* or king) or they lived in its shadow. The Asante empire was one of the most militarily powerful and structurally complex states in all of Africa, and its political union was symbolized by the *Sika Dwa,* the Golden Stool.

Such background helps to explain the activities of Court and his accomplice Tomboy, a Creole. For example, they were assisted in their conspiracy by Obbah (Aba) and Queen, both Akan women who provided critical leadership in facilitating the "Damnation Oath," a ceremony derived from Akan traditions in which the insurrectionists committed themselves by drinking rooster blood, cemetery dirt, and rum, among other elements. Court had been crowned by two thousand of the enslaved as the "king of the Coromantees" (a reference to the Akan), the basis of which was the Akan *ikem* ceremony, a tradition preparing participants for war. Queen, in turn, may have been Court's principal advisor, playing the same role as the queen-mother, or *ohemaa,* in Akan society. Although the conspiracy was exposed before it could be executed, planters were astonished that not only the enslaved but many free blacks and "mulattoes" were also implicated. Some eighty-eight enslaved males were executed and forty-nine expelled from the island.

Of course, religion was important in the lives of the enslaved beyond serving as a basis for insurrection. By religion the enslaved throughout the Americas understood life, death, birth, old age, disease, health, misfortune, and serendipity. This was certainly true of the Yoruba-based religions of the New World, transported from what is now southwestern Nigeria through the Bight of Benin by those whose lives tended to be more centered on their respective towns and therefore urban. The Yoruba *orishas,* or deities, include Olodumare (high god), Oshun (goddess of fresh water and sensuality), Ogun (warrior god of iron), Eshu-Elegba (or Ellegua, trickster god of the crossroads), Shango (god of thunder and lightning), and Yemanja (mother of all *orishas* and goddess of the oceans). The best known of the Yoruba-based religious communities were and are in Brazil and Cuba, though they can be found elsewhere in the Americas. Enslaved Africans entering Brazil borrowed ideas from one another while retaining the concept of distinct ethno-linguistic groupings or communities, or *nações* ("nations"). As the black population became predominantly *crioulo* (Brazilian-born) and stratified along lines of color gradation during the nineteenth century (with *prêtos,* or "blacks," and *pardos,* or intermediate shades, as the basic divisions), persons born in Bahia and elsewhere began to choose a *nação.* This was significant, as those who made such choices were also choosing an African identity and an African religion. The various *nações,* such as the Nagôs (Yoruba) and Jêjes (Aja-Ewe-Fon), maintained distinctive religious traditions, which can collectively be referred to as Candomblé. The various African traditions, associated with specific *nações,* were centered upon sacred spaces known as *terreiros,* where rituals were held. Originating in private houses, the *terreiros* expanded to facilitate the pursuit of Candomblé as a way of life with minimal outside interference. As such, the *terreiros* became epicenters of not only African religion but also African culture. Women were the principal leaders of Candomblé, and perhaps the most famous of the *terreiros* in Bahia, Ilê Iyá Nassô or Engenho Velho, was founded around 1830 by women from the Yoruba town of Ketu.

All of these various Candomblé houses were associated with *irmandades,* brotherhoods and sisterhoods that were mutual aid societies, providing burial benefits, unemployment assistance (for those who were free), and in some instances passage back to Africa. Examples include the Bôa Morte ("Good Death") sisterhood and the Senhor dos Martírios ("Lord of the Martyrs") brotherhood of the Nagôs, and the Bom Jesus das Necessidades e Redenção dos Homens Prêtos ("Good Jesus of the Needs and Redemption of Black Men") of the Jêjes. The affiliation of the brotherhoods/sisterhoods with specific *terreiros* underscores an important feature of Candomblé: its connection to the Catholic Church (more on this below). Other African-centered religions include West Central African *macumba* near Rio de Janeiro, and elsewhere the practice of *umbanda*. Together with Candomblé, these religions feature the common elements of African spiritual entities, sacrifice, drumming and singing, and spirit possession.

The Brazilian experience parallels that of Cuba, where research is revealing the importance of such clandestine religious organizations as the *Abakuá*, a society originating in the Cross River area of southeastern Nigeria and Cameroon. Cuba is also a center of Yoruba or Lucumí influence, apparent in the practice of Santería. Divisions among the African-born and their descendants, which like Brazil eventually became a matter of choice, were equally preserved in Cuba's system of *naciones*, supported as they were by the respective *cabildos*, the functional equivalents of the Brazilian *irmandades*. Yoruba-based religion can also be found in Trinidad in the religion of Shango, in which the Yoruba gods Shango, Yemanja, Eshu, and Ogun are worshiped along with deities of Trinidadian origin.

Christianity Africanized

Mention of Candomblé and Santería provides a segue to the second and third forms of religious activity mentioned at the article's beginning. Practitioners of these African-based religions often functioned as members of the Catholic Church as well. There is debate as to what this actually meant: Some scholars maintain that Catholicism was simply a convenient mechanism by which African religions could be concealed, whereas others argue that practitioners of Candomblé and Catholicism approached the two religions as interrelated and mutually reinforcing. One reason for the ability of worshipers to either merge or conceal their beliefs can be found in the multiplicity of both the *orishas* of Candomblé, such as Eshu, Yemanja, Oshun, and Shango, and the equally numerous saints and principal figures of Catholicism. Furthermore, the areas for which the Catholic saints were responsible and could be petitioned were analogous to those of the *orishas*. Finally, consideration of the long historicity of Yoruba-based religions in Cuba and Brazil, or indeed African religions in Suriname, Haiti, and the Dominican Republic, goes against the common view that African religions decreased in strength with the passing of time. If anything, these religions have grown stronger since slavery ended.

Such correspondences underscore the observation that African religions and Christianity were not necessarily incompatible or significantly divergent. All posited a supreme deity, the existence of a spirit world, the possibility of communication with that world, the belief that witchcraft caused disease and disaster, that some kind of talisman (whether a Muslim amulet or a Christian cross) was necessary and efficacious in combating evil, and so on. But there were also differences, such as the concept of heaven and a summing up of all human history, or the idea that one religion was meant for all of humankind, concepts introduced by Christianity (and Islam).

Consideration of West Central Africa, source of more than one-third of all captives exported via the Atlantic and therefore well represented throughout the Americas, from Brazil to New Amsterdam (New York), raises the point that some Africans (in addition to those in Ethiopia, Nubia, Egypt, and North Africa) had converted to Christianity before their sojourn in the Americas. Communities throughout West Central Africa had long believed in a supreme deity, often referred to as Nzambi a Mpungu, and related spiritual entities. They also embraced the conviction that spirits of the dead who had led good lives resided in *mpemba*, a subterranean realm separated from the living by a large body of water, or *kalunga*. Since the deceased changed color within ten months of their demise, becoming white, they viewed Europeans initially as departed spirits, having crossed the *kalunga* of the Atlantic. Some also came to see Europeans as witches, a judgment equally applied to African rulers complicit in the slave trade.

But by the fifteenth century, a tradition of Christianity had also been established in West Central Africa, the result of Portuguese commercial activities. The social history of seventeenth- and eighteenth-century Kongo, for example, arguably revolved around the exchange between Christianity and Kongolese religion, giving rise to an Africanized Christianity best symbolized by the life of Dona Béatrice Kimpa Vita (1682–1706), leader of a political movement of reconstruction. A prophet-priest, or *kitomi*, her claim to be the incarnation of St. Anthony, combined with her teachings that Jesus, Mary, and the prophets were all Kongolese, are examples of the way Christianity was reconfigured to accommodate West Central African values. She would be burned at the stake for heresy.

The relative percentage of and degree to which those from Kongo and other parts of West Central Africa were Christians is a matter of scholarly contention. What can be safely stated is that some number were practicing Catholics, others knew of Catholicism but were not adherents, and yet others were unaffected by Christianity. The example of Dona Béatrice demonstrates, however, that those who adopted Christianity were deeply informed by antecedent African beliefs. The question becomes, was this yet Christianity, or had it been subsumed by a preceding conceptual framework?

Although at least some in West Central Africa were Christian, it does not follow that the Portuguese, Spanish, or French were heavily invested in the conversion and catechizing of slaves early in the history of slavery in the Americas. Emphasis on the spiritual welfare of the enslaved ebbed and flowed over the centuries, and differences could be noted between urban and rural settings. Evidence from Inquisition records reveals concern over the religious practices of the enslaved in the sixteenth century, as much of it was condemned as *brujería* (witchcraft). Catholicism became more routinized with the passing of centuries and a growing Creole or American-born population of African descent. However, greater familiarity with Catholicism did not necessarily translate into a rejection of African religion, as is evident in the cases of Brazil, Cuba, and elsewhere throughout Latin America.

Likewise, Christianity, predominantly in the form of Protestantism, was slow to make headway among the enslaved in colonial North America. Indeed, there is evidence that slaveholders, who for the most part could hardly be described as faithful churchgoers themselves, were wary of Christianizing their slaves, fearing that conversion would legitimate demands for manumission. By the 1830s, however, southern slaveholders began a systematic campaign to convert the enslaved to a complacent, docile version of Christianity reinforcing slavery, reacting to the use of Christianity as an abolitionist weapon. Blacks who responded to Christianity's appeal preferred its message of liberation, altering the worship style to allow for freedom of movement and the full expression of the Holy Ghost, within which dance and ceremony were in every way consistent with African notions of spirit possession. The ring shout, featuring worshipers moving counterclockwise in an ever-quickening circle, was derivative of West Central African and West African practice and was widespread in North America. In these and other ways, Christianity itself was first converted, facilitating the subsequent conversion of the African to its main tenets. Even so, it has yet to be demonstrated that most blacks in the American South were Christians by 1865. Whereas some may not have subscribed to any religion, others followed traditions derived from Africa, including those designed to improve health and material conditions by manipulating the spiritual world, practices collectively known as *hoodoo*.

The influence of African religions in the English-speaking Caribbean, where Protestantism also prevailed, was even more palpable. There, Christianity was often infused with substantial African content and connected with Obeah, the use of supernatural powers to inflict harm, and Myalism, the employment of spiritual resources and herbs to counteract witchcraft and other evil. The religions of *convince* and *kumina* also developed, the former involving respect for the Christian deity, but also an active veneration of the spirits of African and Maroon ancestors by practitioners known as Bongo men. *Kumina*, otherwise known as *pukumina* or *pocomania*, also venerated ancestors, who rank after sky gods and earth deities. Sacrifice, drumming, and spirit possession were part of these practices.

Beliefs were also shaped by ethno-linguistic groups like the Igbo from the Bight of Biafra (southeastern Nigeria), who made up large percentages of those brought to such places as Jamaica and Virginia. Among the Igbo, Ala (or Ana) the earth mother was functionally the most important deity, although the high creator god was Chineke, or Chukwu, who like the Fon-Ewe's Mawu-Lisa was a blend of male and female components (*chi* and *eke*), and from whom sprang powerful spiritual forces known as the *alusi* or *agbara*, as well as the personal guardian spirit, or *chi*, of each individual. The ancestral dead, the *ndichie*, added to the realm of the disembodied. Likewise, groups from Sierra Leone brought extraordinary ability to organize clandestinely, as they had maintained such "secret societies" as the female Sande or Bundu and the male Poro. Secrecy was critical to slave religion, Christian or not, as it tended to be practiced stealthily, away from slaveholder gaze.

Conclusion

The various religions practiced by enslaved peoples in the Americas were deeply influenced by beliefs and practices initially developed in Africa. Depending upon the precise locale in the Americas, such beliefs would have been continually reinforced throughout the eighteenth and nineteenth centuries with the steady arrival of new African captives. All aspects of life, from such everyday concerns as health and family and subsistence, to spectacular displays of resistance in the form of revolt, were significantly informed by religious considerations. In many ways insistence upon adhering to beliefs and perspectives that were fundamentally African in character and derivation was itself an act of defiance repeatedly undertaken throughout the history of slavery in the Americas.

See also Abakuá; Candomblé; Catholicism in the Americas; Muslims in the Americas; Obeah; Orisha; Religion; Santería; Voodoo; Yoruba Religion and Culture in the Americas

Bibliography

Bastide, Roger. *African Civilizations in the New World.* Translated by Helen Sebba. Baltimore, Md. and London: Johns Hopkins University Press, 1987.

Blassingame, John W. *The Slave Community: Plantation Life in the Antebellum South.* New York: Oxford University Press, 1972.

Butler, Kim D. *Freedoms Given, Freedoms Won: Afro-Brazilians in Post-Abolition São Paulo and Salvador.* New Brunswick, N.J.: Rutgers University Press, 1998.

Eltis, David, Stephen D. Behrendt, David Richardson, and Herbert Klein. *The Trans-Atlantic Slave Trade: A Database on CD-ROM.* Cambridge: Cambridge University Press, 1999.

Franklin, John Hope, and Alfred A. Moss Jr. *From Slavery to Freedom: A History of African Americans,* 7th ed. New York: McGraw-Hill, 1994.

Gaspar, David Barry. *Bondsmen and Rebels: A Case Study of Master-Slave Relations in Antigua, with Implications for Colonial British America.* Baltimore, Md.: Johns Hopkins University Press, 1985.

Gomez, Michael A. *Exchanging Our Country Marks: The Transformation of African Identities in the Colonial and Antebellum South.* Chapel Hill: University of North Carolina Press, 1998.

Miller, Ivor. "A Secret Society Goes Public: The Relationship between Abakua and Cuban Popular Culture." *African Studies Review* 43, no. 1 (April 2000): 161–188.

Palmer, Colin. *Slaves of the White God: Blacks in Mexico, 1570–1650.* Cambridge, Mass.: Harvard University Press, 1976.

Raboteau, Albert J. *Slave Religion: The "Invisible Institution" in the Antebellum South.* New York: Oxford University Press, 1978.

Reis, João José. *Slave Rebellion in Brazil: The Muslim Uprising of 1835 in Bahia.* Translated by Arthur Brakel. Baltimore, Md.: Johns Hopkins University Press, 1993.

Rout, Leslie B., Jr. *The African Experience in Spanish America: 1502 to the Present Day.* Cambridge, U.K.: Cambridge University Press, 1976.

Shepherd, Verene, and Hilary McD. Beckles. *Caribbean Slavery in the Atlantic World: A Student Reader.* Kingston, Jamaica: Ian Randle; Oxford: James Currey; Princeton, N.J.: Markus Weiner, 2000.

Stuckey, Sterling. *Slave Culture: Nationalist Theory and the Foundations of Black America.* New York: Oxford University Press, 1987.

Sweet, James H. *Recreating Africa: Culture, Kinship, and Religion in the African-Portuguese World, 1441–1770.* Chapel Hill: University of North Carolina Press, 2003.

Thornton, John. *The Kongolese Saint Anthony: Dona Beatriz Kimpa Vita and the Antonian Movement, 1684–1706.* Cambridge, U.K.: Cambridge University Press, 1998.

Warner-Lewis, Maureen. *Guinea's Other Suns: The African Dynamic in Trinidad Culture.* Dover, Mass.: Majority Press, 1991.

MICHAEL A. GOMEZ (2005)

Slavery

Slavery is the unconditional servitude of one individual to another. A slave is usually acquired by purchase and legally described as chattel or a tangible form of movable property. For much of human history, slavery has constituted an important dimension of social and occupational organization. The word *slavery* originated with the sale of Slavs to the Black Sea region during the ninth century. Slavery existed in European society until the nineteenth century, and it was the principal source of labor during the process of European colonization.

Some forms of slavery existed among the indigenous societies in the Americas before the arrival of Christopher Columbus. However, the reconstruction of the Americas after 1492 led to a system of slavery quite unprecedented in human experience. Slavery in the Americas was a patently artificial social and political construct, not a natural condition. It was a specific organizational response to a specific labor scarcity. African slavery in the Americas, then, was a relatively recent development in the course of human history—and quite exceptional in the universal history of slave societies.

Slavery was also a form of power relations, so slaves by and large did not have an equal voice in articulating a view of their condition. Their actions, however, spoke loudly of their innermost thoughts and represented their reflections on, and reactions to, the world in which they found themselves. Columbus thought the people he encountered in the Caribbean in 1492 might make good slaves, as he seemed to infer in his log of October 10, 1492, when he wrote: "They ought to make good and skilled servants, for they repeat very quickly whatever we say to them. I think that they can easily be made Christians, for they seem to have no religion. If it pleases Our Lord, I will take six of them to Your Highness when I depart, in order that they may learn our language" (Columbus, p. 77).

Blacks in the New World

Nevertheless, the first Africans who accompanied the early Spanish explorers were not all slaves. Some were free (such as Pedro Alonso Niño, who accompanied Christopher Columbus on his third voyage); and others were servants.

Two little boy slaves. *Children under ten years old comprised about 18 percent of the domestic slave trade. While many were sold with their mothers, one in three children under age fourteen were separated by sale from one or both parents.* PHOTOGRAPHS AND PRINTS DIVISION, SCHOMBURG CENTER FOR RESEARCH IN BLACK CULTURE, THE NEW YORK PUBLIC LIBRARY, ASTOR, LENOX AND TILDEN FOUNDATIONS.

Nuflo de Olano, who accompanied Vasco Nuñez de Balboa across the Isthmus of Panama was, however, a slave. So were Juan Valiente and several others who traveled and fought with Hernán Cortés in Mexico, or the Pizarro brothers in Peru, or Pánfilo de Narváez in Florida. Those blacks who sailed with Columbus on his first voyage to the Americas in 1492 were free men, and their descendants presumably were as free as any other Spanish colonist in the Americas. Other blacks who accompanied the early Spanish *conquistadores* might have been servile, but they were not true slaves as the term was later understood. Estebanico—described as "Andrés Dorantes' black Moorish slave"—accompanied Alvar Nuñez Cabeza de Vaca in his amazing journey around the Gulf of Mexico and overland across the Southwest to Mexico City in the late 1520s and 1530s. Estebanico learned several local Indian languages with consummate ease, and he posed, along with his companions, as holy men gifted with healing powers (Weber, p. 44). The chronicler Bernal Díaz del Castillo describes several "blacks" who accompanied Hernán Cortés to Mexico—one of whom brought wheat to the New World, and another (a follower of Pánfilo de Narváez) who introduced smallpox among the Indians, with lethal results (Castillo, 1979). Of the 168 men who followed Francisco Pizarro to Peru in 1532 and captured the Inca at Cajamarca, at least two were black: Juan García, born in Old Castile, served the expedition as a piper and crier, and Miguel Ruiz, born in Seville, was a part of the cavalry and probably received a double portion of the spoils, as did all those who had horses.

A significant proportion of the nonwhite inhabitants of the American slave societies were not the direct descendants of slaves. That is to say, they were not freedmen, or the descendants of freedmen, but free men and women who could trace their free status through several generations. They comprised a growing segment of the American Creole population. These forever-free people formed an important part of the history of American slave societies, of the constantly negotiated and changing world of masters and slaves.

Less ambiguous was the remarkable case of the slaves and their community of El Cobre in eastern Cuba, described by Olga Portuondo Zúñiga in *La virgen de la Caridad del Cobre: símbolo de cubanía* (1995) and by María Elena Díaz in *The Virgin, The King, and the Royal Slaves of El Cobre* (2000). In El Cobre, the original copper mining company went bankrupt in 1670 and the slaves (as well as the physical property, such as machinery, lands, and buildings) reverted to the monarchy of Castile. The slaves of El Cobre became royal slaves with significant traditional privileges, and apparently they knew these privileges better than the officials at the royal court. The slaves successfully exploited Spanish laws and customs to establish a viable self-governing community in which their town council supervised free people. Surely this was a most anomalous situation in the American slave system: enslaved people with more extensive privileges than freeholders. When the residents eventually lost their autonomy in 1780, a compromise with the copper company established a peculiar category called "wage slaves," and those residents who had not purchased their freedom—or had it purchased for them in the intervening years—fell into this category. The mining company nominally recovered its slaves after more than a hundred years of litigation, but it was forced to pay wages to the slaves as though they were regularly hired free laborers.

Indeed, between 1502 and 1518, Spain shipped hundreds of black slaves from Iberia to the fledgling American colonies. These slaves, called *ladinos,* were born in Iberia, in communities of Africans found between Málaga and Huelva in southern Iberia. As such, they were Roman Catholic in religion and Hispanic in culture. In the Americas they worked in the mines of Hispaniola, Mexico, and Peru; dived for pearls off the Venezuelan coast; helped to build the new cities and towns; and supplemented the faltering Indian population everywhere the Spanish established settlements. From this early population, a growing community of free nonwhite, nonindigenous people developed throughout the Americas. These descendants of various mixtures of population were unique to the colonial experience in the Americas.

The Slave Trade

The transatlantic slave trade formally began in 1518, when King Charles I of Spain sanctioned the direct importation of Africans to his colonies in the Americas, finally acknowledging that the potential supply of indigenous slaves was inadequate to maintain the economic viability of his fledgling overseas colonies. Shortly thereafter, the Portuguese started to import Africans to Brazil to create a plantation society and establish an Atlantic bulwark against other Europeans intruding along the coast. As the demand for labor grew, the number of Africans imported as slaves increased, and manual labor throughout the Americas eventually became virtually synonymous with the enslavement of Africans. The transatlantic slave trade became a lucrative international enterprise, and by the time it ended, around 1870, more than ten million Africans had been forcibly transported and made slaves in the Americas. Many millions more died in Africa or at sea in transit to the Americas.

The slave trade responded to an interrelated series of factors operating across Africa, at the supply side, and also in the Americas, at the market level. The trade can be divided into four phases, strongly influenced by the development of colonialism throughout the hemisphere. In the first phase, lasting to about 1620, the Americas were the domain of the Spanish and the Portuguese. These Iberian powers introduced about 125,000 slaves to the Americas, with some 75,000 (or 27 percent of African slave exports of the period) to the Spanish colonies, and about 50,000 (18 percent of the trade) to Brazil. This was a relatively small flow of about 1,000 slaves per year, most of whom were supplied from Portuguese forts along the West African coast. But slavery in the towns, farms, and mines of the Americas then employed less African slaves (about 45 percent of the total Atlantic trade) than in the tropical African islands of Fernando Po and São Tomé, Europe proper, or the islands of the Madeiras, Cape Verdes, and the Azores (about 55 percent of trade). Indeed, the small island of São Tomé alone received more than 76,000 African slaves during the period, exceeding the entire American market.

The second phase of the transatlantic slave trade lasted from 1620 to about 1700 and saw the distribution of approximately 1,350,000 slaves throughout the Americas, with an additional 25,000 or so going to Europe. During this phase, the Americas became the main destination of enslaved Africans. The trade was marked by greater geographical distribution and the development of a more varied supply pattern. The European component of the trade eventually dwindled to less than 2 percent. Instead, Brazil assumed the premier position as a slave destination, receiving nearly 42 percent of all Africans sold on the western side of the Atlantic Ocean. Spanish America received about 22 percent, distributed principally in Hispaniola, Puerto Rico, Cuba, Mexico, Central America, and the Andean regions of South America. The English Caribbean colonies bought more than 263,000 slaves, or 20 percent of the volume sold in the Americas. The French Caribbean imported about 156,000 slaves, or 12 percent; and the small islands of the Dutch Caribbean bought another 40,000 slaves, or 3 percent of slaves sold throughout the Americas.

During this phase, a social and demographic metamorphosis occurred, brought about by the sugar revolutions in various parts of the tropical Americas. By the end of the period, the Americas were divided between a number of rival European colonies, all successfully establishing plantation colonies for the production and export of tropical staple crops such as cotton, tobacco, sugar, indigo, and rice. Slaves became perhaps the most important commercial commodity in transatlantic trade, as well as the desired form of labor on American plantations.

Even more important, slavery evolved into a complex system of labor, commerce, and society that was legally, socially, and ethnically distinct from other forms of servitude, and that was almost always applied to the condition of nonfree Africans. Two patterns of colonies developed throughout the western hemisphere: colonies designed as microcosms of European societies and colonies designed primarily for the efficient production of export commodities. The first group of colonies constituted the settler colonies. In these colonies, slaves constituted a minority of the population and did not necessarily represent the dominant labor sector. In the second group were exploitation plantation colonies, marked by their overwhelming proportion of nonfree members, and in which slavery formed the dominant labor system.

Slave dealers Price, Birch & Co., Alexandria, Virginia. NATIONAL ARCHIVES AND RECORDS ADMINISTRATION

The period between 1701 and 1810 represented the maturation of the slave system in the Americas. This third phase witnessed the apogee of both the transatlantic slave trade and the system of American slavery. Altogether, nearly six million Africans—amounting to nearly 60 percent of the entire transatlantic slave trade—arrived in American ports. Brazil continued to be the dominant recipient country, accounting for nearly two million Africans, or 31 percent, of the trade during this period. The British Caribbean plantations (mainly on Barbados and Jamaica) received almost a million and a half slaves, accounting for 23 percent of the trade. The French Antilles (mainly Saint-Domingue on western Hispaniola, Martinique, and Guadeloupe) imported almost as many, accounting for 22 percent of the trade. The Spanish Caribbean (mainly Cuba) imported more than 500,000 slaves, or 9.6 percent of the trade. The Dutch Caribbean accounted for nearly 8 percent of the trade, but most of those slaves were re-exported to other areas of the New World. The British North American colonies imported slightly more than 300,000, or slightly less than 6 percent of the trade, while the small Danish colonies of the Caribbean bought about 25,000 slaves, a rather minuscule proportion of the slaves sold in the Americas during this period.

Opposition to Slavery

The eighteenth century formed the watershed in the system of American slavery. Although individuals, and even groups such as the Quakers, had always opposed slavery and the slave trade, general disapproval to the system gained strength during the later eighteenth century, primarily due to the growth of the Enlightenment, with its emphasis on rationality, and British Evangelical Protestantism. Opposition to slavery became increasingly more coordinated in England, and it eventually had a profound impact, with the abolition of the English slave trade in 1807. Before that, prodded by Granville Sharp and other abolitionists, Lord Chief Justice Mansfield declared slavery illegal in Great Britain in 1772, giving enormous impetus to the British antislavery movement. The British legal ruling, in time, freed about 15,000 slaves who were then in Britain with their colonial masters, who estimated their "property loss" at approximately £700,000.

In 1776 the British philosopher and economist Adam Smith declared in his classic study *The Wealth of Nations* that the system of slavery represented an uneconomical use of land and resources, since slaves cost more to maintain than free workers. By the 1780s the British Parliament was considering a series of bills dealing with the legality of the slave trade, and several of the recently independent former North American colonies—then part of the United States of America—began to abolish slavery within their local jurisdictions. After 1808—when Great Britain and the United States legally abolished their component of the transatlantic slave trade—the English initiated a campaign to end all slave trading across the Atlantic, and to replace slave trading within Africa with other forms of legal trade. Through a series of outright bribes, diplomatic pressure, and naval blockades, the trade gradually came to an end around 1870.

But slavery was not only attacked from above. At the same time that European governments contemplated administrative measures against slavery and the slave trade, the implacable opposition of the enslaved in the overseas colonies increased the overall costs of maintaining the system of slavery. Slave revolts, conspiracies, and rumors of revolts engendered widespread fear among owners and administrators. Small bands of runaway slaves formed stable black communities, legally recognized by their imperial powers in difficult geographical locations such as Esmeraldas in Ecuador, the Colombian coastal areas, Palmares in Brazil, and in the impenetrable mountains of Jamaica. Then, in 1791, the slaves of Saint-Domingue/Haiti, taking their cue somewhat from the French Revolution, staged a successful revolt under the leadership of Toussaint Louverture (1743–1803) and a number of other local leaders. The radical French commissioner in the colony, Léger Félicité Sonthonax (1763–1813) saw the futility of trying to defeat the local revolt and declared the emancipation of all slaves and their immediate admission to full citizenship (1793), a move ratified the following year by

Parishes.	Whites.	Free Colored.	Slaves.		Aggregate.	Cotton Bales of 400 lbs. each.
			Black.	Mulatto.		
Ascension..	3,940	168	6,864	512	11,484	684
Assumption	7,189	94	7,041	1,055	15,379	619
Avoyelles..	5,908	74	6,661	524	13,167	20,068
B. Rouge, E.	6,944	532	7,201	1,369	16,046	11,621
B. Rouge, W.	1,859	113	4,890	450	7,312	1,405
Bienville...	5,900	100	4,500	500	11,000	..
Bossier	3,348	..	7,337	663	11,348	40,028
Caddo	4,733	69	6,781	557	12,140	9,385
Calcasieu ..	4,452	305	946	225	5,928	640
Caldwell ...	2,888	..	1,762	183	4,833	7,296
Carroll	4,124	20	12,357	1,551	18,052	84,165
Catahoula..	5,492	46	5,538	575	11,651	25,564
Claiborne..	8,996	4	6,920	928	16,848	18,983
Concordia..	1,242	21	12,205	337	13,805	63,971
De Soto....	4,777	14	7,777	730	13,298	16,554
Feliciana, E.	4,081	23	10,148	445	14,697	23,332
Do. W.	2,036	64	8,363	1,208	11,671	21,331
Franklin...	2,758	2	3,038	364	6,162	9,307
Iberville ...	3,793	188	10,159	521	14,661	179
Jackson....	5,367	..	3,871	227	9,465	10,687
Jefferson...	9,965	287	4,968	152	15,372	..
Lafayette..	4,309	231	3,392	1,071	9,003	11,530
Lafourche..	7,500	149	4,728	1,667	14,044	476
Livingston.	3,120	..	1,240	71	4,431	1,563
Madison ...	1,640	16	11,663	814	14,133	44,870
Morehouse.	3,784	4	5,822	747	10,357	20,982
Natchitoch's	6,306	959	8,806	628	16,699	36,887
Orleans....	149,068	10,939	10,891	3,593	174,491	400
Ouichita...	1,887	..	2,757	83	4,727	8,639
Plaquemine	2,595	514	5,284	101	8,494	..
Pt. Coupee.	4,094	721	11,162	1,741	17,718	28,947
Rapides....	9,711	291	13,486	1,872	25,360	49,168
Sabine.....	4,115	..	1,550	163	5,828	5,052
St. Bernard.	1,771	65	2,020	220	4,076	..
St. Charles.	988	177	3,793	389	5,297	..
St. Helena .	3,413	6	3,453	258	7,130	6,484
St. James ..	3,348	61	7,114	976	11,499	..
St. J. Bapt..	3,037	299	4,079	515	7,930	..
St. Landry .	10,703	965	10,126	1,310	23,104	21,198
St. Martin's	5,605	311	6,361	997	12,674	4,717
St. Mary's .	3,508	251	12,532	525	16,816	142
St. Tam'any	3,153	412	1,636	205	5,406	200
Tensas.....	1,479	7	14,536	56	16,078	141,493
Terre Bonne	5,234	72	6,032	753	12,091	195
Union	6,641	3	3,627	118	10,389	10,843
Vermilion..	3,001	7	1,107	209	4,324	14,405
Washington	2,996	22	1,477	213	4,708	2,735
Winn	5,481	41	1,102	252	6,876	2,993
Total...	357,629	18,647	299,103	32,693	708,002	777,738

1860 Census of Louisiana. *Arranged by parish, the census lists whites, free blacks, and slaves, showing the racial makeup of the population.* PHOTOGRAPHS AND PRINTS DIVISION, SCHOMBURG CENTER FOR RESEARCH IN BLACK CULTURE, THE NEW YORK PUBLIC LIBRARY, ASTOR, LENOX AND TILDEN FOUNDATIONS.

the revolutionary government in Paris, which extended the emancipation to all French colonies. Napoleon Bonaparte revoked the decree of emancipation in 1802, but he failed to make it stick in Saint-Domingue, where the former slaves and their free colored allies declared the independence of Haiti—the second free state in the Americas—in 1804.

The fourth and final phase of the transatlantic trade lasted from about 1810 to 1870. During that phase approximately two million Africans were sold as slaves in a greatly reduced area of the Americas. With its trade legal until 1850, Brazil imported some 1,145,400 Africans, or about 60 percent of all slaves sold in the Americas after 1810. The Spanish Antilles—mainly Cuba and Puerto Rico—imported more than 600,000 Africans (32 percent), the great majority of them illegally introduced to Cuba after an Anglo-Spanish treaty to abolish the Spanish slave trade in 1817. The French Antilles imported approximately 96,000 slaves, about 5 percent of all slaves sold during that period, mainly for the small sugar plantations of Martinique and Guadeloupe. The southern United States also imported about 50,000 slaves, or slightly less than 3 percent of all slaves sold, despite formally agreeing to end their international slave trade in 1807.

Conditions of Slavery

The system of slavery in the Americas was generally restrictive and harsh, but significant variations characterized the daily lives of slaves. The exhaustive demands of the plantation societies in parts of the Caribbean and Brazil, combined with skewed sexual balances among the slaves, resulted in excessively high mortality rates, unusually low fertility rates, and, consequently, a steady demand for imported Africans to maintain the required labor forces. The recovery of the indigenous populations in places such as Mexico and the Andean highlands led to the use of other systems of coerced labor, somewhat reducing the reliance on African slaves in these areas. Frontiers of grazing economies such as the llanos of Venezuela, the southern parts of Brazil, and the pampas of Argentina and Uruguay required only modest supplies of labor, so that African slaves constituted a small proportion of the local population. Only in the United States did the slave population reproduce itself dramatically over the years, supplying most of the internal demand for slave labor during the nineteenth century.

In general, death rates were highest for slaves engaged in sugar production, especially on newly opened areas of the tropics, and lowest among domestic urban workers, except during periodical outbreaks of epidemic diseases.

The Abolition of the Slave Systems

The attack on the slave trade paralleled growing attacks on the system of slavery throughout the Americas. The self-directed abolition from below that occurred in Saint-Domingue in 1793 was not repeated elsewhere, however. Instead, a combination of internal and external events eventually determined the course of abolition throughout the region. The issue of slavery became a part of the struggle for political independence for the mainland Spanish American colonies. Chile (1823), Mexico, and the new Central America States (1824), abolished slavery immediately after their wars of independence from Spain. The British government abolished slavery throughout its empire in 1834, effectively ending the institution in 1838. Uruguay legally emancipated its few remaining slaves in 1842. The French government ended slavery in the French Antilles in 1848. Colombia effectively abolished slavery in 1851, with Ecuador following in 1852, Argentina in 1853, and Peru and Venezuela in 1854. The United States of America abolished slavery after the U.S. Civil War in 1865. Spain abolished slavery in Puerto Rico in 1873 and in Cuba in 1886. Finally, Brazil abolished slavery in 1888.

Slavery Scholarship and the Place of the Slave in the World

The topic of slavery has attracted the attention of a very large number of writers. Before the 1950s, writers tended to view slavery as a monolithic institution. Then, as now, there was much discussion of slavery, and less of the slaves themselves. Standard influential American studies, such as U. B. Phillips's *American Negro Slavery* (1918) and *Life and Labor in the Old South* (1929), Kenneth M. Stampp's *The Peculiar Institution* (1956), and Stanley Elkins' *Slavery: A Problem in American Institutional and Intellectual Life* (1959), misleadingly described slaves as passive participants to their own cruel denigration and outrageous exploitation. In Phillips's world, everyone was sublimely happy. In the world of Stampp and Elkins, they were not happy—but neither could they help themselves. Apparently neither Stampp nor Elkins read much outside their narrow field—or if they did, they discounted it. Certainly the then available scholarship of Eric Williams, C. L. R. James, or Elsa V. Goveia is not evident in their works. Herbert Aptheker in *American Negro Slave Revolts* (1943), Gunnar Myrdal in *An American Dilemma* (1944), and Frank Tannenbaum in *Slave and Citizen* (1946) had tried, in those three intellectually stimulating works, to modify the overall picture, but without much success.

Then, in 1956, Goveia published an outstanding book, *Slave Society in the British Leeward Islands at the End of the Eighteenth Century.* As Francisco Scarano notes of Goveia's work: "Goveia's sensitive and profound study of slave society in the British Leewards . . . is doubtless one of the great works of Caribbean history in any language. The Guyanese historian revealed the ways in which, in a racialized slave society, the imperative of slave subordination permeated all contexts of social interaction, from legal system to education and from religion to leisure. Everything was predicated on the violence necessary to maintain slavocratic order" (Scarano, p. 260). Goveia's approach inculcated the slaves with agency, a fundamental quality of which earlier writers seemed incredibly unaware. Slaves continuously acted in, as well as reacted to, the world in which they existed.

By the 1970s and 1980s, the maturing of Caribbean historiography, combined with the civil rights revolution in the United States, provided a renewed impetus for more sophisticated writings about slaves and slavery across the Americas. The quality of the debate improved noticeably, and comparative history threw refreshing new insights on some of the old problems. Slaves were seen as an inescapable and integral part of the world they fashioned, not some freak sideshow of helpless, subordinated individuals.

From the Caribbean came a rich outpouring of seminal works, all paying inordinate attention to the essential role of slaves in creating the new American experience. A selective list would include: Franklin W. Knight, *Slave Society in Cuba during the Nineteenth Century* (1970); Edward Brathwaite, *The Development of Creole Society in Jamaica, 1770–1820* (1971); Pedro Deschamps Chapeaux, *El Negro en la economía habanera del siglo XIX* (1971); Richard S. Dunn, *Sugar and Slaves: The Rise of the Planter Class in the English West Indies, 1624–1713* (1972); Richard Sheridan, *Sugar and Slavery: An Economic History of the British West Indies, 1623–1775* (1973); José Luciano Franco, *Los palenques de negros cimarrones* (1973); B. W. Higman, *Slave Population and Economy in Jamaica, 1807–1833* (1976); Michael Craton, *Searching for the Invisible Man: Slaves and Plantation Life in Jamaica* (1978); Manuel Moreno Fraginals, *El ingenio. Complejo económico, social cubano del azúcar* (1978); Guillermo Baralt, *Esclavos rebeldes: conspiraciones y sublevaciones de esclavos en Puerto Rico (1795–1873)* (1981); Léo Elizabeth, *L'abolition de l'esclavage à la Martinique* (1983); Hilary Beckles, *Black Rebellion in Barbados: The Struggle against Slavery, 1627–1838* (1984); Rebecca Scott, *Slave Emancipation in Cuba: The Transition to Free Labor* (1984); Barry Gaspar, *Bondmen and Rebels: A Study of Master-Slave Relations in Antigua, with Implications for Colonial British America* (1985); and David Eltis, *Economic Growth and the Ending of the Transatlantic Slave Trade* (1987). In addition to these outstanding monographs, a flood of outstanding articles appeared simultaneously in various journals, especially in *Slavery and Abolition*, and in papers read at annual meetings of the Association of Caribbean Historians.

In the United States, too, the attention given to slavery increased enormously in volume and improved tremendously in sophistication after 1970. Among the new studies were: Carl Degler, *Neither Black nor White: Slavery and Race Relations in Brazil and the United States* (1971); John Blassingame, *The Slave Community* (1972); Robert Fogel and Stanley Engerman, *Time on the Cross: The Economics of American Negro Slavery* (1974); Eugene Genovese, *Roll, Jordan, Roll: The World the Slaves Made* (1974) and *From Rebellion to Revolution* (1979); Peter Wood, *Black Majority: Negroes in Colonial South Carolina from 1670 through the Stono Rebellion* (1974); Edmund S. Morgan, *American Slavery, American Freedom: The Ordeal of Colonial Virginia* (1975); David Brion Davis, *The Problem of Slavery in the Age of Revolution, 1770–1823* (1975); Herbert Gutman, *The Black Family in Slavery and Freedom* (1976); Lawrence Levine, *Black Culture and Black Consciousness: Afro-American Folk Thought from Slavery to Freedom* (1977); Seymour Drescher, *Econocide. British Slavery in the Era of Abolition* (1977); Albert Raboteau, *Slave Religion: The "Invisible Institution" in the Antebellum South* (1978); Daniel Littlefield, *Rice and Slaves: Ethnicity and the Slave Trade in Colonial South Carolina* (1981); James Oakes, *The Ruling Race: A History of American Slaveholders* (1982); Orlando Patterson, *Slavery and Social Death: A Comparative Study* (1982); R. J. M. Blackett, *Building an Antislavery Wall: Black Americans in the Atlantic Abolitionist Movement, 1830–1860* (1983); and Robin Blackburn, *The Overthrow of Colonial Slavery, 1776–1848* (1988).

Giving agency to the slaves allowed for a realization that overt and bloody revolt was not the only, much less the major, form of resistance to the institution of slavery. Just as the poor do not accept their poverty, slaves did not accept slavery. Michael Craton points out, in his *General History of the Caribbean,* that "slave resistance was as inevitable as slavery itself. Slaves 'naturally' resisted their enslavement because slavery was fundamentally *unnatural.* Slave resistance of one kind or another was a constant feature of slavery. Only the forms varied across time and place, according to circumstances and opportunities, mutating in rhythm to an internal dynamic, if not also in relation to the larger historical context. . . . If slave resistance was endemic, it was overt only in special circumstances" (p. 222).

Overt rebellion was, of course, the most dramatic objection to slavery by far as Barry Gaspar and David Geggus illustrate in *A Turbulent Time: The French Revolution and the Greater Caribbean.* Michael Craton provided a detailed catalogue of Caribbean slave revolts in *Testing the Chains: Resistance to Slavery in the British West Indies* (1982), although he retreated and reformulated his original views in his later publication in the UNESCO *General History,* Volume III, which appeared in 1997. Excellent accounts of the various large-scale revolts include: C. L. R James, *The Black Jacobins: Toussaint l'Ouverture and the San Domingo Revolution* (1938), Thomas Ott, *The Haitian Revo-*

Slaves at work in a cotton field. THE LIBRARY OF CONGRESS

lution, 1789–1804 (1973), and David Geggus, *Slavery, War, and Revolution: The British Occupation of Saint Domingue 1793–1798* (1982)—all dealing with Haiti; Emilia Viotti da Costa, *Crowns of Glory, Tears of Blood: The Demerara Slave Rebellion of 1823* (1994), on the largest revolt in the history of Guyana; Robert L. Paquette, *Sugar Is Made with Blood: The Conspiracy of La Escalera and the Conflict between Empires over Slavery in Cuba* (1988); Mary Turner, *Slaves and Missionaries: The Disintegration of Jamaican Slave Society, 1787–1834* (1982); Anne Pérotin-Dumon, *Entre patriote sous les tropiques La Guadeloupe, la colonization et la Révolution* (1985); and Laurent Dubois, *Avengers of the New World: The Story of the Haitian Revolution* (2004) and *A Colony of Citizens: Revolution and Slave Emancipation in the French Caribbean, 1787–1804* (2004).

Most rebellions started with small conspiracies, and planters were often prone to exact tremendous retribution based on their paranoid fear of the ultimate consequences of such revolts. This is exactly what happened in 1843 in Matanzas, Cuba (a place-name that, ironically, translates as "the place of the killings"). It was there that the authorities murdered hundreds of slaves and free people of color, some in cold blood, because they felt that some slaves were about to start a rebellion.

Other forms of resistance were more prevalent, more endemic, than outright revolt. Certainly more pervasive in time and place were deliberate absences from work and running away. This perennial absconding took two forms. The first was a mass desertion of slaves who left deliberately with no intention ever to return. Refugees who followed this course sometimes formed independent communities in the relatively inaccessible hills near plantations and towns, operating in a symbiotic relationship with established colonial society. Such mass desertion was called *gran marronage,* and it gave rise to the various Maroon communities all across the Americas. In Spanish these communities were called *palenques,* and in Brazil they were referred to as *quilombos* or *mocambos*. Some Maroon communities lasted only briefly. Others lasted for centuries, as was the case with the Jamaica Maroons. Determined communities in Bahia and Palmares in Brazil, in Esmeraldas in Ecuador, in Maracaibo in Venezuela, and in Le Maniel in French Saint Domingue lasted for decades.

Concomitant with *gran marronage* was the more individual occurrence called *petit marronage,* the spontaneous decision of an individual slave to leave his master for a short period. *Petit marronage* reflected the strong individual will of the slave to resist forced or unpleasant labor, to procrastinate, or to defy authority. It was never designed to create a viable alternate to the slave society, as was the case with the Maroons. At its most serious, *petit marronage* remained a personal conflict between master and slave.

Other forms of slave resistance were equally personal and vindictive. Suicide among slaves was endemic in the American slave society. Domestic slaves poisoned themselves and their masters. Across the Caribbean, whites spoke often in fear of the magical powers of slaves who they suspected of having cast spells on them. Slaves also malingered and feigned ignorance, pretended not to understand the common plantation language of their drivers, broke farm equipment, killed or maimed cattle, set fires to cane fields at harvest time, destroyed cane carts and milling machinery, or even sold the produce produced on the plantations. By these various forms of industrial action slaves sabotaged the production and productivity of the plantations and increased the overall cost of the system to their owners.

It is extremely difficult to determine what constituted conscious modes of resistance and what actions resulted from the inadvertent consequence of random carelessness on the part of the slaves. But abundant evidence exists to suggest that slaves were largely in command of their world, even when they lacked the force to alter it.

Of course, writers such as Gordon K. Lewis, in *Main Currents in Caribbean Thought,* and Michael Craton, in his contribution in the *General History of the Caribbean,* tend to evaluate all actions of slaves as part of a conscious pattern of resistance. Lewis divides resistance into three categories:

> (1) The category of patterns of accommodation and of habits of learned survival in the daily experience of plantation life: this involved the whole gamut of slave response, short of escape and rebellion, to the general slavery situation, and included everything from feigned ignorance, malingering, sabotage, slowed-down work habits, suicide, and poisoning of masters, on to the endless invention of attitudes that reflected a general war of psychological tensions and stresses between both sides in the master-slave relationship; (2) The category of alternative life-style: this category included the manifold ways whereby the slave populations nourished and developed their own autonomous world of culture—in the areas, variously, of family, religion, language, song and dance, and even economic organization; and (3) The category of escape and open revolt.

Writers such as Lewis and Craton clearly view the entire existence of slave life as a form of resistance—a necessary precondition to a life in freedom, but also a vital manifestation of one's dignity and humanity. As Viotti da Costa writes: "Creating a black community in the slave quarters and holding on to traditions represented resistance to slavery because slavery implied not only the subordination and exploitation of one social group by another, but also the confrontation of two ethnic groups. The slave could resist in different ways: as a slave to his master, as a black man to a white man, and as an African to the Europeans. In the context cultural resistance could be interpreted as a form of social protest" (p. 301).

Nevertheless, viewing the slave systems as merely an enduring inescapable pattern of coercion and resistance is rather narrow and constricting. It fails to do full justice to the dynamic and nuanced world of the American slave systems. Such a narrow view perpetuates an indelible victim mentality and fails to reflect the totality of slavery throughout the Americas. It minimizes the monumental resilience, the astonishing creativity and dynamic contribution of Africans and their descendants in the making of the modern world.

Some of the activities of Africans and their descendants cannot be easily categorized, described, or analyzed within the restrictive bipolar forms of accommodation or resistance. Indeed, a great number of people described as Africans or as African slaves in the Americas were not in any way coerced. Their lot was quite removed from that of plantation field slaves, especially in the later years of the American slave system. The condition of slavery varied too much across the Americas to be neatly categorized. Moreover, it was never a static institution. It changed enormously through time, and even in the same locality.

See also Abolition; Maroon Societies in the Caribbean; Palmares; Runaway Slaves in Latin America and the Caribbean; Runaway Slaves in the United States; Slave Trade; Slavery and the Constitution; Toussaint-Louverture

■ ■ *Bibliography*

Columbus, Christopher. *The Log of Christopher Columbus,* translated by Robert H. Fuson. Camden, Maine: International Marine Publishing Company, 1987.

Craton, Michael. "Forms of Resistance to Slavery." In *General History of the Caribbean,* vol. III, *Slave Societies of the Caribbean,* edited by Franklin W. Knight. New York: UNESCO, 1997.

Díaz del Castillo, Bernal. *The True History of the Conquest of Mexico: Written in the Year 1568,* translated by Maurice Keating. London, 1800. Facsimile edition, La Jolla, Calif.: Renaissance Press, 1979.

Díaz, María Elena. *The Virgin, The King, and the Royal Slaves of El Cobre. Negotiating Freedom in Colonial Cuba, 1670–1780.* Palo Alto, Calif.: Stanford University Press, 2000.

Geggus, David. "Slavery, War, and Revolution in the Greater Caribbean." In *A Turbulent Time: The French Revolution and the Greater Caribbean,* edited by David Gaspar and David Geggus. Bloomington: Indiana University Press, 1997.

Lewis, Gordon K. *Main Currents in Caribbean Thought: The Historical Evolution of Caribbean Society in its Ideological Aspects, 1492–1900.* Baltimore, Md.: Johns Hopkins University Press, 1983.

Lockhart, James. *The Men of Cajamarca. A Social and Biographical Study of the First Conquerors of Peru.* Austin: University of Texas Press, 1972.

Scarano, Francisco A. "Slavery and Emancipation in Caribbean History." In *General History of the Caribbean,* vol. VI, *Methodology and Historiography of the Caribbean,* edited by B. W. Higman. London: UNESCO, 1999.

Viotti da Costa, Emilia. "Slave Images and Realities." In *Comparative Perspectives on Slavery in New World Plantation Societies,* edited by Vera Rubin and Arthur Tuden. New York: New York Academy of Sciences, 1977.

Weber, David J. *The Spanish Frontier in North America.* New Haven, Conn.: Yale University Press, 1992.

West, Steven M. *Though the Heavens May Fall: The Landmark Trial That Led to the End of Human Slavery.* Cambridge, Mass.: Da Capo Press, 2005.

Zúñiga, Olga Portuondo. *La virgen de la Caridad del Cobre: símbolo de cubanía.* Santiago de Cuba: Editorial Oriente, 1995.

FRANKLIN W. KNIGHT (2005)

Slavery and the Constitution

The word *slavery* does not appear in the Constitution, except in the Thirteenth Amendment, which abolishes the institution. Yet slavery was the most divisive constitutional issue in pre–Civil War America.

Constitutional Convention

Throughout the Constitutional Convention of 1787, the delegates heatedly debated the role of slavery under the new form of government. Population-based representation in the new Congress raised the issue of whether to count slaves in allocating representatives. The debates were often blunt and pointed. Gouverneur Morris of Pennsylvania argued against counting slaves for representation because "when fairly explained [it] comes to this; that the inhabitant of Georgia and S.C. who goes to the Coast of Africa, and in defiance of the most sacred laws of humanity tears away his fellow creatures from their dearest connections & damns them to the most cruel bondages, shall have more votes in a Govt. instituted for the protections of the rights of mankind, than the Citizen of Pa. or N. Jersey, who views with a laudable horror, so nefarious a practice." On the other hand, Charles Pinckney of South Carolina declared that slavery was "justified by the example of all the world." Pierce Butler, also of South Carolina, declared that "the security the Southen [sic] States want is that their negroes may not be taken from them which some gentlemen within or without doors, have a very good mind to do." Not surprisingly, James Madison of Virginia believed that the split in the convention was not between the large and the small states, but resulted "principally from their having or not having slaves."

The 1787 Constitution explicitly protected slavery in five ways. The three-fifths clause (Art. I, Sec. 2) gave masters extra representation in Congress for their slaves; the capitation-tax clause (Art. I, Sec. 9, Par. 4) limited the potential taxation of slaves; the migration-and-importation clause (Art. I, Sec. 9, Par. 1) prohibited Congress from ending the African slave trade before 1808; the fugitives-from-labor clause (Art. IV, Sec. 2, Par. 3) provided for the return of fugitive slaves; and the amendment provision (Art. V) gave added protection to the slave trade by prohibiting any amendment of the migration-and-importation clause before 1808. Other clauses strengthened slavery by granting Congress the power to suppress "insurrections," prohibiting taxes on exports (which would have allowed for the taxation on the products of slave labor), and giving the slave states extra votes in the electoral college under the three-fifths clause. The requirement that three-fourths of the states assent to any constitutional amendment guaranteed that the South could always block any proposed amendments. Finally, and most important of all, under the structure of the Constitution the national government had no power to interfere with slavery in the states where it existed.

These clauses led William Lloyd Garrison, America's most famous abolitionist, to call the Constitution a proslavery "covenant with death" and "an agreement in Hell." Southerners also agreed that the document protected their special institution. Shortly after he returned from the Constitutional Convention, Charles Cotesworth Pinckney told the South Carolina legislature, "We have a security that the general government can never emancipate them, for no such authority is granted, and it is admitted on all

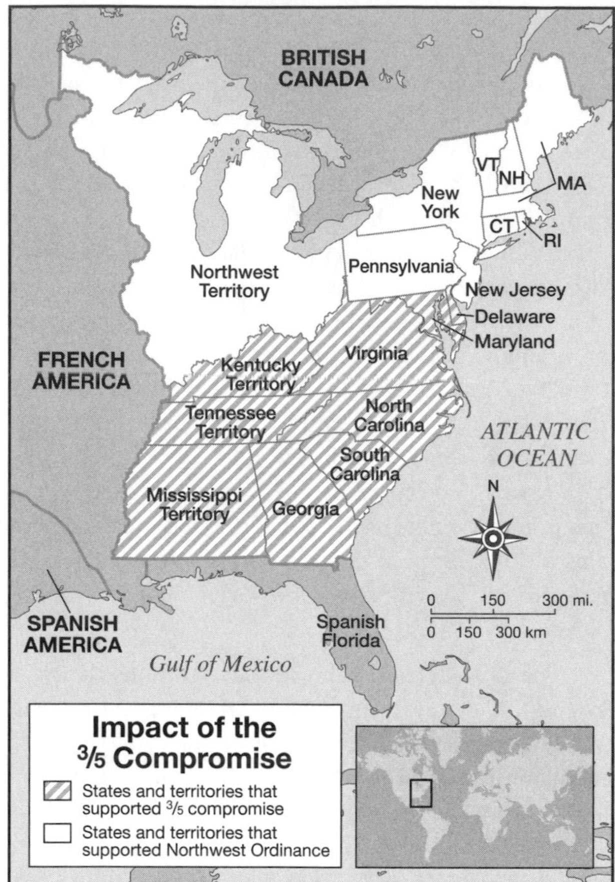

Map of the United States in 1787, showing states and territories that supported the three-fifths compromise and those supporting the Northwest Ordinance. *During the Constitutional Convention that year, southern slaveholding states demanded that slaves be counted in population totals for the purpose of determining representation in Congress. An agreement was reached to count each slave as three-fifths of a person. Meanwhile, the Northwest Ordinance of 1787 forbade slavery in the Northwest territory (Great Lakes region). In effect, these decisions created a nation half slave and half free, leading to a series of further compromises and, ultimately, civil war.* MAP BY XNR PRODUCTIONS. THE GALE GROUP.

hands, that the general government has no powers but what are expressly granted by the constitution; and that all rights not expressed were reserved by the several states."

The Three-fifths Clause and Continuation of the Slave Trade

During the struggle over ratification, a number of northern antifederalists complained about the three-fifths provision and the continuation of the slave trade for at least twenty more years. These two clauses have often been misunderstood.

The three-fifths clause was not an assertion that a black was three-fifths of a person. The clause allocated representation in Congress by adding to the free population three-fifths of the total number of slaves. Free blacks were counted the same as whites, and in a number of states, including Massachusetts, New York, and North Carolina, free blacks voted under the same conditions as whites. The three-fifths rule was a compromise over the allocation of political power in the House of Representatives. Southerners at the convention wanted to count slaves fully for purposes of representation, while northerners did not want to count slaves at all for representation.

The slave-trade clause has been misunderstood to require the end of the trade in 1808. Rather, it only prohibited Congress from ending the trade before that date. If the Deep South had had the political clout, it could have kept the trade legal after 1808.

Supreme Court

Ratification of the Constitution led to Supreme Court decisions on the African slave trade, slaves in interstate commerce, fugitive slaves, federal regulation of slavery in the territories, and the rights of free blacks under the Constitution. With the exception of cases dealing with the African slave trade, the Supreme Court invariably sided with slave owners.

After 1808, the federal courts heard numerous cases involving the importation of slaves from Africa. In the *Antelope* case (1825), Chief Justice John Marshall asserted that the African slave trade was "contrary to the law of nature" but that it was "consistent with the law of nations" and "cannot in itself be piracy." Thus the Court recognized the right of foreigners to engage in the slave trade if their own nations allowed them to do so.

The Court consistently condemned the trade as a violation of natural law and morality, but this did not affect its judgments. In all of the slave-trading cases, the Court enforced concepts of international law; slave traders who violated the laws of their own country could expect no support from the Court. But when foreign nationals participated in the trade, they were protected by their own laws. As Justice Joseph Story noted in a circuit court opinion in *La Jeune Eugénie* (1822), "I am bound to consider the trade an offence against the universal law of society, and in all cases, where it is not protected by a foreign government, to deal with it as an offence carrying with it the penalty of confiscation."

Soon after the adoption of the Constitution, the nation reached an unstated political consensus on the question of slavery and commerce. Although most lawyers would have conceded that after 1808 Congress had the power to regulate the interstate slave trade, the general consensus was that such regulation would be impossible to get through Congress and, in any event, would threaten the Union itself. Arguments of counsel and the opinions of the justices in commerce clause cases recognized the special status of slaves in the general regulation of commerce.

Groves v. Slaughter (1841) was the only major slavery case to come before the Supreme Court that directly raised commerce-clause issues. The Mississippi Constitution of 1832 prohibited the importation of slaves for sale. This was not an antislavery provision, but an attempt to reduce the flow of capital out of the state. In violation of this provision, Slaughter sold slaves in Mississippi and received notes signed by Groves, who later defaulted on the notes, arguing that the sale of slaves in Mississippi was void. The Court ruled that the notes were not void because Mississippi's constitutional prohibition on the importation of slaves was not self-executing, and absent legislation implementing the prohibition, the Mississippi constitutional clause was inoperative. In separate concurrences, northern and southern justices agreed that a state might legally ban the importation of slaves. This principle supported northerners' interest in keeping slaves out of their states and the southern desire to make sure that the federal courts could not interfere with slavery on the local level.

Fugitive Slaves

The jurisprudence surrounding fugitive slaves was the most divisive constitutional issue in antebellum America. The federal and state courts heard numerous cases involving fugitive slaves. While settling the legal issues, none of these cases satisfactorily dealt with the moral and political questions raised when human beings escaped to freedom. Such cases only exacerbated the sectional crisis. Ultimately, these issues were decided not by constitutional arguments and ballots but by battlefield tactics and bullets.

The wording of the fugitive slave clause suggests that the Constitutional Convention did not anticipate any federal enforcement of the law. However, in 1793 Congress passed the first of several fugitive slave laws, which spelled out procedures for the return of runaway slaves. In *Prigg v. Pennsylvania* (1842), Justice Joseph Story upheld the 1793 law and struck down state laws passed to protect free blacks from kidnapping if they interfered with the return of fugitive slaves. Story urged state officials to continue to enforce the 1793 law but concluded that they could not be required to do so. In response to this decision, a number of states passed new personal-liberty laws, prohibiting state officials from participating in the return of fugitive slaves and barring the use of state jails and other facilities for such returns.

Jones v. Van Zandt (1847) was a civil suit over the value of slaves who had escaped from Kentucky to Ohio, where Van Zandt offered them a ride in his wagon. Van Zandt's attorneys, Salmon P. Chase and William H. Seward, unsuccessfully argued that in Ohio all people were presumed free and thus Van Zandt had no reason to know he was transporting runaway slaves. In a harsh interpretation of the 1793 law, the Court concluded that Van Zandt should have known the blacks he befriended were slaves. In essence, this meant that all blacks in the North were presumptively slaves.

Hostility to these decisions led to the Fugitive Slave Act of 1850, which provided for federal commissioners to enforce the law through the United States. These commissioners could call on federal marshals, the military, and "bystanders, or posse comitatus," as necessary. The law provided stiff prison sentences and high fines for people interfering in its enforcement, while not allowing seized blacks to testify on their own behalf or giving them a jury trial. In *Ableman v. Booth* (1859), the Supreme Court upheld this law against a challenge based on the law's violation of the U.S. Constitution and the Wisconsin Constitution.

Slavery in the Territories

In two monumental acts, the Northwest Ordinance (1787; reenacted in 1789) and the Missouri Compromise (1820), Congress prohibited slavery in most of the territories owned by the United States. These acts led to some of the most important, controversial, and complicated cases that ever reached the Supreme Court.

From 1820 until 1850 the issue of slavery in the territories was governed by the Missouri Compromise, which prohibited slavery in almost all of the West. The acquisition of new lands in the Mexican War, and the acceptance throughout the South of a "positive good" theory of slavery, led southerners to demand access to the western territories. In 1854 Congress repealed some of the Missouri Compromise by opening Kansas and Nebraska to slavery under a theory of popular sovereignty. Under popular sovereignty the settlers of a territory would decide for themselves whether to have slavery. Rather than democratizing the west, popular sovereignty led to a mini–Civil War in Kansas, known as Bleeding Kansas, in which free-state and slave-state settlers fought for control of the territorial government. Meanwhile, in the North the newly organized Republican Party gained enormous success campaigning against the spread of slavery. In 1856 this party, which was

Crowds in the U.S. House of Representatives celebrate the passage of the Thirteenth Amendment, January 31, 1865. *Later ratified on December 18 of that same year, the amendment constituted a formal end to slavery, declaring that "neither slavery nor involuntary servitude" shall ever exist in the United States.* HULTON ARCHIVE/GETTY IMAGES

less than two years old, carried all but five northern states in the presidential election.

Dred Scott and the Civil War

This set the stage for the most significant legal case of the antebellum period, if not the entire history of the Supreme Court, *Dred Scott v. Sandford* (1857). The avidly proslavery Chief Justice Roger B. Taney used *Dred Scott* to decide pressing political issues in favor of the South. In his opinion's two most controversial points, Chief Justice Taney ruled that the Missouri Compromise unconstitutionally prohibited citizens from bringing their slaves into federal territories and that free blacks could never be citizens of the United States or sue in federal courts as citizens of the states in which they lived.

This decision, more than anything else, made the constitutionality of slavery into a major political question. In 1860, Abraham Lincoln successfully ran for president by opposing the further expansion of slavery and by attacking Taney and the *Dred Scott* decision. That in turn led to secession, the Civil War, the issuance of the Emancipation Proclamation, and a formal end to slavery through constitutional amendment. Ratified on December 18, 1865, the Thirteenth Amendment pledged that "neither slavery nor involuntary servitude" shall ever exist in the United States.

See also Thirteenth Amendment

Bibliography

Fehrenbacher, Don E. *The Dred Scott Case: Its Significance in American Law and Politics.* New York: Oxford University Press, 1978.

Fehrenbacher, Don E. *The Slaveholding Republic: An Account of the United States Government's Relation to Slavery.* New York: Oxford University Press, 2001.

Finkelman, Paul. "Slavery and the Constitutional Convention: Making a Covenant with Death." In *Beyond Confederation: Origins of the Constitution and American National Identity*, edited by Richard Beeman. Chapel Hill: University of North Carolina Press, 1987, pp. 188–225.

Finkelman, Paul. *Dred Scott v. Sandford: A Brief History with Documents.* New York: St. Martin's, 1997.

Morris, Thomas D. *Free Men All: The Personal Liberty Laws of the North, 1780–1861.* Baltimore, Md.: Johns Hopkins University Press, 1974.

Wiecek, William M. *The Sources of Antislavery Constitutionalism in America, 1760–1848.* Ithaca, N.Y.: Cornell University Press, 1977.

PAUL FINKELMAN (1996)
Updated bibliography

Slave Trade

The Atlantic slave trade was one of the most important demographic, social, and economic events of the Modern Era. Extending over four centuries, it fostered the involuntary migration of millions of African peoples from their homelands to forced labor in the Americas and elsewhere around the globe. In the process, it reshaped African societies; provided much of the raw material for constructing new social, economic, and political structures in the New World; promoted the development of a new industrial order; and furnished essential ingredients of modern world culture. It also left an unfortunate legacy of racism by establishing a connection between servility and barbarity and peoples of African descent.

The eighteenth-century interest in slavery derived from the nature of the mercantilist imperial structures that supported the production of tropical staples through plantation labor. Africa was the source of this labor. Since the material or technological distance between Africa and Europe was not then as great as it was to become later, Europeans approached Africans as approximate equals. European traders were highly dependent upon their African partners and associates to ensure an orderly trade. Since trade frequently depended upon the political vagaries on the African coast, European traders had to be aware of political and social conditions in the areas where they wanted to trade. Consequently, they stationed agents ("factors") where Africans would permit, and these factors collected slaves and forwarded reports on African conditions to mercantile companies in Europe. Although these reports were colored by ethnocentrism, factors made a serious attempt to understand the situations they encountered, mainly because such comprehension was crucial to their ability to offer trustworthy advice. In this way, Europeans disseminated important information about Africa and Africans.

While the circumstances of African migration were unique, neither slavery nor the plantation have been singularly associated with blacks. Slavery maintained a con-

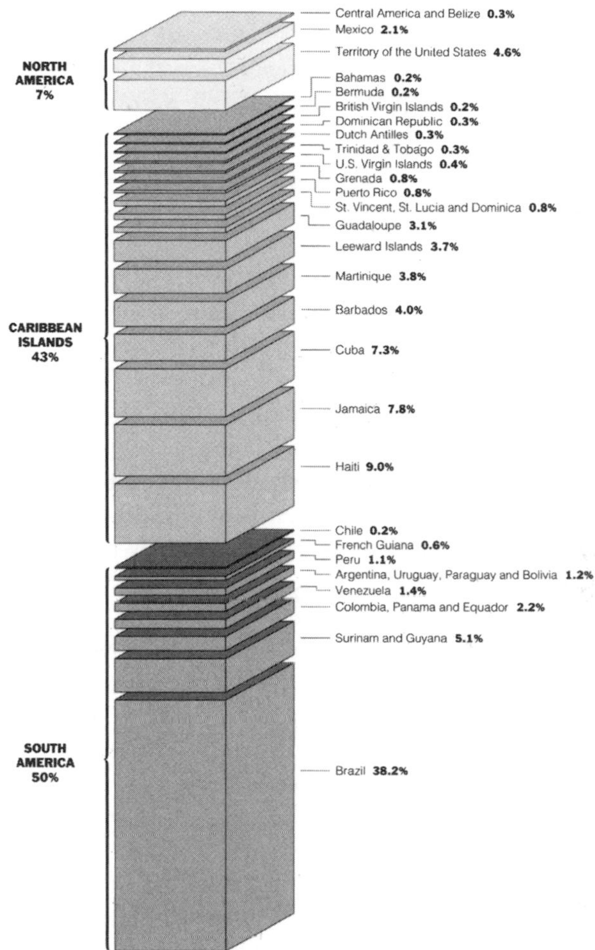

Chart showing the distribution of African slaves in the Americas during the Atlantic Trade, 1450-1870. (Based on information contained in *The African Slave Trade* by Philip Curtin.)

Conservative estimates conclude that upwards of 10 million Africans survived the Middle Passage and were enslaved in the Americas. Indeed, of the first 6.5 million people who crossed the Atlantic and settled in the Americas, 5.5 million were African. Over 90% of these Africans were taken to South America and the Caribbean Islands. Almost as many were sent to the island of Barbados as to the United States, while almost nine times as many were enslaved in Brazil as in the United States.

PHOTOGRAPHS AND PRINTS DIVISION, SCHOMBURG CENTER FOR RESEARCH IN BLACK CULTURE, THE NEW YORK PUBLIC LIBRARY, ASTOR, LENOX AND TILDEN FOUNDATIONS.

tinuous existence in southern Europe from ancient times into the Early Modern Era, and it shaped the attitudes and outlooks of southern Europeans when it was reinvigorated in the New World. In addition, the European-sponsored Atlantic trade was not the only market for bound African labor. Historians have estimated that about six million Africans were taken to Asia and the Middle East, starting as early as the seventh century CE, but reaching a peak between 1750 and 1900. Moreover, an additional eight million slaves were involved in an internal African trade, mostly between 1850 and 1914. But the Atlantic trade, starting as early as the fifteenth century but becoming important after the discovery of America (it reached its height from about 1650 to 1850), carried approximately twelve million people to captivity in the New World. It was the largest mass movement in history up to that time.

The slave trade can be divided into four epochs, determined by source, destination, and the major carriers of slaves. During the era of Iberian domination in the sixteenth century, when Portugal was practically the sole carrier, slaves were taken from Guinea to Spanish colonies and from the Congo-Angola region to Brazil. During this period, slaves were only one of a number of African commodities, all of equal importance. The seventeenth century was a period of transition. The Dutch broke Spanish control of the seas, destroyed the Portuguese monopoly of the African and Indian trades, and established themselves as the leading European maritime nation. Between 1630 and 1650, Dutch control of the sea and of trade was supreme. Dutch ships carried slaves and supplies to Spanish, French, and English colonies, and they transported New World staples from these colonies to Europe. After 1650, England and France moved to establish themselves in Africa and to tighten the mercantilist system in their respective imperial spheres. The eighteenth century thus represented a period of French and English dominance. They took most of their slaves from the Slave Coast (an area along the Bight of Benin), from east of the Volta River, and from the Niger Delta, while maintaining important interests at the peripheries in Upper Guinea and in southern Africa along the Loango Coast. They carried these slaves in British and French ships to their respective possessions in the West Indies and to Spanish America. This represented the height of the period of trade when human cargo was the overriding European interest in Africa. Finally, there was an Iberian epoch in the nineteenth century. Northern Europeans abolished the trade north of the equator and deprecated the practice everywhere, but the demand in Brazil and Cuba continued until the middle of the century.

Captain William Bosman

"Not a few in our country fondly imagine that parents here sell their children, men their wives, and one brother the other. But those who think so, do deceive themselves. . ."

A NEW AND ACCURATE DESCRIPTION OF THE COAST OF GUINEA. LONDON, 1705, P. 363.

The Portuguese Hegemony

Although the acquisition of slaves was not the prime motivating force of the Age of Discovery, it was an early consideration. The era is dated from the Portuguese taking of Ceuta—on the Moroccan coast across the Straits of Gibraltar—in 1415. The first black slaves reached Portugal directly from the Atlantic coast of Africa in 1442, and the first slave trading company was formed in 1444. It obtained slaves through periodic raids. But the Portuguese learned early that trade, whether in slaves or other commodities, proceeded best in cooperation with, rather than in opposition to, Africans. In the fifteenth century, when they laid claim to all of Africa, they divided the western coast into a series of regional monopolies, and the right of exclusive trade in these areas was sold in Lisbon. Some of the Portuguese agents settled in Upper Guinea, intermarried with local peoples, and became middlemen in the trade between Africans and Europeans. These Afro-Portuguese had been joined by a class of Afro-French and Afro-English by the eighteenth century, and these groups operated in competing spheres of influence for the benefit of their respective metropolitan powers. Racially and culturally mixed, they achieved political influence through real or fictitious consanguineous ties to local royalty, and they achieved economic power through their control of trade. Because of their prestige, they—in traditional African fashion—gathered to themselves full-blooded Africans (*grumetes*), who adopted their cultural affectations and became part of a hybrid trade community on the coast. Whereas in the sixteenth century these people were usually in a state of subservience to native chieftains, this condition had reversed by the eighteenth century. By this time they were also able to repel European attempts to circumvent them and establish direct contact with local peoples in those places where they assumed hegemony.

But Portuguese activities were not uniform over all the coast. While a policy of peaceful penetration was adopted in Upper Guinea, in the Gulf of Benin and the coastal regions leading to it a relationship of power politics developed. The Portuguese could not move around freely, but instead were restricted to fortified coastal stations. The most venerable of these, São Jorge da Mina (established in 1482), was important to the Portuguese as a source of gold rather than slaves, with the metal being obtained through barter with local peoples. Africans brought gold from the interior, and because of the long distances they had to travel, they required porters to carry goods secured in trade on the coast to the interior. The slave trade that developed was an internal African trade in which the Por-

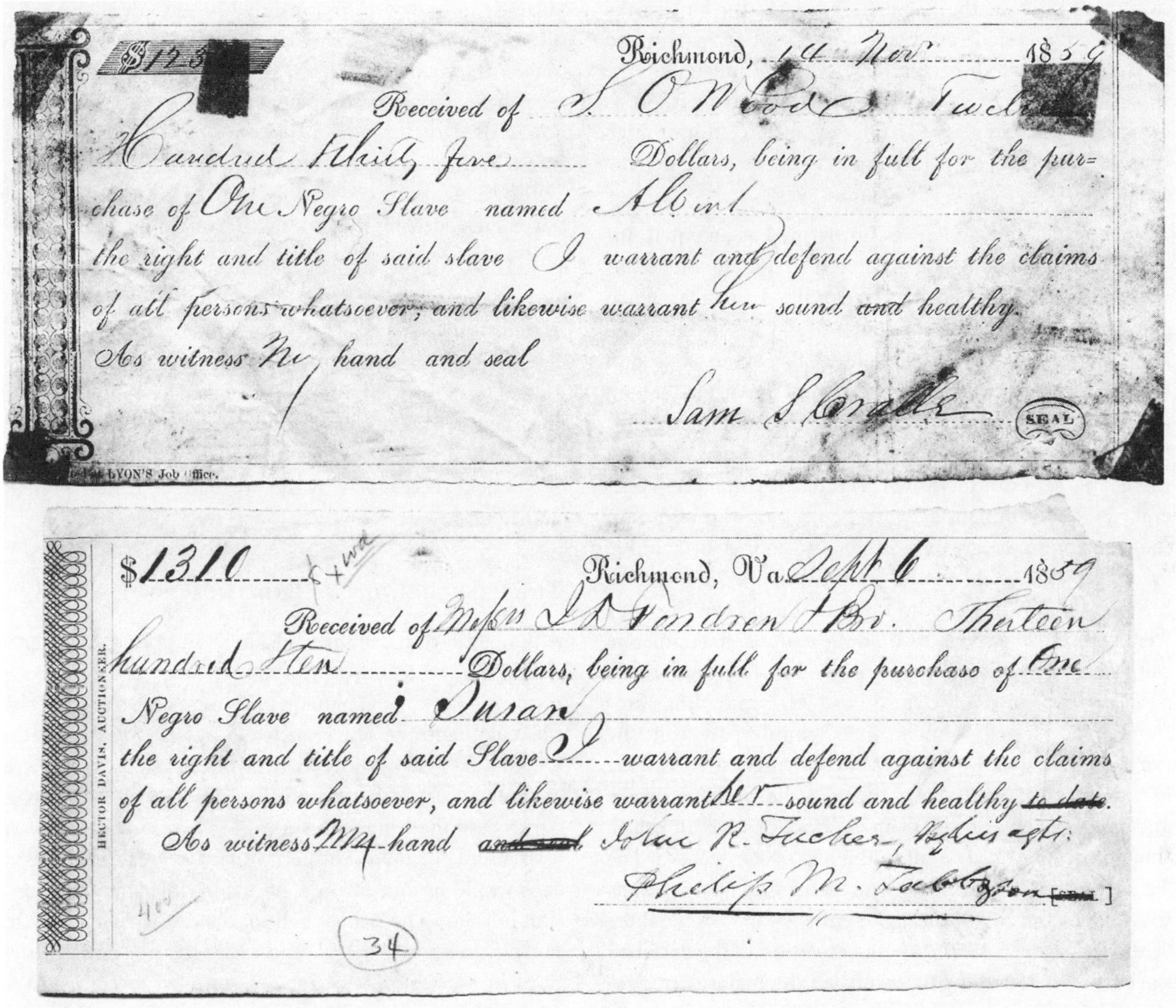
$125 Richmond, 14 Nov 1859

Received of S O Wood ... Twelve Hundred Thirty five Dollars, being in full for the pur-chase of One Negro Slave named Albert

the right and title of said slave I warrant and defend against the claims of all persons whatsoever, and likewise warrant him sound and healthy.

As witness my hand and seal

Sam S Cralle (SEAL)

LYON'S Job Office.

$1310 Richmond, Va Sept 6 1859

Received of Messrs I D Fondren & Bro. Thirteen hundred & ten Dollars, being in full for the purchase of One Negro Slave named Susan

the right and title of said Slave I warrant and defend against the claims of all persons whatsoever, and likewise warrant her sound and healthy ~~to date~~.

As witness my hand ~~and seal~~ Isaac R. Tucker, ... agt.

Philip M. ... [SEAL]

HECTOR DAVIS, AUCTIONEER.

34

Two receipts, or bills of sale, for purchased slaves, Richmond, Virginia, 1859. *These documents guaranteed that the "Negro Slave" being purchased was "sound and healthy." If a slave was later found to be unhealthy or "defective," the buyer could take the seller to court.* MANUSCRIPTS, ARCHIVES AND RARE BOOKS DIVISION, SCHOMBURG CENTER FOR RESEARCH IN BLACK CULTURE, THE NEW YORK PUBLIC LIBRARY, ASTOR, LENOX AND TILDEN FOUNDATIONS.

tuguese participated. They brought slaves from the African kingdom of Benin; from their settlement at São Tomé, an island farther down the coast; and from locations in Upper Guinea to meet the demand. The gold trade was so important that in 1610 the king forbade Portuguese subjects to take captives within several miles of São Jorge da Mina so as not to disturb it.

The fifteenth-century slave trade was basically an Old World affair. The Portuguese utilized Africans in colonial settlements on islands off the African coast, where they produced sugar, and they also supplied them to southern Europe and the Mediterranean. Between 1450 and 1500, about thirty thousand Africans were shipped to Europe. Lisbon now served as entrepot, an intermediary center of trade and transshipment for the Mediterranean trade. In 1551, 10 percent of the city's population was servile, consisting of Moorish and Guinea slaves. At the beginning of the seventeenth century, the servile percentage was about the same, but they were now nearly all black.

During the sixteenth century, the center of major Portuguese slaving activity gradually shifted from Guinea to south-central Africa, in association with the development of a New World plantation system. São Tomé was entrepot for this trade, which for most of the century centered around the Congo. It was here that the first voluntary African attempt at westernization and Christianization played out, as the Portuguese treated the king of the Congo (Manicongo) as an equal and sent craftsmen and missionaries to aid him. But the attempt foundered on the shoals of the slave trade—the Portuguese slaving interests fomented discontent to encourage warfare, from which they secured captives. The kingdom broke up under the strain.

The ruler of Angola was not treated as an equal. Instead, the Portuguese king granted the region to one of his nobles. In 1576 the Portuguese founded Luanda, which supplanted São Tomé as the center of slaving operations—and Angola replaced the Congo as the major source of slaves. Slaving operations were different in Angola than on the Guinea coast. Instead of setting up trading posts, or "factories," to which native chieftains brought captives, merchants sent out their own servants or employees (generally blacks or mulattos) called *pombeiros,* who went into the interior to secure bondsmen by trading or raiding. When captives could not be had, they incited wars or rebellions. Captives were brought to Luanda where they were kept in *barracoons*, or holding stations, to recuperate until ships arrived to take them away. As in Upper Guinea, a racially and culturally hybrid Luso-African trading community developed. Unlike their counterparts on the northern coast, however, the Afro-Portuguese in Angola kept control of their slaves through the Middle Passage and could benefit directly from the price of slaves in Brazil, though they also had to suffer the loss of slaves at sea. The latter consideration caused them to confine their interests to Africa by the end of the eighteenth century. In the three centuries between 1550 and final abolition of the Brazilian slave trade (1850), Angola furnished the majority of Brazil's captive labor.

The Dutch

The Dutch destroyed Portuguese pretensions to an African monopoly. By 1642, Arguim and Gorée in Upper Guinea, São Tomé in the Gulf of Benin, Luanda in Angola, and all the Portuguese forts on the Gold Coast were in Dutch hands. Although Portugal recaptured São Tomé in 1648 and retained the Cape Verde Islands and Cacheu, Holland was the strongest European power in Guinea during the 1650s. The Dutch advantage, however, and their virtual control of the whole European carrying trade for a time, drew the concentrated ire of the English and the French. The latter part of the seventeenth century, therefore, was one of keen competition. Dutch success derived in part from her capitalistic, joint-stock West India Company, formed in 1621. While the Portuguese, claiming all of Africa, granted individual monopolies in various parts of it, the Dutch, claiming parts of Africa, granted a monopoly of trade to one corporation in all of it. Only members of the West India Company were legally enabled to carry slaves or other goods from Africa to Dutch colonies or elsewhere. To better compete, other European nations followed the Dutch model. Most important were the French West Indies Company (1664) and the English Company of Royal Adventurers trading into Africa (1660), which was superceded by the Royal African Company (1672).

The Spanish, largely excluded from African trade but possessing large territories where slaves were useful, resorted to the *asiento*. This slave contract provided exclusive rights to importation of African bondsmen into Spanish colonies for the nation who held it. The movement of this contract from one European nation to another is to some extent a measure of its ascendancy in the slave trade. It was held successively by the Portuguese, Dutch, French, and English.

The French and the English

Although slaves were the single most important trade article by the eighteenth century, gold, ivory, beeswax, rice, camwood, and malaguetta pepper were also traded in significant quantities. The French and English followed in the Dutch wake, establishing their own companies, designated as sole carriers of their countries' trade between Europe, Africa, and the American colonies. These companies were responsible for maintaining factories in areas where Africans would permit in order to secure their nation's position in trade. The British had forts along the Gambia, the French along the Senegal, and each at various other locations in the region, and they all engaged in competition to attract African middlemen. The two nations, along with other Europeans, had outposts along the Gold Coast and adjacent areas, where competition was likewise stiff. The expense of these factories was born by the companies as partial recompense for their monopoly.

The African Input

At the height of the trade in the eighteenth century, the whole coast was regulated on the African side by middlemen who were highly conscious and jealous of their position. They had a monopoly on trade with the interior and insisted that business be conducted through them. Moreover, they refused to be bound by any one European power and insisted on free trade with the outside world. On different parts of the coast, however, different circumstances required distinctive considerations, which changed over time. In Upper Guinea, African polities competed with Afro-Europeans for trade at the posts set up by the French and English in the Senegal and Gambia rivers to

Images of the slave trade: Dutch traders, slaves, and ships, Jamestown, Virginia, 1619. ARCHIVE / GETTY PHOTOS, INC. REPRODUCED BY PERMISSION.

attract commerce. On the leeward coast in the Gulf of Guinea, Akan and Fon kingdoms mediated the trade. In the Niger Delta, various city-states, both monarchies and republics, grew up in response to new opportunities for exchange. Ruled by special political associations, they developed a distinctive trade organization known as the "House system." In *Trade and Politics in the Niger Delta, 1830-1885,* K. Onwuka Dike describes this as "a kind of co-operative trading company based not so much on kinship as on commercial association between the head of a dominant family, his relatives and trading assistants, and all their followers and slaves" (1956, p. 31)—in other words, a creative adaptation to business opportunities. In Congo-Angola, local governments also ruled, though the Portuguese, busily creating a colonial preserve, claimed exclusive rights in parts of the region. These disparate governments and people had their own peculiar requirements in articles, seasons, and methods of trade. Even the trade mediums or units of accounts diverged, with Europeans adopting African practices. In Upper Guinea they used the iron bar; on the leeward coast, the ounce of gold (in the west) and the cowry shell (in the east); in the Niger Delta, the manilla, a bracelet of brass or lead; and in Congo-Angola, a piece of local cloth. For these reasons, European representatives had to be seriously attentive to peoples and conditions at their station or lose trade to their rivals. They had to treat Africans traders with considerable respect.

African Slavery

Early European observers often justified slaving activities by arguing that many, if not most, Africans existed in some form of indigenous servitude, and that the European version was preferable. Later Europeans justified imperialism on the same basis of Africans' widespread enslavement, which they now sought to abolish. Opponents sought to counter these rationales for injustice by contending that few examples of involuntary servitude existed in Africa before European contact, and that where they existed they were of such a nature as to be scarcely comparable to the Western conception let alone the American reality. Where observers stated otherwise, according to these opponents, they were deluded by racism, ethnocentrism, or ignorance. In *Slavery in Africa* (1977), Suzanne Miers

Advertisement for a slave auction, 1780. THE LIBRARY OF CONGRESS

and Igor Kopytoff argue that this confusion results from a misapprehension of the nature of African society. Based on kinship relations that give people social existence to the extent that they belong to or are part of a local lineage, they regard those outside the group as nonpersons. Outsiders, whether slave or free, are nonpersons. Indeed, in some African societies the words for "slave" and "outsider" are the same. There is no dichotomy between slavery and freedom (with its emphasis on autonomy and individualism) as exists in the West, but between nonperson and person (whose identity is found in his association and obligation to the group). Nor are the dichotomies absolute; there are degrees of belonging connected with increasing privileges and acceptability.

Those slaves susceptible of sale (trade slaves) were usually adult males captured in warfare who might never adjust to their captivity and therefore posed a danger to their hosts. At the very least they might run away. They could best serve the community by what they brought in trade. Women and young children, however, were more pliable and less likely to be sold, and therefore were more likely to be absorbed by the local community. The demands of the Atlantic trade were coincident with these African outlooks, in that while Atlantic slavers had more call for adult males, internal African requirements placed more value on women. Consequently, women were not equally available for trade on all parts of the coast, a consideration that slavers had to weigh. Yet Africans who participated in the trade made their decisions within their own contexts and for their own reasons. African slaves were seldom viewed as the simple commodities that capitalism made them in the Americas.

The American Demand

New World planters, thinking of slaves as work units, and being interested in maximum production for the least outlay, ideally desired an adult male in his twenties or thirties. Women, who could also be worked in the fields, were in less demand. Consequently, planters normally asked for slaves in the proportion of two men for every woman. This desire for men was especially great in sugar-producing regions, which had a firm capitalist base by the seventeenth century and considered profit above everything else. Brazilian and Caribbean planters, for example, regarded harsh treatment contributing to high slave mortality in as few as five to seven years after importation to be a more economical management practice than expending either time or money to better the slave's condition and extend his life for labor. They viewed the raising of slave children as equally unprofitable and did not encourage it. Consequently, they had to depend on the slave trade to replenish their labor force for most of the period of slavery's existence in their regions. British planters in North American, raising different crops, computed their finances differently, and while they also asked for slaves in the normal proportions, by the first decades of the eighteenth century they had come to recognize the value of a self-perpetuating labor force. They began to encourage reproduction, an effort that required a more equal balance between males and females. Cargoes containing more males than females, therefore, were likely to find a better market in North America, though such cargoes sold everywhere.

Planters also had distinctive slave preferences, which varied from region to region and over time. The economy of seventeenth-century Brazil was highly dependent on bound labor from Angola, and planters described these laborers as the best that Africa had to offer. In the eighteenth century, both the source and judgment of African labor changed: Brazilian planters now rated "Sudanese" or "Mina" slaves from the leeward coast of West Africa as superior. Indeed, a special relationship developed between the northern Brazilian city of Bahia and the leeward coast, while southern Brazilian traders, centered in Rio de Janeiro, maintained an attachment to Angola. Eighteenth-century Jamaicans exhibited an affinity for Akan-speaking peoples from the Gold Coast, while South Carolina planters desired Senegambians. Virginians expressed no strong likes or dislikes. Traders had to consider these slave fash-

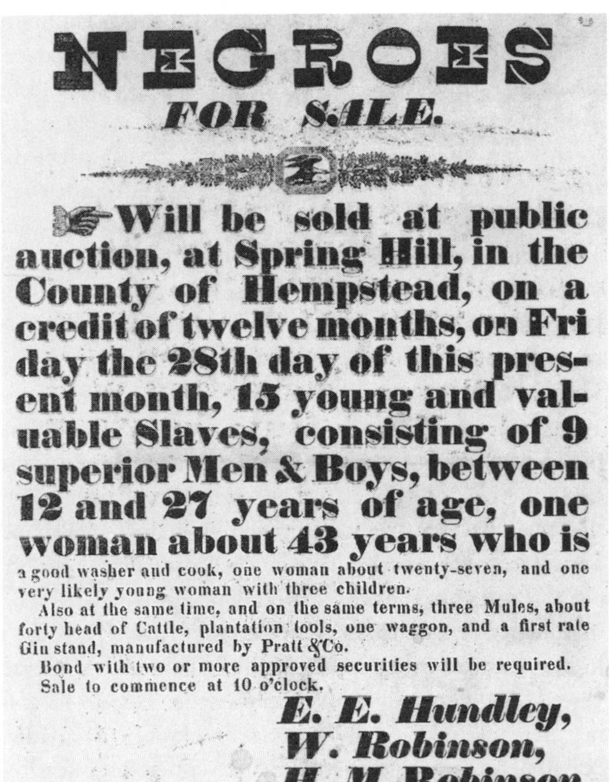

"Negroes for Sale." A bulletin advertising the sale of "15 young and valuable Slaves," as well as one "very likely woman," who has already borne three children. The sale took place in Spring Hill, Arkansas. PHOTOGRAPHS AND PRINTS DIVISION, SCHOMBURG CENTER FOR RESEARCH IN BLACK CULTURE, THE NEW YORK PUBLIC LIBRARY, ASTOR, LENOX AND TILDEN FOUNDATIONS

ions, among other factors, when they planned their voyages. They had also to figure climatological conditions and seasonal variations, since the winter months in North America or the hurricane season in the West Indies could create hazards to trade and sales. Slaves were in greatest demand when they could be put directly to work, and they sold more briskly in some seasons than in others.

Nineteenth-Century Abolition

Humanitarian sentiment against the slave trade grew during the second half of the eighteenth century, supported by economic change in industrializing powers like Great Britain. This sentiment began to have some effects by the century's end. Northern Europeans moved to stop the trade during the nineteenth century's first decade. Denmark outlawed the trade for its citizens effective in 1802, and Great Britain (the largest of slave traders) and the United States followed in 1808. The British government used diplomacy to try to evoke a consensus that the trade was objectionable, and—joined occasionally by the United States, France, and other nations—they sent ships to patrol the African coast to interdict the trade. As the world's strongest naval power, the British attempted to make agreements with other nations that would allow its warships to search vessels suspected of engaging in human commerce, and to seize those that did. Few nations, excluding even the United States, possessed Britain's moral fervor, however, and the struggle continued throughout most of the century.

Iberian nations were conspicuously absent from the developing consensus. Economic expansion in Brazil, Cuba, and Puerto Rico placed a high premium on slaves, and neither Spain nor Portugal regarded the prospect of restricting its labor supply with any enthusiasm. Britain pressured Portugal in 1810 into confining its trade to Portuguese imperial possessions in Africa and America, an agreement that meant that Portuguese subjects could carry slaves only between those regions in Africa where Portugal already had a claim or sphere of influence and other regions within the Lusitanian monarch's realm—most importantly, to Brazil. Portugal agreed to limit the trade to her African possessions below the equator in 1815. That same year, France prohibited the trade. Spain fell into line in 1820, and Brazil, having separated from Portugal, did so in 1830.

These legal prohibitions bore little relationship to reality, however, particularly in Cuba and Brazil. A greater volume of slaves came into Brazil in the first half of the nineteenth century (approximately 1.5 million between 1801 and 1850) than had ever gone to any plantation region, including a half-million or more in the twenty years between its legal cessation and its effective termination by British naval action in 1850. While most of those involved in Brazil's illegal traffic were Brazilian or Portuguese, Spain's replacement of the *asiento* with a free-trade policy in 1789 opened the Cuban market to United States, British, French, and other merchants, and American traders dominated the market after Spain agreed in 1835 to permit Britain the right of search and seizure. By then, the flag of the United States, as the only important seafaring nation to refuse to come to a reciprocal arrangement with Great Britain, provided slavers their sole refuge. Some American traders smuggled slaves into the United States, but the market was better in Cuba and Brazil. Not until the American Civil War did American official attitudes change, effecting the end of the Cuban trade in 1865. Still, by various ruses the trade continued until the end of the century. For example, the French and Portuguese adopted theoretical systems of contract labor that were nothing short of slavery: the indentured, often bought in Africa as slaves and legally freed on the coast, had little or no say

GANG OF 25 SEA ISLAND

COTTON AND RICE NEGROES,

By LOUIS D. DE SAUSSURE.

On *THURSDAY* the 25th Sept., 1852, at 11 o'clock, A.M., will be sold at RYAN'S MART, in Chalmers Street, in the City of Charleston,

A prime gang of 25 Negroes, accustomed to the culture of Sea Island Cotton and Rice.

CONDITIONS.—One-half Cash, balance by Bond, bearing interest from day of sale, payable in one and two years, to be secured by a mortgage of the negroes and approved personal security. Purchasers to pay for papers.

No.	*Age.*	*Capacity.*
1 Aleck,	33	Carpenter.
2 Mary Ann,	31	Field hand, prime.
3—3 Louisa,	10	
4 Abram,	25	Prime field hand.
5 Judy,	24	Prime field hand.
6 Carolina,	5	
7 Simon,	1½	
5—8 Daphne, infant.		
9 Daniel,	45	Field hand, not prime.
10 Phillis,	32	Field hand.
11 Will,	9	
12 Daniel,	6	
13 Margaret,	4	
14 Delia	2	
7—15 Hannah,	2 months.	

No.	*Age.*	*Capacity.*
16 Hannah,	60	Cook.
17 Cudjoe,	22	Prime field hand.
3—18 Nancy,	20	Prime field hand, sister of Cudjoe.
19 Hannah,	34	Prime field hand.
20 James,	13	Slight defect in knee from a broken leg.
21 Richard,	9	
22 Thomas,	6	
5—23 John,	3	
1—24 Squash,	40	Prime field hand.
1—25 Thomas,	28	Prime field hand.

Broadside announcing sale of twenty-five slaves, 1852. *South Carolina advertisement for the sale of a "Gang of 25 Sea Island Cotton and Rice Negroes," listing each individual's name, age, and capacity, as well as the conditions of sale. South Carolina was a major exporter of slaves, with about 65,000 sold and transported out of the state in the 1850s.* MANUSCRIPTS, ARCHIVES AND RARE BOOKS DIVISION, SCHOMBURG CENTER FOR RESEARCH IN BLACK CULTURE, THE NEW YORK PUBLIC LIBRARY, ASTOR, LENOX AND TILDEN FOUNDATIONS.

in the matter and were shipped off to colonial possessions in the Americas and elsewhere. Even the British and the Dutch, who considered themselves enlightened in this regard, adopted similar practices for short periods. Nevertheless, in practice, the Atlantic slave trade essentially came to an end with the closing of the trade to Cuba. Moreover, New World slavery itself was moribund, although it lingered in Cuba and Brazil until the 1880s.

Nineteenth-Century Trade Distinctions

In the process of its long expiration, the nineteenth-century slave trade developed some distinctive features. Economic expansion, together with the prospect of the trade's termination, caused slave prices to rise in the Americas, while the activities of British anti-slave-trade squadrons off the African coast caused them to fall there. At the same time, increased demand and depleted resources near the Congo-Angola coast caused slaves to be brought from regions farther inland, which involved different African middlemen. Although slaves might be smuggled from any part of the coast, slaving was heaviest in this region of west-central Africa—partly because it was a Portuguese preserve and legal there (for Portuguese subjects) until 1836, which permitted smugglers to use the Portuguese flag for cover, and partly because the British naval presence was not as great there as along the northwestern coast. It remained a focus of activity after the 1830s ban. Few Atlantic slavers went to Mozambique in the eighteenth century, but in the nineteenth century the trade there at one point reached a height of twenty-five thousand slaves yearly, encouraged by increased demand and an initial absence of British warships from the eastern coast. Portuguese, Arab, East Indian, and mixed-blood middlemen facilitated the trade and dispensed their human cargo to Spanish, French, Brazilian, and American vessels. The Portuguese edict ending the trade in Angola in 1836 applied equally to Mozambique, but neither ceased before rigorous British action rendered it infeasible after 1850. Slavers maintained their preference for males over females, but they accepted more children than formerly because they occupied less room than adults and more could be carried.

By the nineteenth century, then, the trade had come full circle. The Portuguese, having initiated an Atlantic trade in slaves, were among the last to abandon it. Nevertheless, the nineteenth-century Iberian trade would have been much more difficult without active British and American collaboration. Even while their government sought to abolish it, British merchants continued to invest in Brazilian slave-trading voyages, and British manufacturers continued to produce and forward to Brazilian middlemen goods suitable only for the African market. Americans, meanwhile, furnished speedy ships suitable for evading patrolling squadrons, and they innovated the use of steamships, which could carry larger numbers of slaves, though they did not always carry them better as slaves placed too close to boilers could be burned or scalded. Many of the vessels involved in the West Coast trade, and most of those involved in Mozambique, though manned by citizens of other nations, were constructed in the United States.

In a final irony, the desire to abolish slave trading and establish "legitimate" commerce in Africa furnished the basis for British imperialism there, an example that other Europeans copied. In many places, the forced migration of African peoples from their homelands, either to other parts of Africa or to regions outside of it, was ended by the imperial dictates of western Europeans, though not completely before the twentieth century. By that time, Africans, or peoples with a significant African genetic component, populated much of the globe.

See also Slavery; Slavery and the Constitution

Bibliography

Bethell, Leslie. *The Abolition of the Brazilian Slave Trade: Britain, Brazil, and the Slave Trade Question, 1807-1869.* Cambridge, UK: Cambridge University Press, 1970.

Boxer, Charles. *The Portuguese Seaborne Empire, 1415-1825.* New York: Knopf, 1969.

Conrad, Robert E. *World of Sorrow: The African Slave Trade to Brazil.* Baton Rouge: Louisiana State University Press, 1986.

Curtin, Philip. *The Image of Africa: British Ideas and Action, 1780-1850.* Madison: University of Wisconsin Press, 1964.

Curtin, Philip. *The Atlantic Slave Trade: A Census.* Madison: University of Wisconsin Press, 1969.

Curtin, Philip. *The Rise and Fall of the Plantation Complex: Essays in Atlantic History.* Cambridge, UK: Cambridge University Press, 1990.

Davies, K. G. *The Royal African Company.* New York: Longmans, Green, 1957. Reprint, New York: Octagon, 1975.

Diaz-Soler, Luis M. *Historia de la esclavitud negra en Puerto Rico (1493-1890).* Madrid: Revista de Occidente, 1953.

Dike, E. Onwuka. *Trade and Politics in the Niger Delta, 1830-1885; An Introduction to the Economic and Political History of Nigeria.* Oxford: Clarendon, 1956. Reprint, Westport, Conn.: Greenwood, 1981.

Duffy, James. *Portugal in Africa.* Cambridge, Mass.: Harvard University Press, 1962.

Eltis, David. *The Rise of African Slavery in the Americas.* Cambridge, UK: Cambridge University Press, 2000.

Eltis, David, et al. *The Trans-Atlantic Slave Trade: A Database on CD-ROM.* Cambridge, UK: Cambridge University Press, 1999.

Fage, John D. *A History of West Africa: An Introductory Survey.* Cambridge, UK: Cambridge University Press, 1969.

Gemery, Henry A., and Jan S. Hogendorn, eds. *The Uncommon Market: Essays in the Economic History of the Atlantic Slave Trade.* New York: Academic Press, 1979.

Inikori, J. E., ed. *Forced Migration: The Impact of the Export Slave Trade on African Societies.* New York: Africana, 1982.

Littlefield, Daniel C. "The Colonial Slave Trade to South Carolina: A Profile." *South Carolina Historical Magazine* 91 (1990): 68–99.

Littlefield, Daniel C. "'Abundance of Negroes of That Nation': The Significance of African Ethnicity in Colonial South Carolina." In *The Meaning of South Carolina History: Essays in Honor of George C. Rogers, Jr.*, pp. 19–38. Columbia: University of South Carolina Press, 1991.

Littlefield, Daniel C. *Rice and Slaves: Ethnicity and the Slave Trade in Colonial South Carolina.* Urbana: University of Illinois Press, 1991.

Lovejoy, Paul E. *Africans in Bondage: Studies in Slavery and the Slave Trade.* Madison: University of Wisconsin Press, 1986.

Lovejoy, Paul E. *Transformations in Slavery: A History of Slavery in Africa.* 2d ed. Cambridge, UK: Cambridge University Press, 2000.

Manning, Patrick. *Slavery and African Life: Occidental, Oriental, and African Slave Trades.* Cambridge, UK: Cambridge University Press, 1990.

Mauro, Frédéric. *Le Portugal et L'Atlantic au XVIIe Siècе (1570-1580).* 2d ed. Lisbon and Paris: Fundação Calouste Gulbenkian/Centro cultural portuguès, 1983.

Miers, Suzanne, and Igor Kopytoff, eds. *Slavery in Africa: Historical and Anthropological Perspectives.* Madison: University of Wisconsin Press, 1977.

Miller, Joseph C. *Way of Death: Merchant Capitalism and the Angolan Slave Trade, 1730–1830.* Madison: University of Wisconsin Press, 1988.

Palmer, Colin A. *Human Cargoes: The British Slave Trade to Spanish America.* Urbana: University of Illinois Press, 1981.

Postma, Johannes. *The Dutch in the Atlantic Slave Trade, 1600-1814.* Cambridge, UK: Cambridge University Press, 1990.

Polanyi, Karl. *Dahomey and the Slave Trade: The Study of an Archaic Economic Institution.* Seattle: University of Washington Press, 1966. Reprint, New York: AMS Press, 1991.

Rodney, Walter. "Portuguese Attempts at Monopoly on the Upper Guinea Coast, 1580-1650." *Journal of African History,* 7 (1965): 307–322.

Rodney, Walter. *A History of the Upper Guinea Coast, 1545-1800.* Oxford, UK: Clarendon Press, 1970.

Solow, Barbara, ed. *Slavery and the Rise of the Atlantic System.* Cambridge, Mass.: W. E. B. Du Bois Institute for Afro-American Research, Harvard University, 1991.

Stein, Stanley. *The French Slave Trade in the Eighteenth Century.* Madison: University of Wisconsin Press, 1979.

Thornton, John. *Africa and Africans in the Making of the Atlantic World, 1400-1800.* New York: Cambridge University Press, 1998.

Verger, Pierre. *Flux et Reflux de la Traite des Nègres entre le Golfe de Bénin et Bahia de Todos os Santos du XVIIe au XIXe Siècle.* Paris: Mouton, 1968.

Verlinden, Charles. *L'Esclavage dans l'Europe médiévale.* Brugge, Belgium: De Tempel, 1955.

DANIEL C. LITTLEFIELD (2005)

Sleet, Moneta J., Jr.

February 14, 1926
September 30, 1996

In 1969 Moneta J. Sleet Jr. became the first African American to win a Pulitzer Prize in photography for his now world-renowned image of Coretta Scott King at her husband's funeral, her upturned face shielded by a heavy veil as she embraced her young daughter Bernice. Sleet, although employed by the monthly *Ebony* magazine, became eligible for the prestigious newspaper award when his black-and-white film containing the image was let into a pool for wire-service use and subsequently published in daily newspapers throughout the country.

Sleet's major contribution to photojournalism has been his extensive documentation of the marches, meetings, and rallies of the civil rights movement. He also has a special talent for photographing people. Over the years, he produced sensitive, humanistic, and, on occasion, humorous portraits of celebrities as well as ordinary men, women, and children of America, Africa, and the Caribbean. His photographs are powerful and direct and show a genuine respect for his subjects.

Sleet was born in Owensboro, Kentucky, where he grew up attending the local segregated public schools. His career as a photographer began in boyhood, when his parents gave him a box camera, and continued into high school. Sleet studied photography at Kentucky State College under the tutelage of John Williams, a family friend who was dean of the college and an accomplished photographer. When Sleet interrupted his studies as a business major to serve in World War II, he resolved to enter photography as a profession, though he returned and finished his degree. His mentor moved on to Maryland State College, and in 1948 invited Sleet to set up a photography department there. After a short time in Maryland, Sleet moved to New York, studying at the School of Modern Photography before attending New York University, where he obtained a master's degree in journalism in 1950.

After a brief stint as a sportswriter for the *Amsterdam News,* Sleet joined the staff of *Our World,* a popular black picture magazine. His five years there were training for his photojournalistic sensibility. He and the other staff photographers and writers were subject to the high editorial standards of the publisher, John Davis. It was under Davis's auspices that Sleet produced one of his most engaging stories, a 1953 series on the coal-mining town of Superior, West Virginia.

Our World ceased publication two years later, and Sleet joined the Johnson Publishing Company's New York–based illustrated monthly magazine *Ebony,* where he continued as staff photographer. Publisher John H. Johnson sent him to the far corners of the world on stories. In addition, coverage of the fledgling civil rights movement established the reputation of *Ebony*'s sister publication *Jet,* and in the early years Sleet's photographs appeared in both.

On assignment in 1956, Sleet first met Rev. Dr. Martin Luther King Jr., then a twenty-seven-year-old Atlanta minister, emerging as the leader of the civil rights movement. Their association flourished as the movement dominated the black press, with Sleet covering King's receiving the Nobel Peace Prize in Sweden in 1964, his marching from Selma to Montgomery in 1965, and his funeral in Atlanta following his assassination in April 1968.

Sleet's recollection of the circumstances leading to his memorable Pulitzer Prize–winning photograph of Coretta Scott King was still vivid:

> There was complete pandemonium—nothing was yet organized because the people from SCLC [the Southern Christian Leadership Conference] were all in a state of shock. We had the world press descending upon Atlanta, plus the FBI, who were there investigating.
>
> We were trying to get an arrangement to shoot in the church. They said they were going to "pool it." Normally, the pool meant news services, *Life, Time,* and *Newsweek.* When the pool was selected, there were no black photographers from the black media in it. Lerone Bennett and I got in touch with Mrs. King through Andy Young. She said, "If somebody from Johnson Publishing is not on the pool, there will be no pool." Since I was with Johnson Publishing, I became part of the pool. In those days there weren't many blacks [in journalism], whether writers or photographers.
>
> The day of the funeral, Bob Johnson, the executive editor of *Jet,* had gotten in the church and he beckoned for me and said, Here's a spot right here. It was a wonderful spot. It was then a matter of photographing what was going on. It was so dramatic; everywhere you turned the camera—Daddy King, Vice President Humphrey, Nixon, Jackie Kennedy, Bobby Kennedy, Thurgood Marshall, Dr. Ralph Bunche reading the program with a magnifying glass. I considered myself fortunate to be there documenting everything. If I wasn't there I knew I would be somewhere crying.
>
> We had made arrangements with AP [the Associated Press] that they would process the black-and-white film immediately after the service and put it on the wire. Later I found out which shot they sent out (Taped interview, New York, 1986).

Sleet's career also encompassed the great period of African independence, when in the 1950s autonomous nations emerged from former colonies. His first experience in "pack" journalism abroad came on Vice President Richard Nixon's 1957 trip through Africa, where Sleet photographed in Liberia, Libya, and the Sudan. It was on this trip he photographed Kwame Nkrumah at the moment of Ghana's independence. The results of the trip gained Sleet an Overseas Press Club citation in 1957.

Sleet's long career as a photojournalist took him all over the United States and Africa; he also visited and photographed on assignment in South America, Russia, the West Indies, and Europe. Though photo essays and portrait profiles made up the majority of his output, he also photographed the children who tagged alongside him as he worked. To Sleet, the father of three grown children, these personal portraits were the most rewarding.

In addition to winning a Pulitzer Prize in feature photography and a citation for excellence from the Overseas Press Club of America, Sleet received awards from the National Urban League (1969) and the National Association of Black Journalists (1978). Over the years, his work has appeared in several group exhibitions at museums, including the Studio Museum in Harlem and the Metropolitan Museum of Art. In 1970 solo exhibitions were held at the City Art Museum of St. Louis and the Detroit Public Library. A retrospective exhibition organized by the New York Public Library in 1986 toured nationally for three years. Sleet had just returned from an assignment for *Ebony* at the 1996 Atlanta Olympics when he died on September 30, 1996.

See also King, Martin Luther, Jr.; Photography, U.S.

Bibliography

"Image Maker: The Artistry of Moneta Sleet, Jr." *Ebony* 42 (January 1987): 66–74.

Moneta Sleet, Jr.: Pulitzer Prize Photojournalist. New York, 1986. New York Public Library exhibit brochure.

Saunders, Doris E. *Special Moments in African-American History: 1955–1996: The Photographs of Moneta Sleet, Jr.,* Ebony *Magazine's Pulitzer Prize Winner.* New York: St. Martin's Press, 1998.

JULIA VAN HAAFTEN (1996)
Updated by publisher 2005

SMALLS, ROBERT

APRIL 5, 1839
FEBRUARY 23, 1915

The Civil War navy pilot, politician, and businessman Robert Smalls was born a slave near Beaufort, South Carolina. Smalls moved to Charleston, where he was allowed to hire himself out if he paid his owner $15 a month. The knowledge of coastal waterways that he gained as a boatman made possible one of the Civil War's most daring exploits.

In 1862 the Confederate government made Smalls wheelsman of the steamboat the *Planter* (the title *pilot* was deemed inappropriate for a slave). He learned the signals necessary to pass southern fortifications and the location of mines.

On May 12, 1862, while white crew members were on shore, Smalls steered the ship, containing his family and a small group of other slaves, to Union lines. The news spread across the country. The coup was important militarily and symbolically, demonstrating what slaves—supposedly docile and content in their servitude—could accomplish.

Awarded $1,500 for the armed boat and commissioned as a second lieutenant in the U.S. Colored Troops, Smalls became pilot of the *Planter,* participated in seventeen battles, and recruited for the army. During and after the war he raised funds in the North for black southerners' interests. Doggedly pursuing his own education, he bought schools for freedmen while investing extensively in real estate and companies in his native state.

Dramatic as Smalls's escape was, his later career constituted his greatest legacy. During the twelve years that Reconstruction allowed black southerners political opportunities, Smalls became a South Carolina state congressman and senator and then, for most of the years between 1874 and 1886, a U.S. congressman, known for his repartee. In the state legislature he sponsored bills for free compulsory public education. He attended the 1864 Republican National Convention, helped write the 1868 state constitution, and became a major general of the state militia. In office, he fought not only for freedmen's interests—cheap land prices, continuing eligibility for army enlistment, and enforcement of the Civil Rights Act—but for his general constituency's concerns, including a railroad, reformed penitentiaries, property rights of wives and tenants, and health care for the poor.

When the Compromise of 1877 returned political control to Democrats, they quickly sought to drive out and

372 HARPER'S WEEKLY. [JUNE 14, 1862.

ROBERT SMALLS, CAPTAIN OF THE GUN-BOAT "PLANTER."

THE GUN-BOAT "PLANTER," RUN OUT OF CHARLESTON, S. C., BY ROBERT SMALLS, MAY, 1862.

Robert Smalls and the gun-boat Planter. *Smalls and his fellow black crewman hijacked the Confederate steamer by night in the spring of 1862, sailing the vessel to Union forces and freedom.* PHOTOGRAPHS AND PRINTS DIVISION, SCHOMBURG CENTER FOR RESEARCH IN BLACK CULTURE, THE NEW YORK PUBLIC LIBRARY, ASTOR, LENOX AND TILDEN FOUNDATIONS.

discredit all Republican officeholders. Smalls—who enjoyed the admiration of his African-American constituents for the heroic act he never tired of recounting—did not escape controversy. Despite having consistently attacked governmental extravagance and corruption, he faced a bribery charge, which was ultimately dropped. But staying in office became increasingly difficult, with the Democrats using violence and crooked elections to disfranchise the black population as the federal government lost interest in the former slaves. Smalls won his final congressional election against the viciously racist "Pitchfork" Ben Tillman in 1884.

Even after elected positions were no longer possible, Smalls's loyalty to the Republican Party assured him of patronage jobs. He served as Beaufort's customs collector from 1890 until 1913. He also continued to organize his district's black Republicans and to use his influence for former constituents whenever possible.

See also Civil War, U.S.; Military Experience, African-American

Bibliography

Holt, Thomas. *Black over White: Negro Political Leadership in South Carolina During Reconstruction.* Urbana: University of Illinois Press, 1977.

Miller, Edward A. *Gullah Statesman: Robert Smalls from Slavery to Congress, 1839–1915.* Columbia: University of South Carolina Press, 1995.

Uya, Okon Edet. *From Slavery to Public Service: Robert Smalls, 1839–1915.* New York: Oxford University Press, 1971.

ELIZABETH FORTSON ARROYO (1996)
Updated bibliography

SMITH, ANNA DEAVERE

SEPTEMBER 18, 1950

Born in Baltimore, Maryland, playwright, performance artist, and actress Anna Deavere Smith, a 1996 recipient of the McArthur Foundation "Genius" grant, is noted for developing a unique style of performance art that blends traditional theatrical elements with meticulous journalism to provide social commentary from multiple points of view about controversial events. *Fires in the Mirror: Crown Heights Brooklyn and Other Identities* (1991) and *Twilight: Los Angeles, 1992* (1993), both one-woman shows that Smith premiered to rave reviews and toured around the world, were written as responses to American urban insurrections. The two plays explored themes of racial conflict and racial identity. For *Fires in the Mirror,* Smith received an Obie and a Pulitzer Prize nomination.

Smith's characteristic writing technique involves interviewing people, seeking the "moment when most people say something that nobody else can say." Smith then selects portions of these interviews, arranges them into monologues and dialogues to tell a story, and ends by memorizing and imitating her interviewees' speech and behavior for performance before a live audience. In juxtaposing the thoughts and attitudes of distinctly different people, Smith's plays present a documentary-style cross-section of Americans from the 1980s and 1990s. In 1993, Smith was labeled by *Newsweek* magazine as "the most exciting individual in American Theater." Her technique evolved while teaching theater at Carnegie Mellon University (1978–1979). She has also taught theater in several of America's top dramatic art programs, including the University of Southern California (1982), New York University (1983–1984), Actors Conservatory Theater (1986), Stanford University, where she became the Ann O'Day Maples Professor of the Arts in 1992, and the Tisch School of the Arts at New York University since 2000. Smith's play *House Arrest* premiered in 1997. In 2000 she published the book *Talk to Me: Travels in Media and Politics,* and since 2000 she has worked as a scriptwriter for such television shows as *The Practice* and *West Wing.*

See also Drama; Identity and Race in the United States; Performance Art

Bibliography

"Anna Deavere Smith's *House Arrest.*" *NewYork Metro,* February 10, 2004. Available from <www.newyorkmetro.com/nymetro/arts/theater/reviews/2637>.

Hine, Darlene Clark, ed. *Facts on File Encyclopedia of Black Women in America: Theater Arts and Entertainment.* New York: Facts on File, 1997.

Performing Arts Journal, May–September, 50–51 (1995): 77.

Peterson, Jane T. and Suzanne Bennett. *Women Playwrights of Diversity: A Bio-Bibliographical Sourcebook.* Westport, Conn.: Greenwood Press, 1997.

F. ZEAL HARRIS (2001)
Updated by publisher 2005

Smith, Barbara

November 16, 1946

Barbara Smith is a lesbian writer, publisher, educator, and activist who was born in Cleveland, Ohio. She received her B.A. from Mount Holyoke College in 1969 and her M.A. from the University of Pittsburgh in 1971. In 1974 she cofounded the Combahee River Collective, an early black feminist organization that challenged racism in the gay movement and homophobia in the black community.

Smith was the first to openly address the subject of black lesbian eroticism in the canon of African-American literature. Her well-known 1977 essay, "Toward a Black Feminist Criticism," offered one of the first critical looks at matters of feminism, race, and literature together. Smith was cofounder and publisher of the now defunct Kitchen Table: Women of Color Press. The press was the first to focus on the realities and politics of women and lesbians of color.

Smith's publications include *This Bridge Called My Black: Writings by Radical Women of Color* (1981), *All the Blacks Are Men, But Some of Us Are Brave: Black Women's Studies* (1982), *Home Girls: A Black Feminist Anthology* (1983), *Yours in the Struggle: Three Feminist Perspectives on Anti-Semitism and Racism* (1984), and *The Truth That Never Hurts: Writings on Race, Gender, and Freedom* (1998). Additionally, Smith has lectured and served as writer in residence at numerous colleges and universities, including Radcliffe College, Emerson College, the University of Massachusetts, Boston University, Barnard College, and Mt. Holyoke College. She has remained an outspoken critic of the absence of a discussion of lesbianism within the African-American literary canon.

See also Black Studies; Feminist Theory and Criticism; Intellectual Life; Lesbians

Bibliography

Farajaje-Jones, Elias. Interview by author. April 13, 2000.

"Smith, Barbara." *Contemporary Authors.* Detroit, Mich.: Gale, 1994.

"Smith, Barbara." *Who's Who in Black America,* 6th ed., edited by Iris Loyd. Detroit, Mich.: Gale, 1990.

RACHEL ZELLARS (1996)
Updated by publisher 2005

Smith, Barbara ("B. Smith")

August 24, 1949

Entrepreneur, model, and author Barbara Smith was born in western Pennsylvania and grew up in Everson, a working-class town near Pittsburgh. After developing an interest in modeling, she took weekend classes at the John Robert Powers modeling school in Pittsburgh and graduated just before her high school commencement. When she was nineteen, the slender and attractive Smith was selected to serve as a model for the Ebony Fashion Fair's traveling show. She moved to New York to participate in the fair and begin her modeling career.

Smith's beauty, grace, and intelligence won top spots for her. She appeared on five covers for *Essence,* the first model so honored. In 1976 she became the first African American to appear on the cover of *Mademoiselle.* Since then she has appeared in over fifty print advertisements and television commercials, the most well known of which was a 1990s ad for Oil of Olay.

In the mid-1980s Smith scaled back her modeling to concentrate on the restaurant business, an interest she acquired as a youth watching and assisting her mother and grandmother prepare for family gatherings. Entering a partnership with Ark Restaurant Corporation, she has opened three B. Smith restaurants, two in New York and one in Washington, D.C.

B. Smith, as she prefers to be known, published *B. Smith's Entertaining and Cooking for Friends* in 1995. In 1997 she began hosting *Smith with Style,* a half-hour television show. In late 1999 she launched *B. Smith Style,* a magazine dedicated to her interests in food, fashion, and beauty. That year, too, she published her second book, *B. Smith Rituals and Celebrations,* which won *Food and Wine Magazine*'s 1999 "Best of the Best" Book Award.

See also Entrepreneurs and Entrepreneurship; Hair and Beauty Culture in the United States

Bibliography

B. Smith Web site, <http://www.bsmith.com>.

Current Biography Yearbook 1998. New York: H. W. Wilson, 1998.

Mabubda, L. Mpho, and Shirelle Phelps, eds. *Contemporary Black Biography,* vol. 11. Detroit, Mich.: Gale, 1996.

Reed, Julia. "Can B. Smith Be Martha?" *New York Times Magazine,* August 22, 1999.

JESSIE CARNEY SMITH (1996)
Updated by publisher 2005

Smith, Bessie

April 15, 1894
September 26, 1937

The blues singer Bessie Smith, known as "Empress of the Blues," was the greatest woman singer of urban blues and, to many, the greatest of all blues singers. She was born in Chattanooga, Tennessee, the youngest of seven children of Laura and William Smith. Her father, a part-time Baptist preacher, died while she was a baby, and her early childhood, during which her mother and two brothers died, was spent in extreme poverty. Bessie and her brother Andrew earned coins on street corners with Bessie singing and dancing to the guitar playing of her brother.

The involvement of her favorite brother, Clarence, in the Moses Stokes Show was the impetus for Smith's departure from home in 1912. Having won local amateur shows, she was prepared for the move to vaudeville and tent shows, where her initial role was as a dancer. She came in contact with the singer Gertrude "Ma" Rainey (1886–1939), who was also with the Stokes troupe, but there is no evidence to support the legend that Rainey taught her how to sing the blues. They did develop a friendship, however, that lasted all of Smith's lifetime.

Smith's stint with Stokes ended in 1913, when she moved to Atlanta and established herself as a regular performer at the infamous Charles Bailey's 81 Theatre. By then the Theater Owners Booking Association (TOBA) consortium was developing into a major force in the lives and careers of African-American entertainers, and managers and owners often made the lives of performers miserable through low pay, poor working and living conditions, and curfews. Bailey's reputation in this regard was notorious. Smith became one of his most popular singers, although she was paid only ten dollars a week.

Smith's singing was rough and unrefined, but she possessed a magnificent vocal style and commanding stage presence, which resulted in additional money in tips. With the 81 Theatre as a home base, Smith traveled on the TOBA circuit throughout the South and up and down the eastern seaboard. By 1918 she was part of a specialty act with Hazel Green, but she soon moved on to a solo act as a headliner.

Smith attracted a growing number of black followers in the rural South, as well as recent immigrants to northern urban ghettos who missed the down-home style and sound. She was too raw and vulgar, however, for the Tin Pan Alley black songwriters attempting to move into the lucrative world of phonograph recordings. White record company executives found Smith's (and Ma Rainey's) brand of blues too alien and unrefined to consider her for employment. As a result, Smith was not recorded until 1923, when the black buying public had already demonstrated that there was a market for blues songs, a market the record companies became eager to exploit.

Fortunately, Smith was recorded by the Columbia Gramophone Company, which had equipment and technology superior to any other manufacturer at the time. Columbia touted itself in black newspapers as having more "race" artists than other companies. Into this milieu came Bessie Smith singing "Down Hearted Blues" and "Gulf Coast Blues," the former written (and previously performed) by Alberta Hunter (1895–1984), and the latter by Clarence Williams, a studio musician for Columbia who also played piano on both records. Sales were astronomical. Advertisements in the black newspapers reported her latest releases, and Smith was able to expand her touring range to include black theaters in all of the major northern cities. By 1924, she was the highest-paid African American in the country.

Smith sang with passion and authenticity about everyday problems, natural disasters, the horrors of the workhouse, abuse and violence, unfaithful lovers, and the longing for someone—anyone—to love. She performed these songs with a conviction and dramatic style that reflected the memory of her own suffering, and thus captured the mood of black people who had experienced pain and anguish, drawing listeners to her with empathy and intimacy. The poet Langston Hughes said Smith's blues were the essence of "sadness . . . not softened with tears, but hardened with laughter, the absurd, incongruous laughter of a sadness without even a god to appeal to."

Smith connected with her listeners in the same manner as the southern preacher: They were her flock who came seeking relief from the burdens of oppression, poverty, endless labor, injustice, alienation, loneliness, and love gone awry. She was their spiritual leader who sang away the pain by pulling it forth in a direct, honest manner, weaving the notes into a tapestry of moans, wails, and slides. She addressed the vagaries of city life and its mistreatment of women, the depletion of the little respect women tried to maintain. She sanctioned the power of women to be their own independent selves, to love freely, to drink and party and enjoy life to its fullest, to wail, scream, and lambaste anyone who overstepped boundaries in relationships—all of which characterized Smith's own spirit and life.

Columbia was grateful for an artist who filled its coffers and helped move it to supremacy in the recording industry. Smith recorded regularly for Columbia until 1929, producing 150 selections, of which at least two dozen were her own compositions. By the end of the 1920s, women blues singers were fading in popularity, largely because urban audiences were becoming more sophisticated. Smith appeared in an ill-fated Broadway show, *Pansy,* and received good reviews, but the show itself was weak and she left almost immediately. Her single film, *St. Louis Blues* (1929), immortalized her, although time and rough living had taken a toll on her voice and appearance by then.

Because of the Great Depression, the recording industry was in disarray by 1931. Columbia dismantled its race catalog and dropped Smith along with others. She had already begun to shift to popular ballads and swing tunes in an attempt to keep up with changing public taste. Okeh Records issued four of her selections in 1933. She altered her act and costumes in an attempt to appeal to club patrons, but she did not live to fulfill her hope of a new success with the emerging swing ensembles. On a tour of southern towns, Smith died in an automobile accident.

See also Blues, The; Blueswomen of the 1920s and 1930s; Rainey, Ma; Smith, Mamie; Taylor, Koko

Bibliography

Albertson, Chris. *Bessie.* New York: Stein and Day, 1972. Revised and expanded edition, New Haven, Conn.: Yale University Press, 2003.

Barlow, William. *Looking Up at Down: The Emergence of Blues Culture.* Philadelphia: Temple University Press, 1989.

Harrison, Daphne Duval. *Black Pearls: Blues Queens of the 1920s.* New Brunswick, N.J.: Rutgers University Press, 1988.

Kay, Jackie. *Bessie Smith.* New York: Stewart, Tabori and Chang, 1997.

Manera, Alexandria. *Bessie Smith.* Chicago: Raintree, 2003.

DAPHNE DUVAL HARRISON (1996)
Updated bibliography

SMITH, JAMES MCCUNE

APRIL 18, 1813
NOVEMBER 17, 1865

The physician and abolitionist James McCune Smith was born in New York City, the son of freed slaves. He received his early education at the African Free School, but even with an excellent academic record, he was effectively barred from American colleges because of his race. In 1832 he entered Glasgow University in Scotland, where he earned three academic degrees, including a doctorate in medicine. He also gained prominence in the Scottish antislavery movement as an officer of the Glasgow Emancipation Society.

Following a short internship in Paris, Smith returned to New York City in 1837 and established a medical practice and pharmacy. His distinction as the first degree-holding African-American physician assured him a prominent position in the city's black community. He was involved in several charitable and educational organizations, including the Philomathean Society and the Colored Orphan Asylum.

Smith's intellect, integrity, and lifelong commitment to abolitionism brought him state and national recognition. From the early 1840s, he provided leadership for the campaign to expand black voting rights in New York, although he initially refused to ally with any political party. In the 1850s, Smith continued his suffrage activity through the black state conventions. He eventually gravitated to the political antislavery views of the Radical Abolition Party, and he received the party's nomination for New York secretary of state in 1857.

As a member of the Committee of Thirteen, a group of local black leaders (not to be confused with the U.S. Senate committee formed in 1860 called the Committee of Thirteen) he helped organize local resistance to the Fugitive Slave Act of 1850. He was ranked among the steadfast opponents of the colonization and black emigration movements, affirming instead the struggle for the rights of American citizenship. Although committed to racial integration, he understood the practical and symbolic importance of separate black institutions, organizations, and initiatives. He called for an independent black press, and he worked with Frederick Douglass (1818–1895) in the early 1850s to establish the first permanent national African-American organization—the National Council of the Colored People.

Smith provided intellectual direction as well as personal leadership for the black abolitionist movement. From his critiques of colonization and black emigration in the 1840s and 1850s to his analysis of Reconstruction in the 1860s, his commentary informed the debate on racial identity and the future of African Americans. Smith's published essays include two pamphlets, *A Lecture on the Haytian Revolution* (1841) and *The Destiny of the People of Color* (1843). He wrote several lengthy articles for *Anglo-African Magazine* in 1859, and also provided introductions to Frederick Douglass's second autobiography and Henry Highland Garnet's *Memorial Discourse* (1865). Although he never published his own journal, he assisted other black editors in all phases of newspaper publishing. His letters to Frederick Douglass's paper often appeared under the pseudonym "Communipaw." He contributed as a correspondent or assistant editor to several other journals, including the *Colored American, Northern Star and Freeman's Advocate, Douglass' Monthly,* and *Weekly Anglo-African*. Smith's professional standing, erudition, and community involvement made his life a triumph over racism, and his name was frequently invoked by contemporaries as a benchmark for black intellect and achievement.

See also Abolition; African Free School; Douglass, Frederick

Bibliography

Ripley, C. Peter, et al., eds. *The Black Abolitionist Papers.* Vol. 3, *The United States, 1830–1846.* Chapel Hill: University of North Carolina Press, 1991.

Ripley, C. Peter, et al., eds. *The Black Abolitionist Papers.* Vol. 4, *The United States, 1847–1858.* Chapel Hill: University of North Carolina Press, 1991.

Stauffer, John. *The Black Hearts of Men: Radical Abolitionists and the Transformation of Race.* Cambridge, Mass.: Harvard University Press, 2002.

MICHAEL F. HEMBREE (1996)
Updated bibliography

Smith, James Todd

See L. L. Cool J (Smith, James Todd)

Smith, Mamie

May 26, 1883
September 16, 1946

Many details surrounding the birth of the blues singer Mamie Smith, the first African-American recording star, are uncertain. It is generally conceded that she was born in Cincinnati, Ohio, but it is not clear what her birth name was. Before reaching adulthood she sang, danced, and acted with white and black traveling vaudeville shows, including the Four Dancing Mitchells and the Salem Tutt-Whitney show. She married the singer William "Smitty" Smith in 1912 and came to New York the next year with the Smart Set, a black vaudeville troupe.

In New York, Smith met Perry Bradford (1893–1970), a minstrel performer and popular song composer, who eventually hired her for his show *Made in Harlem* (1918); he also launched her recording career in 1920 when he persuaded technicians at Okeh Records to let her record "That Thing Called Love" and "You Can't Keep a Good Man Down." This disc, one of the earliest known recordings by an African-American popular singer, sold well enough to allow Smith to return to Okeh's studios later that year to record "Crazy Blues," a Bradford composition backed by a jazz band whose members included the pianist Willie "The Lion" Smith (1897–1973). "Crazy Blues" is sometimes considered the first blues recording, but the performance shares less with other classic blues records from the 1920s than with popular musical and vaudeville theater songs of the time. Nonetheless, "Crazy Blues" was a huge success that sold more than one million copies and initiated the blues craze of the 1920s. "Crazy Blues" also inaugurated the "race music" industry, which marketed blues and jazz specifically for African-American audiences.

In the 1920s Smith worked extensively with some of the finest improvisers in blues and jazz, including the trumpet player Bubber Miley on "I'm Gonna Get You" (1922), the saxophonist Coleman Hawkins on "Got to Cool My Doggies Now" (1922), and the saxophonist Sidney Bechet on "Lady Luck Blues" (1923). She also continued to perform in vaudeville and stage acts, including *Follow Me* (1922), *Struttin' Along* (1923), *Dixie Revue* (1924), *Syncopated Revue* (1925), and *Frolicking Around* (1926). Smith became wealthy, lived lavishly, and toured and recorded frequently.

In the 1930s Smith sang at clubs and concerts with the bands of Fats Pichon and Andy Kirk, and with the Beale Street Boys. She also performed in the shows *Sun Tan Follies* (1929), *Fireworks of 1930* (1930), *Rhumbaland Avenue* (1931), and *Yelping Hounds Revue* (1932-1934). Smith's film career began in 1929 with Jailhouse Blues and continued with *Paradise in Harlem* (1939), *Mystery in Swing* (1940), *Murder on Lenox Avenue* (1941), and *Because I Love You* (1943). By the early 1940s, however, Smith had lost much of her wealth. In 1944 she made her last appearance in New York, with Billie Holiday. That year Smith fell ill, and she spent the last two years of her life in Harlem Hospital. Though the generally accepted date of Smith's death is September 16, 1946, it is possible that she died on October 30.

See also Blues, The; Blueswomen of the 1920s and 1930s; Rainey, Ma; Smith, Bessie; Taylor, Koko

Bibliography

Henderson, Ashyia, ed. "Mamie Smith." *Contemporary Black Biography*, vol. 32. Detroit, Mich.: Gale, 2002.

Kunstadt, Len. "Mamie Smith: The First Lady of the Blues." *Record Research* 57 (January 1964): 3–12.

"Mamie Smith." Redhotjazz.com. Available from <http://www.redhotjazz.com/mamie.html>.

Stewart-Baxter, Derrick. *Ma Rainey and the Classic Blues Singers*. New York: Stein and Day, 1970.

BUD KLIMENT (1996)
Updated bibliography

Smith, Venture

c. 1729
September 19, 1805

Venture Smith, a slave, was the author of a memoir titled *A Narrative of the Life and Adventures of Venture, a Native of Africa: But Resident Above Sixty Years in the United States of America, Related by Himself* (1798), one of the earliest American slave narratives and one of the few to include a discussion of African life and of the Middle Passage. Born in Dukandarra, Guinea, as Broteer, son of Prince Saugm, Venture Smith was kidnapped and sold into slavery at the age of eight. Brought first to Barbados, then to North America, he received his names from two owners, a steward and a planter.

Smith spent a dozen years as a slave in Stonington, Connecticut, and Fisher's Island, off Long Island in New York. He was notable in his resistance to slavery. Smith refused to act humble or to accept insults. He grabbed whips away from masters and on one occasion beat his master and his brother after they attacked him. Once he planned an escape in a boat, but he argued with his confederates and the plan collapsed.

During his time in bondage Smith accumulated money through hunting and fishing; he also hired out his labor, chopping large forests of wood on Long Island. He acquired a reputation as a superhuman laborer, a giant man, a combination Paul Bunyan/John Henry figure who weighed three hundred pounds with a six-foot waist. So phenomenal was his strength that, according to legend, he often paddled a canoe forty-five miles across Long Island Sound and back in a single day, between chopping nine cords of wood.

Eventually Smith saved enough money, and in 1765 he bought his freedom for £76. He supported himself by chopping wood, hunting, fishing, trading on merchant ships, whaling, and farming. With the proceeds of his tireless labor he bought freedom for his wife and children and for some friends he had made while in slavery. In 1776 he moved to Haddam Neck, Connecticut, where he bought a house and hired two black indentured servants. He lived there until his death in 1805. In 1798, his *Narrative,* written with Elisha Niles, was printed. Stories of his prowess followed him to Connecticut and survived for a century after his death.

See also Free Blacks 1619–1860; Slave Narratives

Bibliography

Kaplan, Sidney, and Emma Nogrady Kaplan. *The Black Presence in the Era of the American Revolution,* 2d ed. Amherst: University of Massachusetts Press, 1989.

GREG ROBINSON (1996)

Smith, Will

September 25, 1968

Born Willard Christopher Smith Jr. in Philadelphia, Pennsylvania, Will Smith was the second of four children of Caroline and Willard Sr. A graduate of Overbrook High School, Smith declined a scholarship to MIT to focus on his burgeoning musical career. Smith, whose childhood nickname was "Prince," met Jeff Townes at a party, and together they formed the rap duo DJ Jazzy Jeff & the Fresh Prince. In 1987 they issued their first album, *Rock the House*, and had a modest hit with the single "Girls Ain't Nothing But Trouble." Their follow-up album, 1988's *He's the DJ, I'm the Rapper*, achieved double-platinum status and won the first MTV Video Music Award for Best Rap Performance. The duo also won the first Grammy Award for Best Rap Performance in 1989 for the single from that album, "Parents Just Don't Understand." The duo were nominated for Grammys in 1990 and 1991, and won again in 1992 for the song "Summertime" from the album *Homebase*. DJ Jazzy Jeff & the Fresh Prince released their last studio album as a duo with 1993's *Code Red.*

In the meantime, Smith began his acting career on the NBC sitcom *The Fresh Prince of Bel-Air*, which ran from 1990 to 1996 (he served as executive producer for the 1994–1996 seasons). Smith made his film debut in 1992's *Where the Day Takes You* and also had roles in *Made in America* (1993) and *Six Degrees of Separation* (1993). His first major box-office success came costarring with Martin Laurence in the 1995 action film from director Michael Bay, *Bad Boys,* which made more than $145 million worldwide. (A sequel, *Bad Boys II,* was released in 2003.) Smith then went on to star in the summer box-office smashes *Independence Day* (more than $797 million worldwide) in 1996 and *Men in Black* (more than $576 million worldwide) in 1997. He won his first solo Grammy Award for Best Rap Solo Performance for the film's "Men in Black" theme song. Smith also released his first solo album, *Big Willie Style,* that same year.

Smith continued to alternate between music and acting, appearing in the films *Enemy of the State* (1998), *Wild Wild West* (1999), and *The Legend of Bagger Vance* (2000), while releasing the 1999 album *Willennium.* Smith received his fourth Grammy Award in 1999 for the song "Getting' Jiggy Wit It." In 2001, Smith played the role of boxer Muhammad Ali in director Michael Mann's film *Ali,* for which Smith received a 2002 Academy Award nomination as Best Actor as well as a Golden Globe nomination for Best Actor in a Drama. He then went on to star in the films *Men in Black 2* (2002), *I, Robot* (2004), *Shark Tale* (2004), and his first romantic comedy, *Hitch* (2005). Smith also released the albums *Born to Reign* (2002) and *Lost and Found* (2005).

Smith was married to Sheree Smith (with whom he has a son) from 1992 to 1995. He married actress Jada Pinkett Smith (with whom he has a son and daughter) in 1997. The UPN television series *All of Us,* for which the Smiths serve as executive producers, began in 2003 and was inspired by their personal lives.

See also Film in the United States, Contemporary; Rap; Television

Bibliography

Smith, Danyel. "Crazy in Love." Published in *Essence* (February 2005). Available from <http://www.Essence.com>.

Syler, Rene. "Will Smith: From Goofy to Sexy." Interview on *The Early Show* (July 16, 2003). Available from <http://www.cbs.news.com>.

Yarbrough, Marti. "Will Smith." Published in *Jet* (July 19, 2004). Available from <http://www.jetmag.com>.

CHRISTINE TOMASSINI (2005)

SNCC

See Student Nonviolent Coordinating Committee (SNCC)

Sobers, Garfield

July 28, 1936

World-renowned cricket legend Sir Garfield St. Auburn Sobers is regarded as among the most extraordinarily talented all-round players of the sport during the twentieth century. His towering feats at batting, bowling, and fielding were executed at the international level during his twenty-one-year professional career from 1953 to 1974 playing for the West Indies team, whose players are selected from the Anglophone Caribbean countries. Sir Garfield's most spectacular performances were made in test matches against Australian, English, Indian, New Zealand, and Pakistani teams. In the process he set a number of world records that took decades to break, while others have never been broken.

In recognition of his many outstanding cricketing achievements as a player and team captain and of his overall influence on the game, he was knighted by England's Queen Elizabeth II in 1975 and made a National Hero of Barbados in 1998. A larger-than-life statue of him was unveiled in Barbados in 2002, and Barbados's major sports complex is named after him. He has also received numerous awards from groups and organizations in the Caribbean, as well as around the world, including the Black Hall of Fame in the United States.

Sir Garfield was born in the Bay Land, St. Michael, Barbados, the fifth of six children to Sharmont and Thelma Sobers. When Garfield was five years old, his father, a merchant seaman, died on board a Canadian ship that was torpedoed in January 1942 by a German submarine. Young Garfield attended the Bay Street Boys' School near his home but became intensely involved in a wide range of sports from soccer to basketball. By the age of thirteen he exhibited exceptional bowling cricket skills and with limited mentoring rapidly emerged as one of the best youth players in his country. Three years later at age sixteen he was selected by the Barbados Cricket Board to play in his first international competition against the touring team from India in 1953. The following year he made his debut for the West Indies, playing against England's test team, and at seventeen became the second youngest player to represent the region in international cricket.

Over his professional cricketing career, Sobers played almost year-round in league and county games for Nottinghamshire in England and for South Australia. His international test records include taking 235 wickets and scoring 365 undefeated runs in 614 minutes, which remained the highest score in international cricket for thirty-six years until the record was broken by Trinidadian Brian Lara in April 1994. Sir Garfield because the first player in test cricket to score over 8,000 runs, which included making 26 centuries. At bowling, he became the first West Indian player to take over 100 wickets against English test teams. He also set a record in playing in eighty-five consecutive test matches, and he played in thirty-nine consecutive test matches as team captain. During his captaincy, he drew twenty test matches, lost ten and won nine. He still holds a number of records of batting partnerships with other players. Sobers played in ninety-three world test matches, batted in 160 innings, and was not out twenty-one times and made an average of 57.78 runs. As a bowler, he delivered 21,599 balls, had 978 maiden overs, and took 235 wickets for an average of 34.03 runs.

Sobers was first made the captain of his team in March 1964 and led it to victory against three world-class teams from 1965 to 1967. He led the West Indies team to its first-ever test series victory over the Australian team in 1965 to win the Frank Worrell trophy. The following year he led his team over the English team and won the Wisden Trophy, and the year after that he had a victory in the Indian test team series. Sir Garfield's last test match, against England in 1973, was played at the famous Lord's Cricket Grounds and he made 150 runs in one innings.

At the height of his popularity, Sobers married Prudence Kirby of Melbourne, Australia, on September 11, 1969, and later became the father of two sons and a daughter, Matthew, Daniel, and Genevieve.

Sir Garfield's retirement from international professional cricket did not diminish his enthusiasm for the promotion of cricket and other sports. In the early 1980s he coached the Sri Lanka National Cricket Team for two years and assisted it in achieving international playing status. He also worked for various Caribbean organizations promoting improved playing standards in a number of sports. In 1987 he helped establish the Sir Garfield Sobers International Schoolboys Tournament, which still sponsors youth cricket teams from various parts of the Caribbean as well as England, Canada, South Africa, Australia, India, and New Zealand to improve their skills and compete in a series of matches during the summer months.

Additionally, Sir Garfield has remained an ardent promoter of golf throughout the Caribbean. The 2005 Sir Garry Sobers Festival of Golf was held in mid-May in Barbados simultaneously at three major golf courses and attracted 253 golfers from around the Caribbean who participated in a fifty-four-hole event over three days.

See also Headley, George

■ ■ *Bibliography*

Bell, Gordon. *Sir Garfield Sobers.* Kingston, Jamaica: Thomas Nelson Caribbean, 1978.

Carrington, Sean, et al. *A–Z of Barbados Heritage.* Oxford: Macmillan Education Ltd, 2003.

Sobers, Garfield S., with Bob Harris. *Garry Sobers, My Autobiography.* London: Headline Book Publishing, 2003.

GLENN O. PHILLIPS (2005)

Soccer

Soccer is unquestionably a game of the world, but with histories, dimensions, and passions that are more likely to be felt locally. In the context of the Americas, there is no doubt that the legacy of the African diaspora has proven to be a key element in the evolution of the sport from North to South America. Moreover, the result of the African presence can be measured by Brazil's status as the only five-time World Cup champion and its national hero, Pelé, as the greatest player of the world. Thus, while the African presence and influence must be contextualized by region and nation, the connections between Pelé, Brazil, soccer, and the notion of the *jogo bonito* (the "beautiful game") are virtually coextensive. Still, while Brazil and its players are the apex of the sport and the reification of African influence on the game in the new world, the Americas offer other interesting histories of the black experience within soccer.

In the context of Brazil, long rated among the world's soccer powers, the contributions of blacks have been largely felt on the field, beginning with the goal-scoring prowess of Arthur Friedenrich and the contributions of the first great black Brazilian internationals, Domingos and Leonidas, who participated in the 1938 World Cup. Still, the great Brazilian teams from 1950 through 1970 were heavily reliant on the creative talents of a number of black footballers, including Jair, Garrincha, Zizinho, Pelé, and Carlos Alberto. World champions again in 1994, the image of the Brazilian team is now cemented, a multiracial squad engaged in creative work. From the late 1980s to the present, the Brazilian team has competed with a large number of black stars and a succession of key creative and scoring talents (Romario, Rivaldo, Ronaldo, Ronaldinho, Robinho), each of whom has extended the legacy established by the earlier generations of black Brazilian stars. An important part of this legacy is the Brazilian style of play, a reflection of the individual brilliance and inventiveness of black players who have demonstrated an unequaled capacity to create and score.

Notwithstanding the brilliance of such pivotal players, Brazil has also had a brace of defensive players (notably Junior and Cafu). Still, the issue of race has also been in question in Brazil, extending from the early days of the twentieth century when the game was effectively segregated to the almost traditional location of white players in the pivotal role of goalkeeper. This latter fact is perhaps due to the trauma of the Brazilian populace after losing, on home soil, the 1950 World Cup with the unlucky black goalkeeper, Barbosa. Taken as a whole, across several generations, black athletes in Brazil have been central in the nation's ability to secure an unprecedented five FIFA (Federation Internationale de Football Association) World Cups, the quadrennial culmination of regional and international group competitions.

The centrality of blacks, however, is not limited to Brazil. Across many parts of Latin America where generations of forced and unforced immigration have led to significant populations of Afro-Latinos, the presence of blacks has been marked and important. For example, in Peru, a nation with a long history of national and international participation in soccer and a period of punctuated excellence in the early- to mid-1970s, Teofilo Cubillas stands out as the seminal figure within the sport. Similarly, black players have contributed to the successes of Uruguay and, especially, Colombia, the latter having finally produced a run of success through the 1990s based on the talents of midfielder Carlos Valderrama and forwards Freddy Rincon and Faustino Asprilla. Colombia is also notable because of the contributions of coach Francisco Maturana at both the club and national team level. He thus represents the incursions, not yet fully realized, of black managers in the game.

Like their counterparts in Brazil, Peru, and Colombia, various Central American nations (principally Honduras, Costa Rica, and El Salvador) and Caribbean nations (Haiti, Trinidad and Tobago, and Jamaica) have experienced success at the international level and have contributed important black players to the best Latin American and continental professional leagues.

Indeed, the Central American and Caribbean region, which at the international level was regionalized to include the Caribbean islands, Mexico, Canada, and the United States, also has a rich history of black athletes. Costa Rica became highly competitive in the 1990s because of the contributions of players such as Paulo Wanchope (who has played much of his club football in Europe). Similarly, Haiti in 1974, El Salvador and Honduras in 1982, and Jamaica in 1998 have demonstrated the excellence of largely Afro-Latino teams in World Cup competitions. Jamaica is particularly notable because so much of its team was and

Brazilian soccer star Ronaldo, playing in Italy in 1998. PHOTOGRAPH BY LUCA BRUNO. AP/WIDE WORLD PHOTOS. REPRODUCED BY PERMISSION.

remains comprised of the sons of Jamaican immigrants who moved to the United Kingdom. Thus, a large percentage of these players have developed in England's Premier League and the lower divisions of the English Football Association. Likewise, Trinidad and Tobago's team was reliant on expatriates based in the United Kingdom, including Dwight Yorke, a starting striker during the dominant 1990s iterations of Manchester United.

Closer to the United States the impact of such players can be marked by the importance of Pelé in the grassroots popularity of soccer beginning in the mid-1970s with his arrival in the United States to play for the New York Cosmos in the now-defunct North American Soccer League (NASL). Shortly thereafter, other players of high caliber, including Cubillas, the Brazilian Mirandinha, and the Portuguese Eusebio, and a raft of British imports, often with roots in the Caribbean Islands (e.g., Clyde Best, Clive Charles, Godfrey Ingram, and Vince Hilaire), as well as African players (Jomo Sono, Jean-Pierre Tokoto, Andreis Maseko, Ade Coker, Ken Mogojoa, and Ace Ntsolengoe) began appearing for various clubs during the height of the North American Soccer League (1968–1984).

Although black imports like Pelé and Cubillas raised the profile of soccer, this did not necessarily draw African-American youth to the sport in significant numbers. Unlike in Latin America, soccer has long been the sport of the white suburbs and thus the NASL did not connect well with black communities already drawn to baseball, basketball, and football. Within the U.S. national team, which has persisted in regional and international competitions even while an alphabet soup of professional soccer leagues has risen and fallen in the United States, there had been very few black players between 1930, which marked the first U.S. entrance into the World Cup, and 1990, which marked the team's first World Cup appearance since the historic 1950 competition that saw the U.S. team defeat a seemingly all-powerful squad from England. The 1990 team had among its ranks only two African Americans—Jimmy Banks and Desmond Armstrong.

Nevertheless, the emergence of Major League Soccer (MLS) in 1995 also demonstrated a deeper integration of African-American and Afro-Latino players. Thus, apart from bringing such Afro-Latinos as Carlos Valderrama, Eduardo Hurtado, and Jose Dely Valdez to the league, an impressive list of African Americans has emerged. These players have contributed to the league, as well as the development of the national team, which has qualified for each of the last four World Cups (1990–2002), a feat unparalleled in the history of U.S. soccer. Key players in MLS and on the national team have included goalies Tim Howard and Zach Thornton; defenders Eddie Pope and Tony Sanch; midfielders Earnie Stewart, Cobi Jones, and teenage sensation Freddy Adu; and Roy Lassiter and DeMarcus Beasley. Indeed, the caliber of such players is marked by their presence on top-division teams in England, Germany, Holland, and Italy.

For most Americans, the issue of African Americans and sport is dominated by the important social and historical developments within the "big three" of U.S. professional team sports. However, a broader geographical view demonstrates that the historical developments and flows that brought Africans to the shores of the Americas have resulted in profound and spectacular developments across a variety of sports, including soccer. It is impossible to think of the game without its African-American contributors, who have left indelible marks on how the game is played by club and national teams across South, Central, and North America. Undoubtedly, these contributions will continue as the sport moves forward and looks forward to the African continent hosting a World Cup.

See also Pelé (Nascimento, Edson Arantes do); Sports

Bibliography

Bellos, Alex. *Futebol: The Brazilian Way of Life* (spine title: *Futebol: Soccer, the Brazilian Way*). New York: Bloomsbury, 2002.

Lever, Janet. *Soccer Madness: Brazil's Passion for the World's Most Popular Sport.* Chicago: University of Chicago Press, 1983; rev. reissue, Long Grove, Ill.: Waveland, 1995.

Murray, Bill. *The World's Game: A History of Soccer.* Urbana and Chicago: University of Illinois Press, 1996.

Radnedge, Keir, ed. *The Complete Encyclopedia of Soccer.* London: Carlton, 2002.

FERNANDO DELGADO (2005)

Social Dance

One of the most notable aspects of the evolution of American social dance from the late seventeenth century to the end of the twentieth century is the emerging dominance of African-American dance styles. During the first two hundred years the development of a recognizable American dance style progressed slowly through a blending of African and European movement and music forms. By the end of the 1890s, however, a distinct pattern unfolded in which dances created in African-American communities spread out to the American mainstream, moving from the United States to Europe and eventually to other parts of the world, such as the Charleston in the 1920s and the hip-hop/freestyle in the 1970s and 1980s. During the twentieth century the process accelerated. Propelled by the aggressive exportation of American movies, television, records, and videos, African-American dances spread quickly. And since the early 1980s, with worldwide satellite television broadcasting and the consequent expansion of the music-video industry, a world youth culture has developed. Linked together through CDs and music videos and tuned to the latest move, an adolescent in Paris or Tokyo dances to the same beat as a New York hip-hopper. The styles they are trying to master are decidedly African American, and the teenagers dance more like each other than like their parents.

Although American dance has been fused from many different cultural sources over hundreds of years, the two main traditions of movement and music that shaped the way Americans move are those of Western Europe and West Africa. In constant flux, American dance encompasses older traditional dances as well as the newest fads, stage dance and street forms, classical African dances, ballet, square dancing, and the most recent club inventions.

Because popular dances are created democratically by thousands of people over a long period of time and are learned through observation and imitation, traditional movements pass and are recycled from one generation to the next. For example, some of the steps used in hip-hop/rap/freestyle look like updated versions of the fast, slipping footwork of the Charleston, which, in turn, echo the rapid grinding and crisscrossing steps basic to some of the traditional dances of West Africa. The cycle works the other way as well, and contemporary African social dances recycle and retranslate modes of popular American dances.

Because it is nonverbal, dance information can cross temporal and geographic borders. It slips ethnic boundaries, and it blurs the imaginary lines that separate folk art from fine art, popular dance from classical dance. As a result of this flexibility, original functions and forms get altered, movements get reshaped to fit new situations and contexts. Paradoxically—because body language is learned early and strongly and is a fundamental cultural identifier—dance, the most fugitive of artistic expressions, remains one of the most persistent of all cultural retentions.

Carried in the kinetic memories of African slaves and European immigrants, dances arrived whole or in fragmented forms. Subjected in North America to radically different environmental and cultural mixes as well as the harsh conditions of slavery, dances adapted. Circumventing verbal communication, dance (like music) provided a way for Africans from disparate geographic areas to come together, to move together, to bond together in a strange land. Gradually, over time, an African-American style evolved as dances got re-created by those who recalled their dance inheritances whole, those who recalled them only partially, and those of other cultural origins for whom it was not a legacy.

African Traditions in Colonial America

In colonial America the majority of African slaves resided in the middle and southern colonies. The rapid establishment of religious circular dances (grouped under the generic name of "ring shouts") and secular circular dances (called "juba" dances) indicates a probable legacy of compatible movement characteristics shared by the various African groups. These early African Americans also practiced seasonal dances that marked seasonal changes and harvesting and planting times, or dances that celebrated rites of passage such as marriage dances. In addition there seemed to have been a variety of animal dances (probably a fusion of hunting dances and mask-cult or religious dances), and processional dances, used during funeral celebrations.

In the late 1730s slaves were forbidden use of their drums in several colonies, in part because of the 1739 Cato Conspiracy or Stono Rebellion in South Carolina, which led to the subsequent passage of a series of laws forbidding slaves to congregate or to play their big gombe drums. Deprived of their larger percussion instruments, the slaves turned to smaller means of percussion. They used their bodies as musical instruments. Previously used in complementary rhythmic accompaniment, these now became dominant: hand clapping and body slapping (also known as "patting" or hamboneing), and rhythmic footwork. Small percussive instruments, such as tambourines and "bones" (the legbones, ribs, or jawbones of animals played with pieces of wood or metal rasps) became widespread. (At times the bones could be fashioned into two fine, thin, long pieces that were held in the hand and played like castanets.) In both the religious ring shout and the secular juba, the feet slid, tapped, chugged, and stamped in rhythmic harmony with antiphonal singing and clapping as the dancers moved around the circle. The juba and the ring shout shared other characteristics, such as moving counterclockwise, with the dancers in the surrounding circle providing musical, movement, and percussive motifs in a call-and-response pattern with a changing leader. In the juba, individual improvisations occurred in the middle of the circle; in the ring shout, individual ecstatic possession occurred among some of the participants. In the juba especially there was a fluid relationship between the improvisers and the surrounding circle of watchers and music makers. Those in the center would dance until exhausted; then others from the circle would move in to take their places.

Colonial slave masters rarely allowed religious dances to be performed openly, so religious dances continued to be practiced clandestinely. At times they merged with other, more secular dances and continued to exist syncretically. Although these new dances retained many characteristics of those from the Old World, they had become their own distinctive dance forms.

Blending of African and European Traditions

Certainly the most powerful changes were caused by the mixing of African and European dance styles. European dance featured an upright posture with head held high and a still torso with no hip rotations. Arms framed the body and—because European dance was usually performed inside, on floors, in shoes—there was careful placement and articulation of the feet. Men and women danced in couples, and in this partnership, body line and placement, as well as couple cooperation, were emphasized over individual movement. In European "figure" dances, floor patterns were valued above personal invention (in "figure" or "set" dances many couples will move together as a group in specific designs, similar to a modern-day Virginia reel or square dance). Music and dance tempos were organized around simple rhythms with regularly stressed beats and syncopations, and musical compositions emphasized melody. The pervasive dynamics of European dancing were control and erectness.

By contrast, African dance "gets down" in a gently crouched position, with bent knees and flexible spine. Traditional African dance tends to be performed in same-sex groups. Danced in bare feet on the bare earth, it favored dragging, sliding, and stamping steps. The supple upper body, with its flexible relationship to the lower limbs, could physically carry many rhythms simultaneously, mirroring the polyrhythms of the music. A polyrhythmic, multimetered, and highly syncopated percussive dynamic propelled movement and music. Movement often initiated from the pelvis, and pelvis rotations caused a sympathetic undulation in the spine and torso. Animal motions were imitated and quite realistically portrayed on the entire body. Improvisations were appreciated as an integral part of the performance ethos.

These last two qualities would make especially important contributions to the development of African-American dance. First, when the dancer imitates the animal's motions fully, habitual patterns of locomotion and gestures are bypassed. Timing and tempos get altered, usual choices are supplanted by fresh movements, fueling the dance vocabulary with new material, expanding the lexicon of motion. For example, "peckin'" (the head thrusts forward and backward like a bird feeding) and "wings" (the arms are flapped like the wings of a great bird, or sharply bent elbows beat quickly) spiced the larger body movements of the Charleston in the 1920s. The monkey and the pony were popular dances of the 1960s, and breakdancers of the 1980s did the crab and the spider. In the early 1990s, the butterfly (the legs open and close like butterfly wings) became a popular dance in reggae and dance hall styles.

The emphasis on improvisation advanced the evolution of dance styles. The improviser accomplishes two things simultaneously. While staying within the known stylistic parameters (reinforcing traditional patterns), the improviser is an inventor whose responsibility is to add individual flavor to the movement or timing that updates and personalizes the dance. This keeps social dance perpetually on the edge of change and also helps explain why social dance fads come and go so quickly.

The inevitable exchange between European and African styles led to incorporation and synthesis, and what evolved was neither wholly African nor European but something in between. As they served at the masters' balls, slaves observed the cotillions, square dances, and other "set" or "figure" dances. In turn, European-American dances were altered by observation and contact with African-American music and dance. Sometimes black musicians played for the white masters' balls. It was also not uncommon on southern plantations for the children of the slaves to play with the masters' children. It was common practice for the masters to go down to the slave quarters to watch slave dances or to have their slaves dance for them on special occasions. At times, slaves engaged in jig dance competitions, where one plantation would pit its best dancers against the best dancers from another. At first, "jig dance" was a generic term that European Americans gave to different types of African-American step dances where the feet rhythmically played against the floor, because this fancy footwork resembled the jigs of the British Isles. Informal jig dance contests occurred in northern cities on market days, when freedmen and slaves congregated to dance after the market closed (in Manhattan this happened in the Five Points Catherine Square area), and along the banks of the great transportation river highways, where slaves hired out by their masters worked as stevedores alongside indentured or immigrant workers. In New Orleans, "Congo Square" was designated as the place where slaves could congregate and celebrate in song and dance on Sunday.

The majority of the earlier European colonists came from the British Isles, and within that group were large numbers of poor Irish settlers and Irish indentured servants. More than any other ethnic group, the Irish mixed with African slaves doing heavy labor—the Irish as indentured servants, the Africans as slaves—for the master. Later they lived alongside each other in slums of poverty, so that the mutual influence of Irish step dances like the jig and hornpipe and African step dances was early and strong.

General patterns of fusion suggest the following progression. Between the late 1600s and early 1800s, African and African Americans adopted aspects of European dance for their use. For example, they began early to move in male-female couples (mixed couples and body contact in traditional African dance is extremely rare) in European figure dances, such as quadrilles and reels. However, they retained their own shuffling steps and syncopated movements of feet, limbs, and hips. After the 1820s that trend reversed, as Europeans and European Americans began to copy African-American dance styles—a trend still in effect. In general, as the African elements became more formal and diluted, the European elements got looser and more rhythmic. Religious dancing became secular; group dancing gave way to individual couples on the dance floor; and following the rise of urbanization and industrialization and the consequent migration of black workers, rural dances moved to the towns. Since the late 1930s, in reverse, urban dances that became dance crazes spread back to rural communities and out to the world.

The 1890s was the decade that marked the beginning of the international influence of African-American dance. The cakewalk had been developing since the late 1850s, and by the 1890s was well established as an extremely popular dance in both theatrical and nontheatrical contexts. According to ex-slaves, the cakewalk, with its characteristic high-kneed strut walk, probably originated shortly after the mid-1850s. The dance had begun as a parody of the formal comportment and upright posture of the white ballroom dancers as they paraded down the center of the floor, two by two, in the opening figures of a promenade that would have begun the formal balls. The simplicity of this walk made it easy to mimic and exaggerate, it fit easily into the African tradition of satiric song and dance, and the formality of the walk resonated with African processional dances. Apparently the dance had been a "chalkline" dance, where the dancers had to walk a line while balancing containers of water on their heads.

The Cakewalk

By the 1890s the cakewalk had been adapted as a ballroom dance by whites, who grafted the high-kneed walking steps with a simple 2/4 or 4/4 rhythm of early ragtime jazz and blended it with the promenading steps that were already a central motif in many of the schottisches and gallops popular in the ballrooms of the time. The cakewalk quickly translated to the stage and had been regularly performed in the big African-American touring shows since the beginning of the decade, by such troupes as Black Patti and her Troubadours and in shows like *The South Before the War* and *A Trip to Coontown,* among others. The cakewalk was danced on Broadway by excellent black performers in *Clorindy: The Origin of the Cakewalk* (1898). As well, there were numerous cakewalk competitions done regularly by whites (one of the largest annual events took place at Madison Square Garden in Manhattan). The enormous popularity of the dance is clear from even the most cursory perusal of sheet music from 1890 to 1907. A few exhibition dance teams of African-American performers traveled to Europe to perform the dance (the most famous was the husband-and-wife team of Charles Johnson and Dora Dean), and in 1904 the cakewalk received the validation of aristocratic society when the Prince of Wales learned the dance from the comedy-and-dance team of African-American performers Bert Williams and George Walker. The structural framework of the cakewalk had open sections for improvisation that shifted emphasis to the individual's role, changing the focus from the group to the couple and the person. It was the turn of the century, and as the incubator of individual invention, the cakewalk was the perfect artistic catalyst to launch dance into the modernist sensibility of the twentieth century.

A rash of rollicking animal dances gained ascendancy between 1907 and 1914, overlapping the cakewalk and replacing it in the public's favor. The turkey trot, kangaroo hop, and the grizzly bear (three among many) incorporated eccentric animal gestures into the couple-dance format, a blend that had long been practiced by African-American dancers—elbows flapped, heads pecked, dancers hopped—in bits of motion that were derived from such African-American animal dances as the buzzard lope. The rising popularity of these dances paralleled the rise in sheet music publication. For a small investment, people got music and dance instructions, since the song lyrics told how the dance should be done.

A typical example of the instructional song is the well-known ragtime dance *ballin' the jack*, which developed in about 1910. (The meaning of the title is obscure, but it probably originated from railroad slang, with the general meaning of enjoyable, rollicking good times.) As described in 1913 in its published form by two African-American songwriters, Chris Smith and Jim Burris, the dance had the following steps:

> First you put your two knees close up tight, then you sway 'em to the left, then you sway 'em to the right. Step around the floor kind of nice and light, then you twis' around and twis' around with all your might. Stretch your lovin' arms straight out in space, then you do the eagle rock with style and grace, swing your foot way 'round, then bring it back, now that's what I call ballin' the jack.

The Jazz Era

Between 1900 and 1920 a dance fever gripped America. Since the early 1900s couples had been moving closer together, and with the evolution of the slower, more blusey early jazz styles, close-clutching dances like the slow drag, which had always been done at private parties, began to surface in public places. The hip motions and languid gliding feet in such African-American dances as the grind and mooch (both a couple or solo dance) indicate that body contact and postures were already racially shifting. Certainly this prepared the way for the arrival of the tango and its immediate acceptance as a dance craze in 1913. (The tango originated in Argentina. Although its precise origins are quite complex, it was also a likely synthesis of European and African influences.) The tango is a difficult dance to do, necessitating dance lessons, a reality happily exploited by the numerous exhibition tango teams who demonstrated the dance to the eager public, then taught it to them in their studios or at the local dance hall or tango teas. If few could afford this luxury, thousands of people nevertheless danced what they believed to be the tango. In reality, the frank sensuality of thigh and pelvic contact coincided more readily with familiar close-couple African-American dances of the juke joints, small dance halls, and white-and-tan clubs that peppered mixed neighborhoods of every American city.

THEATRICAL DANCE. By the late 1910s a flood of migrating workers moved northward, seeking jobs in urban industries built for the war effort of World War I. As great numbers of African Americans moved into cities, they formed a critical mass of talent that erupted in a variety of artistic expressions. Their energy gave birth to the Harlem Renaissance of the 1920s and turned Harlem—and black neighborhoods in other industrial cities—into crucibles of creativity in the popular and fine arts. The golden years of black Broadway (1921–1929) began with the hugely successful *Shuffle Along* (1921), written, directed, composed, and choreographed by African Americans (its four major creators were Noble Sissle, Eubie Blake, Flournoy Miller, and Aubrey Lyles). This production, and subsequent road shows, brought African-American jazz music and jazz dances to a wide audience. There was little distinction between social dances and stage adaptations, and current popular dances were simply put onstage with few changes. As a result of *Shuffle Along*'s popularity, Broadway dance began to reshape itself, shifting to a jazz mode, as Florenz Ziegfeld and other producer-directors began to copy *Shuffle Along*'s choreography. A spate of new studios opened in the Broadway area to teach this African-American vernacular jazz dance to professional actors and to an eager public (one important instructor was Buddy Bradley, who taught the Astaires and a host of other Broadway and film actors, then went on to choreograph English revues).

THE CHARLESTON. Then with the 1923 Broadway show *Runnin' Wild*, the Charleston burst onstage and into the hearts of the American public, especially through the eponymous song James P. Johnson composed for the show. However, the Charleston had been a popular dance among African Americans long before the 1920s. Although its origins are unclear, it probably originated in the South, as its name suggests, then was brought north with migrating workers. Jazz historian Marshall Stearns reports its existence in about 1904, and the late tap dancer Charles "Honi" Coles said that in about 1916 as a young child he learned a complete version of the dance, which had long been popular in his hometown of Philadelphia.

The Charleston is remarkable for the powerful resurgence of Africanisms in its movements and performance and for shattering the conventions of European partnering. The Charleston could be performed as a solo or a couple dance, or partners could dance together side by side or in the closed-couple position. For women in particular, its wild movements and devil-may-care attitude broke codes of correct deportment and propriety. It was quick and decidedly angular, and the slightly crouched position of the body imparted a quality of alert wildness. The steps (and the early jazz music it was performed to) are syncopated, the knees turn in and out, the feet flick to the side, and a rapid forward-and-backward prancing step alternated with pigeon-toed shuffles and high kicks. As the arms and legs fling in oppositional balance, elbows angled and pumping, the head and hands shake in counterpoint. Knock-kneed, then with legs akimbo, body slightly squatted, this beautiful awkwardness signaled the aesthetic demise of European ideals of symmetry and grace in social dance. The fast-driving rhythms of the music smoothed the flow of broken motions into a witty dance punctuated with shimmies, rubber-legging, sudden stops, and dance elements such as the black bottom, spank the baby, or truckin'. Although these new dances often caused alarm because of their seeming anarchy of motion, and the uncontrolled freedom that that implies, the Charleston in particular roused the ire of the guardians of public morality. Warning that the Charleston would lead to sexual and political dissolution, the dance was condemned by several clerics and was banned in several cities.

Although the Charleston was immediately introduced to Europe by American jazz artists touring there, it was Josephine Baker (she had been a chorus girl in *Shuffle Along*) who personalized the dance. She went to Paris in 1924 and became the darling of the French, and it was Josephine's charming, humorous, and slightly naughty version of the Charleston that caused such a sensation in Europe. The Charleston, and all the bold young women who performed it, came to symbolize the liberated woman of the twenties, and the rubber-legging "flapper" became an icon of the era.

DANCING AT THE SAVOY. Then, in 1926, the Savoy Ballroom opened in New York City's Harlem. Nicknamed "The Track" or "Home of Happy Feet," the Savoy could accommodate up to four thousand people. Because it had the reputation of being the place to go and hear good music and dance, all the best bands wanted to play there. It was the practice to feature two different bands on the same night, playing one after another on two different bandstands placed at opposite ends of the ballroom. This subsequent "battle of the bands" energized dancers to new heights of daring and improvisation. For thirty years the Savoy would be the center of dance in New York City, and there dances were brought to such a level of excellence that the name "the Savoy" was synonymous with the best in dancing. As its reputation grew, the Savoy also became a showplace, a kind of informal stage arena where people could go to watch the finest Savoy dancers as each tried to outdance the other.

Great dancing is inspired by great music, and the history of African-American social dance parallels the history of African-American jazz music. In truth these social dances are most accurately described as "vernacular jazz dance" (from the title and subtitle of Marshall and Jean Stearns's magnificent 1968 historical study of tap and popular dance, *Jazz Dance: The Story of American Vernacular Dance*). The juke joints of the South and the dance halls of the North served as forums where musicians and dancers worked together. The sharing of ideas, rhythms, and the heated excitement of music and movement feeding each other produced an environment of experimentation where the spirit moved and dances got created on the spot. Certainly the arrival of big-band swing music, fathered by the great jazzmen and their groups, all of whom played the Savoy, parented the next great African-American dance as well.

THE LINDY HOP. Existing concurrently with the Charleston and evolving from it, a kind of Savoy "hop" was getting formulated on the floor of the Savoy Ballroom. Then, in 1928 the dance was christened "the lindy hop" by a well-known Savoy dancer, Shorty Snowden, in honor of Charles Lindbergh's 1927 solo flight across the Atlantic. The dance, which would become an international craze and an American classic, contained many ingredients of the Charleston—the oppositional flinging of the limbs, the wild, unfettered quality of the movement, the upbeat tempos, the side-by-side dancing of partners. But the two most outstanding characteristics were the "breakaway," when two partners split apart completely or barely held on to each other with one hand, while each cut individual variations on basic steps (a syncopated box step with an accent on the offbeat) and the spectacular aerial lifts and throws that appeared in the mid-1930s. The tradition of individual improvisation was, of course, well entrenched. However, with the lindy hop, it was the climactic moment of dance, and the aerial work set social dance flying. The lindy hop contained ingredients distilled during the evolution of social dance since the 1890s. It had a wide range of expressive qualities, yet it was grounded in steps and rhythms that were simple enough to be picked up readily and were capable of infinite variations. It would, in fact, become one of the longest lasting of all African-American social dances. Commonly known as the jitterbug in white communities, the dance adapted to any kind of music: There was the mambo lindy, the bebop lindy, and during the 1950s, the lindy/jitterbug changed tempos and syncopations and became known as rock 'n' roll; when looked at carefully, the 1970s "disco hustle" reveals itself as a highly ornamented lindy hop cut down to half time. In the 1980s and '90s, "country-western swing" looks like the lindy hop framed by fancy armwork, and in the South, "the shag" is another regional variation of the lindy hop theme.

On the floor of Harlem's Savoy Ballroom the lindy hop was brought to its highest level of performance, fueled by the big-band swing played by brilliant musicians in orchestras led by such men as Fletcher Henderson, Chick Webb, Al Cooper, Duke Ellington, Earl Hines, Cab Calloway, Count Basie, Billy Eckstine, Benny Goodman, and many more. As the dynamics of swing music heated up to its full musical sound and fast, driving, propulsive "swing" beat, the dancers matched it with ever more athletic prowess. In the mid-1930s the lindy took to the air, and using steps with names such as the hip to hip, the side flip, the snatch, over the back, and over the top, the men tossed the women, throwing them around their bodies, over their heads, and pulling them through their legs until the women seemed to fly, skid-land, then rebound again.

The Savoy lindy hop was renowned for its spectacular speed and aerials. An entrepreneurial bouncer at the club, Herbert White, decided to capitalize on this dancing talent, and he formed "Whitey's Lindy Hoppers." Choosing a large group of lindy hop dancers, the best from the ballroom, White split them into smaller troupes or teams that toured the country, appearing in movies, vaudeville, on Broadway, at the 1939 World's Fair in New York City, and in many other venues. The lindy spread out to the world, first through newsreels and films, and then the dance was carried personally to Europe and Asia by American GIs during the 1940s.

As the language of jazz moved from swing to bebop, rhythmically more complex and harmonically daring, so did the nature of jazz dance. With the passing of the great dance halls, the smaller venues that featured the five- or six-piece jazz combo that was the basic form of bebop became the main site for jazz performance, and though many of these clubs had no space for dancing, bebop-influenced jazz dance nonetheless flourished.

Bebop Influence

Bebop jazz often sounded barely in control with its fast pace and solo improvisations, and bebop dancers mirrored the music. The at-times private, introverted quality of musical performance was reflected by the bebop dancer's performance, which appeared disassociated and inward. Rather than having the movement scattering outward, as in the Charleston and the lindy, the bebop dancers used footwork that slipped and slid but basically stayed in place, the dynamic of the dance was introverted and personal, and the dancer appeared to gather energy into the center of the body.

Like the music, the dance was dominated by males. And if the bebopper used many of the same steps as the lindy hopper, there were enormous stylistic differences in the focus and body language. Bebop was almost the reverse of the lindy: Partners broke away for longer periods of time than they spent together. Bebop dance could be done as a solo, in a couple, or in a small group of three or four. This open relationship was perfect for a dance that placed the strongest significance on individual improvisation and devalued group cooperation. The body rode cool and laid-back on top of busy feet that kept switching dynamics, tempo, flow, timing, direction, impulse, and emphasis. Off-balance and asymmetrical, the dance wobbled at the edge of stability. The dance was filled with slips and rapid splits that broke down to the floor and rebounded right back up, and the bebopper was fond of quick skating-hopping steps that appear to be running very fast while remaining in the same place. Elbows pulled into the body, shoulders hitched up, hands lightly paddled the air. Balanced on a small base—the feet remained rather close together—with swiveling body and hips, the dancer seemed made of rubber. Partners rarely touched each other or looked directly at each other. Bebop dancing influenced the dance styles of rhythm and blues and other black popular music of the 1940s. It is also known as "scat" dancing (the comparison is to the vocal freeflights of the scat singer). James Brown is perhaps the best-known entertainer who dances in bebop mode. Watered down and simplified to rapidly rocking heel-and-toe steps that alternated with pigeon-toed motions in and out, with the occasional splits, bebop lost most of its glittering individualism when translated to the mainstream. Yet the effect of bebop dance was to give the social dancer a new "cool" persona, that of the "hipster," whose sensual slipperiness provided a rest, a contrast, to the heat and speed of the jitterbug lindy. This hip attitude had an enormous effect on Broadway jazz. Bob Fosse, Jerome Robbins, and Jack Cole, three powerful Broadway and film choreographers, would convert the physical language of bebop dance into a style of laid-back, cool jazz that would be viewed as epitomizing the best of Broadway jazz dance.

1950s Rock 'n' Roll

During the 1950s, with the explosion of a "teen culture" and a "teen market," an entertainment industry, led by the record companies, was established to service this market. Bepop dance influenced the dance styles of rock 'n' roll. The record industry, ever quick to seize an opportunity, made the crossover, renaming rhythm and blues rock 'n' roll. The jitterbug got renamed as well, now called by the music's name of rock 'n' roll dance. Partners continued to split apart. With the infusion of the bebop mentality, a slippery smoothness in the footwork calmed down some of the flinging of the older forms of jitterbug, while the twisting hips were beginning to even out the sharp bouncing of the fast-paced Savoy style. Toward the end of the 1950s, gyrating hips (the trademark of Elvis Presley), previously only one movement phrase in the midst of many, would be singled out and made into an individual dance. "The twist," which became another worldwide dance fad, structured an entire dance around a single movement. Its simplicity made it easy to do, and its virtues were promoted in Chubby Checker's beguiling rock 'n' roll song "The Twist" (1960, a close copy of Hank Ballard's 1958 original). Also in the 1950s there was a resurgence of close-clutching couple dances, similar to the older mooch and grind (now known as "dirty dancing"), danced to sweet harmonics of five-part a cappella singing groups who were developing a singing style that became known as doo-wop. It is notable and interesting that in the 1950s, during a period when there was a strong sense of conformity, group line dances such as the stroll and the madison became popular.

Re-Africanization in the 1960s

During the 1960s, the civil rights movement was reflected in a re-Africanization of dance forms in such dances as the Watusi, the monkey, the bugaloo, and a series of spine-whipping, African-inspired dances such as the frug and the jerk. Animal gestures and steps reentered dances with a vengeance, formulated into dances such as the pony, the chicken, and the fish (also known as the swim). Partners did not touch. Instead, they danced face-to-face, but apart, reflecting each other's movements, using a dialogue of movement that was essentially a call-and-response mode of performance.

Motown Choreography

Motown singing groups whose carefully tailored and tasty dance routines were choreographed by Cholly Atkins had an inestimable effect on dance styles. The teenagers who admired these groups and bought their records now watched them perform on television. Then they copied the Motown style, whose choreography was made to underline the message of the song. A variety of pantomimic dances was created in which the words, or story line, of the song were enacted by the dancers. For example, one of the most popular and beautiful of these tunes was Marvin Gaye's "Hitchhiker" (Atkins worked with Gaye on this tune). The major gesture-motif of this dance recurred as the dancer—feet doing little prancing steps, hips swiveling, head bobbing—circled the hand in front of the torso, then swung it off to the side, thumb stuck up, as if he or she were trying to hitch a ride on the road, watching the cars go by.

Disco and Line Dancing

The 1970s disco explosion featured the hustle (if one strips away the ornamentation of multiple turns and sharply pointing arms and poses as the man swings out his partner, the lindy hop becomes visible). The line dance made popular by the movie *Saturday Night Fever* (1976) is actually the old madison, retooled for the 1970s (the same is true for the 1980s' bus stop and the 1990s' electric slide). However, with the explosion of breaking and electric boogie in the Bronx during the late 1970s, and popping in Sacramento and Los Angeles, dance styles underwent a radical change in the United States, then in Europe, Asia, and Africa as the styles spread to the world on television and music videos.

Breakdancing and Hip Hop Culture

Breakdancing was part of a larger cultural movement known as hip-hop, which got established in the South Bronx neighborhood of New York City. Hiphop had a variety of artistic expressions—graphic arts (graffiti or "writing"), spoken poetry (rapping), music (scratchin', which developed into the rap music of the 1980s and 1990s), religion and philosophy (Zulu Nation and the politics put forth in the lyrics of the rap), and dance (breaking, electric boogie, and popping and/or locking). Breakdancing took the structural principle of the breakaway and expanded it into a solo dance form. Accompanying the breakdancers musically were street DJs who were using the techniques of scratchin' (holding the record by its edge, the DJ moves it back and forth on the same groove) and mixing (shifting back and forth between turntables, the DJ replays the same sound bits of a couple of records over and over) to create new syncopations and "breaks" in the old records, thereby improvisationally composing new musical scores. Then, using one or more microphones, rappers would talk rhythmically over the music.

Intensely competitive, breaking was primarily a solo, male dance form that re-Africanized the aesthetics of African-American dance. Visually it retains powerful reverberations of gestures and phrases derived from *capoeira*, the martial-art dance that came to the New World with the slaves captured in the Angola region of southwestern Africa.

Breaking stressed acrobatic fluency in the spins and in the dancer's buoyancy. In fact, bouncing is one of its most obvious characteristics. Performers effortlessly spring from dancing on their feet in an "uprock" style to "breaking" down to twirl on the floor; then they rebound to an upright position. There is little distinction between up and down, and because the breaker moves within a circle, the focus is multidirectional, as a consequence of its bounding-rebounding quality. Breaking seems to defy gravity, to exist almost at the edge of flight.

Popping and locking are other hip-hop dance styles that were performed along with breaking and were developed first on the West Coast. In these styles the body seems to be broken into segments. As motion moved from the fingers of the left arm through the chest and out the fingers of the right arm, the joints "locked" or "popped" into sharp millisecond freezes. The movement looks as if it were a living rendition of a video game, and popping and locking did evolve from an earlier dance known as the robot. A related but more undulating version of popping and locking, called the electric boogie, developed on the East Coast; in this dance the body seemed to move in fluid, increasingly complex minifreezes.

Breaking was the dance of the young and tough hip-hop subcultures of the ghettos, and the rawness of the sounds and the movements made breaking the dance of protest that rallied against the mainstream disco styles of music and movement. Because of its brilliance, its technical display, its physical virtuosity, and its machismo, and because breaking got immediate and near-hysterical media coverage, it became popular worldwide. Breakers sprung up in Tokyo, Rome, Calcutta, Rio de Janeiro, and Paris, and long after it had faded in popularity in the United States (in about 1984), it was still flourishing in the 1990s in other parts of the world. Breaking was the most powerful and early expression of the hip-hop culture, and because of its worldwide success, it prepared the way for the eventual ascendancy of rap, which de-emphasized the dancer for the rapper and was the centerpiece of the hip-hop movement of the 1980s and early 1990s.

In the late 1980s and 1990s, the young adults who were creating the current social dances did little that was reminiscent of traditional European dance and much that was reflective of the ancient African legacy. On the dance floor they gathered in casual circles that randomly arose, then disintegrated. Male/female partnerships, if they existed at all, changed and shifted throughout the night, and a partner was simply another dancer who was focused upon for a while. Dancers moved in loose groupings that may or may not have mixed genders (males often danced together, or there would be a group of females dancing). Though they moved in stylistic harmony, improvisation was highly prized, and each participant brought individual flavor to the movements.

There were many reverberations with traditional African motion. The body was slightly crouched with bent knees, feet flat on the floor. The footwork favored sliding, stamping, or digging steps. When the music was hard-hitting and fast, dancers burst out in vigorous jumps and athletic maneuvers; a phrase may have consisted of diving down to the floor ("breaking" down) in belly slides or shoulder rolls, then smoothly pulling the body upright, swinging back into the beat with fast, sliding steps. Digitalized and engineered, the African drum has been transformed into a sonic bass boom that blasts through the speakers. With volume turned up to the "red zone," the bass power pops the body, vibrating bones, internalizing the beat. The dancers used their torsos as a multiunit instrument with an undulating spine, shimmying shoulders, and swiveling hips. Movement was polyrhythmic, and rippled through the body in waves, or it could lead to very briefly held positions known as freezes. Heads circled and bobbed, arms did not frame the body so much as help it balance. Dances were named for the style of music that is played, such as house, rap, hip-hop or dance hall, or they were called "freestyle" because each dancer improvisationally combined well-known steps as the fancy strikes.

A prime example of an Africanized dance was one performed to Chuck Brown's "The Butt," which hit the top of the commercial pop charts in 1988 and was notable for its bold call-and-response structure. As the title suggests, movement concentrated on shaking buttocks. Dancers "get down" in a deep squat. Placing hands on butts or thighs, they arch their spines, nod their heads, and swivel the pelvis in figure eights. In the early 1990s this same dance remained popular. It was now called "winding," performed by young, urban, black, and white club goers to reggae or go-go (a Washington, D.C., musical style influenced by Jamaican reggae). "Winding" alludes to the circular winding motion of the hips. In 1901 the same moves were called "the funky butt," and in the 1930s they were known as "grinding."

African-American underground club dancers continue to create new dances that will be picked up by the mainstream tomorrow, disseminated through music videos. All music-video dance styles originate in the clubs and on the streets, so one must look at the places of origination to get a glimpse into the dance styles of tomorrow.

Club Dancing and DJs

Club dancers, mostly African American and Latino youth, are the most active, influential, and democratic of the social dance choreographers. The club community is a specialized one, which has coalesced around an action rather than a neighborhood or through bloodlines. Relationships are made because of a shared obsession with dancing. Perhaps the distinguishing characteristic of a real "clubhead" is that dance is passion and possession, and through movement, they experience "going off," a kind of secular spirituality that echoes the spiritual possession of the older African circle dances brought to this country four hundred years ago.

Music is provided by DJs mixing at their consoles with a couple of turntables, merging the sounds of one record into another in a seamless musical flow, composing on the spot. They are musicians of consoles and amplifiers; they are today's bands and orchestras and conductors. Using raw recorded "cuts" that have not been engineered into their final form (this is not the stuff of commercial radio), DJs are the high priests of the clubs who regulate the emotional and physical heat of the dancing. A good DJ knows how to play the songs that inspire movement. He shifts the mood and pace through musical combinations, acting and reacting to what he sees on the floor. Reading ephemeral signals of movement and energy, breath and beat, a constant flow of information is exchanged between dancer and DJ.

In the early 1990s, dance styles fell into rough generational divisions. Hip-hop tended to be done by the younger generation of early through late teens, while lofting (this style of dance is called different names in different parts of the country) and house tended to be done by a slightly older group in their late teens and twenties. Lofting was a softer assimilation of the "old school" breaking, whose immediate predecessors are the lindy hop, and whose older progenitors are the *capoeria* and other African acrobatic dances. The "New Jack" style of hip-hop uses footwork reminiscent of the Charleston and earlier West African step dances. The pose and punch and stylized gestures of voguing exaggerate the syncopated isolations of jazz, and like the cakewalk, voguing makes satiric commentaries on the mannered postures of the monied classes, as represented in the images of models of high-fashion magazines. At the end of the twentieth century and into the new millennium, hip-hop continues to created variations on breakdancing, including popping, uprock, house, and bebop.

Social dance is a structure of movement that is always open to modification. Propelled by improvisational innovation, dancers can transform a recreational participatory event into a performance within a circle. Perhaps the greatest African aesthetic gift was the reverence for improvisation. It keeps social dance democratic, it is not tied to any one institution or controlled by a small elite group who determine who shall perform and who shall observe. Improvisation and individuals keep dance a celebration of imagination, while the flexibility and power of movement itself is what links the past to the present and the community to the person.

See also Breakdancing; Capoeira; Hip Hop; Jazz

Bibliography

Brandman, Russella. "The Evolution of Jazz Dance from Folk Origins to Concert Stage." Ph.D. diss., Florida State University, 1977.

Emery, Lynne F. *Black Dance in the United States from 1619 to 1970,* 2d ed. Pennington, N.J.: Princeton Book Co., 1991.

Franks, Arthur H. *Social Dance.* London: Routledge and Kegan Paul, 1963.

Gorer, Geoffrey. *Africa Dances.* London: Faber and Faber, 1949.

Haskins, James S. *Black Dance in America: A History Through Its People.* New York: Books for Libraries, 1997.

"Jazz Dance, Mambo Dance." *Jazz Review* (November 1958).

Malone, Jacqui. *Steppin' on the Blues: The Visible Rhythms of African American Dance.* Urbana: University of Illinois Press, 1996.

"New Orleans Marching Bands: Choreographer's Delight." *Dance* (January 1958).

"Popular Dance in Black America." *Dance Research Journal* 15, no. 2 (spring 1983). Special issue.

Stearns, Marshall, and Jean. *Jazz Dance: The Story of American Vernacular Dance.* New York: Macmillan, 1968.

Wittke, Carl. *Tambo and Bones.* Durham, N.C.: Duke University Press, 1930.

Yarborough, Camille. "Black Dance in America: The Old Seed." *Black Collegian* (October–November 1980): 46–53.

Yarborough, Camille. "Black Dance in America: The Deep Root and the Strong Branch." *Black Collegian* (April–May 1981): 10–24.

SALLY SOMMER (1996)
Updated by publisher 2005

Social Gospel

Referring generally to a fresh application of the insights of biblical faith to the problems of the social order, historians have usually identified the "social gospel" with the response of reform-minded church men and women to the urban and industrial crises of the post-Reconstruction North. That interpretation runs the risk of truncating the roots of American social Christianity in reform movements of the antebellum period and failing to see the early origins of a distinctive African-American social gospel.

A social gospel began to develop within African-American communities in late eighteenth-century Christian voluntary societies, which commonly combined the functions of church, school, and mutual aid society. These included the Newport, Rhode Island, Free African Union Society, founded in 1780; the Free African Society of Philadelphia, founded in 1787; Charleston, South Carolina's Brown Fellowship Society, founded in 1790; the African Society of Providence, Rhode Island, founded in 1793; and Boston's African Society, founded in 1796. In the same period, the earliest semiautonomous African Baptist congregations were established in the plantation South, first in Virginia and along the Savannah River bordering South Carolina and Georgia.

As these early African-American voluntary societies developed, particularly in the freer setting of the urban North, they articulated a variety of themes within a framework of millennial expectation: economic development and self-help, freedom and social justice, missionary education, and racial nationalism. In the antebellum North, black clergymen such as Henry Highland Garnet, James W. C. Pennington, and Theodore Wright built institutions and networks for organizations that promoted education, social reform, and the freedom of their enslaved southern kinsmen. These activities were the preparation for northern African-American missionaries to move into the South during and after the Civil War. There they established missions as the institutional seeds of rural social settlements, churches and Sunday schools, and schools and colleges for nurturing the former slaves and their children in freedom.

Usually among the race's educated elite in Reconstruction, African-American clergymen gave direction to the social and political aspirations of southern freedmen. They often served in multiple capacities, as pastor, politician, and professor or school administrator. Commonly committed to a conservative theological orthodoxy, they believed in the fatherhood of God, the brotherhood of man, and "uplifting the race." They encouraged the freedman to confirm family ties, acquire property, and get an education. Many of them were active in temperance reform. When male freedmen gained the franchise, some clergymen such as Richard H. Cain, William H. Heard, James W. Hood, Hiram R. Revels, and Henry M. Turner were elected to political office. In state legislatures, for example, their efforts helped to lay the foundations for public school systems in the southern states.

After Reconstruction, black clergymen and laywomen turned to building the institutions of social redemption—churches, schools, and social settlements—within the African-American community. In rural and urban settings, North and South, black churchwomen founded social settlements to "uplift the race." From 1890 to 1908, Janie Porter Barrett founded the Locust Street Settlement at Hampton, Virginia; Margaret Murray Washington founded the Elizabeth Russell Settlement at Tuskegee, Alabama; Victoria Earle Matthews founded New York's White Rose Mission; and Lugenia Burns Hope founded Atlanta's Neighborhood Union.

In urban communities, clergymen built institutional churches to extend the range of church services to migrants from the rural South. Hutchens C. Bishop of New York's St. Philip's Episcopal Church, Henry Phillips of Philadelphia's Episcopal Church of the Crucifixion, Matthew Anderson of Philadelphia's Berean Presbyterian Church, and Henry H. Proctor of Atlanta's First Congregational Church first built institutional churches. Their example was followed by African Methodists Reverdy C. Ransom, Monroe Work, and R. R. Wright Jr. in Chicago. Thereafter, urban Baptist congregations followed suit with remarkable results.

Some churches' pulpits passed from father to son: Washington and Gardner C. Taylor presided at Baton Rouge's Mt. Zion First Baptist Church; Richard H. Bowling, Sr. and Jr., at Norfolk's First Baptist Church; Junius Caesar Austin, Sr. and Jr., at Chicago's Pilgrim Baptist Church; Marshall Shepherd, Sr. and Jr., at Philadelphia's Mt. Olivet Baptist Church; and Adam Clayton Powell, Sr. and Jr., at New York's Abyssinian Baptist Church. These pastors built centers of urban religious, social, and political power. More remarkable is the passage of the pulpit through three generations of William H. Grays, I, II, and III, at Bright Hope Baptist Church in Philadelphia.

Martin Luther King Sr., who succeeded his father-in-law, A. D. Williams, at Atlanta's Ebenezer Baptist Church, would have passed it on to his sons, Martin Luther King Jr., or A. D. Williams King, had their premature deaths not prevented it. Even so, as the heir of many generations of African-American preachers of the social gospel, Rev. Dr. Martin Luther King Jr. had already become its foremost American spokesman in his generation.

See also Brown Fellowship Society; Cain, Richard Harvey; Garnet, Henry Highland; Hood, James Walker; Hope, Lugenia Burns; Pennington, James W. C.; Revels, Hiram

Rhoades; Turner, Henry McNeal; Washington, Margaret Murray; Wright, Theodore Sedgwick

Bibliography

Luker, Ralph E. *The Social Gospel in Black and White: American Racial Reform, 1885–1912.* Chapel Hill: University of North Carolina Press, 1991.

Wheeler, Edward L. *Uplifting the Race: The Black Minister in the New South, 1865–1902.* Lanham, Md.: University Press of America, 1986.

RALPH E. LUKER (1996)

Social Psychology, Psychologists, and Race

There has been substantial disagreement among scholars, educators, and policymakers regarding the degree to which the racial climate in the United States has improved for blacks in the decades following the civil rights era. What is clear is that institutionalized racial inequalities of past eras, such as racially separate schools and voting restrictions, no longer exist, and that social policies such as affirmative action have improved the status of black Americans. The burgeoning black middle class evidences the march toward racial equality.

The second half of the twentieth century was a period of "steady and sweeping movement toward general endorsement of the principles of racial equality and integration" (Bobo, 2001, p. 269). Still, trends in racial attitudes suggest that it was not until the mid-1990s that the vast majority of whites endorsed equal employment access and residential and school integration. Despite this improvement, however, whites still show less support for equality of access to housing and interracial marriage, and remain significantly less likely than blacks to support policies intended to rectify racial differences in access to employment and educational opportunities. Trends in racial attitudes suggest that, for whites, the greatest evidence of increasing endorsement of racial equality and integration is in the most public and impersonal arenas, like schools, public accommodations, and the workplace (Bobo, 2001). Hence, blacks and whites remain at a crossroads with regard to the issues of racial discrimination and the causes of racial inequality.

In their landmark study of black residential segregation, Douglas Massey and Nancy Denton found that "although blacks and whites may share a common commitment to 'integration' in principle, this word connotes very different things to people in the two racial groups. For blacks, residential integration means racial mixing in the range of fifteen to seventy percent black, with fifty percent being most desirable; for whites, it signifies much smaller black percentages" (Massey and Denton, 1993, p. 93).

There is also strong empirical evidence suggesting that racism remains a powerful, damaging force that bars blacks from complete inclusion in American society. Blacks are still the most residentially segregated and economically disadvantaged group in the United States. Massey and Denton's findings show that residential segregation is the "structural linchpin" impeding black progress. The majority of black Americans (irrespective of social class) reside in "hypersegregated areas" replete with poverty and social disorder. Relative to whites, blacks complete fewer years of school, earn less income, and accumulate less wealth.

These patterns of persisting socioeconomic inequality by race feed into whites' negative perceptions of blacks, and thus perpetuate black disadvantage. If blacks and other minority groups cannot get ahead, whites are inclined to perceive it as a consequence of their own lack of motivation or other cultural deficiencies. Research indicates that the more whites' explanations for inequality are rooted in cultural or volitional deficiencies, rather than in structural barriers, the less likely they are to support government intervention.

Laissez-Faire Racism

Lawrence Bobo, a prominent social psychologist who focuses on intergroup relations and inequality, argues that while the modern polity no longer formerly condones institutionalized racism, spurns the belief that blacks are genetically inferior to whites, and discourages overt intolerance, racism remains a durable force in contemporary America. Bobo uses the term *laissez-faire racism* to denote the difference between present-day racism and its predecessor, Jim Crow racism. Laissez-faire racism relies on free-market enterprise, which is opposed to strict government regulation of economic and political affairs. Race-neutral policies are supported and maintained, providing credence to the widely held belief that the United States is a color-blind society in which anyone can succeed. Bobo contends that the historical legacy of Jim Crow racism—the era when state policy was antiblack and most whites believed that blacks were categorically inferior—lives on. A substantial portion of the white population still adheres to patently negative stereotypes of blacks, in addition to blaming them for their own collective disadvantage. Bobo believes that government policy has not been successful in ameliorating race-based inequalities and bringing blacks to the table as equal citizens. Laissez-faire racism, he suggests, relies on "loosely coupled, complex, and permeable" forms of domination (Bobo, et al, 1997, p. 17).

The theory of laissez-faire racism is rooted in the sociologist Herbert Blumer's 1958 thesis that racism is embedded in an historical and collective social order. In this view, racism is seen as a grand integrated structural force within society, perpetually justifying white supremacy, whereas laissez-faire racism is the manifestation of whites' efforts to protect their "sense of group position" and alleviate fears of black encroachment following the collapse of Jim Crow ideology and government-sanctioned segregation.

Psychological Responses to Laissez-Faire Racism

Bobo argues that laissez-faire racism results in certain psychological responses by black Americans and may be damaging to the black psyche. Two theories addressing minority-group responses to their disadvantaged positions are known as *stereotype threat* and *oppositional culture*. In different ways, each of these theories details macro-level responses to laissez-faire racism.

Claude Steele, a professor of psychology at Stanford University, developed the theory of stereotype threat, which asserts that members of certain groups are fearful of fulfilling negative stereotypes about their group's intellectual ability, and is a psychosocial explanation for academic underperformance by black students. Stereotype threat is possible whenever a person is placed in a "risky" situation, when there is a perceived "threat of being viewed through the lens of a negative stereotype or the fear of doing something that would inadvertently confirm that stereotype" (Steele, 1999, p. 46). A risky situation is when an individual feels mistrustful or apprehensive that his or her actions will be perceived as confirming a group stereotype. Black students may do worse on an exam because of fear of confirming the anti-intellectual stereotype of the racial group. All that is necessary is an awareness of the negative stereotypes; whether or not students believe the stereotypes themselves is irrelevant. At least in the short term, the threat of confirming anti-intellectual stereotypes results in performance anxiety that depresses academic performance.

Long-term exposure to stereotype threat can cause affected students to "disidentify" with school as a psychosocial defense mechanism. Academic success is then dropped as a basis for self-esteem. This is a method of self-protection: if students perform poorly, they can fall back on the belief that they did not try as hard as they could have, or that getting an "A" just is not important to them anyway. The theory of stereotype reconciles the seemingly contradictory findings that African-American students have higher academic aspirations and place greater value on education than any other group, consistently underperform academically, and have very high self-esteem.

The theory of oppositional culture, devised by anthropologist John Ogbu, also details the psychosocial responses of black Americans to laissez-faire racism. Ogbu argues that the detrimental effect of racism actually discourages educational and occupational achievement among black Americans. Oppositional-culture theory posits that black Americans underperform at work and school because of racial discrimination and limited socioeconomic possibilities. Blacks are enmeshed in a "blocked opportunities framework" (Kao, 1995) where they occupy a specifically disadvantaged ecological niche that prevents access into high-status (i.e., Eurocentric) social groups, organizations, and institutions.

Ogbu argues that the status of African Americans as involuntary minorities—meaning they were incorporated into U.S. society through enslavement and relegated to a subordinate status—is largely responsible for their development of negative feelings about mainstream values and institutions, as well as their identification of racial and cultural differences as symbols of pride and resistance. Voluntary minorities—those who enter the United States freely to improve their material well-being—would not fall prey to this detrimental cultural orientation because they compare themselves to compatriots in their countries of origin. This theoretical framework presupposes that black Americans cope with their disadvantaged position in society by adopting a "black cultural frame of reference," the appropriation of attitudes and behaviors contrary to mainstream white ideologies (Ogbu, 1991).

Whereas a majority of the oppositional-culture research is based on ethnographic fieldwork with poor black Americans in racially segregated urban schools, some research has validated Ogbu's results with other groups in varied milieus (Solomon, 1991; Waters, 2001). R. Patrick Solomon (1991) found that, despite their voluntary minority status, West Indian students in Toronto exhibit a strong oppositional identity because they have internalized racial discrimination in Canadian society. Findings from Mary Waters's 2001 study of second-generation West Indians in New York City are also somewhat consistent with the oppositional culture framework: those respondents whose reference group was African Americans tended to perform more poorly in school, whereas those who maintained a strong immigrant identity achieved higher educational success.

A black man climbs the stairs to the "colored" entrance of a movie theater in Belzoni, Mississippi, 1939. PHOTOGRAPH BY MARION POST WOLCOTT. PRINTS AND PHOTOGRAPHS DIVISION, LIBRARY OF CONGRESS.

See also Educational Psychology and Psychologists; Psychology and Psychologists: Race Issues

Bibliography

Blumer, Herbert. "Race Prejudice as a Sense of Group Position." *Pacific Sociological Review* 1, no. 1 (1958): 3–7.

Bobo, Lawrence D. "Racial Attitudes and Relations at the Close of the Twentieth Century." In *America Becoming: Racial Trends and Their Consequences,* edited by Neil Smelser, William J. Wilson, and Faith Mitchell, pp. 262–299. Washington, D.C: National Academy Press, 2001.

Bobo, Lawrence D., James Kluegel, and Ryan A. Smith. "Laissez-Faire Racism: The Crystallization of a 'Kinder, Gentler,' Anti-Black Ideology." In *Racial Attitudes in the 1990s: Continuity and Change,* edited by Steven A. Tuch and Jack K. Martin, pp. 93-120. Greenwood, Conn.: Praeger, 1997.

Kao, Grace. "Asian Americans as Model Minorities: A Look at Their Academic Performance." *American Journal of Education* 103 (1995): 121-159.

Massey, Douglas S., and Nancy A. Denton. *American Apartheid: Segregation and the Making of the Underclass.* Cambridge, Mass.: Harvard University Press, 1993.

Ogbu, John. "Minority Coping Responses and School Experiences." *Journal of Psychohistory* 18 (1991): 433–456.

Solomon, R. Patrick. *Black Resistance in High School: Forging a Separatist Culture.* Albany: State University of New York Press, 1991.

Steele, Claude M. "A Threat in the Air: How Stereotypes Shape Intellectual Identity and Performance." *American Psychologist* 52 (1997): 613–629.

Steele, Claude M. "Thin Ice: 'Stereotype Threat' and Black College Students." *Atlantic Monthly* (August 1999): 44-54.

Waters, Mary. *Black Identities: West Indian Immigrant Dreams and American Realities.* Cambridge, Mass.: Harvard University Press, 1999.

CAMILLE Z. CHARLES (2005)
KIMBERLY C. TORRES (2005)

Social Work

Social work and social welfare are intended to help people attain the basic necessities of life—food, clothing, and shelter—as well as to aid them in developing their human potential. Throughout the twentieth century such efforts were often, though not always, carried out in conjunction with programs for social reform. Although social welfare activity initially was the preserve of private services and organizations, over the years government has come to play an increasingly active role. The history of U.S. social work, its relationship to social activism, and its growing importance within government distribution of services have had important implications for the quality of life of African Americans as individuals and as a community.

Mutual Aid

Long before social work emerged as a professional field, African Americans carried out a wide range of cooperative self-help and mutual-aid programs in order to better their lives and their communities. Throughout the eighteenth and nineteenth centuries, free black women and men in the North organized benevolent societies; among the earliest was the Free African Society of Philadelphia, formed in 1787 to provide cradle-to-grave counseling and other assistance, including burial aid. Other groups raised money for educational programs or relief to widows and orphans. Northern blacks not only helped themselves, they extended aid to fugitive slaves and linked their work to a larger effort to improve the standing of African Americans in society.

Following the Civil War, the Freedmen's Bureau, a federal agency, initiated a series of social welfare policies designed to help newly freed black people in their struggle to survive; during Reconstruction many southern states promoted similar relief efforts. But in the context of Emancipation, such economic, educational, and other assistance not only improved the lives of individual African Americans, it posed a challenge to the system of racial inequality itself. After Reconstruction, therefore, most states of the former Confederacy resisted the adoption of programs that would alter the status quo; when local and state government did intervene on behalf of the aged, infirm, and others in need, it did so on a segregated basis.

Largely excluded from such services, African Americans in the North and the South continued to practice the kind of social work that had served them for centuries. Black women were often at the forefront of these efforts, pooling resources and playing a leadership role in establishing orphanages, homes for the poor and aged, educational and health-care services, and kindergartens. The abolitionist Harriet Tubman turned her residence in Auburn, New York, into the Home for Indigent and Aged Negroes, one of perhaps a hundred such facilities by 1915. In urban centers black women organized to aid newly arriving migrant women in finding lodging and employment; among the most prominent of these efforts was New York's White Rose Working Girls Home, founded by Victoria Earle Matthews in 1897.

Professional Social Work and the Black Community

Professional social work emerged around the turn of the twentieth century in response to conditions generated by the processes of industrialization, urbanization, European immigration, and southern migration to the North. Charitable organizations, such as the National Conference of Charities and Corrections, sought to coordinate and professionalize their work, but they continued to emphasize personal misfortune or moral failing instead of larger institutional explanations for the pervasive poverty in urban industrial centers. Before the massive exodus of black people from South to North, most charity workers paid scant attention to the problems of African Americans. With the Great Migration, some charitable reformers came to view black people as another immigrant group needing what they called Americanization, and they found ample support for their moralistic emphasis on thrift and industry from Booker T. Washington's philosophy of individual uplift. Other philanthropists insisted that black people were meant to occupy an inferior station in life and urged that they acquire industrial training suited to their "natural" limitations.

In contrast, settlement workers, who were mostly college-educated white women, sought to learn from immigrants and migrants instead of imposing their own values and assumptions. They proposed to live in impoverished communities, providing services that would help newcomers adjust to urban industrial life without giving up their own beliefs and cultural traditions. Although settlement workers could not always mask their middle-class backgrounds, they did establish job training and placement programs, healthcare services, kindergartens, and recreation facilities. Perhaps the best-known settlement was Chicago's Hull House, founded by Jane Addams and Ellen Gates Starr in 1889.

White activists in the settlement movement were often quicker than charity workers to recognize that poor housing, educational, and job opportunities in the burgeoning black communities of the urban North were the direct result of segregation and racial discrimination. Using scientific methods to identify and analyze social problems, settlement workers pressed for government reforms in such areas as factory and tenement conditions, juvenile justice, child labor, and public sanitation. Their efforts to fuse social work with social reform also extended to race relations; one-third of the signatories of the 1909 call that led to the formation of the National Association for the Advancement of Colored People (NAACP) either were or had been settlement workers.

Advocating racial tolerance and an end to discrimination, however, was not the same as calling for social equality. Many social service agencies in Chicago, New York, and elsewhere either refused help to African Americans outright or offered poor quality assistance on a segregated basis; this was especially true for organizations providing lodging, board, and medical care. The settlement houses were no exception. Many were located in white immigrant communities, but a number of settlements that were easily accessible from black neighborhoods still did not serve the African-American population. Some white reformers pursued alliances with black community leaders in establishing interracial settlements; one notable example was the Frederick Douglass Center, founded in Chicago in 1904. But the center disdained what it called slum work among the black poor. Rather, its leaders, including white minister Celia Parker Wooley and black clubwoman Fannie Barrier Williams, sought to bring together the educated elite, black and white, for lectures, concerts, and other cultural activities.

Funding and Control

It was often African Americans themselves who, seeking to remedy the inequities in social service provision, seized the initiative in addressing individual and social problems in the black community. But such activists were faced with a stark dilemma. Without the assistance of white philanthropists, they could not hope to match white agencies in staffing and programming; indeed, their facilities rarely survived. Between 1900 and 1916 at least nine settlements were established in Chicago's black neighborhoods; by 1919 only one remained. In 1910 renowned antilynching agitator Ida B. Wells-Barnett formed the Negro Fellowship League, which offered recreational services for black men and boys, an employment agency, and later, lodging. But she was forced to disband it for lack of funds.

The alternative—support from white people—usually meant control by white people. Chicago's Wendell Phillips Center, for example, was initiated in 1907 by a group of twenty black activists, and its staff was mostly black; its board, however, was overwhelmingly dominated by whites. White reformers were thus able to limit the autonomy of black community leaders; in so doing, they often contributed to the preservation of the racial status quo and helped shape the kinds of programs that were available; services for black girls, for instance, were more likely to win financial support if they emphasized morality and offered training in domestic work. On the other hand, the very involvement of whites in the creation of services "for blacks" often reflected their desire to maintain segregation in social services.

Social Solutions vs. Personal Solutions

Even when forced to rely on the resources of white philanthropists whose agendas clashed with their own, African Americans often strove to translate their reform activities into a larger program of social action. In 1899 the distinguished Harvard University graduate W. E. B. Du Bois produced *The Philadelphia Negro,* a meticulously researched study of urban African-American life. The project had been commissioned by the College Settlement Association, whose conservative wing was driven by the conviction that black people were somehow ridden with criminality and vice—an early version of the culture-of-poverty argument advanced in the 1960s to explain why economic misery persisted in much of the urban black community. But Du Bois consciously sought to set his findings within a historical and social context that acknowledged the importance of economic and political, not personal, solutions. Du Bois's sociological approach pioneered the use of scientific inquiry into the causes and effects of social problems.

Black Social Workers

The National Urban League—formed in 1910–1911 as a merger of the National League for the Protection of Colored Women, the Committee for Improving Industrial Conditions of Negroes in New York, and the National League on Urban Conditions among Negroes—represented the application of professional social work to the kinds of social services that had long been practiced in the black community. It was founded by George Edmund Haynes, the first black graduate of the New York School of Philanthropy (later the Columbia University School of Social Work), and Ruth Standish Baldwin, a wealthy white reformer. The league offered counseling and other assistance to African Americans in housing, education, employment, health, recreation, and child care. It relied on scientific research techniques to document the exclusion of African Americans and press for greater opportunities.

The league also played an important role in the training and placement of black social workers. Formal social work education made its debut in 1903 with the University of Chicago's School of Civics and Philanthropy, later known as the School of Social Service Administration. In 1917 the National Conference of Charities and Corrections became the National Conference of Social Work. (In 1956 its name was changed to the National Conference on Social Welfare.) But because of racial segregation, blacks were largely barred from social work education and training outside the North until the 1950s, and they were denied full participation in professional bodies.

Through the able leadership of Urban League personnel, historically black educational institutions stepped in to fill the void. Under Haynes's direction, Fisk University developed an undergraduate social service curriculum, including field placement with league affiliates. The Atlanta School of Social Work was founded in 1920 to provide instruction to black students, and it later affiliated with Atlanta University. By 1926 the Urban League itself employed 150 black social workers. Over the years the league continued to preserve important ties to social work education; Whitney M. Young Jr., for example, served as dean of the Atlanta University School of Social Work before becoming the league's executive director in 1961.

Government Involvement

The devastating economic crisis generated by the Great Depression severely strained the capacity of private social service organizations to assist individuals in need. In an extension of the reform impulse of the Progressive period, the federal government under President Franklin D. Roosevelt was forced to intervene with massive programs that placed social work firmly within the public domain. The Social Security Act of 1935 provided old age and survivors' insurance, unemployment insurance (known as entitlement benefits), and public assistance to the aged, the blind, and dependent children.

But for African Americans the impact of government involvement was contradictory, since programs aimed at affected workers automatically excluded large numbers of black people. Nearly half of all African Americans worked in agricultural labor, casual labor, and domestic service, but these occupations were not counted as part of the covered workforce. The Urban League, the NAACP, and others opposed the exclusion, arguing that it would single out black people as a stigmatized, dependent population, but their efforts were unsuccessful. They also openly criticized the unequal distribution of relief and segregated assistance programs.

Impact of the Civil Rights Movement

The civil rights movement of the 1960s, fueled by legal and social gains achieved by African Americans during the previous decade, attacked racism and discrimination on all fronts, and social work was no exception. Concentrated in segregated enclaves, crowded into dilapidated housing, suffering from dramatically high rates of unemployment, black people in the inner cities had not reaped the benefits promised by the advent of civil rights. When Daniel Patrick Moynihan argued in 1965 that the black community was caught in a "tangle of pathology" resulting from "the deterioration of the Negro family," he was articulating a moralistic theme that had persisted in social welfare policy since at least the late nineteenth century. It was activist-oriented African Americans who led the challenge to such interpretations, defending the integrity of the black family and calling for a deeper understanding of the structural causes of poverty.

The antipoverty programs initiated under the Johnson administration's Great Society, while in part a response to Moynihan's analysis, also created new opportunities for contesting it. African-American social workers condemned racism within the profession and demanded a greater commitment to social justice. In 1967, over opposition from the leadership of the National Association of Social Workers, a nondiscrimination amendment to the association's code of ethics was presented on the floor of the delegate assembly, where it passed. The following year, in San Francisco, African Americans founded the National Association of Black Social Workers (NABSW). Although some black individuals gained prominence within existing professional organizations—Whitney Young Jr., for example, became president of the NASW in 1969—many African Americans turned to the NABSW as a vehicle for articulating the goals of effective, responsive service delivery in the black community and an end to racial exclusion and discrimination within the ranks of the profession.

Social work and social welfare programs, although widely believed to provide services on a nondiscriminatory basis, have always been influenced by larger historical trends and conditions. The historical exclusion of African Americans from social work schools and organizations virtually assured that concerned black people would continue to rely on their own methods for improving individual and community life. At the same time, the profession's dominant strategies and methodologies have reflected the racial, sexual, and class biases of the European-American middle class, often to the detriment of those most commonly under the scrutiny of social workers.

Challenging Assumptions

An African-American presence within the social work profession has helped to transform service delivery. Many black social workers have developed innovative models that acknowledge the importance of environmental factors, such as socioeconomic status and citizenship rights, in determining the well-being of African-American people. By asserting positive recognition of extended family formations, they have been able to respond with new flexibility to individual and family concerns. And they have sought to extend these efforts throughout the profession, working to ensure that social work education and training incorporate information about the experiences of people of color. At the same time, many African Americans in social work have rejected the notion of adjustment to the status quo, calling for change in social institutions, laws, and customs that continue to keep African Americans from achieving their full potential.

In the 1990s the assumptions that guided social work theory and practice demanded renewed attention. The problems facing the black community continued to reflect the racism that persisted in employment, health care, education, and other areas. The unemployment rate among African Americans remained twice the national average; the AIDS crisis reached disproportionately into the black community; and drug-addicted children entered an educational system whose capacities were severely constrained by diminishing resources. As in the past, however, the African-American community was left to tap its own potential in order to address these concerns. At the same time, mainstream social workers adopted code words—diversity, multiculturalism, biculturalism—that obscured root causes and so failed to confront deep-seated racism, sexism, and class bias. The challenge facing advocates of social work and social welfare was to respond effectively to these problems by reclaiming a legacy of progressive social reform that would acknowledge the need for structural, not personal, solutions.

See also Du Bois, W. E. B.; National Association for the Advancement of Colored People (NAACP); National Urban League; Wells-Barnett, Ida B.; Young, Whitney M., Jr.

Bibliography

Aptheker, Herbert, ed. *A Documentary History of the Negro People in the United States,* vol. 1. New York: Citadel Press, 1971.

Axinn, June, and Herman Levin. *Social Welfare: A History of the American Response to Need,* 3rd ed. New York: Longman, 1992.

Bell, Howard R. "National Negro Conventions of the Middle 1840s: Moral Suasion vs. Political Action." In *The Making of Black America: Essays in Negro Life and History,* edited by August Meier and Elliott Rudwick, vol. 1. New York: Atheneum, 1969.

Bennett, Lerone, Jr. *The Shaping of Black America.* Chicago: Johnson, 1975.

Bennett, Lerone, Jr. *Before the Mayflower: A History of Black America,* 6th ed. Chicago: Johnson, 1988.

Breul, Frank R., and Steven J. Diner, eds. *Compassion and Responsibility: Readings in the History of Social Welfare Policy in the United States.* Chicago: University of Chicago Press, 1980.

Clark, William E. "The Katy Ferguson Home." *Southern Workman* 52 (1923): 228–230.

Cromwell, Cheryl D. "Black Women as Pioneers in Social Welfare, 1880–1935." *Black Caucus Journal* 7, no. 1 (1976): 7–12.

Franklin, John Hope, and Alfred A. Moss, Jr. *From Slavery to Freedom: A History of Negro Americans,* 6th ed. New York: Knopf, 1988.

Hornsby, Alton, Jr. *The Black Almanac,* 4th rev. ed. Woodbury, N.Y.: Barron's, 1977.

Johnson, Audreye E. "Health Issues and African Americans: Surviving and Endangered." In *Innovations in Health Care Practice,* edited by John S. McNeil and Stanley E. Weinstein. Silver Spring, Md.: National Association of Social Workers, 1988, pp. 34–49.

Johnson, Audreye E. *The National Association of Black Social Workers, Inc.: A History for the Future.* New York, 1988.

Johnson, Audreye E. "The Sin of Omission: African American Women in Social Work." *Journal of Multicultural Social Work* 1, no. 2 (1991): 7–15.

Johnson, Audreye E. "William Still—Black Social Worker: 1821–1902." *Black Caucus Journal* (Spring 1977): 14–19.

Lewis, David Levering. *W. E. B. Du Bois: Biography of a Race, 1868–1919.* New York: Holt, 1993.

Lide, Pauline. "The National Conference on Social Welfare and the Black Historical Perspective." *Social Service Review* 47, no. 2 (June 1973): 171–207.

Philpott, Thomas Lee. *The Slum and the Ghetto: Immigrants, Blacks, and Reformers in Chicago, 1880–1930.* Belmont, Calif.: Wadsworth, 1991.

Ross, Edyth L. *Black Heritage in Social Welfare, 1860–1930.* Metuchen, N.J.: Scarecrow, 1978.

Still, William. *The Underground Railroad* (1872). Chicago: Johnson, 1970.

Weaver, Hilary N. "African-Americans and Social Work: An Overview of the Antebellum through Progressive Eras." *Journal of Multicultural Social Work* 2, no. 4 (1992).

Williams, Leon F. "A Study of Discrimination in Social Work Education Programs." *Black Caucus* 14, no. 1 (Spring 1983): 9–13.

AUDREYE E. JOHNSON (1996)
Updated by publisher 2005

Sociology

This entry consists of two distinct articles. The first by James B. McKee provides an overview of the topic of sociology as it relates to the study of race and African-American culture. The second article by Lawrence D. Bobo examines sociological scholarship in the post–civil rights era.

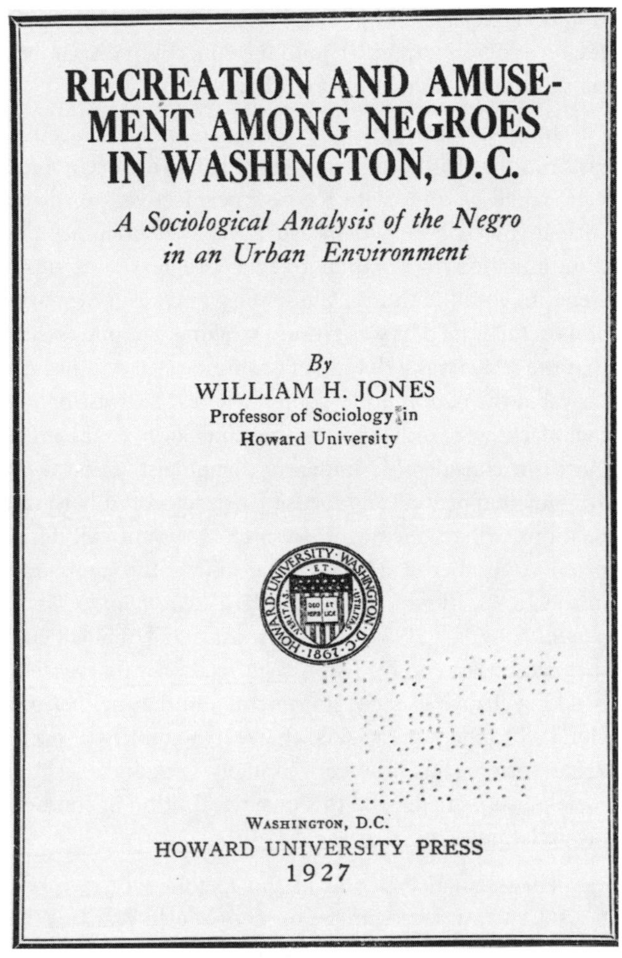

RECREATION AND AMUSEMENT AMONG NEGROES IN WASHINGTON, D.C.

A Sociological Analysis of the Negro in an Urban Environment

By
WILLIAM H. JONES
Professor of Sociology in
Howard University

WASHINGTON, D.C.
HOWARD UNIVERSITY PRESS
1927

Cover of a 1927 sociological study analyzing the various leisure activities pursued by blacks in the nation's capitol. GENERAL RESEARCH AND REFERENCE DIVISION, SCHOMBURG CENTER FOR RESEARCH IN BLACK CULTURE, THE NEW YORK PUBLIC LIBRARY, ASTOR, LENOX AND TILDEN FOUNDATIONS.

Overview

In the last two decades of the nineteenth century, the new discipline of sociology gave little attention to the race problem (or to the Negro problem; the terms were then used interchangeably) and with a very few exceptions accepted uncritically the scientific racism of the day. That racism advanced the claim that the nonwhite races were inferior to the white race by virtue of being endowed by nature with fewer of the attributes required to sustain a civilized society. In the second decade of the twentieth century, however, a new genetics invalidated biology's racial theorizing, and the study of race moved by default to the social sciences. By the 1920s most sociologists had accepted this shift from biology to culture, and a few of them began to study race as a problem in social relations.

At the outset this change in science's understanding of race had no immediate effect beyond the university environment. Racial segregation remained firmly in place, and a racially intolerant white population was unmoved by the collapse of scientific racism and continued to view the nonwhite population as innately inferior and unassimilable. Still, sociologists accepted the scientific judgment that black people were not biologically inferior, but against the arguments of anthropologists, they retained an image of them as culturally inferior. In those two decisions was the beginning of the sociology of race relations.

That beginning was shaped by a perspective rooted in an infrastructure of assumptions and values drawn from sociology's nineteenth-century typology of modern and traditional (premodern) societies, a heritage of social evolutionary thought that was still a central issue for American sociologists in the 1920s. From that perspective came two basic assumptions. The first was the inevitability of modernization —namely, that the historic sweep of urbanization, secularization, and industrialization would wash away all traditional cultures and incorporate into modern society whatever premodern peoples still existed. All people, including the nonwhite races, would need to master the demands of modern civilization.

Their second assumption spelled out the meaning of cultural inferiority: Black people were viewed as a premodern people, culturally backward by modern standards, and still isolated from the socializing currents of modern life. To sociologists that meant they were mostly uneducated, ignorant of the requirements of modern life, and beset with the vices and pathologies peculiar to the poor and ignorant. They were also portrayed as powerless by virtue of white domination and incapable of acting effectively in their own behalf or developing an adequate leadership. Nonetheless, the historic sweep toward modernity made it inevitable that black people would eventually be assimilated.

Given the implacable opposition of white Americans to racial assimilation, however, and the unreadiness of rurally isolated blacks for modern life, sociologists maintained that assimilation would not occur until some unspecified time in the future. It was to be a steady and gradual process, unmarked by large or sudden alterations of existing relations. But there were no immediate prospects of change and no reasons to try to intervene in the structure of racial segregation. Here was a cautious generation's belief in racial progress as a slow but steady process of adjustment and adaptation, not one of conflict and struggle. Until the 1960s such an outlook gave direction and purpose to the sociological study of race; then the events of that decade proved it inadequate.

Studying Race Relations

At the outset, the sociological sense of race relations was expressed by the concepts of assimilation and prejudice. Together they defined the race problem for sociologists in the 1920s: The assimilation of blacks into American society was blocked for the time by the prejudice of the white population, the overwhelming majority of whom regarded blacks as unassimilable.

Neither term was new. Assimilation had been around since the 1850s and was borrowed from sociologists who studied European immigration. Prejudice was first defined as an instinct, but with the decline of the theory of instincts it was redefined as an attitude. But the emphasis then was not on prejudice as an individual attitude (the psychologizing of the term was to come later) but as a group phenomenon; it invoked the idea of a conservative and defensive group consciousness seeking to protect the interests of an advantaged group against the disadvantaged ones.

In 1932 the concept of minority was added, to place under a single covering term the disadvantaged groups —racial, ethnic, and religious—that suffered from the prejudice of the advantaged. It offered the potential for developing an encompassing theory. But the concept was also problematic; in the minds of sociologists, there was an important distinction to be made between the descendants of African slaves and the immigrants from Europe. The two had reached the United States under different historical circumstances, and their futures also seemed to be different. Assimilation was already under way for the recent immigrants but seemed far off for black people. The matter was resolved by the adoption of the paired concepts race and ethnicity.

This also reflected, however, a narrow conception of culture. Although sociologists understood that culture was humanly created, it was nonetheless defined primarily as a social inheritance passed from one generation to the next. Culture is not only inherited, however, it is also created anew under changed circumstances. In their long endurance of slavery and segregation, blacks created themselves as a single people with a distinct culture of their own making. But in the 1920s sociologists, with the exception of Robert Park, had no comprehension of this.

The now familiar concepts of segregation and discrimination entered the sociological vocabulary later. In the 1930s segregation was still constitutionally sanctioned and accepted as the common status of black people. The concept of discrimination was only rarely used, since the unequal treatment of black people was expected and taken for granted. Only later, when segregation and discrimination became legal and political issues, did the terms enter the sociological vocabulary and the concept of discrimination become paired with prejudice.

In the 1930s, with a new vocabulary at hand, sociologists produced a substantial body of work that exemplified what could be done with the new perspective. Consistent with it, they developed measurements of prejudice and discrimination to document racial progress as a steady trendline into the future. While the work was informative and useful, little of it was groundbreaking. Despite the fact that the 1930s was a decade of economic and political upheaval in the nation undergoing the Great Depression and that blacks were moving from the rural South to the urban North in considerable numbers, sociologists resisted examining that process and focused instead on southern race relations, where, they claimed, a caste system still dominated. A number of studies of black life in the rural South in the 1930s, of which John Dollard's *Caste and Class in a Southern Town* (1937) was the most noted, made it clear that race relations were still caste relations, that system-breaking change was not imminent, and that neither precipitate change nor racial conflict seemed likely to occur. A few sociologists, however—notably Park and the black sociologists—challenged this characterization of southern race relations.

This formative period in the sociology of race relations drew to a close with the onset of World War II. What sociology had to say about race relations was summarized in Gunnar Myrdal's mammoth study *An American Dilemma* (1944), undoubtedly the most widely read study on race relations in the United States. Myrdal did three things: He advanced a controversial thesis that race relations were a contradiction between America's democratic ideals and its racial beliefs and practices (that was the "dilemma"); he summarized and assessed what sociologists claimed to know about race relations; and, reflecting his role as a European social democrat and social planner, he criticized American sociologists for not advocating social policies that would change existing race relations. Although Myrdal had little effect on the generation that had produced the work summarized in *An American Dilemma,* he did encourage an oncoming generation that had been raised on the social policies and programs of the New Deal to believe that intervention to change race relations was now possible. It encouraged sociologists, therefore, to move closer to the racial liberals.

Perhaps the least satisfactory aspect of Myrdal's work was his seemingly uncritical acceptance of the denigrating image of the black American from the prevailing sociological literature. While Myrdal did not deny that black people had been culturally innovative, he viewed their innovation as a secondary reaction of the powerless to the primary action of the powerful. But mere reaction did not provide an adequate recognition of the social factors that gave cultural distinctiveness to American blacks. From his reading of the book, the distinguished black novelist Ralph Ellison made this often cited comment in *Shadow and Act* (1964):

> But can a people (its faith in an idealized American Creed nothwithstanding) live and develop for over three hundred years simply by reacting? Are American Negroes simply the creation of white men, or have they at least helped to create themselves out of what they have found around them? Men have made a life in caves and upon cliffs, why cannot Negroes have made a way of life upon the horns of the white man's dilemma?

The Black Sociologists

In the first half of the twentieth century, white sociologists did little to penetrate into the separate communities created by blacks as a consequence of segregation. What was known about blacks came mostly from aggregates of statistical data or from observations of blacks in public, white-controlled places. It became the task of the first black sociologists to reveal the internal structure of black social life and, in doing so, to create a more adequate image of American blacks *as a people.*

The work of black sociologists made evident a perspective on race relations different from that of white sociologists. Although both of them understood that black people wanted the opportunities denied them, white sociologists did not seem to understand what black sociologists knew full well: that black people did not want to so fully assimilate as to disappear as a people; that race pride and a lasting resentment at white oppression had produced a distinctive set of attitudes among black people; and that nationalistic, nonassimilative ideas were emerging among young, educated blacks. Furthermore, black sociologists did not, as did their white colleagues, regard efforts at political reform as illusory; instead, they took them seriously. That was because they were more sensitive than white sociologists to the consequences of economic and demographic change in the United States, in particular the urbanization of black people, for change in race relations. In turn, they viewed the white sociologists' fascination with caste as an illusion of stability in the face of oncoming change.

Two black sociologists, E. Franklin Frazier and Charles S. Johnson, were soon recognized by their white peers as scholars of the first rank. In such books as *The Negro Family in the United States* (1939) and *Negro Youth at the Crossways* (1940), Frazier made a compelling case for understanding black Americans in terms of their life-shaping experiences from slavery to segregation and in the movement from rural South to urban North and not of biology or the residues of an African heritage. For all who would look to see, he revealed the complexity and distinctiveness of black life in the organization of black communities and in the black class structure.

Charles S. Johnson's *Shadow of the Plantation* (1934) provided a compelling study of black rural life in Alabama in the early 1930s, noting that little had changed since slavery and that the harsh conditions of life for black Americans denied the myth of the spontaneous and happy black. In similar fashion, his *Growing Up in the Black Belt* (1941) revealed the growing aspirations of black youth in the Deep South and their deepening resentment at the treatment of them by white people, while his *Patterns of Negro Segregation* (1943) laid bare the harsh reality of racial segregation.

In 1945 a study began in the 1930s provided the first detailed examination of black life in the urban North. In *Black Metropolis,* St. Clair Drake and Horace Cayton described "Bronzeville," the black community of Chicago of the 1930s and '40s. It was a large, inclusive work unlike anything before it, a true classic of the field, and the crowning achievement of the prewar black sociologists.

White sociologists read and appreciated the works of black sociologists, especially those of Johnson and Frazier, but they read them selectively, taking what fitted their perspective on race relations and of blacks as a people. They possessed, in short, a mental outlook that left them unable to grasp the full message of the black sociologists. As a consequence, despite the efforts of black sociologists, an inadequate and selective image of the black American remained a basic feature of the sociology of race relations.

Robert Park: An Unrealized Perspective

At the University of Chicago, Frazier and Johnson were students of Robert Park, whose pioneering work did more to develop the sociology of race relations than that of any other sociologist. Park provided the definitive statement on assimilation, developed his well-known race relations cycle, promoted the idea of prejudice as social attitude, and invented the concept of social distance. Yet these contributions, readily accepted by sociologists, were not all that Park had to offer.

When other sociologists saw black people as a quiescent and backward population not yet ready for modern society, Park saw them as a race-conscious people involved, like the national minorities of Eastern Europe, in a struggle for independence. He placed the American race problem within a world process of racial and ethnic conflict and change, where subject peoples sought independence and self-determination. That made of race relations a continuing field of conflict. For Park, this was not to be deplored because it was a stage in the eventual assimilation of the world's peoples into a common culture and a common historical life.

But all of this was far beyond the parochial worldview of Park's sociological colleagues. As a consequence, a perspective that gave promise of anticipating and better understanding the emergence of a black-led Civil Rights Movement and preparing the nation for significant changes in race relations went unrealized.

The Postwar Sociology of Race Relations

In the 1940s and '50s there was a rush of political and legal actions, neither predicted nor anticipated by sociologists, that changed some basic aspects of race relations and led to expectations of even further changes. Among these were the 1941 March on Washington movement, which led to President Franklin D. Roosevelt's executive order forbidding discrimination in defense industries and which, after the war, stimulated political efforts to promote fair employment practices; the Detroit Riot of 1943 which stimulated the formation of local groups to deal with racial tension in the community; President Harry S. Truman's desegregation of the armed forces; the U.S. Supreme Court's decision rendering restrictive racial convenants illegal and the consequent liberal effort to abolish segregated housing; and the Court's decision in *Brown v. Board of Education of Topeka, Kansas,* to desegregate the public schools. These changes signified that race was finally on the liberal agenda and that the nation was making its first moves to eliminate the established pattern of racial segregation.

In the face of such changes, a new postwar generation of sociologists abandoned the politically detached position of the prewar generation and tried to shift sociology from the "objective" study of race relations to race as a problem in applied research, in service to the liberal activists and the professional practitioners of intergroup relations. It was also an experiment in bringing together scholar and practitioner, in uniting theory and practice.

But it never worked. One reason was that the professionals were too politically constrained by their social agencies; what they could do in practice was limited by what was acceptable to their governing boards. In the public agencies, among a diverse set of politically appointed community representatives, there were always some who were cautious about, if not unsupportive of, decisive action. To work with professional agencies, therefore, was to seek no more change than the civic elite that controlled those agencies was willing to undertake. There was no consideration of organizing a constituency among nonelite groups or of linking the objectives of intergroup relations with other social causes. It was also the case that a sociology that studied social roles in stable structures had difficulty analyzing the more fluid dynamics of racial conflict and change.

The attempt to construct an applied sociology of race relations and to participate in the liberal effort at racial change did not last long. It emerged in the first decade after the war and then vanished almost without a trace with the coming of the black-led civil rights struggle in the 1960s.

Beyond Prejudice

In the 1950s social psychologists went beyond the measurement of prejudice to examine the relation of race to personality. One direction of study saw prejudice in some whites as an expression of a deeply rooted psychological need, which often led to the projection of hostility on a socially acceptable target such as a racial minority. Such individuals exemplified the authoritarian personality: antidemocratic, rigidly inflexible, and admiring of power. A decade of supporting research claimed that these more prejudiced individuals were likely to be people of lesser social status: the less educated, the working class, the lower class. Whereas prewar sociologists had viewed the whole of the white population as prejudiced, a postwar generation saw racial bias differing by social class. An educated middle class, it seemed, was tolerant and racially progressive, while classes below them were not. This quickly became a fixed element in sociological (and liberal) thought.

While research does indeed show that middle-class whites will more readily endorse principles of equal rights, it also finds that, when it comes to implementation, the difference between the middle class and other classes decreases and even disappears. It also declines when the proportion of blacks increases, and it disappears when blacks become a majority. Sociologists' belief in a racially unprejudiced middle class, it now seems, is unwarranted and has provided no basis for a workable strategy of action.

In 1958 the sociologist Herbert Blumer suggested that prejudice is a sense of group position, not a set of feelings the individuals of one group hold toward those of another. A group's position in the racial order, he argued, produced a proprietary claim to privilege and prerogative, and prejudice emerged when that position was threatened. What Blumer had done was return to the earlier idea of prejudice as defense of social advantage. But sociologists made no effort to develop Blumer's conception of prejudice and its promise of a better way to explain race prejudice among social classes.

The relation between prejudice and discrimination and the proclaimed inverse relation between prejudice and social class were easily incorporated into the postwar sociology of race relations. So was another idea: that the firm exercise of authority over recalcitrant whites was necessary to attain racial change. An idea first applied to crowd situations with a potential for violence came to be applied to conflicts over desegregation where, it was believed, the firm exercise of authority would prevent resistance from being effective. Given the fact that sociologists defined the prejudiced person as primarily coming from the working and lower classes, the idea of the firm exercise of authority followed logically.

These were social psychological studies of white people, but sociologists had often commented about the psychological damage done to black people by a racially oppressive environment. In the 1930s one sociologist suggested that blacks suffered from an "oppression psychosis," and in the 1940s another claimed that "personality disorders" were one of the pathologies to be found among black people. The most influential expression of this view came in 1951 when the psychiatrists Abram Kardiner and Lionel Ovesey argued, in *The Mark of Oppression,* that the persistent and pervasive consequence of discrimination had a thoroughly destructive effect on the psychological development of black people.

The image of the black person that emerged from their study was that of a psychological cripple: a mentally unhealthy person given to low self-esteem and self-hatred, to resentment, rage, and an aggression for which there was no safe outlet. Blacks, the authors asserted, lacked any "genuine religiosity," had created no religion of their own, and had been unable to develop their own culture. They bolstered their self-esteem with compensatory activities such as flashy dressing, gambling, taking drugs, and vindictive behavior toward one another.

Perhaps the most damning claim the authors made was that American blacks were incapable of the social cohesion that would enable them to act collectively in their own interests. They traced this back to the severe limitations on personal development imposed by slavery and segregation. The frustrations of childhood, they insisted, produced a distrusting personality lacking confidence in human relations.

Kardiner and Ovesey were not intent on condemning blacks for their deficiencies but on demonstrating the "marks" of oppression under which blacks were forced to live. Nonetheless, their message was that blacks were so victimized by this oppression that they were unable to act in their own behalf and required the assistance of sympathetic whites. Only their oppressors, it seemed, could also be their liberators. For sociologists the book became a seminal work that rounded out their conception of American blacks.

No one can deny that oppression leaves a distorting mark on the human personality. But it is not the case that such oppression can fully and forever cripple the human spirit or leave a people permanently unable to act on its own behalf. Even in the most destructive of environments, a people will create the cultural resources for sustaining hope and preserving a decent sense of their own humanity. From the days of slavery, black Americans did that. Through religion and music they created life-sustaining forces to offset the pain evident in everyday life, while the black church became a force for leadership, for sustaining family, and for building community. But none of this evidence was noted by Kardiner and Ovesey.

Nor did any of this appear in the sociological literature. There was no work to identify and measure cultural resources by which blacks could defend their very humanity against the crippling effects of oppression. Nor did the literature imagine the possibility of black-directed social action. Yet in the 1950s it was already late in the day to be so unaware of the gathering storm already developing in the South.

A Failed Perspective

In the early 1960s that storm of protest and revolt swept through the South and then spread northward, bringing on a decade of black-led civil rights revolution and ending forever the prevailing structure of racial segregation. But the sociologists had provided no warning that such was to occur; a reading of the sociological literature, in fact, would lead one to believe that such was not going to happen. It became painfully obvious to some thoughtful sociologists of race relations that their work could no longer explain what was going on in the world of racial interests and actions. The race relations that appeared in their writings bore little resemblance to the race relations taking shape around them.

Perhaps the greater failure of those writings was their denigrating and inadequate conception of black people as culturally inferior and therefore incapable of acting effectively on their own behalf. The civil rights revolution of the 1960s dispelled that idea once and for all. But it was not until the 1970s that sociologists could acknowledge that blacks were a people with a distinct culture formed in the oppressive heat of slavery and segregation.

Also found wanting was sociology's confident faith that the inevitable outcome of modernization was a steady dissipation of prejudice and discrimination, a gradual assimilation of blacks into the society, and in time, a disappearance of black people as a distinct people. Instead, a heightened race consciousness prevails among black Americans, ethnicity has experienced a worldwide resurgence, and a multicultural movement has arisen to celebrate ethnicity and to seek legal and institutional means to ensure the persistence of ethnic cultures. Furthermore, belief in a progressively more rational social order is now doubted by many and disbelieved by some.

Over the past quarter century sociologists have continued to measure prejudice, discrimination, and still-existing segregation, but they have done little else to inform and educate the citizenry or the political, civic, and educational leadership. Now, late in the twentieth century, the contemporary discourse between white and black and within both races is discordant and without consensus on what to do. New developments, such as the emerging global economy and a new wave of immigration, make more complex the social context in which race relations are embedded. The task for sociologists is to do more than measure prejudice and discrimination, useful as that still is; they must provide analyses that take adequate account of these complexities while finding in them possibilities for racial progress.

See also Cayton, Horace; Drake, St. Clair; Frazier, Edward Franklin; Johnson, Charles Spurgeon; Race, Scientific Theories of; Social Psychology, Psychologists, and Race

Bibliography

Alexander, Rudolph. *Racism, African Americans, and Social Justice.* Lanham, Md.: Rowman & Littlefield, 2005.

Blumer, Herbert. "Race Prejudice as a Sense of Group Position." *Pacific Sociological Review* 1 (1956).

Conyers, James L., and Alva P. Barnett, eds. *African American Sociology: A Social Study of the Pan-African Diaspora.* Chicago: Nelson-Hall Publishers, 1999.

Dollard, John. *Caste and Class in a Southern Town.* New Haven, Conn., 1937. Reprint. New Haven, Conn.: Yale University Press, 1998.

Drake, St. Clair, and Horace R. Cayton. *Black Metropolis: A Study of Negro Life in a Northern City.* New York, 1945. Rev. ed. Chicago: University of Chicago Press, 1993.

Ellison, Ralph. *Shadow and Act.* New York: Vintage International, 1995.

Frazier, E. Franklin. *Negro Youth at the Crossways: Their Personality Development in the Middle States.* Washington, D.C.: American Council on Education, 1940.

Frazier, E. Franklin. *The Negro Family in the United States.* Chicago, 1939. Reprint. South Bend, Ind.: University of Notre Dame Press, 2001.

Hare, Bruce R., ed. *2001 Race Odyssey: African Americans and Sociology.* Syracuse, N.Y.: Syracuse University Press, 2002.

Johnson, Charles S. *Growing Up in the Black Belt: Negro Youth in the Rural South.* Washington, D.C.: American Council on Education, 1941.

Johnson, Charles S. *Patterns of Negro Segregation.* New York: London, Harper & Brothers, 1943.

Johnson, Charles S. *Shadow of the Plantation.* Chicago, 1934. Reprint. New Brunswick, N.J.: Transaction Publishers, 1996.

Kardiner, Abram, and Lionel Ovesey. *The Mark of Oppression: A Psychosocial Study of the American Negro.* New York: Norton, 1951.

McKee, James B. *Sociology and the Race Problem: The Failure of a Perspective.* Urbana: University of Illinois Press, 1993.

Myrdal, Gunnar, with Richard Sterner and Arnold Rose. *An American Dilemma: The Negro Problem and Modern Democracy.* New York, 1944. Reprint. New Brunswick, N.J.: Transaction Publishers, 1996.

Outlaw, Lucius T. Critical *Social Theory in the Interest of Black Folk.* Lanham, Md.: Rowman & Littlefield Publishers, 2005.

Park, Robert. *Race and Culture.* Glencoe, Ill.: Free Press, 1950.

Thompson, Kenneth, ed. *The Early Sociology of Race and Ethnicity.* New York: Routledge, 2005.

Trotter, Joe W., Eral Lewis, Tera W. Hunter, eds. *The African American Urban Experience: Perspectives from the Colonial Period to the Present.* New York: Palgrave Macmillan, 2004.

JAMES B. MCKEE (1996)
Updated bibliography

Scholarship in the Post–Civil Rights Era

Although sociologists did not anticipate the emergence of a sustained nonviolent movement for civil rights, they played pivotal roles in three major sets of public policy discussions launched in the mid to late 1960s. A key case in point is Harvard sociologist (then an advisor to the Lyndon B. Johnson administration) Daniel Patrick Moynihan's infamous report, "The Negro Family: The Case for National Action," issued in 1965. Drawing attention to a growing rate of single-parent female-headed households among blacks, and characterizing this circumstance as correlated with a set of unwanted conditions best understood as "a tangle of pathology," Moynihan ignited a fierce debate on black family life, gender roles, and their influence on issues of black socioeconomic attainment (Rainwater and Yancey, 1967).

In 1966 the massive "Equality of Educational Opportunity" report, prepared under the leadership of sociologist James Coleman and statistician Ernest Campbell, sparked further controversy over the roles of schools and school resources in determining race differences in schooling outcomes. To the surprise of many at the time, the report documented much smaller gaps between black students and white students in school resources and expenditures than anticipated (in part, ironically, because of the NAACP's long-fought and successful legal challenges to "separate but equal" practices, which forced change in many southern states). Moreover, the report undermined the assumption that school expenditures were a key index of school quality, finding instead that family background was much more important to student attainment and achievement.

Then, in 1968, the U.S. National Advisory Commission on Civil Disorders, known as the Kerner Commission after former Illinois governor Otto Kerner (1908–1976), who chaired the commission, issued its extensive assessment of the urban riots that so defined major American cities in the summer of 1967. The report characterized the United States as "two nations, black and white, separate and unequal." It went on to unambiguously fault white racism for the great racial schism in the social fabric.

Both the Moynihan report and the Coleman report, as well as, in a fashion, the Kerner Commission report, occasioned intense controversy, often bitterly acrimonious debate, and reevaluation. The disputes over the theoretical interpretation of social science findings and the remarkable intensity of feeling aroused by the reports also raised doubts about the capacity of social science to directly inform public policy. Emblematic of the intellectual intensity of the times was the influential volume *The Death of White Sociology* (1973), edited by Joyce Ladner. Yet, each of these ambitious reports identified themes, problems, and types of analyses that continue to influence scholarship, and they arguably assumed even greater scholarly importance in the late 1970s and into the present. To wit, this set of studies can be read as defining a still-important spectrum of analyses of racial inequality that sought the main causes of black disadvantage either in the dynamics and function of black families, communities, and culture (Moynihan and Coleman) or in the basic racist structural organization of American society and institutions (Kerner).

Over the course of the 1970s, sociology took a decided turn away from theories of social consensus in general and a focus on prejudice and discrimination in particular as lenses through which to interpret the black experience. Instead, theories of group conflict, internal colonialism, racial oppression, and power and ideology rose to prominence. And sociologists looking at black families and communities increasingly emphasized the resilience and resources of blacks in effectively adapting to the challenges of persistent inequality and racist conditions. Eventually, the research took on a much more structuralist, economy-centered, historical, and often comparative scope. For example, Pierre van den Berghe (1967) and Hubert Blalock (1967) developed important theoretical statements in the 1960s. These came to be focused and amplified in the 1970s by scholars such as Robert Blauner (1972), William Julius Wilson (1973), and Edna Bonacich (1972) who developed analyses of racial antagonism that were focused on the labor market.

This intellectual emphasis on the economy, racism, and structures of racial oppression was decisively reshaped by the publication in 1978 of William Julius Wilson's *The Declining Significance of Race: Blacks and Changing American Institutions.* Adopting a Weberian conception of class and with a focus on the fundamental intersection of the economy and the polity, Wilson boldly declared that the life chances of black Americans were no longer determined by race but rather by the class attributes they brought to the labor market. In a trenchantly argued work, Wilson suggested that three great epochs defined the black experience, with race clearly determining the life chances of most blacks in the first two stages—slavery and the early- and early-modern industrial stages. However, class, rather than race, rose to predominant importance in the third or modern and post-industrial phase.

Wilson's analysis became the subject of misappropriation from academics and others on the right, great praise and respect from a broad interdisciplinary center, and vituperative attack from those on the left, especially the black left. The latter included a regrettable formal vote of censure against Wilson by the Association of Black Sociologists, which reacted mainly against the title rather than the substance of Wilson's argument. The nearly decade-long debate in sociology on "the declining significance of race thesis" did, however, yield important insights about the need to think in terms of the intersection and interaction of race and class, rather than in terms of analyses that afforded one factor transparent primacy over the other.

In 1980 Wilson issued a second edition of the book, which dealt with some of the early criticism of his work. In particular, he took to task those who offered simplistic readings of the complex argument he had made or who treated racism and discrimination in a monolithic fashion that failed to account for the growing class differentiation within the black community. His rejoinder also signaled his next focus—the urban poor in black America—a subject for which he would once again come to redefine the scholarly agenda across the social sciences (Wilson, 1980).

The 1980s saw the rise to the presidency of Ronald Reagan (1911–2004). This ascendancy of conservative Republicans brought a new prominence and influence for scholars and think tanks on the right. Prominent among these right-wing scholars was Charles Murray, who published *Losing Ground: American Social Policy, 1950–1980* (1984), an anti-welfare tract putatively rooted in the canons of social science. Although Murray's analysis became the object of much criticism, the book lent legitimacy to a conservative cultural view of a set of social ills dominating public attention and associated with poor, urban, black communities. These problems included steadily rising rates of single-parent female-headed households, juvenile delinquency, high school dropouts, drug use, violent crime, unemployment, poverty, and long-term welfare dependency. Murray, and such fellow conservatives as political scientist Lawrence Mead (1992), faulted the permissive values and social policies of the 1960s' "Great Society" and "War on Poverty" eras for having undermined individual self-reliance and respect for conventional mainstream values.

Among the significant sociological works to appear in his era was Stanley Lieberson's *A Piece of the Pie: Blacks and White Immigrants Since 1880* (1980). This broad-ranging work took up the "immigrant analogy" hypothesis, which maintained that blacks would experience the same social mobility as European immigrant groups. The argument was read by many as one variant of a conservative position that saw racism, discrimination, and racial inequality as of steadily and inevitably waning importance in the United States. Lieberson's detailed analysis documented the myriad ways in which African Africans in the mid-1800s through the early decades of the twentieth century were more severely disadvantaged and faced more durable barriers to mobility than various southern, central, and eastern European immigrant groups. His work called into question any easy assumption of parallel trajectories of progress.

Despite Lieberson's convincing analysis, the larger conservative framework still dominated. Many scholars sought to challenge these approaches and the influence they exerted in policy-making circles. The most influential such work again came from William Julius Wilson with the publication in 1987 of *The Truly Disadvantaged: The Inner City, the Underclass, and Public Policy*. Wilson spoke directly about issues of crime, out-of-wedlock childbirth, and welfare dependency—the whole complex of problems seen as defining urban inner-city life. Dismissing as outdated the left's analysis from the perspective of racism and discrimination, as well as the right's analysis from the perspective of individual values and culture as ahistorical, factually wrong, and victim-blaming, Wilson developed a three-part argument. He proposed, first, that America's urban centers had witnessed the emergence of a new urban underclass, a truly disadvantaged group. These inner-city black residents, by virtue of historic discrimination, had low skill levels and were not well positioned to respond to profound changes in the structure of the economy.

Second, Wilson argued that inner-city areas were losing the sort of well-paid, low-skill, unionized jobs that once characterized life in the big cities. This was occurring because of the deconcentration of industry as heavy-goods production and manufacturing moved increasingly from proximity to central city cores to suburban and exurban locations. More importantly, this job loss occurred because of the deindustrialization of the American economy, especially in urban centers, as part of a major shift toward service-oriented, information-processing, technology-related high-skill work. This confluence of circumstances resulted in a skills/spatial mismatch wherein low-skill, inner-city blacks were less and less competitive for the high-skill, high-wage jobs (e.g., in banking, finance, law, communications, etc.) available in central city areas. A major consequence of economic restructuring of this kind and scale was a rising rate of black male joblessness, with long-term unemployment and bleak employment prospects becoming commonplace. Joblessness not only heightened the experience of poverty, but it reduced the likelihood of marriage for both black men and women. Wilson argued that men are reluctant to marry when they cannot provide economically for a family, and women do not find men with severely limited employment prospects to be promising marriage partners.

Third, these circumstances resulted in the profound social disorganization of communities, according to Wilson, because the underclass suffered great isolation from mainstream social values. Underclass communities involved areas of extremely high concentrations of poverty, where 40 percent or more of the residents were below the poverty level. Contributing to this growing isolation for the underclass was a greater mobility for middle-class and skilled working-class blacks who were able to leave inner-city ghetto communities due to opportunities afforded by the successes of affirmative action and the civil rights movement. Those left behind were the poorest of the poor. This is the mix that Wilson associated with welfare dependency, out-of-wedlock childbirths, juvenile delinquency, and crime.

The Truly Disadvantaged initiated a wave of research on ghetto poverty; predictably, Wilson's book also garnered intense controversy. Urban ethnographers, theorists, survey researchers, and economists all tackled aspects of Wilson's call for a focus on the new urban poverty. Three aspects of the subsequent research and controversy are worthy of extended consideration in this entry because they came to change the intellectual landscape. One of the first lines of sustained critique of Wilson came from Herbert Gans (1995), who took strong objection to the use of the term *underclass*, suggesting that it was merely another stigmatizing epithet that encouraged focusing on the behavior of individuals rather than the structural circumstance of groups and communities. And certainly there were many commentators on the right who used Wilson's terminology in this fashion, ignoring much of the rich sociological context and argumentation he advanced. Wilson ultimately moved away from using the term *underclass*, preferring instead the *ghetto poor* or *ghetto poverty*, in an effort to emphasize the properties of such structural placements in the economy.

A second major line of criticism faulted Wilson for failing to deal with racial residential segregation. In a major book, *American Apartheid: Segregation and the Making of the Underclass* (1993), sociologists Douglas S. Massey and Nancy A. Denton argued that the racial segregation of communities was the key factor in the rise of concentrated ghetto poverty. On the basis of careful historical, demographic, and econometric simulation analyses, they showed how the emergence and maintenance of racial barriers in the housing market were critical to the development of extremely disadvantaged inner-city communities. As a result, they also pointed out the strong contemporary relevance of racial discrimination in the housing market to larger patterns of modern inequality, thereby resuscitating a focus on processes of discrimination.

A third line of scholarship pointed to the modern potency (not merely historic effects) of racial discrimination in many domains of social life, including the labor market. Ironically, even Wilson's own "Urban Poverty and Family Life Survey of Chicago" (1987) conducted extensive interviews with employers in Chicago and found them to hold clearly negative stereotypes of black workers, especially black men. Employers also engaged in a series of practices to limit or exclude black workers. Careful auditing studies, which involved sending out matched pairs of black job applicants and white job applicants with equivalent resumes, showed significant anti-black (and anti-Latino/a) bias. Sociologist Joe Feagin identified numerous other domains, such as stores, restaurants, and other public spaces, where African Americans reported experiencing racial bias (Feagin and Sikes, 1994; Feagin 2000).

Entrenched ghetto poverty, persistent racial residential segregation and the housing discrimination critical to its maintenance, and ongoing racial bias in the labor market and other spheres of life prompted renewed attention to negative racial attitudes, prejudice, and stereotyping. Thus, a major study carried out by the General Social Survey of the National Opinion Research Center (NORC) at the University of Chicago pointed to the persistence of negative images of blacks among whites (see Bobo, Kluegel, and Smith, 1997), with such negative stereotypes playing an important role in public thinking about how social policy should (or should not) respond to inequality (Bobo and Kluegel, 1993; Gilens, 1999). This survey would be reinforced by scholarship in social psychology pointing to the widespread but deeply implicit and often unconscious basis of negative racial stereotypes.

Another analytical innovation in the 1990s involved renewed attention to matters of wealth inequality as central to the modern problem of racial inequality. The most important and influential work in this area was Melvin Oliver and Thomas Shapiro's *Black Wealth/White Wealth: A New Perspective on Racial Inequality* (1995). Oliver and Shapiro argued that wealth, the accumulated financial assets a person has, is more important to the capacity to maintain a particular standard of living than income or earnings per se. Critically, they documented that, as of the late 1980s, a vast gap of nearly 12-to-1 separated the median financial assets of blacks from those of whites. To wit, for roughly every ten cents of wealth in black hands, whites had slightly more than a dollar. Oliver and Shapiro also reported that in 1989 the median net worth of black households in the United States was approximately $3,700, as compared to $43,800 for white households. The figures for net financial assets, with debts subtracted, were $6,999 for whites and effectively $0 for blacks.

Furthermore, Oliver and Shapiro showed that even young, dual-income black couples lagged far behind whites in wealth (hence, even post–civil rights movement, high-achieving blacks suffered an enormous wealth gap with whites). This was true even though blacks and whites saved at roughly the same rates and even when matched in occupational or educational attainment. The critical reason for this disparity is that much wealth is inherited, not earned via an individual's schooling or wages from work. Oliver and Shapiro attributed the black/white wealth gap to: (1) racialized state policies that systematically excluded African Americans from many opportunities for government-sponsored asset-building opportunities that many whites benefited from (e.g., home mortgage discrimination practices in the 1930s through 1950s); (2) violence and other acts of bias directed at successful black entrepreneurship; and (3) the sedimentation of inequality whereby disadvantages are reinforced and accumulate over time.

Greater attention to theorizing race and racism also started to assume prominence in the later 1980s. A key work here was Michael Omi and Howard Winant's *Racial Formation in the United States* (1986). They suggested that racial phenomena were historically contingent and "made" as part of racializing projects, a theme now broadly resonant in the field. Their work, along with that of other scholars, such as Jonathan Stone and David Theo Goldberg, helped to elevate the examination of race and ethnicity to new theoretical prominence within the discipline.

The 1990s also witnessed the emergence of a whole new line of scholarship focusing on whiteness. Whiteness studies took up historical tracing of the development of whiteness as a privileged social status. Sometimes focused on particular ethnic whites (Ignatiev, 1995), the working class in general (Roediger, 1991), or European ethnics in general (Jacobson, 1998; Allen, 1994 and 1997), scholars traced how would-be peers and allies of blacks embraced the offer of skin-privilege in the American racial hierarchy instead. The work has helped to refocus scholarly attention beyond the circumstances of blacks and black communities to a larger perspective on how race itself is enacted and experienced on both sides of the color line.

Another important trend of the 1990s involved examinations of the place of African Americans in increasingly multiethnic, multiracial urban spaces. To some degree, this work developed in response to instances of overt conflict and tension, such as occurred between African-American communities and immigrant Korean merchants in a number of communities. These tensions were, of course, one of the simmering resentments set aflame in Los Angeles in 1992 following the acquittal of the four white police officers who were video-taped beating black motorist Rodney King. But this expanded scope was also accelerated by such developments as the introduction by the U.S. Census Bureau of the option of identifying with more than one race, arguably lending even greater legitimacy to those attempting to claim a mixed- or multiracial identity. And immigration was also serving to make the country's African-ancestry population more diverse as blacks from the Caribbean and Africa continued to immigrate to the United States.

Over the twentieth century, sociology moved very far from the posture of paying little or no attention to matters of race and offering unreflective acceptance of prevailing racist assumptions. Indeed, matters of race moved to a place of increasing prominence in the discipline, with a number of scholars becoming major students of race and ethnic relations; these scholars included Wilson, Lieberson, Massey, and Feagin, all of whom served as president of the American Sociological Association. Sociology also became one of the primary sites of intellectual analysis and critique of racism. And scholars in the field occupy a far more prominent place in public and policy-making discourse than they typically held in the past.

The study of issues of race, especially the African-American experience, remains a site of controversy. Debates and contestation continue over how to conceptualize race and racism; over the relative weight to attach to prejudice and discrimination as compared to economic, political, and other structural constraints; and, of course, over the extent to which persistent racial inequality is traceable to the choices, behavior, and culture of African Americans as compared to the structures and ideology of racial oppression. While there is no consensus theory of race, the approach to issues of race in sociology is more central, seasoned, empirically grounded, influential, and informed by the work of minority as well as nonminority scholars than ever before. Given other trends in the discipline toward the use of multiple-method designs and comparative scope, there are grounds to be optimistic about future theory development and about the likelihood of sociology having a significant impact on public policy and producing important societal outcomes.

See also Economic Condition, U.S.; Educational Psychology and Psychologists; Education in the United States; Kerner Report; Social Psychology, Psychologists, and Race

Bibliography

Allen, Theodore W. *The Invention of the White Race*, Vol. 1: *Racial Oppression and Social Control*. London and New York: Verso, 1994.

Allen, Theodore W. *The Invention of the White Race*, Vol. 2: *The Origin of Racial Oppression in Anglo-America*. London and New York: Verso, 1997.

Blalock, Hubert M. *Toward a Theory of Minority-Group Relations*. New York: Wiley, 1967.

Blauner, Robert. *Racial Oppression in America*. New York: Harper, 1972.

Bobo, Lawrence D., and James R. Kluegel. "Opposition to Race Targeting: Self-Interest, Stratification Ideology, or Racial Attitudes." *American Sociological Review* 58 (1993): 443–464.

Bobo, Lawrence D., James R. Kluegel, and Ryan A. Smith. "Laissez Faire Racism: The Crystallization of a 'Kinder, Gentler' Anti-Black Ideology." In *Racial Attitudes in the 1990s: Continuity and Change*, edited by Steven A. Tuch and Jack K. Martin. Westport, Conn.: Praeger, 1997.

Bonacich, Edna. "A Theory of Ethnic Antagonism: The Split Labor Market." *American Sociological Review* 37 (1972): 547.

Coleman, James Samuel, et al. *Equality of Educational Opportunity*. Washington, D.C.: U.S. Dept. of Health, Education, and Welfare, Office of Education, 1966.

Feagin, Joe R. *Racist America: Roots, Current Realities, and Future Reparations*. New York: Routledge, 2000.

Feagin, Joe R., and Melvin P. Sikes. *Living with Racism: The Black Middle-Class Experience*. Boston: Beacon, 1994.

Gans, Herbert J. *The War Against the Poor: The Underclass and Antipoverty Policy*. New York: Basic Books, 1995.

Gilens, Martin. *Why Americans Hate Welfare: Race, Media, and the Politics of Antipoverty Policy*. Chicago: University of Chicago Press, 1999.

Goldberg, David Theo. *Racist Culture: Philosophy and the Politics of Meaning*. Oxford and Cambridge, Mass.: Blackwell, 1993.

Ignatiev, Noel. *How the Irish Became White*. New York: Routledge, 1995.

Jacobson, Matthew Frye. *Whiteness of a Different Color: European Immigrants and the Alchemy of Race*. Cambridge, Mass.: Harvard University Press, 1998.

Ladner, Joyce A. *The Death of White Sociology*. New York: Random House, 1973.

Lieberson, Stanley A. *A Piece of the Pie: Blacks and White Immigrants Since 1880*. Berkeley: University of California Press, 1980.

Massey, Douglas S., and Nancy A. Denton. *American Apartheid: Segregation and the Making of the Underclass*. Cambridge, Mass.: Harvard University Press, 1993.

Mead, Lawrence M. *The New Politics of Poverty: The Nonworking Poor in America*. New York: Basic Books, 1992.

Moynihan, Daniel Patrick. *The Negro Family: The Case for National Action*. Washington, D.C.: U.S. Department of Labor, Office of Policy Planning and Research, 1965. Available from <http://www.dol.gov/asp/programs/history/webid-meynihan.htm>.

Murray, Charles A. *Losing Ground: American Social Policy, 1950–1980*. New York: Basic Books, 1984.

National Advisory Commission on Civil Disorders. *The Kerner Report: The 1968 Report of the National Advisory Commission on Civil Disorders*. New York: Pantheon, 1988.

Oliver, Melvin L., and Thomas M. Shapiro. *Black Wealth/White Wealth: A New Perspective on Racial Inequality*. New York: Routledge, 1995.

Omi, Michael, and Howard Winant. *Racial Formation in the United States: From the 1960s to the 1980s*. New York: Routledge & Kegan Paul, 1986.

Rainwater, Lee, and William L. Yancey. *The Moynihan Report and the Politics of Controversy: A Trans-action Social Science and Public Policy Report*. Cambridge, Mass.: MIT Press, 1967.

Roediger, David R. *The Wages of Whiteness: Race and the Making of the American Working Class*. London and New York: Verso, 1991.

van den Berghe, Pierre L. *Race and Racism: A Comparative Perspective*. New York: Wiley, 1967.

Wilson, William Julius. *Power, Racism, and Privilege: Race Relations in Theoretical and Sociohistorical Perspectives*. New York: Macmillan, 1973.

Wilson, William Julius. *The Declining Significance of Race: Blacks and Changing American Institutions*. Chicago: University of Chicago Press, 1978.

Wilson, William Julius. *The Truly Disadvantaged: The Inner City, the Underclass, and Public Policy*. Chicago: University of Chicago Press, 1987.

Wilson, William Julius, et al. "Urban Poverty and Family Life Survey of Chicago." Chicago: Center for the Study of Urban Inequality, National Opinion Research Center, 1987.

LAWRENCE D. BOBO (2005)

Solomon, Patrick

April 12, 1910
August 26, 1997

Patrick Solomon, a government minister, diplomat, and member of the People's National Movement, was born in Port of Spain, Trinidad. He displayed a superior intellect as a child and later excelled at the College Exhibition Examinations, placing first among all primary school students, including Eric Eustace Williams (1911–1981), the future prime minister of Trinidad and Tobago. In secondary school at St. Mary's College, he won a prestigious Island Scholarship in 1928, which allowed him to pursue medical studies at University College, London, and Queen's University in Belfast, Northern Ireland.

Between 1934 and 1939, Solomon practiced medicine in Wales, Scotland, and Ireland. He then returned to the Caribbean, where he served in the Leeward Islands Medical Service until 1942. In 1943 Solomon returned to Trinidad and obtained employment at the Port of Spain General Hospital. That year also marked his entry into politics, as he joined the West Indian National Party (WINP), which was founded in South Trinidad by Dr. David Pitt (1913–1994). Solomon formed a branch of the WINP in Port of Spain and served on its management committee. In 1943 he supported the WINP in its boycott of Victoria County's by-election, an attempt to force the colonial authorities to dissolve the legislature and hold general elections. At the WINP's first party conference on March 19, 1944, Solomon was elected to the party's Central Executive Committee. Three months later, at a meeting of the WINP General Council, Solomon was elected to serve as third vice president.

Within the labor movement, Solomon played a pivotal role but left a transient impression. In 1946 the Seamen and Waterfront Workers' Trade Union (SWWTU) appealed to their employer, the Shipping Association, for a new contract. The association refused and the waterfront workers decided to strike. Solomon intervened, and he not only marched with the disgruntled workers but aired their plight in the Legislative Council in Trinidad and Tobago. The strike eventually ended due to the increasing hunger of the workers, who reluctantly returned to work.

In 1946 Trinidad and Tobago held its first elections under adult suffrage. The United Front was one of the newly formed political parties contesting the election. This was a coalition of individuals and organizations, including the WINP and the Indian National Council. The objectives of the United Front were: (1) full internal self-government; (2) nationalization of the sugar and oil industries; and (3) mass education. Solomon served as secretary of the United Front and was chosen to contest the Port of Spain North seat. In a keenly contested electoral battle, Solomon and two other candidates of the United Front were victorious in the 1946 elections.

The urgency to increase the number of elected members was one of the major factors leading to the formation of the Constitutional Reform Committee in 1947. Solomon submitted a minority report that criticized the nomination system and appealed for a fully elected single chamber (elected on the basis of adult suffrage), an executive elected by and from the legislature, and an executive council to be responsible to the legislature. However, Solomon's suggestions were ignored by Britain. When the new constitution was announced on January 19, 1949, the noteworthy changes were an elected majority of one person in the executive council and the decrease of the nominated element from six to five persons. The House was to be presided over by a speaker chosen from among the elected members.

In the aftermath of the 1946 elections, the high level of racism prompted Solomon to form the Indo-Caribbean Cultural Institute on August 22, 1949. However, due to accusations of promoting Indian racialism, this venture quickly collapsed. Solomon formed the Caribbean Socialist Party to contest the 1950 elections, but he and the party were soundly defeated at the polls. Solomon then briefly withdrew from politics, but he was persuaded by Eric Williams to return to the political arena as one of the founding members of the People's National Movement (PNM). This was a wise move because Solomon apparently had a genuine interest in the political development of the country, and as a professional he was considered an asset to the PNM. Subsequently Solomon was elected as a member of Parliament for Port of Spain South (1956) and Port of Spain West (1961). On September 25, 1959, Solomon put forth a motion in the Legislative Council seeking full internal self-government. This historic appeal finally materialized on August 31, 1962, when the country attained independence.

As a member of the PNM, Solomon faithfully served in various capacities. He served as minister of education and culture (1956–1960), minister of home affairs (1960–1964), and acting prime minister, deputy prime minister, and minister of external affairs (1962–1966). At the international level, Solomon was chosen as vice president of the United Nations General Assembly in 1966 and as High Commissioner for Trinidad and Tobago in London between 1971 and 1976.

In 1978 Solomon was awarded the Trinity Cross, Trinidad and Tobago's highest award for distinguished service. During the 1980s he was no longer in active politics and became a weekly columnist for the *Sunday Express,* a local newspaper.

See also Peoples National Movement; Williams, Eric

Bibliography

Solomon, Patrick. *Solomon: An Autobiography.* Trinidad: Inprint Caribbean, 1981.

Williams, Eric. *History of the People of Trinidad and Tobago.* Port of Spain, Trinidad: PNM, 1962. Reprint, New York: A&B, 2002.

JEROME TEELUCKSINGH (2005)

Sororities, U.S.

According to the National Pan-Hellenic Council, the governing body of black Greek-lettered organizations, there are nine major black fraternities and sororities. Out of the "Divine Nine," four are sororities: Alpha Kappa Alpha, Delta Sigma Theta, Zeta Phi Beta, and Sigma Gamma Rho. They were all founded in the first half of the twentieth century, with a growing, cumulative membership of over 500,000 worldwide. Black sororities place a high emphasis on academic excellence and sisterly unity, and they tend not to "rush" (a Greek term for recruitment). Instead, members are invited by current sisters (soros), and they often learn about these organizations through their churches and high school. Alumni, famous or not, reflect each sorority's commitment to social change through community involvement.

The nation's first sorority was established in 1851 at Wesleyan College but it was not until 1956 that a black woman (Barbara Collier Delany) was invited to join a white sorority. (The Cornell chapter of Sigma Kappa was ordered to rescind Delany's membership; they refused, and headquarters shut down the sorority.) Despite the end of slavery and the guarantee of certain rights, racism continued in the form of Jim Crow. The Fifteenth Amendment granted black men the right to vote in 1870; it would be another fifty years until any woman could do the same. Even then, the remnants of Victorianism and its tenants of "true womanhood"—virtue, piety, domesticity, and obedience—continued to restrict women, particularly black women. Just as black women formed clubs to counter white racist suffragettes, they also formed sororities to combat similar exclusions faced on college campuses. Black women sought to gain equality not *behind* black men or white women, but *beside* them, and social work through sororities afforded them that opportunity.

Inspired by the black fraternity Alpha Phi Alpha (founded in 1906 at Cornell), the first black sorority, Alpha Kappa Alpha (AKA), was founded at Howard University by Ethel Hedgeman Lyle, Beulah E. and Lillie Burke, Margaret Flagg Holmes, Marjorie Hill, Lucy Diggs Slowe, Marie Woolfolk Taylor, Anna Easter Brown, and Lavinia Norman. With their motto, "Service to All Mankind," and their colors of salmon pink and apple green, AKA became official on January 15, 1908. While AKA is considered the oldest black sorority, they are sometimes also seen as the most elite, with accusations ranging from intra-racism (accepting light-skinned blacks only) to classicism (choosing members from the wealthy, professional classes). However, their commitment to social issues affecting the black community, as well as a roster of famous sisters cutting across class and color hues, disputes such criticisms. With chapters in the United States, as well as in the Caribbean, Africa, and Europe, the sorority has continued to stay true to its motto with various education and after-school and weekend projects, such as the Ivy AKAdemy, the On-TRACK Program, and Putting Black Families First, a citizen-awareness program.

Delta Sigma Theta, galvanized by the political atmosphere at the time, was established at Howard on January 13, 1913, by twenty-two former AKA's who sought a name dissimilar to the fraternity Alpha Phi Alpha. The Delta's were ordered by AKA to change their name and come back to the fold. Declining, Delta Sigma Theta created their own colors (crimson and cream), along with a new motto ("Greater Service, Greater Progress") and accompanying song, "The Delta Hymn," penned by Alice Dunbar Nelson and Florence Cole Talbert. Defying their families and Howard University officials, they participated in the 1913 Women's Suffragette March. During the Depression, they were at the forefront of providing various types of academic aid to blacks across the country. Other early projects included the National Library Project, which brought books to a black population hampered by the separate and unequal policies of Jim Crow, and going on record against injustices such as the Scottsboro Boys trial, U.S. involvement in Haiti, and lynching laws. Their commitment to social justice and issues continues with projects such as the Dr. Betty Shabazz Delta Academy, named after their soror and designed for preteen girls to supplement the public-school curriculum; the Delta-funded Thika Memorial Hospital/Mary Sick of the Mission Hospital maternity wing in Kenya; and the "Summit V: Health and Healing—Let It Continue" initiative, which focuses on HIV/AIDS education.

The first official sister organization (to the Phi Beta Sigma fraternity, founded in 1914 at Howard), Zeta Phi Beta, Inc., became the third official black sorority on January 16, 1920, nine months before all women received the right to vote. Founded by Arizona Cleaver, Viola Tyler, Pearl Neal, and Fannie Pettie, Zeta Phi Beta was not only first in being officially and constitutionally bound to a fraternity, but it was also the first black sorority to charter international chapters in West Africa, Germany, the Bahamas, and St. Croix. Among their many highlights is the Finer Womanhood Week, begun in the 1930s, during which each chapter holds a celebration to promote the ideals of "finer womanhood." Stressing community involvement over social background and high grades, the Zetas continue the founders' motto "Scholarship, Service, Sisterhood, and Finer Womanhood," with programs such as: Stork's Nest, which encourages women to seek pre- and postnatal care; the National Education Foundation, which provides scholarships, fellowships, and research grants to eligible women; and the Human Genome Project, whose goal is to raise awareness of genetics among people of color.

While the previously mentioned sororities were founded at Howard, an all-black college located in political and cosmopolitan Washington, D.C., blacks at the predominantly white Butler University in Indiana faced other obstacles. During the 1920s, Indiana was referred to as "Klandania" because it was the Ku Klux Klan's main and strongest base of operation; nearly 30 percent of Indiana's white male population were members. It was not until November 12, 1922, that an all-black sorority was to be established at a white university. Sigma Gamma Rho was founded by Mary Lou Allison Gardner Little, Bessie Mae Downey Rhodes Martin, Hattie Mai Annette Dulin Redford, Nannie Mae Gahn Johnson, Dorothy Hanley Whiteside, Cubena McClure, and Vivan White Marbury, women committed to helping other black women, on campus as well as off, to help other black women. Their motto, "Greater Service, Greater Progress," reflected the political climate for women of the period. During the Depression, they sponsored literacy programs that provided books to young black students; created a National Vocational Guid-

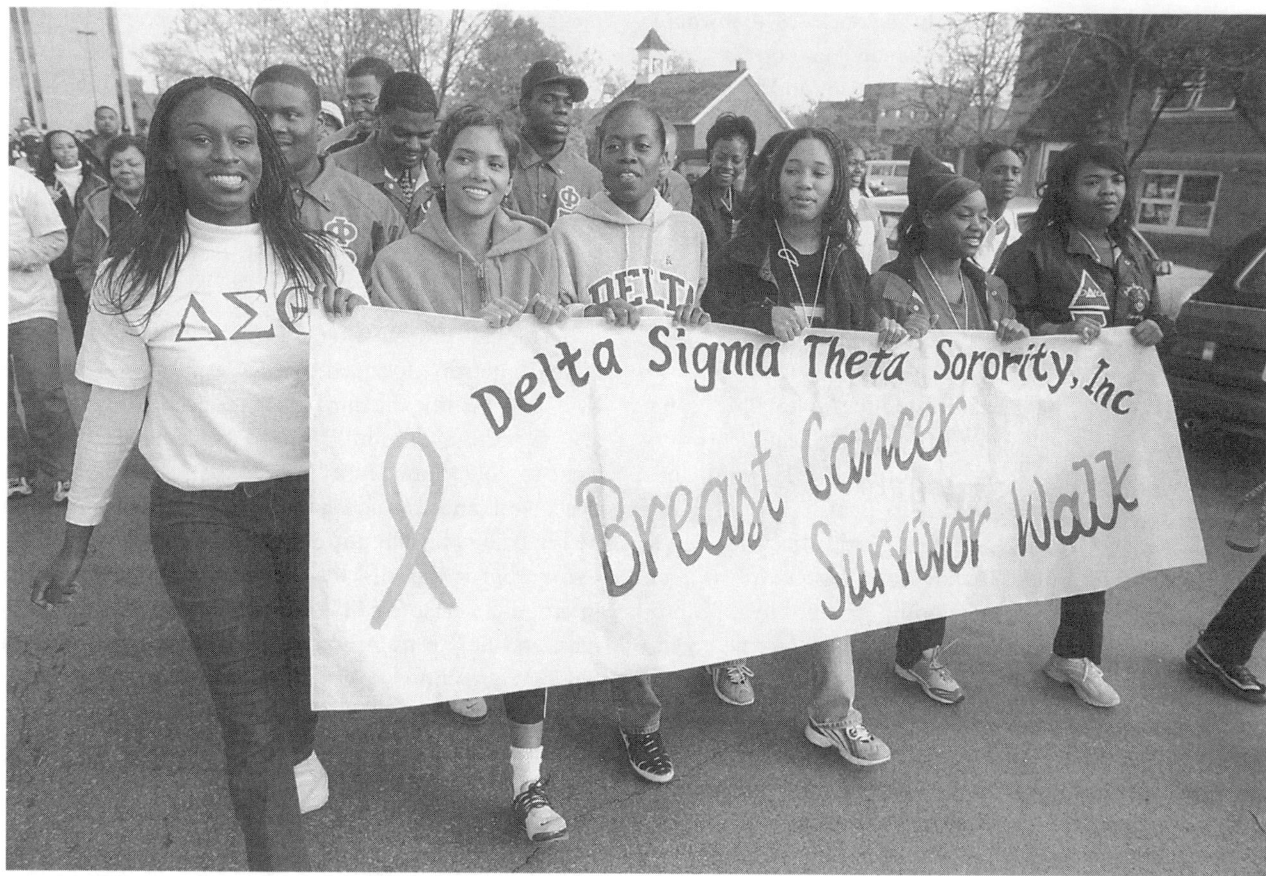

Model and actress Halle Berry, second from left, marches with members of the Delta Sigma Theta sorority at Bowling Green State University, 2000. *The sorority was founded in 1913 by twenty-two women at Washington, D.C.'s Howard University, one of the most prominent black academic colleges in the United States at that time.* J. D. POOLEY/GETTY IMAGES

ance Program; and established the Sigma Gamma Rho Employment Aid Bureau, an early networking system that provided Sigma sisters with life-improving jobs. Continuing the tradition are programs such as Wee Savers, which teaches children six to eighteen years of age about various banking facilities and their services, like investing; Program for Africa, which provides African women with the tools to produce grain more efficiently; and BigBookBag, which provides children in need with school supplies.

Although founded for black women by black women, black sororities accept women from various ethnicities, reflecting the growing diaspora of nonwhite women on American campuses. White membership, however slight, is also increasing, with white soros citing the emphasis of social work over socializing that prompted them to join a black, rather than white, sorority. Black sororities continue to provide a space for black collegians to congregate and network, both socially and professionally, long after members graduate. A brief roster of famous sorors include Mary McLeod Bethune, Johnetta Cole, Ruby Dee, Ella Fitzgerald, Aretha Franklin, Nikki Giovanni, Zora Neale Hurston, Mae Jemison, Barbara Jordan, Hattie McDaniel, Toni Morrison, Rosa Parks, and Mary Church Terrell.

See also Christian Denominations, Independent; Education in the United States; Fraternal Orders; Fraternities, U.S.; Mutual Aid Societies

Bibliography

Ridley, Teresa L., and Carolyn M. Brown. "Black Sororities: Champions of Sisterhood and Good Works." NIA online. Available from <http://www.niaonline.com>.

Ross, Lawrence C. *The Divine Nine: The History of African American Fraternities and Sororities.* New York: Kensington, 2000.

LISE ESDAILE (2005)

Southern Christian Leadership Conference (SCLC)

Initially founded in January 1957 by the Reverend Dr. Martin Luther King Jr. and other young ministers who were active in local civil-rights protest efforts across the South, the Southern Christian Leadership Conference (SCLC) soon became the primary organization through which the southern black church made significant contributions to the black freedom struggle of the 1960s.

Viewed by many as simply the institutional reflection of King's individual role as the civil rights movement's principal symbolic leader, the SCLC in fact served a somewhat larger function. First, beginning in the late 1950s, the SCLC drew together southern ministers who believed that the black church had a responsibility to act in the political arena and who sought an organizational vehicle for coordinating their activism. Second, in the years after 1961, when SCLC possessed a significant full time staff, the organization pulled together important protest campaigns in Birmingham (1963) and Selma, Alabama (1965). These campaigns brought the southern struggle to the forefront of national attention and helped win passage of the landmark Civil Rights Act of 1964 and the Voting Rights Act of 1965. Third, between 1965 and 1968 the SCLC provided the means by which King extended his own national agenda for economic change to include protest campaigns in northern cities such as Chicago (1966) and Cleveland (1967), as well as supplying the institutional basis for the Poor People's Campaign of 1968.

Three principal influences shaped SCLC's founding. The first was the Montgomery, Alabama, bus boycott of 1955 and 1956, a successful local protest effort that brought King to national attention and made him the symbol of new black activism in the South. Second, young ministers in other cities seeking to emulate the Montgomery example launched bus protests in southern cities such as Birmingham, Tallahassee, New Orleans, and Atlanta, and sought a forum for exchanging ideas and experiences. Third, New York–based civil rights activists Bayard Rustin, Ella Baker, and Stanley Levison, who already had helped garner northern funds and publicity for the Montgomery protest, began advocating the formation of a region-wide organization in the South that could spread the influence of Montgomery's mass movement and provide King a larger platform.

Initially labeled the "Southern Negro Leaders Conference on Transportation and Nonviolent Integration" by King and Rustin, the conference met three times in 1957 before finally adopting Southern Christian Leadership Conference as its actual name. Seeking to avoid competition and conflict with the NAACP, SCLC chose to be composed not of individual members but of local organization "affiliates," such as civic leagues, ministerial alliances, and individual churches. Looking for a goal beyond that of desegregating city bus lines, King and the other ministers leading the conference (C. K. Steele of Tallahassee, Fred L. Shuttlesworth of Birmingham, Joseph E. Lowery of Mobile, and Ralph D. Abernathy of Montgomery) focused on the right to vote and sought to develop a program, staff, and financial resources with which to pursue it. Until 1960, however, their efforts largely floundered, in part because of other demands upon King's time and energy, but also because of personnel problems and relatively meager finances.

The transformation of the SCLC into an aggressive, protest-oriented organization began in 1960 with King's own move from Montgomery to Atlanta and his appointment of the energetic Reverend Wyatt Tee Walker as SCLC's new executive director. The coupling of Walker's organizational skills with King's inspirational prowess as a speaker soon brought about a sevenfold expansion of SCLC's staff, budget, and program. While some staff members concentrated on voter registration efforts and citizenship training programs funded by northern foundations, Walker and King set out to design a frontal assault on southern segregation. Stymied initially in 1961 and 1962 in the southwest Georgia city of Albany, Walker and King chose the notorious segregation stronghold of Birmingham, Alabama, as their next target. In a series of aggressive demonstrations throughout April and May of 1963, the SCLC put the violent excesses of racist southern lawmen on the front pages of newspapers throughout the world. Civil rights rose as never before to the top of America's national agenda, and, within little more than a year's time, the Civil Rights Act of 1964 began fundamentally altering southern race relations.

Following King's much-heralded success at the 1963 March on Washington and his receipt of the 1964 Nobel Peace Prize, the SCLC repeated the Birmingham scenario with an even more successful protest campaign in early 1965 in Selma, focusing on the still widely denied right to register and vote. Out of that heavily publicized campaign emerged quick congressional passage of the Voting Rights Act of 1965. With King deeply convinced that the civil rights agenda required an expansion of the southern struggle into the North so as to directly confront nationwide issues of housing discrimination and inadequate education and jobs, the SCLC in early 1966 shifted much of its staff and energies to an intensive organizing campaign in Chicago. Although the "Chicago Freedom Movement" eventually garnered a negotiated accord with Chicago mayor Richard J. Daley, promising new city efforts to root out racially biased housing practices, most observers (and some participants) adjudged the SCLC's Chicago campaign as less than successful.

Following limited 1967 efforts in both Cleveland and Louisville, the SCLC, at King's insistent behest, began planning a massive "Poor People's Campaign" aimed at forcing the country's political elite to confront the issue of poverty in the United States. Following King's assassination on April 4, 1968, however, the SCLC's efforts to proceed with the campaign were marred by widespread organizational confusion. Although the SCLC played an important role in a successful 1969 strike by hospital workers in Charleston, South Carolina, the organization's resources and staff shrank precipitously in the years after King's death. Internal tensions surrounding King's designated successor, the Reverend Ralph D. Abernathy, as well as wider changes in the civil rights movement, both contributed significantly to the SCLC's decline. Only in the late 1970s, when another of the original founders, Joseph E. Lowery, assumed SCLC's presidency, did the conference regain organizational stability. But throughout the 1980s and into the early 1990s, SCLC continued to exist only as a faint shadow of the organization that had played such a crucially important role in the civil rights struggle between 1963 and 1968. In August 2004, Fred Shuttlesworth was elected president of the SCLC. One of his goals upon taking the position was to bring more young people into the organization.

See also Abernathy, Ralph David; Civil Rights Movement, U.S.; King, Martin Luther, Jr.; Lowery, Joseph E.; Montgomery, Ala., Bus Boycott; National Association for the Advancement of Colored People (NAACP); Rustin, Bayard; Shuttlesworth, Fred L.

Bibliography

Fairclough, Adam. *To Redeem the Soul of America: The Southern Christian Leadership Conference and Martin Luther King, Jr.* Athens: University of Georgia Press, 1987.

Garrow, David J. *Bearing the Cross: Martin Luther King, Jr., and the Southern Christian Leadership Conference.* New York: Morrow, 1986.

Manis, Andrew Michael. *A Fire You Can't Put Out: The Civil Rights Life of Birmingham's Reverend Fred Shuttlesworth.* Tuscaloosa: University of Alabama Press, 1999.

DAVID J. GARROW (1996)
Updated by publisher 2005

Southwell, Paul

July 18, 1913
May 18, 1979

Caleb Azariah Paul Southwell is one of the official national heroes of the Caribbean islands of St. Kitts and Nevis. He was born in Dominica and served as a schoolteacher before becoming a member of the Leeward Islands police force in 1938. He left the police force in 1944 and worked as an assistant stock clerk at the St. Kitts Sugar Factory until his dismissal over a wage dispute in 1948. In 1944 he was also recruited into the St. Kitts-Nevis Trades and Labour Union, where he served as part-time organizer until his election in 1947 as union vice-president. Southwell gained tremendous political clout through his participation in militant strikes against the exploitative sugar industry.

Southwell's political ascendancy was accomplished through the struggle for self-government that characterized much of the English-speaking Caribbean during the twentieth century. With the introduction of universal adult suffrage in 1952, Southwell, then the deputy leader of the St. Kitts-Nevis Labour Party, was elected to the St. Kitts Legislature. He was returned to the Legislative Council in 1956 and became minister of communications and works. During his political tenure, Southwell participated with Robert Bradshaw (St. Kitts's foremost political leader) in daring anticolonial protests. In the aftermath of the massive 1950 demonstration against the appointment of Kenneth Blackburne as Leeward Islands governor, Southwell published "The Truth about Operation Blackburne" (1951), a pamphlet explaining his party's frustration over the failure of the British Colonial Office to consult local inhabitants about political appointments.

In sharp contrast to his early years in Bradshaw's shadow, Southwell took the full reins of political leadership on St. Kitts when Bradshaw left to serve in the West Indies Federation (1958–1962). The 1958 strike against sugar industry employers was mounted and settled on his initiative, and he led a delegation to London in 1959 to advocate for further constitutional and electoral reform. He was elected to the Executive Council in 1960 and elevated to the position of chief minister of St. Kitts, Nevis, and Anguilla—a post he held until 1966. When the islands of St. Kitts, Nevis, and Anguilla (before the secession of Anguilla) became a state in association with Great Britain in 1967, Southwell—in deference to Bradshaw's return to the legislature after serving in the parliament of the abortive West Indies Federation—became deputy premier and minister of finance, trade, industry, and tourism. Following Bradshaw's death in 1978, the mantel of premiership passed to Southwell.

Southwell had hoped to ultimately preside over an independent nation, and he figured prominently in the 1970s independence talks in London. He also worked for years to develop the Organization of Eastern Caribbean States and had agreed to serve as its special ambassador. He died suddenly on May 18, 1979, while chairing a meeting of the West Indies Associated States Council of Ministers in St. Lucia. By then, he had set St. Kitts-Nevis well on the way to self-determination.

See also Bradshaw, Robert; West Indies Federation

Bibliography

Browne, Whitman. *From Commoner to King: Robert L. Bradshaw, Crusader for Dignity and Justice in the Caribbean.* Lanham, Md.: University Press of America, 1992.

O'Flaherty, Victoria Borg. *Pioneers of the St. Kitts-Nevis Labour Movement.* Basseterre, St. Kitts: Labour Spokesman Press, 1999.

CARLEEN PAYNE-JACKSON (2005)

Spaulding, Charles Clinton

August 1, 1874
August 1, 1952

Entrepreneur C. C. Spaulding was born in Columbus County, North Carolina. As a youth he worked on his father's farm and attended the local school until 1894, when he went to live with his uncle, Aaron Moore, the first black physician to practice in Durham, North Carolina. In Durham, after graduating from high school in 1898, Spaulding held a variety of jobs before becoming the manager of a cooperative black grocery store. While there, he also sold life insurance policies for the North Carolina Mutual and Provident Association, founded in 1898 by seven black men, including his uncle.

When the Mutual floundered in 1900 and most of the founders resigned their positions, Moore became secretary, and John Merrick, who served as president, hired Spaulding as the general manager. The three men then constituted the board of directors. With the death of Merrick in 1919 and the reorganization of the company as the North Carolina Mutual Life Insurance Company, Spaulding became secretary-treasurer, and with the death of Moore in 1923, president, a position he held until his own death in 1952. Under his leadership, the Mutual became the nation's largest black insurance company, a position it maintains today.

As the head not only of the Mutual but also of its numerous subordinate institutions—banks, a real estate company, and a mortgage company—Spaulding was the most powerful black in Durham and among the most powerful in the nation. His endorsement enabled black initiatives to receive financial support from prominent white foundations, such as the Duke and Rosenwald foundations and the Slater Fund. Spaulding used this power to save such black institutions as Shaw University, Virginia Theological Seminary, and the National Negro Business League from insolvency and to influence the press, church sermons, school curriculums, and the allocation of public funds. With the onset of the Great Depression in 1929, both state and federal governments acknowledged Spaulding's stature, appointing him to relief committees.

In 1933 the National Urban League made him national chair of its Emergency Advisory Council, whose purpose was to obtain black support for the National Recovery Administration (NRA), one of the most important parts of the first phase of President Franklin D. Roosevelt's (1882–1945; served 1933–45) New Deal plan for boosting the economy. The Council's role was to inform blacks about new laws regarding relief, reemployment, and property and to receive complaints of violations against blacks. Spaulding worked enthusiastically in this position, but his early hope that the NRA would bring a new era of fairness for blacks quickly soured.

As with his work for the Emergency Advisory Council, throughout Spaulding's career there was a tension between his desire to address the causes of black poverty and his need to protect his moderate image. In 1933 Spaulding introduced two local lawyers, Conrad Pearson and Cecil A. McCoy, who wanted to integrate the University of North Carolina, to NAACP secretary Walter White. However, as the case, *Hocutt v. North Carolina,* gained more publicity, Spaulding withdrew his essential support and worked instead for reform that did not threaten segregation, such as out-of-state tuition and equal teachers' salaries. But by the middle of the 1930s Spaulding actively supported the return of suffrage to blacks and served as chair of the executive committee of the Durham Committee on Negro Affairs (founded 1935), which was responsible for the registration of thousands of black voters. Because its endorsement on average ensured candidates 80 percent of the black vote, the DCNA was a major political force on Durham.

With the onset of World War II, Spaulding became concerned almost exclusively with unifying blacks and whites in the name of patriotism. He invested much of the Mutual's assets in the war effort, buying $4.45 million in war bonds, and traveled and gave speeches as associate administrator of the War Savings Staff. After the war, Spaulding focused on the threat he believed communism posed to business. An article he wrote for *American Magazine* proclaiming its dangers was incorporated into high school textbooks and was reprinted in a variety of languages.

See also Entrepreneurs and Entrepreneurship; Great Depression and the New Deal; Insurance Companies; National Urban League

Bibliography

Franklin, John Hope, and August Meier. *Black Leaders of the Twentieth Century.* Chicago: University of Illinois Press, 1982.

SIRAJ AHMED (1996)

Spelman College

Spelman College is the oldest black women's college in the United States. Located in Atlanta, Georgia, Spelman is a four-year liberal arts institution that has traditionally offered both the B.A. and B.S. degrees. Renowned for scholastic excellence and community involvement, Spelman was also one of the founding institutions of the Atlanta University Center.

Spelman College was founded in April 1881 as the Atlanta Baptist Female Seminary by Sophia B. Packard and Harriet E. Giles, two New England educators who had long been involved in education for women. While Packard and Giles were conducting a survey on the condition of the freedpersons in the South for the Women's American Baptist Home Mission Society (WABHMS), they became increasingly distressed over the lack of schools for black women. Upon their return to Boston, they were determined to raise the funds necessary to open a school for black girls in the South. After receiving $100 from the First Baptist Church of Medford, Massachusetts, WABHMS finally agreed to sponsor their effort. They arrived in Atlanta, where they met with the Reverend Frank Quarles, who offered the basement of his Friendship Baptist Church as the first home for the new school. When the school opened, there were eleven students; fifteen months later eighty pupils were in regular attendance.

Desperate for financial support, the two women traveled to Cleveland in the summer of 1882 to speak at a church meeting. In attendance at that meeting was John D. Rockefeller, who pledged $250 toward a building for the school. It was the first of his donations toward black education, which eventually totaled millions of dollars.

In 1883 the school moved into what were former Union army officer barracks, which had been purchased by the American Baptist Home Mission Society (ABHMS). The school had grown to 293 students with over thirty boarders. Industrial courses, paid for by a grant from the Slater Fund, were also begun that year. A model school was opened for observation and practice teaching, and as a result, an elementary normal course was introduced.

The buildings were paid off with the help of financial gifts from Rockefeller, and the school continued to grow. In honor of Laura Spelman Rockefeller (John D. Rockefeller's wife), the name of the school was changed to Spelman Seminary in 1884. The school was officially designated for females only and had grown to over 350 day pupils and 100 boarders. The students were taught a traditional New England classical curriculum. Courses included mathematics, English grammar and literature, geography, and natural philosophy. The girls' education was comparable to the education boys were receiving at nearby Atlanta Baptist Seminary, which later became Atlanta Baptist College and (in 1913) Morehouse College. In a spelling match against the boys, the girls from Spelman took top honors. In addition, the girls were also taught cooking, sewing, general housework, and laundry skills.

A printing press was purchased as a result of another gift from the Slater Fund, and the *Spelman Messenger* began publication in March 1885. Students were trained in typesetting and composition and began to contribute articles to the publication. The first six high school graduates of Spelman Seminary completed their work in 1886.

In 1888 Spelman was incorporated and granted a charter from the state of Georgia. Two African Americans were members of the original board, and one was on the executive committee of five. In time, the school was increasingly separated from ABHMS as more and more financial resources were provided by philanthropic organizations.

In 1901 the first baccalaureate degrees were conferred upon two Spelman students who had completed the requirements by taking several college-level courses at Atlanta Baptist College. Spelman continued to grow, new buildings were built, and more lots were purchased. The new buildings led to a constant struggle to stay financially sound, and the board began to seek a source to establish a permanent endowment.

In 1924, after a science building was completed, Spelman was finally in a position to offer a full range of college-level courses. As a result, the name was changed to Spelman College. Sisters Chapel was completed in 1927, and Florence Read became the new president of Spelman. Read placed tremendous emphasis on the development of a strong liberal arts college and greatly increased the college's endowment—from $57,501 in 1928 to $3,612,740 by the time Read retired in 1953. The elementary school was finally abolished in 1928, as was the nurses training department. Cooperation with Morehouse College was expanded in 1928 and 1929. Three members of the faculty were jointly employed, other teachers were exchanged, courses on each campus were opened to juniors and seniors, and the summer school was in joint operation.

Because of constant financial pressures, in 1929 Spelman agreed to a contract of affiliation with Atlanta University and Morehouse College. This allowed them to pool their financial and administrative sources and thus eliminate redundant functions. Part of the agreement required Spelman to eliminate its high school, whose students and function were shifted to Atlanta University, although they were supported by all three affiliates.

Spelman became fully accredited in 1930 by the Association of American Colleges. The Great Depression led to a financial squeeze, but Spelman survived and maintained its standard of excellence. The 1940s saw further growth, both physically and scholastically.

In 1953 Spelman got its first African-American president with the appointment of Albert E. Manley. The contract of affiliation was expanded in 1957 to include other Atlanta area colleges, and the school became part of the Atlanta University Center.

Spelman students were very active in the civil rights movement of the 1960s. They participated in sit-ins at segregated public sites in Atlanta, and several were arrested. Two Spelman students were cofounders of the Student Nonviolent Coordinating Committee, and in 1960 Martin Luther King Jr. delivered the Founder's Day address. In 1961 a non-Western Studies program (in cooperation with Morehouse College) was initiated with the help of a grant from the Ford Foundation. In 1969 a Black Studies program was officially added to the curriculum.

In 1976 Dr. Donald Mitchell Stewart assumed the presidency amid protests from students and faculty, who demanded the appointment of a black woman to that post. That was not to take place until 1987, when Dr. Johnnetta Betsch Cole became the first such president of Spelman College. The following year, $20 million was donated by Bill and Camille Cosby, part of which went into a new building program. In 1992 Spelman had close to two thousand students, 97 percent of whom were African Americans. Cole announced her resignation in 1997.

Beverly Daniel Tatum was inaugurated as the college's ninth president in 2003. In 2004 Spelman partnered with South African University to explore ways of fostering sustainable development.

See also Bethune-Cookman College; Dillard University; Education in the United States; Fisk University; Howard University; Lincoln University; Morehouse College; Spelman College; Tuskegee University

Bibliography

Guy-Sheftall, Beverly, and Jo Moore Stewart. *Spelman: A Centennial Celebration.* Atlanta, Ga., 1981.

Read, Florence. *The Story of Spelman College.* Atlanta, Ga.: Author, 1961.

Roebuck, Julian B., and Komanduri S. Murty. *The Place of Historically Black Colleges and Universities in American Higher Education.* Westport, Conn.: Praeger, 1993.

CHRISTINE A. LUNARDINI (1996)
Updated by publisher 2005

Spingarn Medal

The Spingarn Medal is awarded annually by the National Association for the Advancement of Colored People (NAACP) for "the highest or noblest achievement by an American Negro." It is awarded by a nine-member committee selected by the NAACP board of directors. Nominations are open, and the awards ceremony has traditionally been part of the NAACP annual convention. First awarded in 1915, the Spingarn Medal has gone to African Americans who have made significant contributions in different fields of endeavor. It was for many years considered the highest honor in black America, although its prestige has declined somewhat in recent years because of the NAACP's institution of the Image Awards and perhaps because of the fragmenting of black institutional leadership.

The Spingarn Medal is named for Joel E. Spingarn (1874–1939), who originated the idea of it. Spingarn, who was white, was professor and chair of the Department of Comparative Literature at Columbia University from 1909

Spingarn Medal Winners

1915 Ernest E. Just
1916 Charles Young
1917 Harry T. Burleigh
1918 William S. Braithwhite
1919 Archibald H. Grimké
1920 William E. B. [W. E. B.] Du Bois
1921 Charles S. Gilpin
1922 Mary B. Talbert
1923 George Washington Carver
1924 Roland Hayes
1925 James Weldon Johnson
1926 Carter G. Woodson
1927 Anthony Overton
1928 Charles W. Chesnutt
1929 Mordecai Wyatt Johnson
1930 Henry A. Hunt
1931 Richard Berry Harrison
1932 Robert Russa Moton
1933 Max Yergan
1934 William Taylor Burwell Williams
1935 Mary McLeod Bethune
1936 John Hope
1937 Walter White
1938 No award given
1939 Marian Anderson
1940 Louis T. Wright
1941 Richard Wright
1942 A. Philip Randolph
1943 William H. Hastie
1944 Charles Drew
1945 Paul Robeson
1946 Thurgood Marshall
1947 Percy Julian
1948 Channing H. Tobias
1949 Ralph J. Bunche
1950 Charles Hamilton Houston
1951 Mabel Keaton Staupers
1952 Harry T. Moore (posthumous award)
1953 Paul R. Williams
1954 Theodore K. Lawless
1955 Carl Murphy
1956 Jack Roosevelt (Jackie) Robinson
1957 Martin Luther King Jr.
1958 Daisy Bates and the Little Rock Nine
1959 Edward Kennedy (Duke) Ellington
1960 Langston Hughes
1961 Kenneth B. Clark
1962 Robert C. Weaver
1963 Medgar Wiley Evers (posthumous award)
1964 Roy Wilkins
1965 Leontyne Price
1966 John H. Johnson
1967 Edward W. Brooke III
1968 Sammy Davis Jr.
1969 Clarence Mitchell Jr.
1970 Jacob Lawrence
1971 Leon Howard Sullivan
1972 Gordon Parks
1973 Wilson C. Riles
1974 Damon J. Keith
1975 Henry Aaron
1976 Alvin Ailey
1977 Alexander Palmer (Alex) Haley
1978 Andrew Jackson Young
1979 Rosa L. Parks
1980 Rayford W. Logan
1981 Coleman Alexander Young
1982 Benjamin E. Mays
1983 Lena Horne
1984 Tom Bradley
1985 William H. (Bill) Cosby Jr.
1986 Benjamin Lawson Hooks
1987 Percy Ellis Sutton
1988 Frederick Douglass Patterson
1989 Jesse Jackson
1990 Lawrence Douglas Wilder
1991 Colin Powell
1992 Barbara Jordan
1993 Dorothy I. Height
1994 Maya Angelou
1995 John Hope Franklin
1996 Carl Rowan
1997 Leon Higginbotham
1998 Myrlie Evers-Williams
1999 Earl G. Graves Sr.
2000 Oprah Winfrey
2001 Vernon E. Jordan Jr.
2002 John Lewis
2003 Constance Baker Motley
2004 Robert L. Carter

until 1911, when he resigned over free-speech issues. He became involved in the NAACP because of civil rights abuses in the South. Spingarn joined the NAACP's board of directors in 1913 and helped establish the NAACP's New York office. In 1913 and 1914, while traveling throughout the country organizing the association and speaking for the rights of black people, he noticed that newspaper coverage of African Americans tended to be negative, focusing on black murderers and other criminals. A close collaborator of W. E. B. Du Bois, Spingarn was sensitive to media portrayal of blacks. Independently wealthy, he endowed an award, a medal to be made of gold "not exceeding $100" in value, that would pinpoint black achievement, strengthen racial pride, and publicize the NAACP. To assure that white attention would be directed toward the award, Spingarn set up an award committee consisting of prominent men, including Oswald Garrison Villard (grandson of abolitionist William Lloyd Garrison) and ex-president William Howard Taft. There were thirty nominations for the first medal, which was awarded to biologist Ernest E. Just and presented by the first of the celebrity presenters Spingarn would arrange, New York governor Charles S. Whitman.

Spingarn Medal winners have included ministers, educators, performers (including musicians), popular entertainers, baseball players, military officers, historians, and other professionals and leaders. Beginning with Mary B. Talbert in 1922, eleven women have won the Spingarn Medal. The award has twice been given posthumously.

See also National Association for the Advancement of Colored People (NAACP)

Bibliography

Ross, Barbara Joyce. *J. E. Spingarn and the Rise of the NAACP, 1911–1939.* New York: Atheneum, 1972.

GREG ROBINSON (1996)
Updated by publisher 2005

Spiritual Church Movement

Although some African Americans became involved with Spiritualism in such places as Memphis, Tennessee; Charleston, South Carolina; Macon, Georgia; and New Orleans during the nineteenth century, the Spiritual movement as an institutional form emerged during the first decade of the twentieth century in Chicago—a city that remains the movement's numerical center. Mother Leafy Anderson, who founded the Eternal Life Christian Spiritualist Church in Chicago in 1913, moved to New Orleans sometime between 1918 and 1921 and established an association not only with several congregations there but also with congregations in Chicago; Little Rock, Arkansas; Pensacola, Florida; Biloxi, Mississippi; Houston; and smaller cities.

Mother Anderson accepted elements from Roman Catholicism, and other Spiritual churches also incorporated elements of voodoo. Whereas the number of Spiritual congregations in Chicago and Detroit surpasses the fifty or so reported in New Orleans, in a very real sense the latter continues to serve as the "soul" of the Spiritual church movement.

Like many other African-American religious groups, the Spiritual movement underwent substantial growth during the Great Migration, particularly in northern cities but also in southern ones. In 1923 Father George W. Hurley, a self-proclaimed god like his contemporary, Father Divine, established the Universal Hagar's Spiritual Church in Detroit. On September 22, 1925, in Kansas City, Missouri, Bishop William F. Taylor and Elder Leviticus L. Boswell established the Metropolitan Spiritual Church of Christ, which became the mother church of the largest of the Spiritual associations. Following the death of Bishop Taylor and a succession crisis that prompted a split in the Metropolitan organization, Rev. Clarence Cobbs, pastor of the First Church of Deliverance in Chicago, emerged as the president of the principal faction, the Metropolitan Spiritual Churches of Christ. Cobbs came to symbolize the "gods of the black metropolis" (Fauset, 1971) with his dapper mannerisms and love of the "good life."

The Spiritual religion cannot be viewed simply as a black version of white Spiritualism. Initially, congregations affiliated with the movement referred to themselves as Spiritualist, but by the 1930s and 1940s most of them had contracted this term to Spiritual. As part of this process, African Americans adapted Spiritualism to their own experience. Consequently, much of the social structure, beliefs, and ritual content of Spiritual churches closely resemble that of other religious groups in the black community, particularly the Baptists and Pentecostalists.

In time, the Spiritual movement became a highly syncretic ensemble that incorporated elements from American Spiritualism, Roman Catholicism, African-American Protestantism, and voodoo (or its diluted form known as *hoodoo*). Specific congregations and associations also added elements from New Thought, Ethiopianism, Judaism, and astrology to this basic core.

The Spiritual church movement has no central organization that defines dogma, ritual, and social structure. Many congregations belong to regional or national associations, but some choose to function independently of such ties. An association charters churches, qualifies ministers, and issues "papers of authority" for the occupants of various politico-religious positions. Although associations sometimes attempt to impose certain rules upon their constituent congregations, for the most part they fail to exert effective control.

Instead, the Spiritual movement exhibits an ideology of personal access to power. Theoretically, anyone who is touched by the spirit can claim personal access to knowledge, truth, and authority. Although associations may attempt to place constraints on such claims by requiring individuals exhibiting a "calling" to undergo a process of legitimation, persons can easily thwart such efforts, either by establishing their own congregations or by realigning themselves with some other Spiritual group. The fissioning that results from this process means that Spiritual associations rarely exceed more than one hundred congregations.

Probably more so than even Holiness-Pentecostal (or Sanctified) churches, Spiritual congregations are small, rarely numbering over one hundred. They often meet in storefronts and house churches and have found their greatest appeal among lower- and working-class African Americans. The larger congregations crosscut socioeconomic lines and may be led by relatively well-educated ministers. In addition to the types of offices found in black Protestant churches, Spiritual churches have mediums who are alleged to possess the gift of prophecy—that is, the ability to "read," or tell people about their past, present, and future. For the most part, mediums focus upon the wide variety of problems of living.

Like many other lower-class religious bodies, Spiritual churches are compensatory in that they substitute religious for social status. As opposed to those of many black religious groups, most Spiritual churches permit women to hold positions of religious leadership. Indeed, most of the earliest Spiritual churches in New Orleans were headed by women. Spiritual churches with their busy schedule of religious services, musical performances, suppers, and picnics also offer a strong sense of community for their adherents. Furthermore, they provide their members with a variety of opportunities, such as testimony sessions and "shouting," to ventilate their anxieties and frustrations.

Despite the functional similarities between Spiritual churches and other African-American religious groups, particularly those of the Baptist and Sanctified varieties, the former represent a thaumaturgical response to racism and social stratification in the larger society. The Spiritual church movement provides its adherents and clients with a wide variety of magico-religious rituals, such as praying before the image of a saint, burning votive candles, visualization, and public and private divination by a medium for acquiring a slice of the "American dream." Whereas the majority of Spiritual people are lower class, others—particularly some of those who belong to the larger congregations—are working and middle class. In the case of the latter, the Spiritual religion may serve to validate the newly acquired status of the upwardly mobile.

Most Spiritual people eschew social activism and often blame themselves for their miseries, faulting themselves for their failure to engage in positive thinking. Conversely, they occasionally exhibit overt elements of protest, particularly in remarks critical of business practices, politics, and racism in the larger society. Social protest in Spiritual churches, however, generally assumes more subtle forms, such as the rejection of what Spiritual people term "pie-in-the-sky" religion and a refusal to believe that work alone is sufficient for achieving social mobility.

See also Baptists; Catholicism in the Americas; Judaism; Pentecostalism in North America; Religion; Voodoo

Bibliography

Baer, Hans A. *The Black Spiritual Movement: A Religious Response to Racism.* Knoxville: University of Tennessee Press, 1984.

Baer, Hans A., and Merrill Singer. *African-American Religion in the Twentieth Century: Varieties of Protest and Accommodation.* Knoxville: University of Tennessee Press, 1992.

Fauset, Arthur. *Black Gods of the Metropolis.* Philadelphia: University of Pennsylvania Press, 1971.

Jacobs, Claude F., and Andrew F. Kaslow. *The Spiritual Churches of New Orleans: Origins, Beliefs, and Rituals of an African-American Religion.* Knoxville: University of Tennessee Press, 1991.

HANS A. BAER (1996)
Updated bibliography

Spirituality

Black North American spirituality lies at one end of a topographic continuum, a continuum composed of African diaspora-and-homeland religions and cultures. At the other extreme lie the African homelands of black peoples forcibly relocated to the Americas during almost four hundred years of the Atlantic slave trade. The intermediate sectors of the continuum comprise other cultures of the African diaspora, intermediate because black cultures in South America and the Caribbean exhibit stronger continuity with African traditional religions. Most obvious are Yoruba continuities in Haitian Vodou, Cuban Santería, and Brazilian Candomblé.

In this schema the Atlantic world constitutes the best ethnographic and historical context for understanding the nature and development of African-American spirituality. Europe and Britain are components of this world, too, of course. A triangulation of the Atlantic, then, comprising Africa, the New World, and Europe, represents not only commercial exchanges inaugurated in the slave trade, but also multiple sources of new spiritual traditions.

A minimal set of categories for delineating black North American spirituality, in terms of its multifaceted secular and religious expressions, includes aesthetic, ecstatic, and iconographic or "iconic" features. Compare W. E. B. Du Bois's description of black religion as "the music, the frenzy, and the preacher." The disparate religious traditions involved are predominantly Christian (Protestant and some Catholic), but also Islamic and Hebraic, folk or indigenous, spiritualist and other sectarian traditions, and even neo-African. Some aesthetic features are common throughout the diaspora, while other ecstatic and iconic features are heightened in certain traditions and thus demarcate contrasting modes of spirituality.

Musical expression is so central that it provides paradigms of creativity for other domains of black culture (e.g., improvisation, call-and-response). "It is only in his music," James Baldwin declared, "that the Negro in America has been able to tell his story." That story has multiple "scores," Ralph Ellison has further disclosed: "Often we wanted to share both: the classics and jazz, the Charleston and the Irish reel, spirituals and the blues, the sacred and the profane" (Smith, 1989, pp. 387, 389). Indeed, the desire to link black America with cultural expressions from other sources sometimes transcends even ethnic oppression, and perennially revitalizes spiritual experience.

In addition, such bicultural proficiencies reflect a performance rule characterizing ritual and communication processes in the diaspora. "Style-switching" (Marks, 1974) is the musical alternation between codes that signify black or African cultural contents and codes indicating white or European contents. It can also signal ritual transitions to spirit possession and trance phenomena in both religious and secular contexts. A psychosocial or cognitive basis for this aesthetic feature of African-American spirituality is the "double consciousness" articulated by Du Bois's phenomenon: the intersubjective experience of being both African and American. To generalize: Modes of expression (oral or musical, literary or dramatic, religious or secular) can alternate between forms identified as Afro-American, or "black," and polarized forms identified as Euro-American, or "white."

Spirit possession and ecstatic phenomena typify black religious expression in the New World. Many observers attribute the prominence of ecstatic behaviors in ritual, worship, and everyday life to a common African heritage in which possession "was the height of worship—the supreme religious act" (Mitchell, 1975). Parallel Euro-Christian practices allowed this African predisposition to adapt to the predominantly Protestant ethos of North America through the revival traditions of white Baptists and Methodists. Thus, Albert Raboteau (1978) has described spirit possession as a "two-way bridge" that enabled black Americans to "pass over" from African to Christian ecstatic expression.

A similar claim connects European magical traditions to African-American thaumaturgy and pharmacopoeia (e.g., conjure, as discussed below). Finally, ecstatic phenomena occur in secular performance and ritualized group interactions involving political movements and social and entertainment events. For example, Henry Mitchell (1975) has suggested that possession and trance behavior occur covertly in jazz clubs with comparable cathartic and therapeutic effects. Ecstatic performances by black preachers and other orators are renowned, and bear shamanic commonalities with American revival preaching generally.

On the other hand, not all African-American spirituality is ecstatic in character. Rastafarian spirituality, displacing possession phenomena with revelatory discourse and poetic biblicism, offers a Jamaican exception. Such examples distinguish the other major spiritual dimension expressed by black North Americans: the iconographic or "iconic" dimension. The term connotes the contemplative tradition in Western spirituality, in which not only pictorial but also textual icons—most notably biblical narratives, symbols, and figures—mediate divine significations and transcendent ideals.

African sources of this imagistic propensity comprise a "ritual cosmos" or ancestral worldview, in which "one must see every thing as symbol" (Zuesse, 1979). While (1) an iconic spirituality can be distinguished from (2) emotivist or ecstatic forms of spirituality, it is not necessarily (3) rationalist and discursive in the tradition of the European Enlightenment. Yet it can accompany either of the latter (2, 3) in modes that are iconic-ecstatic (for example, shamanic oratory) or iconic-analytic. Perhaps the spiritual-intellectual discourse of the African-American mystical philosopher Howard Thurman best exemplifies both combinations.

The major instance of iconic expression in black North American spirituality is the figural tradition that improvisationally employs biblical types to configure black experience: Moses (liberator), Exodus (emancipation), Promised Land (destiny). Black religious figuralism emerged in slave religion and bears traces both of Puritan typology and the magical folk healing-and-harming tradition of conjure. Conjure practitioners reenvision and transform reality by performing mimetic (imitative) and medicinal operations (using roots, herbs, etc.) on "material metaphors." Conjurational employment of biblical figures as experiential metaphors operated as recently as the 1960s civil rights movement, in which the Rev. Dr. Martin Luther King Jr. represented himself as a Moses and configured the movement as an exodus.

Secular examples include iconic uses of democratic texts and their ideals as found in the U.S. Constitution and Declaration of Independence. Together these secular and religious vectors account for the "biblical republicanism" that black North Americans share with their compatriots. Even black nationalists and Pan-African political movements (e.g., Ethiopianism and black Zionism) derive from the missionary uses of such Bible figures as Ethiopia and Egypt. Black Muslim and black militant figuration of (Babylonian) exile or captivity in America converge with the Rastafarians' poetic iconography of postcolonial oppression. The iconic dimension, it is evident, conveys liberating and creative energies for future transformations of religion and culture.

See also Candomblé; Religion; Santería; Voodoo; Yoruba Religion and Culture in the Americas

Bibliography

Marks, Morton. "Uncovering Ritual Structures in Afro-American Music." In *Religious Movements in Contemporary America,* edited by Irving Zaretsky and Mark P. Leone, pp. 60–134. Princeton, N.J.: Princeton University Press, 1974.

Mitchell, Henry H. *Black Belief: Folk Beliefs of Blacks in America and West Africa.* New York: Harper & Row, 1975.

Raboteau, Albert J. *Slave Religion: The "Invisible Institution" in the Antebellum South.* New York: Oxford University Press, 1978.

Smith, Theophus H. "The Spirituality of Afro-American Traditions." In *Christian Spirituality III: Post-Reformation and Modern,* edited by Louis K. Dupré and Don Saliers, pp. 372–412. New York: Crossroads, 1989.

Wilmore, Gayraud S. *Black Religion and Black Radicalism: An Interpretation of the Religious History of Afro-American People,* 2d ed. Maryknoll, N.Y.: Orbis, 1983.

Zuesse, Evan M. *Ritual Cosmos: The Sanctification of Life in African Religions.* Athens: Ohio University Press, 1979.

THEOPHUS H. SMITH (1996)

Spirituals

African-American sacred folk songs are known as *anthems, hymns, spiritual songs, jubilees, gospel songs,* or *spirituals,* though the distinctions among these terms are not precise. *Spiritual song* was widely used in English and American tune books from the eighteenth century, but *spiritual* has not been found in print before the Civil War. Descriptions of songs that came to be known by that name appeared at least twenty-five years earlier, however, and African-American distinctive religious singing was described as early as 1819.

Travelers and traders in Africa in the early seventeenth century described the musical elements that later distinguished African-American songs from European folk song: strong, syncopated rhythms reinforced by bodily movement, gapped scales, improvised texts, and the universal call-and-response form in which the leader and responding chorus overlapped. To white contemporaries, the music seemed wholly exotic and barbaric, although later analysts identified elements common to European music, such as the diatonic scale. The performance style of African music, quite distinct from familiar European styles, has persisted in many forms of African-American music to the present day.

Although the music of Africans has been documented in the West Indies and the North American mainland from the seventeenth century, conversion to Christianity was a necessary precondition for the emergence of the spiritual, a distinctive form of African-American religious music. Conversion proceeded slowly. Individual slaves were converted by the families with whom they lived in the seventeenth century, but on southern plantations, where most of the slaves lived, some planters opposed the baptism of their slaves because they believed that baptism would bring freedom. Moreover, plantations were widely separated, missionaries were few, and travel was difficult. Where religious instruction was permitted, however, the slaves responded with enthusiasm.

In the mid-eighteenth century, a few Presbyterian ministers, led by Samuel Davies of Hanover County, Virginia, made special efforts to convert blacks within their neighborhoods, teaching them Isaac Watts's hymns from books sent from England. Davies wrote in 1751, "The Negroes, above all the Human Species that I ever knew, have an Ear for Musick, and a kind of extatic Delight in Psalmody" (Epstein, 1977, p. 104). Whether the blacks injected a distinctive performance style he did not say.

Toward the end of the century, Methodist itinerants like Bishop Francis Asbury—together with his black exhorter, Harry Hosier—held protracted meetings that lasted several days and drew large crowds of blacks and whites. After 1800 the camp meeting developed on the frontier, where settlements were widely scattered. Black worshipers were present at the earliest camp meetings—sometimes seated separately, but in close proximity to whites. In an atmosphere highly charged with emotion, both groups shared songs, parts of songs, and styles of singing in participatory services where large numbers of people needed musical responses they could learn easily and quickly. The call-and-response style of the Africans resembled the whites' time-honored practice of "lining out."

The first documented reports of distinctive black religious singing date from the beginning of the nineteenth century, about twenty years before the first organized missions to plantation slaves. Throughout the antebellum period, spirituals were mentioned in letters, diaries, and magazine articles written by southerners, but to most northerners they were quite unknown. As northern men and women went south during the Civil War, they heard spirituals for the first time. Newspaper reporters included song texts in their stories from the front. Individual songs were published as sheet music, although some editors were well aware that their transcriptions failed to reproduce the music fully. In a letter to the editor of *Dwight's Journal of Music,* Lucy McKim, an early collector and recorder of spirituals, wrote that "the odd turns made in the throat; and the curious rhythmic effect produced by single voices chiming in at different irregular intervals, seem almost as impossible to place on score, as the singing of birds, or the tones of an Æolian Harp" (21 [November 8, 1862]: 254–255).

When a comprehensive collection of songs, *Slave Songs of the United States,* was published in 1867, the senior editor, William Francis Allen, wrote in the introduction: "The best we can do, however, with paper and types . . . will convey but a faint shadow of the original. . . . [T]he intonations and delicate variations of even one singer cannot be reproduced on paper. And I despair of conveying any notion of the effect of a number singing together" (Allen, 1867, pp. iv–v). In effect, the notational system filtered out most of the characteristic African elements, leaving versions that looked like European music. Collectors of these songs had heard the music sung by its creators, and they fully realized how defective their transcriptions were. But they feared that the music would be lost forever if the transcriptions, however unsatisfactory, were not made.

The pattern of transcribing the music in conventional notation was followed in more popular collections of songs transcribed in the 1870s from the singing of the Fisk Jubilee Singers, the Hampton Singers, and other touring groups from black schools in the South. However, these tours of carefully rehearsed ensembles of well-trained singers introduced audiences in the North and Europe to versions of the spirituals that eliminated many of those characteristic elements that had so attracted Lucy McKim and William Allen. The singers had been trained in European music and felt a responsibility to reflect credit on the rising black population.

By the 1890s, spirituals had become widely popular, both in the United States and in Europe, in the versions sung by the college singers. In 1892 a Viennese professor of jurisprudence, Richard Wallaschek, in a book entitled *Primitive Music,* advanced the theory that the spirituals were "mere limitations of European compositions which the negroes have picked up and served up again with slight variations" (p. 60). He never visited the United States or Africa, and his knowledge of the music was wholly derived from the defective transcriptions in *Slave Songs of the United States* and minstrel songs. Never having heard the music, Wallaschek was unaware that there were elements that could not be transcribed, but his ideas were taken seriously by several generations of scholars.

The strongest statement of the white-origins school was made by George Pullen Jackson, a professor of German at Vanderbilt University, who explored with enthusiasm the so-called white spiritual. In his book *White Spirituals of the Southern Uplands* (1933), his discussion of black spirituals was based primarily on an analysis of transcribed versions. He cited priority in publication as certain proof of origin, overlooking the irrelevance of this fact for folk music, most especially for the music of a population kept illiterate by force of law. The white–origins theory is no longer widely accepted. Not until the advent of sound recordings was it possible to preserve the performance itself, including improvised details and performance style, for later study and analysis.

Concert arrangements of spirituals for solo singers and choirs have been made, most notably by Harry T. Burleigh, James Weldon Johnson and J. Rosamund Johnson, and William Levi Dawson. Spiritual thematic materials have permeated diverse genres of American music in the twentieth century.

The musical elements that distinguished African-American spirituals from Euro-American hymnody are virtually impossible to reproduce in standard musical notation. Variable pitches; irregular strong, syncopated rhythms; and freely improvised melodic lines presented insoluble problems to the collector before the age of recording. The performance style also included humming, or "moaning," in response to the solo performer (whether singer or preacher); responsive interjections; and ceaseless physical movement (patting, hand-clapping, foot-tapping, and swaying) in response to the music. The overlapping of leader and responding chorus provided a complex interplay of voice qualities and rhythms. Slurs and slides modified pitch, while turns in the throat, blue notes, microtones, and sighs were equally impossible to notate. Pentatonic scales, however, and flattened fourth or seventh notes could be captured in notation.

Textual elements covered a whole spectrum of concepts, from trials and suffering, sorrow and tribulations, to hope and affirmation. Events from both the Old and the New Testaments were described, including Elijah's chariot and Ezekiel's wheel, along with more common images such as trains, shoes, wings, harps, robes, and ships. Hypocritical preachers and sinners were scorned, while death, heaven, resurrection, and triumph were often invoked.

Besides the purely religious message, there were also hidden meanings in some spirituals, exhorting the singers to resistance or freedom. Songs such as "Steal Away," "Follow the Drinking Gourd," and "Go Down, Moses"—with its refrain, "Let my people go"—could be interpreted in at least two ways. References to crossing Jordan and the trumpet blast could have both religious and secular interpretations.

See also Folk Music; Gospel Music; Music in the United States

Bibliography

Allen, William Francis, Charles Pickard Ware, and Lucy McKim Garrison. *Slave Songs of the United States.* New York: A. Simpson, 1867. Reprint, Bedford, Mass.: Applewood, 1995.

Epstein, Dena J. *Sinful Tunes and Spirituals: Black Folk Music to the Civil War.* Urbana: University of Illinois Press, 1977.

Epstein, Dena J. "A White Origin for the Black Spiritual? An Invalid Theory and How It Grew." *American Music* 1 (1983): 53–59.

Jones, Arthur C. *Wade in the Water: The Wisdom of the Spirituals.* Maryknoll, NY: Orbis Books, 1993.

Krehbiel, Henry Edward. *Afro-American Folksongs: A Study in Racial and National Music.* New York: Schirmer, 1914. Reprint, Portland, Me.: Longwood Press, 1976.

Lovell, John, Jr. *Black Song: The Forge and the Flame—The Story of How the Afro-American Spiritual Was Hammered Out.* New York: Macmillan, 1972.

Marsh, J. B. T. *The Story of the Jubilee Singers; with Their Songs.* London: Hodder and Stoughton, 1875.

Reagon, Bernice Johnson. *If You Don't Go, Don't Hinder Me: The African American Sacred Song Tradition.* Lincoln: University of Nebraska Press, 2001.

Southern, Eileen. *The Music of Black Americans: A History,* 3d ed. New York: Norton, 1997.

Ward, Andrew. *Dark Midnight When I Rise: The Story of the Jubilee Singers, Who Introduced the World to the Music of Black America.* New York: Farrar, Straus and Giroux, 2000.

Spencer, Jon Michael. *Protest and Praise: Sacred Music of Black Religion.* Minneapolis: Fortress Press, 1990.

DENA J. EPSTEIN (1996)
Updated bibliography

SPORTS

Commonly viewed as a social arena in which egalitarian principles of fair conduct determine the outcome of competition, the world of sport is an arena where fortitude of mind and body coalesce into singular focus, actualizing athletic success. While this merit-based view of athletics represents the ethos of sport itself, it is crucial to note that athletic competition, like any social arena, is invariably influenced by the related phenomena of race and racial discrimination. In Donald Spivey's (2004) apt assessment, "The sanctum of sport is premised on the unofficial doctrines of equality of opportunity, sportsmanship, and fair play. It is thus a perfect arena for the exposure of the dual nature of American society, with its paradoxical blend of democracy and inequality" (p. 148). Though Spivey focuses specifically on the contradictions inherent in the pursuit of athletic achievement within the context of American societal racism, critical readers of sport history must also consider the impact of race and racism within a broader diasporic context, for the predominance of scientific racism, the legacy of Jim Crow, and the impact of colonization and decolonization in Africa, Latin America, and the Caribbean have determined modern interpretations of black athletic achievement.

Viewed in this manner, sport becomes a symbolic battleground upon which varying ideological and sociopolitical discourses on race and hegemony have been fought in the twentieth century. The black athlete, consequently, has come to symbolize epochal moments of political consciousness, as his/her political stance falls along a continuum, reflecting varying responses to the dialectic of oppression and resistance that lies at the heart of the African diasporic experience.

To properly contextualize black athletic achievement in the twentieth century, it is crucial to first consider the ideological and social impact of scientific racism. During the mid- to late nineteenth century, scientific racism proved to be the ideological rationalization for the enslavement and colonization of Africans and other "subject" races. Canonized scholars, such as Joseph Arthur, Comte de Gobineau, and Charles Darwin, devoted entire volumes to the hierarchical ranking of the races, which placed Europeans and European civilization at its apex, and African and African civilization at its nadir. Attesting that Gobineau's theories justify the exploitation of slavery and imperialism by proclaiming the unusual stamina of subject peoples, Miller stated:

> Such assertions about European superiority, as strained as they were, also constituted arguments for white supremacy. The ideology of empire thus incorporated the so-called feeble races into elaborate systems of hard labor: the institution of slavery in the United States and colonial workforces elsewhere around the world. Stamina . . . as a kind of brutish endurance, the ability to "bear fatigue" would ultimately be conceived as a trait characteristic of subject peoples who would work on the plantations . . . that fed, clothed and enriched imperialism. (Miller, 2000, p. 331)

In Gobineau's view, subject peoples are able to tolerate fatigue; therefore, their subjugation is not immoral, it is banal.

At the dawn of the twentieth century, racialist theories, seemingly influenced by the earlier work of Gobineau, were used to explain the late-nineteenth-century athletic achievements of blacks. Twentieth-century racial theorists reinterpreted stamina, or brutish strength, as innate athleticism resulting from innate anthropometric difference. These theorized physical differences became common literary fare, as evinced by Miller's citation of a 1900 *Encyclopedia Britannica* entry:

> By 1900 . . . another dimension of scientific racism could be discerned. Rather than simply reinforce prevailing notions of Negro inferiority, experts felt compelled to account for the extraordinary achievements of some black athletes. In the face of an increasing number of victories posted by African Americans, the mainstream culture began to qualify the meanings of excellence in sport. The *Encyclopedia Britannica* had described "the abnormal length of the arm" and "the low instep." Increasingly, these specifications would be advanced as reasons for black success in sports. (p. 331)

Thus, at the dawn of the twentieth century, American society was exposed to social Darwinist thought, which not only discounts the rigor and mental discipline behind black athletic achievement through pseudo-scientific claims of inborn athleticism but also connotes intellectual inferiority as well. Although the commonly held view of innate black athleticism and the anthropometry promulgated by the *Encyclopedia Britannica* would be disproved by African-American scholar W. Montague Cobb's experiments on Jesse Owens in 1935, the early-twentieth-century boxing career of Jack Johnson reveals the sociopolitical impact of racialist theories on African-American athletic achievement.

Johnson's ascendance to the heavyweight throne stirred national controversy on many levels. First and foremost, Johnson refused to placate American society by adhering to white supremacist notions of subservient "negro" behavior. Becoming one of the most vilified public figures in American history, he willfully violated taboo by marrying several white women and adopting a bohemian lifestyle at a time when the Ku Klux Klan terrorized African Americans throughout the country. Of his dangerously unconventional lifestyle, Johnson remarked that he was "not a slave. . . . I have the right to choose who my mate shall be without the dictation of any man. . . . I have eyes and I have a heart . . . and when they fail to tell me who I shall have for mine I want to be put away in a lunatic asylum" (Gilmore, 1975, p. 14).

Johnson's indomitable spirit clearly incurred the wrath of early-twentieth-century American society, and while he is not typically considered an example of revolutionary African-American consciousness, his open defiance of racist norms represents a measure of self-determination atypical of most African Americans in the 1900s. Given Johnson's exceptional confidence and self-possession, it is not surprising that he issued a challenge to then heavyweight titleholder Tommy Burns in 1907, after learning that the Canadian champ would cross the color line unlike the majority of white contenders at the time. Johnson and Burns met for "the fight of the century" in Australia one year later, and predictions of race war made for an intensely charged social climate: "McIntosh announced to the world that Burns and Johnson would fight for the championship. . . . The declaration unleashed an outpouring of racial bigotry. . . . The *Australian Star* offered the opinion that 'this battle may in the future be looked upon as the first great battle of an inevitable race war'" (McCaffrey, 2000, pp. 197–199). Johnson won the match after fourteen rounds, becoming the first man of African descent to win the world heavyweight title.

Johnson's victory over Burns began the search for a "Great White Hope" who could defeat him. In 1909, one year after his title-winning fight against Burns, Johnson easily defeated five white American challengers. Though

Johnson had clearly proven himself to be a formidable boxer, most white Americans did not believe him to be the rightful champion, because he defeated Burns and not the undefeated American champion, Jim Jeffries. Finding himself once again at the center of controversy, Johnson met Jeffries in 1910, and it was this second major bout of Johnson's championship career that revealed the degree to which Americans' acceptance of social Darwinist thought had peaked: "From the very first, it was advertised as a match of civilization and virtue against savagery and baseness. . . . Humanity needed Jeffries. He had inherited the White Man's Burden" (Roberts, 2000, p. 45). Jeffries echoed this sentiment by announcing that he would not "disappoint the public. That portion of the white race that has been looking to defend its athletic superiority may feel assured that I am fit to do my best" (Roberts, 2000, p. 58). Jeffries's proclamations of superior fitness were in vain, for Johnson defeated him and remained world heavyweight champion until 1915.

While Jack Johnson was a youth in the late nineteenth century up until the end of his boxing career in 1915, baseball was thriving in Cuba and among African Americans and Afro-Cubans in the Negro leagues. Numerous baseball teams, referred to as nines, were formed among African Americans in the United States and among Cubans, both in Cuba and in the Negro leagues: "African Americans and Cubans, however, had joined in the baseball fever long before the majors were formed. By 1900 the two peoples had fielded hundreds of nines in their respective communities. Baseball clearly and decisively captured both peoples' imaginations and developed parallel to the game in North America" (Brock and Bayne, 1998, p. 170).

As the American national pastime, baseball's parallel development among African-American and Cuban players may be analyzed through the lens of national identity formation. Continually faced with racial discrimination, African Americans have, according to W. E. B. Du Bois, perceived of their existence from within "the Veil" of "double consciousness." This consciousness of being at once black, subject to the vilest forms at racism, and American creates a bifurcated identity that African Americans ever attempt to reconcile. In their creation of a parallel sphere of baseball, African Americans seemingly reconciled their identities as lovers of the national pastime and as members of a larger African-American community. Barred from participating in the major leagues, African-American baseball players in the Negro leagues gave full expression to their American identity by playing the game among themselves. Interestingly, in Cuba baseball took on nationalistic overtones as Cubans conceptualized the sport as a symbol of Cuban national identity as distinct from their former Spanish colonial identity. These African-American and Cuban players who perceived baseball as a type of national inheritance confounded white American baseball players during off-season exhibition games, known as barnstorming.

As barnstorming brought the exceptional play of African Americans and Cubans to the immediate attention of white players, these exhibition games not only allowed players to hone their skills by playing unfamiliar teams, they also provided baseball players a means of supplementing their incomes. Thus, despite Jim Crow's hold over most team sports, white, African-American, and Cuban players competed against each other. As Lanctot (2000) confirms:

> Organized baseball, despite its unwritten yet unyielding ban on African Americans after 1899, hardly remained isolated from black professional baseball. Eager to supplement their modest salaries, major and minor league players arranged exhibition games against black professional clubs. . . . As early as 1885, the Cuban Giants booked games against the New York Metropolitans and the Philadelphia Athletics . . . and later faced other league clubs, including the St. Louis Browns and Cincinnati Red Stockings as well as . . . the Kansas City Cowboys, Indianapolis Hoosiers, Boston Beaneaters, and Detroit Wolverine. (p. 63)

In addition to barnstorming against African Americans and Cubans on American soil, white American teams also traveled to Cuba during the off-season, continuing their unspoken rivalry with the best Cuban teams: "Since the 1890's, organized baseball teams had traveled to Cuba in the winter to face increasingly stiff local competition. In 1908, the Cincinnati Reds . . . lost seven of eleven games to Cuban teams. . ." (Lanctot, 2000, p. 65).

The undisputed dominance of Cuban baseball players created a conundrum for white American teams adhering to the color line, for most Cuban players were visibly of African descent. New Britain of the Connecticut League signed four light-skinned Cubans, and the Cincinnati Reds signed Armando Marsans and Rafael Almeidau. Darker Cubans, like famed pitcher Jose Mendez, remained unsigned by major and minor league white teams.

Darker skinned Afro-Cubans, however, were eagerly welcomed in the Negro leagues where, "the first team of professional Cubans known to play on the black circuit were the All-Cubans in 1904" (Brock and Bayne, 1998, p. 177). Several other Cuban teams, including the Havana Cubans, the Cuban Stars, and the Cuban Stars-East, were

Cuban sports star Savon, a boxer, is honored by Fidel Castro at an awards ceremony in Havana, 2001. *Savon, a three-time Olympic champion boxer, is presented with a framed certificate honoring him as the most outstanding sportsman of the millennium in Cuba.* © REUTERS/CORBIS

signed to the Negro leagues during the 1900s and 1920s, firmly establishing their incorporation within the Negro leagues. According to one baseball organizer who described the disappointment of African American fans when "the Cuban Stars . . . of Cincinnati . . . did not return to the United States the next year, fans of the west were deprived the privilege of seeing one of the most colorful clubs, and one of the strongest baseball clubs ever assembled in any league" (Brock and Bayne, 1998, p. 182).

Ironically, at the same time that African-American and Cuban baseball players thrived in the segregated, parallel sphere of the Negro leagues in 1918, Paul Robeson, an African-American student at Rutgers University, broke the color-line in football, becoming the first African American selected to the All-American football team. After he graduated Phi Beta Kappa from Rutgers and attended Columbia University Law School, Robeson's athletic career featured brief stints with the Akron Pros and the Milwaukee Badgers. Though Robeson's professional athletic career was brief, it is highly significant that Robeson was a former athlete who transitioned into two careers—theater and international political activism—that were ostensibly distinct from athletics. Although Robeson's selection onto the All-American teams represents an exception to the color line in sports, America was not alone in its racialist practices; racial segregation was also prevalent in Brazil. Only there, the national game in question was soccer.

In the late nineteenth and early twentieth centuries, soccer in Brazil was the sport of the country's European colonial elite; these Europeans and Euro-Brazilians maintained de facto segregation in soccer through the establishment of soccer clubs. These clubs provided recreation for Brazil's upper classes; businessmen, professionals, and politicians socialized together and competed against one another. Like most social sporting clubs of this nature, Brazilian soccer clubs came to symbolize class and privilege, its members both wealthy and white. In order to join these clubs, Afro-Brazilians were forced to find patrons willing to sponsor their membership; needless to say, this sponsorship clause was merely used as a ploy, ostensibly proving that Brazilian soccer clubs did not officially practice racial segregation. The exclusion of Afro-Brazilian players thus reinforced extant race, caste, and class hierarchies within Brazil's colonial society and led to the formation of parallel soccer clubs reflective of the players' respective social positions:

> The clubs . . . represented and dramatized other social differences . . . in Rio, Fluminese was associated with the old, high-status families, Flamengo the team of the poor and the blacks, Vasco da Gama supported by Portuguese migrants and their Brazilian-born descendants while Botafogo attracted the modern middle class. (Mason, 1995, p. 97)

The late 1920s and early 1930s would prove to be a significant era in the growth of Brazilian soccer. On May 13, 1927, a black-versus-white soccer match was held in celebration of Abolition Day; Afro-Brazilians won the first two matches, proving themselves worthy opponents undeserving of strictures limiting their potential range of competitors. This competition may have catalyzed the integration of Brazil's elite soccer clubs. Brazilian soccer clubs were beginning to integrate; nevertheless, racism was maintained in the Liga Metropolitana de Desportos Terrestres (LMDT). The LMDT instituted exclusionary practices similar to those of the late-nineteenth-century elite soccer clubs. Though it did not formally ban blacks, the LMDT instituted a type of literacy test that would prevent both black and poor soccer players from competing:

> . . . in an astonishing attempt to . . . keep top football for the better-off player they introduced the

> AMEA card. Before each game every player had to complete one in the presence of officials and include the name, nationality, date of birth, place of study and workplace of the player. In a country where neither education nor literacy was widespread this was a test intended to exclude the poor white as well as the black player. (Mason, 1995, p. 50)

Thus, as white soccer clubs became increasingly aware of black soccer talent, the Brazilian sporting establishment seemed dedicated to maintaining a degree of racial segregation in soccer.

The 1930s—the Vargas era—represent a period in Brazilian history when nation building was of utmost importance; soccer was recognized as integral to this process of national and cultural identification:

> The Vargas era was a turning point in the relationship between football and politics. From this time not only the Federal Government but individual politicians would try to associate themselves with what was becoming an increasing powerful manifestation of Brazilian popular culture . . . the success of Brazilian football abroad, both at the club and international level, illuminated the name of Brazil for the rest of the world to see. (Mason, 1995, p. 63)

Clearly, the Brazilian government viewed soccer as a means of glorifying its country's presence on the world stage; as national propaganda became a priority, it followed that the government would encourage the recruitment of the best players onto its teams. As a result, those Afro-Brazilian players who excelled would be selected by soccer clubs, so that their outstanding play abroad would become synonymous with Brazil's greatness as a nation. It is not surprising, then, that "Fausto, one of the great black attacking centre-halves . . . compared himself to an orange which would one day be left as pulp by his white bosses" (Mason, 1995, p. 56). Fausto's experience of exploitation, however unfortunate, is indicative of widespread institutionalized discrimination against Afro-Brazilians. In Moore's study of institutionalized racism in Brazilian society from 1964 to 1985, Fauso's claims of exploitation may be substantiated by statistics revealing that semi-professional and professional soccer in Brazil offered socio-economic opportunity for Afro-Brazilians living in poverty. In Moore's estimation, "Afro-Brazilians are faced with tremendous disadvantages in the arena of education, and nowhere is this more telling than in the area of illiteracy. . . . Blacks had two times more chances than Whites of being illiterate, and Whites had four times more opportunities of going to the university than Blacks." (p. 402). Given that illiteracy remained a serious impediment to acquiring a college degree for Afro-Brazilians, it is not surprising that many viewed soccer as an opportunity for greater socio-economic mobility.

As Afro-Brazilians became more visible in soccer during the 1930s, African-American athletes were steeling themselves against domestic and international pressure to boycott the 1936 Olympic Games in Berlin. The Amateur Athletic Union (AAU), along with several international and domestic human rights groups, grew increasingly vocal against the Nazi regime's racialist ideology of Aryan supremacy and its anti-Semitism. A widespread media campaign, involving several of the nation's leading newspapers, debated the issue of American, and particularly African-American, participation in the Games. While a relatively small number of African-American Olympians supported the boycott movement, the majority of athletes resented the AAU's sudden interest in the plight of Jews, when the organization had done nothing to assist its American athletes of African descent: "The most powerful of American amateur sport bodies continually rallied against the cruelties inflicted by the Hitler government but generally did nothing to improve the plight of black athletes in America." (Wiggins, 1997, p. 69).

Jesse Owens' historic four-gold-medal performance was one of several outstanding track-and-field performances of African Americans that earned a staggering half of the American Olympic team's total of 167 medals. Other African American medalists in track and field included Ralph Metcalfe, Mack Robinson (Jackie Robinson's older brother), Archie Williams, James Luvalle, John Woodruff, Cornelius Johnson, David Albritton, and Fritz Pollard, Jr. Thus, in a single Olympiad, African American athletes had disproved Hitler's theory of Aryan supremacy, which only months earlier had seemingly been substantiated by Max Schmeling's defeat of Joe Louis.

The symbolism of Joe Louis's rematch against Schmeling in 1938, consequently, took on epic proportions. Unlike the Johnson-Jeffries bout in which Social Darwinist theories of racial superiority were tested, the Louis-Schmeling match became a struggle that not only tested racial fitness; it became a battle between opposing political philosophies: democracy and justice versus fascism and oppression, with Louis and Schmeling as warring political icons: "The political mood of the country had changed dramatically in the brief two-year span between their first meeting in 1936. . . . With the increasing militaristic tension of the times, both fighters became living symbols of their respective countries' fundamental beliefs" (William Wiggins, 2004, p. 138). Louis's victory announced the perpetuity of American democratic values; furthermore, his subsequent acts of patriotism—donating a combined total of $82,000 to the Army and Navy Relief Funds, and enlisting in the Army—enshrined him as a national hero whose broad based appeal was unmatched by any other athlete in history.

While Joe Louis's triumph over Max Schmeling was an inspiration to millions of Americans, the sport of boxing was intensely scrutinized among British colonial officials in Rhodesia (now Zimbabwe). Chief Native Commissioner Bullock strongly believed that in order to maintain British imperial order, colonial subjects should not be encouraged to take up the sport, believing that, "boxing would make urban Africans aggressive" (Ranger, 1997, p. 203). Aggressive Africans would be more difficult to rule, more confrontational, less willing to maintain their prescribed subject positions. In addition to fearing widespread African recalcitrance, Bullock was also wary of the tribal linkages that could potentially be strengthened through the event of national boxing tournaments, linkages among Africans that could potentially threaten British colonial rule: "Bullock . . . was himself most worried by the far-ranging tribal networks that underlay the boxing factions of Salisbury" (Ranger, 1997, p. 203). Thus, in boxing, England's chief colonial officer saw something far more troubling than the pursuit of athleticism; Bullock saw the potential for national consciousness and self-determination, the necessary components for decolonization, which directly threatened British hegemony in Rhodesia and on the greater African continent.

As Joe Louis continued to dominate boxing and African men in Rhodesia were prevented from doing so, African-American women were beginning to emerge as international track-and-field stars. Just one year after Jackie Robinson's historic integration of the major leagues, Alice Coachman became the first woman of African descent to win a gold medal at the 1948 London Olympics. Dominating the high jump, Coachman also became the first American woman to win an individual track-and-field medal at the Games. Despite the groundbreaking nature of Coachman's achievement, she did not become famous as Owens had only twelve years earlier and as Jackie Robinson had one year before. Coachman, like other African-American women athletes, remained a relatively obscure figure whose accomplishments were never properly acknowledged by the white media. Explaining the white American media's disregard for Coachman's achievement, Cahn (2000) writes:

> For the most part black women athletes were simply ignored by the white media. Figures like Alice Coachman . . . or Mildred McDaniel, the only American woman to win an individual gold medal in the 1956 Olympic track-and-field competition, did not become national celebrities . . . or even the subject of magazine feature stories. The most striking feature of the historical record on black women athletes is neglect. (p. 220)

Though the triumphs of African-American female track-and-field athletes were ignored by white American society, these women—like the Negro league players of the 1900s—honed their skills in the parallel sphere of historically black colleges where young African-American women were encouraged to participate in track-and-field events. At Tuskegee Institute, where the first collegiate women's track meet was held as early as 1929, Coachman traveled with her teammates throughout the South to compete in track meets in the 1930s. Traveling through the Jim Crow South, away from the haven of Tuskegee, these young women were exposed to the harsh realities of American racism.

As American society in the 1930s and 1940s saw the rise of Joe Louis as a symbol of democracy and justice, British colonial subjects in Trinidad began to view their native cricketers as national heroes. In *Beyond a Boundary*, noted Trinidadian scholar C.L. R. James underscores the manner in which the British colonial hierarchy created racial, caste, and class divisions in cricket, and the society at-large, engendering widespread discrimination against Trinidadians of African descent. Of famous Afro-Trinidadian batsman Wilton St. Hill's outstanding play and his subsequent failure to be selected for the Trinidadian team in 1923, James writes:

> to tens of thousands of coloured Trinidadians the unquestionable glory of St. Hills batting conveyed the sensation that here was one of us, performing in excelsis. . . . It was a demonstration that atoned for a pervading humiliation, and nourished pride and hope. . . . Wilton St. Hill was our boy. . . . We became convinced . . . that St. Hill was the greatest of all West Indian batsmen and on English wickets this coloured man would infallibly put all white rivals in the shade. And they too were afraid of precisely the same thing. (p. 93)

That St. Hill was deemed a Trinidadian national hero is significant, for in embracing St. Hill as a hero, Trinidadians broke the long-standing colonial tradition of idealizing, and idolizing, British culture and British heroes. What is more, St. Hill's superior play refuted theories of inherent British superiority. If St. Hill could beat the British at their own game, surely an entire nation of Trinidadians could direct the destiny of their own country. Thus, among Trinidadians a burgeoning sense of national consciousness was born, and though they were still colonial subjects they were beginning to experience the stirrings of national pride, a crucial element of national self-definition and self-determination.

Throughout the 1920s and 1930s, James established a career as a noted cricket writer who continually advocated for the inclusion of Afro-Trinidadian players on the country's national teams. As his editorial agitation for these players' recognition intensified, so did his political beliefs, and in 1932 James penned the influential text, *The Case for West Indian Self-Rule*. This seminal text, according to James, was partially responsible for the politicization of oilfield workers throughout the Caribbean, who were used as an exploited colonial labor force to supply England with an inexpensive oil supply. On *The Case for West Indian Self-Rule's* influence on West Indian colonial laborers, James (1983) writes:

> Trinidad workers in the oilfields moved. They were followed by masses of people in all the other islands, closing one epoch in West Indian history and opening another. . . . When the upheavals did take place these books were high on the list of those few that helped them to make the mental and moral transition which the new circumstances required. (p. 121)

The closing epoch of which James writes is that of colonialism; the emerging one is that of decolonization. Thus, through his and the Trinidadians' love of cricket an independent national consciousness was born; it was a consciousness that allowed James to launch his unflinching assault on the racist colonial practices inherent to the game itself, and intrinsic to Trinidadian colonial society.

West Indian decolonization of the 1960s mirrored the national liberation movements on the African continent, and the American civil rights and Black Power movements. The seeds of dissent and self-determination germinated throughout the African diaspora, and its athletes, from Ethiopia to America, became symbols of black liberation. With Ethiopian runner Abebe Bikila's historic marathon victory in Rome, the 1960 Olympics seemed to herald both the arrival of the African athlete and the age of African nationalism: "Finally, in 1960 Abebe Biklila of Ethiopia ran the marathon barefoot through the streets of Rome to claim the first gold medal for a black African nation" (Baker, 1987, p. 275). Bikila's gold-medal performance marked the beginning of African runners' more than forty-year dominance of distance running that, to date, shows no sign of waning. Although the historical significance of Bikila's marathon win is unquestionable, the athlete that would most famously come to symbolize black people's struggle for self-determination would be former heavyweight champion Muhammad Ali.

In 1964, during the height of the civil rights movement and the pinnacle of Malcolm X's ministry with the Nation of Islam, Muhammad Ali publicly announced his conversion from Christianity to the Black Muslim faith. Formerly known as Cassius Clay, a patriot, Ali shocked America by joining a religious order known for its interrelated doctrines of racial separatism, African-American self-reliance, and African-American pride. Ali took a political stance in joining the Black Muslim order, and it was a stance that many Americans deemed far too radical: "Ali's conversion from Christian to Muslim seemed to some whites much like going from Stepin Fetchit to Nat Turner. The change broke a compact that Americans had forged with their black athletes—'be good negroes and enjoy the fruits of athletic success'" (Zang, 2000, p. 290). In deciding to chart the course of his own sociopolitical destiny as an African American, Ali, like Jack Johnson before him, defied white Americans' preconceived notions of acceptable black behavior.

In 1966 Ali became a conscientious objector to the Vietnam War, famously remarking, "Man, I ain't got no quarrel with them Vietcong" (Zang, 2000, p. 294). The following year, Ali was stripped of his heavyweight title for failing to report for military duty. Though he would not regain his title until 1974, his act of conscience inspired the birth of the 1968 Olympic Project for Human Rights (OPHR), led by San Jose State College professor Harry Edwards, which called for African-American athletes to boycott the 1968 Games in Mexico City. The OPHR's principal demands included the

> restoration of Muhammad Ali's title and right to box in this country; removal of the anti-semitic and anti-black personality Avery Brundage from . . . the International Olympic Committee; curtailment of participation of all-white teams . . . from the Union of South Africa and Southern Rhodesia in all United States and Olympic Athletic Events. . . . (Edwards, 1970, p. 59)

The Olympic Committee did, in fact, bar South Africa from competing in the games; as a result African-American athletes did not boycott the Games. Rather, they participated and symbolically displayed their solidarity with the growing Black Power movement: "Tommie Smith and John Carlos startled the world on October 16 when they bowed their heads in defiance and raised black-gloved fists high in the air while on the Olympic victory stand. . ." (Wiggins, 1997, p. 110).

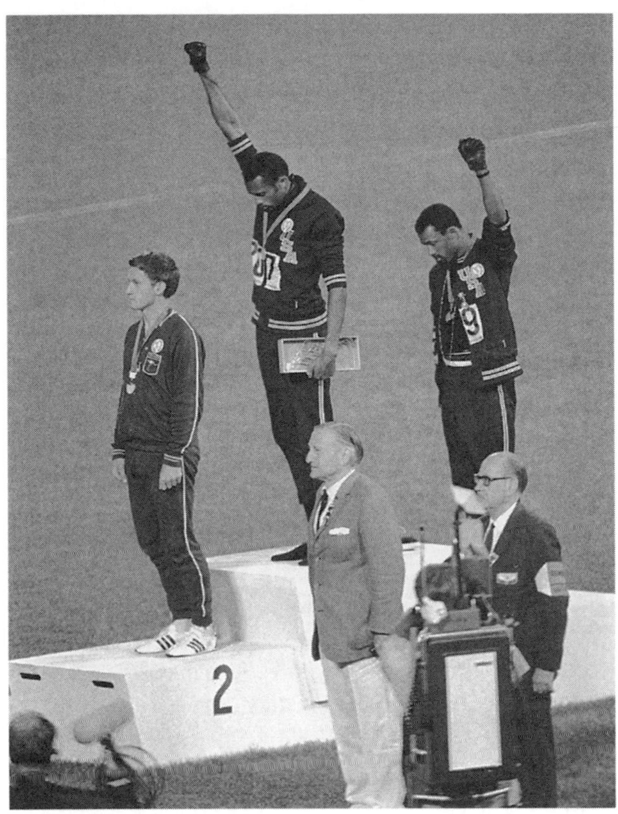

Tommy Smith (center) and John Carlos (right) at the 1968 Summer Olympics in Mexico City. *Amid the racial tensions of the 1960s, Smith and Carlos, who finished first and third, respectively, in the 200-meter finals, showed their solidarity with the Black Power movement by raising their black-gloved fists on the victory stand during the playing of the "Star Spangled Banner."* AP/WIDE WORLD PHOTOS. REPRODUCED BY PERMISSION.

While Smith and Carlos's display ignited strong reactions both within the Olympic Village and without, the 1972 Munich Games found yet another black athlete asserting his socio-political identity. Teofilo Stevenson, an Afro-Cuban boxer, competed for the Olympic heavyweight title. Following his gold-medal win, "Stevenson rejected a one million dollar offer to defect from Cuba and fight Ali" (Sugden, p. 191). Stevenson declined the offer, explaining: "not any money in the world is worth losing the love of millions of Cubans" (Sugden, p. 146).

Clearly, Stevenson privileged his national identity as a Cuban above his identity as an athlete; more significant to him than material wealth was his membership within the greater political collective of his native country. It is important to consider that Stevenson grew up during the Cuban Revolution, when anti-American imperialist sentiment ran high. As Sugden emphasizes: "After the revolution the deepening hostility in relations between Castro's government and the United States increased nationalism within Cuba" (Sugden, 1996, p. 150). Given that Stevenson was a young boy inculcated into nationalistic, revolutionary doctrine, his refusal of monetary gains is not surprising. In this manner, Stevenson was seemingly fulfilling his duties as a revolutionary Cuban. As Sugden (1996) further argues: "Olympic achievement provided a showcase for Castro's and Che Guevara's vision of the 'new Cuban' athletic hero who was nurtured through socialism and who participates purely for the love of his country" (p. 150). Stevenson's love of country was evident; regardless of his political indoctrination, he flatly refused a great deal of money that would have ensured him a life of comfort and ease. His rejection of the offer seemingly marked the end of an era, for in the coming decades, lucrative athletic contracts and endorsements would become much more common among black athletes than would acts of political conscience.

In 1984, Michael Jordan was not yet a household name; however, his relative anonymity would prove to be short-lived as the then National Basketball Association rookie would be catapulted into worldwide fame both on and off the court. Jordan's incomparable skills and daring play became well known to basketball fans: "There seemed to be nothing that Jordan could not do on the basketball court. His slam-dunk is legendary and he seems to defy gravity as he flies through the air" (Kellner, p. 309). As he continued to thrill spectators on the court, his lucrative contracts also became the subject of great discussion. During his rookie year with the Chicago Bulls, Jordan entered into his first highly profitable contract with Nike; over the next decade several others followed. Because Jordan's earning power seemed infinite, he opened the door for African-American athletes to obtain lucrative endorsement deals: "It is generally acknowledged that he was one of the first African American athletes to break advertising's color barrier, paving the way for lucrative contracts for the next generation of black athletes" (Kellner, p. 310). Unlike post–World War I and World War II athletes for whom a color barrier connoted Jim Crow segregation, which barred them from competition, in the post–civil rights era, the only color barrier that Jordan had to cross was one of potential earning power, a far cry from being unable to compete, or being underpaid because of race. Because of trailblazers like Harry Edwards and Bill Russell, who spoke out on the professional sports worlds' consistent underpayment of African-American athletes, Jordan did not have to concern himself with worries over equal pay. On the contrary, Jordan's 1984 Nike contract was unprecedented for a rookie player (Kellner, p. 311). Thus, the 1990s found Jordan unstoppable on the court as well as in the boardrooms.

When Jordan's unstoppable play and mounting endorsements created a one-man media frenzy in the early 1990s, Tiger Woods and Venus and Serena Williams were teenage prodigies, already showing signs that they would revolutionize golf and tennis.

As an African-American golfer of extraordinary talent, it is widely acknowledged that Tiger Woods completely changed the game. Prior to Woods, the game had maintained its reputation as the sport of America's white elite; however, once Woods became a force to be reckoned with, African Americans' historical exclusion from America's fairways seemed to have been vindicated: "Most astonishing of all, Woods has taken the most shameful theme of golf's history . . . and turned it inside out. For a hundred years, golf in American has stood as a potent symbol of exclusion and racial intolerance" (Owen, 2001, p. 177). Indeed, Woods' mastery of the game does provide a degree of retribution to black golfers. However, one must also consider that early-twentieth-century African-American golfers, like their fellow sportsmen in the Negro leagues, also established the parallel realm of the United States Colored Golf Association (USCGA), later renamed the (UGA). Equally worthy of note is that the first man to patent the golf tee was an African American by the name of Dr. George Franklin Grant, a dentist from Boston (Sinette, pp. 7–11). Woods's accomplishments in golf are too numerous to list here; suffice it to say that his stellar play not only vindicates African-American exclusion from the sport; it also honors those African American pioneers in golf, like Dr. Grant, who came before him.

Similar to Woods, the Williams sisters transformed the country club sport of tennis. Unconventionally coached by their father, who learned the game by watching instructional videos and reading tennis books, Venus and Serena Williams perfected their game on the asphalt courts of Compton, California, a neighborhood known for widespread drug and gang activity. From the moment Venus turned professional in 1994, and Serena in 1995, the Williams sisters established themselves as athletic virtuosos able to prove that they would—just as they had predicted early into their careers—forever change the game of women's tennis.

Since the dawn of the twentieth century, the black athletic achievement in the African diaspora has come to symbolize various historical and ideological struggles. As a result, black athletes in America, Africa, and the Caribbean have been alternately vilified and lionized by their respective societies. Dramatically altering the black athlete's past political activism, however, have been sociopolitical and socio-economic gains made possible by the national independence struggles in Africa and the Caribbean, and the civil rights and Black Power movements in the United States.

The one societal factor that remains unchanged, that is, remains endemic to the interpretation of black athletic achievement, however, is racism. As recently as the 1980s two well-known sports personalities, Al Campanis, a former Major League Baseball official, and Jimmy "The Greek" Snyder, revealed the extent to which the tenets of scientific racism and social Darwinism are still followed. Campanis remarked that: "blacks performed well on the field but lacked 'the necessities' to occupy managerial positions . . . in the front offices of sports organizations" (Miller, p. 338). In this statement Campanis not only revealed his belief in the intellectual inferiority of blacks; he also revealed his ignorance. Former Celtic Bill Russell coached the Boston Celtics from 1966 to 1969, at which time he led the Celtics to two NBA championships; the Seattle Supersonics from 1973 to 1977; and the Sacramento Kings from 1987 to 1988. Campanis's ideological partner in crime, Jimmy "The Greek," expostulated on Darwinian evolutionary theory, stating: "The slave owner would breed his big black with his big woman so that he could have a big black kid" (Miller, p. 338). The big black kid of whom The Greek so crudely speaks is the black athlete.

Over a century has passed since the works of Gobineau and Darwin were published, and it remains painfully obvious that racialist theories of innate black athleticism and deficient black intelligence are still accepted as truth. The fact that these theories have been repeatedly disproved throughout the twentieth century is, apparently, of no interest to the believers, because as recently as 2000 the latest addition to the canon of racialist theory was published: John Entine's *Taboo: Why Black Athletes Dominate Sport and Why We're Afraid to Talk About It.* It is unclear why Entine thinks the subject of black athletic achievement is taboo. Black athletic achievement has been debated for over two centuries and, as Entine has shown, the accomplishments of black athletes will continue to ignite sociopolitical discourse on either side of the ideological divide.

See also Ali, Muhammad; Baseball; Basketball; Boxing; Gibson, Althea; Johnson, Jack; Jordan, Michael; Louis, Joe; Olympians; Owens, Jesse; Robeson, Paul; Robinson, Jackie; Soccer; Tennis; Williams, Venus and Serena; Woods, Tiger

Bibliography

Baker, William J. "Political Games: The Meaning of International Sport for Independent Africa." In *Sport in Africa: Es-*

says in Social History, edited by William J. Baker and James A. Managan. New York: Holmes & Meir-Africana Publishing Company, 1987.

Brock, Lisa, and Bijan Bayne. "Not Just Baseball: African-Americans, Cubans, and Baseball." In *Between Race and Empire: African-Americans and Cubans Before the Revolution,* edited by Lisa Brock and Digna Castaneda Fuentes. Philadelphia: Temple University Press, 1998.

Cahn, Susan. "'Cinderallas' of Sport: Black Women in Track and Field." In *Sport and the Color Line: Black Athletes and Race Relations in Twentieth Century America,* edited by Patrick B. Miller and David K. Wiggins. New York: Routledge, 2004.

Du Bois, W. E. B. *The Souls of Black Folk.* New York: Vintage Books–Library of America, 1990.

Edwards, Harry. *The Revolt of the Black Athlete.* New York: Macmillan/The Free Press, 1970.

Gilmore, Al-Tony. *Bad Nigger! The National Impact of Jack Johnson.* Port Washington, N.Y.: Kennikat Press, 1975.

Hoberman, John. *Darwin's Athletes: How Sport Has Damaged Black America and Preserved the Myth of Race.* Boston: Houghton Mifflin, 1997.

James, C. L. R. *Beyond a Boundary.* Durham, N.C.: Duke University Press, 1983.

Kellner, Douglas. "The Sports Spectacle, Michael Jordan, and Nike." In *Sport and the Color Line: Black Athletes and Race Relations in Twentieth Century America,* edited by Patrick B. Miller and David K. Wiggins. New York: Routledge, 2004.

Lanctot, Neil. "'A General Understanding': Organized Baseball and Black Professional Baseball, 1900–1930." In *Sport and the Color Line: Black Athletes and Race Relations in Twentieth Century America,* edited by Patrick B. Miller and David K. Wiggins. New York: Routledge, 2004.

Mason, Tony. *Passion of the People? Football in South America.* London: Verso, 1995.

McCaffrey, Dan. *Tommy Burns: Canada's Unknown World Heavyweight Champion.* Toronto: James Lorimer, 2000.

Miller, Patrick B. "The Anatomy of Scientific Racism." In *Sport and the Color Line: Black Athletes and Race Relations in Twentieth Century America,* edited by Patrick B. Miller and David K. Wiggins. New York: Routledge, 2004.

Moore, Zelbert L. "Out of the Shadows: Black and Brown Struggles for Recognition and Dignity in Brazil, 1964–1985." *Journal of Black Studies* 19, no. 4 (June 1989): 394–410.

Owen, David. *The Chosen One: Tiger Woods and the Dilemma of Greatness.* New York: Simon and Schuster, 2001.

Perez, Louis Jr. "Between Baseball and Bullfighting: The Quest for National Identity in Cuba, 1868–1898." *Journal of American History* 81 (September 1994): 494.

Ranger, Terence. "Pugilism and Pathology: African Boxing and the Black Experience in Southern Rhodesia." In *Sport in Africa: Essays in Social History,* edited by William J. Baker and James A. Managan. New York: Holmes & Meier-Africana Publishing Company, 1997.

Roberts, Randy. "Year of the Comet: Jack Johnson versus Jim Jeffries, July 4, 1910." In *Sport and the Color Line: Black Athletes and Race Relations in Twentieth Century America,* edited by Patrick B. Miller and David K. Wiggins. New York: Routledge, 2004.

Sinette, Calvin H. *Forbidden Fairways: African Americans and the Game of Golf.* Chelsea, Mich.: Sleeping Bear Press, 1998.

Spivey, Donald. "'End Jim Crow in Sports': The Leonard Bates Controversy and Protest at New York University, 1940–1941." In *Sport and the Color Line: Black Athletes and Race Relations in Twentieth Century America,* edited by Patrick B. Miller and David K. Wiggins. New York: Routledge, 2004.

Stewart, Mark. *Venus and Serena Williams: Sisters in Arms.* Brookfield, Conn.: Millbrook Press, 2000.

Sugden, John. *Boxing and Society: An International Analysis.* Manchester, England: Manchester University Press, 1996.

Wiggins, David K. "The Notion of Double Consciousness and the Involvement of Black Athletes in American Sport." In *Ethnicity and Sport in North American History and Culture,* edited by George Eisen and David K. Wiggins. Westport, Conn.: Greenwood Press, 1994.

Wiggins, David K. *Glory Bound: Black Athletes in a White America.* Syracuse, N.Y.: Syracuse University Press, 1997.

Wiggins, William H. "Joe Louis: American Folk Hero." In *Sport and the Color Line: Black Athletes and Race Relations in Twentieth Century America,* edited by Patrick B. Miller and David K. Wiggins. New York: Routledge, 2004.

Zang, David K. "The Greatest: Muhammad Ali's Confounding Career." In *Sport and the Color Line: Black Athletes and Race Relations in Twentieth Century America,* edited by Patrick B. Miller and David K. Wiggins. New York: Routledge, 2004.

LAROSE PARRIS (2005)

Stepin Fetchit (Perry, Lincoln)

May 30, 1902
November 19, 1985

Lincoln Theodore Monroe Andrew Perry, named after four U.S. presidents, became a major star as Stepin Fetchit and the center of a still-ongoing controversy. His supporters see him as a pioneering black comic actor who had a pathbreaking Hollywood career; his detractors see him as one who profited through his demeaning depictions of African Americans.

Perry was born and raised in Key West, Florida, and left home in 1914 after a stint at St. Joseph's College (a Catholic boarding school) to pursue a career in show business, joining the Royal American Shows plantation minstrel revues. With comic Ed Lee, he developed a vaudeville act entitled "Step 'n' Fetchit: Two Dancing Fools from Dixie." When Perry and Lee split, he adopted the name "Stepin Fetchit" as his own.

Stepin Fetchit spent years on the TOBA (Theater Owners Booking Association) vaudeville circuit, developing his stage persona as a lazy, dim-witted, slow, shuffling black servant, where he performed for primarily black audiences to great success. Stepin Fetchit came to Hollywood in the 1920s, and his first appearance in the 1927 film *In Old Kentucky,* playing his stereotyped black persona, earned him a positive mention in *Variety*. The next two films in which he appeared—*Salute* (1929) and *Hearts of Dixie* (1929), the first all-black film musical—brought Stepin Fetchit considerable press attention.

Stepin Fetchit went on to make more than forty films from 1927 to 1976, becoming one of the first black Hollywood stars. He was a favorite of director John Ford, with whom he made five films: *Salute* (1929), *The World Moves On* (1934), *Judge Priest* (1934), *Steamboat Round the Bend* (1935), and *The Sun Shines Bright* (1954). In *Steamboat Round the Bend* and *Judge Priest,* Ford teamed him up with Will Rogers, with whom he had worked years earlier on the vaudeville circuit. The finale of *Judge Priest* consisted of Fetchit's leading a street parade in a top hat to the tune of "Dixie," and thereby stealing the show.

Nonetheless, Stepin Fetchit's main Hollywood career came to an end in the late 1930s. Black audiences were uncomfortable with the caricatures, and white audiences became tired of them. Stepin Fetchit left Hollywood in the early 1940s bankrupt, having reportedly squandered $1 million, and moved to Chicago, where he made occasional nightclub appearances. In the 1950s he reemerged, appearing in *Bend of the River* (1952) and *The Sun Shines Bright* (1954), but neither film succeeded in reviving his career. It was not until the late 1960s that he resurfaced as a member of Muhammad Ali's entourage and as the litigant in a 1970 $3 million lawsuit against CBS for, Stepin Fetchit claimed, "taking me, a Negro hero, and converting me into a villain," in a television show on black history. The suit was eventually dismissed.

In 1972 Stepin Fetchit was awarded a Special Image Award by the Hollywood chapter of the NAACP. He also received the Bethune-Cookman Award for Black Leadership (1972), and in 1978 he was presented with the Black Filmmakers' Hall of Fame Award. Stepin Fetchit died in Los Angeles in 1985.

See also Comedians; Film in the United States; Minstrels/Minstrelsy; Musical Theater

Bibliography

Bogle, Donald. *Toms, Coons, Mulattoes, Mammies and Bucks: An Interpretive History of Blacks in American Films.* New York: Viking, 1973.

Bogle, Donald. *Blacks in American Films and Television.* New York: Simon and Schuster, 1988.

"Comeback in Movies." *Ebony* (February 1952): 64–67.

"Stepin Fetchit." *Contemporary Black Biography,* vol. 32. Detroit, Mich.: Gale, 2002.

SUSAN MCINTOSH (1996)
Updated bibliography

STILL, WILLIAM

1821
JULY 14, 1902

Abolitionist William Still was the eighteenth and last child born to former slaves near Medford, Burlington County, New Jersey. His mother had escaped from a plantation in Maryland, and his father had bought his own freedom. Still worked on his family's farm until he was twenty, when he went to work for neighboring farmers. He had little formal education and was largely self-taught. In 1844 he left for Philadelphia, where he spent three years working at a number of odd jobs.

Still became involved with the abolitionist movement in 1847, when he was employed by the Pennsylvania Society for the Abolition of Slavery. Three years later he was named chair of the Philadelphia Vigilance Committee, the clandestine wing of the Abolition Society that organized the city's Underground Railroad. Still and the committee helped shelter fugitive slaves stopping in Philadelphia on the way to Canada. One of the slaves he helped was his brother, Peter Still, who had been left behind by his mother during her escape.

While working with the Pennsylvania Society, Still gave material aid to John Brown's raid on Harpers Ferry and housed Brown's wife after the raid. Still also worked as the Philadelphia distribution agent for the national abolitionist paper the *Provincial Freeman*. He discontinued his abolitionist work in 1861 but remained affiliated with the society for the remainder of his life.

During the Civil War Still devoted himself to business ventures; he opened a store that sold stoves, he sold provisions to black soldiers stationed at nearby Camp William Penn, and he started a successful coal business. In the late 1860s he led a successful campaign to end discrimination on Philadelphia streetcars, helped organize a research organization to collect data about African Americans, and played for the all-black Philadelphia Pythians baseball team, which was denied entry into a white league.

In 1872 Still published an extensive account of his work with fugitive slaves, *The Underground Railroad,* one of the few memoirs of this kind written by an African

American after Emancipation. The book portrays the runaway slaves as courageous, even heroic figures and their escape to freedom as an act of self-determination. Still's work was published in three editions and was the most widely circulated nineteenth-century history of the Underground Railroad.

In the late nineteenth century Still developed several modestly successful businesses and continued to devote himself to black social causes. In the 1870s and 1880s he supported local reform candidates, organized a YMCA branch for black youth, served on the Freedmen's Aid Commission, and helped manage homes for African-American elderly and orphans.

In the early 1880s Still was one of a group of older black leaders in the Northeast who left the Republican Party to encourage black political independence and support of Democratic candidates when such support was advantageous to African Americans. Despite his extensive political activities, Still advocated economic self-improvement over politics as the best course for black advancement.

In 1888 Still and his son-in-law, Matthew Anderson, a prominent black minister and businessman in Philadelphia, founded the Berean Building and Loan Association, which provided loans to black home buyers. Still served as the association's first president. From 1896 to 1901 he also served as president of the Pennsylvania Society for the Abolition of Slavery, which after 1865 continued to work for African-American rights and added "and for Improving the Condition of the African Race" to its title. Still died in Philadelphia in 1902.

See also Abolition; Underground Railroad

Bibliography

Buckmaster, Henrietta. *Let My People Go: The Story of the Underground Railroad and the Growth of the Abolition Movement* (1941). Columbia: University of South Carolina Press, 1992.

Hendrick, George, and Willene Hendrick. *Fleeing for Freedom: Stories of the Underground Railroad As Told by Levi Coffin and William Still.* Chicago: Ivan R. Dee, 2004.

Lane, Roger. *William Dorsey's Philadelphia and Ours: On the Past and Future of the Black City in America.* New York: Oxford University Press, 1991.

Still, William. *The Underground Railroad* (1872). New York: Arno Press, 1968.

THADDEUS RUSSELL (1996)
Updated bibliography

Still, William Grant

May 11, 1895
December 3, 1978

Although he was born in Woodville, Mississippi, composer William Grant Still grew up in Little Rock, Arkansas. He attended Wilberforce University and Oberlin College. His private studies in composition were with George Whitefield Chadwick in Boston and Edgard Varèse in New York.

Still's musical style is perhaps best described as nationalist, successfully blending indigenous American musical elements, African-American folk materials, and the blues idiom into a range of musical genres: symphonic and operatic compositions, chamber music, and art songs. Many of his compositions were inspired by the black experience in America. Over the years he developed an eloquent musical expressiveness in his works. An outstanding achievement was his handling of melody in his strongly lyrical pieces.

Because he was an excellent orchestrator, Still was engaged by such celebrities as Paul Whiteman, Don Voorhees, Sophie Tucker, Willard Robison, and Artie Shaw to prepare orchestral arrangements. In his early years he played in various dance orchestras and pit orchestras for musicals. Still was associated in the music industry with W. C. Handy, Harry Pace and his Black Swan Phonograph Company, the *Deep River Hour* on CBS Radio, and Columbia Pictures.

Still composed over 150 musical works. His most significant symphonic compositions are the Afro-American Symphony (1930), Symphony No. 2 in G Minor (1937), *Festive Overture* (1944), *Plain-Chant for America* (1941, revised 1968), *From the Black Belt* (1926), *And They Lynched Him on a Tree* (1940), and *Darker America* (1924). Still composed ten operas, including *Highway 1, U.S.A.* (1962), *Troubled Island* (1941), and *A Bayou Legend* (1941). His ballets include *Sadhji* (1930), *Lenox Avenue* (1937), and *La Guiablesse* (1927). Verna Arvey, his wife, collaborated as a librettist in the writing of many of his works.

Still received many commissions, awards, prizes, and honorary degrees, as well as Guggenheim and Rosenwald Fellowships. His contributions to African-American music are significant: He was the first African-American composer to have a symphony played by a major American orchestra (*Afro-American Symphony*), the first to have an opera performed by a major company, the first to conduct a major orchestra, and one of the first to write for radio, films, and television.

See also Music in the United States; Opera

Bibliography

Arvey, Verna. *In One Lifetime.* Fayetteville: University of Arkansas Press, 1984.

Southern, Eileen. "William Grant Still." In *Biographical Dictionary of Afro-American and African Musicians.* Westport, Conn.: Greenwood Press, 1982.

LUCIUS R. WYATT (1996)

Stokes, Carl Burton

June 21, 1927
April 3, 1996

Lawyer and politician Carl Stokes was born and raised in Cleveland, Ohio. He attended West Virginia State College from 1947 to 1948 and Cleveland College of Western Reserve University from 1948 to 1950. He left college to take a job with the enforcement division of the Ohio State Department of Liquor Control. In 1952 Stokes enrolled in the University of Minnesota at Minneapolis, receiving a B.S. degree in law in 1954. He then entered the Cleveland Marshall School of Law, and in 1956 received an LL.B. degree. That year he and his brother, Louis Stokes, opened the law firm of Minor, McCurdy, Stokes & Stokes in Cleveland.

In 1958 Stokes began his career in government when Cleveland's Mayor Anthony J. Celebrezze appointed him as an assistant city prosecutor. In the late 1950s Stokes became involved in the civil rights movement, and in 1958 he was elected to the executive committee of the Cleveland branch of the National Association for the Advancement of Colored People (NAACP). In 1962 he entered electoral politics, becoming the first black Democrat elected to the Ohio General Assembly. He was reelected twice and served through 1967.

In 1965, while serving as a legislator, Stokes ran unsuccessfully for mayor of Cleveland as an independent Democrat in a general election decided by fewer than three thousand votes. In 1967 he ran again, this time in the Democratic primary election and, with the help of voter registration drives conducted by the Southern Christian Leadership Conference (SCLC) and the Congress of Racial Equality (CORE), defeated his two opponents, including incumbent candidate Ralph Locher. In the general election Stokes easily defeated his Republican opponent, Seth C. Taft, to become the first elected black mayor of a major American city. He was reelected in 1969 but decided not to run for a third term in 1971.

Stokes's tenure as mayor was marked by his efforts to conciliate Cleveland's white and conservative populations while accommodating the demands of a restive black community. His administration succeeded in raising the city income tax to increase spending for schools, welfare, street improvement, the city zoo, and water purification. Stokes faced his greatest challenge in the summer after his election, when a black nationalist group ambushed and killed several city police officers, sparking a nightlong shoot-out and five days of rioting in the predominantly African-American neighborhood of Glenville. Stokes initially responded by mandating that only black police officers patrol the area, but after several days of rioting, he called in the National Guard, finally quelling the uprising. Stokes's administration was rocked the following spring when it was revealed that funds provided by the mayor's "Cleveland: Now!" urban rehabilitation program had been used without approval to purchase the weapons used in the Glenville shoot-out. Resulting conflicts with the police department, as well as the voters' refusal to raise the city income tax again, compelled Stokes to leave office after his second term.

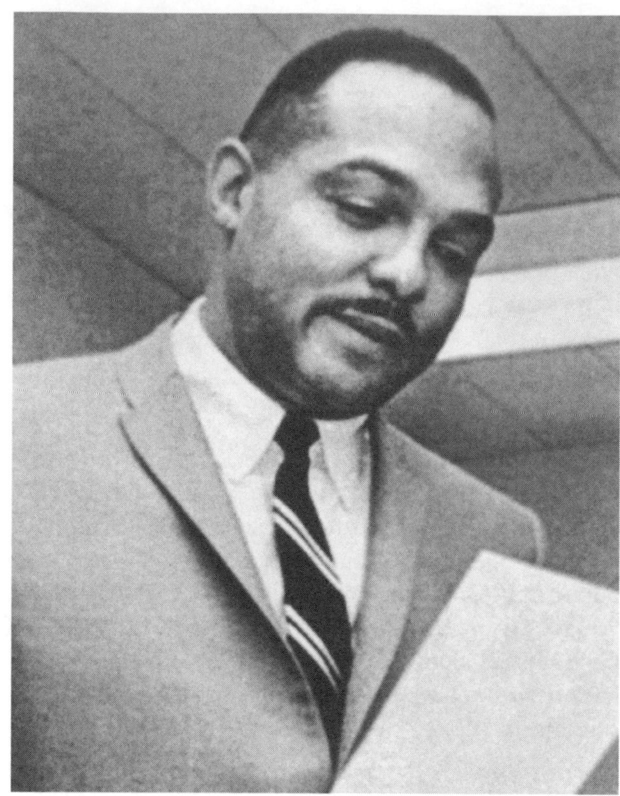

Carl Burton Stokes (1997–1996). *Elected mayor of Cleveland, Ohio, in 1967, Stokes was the first elected black mayor of a major American city.* THE LIBRARY OF CONGRESS

In 1972 Stokes moved to New York City to work as a reporter and anchor for WNBC-TV, an NBC station. In 1980 he returned to Cleveland to serve as a senior partner in the labor law firm of Green, Schiavoni, Murphy, Haines & Sgambati. Three years later Stokes successfully ran for a seat as Cleveland municipal court judge, a position he held through the early 1990s. In 1994 President Bill Clinton appointed him U.S. ambassador to the Seychelles. Suffering from poor health, he took an extended leave of absence from his post and died in 1996.

See also Politics in the United States

Bibliography

Moore, Leonard N. *Carl B. Stokes and the Rise of Black Political Power.* Urbana: University of Illinois Press, 2002.

Van Tassel, David D., and John J. Grabowski. *The Encyclopedia of Cleveland History*. Bloomington: Indiana University Press, 1987.

Wilkerson, Isabel. "Past Glory Has Faded for Stokes." *New York Times,* December 3, 1989, p. 34.

THADDEUS RUSSELL (1996)
Updated by publisher 2005

Stono Rebellion

The Stono Rebellion of 1739 was the largest uprising of enslaved African Americans to take place in Britain's mainland colonies before the American Revolution. South Carolina's black majority outnumbered whites by nearly two to one and by far more in the coastal low country where West African rice-growing skills were providing planters with enormous profits. Although suppressed by local authorities, the revolt came close to succeeding in ways that could have made it a dramatic turning point in American history.

Despite harsh conditions and diverse languages, underground information networks allowed black Carolinians to communicate. Many were aware of recent resistance in other colonies and knew of the Spanish crown's 1733 offer of freedom to fugitive slaves reaching Florida. Harvest pressures upon blacks and seasonal sickness among whites made September a likely time to rebel, and planners selected Sunday morning because most whites still attended church unarmed and most slaves were released from work on the Sabbath. Much of the leadership came from Angolans, who represented the largest proportion of recently arrived slaves and who brought military experience from Africa.

Led by a man named Jemmy and no doubt spurred by news that the so-called War of Jenkins' Ear had erupted between England and Spain, a score of black Carolinians met near the west branch of the Stono River about twenty miles southwest of Charleston early on Sunday, September 9, 1739. At Stono Bridge they broke into Hutcheson's store, killing the two storekeepers and taking guns and powder. With cries of "Liberty" and beating of drums, the rebels raised a standard and headed south toward Spanish St. Augustine, where escaping Carolina slaves had been granted freedom at Fort Mose. Along the road they gathered black recruits, burned houses, and killed white opponents, sparing one innkeeper who was "kind to his slaves."

By chance Lt. Gov. William Bull glimpsed the insurgents and alerted white parishioners. Late Sunday afternoon, planters on horseback caught up with the band of sixty to one hundred rebels in an open field, where they had paused hoping news of their action would inspire further support. In the ensuing encounter some rebels surrendered or were captured; others were wounded or killed. Several dozen managed to escape, but the organized march southward had been broken up. In the next two days, by one account, militiamen and Indians "kill'd twenty odd more, and took about 40; who were immediately some shot, some hang'd, and some Gibbeted alive." Others remained at large for months.

More than twenty whites and nearly twice as many blacks were killed in the uprising, which led quickly to a harsher slave code and a moratorium on slave imports, as the white minority debated their precarious situation. Had the rebels managed to travel farther, spread word faster, and delay a confrontation a bit longer, their brave attempt might have spiraled into a successful rebellion that challenged the logic and stability of the emerging slave system. But the tide flowed the other way. By the 1750s the neighboring colony of Georgia had legalized African slavery, and a decade later the English had taken over Florida from the Spanish. Occupants of the Carolina gulag would have to wait generations for a plausible opportunity to strike a blow for their release from bondage.

See also Christiana Revolt of 1851; Demerara Revolt; Nat Turner's Rebellion

Bibliography

Thornton, John K. "African Dimensions of the Stono Rebellion." *American Historical Review* 96 (October 1991): 1101–1113.

Wax, Darold D. " 'The Great Risk We Run': The Aftermath of Slave Rebellion at Stono, South Carolina, 1739–1745." *Journal of Negro History* 67 (1982): 136–147.

Wood, Peter H. *Black Majority: Negroes in Colonial South Carolina from 1670 through the Stono Rebellion.* New York: Knopf, 1974.

PETER H. WOOD (1996)

Stout, Reneé

1958

Reneé Stout was born in Junction City, Kansas, and grew up in Pittsburgh, Pennsylvania. When she was ten years old, Stout attended Saturday art classes at the Carnegie Museum of Art, where she encountered an object in the museum collection that, combined with her fascination with a mysterious spiritualist who had a consultation space in her neighborhood, had a profound effect upon the nature of her mature artwork. The object was an African nail figure by the Bakongo (or Kongo) people of Central Africa called a *nkisi nkondi.* The spiritualist was Madam Ching, and though Stout never actually talked with her, the mystery of Madam Ching ignited Stout's imagination and became a trope for spirit workers and mediators of transformation in Stout's work.

Stout received her B.F.A. degree from Carnegie-Mellon University in Pittsburgh in 1980. In 1984 she received a residency in the Afro-American Master Artist Program at Northeastern University in Boston, and six months later she moved to Washington, D.C., where she began creating her mature work.

Stout's early work was photorealistic painting, but the work that first garnered national attention for her in art circles was sculpture informed by the *nkisi* (pl. *minkisi*) she saw at the Carnegie Museum and the ideas associated with Kongo objects. *Minkisi,* whether figurative or not, are sacred Kongo objects that are believed to make things happen, and Stout adapted this notion to the creation of art objects that seemed to be ritual works. Most of Stout's works suggest an intervention in one's love life, while some work for protection. In one of her most notable works, *Fetish No. 2* (1988, collection of the Dallas Museum of Art), Stout created a life-size self-portrait as an *nkisi nkondi* ritual object. This work was firmly placed on the national stage when it was shown at the exhibition *Black Art, Ancestral Legacy: The African Impulse in African American Art,* which originated at the Dallas Museum of Art in 1989 and traveled the country for several years. She gained further attention from the 1993 exhibition *Astonishment and Power: Kongo Minkisi and the Art of Renee Stout,* at the National Museum of African Art in Washington, D.C., a two-part show pairing her work with a number of *minkisi* power objects from Kongo.

In the 1990s Stout began creating work that reflected influences from the Yoruba culture of West Africa, and she showed an increasing interest in the American cultural forms and spiritual practices of New Orleans and the Mississippi Delta region. An installation titled *Dear Robert, I'll See You at the Crossroads* (1995) was inspired by the life of bluesman Robert Johnson, who, according to legend, encountered the devil at a crossroads and sold his soul for the ability to play the blues better than anyone else. This legend emerges from folklore that transformed the Yoruba trickster deity Eshu Elegba into Papa Legba in the New World. Both are encountered at "the crossroads" because they carry messages and prayers from the human side to the spiritual side.

Reneé Stout's work is in museums and collections all over the United States, and she has received important commissions, including *Houses of Spirit/Memories of Ancestors,* an installation at the Woodlawn Cemetery (an African slave burial site) in the Bronx in New York. She continues to live and work in Washington, D.C.

See also Central African Religions and Culture in the Americas; Contemporary Art in the United States; Painting and Sculpture

Bibliography

Berns, Marla C. *Dear Robert, I'll See You at the Crossroads: A Project by Reneé Stout.* Santa Barbara, Calif.: University Art Museum, University of California, 1995.

McGaffey, Wyatt, and Michael D. Harris. *Astonishment and Power: Kongo Minkisi and the Art of Renee Stout.* Washington, D.C.: Smithsonian Institution Press, 1993.

Riggs, Thomas, ed. *The St. James Guide to Black Artists.* Detroit, Mich.: St. James Press, 1997.

MICHAEL D. HARRIS (2005)

Student Nonviolent Coordinating Committee (SNCC)

After an initial protest on February 1, 1960, that attempted to integrate a Woolworth lunch counter in Greensboro, North Carolina, black college students spearheaded a sit-in movement that spread rapidly through the South. Reacting to this upsurge of student activism, Southern Christian Leadership Conference (SCLC) official Ella Baker invited student protest leaders to an Easter weekend conference in Raleigh, North Carolina. The student leaders, believing that existing civil rights organizations were overly cautious, agreed to form a new group, the Student Nonviolent Coordinating Committee (SNCC, or "Snick"), and elected Fisk University graduate student Marion Barry as chair.

Originally a means of communication among autonomous local student protest groups, SNCC gradually assumed a more assertive role in the southern civil rights movement. In February 1961, four students affiliated with SNCC traveled to Rock Hill, South Carolina, to join a group of protesters arrested at a segregated lunch counter. The arrested students utilized a "jail-no-bail" strategy that was designed to demonstrate their militancy and independence from the NAACP and its legal-assistance staff. In May 1961, after a group of Freedom Riders organized by the Congress of Racial Equality (CORE) encountered violence in Alabama, SNCC activists insisted on continuing the protests against segregated transportation facilities. Dozens of black students rode buses from Alabama to Jackson, Mississippi, where they were arrested, quickly convicted of violating segregation norms, and then incarcerated in Parchman Prison.

From the fall of 1961 through the spring of 1966, SNCC shifted its focus from nonviolent desegregation protests to long-term voting rights campaigns in the Deep South. Full-time SNCC field secretaries—many of them veterans of the Mississippi Freedom Rides—gradually displaced representatives of local protest groups as the organization's principal policymakers. Initially dominated by advocates of Christian Gandhiism, SNCC increasingly became composed of secular community organizers devoted to the development of indigenous black leaders and local institutions.

SNCC's ability to work closely with local leaders was evident in the Albany, Georgia, protests of 1961 and 1962. Under the leadership of former Virginia Union University student Charles Sherrod, SNCC workers in Albany mobilized black student protesters and spearheaded marches that resulted in hundreds of arrests. Neither the group's brash militancy nor the more cautious leadership of the Reverend Dr. Martin Luther King Jr. overcame segregationist opposition in Albany, however, and SNCC's voter-registration campaign in nearby rural areas also achieved few gains in the face of violent white resistance. By 1963, SNCC staff members in southwest Georgia and elsewhere had become dissatisfied with the failure of the federal government to protect them. John Lewis, who replaced Barry as chair, expressed this growing disillusionment in a controversial speech given at the massive 1963 March on Washington.

By the time of the march, SNCC's most substantial projects were in Mississippi, where its community-organizing efforts encountered fierce white resistance. After launching the Mississippi effort in McComb in 1961, Bob Moses, a former Harvard University graduate student, became voter-registration director of the Council of Federated Organizations (COFO), a SNCC-dominated coalition of civil rights groups. Although SNCC's staff was composed mainly of native Mississippians, the campaign for voting rights in the state attracted increasing support from northern whites. Acknowledging the need for more outside support, COFO sponsored a summer project in 1964 that was designed to bring hundreds of white students to Mississippi. The murder of three civil rights workers, two of them white, during the early days of the project brought unprecedented national attention to the suppression of black voting rights in the Deep South. SNCC staff members, however, became ever more disillusioned with their conventional liberal allies. In August, this disillusionment increased when leaders at the Democratic National Convention refused to back the Mississippi Freedom Democratic Party's effort to take the seats of the all-white regular Democratic Party delegation.

During 1965 and 1966, the gulf grew larger between SNCC and its former liberal allies. A major series of voting rights protests in Alabama during the spring of 1965 exposed the group's increasing tactical differences with the SCLC. After the killing of Jimmy Lee Jackson in Marion, and a brutal police attack in March on a group marching from Selma to the state capitol in Montgomery, SNCC militants severed many of their ties to the political mainstream. Stokely Carmichael and other SNCC organizers helped establish an independent political entity, the Lowndes County Freedom Organization. In May 1966, SNCC workers' growing willingness to advocate racial separatism and radical social change led to a shift in the group's leadership, with Carmichael replacing Lewis as chair. The following month, Carmichael publicly expressed SNCC's new political orientation when he began using the Black Power slogan on a voting rights march through Mississippi. The national controversy surrounding his Black Power speeches further separated SNCC from the SCLC, the NAACP, and other elements of the coalition supporting civil rights reform.

Confronting increasing external opposition and police repression, SNCC also endured serious internal conflicts that made it more vulnerable to external attack. In 1967, executive director Ruby Doris Robinson's death from illness further weakened the organization. After H.

Rap Brown became the new chair in June 1967, Carmichael traveled extensively to build ties with revolutionary movements in Africa and Asia. Upon his return to the United States, he led an abortive effort to establish an alliance between SNCC and the California-based Black Panther Party. The two groups broke their ties in the summer of 1968, however, and Carmichael remained with the Panthers, leaving James Forman as SNCC's dominant figure. By this time, however, SNCC's Black Power rhetoric and support for the Palestinian struggle against Israel had alienated many former supporters. In addition, its leaders' emphasis on ideological issues detracted from long-term community-organizing efforts. SNCC did not have much impact on African-American politics after 1967, although it remained in existence until the early 1970s.

See also Al-Amin, Jamil Abdullah; Barry, Marion; Black Panther Party for Self-Defense; Black Power Movement; Carmichael, Stokely; Congress of Racial Equality (CORE); Freedom Rides; Lewis, John; Lowndes County Freedom Organization; Moses, Robert Parris; Southern Christian Leadership Conference (SCLC)

Bibliography

Carson, Clayborne. *In Struggle: SNCC and the Black Awakening of the 1960s.* Cambridge, Mass.: Harvard University Press, 1981.

Forman, James. *The Making of Black Revolutionaries.* New York: Macmillan, 1972. Reprint, Seattle: University of Washington Press, 1997.

Greenberg, Cheryl Lynn, ed. *A Circle of Trust: Remembering SNCC.* New Brunswick, N.J.: Rutgers University Press, 1998.

Lewis, John, with Michael D'Orso. *Walking with the Wind: A Memoir of the Movement.* New York: Simon & Schuster, 1998.

Sellers, Cleveland, with Robert Terrell. *The River of No Return: The Autobiography of a Black Militant and the Life and Death of SNCC.* New York: William Morrow, 1973. Reprint, Jackson: University Press of Mississippi, 1990.

CLAYBORNE CARSON (1996)
Updated bibliography

Sullivan, Leon Howard

October 16, 1922
April 24, 2001

Civil rights teacher Leon Sullivan was born in Charleston, West Virginia. As a young man he was encouraged by his grandmother to improve the lives of the disadvantaged; after receiving a B.A. from West Virginia State College in 1943, he decided he could do this best by entering the ministry. That year he moved to New York and, on a scholarship, enrolled in the Union Theological Seminary, where he came to the attention of Rev. Adam Clayton Powell Jr. Powell hired Sullivan as an assistant minister at the Abyssinian Baptist Church in Harlem. Another mentor, A. Philip Randolph, instructed Sullivan in community mobilization tactics. These lessons stood Sullivan in good stead when, after receiving his seminary degree in 1945 and an M.A. from Columbia University in religious education in 1947, he worked as a community organizer in South Orange, New Jersey.

In 1950 Sullivan was named pastor of the Zion Baptist Church in Philadelphia. A small church of six hundred members, it had grown to a membership of three thousand by the time Sullivan retired and became pastor emeritus in 1988. He was active in numerous efforts in the late 1950s and early 1960s to encourage local businesses to hire minorities, although he came to the conclusion that many African Americans were unprepared for a number of employment opportunities. To address that need, Sullivan founded Opportunities Industrialization Centers of America (OIC) in 1964. "Integration without preparation is frustration," he claimed. A not-for-profit organization that provided motivation and job training to unskilled workers of all races, OIC grew by 1980 into a network of nationwide comprehensive training centers with 140 affiliates and funding of over $130 million a year. With the advent of the Reagan administration, however, federal funding for OIC dwindled, and the organization was forced to make deep cuts in its programs and budget. Nevertheless, by 1993 the OIC still had training programs in eighty cities, had trained a total of one million men and women for jobs, and had established branches in at least thirteen sub-Saharan African countries.

Sullivan is probably best known, however, for formulating what became known as the Sullivan Principles, a set of guidelines for American corporations doing business in South Africa aimed at obtaining fair treatment of black South African workers. Using his prominent position as the first black director of General Motors (he was appointed to that post in 1971), Sullivan enumerated the principles in 1977. The original six called for nonsegregation of the races in all eating, comfort, and work facilities; equal and fair employment practices for all employees; equal pay for all employees doing equal or comparable work for the same period of time; initiation and development of training programs to prepare substantial numbers of blacks and other nonwhites for supervisory, administrative, clerical, and technical jobs; increasing the number of blacks and other nonwhites in supervisory positions; and improving the quality of employees' lives outside the work environment in such areas as housing, transportation, schooling, recreation, and health facilities.

In 1984 the principles were revised to require American corporations doing business in South Africa to work to overturn the country's racial policies, to allow black workers freedom of mobility in order to take advantage of work opportunities wherever they existed, and to provide adequate housing for workers close to the workplace. By this time, about 150 of the 350 American corporations with investments in South Africa were voluntarily complying with the principles.

From the beginning, however, the principles were controversial. Some South African trade unionists and many Americans who favored complete corporate disinvestment in South Africa claimed that the principles enabled corporations to say they were fighting racism while profiting from apartheid. But Sullivan claimed that without the principles, the enormous leverage of American corporate power could not create changes in the lives of black South Africans.

Nevertheless, in 1987 Sullivan declared that the principles had failed to undermine apartheid. He called on American corporations to sell their investments in South Africa and on the Reagan administration to sever all diplomatic ties. He also urged a complete trade embargo with South Africa.

At the same time, Sullivan was expanding his self-help and educational efforts in Africa. In 1983 he established the International Foundation for Education and Self-Help (IFESH) to fight illiteracy, hunger, and unemployment in fifteen sub-Saharan African countries alongside the OIC. In the 1990s he was the moving force behind a series of African–African American Summits held successively in South Africa, Gabon, Senegal, and Ghana. The last summit, in 1999, drew 3,500 people, including 1,000 prominent African Americans. The purpose of the summits was to focus on ways to improve the living conditions of Africans.

Sullivan received numerous awards and honorary degrees. The NAACP awarded him the Spingarn Medal in 1971 for training inner-city workers for new job opportunities. In 1991 he received the highest U.S. civilian award, the Presidential Medal of Freedom, for his life's work in helping the poor and disadvantaged in both America and Africa. That same year he received the Ivory Coast's highest honor, the Distinguished Service Award, in recognition of his efforts to improve the lives of sub-Saharan Africans.

See also Abyssinian Baptist Church; Anti-Apartheid Movement; Civil Rights Movement, U.S.; Randolph, Asa Philip

Bibliography

"Leon H. Sullivan." In *Contemporary Black Biography,* vol. 30, edited by Ashyia Henderson. Detroit, Mich.: Gale, 2001.

"Negro on G.M. Board Ready for Challenge." *New York Times,* January 9, 1975, p. 35.

"Rev. Sullivan Steps Up." *New York Times,* November 6, 1983, Sec. 4, pp. 12–13.

Sullivan, Leon. *Build, Brother, Build.* Philadelphia: Macrae Smith, 1969.

Walker, Jim. "Interview: Elton Jolly." *Crisis* (April 1985): 34–48.

MICHAEL PALLER (1996)
Updated by publisher 2005

Sullivan, Louis

November 3, 1933

Louis Sullivan, a physician and member of President George H. W. Bush's cabinet, was born in Atlanta, Georgia, to undertaker Walter Wade Sullivan and Lubirda Elizabeth Sullivan, a schoolteacher. Sullivan's parents moved to Blakely, Georgia, where they later founded the Blakely chapter of the National Association for the Advancement of Colored People (NAACP). Louis stayed in Atlanta with relatives because of its better educational opportunities and graduated from Morehouse College in 1954. Winning a scholarship to Boston University Medical School, he graduated cum laude as the only black member of his class in 1958. He finished his internship and residency at New York Hospital–Cornell Medical Center in New York City in 1960 and subsequently won a fellowship in pathology at Massachusetts General Hospital in Boston. In 1961 he was awarded a research fellowship to the Thorndike Memorial Laboratory at Harvard Medical School, where he was named instructor of medicine in 1963. From 1964 to 1966, he served as assistant professor of medicine at the New Jersey College of Medicine. He returned to Boston University in 1966 and became assistant professor of medicine at the medical school as well as codirector of hematology at the medical center. In 1974 he became a full professor of medicine and physiology.

In 1978 Sullivan helped found a new medical school, Morehouse School of Medicine (affiliated with Morehouse College yet independent of it), to train African-American doctors to practice in the South. With Sullivan as its first dean and president, Morehouse School of Medicine became accredited in 1981. Sullivan received personal support for his school from Vice President George Bush and his wife, Barbara Bush. Mrs. Bush became a trustee of the school in 1983, and following her husband's election to the presidency five years later, she led the effort to secure Sullivan's nomination as secretary of health and human services. Despite a moderate position on abortion, Sullivan was nominated by Bush and confirmed in 1989 after calling for the reversal of the U.S. Supreme Court *Roe v. Wade* abortion decision.

As secretary, Sullivan devoted most of his attention to minority health care and preventive medicine and opposed further cutbacks in Medicare. He encouraged Congress to reverse the Reagan administration's budget cuts for medical education, and he initiated a program to curtail the spread of tuberculosis. Sullivan incurred controversy when he initially supported needle exchanges with drug users to prevent the spread of AIDS; he later reversed his position.

After Bush left the White House in 1993, Sullivan returned to full-time service as president of the Morehouse School of Medicine. He left the presidency of Morehouse in 2000 but remained as president emeritus and professor. He was named to the *Georgia Trend* Hall of Fame in 2003.

See also Politics in the United States

Bibliography

"Influence That Lasts." *Georgia Trend* 18, no. 5 (January 2003): 29.

Jensen, Kris. "Emerge Profiles Morehouse's Sullivan," *Atlanta Constitution*, December 7, 1993, sec. F, p. 3.

"Louis Sullivan's Record." *Boston Globe*, December 15, 1992, p. 22.

DURAHN TAYLOR (1996)
Updated by publisher 2005

Sun Ra (Blount, Herman "Sonny")

May 1914
May 30, 1993

The jazz bandleader and pianist Herman "Sonny" Blount was born in Birmingham, Alabama, played piano as a child, and led his own band while still in high school. He studied music education at Alabama A & M University and studied classical piano with Willa Randolph. Blount moved to Chicago while still in his teens, and in the mid-1930s he toured with John "Fess" Whatley's band. He gradually gained a reputation as a sideman and arranger for shows. From 1946 to 1947, Blount worked at Chicago's Club de Lisa, leading his own group and also serving as pianist and arranger for Fletcher Henderson.

In the late 1940s Blount completely reinvented himself, changing his name to Sun Ra and claiming the planet Saturn as his birthplace. Thereafter his music carried strong science fiction overtones, and he took as his motto "Space Is the Place." At the same time, he also began to turn to ancient Egypt and Ethiopia for his spiritual outlook and sartorial style. In 1953 he formed a big band called the Arkestra, and over the next forty years the group pioneered the use of modern collective improvisation and exemplified the anarchic spirit of free jazz (*Sound of Joy*, 1957). Sun Ra also established a core of remarkable soloists, including saxophonists Marshall Allen, John Gilmore, and Pat Patrick. Sun Ra was himself an accomplished pianist capable of contemplative modal moments as well as roiling solos, never losing the energetic drive of his stride piano roots. He was a pioneer in the use of electric instruments, playing the electric piano as early as 1956. He also gained renown as a composer of songs such as "A Call for All Demons" (1956) and "Cosmic Chaos" (1965).

While in Chicago in the 1950s, Sun Ra found his music rejected by established jazz musicians, but he proved enormously influential to the new generation of avant-garde musicians. In the late 1950s he started Saturn Records, which released dozens of his albums during the next few decades. In the early 1960s, the Arkestra set up communal living quarters in New York and thereafter became a mainstay in avant-garde jazz (*The Heliocentric Worlds of Sun Ra*, 1965; *Nothing Is*, 1966). They participated in Bill Dixon's October Revolution series of concerts in 1964 and joined the cooperative Jazz Composers Guild. In the late 1960s and throughout the 1970s, the Arkestra continued to record (*The Solar Myth Approach*, 1970–1971) and tour.

Although Sun Ra's work was always heavily influenced by Henderson's work, it was not until the late 1970s, when the Arkestra moved to Philadelphia, that Sun Ra began to incorporate traditional arrangements of tunes by Henderson, Jelly Roll Morton, Duke Ellington, and Thelonious Monk into its repertoire. Nonetheless, the Arkestra never lost its futuristic eccentricity. During this time, Sun Ra directed circuslike concerts, complete with dancers and spectacular costumes, chants of "next stop Mars!" space-age prophecy, and tales of intergalactic travel (*Live at Montreux*, 1976; *Sunrise in Different Dimensions*, 1980). By the 1980s Sun Ra had become an internationally acclaimed figure, recording frequently (e.g., *Blue Delight*, 1989) and taking his extravagant show on tours of Europe and Asia. The subject of two documentary films, *The Cry of Jazz* (1959) and *Sun Ra: A Joyful Noise* (1980), Sun Ra died in 1993 in Birmingham, Alabama.

See also Jazz; Music in the United States

Bibliography

Litweiler, John. *The Freedom Principle: Jazz after 1958.* New York: W. Morrow, 1984.

Pekar, Harvey. "Sun Ra." *Coda* 139 (1975): 2.

Szwed, John F. *Space Is the Place: The Lives and Times of Sun Ra.* New York: Pantheon, 1997.

Wilmer, Valerie. *As Serious as Your Life: The Story of the New Jazz.* Westport, Conn.: L. Hill, 1980.

ERNEST BROWN (1996)
Updated bibliography

Supremes, The

The female soul vocal trio called the Supremes was one of Motown's most successful rhythm-and-blues acts and one of the most successful recording groups of all time. They earned twelve number-one hits and sold over twenty million records; their rise to national fame signaled the elimination of the color barrier in the pop market.

Originally a quartet known as the Primettes, the Detroit-based group had several personnel changes during its eighteen-year history. At the height of its popularity (1962–1967), the group included Diana Ross, Florence Ballard, and Mary Wilson. Their hits included "Where Did Our Love Go," "Baby Love," "Come See About Me," "Stop! In the Name of Love" (no. 1, *Billboard* charts 1965), "Back in My Arms Again" (no. 1, 1965), and "I Hear a Symphony" (no. 1, 1965), written by Motown's Holland-Dozier-Holland songwriting team. The Supremes' earliest recordings featured Ballard's strong lead vocals (produced by Smokey Robinson), but the hits from 1964 and 1965 featured Ross's bright, cooing vocals.

In 1967 Cindy Birdsong (formerly with Patti Labelle and the Blue Belles) replaced Ballard, and the group was billed as Diana Ross and the Supremes. Their hits included "Love Child" (no. 1, 1968), "Someday We'll Be Together" (no. 1, 1969), and, with the Temptations, "I'm Gonna Make You Love Me" (no. 2, 1968). In 1970 Ross departed for a solo career and Jean Terrell led the trio, but their popularity declined by 1973. The 1981 Broadway show *Dreamgirls* supposedly depicts Ballard's perspective on the group, and in 1984 Wilson published her own memoir, *Dreamgirl: My Life as a Supreme*. In 2000 a reunion tour was launched, but Mary Wilson, citing displeasure with the financial arrangements, declined to participate. The tour thus began in controversy, and when ticket sales were poor, the remainder of the tour was canceled.

See also Ross, Diana; Music in the United States

Bibliography

George, Nelson. *Where Did Our Love Go? The Rise and Fall of the Motown Sound.* New York: St. Martin's Press, 1985.

Ross, Diana. *Upside Down: Wrong Turns, Right Turns, and the Road Ahead.* New York: Regan Books, 2005.

KYRA D. GAUNT (1996)
Updated by publisher 2005

Sutton, Percy Ellis

November 24, 1920

The politician and media businessman Percy Ellis Sutton was born in San Antonio, Texas. His parents, Samuel J. Sutton and Lillian Smith, were educators and philanthropists. Percy Sutton graduated from Phillis Wheatley High School in San Antonio and subsequently attended Prairie View Agricultural and Mechanical College, Tuskegee Institute, and Hampton Institute. When he attempted to join the Army Air Force in Texas during World War II, he was rejected for reasons having to do with his racial background. He then successfully enlisted in New York City. As an intelligence officer with the black Ninety-ninth Fighter Squadron serving in the Italian and Mediterranean theaters, Sutton earned combat stars and rose to the rank of captain.

After the war, Sutton completed his education under the G.I. Bill, graduating from Brooklyn Law School in 1950. During the Korean War, Sutton reentered the Air Force as an intelligence officer and trial judge advocate. When the war ended, in 1953, Sutton opened a law partnership in Harlem with his brother Oliver and George Covington and worked with the National Association for the Advancement of Colored People (NAACP) on several civil rights cases throughout the 1950s. In addition to its work with the NAACP, the firm served other clients, such as Malcolm X and the Baptist Ministers Conference of Greater New York.

From 1961 to 1962 Sutton served as branch president of the New York City NAACP, participating in demonstrations and Freedom Rides in the South. During the winter of 1963–1964, Sutton and Charles Rangel cofounded the John F. Kennedy Democratic Club, later known as the Martin Luther King Jr. Club. Sutton was elected to the New York State Assembly in 1964. In 1966, after Manhattan borough president Constance Baker Motley accepted an appointment as a federal judge, the New York City Council chose Sutton to finish Motley's term. Sutton was reelected in his own right later that year and was subsequently reelected in 1969 and 1973. As borough president, Sutton focused on decentralizing the municipal bureaucracy, cutting city spending, and addressing the broader social causes of urban crime and poverty.

In 1970 Sutton endorsed Rangel's campaign to replace Adam Clayton Powell Jr. as congressman from Harlem. Rangel's victory marked the ascendancy of a new black political coalition in Harlem, a coalition that included not only Percy Sutton but also future New York City mayor David Dinkins. In 1971, while still Manhattan borough president, Sutton set out to purchase several black-owned media enterprises, beginning with the New York *Amsterdam News* (which he sold in 1975) and radio station WLIB-AM. In 1977 Sutton became owner and board chair of the Inner-City Broadcasting Company, a nationwide media corporation, and through the corporation he subsequently purchased radio stations in New York, California, and Michigan. He also formed Percy Sutton International, Inc., the investments of which encouraged agriculture, manufacturing, and trade in Africa, Southeast Asia, and Brazil.

In September 1977 Sutton was an unsuccessful candidate for the nomination for mayor. He retired from public office after finishing his second full term as borough president in December 1977, but he continued to advise Rangel, Dinkins, and other black politicians on electoral strategy and urban policy. In 1981 he acquired Harlem's Apollo Theater as a base for the production of cable television programs. By the end of the decade Sutton's estimated net worth was $170 million. In 1990 he was succeeded as head of Inner-City Broadcasting by his son, Pierre Montea ("PePe"), who raised the company's net worth to $28 million by 1992.

Sutton has been a guest lecturer at many universities and corporations and has held leadership positions in the Association for a Better New York, the National Urban League, the Congressional Black Caucus Foundation, and several other civil rights organizations. A founding member and director of Operation PUSH (People United to Save Humanity), Sutton was also a close adviser to Rev. Jesse Jackson. He was awarded the NAACP's Spingarn Medal in 1987 at the Apollo Theater, which under Sutton's management had been restored as a major Harlem cultural center and landmark.

In 2002 Sutton cofounded Synematics, of which he is the chief executive officer. In 2004 he was named to the *Broadcasting & Cable* Hall of Fame.

See also Apollo Theater; Dinkins, David; Harlem, New York; Jackson, Jesse; Malcolm X; National Association for the Advancement of Colored People (NAACP); National Urban League; Operation PUSH (People United to Serve Humanity); Rangel, Charles Bernard; Spingarn Medal

Bibliography

Green, Charles. *The Struggle for Black Empowerment in New York City: Beyond the Politics of Pigmentation.* New York: Praeger, 1989.

"Hall of Fame." *Broadcasting & Cable* 134, no. 15 (2004): 62.

Lewinson, Edwin R. *Black Politics in New York City.* New York: Twayne, 1974.

DURAHN TAYLOR (1996)
Updated by publisher 2005

SWEATT V. PAINTER

Through much of the 1930s and 1940s, the legal staff of the National Association for the Advancement of Colored People (NAACP) pursued an "indirect" strategy against segregation in public education. The NAACP reasoned that black exclusion from white schools might be most immediately challenged in graduate and professional schools, because separate black facilities had not generally been provided by states enforcing segregation—and would likely prove too expensive to provide. Accordingly, in 1946 the organization backed Heman Sweatt, an African-American postal employee from Houston, in a suit to compel his admission to the University of Texas School of Law. Segregation in education had been mandated by the state constitution and endorsed in *Plessy v. Ferguson,* but no black law school existed in Texas. Rather than force university president T. S. Painter to admit Sweatt, however, state courts allowed Texas to make efforts to provide "substantially equal" segregated facilities. The state authorized its black college to expand professional programs, provided for the establishment of a new black university and law school, and, as a stopgap measure, opened a temporary law school for blacks in an Austin basement.

In response, NAACP lawyers, led by Thurgood Marshall, more directly attacked separate-but-equal doctrine. They argued that no newly minted Jim Crow school could offer an education comparable to that of a longstanding and prestigious state institution, but also that segregation itself was intellectually indefensible. Though state appellate courts denied Sweatt's petitions, the U.S. Supreme Court ruled in June 1950 that the Fourteenth Amendment's "equal protection" language required his admission to the University of Texas. Blacks could not receive a substantially equal legal education in existing segregated facilities, because they did not compare to the University of Texas School of Law either in material resources or in less tangible realms, such as reputation and prestige. Though the Court did not thereby abandon the separate-but-equal precedent, it made it more difficult to apply. More important, Sweatt foreshadowed the more exacting definitions of equality that would shape the 1954 *Brown v. Board of Education* decision.

See also *Brown v. Board of Education of Topeka, Kansas*; Fourteenth Amendment; Marshall, Thurgood; *Plessy v. Ferguson*

Bibliography

Gillette, Michael. "Herman Marion Sweatt: Civil Rights Plaintiff." In *Black Leaders: Texans for Their Times,* edited by Alwyn Barr and Robert Calvert. Austin: Texas State Historical Association, 1981.

PATRICK G. WILLIAMS (1996)

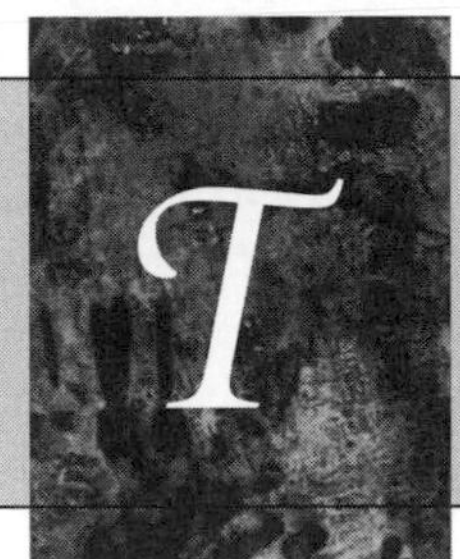

Tailor's Revolt

Liberty, fraternity, and equality were ideas of the French Revolution spread throughout the Atlantic world. In late-eighteenth-century Brazil, intellectuals read the *philosophes*, Enlightenment thinkers whose writing inspired the Age of Revolution. At fashionable salons, the *letrados*, or intellectuals, gathered to discuss philosophy and the torrent of events unfolding outside of Brazil. Educated in Coimbra, Portugal, alongside the sons of Brazil's wealthiest sugar planters, the *letrados* understood the ideas of the revolution in largely intellectual terms. Their position of privilege within Brazil's slave society limited the extent to which they questioned the colonial compact. The influence of the French Revolution, however, spread beyond the propertied few with access to university education. Like the slaves and mulattoes of Haiti, working people in the northeastern Brazilian city of Salvador da Bahia interpreted ideas of liberty and equality in profoundly radical terms. In August 1798 a group of free mulattoes, black slaves, and white artisans took part in a movement that sought to actualize on Brazilian soil the goals of the French Revolution.

The Tailor's Revolt, named for the profession of a number of its conspirators, was one of a series of plots that signaled the disintegration of the colonial system that bound Brazil to Portugal. Under the great administrator of the Portuguese empire, the Marquis de Pombal, and his less able successor, Martinho de Melo e Castro, the Portuguese crown carried out a program of imperial reorganization intended to make more efficient the extraction of wealth from its overseas dominions, of which Brazil was the crowning jewel. In the gold mining captaincy of Minas Gerais, the reforms spawned in February 1789 an independence movement led by some of the region's most prominent men, angered over the crown's relentless efforts to collect back taxes in the face of declining gold deposits. Colonial authorities managed to uncover the plot before it was executed and forestalled further discontent by loosening fiscal demands. The Minas conspirators sought free trade and independence from Portugal. The propertied men central to the plot offered freedom to Brazilian-born slaves who would join the insurrectionist forces, but they did not propose an end to the transatlantic trade or slavery itself. Following the outbreak of both the French and Haitian revolutions, the Bahian tailors would envisage far more profound social changes: the abolition of slavery and an end to racial discrimination, goals that extended the ideals of liberty and equality in ways that wealthy slaveholders found untenable.

In August 1798 broadsides announcing revolutionary plans appeared affixed to churches and other public walls throughout the city of Salvador. The tailors' manifestos called out to the "Republican Bahian people" and in the "name of the supreme tribunal of Bahian democracy." They publicly displayed their plans to overturn "the detestable metropolitan yoke of Portugal." Most dangerously, the rebels proclaimed that theirs would be a republic in which "all citizens, especially mulattoes and blacks" would enjoy equal protection: "all will be equal, there will be no difference." The conspirators' cries for "freedom, equality, and fraternity" took on an especially subversive meaning in a slave society. Unlike the wealthy men who planned the Minas conspiracy, the Bahian rebels imagined far more than political independence from Portugal. They demanded true social change: "all black and brown slaves are to be free, so that there will be no slaves whatsoever." The tailors further appealed to the free poor, hurt by rising prices that accompanied the economic resurgence of the sugar economy following the Haitian Revolution. They demanded lower food prices, for manioc and meat in particular. They also called for free trade and an opening of ports to trade with France and other foreign powers.

Public authorities countered swiftly the tailors' open display of revolutionary ideas. Domingos de Silva Lisboa, a professional scribe, quickly faced arrest. When manifestos continued to appear in public, police attention focused on Luís Gonzaga das Virgens, a soldier in the mulatto regiment. On August 26 authorities apprehended forty-seven suspected revolutionaries, among them five women, nine slaves, ten whites, and the rest mulattoes, including João de Deus do Nascimento, a tailor of meager means. Investigations failed to uncover a revolutionary plot. Although several detainees were members of a mulatto regiment, they appeared to have formulated no military plan. If, as authorities feared, the tailors had intended to mount a French-style revolution, they had not progressed beyond hanging manifestos throughout the city. Yet the mere dissemination of revolutionary ideas was enough to convict the conspirators. Governor Fernando José de Portugal denounced the "abominable Jacobin ideas," especially dangerous "in a country with so many slaves." On November 8, 1799, four leaders were publicly hanged in the center of the city. Free mulattoes Lucas Dantes, João de Deus, and Manuel Faustas were beheaded and quartered. Authorities displayed their severed body parts for two days until the superintendent of health petitioned to have the rotting flesh taken down due to public health concerns. Two slaves and five free men of color were publicly whipped and compelled to watch the executions. Together with sixteen other defendants, they were deported to the African coast and forbidden from setting foot ever again in Portuguese territory.

The fact that the Bahian conspirators imagined a world free from slavery and racial discrimination made their plot far more threatening than other pre-independence conspiracies in, for example, Minas Gerais and Pernambuco. The Portuguese secretary of state for overseas dominion, Rodrigo de Sousa Coutinho, expressed concern that "the abominable French principles" had "infected" even "the principal people of the city." Authorities, however, quickly exonerated white Bahian *letrados* found with the same French writings that had cost men of color their lives. The Bahian governor assured the crown that only those of "the lowest orders" had been guilty of treason. "Liberty, fraternity, and equality" took on subversive connotations when voiced by slaves and free men of color. Equality and slavery could not coexist.

See also Haitian Revolution

Bibliography

Allen, Judith Lee. "Tailors, Soldiers, and Slaves: The Social Anatomy of a Conspiracy." M.A. thesis, University of Wisconsin, Madison, 1987.

Maxwell, Kenneth R. *Conflicts and Conspiracies: Brazil and Portugal, 1750–1808.* Cambridge, U.K.: Cambridge University Press, 1974.

Morton, F. W. O. "The Conservative Revolution of Independence: Economy, Society, and Politics in Bahia, 1790–1840." Ph.D. diss., Oxford University, Oxford, U.K., 1974.

Ramos, Donald. "Social Revolution Frustrated: The Conspiracy of the Tailors in Bahia, 1798." *Luso-Brazilian Review* 13, no. 1 (summer 1976): 74–90.

ALEXANDRA K. BROWN (2005)

Tanner, Benjamin Tucker

December 25, 1835
January 14, 1923

The African Methodist Episcopal (AME) Church bishop and editor Benjamin Tucker Tanner was born in Pittsburgh, Pennsylvania, and worked as a barber while he attended Avery College (1852–1857) and Western Theological Seminary (1857–1860). In 1860 he was ordained a deacon and then an elder in the AME Church. In 1867 Tanner became the principal of the AME Conference

School in Frederickstown, Maryland. Later he was appointed to Bethel Church in Philadelphia. From 1868 to 1884 Tanner edited the *Christian Recorder,* an AME publication. During the 1870s he was awarded a master's degree from Avery and an honorary doctor of divinity degree from Wilberforce. In 1884 Tanner founded the *A.M.E. Church Review,* a quarterly journal focusing on African-American issues. Tanner became known as the king of the Negro editors. A black nationalist, he believed that racial solidarity was needed to combat racial injustice and he encouraged black-owned business. In 1888 Tanner was consecrated a bishop. In 1901 he served as dean of Payne Theological Seminary at Wilberforce University. Tanner retired in 1908 at the AME General Conference. He and his wife, Sarah Miller, whom he had married in 1858, had seven children, including the painter Henry Ossawa Tanner. Benjamin Tanner wrote several books, including *An Apology for African Methodism* (1867).

See also African Methodist Episcopal Church; Tanner, Henry Ossawa

Bibliography

Bowden, Henry Warner. *Dictionary of American Religious Biography,* 2d ed. Westport, Conn.: Greenwood, 1993, pp. 538–539.

Seraile, Willam. *Fire in His Heart: Bishop Benjamin Tucker Tanner and the A.M.E. Church.* Knoxville: University of Tennessee Press, 1998.

SASHA THOMAS (1996)
Updated bibliography

Tanner, Henry Ossawa

**June 21, 1859
May 25, 1937**

Henry Tanner was a painter and illustrator. His father, Benjamin Tucker Tanner (1835–1923) and his mother, Sarah Elizabeth Miller (1840–1914), lived in Pittsburgh at the time of Henry's birth. They gave their son the middle name Ossawa, after the Kansas town of Osawatomie, where white abolitionist John Brown had started an antislavery campaign in 1856. After entering the ministry in 1863, Tanner's father rose to the rank of bishop in the African Methodist Episcopal Church in 1888. The Reverend Tanner relocated the family to Philadelphia in 1868 so that he could serve as editor of the *Christian Recorder.* Tanner attended Lombard Street School for Colored Students in 1868. The next year he enrolled at the Robert Vaux Consolidated School for Colored Students, then the only secondary school for black students in Philadelphia, which was renamed Robert Vaux Grammar School the year before Tanner graduated as valedictorian in 1877.

Tanner began painting when he was thirteen years old, and although his parents supported his early efforts, he did not receive formal training until 1880, studying with Thomas Eakins at the Pennsylvania Academy of the Fine Arts until 1885. During his academy years and through 1890, Tanner was primarily a painter of seascapes, landscapes, and animal life. Many of his paintings engaged a particular technical challenge in representing natural phenomena such as waves breaking on rocks in stormy seas (*Seascape-Jetty,* 1876–1879), rippling autumn foliage (*Fauna,* 1878–1879), or the light in a lion's mane at the Philadelphia Zoo (*Lion Licking Its Paw,* 1886). While his work in each genre was influenced by numerous lesser-known local artists, Tanner was developing his own style and becoming skilled at controlling effects of light, giving objects form through a subdued color scheme and a subtle sense of tonality, and creating decorative effects with tiny flecks of color. Tanner strategically organized space by surrounding central figures with vast areas of opaque color—representing grass or sky, for example—and using the emptiness to draw the viewer's attention to the locus of dramatic activity.

Although Tanner met with some critical success as a landscape painter during his academy years, he was unable to support himself by painting and worked for a flour business owned by friends of his family. In 1889 he relocated to Atlanta, where he taught at Clark University and worked for a year as a photographer. There was a lull in Tanner's painting from 1889 to 1890, but he used some photographs from this year, taken on a trip to North Carolina, as studies for paintings such as his well-known work *The Banjo Lesson* (1893).

In Atlanta, Tanner met Joseph Crane Hartzell, a white Methodist Episcopal bishop, and his wife. They became his patrons, sponsoring the first exhibition of his work in Cincinnati in 1890. They supported Tanner when he traveled to Europe in 1891 and set up a studio in Paris, where he began studying with Jean-Joseph Benjamin Constant and Jean-Paul Laurens. Tanner returned to Philadelphia in 1893, although he found the racial restrictions onerous and soon returned to Paris. In 1899 he married Jessie Macauley Olssen (1873–1925), a white American of Swedish descent who was living abroad in Paris. The two remained happily married and lived in France for most of their lives,

The Banjo Lesson (Henry Ossawa Tanner, 1893). *The first African-American artist to receive national and international recognition for his work, Tanner turned to depictions of African-American life in his paintings of the 1890s.* © HAMPTON UNIVERSITY MUSEUM, VIRGINIA. REPRODUCED BY PERMISSION.

except for the years Tanner spent at an artists' colony in Mount Kisco, New York, from 1901 to 1904. Tanner's Paris studio became a hub of activity for visiting African-American artists and other visitors from abroad in the early part of twentieth century.

During the 1890s Tanner's work shifted from landscape painting to genre scenes depicting black life in America. The change has been attributed to Tanner's 1893 participation as a speaker in the Columbian Exposition's Congress on Africa, where he asserted the achievements of African-American artists and listened to speakers give an overview of post-Emancipation black leadership across the nation. With his thoughts focused on issues of black identity and productivity, Tanner began depicting genre scenes of African-American life. Though he painted relatively few genre scenes, some of them, such as *The Banjo Lesson* and *The Thankful Poor* (1894), are among his best-known paintings. *The Banjo Lesson* depicts one of the acclaimed themes in American genre painting, an older musician teaching his art to a young boy. *The Thankful Poor* also features an old man and a boy to show how the black family passed on moral and spiritual lessons to its children.

Tanner's style during his genre period had several influences. In 1889 Tanner spent time in the Brittany region of France, involved in the impressionist and postimpressionist movements, particularly those in the circle of Gauguin. Whereas some critics have noted that Tanner borrowed the impressionists' techniques and was influenced by their use of color and spatial organization to communicate mood, the overall character of his work was shaped by academic romantic realism.

Tanner's illustrations appeared in American journals such as *Harper's Young People* and *Our Continent,* as well as in exhibition catalogs at the Pennsylvania Academy of the Fine Arts. His work was seen in exhibitions at the academy in 1888, 1889, 1898, and 1906 and was frequently shown at the prestigious Salon de la Société des Artistes Français in Paris during the period 1894 to 1914.

In the later stages of his career, Tanner was most active as a religious painter, and though these works were based on biblical stories and did not directly address issues of black life, they were continually concerned with broad themes of social justice in the earthly world, using the stories as metaphors for more contemporary issues such as slavery and emancipation in America. An early representation of *Daniel in the Lions' Den* (1896), one of his two known paintings of this well-known religious theme, was exhibited at the salon, where it received honorable mention. In 1897, shortly after he painted *Daniel in the Lions' Den,* Tanner traveled to the Middle East to observe the people and geography of the ancient lands and to enhance the historical accuracy of his paintings with biblical themes. Among the most celebrated religious compositions was *The Raising of Lazarus* (1896), now located at the Musée d'Orsay in Paris. Other paintings on sacred subjects included *Nicodemus Visiting Jesus* (1899), *Flight into Egypt* (1899), *Mary* (1900), *Return of the Holy Women* (1904), *Christ at the Home of Mary and Martha* (1905), *Two Disciples at the Tomb* (1906), *The Holy Family* (1909–1910), *Christ Learning to Read* (1910), *The Disciples on the Sea of Galilee* (1910), and *The Good Shepherd* (1922).

Tanner's religious work went through multiple stylistic phases and had diverse influences, including Velázquez's portraiture, El Greco's elongated figures, David's scale of historical paintings, and Georges Rouault's use of color in contemporary religious paintings. The style of his paintings after 1920 was marked by an overall conservatism. He remained uninfluenced by contemporary developments. Despite some brilliant coloristic effects, the overall impact of his religious compositions, with their limited range of tonality and virtually absent source of light, is a brooding, somber, and contemplative mood.

Tanner exhibited widely in the United States after 1900, with paintings appearing at the Pan-American Exposition (Buffalo, New York) in 1901, the Louisiana Purchase Exposition in 1904, the St. Louis Exposition in 1904, the Carnegie Institute Annual Exhibition in Pittsburgh in 1906, the Anglo-American Art Exhibition (London) in 1914, the Panama-Pacific Exposition (San Francisco) in 1915, the Los Angeles County Museum in 1920, and the Grand Central Art Galleries in New York in 1920. Since 1968 Tanner's works have been shown in major United States exhibitions celebrating the accomplishments of American artists of African descent.

Tanner served his country during World War I as a lieutenant in the American Red Cross in the Farm Service Bureau. In 1918 he worked in the Bureau of Publicity as resident artist. Although his academic style was increasingly out of fashion, in his later years he was given many honors. He received the coveted Légion d'Honneur (Legion of Honor) from the French government in 1923. Tanner's son Jesse graduated from Cambridge University in 1924 and became an engineer upon his return to France. In 1927 Tanner became the first African American elected to full membership in the National Academy of Design. He continued to work as a painter until his death in Paris.

See also African Methodist Episcopal Church; Painting and Sculpture

Bibliography

Driskell, David C. *Two Centuries of Black American Art.* New York: Knopf, 1976.

Driskell, David C. *Hidden Heritage: Afro-American Art 1800–1950.* San Francisco: Art Museum Association of America, 1985.

Matthews, Marcia M. *Henry Ossawa Tanner, American Artist.* Chicago: University of Chicago Press, 1969.

Mosby, Dewey F., Darrel Sewell, and Rae Alexander-Minter. *Henry Ossawa Tanner.* Philadelphia: Philadelphia Museum of Art, 1991.

DAVID C. DRISKELL (1996)

TAP DANCE

Tap is a form of American percussive dance that emphasizes the interplay of rhythms produced by the feet. Fused from African and European music and dance styles, tap evolved over hundreds of years, shaped by the constant exchanges and imitations that occurred between the black and white cultures as they converged in America. However, since it is jazz syncopations that distinguish tap's rhythms and define its inflections, the heritage of African percussive sensibilities has exerted the strongest influence on tap's evolution.

Unlike ballet, whose techniques were codified and taught in the academies, tap developed informally from black and white vernacular social dances, from people watching each other dance in the streets and dance halls. As a result of the offstage challenges and onstage competitions where steps were shared, stolen, and reinvented, tap gradually got fashioned into a virtuosic stage dance. Because tap must be heard, it must be considered a musical form as well as a dance form, one that evolved as a unique percussive expression of American jazz music. Tappers consider themselves musicians and describe their feet as a set of drums—the heels playing the bass, the toes the melody. Like jazz, tap uses improvisation, polyrhythms, and a pattern of rhythmic accenting to give it a ropulsive (swinging) quality. Many of tap's choreographic structures reflect the formal musical structures of blues, ragtime or Dixieland, swing, bebop, and cool jazz.

Perhaps the most distinguishing characteristic of tap is the amplification of the feet's rhythms. Early styles of tapping utilized boards laid across barrels, sawhorses, or cobblestones; hard-soled shoes, wooden clogs, hobnailed boots, hollow-heeled shoes, as well as soft-soled shoes (and even heavily calloused feet) played against a wooden, oily, or abrasive surface, such as sand. Specially made metal plates attached to the heel and toe of the shoes did not commonly appear until the early 1910s, in chorus lines of Broadway shows and revues.

Opportunities for whites and blacks to watch each other dance began in the early 1500s when enslaved Africans were shipped to the West Indies. During the infamous "Middle Passage" across the Atlantic, slaves were brought to the upper decks and forced to dance (or "exercise"). Without traditional drums, slaves played on upturned buckets and tubs. Thus, the rattle and restriction of chains and the metallic thunk of buckets were some of the first changes in African dance as it evolved toward an African-American style. Sailors witnessing these events set an early precedent of the white observers who would serve as social arbiters, onlookers, and participants at urban slave dances and plantation slave "frolicks." Upon arriving in North and South America and the West Indies, some Africans had been exposed to European court dances like the quadrille, cotillion, and contredanse, and they adopted these dances, keeping the patterns and figures but retaining their African rhythms.

Slaves purchased on the stopover in the Caribbean islands came into contact with thousands of Irishmen and Scotsmen who were deported, exiled, or sold in the new English plantation islands. The cultural exchange between first-generation enslaved Africans and indentured Irishmen—with Ibo men playing fiddles and Kerrymen learning how to play jubi drums—continued through the late 1600s on plantations and in urban centers during the transition from white indentured servitude to African slave labor.

In colonial America, a new percussive dance began to fuse from a stylistic meld of two great dance traditions. The African-American style tended to center movement in the hips and favored flat-footed, gliding, dragging, stamping, shuffling steps, with a relaxed torso gently bent at the waist and the spine remaining flexible. Gradually, that style blended with the British-European style, which centered movement in dexterous footwork that favored bounding, hopping, precisely placed toe-and-heel work, and complicated patterns, with carefully placed arms, an upright torso and erect spine, and little if any hip action.

Between 1600 and 1800, the new American tap-hybrid slowly emerged from British step dances and a variety of secular and religious African step dances labeled "juba" dances and "ring-shouts." The Irish jig, with its rapid toe and heelwork, and the Lancashire clog, which was danced in wooden-soled shoes, developed quickly. The clog involved faster and more complex percussive techniques, while the jig developed with a range of styles and functions that extended from a ballroom dance of articulate footwork and formal figures to a fast-stomping competitive solo performed by men on the frontier.

By contrast, the African-American juba (derived from the African djouba), moved in a counterclockwise circle and was distinguished by its rhythmically shuffling footwork; the clapping of hands; "patting," or "hamboning" (the hands rhythmically slap the thighs, arms, torso, cheeks, playing the body as if it were a large drum); the use of call-and-response patterning (vocal and physical); and solo or couple improvisation within the circle. The religious ring-shout, a similar countercircle dance driven by singing, stomping, and clapping, became an acceptable mode of worship in the Baptist church as long as dancers did not defy the ban against the crossing of the legs. With the arrival of the slave laws of 1740 prohibiting the beating of drums came substitutes for the forbidden drum: bone clappers, jawbones, tambourines, hand-clapping, hamboning, and the percussive footwork that was so crucial in the evolution of tap.

By 1800, "jigging" was a term applied to any black style of dancing in which the dancer, with relaxed and responsive torso, emphasized movement from the hips down with quickly shuffling feet beating tempos as fast as trip-hammers. Jigging competitions that featured buck-and-wing, shuffling ring dances, and breakdowns abounded on plantations and urban centers where freedmen and slaves congregated.

Though African-Americans and European-Americans both utilized a solo, vernacular style of dancing, there was a stronger and earlier draw of African-American folk material by white performers. By the 1750s, "Ethiopian delineators," most of them English and Irish actors, arrived in America. John Durang's 1789 "Hornpipe," a clog dance that mixed ballet steps with African-American shuffle-and-wings, was performed in blackface. By 1810 the singing and dancing "Negro boy" was an established stage character of blackface impersonators who performed jigs and clogs to popular songs. Thomas Dartmouth Rice's "Jump Jim Crow"—which was less a copy of an African-American dance than it was Rice's "black" version of the Irish jig that appropriated a Negro work-song and dance—was a phenomenal success in 1829. After Rice, Irishmen George Churty and Dan Emmett organized troupes of blackface minstrelmen who brought their Irish-American interpretations of African-American song and dance styles to the minstrel stage. By 1840, the minstrel show as a blackface act of songs, fast-talking repartee in black dialects, and shuffle-and-wing tap dancing became the most popular form of entertainment in America.

That the oddly cross-bred and newly emerging percussive dance was able to retain its African-American integrity is due, in large measure, to William Henry Lane (c. 1825–1852). Known as Master Juba, he was perhaps the most influential single performer in nineteenth-century American dance. Born a free man in Rhode Island, Lane grew up in the Five Points district of Manhattan (now South Street Seaport). An accomplished Irish jig dancer, Lane was unsurpassed in grace and technique, popular for his imitations of famous minstrel dancers, and famous as the undisputed champion of fierce dance competitions. This African-American dancer broke the whites-only barrier of the major minstrel companies, and as a young teenager he toured as the featured dancer with four of the biggest troupes. Lane was an innovator who grafted authentic African-American performance styles and rhythms onto the exacting techniques of jig and clog dancing. Because of his excellence, he influenced the direction of tap, and because he was so admired and imitated during his life and after his death, he fostered the spread of this new dance style.

When black performers finally gained access to the minstrel stage after the Civil War, the tap vocabulary was infused with a variety of fresh new steps and choreographic structures that spurred its growth. The "Essence of Old Virginia," originally a rapid, pigeon-toed sliding step, got slowed down and popularized in the 1870s by Billy Kersands, then refined by George Primrose in the 1890s to a graceful soft shoe. From the minstrel show came the walk-around finale, dances that included competitive and improvisatory sections, and a format of performance that combined songs, jokes, and specialty dances. By the late 1800s, big touring shows such as *Sam T. Jack's Creole Company* and *South Before the War* brought black vernacular dance to audiences across America. With the success of *Clorindy* (1898), which featured a small chorus line of elegant and fashionably dressed women,, and the *Creole Show* (1889), which replaced the usual blackface comedians with stylish cakewalk teams like Johnson and Dean, the stereotypes set by minstrelsy began to be displaced, and new images of the black performer were formed.

Turn-of-the-century medicine shows, gillies, carnivals and circuses helped establish the black dancer in show business and provided seeds for the growth of professional dancing. During the late 1890s, touring road shows like *In Old Kentucky* featured Friday night "buck dance" contests (another early term for tap dancing). Black Patti's Troubadours featured cakewalkers and buck-and-wing specialists, while the "jig top" circus tent had chorus lines and comedians dancing an early jazz style that combined shuffles, twists, grinds, struts, flat-footed buck, and eccentric dancing. Tap dance incorporated rubber-legging, the shimmy, and animal dances (peckin', camel-walk, scratchin') from social dance, as well as an entire vocabulary of wings, slides, chugs, and drags.

Performing opportunities increased with the rise of vaudeville (a kind of variety show). Vaudeville, which began in the 1880s, was the most popular form of stage entertainment in America by 1900. It was controlled by syndicates that brought together large numbers of theaters under a single management, which hired and toured the various acts. Because of racist policies, however, two separate vaudevilles developed, one black and one white.

Because of the nature of vaudeville, where performers spent years perfecting their acts before audiences, tap artists were able to refine the steps and styles that expanded tap's vocabulary. The black vaudeville syndicate, the Theatre Owners Booking Association (TOBA), offered grueling schedules and hard-earned but widespread exposure for such artists as the Whitman Sisters and the Four Covans. Although many black artists—such as "Covan and Ruffin," "Reed and Bryant" and "Greenlee and Drayton"—crossed over to appear on the white vaudeville circuits, they were bound by the "two colored" rule, which restricted blacks to pairs.

Rising from the minstrel show and vaudeville, "Williams and Walker" (Bert Williams and George Walker) introduced a black vernacular dance style to Broadway that was an eccentric blend of the shuffle, strut-turned cakewalk and grind, or mooch. Other important contributions were made by younger tap stylists, such as Ulysses "Slow Kid" Thompson and Bill Bailey, whose styles were descendants of the flat-footed hoofing of King Rastus Brown. The combined contributions of many such artists added to tap's endowment and, equally important, helped shape another stage dance, Broadway jazz.

The *Darktown Follies* (1913) serves as an example of how black shows disseminated African-American dance styles to the wider culture. Opening in Harlem's Lafayette Theater, *Darktown Follies* introduced the Texas Tommy, forerunner of the lindy hop, and tap dancer Eddie Rector's smooth style of "stage dancing," Toots Davis's "over-the-top" and "through-the-trenches" (high-flying air steps that would become the tap act's traditional flash finale). Then the black musicals *Shuffle Along* (1921) and *Runnin' Wild* (1923) on Broadway created rapid-fire tapping by chorus lines dancing to ragtime jazz, combining tap and stylish vernacular dances such as the Charleston, while the speciality solo and duo tappers blended tap with flips, somersaults, and twisting shimmies.

Bill "Bojangles" Robinson gained wide public attention on Broadway in Lew Leslie's *Blackbirds of 1928* at the age of fifty, although he had performed in vaudeville houses since 1921. Wearing wooden, split-soled shoes that gave mellow tones to his tapping, Robinson was known for bringing tap up on its toes, dancing upright and swinging. The 1920s also saw the rise of John "Bubbles" Sublett, credited with inventing "rhythm tap," a fuller and more dimensional rhythmic concept that utilized the dropping of the heels as bass accents and added more taps to the bar. The team of "Buck and Bubbles," formed with Ford Lee "Buck" Washington, was a sensation in the *Ziegfield Follies of 1931.* White Broadway stars had African-American dance directors, such as Clarence "Buddy" Bradley, who created routines that blended easy tap with black vernacular dance and jazz accenting. Bradley coached such stars as Ruby Keeler, Adele and Fred Astaire, Eleanor Powell and Paul Draper.

While white dancers learned tap in the classroom, black dancers developed on their own, often on street corners where dance challenges were hotly contested events. If tap had an institution of learning and apprenticeship, it was the Hoofers Club, next to the Lafayette Theatre in Harlem, where rookie and veteran tappers assembled to share, steal, and compete with each other. During the 1930s, tap dancers were often featured performing in front of swing bands in dance halls like Harlem's Savoy Ballroom. The swinging 4/4 bounce of the music of bands such as those of Count Basie and Duke Ellington proved ideal for hoofers, while the smaller vaudeville houses and intimate nightclubs, such as the Cotton Club, featured excellent tap and specialty dancers and small (six- to eight-member) tap chorus lines like the Cotton Club Boys.

Tap was immortalized in the Hollywood film musicals of the 1930s and 1940s, which featured Bill Robinson, Robinson and Shirley Temple, Buck and Bubbles, the Nicholas Brothers, and the Berry Brothers. However, these were exceptions, and for the most part, black dancers were denied access to the white film industry. Because of continued segregation and different budgets, a distinction in tap styles developed. In general, black artists like John Bubbles kept the tradition of rhythm-jazz tapping with its flights of percussive improvisation, while white artists like Fred Astaire polished the high style of tapping seen on films, where rhythms were often less important than the integration of choreography with scenography.

As tap became the favorite form of American theatrical dance, its many stylistic genres got bunched into loose categories: The Eccentric style was comedic, virtuosic, and idiosyncratic, exemplified by the routines (progenitors of later breakdancing moves) of Jigsaw Jackson, who circled and tapped while keeping his face against the floor; or the tapping of Alberta Whitman, who executed high-kicking legomania as a male impersonator. A Russian style, pioneered by Ida Forsyne in the 1910s, popularized Russian "kazotsky" kicks. This style was taken to Broadway by Dewey Weinglass and Ulysses "Slow Kid" Thompson. (A profusion of similar kicks and twisting, rubbery legs reemerged in hip-hop dance).

The Acrobatic style made famous by Willie Covan, Three Little Words, and the Four Step Brothers, featuring flips, somersaults, cartwheels, and splits. A cousin of this form, the Flash Act—brought to a peak of perfection by the Nicholas Brothers (Harold and Fayard)—combined elegant tap dancing with highly stylized acrobatics and precision-timed stunts.

Comedy Dance teams such as Slap and Happy, Stump and Stumpy, Chuck and Chuckles, and Cook and Brown inculcated their tap routines with jokes, knockabout acrobatics, grassroots characterizations, and rambunctious translations of vernacular dance in a physically robust style.

The Class Act brought the art of elegance and nuance, complexity and musicality to tap. From the first decades of the century, the debonair song-and-dance teams of Johnson and Cole and Greenlee and Drayton, as well as soloists such as Maxie McCree, Aaron Palmer, and Jack Wiggins, traversed the stage, creating beautiful pictures with each motion. Eddie Rector dovetailed one step into another in a graceful flow of sound and movement, while the act of Pete, Peaches, and Duke brought precision and unison work to a peak. Coles and Atkins (Charles "Honi" Coles and Cholly Atkins), certainly the most famous of the Class Act tappers of the 1930s to 1960s, combined flawless, high-speed rhythm-tapping with the slowest soft shoe in the business. Lena Horne said that Honi Coles made butterflies seem clumsy.

By the mid-1940s, big bands were being replaced by smaller, streamlined bebop groups whose racing tempos and complex rhythms were too challenging for most tappers, who were accustomed to the clear rhythms of swing. However, led by the greatly admired "Baby" Laurence, who meshed into bop combos by improvising and using tap as another percussive voice within the combo, many younger tappers took flight with bop and made the transition. These early tap bopsters of the 1940s and 1950s broke ground for the rapid and dense tap style that gained popularity in the 1990s.

By the 1950s, tap was in a sharp decline. This has been attributed to various causes: (1) the demise of vaudeville and the variety act; (2) the devaluing of tap dance on film; (3) the shift toward ballet and modern dance on the Broadway stage; (4) the imposition of a federal tax on dance floors which closed ballrooms and eclipsed the big bands; and (5) the advent of the jazz combo and the desire of musicians to play in a more intimate and concertized format. "Tap didn't die," says tap dancer Howard "Sandman" Sims, "it was just neglected." In fact the neglect was so thorough that this indigenous American dance form was almost lost, except for television reruns of old Hollywood musicals.

Those hoofers who lived through tap's lean years reveled in tap's resurgence. Jazz and tap historian Marshall Stearns, recognizing the danger of tap's imminent demise, arranged for a group of tap masters to perform at the 1962 Newport Jazz Festival. It was viewed as the last farewell, but it actually marked a rebirth that continued with Leticia Jay's historic *Tap Happening* (1969) at the Hotel Dixie in New York.

By the mid-1970s, young dancers began to seek out elder tap masters to teach them. Tap dance—previously ignored as art and dismissed as popular entertainment—now made one of the biggest shifts of its long history and moved to the concert stage. The African-American aesthetic fit the postmodern dance taste: it was a minimalist art that fused musician and dancer; it celebrated pedestrian movement and improvisation; its art seemed casual and democratic; and tap could be performed in any venue, from the street to the stage. Enthusiastic critical and public response placed tap firmly within the larger context of dance as art, fueling the flames of its renaissance.

The 1970s produced a number of video documentaries on tap, such as *Jazz Hoofer: The Legendary Baby Laurence, Great Feats of Feet,* and *No Maps On My Taps,* while the 1980s exploded with the films *White Nights, The Cotton Club and Tap;* tap festivals across the country; and the musical *Black and Blue* on Broadway. On television, *Tap Dance in America,* hosted by Gregory Hines and featuring tap masters and young virtuosos such as Savion Glover, bridged the gap between tap and mainstream entertainment.

In the 1990s, tap dance became concertized art form, danced, though not exclusively, to jazz music and infused with upper-body shapes of jazz dance and new spatial forms from modern dance. Incorporating new technologies for amplifying sounds and embellishing rhythms, new generations of tap artists are not only continuing tap's heritage, but forging new styles for the future.

See also Davis, Sammy, Jr.; Glover, Savion; Hines, Gregory; Minstrels/Minstrelsy; Robinson, Bill "Bojangles"; Social Dance

Bibliography

Emery, Lynne Fauley. *Black Dance: From 1619 to Today,* 2d ed. Princeton, N.J.: Princeton Book Company, 1988.

Fletcher, Beverly. *Tapworks: A Tap Dictionary and Reference Manual,* 2d ed. Hightstown, N.J.: Princeton Book Company, 2002.

Fletcher, Tom. *100 Years of the Negro in Show Business: The Tom Fletcher Story.* New York: Burdge, 1954. Reprint, New York: Da Capo, 1986.

Knowles, Mark. *Tap Roots: The Early History of Tap Dancing.* Jefferson, N.C.: McFarland, 2002.

Nathan, Hans. *Dan Emmett and the Rise of Early Negro Minstrelsey.* Norman: University of Oklahoma Press, 1962.

Sloan, Leni. "Irish Mornings and African Days On the Old Minstrel Stage." *Callahan's Irish Quarterly* 2 (Spring 1982): 50–53.

Sommer, Sally. "Feet, Talk to Me!" *Dance Magazine* (September 1988): 56–60.

Stearns, Marshall, and Jean Stearns. *Jazz Dance: The Story of American Vernacular Dance.* New York: Macmillan, 1968. Updated edition, New York: Da Capo Press, 1994.

Szwed, John, and Morton Marks. "The Afro-American Transformation of European Set Dances and Dance Suites." *Dance Research Journal* 20, no. 1 (Summer 1988): 29–36.

Toll, Robert. *Blacking Up: The Minstrel Show in Nineteenth Century America.* New York: Oxford University Press, 1974.

Williams, Joseph J. *Whence the "Black Irish" of Jamaica?* New York: Dial Press, 1932.

Winter, Maria Hannah. "Juba and American Minstrelsey." In *Chronicles of the American Dance: From the Shakers to Martha Graham,* edited by Paul Magriel. New York: Da Capo Press, 1978.

Woll, Allen. *Black Musical Theatre: From Coontown to Dreamgirls.* Baton Rouge: Louisiana State University Press, 1989.

CONSTANCE VALIS HILL (1996)
SALLY SOMMER (1996)
Updated by publisher 2005

Taylor, Koko

September 28, 1935

The 1920s witnessed the musical ascendance of black women blues artists. Mamie Smith's 1920 recording of "Crazy Blues" ushered in the "classic blues" era, facilitating the recording industry's entree into an untapped black market. Ida Cox, Alberta Hunter, Sippie Wallace, Ethel Waters, Bessie Smith, Gertrude "Ma" Rainey, and many others actively toured and recorded throughout the decade. However, the 1929 stock market crash marked a turn in recording company priorities. Country blues, performed by black men, moved to the forefront. The lower cost of scouting and recording a single man with a guitar (or sometimes a piano or harmonica) was more appealing to record company owners than the full rhythm-section sound of classic blues.

Koko Taylor, known as the "Queen of the Blues," was born into a Memphis, Tennessee, sharecropping family during this blues transition. Taylor (née Cora Walton) was the youngest of William and Annie Mae Walton's six children. Her early musical training was in a country Baptist church choir, the cotton fields of the family farm, and impromptu jam sessions with her siblings. The family radio also contributed to Taylor's musical development, particularly the broadcasts of Memphis disc jockeys (and later blues greats) Rufus Thomas and B. B. King. Bessie Smith, Memphis Minnie, and Sonny Boy Williamson were some of her early musical influences.

Taylor's mother passed away when she was four years old, and her father died when she was eleven. In 1953, at age eighteen, she moved to Chicago with her soon-to-be husband, Robert "Pops" Taylor. She did domestic work in the wealthy suburbs while Pops worked in the slaughterhouses. They frequented the South Side and West Side blues clubs and juke joints, with Pops playing guitar and Taylor singing. It was during this time that Taylor began musical relationships with bluesmen such as Howlin' Wolf, Magic Sam, Buddy Guy, Junior Wells, and Muddy

Waters, whom she credits as her greatest influence. In 1963 she recorded her first single for the USA label. However, it was her introduction to the incomparable Willie Dixon that altered the course of her career. In 1965 Dixon produced Taylor's rendition of his "Wang Dang Doodle" for the Checker label, a subsidiary of Chess Records. As Chess's last big hit, the million-selling single moved beyond black radio and broke into the national charts, becoming a signature song for Taylor.

Between 1980 and 2002 Taylor received twenty-two W. C. Handy Awards in a number of categories, including Contemporary Female Artist of the Year, Traditional Female Artist of the Year, Vocalist of the Year, and Entertainer of the Year. She has received multiple Grammy nominations, and she won a Grammy in 1984 for Best Traditional Blues Recording (for *Blues Explosion*). In 1993 Chicago mayor Richard M. Daley proclaimed March 3 "Koko Taylor Day." She has been inducted into the Blues Hall of Fame twice—in 1995 for her classic single "Wang Dang Doodle," and in 1997 as a performer.

Taylor's gritty and powerful "Mississippi blues" sound, coupled with her articulation of female sensibilities and concerns, link classic blues women and country blues men in an unparalleled fashion. Her distinct sound and mesmerizing stage presence have taken her around the world. She has made numerous national television appearances and is the subject of a documentary. In 2003 the Rhythm & Blues Foundation, recognizing Taylor's lifetime contribution to the development of rhythm and blues music, honored her with the Pioneer Award.

See also Blues, The; Blueswomen of the 1920s and 1930s; Rainey, Ma; Smith, Bessie; Smith, Mamie

Bibliography

Carter, Dick, and Sherry Wormser, prod. and dir. *Koko Taylor: Queen of the Blues.* MPI Home Video, 1992.

Davis, Angela Y. *Blues Legacies and Black Feminism: Gertrude "Ma" Rainey, Bessie Smith, and Billie Holiday.* New York: Pantheon, 1998.

Plath, James. "Queen of the Blues: Koko Taylor Talks About Her Subjects." Illinois Wesleyan University, 1994. Available from <http://titan.iwu.edu/~jplath/taylor.html>. Originally published in *Clockwatch Review* 9, nos. 1–2 (1994–1995): 117–131.

JUDITH CASSELBERRY (2005)

Television

The growing participation of African Americans in television, both in front of and behind the camera, has coincided with the radical restructuring of race relations in the United States from the end of World War II to the present day. Throughout this period, the specific characteristics of the television industry have complicated the ways in which these changing relations have been represented in television programming.

Television was conceived as a form of commercialized mass entertainment. Its standard fare—comedy, melodrama, and variety shows—favors simple plot structures, family situations, light treatment of social issues, and reassuring happy endings, all of which greatly delimit character and thematic developments. Perhaps more than any other group in American society, African Americans have suffered from the tendencies of these shows to depict one-dimensional character stereotypes.

Because commercial networks are primarily concerned with the avoidance of controversy and the creation of shows with the greatest possible appeal, African Americans were rarely featured in network series during the early years of television. Since the 1960s, the growing recognition by network executives that African Americans are an important group of consumers has led to greater visibility; however, in most cases, fear of controversy has led programmers to promote an unrealistic view of African-American life. Black performers, writers, directors, and producers have had to struggle against the effects of persistent typecasting and enforced sanitization in exchange for acceptance in white households. Only when African Americans made headway into positions of power in the production of television programs were alternative modes of representing African Americans developed.

Although experiments with television technology date back to the 1880s, it was not until the 1930s that sufficient technical expertise and financial backing were secured for the establishment of viable television networks. The National Broadcasting Company (NBC), a subsidiary of the Radio Corporation of America (RCA), wanted to begin commercial television broadcasting on a wide scale but was interrupted by the outbreak of World War II, and the television age did not commence in earnest until after peace was declared.

In 1948 the three major networks—the National Broadcasting Company (NBC), the Columbia Broadcasting System (CBS), and the American Broadcasting Company (ABC)—began regularly scheduled prime-time programming. That same year, the Democratic Party adopted

***Cicely Tyson and Maya Angelou in a scene from the groundbreaking 1977 television miniseries* Roots.** *The film adaptation of Alex Haley's novel was nominated for a record 37 Emmys.* AP/WIDE WORLD PHOTOS. REPRODUCED BY PERMISSION.

a strong civil rights platform at the Democratic convention, and the Truman administration issued a report entitled *To Secure These Rights*, the first statement made by the federal government in support of desegregation. Yet these two epochal revolutions—television and the civil rights movement—had little influence on one another for many years. While NBC, as early as 1951, stipulated that programs dealing with race and ethnicity should avoid ridiculing any social or racial group, most network programming rarely reflected the turbulence caused by the agitation for civil rights, nor did activists look to television as a medium for effecting social change. The effort to obtain fair and honest representation of African Americans and African-American issues on television remains a complex and protracted struggle.

In the early years of television, African Americans appeared most often as occasional guests on variety shows. Music entertainment artists, sports personalities, comedians, and political figures of the stature of Ella Fitzgerald, Lena Horne, Sarah Vaughan, Louis Armstrong, Duke Ellington, Cab Calloway, Pearl Bailey, Eartha Kitt, the Harlem Globetrotters, Dewey "Pigmeat" Markham, Bill "Bojangles" Robinson, Ethel Waters, Joe Louis, Sammy Davis Jr., Ralph Bunche, and Paul Robeson appeared in such shows as Milton Berle's *Texaco Star Theater* (1948–1953), Ed Sullivan's *Toast of the Town* (1948–1955), the *Steve Allen Show* (1950–1952; 1956–1961), and *Cavalcade of Stars* (1949–1952). Quiz shows like *Strike It Rich* (1951–1958), amateur talent contests like *Chance of a Lifetime* (1950–1953; 1955–1956), and shows concentrating on sporting events (particularly boxing matches), like *The Gillette Cavalcade of Sports* (1948–1960), provided another venue in which prominent blacks occasionally took part.

Rarely did African Americans host their own shows. Short-run exceptions included *The Bob Howard Show* (1948–1950); *Sugar Hill Times* (1949), an all-black variety show featuring Willie Bryant and Harry Belafonte; the *Hazel Scott Show* (1950), the first show featuring a black female host; the *Billy Daniels Show* (1952); and the *Nat "King" Cole Show* (1956–1957). There were even fewer all-black shows designed to appeal to all-black audiences or shows directed and produced by blacks. Short-lived local productions constituted the bulk of the latter category. In the early 1950s, a black amateur show called *Spotlight on Harlem* was broadcast on WJZ-TV in New York City; in 1955, the religious *Mahalia Jackson Show* appeared on Chicago's WBBM-TV.

Comedy was the only fiction-oriented genre in which African Americans were visible participants. Comedy linked television with the deeply entrenched cultural tradition of minstrelsy and blackface practices dating back to the antebellum period. In this cultural tradition, the representation of African Americans was confined either to degrading stereotypes of questionable intelligence and integrity (such as coons, mammies, Uncle Toms, or Stepin Fetchits) or to characterizations of people in willingly subservient positions (maids, chauffeurs, elevator operators, train conductors, shoeshine boys, handypeople, and the like). Beginning in the 1920s, radio comedies had perpetuated this cultural tradition, tailored to the needs of the medium.

The dominant television genre, the situation comedy, was invented on the radio. Like its television successor, the radio comedy—self-contained fifteen-minute or half-hour episodes with a fixed set of characters, usually involving minor domestic or familial disputes, and painlessly resolved in the allotted time period—lent itself to caricature. Since all radio comedy was verbal, it relied for much of its humor on the misuse of language, such as malapropisms or syntax error; and jokes made at the expense of African Americans (and their supposed difficulties with the English language) were a staple of radio comedies.

The first successful radio comedy, and the series that in many ways defined the genre, was *Amos 'n' Andy*, (1929–1960), which employed white actors to depict unflattering black characters. *Amos 'n' Andy* featured two white comedians, Freeman Gosden and Charles Correll, working in the style of minstrelsy and vaudeville. Another radio show that was successfully transferred to television was *Beulah* (1950–1953). The character Beulah was originally created for a radio show called *Fibber McGee and Molly* (1935–1957), in which Beulah was played by Marlin Hurt, a white man. These two shows, which adopted an attitude of contempt and condescending sympathy toward the black persona, were re-created on television with few changes, except that the verisimilitude of the genre demanded the use of black actors rather than whites in blackface and "blackvoice." As with *Amos 'n' Andy* (1951–1953)—in its first season the thirteenth most-watched show on television—the creators of *Beulah* had no trouble securing commercial support; both television shows turned out to be as popular as their radio predecessors, though both were short-lived in their network television incarnations.

Beulah (played first by Ethel Waters, then by Louise Beavers) developed the story of the faithful, complacent Aunt Jemima who worked for a white suburban middle-class nuclear family. Her unquestioning devotion to solving familial problems in the household of her white employers, the Hendersons, validated a social structure that forced black domestic workers to profess unconditional fidelity to white families, while neglecting their personal relations to their own kin. When blacks were included in Beulah's personal world, they appeared only as stereotypes. For instance, the neighbor's maid, Oriole (played by Butterfly McQueen), was an even more pronounced Aunt Jemima character; and Beulah's boyfriend, Bill Jackson (played by Percy Harris and Dooley Wilson), the Henderson's handyperson, was a coon. The dynamics between the white world of the Hendersons and Beulah's black world were those of the perfect object with a defective mirror image. The Hendersons represented a well-adjusted family, supported by a strong yet loving working father whose sizable income made it possible for the mother to remain at home. In contrast, Beulah was condemned to chasing after an idealized version of the family because her boyfriend did not seem too interested in a stable relationship; she was destined to work forever because Bill Jackson did not seem capable of taking full financial responsibility in the event of a marriage. As the show could only exist as long as Beulah was a maid, it was evident that her desires were never to be fulfilled. If Beulah seemed to enjoy channeling all her energy toward the solution of a white family's conflicts, it was because her own problems deserved no solution.

Amos 'n' Andy, on the other hand, belonged to the category of folkish programs that focused on the daily life and family affairs of various ethnic groups. Several such programs, among them *Mama* (1949–1956), *The Goldbergs* (1949–1955), and *Life with Luigi* (1952–1953)—depicting the lives of Norwegians, Jews, and Italians, respectively—were popularized in the early 1950s. In *Amos 'n' Andy*, the main roles comprised an assortment of stereotypical black characters. Amos Jones (played by Alvin Childress) and his wife, Ruby (played by Jane Adams), were passive Uncle Toms, while Andrew "Andy" Hogg Brown (played by Spencer Williams) was gullible and half-witted. George "Kingfish" Stevens (played by

Tim Moore) was a deceiving, unemployed coon, whose authority was constantly being undermined by his shrewd wife Sapphire (played by Ernestine Wade) and overbearing mother-in-law, "Mama" (played by Amanda Randolph). "Lightnin'" (played by Horace Stewart) was a janitor, and Algonquin J. Calhoun (played by Johnny Lee) was a fast-talking lawyer. These stereotypical characters were contrasted, in turn, with serious, level-headed black supporting characters, such as doctors, business people, judges, law enforcers, and so forth. The humorous situations created by the juxtapositions of these two types of characters—stereotypical and realistic—made *Amos 'n' Andy* an exceptionally intricate comedy and the first all-black television comedy that opened a window for white audiences on the everyday lives of African-American families in Harlem.

Having an all-black cast made it possible for *Amos 'n' Andy* to neglect relevant but controversial issues like race relations. The Harlem of this show was a world of separate but equal contentment, where happy losers, always ready to make fools of themselves, coexisted with regular people. Furthermore, the show's reliance on stereotypes precluded both the full fledged development of its characters and the possibility of an authentic investigation into the pathos of black daily life. Even though the performers often showed themselves to be masters of comedy and vaudeville, it is unfortunate that someone like Spencer Williams, who was also a prolific maker of all-black films, would only be remembered by the general public as Andy.

While a number of African Americans were able to enjoy shows like *Beulah* and *Amos 'n' Andy*, many were offended by their portrayal of stereotypes, as well as by the marked absence of African Americans from other fictional genres. Black opposition had rallied without success to protest the airing of this kind of show on the radio in the 1930s. Before *Amos 'n' Andy* aired in 1951, the National Association for the Advancement of Colored People (NAACP) began suing CBS for the show's demeaning depiction of blacks, and the organization did not rest until the show was canceled in 1953. Yet the viewership of white and black audiences alike kept *Amos 'n' Andy* in syndication until 1966. The NAACP's victory in terminating *Amos 'n' Andy* and *Beulah* also proved somewhat pyrrhic, since during the subsequent decade the networks produced no dramatic series with African Americans as central characters, while stereotyped portrayals of minor characters continued.

Many secondary comic characters from the radio and cinema found a niche for themselves in television. In the *Jack Benny Show* (1950–1965), Rochester Van Jones (played by Eddie "Rochester" Anderson) appeared as Benny's valet and chauffeur. For Anderson, whose Rochester had amounted to a combination of the coon and the faithful servant in the radio show, the shift to television proved advantageous, as he was able to give his character greater depth on the television screen. Indeed, through their outlandish employer-employee relationship, Benny and Anderson established one of the first interracial onscreen partnerships in which the deployment of power alternated evenly from one character to the other. The same may not be said of Willie Best's characterizations in shows like *The Stu Erwin Show* (1950–1955) and *My Little Margie* (1952–1955). Best tended to confine his antics to the Stepin Fetchit style and thereby reinforced the worst aspects of the master-slave dynamic.

African-American participation in dramatic series was confined to supporting roles in specific episodes in which the color-line tradition was maintained, such as the Philco *Television Playhouse* (1948–1955), which featured a young Sidney Poitier in "A Man Is Ten Feet Tall" in 1955; the *General Electric Theater* (1953–1962), which featured Ethel Waters and Harry Belafonte in "Winner by Decision" in 1955; and *The Hallmark Hall of Fame* (1952–) productions in 1957 and 1959 of Marc Connelly's "Green Pastures," a biblical retelling performed by an all-black cast. African Americans also appeared as jungle savages in such shows as *Ramar of the Jungle* (1952–1953), *Jungle Jim* (1955), and *Sheena, Queen of the Jungle* (1955–1956). The television western, one of the most important dramatic genres of the time, almost entirely excluded African Americans, despite their importance to the real American West. In the case of those narratives set in contemporary cities, if African Americans were ever included, it was only as props signifying urban deviance and decay. A rare exception to this was *Harlem Detective* (1953–1954), an extremely low-budget, local program about an interracial pair of detectives (with William Marshall and William Harriston playing the roles of the black and white detectives, respectively) produced by New York's WOR-TV.

Despite the sporadic opening of white households to exceptional African Americans and the effectiveness of the NAACP's action in canceling *Amos 'n' Andy*, the networks succumbed to the growing political conservatism and racial antagonism of the mid-1950s. The cancellation of the *Nat "King" Cole Show* exemplifies the attitude that prevailed among programmers during that time. Nat "King" Cole had an impeccable record: his excellent musical and vocal training complemented his noncontroversial, delicate, and urbane delivery; he had a nationally successful radio show on NBC in the 1940s; and over forty of his recordings had been listed for their top sales by *Billboard* magazine between 1940 and 1955. Cole's great popularity was demonstrated in his frequent appearances as guest or host on the most important television variety shows. NBC first backed Cole completely, as is evidenced by the network's willingness to pour money into the show's budget, to increase the show's format from fifteen to thirty minutes, and to experiment with different time slots. Cole also had the support of reputable musicians and singers who were willing to perform for nominal fees. His guests included Count Basie, Mahalia Jackson, Pearl Bailey, and all-star musicians from "Jazz at the Philharmonic." Yet the Nat "King" Cole Show did not gain enough popularity among white audiences to survive the competition for top ratings; nor was it able to secure a stable national sponsor. After about fifty performances, the show was canceled.

African Americans exhibited great courage in these early years of television by supporting some shows and boycotting others. Organizations such as the Committee on Employment Opportunities for Negroes, the Coordinating Council for Negro Performers, and the Committee for the Negro in the Arts constantly fought for greater and fairer inclusion. During the height of the civil rights movement, the participation of African Americans in television intensified. Both Africans and African Americans became the object of scrutiny for daily news shows and network documentaries. The profound effects of the radical recomposition of race relations in the United States and the independence movement in Africa could not go unreported. "The Red and the Black" (January 1961), a segment of the *Close Up!* documentary series, analyzed the potential encroachment of the Soviet Union in Africa as European nations withdrew from the continent; "Robert Ruark's Africa" (May 1962), a documentary special shot on location in Kenya, defended the colonial presence in the continent. The series *See It Now* (1951–1958) started reporting on the civil rights movement as early as 1954, when the U.S. Supreme Court ruled to desegregate public schools, and exposed the measures that had been taken to hinder desegregation in Norfolk high schools in an episode titled "The Lost Class of '59," aired in January 1959. *CBS Reports* (1959–) examined, among other matters, the living conditions of blacks in the rural South in specials such as "Harvest of Shame" (November 1960). In December 1960 *NBC White Paper* aired "Sit-In," a special report on desegregation conflicts in Nashville. "Crucial Summer" (which started airing in August 1963) was a five-part series of half-hour reports on discrimination practices in housing, education, and employment. It was followed by "The American Revolution of '63" (which started airing in September 1963), a three-hour documentary on discrimination in different areas of daily life across the nation.

However, the gains made by the airing of these programs were offset by the effects of poor scheduling, and they were often made to compete with popular series programs and variety and game shows from which blacks had been virtually erased. As the civil rights movement gained momentum, some southern local stations preempted programming that focused on racial issues, while other southern stations served as a means for the propagation of segregationist propaganda.

As black issues came to be scrutinized in news reports and documentaries, African Americans began to appear in the growing genre of socially relevant dramas, such *as The Naked City* (1958–1963), *Dr. Kildare* (1961–1966), *Ben Casey* (1961–1966), *The Defenders* (1961–1965), *The Nurses* (1962–1965), *Channing* (1963–1964), *The Fugitive* (1963–1967), and *Slattery's People* (1963–1965). These shows, which usually relied on news stories for their dramatic material, explored social problems from the perspective of white doctors, nurses, educators, social workers, or lawyers. Although social issues were seriously treated, their impact was much diminished by the easy and felicitous resolution with which each episode was brought to a close. Furthermore, the African Americans who appeared in these programs—Ruby Dee, Louis Gossett Jr., Ossie Davis, and others—were given roles in episodes where topics were racially defined, and the color line was strictly maintained.

The short-lived social drama *East Side/West Side* (1963–1964) proved an exception to this rule. It was the first noncomedy in the history of television to cast an African American (Cicely Tyson) as a regular character. The program portrayed the dreary realities of urban America without supplying artificial happy endings; on occasion, parts of the show were censored because of their liberal treatment of interracial relations. *East Side/West Side* ran into difficulties when programmers tried to obtain commercial sponsors for the hour during which it was aired; eventually, despite changes in format, it was canceled after little more than twenty episodes.

Unquestionably, the more realistic television genres that evolved as a result of the civil rights movement served as powerful mechanisms for sensitizing audiences to the predicaments of those affected by racism. But as television grew to occupy center stage in American popular entertainment, the gains of the civil rights movement came to be ambiguously manifested. By 1965, a profusion of top-rated programs had begun casting African Americans both in leading and supporting roles. The networks and commercial sponsors became aware of the purchasing power of African-American audiences, and at the same time they discovered that products could be advertised to African-American consumers without necessarily offending white tastes. Arguably, the growing inclusion of African Americans in fiction-oriented genres was premised on a radical inversion of previous patterns. If blacks were to be freed from stereotypical and subservient representation, they were nevertheless portrayed in ways designed to please white audiences. Their emergence as a presence in television was to be facilitated by a thorough cleansing.

A sign of the changing times was the popular police comedy *Car 54, Where Are You?* (1961–1963). Set in a rundown part of the Bronx, this comedy featured black officers in secondary roles (played by Nipsey Russell and Frederick O'Neal). However, the real turning point in characterizations came with *I Spy* (1965–1968), a dramatic series featuring Bill Cosby and Robert Culp as Alexander Scott and Kelly Robinson, two secret agents whose adventures took them to the world's most sophisticated spots, where racial tensions did not exist. In this role, Cosby played an immaculate, disciplined, intelligent, highly educated, and cultured black man who engaged in occasional romances but did not appear sexually threatening and whose sense of humor was neither eccentric nor vulgar. While inverting stereotypical roles, *I Spy* also created a one-to-one harmonious interracial friendship between two men.

I Spy was followed by other top-rated programs. In *Mission Impossible* (1966–1973), Greg Morris played Barney Collier, a mechanic and electronics expert and member of the espionage team; in *Mannix* (1967–1975), a crime series about a private eye, Gail Fisher played Peggy Fair, Mannix's secretary; in *Ironside* (1967–1975), Don Mitchell played Mark Sanger, Ironside's personal assistant and bodyguard; and in the crime show *Mod Squad* (1968–1973), Clarence Williams III played Linc Hayes, one of the three undercover police officers working for the Los Angeles Police Department. This trend was manifested in other top-ranked shows: *Peyton Place* (1964–1969), the first prime-time soap opera, featured Ruby Dee, Percy Rodriguez, and Glynn Turman as the Miles Family; in *Hogan's Heroes* (1965–1971), a sitcom about American prisoners in a German POW camp during World War II, Ivan Dixon played Sergeant Kinchloe; in *Daktari* (1966–1969), Hari Rhodes played an African zoologist; in *Batman* (1966–1968), Eartha Kitt appeared as Catwoman; in *Star Trek* (1966–1969), Nichelle Nichols was Lieutenant Uhura; in the variety show *Rowan and Martin's Laugh-In* (1966–1973), Chelsea Brown, Johnny Brown, and Teresa Graves appeared regularly; and in the soap opera *The Guiding Light* (1952–), Cicely Tyson started appearing regularly after 1967.

Julia (1968–1971) was the first sitcom in over fifteen years to feature African Americans in the main roles. It placed seventh in its first season, thereby becoming as popular as *Amos 'n' Andy* had been in its time. Julia Baker (played by Diahann Carroll) was a middle-class, cultured widow who spoke standard English. Her occupation as a nurse suggested that she had attended college. She was economically and emotionally self-sufficient; a caring parent to her little son Corey (played by Marc Copage); and equipped with enough sophistication and wit to solve the typical comic dilemmas presented in the series. However, many African Americans criticized the show for neglecting the more pressing social issues of their day. In Julia's suburban world, it was not so much that racism did not matter, but that integration had been accomplished at the expense of black culture. Julia's cast of black friends and relatives (played by Virginia Capers, Diana Sands, Paul Winfield, and Fred Williamson) appeared equally sanitized. Ironically, Julia perpetuated some of the same misrepresentations of the black family as *Beulah*—for despite its elegant trappings, Julia's was yet another female-headed African-American household.

As successful as *Julia* was the *Bill Cosby Show* (1969–1971), which featured Bill Cosby as Chet Kincaid, a single, middle-class high school gym teacher. In contrast to *Julia*, however, this comedy series presented narrative conflicts that involved Cosby in the affairs of black relatives and inner-city friends, as well as in those of white associates and suburban students. The *Bill Cosby Show* sought to integrate the elements of African-American culture through the use of sound, setting, and character: African-American music played in the background, props reminded one of contemporary political events, Jackie "Moms" Mabley and Mantan Moreland appeared frequently as Cosby's aunt and uncle, and Cosby's jokes often invested events from black everyday life with comic pathos. A less provocative but long-running sitcom, *Room 222* (1969–1974), concerned an integrated school in Los Angeles. Pete Dixon (played by Lloyd Haynes), a black history teacher, combined the recounting of important events of black history with attempts to address his students' daily problems. Another comic series, *Barefoot in the Park* (1970–1971)—with Scoey Mitchell, Tracey Reed, Thelma Carpenter, and Nipsey Russell—was attempted, but failed after thirteen episodes; it was an adaptation of the film by the same name but with African Americans playing the leading roles.

By the end of the 1960s, many of the shows in which blacks could either demonstrate their decision-making abilities or investigate the complexities of their lives had been canceled. Two black variety shows failed due to poor scheduling and lack of white viewer support: *The Sammy Davis Jr. Show*, the first variety show hosted by a black person since the *Nat "King" Cole Show* (1966); and *The Leslie*

Uggams Show (1969), the first variety show hosted by a black woman since Hazel Scott. A similar fate befell *The Outcasts* (1968–1969), an unusual western set in the period immediately following the Civil War. The show, which featured two bounty hunters, a former slave and a former slave owner, and addressed without qualms many of the same controversial themes associated with the civil rights movement, was canceled due to poor ratings. Equally short-lived was *Hawk* (1966), a police drama shot on location in New York City, which featured a full-blooded Native American detective (played by Burt Reynolds) and his black partner (played by Wayne Grice). An interracial friendship was also featured in the series *Gentle Ben* (1967–1969), which concerned the adventures of a white boy and his pet bear; Angelo Rutherford played Willie, the boy's close friend. While interracial friendships were cautiously permitted, the slightest indication of romance was instantly suppressed: The musical variety show *Petula* (1968) was canceled because it showed Harry Belafonte and Petula Clark touching hands.

Despite these limitations, the programs of the 1960s, 1970s, and 1980s represented a drastic departure from the racial landscape of early television. In the late 1940s, African Americans were typically confined to occasional guest roles; by the end of the 1980s, most top-rated shows featured at least one black person. It had become possible for television shows to violate racial taboos without completely losing commercial and viewer sponsorship. However, greater visibility in front of the camera did not necessarily translate into equal opportunity for all in all branches of television: the question remained as to whether discriminatory practices had in fact been curtailed, or had simply survived in more sophisticated ways. It was true that the presence of blacks had increased in many areas of television, including, for example, the national news: Bryant Gumbel co-anchored *Today* (1952–) from 1982 to 1997; Ed Bradley joined *60 Minutes* (1968–) in 1981; Carole Simpson was a weekend anchor for *ABC World News Tonight*, where she had started as a correspondent in 1982, from 1988 to 2003.

Nevertheless, comedy remained the dominant form for expressing black lifestyles. Dramatic shows centering on the African-American experience have had to struggle to obtain high enough ratings to remain on the air—the majority of the successful dramas have been those where blacks share the leading roles with other white protagonists.

During the 1970s and 1980s, the number of social dramas, crime shows, or police stories centering on African Americans or featuring an African American in a major role steadily increased. Most of the series were canceled within a year. These included *The Young Lawyers* (1970–1971), *The Young Rebels* (1970–1971), *The Interns* (1970–1971), *The Silent Force* (1970–1971), *Tenafly* (1973–1974), *Get Christie Love!* (1974–1975), *Shaft* (1977), *Paris* (1979–1980), *The Lazarus Syndrome* (1979), *Harris & Co.* (1979), *Palmerstown, USA* (1980–1981), *Double Dare* (1985), *Fortune Dane* (1986), *The Insiders* (1986), *Gideon Oliver* (1989), *A Man Called Hawk* (1989), and *Sonny Spoon* (1988). The most popular dramatic series with African-American leads were *Miami Vice* (1984–1989), *In the Heat of the Night* (1988–1994), and *The A-Team* (1983–1987). On *Miami Vice* and *In the Heat of the Night*, Philip Michael Thomas and Howard Rollins, the black leads, were partnered with better-known white actors who became the most identifiable character for each series. Perhaps the most popular actor on a dramatic series was the somewhat cartoonish Mr. T, who played Sergeant Bosco "B.A." Baracus on *The A-Team*, an action-adventure series in which soldiers of fortune set out to eradicate crime. Although in the comedy *Barney Miller* (1975–1980) Ron Glass played an ambitious middle-class black detective, the guest spots or supporting roles in police series generally portrayed African Americans as sleazy informants, such as Rooster (Michael D. Roberts) on *Baretta* (1975–1978), or Huggy Bear (Antonio Fargas) on *Starsky and Hutch* (1975–1979).

In prime-time serials, African Americans appeared to have been unproblematically assimilated into a middle-class lifestyle. *Dynasty* (1981–1989) featured Diahann Carroll as one of the series' innumerable variations on the "rich bitch" persona; while *Knots Landing* (1979–1993), *L.A. Law* (1986–1994), *China Beach* (1988–1990), and *The Trials of Rosie O'Neal* (1991–1992) developed storylines with leading black roles as well as interracial romance themes. Later dramatic series featuring African Americans in regularly occurring roles included *Homicide: Life on the Street* (1993–1999), *NYPD Blue* (1993–2005), *Oz* (1997–2003), *The Practice* (1997–2004), *Third Watch* (1999–2005), *Boston Public* (2000–2004), and *Six Feet Under* (2001–2005), as well as *ER* (1994–), *"24"* (2001–), *The Wire* (2002–), *Without a Trace* (2002–), *Law & Order* (1990–) and its spin-offs *Law & Order: Special Victims Unit* (1999–) and *Law & Order: Criminal Intent* (2001–), and *CSI: Crime Scene Investigation* (2000–) and its spin-offs *CSI: Miami* (2002–) and *CSI: New York* (2004–).

MTM Enterprises produced some of the most successful treatments of African Americans in the 1980s. In their programs, which often combined drama and satire, characters of different ethnic backgrounds were accorded full magnitude. *Fame* (1982–1983) was an important drama about teenagers of different ethnicities coping with the complexities of contemporary life. *Frank's Place* (1987–1988), an offbeat and imaginative show about a professor who inherits a restaurant in a black neighborhood in New Orleans, provided viewers with a realistic treatment of black family affairs. Though acclaimed by critics, *Frank's Place* did not manage to gain a large audience, and the show was canceled after having been assigned four different time slots in one year.

African Americans have been featured in relatively minor and secondary roles on science fiction series. *Star Trek*'s communications officer Lieutenant Uhura (played by Nichelle Nichols) was little more than a glorified telephone operator. *Star Trek: The Next Generation* (1987–1994) featured LeVar Burton as Leiutenant Geordi La Forge, a blind engineer who can see through a visor. A heavily made-up Michael Dorn was cast as Lieutenant Worf, a horny-headed Klingon officer, and Whoopi Goldberg appeared frequently as the supremely empathetic, long-lived bartender Guinan. In *Deep Space 9* (1992–1999), the third *Star Trek* series, a major role was given to Avery Brooks as Commander Sisko, head of the space station on which much of the show's action takes place, while *Star Trek: Voyager* (1995–2001) featured Tim Russ as Vulcan security officer Tuvok. *Enterprise* (2001–2005), the fifth *Star Trek* series, featured Anthony Montgomery as Ensign Travis Mayweather.

Until recently, blacks played an extremely marginal role in daytime soap operas. In 1966, *Another World* became the first daytime soap opera to introduce a storyline about a black character, a nurse named Peggy Harris Nolan (played by Micki Grant). In 1968, the character of Carla Hall was introduced as the daughter of housekeeper Sadie Gray (played by Lillian Hayman). Embarrassed by her social and ethnic origins, Carla was passing for white in order to be engaged to a successful white doctor. Some network affiliates canceled the show after Carla appeared. Since then, many more African Americans have appeared in soap operas, including Al Freeman Jr., Darnell Williams, Phylicia Rashad, Jackée, Blair Underwood, Nell Carter, Billy Dee Williams, Cicely Tyson, and Ruby Dee. In most cases, character development has been minor, with blacks subsisting on the margins of activity, not at the centers of power. An exception was the interracial marriage between a black woman pediatrician and a white male psychiatrist on *General Hospital* in 1987. *Generations*, the only soap opera that focused exclusively on African-American family affairs, was canceled in 1990 after a yearlong run. However, *The Young and the Restless* (1973–) has featured such African-American actors as Kristoff St. John, Victoria Rowell, Shemar Moore, and Tonya Lee Williams in long-running storylines. In addition, black actor James Reynolds joined the cast of *Days of Our Lives* (1965–) in 1982 as police commander Abe Carver, and continued in the role for more than twenty years, with a short break in the early 1990s to star in *Generations*. Reynold's Abe Carver has become one of television's longest-running black characters.

The dramatic miniseries *Roots* (1977) and *Roots: The Next Generation* (1979)—more commonly known as *Roots II*—were unusually successful. For the first time in the history of television, close to 130 million Americans dedicated almost twenty-four hours to following a 300-year saga chronicling the tribulations of African Americans in their sojourn from Africa to slavery and, finally, to emancipation. Yet *Roots* and *Roots II* were constrained by the requirements of linear narrative, and characters were seldom placed in situations where they could explore the full range of their historical involvement in the struggle against slavery. The miniseries *Beulah Land* (1980), a reconstruction of the southern experience during the Civil War, attempted to recapture the success of *Roots*, but ended up doing no more than reviving some of the worst aspects of *Gone with the Wind*. Other important but less commercially successful dramatic historical reconstructions include *The Autobiography of Miss Jane Pittman* (1973), *King* (1978), *One in a Million: The Ron LeFlore Story* (1978), *A Woman Called Moses* (1978), *Backstairs at the White House* (1979), *Freedom Road* (1979), *Sadat* (1983), and *Mandela* (1987). There are also a number of made-for-television movies based on the civil rights movement, including *The Ernest Green Story* (1993), *Mr. & Mrs. Loving* (1996), *The Color of Courage* (1998), *Ruby Bridges* (1998), *Selma, Lord, Selma* (1999), *Freedom Song* (2000), *Boycott* (2002), and *The Rosa Parks Story* (2002).

A number of miniseries and made-for-television movies about black family affairs and romance were broadcast in the 1980s. *Crisis at Central High* (1981) was based on the desegregation dispute in Little Rock, Arkansas, while *Benny's Place* (1982), *Sister, Sister* (1982), *The Defiant Ones* (1985), and *The Women of Brewster Place* (1989) were set in various African-American communities. Other more recent examples include *The Josephine Baker Story* (1990), *The Temptations* (1998), *Introducing Dorothy Dandridge* (1999), *The Corner* (2000), *Carmen: A Hip Hopera* (2001), *The Old Settler* (2001), *Lackawanna Blues* (2005), and *Their Eyes Were Watching God* (2005).

The 1970s witnessed the emergence of several television sitcoms featuring black family affairs. In these shows, grave issues such as poverty and upward mobility were embedded in racially centered jokes. A source of inspiration for these sitcoms may have been *The Flip Wilson Show* (1970–1974), the first successful variety show hosted by an

The **Oprah Winfrey Show,** *so named in 1985 after Winfrey successfully assumed anchor duties for its failing precursor,* **A.M. Chicago,** *the previous year, is the most-watched television talk show in the United States.* AP/WIDE WORLD PHOTOS. REPRODUCED BY PERMISSION.

African American. The show, which featured celebrity guests like Lucille Ball, Johnny Cash, Muhammad Ali, Sammy Davis Jr., Bill Cosby, Richard Pryor, and B. B. King, was perhaps best known for the skits Wilson performed. The skits were about black characters (Geraldine Jones, Reverend Leroy, Sonny the janitor, Freddy Johnson the playboy, and Charley the chef) who flaunted their outlandishness to such a degree that most viewers were unable to determine whether they were meant to be cruel reminders of minstrelsy or parodies of stereotypes.

A number of family comedies, mostly produced by Tandem Productions (Norman Lear and Bud Yoking), became popular around the same time as *The Flip Wilson Show*: these included *All in the Family* (1971–1983), *Sanford and Son* (1972–1977), *Maude* (1972–1978), *That's My Mama* (1974–1975), *The Jeffersons* (1975–1985), *Good Times* (1974–1979), and *What's Happening* (1976–1979). On *Sanford and Son*, Redd Foxx and Demond Wilson played father-and-son Los Angeles junk dealers. *Good Times*, set in a housing development on the South Side of Chicago, portrayed a working-class black family. Jimmie Walker, who played J.J., became an overnight celebrity with his "jive-talking" and use of catchphrases like "Dy-No-Mite." On *The Jeffersons*, Sherman Hemsley played George Jefferson, an obnoxious and upwardly mobile owner of a dry-cleaning business. As with *Amos 'n' Andy*, these comedies relied principally on stereotypes—the bigot, the screaming woman, the grinning idiot, and so on—for their humor. However, unlike their predecessor of the 1950s, the comedies of the 1970s integrated social commentary into the joke situations. Many of the situations reflected contemporary discussions in a country divided by, among other things, the Vietnam War. And because of the serialized form of the episodes, most characters were able to grow and learn from experience.

By the late 1970s and early 1980s, the focus of sitcoms had shifted from family affairs to nontraditional familial arrangements. *The Cop and the Kid* (1975–1976), *Diff'rent Strokes* (1978–1986), *The Facts of Life* (1979–1988), and *Webster* (1983–1987) were about white families and their adopted black children. Several comic formulas were also reworked, as a sassy maid (played by Nell Carter) raised several white children in *Gimme a Break!* (1981–1987), and a wise-cracking and strong-willed butler (played by Robert Guillaume) dominated the parody *Soap* (1977–1981). Guillaume later played an equally daring budget director for a state governor in *Benson* (1979–1986). Several less successful comedies were also developed during this time, including *The Sanford Arms* (1976), *The New Odd Couple* (1982–1983), *One in a Million* (1980), and *The Red Foxx Show* (1986).

The most significant comedies of the 1980s were those in which black culture was explored on its own terms. The extraordinarily successful *The Cosby Show* (1984–1992), the first African-American series to top the annual Nielsen ratings, featured Bill Cosby as Cliff Huxtable, a comfortable middle-class paterfamilias to his Brooklyn family, which included his successful lawyer wife Clair Huxtable (played by Phylicia Rashad) and their six children. The series *227* (1985–1990) starred Marla Gibbs, who had previously played a sassy maid on *The Jeffersons,* in a family comedy set in a black section of Washington, D.C. *A Different World* (1987–1993), a spin-off of *The Cosby Show,* was set in a black college in the South. *Amen* (1986–1991), featuring Sherman Hemsley as Deacon Ernest Frye, was centered on a black church in Philadelphia. In all of these series, the black-white confrontations that had been the staple of African-American television comedy were replaced by situations in which the humor was provided by the diversity and difference within the African-American community.

Some black comedies—*Charlie & Company* (1986), *Family Matters* (1989–1998), *Fresh Prince of Bel Air* (1990–1996), and *True Colors* (1990–1992)—followed the style set by *The Cosby Show.* Others like *In Living Color* (1990–1994) took the route of reworking a combination of variety show and skits in a manner reminiscent of *The Flip Wilson Show.* Other popular variety and sketch comedy series starring African-American comedians included HBO's *The Chris Rock Show* (1997–2000) and Dave Chappelle's *Chappelle's Show* (2003–2005) on Comedy Central. Much of the originality and freshness of these comedies is due to the fact that some of them were produced by African Americans (*The Cosby Show, A Different World, Fresh Prince of Bel Air,* and *In Living Color*). *Carter Country* (1977–1979), a sitcom that pitted a redneck police chief against his black deputy (played by Kene Holliday), inspired several programs with similar plot lines: *Just Our Luck* (1983), *He's the Mayor* (1986), *The Powers of Matthew Star* (1982–1983), *Stir Crazy* (1985), *Tenspeed and Brown Shoe* (1980), and *Enos* (1980–1981).

UPN, launched as the United Paramount Network in 1995, has made a staple of programming situation comedies featuring primarily African-American casts, including *Moesha* (1996–2001), *The Parkers* (1999–2004), *Girlfriends* (2000–), *One on One* (2001–), *Half & Half* (2002–), *All of Us* (2003–), *Eve* (2003–), and *Second Time Around* (2004–2005). The actor Taye Diggs produced and starred as a hotshot attorney in the UPN dramatic series *Kevin Hill* (2004–). The Fox network offered the comedy *Living Single* (1992–1998), starring Queen Latifah, and *The Bernie Mac Show* (2001–), while the WB had actors Jaime Foxx in *The Jaime Foxx Show* (1996–2001) and Steve Harvey in *Steve Harvey's Big Time* (2003–2005). ABC's comedies included *The Hughleys* (1998–2002), starring D. L. Hughley, and *My Wife and Kids* (2001–2005), starring Damon Wayans, while cable station Showtime offered a series adaptation of the movie *Soul Food* (2000–2004). Reality series such as *Survivor* (2000–), *The Amazing Race* (2001–), *American Idol* (2002–), and *The Apprentice* (2004–) featured African Americans among their participants. The UPN's popular reality show *America's Next Top Model* (2001–) also featured black participants, as well as an African-American host and producer, Tyra Banks.

Alternatives

Local stations, public television outlets, syndication, and cable networks have provided important alternatives for the production of authentic African-American programming. In the late 1960s, local television stations began opening their doors to the production of all-black shows and the training of African-American actors, commentators, and crews. Examples of these efforts include *Black Journal*—later known as *Tony Brown's Journal*—(1968–1976), a national public affairs program; *Soul* (1970–1975), a variety show produced by Ellis Haizlip at WNET in New York; *Inside Bedford-Stuyvesant* (1968–1973), a public affairs program serving the black communities in New York City; and *Like It Is*, a public affairs show featuring Gil Noble as the outspoken host.

At the national level, public television has also addressed African-American everyday life and culture in such series and special programs as *History of the Negro People* (1965), *Black Omnibus* (1973), *The Righteous Apples* (1979–1981), *With Ossie and Ruby* (1980–1981), *Gotta Make This Journey: Sweet Honey and the Rock* (1984), *The Africans* (1986), *Eyes on the Prize* (1987), and *Eyes on the Prize II* (1990). The Public Broadcasting Service (PBS) documentary series *American Masters* (1986–) featured a number of episodes on African-American artists, including Louis Armstrong, James Baldwin, Duke Ellington, Lena Horne, Sidney Poitier, and others. *The American Ex-*

perience (1988–), another documentary series on PBS, included episodes on the careers of Ida B. Wells, Adam Clayton Powell, Malcolm X, Marcus Garvey, and other important African Americans, along with episodes on topics in black culture and history, including "Roots of Resistance: The Story of the Underground Railroad" (1995), "Scottsboro: An American Tragedy" (2000), and "The Murder of Emmett Till" (2003). In addition, black journalist Gwen Ifill became the moderator of *Washington Week* (1967–) and senior correspondent for *The NewsHour with Jim Lehrer* (1995–) on PBS in 1999. Ifill also moderated the first televised debate between the candidates for vice president during the 2004 presidential campaign.

Syndication, the system of selling programming to individual stations on a one-to-one basis, has been crucial for the distribution of shows such as *Soul Train* (1971–), *Solid Gold* (1980–1988), *The Arsenio Hall Show* (1989–1994), *The Oprah Winfrey Show* (1986–), and *The Montel Williams Show* (1991–). A wider range of programming has also been made possible by the growth and proliferation of cable services. Robert Johnson took a personal loan for $15,000 in the early 1980s to start a cable business—Black Entertainment Television (BET)—catering to the African Americans living in the Washington, D.C., area. At that time BET consisted of a few hours a day of music videos. By the early 1990s, the network had expanded across the country, servicing about 25 million subscribers, and had a net worth of more than $150 million. (Its programming had expanded to include black collegiate sports, music videos, public affairs programs, and reruns of, among others, *The Cosby Show* and *Frank's Place*.) The Black Family Channel, founded in 1999 as MBC Network, is a black-owned and operated cable network for African-American families with children's programs, sports, news, talk shows, and religious programming.

Children's Programming

As late as 1969, children's programming did not include African Americans. The first exceptions were *Sesame Street* (1969–) and *Fat Albert and the Cosby Kids* (1972–1989). These two shows were groundbreaking in content and format; they emphasized altruistic themes, the solution of everyday problems, and the development of reading skills and basic arithmetic. Other children's shows that focused on or incorporated African Americans include *The Jackson Five* (1971), *ABC After-School Specials* (1972–), *The Harlem Globetrotters Popcorn Machine* (1974–1976), *Rebop* (1976–1979), *30 Minutes* (1978–1982); *Reading Rainbow* (1983–2004), *Pee-Wee's Playhouse* (1986–1991); *Saved by the Bell* (1989–1993), *Saved by the Bell: The New Class* (1993–2000), and *Where in the World Is Carmen San Diego* (1991–1996).

Conclusion

Although African Americans have had to struggle against both racial tension and the inherent limitations of television, they have become prominent in all aspects of the television industry. As we enter the twenty-first century, the format and impact of television programming will undergo some radical changes, and the potential to provoke and inform audiences will grow. Television programs are thus likely to become more controversial than ever, but they will also become an even richer medium for effecting social change. Perhaps African Americans will be able to use these technical changes to allay the racial discord and prejudice that persists off-camera in America.

This article primarily explores the racial issues that impacted on television in its golden years right up to the current century. The arrival of digital delivery systems that have enhanced satellite, cable, DVD and even the internet has reduced the power and reach of broadcast television. Nevertheless, African Americans continue to be short-changed by the medium even with the huge success of Oprah Winfrey, Chris Rock, and a few other Black super stars. The more the technology changes the more it stays the same.

See also Black Entertainment Television (BET); Carroll, Diahann; Cosby, Bill; Davis, Ossie; Dee, Ruby; Film in the United States; Gossett, Louis, Jr.; Minstrels/Minstrelsy; Poitier, Sidney; Radio; Tyson, Cicely; Wilson, Flip

Bibliography

Allen, Robert C., ed. *Channels of Discourse, Reassembled: Television and Contemporary Criticism,* 2d ed. Chapel Hill: University of North Carolina Press, 1992.

Bogle, Donald. *Blacks in American Films and Television: An Encyclopedia.* New York: Garland, 1988.

Bogle, Donald. *Primetime Blues: African Americans on Network Television.* New York: Farrar, Strauss Giroux, 2001.

Brooks, Tim, and Earle Marsh, eds. *The Complete Directory to Prime Time Network and Cable TV Shows, 1946–Present.* 8th ed. New York: Ballantine, 2003.

Dates, Jannette L., and William Barlow, eds. *Split Image: African Americans in the Mass Media,* 2d ed. Washington, D.C.: Howard University Press, 1993.

Gray, Herman S. *Cultural Moves: African Americans and the Politics of Representation.* Berkeley: University of California Press, 2005.

Hunt, Darnell M., ed. *Channeling Blackness: Studies on Television and Race in America.* New York: Oxford University Press, 2005.

Lommel, Cookie. *African Americans in Film and Television.* Philadelphia: Chelsea House, 2003.

MacDonald, J. Fred. *Blacks and White TV: Afro-Americans in Television Since 1948,* 2d ed. Chicago: Nelson-Hall, 1992.

McNeil, Alex. *Total Television: A Comprehensive Guide to Programming from 1948 to the Present,* 4th ed. New York: Penguin, 1996.

Means Coleman, Robin R. *African American Viewers and the Black Situation Comedy: Situating Racial Humor.* New York: Garland, 1998.

Neale, Stephen, and Frank Krutnik. *Popular Film and Television Comedy.* London and New York: Routledge, 1990.

Pulley, Brett. *The Billion Dollar BET: Robert Johnson and the Inside Story of Black Entertainment Television.* Hoboken, N.J.: Wiley, 2004.

Torres, Sasha, ed. *Living Color: Race and Television in the United States.* Durham, N.C.: Duke University Press, 1998.

Torres, Sasha. *Black, White, and in Color: Television and Black Civil Rights.* Princeton, N.J.: Princeton University Press, 2003.

White, Mimi. "What's the Difference? 'Frank's Place' in Television." *Wide Angle* 13 (1990): 82–93.

Zook, Kristal Brent. *Color by Fox: The Fox Network and the Revolution in Black Television.* New York: Oxford University Press, 1999.

CHARLES HOBSON (1996)
CHRIS TOMASSINI (2005)

Temptations, The

During their more than three decades of entertaining, the rhythm-and-blues quintet has seen a number of replacements involving twenty-one group members and fifty-seven albums. Formed from the merger of the Primes and the Distants, based in Detroit in 1960, the original Temptations included Eldridge Bryant (baritone, replaced by David Ruffin in 1963; Ruffin was replaced by Dennis Edwards in 1968; Edwards by Louis Price in 1977; Price by Ali-Ollie Woodson in 1983; Woodson by Edwards in 1987; Edwards by Woodson in 1988; and Woodson was replaced by Terry Weeks in 2003), Eddie Kendricks (first tenor; replaced by Ricky Owens for one show only in 1971; Owens was replaced by Damon Harris that year; Harris by Glenn Leonard in 1975; and Leonard by Ron Tyson in 1983), Paul Williams (second tenor; replaced by Richard Street in 1971; Street by Theo Peoples in 1992; Peoples later joined the Four Tops and was replaced by Barrington Henderson in 1998; and Henderson was replaced by G. C. Cameron in 2003), Otis Williams (baritone; the only remaining original member and of no relation to Paul), and Melvin Franklin (bass; after his sudden death, he was replaced by Parliament/Funkadelic's Ray Davis in 1995; Davis was replaced by Harry McGillberry in 1996; and McGillberry by Joe Herndon in 2003). The original quintet was signed by Berry Gordy to the Motown label in 1960. It was barely noticed when the group released material as The Pirates in 1962.

The group's major successes are defined by three distinct periods. First, featuring a crossover doo-wop style with various lead singers and trademark choreography by Cholly Atkins that resulted in several hit singles, including "The Way You Do the Things You Do" (number eleven, 1964), "My Girl" (number one, 1965), and "Ain't Too Proud to Beg" (number thirteen, 1966). Kendricks's smooth falsetto and David Ruffin's rugged baritone marked this classic lineup from 1964 to 1968.

The second period, beginning in 1966, featured producer Norman Whitfield arranging Grammy-award winning songs for five distinct lead singers rather than one lead and a doo-wop chorus. He introduced the "psychedelic soul" sound with its tight brass and engaging social commentary. This style produced "Cloud Nine" (number six, 1969; Grammy for Best Rhythm & Blues Performance by a Duo or Group), "Psychedelic Shack" (number seven, 1970), "Ball of Confusion" (number three, 1970), and "Papa Was a Rolling Stone" (number one, 1972), a powerful, double-platinum-selling anthem depicting the urban story of a deadbeat dad that sold two million copies. "Papa Was a Rolling Stone" won two Grammies in 1972; one for Best R&B Vocal Performance by a Duo, Group, or Chorus and the other for Best R&B Instrumental Performance featuring the Temptations and orchestral arranger Paul Riser.

The Temptations broke with Motown in 1975 and spent an unsuccessful span signed to Atlantic Records (1977-1979) trying to tap into the disco market. In 1980, they returned to Motown releasing the hit "Power." That same year, there was a failed attempt to reunite the original group. They reunited, more or less, in 1982 when Ruffin and Kendricks joined the five current members for the *Reunion* album and the Tribute to the Temptations national tour, but Ruffin's no-shows and problems with Motown sullied the tour. The group was of course featured in the televised Motown 25 Special in 1987 and they earned their induction into the Rock and Roll Hall of Fame in 1989.

Performing on the oldies circuit with groups like the Four Tops and the O'Jays, the third phase of their career was marked by the influence of retro television, online sales, and sampling. The Temptations were the subject of an NBC mini-series in 1998 that was number one in its time-slot. That year they released the album *Anthology: The Best of the Temptations*, which jumped from number fourteen-hundred to number four on Amazon.com, the likely result of their exposure on NBC. Then, in 2000, the biggest-selling album of their career, *Phoenix Rising,* put the group back on the radar. The album received a Grammy nomination for Traditional R&B Vocal Performance, and the platinum single, "Stay," featuring a sample from the Temps' own 1965 number one hit "My Girl," also was nominated for Best R&B Vocal Performance by a Duo or Group. With the release of *Ear-Resistable,* their fifty-sixth album, featuring R&B crooner Joe and Gerald Lavert as producers, the Temptations garnered their fourth Grammy for Best Traditional R&B Vocal Album almost thirty years after their previous award. Their fifty-seventh album, released in 2004, was aptly titled *Legacy.*

See also Gordy, Berry; Music in the United States; Rhythm and Blues

Bibliography

Ankeny, Jason. "The Temptations (biography)." *The All Music Guide.* Available from <http://www.allmusic.com>.

George, Nelson. *Where Did Our Love Go? The Rise and Fall of the Motown Sound.* New York: St. Martin's, 1985.

Otis Williams' Homepage. "History." Available from <http://otiswilliams.net/history.aspx>.

Porter, David. "Ray Davis, founding member of Parliament-Funkadelic." *Boston Globe.* July 8, 2005. Available from <http://www.boston.com/news/globe/obituaries>.

Rosen, Craig. "Temptations Sample Themselves." 08/18/1998 9:00pm, *LAUNCH.* Available from <http://music.yahoo.com/read/news/12049430> .

The Temptations.com. Available at <http://www.thetemptations.com>.

Williams, Otis, with Patricia Romanowski. *Temptations.* Updated ed. New York: Cooper Square Press, 2002.

KYRA D. GAUNT (1996)
Updated by author 2005

Tennis

A Bermuda socialite, Mary Outerbridge, brought tennis to America in 1874, and national tournaments restricted to whites began in 1881. But enterprising black players organized local tournaments as early as 1895 at Tuskegee Institute in Alabama. In the early twentieth century, varsity teams were formed at Howard University, Lincoln University, Tuskegee Institute, Atlanta University, and Hampton Institute. On the eve of World War I, tennis was firmly rooted in black communities in the Northeast, South, and northern California.

In 1916 a group of black tennis enthusiasts formed the American Tennis Association (ATA). The ATA is the oldest continuously operated independent black sports organization in the United States. The first ATA National Championships were held in 1917 at Druid Hill Park in Baltimore. The first ATA women's champion, Lucy D. Slowe, became the first black female national titleholder in any sport.

The ATA has formed the backbone of black tennis participation in the United States, the Caribbean, and Bermuda. It sponsored traveling tours by good players and sought assistance for top black college players. The ATA began serious junior development programs in the late 1930s. Hundreds of tennis courts were built by the federal government during the Great Depression to help provide work, and the ATA wanted to take advantage of these public facilities, as well as ensure a steady flow of players for its events.

Tuskegee Institute sisters Margaret "Pete" Peters and Matilda Roumania "Repeat" Peters (Pete and Repeat) won a record fourteen ATA doubles championships on two streaks from 1938 to 1941 and 1944 to 1953. Roumania Peters also won ATA singles titles in 1944 and 1946, making her and her sister the first set of African-American siblings to make tennis history. In the 1946 tournament, Roumania defeated another woman who would make international tennis history, Althea Gibson.

In September 1950 Althea Gibson became the first black player to compete at the West Side Tennis Club in Forest Hills, New York, the site of the United States Tennis Association (USTA) National Championships. In addition to winning the ATA junior and senior singles and doubles titles, Gibson also captured the French singles and doubles (1956), the Wimbledon singles crown (twice, in 1957 and 1958), and the United States singles title (twice, in 1957 and 1958), as well as the Australian mixed doubles event (1957). After Gibson's initial appearance at Forest Hills in 1950, the USTA and the ATA announced that they had arrived at an arrangement whereby for twenty years to come the ATA would nominate black players who would be automatically entered in the main draw.

Althea Gibson's coach, Robert W. Johnson, led the ATA junior development effort, while his son, Robert Johnson Jr., provided much of the on-court expertise. One of the products of the program was Arthur Ashe Jr., who from 1955 to 1962 won eleven ATA titles. Ashe went on to capture singles crowns in the U.S. Open in 1968, in the Australian Open in 1970, and at Wimbledon in 1975. He was co-ranked number one in the world in 1968 and again in 1975, and was a member of the American Davis Cup team in 1963, 1965 to 1970, 1975, 1977, and 1978. He served as team captain from 1981 to 1985.

The era of "open" tennis (with amateurs and professionals playing together) began in 1968, and black players, schools, and coaches responded with growing numbers and excellence. The 1990s witnessed the development of African-American tennis stars such as Zina Garrison, who in 1990 at Wimbledon became the first African-American woman to reach a Grand Slam final since Althea Gibson thirty-two years earlier. In Garrison's fifteen-year professional career she won fourteen singles titles and twenty doubles crowns. Like Garrison, MaliVai Washington, who won four career singles titles, has transformed tennis success into philanthropic ventures supporting young African Americans. Chanda Rubin, who first gained international recognition in the 1990s, has earned at least seven singles titles. In addition, the number of people of African descent on the tour increased dramatically during the 1990s and early 2000s.

Perhaps the most famous African-American women in tennis history, Venus and Serena Williams have transformed women's tennis in the twenty-first century, turning it into a game requiring far more fitness, agility, speed, and power. They have repeatedly made history, each of them earning dozens of singles and doubles titles, as well as numerous grand slam championships, and often being "first" in everything from service speed to sisters facing each other as finalists in multiple major tennis events.

The success of the Compton, California-reared Williams sisters inspired growing numbers of African Americans to play tennis and encouraged the USTA to invest in developing tennis programs in urban centers. Although great strides have been made in tennis for African Americans, history is still being made. In 2004 eighteen-year-old Scoville Jenkins became the first African American to win the USTA boys title in the event's eighty-nine year history.

See also American Tennis Association; Ashe, Arthur; Gibson, Althea; Williams, Venus and Serena

Bibliography

Ashe, Arthur R., Jr. *Off the Court.* New York: New American Library, 1981.

Ashe, Arthur R., Jr. *A Hard Road to Glory: A History of the African-American Athlete,* 3 vols. New York: Warner, 1988.

Djata, Sundiata A. K. *Blacks in Tennis: A Global History of "White Sport" and Its Colorful Players.* Princeton, N.J.: Markus Wiener, 2002.

Smith, Doug. *Whirlwind, the Godfather of Black Tennis: The Life and Times of Dr. Robert Walter Johnson.* Washington, D.C.: Blue Eagle, 2004.

ARTHUR R. ASHE JR. (1996)
IMANI PERRY (2005)

Terrell, Mary Eliza Church

September 26, 1863
July 24, 1954

The civil rights activist and women's rights advocate Mary Eliza Church Terrell was born in Memphis, Tennessee, into a prosperous family of former slaves; she graduated from Oberlin College (1884) at the head of her class, then taught at Wilberforce University (1885–1887) and briefly in a high school in Washington, D.C. After receiving an M.A. from Oberlin (1888), she traveled in Europe for two years, studying French, German, and Italian. In 1891 she married Robert Terrell, who was appointed judge of District of Columbia Municipal Court in 1901.

The overlapping concerns that characterized Terrell's life—public-education reform, women's rights, and civil rights—found expression in community work and organizational activities. She served as the first woman president of Bethel Literary and Historical Association (1892–1893) and was the first black woman appointed to the District of Columbia Board of Education (1895–1901, 1906–1911).

In spite of elements of racism and nativism in the National American Woman Suffrage Association, Terrell was an active member and addressed its conventions in 1898 and 1900. She joined the Woman's Party picket line at the White House, and after the achievement of suffrage was active in the Republican Party.

Women's international affairs involved her as well. She addressed the International Council of Women (Berlin, 1904) in English, German, and French, the only American to do so; was a delegate to the Women's International League for Peace and Freedom (Zurich, 1919); was a vice president of the International Council of Women of the Darker Races; and addressed the International Assembly of the World Fellowship of Faiths (London, 1937).

Terrell participated in the founding of the National Association for the Advancement of Colored People (NAACP) and was vice president of the Washington, D.C., branch for many years. Her various causes coalesced around her concern with the quality of black women's lives. In 1892 she helped organize and headed the National League for the Protection of Colored Women, in Washington, D.C.; she was the first president of the National Association of Colored Women, serving three terms (1896–1901) before being named honorary president for life and a vice president of the National Council of Negro Women.

Terrell worked for the unionization of black women and for their inclusion in established women's affairs. In 1919 she campaigned, unsuccessfully, for a colored women's division within the Women's Bureau of the Department of Labor, and to have the First International Congress of Working Women directly address the concerns of black working women.

Age did not diminish Terrell's activism. Denied admission to the Washington chapter of the American Association of University Women in 1946 on racial grounds, she entered a three-year legal battle that led the national group to clarify its bylaws to read that a college degree was the only requirement for membership. In 1949 Terrell joined the sit-ins that challenged segregation in public accommodations and a landmark civil rights case, as well as serving as chair of the Coordinating Committee for the Enforcement of the District of Columbia Anti-Discrimination Laws.

In addition to her picketing and sit-ins, Terrell wrote many magazine articles treating disfranchisement, discrimination, and racism, as well as an autobiography, *A Colored Woman in a White World* (1940).

See also Civil Rights Movement, U.S.; National Association for the Advancement of Colored People (NAACP); National Association of Colored Women; National Council of Negro Women

■ ■ *Bibliography*

Sterling, Dorothy. "Mary Eliza Church Terrell." In *Notable American Women: The Modern Period,* edited by Barbara Sicherman et al. Cambridge, Mass.: Belknap, 1980, pp. 678–680.

QUANDRA PRETTYMAN (1996)

TESHEA, ISABEL

JULY 24, 1911
APRIL 14, 1981

Isabel Ursula Teshea was the first woman elected to Trinidad and Tobago's Parliament. Hers was a humble home; her father, Thomas Cadogan, was a tailor, her mother, a homemaker. From early on young Isabel displayed the qualities of leadership and drive that would propel her into politics and two overseas ambassadorships. Always involved in social and community work even as a teaching assistant, in her early forties she founded a boys club in her neighborhood of Princes Town to keep the young out of mischief.

After an unsatisfactory marriage in 1938, and with no children of her own, in the 1950s Teshea turned her attention to the political scene, becoming an ardent supporter of nationalist leader Eric Williams, who would turn the country's colonialist machinery on its head. Her innate organizational and speaking skills, coupled with her links to village councils, quickly became a key factor in the formation of party groups for Trinidad and Tobago's first modern political party, the People's National Movement (PNM).

Teshea never missed a meeting, where throngs of people, most with no formal education, gathered to listen to "university dishes served with political sauce" à la Eric Williams, whose paramount mission was to "teach the people what one French writer of the 18th century saw as the greatest danger, that they had a mind" (Williams, 1969, p. 133).

By 1956 and in recognition of her sterling efforts, Teshea had been elected lady vice-chair of the PNM and, therefore, the first chairwoman of the PNM Women's League. She worked tirelessly to craft a passionate, vibrant, effective women's arm, which helped to ensure the party's success in general elections for six consecutive terms.

In 1961 Teshea served as parliamentary secretary in the Ministry of Local Government and Community Development and two years later was promoted to Minister of Health and Housing. By 1967 these two ministries had been divided, but she continued to hold the latter portfolio until 1970, when she was appointed Trinidad and Tobago's ambassador to Ethiopia and to the Organization of African Unity (in 1964, she had accompanied Trinidad and Tobago's prime minister, Eric Williams, on a tour of major African states).

A self-effacing yet charming individual, Isabel Teshea earned the respect of all who knew and worked with her. During her decades-long tenure as a government official, she addressed several areas of global, national, and regional concern, notably the 1972 United Nations population conference in Romania. As Trinidad and Tobago's high commissioner to Guyana from 1974 to 1977, she participated in the regional unification negotiations that resulted in the creation of CARICOM, the Caribbean Community and Common Market.

Retiring in 1977 and shunning further spotlight, Teshea passed away quietly. Her stellar example of public service and community spirit resulted in the 1981 posthumous award of her country's highest honor, the Trinity Cross. To the extent that she blazed a trail for her nation's modern women at a time when such a path was deemed unthinkable at best, Isabel Ursula Teshea's life remains a beacon of both hope and possibility.

See also Caribbean Community and Common Market (CARICOM); Peoples National Movement; Williams, Eric

Bibliography

Williams, Eric. *Inward Hunger: The Education of a Prime Minister.* London: Deutsch, 1969.

ERICA WILLIAMS CONNELL (2005)

TEXTILES, DIASPORIC

When African religious ideas appeared in the New World, they often assumed new forms and meanings and were transmitted in unprecedented ways. As essential tools for survival, these ideas were encoded in arts in a multiplicity of forms, including architecture, dance, funerary practices, narratives, rituals, speech, music, and other visual arts, especially textiles. Arts preserve cultural traditions even when the social context of traditions changes; yet the codes are neither simple nor easy to decipher.

Sometimes forms endure while the meanings once associated with them shift; in other instances, meanings persist and the shapes evolve. Knowledge of ideas and techniques for creating arts are not necessarily verbalized, written down, or expressly transmitted within a family, nor are all levels of meaning always known to everyone in a community. Some African Americans, and most Americans in general, are thoroughly unaware of many of these cultural traditions. One challenge is to examine which ideas can be traced back to African cultures. A bigger challenge is to understand the transmutations and creolizations that occur as each generation improvises upon previous visual traditions.

Africans who came to the Americas brought with them many memories: memories of social organizations, religious values, and technological skills. But this knowledge was often hidden, encoded in decorative arts, arts that were appreciated and continued for their decorative qualities. Often the meanings originally associated with the symbols were lost over time.

Scholars are just beginning to unravel the numerous ways in which valuable African skills, values, and ways of organizing ideas were and are encoded in many art forms. They are learning to read symbolic elements that have been passed on from one generation to the next, not through genes, but through cultural memories. Quilts were one of many media used to encode cultural knowledge. Three themes can be explored to explain continuities

Banner of a Dahomean Society, collected by anthropologist Melville Herskovits. *When African societies of a social character were formed, each acquired a flag featuring applique designs sewed on cloth and recounting some of the exploits of its members.* MELVILLE J. AND FRANCES S. HERSKOVITS PHOTOGRAPH COLLECTION, ART AND ARTIFACTS DIVISION, SCHOMBURG CENTER FOR RESEARCH IN BLACK CULTURE, THE NEW YORK PUBLIC LIBRARY, ASTOR, LENOX AND TILDEN FOUNDATIONS.

between African-American quilting and African cultural knowledge: technical skills, secret scripts, and charm-making traditions. As William Arnett wrote in *Souls Grown Deep*:

> Every great quilt, whether it be a patchwork, appliqué, or strip quilt, is a potential Rosetta stone. Quilts represent one of the most highly evolved systems of writing in the New World. Every combination of colors, every juxtaposition or intersection of line and form, every pattern, traditional or idiosyncratic, contain data that can be imparted in some form or another to anyone. All across Africa, geometric designs, the syntax of quilt tops, have been used to encode symbolic or secret knowledge. Bodily decoration and costumes, architectural ornamentation (including painting), and relief carving have been primary media. (Arnett, et al, 2000).

In the ways in which quilts are put together, we find information about how West African textiles were constructed, mainly from narrow strips, about the width of a human hand. Men wove these strips on narrow portable looms, and then the strips were sewn together in symmetrical or asymmetrical arrangements, or strips with different patterns were sewn together to create the most prestigious textiles. In the ways in which designs were borrowed, improvised upon, and jazzed up, scholars find clues to secret African symbol systems, which are also seen in African-American vernacular arts.

African secret society signs and symbols are still hidden in decorative textile designs. Examples include Bogolanfini cloth painted by Bamana women in Mali; Adinkra cloth stamped by Ashanti men in Ghana; Adire cloth painted with starch and dyed by Yoruba women with designs said to have been given to them by Oshun, the goddess of wealth and fertility, in Nigeria; Ekpe (Leopard) society cloth resist dyed by Ejagham women with Nsibidi secret society signs in Nigeria; and Kuba cloth woven by men and embroidered by women with designs that allude to the Central African Kongo cosmogram, a diamond or a cross that represents the four moments of the sun or the soul: birth, life, death, and rebirth in a watery ancestral realm. Scripts are also considered protective and thus bits of writing—Christian, Islamic, or indigenous secret signs—are enclosed in West African charms.

This tradition of encoding secret signs in textile designs, mostly done by women, continued in the New World, where remembered African signs were combined to create unique new creolized symbol systems. Examples include a Brazilian cloth embroidered with designs called *points* for a Yoruba god, Ogun, as well as Surinamese capes embroidered by women with designs derived from a Djuka script called Afaka, which is based on Adinkra symbols from Ghana and Nsibidi signs from Nigeria. Cuban Abakua society costumes are based on Nigerian ones with light and dark squares to represent leopard spots and valued religious principles of leadership. Haitian Vodou flags are decorated with sequins arranged in *veve* signs, which refer to various remembered Yoruba and Fon gods.

Throughout the southern United States, as insulation against the cold, people decorated the interior walls of their home with cutouts from books, newspapers, and magazines. Some African-American quilts look like those walls, because for many there was an additional religious meaning associated with those multiple images. Unhappy, neglected ancestral spirits could be thwarted from their mischievous ways because they would be distracted by, and need to read and decipher, all the chopped up and discontinuous text before they could do any harm. In much the same way that quilts provided physical warmth and spiritual safety, the wall collages linked African Americans' most corporeal needs with their most metaphysical ones. These practices can be traced to the African belief that writing is considered protective and is thus enclosed in charms. The form has changed but the protective idea persists. Romare Bearden drew upon this African-American tradition of collaging walls with protective images in his famous collaged art. Quilters drew on this collage tradition in their improvised quilts, which feature multiple patterns and thus function as protective bedcovers in several ways.

African-American quilts feature narrow strips, bright contrasting colors, large patterns, multiple patterns, asymmetrical designs, and symbolic designs. All these aesthetic principles can be traced back to African textiles, which feature these same aesthetic values, but often for different reasons. Most African textiles are made by men, to sell, commissioned for special events, or for family use, in cultures that understand the improvised aesthetic and the symbols. Most African-American textiles are made by women for family use; a few women make quilts to sell, and they often make quilts in both the symmetrical Anglo-American tradition and in the improvised African-American traditions. In addition to their technical skills of piecing and appliqué, scholars admire their ability to manipulate and hide symbols.

In the United States, various African and African Latin American and Caribbean signs appear in historic and contemporary African-American quilts. Recent research by Maude Southwell Wahlman concentrates on the convergence of secret African symbols and Masonic signs that were used to run the Underground Railroad. Women sewed Masonic aprons and other textiles and knew of the multiple levels of meaning attached to the symbols. The nineteenth-century quilter and Eastern Star society leader Harriet Powers used these symbols in her Masonic apron and in her quilts, where one can see references to her control of Fon symbols from the Republic of Benin in West Africa, Kongo symbols from Central Africa, Christian symbols, and Masonic signs. Her own Masonic apron features an embroidered cross (the cosmogram of the Kongo people) and an appliquéd light-colored sun for life, as well as a dark-colored "midnight" sun for the undersea world of Kongo ancestors. She may not have known about Kongo or Fon religions, but she did know the symbols.

Hidden in Plain View (2000) by Jacqueline Tobin and Raymond Dobard validates the many African traditions of women encoding secret signs in textile designs. In addition, many abolitionists were Masons, and Tobin and Wahlman have found more and more documentation for cooperation between members of African-American and Anglo-American Masonic societies. Many African-American families have retained knowledge of how artifacts were encoded with secret signs that were used to communicate vital information on how to proceed on the Underground Railroad to freedom.

In the ways in which symbolic designs were included in decorative pieced patterns and appliqués, there is evidence of remembered charm-making traditions, which also persist in African-American vernacular sculpture and textiles. The African-American protective charm, called a *mojo* or a *hand*, is often a small square made of red flannel, which is carried in a pocket or worn around the neck. The writer and folklorist Zora Neale Hurston recorded numerous instructions for how to make these charms. One also sees them on numerous African-American quilts, particularly those using a nine-patch pattern. Sarah Mary Taylor, a noted Mississippi folk artist, even made a quilt with both blue hands and red squares, indicating her mastery of these symbols. The "vodou dolls" seen on African-American quilts made by Taylor and Mississippi-born quilter Pearlie Posey can be traced back to the cloth Pacquet Kongo charms brought to Haiti by the Kongo peoples of Central Africa, where they are referred to as *minkisi*, or "the medicines of God."

Contemporary African-American fine artists, such as Betye Saar, Joyce Scott, and Renée Stout, incorporate folk art traditions and family oral histories into their arts, particularly their textiles. Stout's *Conjuring Vest* (1995) includes references to West African cloth charms. Both fine and folk (or vernacular) African-American arts possess sophisticated levels of meaning that one has to learn to read. If scholars and students are persistent and attentive, they will find many examples of hidden codes in African-American textiles and other arts. In addition, young people must interview their grandparents before this knowledge is lost. According to an old African proverb, often repeated by folklorist William Ferris, "in Africa when an older person dies, a library burns." That can also be said for elders in African-American cultures.

See also Beardon, Romare; Folk Arts and Crafts; Powers, Harriet

Bibliography

Arnett, Paul, William Arnett, Theophus Smith, and Maude Southwell Wahlman, eds. *Souls Grown Deep: African American Vernacular Art of the South.* Atlanta: Tinwood; New York: Schomburg Center for Research in Black Culture, 2000.

Fry, Gladys-Marie. *Stitched from the Soul: Slave Quilts from the Ante-Bellum South.* New York: Dutton, 1990.

Leon, Eli. *Models in the Mind: African Prototypes in American Patchwork.* Winston-Salem, N.C.: Winston-Salem State University, 1992.

Picton, John, and John Mack. *African Textiles.* New York: Harper, 1989.

Thompson, Robert Farris. *Flash of the Spirit: African and Afro-American Art and Philosophy.* New York: Random House, 1983.

Tobin, Jacqueline, and Raymond Dobard. *Hidden in Plain View: The Secret Story of Quilts and the Underground Railroad.* New York: Doubleday, 1999.

Vlach, John Michael. *The Afro-American Tradition in Decorative Arts.* Cleveland, Ohio: Cleveland Museum of Art, 1978.

Wahlman, Maude. *Signs and Symbols: African Images in African American Quilts.* New York: Penguin, 1993.

MAUDE SOUTHWELL WAHLMAN (2005)

Tharpe, "Sister" Rosetta

March 20, 1915
October 9, 1973

The gospel singer and guitarist Sister Rosetta Tharpe was born Rosetta Nubin in Cotton Plant, Arkansas. She began her musical apprenticeship playing guitar and singing in the Church of God in Christ, a Pentecostal church, and she gained professional experience traveling with her mother, Katie Bell Nubin, a missionary. In her teens she followed her mother to Chicago. It is not clear whether she took a new last name as the result of a marriage, but it was as Sister Rosetta Tharpe that she came to prominence in 1938 in New York. At first she was known for performing in secular venues, a controversial practice for a gospel singer. In 1938 she performed at Harlem's Cotton Club with bandleader Cab Calloway and at the famous "Spirituals to Swing" concert at Carnegie Hall. Those performances helped her land a contract with Decca Records, making her the first gospel singer to record for a major label. In 1943 she performed at the Apollo Theater, the first time that a major gospel singer had appeared there. Her 1944 rendition of "Strange Things Happen Every Day" was widely popular.

Starting in the 1940s, Tharpe performed in churches, concert halls, nightclubs, on the radio, and later even on television. She gained fame not only because of her practice of playing secular venues, a practice she defended by calling all of her music evangelical, but also because of her jazz and blues–influenced guitar playing. Tharpe, who recorded "Daniel in the Lion's Den" in 1949 with her mother, eventually toured with such jazz and blues groups as those led by Benny Goodman, Count Basie, Muddy Waters, Sammy Price, and Lucky Millinder, as well as with gospel groups such as the Caravans, the James Cleveland Singers, the Dixie Hummingbirds, the Richmond Harmonizing Four, and the Sally Jenkins Singers, with whom she recorded "I Have Good News to Bring" in 1960. Tharpe, who was the first major gospel singer to tour Europe, was also widely known for her live performances and recordings of "That's All," "I Looked Down the Line," "Up Above My Head," and "This Train." She died in Philadelphia. Tharpe was honored in 1998 by having her image appear on a U.S. postage stamp.

See also Gospel Music; Music in the United States

Bibliography

Broughton, Viv. *Black Gospel: An Illustrated History of the Gospel Sound.* Poole, Dorset, U.K.: Blandford Press, 1985.

Gilmore, Lea. "Sister Rosetta Tharpe: The Original Soul Sister." *Sing Out!* 47, no. 4 (Winter 2004): 47.

Heilbut, Tony. *The Gospel Sound: Good News and Bad Times.* Garden City, N.Y.: Anchor Press, 1975.

IRENE V. JACKSON (1996)
Updated by publisher 2005

Theater

See Caribbean Theater, Anglophone; Drama; Experimental Theater; Musical Theater

Theatrical Dance

Africans who came to the Americas brought with them a rich tradition in instrumental music, song, and dance. By the early 1800s, not long after the official creation of the United States as a country, white men were carrying their versions of slave dances to the minstrel stage, arguably America's first indigenous theater form. According to Robert Toll, the arena in which early minstrelsy showed the strongest debt to African Americans was that of dance.

Several African-American minstrel performers were international stars and extraordinary dancers. William Henry Lane, known as Master Juba, ingeniously combined the Irish jig and reel with African derived movements and rhythms to lay the foundation for what is known as American tap dance. Billy Kersands, who introduced the Virginia Essence, was both an excellent dancer and black minstrelsy's most famous comedian. Black minstrel men and women brought fresh and original dance material to the American stage: stop time dances, various trick dances, and authentic exhibitions of the jig, the cakewalk, and the buck-and-wing.

During the last quarter of the nineteenth century, white road shows generally did not open their stages to black actors and actresses. During those same years, however, such shows as Uncle Tom's Cabin and In Old Kentucky often featured black dancers and choral groups. Some nineteenth-century traveling shows attracted new talent by holding weekly dance contests.

Many touring shows began and ended in New York City around the turn of the twentieth century. With more theaters than any other American city and a solid theatrical tradition for black artists, it was a logical place to plant seeds for the development of black musical theater. Bob Coles and Billy Johnson's production of *A Trip to Coontown* (1898) was the first musical play organized, managed, produced, and written by African Americans. An excellent dancer, Coles staged several specialty acts that included dance. Will Marion Cook's *Clorindy: The Origin of the Cakewalk* (1898) closely followed *A Trip to Coontown. Clorindy* set a new standard for the Broadway stage by introducing exuberant dancing and "Negro syncopated music." Cook's model was adapted for the white stage by George Lederer, who produced *Clorindy* at the Casino Roof Garden.

At the end of the nineteenth century, the cakewalk became the rage of Manhattan, with Bert Williams and George Walker the dancing masters of white New York society. The Williams and Walker musical comedy *In Dahomey* (1902) lifted the cakewalk to the status of an international dance craze after the show's smashing London run of 1903. Walker's wife, Aida Overton Walker, was America's leading black female singer and dancer of that era. She played the female lead in and created most of the choreography for *In Dahomey* and the shows that followed and was probably the first woman to receive program credit as choreographer.

A strong influence on many twentieth-century dance steps, the cakewalk initiated the evolution of American social and theatrical dances that would upstage and then replace the nineteenth-century cotillions, schottisches, and waltzes. The long-standing impact of the cakewalk led James Weldon Johnson to observe in 1930: "The influence [of the cakewalk] can be seen today on any American stage where there is dancing. . . . Anyone who witnesses a musical production in which there is dancing cannot fail to notice the Negro stamp on all the movements."

Between 1910 and 1920 black theatrical development in New York took place away from Broadway, allowing African-American musical theater to develop without the constraints of white critics. *Darktown Follies* (1913), the most important musical of the decade leading into the twenties, exploded with such dances as ballin' the jack, tap air steps, the Texas Tommy, the cakewalk, and the tango. Several critics shared the New York World's claim that the dancing was the best New York had ever seen. Astounded by the energy, vitality, and dynamic dancing of the cast, these critics eventually lured downtown visitors to Harlem. Florenz Ziegfeld, one such visitor, bought the rights to "At the Ball," the *Darktown Follies*' finale, and put it in his Follies of 1914.

In 1921 Eubie Blake, Noble Sissle, Flourney Miller and Aubrey Lyles joined forces and created the most im-

Portrait of J. Leubrie Hill and his Darktown Follies. *The Darktown Follies, beginning in 1913, introduced new and energetic dances to African Americans in Harlem.* PHOTOGRAPHS AND PRINTS DIVISION, SCHOMBURG CENTER FOR RESEARCH IN BLACK CULTURE, THE NEW YORK PUBLIC LIBRARY, ASTOR, LENOX AND TILDEN FOUNDATIONS.

portant black musical comedy of the 1920s, *Shuffle Along.* The dancing in *Shuffle Along* included buck-and-wing, slow-motion acrobatics, tap air steps, eccentric steps, legomania, the soft shoe, and high kicking. Several members of the cast later became international stars, notably Josephine Baker and Florence Mills.

Shuffle Along's greatest contribution and innovation was the dancing of its sixteen-woman chorus line. According to Marshall and Jean Stearns, "musical comedy took on a new and rhythmic life and [white] chorus girls began learning to dance to jazz." Numerous white stars of the theater learned jazz routines from downtown and uptown African-American dance instructors.

Shuffle Along was followed by a wave of African-American cast shows that continued to feature exciting dance. *Runnin' Wild* (1923) introduced the Charleston, *Dinah* (1924) introduced the Black Bottom, and *Chocolate Dandies* (1924), starring Josephine Baker, featured a female chorus line that presented swinging and complex ensemble tap sequences, a new development created by choreographer Toots Davis.

The opening of white producer Lew Leslie's *Dixie to Broadway* (1924) helped stabilize a trend that stifled the evolution of black musicals for years to come: All the performers were black, but all the producers and off-stage creative talents were white. White dance directors were often credited with choreography created by black dancers. Leslie's *Blackbirds of 1928* showcased the talents of Bill "Bojangles" Robinson and Earl "Snake Hips" Tucker, and

Blackbirds of 1930 featured Buck and Bubbles, the Berry Brothers, and "Jazzlips" Richardson.

The musical comedy hit of 1929 was *Hot Chocolates*, which began as a revue at Connie's Inn, a Harlem cabaret. Fats Waller, Andy Razaf, and Harry Brooks provided the music and lyrics; Leroy Smith's band played in the orchestra pit; and for part of the show's run, Louis Armstrong played his trumpet during intermission. Even with all the musical talent on hand, however, it was the dancing of the Six Crackerjacks, tap dancer Roland Holder, and "Jazzlips" Richardson that prevailed in the reviews. Cecil Smith commented in 1950 that "the rhythm of Broadway musical comedies is suffused with syncopations and figures which became rooted in our national consciousness in the 1920s."

While black musicals of the twenties were revolutionizing American theatrical dance on Broadway, African-American vaudevillians were impressing theater audiences throughout the country. Since the early 1900s black dance teams were rising in popularity on vaudeville stages, and many original and inventive combinations of comic, tap, and acrobatic routines thrilled audiences and inspired emerging artists. Although some black dancers performed on white theater circuits, most were restricted to black theaters. Jack Wiggins, Bill Robinson, Eddie Rector, the Berry Brothers, and a host of other star dancers served their apprenticeships on the Theater Owners Booking Association (TOBA), the black circuit. Free of the constraints imposed on aspiring artists in schools and studios, black artists in this setting could experiment and advance the development of vernacular dance at breakneck speed. The Whitman Sisters troupe (1900-1943), the greatest developer of black dancing talent, toured on the TOBA circuit for many years.

While TOBA and black musicals were enjoying their golden years, Harlem was fast establishing itself as one of the entertainment centers of the world. In Harlem cabarets and night clubs, dancers, musicians, and singers participated jointly in revues that rivaled Broadway shows. Business was booming in Connie's Inn, Smalls Paradise, and the Cotton Club, where revues were usually built around popular dance fads. Many of America's most exciting dancers appear on the roll call of Cotton Club dancers: the Berry Brothers, Cora La Redd, the Nicholas Brothers, Peg Leg Bates, Bill Robinson, the Four Step Brothers, Buck and Bubbles, Whitey's Lindy Hoppers, the Three Chocolateers, Bessie Dudley, and Earl "Shakehips" Tucker.

The early 1930s saw American vernacular dance slowly disappear from Broadway shows. Between the late 1930s and the late 1950s there were only occasional shows that featured leading dancers of authentic jazz dance: *The Hot Mikado* (1939) showcased the fancy footwork of Bill "Bojangles" Robinson and Whitey's Lindy Hoppers; the short-lived *Swingin' the Dream* (1939) presented Whitey's Lindy Hoppers, including Norma Miller and Frankie Manning; Avon Long played the role of Sportin' Life in a revival of *Porgy and Bess* (1941); and Cholly Atkins and Honi Coles stole the show every night in *Gentlemen Prefer Blondes* (1949). In addition, modern dance pioneer Katherine Dunham included African indigenous dances in some of her revues. For the most part, however, it was during this period that the American theater turned its back on indigenous dance.

A new performance format called "presentation" evolved in the early 1930s, as vaudeville theaters slowly converted to movie theaters. By this time, radio broadcasts helped create a demand for jazz bands throughout the country at hotels, supper clubs, theaters, nightclubs, and dance halls. Big bands took center stage, and many showcased two or three dancing acts. Tap dancer Honi Coles reported that during the late 1920s through the early 1940s, there were as many as fifty topflight dance acts. There was also a diversity of tap dancing acts, among them: eccentric dancing, a catchall term to describe dancers' use of individual styles and movements; flash dancing, which uses acrobatic combinations and fast-paced syncopations; adagio dancing, which features a slow style; comedy dancing, which includes singing, dancing, and dialogue; and acrobatic dancing, which includes somersaults, cartwheels, flips, and spins.

The fruitful years that dancers had enjoyed with jazz musicians and singers were brought to a halt in the mid-1940s. Although several factors led to the separation of jazz music and classic jazz dance, the single most detrimental factor was the imposition of a 20 percent tax against dancing nightclubs by federal, state, and city governments. Many theatrical dancers turned to other jobs, such as choreographing stage routines for pop musicians. With the help of choreographer and tap dancer Cholly Atkins, these artists became the new disseminators of vernacular dance on stage. Dancing singers appeared primarily on television, in films, and in rhythm-and-blues concerts in the United States and abroad. In the 1990s dancing singers continue to have a major impact on American vernacular dance from the Cadillacs through James Brown, the Temptations, the O'Jays, and Michael Jackson, to the hip-hop generation.

During the 1960s vernacular dance was kept alive in part by such television variety shows as *The Ed Sullivan Show, The Lawrence Welk Show, Hollywood Palace, The Tonite Show,* and *American Bandstand.* On Broadway there remained an implied African-American presence in the work of Broadway choreographers who combined ballet and modern dance with elements of their own particular interpretations of classic jazz dance. On the concert dance stage, black choreographers Alvin Ailey, Talley Beatty, Eleo Pomare, and Donald McKayle successfully presented works influenced by jazz dance. Ailey collaborated with Duke Ellington on several projects, and in 1976 the Alvin Ailey American Dance Theater presented "Ailey Celebrates Ellington," featuring fifteen new ballets set to his music.

Fueled by the appearance of several tap masters at the 1962 Newport Jazz festival, jazz music critics began to write about rhythm tap as an art form. By the seventies, Broadway was once again embracing this genre. Tapping feet figured prominently in musicals of the 1970s and 1980s: *No! No! Nanette!* (1971), *The Wiz* (1975), *Bubbling Brown Sugar* (1976), *Eubie!* (1978), *Black Broadway* (1980), *Sophisticated Ladies* (1981), *Tap Dance Kid* (1983), and *My One and Only* (1983), which featured tap master Honi Coles. Cholly Atkins, Frankie Manning, Henry LeTang, and Fayard Nicholas won Tony Awards for their tap and jazz choreography in *Black and Blue* (1989), a musical revue that also featured tap artists Bunny Briggs, Ralph Brown, Lon Chaney, Jimmy Slyde, Dianne Walker, and the talented young dancer Savion Glover.

As Americans danced through the 1990s, African-American vernacular dance took center stage on television, in films, and in American musical theater. The last jazz music critic Martin Williams made this observation in *Jazz Heritage* (1985):

> Most of the characteristics that we think of as "American" in our musicals are Afro-American. . . .The same sort of thing is true of our theatrical dance. Tap dancing is obvious enough. . . . But actually, almost any dancing in which the body moves with hips loose and flexible, with easy horizontal body movement below the waist, is Afro-influenced.

On the North-American continent African-American culture has been a wellspring of new creations in music, dance, comedy, and pantomime. For well over a century, African-American theatrical dancers have graced the stages of the United States and infused American culture with elegance in movement and an unmistakable style that has been embraced worldwide.

See also Baker, Josephine; Robinson, Bill "Bojangles"; Minstrels/Minstrelsy; Musical Theater; Social Dance; Tap Dance; Walker, George; Williams, Bert

Bibliography

Boskin, Joseph. *Sambo.* New York, 1986.

Coles, Honi. "The Dance." In *The Apollo Theater Story.* New York, 1966.

Dixon-Stowell, Brenda. "Popular Dance in the Twentieth Century." In Lynne Fauley Emery, ed. *Black Dance from 1619 to Today.* 1972. Reprint. Princeton, N.J., 1988.

Epstein, Dena J. *Sinful Tunes and Spirituals: Black Folk Music to the Civil War.* Chicago, 1977.

Fletcher, Tom. *100 Years of the Negro in Show Business.* New York, 1954.

Haskins, James. *The Cotton Club.* New York, 1977.

Isaacs, Edith J. R. *The Negro in American Theater.* New York, 1947.

Johnson, James Weldon. *Black Manhattan.* 1930. Reprint. New York, 1968.

Long, Richard A. "A Dance in the Jazz Mode." In *100 Years of Jazz & Blues* [festival booklet]. New York, 1992.

Malone, Jacqui. "Let the Punishment Fit the Crime: The Vocal Choreography of Cholly Atkins." *Dance Research Journal* (Summer 1988): 11-18.

Riis, Thomas. *Just Before Jazz.* Washington, D.C., 1988.

Sommer, Sally. "Tap and How It Got That Way; Feet Talk to Me!" *Dance Magazine* (September 1988).

Stearns, Marshall, and Jean Stearns. *Jazz Dance: American Vernacular Dance.* New York, 1968.

Toll, Robert C. *Blacking Up: The Minstrel Show in Nineteenth-Century America.* New York, 1974.

Toll, Robert C. *On with the Show.* New York, 1976.

Williams, Martin. "Cautions and Congratulations: An Outsider's Comments on the Black Contribution to American Musical Theater." In *Jazz Heritage.* New York, 1985.

Woll, Allen. *Black Musical Theater: From Coontown to Dreamgirls.* Baton Rouge, La., 1989.

JACQUI MALONE (1996)

THEOLOGY, BLACK

The phrase "black theology" was first used by a small group of African-American ministers and religious leaders in the late 1960s. It referred to their rejection of the dominant view of Christianity as passive and otherworldly and their definition of Christianity as a religion of liberation, consistent with black people's political struggle for justice in America and their cultural identification with Africa. The origin of black theology has two contexts: the civil rights movement of the 1950s and 1960s, largely associated with the Rev. Dr. Martin Luther King, Jr., and the rise of the Black Power movement, strongly influenced by Malcolm X's philosophy of black nationalism.

All those who advocated the need for a black theology were deeply involved in the civil rights movement, and they participated in the protest demonstrations led by King. Unlike most theological movements in Europe and North America, black theology's origin did not take place in the seminary or university. It was created in the context of black people's struggle for racial justice, organized in the churches, and often led by ministers.

From the beginning, black theology was understood by its interpreters as a theological reflection upon the black struggle for liberation, defined primarily by King's ministry. When King and other black church people began to connect the Christian gospel with the struggle for racial justice, the great majority of the white churches and their theologians denied that such a connection existed. Conservative white Christians said that religion and politics did not mix. Liberals, with few exceptions during the 1950s and early 1960s, remained silent or advocated a form of gradualism that questioned the morality of boycotts, sit-ins, and freedom rides.

Contrary to popular opinion, King was not well received by the white church establishment when he and other blacks inaugurated the civil rights movement with the Montgomery bus boycott in 1955. Because black clergy received no theological support from white churches, they searched African-American history for the religious basis of their prior political commitment to fight for justice alongside the black poor. They found support in Henry Highland Garnet, Nat Turner, Sojourner Truth, Harriet Tubman, Henry McNeal Turner, and many other pre- and post-Civil War black Christians. They discovered that the black freedom movement did not begin in the 1950s but had roots going back many years. Black Christians played major leadership roles in the abolition movement, always citing their religious faith as the primary reason for their political commitment. They claimed that the God of the Bible did not create them to be slaves or second-class citizens in the United States. In order to give an intellectual account of this religious conviction, black clergy radicals created a black theology that rejected racism and affirmed that the struggle for black liberation was supported by the gospel of Jesus.

After the March on Washington in August 1963, the integration theme began to lose ground to the black nationalist philosophy of Malcolm X. The riots in the ghettoes of U.S. cities were evidence that many blacks agreed with Malcolm's contention that their status in America was the subject not of a dream but of a nightmare. It was not until the summer of 1966, however, after Malcolm's assassination (1965), that the term *Black Power* began to replace the word *integration* among many civil rights activists. The occasion was the continuation of James Meredith's 1966 March against Fear (in Mississippi) by King, Stokely Carmichael, and other civil rights activists. Carmichael seized the occasion to proclaim the Black Power slogan, and it was heard throughout the United States.

The rise of Black Power had a profound effect on the appearance of black theology. When Carmichael and other radicals separated themselves from King's absolute commitment to nonviolence by proclaiming Black Power, white liberal Christians, especially clergymen, urged black clergy to denounce Black Power as unchristian. To the surprise of these white Christians, a small but significant group of black ministers refused to condemn Black Power. Instead they embraced it and wrote a "Black Power" statement that was published in the *New York Times* on July 31, 1966.

The publication of the "Black Power" statement was the beginning of the conscious development of a black theology. While blacks have always recognized the ethical heresy of white Christians ("Everybody talking about heaven ain't going there"), they still assumed that whites had the correct understanding of the Christian faith. However, the call for a black theology meant that black ministers, for the first time since the founding of black churches in the late eighteenth and early nineteenth centuries, recognized that white people's privilege in society created a defect not only in their ethical behavior but also in their theological reflections.

No longer able to accept white theology, which was silent on black oppression, black theologians began to make their own theology by rereading the Bible in the context of their participation in the liberation struggles of the black poor. They denounced white theology as racist and were unrelenting in their attack on the manifestations of racism in white denominations. Black clergy also created an ecumenical organization called the National Conference of Black Churchmen, as well as black caucuses in the National Council of Churches and in nearly all the white denominations. It was in this context that the phrase "black theology" emerged.

It was one thing to proclaim the need for a black theology, however, and another to define its intellectual content. Nearly all white ministers and theologians initially dismissed it as ideological rhetoric having nothing to do with real Christian theology. Since white theologians controlled public theological discourse in seminaries and university departments of religion, they made many blacks feel that only Europeans and persons who think like them could define what theology is. In order to challenge the white monopoly on the definition of theology, many young black scholars realized that they had to carry the fight on to the seminaries and universities where theology was being taught and written.

The first book on black theology was written in 1969 by James H. Cone under the title *Black Theology and Black Power.* That study identified the liberating elements of black power with the Christian gospel. Cone's second book, *A Black Theology of Liberation* (1970), made the liberation of the poor from oppression the organizing center of the author's theological perspective.

After Cone's works appeared, other black theologians joined him, supporting his theological project and also pointing to what they believed to be some of the limitations of his conclusions. In his *Liberation and Reconciliation: A Black Theology* (1971), J. Deotis Roberts, while supporting Cone's accent on liberation, claimed that Cone overlooked reconciliation as central to the gospel in black-white relations. Other black scholars argued that Cone's view of black theology was too dependent on the white European theology he claimed to have rejected, and thus not sufficiently aware of the African origin of black religion. This position was taken by Gayraud S. Wilmore, the author of *Black Religion and Black Radicalism* (1972).

While black scholars debated about black theology, they agreed that liberation is the central core of the gospel as found in the scriptures and the religious history of the African Americans. They claimed that the political meaning of the gospel is best illustrated in the Exodus, and its spiritual meaning is found in the ministry, death, and resurrection of Jesus. The Exodus was interpreted as analogous to Nat Turner's slave insurrection, Harriet Tubman's liberation of an estimated 300 slaves, and the Black Power revolution of the 1960s. Slave spirituals, sermons, prayers, and the religious fervor and suffering (including martyrs) that characterized the contemporary civil rights movement expressed the spiritual character of liberation found in the ministry, death, and resurrection of Jesus.

During the early part of the 1970s, black theology in the United States influenced the development of black theology in South Africa. Black theologians in the United States also began to have contact with theologians of liberation in Latin America and Asia. Although Latin-American theologians emphasized classism, in contrast to black theologians' accent on racism, they became partners in their opposition to the dominant theologies of Europe and the United States and in their identification of the gospel with the liberation of the poor. A similar partnership occurred with Asians regarding the importance of culture in defining theology.

In the late 1970s, a feminist consciousness began to emerge among black women as more women entered the ministry and the seminaries. Their critique of black theology as sexist led to the development of a "womanist theology." The term *womanist* was derived from Alice Walker's *In Search of Our Mothers' Gardens: Womanist Prose* (1983), and it was applied to theology by Delores Williams, Katie G. Cannon, Jacquelyn Grant, Kelly Brown-Douglas, and other black women scholars. It has been within the context of black theologians' dialogue with women and Third World peoples that the theological meaning of liberation has been enlarged and the universal character of the Christian faith reaffirmed. The enlargement of black theology's vision has been developed by a "second generation" of black theologians who have incorporated not only race but gender, class, and sexuality into their discourse. They include Dwight Hopkins, Anthony Pinn, and JoAnne Terrell.

See also Black Power Movement; Carmichael, Stokely; Cone, James H.; Garnet, Henry Highland; King, Martin Luther, Jr.; Liberation Theology; Malcolm X; Meredith, James H.; Nat Turner's Rebellion; Tubman, Harriet; Turner, Henry McNeal; Walker, Alice

Bibliography

Cone, James H. *God of the Oppressed.* New York: Seabury Press, 1975.

Cone, James H. *For My People: Black Theology and the Black Church.* Maryknoll, N.Y.: Orbis Books, 1984.

Cone, James H., and Gayraud S. Wilmore, eds. *Black Theology: A Documentary History. Vol. One: 1966–1979.* Rev. ed. Maryknoll, N.Y.: Orbis Books, 1992.

Cone, James H., and Gayraud S. Wilmore, eds. *Black Theology: A Documentary History. Vol. Two: 1980–1992.* Maryknoll, N.Y., 1992.

Cone, James H. *Risks of Faith: The Emergence of a Black Theology of Liberation, 1968–1998.* Boston, Mass.: Beacon Press, 1999.

Evans, James H., Jr. *Black Theology: A Critical Assessment and Annotated Bibliography.* New York: Greenwood Press, 1987.

Jones, William R. *Is God a White Racist? A Preamble to Black Theology.* Garden City, N.Y.: Anchor Press, 1973.

JAMES H. CONE (1996)
Updated bibliography

Third World Women's Alliance

The Third World Women's Alliance was a collective founded in 1971 as the Women's Liberation Committee of the Student Nonviolent Coordinating Committee (SNCC). Under the leadership of founding member Frances Beale, the group later became autonomous, with a mandate to work for African Americans and other minority communities by exposing the relationship between racism, economic exploitation, and sexual oppression. The organization saw the creation of a socialist society as a necessary part of this process.

Although the Third World Women's Alliance's focus was an international one, the issues of racism and sexism in the United States played an integral part in their work. The magazine produced by the group, *Triple Jeopardy,* carried articles about African-American and Hispanic women in the United States. The journal explored topics such as black women's role in Vietnam protests, the sterilization of women of color in the United States, and the relationship between feminism and the black liberation movement.

During the early 1970s the group, which was based in New York City, established several chapters across the country. By the 1980s it was the last surviving part of its parent organization, SNCC.

See also Student Nonviolent Coordinating Committee (SNCC)

Bibliography

King, Deborah K. "Multiple Jeopardy, Multiple Consciousness: The Context of a Black Feminist Ideology." *Signs: Journal of Women in Culture and Society* 14, no. 1 (1988): 42–72.

MARIAN AGUIAR (1996)

Thirteenth Amendment

The Thirteenth Amendment to the U.S. Constitution, ratified in 1865, abolished slavery. Its first section states that "neither slavery nor involuntary servitude" should exist within the United States or in any place subject to its jurisdiction. The second section grants Congress the power to "enforce this article by appropriate legislation."

Early in the Civil War, President Abraham Lincoln repeatedly assured "loyal" planters that they would be able to keep their slaves, and the Emancipation Proclamation, issued in 1863, specifically exempted most slaves held in areas already under federal military occupation and in the loyal border states. Yet, by encouraging abolitionist sentiment and authorizing the enlistment of African Americans in the Union Army, the Emancipation Proclamation also changed the focus of the war into a struggle against slavery itself—regardless of where it existed.

Because the Emancipation Proclamation had been issued as a war measure, some feared that it might be judged unconstitutional after the war's end. Lincoln came under increasing political pressure from within his Republican Party to resolve the issue with a constitutional amendment abolishing slavery. The Republican platform of 1864 strongly supported such an amendment, and when Lincoln was re-elected in November, he began an aggressive attempt to win passage from the "lame duck" Congress in early 1865. Though the Democratic opposition had the votes to prevent passage of the amendment in the House of Representatives, Lincoln's electoral mandate served to undermine their unity. Furthermore, secret promises of administration patronage, approaching outright bribery, secured sufficient Democratic votes and absences to allow passage by a vote of 119 to 56—two votes above the required two-thirds margin.

After passage, the proposed amendment then required endorsement by three-quarters of the state legislature for ratification. It was rapidly passed by most of the northern states, and so its ratification rested with the actions of the southern states, then in constitutional limbo after the collapse of the Confederacy in April 1865. President Andrew Johnson, eager to readmit the southern states to the Union under the "lenient" terms of Reconstruction, told southern legislatures that ratification of the amendment was a prerequisite for restoration to the Union. The southern constitutional conventions were very uncomfortable with this condition, especially the second section of the amendment, which apparently legitimated federal intervention to secure civil rights against state intrusion. Mississippi refused to ratify the amendment altogether, but most southern states complied with the president's emphatic instruction, and the amendment was declared ratified on December 18, 1865. Despite the end of the war, the border states of Kentucky and Delaware had refused to emancipate their slaves, so the amendment had a direct and practical effect in those states. In Oklahoma, slavery was abolished in 1866 by a treaty with the Cherokee Nation, thus bringing a formal end to the institution in the entire United States.

The legal interpretation of the Thirteen Amendment engenders continuing controversy, specifically the section granting Congress enforcement powers. Many proponents of the legislation have offered an expansive view of the amendment, maintaining that it gives Congress the power to overturn all state legislation inconsistent with basic civil liberties. Others have taken a more restrained, narrowly defined view of the powers it grants, arguing that its only purpose is to outlaw slavery.

See also Emancipation in the United States; Slavery; Slavery and the Constitution

Bibliography

Cox, LaWanda, and John H. Cox. *Politics, Principle, and Prejudice, 1865–1866: Dilemma of Reconstruction America.* New York: Free Press, 1969.

Hyman, Harold M. *A More Perfect Union: The Impact of the Civil War and Reconstruction on the Constitution.* Boston: Houghton Mifflin, 1975.

Maltz, Earl M. *Civil Rights, the Constitution, and Congress, 1863–1869.* Lawrence: University Press of Kansas, 1990.

Vorenberg, Michael. *Final Freedom: The Civil War, the Abolition of Slavery, and the Thirteenth Amendment.* Cambridge, UK: Cambridge University Press, 2001.

MICHAEL W. FITZGERALD (1996)
Updated bibliography

THOMAS, CLARENCE

JUNE 23, 1948

Born in Pin Point, Georgia, U.S. Supreme Court Justice Clarence Thomas was the second of three children of M. C. and Leola (Anderson) Thomas. M. C. Thomas left when his son was two, and Leola Thomas supported the family. They had little money, and after the family house burned down, Clarence Thomas went to live with grandparents in Savannah, Georgia. Thomas attended Catholic schools, whose teachers he later credited with giving him hope and self-confidence.

In 1967 Thomas entered the Immaculate Conception Seminary in Conception, Missouri, intending to become a Catholic priest. He decided to leave after hearing white classmates happily report the assassination of the Reverend Dr. Martin Luther King Jr. Thomas transferred to Holy Cross College in Worcester, Massachusetts, on the school's first Martin Luther King Scholarship. At Holy Cross Thomas majored in English literature, graduating cum laude in 1971. An admirer of Malcolm X, Thomas helped form the Black Students League, joined the Black Panther Party, and ran a free-breakfast program for black children.

Rejected for military service on medical grounds, Thomas entered Yale University Law School in the fall of 1971 under the university's affirmative action program. He was admitted to the bar in 1974, then accepted a position as an aide to John Danforth, Missouri's attorney general. Shortly thereafter, he read the conservative African-American economist Thomas Sowell's book *Race and Economics* (1975), which he later claimed as his intellectual "salvation." Thomas adopted Sowell's pro-market, anti-affirmative action theories. In 1977 Thomas became a staff attorney for the Monsanto Company in St. Louis. In 1979 he joined Danforth, by that time a U.S. senator, as an energy and environmental specialist on his staff.

In 1980 Thomas spoke at the Fairmount Conference in San Francisco, a meeting of black conservatives. He denounced the social welfare system for fostering dependency. The publicity Thomas's conservative views received won him the interest of the Reagan administration. In 1981, despite his reluctance to be "typed" as a civil rights specialist, Thomas was named assistant secretary for Civil Rights in the Department of Education, where he drew criticism for refusing to push integration orders on southern colleges. In 1982 he was appointed chair of the Equal Employment Opportunity Commission. Reappointed in 1986, he served until 1990. His tenure was controversial. An opponent of activist judicial action, he refused to press pending class-action suits and opposed the use of comparable-worth guidelines in gender discrimination cases. The commission allowed thousands of age-discrimination lawsuits to lapse through what he claimed was "bad management." Yet Thomas opposed efforts to secure tax-exempt status for racially discriminatory colleges, and in 1983 he secured an important affirmative action agreement with General Motors.

In 1989 President George H. W. Bush nominated Thomas for a seat on the U.S. Circuit Court of Appeals for the District of Columbia. The appointment was widely understood as preliminary to a possible Supreme Court appointment as a replacement for aging African-American justice Thurgood Marshall. Thomas was easily confirmed for the district court in February 1990. In July 1991 Marshall retired, and Bush nominated Thomas as his successor. Bush claimed race had nothing to do with the nomination and that Thomas was the "most qualified candidate" to succeed Marshall, an assertion widely viewed as disingenuous. Nevertheless, many blacks who opposed Thomas's conservative ideas initially felt torn by the nomination and supported him or remained neutral on racial grounds.

Thomas's confirmation hearings were acrimonious. He denounced the reasoning of the Court's *Brown v. Board of Education* (1954) desegregation case as "dubious social engineering." He refused to take a position on the *Roe v. Wade* (1973) abortion decision and aroused doubts by his assertion that he had never discussed it, even in private conversation. On September 27, 1991, the Senate Judiciary Committee deadlocked on Thomas's nomination and sent it to the Senate floor without recommendation. Shortly thereafter, testimony by Anita Hill, Thomas's former assistant who claimed he had sexually harassed her, was leaked to media sources. The committee reopened hearings to discuss the issue. The questioning of Hill and Thomas became a national television event and a source of universal debate over issues of sexual harassment and Hill's truthfulness. Despite the damaging allegations, on October 15, Thomas was confirmed by a vote of 52–48.

In his first years on the Supreme Court, Thomas voted consistently with the Court's conservative wing. His decisions narrowed the scope of the 1965 Voting Rights Act, upheld new limits on abortion rights (he pronounced himself ready to overturn *Roe v. Wade*), and curbed affirmative action policies. In *Hudson v. McMillian* (1992), perhaps his most controversial opinion, Thomas held that the Eighth Amendment did not proscribe beating of prison inmates by guards. Thomas sometimes spoke about the treatment he had received during his confirmation process. In 1993 he gave a controversial speech linking society's treatment of conservative African-American intellectuals to lynching. During the early 1990s he regularly voted with his conservative colleagues on the Court in cases involving affirmative action, abortion, educational opportunity, the death penalty, and civil rights for gays and lesbians.

Since 1994 Thomas has increasingly become the deciding vote in numerous controversial cases, often those dealing with issues of race and free speech. He continues to make decisions that are not popular in the African-American community but that have helped him gain the respect of many people in the field. In 2003 Thomas signed a contract with book publisher HarperCollins to publish his memoirs, documenting his rise to the Supreme Court. The book is expected to be released in 2005.

See also Affirmative Action; Hill-Thomas Hearings

Bibliography

Comiskey, Michael. *Seeking Justices: The Judging of Supreme Court Nominees.* Lawrence: University Press of Kansas, 2004.

Court of Appeal: The Black Community Speaks Out on the Racial and Sexual Politics of Thomas v. Hill, eds. Robert Chrisman and Robert L. Allen. New York: Ballantine Books, 1992.

Foskett, Ken. *Judging Thomas: The Life and Times of Clarence Thomas.* New York: Morrow, 2004.

Morrison, Toni, ed. *Race-ing Justice, Engendering Power.* New York: Pantheon Books, 1992.

Phelps, Timothy, and Helen Winternitz. *Capitol Games.* New York: Hyperion, 1992.

Toobin, Jeffrey. "The Burden of Clarence Thomas." *New Yorker* (September 27, 1993): 38–51.

CLARENCE E. WALKER (1996)
Updated by publisher 2005

Thurman, Howard

November 18, 1900
April 10, 1981

Minister and educator Howard Thurman, whose career as pastor, scholar, teacher, and university chaplain extended over fifty years, was the author of over twenty books. One of the most creative religious minds of the twentieth century, Thurman touched the lives of many cultural leaders within and beyond the modern civil rights movement, including Martin Luther King, Jr., A. Philip Randolph, Alan Paton, Eleanor Roosevelt, Mary McLeod Bethune, Mordecai Wyatt Johnson, Rabbi Alvin Fine, and Arthur Ashe. "The search for common ground" was the defining motif of Thurman's life and thought. This vision of the kinship of all peoples, born of Thurman's own personal struggles with the prohibitions of race, religion, and culture, propelled him into the mainstream of American Christianity as a distinctive interpreter of the church's role in a pluralistic society.

The grandson of slaves, Thurman was born in Daytona, Florida, and raised in its segregated black community. He was educated in the local black school, where he was the first African American to complete the eighth grade. He attended high school at Florida Baptist Academy (1915–1919), one of only three public high schools for blacks in the state. Upon graduation, Thurman attended Morehouse College (1919–1923) and Rochester Theological Seminary (1923–1926). After serving as pastor of Mt. Zion Baptist Church in Oberlin, Ohio, for two years (1926–1928), he studied with the Quaker mystic Rufus Jones in the spring of 1929. He served as director of religious life and professor of religion at Morehouse and Spelman Colleges (1929–1930), and dean of Rankin Chapel and professor of religion at Howard University (1932–1944).

Thurman was cofounder and copastor of the pioneering interracial, interfaith Fellowship Church for All Peoples in San Francisco from 1944 to 1953. In 1953 he assumed the dual appointment of professor of spiritual resources and disciplines and dean of Marsh Chapel at Boston University. He founded the Howard Thurman Educational Trust in San Francisco in 1961, which he administered after his retirement in 1965 until his death in 1981.

See also Christian Denominations, Independent; Civil Rights Movement, U.S.

Bibliography

The Faith Project. Public Broadcasting Service. "This Far by Faith," April 2003. Available from <http://www.pbs.org/thisfarbyfaith/people/howard_thurman.html>.

Fluker, Walter, and Catherine Tumber, eds. *A Strange Freedom: The Best of Howard Thurman on Religious Experience and Public Life.* Boston: Beacon Press, 1998.

Mitchell, Mozella Gordon. *Spiritual Dynamics of Howard Thurman's Theology.* Bristol, Ind.: Wyndham Hall Press, 1985.

Smith, Luther E. *Howard Thurman: The Mystic as Prophet.* Washington, D.C.: University Press of America, 1981.

WALTER EARL FLUKER (1996)
Updated bibliography

Thurman, Wallace

August 16, 1902
December 22, 1934

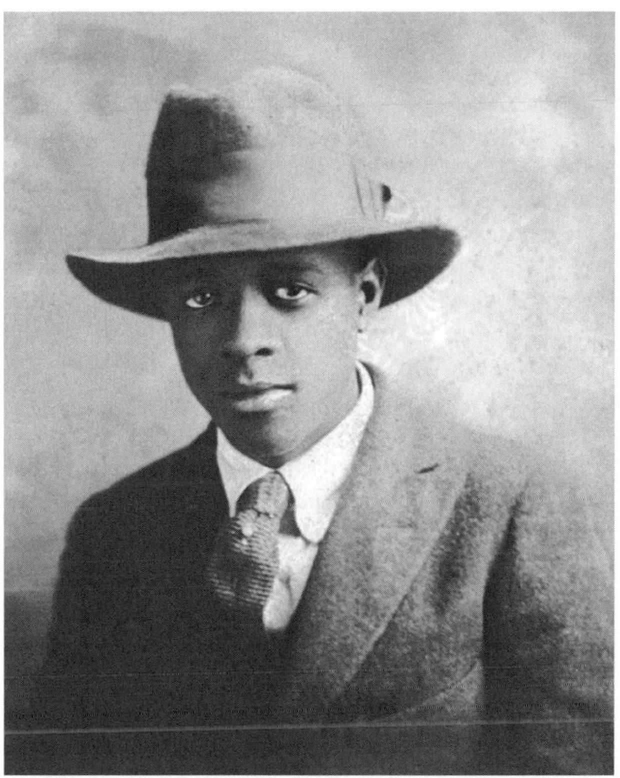

Wallace Thurman. *One of the most gifted editors of the Harlem Renaissance, Thurman became one of the movement's most virulent critics.* REPRODUCED BY PERMISSION OF THE BEINECKE RARE BOOK AND MANUSCRIPT LIBRARY.

Writer Wallace Thurman was born in Salt Lake City, Utah. His literary career began shortly after he left the University of Utah to study at the University of Southern California. Although his intent was to study medicine, Thurman soon rediscovered an earlier enthusiasm for writing. According to Arna Bontemps, whom he first met during this period, Thurman "lost sight of degrees" and began to pursue courses related to his interest in literature and writing. In Los Angeles he also wrote a column called "Inklings" for a local black newspaper. Having heard about the New Negro movement in New York, Thurman attempted to establish a West Coast counterpart to the Harlem Renaissance and began editing his own literary magazine, the *Outlet.* The publication lasted for only six months but was described by his friend Theophilus Lewis, the Harlem theater critic, as Thurman's "first and most successful venture at the editorial desk."

Dissatisfied, Thurman left for New York where, as he put it, he "began to live on Labor Day, 1925." Later he became known for his declaration that he was a man who hated "every damned spot in these United States outside of Manhattan Island." In New York Thurman secured his first position, as an editorial assistant at the *Looking Glass,* another small, short-lived review. His first important position was as temporary editor for the leftist *Messenger*, published by A. Philip Randolph and Chandler Owen. When the managing editor, George Schuyler, went on leave, Thurman's role provided him with a forum not only for his own work but for that of other nascent Renaissance talent, including Langston Hughes, Arna Bontemps, Zora Neale Hurston, and Dorothy West.

When Schuyler returned, Thurman became associated with a white publication, the *World Tomorrow,* and at the same time joined a group of young black writers and artists—Hurston, Hughes, Aaron Douglas, John P. Davis, Bruce Nugent, and Gwendolyn Bennett—to launch "a new experimental quarterly," *Fire,* in 1926. The purpose of *Fire,* according to its founders, was to "burn up a lot of the old, dead conventional Negro-white ideas of the past, épater la bourgeoisie into the realization of the existence of the younger Negro writers and artists." Yet Thurman's enduring ambition to become editor of "a financially secure magazine" seemed ill fated. *Fire* itself became a casualty of a real fire in a basement where several hundred copies had been stored, and the disaster led to its demise after the first issue. Thurman's next editorial venture came two years later, when he began publishing *Harlem, a*

Forum of Negro Life. Although the magazine lasted a little longer than its predecessor, it too folded due to a lack of funds.

Thurman also wrote critical articles on African-American life and culture for such magazines as the *New Republic,* the *Independent,* the *Bookman,* and *Dance Magazine.* The black writer, he contended, had left a "great deal of fresh, vital material untouched" because of his tendency to view his own people as "sociological problems rather than as human beings." Like Hughes, he criticized those writers who felt "that they must always exhibit specimens from the college rather than from the kindergarten, specimens from the parlor rather than from the pantry." He exhorted black writers to exploit those authentic and unique aspects of black life and culture ignored by writers who suppressed the seamy or sordid or low-down, common aspects of black existence.

Thurman published his first novel, *The Blacker the Berry* (1929) while on the staff of MacFadden Publications. Although the book was acclaimed by the critics, the author remained characteristically skeptical of his own efforts. Doubtless invoking some of his own experiences, Thurman's novel deals with the problems of a dark-skinned woman who struggles with intraracial schisms caused by colorism. Later that same year Thurman collaborated with a white writer, William Jourdan Rapp, on the play *Harlem,* which opened at the Apollo Theater. Thurman based the plot and dialogue on his short story "Cordelia the Crude," which was originally published in *Fire.* The play was described by Hughes as "a compelling study . . . of the impact of Harlem on a Negro family fresh from the south." After its production Thurman continued to write prolifically, sometimes ghostwriting popular "true confessions" fiction.

In 1932 Thurman published his second novel, *Infants of the Spring,* an autobiographical roman à clef, documenting the period from a contemporary perspective. The novel is a biting satire and poignant critique of the Harlem Renaissance. For Thurman, the failure of the movement lay in the race consciousness emanating from the literary propagandists on the one hand and the assimilationists on the other, both undermining any expression of racial authenticity and individuality.

His final novel, *The Interne,* written in collaboration with Abraham L. Furman, was also published in 1932. It was a muckraking novel exposing the corrupt conditions in City Hospital in New York. Both of these novels were published by Macaulay, where Thurman became editor in chief in 1932. Two years later he negotiated a contract with Foy Productions to write scenarios for two films, *High School Girl* and *Tomorrow's Children.* But the strain of life in Hollywood took its toll on Thurman, who became ill and returned to New York in the spring of 1934. Not only had he been marked by a certain physical fragility, he had also been plagued with chronic alcoholism. Shortly after his return Thurman was taken to City Hospital, the very institution he had written about in *The Interne.* After remaining for six months in the incurable ward, he died of consumption on December 22, 1934.

Thurman had arrived in New York in 1925 at the peak of the Harlem Renaissance, whose rise and ebb paralleled his own life and career. He early became one of the leading critics of the older bourgeoisie, both black and white; his lifestyle and literary criticism were calculated to outrage their sensibilities and articulate a New Negro attitude toward the black arts. His importance to the Harlem Renaissance can be measured in terms of both his literary contributions and his influence on younger and perhaps more successful writers of the period. His criticism also set a standard of judgment for subsequent scholars of the Harlem Renaissance. Perhaps his evaluation of Alain Locke's *The New Negro* (1925), a collection inaugurating the movement, best summarizes his own life and contribution: "In [*The New Negro*] are exemplified all the virtues and all the faults of this new movement." Thurman's life itself became a symbol of the possibilities and limitations of the Harlem Renaissance.

See also Bontemps, Arna; Harlem Renaissance; Hughes, Langston; Hurston, Zora Neale; New Negro; Owen, Chandler; Randolph, Asa Philip; Schuyler, George S.; West, Dorothy

Bibliography

Beckman, Wendy Hart. *Artists and Writers of the Harlem Renaissance.* Berkeley Heights, N.J.: Enslow, 2002.

Bloom, Harold, ed. *The Harlem Renaissance.* Philadelphia: Chelsea House, 2004.

Huggins, Nathan I. *Harlem Renaissance.* New York: Oxford University Press, 1971.

Huggins, Nathan I., ed. *Voices from the Harlem Renaissance.* New York: Oxford University Press, 1976.

Lewis, David Levering. *When Harlem Was in Vogue.* New York: Vintage, 1981.

MAE G. HENDERSON (1996)
Updated bibliography

Tia Ciata

April 23, 1854
April 11, 1924

Hilária Batista de Almeida, known as Tia ("Aunt") Ciata (sometimes written Assiata, Siata, Aciata, or Asseata), became a living icon of Afro-Brazilian culture in Rio de Janeiro, then the nation's capital, during a time of accelerating urban growth and cultural ferment in the late nineteenth and early twentieth centuries. As a cook, entrepreneur, spiritual leader, and matriarch within the city's African-descended community, she made her home into the headquarters of the section of Rio de Janeiro known as "Little Africa."

Ciata, never a slave, was born in Salvador, the capital of the northeastern province of Bahia. In 1874, she and her daughter Isabel became part of a massive flow of Brazilians of African descent from the country's northeast southward to Rio de Janeiro. Estranged from the father of her daughter, Ciata married João Batista da Silva, a fellow Bahian who was well situated in Rio's Afro-Brazilian community. She eventually rented a house at 117 Visconde de Itaúna Street in the neighborhood called Cidade Nova, near Praça Onze (de Junho). Here, Ciata settled within a thriving Afro-Brazilian colony populated by former slaves from Bahia and elsewhere in the northeast, free people of color, and (until abolition) slaves from Rio. Praça Onze served as the unofficial "capital" of Little Africa.

Rio's Afro-Brazilian community maintained its vibrant culture largely through religious practice, and Tia Ciata's prominence derived partly from her active participation in Afro-Brazilian religion (Candomblé), a practice in which she had already been initiated in Bahia. Once in Rio, Ciata associated herself with the *terreiro* (religious community) of the African-born João Alabá. She became *mãe-pequena*—literally "little mother" (or Iyá Kekerê)—the second highest position in the Candomblé hierarchy. Among Rio's numerous Bahian matriarchs affectionately called "Tia" at the time, Ciata was the most famous.

A skilled confectioner, Tia Ciata made sweets and other Bahian delicacies in her home and sold them on the street. She also started a successful business renting out the traditional white festive costumes of her native Bahia for carnival and theatrical events, and she set up a food stand at the Festa da Penha, an annual religious festival. This traditionally Portuguese event attracted a diverse crowd of devotees and spectators, and it slowly became Africanized throughout the late nineteenth and early twentieth centuries, as proto-samba associations (*ranchos*) and costumed groups competed for space with the penitent pilgrims. Here, Ciata became an important catalyst for the advancement of the nascent musical genre of samba, as she made her market stall into a meeting place for musicians, composers, and interested audiences.

As other Bahian "tias" did, Tia Ciata threw parties in her home on Visconde de Itaúna Street that served both spiritual and entertainment purposes. Her charisma, famous cooking, and exciting parties drew politicians, literary figures, musicians, composers, fellow devotees of Candomblé, and others. Popular memory holds her house as the birthplace of samba, a music and dance style descended from African-derived *lundu* and *maxixe*, European waltzes and polkas (which were then circulating in Rio de Janeiro), and the Portuguese-Brazilian *modinha*. Ciata united the most important popular musicians and composers of her time, such as Donga, Sinhô, Pixinguinha, Hilário Jovino Ferreira, João da Baiana, and Heitor dos Prazeres. Her distinctive manner of bringing together samba musicians may have influenced the genre's typically collective composition and performance style in Rio de Janeiro. In addition, some have speculated that Tia Ciata managed to avoid police interference at her parties because of her husband's position on the staff of the chief of police.

Participants in one of the sessions at Ciata's house collectively authored the song "Pelo telefone" ("On the telephone"), which a group called Banda Odeon recorded in 1917, a song later recorded by Donga and Mauro de Almeida and registered with the Brazilian National Library under Donga's name. While not the first recorded samba rhythm, as commonly believed, "Pelo telefone" was indeed the first one to enjoy enormous success. The song's controversial theme parodied police persecution of—and involvement in—illicit gambling.

Rio's *belle époque* is often understood as characterized by a stark separation between elite and popular culture, and by elite attempts to extinguish African culture in the name of modernity. Yet historians have pointed to Tia Ciata's house as an example of the cultural mixing that also occurred. Bahian immigrants, of which Tia Ciata was among the most active, productive, and famous, were enormously important in bringing Bahian culture to the capital, thus making such forms of Afro-Brazilian expression as samba so central to Brazilian national culture, a process that really only began in earnest in the late 1920s and 1930s, after the end of Tia Ciata's life.

Upon her death in 1924, Tia Ciata was survived by her fifteen children. Her legendary house at 117 Visconde de Itaúna Street no longer stands, a sacrifice to the demolitions that tore down whole blocks of the Cidade Nova in the middle of the twentieth century. The Escola Municipal

Tia Ciata, an experimental public school near the site where her famous house stood, bears her name.

See also Candomblé; Samba

Bibliography

Lopes, Antonio Herculano, ed. *Entre Europa e África: A invenção do carioca.* Rio de Janeiro: Fundação Casa de Rui Barbosa, Topbooks, 2000.

Moura, Roberto. *Tia Ciata e a Pequena África no Rio de Janeiro,* 2d ed. Rio de Janeiro: Coleção Biblioteca Carioca, 1995.

Sandroni, Carlos. *Feitiço Decente: Transformações do samba no Rio de Janeiro (1917–1933).* Rio de Janeiro: Jorge Zahar, 2001.

Silva, Eduardo. *Prince of the People: The Life and Times of a Brazilian Free Man of Color,* translated by Moyra Ashford. New York: Verso, 1993.

Vianna, Hermano. *The Mystery of Samba: Popular Music and National Identity in Brazil.* Edited and translated by John Charles Chasteen. Chapel Hill: University of North Carolina Press, 1999.

AMY CHAZKEL (2005)

Till, Emmett

July 25, 1941
August 28, 1955

Emmett Louis Till was born and raised in Chicago, Illinois. When he was fourteen, his parents sent him to LeFlore County, Mississippi, to visit his uncle for the summer. That summer Till bragged to his friends about northern social freedoms and showed them pictures of a white girl he claimed was his girlfriend. His friends, schooled in the southern rules of caste based on black deference and white supremacy, were incredulous. One evening they dared Till to enter a store and ask the white woman inside, Carolyn Bryant, for a date. Till entered the store, squeezed Bryant's hand, grabbed her around the waist, and propositioned her. When she fled and returned with a gun, he wolf-whistled at her before being hurried away by his friends.

Till's act of youthful brashness crossed southern social barriers that strictly governed contact between black men and white women. In Mississippi, where the Ku Klux Klan was newly revived and African Americans were impoverished and disfranchised, these barriers were strictly enforced by the threat of social violence. On August 28, 1955, Carolyn Bryant's husband, Roy, and his half brother, J. W. Milam, abducted Till from his uncle's home, brutally beat him, shot him in the head, and then dumped his naked body in the Tallahatchie River. Till's mangled and decomposed body was found three days later, and his uncle named both men as the assailants. Bryant and Milam were tried for murder. Despite the fact that the two men had admitted abducting Till, they were acquitted on September 23 by an all-white jury because the body was too mangled to be definitively identified.

The verdict unleashed a storm of protest. Till's mother, Mamie Till, had insisted on an open-casket funeral, and pictures of Till's disfigured body featured in *Jet* magazine had focused national attention on the trial. Till's age, the innocence of his act, and his killers' immunity from retribution represented a stark and definitive expression of southern racism to many African Americans. Demonstrations were organized by the National Association for the Advancement of Colored People (NAACP), and the Brotherhood of Sleeping Car Porters and black leaders such as W. E. B. Du Bois demanded antilynching legislation and federal action on civil rights.

Emmett Till's lynching was a milestone in the emergent civil rights movement. Outrage over his death was key to mobilizing black resistance in the Deep South. In addition, black protest over the lack of federal intervention in the Till case was integral to the inclusion of legal mechanisms for federal investigation of civil rights violations in the Civil Rights Act of 1957.

In 1959 Roy and Carolyn Bryant and Milam told their stories to journalist William Bradford Huie. Only Milam spoke for the record, but what he revealed was tantamount to a confession. Huie's interviews were subsequently published in 1959 as a book titled *Wolf Whistle.* The NAACP, Mamie Till, and other civil rights leaders continued to call for justice and in May 2004, after new evidence was uncovered by documentary filmmaker Keith Beauchamp, the Justice Department reopened the Till case. Till's body was exhumed for autopsy on June 1, 2005.

See also Civil Rights Movement, U.S.; Lynching; National Association for the Advancement of Colored People (NAACP); United States Commission on Civil Rights

Bibliography

Metress, Christopher. *The Lynching of Emmett Till: A Documentary Narrative.* Charlottesville: University of Virginia Press, 2002.

Whitfield, Stephen J. *A Death in the Delta: The Story of Emmett Till.* New York: Free Press, 1988.

ROBYN SPENCER (1996)
Updated by author 2005

TOLSON, MELVIN B.

FEBRUARY 6, 1898
AUGUST 29, 1966

The poet and educator Melvin Beaunorus Tolson was born in Howard County, Missouri, to Alonzo Tolson, a Methodist minister, and Lera Tolson. He attended Lincoln High School in Kansas City, Missouri, spent a year (1918) at Fisk University in Nashville, and then transferred to Lincoln University in Pennsylvania, where he received his B.A. With his wife, Ruth, whom he married in 1922, he would raise several highly successful children. In 1923, Tolson secured a post at Wiley College in Marshall, Texas, where he taught English literature and coached one of the country's most successful debating teams.

As early as 1917, Tolson had begun to write poems and short tales that reveal and foreshadow the intensity of his intellectual life and his preoccupation with esoteric knowledge. His poetic interests took off, however, while he was attending Columbia University on a Rockefeller Foundation scholarship during 1931 and 1932, the dimming of the so-called Harlem Renaissance. His M.A. thesis presents a somewhat brief but accurate portrait of some of the leading figures of the Renaissance, including Langston Hughes (1902–1967), whom he knew fairly well. The fervor and ferment of the Harlem community inspired Tolson in 1932 to write a sonnet about Harlem's denizens. This sonnet was the germ of an extended poetic work, which was published posthumously as *A Gallery of Harlem Portraits* (1979). Lyrics from the blues and spirituals freely intermix with conventional poetic language to create stylized "portraits" of Harlemites of the 1930s and 1940s. Several years after his return to Wiley College, Tolson's enormous success as a debating coach prompted the *Washington Tribune* in 1938 to request that he write a guest column, which for almost seven years flourished as a regular feature titled "Caviar and Cabbages."

With the publication of "Dark Symphony" in the *Atlantic Monthly* (1941), Tolson demonstrates his earliest preoccupation with, and mastery of, the poetic sequence. Constructed around the personalities of major historical black figures, the poem won first prize at the American Negro Exposition in Chicago in 1940. The award assisted Tolson in getting *Rendezvous with America* (1944)—his first major poetic composition—published.

In his early phase Tolson's poems, which appeared in magazines such as the *Atlantic Monthly* and *Prairie Schooner,* were fairly accessible and transparent. But the poems of his second phase became more esoteric and highly allusive. His work then began appearing in magazines such as the *Modern Quarterly,* the *Arts Quarterly,* and *Poetry*. In the intervening years, Tolson was elected four times as mayor of Langston, Oklahoma. In 1947 the government of Liberia commissioned him to write a work to be read at the International Exposition in Liberia, commemorating the country's centennial, and simultaneously made him their poet laureate. To celebrate the ideals upon which Liberia was founded, Tolson wrote *Libretto for the Republic of Liberia* (1953), a difficult and enormously complex work about intellectual freedom and international brotherhood—a virtual constant in his writings. The primary work upon which Tolson's fame rests, however, is *Harlem Gallery* (1965), a lengthy poetic sequence of portraits or odes devoted as much to the modern Anglo-American poetic tradition as to African-American culture. *Harlem Gallery* is primarily concerned, for example, with the integrity of the black artist and his cultural allegiances.

Although Tolson is often grouped with the major poetic figures of the 1950s and early 1960s, such as Gwendolyn Brooks and Robert Hayden, his reputation remains far behind those of his peers, and readers and scholars alike are kept at bay by the erudition and monumentality of his work.

See also Harlem Renaissance; Hughes, Langston; Poetry, U.S.

Bibliography

Farnsworth, Robert M. *Melvin B. Tolson, 1898-1966, Plain Talk and Poetic Prophecy*. Columbia: University of Missouri Press, 1984.

Flasch, Joy. *Melvin B. Tolson*. New York: Twayne, 1972.

Russell, Mariann. *Melvin B. Tolson's "Harlem Gallery": A Literary Analysis*. Columbia: University of Missouri Press, 1980.

Thompson, Gordon, E. *Charles W. Chesnutt, Zora Neale Hurston, Melvin B. Tolson: Folk and Non-Folk Representation of the Fantastic*. Ph.D. diss. Yale University, 1987.

GORDON THOMPSON (1996)

TOOMER, JEAN

DECEMBER 26, 1894
MARCH 30, 1967

Writer Jean Toomer was born Nathan Pinchback Toomer in Washington, D.C. (He changed his name to Jean Toomer in 1920.) His maternal grandfather, Pinckney Benton Stewart Pinchback, a dominant figure in Toomer's childhood and adolescence, was acting governor of Louisiana for about five weeks in 1872 and 1873. Because Toomer's father Nathan deserted his wife and child in 1895, and his mother Nina died in 1909, Toomer spent much of his youth in the home of his Pinchback grandparents in Washington, D.C. After graduating from Dunbar High School in 1914, Toomer spent about six months studying agriculture at the University of Wisconsin. During 1916 and 1917 he attended classes at various colleges, among them the American College of Physical Training in Chicago, New York University, and the City College of New York.

By 1918 Toomer had written "Bona and Paul," a story that became part of *Cane,* his masterpiece. This early story signaled a theme that Toomer was preoccupied with in most of his subsequent writing: the search for and development of personal identity and harmony with other people. Throughout his life, Toomer, who had light skin, felt uncomfortable with the rigid racial and ethnic classifications in the United States. He felt such classifications limited the individual and inhibited personal psychic development. Having lived in both white and black neighborhoods in Washington, D.C., and having various racial and ethnic strains within him, he thought it ridiculous to define himself simplistically.

Two events early in Toomer's literary career were of great importance to his development as a writer. In 1920 he met the novelist and essayist Waldo Frank, and in 1921 he was a substitute principal at the Sparta Agricultural and Industrial Institute in Georgia. Toomer and Frank became close friends, sharing their ideas about writing, and Frank, the established writer, encouraged Toomer in his fledgling work. However, it was in Georgia that Toomer became most inspired. He was moved and excited by the rural black people and their land. He felt he had found a part of himself that he had not known well, and perhaps for the first time in his life truly identified with his black heritage. The result was an outpouring of writing, bringing forth most of the southern pieces that would be in *Cane.*

Cane, stylistically avant-garde, an impressionistic collection of stories, sketches, and poems, some of which had been previously published in *Crisis, Double Dealer, Liberator, Modern Review,* and *Broom,* was published in 1923. Though only about a thousand copies were sold, it received mostly good reviews and was proclaimed an important book by the writers who were then establishing what was to become the Harlem Renaissance. Alain Locke praised *Cane*'s "musical folk-lilt" and "glamorous sensuous ecstasy." William Stanley Braithwaite called Toomer "the very first artist of the race, who . . . can write about the Negro without the surrender of compromise of the artist's vision. . . . Toomer is a bright morning star of a new day of the race in literature." A review in *The New Republic* lauded Cane for its unstereotyped picture of the South, and Allen Tate compared Toomer's avant-garde style favorably to other modern works.

However, despite the critical praise for *Cane,* by 1924 Toomer was feeling restless and unhappy with himself. His struggle with personal identity continued. He went to France to study at Georges I. Gurdjieff's Institute for the Harmonious Development of Man at Fontainebleau. Gurdjieff believed that human beings were made up of two parts: "personality" and "essence." Personality is superficial, created by social environment. It usually obscures essence, which is one's true nature and the core of one's being. Gurdjieff claimed that he could help people discover their essence. Toomer soon embraced Gurdjieff's ideas of personal development, and when he returned to the United States, he became an advocate of Gurdjieff's philosophy, leading Gurdjieff workshops at first briefly in Harlem and then in Chicago until 1930.

Due to Gurdjieff's influence and Toomer's continuing search for a meaningful identity, after 1923 he largely abandoned the style and subject matter he had used in *Cane.* To a great extent he abandoned black writing. From 1924 until his death, he wrote voluminously, but with little critical or publishing success. He wrote in all genres: plays, poems, essays, stories, novels, and autobiographies. Whereas his writing became noticeably more didactic, some of it was not without interesting stylistic experimentation, especially his expressionistic drama, most notably *The Sacred Factory,* published posthumously in 1980. During this period, Toomer also wrote a number of autobiographies and provocative social, political, and personal essays, some of which were published posthumously. Works that Toomer did publish after *Cane* include: *Balo* (1927), a play of Southern rural black life, written during the *Cane* period; "Mr. Costyve Duditch" and "Winter on Earth," stories published in 1928; "Race Problems and Modern Society" (1929), an important essay on the racial situation in the United States that complements "The Negro Emergent," published posthumously in 1993; and "Blue Meridian" (1936), a long poem in which Toomer depicts the development of the American race as the coming together of the black, red, and white races.

A decade after the publication of *Cane,* Toomer had dropped into relative obscurity. It was not until the 1960s and the renewed interest in earlier African-American writing and the republication of *Cane* that Toomer began to have a large readership and an influence on the young black writers of the day. Since then, four posthumous collections of mostly previously unpublished material have appeared: *The Wayward and the Seeking* (ed. Darwin T. Turner, 1980); *The Collected Poems of Jean Toomer* (ed. Robert B. Jones and Margery Toomer Latimer, 1988); *Essentials* (ed. Rudolph P. Byrd, 1991, a republication of a collection of aphorisms originally privately printed in 1931); and *A Jean Toomer Reader: Selected Unpublished Writings* (ed. Frederik L. Rusch, 1993).

Toomer had two wives. He married Margery Latimer in 1931, but she died the following year giving birth to their daughter, also named Margery. In 1934 he married Marjorie Content. From 1936 to his death, Toomer resided in Bucks County, Pennsylvania.

See also Harlem Renaissance; Literature of the United States

Bibliography

Byrd, Rudolph P. *Jean Toomer's Years with Gurdjieff: A Portrait of an Artist, 1923–1936.* Athens: University of Georgia Press, 1990.

Griffin, John Chandler. *Biography of American Author Jean Toomer, 1894–1967.* Lewiston, N.Y.: Edwin Mellen Press, 2002.

Kerman, Cynthia Earl, and Richard Eldridge. *The Lives of Jean Toomer: A Hunger for Wholeness.* Baton Rouge: Louisiana State University Press, 1987.

McKay, Nellie Y. *Jean Toomer, Artist: A Study of His Life and Work, 1894–1936.* Chapel Hill: University of North Carolina Press, 1984.

FREDERIK L. RUSCH (1996)
Updated bibliography

Toussaint, Pierre

c. 1766
June 30, 1853

Businessman, philanthropist, and candidate for canonization Pierre Toussaint was probably born in Haiti in 1766, the slave of a planter, Jean Berard. Toussaint, a house servant, was looked upon affectionately by the Berards and treated as a member of the family. His grandmother taught him to read and his master permitted him use of the home library. In 1787, during the early stages of a slave revolt, the Berards fled Haiti to go to New York City, taking Toussaint and his sister with them. Toussaint remained loyal to his masters throughout the unrest and rebellion. After arriving in New York, he was apprenticed to a hairdresser and, while still a slave, was able to set up a successful business of his own. His services were desired by many of the wealthiest and most distinguished women in the city. As a hairdresser he earned enough to become quite wealthy and to support his mistress after his master died. Although he had the means to purchase his own freedom, he chose to remain with his mistress even after she remarried.

In 1809, on her deathbed, Madame Berard granted Toussaint his freedom. His loyalty did not end with his manumission, however, and he continued to support Madame Berard's daughter for several years. With his considerable wealth he was able to purchase the freedom of his sister, Rosalie, and his future wife, Juliette Noel, in 1811. Three years later he purchased the freedom of his niece, Euphemia, and cared for and educated her. Following Euphemia's death of tuberculosis in 1829, the grief-stricken Toussaint turned to benevolent activities.

Toussaint had been a devout Roman Catholic since he was a child, and after arriving in New York he attended mass every day for sixty-six years at Saint Peter's Roman Catholic Church in lower Manhattan. He was the most notable black layperson in the antebellum Roman Catholic Church in New York City. The kindhearted Toussaint was also generous and charitable. He and his wife took black orphans into their home and raised money in support of the Catholic Orphan Asylum for white children. In 1841 he was the first person to respond to the request of Monsignor de Forbin-Jasson for donations to erect a Roman Catholic church for French speakers (now Saint Vincent de Paul's) with what was then a considerable contribution of one hundred dollars. When Toussaint died in 1853, he was buried beside his wife in Saint Patrick's Cemetery.

In response to the many voices that called for recognition of Toussaint's exemplary piety, in the early 1990s the New York archdiocese began the process of canonizing him as a saint. This effort led to some conflict and disagreement within the church. New York's John Cardinal O'Connor and other Catholics, black and white, regarded Toussaint as a model of faith and charity who deserved the honor of sainthood. Others saw his career as marked by passivity and servility and therefore unworthy of veneration. The canonization is to be decided by a commission in Rome. Despite the controversy surrounding Toussaint's legacy, he remains an important figure within nineteenth-century African-American history.

See also Catholicism in the Americas

Bibliography

Lee, Hannah Farnham. *Memoir of Pierre Toussaint: Born a Slave in St. Domingo*. Boston: Crosby, Nichols and Co., 1854.

Ottley, Roi, and William J. Weatherby, eds. *The Negro in New York*. New York: New York Public Library, 1967.

Tarry, Ellen. *The Other Toussaint: A Modern Biography of Pierre Toussaint, a Post-Revolutionary Black*. Boston: St. Paul Editions, 1981.

WILLIAM J. MOSES (1996)

Toussaint-Louverture

1743
April 7, 1803

Toussaint-Louverture, born François Dominique Toussaint Bréda, was born a black slave on the Bréda sugar plantation in Saint Domingue (or Santo Domingo, modern Haiti) on May 20, 1743. His death in a French prison in 1803 marked the end of an unparalleled career as a statesman, military general, and leader of the largest and, ultimately, most successful slave revolt in modern history. Some of this success was, no doubt, attributable to his position in the colonial society of Saint Domingue and his ability to move between the white, free colored, and slave populations with ease. He is thought to have spoken the Aja-Fon language of his African father (said to be of a royal lineage), and he certainly spoke the slave vernacular (Haitian) he learned as a child. He later acquired some proficiency in written and spoken French.

As a Creole slave, Toussaint held a privileged position as a coachman and a horse doctor, thus avoiding the awful realities experienced by the *bossales*, or African-born slaves. Although he is often believed to have been an elite slave at the outbreak of the 1791 slave insurrection, records show that he had been a black freedman, or Creole, for some time, possibly twenty years. His free status is of interest because his contemporaries thought he was a slave. He did nothing to disabuse them of this notion, however, and clearly used it to his advantage. And, like many of the free colored of the period, he owned and rented slaves.

A number of scholars have argued that Toussaint was one of the principal organizers of the August 1791 revolt, but he most likely maintained a low profile until several months after the rebellion began, continuing to live on the Bréda plantation (owned by the French Comte de Noé) with his family. Following his entry into the insurrection, he worked his way up the ranks of the rebel fighting force, later becoming the leader of his own army.

In the spring of 1793 Toussaint allied himself with the Spanish, who intended to take over the French colony, and distinguished himself as a leader and battlefield commander. About a year later—and not long after the Jacobin government officially abolished slavery in all the French colonies—he abandoned the Spanish army and joined forces with the French Republicans. It was in this period that he took on the name Louverture—meaning "the opening"—and dropped the name Bréda.

For the next seven years, Toussaint displayed a formidable political and military prowess in what could be described as a relentless quest for power. He brilliantly outmaneuvered successive French administrators and generals, and by August 1800 emerged the victor in the bloody War of the South against André Rigaud, the last leader in Toussaint's way toward complete domination of the island. Rigaud was a light-skinned free colored general from the South. The war (1799-1800) known as the War of the South or the War of Knives, ended with the defeat of Rigaud and his flight to France. The cause of the conflict is highly debated; some say it was a racial conflict and others a regional conflict. In his July 1801 constitution, Toussaint named himself governor for life, but in so doing he attracted the wrath of Napolean Bonaparte, who sent an expedition under General Charles Leclerc to wrest the colony from his control. With Leclerc's conquest of the colony completed by May 1802, Toussaint surrendered and retired to his plantations in the north. The French, however, viewed him as a threat and he was soon detained, deported to France, and held in the Fort de Joux prison in Jura where he later died, probably from pneumonia.

Historians disagree in their evaluation of Toussaint. To some he was an opportunist who sought power and glory; for others he remains one of the Americas' great political visionaries. Even though he might best be described as enigmatic, it is difficult to dismiss his impact as a leader and the success he achieved politically. Nor is it possible to deny his contribution to the creation, training, and maintenance of an army that eventually defeated the French at Vertières on November 18, 1803, under the leadership of Jean-Jacques Dessalines, a victory that culminated in the declaration of Haitian Independence on January 1, 1804.

Toussaint-Louverture's historical significance is wide-ranging. He has been, and continues to be, the subject of a large body of work. Caribbean scholars, in particular, have linked his contributions to the emancipation of the enslaved populations of the Caribbean, and he has been immortalized by authors such as Aimé Césaire and Edouard Glissant. Despite his many contradictions, Toussaint-Louverture remains one of the most important historical actors in the formation of the modern Caribbean, and he remains a powerful symbol of the region's ongoing search for political, economic, and cultural autonomy.

See also Christophe, Henri; Dessalines, Jean-Jacques; Haitian Revolution

Bibliography

James, Cyril Lionel Robert. *The Black Jacobins: Toussaint Louverture and the San Domingo Revolution.* 1938, 2d ed., rev., New York: Vintage, 1963; reprint, 1989.

Geggus, David P. *Haitian Revolutionary Studies.* Bloomington: University of Indiana Press, 2002.

Pluchon, Pierre. *Toussaint Louverture: Un Révolutionnaire noir d'ancien régime.* Paris: Fayard. 1989.

THORALD M. BURNHAM (2005)

Townsend, Fannie Lou

See Hamer, Fannie Lou (Townsend, Fannie Lou)

Track and Field

See Olympians; Sports

TransAfrica Forum

TransAfrica was the African-American lobby for Africa and the Caribbean. Incorporated in September 1977, it became the first national advocacy organization to exist solely for the purpose of articulating an African-American voice in the formulation of U.S. foreign policy. TransAfrica Forum, the lobby's research and educational affiliate, was established in 1981. It published the journal *TransAfrica Forum*, sponsored an annual foreign policy conference, and administered a library and resource center. Operating in tandem under a shared executive director, the parent body and its educational offshoot promoted progressive, nonracialist policies to address political, economic, and humanitarian concerns in the black world.

The history of African-American activism in foreign policy predates the Civil War. Indeed, while slavery was still practiced on American soil, abolitionists, among them Frederick Douglass, pressed for official recognition of the independent black republics of Haiti and Liberia. African-Americans opposed the U.S. invasion and occupation of Haiti (1915–1934); tried at the end of World War I to petition the Versailles Peace Conference on behalf of colonial populations; mobilized to circumvent the U.S. federal government's neutrality toward the Italian invasion of Ethiopia in 1934; and criticized U.S. policy toward the Belgian Congo in the 1960s.

The impact of these early campaigns, however, was largely symbolic. Not until the 1970s—in the aftermath of the civil rights movement and the emergence of a critical mass of black elected officials—did African Americans command the political resources necessary to promote a foreign policy agenda.

The decision to institutionalize a foreign policy lobby was the direct result of a Leadership Conference convened by the Congressional Black Caucus under the direction of congressmen Charles Diggs (Dem-Michigan) and Andrew Young (Dem-Georgia). On September 25, 1976, leaders from civil rights organizations and church, labor, business, and community development groups, as well as academics and elected officials, gathered in Washington, D.C., to discuss Africa policy. Their immediate concern was Secretary of State Henry Kissinger's maneuvers to protect white minority interests in Southern Rhodesia (now Zimbabwe), which was moving rapidly toward black majority rule. The conferees issued an "African-American Manifesto on Southern Africa" and pledged to mobilize a constituency for Africa. TransAfrica formed one year later, with Randall Robinson as its executive director.

Emerging out of support for liberation movements in Southern Africa, TransAfrica quickly developed an image as an antiapartheid group. This perception was further enhanced in 1985 by the success of its yearlong civil disobedience campaign in front of the South African embassy in Washington, D.C. The demonstrations drew thousands of protesters from around the country and culminated with the passage—over President Ronald Reagan's veto—of the Comprehensive Anti-Apartheid Act of 1986, which imposed sanctions on South Africa.

TransAfrica targeted aspects of policy that affect Africa and the Caribbean: development aid, debt relief, human rights and democratization, refugee issues, famine assistance, covert operations, the drug war, and advocacy for a postapartheid South Africa. In 1990 the forum began an International Careers Program to prepare black students for the foreign service exam. The Washington, D.C.–based lobby had chapters in Boston, the District of Columbia, Chicago, Detroit, and Cincinnati.

In 2004 the organization decided to focus its efforts on researching U.S. foreign policy and educating and informing the general public, government officials, and political officials. A name change to TransAfrica Forum signaled this decision.

See also Anti-Apartheid Movement; Haitian Revolution, American Reaction to the; Politics in the United States

Bibliography

Challenor, Herchelle Sullivan. "The Influence of Black Americans on U.S. Foreign Policy Toward Africa." In *Ethnicity and U.S. Foreign Policy*, rev. ed., edited by Abdul Aziz Said. New York: Praeger, 1981.

TransAfrica Forum. *A Retrospective: Blacks in U.S. Foreign Policy*. Washington, D.C.: Author, 1987.

PEARL T. ROBINSON (1996)
Updated by publisher 2005

Trindade, Solano

July 24, 1908
February 19, 1974

Together with Abdias do Nascimento, the poet and playwright Solano Trindade stands out as one of the most influential black Brazilian activists and intellectuals of the twentieth century. A native of Recife, Pernambuco, Francisco Solano Trindade migrated to Rio de Janeiro, where he would stand apart with other important black intellectuals in the rich cultural and political environment of the time. Before leaving Pernambuco, he participated in the formation of the Frente Negra Pernambucana (Pernambuco Black Front) in 1936. In 1937, with Vicente Lima and others, he established the Afro-Brazilian Cultural Center in Recife, which offered seminars, artistic productions, child education projects, women's support groups, and medical and dental assistance. The center also supported important publications, such as *Xangô*, a book by Vicente Lima. In 1934 and 1937 Trindade participated in the first and second Afro-Brazilian Congresses, held in Recife and in Salvador. Also during this time he traveled to Belo Horizonte and later to Pelotas, where he founded popular art groups.

Trindade settled in Rio de Janeiro in 1942. There was a vibrant debate over the racial question in Brazil, linking intellectuals, activists, and diverse political sectors. Trindade had—together with others—an important role in this political atmosphere. His close affiliations with the Communist Party and communist intellectuals, along with his poems of strong social critique, immediately made him a standout activist, fundamentally denouncing racism and the living conditions of the Afro-Brazilian population. His poems had a strong impact during the period, and with the unfolding of events in the 1970s and 1980s, when left-leaning artists and intellectuals found themselves repressed by the military government, they inspired new generations of intellectuals and popular artists. In the 1940s he also worked in the founding of the Afro-Brazilian Democratic Committee in Rio de Janeiro, where black intellectuals of various political-ideological convictions came together as neighbors and friends—such people as Alberto Guerreiro Ramos, Raimundo de Souza Dantas, Edison Carneiro, Sebastião Rodrigues Alves, and Abdias do Nascimento.

In the 1950s, together with his wife Margarida and others, he created the Brazilian Popular Theater. His theater had important repercussions, attracting black artists and addressing themes from Afro-Brazilian music, dance, and culture. Later, he rooted himself in São Paulo, specifically in the city of Embú, developing a hub of Afro-Brazilian culture and traditions, a movement that still exists under the direction of his daughter, Raquel Trindade.

Beyond his political activity, Solano Trindade stands apart in his artistic work—poems, re-adaptations of folklore, and paintings. He continued working in the city of Duque de Caxias—where his name is still remembered by the poor and black communities—until his death at age sixty-five.

See also Frente Negra Brasileira; Nascimento, Abdias do

Bibliography

Barcelos, Luiz Claúdio. "Mobilização Racial no Brasil: Uma Revisão Crítica." *Afro-Ásia* 17 (1996): 187-212.

Leite, José Correia. *E Disse o Velho Militante José Correia Leite: depoimentos e artigos/José Correia Leite, organização e textos Cuti.* São Paulo: Secretaria Municipal de Cultura, 1992.

Nascimento, Abdias do. *Genocídio do Negro Brasileiro.* Rio de Janeiro: Paz e Terra, 1978.

Nascimento, Abdias do. *O Negro Revoltado.* Rio de Janeiro: Vozes, 1982.

FLÁVIO GOMES (2005)
Translated by James H. Sweet

Tropical Diseases

The field of tropical medicine was first defined by European colonial explorers and settlers whose morbidity and mortality rates skyrocketed in areas such as West Africa and the Caribbean. Malaria, cholera, yellow fever, dysentery, leprosy, yaws, and elephantiasis were among the most common afflictions. In some cases, notably the use of quinine among the Incas, indigenous medical systems provided an important basis for therapy. Theories surrounding the origin and proliferation of these diseases focused on local climatic factors until the late nineteenth century, when scientists established the germ theory (Robert Koch and Louis Pasteur) and the transmissibility of infection by insect vectors (Patrick Manson).

With the increasing mobility of populations in the twentieth century, the notion of tropical disease broadened beyond geographic considerations to include biological, social, and cultural factors as well. The role of nutrition and sanitation in the spread (and control) of disease became clear. Studies undertaken by the National Medical Association (NMA) among selected black populations in the United States during the 1910s helped draw attention to these crucial environmental influences. The NMA's commissions on pellagra, hookworm, and tuberculosis performed investigations and issued annual reports. A prime mover in these studies was H. M. Green, a black physician from Knoxville, Tennessee, who cofounded the National Hospital Association in 1923. Another black physician, Hildrus A. Poindexter, became a specialist in tropical medicine and produced numerous epidemiological studies between 1931 and 1970. The work of such researchers became a prototype for the use of objective scientific criteria, rather than racial or geographic stereotypes, in the study of disease.

See also Mortality and Morbidity

Bibliography

Curtin, Philip D. *Disease and Empire: The Health of European Troops in the Conquest of Africa.* New York: Cambridge University Press, 1998.

Green, H. M. "Report of the Pellagra Commission." *Journal of the National Medical Association* 9 (October–December 1917): 223–227.

Haynes, Douglas M. *Imperial Medicine: Patrick Manson and the Conquest of Tropical Disease.* Philadelphia: University of Pennsylvania Press, 2001.

Poindexter, Hildrus A. *My World of Reality.* Detroit: Balamp, 1973.

PHILIP N. ALEXANDER (1996)
Updated bibliography

Trotter, James Monroe

February 7, 1842
February 26, 1892

The politician and author James Monroe Trotter was born in Grand Gulf, Mississippi, to Letitia, a slave, and Richard S. Trotter, her owner. Around 1854 Trotter sent Letitia and her children to the free city of Cincinnati, Ohio, where James attended the Gilmore School for former slaves. He continued his education in Hamilton and Athens, specializing in music and art, and he taught school in the area.

During the Civil War, Trotter enlisted as a private in the all-black 55th Massachusetts Regiment. Although initially the officers were white, Trotter rose rapidly through the ranks; by April 1864 he was a second lieutenant. The U.S. War Department, however, was slow to recognize the field commissions granted to Trotter and several other black men, and Trotter openly protested this discrimination. He also participated in the struggle for equal pay. In both the North and the South, black Union soldiers insisted on the same recognition that their white counterparts received. To Trotter and many of his fellow troops, the principle of racial justice was more important than immediate gratification; the two black regiments in Massachusetts went without pay for a full year before the U.S. Congress approved equal compensation.

After the war, Trotter moved to Boston and was appointed as a clerk in the U.S. Post Office. In 1868 he married Virginia Isaacs of Chillicothe, Ohio. The Trotters intended to demonstrate that black people could achieve the highest standards set by white society; thus they settled in a white neighborhood and sent their children to white schools. At the same time, they remained deeply committed to their racial identity, and they associated with prominent black families steeped in the abolitionist tradition. In 1878 Trotter realized his aims through the publication of *Music and Some Highly Musical People,* a pioneering tribute to African-American musical talent that employed a European model of artistic quality. The book sold more than seven thousand copies.

Trotter, like most African Americans during this period, was a Republican. He had been dismayed, however, by the Republicans' withdrawal of federal troops from the South in 1877. Personal evidence of the party's indifference to racial justice came in 1882, when Trotter himself was passed over for a promotion in favor of a white man. Trotter resigned from the post office and broke openly with the Republican Party. He became active in Democratic Party politics, campaigning for a successful gubernatorial candidate in 1883 and organizing a conference of black Democrats in Boston in 1886.

Meanwhile, Trotter pursued a variety of employment strategies, ranging from musical promotion to real estate. His shift in political allegiances, though, brought unexpected rewards. In 1887 President Grover Cleveland nominated Trotter as U.S. recorder of deeds, a position formerly held by Frederick Douglass. Although a U.S. Senate committee voted narrowly against confirmation, Trotter's appointment was approved by a majority in the full Senate, due largely to Republican support. He served the administration until 1889, when the Republicans were returned to the presidency.

Trotter died in February 1892 of the effects of tuberculosis. As a result of his lucrative recordership, he was able to leave substantial property to his family. His son, William Monroe, absorbed James Trotter's legacy of militancy and his commitment to integration and racial equality.

See also Civil War, U.S.; Douglass, Frederick; Military Experience, African-American

Bibliography

Berlin, Ira, ed. *Freedom: A Documentary History of Emancipation, 1861–1867.* Series II: *The Black Military Experience.* Cambridge, U.K.: 1982.

Fox, Stephen B. *The Guardian of Boston: William Monroe Trotter.* New York: Atheneum, 1970.

TAMI J. FRIEDMAN (1996)

Trotter, William Monroe

April 7, 1872
April 7, 1934

William Monroe Trotter, a newspaper editor and civil rights activist, was born in 1872 in Chillicothe, Ohio, the son of James Monroe Trotter and Virginia Isaacs Trotter. Raised in a well-to-do white Boston neighborhood, young Trotter absorbed the militant integrationism of his politically active father, a tradition that he carried on throughout his own life.

Elected president of his senior class by his white high school classmates, Trotter worked briefly as a clerk and entered Harvard College in the fall of 1891. He graduated magna cum laude in June 1895, and moved easily into Boston's elite black social set. In June 1899 he married Geraldine Louise Pindell. That same year he opened his own real estate firm.

By the turn of the century, Trotter and his peers were deeply concerned about worsening race relations in the South and signs of growing racial antagonism in the North. In March 1901 Trotter helped form the Boston Literary and Historical Association, which fostered intellectual debate among prosperous African Americans; he also joined the more politically active Massachusetts Racial Protective Association (MRPA). These organizations served as early forums for his denunciation of the virtually undisputed accommodationist leadership of Booker T. Washington. In contrast to Washington, Trotter defended liberal arts education for black people, championed electoral participation as a means of securing basic rights, and counseled agitation on behalf of racial justice. With fellow MRPA member George W. Forbes, Trotter embarked on what became his life work: the uncompromising advocacy of civil and political equality for African Americans, through the pages of the *Guardian.*

The *Guardian* newspaper, which began weekly publication in November 1901, offered news and analysis of the African-American condition. At the same time, it served as a base for independent political organizing led by Trotter himself. The "Trotterites" not only vilified their enemies in the pages of the *Guardian,* they also resorted to direct confrontation. On several occasions, Trotter and his supporters attempted (without success) to wrest control of the Afro-American Council from the pro–Booker T. Washington camp. More effective was their disruption of a speech Washington himself was scheduled to deliver in July 1903. Amid the fracas, Trotter delivered a litany of accusations and demanded of Washington, "Are the rope and the torch all the race is to get under your leadership?" He served a month in jail for his role in what was dubbed the "Boston Riot." After the incident, Trotter founded the Boston Suffrage League and the New England Suffrage League, through which he called for federal anti-lynching legislation, enforcement of the Fifteenth Amendment, and the end of racial segregation.

Although Trotter's editorial belligerence and unorthodox tactics were often disapproved of, many nonetheless respected his unswerving commitment to the cause of racial equality. They rose to Trotter's defense in the aftermath of the "riot" when Washington launched a malicious campaign—including surveillance, threats of libel, and the secret financing of competing publications—to intimidate and silence the *Guardian* and its editor. In this sense, Trotter's actions, and Washington's heavy-handed efforts to squelch them, helped crystallize the growing disaffection with Washington into an organizational alternative. Trotter was able to forge a successful, if temporary, alliance with W. E. B. Du Bois and other proponents of racial integration, and he participated in founding the Niagara Movement in 1905.

Trotter's political independence and confrontational style went beyond the fight against Booker T. Washington, however. He clashed repeatedly with the Niagara Movement over questions of personality and leadership, and he resolved to wage the fight for racial justice under the auspices of his own virtually all-black organization, the National Equal Rights League (NERL; originally founded as the Negro-American Political League in April 1908). Though Trotter attended the founding convention of the National Association for the Advancement of Colored People (NAACP) in May 1909, he kept his distance from the white-dominated association. Relations between NERL and the NAACP remained cool over the years, with occasional instances of cooperation to achieve common goals.

Trotter's zeal for direct action remained undiminished through the 1910s and 1920s. In a much-celebrated audience with Woodrow Wilson in 1914, Trotter challenged the president's segregationist policies. Wilson, viewing his adversary's candor as insolent and offensive, ordered the meeting to a close. The following year, Trotter led public protests against the showing of the film *The Birth of a Nation;* as a result of his renewed efforts in 1921, the movie was banned in Boston. In early 1919, denied a passport to travel to the Paris Peace Conference, he made his way to France disguised as a ship's cook, hoping to ensure that the Treaty of Versailles contained guarantees of racial equality; unable to influence the proceedings, he later testified against the treaty before the U.S. Congress. In 1926 Trotter again visited the White House to make the case against segregation in the federal government, this time before President Calvin Coolidge.

The *Guardian,* however, remained the primary outlet for Trotter's political convictions. Dependent largely on the contributions of black subscribers, the paper was often on shaky financial ground. It not only absorbed Trotter's time and energy, it also drained his assets: Having abandoned the real estate business early on in order to devote himself entirely to the *Guardian*, he gradually sold off his property to keep the enterprise afloat. By 1920, with Trotter's standing as a national figure eclipsed by both the NAACP and the Garvey movement, publication of the *Guardian* became even more difficult to sustain.

Over the years, the impassioned advocacy of militant integrationism remained the hallmark of Trotter's *Guardian*. Back in 1908, Trotter, rather than supporting the black community's creation of its own hospital, had called for integration of Boston's medical training facilities. He had insisted that short-term benefits could not outweigh the "far more ultimate harm in causing the Jim Crow lines to be drawn about us." Trotter was driven by that philosophy throughout his life, even in the face of opposition from other African Americans.

On April 7, 1934, Trotter either fell or jumped to his death from the roof of his apartment building. Although he no longer enjoyed a mass following, he was remembered as one who had made enormous personal sacrifices for the cause of racial equality.

See also Civil Rights Movement, U.S.; Du Bois, W. E. B.; Fifteenth Amendment; Garvey, Marcus; *Guardian, The*; Lynching; National Association for the Advancement of Colored People (NAACP); Niagara Movement; Washington, Booker T.

Bibliography

Bennett, Lerone, Jr. *Pioneers in Protest.* Baltimore: Johnson Publishing, 1968.

Fox, Stephen R. *The Guardian of Boston: William Monroe Trotter.* New York: Atheneum, 1970.

Harlan, Louis R. *Booker T. Washington: The Wizard of Tuskegee, 1901–1915.* New York: Oxford University Press, 1983.

TAMI J. FRIEDMAN (1996)

Troupe, Quincy

July 22, 1939

Quincy Thomas Troupe Jr. has successfully bridged literary and popular culture as a poet, performer, editor, publisher, biographer, scholar, educator, children's writer, screenwriter, art and music critic, and community arts activist. His career has been unified by a deeply rooted sense of place, a grounding in the blues/jazz matrix, a mediation between local and diasporic black experiences, and a commitment to honor what he calls "the continuum of African spirituality."

Troupe was born in St. Louis, Missouri, to Dorothy Marshall Smith Troupe and Quincy Troupe Sr., a catcher and manager for the Cleveland Buckeyes and, for six months, the Cleveland Indians. Quincy Troupe Jr. was raised in St. Louis in a politically active family, and as a boy he was an avid reader, a talented athlete, and a member of the church choir. He attended Grambling College in Louisiana, and he played for the Army basketball team in Europe for two years. A knee injury sent him home, and he then moved to Los Angeles, where he received an A.A. degree in journalism from Los Angeles City College in 1967.

Troupe joined the Watts Writers' Workshop, and during this fertile and volatile time he taught community-based creative writing workshops and black literature classes at the University of California, Los Angeles and the University of Southern California. He also co-edited *Shrewd* magazine, directed the Malcolm X Center in Los Angeles, and ran the John Coltrane Summer Festival. He went on to teach at Ohio University; Richmond College (in Staten Island, New York); the University of California, Berkeley; California State University, Sacramento; and the University of Ghana. Troupe spent many years in New York City, teaching at the College of Staten Island and Columbia University's Graduate Writing Program. He returned to the West Coast in 1990 to teach literature and creative writing at the University of California, San Diego.

While in Los Angeles, Troupe began his lifelong commitment to promoting the work of black writers and musicians by publishing the anthology *Watts Poets and Writers: A Book of New Poetry and Essays* (1968). In 1970 Troupe founded *Confrontation: A Journal of Third World Literature,* which led to one of his most significant contributions as an editor, *Giant Talk: An Anthology of Third World Writings* (1975). Troupe's other works include *The Inside Story of TV's "Roots"* (1978), written with David L. Wolper, which sold over a million copies. He paid tribute to his friend James Baldwin by soliciting essays for *James Baldwin: The Legacy* (1989), and he gained notoriety through his collaboration with Miles Davis on *Miles: The Autobiography* (1989) and the more personal *Miles and Me* (2000).

As a poet, Troupe fuses an international poetic sensibility with black American vernacular language and culture. His books include *Embryo Poems 1967–1971* (1972); *Snake-Back Solos: Selected Poems, 1969–1977* (1978); *Skulls Along the River* (1984); *Weather Reports: New and Selected Poems* (1991); *Avalanche: Poems* (1996); *Choruses: Poems* (1999); and *Transcircularities: New and Selected Poems* (2002). Troupe's densely packed, fast-moving poems are rooted in the cadences of black speech, shaped by the driving, improvisatory energy of jazz, and informed by irony, humor, and political anger. Described as "urbane and at times profane," Troupe is also a riveting performer who riffs like a horn soloist and personally engages his audience.

Troupe is the recipient of numerous grants and awards, including two American Book Awards. On June 11, 2002, Troupe was appointed California's first official poet laureate. However, he resigned this post and retired from his teaching position after it was revealed that he had falsified a B.A. degree from Grambling College.

See also Poetry, U.S.

Bibliography

Troupe, Quincy. *Root Doctor* (audio CD). New Alliance Records, 1995.

Turner, Douglas. "Miles and Me: An Interview with Quincy Troupe." *African American Review* 36, no. 3 (2002): 429–434.

LORRIE N. SMITH (2005)

Truth, Sojourner

c. 1797
November 26, 1883

Abolitionist, suffragist, and spiritualist Sojourner Truth was born Isabella Bomefree in Ulster County, New York, the second youngest of thirteen children born in slavery to Elizabeth (usually called Mau-Mau Bett) and James Bomefree. The other siblings were either sold or given away before her birth. The family was owned by Johannes Hardenbergh, a patroon and Revolutionary War patriot, the head of one of the most prominent Dutch families in late eighteenth-century New York.

Mau-Mau Bett was mystical and unlettered but imparted to her daughter strong faith, filial devotion, and a strong sense of individual integrity. Isabella Bomefree, whose first language was Dutch, was taken from her parents and sold to an English-speaking owner in 1808, who maltreated her because of her inability to understand English. Through her own defiance—what she later called her "talks with God"—and her father's intercession, a Dutch tavern keeper soon purchased her. Kindly treated but surrounded by the rough tavern culture and probably sexually abused, the girl prayed for a new master. In 1810 John I. Dumont of New Paltz, New York, purchased Isabella Bomefree for three hundred dollars.

Isabella remained Dumont's slave for eighteen years. Dumont boasted that Belle, as he called her, was "better to me than a man." She planted, plowed, cultivated, and harvested crops. She milked the farm animals, sewed, weaved, cooked, and cleaned house. But Mrs. Dumont despised and tormented her, possibly because Dumont fathered one of her children.

Isabella had two relationships with slave men. Bob, her first love, a man from a neighboring estate, was beaten senseless for "taking up" with her and was forced to take another woman. She later became associated with Thomas, with whom she remained until her freedom. Four of her five children survived to adulthood.

Although New York slavery ended for adults in 1827, Dumont promised Isabella her freedom a year earlier. When he refused to keep his promise, she fled with an infant child, guided by "the word of God," as she later related. She took refuge with Isaac Van Wagenen, who purchased her for the remainder of her time as a slave. She later adopted his family name.

Isabella Van Wagenen was profoundly shaped by a religious experience she underwent in 1827 at Pinkster time, the popular early summer African-Dutch slave holiday. As she recounted it, she forgot God's deliverance of his people from bondage and prepared to return to Dumont's farm for Pinkster: "I looked back in Egypt," she said, "and everything seemed so pleasant there." But she felt the mighty, luminous, and wrathful presence of an angry God blocking her path. Stalemated and momentarily blinded and suffocated under "God's breath," she claimed in *Narrative of Sojourner Truth,* Jesus mercifully intervened and proclaimed her salvation. This conversion enabled Isabella Van Wagenen to claim direct and special communication with Jesus and the Trinity for the remainder of her life, and she subsequently became involved with a number of highly spiritual religious groups.

A major test of faith followed Isabella Van Wagenen's conversion when she discovered that Dumont had illegally sold her son, Peter. Armed with spiritual assurance and a mother's rage, she scoured the countryside, gaining moral and financial support from prominent Dutch residents, antislavery Quakers, and local Methodists. She brought suit, and Peter was eventually returned from Alabama and freed.

In 1829 Isabella, now a Methodist, moved to New York City. She joined the African Methodist Episcopal Zion Church, where she discovered a brother and two sisters. She also began to attract attention for her extraordinary preaching, praying, and singing, although these talents were mainly employed among the Perfectionists (a sect of white radical mystics emerging from the Second Great Awakening who championed millennial doctrines and who equated spiritual piety with morality, social justice with true Christianity). As housekeeper for Perfectionist Elijah Pierson, Isabella was involved in "the Kingdom," a sect organized by the spiritual zealot Robert Matthias. Among other practices he engaged in "spirit-matching," or wife swapping, with Ann Folger, wife of

"Ar'n't I a Woman" Truth or Myth?

Nell Irvin Painter stunned many Americans when she published her iconoclastic 1996 biography, *Sojourner Truth: A Life, A Symbol.* Therein Painter struggled relentlessly to distinguish the actual life history of Sojourner Truth. In particular, Painter argued that though Truth is now widely credited with making her famed "Ar'n't I a Woman?" speech at an 1851 Akron Ohio women's rights convention, the historical record does not fully support the validity of this mythic moment.

Marius Robinson produced a straightforward report of Truth's comments at the Akron convention soon after it took place in 1851. His report differs quite significantly from Frances Dana Gage's 1863 article in the New York *Independent*, which eventually became the standard treatment of Truth's speech. Nowhere does Robinson suggest that the Akron auditorium was filled with women who were unskilled at public speaking, women who needed to be saved by a more self-confident Truth. Gage reported that Truth said, "'twixt all the niggers of de South and de women at the Norf, all a-talking 'bout rights, de white men will be in a fix pretty soon," at the beginning of her comments. Robinson placed this sentence at the end. It is also unclear, as Gage suggested, that Truth lost thirteen children to the slave trade. Most importantly, however, Robinson never recounted Truth having asked the question, "Ar'n't I a woman?," a phrase that is repeated four times in Gage's version of the speech. Though historians have known for some time that there were significant discrepancies between Gage's depiction of Truth's 1851 comments and Robinson's, Gage's narrative has become standard. Nell Painter argued that this has more to do with the fact that Gage's more dramatic comments serve contemporary interests better than do Robinson's more mundane words.

ROBERT REID-PHARR (2005)

Pierson's business partner. Elijah Pierson's unexplained death brought public outcries of foul play. To conceal Ann Pierson's promiscuity, the Folgers suggested that there had been an erotic attachment between Matthias and Isabella Van Wagenen and that they murdered Pierson with poisoned blackberries. Challenging her accusers, Isabella Van Wagenen vowed to "crush them with the truth." Lack of evidence and prejudice about blacks testifying against whites led to dismissal of the case. Isabella Van Wagenen triumphed by successfully suing the Folgers for slander. Although chastened by this experience with religious extremism, the association with New York Perfectionists enhanced her biblical knowledge, oratorical skills, and commitment to reform.

Isabella Van Wagenen encouraged her beloved son Peter to take up seafaring to avoid the pitfalls of urban crime. In 1843 his vessel returned without him. Devastated by this loss, facing (at forty-six) a bleak future in domestic service, and influenced by the millennarian (known as the Millerite movement) ferment sweeping the Northeast at the time, she decided to radically change her life. She became an itinerant preacher and adopted the name Sojourner Truth because voices directed her to sojourn the countryside and speak God's truth. In the fall of 1843 she became ill and was taken to the Northampton utopian community in Florence, Massachusetts, where black abolitionist David Ruggles nursed her at his water-cure establishment. Sojourner Truth impressed residents, who included a number of abolitionists, with her slavery accounts, scriptural interpretations, wit, and simple oral eloquence.

By 1846 Sojourner Truth had joined the antislavery circuit, traveling with Abby Kelly Foster, Frederick Douglass, William Lloyd Garrison, and British member of Parliament George Thompson. An electrifying public orator, she soon became one of the most popular speakers for the abolitionist cause. Her fame was heightened by the publication of her *Narrative* in 1850, related and transcribed by Olive Gilbert. With proceeds from its sale she purchased a Northampton home. In 1851, speaking before a National Women's Convention in Akron, Ohio, Sojourner Truth defended the physical and spiritual strength of women, in her famous "Ain't I a Woman?" speech. In 1853 Sojourner's antislavery, spiritualist, and temperance advocacy took her to the Midwest, where she settled among spiritualists in Harmonia, Michigan.

"I cannot read a book," said Sojourner Truth, "but I can read the people." She dissected political and social issues through parables of everyday life. The Constitution, silent on black rights, had a "little weevil in it." She was known for her captivating one-line retorts. An Indiana audience threatened to torch the building if she spoke. Sojourner Truth replied, "Then I will speak to the ashes." In the late 1840s, grounded in faith that God and moral suasion would eradicate bondage, she challenged her despairing friend Douglass with "Frederick, is God dead?" In 1858, when a group of men questioned her gender, claiming she wasn't properly feminine in her demeanor, Sojourner Truth, a bold early feminist, exposed her bosom to the entire assembly, proclaiming that shame was not hers but theirs.

During the Civil War Sojourner Truth recruited and supported Michigan's black regiment, counseled freedwomen, set up employment operations for freedpeople willing to relocate, and initiated desegregation of streetcars in Washington, D.C. In 1864 she had an audience with Abraham Lincoln. Following the war Sojourner Truth moved to Michigan, settling in Battle Creek, but remained active in numerous reform causes. She supported the Fifteenth Amendment and women's suffrage.

Disillusioned by the failure of Reconstruction, Sojourner Truth devoted her last years to the support of a black western homeland. In her later years, despite decades of interracial cooperation, she became skeptical of collaboration with whites and became an advocate of racial separation. She died in 1883 in Battle Creek, attended by the famous physician and breakfast cereal company founder John Harvey Kellogg.

See also Abolition; African Methodist Episcopal Zion Church; Free Blacks, 1619–1860

Bibliography

Fauset, Arthur H. *Sojourner Truth*. Chapel Hill: University of North Carolina Press, 1938.

Washington, Margaret, ed. *Narrative of Sojourner Truth*. New York: Vintage, 1993.

Yellin, Jean Fagan. *Women and Sisters: The Antislavery Feminists in American Culture*. New Haven, Conn.: Yale University Press, 1989.

MARGARET WASHINGTON (1996)

Tubman, Harriet

c. 1820

March 10, 1913

The abolitionist, nurse, and feminist Harriet Ross—later Harriet Ross Tubman—was one of eleven children born

Harriet Tubman at her home in Auburn, New York, 1911. *An escaped slave from Maryland, Tubman became the best-known leader of rescue expeditions on the Underground Railroad, bringing more than two hundred persons to freedom on at least fifteen trips to the South. Well before the Civil War, she had attained a legendary status among both slaves and abolitionists.* THE LIBRARY OF CONGRESS.

to the slaves Benjamin Ross and Harriet Green. She was born about 1820 in Dorchester County, Maryland. Although she was known on the plantation as Harriet Ross, her family called her Araminta, or Minty, a name given to her by her mother.

Early Years

Like most slaves, Ross had no formal education and began work on the plantation as a child. When she was five years old, her master rented her out to a neighboring family, the Cooks, as a domestic servant. At age thirteen, Ross suffered permanent neurological damage after either her overseer or owner struck her in the head with a two-pound lead weight when she placed herself between her master and a fleeing slave. For the rest of her life, she experienced sudden blackouts.

In 1844 she married John Tubman, a free black who lived on a nearby plantation. Her husband's free status, however, did not transfer to Harriet through marriage. Between 1847 and 1849, after the death of her master, Tubman worked in the household of Anthony Thompson, a physician and preacher. Thompson was the legal guardian of Tubman's new master, who was still too young to operate the plantation. When the young master died, Tubman faced an uncertain future, and rumors circulated that Thompson would sell slaves out of the state.

In response, Tubman escaped from slavery in 1849, leaving behind her husband, who refused to accompany her. She settled in Philadelphia, where she found work as a scrubwoman. She returned to Maryland for her husband two years later, but John Tubman had remarried.

Underground Railroad

Tubman's successful escape to the free state of Pennsylvania, however, did not guarantee her safety, particularly after the passage of the Fugitive Slave Law of 1850, which facilitated southern slaveholders' efforts to recover runaway slaves. Shortly after her escape from slavery, Tubman became involved in the abolitionist movement, forming friendships with one of the black leaders of the Underground Railroad, William Still, and white abolitionist Thomas Garrett. While many of her abolitionist colleagues organized antislavery societies, wrote and spoke against slavery, and raised money for the cause, Tubman's activities were more directly related to the actual freeing of slaves through the Underground Railroad. She worked as an agent on the railroad, assuming different disguises to assist runaways in obtaining food, shelter, clothing, cash, and transportation. Tubman might appear as a feeble old woman or as a demented, impoverished man, and she was known for the rifle she carried on rescue missions, both for her own protection and to intimidate fugitives who might become fainthearted along the journey.

Tubman traveled to the South nineteen times to rescue approximately three hundred African-American men, women, and children from bondage. Her first rescue mission was to Baltimore, Maryland, in 1850 to help her sister and two children escape. Her notoriety as a leader of the Underground Railroad led some Maryland planters to offer a $40,000 bounty for her capture. Having relocated many runaways to Canada, Tubman herself settled in the village of Saint Catharines, Canada West (now Ontario), in the early 1850s. She traveled to the South in 1851 to rescue her brother and his wife, and returned in 1857 to rescue her parents, with whom she resettled in Auburn, New York, shortly thereafter.

Tubman's involvement in the abolitionist movement placed her in contact with many progressive social leaders in the North, including John Brown, whom she met in 1858. She helped Brown plan his raid on Harpers Ferry, Virginia, in 1859, but illness prevented her from participating. Tubman's last trip to the South took place in 1860, after which she returned to Canada. In 1861, she moved back to the United States as the last of eleven southern states seceded from the Union.

Civil War and Thereafter

When the Civil War broke out, Tubman served in the Union army as a scout, spy, and nurse. In 1862 she went to Beaufort, South Carolina, where she nursed both white soldiers and black refugees from neighboring plantations. Tubman traveled from camp to camp in the coastal regions of South Carolina, Georgia, and Florida, using her nursing skills wherever they were needed. Tubman also worked as a scout for the Union army, traveling behind enemy lines to gather information and recruit slaves. She supported herself by selling chickens, eggs, root beer, and pies. After returning briefly to Beaufort, Tubman worked during the spring and summer of 1865 at a freedman's hospital in Fortress Monroe, Virginia.

After the war ended, Tubman eventually returned to Auburn to care for her elderly parents. Penniless, she helped support her family by farming. In 1869 Tubman married Nelson Davis, a Civil War veteran. That same year, she published *Scenes in the Life of Harriet Tubman,* written for her by Sarah H. Bradford and printed and circulated by Gerrit Smith and Wendell Phillips. Tubman received some royalties from the book, but she was less successful in her effort to obtain financial compensation for her war work. She agitated for nearly thirty years for $1,800 compensation for her service as a Civil War nurse and cook. In 1890, Congress finally awarded Tubman a monthly pension of $20, not for her own work but because she was the widow of a war veteran.

Tubman's activism continued on many fronts after the Civil War. She was an ardent supporter of women's suffrage and regularly attended women's rights meetings. To Tubman, racial liberation and women's rights were inextricably linked. Tubman formed close relationships with Susan B. Anthony and other feminists. She was a delegate to the first convention of the National Federation of Afro-American Women in 1896 (later called the National Association of Colored Women). The following year, the New England Women's Suffrage Association held a reception in Tubman's honor.

While living in Auburn, Tubman continued her work in the black community by taking in orphans and the elderly, often receiving assistance from wealthier neighbors. She helped establish schools for former slaves and wanted to establish a permanent home for poor and sick blacks. Tubman secured twenty-five acres in Auburn through a bank loan but lacked the necessary funds to build on the land. In 1903, she deeded the land to the African Methodist Episcopal Zion Church, and five years later the congregation built the Harriet Tubman Home for Indigent and Aged Negroes, which continued to operate for several years after Tubman's death and was declared a National Historic Landmark in 1974.

Tubman died on March 10, 1913, at the age of ninety-three. Local Civil War veterans led the funeral march. The National Association of Colored Women later paid for the funeral and for the marble tombstone over Tubman's grave. A year after her death, black educator Booker T. Washington delivered a memorial address in celebration of Tubman's life and labors and on behalf of freedom. In 1978, the United States Postal Service issued the first stamp in its Black Heritage series to honor Tubman.

Tubman was called the Moses of her people and had attained legendary status in the African-American community within ten years of her escape to freedom. Perhaps more than any other figure of her time, she personified resistance to slavery, and she became a symbol of courage and strength to African Americans, both slave and free. The secrecy surrounding Tubman's activities on the Underground Railroad and her own reticence about her role contributed to her mythic status. Heroic images of the rifle-carrying Tubman have persisted into the twentieth-first century, when she continues to be the leading symbol of the Underground Railroad.

See also Abolition; National Association of Colored Women; Runaway Slaves in the United States; Slave Narratives; Still, William; Underground Railroad

▪▪ *Bibliography*

Bradford, Sarah. *Harriet Tubman: The Moses of Her People* (1886). New York: Corinth Books, 1961.

Clinton, Catherine. *Harriet Tubman: The Road to Freedom.* Boston: Little, Brown, 2004.

Conrad, Carl. *Harriet Tubman.* Washington, D.C.: Associated, 1943.

Larson, Kate Clifford. *Bound for the Promised Land: Harriet Tubman, Portrait of an American Hero.* New York: Ballantine, 2004.

Litwack, Leon, and August Meier. *Black Leaders of the Nineteenth Century.* Urbana: University of Illinois Press, 1988.

LOUISE P. MAXWELL (1996)
Updated bibliography

Turner, Benjamin Sterling

March 17, 1825
March 21, 1894

Born into slavery near Weldon, North Carolina, congressman and merchant Benjamin S. Turner was taken by his owner, a widow, to Alabama when he was five. Allegedly taught by his owner's children to read, Turner was sold when he was twenty. His new master permitted him to hire his own time. As a result, Turner became a successful merchant and ran a thriving livery stable. After the Civil War he ran an omnibus company and accumulated property in Selma, Alabama.

Turner became involved in local politics, serving as a tax collector for Dallas County and later on the city council of Selma. In 1870 he was easily elected to Congress. While he never addressed the floor, two of Turner's eloquent speeches were read into the *Congressional Record*. One speech called for a refund of the cotton tax levied on the South, which Turner claimed was economically crippling to blacks and whites alike. The other, much less controversial, proposed federal grants to help rebuild government buildings in Selma destroyed by the war.

Turner was generally loyal to the Republican Party, almost always voting the party line on such issues as education, the test oath, and civil rights. A proponent of reconciliation, Turner also urged amnesty for ex-Confederates. In 1872 Turner faced freeborn African American Philip Joseph for the nomination. Both candidates ran anyway, split the vote, and the Democrat won. In March 1873, Turner returned to Alabama and his business. Although he participated in Republican conventions, he never again ran for office. After losing much of his fortune during the recession in the 1870s, he returned to farming and died in Alabama in 1894 in relative poverty and obscurity.

See also Entrepreneurs and Entrepreneurship; Free Blacks, 1619–1860; Politics in the United States

Bibliography

Christopher, Maurine. *Black Americans in Congress.* New York: Crowell, 1976.

Foner, Eric. *Freedom's Lawmakers: A Directory of Black Officeholders during Reconstruction.* New York: Oxford University Press, 1993.

McFarlin, Annjennette Sophie. *Black Congressional Reconstruction Orators and their Orations, 1869–1879.* Metuchen, N.J.: Scarecrow Press, 1976.

ALANA J. ERICKSON (1996)

Turner, Henry McNeal

February 1, 1834
May 8, 1915

Born free in Newberry Courthouse, South Carolina, Henry McNeal Turner, a theologian and African colonizationist, worked picking cotton during his youth. He experienced an emotional conversion at a camp meeting as a teenager. Licensed to preach by the Methodist Episcopal Church–South in 1853, he took to the road as a traveling evangelist. In 1858 he joined the African Methodist Episcopal (AME) Church in St. Louis and spent the next five years as an AME pastor in Baltimore and in Washington, D.C. In 1863 he organized the first regiment of the U.S. Colored Troops in his churchyard and was commissioned as chaplain, becoming probably the first African-American army chaplain. He was present at battles in Petersburg, Virginia, and Fort Fisher, North Carolina.

After the Civil War Turner traveled to Georgia, where he was briefly a Freedmen's Bureau agent. Appointed presiding elder of AME missions in Georgia, Turner was largely responsible for the tremendous growth of the AME Church in the state. In 1867 he was elected a delegate to the Georgia constitutional convention. There he primarily supported conservative and elitist positions, such as a clemency petition for Jefferson Davis and opposition to land reform and tax sales of planter property, although he supported the creation of public schools. In 1868 he was elected to the Georgia legislature. The following year, all African-American representatives were illegally expelled from the legislature. Turner was then named postmaster in Macon, Georgia, but resigned after white Macon residents exposed his association with a prostitute. In 1870 he returned to the legislature. His political career was marked by growing distrust for whites and support for problack measures such as protection for sharecroppers.

Turner largely abandoned politics in the early 1870s, although he was a candidate to the national convention of the Prohibition Party in the mid-1880s. He did continue to speak out on issues, however. He was an outspoken advocate of the Civil Rights Act of 1875 and strongly denounced the U.S. Supreme Court for voiding most of that legislation eight years later. During the late 1890s he was a passionate opponent of imperialist measures, such as the U.S. annexation of Hawaii, and he called the takeover of the Philippines "the crime of the century." In 1906 Turner joined with W. E. B. Du Bois and others in founding the Georgia Equal Rights League.

In 1876 Turner was named manager of the AME Book Concern in Philadelphia. During the following years, he published the *Christian Recorder* journal, compiled a hymnbook, wrote *The Genius of Methodist Polity* (1885), and put together a catechism of the AME Church. In 1880 he was elected a bishop in the AME Church, one of the first southerners to become a church leader, although his election was opposed by several northern bishops. He soon became a controversial figure in the church as a result of his advocacy of services with elaborate vestments and rituals along with his emotional preaching style. Turner believed it was the church's duty to instill pride and self-respect in its members. A forerunner of the black theology movement, he rejected white teachings of black inferiority. Explaining that blacks had no less right than whites to depict the Creator in their own image, he called for a black translation of the Bible and often stated that "God is a Negro." In 1885 Turner became the first minister to ordain a woman, Sarah Ann Hughes, to the ministry. His act was later rescinded by Bishop Jabez Campbell at the 1887 North Carolina Annual Conference of Bishops. In 1890 he was named chair of the board of Atlanta's Morris Brown College, which in 1900 founded the Turner Theological Seminary in his honor. In 1892 he became editor of the monthly AME magazine, *Voice of Missions,* and published articles on discrimination, black history, and other issues. In 1900 Turner left the journal and began his own organ, *Voice of the People.*

Turner is best known for his black nationalist ideas and advocacy of African colonization. As early as 1866 he had expressed interest in emigration, and in 1876 he drew widespread black criticism by serving as vice president of the American Colonization Society, still despised by many blacks as a racist group. By the 1880s he had become convinced that there was no future for blacks in the United States, and in 1893 he organized an Afro-American convention in Cincinnati, where he strongly urged blacks to emigrate to Africa in order to Christianize the continent and to build up black businesses and governments. He insisted that the federal government finance the project as reparation for slavery.

Turner himself made four trips to Africa during the 1890s. In 1891 he traveled to Liberia to found schools and to convert Liberians to Christianity. He founded annual conferences there, in Sierra Leone, in British South Africa (where he named a "vicar-bishop"), and in the Transvaal. His opponents attacked him for his overly positive depiction of life in Africa and his unrealistic plans for mass emigration. His conservatism and belief in building separate black institutions led him, on occasion, like Marcus Garvey in a later generation, into questionable alliances with race-baiting white politicians.

In the mid-1890s two boatloads of African Americans left for Liberia, but they faced hardship and many later returned. The failure of this mission helped discredit Turner's emigration program. His influence waned after 1900, but he remained active. In 1915, while in Windsor, Ontario, for a church function, he died of a stroke. Despite some idiosyncrasies, Turner was a passionate defender of the cultural and political independence of African Americans and was the most influential black nationalist of the second half of the nineteenth century.

See also African Methodist Episcopal Church; Bureau of Refugees, Freedmen, and Abandoned Lands; Nationalism in the United States in the Nineteenth Century

Bibliography

Angell, Stephen Ward. *Bishop Henry McNeal Turner and African-American Religion in the South.* Knoxville: University of Tennessee Press, 1992.

Redkey, Edwin. *Black Exodus: Black Nationalist and Back-to-Africa Movements, 1890–1910.* New Haven, Conn.: Yale University Press, 1969.

Redkey, Edwin, ed. *Respect Black: The Writings and Speeches of Henry McNeal Turner.* New York: Arno Press, 1971.

STEPHEN W. ANGELL (1996)

Turner, Lorenzo Dow

January 1895
February 10, 1972

Linguist and ethnologist Lorenzo Dow Turner, the first important African-American linguist, is best known for the book *Africanisms in the Gullah Dialect* (1949) and for scholarly articles tracing the influence of African languages on African-American speech. He was born in Elizabeth City, North Carolina. He attended Howard University Academy, graduating in 1910, then entered Howard University, where he received his bachelor's degree in 1914.

He then attended Harvard University, where he received a master's degree in English in 1917. The same year, Turner was hired as chair of the English Department of Howard University. During his time at Howard Turner studied for a doctoral degree in English at the University of Chicago, receiving his Ph.D. in 1926. His thesis, "Anti-Slavery Sentiment in American Literature Prior to 1865," was published in 1929.

In 1928 Turner left Howard University, and he and his brother Arthur began a short-lived newspaper, the *Washington Sun,* with Turner serving as editor. After the paper's demise, Turner accepted a position as head of the English Department at Fisk University in Nashville, Tennessee. In addition to teaching, Turner was coeditor with Otelia Cromwell and Eva Dykes of a literary textbook, *Readings from Negro Authors for Schools and Colleges* (1931).

During the period Turner taught summer courses at various black colleges. Through his work he became interested in rural southern black English dialects. In 1929 he first heard and became interested in the Gullah dialect. The following year, he began to attend summer Institutes of the Linguistics Society (of which he became the first African-American member in 1931), and from 1932 through 1935 he did field work and collected data for the Linguistics Atlas Project on Gullah and Louisiana Creole. Turner and other scholars, notably Melville Herskovits, rebutted the popular assumption that no artifacts of African culture had survived in the New World. Having studied Gullah, Turner began to study African languages to find similarities. In the late 1930s he received a series of grants that allowed him to study African languages in England and France. In 1940 he spent a year in Brazil, where he compiled large amounts of data on customs and language. In the years following his return he published a series of articles based on his research. His research culminated in a book, *Africanisms in the Gullah Dialect* (1949). In this work Turner presented transcribed texts and word lists and explained the relationship between Gullah and African languages of the Niger-Kordofanian family in terms of etymology, syntax, grammar, and pronunciation. His work inspired linguistic studies of Creole dialects, a reevaluation of the role of Black English, and more generally, the nature of African retentions in southern African-American cultures.

In 1944 Turner moved from Fisk's English department to become director of its Inter-Departmental Curriculum in African Studies. Two years later he accepted an invitation to join the faculty of Roosevelt College, an experimental integrated college in Chicago, as professor of English and lecturer in African culture. Turner remained at Roosevelt until his death. During these years he published articles on jazz, Zulu culture, Western education in Africa, and African-American literature. His expertise in African linguistics served him well when he was made Peace Corps Faculty Coordinator at Roosevelt in the early 1960s. He prepared two works dealing with the Krio language, spoken in Sierra Leone, for Peace Corps volunteers assigned there: *An Anthology of Krio Folklore and Literature with Notes and Inter-linear Translations in English* (1963) and *Krio Texts: With Grammatical Notes and Translations in English* (1965). Turner died in Chicago.

See also Africanisms; English, African-American; Gullah

Bibliography

Turner, Lorenzo Dow. *Africanisms in the Gullah Dialect* (1949). Ann Arbor: University of Michigan Press, 1974.

Wade-Lewis, Margaret. "Lorenzo Dow Turner: Pioneer African-American Linguist." *Black Scholar* 21, no. 4 (Fall 1991): 10–24.

GREG ROBINSON (1996)

Turner, Nat

See Nat Turner's Rebellion

Tuskegee Syphilis Experiment

In the early twentieth century, African Americans in the South faced numerous public health problems, including tuberculosis, hookworm, pellagra, and rickets; their death rates far exceeded those of whites. The public health problems of blacks had several causes—poverty, ignorance of proper health procedures, and inadequate medical care—all compounded by racism that systematically denied African Americans equal services. In an effort to alleviate these problems, in 1912 the federal government united all of its health-related activities under the Public Health Service (PHS). One of the primary concerns of the PHS was syphilis, a disease that was thought to have a moral as well as a physiological dimension. In 1918 a special Division of Venereal Diseases within the PHS was created.

In the late 1920s the PHS joined forces with the Rosenwald Fund (a private philanthropic foundation based in Chicago) to develop a syphilis control program for blacks in the South. Most doctors assumed that blacks suffered a much higher infection rate than whites because blacks abandoned themselves to promiscuity. And once infected, the argument went, blacks remained infected because they were too poor and too ignorant to seek medical care. To test these theories, PHS officers selected communities in six different southern states, examined the local black populations to ascertain the incidence of syphilis, and offered free treatment to those who were infected. This pilot program had hardly gotten underway, however, when the stock market collapse in 1929 forced the Rosenwald Fund to terminate its support, and the PHS was left without sufficient funds to follow up its syphilis control work among blacks in the South.

Macon County, Alabama, was the site of one of those original pilot programs. Its county seat, Tuskegee, was the home of the famed Tuskegee Institute. It was in and around Tuskegee that the PHS had discovered an infection rate of 35 percent among those tested, the highest incidence in the six communities studied. In fact, despite the presence of the Tuskegee Institute, which boasted a well-equipped hospital that might have provided low-cost health care to blacks in the region, Macon County was home not only to the worst poverty but the most sickly residents the PHS uncovered anywhere in the South. It was precisely this ready-made laboratory of human suffering that prompted the PHS to return to Macon County in 1932. Since they could not afford to treat syphilis, the PHS officers decided to document the damage to its victims by launching a study of the effects of untreated syphilis on black males. Many white southerners (including physicians) believed that although practically all blacks had syphilis, it did not harm them as severely as it did whites. PHS officials, however, knew that syphilis was a serious threat to the health of black Americans, and they intended to use the results of the study to pressure southern state legislatures into appropriating funds for syphilis control work among rural blacks.

Armed with these good motives, the PHS launched the Tuskegee Study in 1932. It involved approximately four hundred black males who tested positive for the disease, as well as two hundred nonsyphilitic black males to serve as controls. In order to secure cooperation, the PHS told the local residents that they had returned to Macon County to treat people who were ill. The PHS did not inform the study subjects that they had syphilis. Instead, the men were told they had "bad blood," a catchall phrase rural blacks used to describe a host of ailments.

Although the PHS had not intended to treat the men, state health officials demanded, as the price of their cooperation, that the men be given at least enough medication to render them noninfectious. Consequently, all of the men received a little treatment. No one worried much about the glaring contradiction of offering treatment in a study of untreated syphilis because the men would not receive enough treatment to cure them. Thus, the experiment was scientifically flawed from the outset.

Although the original plan called for a one-year experiment, the Tuskegee Study continued until 1972, partly because many of the health officers became fascinated by the scientific potential of a long-range study of syphilis. No doubt others rationalized the study by telling themselves that the men were too poor to afford proper treatment, or that too much time had passed for treatment to be of any benefit. The health officials, in some cases, may have seen the men as clinical material rather than human beings.

At any rate, as a result of the Tuskegee Study approximately one hundred black men died of untreated syphilis, scores went blind or insane, and still others endured lives of chronic ill health from syphilis-related complications. Throughout this suffering, the PHS made no effort to treat the men, and on several occasions steps were taken to prevent them from getting treatment on their own. As a result, the men did not receive penicillin when it became widely available after World War II.

During those same four decades, civil protests raised America's concern for the rights of black people, and the ethical standards of the medical profession regarding the treatment of nonwhite patients changed dramatically. These changes had no impact, however, on the Tuskegee Study. PHS officials published no fewer than thirteen scientific papers on the experiment (several of which appeared in the nation's leading medical journals), and the PHS routinely presented sessions on it at medical conventions. The Tuskegee Study ended in 1972 because a whistle-blower in the PHS, Peter Buxtun, leaked the story to the press. At first, health officials tried to defend their actions, but public outrage quickly silenced them, and they agreed to end the experiment. As part of an out-of-court settlement, the survivors were finally treated for syphilis. In addition, the men, and the families of the deceased, received small cash payments.

The forty-year deathwatch had finally ended, but its legacy can still be felt. In the wake of its hearings, Congress enacted new legislation to protect the subjects of human experiments. The Tuskegee Study left behind a host of unanswered questions about the social and racial attitudes of the medical establishment in the United States. It served as a cruel reminder of how class distinctions and racism could negate ethical and scientific standards.

See also Race and Science

Bibliography

Jones, James H. *Bad Blood: The Tuskegee Syphilis Experiment,* expanded edition. (Originally published in 1981.) New York: Free Press, 1993.

Reverby, Susan M., ed. *Tuskegee's Truths: Rethinking the Tuskegee Syphilis Study*. Foreword by James H. Jones. Chapel Hill: University of North Carolina Press, 2000.

"The Tuskegee Study." 3 parts. *Jet,* November 9, 16, 23, 1972.

University of Virginia Health System. "Bad Blood: The Troubling Legacy of the Tuskegee Syphilis Study." Available from http://hsc.virginia.edu/hs-library/historical/apology.

JAMES H. JONES (1996)
Updated bibliography

TUSKEGEE UNIVERSITY

Tuskegee University was founded in 1881 as the Normal School for colored teachers at Tuskegee in Alabama's Macon County, as the result of a political deal made between local white politicians and Lewis Adams, a leading black citizen. In exchange for black votes, Arthur Brooks and Col. Wilbur Foster, candidates for the Alabama legislature, promised to seek state appropriation for a black normal school in Tuskegee. Adams successfully rallied black support, and on February 10, 1881, House Bill No. 165 was passed, appropriating $2,000 annually for a black state and normal school in Tuskegee. The act prohibited the charge of tuition and mandated a minimum of twenty-five students to open.

Booker T. Washington was recommended to organize the school by his mentor, Gen. Samuel Chapman Armstrong, the founder of Virginia's Hampton Institute, although Tuskegee's trustees had specifically requested a white man. Washington had been Armstrong's best student at Hampton, where he fully accepted Armstrong's philosophy that the first step for blacks was economic and moral uplift.

When Booker T. Washington arrived at Tuskegee on June 24, 1881, there was no actual school to open, just an appropriation and authorization by the Alabama state legislature. Before selecting a location, Washington met with local white supporters, toured the area to recruit students, and investigated existing living and educational conditions for Tuskegee's black population. Washington selected a shack next to Butler Chapel, the African Methodist Episcopal Church on Zion Hill, where Lewis Adams was superintendent, as the site for the school. The school officially opened on July 4, 1881, as a secondary normal school with thirty students.

By July 14, 1881, Tuskegee Normal School had more than forty students ranging in age from sixteen to forty, most of whom were already public school teachers in Macon County. As enrollment increased, Washington recruited other Hampton and Fisk graduates to teach, including Olivia A. Davidson (who served as lady principal from 1881 until her death in 1889 and who married Washington in 1886). He decided that a larger facility would soon be needed. He wrote to J. F. B. Marshall, the treasurer of Hampton Institute, and requested a loan of $200 to purchase a new farm site. Although the school could not make such loans, Marshall personally loaned Washington the money, enabling him to make a down payment on the Bowen estate.

The Bowen estate, owned by William B. Bowen, was located one mile south of town. The main house had been burned down during the Civil War, leaving two cabins, a stable, and a chicken house. In keeping with his philosophy of self-knowledge, self-help, and self-control, Washington required students to clean and rebuild the Bowen estate while attending classes. By requiring such manual labor of his students, Washington was attempting to demonstrate that others were willing to help them—provided that they help themselves.

The money acquired to complete the payments on the Bowen estate came from many sources, including northern philanthropy and student fund-raisers, such as benefit suppers and student "literary entertainments," organized by Olivia Davidson. Payments on the Bowen estate were completed in April 1882.

Washington's philosophy of industrial education made Tuskegee Normal School a controversial model of black progress. Washington supported the use of manual labor as a moral training device, and he believed that manual labor would build students' character and improve their minds. In implementing a program of mandatory labor and industrial education, Washington had four basic objectives: to teach the dignity of labor, to teach the trades, to fulfill the demand for trained industrial leaders, and to offer students a way to pay expenses while attending the school (although no student, regardless of his or her economic standing, was exempt from this labor requirement). Washington also considered industrial education to be valuable because it trained students in specific skills that would prepare them for jobs. However, Tuskegee's graduates primarily became members of the teaching profession. Instructors also offered academic and normal courses in botany, literature, rhetoric, astronomy, and geography in addition to the much publicized industrial courses.

Tuskegee expanded steadily over the years with money acquired from the northern speaking tours of Olivia Davidson and Booker T. Washington. Davidson began touring New England in spring 1882, soliciting support door to door on weekdays and speaking in churches and Sunday schools during the evenings and on weekends. Washington began his own fund-raising tour on May 1, 1882, in Farmington, Connecticut. He traveled through the North with letters of introduction from such prominent southern officials as Henry Clay Armstrong, the state superintendent, and Gov. Rufus W. Cobb. By the end of May, they had collected more than $5,000 for the expansion of Tuskegee Normal and Industrial Institute.

Porter Hall was the first new building erected, named in honor of a generous Brooklyn businessman, Alfred Haynes Porter. The three-story building housed recitation rooms on the first floor, a chapel and library on the second floor, and the girls' dormitory on the third floor. Up to this time the boys stayed with neighboring black families. Shortly after Porter Hall was completed, Washington arranged to rent several nearby cottages to house the boys, until their three-story dormitory, Armstrong Hall, was completed in 1888.

State funding for Tuskegee was increased in 1883 when the Alabama state legislature approved an additional $1,000 appropriation. The school also began receiving a $500 annual appropriation from the Peabody Fund in 1883 and $1,000 annual awards from the Slater Fund in 1884. Philanthropic funding to Tuskegee Normal and Industrial Institute signified the extent of northern support for black industrial education.

In addition to fund-raisers, grants, and philanthropic support, money was raised for Tuskegee through brick making, which Washington began at the school in 1883, though its long-term contribution to Tuskegee's financial health was more symbolic than practical.

In 1892 the Alabama legislature adopted an act to incorporate Tuskegee Normal and Industrial Institute, legally changing the school's name. After 1895 new buildings replaced those built from northern philanthropy. With names like Rockefeller, Huntington, and Carnegie, these buildings indicated support from the northern, chiefly New York–based business community. Such support increased Tuskegee's property value to more than $300,000 by 1901 and facilitated the growth of the faculty and student body.

On April 1, 1896, Booker T. Washington wrote to George Washington Carver, an agricultural chemist who had just completed his M.A. at Iowa State College of Agricultural and Mechanical Arts, and offered him a position as the head of the agriculture department at a salary of $1,500. Carver arrived shortly thereafter and established the Agriculture Experiment Station, where research was conducted in crop diversification. Carver taught Tuskegee's students, emphasizing the need for improved agricultural practices and self-reliance, and also made a great effort to educate Tuskegee's black residents. He garnered national and international fame in the 1920s for his experiments with sweet potatoes, cowpeas, and peanuts.

Both Carver and Washington left a powerful legacy of manual and agricultural training at Tuskegee. Their educational philosophies had a lasting impact upon Tuskegee's curriculum and continued to influence the school's direction. After Washington's death in 1915, it had become apparent to many that Tuskegee's industrial training was increasingly obsolete in the face of rapid technological transformation in American business. The school thus entered a new era, shifting its emphasis from industrial to vocational education.

In 1915 Robert R. Moton became the second principal of Tuskegee, and although he practiced Washington's accommodationist style, he moved the school forward in directions that Washington had refused to move. Despite white opposition, Moton was instrumental in bringing a veterans' hospital to Tuskegee in 1923. He ensured that the institution, like Tuskegee Normal and Industrial Institute, was staffed entirely by blacks. Under Moton's direction, a college curriculum was developed in 1927. Two years later, Tuskegee's students demanded a shift away from "Washington's education." Moton heeded their voices and coordinated a new emphasis on science and technology.

Robert R. Moton was succeeded by Frederick D. Patterson in 1935. Patterson's administration also brought fundamental changes to the school, reflected in the name change to Tuskegee Institute in 1937. During World War II Patterson pursued the placement of a program for the segregated training of black pilots in Tuskegee, an action that was criticized by the NAACP. From 1939 to 1943 the air force trained more than nine hundred black pilots at Tuskegee, establishing the Tuskegee Army Airfield in 1941. Patterson also obtained significant state funding for the establishment of a graduate program (1943), a school of veterinary medicine (1945), and a school of nursing (1953).

In its entire history, Tuskegee has had only five presidents. Subsequent presidents have included Luther H. Foster (1953–1981) and Benjamin F. Payton (1981–). Foster modernized and expanded Washington's emphasis on the trade industry and established the College of Arts and Sciences and the School of Business. He led Tuskegee through the civil rights movement, when in 1968, Tuskegee students briefly held members of the board of trustees hostage in an attempt to force changes in campus policies. When Benjamin E. Payton assumed control of the school in its centennial anniversary, Tuskegee boasted five thousand acres, 150 buildings, and an endowment of more than $22 million. Payton presided over the school's name change to Tuskegee University in 1985, and in 1989 he also undertook a major fund-raising effort for the school, the largest ever attempted by a black college.

Although the school's curriculum and focus shifted over the years, the school continued to emphasize business, scientific, and technical instruction, a legacy of both Washington and Carver. In 1994 Tuskegee University had 3,598 students; the number had dropped to about 3,000 in 2004, but that year's record-setting entering class included over a thousand students. It offered fifty programs of study, twenty-one master's degrees, and a doctor of veterinary medicine degree—the only historically black college to grant such a degree. Distinguished alumni include novelist Ralph Ellison, actor Keenan Ivory Wayans, and Arthur W. Mitchell, the first black Democratic congressman.

See also Carver, George Washington; Education in the United States; Fisk University; Howard University; Lincoln University; Moton, Robert Russa; Washington, Booker T.

Bibliography

Anderson, James. *The Education of Blacks in the South, 1865–1935*. Chapel Hill: University of North Carolina Press, 1988.

Bowman, J. Wilson. *America's Black Colleges: The Comprehensive Guide to Historically and Predominantly Black 4-Year Colleges and Universities*. Pasadena, Calif.: J. Wilson Bowman,1992.

Harlan, Louis R. *Booker T. Washington: The Wizard of Tuskegee, 1901–1915*. New York: Oxford University Press, 1983.

Homan, Lynn M., and Thomas Reilly. *Black Knights: The Story of the Tuskegee Airmen*. Gretna, La.: Pelican, 2001.

Manber, David. *Wizard of Tuskegee: The Life of George Washington Carver*. New York: Crowell-Collier, 1967.

Marable, Manning. "Tuskegee Institute in the 1920s." *Negro History Bulletin* 40 (November–December 1977): 64–68.

Norrell, Robert J. *Reaping the Whirlwind: The Civil Rights Movement in Tuskegee*, 2d ed. Chapel Hill: University of North Carolina Press, 1998.

LISA MARIE MOORE (1996)
Updated by publisher 2005

Twilight, Alexander

September 26, 1795
June 1857

Born free in Corinth, Vermont, in 1795, Alexander Lucius Twilight, an educator and legislator, was the third of six children of Mary and Ichabod Twilight. Indentured to a local farmer, Twilight worked in his spare time and eventually saved enough to purchase the last year of his indenture in 1815. Twilight went on to attend Randolph Academy and in 1821 graduated with the equivalent of a high school degree and two years of college. He then entered Middlebury College and in 1823 received his B.A. degree. Twilight was probably the first African American to graduate from an American college.

After completing college, Twilight accepted a teaching position in Peru, New York. He studied theology and was granted a license to preach by the Champlain Presbytery of Plattsburgh, New York. In 1829 he moved to Brownington, Vermont, where he took over as principal of the Orleans County Grammar School as well as minister of the local congregation, which prayed in the school building. Twilight began a campaign to raise money for a new, larger school building to house an intermediate school, Brownington Academy. He received little funding either from public or private sources, but he supervised the construction of Athenian Hall, a three-story granite structure with sufficient room.

Twilight became so popular through his various activities that in 1836 he was elected by the village to a one-year term in the Vermont state legislature in Montpelier. He thus became the first African-American state representative and probably the first black elected official in America. His term of office was unexceptional, and at its close Twilight returned to Brownington Academy. In 1847 he left Brownington to teach in other villages, but he returned to his ministerial and educational functions in Brownington in 1852. He retired in 1855, following a stroke, and died in June 1857.

See also Free Blacks, 1619–1860; Politics in the United States

Bibliography

Hileman, Gregor. "The Iron-Willed Black Schoolmaster and His Granite Academy." *Middlebury College News Letter* (spring 1974): 6–26.

GREG ROBINSON (1996)

TYSON, CICELY

DECEMBER 19, 1939

Born to immigrant parents from Nevis, one of the Leeward Islands in the Caribbean, television, screen, and stage actress Cicely Tyson grew up in East Harlem in New York City. Her father worked as a carpenter, at times selling fruit and vegetables from a pushcart, while her mother worked as a domestic. After the divorce of her parents she lived with her mother, who forbade secular theatrical entertainment such as movies. It was in Saint John's Episcopal Church in Harlem, where she sang and played the organ, that Tyson's theatrical talents surfaced.

After graduating from high school and taking a job as a secretary with the American Red Cross, Tyson was asked to model hairstyles by her hairdresser. He encouraged her to enroll in the Barbara Watson Modeling School, where she met *Ebony* fashion editor Freda DeKnight. Soon she was appearing on the covers of the major fashion magazines in the United States, such as *Vogue* and *Harper's Bazaar.*

In 1957 Tyson had a small part in the film *Twelve Angry Men* with Henry Fonda. Two years later she made her stage debut, starring in *Dark of the Moon* directed by Vinnette Carroll and produced by the Harlem YMCA's Drama Guild. In 1962 she appeared in both *Moon on the Rainbow Shawl* and Jean Genet's *The Blacks,* for which she received a Vernon Rice Award.

Tyson was recruited in 1963 for a lead role in the CBS television series *East Side, West Side,* becoming the first African-American actress to be a regular on a dramatic television series. The same year she appeared on stage with Alvin Ailey in the Broadway production of *Tiger, Tiger, Burning Bright* and in the Off-Broadway production of *The Blue Boy in Black,* playing opposite Billy Dee Williams. In 1968 she appeared in the film *The Heart Is a Lonely Hunter,* for which she received critical and public acclaim for her performance.

Tyson waited four years before doing film work again because of her decision not to accept roles that added to the negative stereotypes of African Americans. Then, in 1972 she accepted the role of Rebecca in the film *Sounder.* Her performance earned her an Academy Award nomination for best actress.

In 1974 Tyson received two Emmy Awards—one for best lead actress in a drama and the other for actress of the year—for her portrayal of aged ex-slave Jane Pittman in *The Autobiography of Miss Jane Pittman.* She went on to play other socially conscious roles for television, including the part of Harriet Tubman in *A Woman Called Moses* (1976), Kunte Kinte's mother in *Roots* (1977), and Coretta Scott King in *King* (1978).

On Thanksgiving Day 1981 Tyson married jazz trumpeter Miles Davis. Davis's third attempt at marriage and Tyson's first, the arrangement lasted seven years. Tyson continues to be active in film and television, appearing with Oprah Winfrey in the television miniseries *The Women of Brewster Place* in 1989 and in the film *Fried Green Tomatoes* in 1991. In 1994 she won an Emmy for her performance in *The Oldest Living Confederate Widow Tells All,* and in 1999 she appeared in the highly regarded television movie *A Lesson Before Dying.* She sponsors the Cicely Tyson School for the Performing Arts in East Orange, New Jersey. Scheduled for 2005 is *The Diary of a Mad Black Woman,* in which she appears as the character Myrtle.

See also Film in the United States, Contemporary; Television

Bibliography

Davis, Miles, with Quincy Troupe. *Miles: The Autobiography.* New York: Simon and Schuster, 1989.

Hine, Darlene Clark. *Black Women in America.* Brooklyn, N.Y.: Carlson, 1993.

Mapp, Edward, ed. *Directory of Blacks in the Performing Arts.* Metuchen, N.J.: Scarecrow Press, 1990.

JOSEPH E. LOWNDES (1996)
SABRINA FUCHS (1996)
Updated by publisher 2005

TYSON, MIKE

JUNE 30, 1966

In 1986 Mike Tyson became the youngest boxer ever to win a world heavyweight championship title. Dubbed "Iron Mike" by the press because his physique made him seem invincible, he was hailed as the long-awaited successor to Muhammad Ali. He was later demonized in the same media after a series of personal and legal problems made headlines. Though he was considered one of boxing's most promising talents, mastering the fortune and fame that came with success proved to be Tyson's toughest challenge in life.

Born in the summer of 1966 in the Bedford-Stuyvesant neighborhood of Brooklyn, Tyson later moved

Mike Tyson with flamboyant boxing promoter Don King. AP/WIDE WORLD PHOTOS. REPRODUCED BY PERMISSION.

with his mother to the Brownsville section of the borough during his early years. He knew who his father was but had little contact with him. By fifth grade, the future icon was a habitual truant and could barely read. He was also large and powerful for his age and became known for being able to knock down full-fledged teenagers in street fights. He fell into a bad crowd and compiled a lengthy juvenile record for armed robbery and other transgressions.

The turning point in Tyson's life came around 1980, after he had spent two years at a facility for juvenile offenders in upstate New York. A teacher there introduced him to a local septuagenarian and legendary boxing manager, Constantine "Cus" D'Amato. D'Amato recognized Tyson's promise, and the teen began training in earnest for the ring. D'Amato also became a father figure for the teen, and even his official legal guardian after his mother died. When Tyson failed to win a spot on the 1984 U.S. Olympic boxing team, he decided to turn professional in early 1985. Over the next year, he knocked out seven other fighters in the first round. He became boxing's youngest heavyweight champion when he won a World Boxing Council (WBC) match against Trevor Berbick in November 1986. Four months later, he won the World Boxing Association (WBA) belt, and later in 1987 took an International Boxing Federation (IBF) title.

Tyson successfully defended his title as the world heavyweight champion in 1988 and 1989. The celebrity that came with his new life, however, seemed to prove a deadlier adversary for him. After a whirlwind courtship, he wed actress Robin Givens in 1988, who later that year told television personality Barbara Walters that her husband suffered from manic depression and could sometimes frighten her and become physically violent. The couple filed for divorce two weeks later. The deaths of D'Amato and a subsequent manager left Tyson adrift professionally, and he fell into the orbit of boxing promoter Don King. His first serious professional loss came in February 1990 in a match with James "Buster" Douglas, to whom he ceded the world heavyweight title. Tyson seemed sluggish in the ring, and rumors arose that he was taking mood-stabilizing medication.

Tyson's fortunes continued to sink, and rapidly. In early 1992, he was convicted of the sexual assault of a Miss Black America contestant in a case that seemed shaky at best, and served three years in an Indiana prison. During his incarceration, Tyson took remedial math classes and converted to Islam. He returned to the ring in 1996, handily beating a string of lesser opponents, and won back his WBA championship belt in September of that year. He lost it two months later to Evander Holyfield, who had not been favored to beat Tyson. In June 1997 the two met again in a massively hyped event, and Tyson bit off a part of Holyfield's ear. Boxing authorities initially banned him from the sport for life because of the transgression, but he was later reinstated.

Tyson made his third comeback in 1999 after he broke professional ties with Don King, but was deeply mired in financial troubles and more than one lawsuit by then. In January 2002, before a press conference to announce a bout with heavyweight champion Lennox Lewis, Tyson rushed at the British boxer and the two brawled for nearly five minutes. Tyson lost their June fight and filed for bankruptcy the following year. He claimed to have racked up thirty-eight million dollars in debt. In July 2004 he lost to another British boxer, Danny Williams, in the fourth round. Sportswriters and boxing fans predicted Tyson's career was over, for at age thirty-eight he was considered well past his athletic prime.

See also Boxing

Bibliography

Hoffer, Richard. "Bottomed Out: Mike Tyson's Latest Comeback—and Most Likely His Career—Ended in a Stunning Knockout by a Handpicked Opponent." *Sports Illustrated* (August 9, 2004): 72.

O'Connor, Daniel, ed. *Iron Mike: A Mike Tyson Reader.* New York: Thunder's Mouth Press, 2002.

CAROL BRENNAN (2005)

Underground Railroad

Few aspects of the antislavery movement have been more shrouded in myth and misunderstanding than the Underground Railroad. Although white abolitionists, including Quakers, played an important role in helping to free thousands of African Americans, the degree of their involvement has been overemphasized. In the years before the Civil War, the Underground Railroad was primarily run, maintained, and funded by African Americans. Black working-class men and women collected the bulk of money, food, and clothing and provided the shelter and transportation for the fugitives. Wealthier, better educated blacks such as Pennsylvania's Robert Purvis and William Whipper arranged for legal assistance and offered leadership, financial support, and indispensable contacts among sympathetic and influential white political leaders. Philadelphia's William Still, who ran the city's vigilance committee and later recorded the stories of many of the people he helped, managed the pivotal point in the North's most successful underground system. He personally assisted thousands of escaping slaves and helped settle them in northern African-American communities or in Canada. As one white abolitionist leader admitted about the Underground Railroad in 1837, "Such matters are almost uniformly managed by the colored people."

Although the origins of the term Underground Railroad are uncertain, by 1850 both those who participated in it and those who sought to destroy it freely employed metaphors from the railroad business to describe its activities. More important, northerners and southerners understood both its symbolic and its real meanings. The numbers of African Americans who fled or were smuggled out of the South were never large enough to threaten the institutional stability of slavery. Yet the number actually freed was, in a way, less important than what such activities said about the institution of slavery and the true character of southern slaves. Apologists for slavery described blacks as inferior, incapable of living in freedom, and content in their bondage. Those who escaped from the South, and the free African Americans who assisted them, undermined slavery by irrefutably disproving its racist ideology.

Most slaves who reached freedom in the North initiated their own escapes. After their initial flight, however, fugitives needed guidance and assistance to keep their hard-won liberty. Many did not have to travel far before finding help. Although the black underground's effectiveness varied over time and place, an astonishingly large

Children pose for a class picture outside the doors of a "colored" school in Buxton, Ontario, Canada, 1910. *Both black and white children attended the school, one of the few in North America to offer a "classical" curriculum. The town of Buxton was founded as the Elgin settlement, a destination community for escaped slaves seeking refuge via the Underground Railroad.* © REUTERS/CORBIS

number of semiautonomous networks operated across the North and upper South. They were best organized in Ohio, Pennsylvania, and New York, but surprisingly efficient networks, often centered in local black churches, existed in most northern and border states, and even in Virginia. At hundreds of locations along the Ohio River, where many former slaves lived, fugitives encountered networks of black underground laborers who offered sanctuary and passed them progressively northward to other black communities. African-American settlements from New Jersey to Missouri served as asylums for fugitive slaves and provided contacts along well-established routes to Michigan, Ohio, Pennsylvania, and New York for easy transit to Canada.

Urban vigilance committees served as the hub for most of the black undergrounds. Along the East Coast, where the black underground was most effective, the Philadelphia and New York vigilance committees operated as central distribution points for many underground routes. Committee leaders such as William Still and David Ruggles directed fugitives to smaller black "stations," such as that of Stephen A. Myers in Albany, New York, who in turn provided transportation directly to Canada or farther west to Syracuse. Vigilance committees also warned local blacks of kidnapping rings, and members hazarded their lives in searching vessels for illegal slaves. Such black leaders also maintained contacts among influential whites who covertly warned of the movement of slave owners and federal marshals. Where formal committees did not exist, ad hoc ones functioned, supplied with information from, for example, black clerks who worked in hotels frequented by slave catchers. Black leaders such as William Still, who helped finance the famous exploits of Harriet Tubman, employed the latest technology to facilitate their work; during the 1850s these committees regularly used the telegraph to communicate with far-flung "stations."

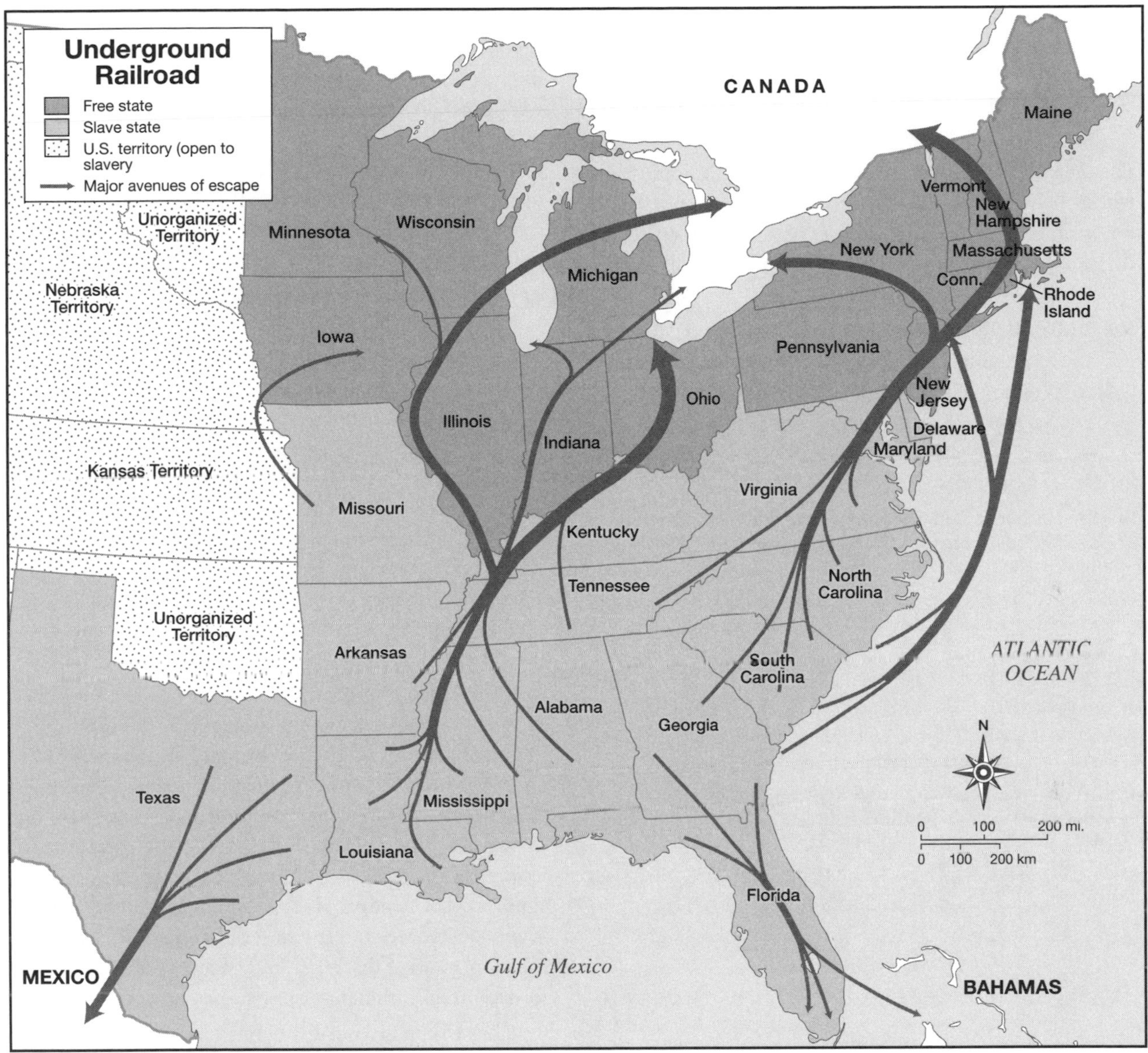

Map of the Underground Railroad, showing primary routes of escape. *Working class African Americans generally provided asylum and contacts for fugitive slaves along well-established routes to northern states and Canada.* MAP BY XNR PRODUCTIONS. THE GALE GROUP.

The most daring and best-organized "station" toiled in the very shadow of the U.S. Capitol. Run by free blacks from Washington, D.C., and Baltimore, this underground network rescued slaves from plantations in Maryland and Virginia, supplied them with free papers, and sent them north by a variety of land and water routes. These free blacks used their good standing among whites—as craftsmen, porters, and federal marshals' assistants—to facilitate their work. One free black used his painting business as a cover to visit plantations and arrange escapes; another employed his carriage service to transport slaves; others sustained the charges of slave owners and used their positions as plantation preachers and exhorters to pass escape plans to their "parishioners." When stealth and secrecy failed, heroic members of the Washington, D.C., "station" successfully attacked a slave pen to free some of its captives.

Members of this eastern network occasionally worked with white abolitionists such as Charles T. Torrey and the Quaker leader Thomas Garrett. But they primarily worked with other blacks, sending fugitives to Philadelphia where, either singly or in large groups, the escapees were directed to New York City and dispersed along many routes reaching into New England and Canada or toward western New York. This network was temporarily disrupted during the 1840s, when race riots in northern cities and escalated southern surveillance forced the removal of Washington's most active agents. Nevertheless, by one estimate, between 1830 and 1860 over nine thousand fugitive slaves passed through Philadelphia alone on their way to freedom.

The Underground Railroad never freed as many slaves as its most vocal supporters claimed, and far fewer whites helped than the mythology suggests. Undeniably, however, the existence and history of the system reflect the African-American quest for freedom and equality.

See also Abolition; Free Blacks, 1619–1860; Ruggles, David; Runaway Slaves in the United States; Slavery; Still, William; Tubman, Harriet

Bibliography

Blockson, Charles L. *The Underground Railroad: First Person Narratives of Escapes to Freedom in the North.* New York: Prentice-Hall, 1987.

Gara, Larry. *The Liberty Line: The Legend of the Underground Railroad.* Lexington: University of Kentucky Press, 1961.

Ripley, C. Peter, et al., eds. *The Black Abolitionist Papers.* Vol. 3, *The United States.* Chapel Hill: University of North Carolina Press, 1991.

Siebert, Wilbur H. *The Underground Railroad: From Slavery to Freedom.* New York: Macmillan, 1898.

Still, William. *The Underground Railroad.* Philadelphia: Porter and Coates, 1872. Reprint, Chicago: Johnson Publishing, 1970.

DONALD YACOVONE (1996)

UNIA

See Universal Negro Improvement Association

Union League of America

The Union League (or Loyal League) was the first mass-based African-American political organization. During congressional Reconstruction it was the vehicle for mobilizing the newly enfranchised voters for the Republican Party. The league was severely maligned by historians of the late nineteenth and early twentieth centuries, but recently scholars have taken a more favorable view.

The Union League originated during the Civil War as a white patriotic organization supporting the Union war effort. Under its longtime president James M. Edmunds, it spawned both the patrician Union League Clubs and many mass organizations in the northern states, and these were generally secret and oath-bound. With the end of the war, Republican leaders decided that the clandestine character of the organization made it appropriate for southern operations, and during presidential Reconstruction thousands of white Unionists, particularly in the mountains, joined the order.

With the passage of the Military Reconstruction acts in March 1867, Republican leaders turned their attention to the freedpeople. Republican donors underwrote an organizing campaign, and paid speakers, black and white, swept through the southern states. Encouraged by a sympathetic Freedmen's Bureau and other government officials, hundreds of thousands of blacks joined in the spring and summer of 1867. This mobilization was the freedpeople's first introduction to partisan politics and the mechanics of voting, and it was instrumental in the overwhelming vote they gave the Republican Party. The league thus helped "reconstruct" southern governments under the congressional plan.

The social impact of the movement was pronounced as well, coming at a critical moment in the evolution of the plantation system. After the war, planters tried to reconstruct production on familial lines: gang labor, physical coercion, tight supervision, and women and children in the work force. The vigorous black response to the league can be seen as a measure of frustration with the similarity the freedpeople's condition still bore to slavery. Their politicization around egalitarian slogans undermined plantation discipline and encouraged the transition to decentralized tenant farming and sharecropping.

The Union League was repressed by the Ku Klux Klan in 1868 and after, and consciously demobilized by the Republican leadership as a conciliatory gesture. Its influence on black voting patterns and on the plantation system was to prove more enduring.

See also Politics in the United States

Bibliography

Fitzgerald, Michael W. *The Union League Movement in the Deep South: Politics and Agricultural Change during Reconstruction.* Baton Rouge: Louisiana State University Press, 1989.

Foner, Eric. *Reconstruction: America's Unfinished Revolution, 1863–1877.* New York: Harper and Row, 1988, pp. 281–345.

Lawson, Melinda. "'A Profound National Devotion': The Civil War Union Leagues and the Construction of a New National Patriotism." *Civil War History* 48, no. 4 (December 2002): 338.

Silvestro, Clement Mario. *None but Patriots: The Union Leagues in Civil War and Reconstruction.* Ph.D. diss., University of Wisconsin, 1959.

MICHAEL W. FITZGERALD (1996)
Updated bibliography

Unions

See Labor and Labor Unions

United Negro College Fund

The United Negro College Fund, an alliance of forty-one black colleges and institutions of higher education, is a philanthropic enterprise established to fund black education. It was created during World War II, at a time when almost all black colleges were in dangerously poor financial shape. The Great Depression and wartime shortages had cut deeply into charitable donations, and many students were unable to pay their own tuition. In 1943 Tuskegee Institute president Frederick Douglass Patterson wrote an article in the *Pittsburgh Courier,* proposing that black colleges streamline their fund-raising by uniting in a joint funding appeal. The next year, presidents of twenty-seven colleges met and agreed to support a united mass fund-raising campaign, the proceeds of which they would divide among their colleges. With the aid of donations from the Julius Rosenwald Fund and the Rockefeller-based General Education Board, the organization, named the United Negro College Fund (UNCF) and based in New York, was founded. It was composed of privately supported (largely southern) black colleges, which authorized the UNCF to raise all funds for operating expenses such as scholarships, teachers' salaries, and equipment. Each college president agreed to serve revolving thirty-day terms leading UNCF efforts. William Trent, a manager trained at the University of Pennsylvania's Wharton School, was its first executive director.

In 1944 the UNCF inaugurated its first national campaign. It was an enormous success: the organization raised $765,000, three times the combined amount that its member colleges had collected in the previous year. Fueled by its rapid success, the UNCF soon grew, hiring a permanent independent staff. In 1951 the UNCF began a separate capital campaign, the National Mobilization of Resources, for the United Negro Colleges to pay for building and endowment funds, and raised $18 million in four years with the help of John D. Rockefeller Jr. In 1963 the UNCF, with the support of President John F. Kennedy and the Ford Foundation, began an additional appeal for funds for long-neglected maintenance and expansion of campus physical plants, and raised $30 million in a single year.

In 1964 Trent resigned. As it struggled to redefine its mission and to promote the legitimacy of black college education in the face of mainstream university desegregation, the UNCF went through six presidents, beginning with Patterson, in the next ten years. The turbulence of the civil rights movement scared away potential donors, and funding levels dropped.

In 1972 the UNCF was accepted by the Advertising Council, and television and radio advertising became a major avenue for fund-raising. The UNCF's slogan, "A mind is a terrible thing to waste," became so well known it was included in *Bartlett's Familiar Quotations.* Under the leadership of Christopher Edley (president from 1973 to 1990), the UNCF's annual campaign receipts went from $11.1 million to $48.1 million, and its membership grew to forty-one colleges. In 1978 the UNCF inaugurated a Capital Resources Development Program, which raised $60 million for its member institutions, and a College Endowment Funding Program, designed by Patterson to reduce college dependence on federal funding for permanent expenses. In 1980 the UNCF also began a yearly fund-raising telethon, "The Lou Rawls Parade of Stars."

In 1990 Christopher Edley resigned, and the following year, U.S. House Majority Whip William Gray III left his seat in Congress to become the UNCF's new president, underlining its importance in the black community. That year the UNCF started "Campaign 2000," a drive to raise $250 million by the year 2000. With the support of President George H. W. Bush and a $50 million gift from media magnate Walter Annenberg, it raised $86 million in its first year.

The United Negro College Fund remains the premier nongovernmental funding source for historically black colleges. Its narrow goal of endowment fund-raising and appeal to donors across the political spectrum has brought it a certain amount of criticism as a politically "safe" charity. However, its defenders have emphasized that quality black colleges remain a necessary alternative for students seeking higher education, and the UNCF's efforts have assured the survival and growth of these institutions.

In 2003, after transforming the UNCF into a powerful philanthropic organization, Gray announced that he would step down as president. In 2004 Dr. Michael L. Lomax became president and CEO.

See also Education in the United States; Gray, William H., III

Bibliography

Patterson, Frederick Douglass. *Chronicles of Faith: The Autobiography of Frederick Douglass Patterson.* Tuscaloosa: University of Alabama Press, 1991.

GREG ROBINSON (1996)
Updated by publisher 2005

United States Commission on Civil Rights

The Commission on Civil Rights was established as part of the Civil Rights Act of 1957. Originally known as the President's Commission on Civil Rights, it was intended to be a temporary commission. The commission's purpose was to investigate complaints about voting rights infringement because of race, color, religion, or ethnicity; to compile information on the denial of equal protection under the law that could be used in further civil rights protection; to serve as a clearinghouse of information on equal protection in the United States; and to submit a final report and recommendations to Congress and the president within two years.

Of the first six commissioners appointed by the president and Congress, only one was black—J. Ernest Wilkins, an assistant secretary of labor in the Eisenhower administration. The first chair was Stanley Reed, a former U.S. Supreme Court Justice who resigned almost immediately, citing "judicial improprieties" in the commission's charter. Reed was replaced by Dr. John Hannah, who served as chair until 1969. The commission, which had its mandate extended by the Civil Rights Act of 1960, served to focus attention on the U.S. government's responsibilities regarding civil rights. The commission was also a place to which African Americans could bring complaints about legislative and extralegal, violent attempts to keep them from voting. In February 1963 the commission issued *Freedom to the Free,* a report marking the centennial of the Emancipation Proclamation. It pointed out that while the problem in the South remained de jure segregation and discrimination, in the North it was de facto: "The condition of citizenship is not yet full-blown or fully realized for the American Negro. . . . The final chapter in the struggle for equality has yet to be written." The commission's powers were enlarged and its existence extended by the 1964 Civil Rights Act to encompass investigation of allegations of denial of equal protection of any kind. Its two-volume report, *Racial Isolation in the Public Schools* (1967), pointed out increasing racial segregation in schools, especially in metropolitan areas, as whites left the cities for the suburbs, laying responsibility at the feet of housing discrimination as practiced by private citizens and local, state, and federal government. In 1969 Rev. Theodore Hesburgh of the University of Notre Dame, a noted liberal on civil rights and segregation issues, succeeded Hannah as chair.

During the busing crisis of the early 1970s, the commission reaffirmed the view that Congress had the responsibility for establishing a "uniform standard to provide for the elimination of racial isolation." It chided President Richard Nixon for being overly cautious about ending de facto segregation in the North in a 1970 report. Largely because of this, Nixon forced Chairman Hesburgh to resign in 1972 and replaced him with the more conservative Arthur S. Fleming the following year. The fifth report of the commission, released in November 1974, documented the failure of the government to fulfill its obligations to blacks in employment. The commission's term was extended by the Civil Rights Commission Authorization Act of 1978, as it had been previously extended every time its term was up.

During Ronald Reagan's administration, the commission became the stage for a debate about affirmative action. In 1980 it endorsed racially based employment quotas in a report titled "Civil Rights in the 1980s: Dismantling the Process of Discrimination." However, in 1981 President Reagan fired Chairman Arthur Fleming and replaced him with Clarence Pendleton Jr., an archconservative and the first African American to serve as chair; all subsequent chairpersons have also been African American. In 1983 Reagan dismissed three other commissioners because they were critical of his administration's civil rights policies. One of the dismissed members, noted African-American historian Mary Frances Berry, successfully sued the Reagan administration to retain her position on the board, citing the commission's loss of independence. Following several months of negotiations involving the administration, Congress, and the commission itself, a compromise was reached and the body was reconstituted as the U.S. Commission on Civil Rights, with the president and Congress each appointing half the members, now numbering eight. More importantly, commissioners now had eight-year terms that could be terminated "only for neglect of duty or malfeasance in office."

In 1985 Chairman Pendleton declared that affirmative action programs should be ended and the commission ultimately abolished. The next year he proposed that minority contract set-asides should be ended; the rest of the commission disagreed with him, as did the National Black Republican Council, so the plan did not go forward. During the George H. W. Bush administration, the debate over quotas continued. Pendleton died in 1988 and was replaced by William Barclay Allen, an African American, who was forced to resign in October 1989 following the disclosure that he had been arrested for kidnapping a fourteen-year-old girl in a child custody battle. The commission's authorization expired September 30, 1989, and the reauthorization process was an occasion for Congress to examine the body's composition and future. Its new chair, Arthur A. Fletcher, former executive director of the National Urban League, appointed in February 1990, vowed to be more active than his predecessors and to make the commission the nation's conscience once again. In August 1991 the commission issued its first significant report on discrimination on six military bases in Germany, and followed it six months later with a report on pervasive discrimination against Asians, based on barriers of language and culture. The Civil Rights Commission was stalled through much of the mid-1990s by a battle between the Clinton administration and the Republican Congress over Bill Lann Lee, a former Inc. Fund attorney who was appointed commission chair in 1995. When Congress filibustered on the nomination because of Lee's support for racial preferences, Clinton appointed Lee as a recess appointment.

In 2001 the Civil Rights Commission called for a probe of the 2000 presidential election, stating that thousands of African American voters had their votes rejected as a result of faulty voting machines in areas highly populated by African Americans.

See also Affirmative Action; Civil Rights Congress; Civil Rights Movement, U.S.; Politics in the United States

Bibliography

Blaustein, Albert P., and Robert L. Zangrando, eds. *Civil Rights and the American Negro: A Documentary History*. New York: Trident Press, 1968.

Lowery, Charles D., and John F. Marszalek, eds. *Encyclopedia of African-American Civil Rights: From Emancipation to the Present.* New York: Greenwood Press, 1992.

Ploski, Harry A., and James Williams, eds. *The Negro Almanac: A Reference Work on the African American,* 5th ed. Detroit, Mich.: Bellwether, 1989.

ALANA J. ERICKSON (1996)
Updated by publisher 2005

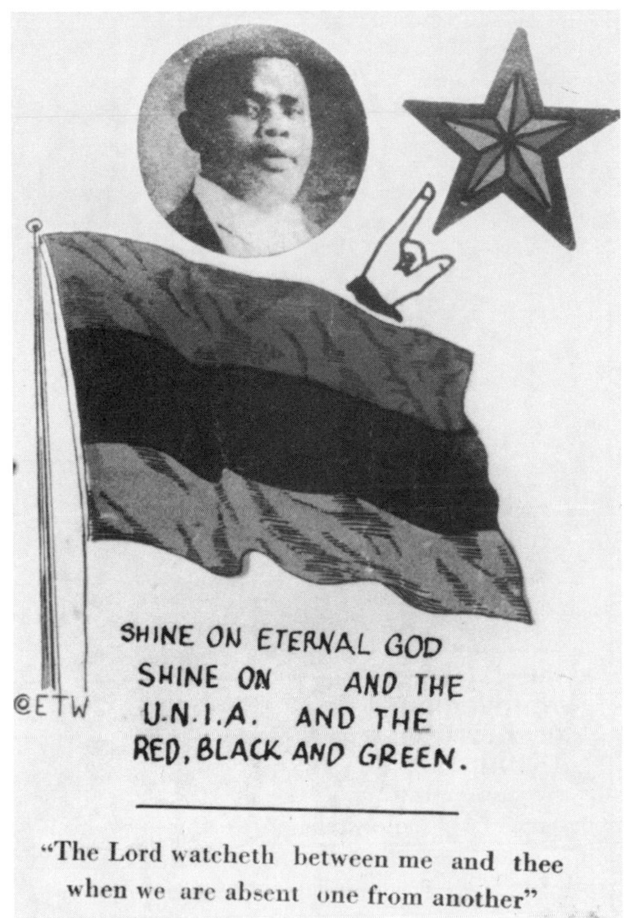

Universal Negro Improvement Association hand card, bearing a portrait of Marcus Garvey along with the UNIA flag. PHOTOGRAPHS AND PRINTS DIVISION, SCHOMBURG CENTER FOR RESEARCH IN BLACK CULTURE, THE NEW YORK PUBLIC LIBRARY, ASTOR, LENOX AND TILDEN FOUNDATIONS.

Universal Negro Improvement Association

The Universal Negro Improvement Association (UNIA), with its motto "One God, One Aim, One Destiny," stands as one of the most important political and social organizations in African-American history. It was founded by Marcus Garvey in July 1914, in Kingston, Jamaica, in the West Indies.

At the time of its establishment, its full name was the Universal Negro Improvement and Conservation Association and African Communities (Imperial) League (ACL). Originally organized as a mutual benefit and reform association dedicated to racial uplift, the UNIA and ACL migrated with Garvey to the United States in 1916. Incorpo-

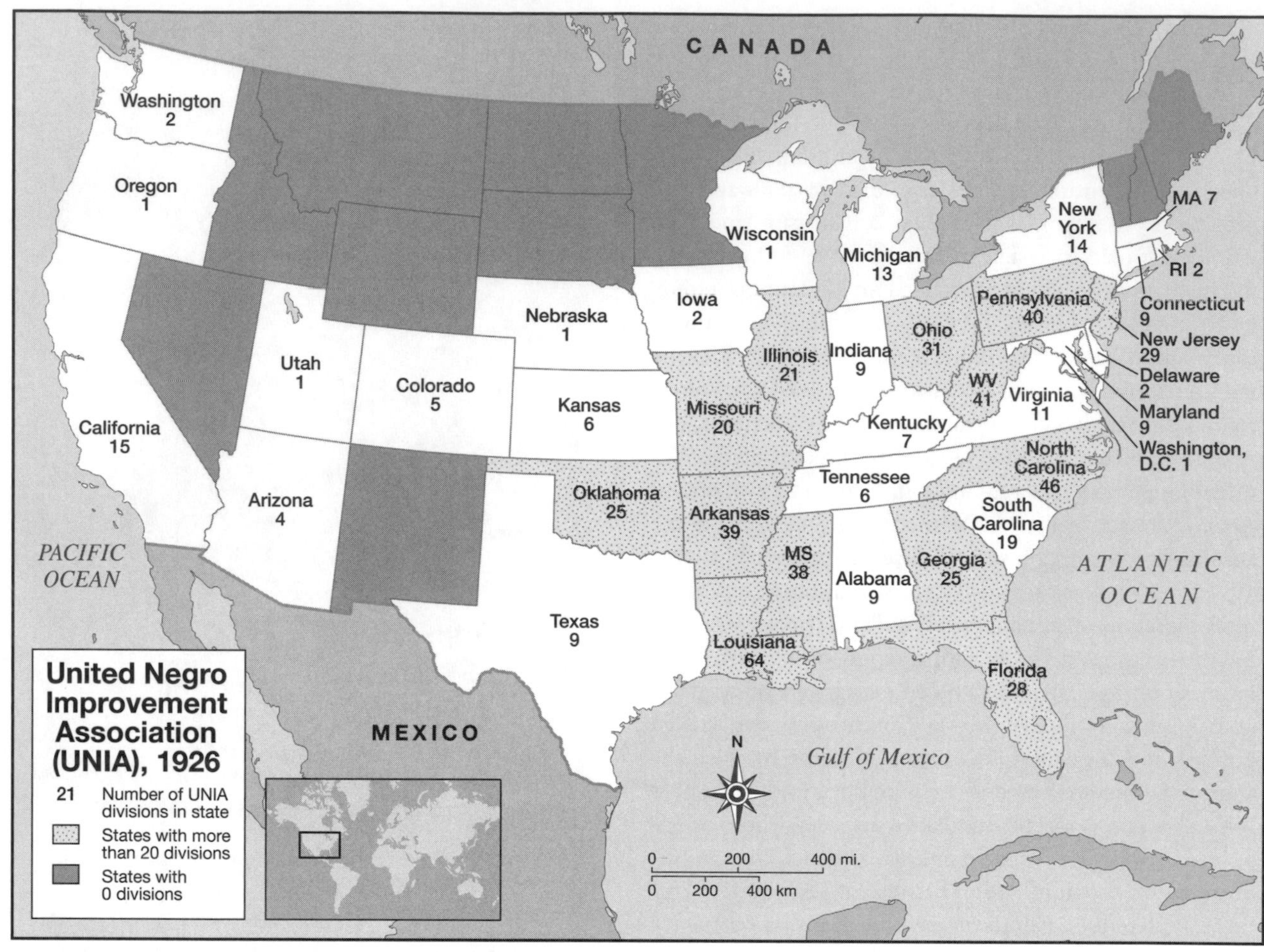

Map showing the growth of the Universal Negro Improvement Association (UNIA) in the United States 1926. *Marcus Garvey began the association in his homeland of Jamaica in 1914. Two years later, he moved to Harlem, preaching black nationalism and expanding his remarkably fast-growing all-black organization. The UNIA became so popular that by 1926, there were chapters in thirty-seven states plus the District of Columbia, as well as branches in most of the nations of the Caribbean and Central America.* MAP BY XNR PRODUCTIONS. THE GALE GROUP.

rated in New York in 1918, the UNIA gradually began to give voice to the rising mood of New Negro radicalism that emerged within the African-American population following the signing of the armistice ending World War I in November 1918.

The UNIA experienced a sudden massive expansion of membership beginning in the spring of 1919, spearheaded by the spectacular success of the stock-selling promotion of the Black Star Line (BSL). Together with the Negro Factories Corporation and other commercial endeavors, all of which were constituted under the ACL, the BSL represented the heart of the movement's economic program.

Outfitted with its own flag, national anthem, Universal African Legion and other uniformed ranks, official organ (the *Negro World*), African repatriation and resettlement scheme in Liberia, constitution, and laws, the UNIA attempted to function as a sort of provisional government of Africa. The result was that by 1920–1921 the UNIA had become the dominant voice advocating black self-determination under its irredentist program of African Redemption. Accompanied by spectacular parades, annual month-long conventions were held at Liberty Hall in Harlem, in New York City, between 1920 and 1924, at all of which Garvey presided. The document with the greatest lasting significance was the "Declaration of the Rights of the Negro Peoples of the World," passed at the first UNIA convention in August 1920.

Nearly a thousand local divisions and chapters of the UNIA were established by the mid-1920s in the United States, Canada, the West Indies, Central and South America, Africa, and the United Kingdom, causing the influence of the UNIA to be felt wherever peoples of African descent lived. With actual membership running into the hundreds of thousands, if not millions, the UNIA is reputed to have been the largest political organization in African-American history.

After Garvey's 1923 conviction on charges of mail fraud following the collapse of the Black Star Line and his incarceration in the Atlanta Federal Penitentiary starting in 1925, membership in the UNIA declined rapidly. When President Calvin Coolidge commuted Garvey's sentence and he was deported from the United States in 1927, the organization found itself racked by increasing factionalization.

Garvey incorporated a new UNIA and ACL of the World in Jamaica at the August 1929 convention, competing with the New York–based UNIA parent body headed at the time by Fred A. Toote, who was succeeded by Lionel Francis in 1931. With the worldwide economic collapse that followed the 1929 stock market crash, the UNIA went into further decline as members' resources dwindled, making it difficult to support two separate wings of the movement. Demoralization also set in as a result of the UNIA leadership's increasing fragmentation. Garvey was able to retain the loyalty of only a part of the movement, notably the Garvey Club and the Tiger division of the New York UNIA.

When Garvey moved his headquarters in 1935 from Jamaica to London, he tried once again to revive the movement but soon found himself confronting considerable opposition by members who were in the forefront of the campaign to support Ethiopia during the Italian–Ethiopian War of 1935. These members repudiated the criticisms Garvey leveled against Ethiopia's Emperor, Haile Selassie I, following the invasion by Mussolini and the Fascist Italian Army.

After Garvey's death in 1940, loyalists moved the headquarters of the organization to Cleveland, Ohio, under the leadership of its new president general, James Stewart, who thereafter relocated with it to Liberia. By the 1940s and 1950s, the UNIA had a mere shadow of its former strength, but it still continues to function into the twenty-first century.

See also Garvey, Marcus; Pan-Africanism

Bibliography

Hill, Robert A., ed. *The Marcus Garvey and Universal Negro Improvement Association Papers,* vols. 1–7. Berkeley: University of California Press, 1983–1991.

Hill, Robert A., and Barbara Bair. *Marcus Garvey: Life and Lessons.* Berkeley: University of California Press, 1987.

ROBERT A. HILL (1996)

University of the West Indies

The University of the West Indies comprises three campuses: Mona in Jamaica, St. Augustine in Trinidad, and Cave Hill in Barbados. There are also university centers located in noncampus countries. These constitute the outreach arm of the university, providing classroom teaching and enabling the delivery of some courses via the Distance Education Programme. The university also maintains working relations with a number of tertiary-level affiliated institutions. More recently it has forged alliances in some islands with selected teachers colleges and community colleges that register students for courses approved by the university. Certification in such courses comes from the university.

The university has seven faculties (Agriculture, Humanities and Education, Engineering, Law, Medicine, Pure and Applied Science, and Social Sciences). Only the faculties of Agriculture and Engineering are specific to one campus (St. Augustine); the others are duplicated on all the campuses. The total on-campus student population in the academic year 2002–2003 stood at 22,463 (Mona, 9,440; St. Augustine, 8,644; Cave Hill, 4,359). There were 1,095 full-time academic staff altogether in 2002–2003 (706 males and 389 females).

From about 1926 the British government responded in piecemeal fashion to separate inquiries about the possibilities of university education from the West Indies, Singapore, East Africa, and Malaya. The onset of World War II made it more urgent to promise the colonies a better deal after the fighting and to impress world opinion that Britain was an enlightened imperial power. The social conditions in the colonies had to be drastically improved and more liberal political goals—self-government, for example—agreed on. Not only primary and secondary education but also university education became a matter of importance, if only to control the new colonial elite. In the case of the West Indies, before an aid agency of British advisers implanted in the West Indies (Colonial Development and Welfare) could set in motion British-funded improvements in primary and secondary education, another set of advisers (the Irvine Committee) was set up for funding a scheme of university education for the islands.

The Asquith Commission was a landmark in the evolution of British government support for university education in the colonies. A branch of it, the Irvine Committee, was sent to the West Indies in 1944 to investigate and report. After a tour of major colonies this committee recommended that a small single-campus residential university allied with the University of London, which would issue degrees in its name, should be established in Jamaica. A major issue before the committee was whether a centralized university, meaning a single-campus university, or a decentralized university, meaning a university of colleges scattered over more than one island, should be set up.

The evidence provided by witnesses, except in Jamaica, suggested that the islands would have been more comfortable with a decentralized university, but the Irvine Committee was convinced that in order to cultivate a West Indian outlook two requirements were nonnegotiable: the university should be residential and it should be centralized on one campus.

With funds for buildings from the British government and commitments from West Indian governments to meet recurrent expenses, such a centralized university college came to life in Jamaica in October 1948, with teaching first in medicine, followed by natural sciences (1949) and arts (1950). Extramural staff to develop adult education and West Indian cultural activities were placed on noncampus islands, but this was not thought to detract from the principle of a centralized university. However, after about twelve years this centralized single-campus residential model was found inadequate to guarantee rapid expansion or to satisfy insular nationalistic drives to possess a part of the university. In 1960 the Imperial College of Tropical Agriculture, a tertiary-level institution in Trinidad founded in 1922, merged with the University College and became its Faculty of Agriculture.

Two years later (1962) a Faculty of Engineering, with much funding from the government of Trinidad, started at St. Augustine, and the next year (1963) teaching in arts and natural sciences commenced at St. Augustine and Cave Hill. The university had begun its journey to decentralization.

The history of the University College (which became the University of the West Indies in 1962, having claimed its independence from the University of London) may be conveniently divided into three periods: first 1948 to 1960, when it was a residential single-campus centralized University College; then 1960 to 1984, when the struggles to find a new nonresidential, decentralized, multicampus model was most pronounced; and finally 1984 to the present, when a highly satisfactory decentralized model was agreed on, first in 1984 and then refined in the mid-1990s by a new governance system. At this point, for instance, each faculty on each campus got its own dean. The university grew from thirty-three medical students in 1948 to 970 students in 1960, and despite repeated difficulties in raising recurrent financing, it did succeed largely by a mix of students from different territories in creating the West Indian outlook the Irvine Committee dreamed of. However, this outlook was subsequently impaired, though not lost, by a number of developments. West Indian leaders failed to create a national state; the Federation of the West Indies lasted only from 1958 to 1962; territorial nationalism grew; some territories, starting with Jamaica and Trinidad, became independent after 1962; and Guyana withdrew from the university in 1962. Eventually the university authorities found that instead of dealing with seven governments as at the start, they were dealing with fourteen. The university was financed for limited periods, usually for nine years at a time, and it was not until 1989 that the West Indian governments declared their commitment to keeping it as a regional institution in perpetuity. Most of the islands could not seriously think of financing their own university apart from the University of the West Indies, but two islands, Jamaica and Trinidad, because of their greater size and greater resources, talked as if they could establish their own university. The more credible threat came in the mid-1970s from Trinidad, which had surplus oil revenues. But using hindsight now it seems as if all the threats of the leading politicians were only negotiating positions in the struggle to locate faculties and programs in their territories or to have more local power over the university.

From decentralization through two specialized faculties (Agriculture and Engineering at St. Augustine), the university duplicated faculties and programs on any campus that could afford them. It took some twenty years for the management structures of the single-campus centralized university to be adjusted to fit a decentralized university model. By 1984 a university center headed by the vice chancellor assisted by a number of pro–vice chancellors had successfully claimed authority over enough administrative, academic, and financial functions to hold the university together as a regional institution, but large areas of autonomy were allowed to the local campuses.

With the abandonment of a single-campus residential model, student numbers rose sharply from the 1960s onwards. The addition of evening programs boosted numbers especially in the Arts and Social Science faculties on all three campuses. Mona stayed ahead with 3,735 and 7,503 students in 1974 and 1994, respectively; followed by St. Augustine with 2,202 and 5,231 students in 1974 and 1994, respectively; and then Cave Hill with 991 and 2,870 students in 1974 and 1994, respectively. But the proportion of university students was still small and in most faculties applicants outnumbered matriculants. Although the level of financial support offered to students varied from campus to campus, the general trend has been to put more of the real cost of their education on the shoulders of the students. There were never enough scholarships, and presently there is a conviction that students, not the general taxpayers, should pay for university education. Since the 1990s, in the spirit of globalization several overseas universities, especially from the United States, have offered degree, diploma, or certificate programs in Jamaica, Trinidad, and Barbados, usually in association with a local college but in competition with the University of the West Indies. The university now has to fight to preserve its place as the leading tertiary institution in the West Indies.

The West Indianization of the staff of the university began from the first period of its existence, and as the university established successful graduate programs, some of its bright graduates were able to join the staff. Because West Indian staff members tended to have research interests in West Indian fields, the West Indianization of the staff enabled the university to bring its expertise to bear on West Indian problems. So little research prior to 1948 had been done on West Indian problems that the staff had a wide-open field for research in every discipline. From the start the university aspired to place much emphasis on research, and with the addition of public service to government or nongovernmental agencies as further fields of academic action, those staff members so minded could find ample scope for action outside teaching. While politicians have occasionally complained that research done at the university was irrelevant to some perceived needs, the university has a history of responding favorably to all requests from governments for special help with national projects.

The University of the West Indies has been a serious contributor to the growth of the professions in the islands over the last half of the twentieth century. The rapid expansion of secondary education in the islands, one of the most democratizing social developments of the last fifty years, would have been impossible without the humanities and science graduates from the university. The creation of independent states demanded highly trained public servants, social scientists, economists, and other professionals. The public hospitals are staffed to a significant extent by medical graduates from the university. The university has the largest core of intellectuals in the islands and is the source from which the grand theories of West Indian societies emanate.

A source of much comment is the large number of female students and graduates in most faculties. This trend only started in the mid-1980s. No doubt it has its source in similar movements at the level of the secondary schools. Whether male or female, the student of the university still has the challenge of the Irvine Committee to face: how to nurture a West Indian outlook in a regional institution. The decentralization has lowered the level of the mix of students from different islands on each campus. Cave Hill has a better mix than St. Augustine, and the latter has a better mix than Mona. While the Mona campus in Jamaica was certainly not Jamaican in the early years from 1948 to 1960, it is decidedly Jamaican at present. The cultivation of the West Indian outlook now depends largely on West Indian curricula and a mix of West Indian staff, but even the latter has suffered some dilution. The inherent insular pressures of the decentralized university require constant efforts from the university center, led by the vice chancellor, to mitigate, if not reverse them.

See also Education in the Caribbean

Bibliography

Campbell, Carl. "The University of Our Dreams: Centralisation versus Decentralisation in the Planning of the University of the West Indies 1943/1944." *Jamaica Historical Review* 16 (1988): 17–32.

Hall, Douglas. *The University of the West Indies. A Quinquagenary Calendar 1948–1998.* Kingston, Jamaica: University of the West Indies Press, 1998.

Payne, Anthony. "One University, Many Governments: Regional Integration, Politics, and the University of the West Indies." *Jamaica Historical Review* 16 (1988): 33–53.

Report of the West Indies Committee of the Commission on Higher Education in the Colonies. (Also known as the *Irvine Report.*) CMD 6654. London: H.M. Stationery Office, 1945.

Sherlock, Philip, and Rex Nettleford. *The University of the West Indies. A Caribbean Response to the Challenge of Change.* London: Macmillan, 1990.

CARL C. CAMPBELL (2005)

URBAN CINEMA

Urban Cinema describes a wave of city-based, feature-length films by African-American directors that began in the mid-1980s and that were dominated by action movies and youth dramas. In urban cinema, social and economic injustices, along with the conditions and relationships they produce, function as essential elements that directly motivate a film's characters, plot, dialogue, action, and aesthetics.

Many films within urban cinema have been influenced by hip-hop culture and reflect what S. Craig Watkins calls "the ghettocentric imagination" (1998). In addition to featuring rap-dominated sound tracks, urban cinema sometimes features rap stars in leading roles and often presents the points of view and experiences of young

Ice-T (standing) and Chris Rock in a scene from the 1991 film New Jack City, *directed by Mario Van Peebles.* WARNERS BROS./THE KOBAL COLLECTION

African-American men in the direct, sincere, and fearless style popularized by hip-hop. Early urban films like *Beat Street* (1984) and *Krush Groove* (1985) placed hip-hop culture itself at the center of the drama.

Contemporary urban cinema is also inspired by 1970s "blaxploitation" films, which focused on urban landscapes and celebrated black action heroes and heroines. Much, though not all, contemporary urban cinema abandons the blaxploitation genre's focus on superhuman characters and instead applies the hip-hop ethic of "keeping it real" to film. The result is a cinema that claims to represent the lived experience of young, usually poor, city-dwelling African Americans and/or to expose African-American "gangsta culture." Many argue, however, that the "gangstas" in urban cinema are directly informed by Latino and Italian gangster characters in mainstream movies like *Scarface* (1983) and the *Godfather* films of the 1970s.

Most African-American urban films have been written and directed by African-American men. Urban cinema coincides historically with the growing numbers of African-American men who directed feature films after the success of Spike Lee's *She's Gotta Have It* (1986) and *Do the Right Thing* (1989). From 1990 to 1995 more than forty feature films by African-American directors were released nationally, more than ever before in film history. Through them, modern urban cinema was born.

In 1991 three films were released that established urban cinema's two main sub-genres of crime-driven action films and tragedy-tinged youth dramas. *New Jack City*, directed by Mario Van Peebles, son of legendary blaxploitation director Melvin Van Peebles, resurrected blaxploitation cinema's themes of action, crime, and violence. That same year, John Singleton's *Boyz N the Hood*, which was nominated for two Academy Awards, and nineteen-year-old Matty Rich's *Straight Out of Brooklyn* established somber, socially conscious youth dramas as a foundation of urban cinema.

These films were soon joined by Ernest Dickerson's *Juice* (1992); The Hughes Brothers's *Menace II Society* (1993); Leslie Harris's *Just Another Girl on the IRT* (1993) and Darnell Martin's *I Like It Like That* (1994), two of the only films in the genre directed by women and among the few, along with Singleton's *Poetic Justice* (1993), that feature female leads; and Spike Lee's masterful *Clockers* (1995). This period also saw successful urban comedies such as *House Party* (1990), *Friday* (1995), and the comedy-action hybrid *Bad Boys* (1995), all of which were followed by sequels. Not long after came the urban cinema spoof *Don't Be a Menace to South Central While Drinking Your Juice in the Hood* (1996) and the sexual satire *Booty Call* (1997). From 1996 to 2000, the number of feature films directed by African Americans dropped by almost half, and as a result, urban cinema also declined. Films that sustained the genre included *Set It Off* (1996), *Gridlock'd* (1997), *Belly* (1998), and a remake of *Shaft* (2000).

Since 2001 African-American directors have produced a handful of feature films each year but have never replicated their previous numbers. Urban cinema continued with films like *Prison Song* (2001), *Baby Boy* (2001), and *Never Die Alone* (2004). However, action-driven films like *Bad Boys* (1995), *2 Fast 2 Furious* (2003), and *Four Brothers* (2005) have frequently attracted more attention than personal dramas. Antoine Fuqua's interracial crime thriller, *Training Day* (2001), brought Denzel Washington his first best-actor Oscar. *8 Mile* (2002) successfully mimicked the formula of earlier youth dramas but replaced the unknown African-American leads that anchored those films with white rap star Eminem. In 2005, *Hustle and Flow*, produced by urban-cinema auteur John Singleton and featuring an acclaimed performance by Terrence

Dashon Howard, attempted to renew urban cinema by moving it to the South and by merging contemporary hip-hop themes with the classical blaxploitation plot of a pimp, in the spirit of *Superfly* (1972), who is desperate to escape the streets.

Debates within urban cinema echo debates about the hip-hop culture that has always influenced it. Advocates of urban cinema celebrate its focus on the marginalized lives of young African-American men and its role in the artistic achievements of African-American filmmakers and performers. Its critics claim that urban cinema glorifies violence, demeans women, and perpetuates negative stereotypes. Other critics challenge its emphasis on "authentic" representations of African Americans, arguing that urban films pretend to represent "gritty," "ghetto" realities when they are actually well-constructed cinema fantasies. However, the final judgment of urban cinema rests in the hands of its young African-American consumers whose profound longing to see any version of their lives reflected on screen has always served as the soul of the genre.

See also Blaxploitation Films; Film in the United States; Film in the United States, Contemporary; Filmmakers, Los Angeles School of; Lee, Spike; Singleton, John

Bibliography

Boyd, Todd. *Am I Black Enough for You?: Popular Culture from the 'Hood and Beyond.* Bloomington: Indiana University Press, 1997.

Dent, Gina, ed. *Black Popular Culture.* New York: The New Press, 1998.

Dyson, Michael Eric. "Out of the Ghetto." *Sight and Sound* (1992) 2:6, 18–21.

Grant, William R. *Post-Soul Black Cinema: Discontinuities, Innovations, and Breakpoints, 1970–1995.* New York: Routledge, 2004.

Jones, Jacquie. "The New Ghetto Aesthetic." In *Mediated Messages and African American Culture: Contemporary Issues,* edited by V. Berry and C. Manning-Miller. Thousand Oaks, Calif.: Sage Publications, 1996.

Reid, Mark A. *Black Lenses, Black Voices: African American Film Now.* Lanham, Md.: Rowman & Littlefield, 2005.

Watkins, S. Craig. *Representing: Hip-hop Culture and the Production of Black Cinema.* Chicago: University of Chicago Press, 1998.

DIONNE BENNETT (2005)

Urban Poverty in the Caribbean

In a global environment defined by great upheaval and disorder, the small-island states of the Caribbean have largely been spared the worst aspects of the upheaval and violence afflicting other parts of the world. Indeed, in a world where war, social violence, genocide, state collapse, and terror are commonplace, the English-speaking and politically independent states of the Caribbean remain exceptional for their low levels of social disorder, high levels of human development, and unity of democratic governance. The stereotype of the Caribbean as an idyllic tropical paradise where tourists and visitors can enjoy their leisure time in politically free and fairly well-governed societies is in fact not too far from the truth. Political stability, democracy, and high levels of social well-being remain defining features of the region.

It is also true, however, that upheaval in the economic, political, and cultural structures of world society is dramatically undermining these positive inheritances and altering this condition of Caribbean exceptionalism. For example, North American media images depicting dissident youth cultures, hedonistic lifestyles, and the subversion of conventional values are now common fare in the Caribbean. Television commercials and media programming celebrating leisure, sex, and conspicuous consumption helped undermine commitment to thrift, personal modesty, and the value of education and hard work. Consequently, for Caribbean youths today, prize-winning high school students are no longer the role models; they have been replaced by the gold chain-wearing drug dealer and the gangster with a fancy car. The emulation of these role models by unemployed youth, along with the easy availability of drugs and guns, has led to an increase in antisocial behaviors by youths across the region.

This contagion is apparent in the explosion in urban street crime. Kidnappings, armed robberies, extortion, and murder are now commonplace in the larger islands of the Caribbean. For example, Jamaica, with a population of 2.6 million, had more than 1,200 murders in 2004—one of the highest rates in the western hemisphere. That same year there were 164 kidnappings in Trinidad, a record for that country. That the smaller islands with tiny populations had fewer incidents of crime did little to diminish concern about this epidemic of violence and its destructive effects on urban communities.

While the link between poverty and crime remains complicated, there is little doubt that globalization is influencing both crime and urban poverty across the English-speaking Caribbean. Indeed, because of the highly interactive nature of the globalization process, both the dynamics of Caribbean societies and the ecology of their inner cities resemble patterns in the advanced industrial societies of western Europe and North America.

Today, inner-city Caribbean communities duplicate almost exactly the sociology of urban poverty in the United States. For example, the city of Kingston, Jamaica, particularly its western precincts, is known for its intense poverty, especially among youths aged fifteen to twenty-four. Lacking education and bereft of skills, urban youths in Jamaica make up a significant proportion of the 18 percent of the population that fell below the poverty line in 2002.

Furthermore, having lost the diverse class composition of earlier decades—in which the unemployed poor lived in the same neighborhoods with unionized workers, domestics, and middle-class professionals—whole areas of West Kingston have been transformed into segregated ghettos in which the poor are cut off from the wider society.

The same is true of Port-of-Spain, Trinidad, and its poorer eastern precincts, where joblessness, crime, and poverty afflict residents, most of whom are deprived of family and community ties. Decrepit housing, poor drainage, and squalor in impoverished hillside communities such as Levantville only aggravate this situation.

Much like the physical and social isolation of urban ghetto residents in the United States, chronic joblessness of poor residents, the collapse of family and community life, and the erosion of conventional values are now pervasive features of urban poverty in the Caribbean. Global upheaval, and its nexus with the political economy of these dynamic islands, has made Caribbean societies—and particularly the disadvantaged populations in the capital cities—poorer, more violent, and more ungovernable than they were a generation ago. Reports indicate that poverty in the Caribbean persists despite significant economic growth in countries like Trinidad and Barbados. Paradoxically, Trinidad's current oil boom and double-digit economic growth rate have done little to reduce high unemployment and poverty rates there.

Although the incidence of poverty is greatest in the Caribbean countryside, poverty is felt much more intensely in the urban areas, particularly in the capital cities of Kingston, Jamaica; Georgetown, Guyana; and Port-of-Spain, Trinidad. In these and other islands, poverty rates remain high. Surveys indicate that even though the rate of poverty has declined in recent years, 21 percent of the population in Trinidad and Tobago lived below the poverty line in 2003. In Guyana, the poorest country in the Anglophone Caribbean, the rate was 35 percent.

Failing economies have been a major cause of poverty in the region. Low worker productivity, low educational achievement, limited economic diversification, and scarcity of productive investment beyond a few economic enclaves have historically restricted economic growth and curbed employment in the region. As economic growth lagged in the late 1970s, and as export earnings fell in the 1980s and after, Caribbean governments typically resorted to deficit spending and high levels of borrowing. But due to poor export earnings and an increased debt load, deficit spending became unsustainable. The result throughout the region was an imposition of austerity measures and the adoption of structural adjustment policies.

This retrenchment proved to be a double-edged sword, however. Fiscal discipline certainly helped cut ballooning deficits and reduced inflation rates, but because of high interest rates and cuts in state spending, these very measures also curbed investment, dampened economic growth, fed unemployment, and spurred poverty rates across the region. Thus, throughout the region, tight fiscal management did not result in new jobs or economic growth. In instances of extreme structural adjustment, as in Jamaica and Guyana, such measures merely drove more persons into poverty and crime.

In an increasingly competitive global environment, the structural dependence of Caribbean economies and low worker productivity contributed to these worsening social conditions. Lagging income from agricultural exports and rising prices for critical imports, such as oil and manufactured goods, highlight Caribbean dependence in the international economy. Poor export earnings in turn hamper investment in equipment and human resources, and these together lower wages and employment. The result is low worker productivity that reinforces this vicious cycle. This nexus of structural dependence and low worker productivity is the proximate source of urban poverty in the Caribbean. While poor governance, undeveloped human capital, and a lack of institutional capacity have aggravated the incidence of poverty in the region, the key determinants were economic. In sum, poorly performing economies within a global context of increased competition fed and sustained poverty in the Caribbean.

Nevertheless, this erosion in the quality of life of Caribbean populations did not lead to gross malnutrition or starvation, as is the case in some poverty-stricken parts of the world. Rather, the extent of urban poverty and the profile of the urban poor in the Anglophone Caribbean reveal a far more ambiguous and nuanced condition.

For example, successive annual reports on human development in the world have repeatedly placed English-speaking Caribbean nations in the ranks of countries with high human development because of their low levels of poverty, as well as high literacy and life expectancy rates. These countries made investments in human development in such areas as health and education and had enough economic growth to afford their populations both longevity and a decent standard of living. Barbados, for example, has for several years been the best performer in the Anglophone Caribbean on the United Nations Human Development Index.

Yet, despite this achievement, countries in the Anglophone Caribbean are neither wealthy nor immune to having populations living in abject poverty. Data on these economies reveal that despite a gross domestic product (GDP) per capita of US$16,691 in the Bahamas in 2003 and US$15,290 in Barbados in 2004, the region's average GDP per capita in 2003 was a mere US$5,366. After Haiti, Guyana was the poorest country in the wider Caribbean, with a per capita GDP of US$911 in 2003. (This did mark an increase from the low of US$300 in 1992.) Indeed, dire poverty and unsustainable debt in Guyana qualified this country for relief under the Highly Indebted Poor Countries Initiative, established by the World Bank and the International Monetary Fund in 1996.

These variations point to the wide gap between prosperity and want in a region full of paradoxes. Thus, for example, Trinidad—with its booming oil and petrochemical sectors—experienced record economic growth rates in the early twenty-first century. Yet despite a spectacular rate of growth of over 10 percent in 2004, with huge revenues generated by the oil and petrochemicals industries, these breakthroughs did not create jobs or reduce the incidence of poverty. As in Trinidad, improved inflows of revenue based on exports and investments (the Holy Grail of Caribbean development) have done little to alleviate poverty and unemployment in the region.

In the early twenty-first century, then, the region has experienced rising but comparatively moderate rates of poverty, with inner-city communities and blighted urban areas experiencing harsh conditions. Women, children, and young people have been the victims, as they make up a high proportion of those trapped in poverty. Throughout the region, the fifteen to twenty-five age group has had the lowest level of educational achievement and the highest rate of unemployment. Though better off when compared with poverty-stricken nations elsewhere, the Anglophone Caribbean has several countries with particularly deep pockets of urban poverty.

But even here, paradox is apparent: the level of material want in the Caribbean has been buffered by protective circumstances that rescue the poor-but-not-indigent urban population from great material want. These alleviating circumstances include massive poverty-relief programs throughout the region, significant remittances from relatives abroad, and poor people turning to crime and petty entrepreneurship in the informal, underground economy. Together with extensive migration away from the region, these measures have tempered the worst effects of poverty and economic hardship in the Caribbean.

See also Caribbean Commission; Caribbean Community and Common Market (CARICOM); International Relations of the Anglophone Caribbean; Media and Identity in the Caribbean; Mortality and Morbidity, Latin America and the Caribbean

Bibliography

Green, Charles, ed. *Globalization and Survival in the Black Diaspora: The New Urban Challenge.* Albany: State University of New York Press, 1997.

Moser, Caroline, and Jeremy Holland. *Urban Poverty and Violence in Jamaica.* Washington, D.C.: World Bank, 1997. Available from <http://poverty.worldbank.org>.

Robotham, Don. "A Challenge for the Whole Society." *Jamaica Gleaner Online,* October 19, 2003. Available from <http://www.jamaica-gleaner.com>.

Sahay, Ratna. "Stabilization, Debt, and Fiscal Policy in the Caribbean." Paper presented at a high-level seminar on Developmental Challenges Facing the Caribbean, June 11–12, 2004, Port-of-Spain, Trinidad and Tobago. Available from <http://www.imf.org>.

Wilson, William Julius. *When Work Disappears: The World of the New Urban Poor.* New York: Vintage, 1996.

World Bank. *Guyana Poverty Reduction Strategy Paper.* Washington, D.C.: World Bank, 2002. Available from <http://poverty.worldbank.org>.

World Bank. *Trinidad and Tobago: Poverty and Unemployment in an Oil-Based Economy.* Washington, D.C.: World Bank, 1995. Available from <http://wbln0018.worldbank.org>.

OBIKA GRAY (2005)

URBAN RIOTS

See Riots and Popular Protests

VanDerZee, James

June 29, 1886
May 15, 1983

Photographer James Augustus VanDerZee was born in Lenox, Massachusetts, the eldest son and second child of Susan Brister and John VanDerZee. He grew up in Lenox and attended the public schools there. In 1900 he won a small box camera as the premium for selling packets of sachet powder. Shortly afterward he purchased a larger camera and began photographing family members, friends, and residents in Lenox. Thus began his lifelong commitment to photography. In 1906 VanDerZee and his brother Walter moved to New York City to join their father, who was working there. By this time VanDerZee was already an accomplished photographer; however, his first New York job was waiting tables in the private dining room of a bank. In New York he met his first wife, Kate L. Brown, whom he married in 1907. The next year he and Kate moved to Phoebus, Virginia, then a small resort town near her home at Newport News. He worked as a waiter at the popular Hotel Chamberlin, a favored resort for the wealthy in Hampton. While in Virginia, VanDerZee continued photographing and made some of his most notable early images: photographs of the faculty and students of the Whittier School, a preparatory academy for Hampton Institute.

In 1908, after the birth of their first child Rachel, the family returned to New York. VanDerZee continued working at a variety of jobs, including photography. For a brief period he commuted to Newark, New Jersey, where he operated the camera in a department-store portrait studio. In 1910, a son, Emile, was born. At the end of the first quarter-century of his life, James VanDerZee had much to celebrate—he was twice a father, happily married, and a success in the economically competitive world of pre–World War I New York. But this period of happiness did not last long. Emile died in 1911, and the following year, VanDerZee and Kate separated.

VanDerZee had recovered sufficiently by 1916 to open his first photography portrait studio. It was in Harlem, on 135th Street at Lenox Avenue. He also had a partner in the enterprise, his new wife, Gaynella Greenlee Katz. From 1916 to 1931 VanDerZee stayed at this location, and the studio became one of Harlem's most prominent photographic operations. He specialized in portraits and wedding photographs but also took on assignments away from the studio. Among these assignments was his work for Marcus Garvey in 1924. It was also during these years that

VanDerZee began his experimental photomontage assemblages.

VanDerZee and his wife weathered the Great Depression, and in 1943, in the midst of World War II (1939–45), they purchased the building they had been renting at 272 Lenox Avenue. For the rest of the decade he continued his portrait work and took assignments for a variety of Harlem customers. However, a decline in business began to set in during the early 1950s. Ultimately, all he could maintain was a mail-order restoration business. Through a complicated series of loans and second mortgages, the VanDerZees were able to keep their property until 1969, when they were evicted. Ironically, VanDerZee's greatest fame and success as a photographer were yet to come.

Two years before his eviction, VanDerZee had met Reginald McGhee, who was a curator for the Metropolitan Museum exhibition *Harlem on My Mind*. Through McGhee's efforts, his work of the previous four decades became the central visual focus of the exhibition. The photographs became some of the most written-about images in the history of photography, while their maker was reduced to living on welfare. VanDerZee's fame grew when in 1969 McGhee and other young black photographers formed the James VanDerZee Institute, which showed his work in the United States and abroad. His photographs became even more widely known when three monographs were published during the 1970s. By the second half of that decade, VanDerZee's work was being sought out by both institutional and individual collectors. By the time Gaynella died in 1976, VanDerZee had become a symbol of artistry and courage to the Harlem community. He resumed making portraits, spoke at conferences, and gave countless interviews. In 1978, he was named the first recipient of the New York Archdiocese Pierre Toussaint Award. That year he married for the third time, to Donna Mussendon, a woman sixty years his junior.

In 1980, with his wife's help, VanDerZee began a series of portraits of African-American celebrities. Among his sitters were Eubie Blake, Miles Davis, Cicely Tyson, and Muhammad Ali. He made his last portrait, for art historian Reginia Perry, in February 1983. VanDerZee died on May 15, 1983. That day he had received an honorary doctorate of humane letters at the Howard University commencement. He was ninety-six years old.

See also Harlem, New York; Harlem Renaissance; Photography, U.S.

Bibliography

De Cock, Liliane, and Reginald McGhee. *James VanDerZee.* New York, 1973.

McGhee, Reginald. *The World of James VanDerZee: A Visual Record of Black Americans.* New York: Grove Press, 1969.

VanDerZee, James, et al. *The Harlem Book of the Dead.* New York: Morgan and Morgan, 1978.

Westerbeck, Colin, ed. *The James VanDerZee Studio.* Chicago: Art Institute of Chicago, 2004.

RODGER C. BIRT (1996)
Updated bibliography

Van Peebles, Melvin

August 21, 1932

Filmmaker Melvin Van Peebles was born on the South Side of Chicago in 1932. He grew up in Phoenix, Illinois, a middle-class suburb of Chicago. He attended West Virginia State College in Institute, West Virginia, and Ohio Wesleyan University in Delaware, Ohio, where he received a B.A. degree in literature in 1953.

After graduation, Van Peebles enlisted in the U.S. Air Force, where he spent three and a half years as a flight navigator. Facing a lack of employment opportunities for blacks at commercial airlines, Van Peebles was unable to continue this career after his military service. Instead, he became a cable-car gripman in San Francisco. In 1957 he published *The Big Heart,* a sentimental portrait of the cable cars illustrated with photographs by Ruth Bernard. Shortly afterward, he was fired from his job.

Van Peebles spent the next two years making a number of short films in an unsuccessful attempt to interest Hollywood in his ideas. Frustrated, he emigrated to the Netherlands, where he studied with the Dutch National Theatre and toured as an actor in Brendan Behan's play *The Hostage*. Van Peebles then moved to Paris to continue his attempt to get his work produced. He discovered that the French film directors' union would grant a union card to any writer who wished to make a film on his or her own. He wrote five works of fiction that were published in French: the novels *Un Ours pour le FBI* (translated as *A Bear for the FBI,* 1968); *Un Americain en enfer* (1965; translated as *The American: A Folk Fable,* 1965); *La Fête à Harlem* and *La Permission* (published jointly, 1965; the former translated as *Don't Play Us Cheap: A Harlem Party,* 1973); and a collection of short stories, *Le Chinois du XIVe* (1966). He filmed *La Permission,* under the title of *The Story of a Three Day Pass,* in 1967 for $200,000. The film concerns a black U.S. serviceman and the harassment he experiences when his army buddies discover that he has a white girlfriend. It was shown at the 1967 San Francisco

Film Festival, where it won the Critics Choice award for best film. The film garnered sufficient attention to earn Van Peebles a studio contract with Columbia Pictures.

In 1969, Van Peebles directed *Watermelon Man,* a farce about a white racist insurance salesman who wakes up one morning to discover that he has become black. Though the film was a moderate success, Van Peebles found that he disliked working in the studio system. He set out to make his next film, *Sweet Sweetback's Baadasssss Song* (1971), without studio financing. By employing non-union technicians, investing his own money, and receiving financial support from friends and investors, Van Peebles was able to shoot the film for $500,000. Although *Sweetback,* an unconventional fantasy film about a pimp-turned-revolutionary avenger, had difficulty finding distribution through mainstream sources, Van Peebles successfully promoted the film, and it had a large black audience. *Sweetback* became one of the top-grossing independently produced features, and its success proved that there was a large black audience ready for something other than mainstream films. Along with *Shaft,* released later in the same year, *Sweetback* inaugurated the era of the blaxploitation film. By portraying kinetic and picaresque black heroes in opposition to the white establishment, these films played out contemporary urban black fantasies of power and retribution.

The financial success of *Sweetback* made it possible for Van Peebles to open his musical play *Ain't Supposed to Die a Natural Death* on Broadway in 1972. The play's gritty portrayal of life in the black ghetto included frank and controversial discussions of lesbians and prostitution. When the play had difficulty attracting an audience, Van Peebles employed the same kind of tactics he had used to promote *Sweetback,* including the recruitment of black celebrities to attend the performances. Van Peebles's vigorous promotion efforts expanded the play's Broadway run to 325 performances.

While this show was still running, Van Peebles was able to mount another Broadway production, *Don't Play Us Cheap* (1972), adapted from his novel *A Harlem Party* (1973). A few months later, he shot a film version of *Don't Play Us Cheap.*

In 1973 Van Peebles went on tour throughout the United States with his one-man show *Out There by Your Lonesome,* his last stage work of the 1970s. In the middle of the 1970s he shifted to television, writing two scripts that were produced as television films for NBC. *Just an Old Sweet Song* was broadcast in 1976, and the highly regarded *Sophisticated Gents,* filmed in 1979, was broadcast in 1981. In 1982 Van Peebles returned to the stage to appear with his son Mario in his own *Waltz of the Stork.*

After *Waltz of the Stork* ended its run, Van Peebles temporarily set aside entertainment in favor of business, becoming an options trader on the floor of the American Stock Exchange in 1983. At the time, he was the only black trader at the exchange. In the middle of the decade, he followed up on his success in options trading with two books, *Bold Money: A New Way to Play the Options Market* (1986) and *Bold Money: How to Get Rich in the Options Market* (1987).

At the end of the decade, Van Peebles returned to entertainment to direct *Identity Crisis* (1989), a comedy film written by and starring his son Mario. He later acted in another of his son's films, *Posse* (1993), an all-black Western, as well as in such films as *Terminal Velocity* (1994), *Panther* (1995), and *Time of Her Time* (1999). In 2000 he released *Bellyful,* a film written thirty years earlier. In the mid-1990s he co-created two made-for-television films, *Gang in Blue* and *Riot.* He also resurrected his musical career with *Ghetto Gothic* in 1995.

In the 1990s Van Peebles's work received renewed attention as an influence on the second wave of black filmmaking. His films have been featured at several film festivals. In 1990 the Museum of Modern Art honored him with a retrospective showing of his film oeuvre.

See also Blaxploitation Films; Film in the United States, Contemporary

Bibliography

Cripps, Thomas. "Sweet Sweetback's Baadasssss Song and the Changing Politics of Genre Film." In Peter Lehman, ed. *Close Viewings: Recent Film.* Tampa, Fla., 1990.

"Melvin Van Peebles." *Encyclopedia of World Biography Supplement,* vol. 21. Detroit, Mich.: Gale, 2001. Reproduced in *Biography Resource Center.* Farmington Hills, Mich.: Thomson Gale, 2005. Available from <http://galenet.galegroup.com/servlet/BioRC>.

Parrish, James Robert, and George C. Hill. *Black Action Films.* Chapel Hill, N.C., 1989.

ELIZABETH V. FOLEY (1996)
Updated by publisher 2005

Varick, James

1750
July 22, 1827

The church founder, bishop, and abolitionist James Varick was born near Newburgh, New York, to a slave mother (manumitted when Varick was a small boy) and a free father. When he was sixteen, he joined the John Street Methodist Episcopal Church in New York City, where he was eventually licensed to preach. He learned shoemaking and had opened his own business by 1783. In 1790 he married Aurelia Jones and they had seven children, four of whom lived to adulthood.

As black membership in the John Street Church grew, segregation was introduced and black members had to sit in the back pews. In 1796, in response, a small group of black men, led by Varick, obtained church approval to hold separate services for the black congregation. By 1800 they had purchased a lot and built their own church and they secured an independent charter in 1801. This church, the African Methodist Episcopal (AME) Zion Church, became the mother church of the AME Zion Church movement.

In 1806 Varick and two others were ordained as the first black deacons in New York. Varick's intelligence, oratorical skills, and piety were well known and he became a spokesperson for African Americans and a pioneer in the independent black church movement. He assisted in and encouraged the formation of the Zion Church in New Haven in 1818, and in Philadelphia in 1820. He also fought for twenty years to free his church from white Methodist Episcopal control. In 1820 Varick led his congregation to adopt resolutions (which he had written) that would formally separate the Zion church from the white denomination. Not only was he able to formally charter this new denomination based on Wesleyan Methodist doctrines (and not to be confused with the African Methodist Episcopal Church founded in 1816 by Richard Allen), but he made sure that the church maintained undisputed rights to its finances and properties. In 1821 he was elected district elder during a conference with other black Methodist leaders. And after a two-year struggle with the white church hierarchy, he was finally ordained as the first black bishop of the independent African Methodist Episcopal Zion Church in 1822.

Varick was a gifted preacher, but black preachers were paid little or nothing. During the twenty-year struggle to break away from white control, the white pastor of his church made a full-time salary while Varick was forced to continue in the shoemaking trade and also taught classes out of his home. Yet this did not slow his efforts for equality. He was named the first chaplain of the New York African Society for Mutual Relief in 1810. In 1817 he became one of the vice presidents of the New York African Bible Society. Having been deeply influenced by the spirit of the revolution, in 1821 he joined a group of black businessmen and clergy and petitioned the New York State Constitutional Convention for black suffrage. He was strongly opposed to the colonization movement and worked to enlighten white supporters as to its unfairness.

Shortly before his death in his home in 1827, Varick became one of the founders of the first black newspaper in the United States, *Freedom's Journal.* His commitment to freedom for all and to universal dignity were in evidence in all the articles he contributed.

In 1996, the AME Zion Church held its bicentennial. More than 15,000 members converged on Washington, D.C., in July, and a celebration was held in New York in October. In addition to the festivities, an exhibit of AME archives was on display at the Schomburg Center for Research and Black Culture.

See also African Methodist Episcopal Zion Church; *Freedom's Journal*

Bibliography

Logan, Rayford W., and Michael R. Winston, eds. *Dictionary of American Negro Biography.* New York: Norton, 1982.

Washington, Joseph R., Jr. *Black Religion.* Boston: Beacon Press, 1964.

Wilmore, Gayraud S. *Black Religion and Black Radicalism.* New York: Doubleday, 1972.

SASHA THOMAS (1996)
DEBI BROOME (1996)
Updated by publisher 2005

VASSA, GUSTAVUS

See Equiano, Olaudah

VAUGHAN, SARAH

MARCH 29, 1924
APRIL 3, 1990

Nicknamed "Sassy" and "the Divine One," Sarah Vaughan is considered one of America's greatest vocalists and part of the triumvirate of women jazz singers that includes Ella Fitzgerald (1917–1996) and Billie Holiday (1915–1959). A unique stylist, she possessed vocal capabilities—lush tones, perfect pitch, and a range exceeding three octaves—that were matched by her adventurous, sometimes radical sense of improvisation. Born in Newark, New Jersey, she began singing and playing organ in the Mount Zion Baptist Church when she was twelve.

In October 1942, Vaughan sang "Body and Soul" to win an amateur-night contest at Harlem's Apollo Theater. Billy Eckstine (1914–1993), the singer for Earl "Fatha" Hines's big band, happened to hear her and was so impressed that he persuaded Hines to hire Vaughan as a second pianist and singer in early 1943. Later that year, when Eckstine left Hines to organize his own big band, Vaughan went with him. In his group, one of the incubators of bebop jazz, Vaughan was influenced by Eckstine's vibrato-laced baritone, and by the innovations of such fellow musicians as Dizzy Gillespie and Charlie Parker. Besides inspiring her to forge a personal style, they instilled in her a lifelong desire to improvise. ("It was just like going to school," she said.)

Vaughan made her first records for the Continental label on New Year's Eve 1944, and she began working as a solo act the following year at New York's Cafe Society. At the club she met the trumpeter George Treadwell, who became her manager and the first of her four husbands. Treadwell promoted Vaughan and helped create her glamorous image. Following hits on Musicraft (including "It's Magic" and "If They Could See Me Now") and Columbia ("Black Coffee"), her success was assured. From 1947 through 1952, she was voted Top Female Vocalist in polls in *Down Beat* and *Metronome* jazz magazines.

Throughout the 1950s, Vaughan recorded pop material for Mercury Records, including such hits as "Make Yourself Comfortable" and "Broken-Hearted Melody" and songbooks (like those made by Ella Fitzgerald) of classic American songs by George Gershwin and Irving Berlin; she also recorded jazz sessions on the EmArcy label (Mercury's jazz label) with trumpeter Clifford Brown, the Count Basie Orchestra, and other jazz musicians. By the mid-1960s, frustrated by the tactics of record companies trying to sustain her commercially, Vaughan took a five-year hiatus from recording. By the 1970s, her voice had become darker and richer.

Vaughan was noted for a style in which she treated her voice like a jazz instrument rather than as a conduit for lyrics. A contralto, she sang wide leaps easily, improvised sometimes subtle, sometimes dramatic melodic and rhythmic lines, and made full use of timbral expressiveness—from clear tones to bluesy growls with vibrato. By the end of her career, she had performed in more than sixty countries, in small boîtes and in football stadiums, with jazz trios as well as symphony orchestras. Her signature songs, featured at almost all of her shows, included "Misty," "Tenderly," and "Send In the Clowns." She died of cancer in 1990, survived by one daughter.

See also Fitzgerald, Ella; Holiday, Billie; Jazz; Jazz Singers

Bibliography

Azrai, Ahmad. "Sublimely 'Sassy'." *Asia Africa Intelligence Wire*, July 1, 2003.

Giddins, Gary. "Sarah Vaughan." In *Rhythm-a-Ning: Jazz Tradition and Innovation in the '80s.* New York: Oxford University Press, 1985, pp. 26–34.

Jones, Max. "Sarah Vaughan." In *Talking Jazz* New York: W. W. Norton, 1988, pp. 260–265.

"Sarah Vaughan." *Contemporary Black Biography*, vol. 13. Detroit, Mich.: Gale, 1996.

BUD KLIMENT (1996)
Updated bibliography

Vernacular Architecture

See Architecture: Vernacular Architecture

Vietnam War

See Military Experience, African-American

Vodou

See Voodoo

Voodoo

Voodoo, also spelled Vodou (following the official Haitian Creole orthography) or vodoun, refers to traditional religious practices in Haiti and in Haitian-American communities such as the sizable ones in New York City and Miami. New Orleans has the oldest Haitian immigrant community, dating from the eighteenth century. In New Orleans priests and priestesses are sometimes called "voodoos," and throughout the southern United States the term is also used as a verb, to "voodoo" someone, meaning to bewitch or punish by magical means. More frequently "voodoo," or "hoodoo"—as well as "conjure," "rootwork," and "witchcraft"—is a term used to refer to a diverse collection of traditional spiritual practices among descendants of African slaves in the United States.

Haiti, a small, mountainous, and impoverished West Indian country, was a French slave colony and a major sugar producer during the eighteenth century. The strongest African influences on Haitian Vodou came from the Fon and Mahi peoples of old Dahomey (now the Republic of Benin); the Yoruba peoples, mostly in Nigeria; and the Kongo peoples of Angola and Zaire. The term *vodun* is West African, probably Ewe, in origin and came to the Western Hemisphere with Dahomean slaves. Today, "vodun" is the most common Fon term for a traditional spirit or deity.

Haitian Vodou is said to have played a key role in the only successful slave revolution in the history of transatlantic slavery, the plotters being bound to one another by a blood oath taken during a Vodou ceremony. The ceremony, conducted by the legendary priest Makandal, took place in Bois Cayman in northern Haiti. It is also claimed that word of the uprising spread via Vodou talking drums, and Vodou charms gave strength and courage to the rebels.

Haiti declared its independence in 1804, when the United States and much of Europe still held slaves. For approximately fifty years the Catholic Church refused to send priests to Haiti, and for nearly a century the struggling black republic was economically isolated from the larger world. Political concerns played a major role in shaping the negative image of Haitian Vodou in the West. Vodou has been caricatured as a religion obsessed with sex, blood, death, and evil. The reality of Haitian Vodou, a religion that blends African traditions with Catholicism, is strikingly different from the stereotypes.

Following independence, large numbers of Haitians acquired small plots of land and became subsistence farmers. This agricultural base distinguishes Vodou from other New World African religions. Central to Vodou are three loyalties: to land (even urban practitioners return to conduct ceremonies on ancestral land), to family (including the dead), and to the Vodou spirits. Most Haitians do not call their religion Vodou, a word that more precisely refers to one style of drumming and dancing. Haitians prefer a verbal form. "Li sevi lwa-yo," they say, "he (or she) serves the spirits." Most spirits have two names, a Catholic saint's name and an African name. Daily acts of devotion include lighting candles and pouring libations. Devotees wear a favored spirit's color and observe food and behavior prohibitions the spirits request. When there are special problems, they make pilgrimages to Catholic shrines and churches and undertake other trials. Most important, they stage elaborate ceremonies that include singing, drumming, dancing, and sumptuous meals, the most prestigious of which necessitate killing an animal. Possession, central in Vodou, provides direct communication with the *lwa,* or spirits. A devotee who becomes a "horse" of one of the spirits turns over body and voice to that *lwa*. The spirit can then sing and dance with the faithful, bless them, chastise them, and give advice. In Vodou persons are defined by webs of relationship with family, friends, ancestors, and spirits. The central work of Vodou ritual, whether performed in a community setting or one-on-one, is enhancing and healing relationships. Gifts of praise, food, song and dance are necessary to sustain spirits and ancestors and to enable them to reciprocate by providing wisdom and protection to the living.

The large Haitian immigrant communities that have grown up in the United States over the last forty years are thriving centers for Vodou practice. Hundreds of Vodou healers serve thousands of clients who are taxi drivers, restaurant workers, and nurse's aides. Most of the rituals performed in Haiti are now also staged, albeit in truncated form, in living rooms and basements in New York and Miami. Vodou "families" provide struggling immigrants with connections to Haitian roots and an alternative to American individualism.

Voodoo in New Orleans is more distant from its Haitian roots. Scholars believe there were three generations of women called Marie Laveau who worked as spiritual counselors in New Orleans. The first was a slave brought from Haiti to Louisiana during the time of the slave revolution. The most famous Marie Laveau, the "voodoo queen of New Orleans," born in 1827, was the granddaughter of this slave woman. The religion she practiced was a distillation of Haitian Vodou. She kept a large snake on her altar (a representative of the spirit Danbala Wedo), went into possession while dancing in Congo Square, presided over an elaborate annual ceremony on the banks of Lake Pontchartrain on St. John's Eve (June 24), and above all, worked with individual clients as a spiritual adviser, healer, and supplier of charms, or *gris-gris.* Contemporary New Orleans voodoo is largely limited to these last activities.

Hoodoo, or voodoo as practiced throughout the American South, is similarly limited to discrete client/practitioner interactions. This type of voodoo is not a child of Haiti but the legacy of Dahomean and Kongo persons among North American slaves. As with Haitian Vodou, engagement with hoodoo has typically worked as a supplement to Christianity, most likely because hoodoo addresses issues Christianity ignores—issues of spiritual protection, romantic love, and luck. Harry M. Hyatt (1970) said it well: "To catch a spirit or to protect your spirit against the catching or to release your caught spirit—this is the complete theory and practice of hoodoo." The spiritual powers used in voodoo or hoodoo are morally neutral (e.g., souls of persons not properly buried) and can therefore be used constructively or destructively. Yet clear moral distinctions in how they are used are not always easy to make.

In hoodoo the illness in one person may be traced to an emotion in another, jealousy being the most destructive. In such a case, attacking the jealous person may be the only way to a cure. A related dynamic emerges in love magic, a very common type of healing that inevitably tries to control another's will. Zora Neale Hurston collected this cure for a restless husband: "Take sugar, cinnamon and mix together: Write name of a husband and wife nine times. Roll paper . . . and put in a bottle of holy water with sugar and honey. Lay it under the back step." There have been root doctors—conjure men and women—who have used their powers unethically and maliciously, but hoodoo's fear-provoking reputation is unmerited. Most hoodoo or voodoo is of the type described in Hurston's example.

See also Candomblé; Central African Religions and Culture in the Americas; Divination and Spirit Possession in the Americas; Myal; Orisha; Religion; Santería; Slave Religions; Yoruba Religion and Culture in the Americas

Bibliography

Brown, Karen McCarthy. "The Power to Heal: Reflections on Women, Religion, and Medicine." In *Shaping New Vision: Gender and Values in American Culture*, edited by Clarissa W. Atkinson, Constance H. Buchanan, and Margaret R. Miles, pp. 123–141. Ann Arbor: University of Michigan Press, 1987.

Brown, Karen McCarthy. *Mama Lola: A Vodou Priestess in Brooklyn*. Los Angeles and Berkeley: University of California Press, 1991.

Deren, Maya. *Divine Horsemen: The Voodoo Gods of Haiti*. 1970. Reprint, New Paltz, N.Y.: McPherson, 1983.

Herskovits, Melville. *Life in a Haitian Valley*. Garden City, N.Y.: Anchor Books, 1971.

Hurston, Zora Neale. "Hoodoo in America." *Journal of American Folklore* 44 (1931): 316–417.

Hurston, Zora Neale. *Mules and Men*. New York: Harper & Row, 1970.

Hyatt, Harry Middleton. *Hoodoo-Conjuration-Witchcraft-Rootwork: Beliefs Accepted by Many Negroes and White Persons, These Being Orally Recorded Among Blacks and Whites*. Hannibal, Mo.: Western Publishing, 1970.

Laguerre, Michel S. *American Odyssey: Haitians in New York City*. Ithaca, N.Y.: Cornell University Press, 1984.

McAlister, Elizabeth A. *Rara: Vodou, Power, and Performance in Haiti and Its Diaspora*. Berkeley: University of California Press, 2002.

Metraux, Alfred. *Voodoo in Haiti*, trans. by Hugo Charteris. New York: Oxford University Press, 1972.

KAREN MCCARTHY BROWN (1996)
Updated bibliography

Voting Rights Act of 1965

The Voting Rights Act of 1965, signed into law by President Lyndon B. Johnson on August 6, 1965, was intended to reverse the historic disenfranchisement of the black electorate, which had been the hallmark of southern politics since the end of Reconstruction. It applied to states and counties in which a test or other device was used to determine voter eligibility, and where voter registration or turnout for the 1964 presidential election had been less than 50 percent of potentially eligible voters. In those "covered jurisdictions," it suspended literacy and other racially discriminatory tests; authorized federal examiners to replace or supplement local registrars; allowed federal observers at polling sites; and required advance federal approval for changes in election laws and voting procedures. It also expanded the voting rights of non-English-speaking citizens.

Although the Fifteenth and Nineteenth Amendments to the U.S. Constitution had conferred voting rights on black men and black women, respectively, violence and economic reprisals, as well as more subtle methods, had effectively barred African Americans from the election rolls for generations. Although the Civil Rights Acts of 1957, 1960, and 1964 contained some voting rights provisions, their enforcement depended on the cooperation of recalcitrant southerners and on appeals through a slow, cumbersome judicial process.

In the context of rising demands for more substantive redress of race-based discrimination, the Johnson administration proposed to restore suffrage by a more direct route. In Selma, Alabama, black people had tried to register to vote in the early 1960s; obstructed from doing so, they appealed to the Justice Department for support. By late 1964, the Southern Christian Leadership Conference (SCLC) decided to launch an all-out campaign in Selma aimed at winning new federal voting-rights legislation. Their efforts were met with police attacks and mass arrests, which culminated in a brutal assault on peaceful demonstrators marching to Montgomery on March 7, 1965. Even though "Bloody Sunday" was not the direct catalyst for Johnson's initiative, it proved decisive for rallying public and congressional sentiment around his plan.

Congressional passage of the bill was marked by intense controversy, however. The Johnson administration successfully resisted efforts to impose an outright ban on poll taxes (although the Supreme Court struck down the poll tax in 1966), and House Republican leaders and southern Democrats failed in their bid to weaken the legis-

FIGURE 3

Voting-age population, percent reporting registered, 1976–2004

	Population (in millions)		% Registered				% Voted			
			Presidential election years		Congressional election years		Presidential election years		Congressional election years	
Year	Total	Black	Total	Black	Total	Black	Total	Black	Total	Black
1976	146.5	14.9	66.7	58.5	—	—	59.2	48.7	—	—
1978	151.6	15.6	—	—	62.6	57.1	—	—	45.9	37.2
1980	157.1	16.4	66.9	60.0	—	—	59.2	50.5	—	—
1982	165.5	17.6	—	—	64.1	59.1	—	—	48.8	43.0
1984	170.0	18.4	68.3	66.3	—	—	59.9	55.8	—	—
1986	173.9	19.0	—	—	64.3	64.0	—	—	46.0	43.2
1988	178.1	19.7	66.6	64.5	—	—	57.4	51.5	—	—
1990	182.1	20.4	—	—	62.2	58.8	—	—	45.0	39.2
1992	185.6	n.a.	68.2	63.9	—	—	61.3	54.0	—	—
1994	190.2	n.a.	—	—	62.5	58.5	—	—	45.0	37.1
1996	193.6	n.a.	65.9	63.5	—	—	54.2	50.6	—	—
1998	198.2	22.6	—	—	62.1	60.9	—	—	41.9	40.0
2000	202.6	23.6	63.9	64.3	—	—	54.7	54.1	—	—
2002	210.4	24.4	—	—	60.9	58.5	—	—	42.3	39.7
2004	215.7	24.9	65.9	64.4	—	—	58.3	56.3	—	—

SOURCE: U.S. Bureau of the Census, *Current Population Reports.*

lation. Still, in its final form, the measure was overwhelmingly approved, by a vote of 328 to 74 in the House and 79 to 18 in the Senate.

In the immediate aftermath of the act's passage, impressive gains were made by federal authorities; in the first six months, they registered more than 100,000 southern blacks, while local officials, aware of the new threat of federal action, added another 200,000. In 1965, some 2 million African Americans were registered to vote in the South; by mid-1970, that figure had jumped to 3.3 million.

But the Justice Department preferred voluntary compliance with the new directives; moreover, since enforcement depended on the department's own vigorous commitment, during the Nixon and Ford years it was significantly weaker than in the early period. The Nixon administration, in fact, sought to dramatically curtail the act's powers when it came up for Congressional extension in 1970.

Many southern officials resisted the Voting Rights Act, challenging its constitutionality in court and continuing to withhold the ballot through arbitrary means. They also adopted new mechanisms that, although not directly denying the right to register and vote, diluted the black community's electoral power. Using a variety of techniques—redrawing districts to break up black majorities (racial gerrymandering), imposing new restrictions and property qualifications on candidates, and holding at-large races in which an expanded electoral base ensured a white majority—southern politicians made it difficult for black candidates to run for and win office. These measures were contested by civil rights advocates in litigation that lasted well into the 1980s. In the case of *Mobile v. Bolden* in 1980, the Supreme Court upheld the use of at-large elections, arguing that their practical effect—preventing minority black populations from electing their own candidates—was not the same as discriminatory intent.

The Voting Rights Act has been extended three times since its initial passage. Originally, its targets included Alabama, Georgia, Louisiana, Mississippi, South Carolina, Virginia, parts of North Carolina, and Alaska. In 1970 the ban on literacy tests was expanded nationwide and the formula for identifying covered areas was altered to broaden its scope. It was again extended in 1975, with less southern resistance than in the past. In 1982 the Reagan administration fought vigorously against another extension. But it was not only extended, it was also amended to address the wide range of strategies designed to circumvent its authority, effectively nullifying the Mobile decision. By 1989, a total of 7,200 African-Americans held elected office in the United States (compared to just 500 in 1965); of these, 67 percent were in the South.

See also Civil Rights Movement, U.S.; King, Martin Luther, Jr.; Politics in the United States; Southern Christian Leadership Conference (SCLC)

Bibliography

Davidson, Chandler, and Bernard Grofman, eds *The Quiet Revolution: The Impact of the Voting Rights Act in the South, 1965–1990.* Princeton, N.J.: Princeton University Press, 1994.

Garrow, David J. *Protest at Selma: Martin Luther King, Jr., and the Voting Rights Act of 1965.* New Haven, Conn.: Yale University Press, 1978.

Parker, Frank R. *Black Votes Count: Political Empowerment in Mississippi after 1965.* Chapel Hill: University of North Carolina Press, 1990.

Pildes, Richard H. "Diffusion of Political Power and the Voting Rights Act." *Harvard Journal of Law & Public Policy* 24, no. 1 (2000): 119.

Weisbrot, Robert. *Freedom Bound: A History of America's Civil Rights Movement.* New York: Norton, 1990.

Valelly, Richard. "Voting Rights in Jeopardy." *The American Prospect* 10, no. 46 (September 1999): 43.

Valelly, Richard. *The Two Reconstructions: The Struggle for Black Enfranchisement.* Chicago: University of Chicago Press, 2004.

MICHAEL PALLER (1996)
TAMI J. FRIEDMAN (1996)
Updated bibliography

Walcott, Derek Alton

January 23, 1930

The poet, playwright, and essayist Derek Walcott is the son of Warwick Walcott, a civil servant and skilled painter in watercolor who also wrote verse, and Alix Walcott, a schoolteacher who took part in amateur theater. He and his twin brother Roderick were born in Castries, Saint Lucia, a small island in the Lesser Antilles of the West Indies. He grew up in a house he describes as haunted by the absence of a father who had died quite young, because all around the drawing room were his father's watercolors. He regards his beginnings as an artist, therefore, as a natural and direct inheritance: "I feel that I have continued where my father left off." After completing his studies at St. Mary's College in his native Saint Lucia, he continued his education at the University of the West Indies in Kingston, Jamaica.

His literary career began in 1948 with his first book of verse, *25 Poems* (1948), followed not long thereafter by *Epitaph for the Young, XII Cantos* (1949), and *Poems* (1951), all privately published in the Caribbean. The decade of the 1950s, however, marked his emergence as a playwright-director in Trinidad. His first theater piece, *Henri Cristophe* (1950), a historical play about the tyrant-liberator of Haiti, was followed by a series of well-received folk-dramas in verse. *The Sea at Dauphin* (1954), *Ione* (1957), and *Ti-Jean and His Brothers* (1958) are usually cited among the most noteworthy, along with his most celebrated dramatic work, *Dream on Monkey Mountain* (an Obie Award winner), which he began in the late 1950s but did not produce until 1967 in Toronto. After a brief stay in the United States as a Rockefeller Fellow, Walcott returned to Trinidad in 1959 to become the founding director of the Trinidad Theatre Workshop. He continues to work as a dramatist, contributing a libretto for the Paul Simon Broadway musical *Capeman* (1997), and is still more likely to be identified by a West Indian audience as a playwright.

Walcott debuted internationally as a poet with *In a Green Night: Poems 1948–1960* (1962), followed shortly thereafter by *Selected Poems* (1964). These volumes established the qualities usually identified with his verse: virtuosity in traditional, particularly European literary forms; enthusiasm for allegory and classical allusion—for which he is both praised and criticized; and the struggle within himself over the cruel history and layered cultural legacy of Africa and Europe reflected in the Caribbean landscape, which some critics have interpreted as the divided con-

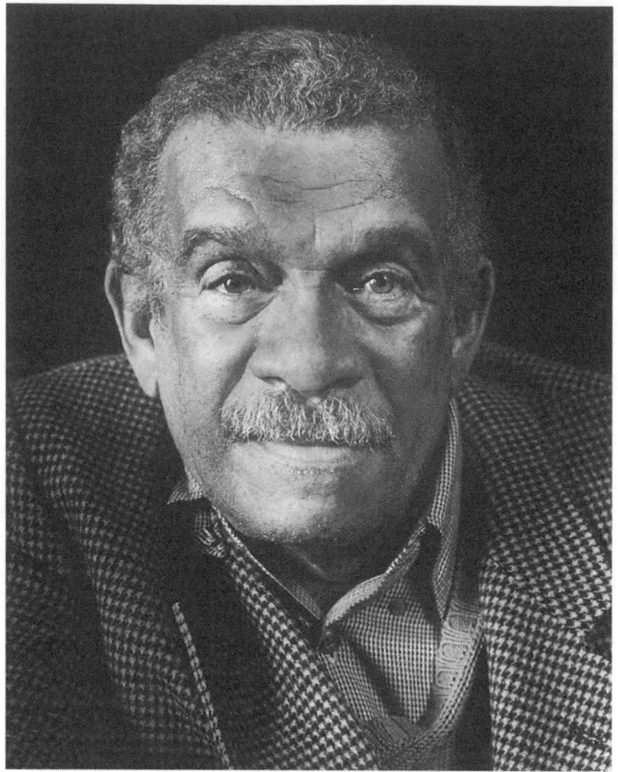

Playwright and poet Derek Walcott. *Walcott, born in St. Lucia, became the first native West Indian writer to win the Nobel Prize for Literature in 1992.* © CHRISTOPHER FELVER/CORBIS

sciousness of a Caribbean ex-colonial in the twilight of empire. A prolific quarter-century of work was shaped by recurrent patterns of departure, wandering, and return—in his life as well as in his poetry—and a powerful preoccupation with the visual imagery of the sea, beginning with *Castaway and Other Poems* (1965), in which he establishes an imaginative topography (e.g., of "seas and coasts as white pages"), and a repertory of myths, themes, and motifs (e.g., of "words like migrating birds") for the titular exile, a repertory that recurs in later volumes.

In *The Gulf and Other Poems* (1969), reprinted with *Castaway and Other Poems* in a single volume titled *The Gulf* (1970) in the United States, he sounds an ever more personal note as he considers the Caribbean from the alienating perspective of the political turbulence of the late 1960s in the southern and Gulf states of the United States. In *Another Life* (1973), his book-length self-portrait (dealing with his life both as a young man and at age forty-one), he contemplates the suicide of his mentor and the attempted suicide of a close childhood companion with whom he discovered the promise, and the disappointment, of their lives dedicated to art. In *Sea Grapes* (1976), he identifies the Caribbean wanderer as caught up in the same ancient and unresolved dilemmas as the exiles Adam and Odysseus, whose pain the poems of a West Indian artist, like the language of the Old Testament and the Greek and Latin classics, can console but never cure.

At his most eloquent in *The Star-Apple Kingdom* (1979), Walcott fingers the rosary of the Antilles in the title poem in order to expose the inhumanity and corruption belied by the gilt-framed Caribbean pastoral of the colonialist's star-apple kingdom, so named for a native fruit tree found in the West Indies. In the volume's other verse narrative, "The Schooner Flight," he finds a powerful voice in the West Indian vernacular of the common man endowed with "no weapon but poetry and the lances of palms of the sea's shiny shields." In *The Fortunate Traveler* (1981) he sounds repeated and painful notes of exhaustion, isolation, and disappointment of the peripatetic poet in exile and at home, perhaps most sharply in the satirical mode of the *kaiso* (a Trinidadian term for calypso) vernacular of "The Spoiler Returns."

In *Midsummer* (1984), published in his fifty-fourth year, he probes the situation of the poet as prodigal, *nel mezzo del camin* (in the middle of the journey) of exile in fifty-four untitled stanzas of elegiac meter. In *The Arkansas Testament* (1987), divided into the sections "Here" and "Elsewhere" (recalling the divisions of "North" and "South" of *The Fortunate Traveler*), he succumbs once again to pangs of art's estrangement. However, in *Omeros* (1990), his most ambitious verse narrative yet, he overlays his problematic but richly figured Caribbean environment with Homer's transformative Mediterranean domain, weaving together the myths, themes, motifs, and imaginary geography of a prolific career to attempt a consummation and reconciliation of the psychic divisions and the spiritual and moral wounds of history and exile.

In 1992 Walcott was awarded the Nobel Prize for literature. In the following decade he published three books of poetry: *The Bounty* (1997), *Tiepolo's Hound* (2000), and *The Prodigal* (2004). He has explored, in different registers, the arc of a lifetime, and a heightened sense of mortality—brought on by the deaths of his mother, Alix; his brother Roderick; and many friends—inflects his work as he addresses his personal sunset in the twilight of empire. "This is how people look at death / and write a literature of gliding transience / as the sun loses its sight, singing of islands" (*The Prodigal*, p. 54). Themes, phrases, and motifs established earlier—the mysteries of language, the writer's vocation, exile and homecoming, and the echoes of his beloved Caribbean—are evoked and reworked together (often "blent" together, to use a favored Walcott word) in a single verbal flourish. A singular image of the prodigal sitting like Oedipus on his plinth at Colonus awaiting transformation catches the spirit of Walcott's new mood in these works.

Although he has described himself as a citizen of "no nation but the imagination," and has lived as an international bard, directing plays, creating poetry, and teaching at a number of colleges and universities, he has remained faithful to the Caribbean as his normative landscape. His affirmation of identity and of the significance of myth over history for the poetic imagination is inseparable from a discussion of the historic drama played out over recent centuries across the islands of the Caribbean, and from which the Odyssean wayfarer ventures in a lifelong cycle of escape and return. This profound engagement with the Caribbean, explored in a series of early essays—"What the Twilight Says: An Overture," "Meanings," and "The Muse of History"—and restated in his Nobel lecture *The Antilles: Fragments of Epic Memory,* is summed up in a particularly poignant credo: "I accept this archipelago of the Americas. I say to the ancestor who sold me, and to the ancestor who bought me . . . and also you, father in the filth-ridden gut of the slave ship . . . to you inwardly forgiven grandfathers, I like the more honest of my race, give a strange thanks. I give the strange and bitter and yet ennobling thanks for the monumental groaning and soldering of two great worlds, like the halves of a fruit seamed by its own bitter juices, that exiled from your own Edens you have placed me in the wonder of another, that was my inheritance and your gift."

See also Caribbean/North American Writers (Contemporary); Literature of the English-Speaking Caribbean

Bibliography

Baugh, Edward. "Derek Walcott and the Centering of the Caribbean Subject." *Research in African Literatures* 34, no. 1 (2003): 151–159.

Breslin, Paul. *Nobody's Nation: Reading Derek Walcott.* Chicago: University of Chicago Press, 2001.

Burnett, Paula. *Derek Walcott: Politics and Poetics.* Gainesville: University Press of Florida, 2000.

Dabydeen, David. "Derek Walcott in Conversation with David Dabydeen." *Wasafiri: The Transnational Journal of International Writing* 42 (2004): 37–41.

Hanner, Robert D. *Epic of the Dispossessed: Derek Walcott's Omeros.* Columbia: University of Missouri Press, 1997.

Thieme, John. *Derek Walcott.* Manchester, UK: Manchester University Press, 1999.

Walcott, Derek. *The Antilles: Fragments of Epic Memory: The Nobel Lecture.* New York: Farrar, Straus, & Giroux, 1993.

Walcott, Derek. *The Prodigal.* New York: Farrar, Straus, & Giroux, 2004.

JAMES DE JONGH (1996)
Updated by author 2005

Walcott, Frank

September 16, 1916
February 24, 1999

Frank Leslie Walcott was born in the parish of St. Peter on Barbados. His father died during Frank's infancy, and his mother, Marian Walcott, was a plantation worker who later migrated to the capital city of Bridgetown, where she worked as a domestic helper. After attending the Wesley Hall Boys' School, Walcott worked in two merchant houses in Bridgetown, where he observed the harsh conditions under which the Barbadian working class labored. Membership in the Weymouth Debating Club helped to round out his education, developed his talent for debate, and enabled him to establish contacts that would be important in later life.

In 1945 Walcott became an assistant to Hugh Springer, the general secretary of the Barbados Workers' Union (BWU) and a fellow member of Weymouth. In 1947, following Springer's resignation, Walcott acted as general secretary until he was formally elected to the post in 1948. He continued organizing as many sectors of the Barbadian working class as possible under the union's umbrella, increasing its social and political influence.

Walcott articulated the union's position on all social issues. The union helped to institutionalize industrial relations, successfully lobbied for labor and social legislation, established a credit union, strengthened its bureaucracy, and constructed modern physical facilities, a labor college, and housing for its membership.

Walcott was a member of the House of Assembly and, after breaking with Grantley Adams, premier and leader of the government and the Barbados Labour Party, in 1954, he became an independent. Later, he joined the Democratic Labour Party (DLP). He also served as president of the senate, wrote a newspaper column, and was Barbados's first ambassador to the United Nations. The BWU came of age during the era of British West Indian nationalism and economic modernization. In this, Walcott put the union's weight behind Barbados's national leadership.

Walcott remained a servant of the regional and international working class. Before ill health forced his retirement from public life in 1991, he was general secretary of the BWU for forty-three unbroken years and a longstanding member of regional and international labor organizations. He received an honorary Doctor of Laws degree from the University of the West Indies in 1987 and was made a Knight of St. Andrew in 1988. In 1998 he was declared a National Hero of Barbados. His work with the National Insurance Scheme was honored by the naming of its new complex in his honor. In a long, distinguished public career, he rose from the depths of the Barbadian working class and made the Barbados Workers' Union, and himself, respected both at home and abroad.

See also West Indies Democratic Labour Party

Bibliography

Mark, Francis. *The History of the Barbados Workers' Union.* Bridgetown: Barbados Workers' Union, c. 1966.

Morris, Robert, Leonard Shorey, and Ronnie Hughes. "Rt. Excellent Sir Frank Walcott, K.A. O.B.E. LL.D. The Days of the 'Boss' System Are Over." In *For Love of Country: The National Heroes of Barbados,* edited by Hilary McD. Beckles. St. Michael, Barbados: Foundation Publishing, 1998.

National Heroes of Barbados. Bridgetown: Barbados Government Information Service, 1998.

C. M. JACOBS (2005)

Walcott, Jersey Joe

January 13, 1914
February 25, 1994

Boxer Jersey Joe Walcott was born Arnold Raymond Cream and raised in Merchantville, near Camden, New Jersey, one of twelve children of Ella and Joseph Cream. His father, an immigrant from Barbados, died when Arnold was fourteen. To help support the family, the boy began working in a soup factory and did odd jobs. He also began to train as a boxer. In 1930 he started his professional career as a lightweight. Soon after, he took the name "Jersey Joe Walcott" in honor of Joe Walcott, a well-known Barbadian welterweight champion.

Walcott fought, largely in obscurity, for fifteen years before becoming a championship contender. In 1933, after growing into the light-heavyweight class, Walcott knocked out Al King to become the light-heavyweight champion of South Jersey. In 1936, in a heavyweight bout at Coney Island in Brooklyn, New York, Walcott attracted significant attention for the first time by knocking out Larry LaPage in three rounds. Unable to support himself and his family on his small boxing earnings, he worked in a number of manual labor jobs, fighting only sporadically.

In 1945, after a two-year stint working at the Camden shipyards, Walcott returned once more to boxing. Over the following two years, he won eleven of fourteen fights, including seven by knockouts. On December 5, 1947, he fought a heavyweight bout against champion Joe Louis. Although he knocked Louis down twice, he lost in a split decision. Many commentators felt that Walcott had defeated the champion, and he appealed the ruling unsuccessfully to the New York Athletic Commission. On June 25, 1948, he and Louis fought again. Although Walcott floored Louis, Louis knocked him out in the eleventh round.

The following year, Louis retired, and Walcott signed to box Ezzard Charles for the championship. On June 22, 1949, Charles beat Walcott in a fifteen-round decision for the title, then defeated him again in March 1951. Undaunted, Walcott signed to face Charles a third time. On July 18, 1951, in Pittsburgh, Pennsylvania, Walcott knocked Charles out in the seventh round, thus becoming the oldest man to that time to hold the heavyweight title. On June 15, 1952, Walcott successfully defended his title in a rematch with Charles. However, on September 23, 1952, Walcott fought Rocky Marciano, who knocked him out to take the heavyweight championship. Walcott met Marciano in a rematch on May 15, 1953, but was knocked out in the first round. He retired after the fight.

After retiring, Walcott worked as a fight referee and acted in the 1956 film *The Harder They Fall.* In 1972 he became sheriff of Camden County, New Jersey, and in 1975 he was made chair of the New Jersey State Athletic Commission. Following his retirement in 1984, he spent his time working with children for the New Jersey Department of Community Affairs. A longtime diabetic, he died in Camden in 1994 of complications resulting from the disease.

See also
Boxing; Louis, Joe

Bibliography

"Jersey Joe Walcott, Boxing Champion, Dies at 80." *New York Times,* February 26, 1994.

GREG ROBINSON (1996)

Walker, Aida Overton

1880

October 11, 1914

Aida Overton Walker was the leading African-American female performing artist at the turn of the twentieth century. Unsurpassed as a ragtime singer and cakewalk dancer, she became a national, then international, star at a time when authentic black folk culture was replacing minstrelsy and making a powerful and permanent impact on American vernacular entertainment. Born in New York City, Walker began her career in the chorus of "Black Patti's Troubadours." She married George William Walker, of the vaudeville comedy team Williams and Walker, and soon became the female lead in their series of major musical comedies: *The Policy Players, Sons of Ham, In Dahomey, Abyssinia,* and *Bandanna Land.*

In Dahomey played London in 1903, including a command performance before the royal family on the lawn of Buckingham Palace. Walker also choreographed these shows, perhaps the first woman to receive program credit for doing so. Among her best-known songs were "Miss Hannah from Savannah," "A Rich Coon's Babe," and "Why Adam Sinned." At George Walker's death she continued in musical theater and vaudeville, playing the best houses, including Hammerstein's Victoria Theater in New York, where she performed *Salome* in 1912. She died in New York in 1914, at the age of thirty-four. Critics considered Walker a singer and dancer superior to both of her better-known successors, Florence Mills and Josephine Baker.

See also Musical Theater; Social Dance; Theatrical Dance

Bibliography

"Aida Overton Walker Is Dead." *New York Age.* October 15, 1914.

Riis, Thomas Laurence. *Just Before Jazz: Black Musical Theater in New York, 1890–1915.* Washington, D.C.: Smithsonian Institution Press, 1989.

RICHARD NEWMAN (1996)

Walker, A'Lelia

June 6, 1885

August 17, 1931

Through the lavish parties she hosted, entrepreneur A'Lelia Walker made herself the center of elite social life during the Harlem Renaissance. She was born Lelia Walker to Sarah and Moses McWilliams in Vicksburg, Mississippi. (She changed her name to "A'Lelia" as an adult.) After her father died when she was two, her mother took her to St. Louis. She attended public schools there and graduated from Knoxville College, a private black school in Knoxville, Tennessee.

She and her mother then moved to Denver, where her mother married C. J. Walker, from whom they took their surnames. A'Lelia also married, but although she took the surname Robinson from her husband, she only occasionally used it, and the marriage was as short-lived as two subsequent unions. While in Denver, the Walkers began their hair-care business. Madam C. J. Walker developed products that straightened and softened African-American women's hair, and assisted by her daughter, she quickly created a vast empire. She moved parts of her operations and her residence to Pittsburgh and Indianapolis before finally settling in New York. In 1917 the Walkers built a thirty-four-room mansion in Irvington-on-Hudson, New York, which A'Lelia's friend, the opera singer Enrico Caruso, dubbed "Villa Lewaro" (short for Lelia Walker Robinson).

With her mother's death on May 25, 1919, A'Lelia inherited the bulk of her mother's estate, including Villa Lewaro and two twin brownstones at 108–110 West 136th Street in Harlem. Soon after her mother's death, Walker also bought an apartment at 80 Edgecombe Avenue in Harlem. While she was the titular director of the Walker business interests, A'Lelia Walker devoted most of her money and attention to social life. She threw parties at Villa Lewaro and in Harlem. She established "at-homes" at which she introduced African-American writers, artists, and performers to each other and to such white celebrities as photographer Carl Van Vechten. Her "salon" was regarded as a place where artistic people, particularly male and female homosexuals, could go to eat, drink, and hear music. In 1927 and 1928, she turned part of the brownstones into a nightclub, which she named "The Dark Tower."

When the Depression came, Walker experienced grave financial difficulties. She was forced to close her nightclub, and she mortgaged Villa Lewaro. When she died suddenly on August 17, 1931, poet Langston Hughes wrote that this "was really the end of the gay times of the New Negro era in Harlem." The National Association for the Advancement of Colored People (NAACP), to which Walker had willed Villa Lewaro, was unable to keep up the payments on the estate and ended up putting it on the auction block.

See also Hair and Beauty Culture in the United States; Harlem Renaissance; Walker, Madam C. J.

Bibliography

Hughes, Langston. *The Big Sea: An Autobiography.* New York: Alfred A. Knopf, 1940.

Lewis, David Levering. *When Harlem Was in Vogue.* New York: Knopf, 1981.

Neihart, Ben. *Rough Amusements: The True Story of A'Lelia Walker, Patroness of the Harlem Renaissance's Down-Low Culture.* New York: Bloomsbury, 2003.

SIRAJ AHMED (1996)
Updated bibliography

WALKER, ALICE

FEBRUARY 9, 1944

Novelist Alice Walker was born in Eatonton, Georgia, the eighth child of sharecroppers Willie Lee and Minnie Lou Grant Walker. The vision in Walker's right eye was destroyed when she was eight years old by a brother's BB gun shot, an event that caused her to become an introverted child. Six years later Walker's self-confidence and commitment to school increased dramatically after a minor surgical procedure removed disfiguring scar tissue from around her injured eye. Encouraged by her family and community, Walker won a scholarship for the handicapped and matriculated at Spelman College in 1961.

After two years Walker transferred to Sarah Lawrence College because she felt that Spelman stifled the intellectual growth and maturation of its students, an issue she explores in the novel *Meridian.* At Sarah Lawrence, Walker studied works by European and white American writers, but the school failed to provide her with an opportunity to explore the intellectual and cultural traditions of black people. Walker sought to broaden her education by traveling to Africa during the summer before her senior year. During her stay there Walker became pregnant, and the urgency of her desire to terminate the pregnancy (she was prepared to commit suicide had she not been able to get an abortion), along with her experiences in Africa and as a participant in the civil rights movement, became the subject of her first book, a collection of poems entitled *Once* (1968).

Walker moved to Mississippi in 1965, where she taught, worked with Head Start programs, and helped to register voters. There she met and married Melvyn Leventhal, a civil rights lawyer whom she subsequently divorced (a daughter, Rebecca, was born in 1969), and wrote her first novel, *The Third Life of Grange Copeland* (1970), a chilling exploration of the causes and consequences of black intrafamilial violence. While doing research on black folk medicine for a story that became "The Revenge of Hannah Kemhuff," collected in *In Love and Trouble* (1973), Walker first learned of Zora Neale Hurston.

In Hurston, Walker discovered a figure who had been virtually erased from American literary history in large part because she held views—on the beauty and complexity of black southern rural culture; on the necessity of what Walker termed a "womanist" critique of sexism; and on racism and sexism as intersecting forms of oppression—for which she had herself been condemned. In Hurston, Walker found legitimacy for her own literary project. Walker obtained a tombstone for Hurston's grave, which proclaimed her "A Genius of the South," and focused public attention on her neglected work, including the novel *Their Eyes Were Watching God.*

In her influential essay "In Search of Our Mothers' Gardens" Walker asked, with Hurston and other marginalized women in mind, "How was the creativity of the black woman kept alive, year after year and century after century?" Some of the most celebrated of Walker's works—from the short stories "Everyday Use" and "1955" to the novel *The Color Purple* (1982)—explore this question. By acknowledging her artistic debt to such writers as Phillis Wheatley, Virginia Woolf, and Hurston, as well as to her own verbally and horticulturally adept mother, Walker encouraged a generation of readers and scholars to question traditional evaluative norms.

After *In Love and Trouble,* Walker published several novels (including *Meridian, The Temple of My Familiar,* and *Possessing the Secret of Joy*), volumes of poetry (including *Horses Make a Landscape Look More Beautiful*), collections of essays, and another short story collection, *You Can't Keep a Good Woman Down* (1981). In all these works, she examined the racial and gendered inequities that affect black Americans generally and black women in particular. The most celebrated and controversial of these works is her Pulitzer Prize– and National Book Award–winning epistolary novel, *The Color Purple,* which explores, among other matters, incest, marital violence, lesbianism, alternative religious practices, and black attitudes about gender.

Walker continues to add to an acclaimed and varied body of work that challenges and inspires its readers, including a volume of new poetry, *Absolute Trust in the Goodness of the Earth* (2003), and her novel *Now Is the Time to Open Your Heart* (2004). In 2003 Walker was arrested, along with other members of a group called CodePink, while protesting the war in Iraq.

See also Caribbean/North American Writers (Contemporary); Hurston, Zora Neale; Literature of the United States

Bibliography

Awkward, Michael. *Inspiriting Influences: Tradition, Revision, and Afro-American Women's Novels.* New York: Columbia University Press, 1989.

Bloom, Harold, ed. *Alice Walker.* Philadelphia: Chelsea House, 2002.

White, Evelyn C. *Alice Walker: A Life.* New York: Norton, 2004.

MICHAEL AWKWARD (1996)
Updated by publisher 2005

WALKER, DAVID

c. 1785
June 28, 1830

The civil rights activist and pamphleteer David Walker was born free in Wilmington, North Carolina, the son of a free white mother and a slave father. He traveled extensively in the South and observed the cruelty of slavery firsthand. Little is known about his life until he settled in Boston, where he was living as early as 1826. A tall, dark-complexioned mulatto, he operated a clothing store, selling both new and secondhand clothes, and became a leader in Boston's black community. Walker was a member of Father Snowden's Methodist Church and was active in the Massachusetts General Colored Association, formed in 1826. He was a contributor of funds to emancipate George M. Horton, a slave poet in North Carolina, and also served as an agent for *Freedom's Journal* (New York), established in 1827. Walker and his wife, Eliza, had one son, Edwin G. Walker, who later became the first black elected to the Massachusetts legislature.

Walker represented a new generation of black leaders forged by the experience of creating the first extensive free black communities in urban centers of the United States in the half-century after the American Revolution. The achievement of African Americans in establishing institutions (churches, schools, and mutual aid and fraternal societies) and in producing leaders (ministers, educators, businessmen) emboldened some in Walker's generation to challenge the reigning view among whites that African Americans, even if freed, were destined to remain a degraded people, a caste apart, better served by the removal of free blacks to Africa, which became the objective of the American Colonization Society (ACS), formed in 1817 by leading statesmen and clergy.

In an address in 1828 delivered before the Massachusetts General Colored Association, Walker laid out a strategy of opposition. Overcoming resistance to organization from within the black community, Walker and others recognized the need for a formal association to advance the race by uniting "the colored population, so far, through the United States of America, as may be practicable and expedient; forming societies, opening, extending, and keeping up correspondences" (*Freedom's Journal*, December 19, 1828). Presaging his famous *Appeal to the Colored Citizens of the World,* Walker sought to arouse blacks to mutual aid and self-help, to cast off passive acquiescence in injustice, and to persuade his people of the potential power that hundreds of thousands of free blacks possessed, once mobilized.

Published in 1829, Walker's *Appeal* aimed at encouraging black organization and individual activism. It went through three editions in two years, each one longer than the previous one, the final version reaching eighty-eight pages. For many readers, the most startling aspect of the *Appeal* was its call for the violent revolt of slaves against their masters. But Walker was also vitally concerned with the institutions of free blacks in the North. Walker understood that the formation of organizations such as the Massachusetts General Colored Association and the appearance of *Freedom's Journal* in 1827 were evidence of a rising tide of black opposition to slavery and racism. Walker, along with many African-American activists of his era, was profoundly opposed to the African colonization schemes of the American Colonization Society. Colonizationists ignored and suppressed the prevailing black opposition and sought support among African Americans. For Walker, colonization represented an immediate threat to any long-term hopes of black advancement, since its cardinal assumption was that such advancement was impossible.

Walker's *Appeal* was thus much more than a cry of conscience, for all its impassioned rhetoric. Despite its rambling organization, its prophetic denunciations of injustice and apocalyptic predictions, the *Appeal* forms a

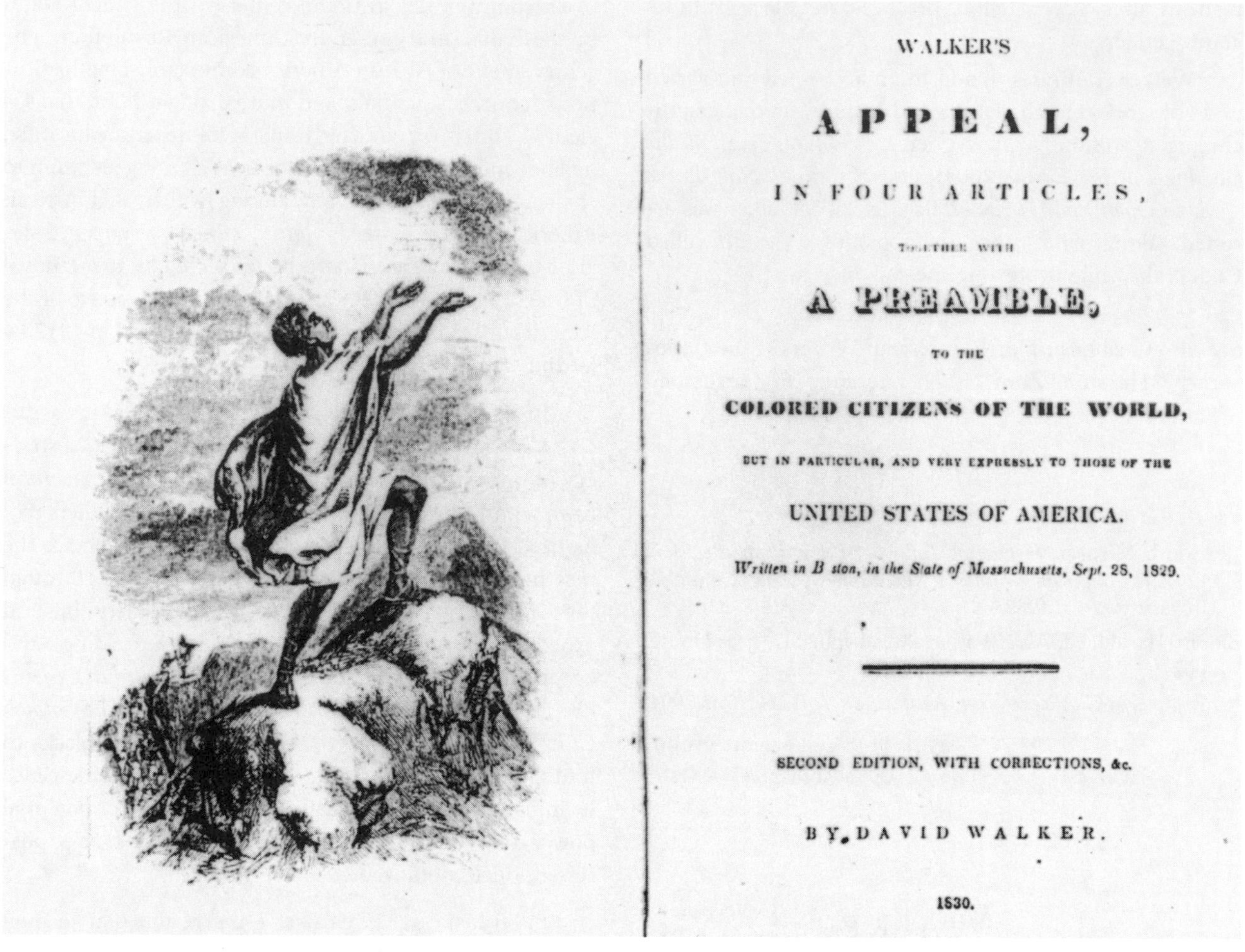

WALKER'S

APPEAL,

IN FOUR ARTICLES,

TOGETHER WITH

A PREAMBLE,

TO THE

COLORED CITIZENS OF THE WORLD,

BUT IN PARTICULAR, AND VERY EXPRESSLY TO THOSE OF THE

UNITED STATES OF AMERICA.

Written in Boston, in the State of Massachusetts, Sept. 28, 1829.

SECOND EDITION, WITH CORRECTIONS, &c.

BY DAVID WALKER.

1830.

Title page and frontispiece for the second edition of David Walker's* Appeal, *published in 1830. *Walker sought in his impassioned essay to persuade blacks to struggle with whites, abandoning colonization schemes and striving instead toward a society of racial equality. He published three editions of the work beginning in 1829, each expanding upon ideas presented in the previous iteration.* MANUSCRIPTS, RARE BOOKS AND ARCHIVES DIVISION, SCHOMBURG CENTER FOR RESEARCH IN BLACK CULTURE, THE NEW YORK PUBLIC LIBRARY, ASTOR, LENOX AND TILDEN FOUNDATIONS.

David Walker

"This country is as much ours as it is the whites', whether they will admit it now or not, they will see and believe it by and by … Their prejudices will be obliged to fall lightning to the ground, in succeeding generations."

DAVID WALKER'S APPEAL. REVISED EDITION, NEW YORK: HILL AND WANG, 1995.

complex, cogent argument with political purpose: to persuade blacks to struggle with whites to abandon colonization and to strive toward racial equality. The essay culminates in an attack on colonization and concludes with an affirmation of the *Declaration of Independence*.

Walker aimed the *Appeal* at two audiences simultaneously. His first target was blacks, whose achievements in history, Walker argued, rebutted the degraded view popularized by colonizationists and the "suspicion" of Thomas Jefferson of inherent black intellectual inferiority. Walker insisted on the importance of black self-help through rigorous education and occupational training to refute Jefferson and others. He was also unsparing in his condemnation of the ignorance and passivity of free blacks and the complicity of the enslaved—of their acquiescence in helping to sustain the American racial regime. Yet in justifying physical resistance—the element which most alarmed many readers in his own day and since—Walker carefully qualified his views. He relied primarily on the power of persuasion to convince white people to recognize that slavery and racism perverted Christianity and republicanism, though his apocalyptic warnings undoubtedly were designed to stir fear in the hearts of tyrants.

Indeed, Walker succeeded in creating this fear. He circulated copies of the *Appeal* through the mails and via black and white seamen who carried them to southern ports in Virginia, North Carolina, Georgia, and Louisiana. Southern leaders became alarmed and adopted new laws against teaching free blacks to read or write, demanding that Mayor Harrison Gray Otis of Boston take action against Walker. Otis gave assurances that Walker's was an isolated voice, without sympathy in the white community, but Walker had violated no laws. Georgians, however, placed a large sum on Walker's head. In 1830, Walker died from unknown causes amid suspicion, never confirmed, of foul play.

Few documents in American history have elicited such diverse contemporary and historical evaluations as Walker's *Appeal.* Benjamin Lundy, the pioneer abolitionist, condemned it as incendiary. The abolitionist William Lloyd Garrison (1805–1879) admired the *Appeal*'s "impassioned and determined spirit," and its "bravery and intelligence," but thought it "a most injudicious publication, yet warranted by the creed of an independent people." The black leader Henry Highland Garnet (1815–1882) in 1848 proclaimed it "among the first, and . . . the boldest and most direct appeals in behalf of freedom, which was made in the early part of the Antislavery Reformation." In 1908 a modern white historian, Alice D. Adams, deemed it "a most bloodthirsty document," while in 1950 the African-American scholar Saunders Redding thought "it was scurrilous, ranting, mad—but these were the temper of the times." In their biography of their father, the Garrison children probably came closest to the truth about Walker: "his noble intensity, pride, disgust, fierceness, his eloquence, and his general intellectual ability have not been commemorated as they deserve."

See also Abolition; Civil Rights Movement, U.S.; Free Blacks, 1619–1860; *Freedom's Journal;* Slavery

Bibliography

Aptheker, Herbert. *"One Continual Cry": David Walker's Appeal to the Colored Citizens of the World (1829–1830).* New York: Humanities Press, 1965.

Garrison, W. P., and F. J. Garrison. *William Lloyd Garrison, 1805–1879. The Story of His Life, Told by His Children,* vol. 1. New York: The Century Company, 1885.

Horton, James O., and Lois E. Horton. *Black Bostonians: Family Life and Community Struggle in the Antebellum North.* New York: Holmes & Meier, 1979. Revised edition, 1999.

Litwack, Leon F. *North of Slavery: The Negro in the Free States, 1790–1860.* Chicago: University of Chicago Press, 1961.

Peters, James S., II. *The Spirit of David Walker: The Obscure Hero.* Lanham, Md.: University Press of America, 2002.

PAUL GOODMAN (1996)
Updated bibliography

WALKER, GEORGE WILLIAM

1873
JANUARY 6, 1911

Entertainer George William Walker was born in Lawrence, Kansas. While still a teenager he joined a traveling "medicine-man" show in which he rattled bones, shook a tambourine, and mugged for the audience. The show took Walker to San Francisco, where he settled in the early 1890s to look for theater work. There, in 1893, Walker met Bert Williams, a comedian with whom he began a sixteen-year stage career.

The Williams and Walker comedy team found little success in San Francisco, but in 1895 the pair gained popular acclaim when they appeared in Chicago with John Isham's Octoroons, a black vaudeville company. During that production the two developed their act into the classic minstrel interaction between the slapstick buffoon—played by Williams—and the cocky, flamboyant huckster—played by Walker.

In 1896 Williams and Walker came into their own at Koster and Bial's Music Hall, then New York's most important vaudeville theater. Billed as "The Two Real Coons," the duo introduced their famous "cakewalk" routine during their highly successful forty-week run at Koster and Bial's. Having established themselves as a major Broadway attraction, the comedy team went on to perform in a number of major musicals, including *Clorindy, The Origin of the Cakewalk* in 1898.

Williams and Walker became major entertainment figures over the first decade of the twentieth century with a series of Broadway shows in which they were the featured attraction. Their successful, all-black shows included *The Policy Players* (1900), *Sons of Ham* (1900), *In Dahomey* (1902), *Abyssinia* (1906), and *Bandanna Land* (1908). *In Dahomey* was the first all-black production in a major Broadway theater. In these productions the pair's roles evolved from two-dimensional parodies of African Americans into more human, complex, and often tragic characterizations. During the production of *Bandanna Land* Walker began to show symptoms of the final stage of syphilis and was forced to leave the cast in February 1909. Over the next two years Walker gradually and painfully deteriorated from the disease. He died in Islip, New York, in 1911. Bert Williams went on to a highly successful solo career on Broadway.

See also Minstrels/Minstrelsy; Williams, Bert

Bibliography

Riis, Thomas Laurence. *Just Before Jazz: Black Musical Theater in New York, 1890–1915*. Washington, D.C.: Smithsonian Institution Press, 1989.

Riis, Thomas Laurence. *More Than Just Minstrel Shows: The Rise of Black Musical Theatre at the Turn of the Century*. Brooklyn, N.Y.: Brooklyn College of the City University of New York, 1992.

Sampson, Henry T. *Blacks in Blackface: A Source Book on Early Black Musical Shows*. Metuchen, N.J.: Scarecrow Press, 1980.

Smith, Eric Ledell. *Bert Williams: A Biography of the Pioneer Black Comedian*. Jefferson, N.C.: McFarland, 1992.

Woll, Allen. *Black Musical Theatre: From Coontown to Dreamgirls*. Baton Rouge: Louisiana State University Press, 1989.

THADDEUS RUSSELL (1996)

Walker, Kara

November 26, 1969

Since being awarded a coveted John D. and Catherine T. MacArthur Foundation "genius" grant in 1997, Kara Walker has become one of the most celebrated and controversial African-American women artists of her generation. Best known for life-size cut paper silhouette installations that feature ribald and provocative scenes of antebellum plantation life and interracial cultural farce, Walker is also an accomplished draftsperson whose drawings, prints, and paintings in various media—from gouache watercolor to Colombian coffee—are owned by numerous institutions and private collectors.

Kara Elizabeth Walker was born in Stockton, California, where she lived until the age of thirteen, when her family moved to the Atlanta suburb of Stone Mountain, Georgia. The artist has often credited her coming-of-age in a community steeped in a southern culture dominated by the lore of *Gone with the Wind* as being pivotal to her work. Following high school, Walker attended the Atlanta College of Art and then enrolled as a graduate student at the Rhode Island School of Design. While working on her master's degree, she became interested in the silhouette, a medium that she felt was uniquely able to communicate complicated sociohistorical and psychoracial issues within a deceptively simple yet visually complex form.

In 1994 Walker's work received much critical acclaim when it was featured in a group show at The Drawing Center in New York City. Following this auspicious debut, many of her silhouettes and drawings that skewer uncannily familiar historical subject matter were exhibited nationally and internationally. In 1997 the ambitious installation *The End of Uncle Tom and the Grand Allegorical Tableau of Eva in Heaven* (1995), measuring up to 50 feet and covering three gallery walls and inspired by Harriet Beecher Stowe's 1852 abolitionist novel *Uncle Tom's Cabin,* was included in the Biennial at the Whitney Museum of American Art.

Whereas Walker's work has been celebrated by the mainstream art world for its technical virtuosity and its biting racial satire, it has also received a great deal of negative criticism from well-established, often older, African-American artists and scholars. Many of these critics fought actively during the 1960s and 1970s to open up an often resistant and blatantly racist art establishment that excluded artists of color (such as the artist's own father, the painter Larry Walker) from exhibition opportunities in the museums and high-profile galleries that are essential to an artist's career. One of the most visible critiques of Walker's work came in 1998 when the assemblage artist Betye Saar, who saw Walker's use of negatively charged racial stereotypes as being at odds with the goals and achievements of the previous generation, mounted a letter-writing campaign to pressure potential exhibition venues to withdraw the artist's work from view.

Despite this limited domestic dissent, or perhaps because of it, Walker's art has been warmly received in many international venues; solo exhibitions have been mounted in Austria (1998 and 2002), Sweden (1999), Switzerland (2000), Israel (2001), Tokyo (2001), Brazil (2002), and Germany (2002). And as Walker's geographic reach has increased, so too has the scope of her work, evolving from the ubiquitous life-size, black-and-white silhouettes of the 1990s into theatrical, transparent, multicolored light-projection installations. One such work, *Insurrection!* (2000), actively incorporates the viewer into the scene through the use of projectors that have been sequestered in the corners of the gallery walls, thereby making the would-be witness of the static tableau an active participant in the drama.

Slavery! Slavery! presenting a GRAND and LIFELIKE Panoramic Journey into Picturesque Southern Slavery, or Life at Ol' Virginny's Hole (sketches from Plantation Life) ***(Kara Walker, 1997).*** *Walker's installation, featuring silhouettes in a panorama, combines a nineteenth century style of art with an uncensored modern perspective, highlighting the full range of physical and sexual exploitation of blacks during the antebellum era.* PHOTOGRAPH BY BRENT SIKKEMA, NEW YORK CITY. REPRODUCED BY PERMISSION.

Two major exhibitions, accompanied by large catalogs, of Walker's work appeared in university art museums in 2002 (University of Michigan, Ann Arbor) and 2003 (Skidmore College and Williams College), solidifying her presence within academia as well as the mainstream art world—a world that her father's generation had fought hard to open to the work of African-American artists.

See also Art in the United States, Contemporary; Painting and Sculpture

Bibliography

Berry, Ian, Darby English, Vivian Patterson, and Mark Reinhardt, eds. *Kara Walker: Narratives of a Negress* (exhibition catalog). Cambridge, Mass.: Tang Teaching Museum at Skidmore College, Williams College Museum of Art, and MIT Press, 2003. Essays by Darby English, Mark Reinhardt, Anne M. Wagner, and Michele Wallace. Writings by Kara Walker.

Dixon, Annette. *Pictures from Another Time* (exhibition catalog). Ann Arbor: University of Michigan Museum of Art, 2002. Essay by Robert Reid-Pharr; interview by Thelma Golden.

Shaw, Gwendolyn DuBois. *Seeing the Unspeakable: The Art of Kara Walker.* Durham, N.C.: Duke University Press, 2004.

GWENDOLYN DUBOIS SHAW (2005)

Walker, Madame C. J.

December 23, 1867
May 25, 1919

Madame C. J. Walker was an entrepreneur, hair-care industry pioneer, philanthropist, and political activist. Born Sarah Breedlove to ex-slaves Owen and Minerva Breedlove on a Delta, Louisiana cotton plantation, she was orphaned by age seven. She lived with her sister, Louvenia, in Vicksburg, Mississippi, until 1882, when she married Moses McWilliams, in part to escape Louvenia's cruel husband. In 1887, when her daughter, Lelia (later known as A'Lelia Walker), was two years old, Moses McWilliams died. For the next eighteen years she worked as a laundress in St. Louis. But in 1905, with $1.50 in savings, the thirty-seven-year-old McWilliams moved to Denver to start her own business after developing a formula to treat her problem with baldness—an ailment common among African-American women at the time, brought on by poor diet, stress, illness, damaging hair-care treatments, and scalp disease. In January 1906 she married Charles Joseph Walker, a newspaper sales agent, who helped design her advertisements and mail-order operation.

Although Madam Walker is often said to have invented the "hot comb," it is more likely that she adapted metal implements popularized by the French to suit black women's hair. Acutely aware of the debate about whether black women should alter the appearance of their natural hair texture, she insisted years later that her Walker System was not intended as a hair "straightener" but rather as a grooming method to heal and condition the scalp to promote hair growth and prevent baldness.

From 1906 to 1916 Madam Walker traveled throughout the United States, Central America, and the West Indies promoting her business. She settled briefly in Pittsburgh, establishing the first Lelia College of Hair Culture there in 1908, then moved the company to Indianapolis in 1910, building a factory and vastly increasing her annual sales. Her reputation as a philanthropist was solidified in 1911, when she contributed one thousand dollars to the building fund of the Indianapolis YMCA. In 1912 she and C. J. Walker divorced, but she retained his name. Madam Walker joined her daughter, A'Lelia, and A'Lelia's adopted daughter, Mae (later Mae Walker Perry), in Harlem in 1916. She left the daily management of her manufacturing operation in Indianapolis to her longtime attorney and general manager, Freeman B. Ransom, factory forewoman Alice Kelly, and assistant general manager Robert L. Brokenburr.

Madam Walker's business philosophy stressed economic independence for the twenty thousand former maids, farm laborers, housewives, and schoolteachers she employed as agents and factory and office workers. To further strengthen her company, she created the Madam C. J. Walker Hair Culturists Union of America and held annual conventions.

During World War I Walker was among those who supported the government's black recruitment efforts and war bond drives. But after the bloody 1917 East St. Louis riot, she joined the planning committee of the Negro Silent Protest Parade, traveling to Washington, D.C., to present a petition urging President Woodrow Wilson to support legislation that would make lynching a federal crime. As her wealth and visibility grew, Walker became increasingly outspoken, joining those blacks who advocated an alternative peace conference at Versailles after the war to monitor proceedings affecting the world's people of color. She intended her estate in Irvington-on-Hudson, New York—Villa Lewaro, which was designed by black architect Vertner W. Tandy—not only as a showplace but as an inspiration to other blacks.

During the spring of 1919, aware that her long battle with hypertension was taking its final toll, Madam Walker revamped her will, directing her attorney to donate five thousand dollars to the National Association for the Advancement of Colored People's antilynching campaign and to contribute thousands of dollars to black educational, civic, and social institutions and organizations.

When she died at age fifty-one, at Villa Lewaro, Walker was widely considered the wealthiest black woman in America and was reputed to be the first African-American woman millionaire. Her daughter, A'Lelia Walker—a central figure of the Harlem Renaissance—succeeded her as president of the Mme. C. J. Walker Manufacturing Company.

Walker's significance is rooted not only in her innovative (and sometimes controversial) hair-care system but also in her advocacy of black women's economic independence and her creation of business opportunities at a time when most black women worked as servants and sharecroppers. Her entrepreneurial strategies and organizational skills revolutionized what would become a multibillion-dollar ethnic hair-care and cosmetics industry by the last decade of the twentieth century. Having led an early life of hardship, she became a trailblazer of black philanthropy, using her wealth and influence to leverage social, political, and economic rights for women and blacks. In 1992 Madam Walker was elected to the National Business Hall of Fame.

See also Entrepreneurs and Entrepreneurship; Hair and Beauty Culture in the United States; Walker, A'Lelia

Bibliography

Bundles, A'Lelia Perry. *Madam C. J. Walker—Entrepreneur.* New York: Chelsea House, 1991.

Bundles, A'Lelia Perry. *On Her Own Ground: The Life and Times of Madam C. J. Walker.* New York: Scribner, 2001.

Giddings, Paula. *When and Where I Enter: The Impact of Black Women on Race and Sex in America.* New York: Morrow, 1984.

Lowry, Beverly. *Her Dream of Dreams: The Rise and Triumph of Madam C. J. Walker.* New York: Knopf, 2003.

A'LELIA PERRY BUNDLES (1996)
Updated bibliography

Walker, Margaret

July 7, 1915
October 1998

The writer Margaret Abigail Walker was born in Birmingham, Alabama. She received her early education in New Orleans and completed her undergraduate work at Northwestern University at the age of nineteen. Although Walker had published some of her poems before she moved to

Chicago, it was there that her talent matured. She wrote as a college student and as a member of the federal government's Works Project Administration, and she shared cultural and professional interests with black and white intellectuals in Chicago, the best known of whom was the writer Richard Wright (1908–1960). Wright and Walker were close friends until Walker left Chicago for graduate work at the University of Iowa in 1939, by which time she was on her way to becoming a major poet.

In 1942 Walker completed the manuscript of a collection of poems entitled *For My People,* the title poem of which she had written and published in Chicago in 1937. The book served as her master's thesis at the Iowa Writers Workshop, and it won a measure of national literary prominence. In 1942 *For My People* won the Yale Younger Poets Award. About the same time, Walker began work on a historical novel based on the life of her grandmother, Elvira Dozier Ware, a work she did not finish until she returned to Iowa in the 1960s to complete her Ph.D. In the interim, she joined the faculty at Jackson State University in Jackson, Mississippi, where she and her husband, Firnist James Alexander, raised their four children.

Walker played an active role in the civil rights movement in Mississippi, while continuing to write. The novel she created from her grandmother's stories was published in 1966 as *Jubilee,* and it received the Houghton Mifflin Literary Award. It was translated into seven languages and enjoyed popularity as one of the first modern novels of slavery and the Reconstruction South told from an African-American perspective. Other books followed: *Prophets for a New Day* (1970), *How I Wrote Jubilee* (1972), *October Journey* (1973), and *A Poetic Equation: Conversations Between Nikki Giovanni and Margaret Walker* (1974). Throughout her long career, Walker received numerous awards and honors for her contribution to American letters. She received several honorary degrees, and in 1991 she received a Senior Fellowship from the National Endowment for the Arts.

Walker retired from full-time teaching in 1979. She remained in Jackson and worked on several projects, especially a controversial biography of Richard Wright, published in 1988 as *Richard Wright: Daemonic Genius.* In 1989 Walker brought together new and earlier poems in *This Is My Century: New and Collected Poems.* A year later she published her first volume of essays, *How I Wrote Jubilee and Other Essays on Life and Literature.*

In all her work, Walker incorporated a strong sense of her own humanistic vision, together with an autobiographical recall of her own past and cogent themes from black history. Her artistic vision recognized the distinctiveness of black cultural life and the values associated with it. She was also outspoken on matters of political justice and social equality, for women as well as for men.

Jubilee tells the story of Vyry, a slave on an antebellum Georgia plantation who aspires to freedom. The unacknowledged daughter of the master, she marries a fellow slave and assumes responsibility for the plantation during the Civil War. After the war she moves away and discovers that her courage and determination make it possible for her to triumph over numerous adversities. In a 1992 interview, Walker stated, "The body of my work springs from my interest in the historical point of view that is central to the development of black people as we approach the twenty-first century."

See also Caribbean/North American Writers (Contemporary); Literature of the United States; Poetry, U.S.

Bibliography

Graham, Maryemma. *Fields Watered with Blood: Critical Essays on Margaret Walker.* Athens: University of Georgia Press, 2001.

Walker, Margaret. *How I Wrote Jubilee and Other Essays on Life and Literature.* Edited by Maryemma Graham. New York: Feminist Press at the City University of New York, 1990.

Walker, Margaret. *Conversations With Margaret Walker.* Edited by Maryemma Graham. Jackson: University Press of Mississippi, 2002.

MARYEMMA GRAHAM (1996)
Updated by publisher 2005

WALKER, WYATT TEE

AUGUST 16, 1929

Born in Brockton, Massachusetts, minister and civil rights activist Wyatt Walker was educated at Virginia Union University in Richmond, Virginia (B.S., 1950, M.Div., 1953). He received a D.Min. from Colgate Rochester Bexley Hall/Crozer in 1975. Walker was minister of Gillfield Baptist Church in Petersburg, Virginia, from 1953 to 1960. In 1960, with his wife, two children, and several followers, Walker entered Petersburg's segregated public library and asked for the first volume of Douglas Southall Freeman's biography of Robert E. Lee. Arrested for trespassing, Walker refused to post bail and spent three days in jail. This event attracted the attention of Martin Luther King Jr., who invited Walker to join him in Atlanta.

From 1960 to 1964 Walker worked closely with King as executive director of the Southern Christian Leadership

Conference (SCLC). Combining an intense personality with strong tactical skills, Walker was at the forefront of the civil rights movement. In addition to his administrative duties he was often on the frontline of the protests, enduring police beatings and arrests. On June 16, 1961, Walker was one of the delegates from the Freedom Ride Coordinating Committee to meet with Attorney General Robert Kennedy. Walker is credited with organizing "Project C," the detailed plan for the Birmingham campaign in April 1963. He controlled the marches and sit-ins by walkie-talkie all day, and stayed up at night personally typing King's famous "Letter from Birmingham Jail" as it was smuggled to him in installments.

In the summer of 1964 Walker resigned his position with the SCLC and moved to New York City, where, as assistant to Adam Clayton Powell Jr., he served as pulpit minister at the Abyssinian Baptist Church. He was also vice president of American Education Heritage, publishers of a multivolume series on the history and culture of black America. In 1966 he was appointed assistant on urban affairs to Gov. Nelson Rockefeller. In 1967, having left Abyssinian, he became minister (and subsequently senior pastor) of the Canaan Baptist Church of Christ in Harlem. From this pulpit Walker continued to work on behalf of the African-American community into the 1990s. As CEO of the Church Housing Development Fund, Walker supervised the construction of housing for the elderly known as the Wyatt Tee Walker Apartments. From 1977 to 1987 he was director of the Freedom National Bank, which later failed. In August 1979 he was a member of the controversial SCLC delegation that met with the UN Representative of the Palestinian Liberation Organization in order to promote peace in the Middle East. He served as an advisor to Jesse Jackson and was National Coordinator for Church and Clergy during Jackson's 1984 and 1988 presidential bids. An expert in black gospel music, in February 1985 Walker participated in "Thank God!" a four-part TV "docu-drama" about black church music.

In the early 1990s Walker was active in the Consortium for Central Harlem Development, a group of religious, civic and business leaders working to improve living conditions for the needy; as National Chairman of the Religious Action Network of the American Committee on Africa, Walker raised funds for Nelson Mandela and the African National Conference.

Walker has authored numerous books, including *Somebody's Calling My Name: Black Sacred Music and Social Change* (1979); *Road to Damascus* (1985), which tells of the group he and Jesse Jackson led to Syria in 1984 to obtain the freedom of a black Navy flier, Lt. Robert O. Goodman, held hostage there; and most recently *My Stroke of Grace: A Testament of Faith Renewal* (2002).

See also Abyssinian Baptist Church; Civil Rights Movement, U.S.; Freedom Rides; Gospel Music; Southern Christian Leadership Conference (SCLC)

Bibliography

Cloyd, Iris, and William C. Matney Jr., eds. *Who's Who Among Black Americans*, 6th ed. Detroit, Mich.: Gale, 1990.

Colaiaco, James A. *Martin Luther King, Jr.: Apostle of Militant Nonviolence.* New York: St. Martin's Press, 1988.

LYDIA MCNEILL (1996)
Updated by publisher 2005

Wallace, Ruby Ann

See Dee, Ruby

Walrond, Eric Derwent

1898
1966

The writer Eric Walrond was born in Georgetown, British Guiana. He immigrated to Barbados in 1906, and in 1910 he left for the Panama Canal Zone, where he worked as a clerk for the health department of the Panama Canal Commission. From 1916 to 1918 he worked as a reporter and sportswriter for the Panama *Star and Herald*. In 1918 Walrond moved to New York, where he attended the College of the City of New York until 1921. During this time he also worked as an associate editor of Marcus Garvey's *Negro World*. Walrond soon broke with Garvey's Universal Negro Improvement Association, and he eventually became one of its chief African-American critics. From 1922 to 1924 Walrond took writing classes at Columbia University. He contributed fiction and nonfiction to magazines such as the *New Republic*, the *Messenger*, *Vanity Fair*, and the *New Age*. His short story "The Palm Porch" was included in the well-known 1925 anthology edited by Alain Locke, *The New Negro*.

From 1925 to 1927 Walrond served as the business manager for the Urban League's *Opportunity: Journal of Negro Life*. He also published a critically acclaimed collection of short stories, *Tropic Death* (1926), about life in Barbados, the Canal Zone, and British Guiana. Using native dialects and an impressionistic style, Walrond addressed the problems of physical suffering and discrimination facing African Americans in the tropics. His work was anthologized in *The American Caravan* (1927).

In 1928 Walrond received a Guggenheim Fellowship and became a Zona Gale scholar at the University of Wisconsin. That same year he moved to Europe. Although Walrond had been considered one of the brightest young voices of the Harlem Renaissance, when interest in black literature waned in the 1930s, he disappeared from American literary life. In the late 1930s, when Walrond and Garvey were both living in London, the two grew close again, and Walrond contributed to a Garveyite magazine, *Black Man.* His contributions included a short story and articles that dealt with American literature and politics. Thereafter, Walrond virtually ceased writing. He traveled throughout Europe, and lived for several years in France before settling again in London. He was at work on a novel set in the Panama Canal region when he died in England in 1966.

See also *Negro World*; Garvey, Marcus

Bibliography

Beckman, Wendy Hart. *Artists and Writers of the Harlem Renaissance.* Berkeley Heights, N.J.: Enslow Publishers, 2002.

Martin, Tony. *Literary Garveyism: Black Arts and the Harlem Renaissance.* Dover, Mass.: Majority Press, 1983.

JONATHAN GILL (1996)
Updated bibliography

War Between the States

See Civil War, U.S.

Ward, Samuel Ringgold

October 17, 1817
c. 1866

Abolitionist and clergyman Samuel Ward was born on Maryland's Eastern Shore. His parents, believed to have been William Ward and Anne Harper, escaped from slavery to Greenwich, New Jersey in 1820 and moved to New York City in 1826. Samuel Ward attended the African Free School, where Alexander Crummell and Henry Highland Garnet were fellow students.

Ward taught in black schools in Newark, New Jersey, until 1839, when he was ordained by the New York Congregational (General) Association. From 1841 to 1843 he served as pastor to a white congregation in South Butler, New York, and from 1846 to 1851 to a white congregation in Cortland, New York. During a period of poor health between the two ministries, he studied medicine and law.

In 1839 Ward was also appointed an agent of the American Anti-Slavery Society, and he embarked upon a career as an orator in abolition and party politics, for which he became known as "the black Daniel Webster." Active in the Liberty Party from its establishment in 1840, he addressed its convention in 1843 and lectured under its auspices, having particular effect in the defeat of Henry Clay in New York State. In 1846 Ward served as a vice president of the American Missionary Association, an abolition-oriented missionary group.

Ward fled to Canada in 1851 because of his involvement in the rescue of the "fugitive slave" William ("Jerry") Henry. From 1851 to 1866 he served as an agent of the Anti-Slavery Society of Canada, as well as a member of its executive committee, lecturing against slavery as he had done in the United States. Under its auspices he traveled to England seeking aid for exiled and immigrant former slaves. He addressed the British and Foreign Anti-Slavery Society in 1853 and 1854.

Ward was associated as agent or editor with a number of black periodicals, including *The True American and Religious Examiner* and the *Impartial Citizen;* in Canada he was the nominal editor of the *Provincial Freeman.* Ward also was the author of *The Autobiography of a Fugitive Slave: His Anti-Slavery Labours in the United States, Canada, & England* (London, 1855) and an account of the Jamaica Rebellion of 1865, *Reflections upon the Gordon Rebellion* (1866).

Ward was given land in Jamaica by an English Quaker and moved there in 1855, serving as a Baptist minister in Kingston. Little is known of his last years.

See also Abolition; Free Blacks, 1619–1860; Missionary Movements; Runaway Slaves in the United States

Bibliography

Winks, Robin. "Samuel Ringgold Ward." In *Dictionary of Canadian Biography*, vol. 9. Toronto, Ontario, Canada: University of Toronto Press, 1976.

QUANDRA PRETTYMAN (1996)

Washington, Booker T.

c. 1856
November 14, 1915

Founder of Tuskegee Institute in Alabama and prominent race and education leader of the late nineteenth and early twentieth centuries, Booker Taliaferro Washington was born a slave on the plantation of James Burroughs near Hale's Ford, Virginia. He spent his childhood as a houseboy and servant. His mother was a cook on the Burroughs plantation, and he never knew his white father. With Emancipation in 1865, he moved with his family—consisting of his mother, Jane; his stepfather, Washington Ferguson; a half-brother, John; and a half-sister, Amanda—to West Virginia, where he worked briefly in the salt furnaces and coal mines near Malden. Quickly, however, he obtained work as a houseboy in the mansion of the wealthiest white man in Malden, General Lewis Ruffner. There, under the tutelage of the general's wife, Viola Ruffner, a former New England schoolteacher, he learned to read. He also attended a local school for African Americans in Malden.

From 1872 to 1875 Washington attended Hampton Institute, in Hampton, Virginia, where he came under the influence of the school's founder, General Samuel Chapman Armstrong, who inculcated in Washington the work ethic that would stay with him his entire life and that became a hallmark of his educational philosophy. Washington was an outstanding pupil during his tenure at Hampton and was placed in charge of the Native American students there. After graduation he returned to Malden, where he taught school for several years and became active as a public speaker on local matters, including the issue of the removal of the capital of West Virginia to Charleston.

In 1881 Washington founded a school of his own in Tuskegee, Alabama. Beginning with a few ramshackle buildings and a small sum from the state of Alabama, he built Tuskegee Institute into the best-known African-American school in the nation. While not neglecting academic training entirely, the school's curriculum stressed industrial education, training in specific skills and crafts that would prepare students for jobs. Washington built his school and his influence by tapping the generosity of northern philanthropists, receiving donations from wealthy New Englanders and some of the leading industrialists and businessmen of his time, such as Andrew Carnegie, William H. Baldwin Jr., Julius Rosenwald, and Robert C. Ogden.

In 1882 Washington married his childhood sweetheart from Malden, Fanny Norton Smith, a graduate of Hampton Institute, who died two years later as a result of injuries suffered in a fall from a wagon. Subsequently Washington married Olivia A. Davidson, a graduate of Hampton and the Framingham State Normal School in Massachusetts, who held the title of lady principal of Tuskegee. She was a tireless worker for the school and an effective fund-raiser in her own right. Always in rather frail health, Davidson died in 1889. Washington's third wife, Margaret James Murray, a graduate of Fisk University, also held the title of lady principal and was a leader of the National Association of Colored Women's Clubs and the Southern Federation of Colored Women's Clubs.

Washington's reputation as the principal of Tuskegee Institute grew through the late 1880s and the 1890s; his school was considered the exemplar of industrial education, viewed as the best method of training the generations of African Americans who were either born in slavery or were the sons and daughters of freed slaves. His control of the pursestrings of many of the northern donors to his school increased his influence with other African-American schools in the South. His fame and recognition as a national race leader, however, resulted from the impact of a single speech he delivered before the Cotton States and International Exposition in Atlanta in 1895. This important speech, often called the Atlanta Compromise, is the best single statement of Washington's philosophy of racial advancement and his political accommodation with the predominant racial ideology of his time. For the next twenty years, until the end of his life, Washington seldom deviated publicly from the positions taken in the Atlanta address.

In his speech Washington urged African Americans to "cast down your bucket where you are"—that is, in the South—and to accommodate to the segregation and discrimination imposed upon them by custom and by state and local laws. He said the races could exist separately from the standpoint of social relationships but should work together for mutual economic advancement. He advocated a gradualist advancement of the race, through hard work, economic improvement, and self-help. This message found instant acceptance from white Americans, north and south, and almost universal approval among African Americans. Even W. E. B. Du Bois, later one of Washington's harshest critics, wrote to him immediately after the Atlanta address that the speech was "a word fitly spoken."

Whereas Washington's public stance on racial matters seldom varied from the Atlanta Compromise, privately he was a more complicated individual. His voluminous

Booker T. Washington (seated, third from left) with some of the teachers and trustees of the Tuskegee Institute, 1906. PHOTOGRAPHS AND PRINTS DIVISION, SCHOMBURG CENTER FOR RESEARCH IN BLACK CULTURE, THE NEW YORK PUBLIC LIBRARY, ASTOR, LENOX AND TILDEN FOUNDATIONS.

private papers, housed at the Library of Congress, document an elaborate secret life that contradicted many of his public utterances. He secretly financed test cases to challenge Jim Crow laws. He held great power over the African-American press, both north and south, and secretly owned stock in several newspapers. While Washington himself never held political office of any kind, he became the most powerful African-American politician of his time as an adviser to presidents Theodore Roosevelt and William Howard Taft and as a dispenser of Republican Party patronage.

Washington's biographer, Louis R. Harlan, called the Tuskegean's extensive political network "the Tuskegee Machine" for its resemblance to the machines established by big-city political bosses of the era. With his network of informants and access to both northern philanthropy and political patronage, Washington could make or break careers, and he was the central figure in African-American public life during his heyday. Arguably no other black leader, before or since, has exerted similar dominance. He founded the National Negro Business League in 1900 to foster African-American business and create a loyal corps of supporters throughout the country. Indirectly he influenced the National Afro American Council, the leading African-American civil rights group of his day. The publication of his autobiography, *Up from Slavery,* in 1901 spread his fame even more in the United States and abroad. In this classic American tale, Washington portrayed his life in terms of a Horatio Alger success story. Its great popularity in the first decade of the twentieth century won many new financial supporters for Tuskegee Institute and for Washington personally.

Washington remained the dominant African-American leader in the country until the time of his death from exhaustion and overwork in 1915. But other voices rose to challenge his conservative, accommodationist leadership. William Monroe Trotter, the editor of the *Boston Guardian,* was a persistent gadfly. Beginning in 1903 with the publication of Du Bois's *The Souls of Black Folk,* and continuing for the rest of his life, Washington was criticized for his failure to be more publicly aggressive in fighting the deterioration of race relations in the United States, for his avoidance of direct public support for civil rights legislation, and for his single-minded emphasis on industrial education as opposed to academic training for a "talented tenth" of the race. Washington, however, was adept at outmaneuvering his critics, even resorting to the use of spies to infiltrate organizations critical of his leadership, such as the Niagara Movement, led by Du Bois. His intimate friends called Washington "the Wizard" for his mastery of political intrigue and his exercise of power.

Washington's leadership ultimately gave way to new forces in the twentieth century, which placed less emphasis on individual leadership and more on organizational power. The founding of the National Association for the Advancement of Colored People (NAACP) in 1909 and of the National Urban League in 1911 challenged Washington in the areas of civil rights and his failure to address problems related to the growth of an urban black population. The defeat of the Republican Party in the presidential election of 1912 also spelled the end of Washington's power as a dispenser of political patronage. Nevertheless, he remained active as a speaker and public figure until his death, in 1915, at Tuskegee.

Washington's place in the pantheon of African-American leaders is unclear. He was the first African American to appear on a United States postage stamp (1940) and commemorative coin (1946). Although he was eulogized by friend and foe alike at the time of his death, his outmoded philosophy of accommodation to segregation and racism in American society caused his historical reputation to suffer. New generations of Americans, who took their inspiration from those who were more outspoken critics of segregation and the second-class status endured by African Americans, rejected Washington's leadership role. While much recent scholarship has explored his racial philosophy and political activity in considerable depth, he remains a largely forgotten man in the consciousness of the general public, both black and white. In recent years, however, there has been some revival of interest in his economic thought by those who seek to develop African-American businesses and entrepreneurial skills. Indeed, no serious student of the African-American experience in the United States can afford to ignore the lessons that can be gleaned from Washington's life and from the manner in which he exercised power.

See also Atlanta Compromise; Autobiography, U.S.; Civil Rights Movement, U.S.; Du Bois, W. E. B.; Intellectual Life; Tuskegee University; Washington, Margaret Murray

Bibliography

Harlan, Louis R. *Booker T. Washington: The Making of a Black Leader, 1856–1901.* Urbana: University of Illinois Press, 1972.

Harlan, Louis R. *Booker T. Washington: The Wizard of Tuskegee, 1901–1915.* Urbana: University of Illinois Press, 1983.

Harlan, Louis R., and Raymond W. Smock, eds. *The Booker T. Washington Papers,* 14 vols. Urbana: University of Illinois Press, 1972–1989.

Meier, August. *Negro Thought in America: Racial Ideologies in the Age of Accommodation, 1880–1915.* Ann Arbor: University of Michigan Press, 1963.

Smock, Raymond W., ed. *Booker T. Washington in Perspective: The Essays of Louis R. Harlan.* Jackson: University Press of Mississippi, 1988.

Washington, Booker T. *Up from Slavery: An Autobiography.* New York: Doubleday, 1901.

RAYMOND W. SMOCK (1996)

Washington, Denzel

December 28, 1954

Born into a middle-class family in Mount Vernon, New York, actor Denzel Washington is one of three children of a Pentecostal minister and a beauty shop owner. His parents divorced when he was fourteen, and Washington went through a rebellious period. Consequently, his mother sent him to boarding school at Oakland Academy in Windsor, New York. He went on to matriculate at Fordham University in New York City.

Washington became interested in acting while at college. When he was a senior at Fordham, he won a small role in the television film *Wilma,* the story of Olympic track star Wilma Rudolph. After graduating with a B.A. in journalism in 1978, Washington spent a year at San Francisco's American Conservatory Theater.

Washington's first film, *Carbon Copy* (1981), received little notice. However, his portrayals of Malcolm X in *When the Chickens Come Home to Roost* by Laurence Holder (Audelco Award, 1980) and Private Peterson in *A*

Soldier's Play by Charles Fuller (Obie Award, 1981) brought him to the attention of New York's theater critics. After refusing to take roles that he deemed degrading, Washington took the part of the idealistic surgeon Dr. Philip Chandler on the popular hospital television drama series *St. Elsewhere* (1982–1988). In 1984, accompanied by most of the original stage cast, Washington reprised his role as Private Peterson in *A Soldier's Story,* the film version of *A Soldier's Play.*

Despite his consistently powerful performances, it was not until the end of the 1980s that Washington was acknowledged as one of America's leading actors. He appeared as martyred South African activist Stephen Biko in *Cry Freedom* (1987), a policeman in *The Mighty Quinn,* and the embittered ex-slave and Union soldier Trip in *Glory,* both in 1989. Washington received an Academy Award nomination for his work in *Cry Freedom* and in 1990 won an Academy Award for best supporting actor for his performance in *Glory.* That same year he played the title role in *Richard III* in the New York Shakespeare Festival.

In 1990 Washington starred as a jazz musician in director Spike Lee's film *Mo' Better Blues.* He teamed with Lee again in 1992, playing the title role in the controversial film *Malcolm X.* The film received mixed reviews, but Washington's performance as the black nationalist was a critical success, and he received an Oscar nomination as best actor. The following year he appeared in leading roles in three films to much acclaim. He portrayed Don Pedro, Prince of Aragon, in Kenneth Branagh's version of the Shakespearean comedy *Much Ado About Nothing,* an investigative reporter in the thriller *The Pelican Brief,* and a trial lawyer in *Philadelphia.* In 1995 he starred with Gene Hackman in *Crimson Tide.* His starring roles since then have included *Devil in a Blue Dress* (1995), an adaptation of Walter Mosley's novel; *Courage Under Fire* (1996); *The Preacher's Wife* (1997); *Love Jones* (1997); *Fallen* (1998); *He Got Game* (1998); *The Siege* (1998); *Remember the Titans* (2000); *John Q* (2002); *Antwone Fisher* (2002); *Out of Time* (2003); *Man on Fire* (2004); and *The Manchurian Candidate* (2004).

Washington won a Golden Globe for Best Actor for his role in *The Hurricane* (1999) and an Academy Award for Best Actor for his role in *Training Day* (2001).

See also Film in the United States, Contemporary

Bibliography

Brode, Douglas. *Denzel Washington: His Films and Career.* Secaucus, N.J.: Carol, 1997.

Davis, Thulani. "Denzel in the Swing." *American Film* (August 1990): 26–31.

Hoban, Phoebe. "Days of Glory: Denzel Washington—From Spike Lee's Blues to Richard III." *New York Magazine* (August 13, 1990): 35–38.

Randolph, Laura B. "The Glory Days of Denzel Washington." *Ebony* (September 1990): 80–82.

JANE LUSAKA (1996)
Updated by publisher 2005

WASHINGTON, HAROLD

APRIL 15, 1922
NOVEMBER 25, 1987

The politician Harold Washington was born on the South Side of Chicago to Bertha and Roy Lee Washington Sr. His parents separated, and Washington's father, a stockyard worker, raised the children; he also earned a law degree at night and became a Democratic party precinct captain in the Third Ward.

Harold Washington attended DuSable High School but dropped out after his junior year. He was drafted during World War II and while in the army earned a high school equivalency diploma. In 1941 he married Dorothy Finch; they divorced in 1950.

After the war, Washington entered Roosevelt University in Chicago, where he was the first black student to be elected senior class president. He graduated in 1949 with a degree in political science. He completed law school at Northwestern University in 1952—by "quota" the only black student in his class.

When Roy Washington died in 1953, Ralph Metcalfe, an alderman and Democratic party committeeman, invited Harold Washington to take over his father's precinct. Washington proved to be a talented organizer, successfully mobilizing votes for Metcalfe and training new Democratic party leadership. He was also involved in independent black political organizations.

Washington served in the Illinois House of Representatives from 1965 to 1976, and in the state senate from 1976 to 1980. In office, he selectively dissented from "machine" policies, incurring special wrath in the late 1960s by calling for a police review board with civilian participation. In 1969, he helped organize the Illinois Legislative Black Caucus. He fought for consumer protection for the poor and elderly, supported the Equal Rights Amendment, and strengthened the Fair Employment Practices Act.

In 1977, Washington openly broke with the machine, running for mayor of Chicago in the special election that followed Richard J. Daley's death. He lost the Democratic primary but won 10.7 percent of the vote. A year later, Washington returned to the state senate despite a machine-orchestrated challenge. In 1980 he was elected to the U.S. Congress, where he demonstrated leadership on issues important to blacks and Latinos. Washington played a key role in the 1982 fight to extend the 1965 Voting Rights Act, and he was secretary of the Congressional Black Caucus. He also supported a nuclear freeze and a 20 percent cut in defense spending.

Shortly after Washington's election, he was approached by independent political and community groups hoping to draft a black candidate for mayor of Chicago. After a massive campaign that registered at least 20,000 new voters by October 1982, Washington agreed to run. The media slighted his candidacy, casting the Democratic primary as a contest between incumbent mayor Jane Byrne and State's Attorney Richard M. Daley, son of the former mayor. But Washington's overwhelming support in the black community, his debate performance, and a high level of grassroots mobilization tipped the balance in his favor. He won with a plurality of 38 percent.

In the 1983 general election, many white Democrats, including some key party leaders, backed Republican Bernard Epton. The campaign was volatile and racially charged, as whites jeered Washington and hurled accusations of personal impropriety. Still, he prevailed with 51.5 percent of the vote due to record-breaking turnouts and support in the black community, and to strong support from Latino and liberal white neighborhoods.

Washington's first term was marred by opposition on the city council, led by Democratic Party–machine stalwarts Edward Vrydolyak and Ed Burke. Washington lacked majority support on the council, and his initiatives often were defeated. The "Council Wars" raged from 1983 through 1986, when a federal court ruled the ward map was racially biased. When Washington sought re-election in 1987, he was challenged by former mayor Jane Byrne in the primary and by Vrydolyak, running as an independent, in the general election. He outpolled his rivals, garnering 99.6 percent of the black vote and significant backing among gays, Latinos, and Asian Americans.

Despite resistance, Washington's structural and programmatic reforms were substantial. He signed the Shakman Decree, which outlawed patronage hiring and firing, and he imposed a $1,500 cap on campaign contributions from companies doing business with the city. He increased racial and ethnic diversity in the city administration, and he aided women and minorities in competing with white male contractors. He appointed Chicago's first black police chief and sought to provide city services more equitably in the black community.

On November 25, 1987, Washington suffered a heart attack at his desk in city hall. He died later that day, mourned by many who believed his career had both reflected and helped to create new avenues for political participation among African Americans.

See also Congressional Black Caucus; Metcalfe, Ralph; Politics in the United States; Voting Rights Act of 1965

Bibliography

Carl, Jim. "Harold Washington and Chicago's Schools Between Civil Rights and the Decline of the New Deal." *History of Education Quarterly,* 41, no. 3 (2001), pp 311–343.

Clavel, Pierre and Wim Wiewel, eds. *Harold Washington and the Neighborhoods: Progressive City Government in Chicago, 1983–1987.* New Brunswick, N.J.: Rutgers University Press, 1991.

Gove, Samuel K., and Louis A. Masotti, eds. *After Daley: Chicago Politics in Transition.* Urbana: University of Illinois Press, 1982.

Kleppner, Paul. *Chicago Divided: The Making of a Black Mayor.* DeKalb, Ill.: Northern Illinois University Press, 1985.

Miller, Alton. *Harold Washington: The Mayor, The Man.* New York: Random House Value, 1995.

Rivlin, Gary. *Fire on the Prairie: Chicago's Harold Washington and the Politics of Race.* New York: Henry Holt, 1993.

Travis, Dempsey J. *An Autobiography of Black Politics.* Chicago, Ill.: Urban Research Institute, 1987.

DIANNE M. PINDERHUGHES (1996)
Updated bibliography

Washington, Margaret Murray

c. 1861
June 4, 1925

The child of a black mother, Lucy Murray, and a white father, educator and clubwoman Margaret Murray was born in Macon, Mississippi. March 9, 1865, is inscribed on her gravestone as her birthday, but she was listed as being nine years old in the census of 1870. She may have lowered her age in 1881, when she began attending Fisk Preparatory School in Nashville, Tennessee. Taken in by a Quaker brother and sister after her father's death when she was seven, Washington was educated by them, and it was they who suggested she become a teacher.

Margaret Murray became Booker T. Washington's third wife. After completing her Fisk University education in 1889, she joined the Tuskegee faculty and the next academic year became dean of the women's department. Washington, who was recently widowed and had three small children, proposed to her in 1891 and they married on October 12, 1892. Margaret Murray Washington advised her husband in his speaking and fund-raising work, and she shared his advocacy of accommodation with whites while uplifting the black race. As an educated woman, Margaret Washington believed she had a responsibility to help those of her race who had fewer opportunities. She pursued her own work at Tuskegee and was a leader in the black women's club movement.

Washington was the director of the Girls' Institute at Tuskegee, which provided courses in laundering, cooking, dressmaking, sewing, millinery, and mattress making, skills that students were to use in maintaining healthy, efficient, and gracious homes. She founded the women's club at Tuskegee for female faculty and faculty wives, which was active, especially in the temperance movement. She also worked with people in the surrounding rural area on self-improvement. By 1904 nearly three hundred women had attended her mothers' meetings each Sunday. Especially concerned about high rates of black mortality and illegitimate births, Washington instructed the women on diet and personal hygiene for better health and urged them to set good moral examples at home for both boys and girls.

These sentiments found expression in the motto of the influential National Association of Colored Women's Clubs (NACW)—"Lifting as we climb." Washington was one of the women invited by Josephine St. Pierre Ruffin to meet in Boston in July 1895 to form the National Federation of Afro-American Women. She became vice president and then, in 1896, president of the federation, which was now sixty-seven clubs strong; it joined with the Colored Women's League to form the NACW that year. In 1914 Washington was elected president of the NACW after holding numerous other offices and served two terms. She also edited the NACW's *National Notes* until her death.

President of the Alabama Association of Women's Clubs (AAWC) from 1919 until her death in 1925, Margaret Murray Washington led the movement to establish a boys' reform school as an alternative to prison, and later the Rescue Home for Girls, both in Mt. Meigs, Alabama. Through the AAWC she worked with the Commission on Interracial Cooperation to provide educational opportunities for blacks in Alabama. A lifelong friend of W. E. B. Du Bois, in 1920 Margaret Washington helped found the International Council of Women of the Darker Races to promote race pride through knowledge of black culture around the world.

See also Black Women's Club Movement; Education in the United States; National Association of Colored Women; National Federation of Afro-American Women; Washington, Booker T.

Bibliography

Hall, Jacquelyn Dowd. *Revolt Against Chivalry: Jessie Daniel Ames and the Women's Campaign Against Lynching.* New York: Columbia University Press, 1974.

Johns, Robert L. "Margaret Murray Washington." In *Notable Black American Women*, edited by Jessie Carney Smith. Detroit, Mich.: Gale, 1992.

Moton, Jennie B. "Margaret M. Washington." In *Homespun Heroines and Other Women of Distinction*, edited by Hallie Q. Brown. New York: Oxford University Press, 1988.

ALANA J. ERICKSON (1996)

Waters, Ethel

October 31, 1896?
September 1, 1977

Singer and actress Ethel Waters was born in Chester, Pennsylvania, to a musical family; her father played piano, and her mother and maternal relatives sang. Her first public performance was as a five-year-old billed as Baby Star in a church program. Waters began her singing career in Baltimore with a small vaudeville company where she sang W. C. Handy's "St. Louis Blues," becoming, apparently, the first woman to sing the song professionally. She was billed as Sweet Mama Stringbean.

About 1919 Waters moved to New York and became a leading entertainer in Harlem, where her first engagement was at a small black club, Edmond's Cellar. As an entertainer she reached stardom during the Harlem Renaissance of the 1920s. In 1924 Earl Dancer, later the producer of the Broadway musical *Africana,* got her a booking in the Plantation Club as a replacement for Florence Mills, who was on tour. When Mills returned, Waters toured in Dancer's *Miss Calico*. By then she had begun to establish herself as an interpreter of the blues with such songs as Perry Bradford's "Messin' Around." In 1921 she recorded "Down Home Blues" and "Oh Daddy" for Black Swan Records. The success of her first recording led her to embark on one of the first personal promotion tours in the United States.

In 1932 and 1933 Waters recorded with Duke Ellington and Benny Goodman, respectively. Her renditions of "Stormy Weather," "Taking a Chance on Love," and

"Lady Be Good" were closer stylistically to jazz than to popular music. She sang with the swing orchestra of Fletcher Henderson, who was her conductor on the Black Swan tours. Although her performances were unquestionably potent, many critics did not consider her a real jazz performer but rather a singer who possessed a style that was more dramatic and histrionic than jazz oriented. However, Waters, along with Billie Holiday and Louis Armstrong, significantly influenced the sound of American popular music. Though generally regarded as blues or jazz singers, all of them sang the popular songs of their day like no other singers of the period.

"Dinah" (first performed in 1925), "Stormy Weather," and "Miss Otis Regrets" were among Waters's most popular songs. Later she recorded with Russell Wooding and Eddie Mallory, among others. Beginning in 1927 she appeared in Broadway musicals, including *Africana* (1927), Lew Leslie's *Blackbirds* of 1930, *Rhapsody in Black* (1931), *As Thousands Cheer* (1933), *At Home Abroad* (1936), and *Cabin in the Sky* (1940). All these roles primarily involved singing.

It was not until the Federal Theatre Project (FTP) that she had the chance to do more serious and dramatic roles. Waters received excellent reviews for her performance in Shaw's *Androcles and the Lion,* which led to her being cast as Hagar in Dubose and Dorothy Heyward's *Mamba's Daughters* (1939), for which she again received good notices. Ten years later, she was acclaimed for her performance as Berenice in Carson McCullers' *The Member of the Wedding* (which won the Drama Critics Circle Award for Best American Play of the Year in 1950).

Waters appeared in nine films between 1929 and 1959, the most popular being *Pinky,* which garnered her an Academy Award nomination as Best Supporting Actress (1949). From 1957 to 1976 she toured with evangelist Billy Graham's religious crusades in the United States and abroad and became celebrated for singing "His Eye Is on the Sparrow." This song became the title of her first autobiography, which was published in 1951. A second autobiography, *To Me It's Wonderful,* was published in 1972. Waters died in 1977 following a long bout with cancer.

See also Blueswomen of the 1920s and 1930s; Drama; Jazz Singers; Musical Theater

Bibliography

Haskins, James. *Black Theater in America.* New York: Crowell, 1982.

JAMES E. MUMFORD (1996)

Waters, Maxine Moore

August 15, 1938

Maxine Moore, the daughter of Remus Carr and Velma Moore, was born in Saint Louis, Missouri, and eventually became a congresswoman. She attended the public schools in Saint Louis and married Edward Waters immediately upon graduation from high school. In 1961 she moved with her husband and two children to the Watts section of Los Angeles. After working at a garment factory and as an operator for Pacific Telephone, Waters was hired in 1966 as an assistant teacher in a local Head Start program and was later promoted to supervisor.

In 1971 Waters received her bachelor's degree in sociology from California State University at Los Angeles. She became active in local and state politics, serving as a chief advisor for David S. Cunningham's successful race for a city council seat in 1973. After Cunningham's election, Waters became his chief deputy.

In 1976 Waters was elected to the California State Assembly, where she served for fourteen years. She represented the Watts area and was a noted spokesperson for women's issues. In 1978 she cofounded the Black Women's Forum, a national organization designed to provide a platform for the discussion of issues of concern to black women—programs for the poor and minorities, and divestiture of investments in South Africa. Among her many achievements, Waters helped establish the Child Abuse Prevention Training Program and sponsored legislation to protect tenants and small businesses, to impose stringent standards on vocational schools, and to limit police strip-and-search authority. Waters served as the assembly's first black female member of the Rules Committee and the first Judiciary Committee member who was not a lawyer.

In 1990 Waters was elected to represent a wide area of South Central Los Angeles in the United States House of Representatives. In the ensuing years, she voiced her criticism of U.S. involvement in the Persian Gulf War and advocated a number of reintegration services for black troops on their return home.

Following the outbreak of riots in her Los Angeles district after the acquittal of the police officers charged in the Rodney King case in April 1992, Waters received national attention for her statements about the root social causes of the riots. In 1993 Waters proposed legislation for the Youth Fair Chance Program, an inner-city job training program, and supported passage of AIDS and abortion-rights legislation. Over the course of her first two terms, Waters rapidly emerged as a major spokesperson for the black community and one of the most prominent women in Congress. In 1998 she distinguished herself as a defender of President Bill Clinton, and she voted against impeachment as a member of the House Judiciary Committee.

In the early 2000s, Waters worked with various hip-hop artists to reclaim hip-hop from what she felt was co-opting by and racism on the part of the white music industry. In 2004 Waters sponsored a resolution in Congress to provide assistance to the ravaged country of Haiti.

See also Politics in the United States

Bibliography

Mathews, Jay. "California Freshman Brings a Warm Touch to Her Firm Stance." *Washington Post,* February 19, 1991.

Newman, Maria. "Lawmaker from Riot Zone Insists on a New Role for Black Politicians." *Washington Post,* May 19, 1992.

LOUISE P. MAXWELL (1996)
Updated by publisher 2005

Watts, J. C.

November 18, 1957

Julius Caesar Watts Jr., a leading Republican in the U.S. House of Representatives, was born in Eufaula, Oklahoma, the son of a policeman. He later described his childhood poverty, noting that he had only two pairs of pants, both patched. Watts attended the University of Oklahoma in Norman on a football scholarship, and he received a B.A. degree in journalism in 1981. As quarterback for the powerful Sooners, Watts led the team to victories in the Orange Bowl in 1980 and 1981 and was named Most Valuable Player of both bowls. After graduation, Watts joined the Ottawa Roughriders of the Canadian Football League. In his rookie year he led the Roughriders to the Grey Cup and was named Most Valuable Player of the Cup game. He retired after four years with Ottawa and a year with the Toronto Argonauts.

Following his retirement from football, Watts returned to Norman, where he formed the Watts Energy Corporation. An ordained minister, Watts also became the youth director of Sunnylane Baptist Church in nearby Del City. In 1994, relying on his football celebrity and conservative Republican politics, Watts campaigned for Congress. That fall, he was elected to the U.S. House of Representatives from Oklahoma's largely white fourth district, and he was easily reelected in 1996 and 1998. As the sole black Republican in Congress during the late 1990s, Watts cultivated a color-blind image, declining to join the Congressional Black Caucus and calling for an end to affirmative action and welfare programs. In 1997 Watts was selected by House Republicans to respond to the president's State of the Union Address, and in November 1998 he was named chair of the congressional Republican Conference.

Watts published his autobiography in 2002. In 2003 he left Congress and became chairman of FN Policy Focus, a government-sponsored enterprise.

See also Politics in the United States

Bibliography

Watts, J. C., with Chriss Winston. *What Color Is a Conservative: My Life and My Politics.* New York: HarperCollins, 2002.

GREG ROBINSON (1996)
Updated by publisher 2005

Waymon, Eunice Kathleen

See Simone, Nina

Weaver, Robert Clifton

December 29, 1907
July 19, 1997

Economist Robert Weaver's maternal grandfather, Robert Tanner Freeman, the son of a slave who bought freedom for himself and his wife in 1830 and took his surname as the badge of his liberty, graduated from Harvard University in 1869 with a degree in dentistry, the first African American to do so. His daughter Florence attended Virginia Union University, then married Mortimer Grover Weaver, a Washington, D.C., postal clerk, and gave birth to Robert Weaver. Raising Robert and his older brother, Mortimer Jr., in a mostly white Washington neighborhood, Florence Weaver repeatedly emphasized to her sons that "the way to offset color prejudice is to be awfully good at whatever you do."

The Weaver boys did exceptionally well in Washington's segregated school system: Mortimer went on to Williams College and then to Harvard for advanced study in English; Robert joined him at Harvard as a freshman, and when he was refused a room in the dormitory because he was African American, he lived with his brother off campus. Robert Weaver graduated cum laude in 1929, the year his brother died of an unexplained illness, and stayed at Harvard to earn his master's degree in 1931 and doctorate in economics in 1934. In 1933, with the advent of the New Deal, Weaver was hired by Secretary of the Interior Harold Ickes to be the race-relations adviser in the Housing Division. While holding that post, Weaver helped desegregate the cafeteria of the Interior Department and became an active member of the "Black Cabinet," an influential group of African Americans in the Roosevelt administration who met regularly to combat racial discrimination and segregation in New Deal programs and within the government itself.

In 1935 Weaver married Ella V. Haith, a graduate of Carnegie Tech, and from 1937 to 1940 he served as special assistant to the administrator of the U.S. Housing Authority. During World War II he held positions on the National Defense Advisory Committee, the War Manpower Commission, and the War Production Board. In 1944 he left the government to direct the Mayor's Committee on Race Relations in Chicago, and then the American Council on Race Relations. After the war, he worked for the United Nations Relief and Rehabilitation Administration, headed a fellowship program for the John Hay Whitney Foundation, and published two critical studies of discrimination against African Americans—*Negro Labor: A National Problem* (1946) and *The Negro Ghetto* (1948)—before being chosen by New York's Democratic governor, Averell Harriman, in 1955 as the state rent commissioner, the first African American to hold a cabinet office in the state's history.

This was followed by Weaver's appointment by President John F. Kennedy after the 1960 election to be director of the U.S. Housing and Home Finance Agency, at the time the highest federal position ever held by an African American. While heading what he termed an "administrative monstrosity," Weaver authored the acclaimed *The Urban Complex* (1964) and *Dilemmas of Urban America* (1965), which focused attention on the inadequate public services and the inferior schools in lower-class inner cities, but he achieved only minor successes in his endeavors to stimulate better-designed public housing, provide housing for families of low or moderate incomes, and institute federal rent subsidies for the ailing and the elderly.

Kennedy had promised in 1960 to launch a comprehensive program to assist cities, run by a cabinet-level department. But because of his intention to select Weaver as department secretary, and thus the first African-American cabinet member, Congress twice rebuffed Kennedy's plan. Southern Democrats opposed Weaver because of his race and his strong support of racially integrated housing. Following the landslide election of Lyndon B. Johnson in 1964, however, Congress approved a bill to establish a new Department of Housing and Urban Development (HUD) in 1965, and, because of Johnson's influence, confirmed his choice of Weaver to head it. By then, Weaver's moderation and reputation for being professionally cautious had won over even southern Democrats who had formerly voted against him, like Senator A. Willis Robertson of Virginia, who claimed: "I thought he was going to be prejudiced. But I have seen no evidence of prejudice."

Weaver ably administered HUD's diffuse federal programs and the billions of dollars spent to attack urban blight, but innovative policies and plans, such as those in the Demonstration Cities and Metropolitan Development Act, soon fell victim to the escalating expenditures for the Vietnam War and to the conservative backlash fueled by ghetto rioting from 1965 to 1968. In 1969, after more than a third of a century of government service, Weaver left Washington to preside over the City University of New York's Baruch College for two years and then to be Distinguished Professor of Urban Affairs at CUNY's Hunter College until 1978, when he became professor emeritus. He stayed busy during his retirement, serving on the boards of the Metro Life Insurance Company, the Bowery Savings Bank, and Mount Sinai Hospital and Medical School, and he was active in the American Jewish Congress, the Citizens Committee for Children, and the New York Civil Liberties Union.

Although never an active frontline fighter in the civil rights movement, Weaver chaired the board of directors of the NAACP (National Association for the Advancement of Colored People) in 1960, served on the executive committee of the NAACP Legal Defense Fund from 1973 to 1990, and was president of the National Committee against Discrimination in Housing from 1973 to 1987. He received numerous awards, including the Spingarn Medal of the NAACP (1962), the New York City Urban League's Frederick Douglass Award (1977), the Schomburg Collection Award (1978), and the Equal Opportunity Day Award of the National Urban League (1987), and he was the recipient of more than thirty honorary degrees from colleges and universities before his death in 1997. In 2000 the Housing and Urban Development headquarters in Washington, D.C., was named in his honor, the first building in the nation's capital to be named after an African American.

See also Politics in the United States

Bibliography

"New Cabinet Member." *Crisis* (February 1966): 76, 120ff.

"Robert C. Weaver." *Contemporary Black Biography*. Vol. 46. Detroit, Mich.: Thomson Gale, 2005.

Weaver, Robert C. "The Health Care of Our Cities." *National Medical Association Journal* (January 1968): 42–46.

HARVARD SITKOFF (1996)
Updated by publisher 2005

Webb, Frank J.

March 21, 1828
May 7, 1894

Novelist, newspaperman, and educator Frank Johnson Webb was named after an internationally popular black orchestra leader in Philadelphia. His proud, striving family apparently provided a classical education. In 1845 Webb married Mary E., the similarly educated daughter of a fugitive Virginia slave and reputed Spanish nobleman. Before Frank and Mary launched their artistic careers, the Webbs' Philadelphia cloth and clothing designing business failed in 1854, despite winning prizes in Philadelphia for its products in the early 1850s.

Early in the spring of 1855 Mary set out to become a dramatic reader with Frank as her manager. She gained encouragement and training assistance from Harriet Beecher Stowe, who dramatized selections from *Uncle Tom's Cabin* precisely for Mary. John Greenleaf Whittier, Henry Wadsworth Longfellow, and others commended her efforts. Through May 1856, she performed from Washington, D.C., to Cleveland, Ohio. Nearly everywhere, however, the Webbs faced racial restrictions and condescension. Frank publicly and independently spoke out in favor of black emigration and martial training. In September 1855 the Webbs sought passage to Brazil but were denied because, as Mary said in a private letter, her husband was "somewhat more brown" than she.

Believing they might be treated better in England, they encouraged Stowe to write introductions and were well received there by friendly nobility in July 1856. Mary's readings and Frank's well-written, groundbreaking novel *The Garies and Their Friends,* published in London in September 1857, both enjoyed generally positive reviews. The modest adventures of the novel's black hero, Charlie Ellis, and those of mixed-race peers in and around racist Philadelphia suggest the author's own experiences. Stowe's hasty preface may have encouraged sales, but did not throw any light on the novel or its little-known author. By that September Mary's consumption had also been noted; the Webbs went to southern France for her health through January 1858. English friends then arranged for a clerk's position in the post office for Frank in Kingston, Jamaica.

Despite their English successes, the couple's short stop in Philadelphia before heading for Jamaica was disappointing. A dramatic reading was not well attended, and no American offered to publish Frank's novel. Stowe abandoned them. She wrote to friends that she had been "worn down" attempting to guide the Webbs and other African Americans in England. No English person had noticed this burden—nor did Stowe's sister, who admired the Webbs' refinement.

In March the Webbs moved to Jamaica, where Mary died in June 1859. Five years later Frank married Jamaican Mary Rosabell Rodgers, and together they had six children. In 1869 he moved to Washington, D.C., worked as a Freedman's Bureau clerk, studied law at Howard University, and contributed two stories with male characters like his novel's hero further refined, but white; three short race-defending commentaries; and two love poems. He also attempted, unsuccessfully, to find a publisher for another novel.

Late in 1870 the reunited Webb family moved to Galveston, Texas. Frank edited and published the assertively black *Galveston Republican* newspaper from January to August 1871. Between 1872 and 1878 he clerked in a post office and strove to create a Republican Party that respected blacks. From 1881 through 1894 he was a teacher, and he served as a high school principal through his remaining years. His wife lectured and wrote race-lifting papers. His eldest son was also a writer and newspaperman.

Bibliography

Crockett, Rosemary F. "'The Garies and Their Friends': A Study of Frank J. Webb and His Novel." Ph.D. diss., Harvard University, 1998.

Gardner, Eric, "'A Gentleman of Superior Cultivation and Refinement': Recovering the Biography of Frank J. Webb." *African American Review* 35 (2001): 297–308.

ALLAN D. AUSTIN (1996)
Updated by author 2005

WEEMS, CARRIE MAE

APRIL 20, 1953

The photographer Carrie Mae Weems was born in Portland, Oregon, and began taking pictures in 1976, after a friend gave her a camera as a gift. Weems worked as a professional modern dancer and also held odd jobs on farms and in restaurants and offices until 1979, when she began taking classes in art, folklore, and literature at the California Institute of the Arts (B.F.A., 1981). She traveled to Mexico and Fiji, and then studied photography at the University of California, San Diego, where she worked with Fred Lonidier (M.F.A., 1984).

In 1978 Weems began taking her first series of images, *Environmental Profits,* which focused on life in Portland. Weems continued to develop her interest in autobiographical images in *Family Pictures and Stories* (1978–1984), which took the format of a family photo album and featured images of relatives at their jobs and at home, often with accompanying narrative text and audio recordings. *Family Pictures* was Weems's response to the Moynihan Report of ten years earlier, which claimed that a matriarchal system of authority was responsible for a systemic crisis in the black family. Images in the series, one of which is titled "Mom at Work," were arranged to look like snapshots of ordinary moments to show that the process of passing on family history is an aspect of everyday life.

Weems's work on *Family Pictures* intensified her interest in folklore, and she took graduate classes in the folklore program at University of California, Berkeley, from 1984 to 1987. Her work *Ain't Jokin* (1987–1988), which grew out of her studies at the university, was a series of captioned photographs that prompts viewers to question racial stereotypes ("Black Woman with Chicken").

In 1990 Weems explored the conflict between a woman's political ideals and her emotional desires in "Untitled" (*Kitchen Table Series*). Shot with a large-format camera, the images record episodes in the relationship between a woman and man; they are taken from a single vantage point in front of the receding kitchen table.

In the same year, Weems completed *Then What? Photographs and Folklore,* a collection of images that illustrates or comments upon folk sayings, signs, and omens. Weems's image of a coffee pot highlights a superstition by quoting parents who tell their child not to drink coffee because "coffee'll make you black." *Then What?* also includes *Colored People* (1989–1990), a series of front- and side-view mug shots of girls and boys that explores the process of color stereotyping.

In 1991, Weems began creating large-scale color still lifes and portraits that were included in *And 22 Million Very Tired and Angry People* (1992). Selecting a title that echoes Richard Wright's 1941 *12 Million Black Voices,* Weems combines photos of ordinary objects such as an alarm clock ("A Precise Moment in Time"), a fan ("A Hot Day"), and a typewriter ("An Informational System") with text from thinkers such as Ntozake Shange, Malcolm X, and Fannie Lou Hamer, to educate viewers about historical causes of political change. In 1992, Weems exhibited a series of images on the Gullah culture of the Sea Islands, located off the coast of South Carolina and Georgia, at the P.P.O.W. Gallery in New York City. Weems also traveled to West Africa during this period, producing her "Africa" series (1990–1993), a selection of photos taken around Djenne, one of the oldest cities of sub-Saharan Africa. In this historical venue, Weems explored themes of myth, history, and the quest for origins, retelling the story of Adam and Eve with an African setting.

In 1995, the artist began work on her 32–piece installation "From Here I Saw What Happened and I Cried," an emotional response to Getty Museum's "Hidden Witness" exhibition depicting African-American life in the decades preceding the Civil War. Weems explored the relation between art and politics in two significant 1998 installations, "Who What When Where" and "Ritual and Revolution." Turning again to historical subjects, she was commissioned by Tulane University to create a new series of images to celebrate the bicentennial of the Louisiana Purchase in 2003. That same year, the artist produced two more installations, "May Days Long Forgotten" and "Dreaming in Cuba," offering perspectives on social history in twentieth-century America and the Caribbean.

Weems has taught photography at institutions such as San Diego City College in California (1984); Hampshire College in Amherst, Massachusetts (1987–1992), Hunter College in New York City (1988–1989), and California College of Arts and Crafts in Oakland (1991). She has been artist-in-residence at the Visual Studies Workshop in Rochester, New York (1986); Rhode Island School of Design in Providence (1989–1990); and the Art Institute of Chicago (1990).

Weems's work has been shown in solo exhibitions at the Alternative Space Gallery, San Diego, California (1984); Hampshire College Art Gallery (1987); CEPA Gallery, Buffalo, New York (1990); P.P.O.W. Gallery, New York City (1990, 1992, 2003); New Museum of Contemporary Art, New York City (1991); National Museum of Women in the Arts, Washington, D.C. (1993); Everson Museum of Art, Syracuse (1999); Williams College Museum of Art, Williamstown, Massachusetts (2001); the International Center of Photography, New York, New York (2001); and the Newcomb Art Gallery, Tulane University, New Orleans, Louisiana (2003).

See also Art in the United States, Contemporary; Photography, U.S.

Bibliography

Kirsh, Andrea, and Susan Fisher Sterling. *Carrie Mae Weems.* Washington, D.C.: National Museum of Women in the Arts, 1993.

Patterson, Vivian. *Carrie Weems: The Hampton Project.* New York: Aperture, 2000.

Weems, Carrie Mae. *Then What? Photographs and Folklore.* Buffalo, N.Y.: CEPA Gallery, 1990.

Weems, Carrie Mae. *And 22 Million Very Tired and Angry People.* San Francisco, Calif.: San Francisco Art Institute, 1992.

Weems, Carrie Mae. *Carrie Mae Weems: Recent Work.* New York: Braziller, 2003.

RENEE NEWMAN (1996)
Updated by publisher 2005

WELLS-BARNETT, IDA B.

JULY 6, 1862
MARCH 25, 1931

Ida B. Wells-Barnett (1862–1931). *Born a slave in Mississippi, Wells-Barnett used the power of the pen to fight for civil rights, particularly in her unflagging campaign against lynching.* PHOTOGRAPHS AND PRINTS DIVISION, SCHOMBURG CENTER FOR RESEARCH IN BLACK CULTURE, THE NEW YORK PUBLIC LIBRARY, ASTOR, LENOX AND TILDEN FOUNDATIONS.

The journalist and civil rights activist Ida Bell Wells was born in Holly Springs, Mississippi, the first of eight children of Jim and Elizabeth Wells. Her father was a slave—the son of his master and a slave woman—and worked as a carpenter on a plantation. There he met his future wife, who served as a cook. After emancipation, Jim Wells was active in local Reconstruction politics.

Young Ida Wells received her early education in the grammar school of Shaw University (now Rust College) in Holly Springs, where her father served on the original board of trustees. Her schooling was halted, however, when a yellow fever epidemic claimed the lives of both her parents in 1878 and she assumed responsibility for her siblings. The next year, the family moved to Memphis, Tennessee, to live with an aunt, and Ida found work as a teacher. She later studied at Fisk University and Lemoyne Institute.

A turning point in Wells's life occurred on May 4, 1884. While riding a train to a teaching assignment, she was asked to leave her seat and move to a segregated car. Wells refused, and she was physically ejected from the railway car. She sued the railroad, and though she was awarded $500 by a lower court, the Tennessee Supreme Court reversed the decision in 1887. In the same year, she launched her career in journalism, writing of her experiences in an African-American weekly called the *Living Way.* In 1892 she became the co-owner of a small black newspaper in Memphis, the *Free Speech.* Her articles on the injustices faced by southern blacks, written under the pen name "Iola," were reprinted in a number of black newspapers, including the *New York Age,* the *Detroit Plain-Dealer,* and the *Indianapolis Freeman.*

In March 1892, the lynching of three young black businessmen, Thomas Moss, Calvin McDowell, and Henry Steward, in a suburb of Memphis focused Wells's attention on the pressing need to address the increasing prevalence of this terrible crime in the post-Reconstruction South. Her approach was characteristically forthright. She argued that though most lynchings were fueled by accusations of rape, they actually were prompted by economic competition between whites and blacks. Wells infuriated most whites by asserting that many sexual liaisons between black men and white women were not rape but mutually consensual.

She urged African Americans in Memphis to move to the West (where, presumably, conditions were more fa-

> *Ida B. Wells-Barnett*
>
> "Our country's national crime is lynching. It is not the creature of an hour, the sudden outburst of uncontrolled fury, or the unspeakable brutality of an insane mob. It represents the cool, calculating deliberation of intelligent people who openly avow that there is an 'unwritten law' that justifies them in putting human beings to death without complaint under oath, without trial by jury, without opportunity to make defense, and without right of appeal."
>
> "LYNCH LAW IN AMERICA," THE ARENA 23.1 (JANUARY 1900): 15-24.

vorable) and to boycott segregated streetcars and discriminatory merchants. Her challenges to the prevailing racial orthodoxy of the South were met by mob violence, and in May 1892, while she was out of town, the offices of the *Free Speech* were destroyed by an angry throng of whites.

Wells then began to work for the *New York Age*, and she continued to write extensively on lynching and other African-American issues. She penned exposés of southern injustice and decried the situation before European audiences in 1893 and 1894. During these European tours, she criticized some white American supporters of black causes for their halfhearted opposition to lynching. Wells's most extended treatment of the subject, *A Red Record: Tabulated Statistics and Alleged Causes of Lynchings in the United States,* appeared in 1895. This was the first serious statistical study of lynchings in the post-Emancipation South. She continued this work for the rest of her life. Some of her more widely read articles in this area include "Lynching and the Excuse for It" (1901) and "Our Country's Lynching Record" (1913). Perhaps her greatest effort in this arena was her tireless campaign for national antilynching legislation. In 1901 she met with President William McKinley to convince him of the importance of such legislation. Her appeal was to no avail.

Another issue that provoked Wells's ire was the decision not to permit an African-American pavilion at the 1893 World's Fair. Wells, with the financial support of Frederick Douglass, among others, published a widely circulated booklet entitled *The Reason Why the Colored American Is Not in the World's Exposition* (1893).

In 1895 Wells married Ferdinand L. Barnett, a lawyer and editor from Chicago who was appointed assistant state attorney for Cook County in 1896. The couple had four children, and Chicago would remain their home for the rest of their lives. While Wells-Barnett was a devoted mother and homemaker, her political and reform activities were unceasing. She served as secretary of the National Afro-American Council from 1898 to 1902 and headed its Antilynching Speakers Bureau. She played an important role in the founding of the National Association of Colored Women in 1896, and in 1910 she founded the Negro Fellowship League, which provided housing and employment for black male migrants. The Barnetts challenged restrictive housing covenants when they moved to the all-white East Side of Chicago around 1910. Her concern for the welfare of Chicago's black community led Wells-Barnett to become, in 1913, the first black woman probation officer in the nation. She lost her appointment in 1916, when a new city administration came to power.

Wells-Barnett was also active in the fight for women's suffrage. In 1913 she organized the Alpha Suffrage Club, the first black women's suffrage club in Illinois. That year, and again in 1918, she marched with suffragists in Washington, D.C. On the former occasion she insisted on marching with the Illinois contingent, integrating it over the objection of many white women marchers.

Wells-Barnett's militant opposition to the southern status quo placed her at odds with Booker T. Washington and his strategy of accommodationism. She was much more sympathetic to the ideology of W. E. B. Du Bois, and in 1906 she attended the founding meeting of the Niagara Movement. She was also a member of the original Executive Committee of the National Association for the Advancement of Colored People (NAACP) in 1910. She was, however, uneasy about the integrated hierarchy at the organization, believing that their public stance was too tempered, and she ceased active participation in 1912.

In 1916 Wells-Barnett began an affiliation with Marcus Garvey's Universal Negro Improvement Association (UNIA). In December 1918, at a UNIA meeting in New York, Wells-Barnett was chosen, along with A. Philip Randolph (1889-1979), to represent the organization as a delegate to the upcoming Versailles Conference. Both representatives were repeatedly denied U.S. State Department clearance, however, so they never attended the meeting. Wells-Barnett did speak on behalf of the UNIA at Bethel AME Church in Baltimore at the end of December 1918, but her continued affiliation with the organization after this was less public.

In the last decades of her life, Wells-Barnett continued to write about racial issues and American injustice.

The East St. Louis race riot of July 1917 and the Chicago riot of July and August 1919 provided the impetus for impassioned denunciations of the treatment of African Americans in the United States. She wrote *The Arkansas Race Riot* in 1922 in response to the accusation of murder aimed at several black farmers, an accusation that was said to have instigated the disturbance. Most of her later work targeted social and political issues in Chicago. In 1930, Wells-Barnett ran unsuccessfully as an independent candidate for the U.S. Senate from Illinois.

Ida Wells-Barnett died on March 25, 1931. In 1941 the Chicago Housing Authority named one of its first low-rent housing developments the Ida B. Wells Homes. In 1990 the U.S. Postal Service issued an Ida B. Wells stamp.

See also Abolition; Douglass, Frederick; Du Bois, W. E. B.; Garvey, Marcus; Journalism; Lynching; National Association for the Advancement of Colored People (NAACP); Niagara Movement; Randolph, Asa Philip; Universal Negro Improvement Association; Washington, Booker T.

Bibliography

Burt, Olive W. *Black Women of Valor.* New York: J. Messner, 1974.

McMurry, Linda O. *To Keep the Waters Troubled: The Life of Ida B. Wells.* New York: Oxford University Press, 1998.

Royster, Jacqueline Jones, ed. *Southern Horrors and Other Writings: the Anti-Lynching Campaign of Ida B. Wells, 1892–1900.* Boston: Bedford Books, 1997.

Sterling, Dorothy. *Black Foremothers.* Old Westbury, N.Y.: Feminist Press, 1979.

Wells-Barnett, Ida B. *Crusade for Justice: The Autobiography of Ida B. Wells,* edited by Alfreda Duster. Chicago: University of Chicago Press, 1970.

MARGARET L. DWIGHT–BARRETT (1996)
Updated bibliography

Wesley, Charles Harris

December 2, 1891
August 16, 1987

Historian, educator, and minister Charles H. Wesley was a native of Louisville, Kentucky, where he attended public schools. He received a B.A. from Fisk University in 1911, an M.A. from Yale University in 1913, and a Ph.D. from Harvard University in 1925. He was the third black American to receive a Ph.D. in history from Harvard, following W. E. B. Du Bois and Carter G. Woodson.

Upon graduation Wesley accepted a position on the faculty of Howard University, where he served from 1913 to 1942 (leaving briefly, from 1920–1921, to attend Harvard). Wesley rose from the position of instructor to that of professor, then to chair of the history department and finally to dean of the graduate school. In 1930 he was the first black historian to receive a Guggenheim Fellowship, and he spent the following year in England studying slave emancipation in the British Empire.

Wesley was an ordained minister and a presiding elder of the African Methodist Episcopal church (1914–1937). He was also general president of the black fraternity Alpha Phi Alpha (1931–1946), about which he wrote *The History of Alpha Phi Alpha* (1953). He was one of Carter G. Woodson's principal associates at the Association for the Study of Negro Life and History (ASNLH), with which he was involved from 1916 to 1987. Wesley worked with Woodson on several important research projects. He was also cofounder of the Association of Social Science Teachers at Negro Colleges (1936).

Wesley's *Negro Labor in the United States, 1850–1925* (1927) grew out of his dissertation at Harvard and was the first comprehensive historical study of black workers. It is still one of the basic works on the subject, and was pioneering in its use of economic and social analysis for black history. *The Collapse of the Confederacy* (1937) established Wesley's expertise in southern history, and his scholarly articles on subjects ranging from black abolitionists to the diplomatic history of Haiti and Liberia helped to legitimize and popularize the emerging discipline of black history. Wesley also wrote several other histories of black organizations and their leaders, such as *Richard Allen, Apostle of Freedom* (1935), *History of the Improved Benevolent and Protective Order of Elks of the World* (1955), and *Prince Hall: Life and Legacy* (1977).

Wesley was a vocal critic of the limited curriculum and paternalistic procedures at black colleges. In 1942 he was elected president of Wilberforce University in Ohio, an AME church-supported school. In the spring of 1947 church trustees, led by his former mentor Bishop Reverdy Ransom, dismissed Wesley. Student protests followed, and afterward an acrimonious legal battle between the university and the state of Ohio, which provided funds for the School of Education. The school was permanently split into two institutions, and Wesley became the first president of Wilberforce State College (later renamed Central State University). Wesley upgraded the faculty, integrated the student body, and introduced new programs such as African Studies.

During this period Wesley also served as president of the ASNLH (1950–1965), and when he retired as president of Central State University in 1965, he assumed the executive directorship of the association. He continued to write histories of African Americans, including *Neglected History: Essays in Negro History by a College President* (1965), *In Freedom's Footsteps, From the African Background to the Civil War* (1968), *The Quest for Equality: From Civil War to Civil Rights* (1968), and a new introduction for Woodson's treatise, *The Mis-Education of the Negro* (1969). In 1972 Wesley resigned his position as executive director of the ASNLH.

Wesley came out of retirement in 1974 to direct the new Afro-American Historical and Cultural Museum in Philadelphia, serving until 1976. In 1979 Wesley, a widower of six years, married Dorothy B. Porter, a librarian and bibliographer. He continued to write in his later years, publishing his last book, *The History of the National Association of Colored Women's Clubs: A Legacy of Service*, in 1984 at the age of ninety-two. He died in Washington, D.C., three years later.

See also Association for the Study of African American Life and History; Historians/Historiography; Howard University; Wilberforce University; Woodson, Carter G.

Bibliography

Meier, August, and Elliot Rudwick. *Black History and Historical Profession, 1915–1980.* Urbana: University of Illinois Press, 1986.

Wesley, Charles H. *Negro Labor in the United States, 1950–1925.* New York: Vanguard, 1927.

FRANCILLE RUSAN WILSON (1996)

West, Cornel

June 2, 1953

Cornell Ronald West, an educator, was born in Tulsa, Oklahoma. He graduated magna cum laude from Harvard and received an M.A. and Ph.D. from Princeton. He taught at Union Seminary, Yale, the University of Paris, and Princeton, where he was director of the Afro-American Studies Program. In 1994 he moved to Harvard, where he took a position as Alphonse Fletcher Jr. University Professor.

West is one of the leading contemporary African-American intellectuals and activists at the beginning of the twenty-first century. The author or editor of more than fifteen books, he is also a popular public speaker. West's work ranges over the fields of philosophy, literature, religion, music, and black history, and focuses on social thought, cultural and political criticism, modern philosophy, and issues of social justice. West has deep roots in the Baptist church, the source of his preaching style. His intellectual foundation combines democratic socialism, Christian compassion, the modernity of Franz Kafka, and black music. His intellectual heroes include Anton Chekhov and John Coltrane.

A list of his books begins with professional works of scholarship, such as *The American Evasion of Philosophy: A Generation of Pragmatism* (1989) and *The Ethical Dimensions of Marxist Thought* (1991). West became a national figure with *Race Matters* (1993), a collection of essays that made the best-seller list. His later books, *Keeping Faith* (1993) and *Restoring Hope* (1997), were followed by a large compendium of his work, *The Cornel Reader* (1999). With Jack Salzman and David Lionel Smith, he coedited the first edition of the *Encyclopedia of African-American Culture and History.* He has also edited two books dealing with black-Jewish relations: *Jews and Blacks: A Dialogue on Race, Religion and Culture in America* (with Michael Lerner), and *Struggles in the Promised Land: Toward a History of Black-Jewish Relations* (with Jack Salzman), 1997. West made his first major foray into national politics during the 2000 presidential primaries when he worked for Democrat Bill Bradley as an adviser and as cochair of Bradley's Massachusetts campaign.

After a falling out with Harvard president Lawrence Summers in 2002, West left Harvard for Princeton University.

See also Black Studies; Intellectual Life

Bibliography

Emerge, March 1993.

Hooks, Bell, and Cornel West. *Breaking Bread: Insurgent Black Intellectual Life.* Boston, Mass.: South End Press, 1991.

West, Cornel. *The American Evasion of Philosophy: A Genealogy of Pragmatism.* Madison: University of Wisconsin Press, 1989.

RICHARD NEWMAN (1996)
Updated by publisher 2005

West, Dorothy

June 2, 1907
August 16, 1998

Writer Dorothy West was born to Rachel Pease West and Isaac Christopher West in Boston, where she attended Girls' Latin School and Boston University. Hers was a long and varied writing career that spanned over eighty years, beginning with a short story she wrote at age seven. When she was barely fifteen, she was selling short stories to the *Boston Post.* And before she was eighteen, already living in New York, West had won second place in the national competition sponsored by *Opportunity* magazine, an honor she shared with Zora Neale Hurston. The winning story, "The Typewriter," was later included in Edward O'Brien's *The Best Short Stories of 1926.*

As a friend of such luminaries as Countee Cullen, Langston Hughes, Claude McKay, and Wallace Thurman, Dorothy West judged them and herself harshly for "degenerat[ing] through [their] vices" and for failing, in general, to live up to their promise. Thus, in what many consider the waning days of the Harlem Renaissance and in the lean years of the Depression, West used personal funds to start *Challenge,* a literary quarterly, hoping to recapture some of this failed promise. She served as its editor from 1934 until the last issue appeared in the spring of 1937. It was succeeded in the fall of that year by *New Challenge.* The renamed journal listed West and Marian Minus as coeditors and Richard Wright as associate editor, but West's involvement with the new project was short-lived.

The shift from *Challenge* to *New Challenge* is variously explained but can perhaps be summed up in Wallace Thurman's observation to West that *Challenge* had been too "high schoolish" and "pink tea." Whether *Challenge* was to *New Challenge* what "pink tea" was to "red" is debatable, but West admitted that *New Challenge* turned resolutely toward a strict Communist Party line that she found increasingly difficult to toe. Despite her resistance to this turn in the journal's emphasis, *Challenge,* under West's editorship, succeeded in encouraging and publishing submissions that explored the desperate conditions of the black working class.

Because of her involvement with *Challenge* and her early associations with the figures and events that gave the period its singular status and acclaim, West in the 1990s was generally designated the "last surviving member of the Harlem Renaissance." The bulk of her writing, however, actually began to be published long after what most literary historians consider the height of the movement.

In the more than sixty short stories written throughout her career, West showed that form to be her forte. Many of these stories were published in the *New York Daily News.* The first to appear there was "Jack in the Pot" (retitled "Jackpot" by the editors), which won the Blue Ribbon Fiction contest and was anthologized in John Henrik Clarke's 1970 collection *Harlem: Voices from the Soul of Black America.* Another story, "For Richer, for Poorer," has been widely anthologized in textbooks and various collections.

Although the short story was the mainstay of her career, West is best known for her novel, *The Living Is Easy.* Published in 1948, the novel has been praised for its engaging portrayal of Cleo Judson, the unscrupulous and manipulative woman who brings ruin on herself as well as on family members who fall under her domination and control. But the novel also earned West high marks for its treatment of the class snobbery, insularity, and all-around shallowness of the New England black bourgeoisie, whom West termed the "genteel poor." Whereas Mary Helen Washington (1987) commends *The Living Is Easy* for its array of feminist themes—"the silencing of women, the need for female community, anger over the limitations and restrictions of women's lives" in the final analysis she faults it for silencing the mother's voice.

In the last decades of her life Dorothy West lived on Martha's Vineyard, contributing after 1968 a generous sampling of occasional pieces and columns to its newspaper, the *Vineyard Gazette.* In 1995 she published *The Wedding,* which dealt with blacks on Martha's Vineyard and was turned into a television movie in 1998 by director Charles Burnett.

See also Harlem Renaissance; Literary Magazines

Bibliography

Washington, Mary Helen. *Invented Lives: Narratives of Black Women 1860–1960.* New York: Anchor Press, 1987.

DEBORAH MCDOWELL (1996)
Updated by publisher 2005

Westerman, George

February 22, 1910
August 30, 1988

George Washington Westerman was an autodidact, tennis champion (1936–1938), journalist, diplomat, advisor to several Panamanian presidents, defender of human rights, friend of the United States, and a moderate Panamanian nationalist. The fifth child of George Benjamin Westerman and Marie Josephine Rosena Bridget, he was born in Coolie Town, on the Atlantic Coast of the Republic of Panama. His father was born in Barbados but traveled to Panama in 1905 with his wife and four daughters. Like tens of thousands of West Indians, he found work in the Canal Zone, contributing significantly to the successful building of the Panama Canal, which was completed in 1914.

Westerman became one of the best chroniclers of West Indian participation in the building and maintenance of the waterway. He started his journalism career at the age of sixteen with the *Panama American,* and in 1928 he joined the *Panama Tribune.* In 1959, Westerman became the editor and publisher of the *Tribune,* and over the years, he wrote hundreds of articles and editorials, dozens of pamphlets, and several published and unpublished books on isthmian West Indians and their progeny.

Although Westerman wrote on many topics and themes, his journalistic and literary production was primarily driven by his concern for the civil and human rights of minorities in the Canal Zone and Panama. During the 1940s and 1950s he wrote incessantly in defense of non-U.S. citizens in the Panama Canal Zone who were victims of segregation. In Panama, he organized the National Civic League in 1944 to lobby the Panamanian government to return citizenship rights to children of West Indian parents.

Westerman's success as a defender of minority rights on the Isthmus of Panama, and as a diplomat, was due to his reputation as a fair and objective journalist, his moderate nationalism and admiration of U.S.-style democracy, and his many support networks among the Panamanian elite and within African-American literary, artistic, and political circles. His penchant for chronicling the West Indian experience on the isthmus and in defending the group's labor interest in the Canal Zone (and their cultural and political rights in Panama) was shaped by his understanding of their many contributions to the United States and to the Republic of Panama.

On several occasions during the 1950s, Westerman was approached to run for political office. He declined, however, and supported other West Indian-Panamanian candidates. In 1952 he endorsed the successful candidacy of Alfredo Cragwell, who became the first of his ethnic group to serve in the national Legislative Assembly. On the other hand, Westerman was very interested in behind-the-scenes politics as well as in diplomatic affairs.

In 1952, West Indian-Panamanians supported the presidential candidacy of Colonel José Antonio Remón Cantera, who was put forward by the National Patriotic Coalition (Coalición Patriótico Nacional, or CPN), a political coalition of five parties, including the Partido Renovador, a liberal party with which Westerman was affiliated. Between 1952 and 1955, Westerman played several important roles in the CPN and in the Remón government. For example, as the United States and Panama negotiated the 1955 Eisenhower-Remón Treaty, President Remón called on Westerman to advise the Panamanian negotiating team on Canal Zone labor issues, a task that prepared him for a larger diplomatic role during the 1956–1960 presidency of Ernesto de la Guardia Jr.

As a friend, colleague, and political partisan of the president, Westerman was appointed to the United Nations (UN) in each of the four years that de la Guardia served as president of Panama. By all accounts, Westerman did a great job promoting the president's agenda and Panama's national interests. He served with distinction on the Fourth Committee, which won him much acclaim and a brief mention to succeed Dag Hammarksjold as UN Secretary-General.

Despite his success on the international diplomatic stage, Westerman will be most remembered for single-handedly tackling segregation in the U.S. Canal Zone in the 1940s and 1950s, and for denouncing prejudice and the cultural exclusion of West Indians in Panama during the same period.

See also Panama Canal

Bibliography

Priestley, George. "Raza y Nacionalismo en Panamá: George Westerman y la 'cuestión' Antillana." In *Piel Oscura Panamá: Ensayos y reflexiones al filo del Centenario,* edited by Alberto Barrow and George Priestley. Panama: Universidad de Panama, 2003.

GEORGE PRIESTLEY (2005)

West Indies Democratic Labour Party

The West Indies Democratic Labour Party (WIDLP) was formed in 1958 and led by Alexander Bustamante, a Jamaican who was also leader of the Jamaica Labour Party (JLP, formed in 1943). The WIDLP was formed to contest the 1958 federal elections. The party ceased to exist in

1962, when the West Indies Federation collapsed. While it lasted, it was an alliance of political parties from the twelve member countries of the West Indies Federation, and it became the opposition party in the federation, having narrowly lost the first and only federal elections, which were won by the West Indies Federal Labour Party. The WIDLP's affiliates, including the JLP, were opposition parties in the territories of the West Indies Federation, with the exception of Saint Vincent. The party itself existed more as a label than as an organization with a strong center. It had no constitution and offered no manifesto in contesting the federal elections.

The WIDLP won twenty of the forty-five seats contested in the federal elections. Its strength lay in three territories where it won the majority of seats: Jamaica (twelve), Trinidad and Tobago (six), and Saint Vincent (two). Bustamante's JLP was the strongest affiliate, and he was the dominant labor personality in the West Indies. The party moderately supported federation, preferring a gradual and cautious approach to such issues as the creation of a customs union and freedom of movement, as well as a weak federal center.

The fate of the party rested on Bustamante's political ambitions in Jamaica, and he was more nationalist than regionalist. He did not offer himself as a candidate in the federal elections; did not try to establish close personal links in the Eastern Caribbean, where he was not popular; feared that Jamaica would be asked to subsidize the less-developed Eastern Caribbean countries; and feared Trinidad and Tobago's competition with Jamaica's manufacturing sector. Bustamante eventually led a successful secession from the federation when the JLP won a 1961 referendum in Jamaica, which was the largest member.

The WIDLP lacked distinct foundations in doctrine, traditional themes, and structures around which leaders of diverse territorial parties could rally. Furthermore, communication across the Caribbean was difficult. Leaders in the Eastern Caribbean could hardly tell what Jamaica's leaders were planning. The politics of Bustamante and the WIDLP often reflected the competitive politics of the JLP and its rival Peoples National Party (PNP) in Jamaica. It failed to consolidate itself during the four-year life of the federation. The reason is captured by Bustamante's statement that he would sacrifice the WIDLP and the federation if he thought they might hurt Jamaica's interest. In the end, he did.

See also Bustamante, Alexander; Jamaica Labour Party; West Indies Federal Labour Party; West Indies Federation

Bibliography

Mordecai, John. *The West Indies: The Federal Negotiations.* London: Allen and Unwin, 1968.

ROBERT MAXWELL BUDDAN (2005)

West Indies Federal Labour Party

Throughout its existence, the West Indies Federal Labour Party (WIFLP) was led by Jamaican Norman Manley, who was also president of Jamaica's People's National Party (PNP, formed in 1938). The WIFLP was formed in 1956 and its leaders were among the strongest proponents of the West Indies Federation (1958–1962). The opposing party within the federation was the West Indies Democratic Labour Party (WIDLP), led by Alexander Bustamante, also a Jamaican, who was also leader of the Jamaica Labour Party (JLP, formed in 1943).

The WIFLP had twelve affiliate parties from the territories of the West Indies Federation. It also had a constitution and presented a manifesto for the federal elections of 1958. It required affiliated territorial parties to declare themselves socialist. However, it was forced to accept some parties as affiliate members that had not so declared themselves. The WIFLP and its affiliates were therefore socialist more in name than in program.

The WIFLP narrowly defeated its rival WIDLP by winning twenty-two (to the latter's twenty) of the forty-five federal seats in the elections of March 1958. Its minority government was generally supported by three independent members. The party's narrow victory was surprising considering the prestige of its leaders. Norman Manley was the region's most prestigious political leader, followed by Grantley Adams of Barbados and Eric Williams of Trinidad and Tobago. The party also had the advantage that eleven of its affiliates formed territorial governments in the federation's member countries.

The WIFLP affiliates faced strongest antifederal sentiments in the largest and most important countries: Jamaica and Trinidad and Tobago. The federal election was conducted under local election laws. The WIFLP's largest affiliate, the PNP of Jamaica, won only five of the seventeen seats allocated to Jamaica. The WIFLP also suffered a major defeat when the People's National Movement of Trinidad and Tobago, led by Eric Williams, failed to secure a majority of seats allocated to that island.

This meant that two of the strongest affiliates of the WIFLP had relatively few representatives in the federal parliament, and neither Manley nor Williams contested seats to that parliament. The strongest support for the WIFLP came from Barbados and the eastern Caribbean. The first prime minister of the federation was Grantley Adams, but his Barbados Labour Party lost national elections in 1961, denying him much prestige at the federal level.

This meant that, although the parliamentary group of the WIFLP represented eight islands altogether, more than two-thirds of the MPs were from Barbados and the Leeward and Windward islands of the eastern Caribbean. The opposition WIDLP's parliamentary group came entirely from four islands: Jamaica, Trinidad and Tobago, and Saint Vincent. Furthermore, neither of the leaders of the two federal parties contested elections and so none were members of the federal parliament.

Sir John Mordecai raised the question of how truly federal the two parties were. He writes, "Both the WIFLP and the DLP were contrived in expediency—both lacking distinct foundations in doctrine, traditional themes and standards around which leaders of territorial Federal Parties, so diverse in pattern and status, could rally. The fact of each alliance being headed by the founders of the two Jamaican Parties for twenty years at 'war' with each other, also contributed to the weakness of both Federal Parties" (p. 85).

At the outset, the WIFLP favored a relatively strong central government and the rapid development of a customs union. However, nationalist politics and regional fragmentation undermined the party's leadership of the federal government and its policies. Norman Manley, for instance, had decided to remain as head of the Jamaican government rather than become prime minister of the federation in order to fight the antifederal tendencies in Jamaica. This undermined both his regional stature and that of the federation itself.

Furthermore, the WIFLP suffered from the fragmentation of the West Indian islands and the long distances between them, especially between Jamaica and the eastern Caribbean. Communication systems were weak and travel was irregular. This affected the coherence of the WIFLP and its ability to consolidate its regional organization. Manley's PNP, being the largest affiliate of the WIFLP, lost a referendum in 1961 on whether Jamaica should remain in the federation and this forced the country to withdraw, which led to the demise of the federation and the WIFLP in 1962.

See also Barbados Labour Party; Jamaica Labour Party; West Indies Democratic Labour Party; West Indies Federation

Bibliography

Eaton, George. *Alexander Bustamante and Modern Jamaica.* Kingston, Jamaica: Kingston Publishers, 1995.

Mordecai, Sir John, *The West Indies: The Federal Negotiations.* London: Allen and Unwin, 1968.

ROBERT BUDDAN (2005)

West Indies Federation

The federal idea evolved from Britain's desire for administrative convenience in managing her colonial empire since its beginnings in the seventeenth century. From William Stapleton's General Assembly of the Leeward Islands of 1674 to the establishment of Robert Melvill's Government of Grenada of 1763, to John Pope-Hennessy's Confederation of the Windward Islands of 1876, Britain had, throughout the centuries, sought to rationalize the administration of her possessions in the West Indies. These attempts to impose federation by imperial fiat all ended in failure.

There was, however, an unofficial but no less real sense of unity among ordinary Caribbean people, particularly in the eastern Caribbean. They impeded the advance of European colonialism for the two centuries before 1763 and participated in each other's anticolonial, antislavery, proto-nationalist struggles at the end of the eighteenth century. Close bonds of friendship, trade, and consanguinity developed among them, despite the continued insularity and parochialism of the elites of their respective colonies. Few such relationships developed between the people of the eastern Caribbean and those of Jamaica, more than a thousand miles to the northwest, despite their common history of British colonial rule.

The experiences of Afro-Caribbean soldiers during World War I, leading to the formation of a "Caribbean League," brought about some semblance of a West Indian ethos to the forefront of the collective consciousness of the ordinary people. No less important was the granting of test status to the West Indies cricket team in 1928. By then, Britain had already regarded her West Indies possessions as a single unit. By the middle 1920s the British had also begun the gradual process of dismantling colonial rule by granting increasing degrees of self-government to the colonial constitutions.

By the 1930s the federation's chief ideologue was T. Albert Marryshow, the Grenadian editor of *The West Indian* newspaper, which carried the masthead, "The West In-

The inauguration of the West Indies Federation (1958–1962), April 22, 1958, Governor General's House, Port-of-Spain, Trinidad. *Pictured are Princess Margaret, who presided over the ceremony, and to her left, Lord Hailes, Governor General of the newly formed Federation. The short-lived Federation held most of Britain's West Indian colonies under a single administration, suggesting the promise of a future unified West Indian nation.* © BETTMANN/CORBIS

dies must be West Indian." He used the paper to popularize both the causes of West Indian self-government and federation. A conference of British West Indies labor leaders in Dominica in 1932 then called for a West Indies federation. The cause was strengthened in 1933 by the West Indian intellectual C. L. R. James, who argued persuasively in his essay, *The Case for West Indian Self-Government*, for the British West Indies to be granted self-government, even if it meant freedom to make their own mistakes.

After 1945 the federal idea was entrenched—somewhat—among ordinary West Indians, and somehow synchronized with Britain's post–World War II exhaustion and a newfound disposition to relinquish her colonial empire. In cricket, the West Indies won its first ever series victory over England in 1950. Cricket had, by then, become a major theater in which the struggle for West Indian nationhood was fought. The West Indians' mastery of this complex, quintessentially British game demonstrated their ability to manage their own affairs.

In 1948 the University College of the West Indies was established, with a single campus at Mona, Jamaica. It was in a special relationship with the University of London. This brought the region's tertiary students together at a university in the Caribbean for the first time, and also brought together some of the region's best intellectual talent for teaching and research on primarily West Indian subjects and issues. It was not an independent degree-granting institution at the time.

The 1947 Montego Bay, Jamaica, Conference of colonial leaders produced the Closer Union Committee and the Regional Economic Committee. The former produced a draft constitution for a British West Indies federation that was accepted by all British colonies except the British Virgin Islands, British Honduras, and British Guiana, which eventually opted out of membership of the proposed body. This left a body of ten member units, all island colonies.

Follow-up conferences in London in 1953, 1955, and 1956 worked out the general details. The British Parliament then passed the British Caribbean Federation Act. Britain retained powers over external affairs, defense, and general financial affairs in the colonial federation. The constitution established a bicameral legislature, with a governor-general vested with significant executive powers. The forty-five-member House of Representatives was elected by universal adult suffrage, and the Senate comprised nineteen nominated members. The executive was a "Council of State," composed of and presided over by the governor-general, prime minister, and ten ministers. A supreme court and a civil service were also established. Chaguaramas, an American World War II naval base on the northwestern peninsula of Trinidad and Tobago, was chosen as the site for the federal capital.

The British continued the gradual constitutional decolonization in the major colonies, to the extent that the 1958 federal constitution lagged behind those of Jamaica, Trinidad and Tobago, and Barbados, all of which then possessed varying degrees of self-government. This policy was, however, not consistently followed in the eastern Caribbean. This continued after 1958, a policy that ultimately helped to undermine the federal body itself.

In the 1958 federal elections, the West Indies Federal Labour Party, an association of political parties with a socialist outlook, won twenty-six seats, with the Democratic Labour Party winning seventeen. Norman Manley and Eric Williams, two of the most prominent figures in British West Indian politics, refused to stand for election to the federal parliament. Their absence lowered the federation's legitimacy for many West Indians. This left them free to criticize the federation from the sidelines, while simultaneously pursuing their respective colony's particular interests independent of the federation's official authority.

In any event, the political arrangement after the elections left Jamaica and Trinidad and Tobago underrepresented in the federal government, while the eastern Caribbean was overrepresented. Lord Hailes was appointed governor-general. The Barbadian Grantley Adams became prime minister, with most ministers from the eastern Caribbean.

The first British West Indian parliament was inaugurated by Her Royal Highness Princess Margaret at Governor General's House, Port-of-Spain, Trinidad and Tobago, on April 22, 1958. Marryshow's death on October 19, 1958, boded ill for the fledgling federation. A member of the federal Senate and the "Father of Federation," Marryshow may have died happy in seeing his dream realized in his lifetime, but the federation was constituted contrary to his declared wish that self-government should be granted before federation.

Outside of the West Indies Welfare Fund, the University College of the West Indies, the Federal Supreme Court, and the West India Regiment, the federation's powers did not extend very far. In addition, its revenue base was narrow, largely due to the colonial legislatures' refusal to surrender the powers of taxation to the federal parliament. It could contribute little to real development, as such matters as education and economic development remained the preserve of the individual colonies.

Jamaica and Trinidad and Tobago, the two largest colonies and major contributors to the federation's operating costs, prevailed upon the British to overrule the eastern Caribbean representatives' objections and revise the constitution at a conference in September 1959—well ahead of schedule—with a view to making the federal parliament more representative of these colonies' size and contribution. The membership of the House of Representatives was increased to sixty-four, with Jamaica and Trinidad and Tobago allocated thirty and fifteen seats respectively. Cabinet government was granted and the governor-general's powers reduced. Overall, the federal constitution was brought on par with those of Barbados, Jamaica, and Trinidad and Tobago.

The conference that produced these constitutional advances could not repair the serious rift that developed over the two dominant colonies' rival and opposing concepts of federation. Trinidad and Tobago, or at least Eric Williams, wanted a strong centralized federation with powers over taxation and economic development and a customs union. Jamaica, or at least Manley, wanted a loose, weak union leaving economic development to the individual territories. The Jamaican delegation all but walked out of the 1959 conference and the federation itself.

Other tensions arose, particularly when Williams successfully negotiated with the U.S. government for the return of Chaguaramas to Trinidad and Tobago, independent of the federal authorities and despite the protests of the federal officials. There were also strong disagreements, particularly between Trinidad and Tobago and the eastern Caribbean territories, over the question of freedom of movement of people in the federation. The smaller, poorer, and densely populated member colonies desired freedom of movement, particularly after Britain imposed restrictions on immigration to the United Kingdom itself. Trinidad and Tobago, however, strongly resisted this measure.

The question of the free movement of goods was another issue. Trinidad and Tobago was in favor of the free movement of goods within the free trade area created by the federation and a system of uniform tariffs outside of it. Jamaica, whose government revenues depended heavily on customs duties, strongly opposed this.

Perhaps the greatest difficulty in the federation was that of economic development. The federal parliament desired control over the economic development of the federation as a whole. Jamaica opposed this on the grounds that this might be achieved at the expense of her own development. This was a crucial factor in Jamaica's eventual withdrawal from the federation.

Both the Jamaicans and Trinidadians were convinced that in granting federation, Britain had in fact transferred her liability for the eastern Caribbean to their colonies, which they saw was adversely affecting their own development. The passage of the Commonwealth Immigrants Act by the British Parliament, enacted to control immigration from Commonwealth countries, and Britain's decision to become a member of the European Common Market seemed to vindicate their concerns.

Unless some compromise was worked out, the federation was doomed. Unofficial discussions between Trinidad and Tobago and Jamaica failed to produce a satisfactory solution. In a September 1961 referendum, Jamaica voted to secede from the federation, prompting Williams's calculation that "1 from 10 leaves 0." Ignoring all entreaties to continue a rump, Jamaica-less federation composed effectively of the eastern Caribbean—virtually integrated already—Williams followed Jamaica's lead. The British Parliament dissolved the federation effective May 1962. Jamaica and Trinidad and Tobago proceeded to independence in August 1962, leaving the smaller colonies to work out their future individual relationships with Britain.

From 1958 to 1962 Britain held most of her West Indian colonies under a single administration, and for a brief moment their peoples glimpsed the possibilities of a West Indian nation. Representatives of the entire Caribbean with a common history of British rule met in one place and under one authority to address the issues that concerned them. The British West Indies received diplomatic recognition from the rest of the British Commonwealth and the United States. The federation's sportsmen participated in international events as a single unit.

The collapse of the British West Indies Federation was the result of many deep-seated causes. Perhaps the most important was the intercolonial rivalries, insularity, and parochialism that have characterized British West Indian politics for three centuries. For most West Indians, the island was the unit that held the first claim to their allegiance. Whereas in the eastern Caribbean, profederation sentiment seemed to have always been strong, it was not uniformly so in the rest of the Caribbean. This was particularly so in the case of Jamaica, which had more in common with her neighbors and North America than the eastern Caribbean.

Perhaps most of all, the British West Indies Federation was still a collection of British colonies not yet granted full self-government, and for which the United Kingdom retained ultimate control. There were left too many fundamental issues to be worked out between politicians who had no significant history of working together for a common purpose and who were more inclined to place the interests of their individual territories before those of a federated whole.

The British West Indies Federation was a shattered dream to many West Indian people. In the decades that followed its collapse, the West Indies cricket team and The University of the West Indies, which received its independence in 1962, have remained the most visible manifestations of the dream of a West Indian nation.

See also Adams, Grantley; Williams, Eric; West Indies Democratic Labour Party; West Indies Federal Labour Party

Bibliography

Greenwood, R., and S. Hamber. *Caribbean Certificate History: Development and Decolonisation.* London and Oxford: Macmillan Education, 1981.

Grimshaw, Anna, ed. *The C. L. R. James Reader.* Oxford, U.K. and Cambridge, Mass.: Blackwell, 1992.

Meighoo, Kirk Peter. *Politics in a "Half Made Society": Trinidad and Tobago 1925–2001.* Kingston, Oxford, and Princeton: Ian Randle Publishers, James Currey Publishers, and Marcus Wiener Publishers, 2003.

Parry, J. H., and Philip Sherlock. *A Short History of the West Indies.* London and Basingstoke, N.J.: Macmillan, 1981.

Steele, Beverley A. *Grenada: A History of Its People.* Oxford: Macmillan Education, 2003.

Williams, Eric. *Inward Hunger: The Education of a Prime Minister.* London: Andre Deutsch, 1969.

C. M. JACOBS (2005)

Wheatley, Phillis

c. 1753
December 5, 1784

The poet Phillis Wheatley was born, according to her own testimony, in Gambia, West Africa, along the fertile lowlands of the Gambia River. She was abducted at the age of seven or eight, and then sold in Boston to John and Susanna Wheatley on July 11, 1761. The horrors of the Middle Passage very likely contributed to the persistent asthma that plagued her throughout her short life. The Wheatleys apparently named the girl, who had nothing but a piece of dirty carpet to conceal her nakedness, after the slave ship *Phillis,* which had transported her. Nonetheless, unlike most slave owners of the time, the Wheatleys permitted Phillis to learn to read, and her poetic talent soon began to emerge.

Her earliest known piece of writing was an undated letter from 1765 (no known copy now exists) to Samson Occom, a Native American Mohegan minister and one of Dartmouth College's first graduates. The budding poet first appeared in print on December 21, 1767, in the *Newport Mercury* newspaper, when the author was about fourteen. The poem, "On Messrs. Hussey and Coffin," relates how the two gentlemen of the title narrowly escaped being drowned off Cape Cod in Massachusetts. Much of her subsequent poetry also dealt with events occurring close to her Boston circle. Of her fifty-five extant poems, for example, nineteen are elegies; all but the last of these are devoted to commemorating someone known by the poet. Her last elegy is written about herself and her career.

In early October 1770, Wheatley published an elegy that was pivotal to her career. The subject of the elegy was George Whitefield, an evangelical Methodist minister and privy chaplain to Selina Hastings, Countess of Huntingdon. Whitefield made seven journeys to the American colonies, where he was known as "the Voice of the Great Awakening" and "the Great Awakener." Only a week before his death in Newburyport, Massachusetts, on September 30, 1770, Whitefield preached in Boston, where Wheatley very likely heard him. As Susanna Wheatley regularly corresponded with the countess, she and the Wheatley household may well have entertained the Great Awakener. Wheatley's vivid, ostensibly firsthand account in the elegy, replete with quotations, may have been based on an actual acquaintance with Whitefield. In any case, Wheatley's deft elegy became an overnight sensation and was often reprinted.

It is almost certain that the ship that carried news of Whitefield's death to the countess also carried a copy of Wheatley's elegy, which brought Wheatley to the sympathetic attention of the countess. Such an acquaintance ensured that Wheatley's elegy was also reprinted many times in London, giving the young poet the distinction of an international reputation. When Wheatley's *Poems on Various Subjects, Religious and Moral* was denied publication in Boston for racist reasons, the Countess of Huntingdon generously financed its publication in London.

Wheatley's support by Selina Hastings, and her rejection by male-dominated Boston, signaled her nourishment as a literary artist by a community of women. All these women—the countess, who encouraged and financed the publication of her *Poems* in 1773; Mary and Susanna Wheatley, who taught her the rudiments of reading and writing; and Obour Tanner, who could empathize probably better than anyone with her condition as a slave—were much older than Wheatley and obviously nurtured her creative development.

During the summer of 1772, Wheatley actually journeyed to England, where she assisted in the preparation of her volume for the press. While in London she enjoyed considerable recognition by such dignitaries as Lord Dartmouth, Lord Lincoln, Granville Sharp (who escorted Wheatley on several tours about London), Benjamin Franklin, and Brook Watson, a wealthy merchant who presented Wheatley with a folio edition of John Milton's *Paradise Lost* and who would later become lord mayor of London. Wheatley was to have been presented at court when Susanna Wheatley became ill. Wheatley was summoned to return to Boston in early August 1773. Sometime before October 18, 1773, she was granted her freedom, according to her own testimony, "at the desire of my friends in England." It seems likely, then, that if Selina Hastings had not agreed to finance Wheatley's *Poems* and if the poet had not journeyed to London, she would never have been manumitted.

As the American Revolution erupted, Wheatley's patriotic feelings began to separate her even more from the Wheatleys, who were loyalists. Her patriotism is clearly underscored in her two most famous Revolutionary War poems. "To His Excellency General Washington" (1775) closes with this justly famous encomium: "A crown, a mansion, and a throne that shine, / With gold unfading WASHINGTON! be thine." "Liberty and Peace" (1784), written to celebrate the Treaty of Paris (September 1783), declares: "And new-born Rome [i.e., America] shall give Britannia Law."

Phillis Wheatley's attitude toward slavery has also been misunderstood. Because some of her antislavery statements have been recovered only in the 1970s and 1980s, she has often been criticized for ignoring the issue.

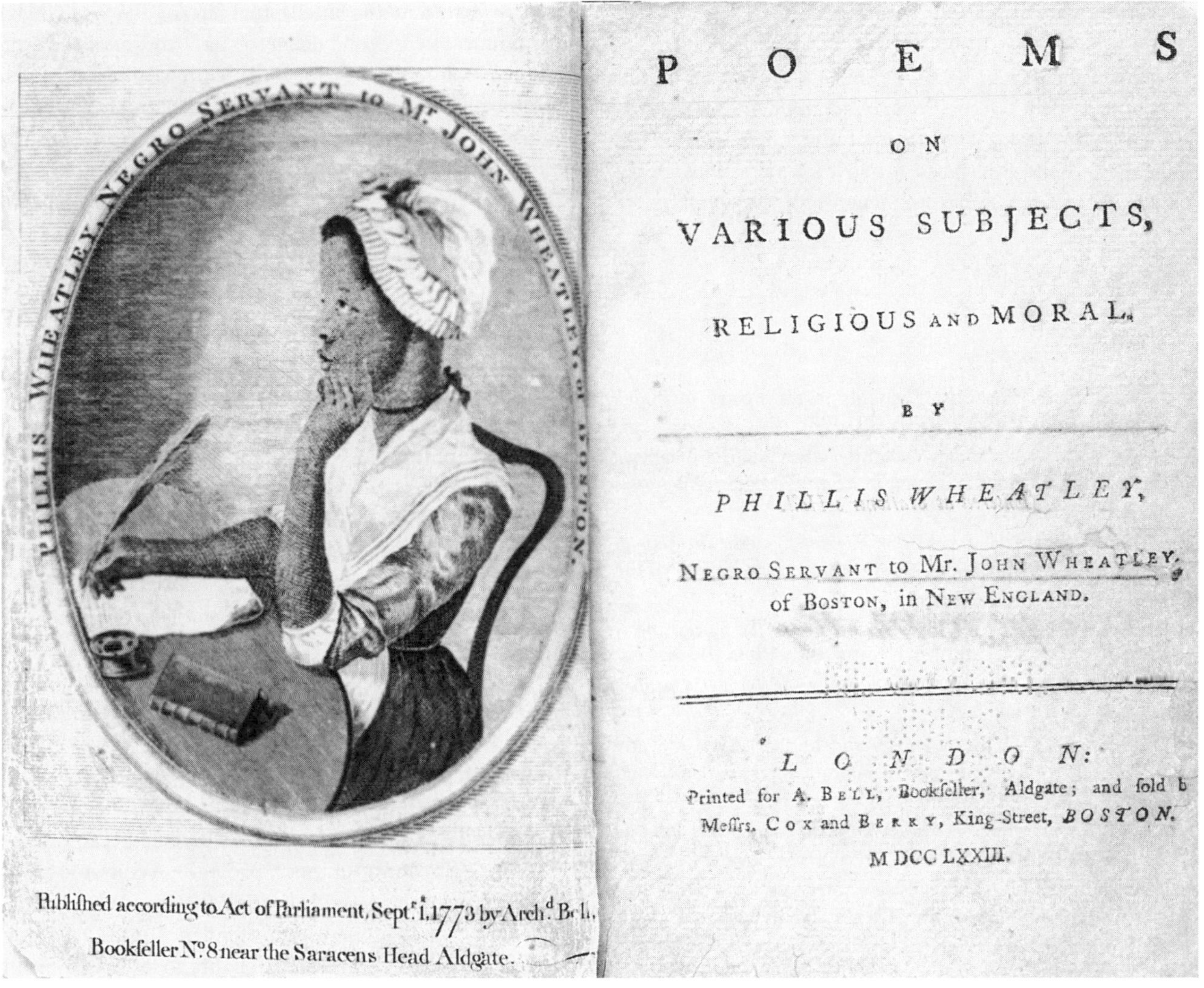
PHILLIS WHEATLEY, NEGRO SERVANT to MR. JOHN WHEATLEY, of BOSTON.

Publifhed according to Act of Parliament, Sept. 1, 1773 by Arch.d Bell, Bookfeller No. 8 near the Saracens Head Aldgate.

P O E M S

ON

VARIOUS SUBJECTS,

RELIGIOUS AND MORAL.

BY

PHILLIS WHEATLEY,

NEGRO SERVANT to Mr. JOHN WHEATLEY, of BOSTON, in NEW ENGLAND.

LONDON:

Printed for A. BELL, Bookfeller, Aldgate; and fold by Meffrs. COX and BERRY, King-Street, BOSTON.

MDCCLXXIII.

Title page and frontispiece for Wheatley's* Poems *(1773). *Because she was a slave, Wheatley's book was not printed in the United States, but support from a number of Boston women led to the volume being published in London. As a result, Wheatley became the first published African American author.* MANUSCRIPTS, ARCHIVES AND RARE BOOKS DIVISION, SCHOMBURG CENTER FOR RESEARCH IN BLACK CULTURE, THE NEW YORK PUBLIC LIBRARY, ASTOR, LENOX AND TILDEN FOUNDATIONS.

But her position was clear: In February 1774, for example, Wheatley wrote to Samson Occom that "in every human breast, God has implanted a Principle, which we call Love of Freedom; it is impatient of Oppression, and pants for Deliverance." This letter was reprinted a dozen times in American newspapers over the course of the next twelve months. Certainly Americans of Wheatley's time never questioned her attitude toward slavery after the publication of this letter.

In 1778 Wheatley married John Peters, a free African American who was a jack-of-all-trades, serving in various capacities from storekeeper to advocate for African Americans before the courts. But given the turbulent conditions of a nation caught up in the Revolution, Wheatley's fortunes began to decline steadily. In 1779 she published "Proposals for Printing by Subscription," a solicitation for funds for a new volume of poems. Although this failed to attract subscribers, it attests that the poet had been diligent with her pen since the 1773 *Poems,* and that she had indeed produced some three hundred pages of new poetry. This volume never appeared, however, and most of its poems are now lost.

Phillis Wheatley Peters and her newborn child died in a shack on the edge of Boston on December 5, 1784. Preceded in death by two other young children, Wheatley's tragic end resembles her beginning in America. Yet Wheatley has left to her largely unappreciative country a legacy of firsts: She was the first African American to publish a book, the first woman writer whose publication was urged and nurtured by a community of women, and the first American woman author who tried to earn a living by means of her writing.

On February 4, 1999, a long-lost poem by Phillis Wheatley, titled "Ocean," was read publicly for the first time in 226 years. The copy of the poem, written in Wheatley's hand, was part of the Newseum's 1999 special exhibition *African American Newspeople, Newsmakers.*

See also Poetry, U.S.

Bibliography

Davis, Arthur P. "Personal Elements in the Poetry of Phillis Wheatley." *Phylon* 13 (1953): 191–198.

O'Neale, Sondra A. "A Slave's Subtle War: Phillis Wheatley's Use of Biblical Myth and Symbol." *Early American Literature* 21 (1986): 144–165.

Robinson, William H. *Black New England Letters: The Uses of Writing in Black New England.* Boston: Public Library of the City of Boston, 1977.

Robinson, William H., ed. *Phillis Wheatley in the Black American Beginnings.* Detroit, Mich.: Broadside Press, 1975.

Robinson, William H., ed. *Critical Essays on Phillis Wheatley.* Boston: G. K. Hall, 1982.

Shields, John C. "Phillis Wheatley and Mather Byles: A Study of Literature Relationship." *College Language Association Journal* 23 (1980): 377–390.

Shields, John C. "Phillis Wheatley's Use of Classicism." *American Literature* 52 (1980): 97–111.

Shields, John C. "Phillis Wheatley's Struggle for Freedom in Her Poetry and Prose." In *The Collected Works of Phillis Wheatley,* edited by John C. Shields. New York: Oxford University Press, 1988.

Shields, John C. "Phillis Wheatley." In *African American Writers,* edited by Valerie Smith. New York: Scribner's, 1991.

JOHN C. SHIELDS (1996)

Whipper, William

c. February 22, 1804
March 9, 1876

The moral reformer and businessman William Whipper was born in Little Britain Township, in Lancaster County, Pennsylvania. Although the inscription on Whipper's tombstone gives 1804 as his date of birth, census data list his year of birth as 1806. Little is known about Whipper's early life, but by 1830 he was living in Philadelphia and working as a steam scourer, cleaning clothing with a steam process.

By the early 1830s, Whipper, who was operating a "free labor and temperance grocery" in Philadelphia, had become active in the intellectual life of the city's black community. In 1828 he delivered an "Address Before the Colored Reading Society of Philadelphia," and in 1833 he was selected to deliver a public eulogy on the British abolitionist William Wilberforce. That same year, he was among the nine founders of the Philadelphia Library of Colored Persons.

Whipper attended every annual National Negro Convention from 1830 to 1835 and was chosen to help draft the movement's declaration of sentiments. In 1834, Whipper, who had earned a reputation among Philadelphia's black elite for his support of moral reform, delivered an address to the Colored Temperance Society of Philadelphia that emphasized the importance of virtue in promoting racial uplift.

At the 1835 national convention, Whipper spearheaded the movement to form the American Moral Reform Society (AMRS), an interracial organization with a broad reform agenda that did not focus exclusively on slavery. Whipper was appointed to the committee to draft the society's constitution, was elected as secretary, and delivered the address "To the American People" at the society's first annual meeting in Philadelphia in 1837. Whipper also helped establish and served as editor of the society's journal, the *National Reformer* (1838–1839).

By 1835 Whipper had moved to Columbia, Pennsylvania, on the Susquehanna River, where he became active in the Underground Railroad, providing economic aid to fugitive slaves who passed through the city. While in Columbia, Whipper joined with Stephen Smith, a wealthy African-American lumber merchant, to establish Smith and Whipper, a lucrative lumber business with operations in Philadelphia and Columbia.

The AMRS lost most of its support in the late 1830s, and with its collapse in 1841 Whipper's public career began to fade. Whipper focused his attention on his lumber company, although he continued to participate in the activities of the northern black leadership. In 1848, he attended the state convention in Philadelphia, reversing his previous denunciation of "complexional" gatherings, and participated in the national conventions of 1853 (Rochester, New York) and 1855 (Philadelphia).

After the passage of the Fugitive Slave Act of 1850, Whipper became interested in emigration to Canada West (now Ontario), shifting his longtime opposition to emigrationist schemes. In 1853 Whipper traveled to Canada and decided to purchase property in the town of Dresden. He was on the verge of moving his family there in 1861 when the outbreak of the Civil War caused him to abandon his plans.

Whipper moved to New Brunswick, New Jersey, in 1868, but he retained his residence in Philadelphia. In

1870 he was appointed a cashier in the Philadelphia branch of the Freedmen's Savings Bank and two years later he relocated to that city. When the bank collapsed in 1873, Whipper apparently lost a large portion of his substantial personal savings. He died at his home in Philadelphia.

See also American Moral Reform Society; Entrepreneurs and Entrepreneurship; Free Blacks, 1619–1860; Freedman's Bank; Underground Railroad

Bibliography

McCormick, Richard P. "William Whipper: Moral Reformer." *Pennsylvania History* 43 (January 1976): 22–46.

Still, William. *The Underground Railroad.* Philadelphia: People's Publishing, 1879.

LOUISE P. MAXWELL (1996)

White, Walter Francis

July 1, 1893
March 21, 1955

Civil rights leader Walter White, executive secretary of the National Association for the Advancement of Colored People (NAACP) from 1931 to 1955, was born in Atlanta, Georgia. Blond and blue-eyed, he was an African American by choice and social circumstance. In 1906, at age thirteen, he stood, rifle in hand, with his father to protect their home and faced down a mob of whites who had invaded their neighborhood in search of "nigger" blood. He later explained: "I knew then who I was. I was a Negro, a human being with an invisible pigmentation which marked me a person to be hunted, hanged, abused, discriminated against, kept in poverty and ignorance, in order that those whose skin was white would have readily at hand a proof of their superiority, a proof patent and inclusive, accessible to the moron and the idiot as well as to the wise man and the genius."

In 1918, when the NAACP hired White as assistant executive secretary to investigate lynchings, sixty-seven such crimes were committed that year in sixteen states. By 1955, when he died, there were only three lynchings, all in Mississippi, and the NAACP no longer regarded the problem as its top priority. White investigated forty-two lynchings, mostly in the Deep South, and eight race riots in the North that developed between World War I and after World War II in such cities as Chicago, Philadelphia, Washington, D.C., Omaha, and Detroit.

In August 1946 White helped to create a National Emergency Committee Against Mob Violence. The following month, he led a delegation of labor and civic leaders in a visit with President Harry S. Truman to demand federal action to end the problem. Truman responded by creating the President's Committee on Civil Rights, headed by Charles E. Wilson, chair and president of General Electric. The committee's report, *To Secure These Rights,* provided the blueprint for the NAACP legislative struggle.

The NAACP's successful struggle against segregation in the armed services was one of White's major achievements. In 1940, as a result of the NAACP's intense protests, President Franklin D. Roosevelt appointed Judge William H. Hastie as civilian aide to the secretary of war, promoted Colonel Benjamin O. Davis, the highest-ranking black officer in the Army, to brigadier general, and appointed Colonel Campbell Johnson as special aide to the director of Selective Service. As significant as these steps were, they did not satisfy White because they were woefully inadequate. So he increasingly intensified the NAACP's efforts in this area.

White then attempted to get the U.S. Senate to investigate employment discrimination and segregation in the armed services, but the effort failed. He therefore persuaded the NAACP board to express its support for the threat by A. Philip Randolph, president of the Brotherhood of Sleeping Car Porters, to lead a march on Washington to demand jobs for blacks in the defense industries and an end to segregation in the military. To avoid the protest, President Roosevelt on June 25, 1941, issued Executive Order 8802, barring discrimination in the defense industries and creating the Fair Employment Practice Committee. That was the first time a U.S. president acted to end racial discrimination, and the date marked the launching of the modern civil rights movement. Subsequently, the NAACP made the quest for presidential leadership in protecting the rights of blacks central to its programs.

As a special war correspondent for the *New York Post* in 1943 and 1945, White visited the European, Mediterranean, Middle Eastern, and Pacific theaters of operations and provided the War Department with extensive recommendations for ending racial discrimination in the military. His book *A Rising Wind* reported on the status of black troops in the European and Mediterranean theaters.

White was as much an internationalist as a civil rights leader. In 1921 he attended the second Pan-African Congress sessions in England, Belgium, and France, which were sponsored by the NAACP and led by W. E. B. Du Bois. While on a year's leave of absence from the NAACP in 1949 and 1950, he participated in the "Round the World Town Meeting of the Air," visiting Europe, Israel, Egypt, India, and Japan.

In 1945 White, Du Bois, and Mary McLeod Bethune represented the NAACP as consultants to the American delegation at the founding of the United Nations in San Francisco. They urged that the colonial system be abolished, that the United Nations recognize equality of the races, that it adopt a bill of rights for all people, and that an international agency be established to replace the colonial system. Many of their recommendations were adopted by the United Nations.

White similarly protested the menial roles that blacks were forced to play in Hollywood films and sought an end to the harmful and dangerous stereotypes of the race that the industry was spreading. He enlisted the aid of Wendell Willkie, the Republican presidential candidate who was defeated in 1940 and who had become counsel to the motion picture industry, in appealing to Twentieth Century Fox, Warner Brothers, Metro-Goldwyn-Mayer, and other major studios and producers for more representative roles for blacks in films. He then contemplated creating an NAACP bureau in Hollywood to implement the organization's programs there. Although the bureau idea fizzled, the NAACP did create a Beverly Hills–Hollywood branch in addition to others in California.

During White's tenure as executive secretary, the NAACP won the right to vote for blacks in the South by getting the U.S. Supreme Court to declare the white Democratic primary unconstitutional, opposed the poll tax and other devices used to discriminate against blacks at the polls, forged an alliance between the organization and the industrial trade unions, removed constitutional roadblocks to residential integration, equalized teachers' salaries in the South, and ended segregation in higher education institutions, in addition to winning the landmark *Brown v. Board of Education* decision in 1954, overturning the Supreme Court's "separate but equal" doctrine. Overall, White led the NAACP to become the nation's dominant force in the struggle to get the national government to uphold the Constitution and protect the rights of African Americans.

White was a gregarious, sociable man who courted on a first-name basis a vast variety of people of accomplishment and influence, including Willkie, Eleanor Roosevelt, Harold Ickes, and Governor Averell Harriman of New York. In 1949 he created a furor by divorcing his first wife, Gladys, and marrying Poppy Cannon, a white woman who was a magazine food editor.

In addition to his many articles, White wrote two weekly newspaper columns. One was for the *Chicago Defender,* a respected black newspaper, and the other for white newspapers such as the Sunday *New York Herald-Tribune.* He wrote two novels, *The Fire in the Flint* (1924) and *Flight* (1926); *Rope and Faggot* (1929, reprint 1969), an exhaustive study of lynchings; *A Man Called White* (1948), an autobiography; and *A Rising Wind* (1945). An assessment of civil rights progress, *How Far the Promised Land?* was published shortly after White's death in 1955.

See also *Brown v. Board of Education of Topeka, Kansas;* Civil Rights Movement, U.S.; Lynching; National Association for the Advancement of Colored People (NAACP)

Bibliography

Janken, Kenneth Robert. *White: The Biography of Walter White, Mr. NAACP.* New York: The New Press, 2003.

Report of the Secretary to the NAACP National Board of Directors, 1940, 1941, 1942.

Sitkoff, Harvard. *A New Deal for Blacks, The Emergence of Civil Rights as a National Issue: The Depression Decade.* New York: Oxford University Press, 1978.

Watson, Denton L. *Lion in the Lobby, Clarence Mitchell, Jr.'s Struggle for the Passage of Civil Rights Laws.* New York: William Morrow, 1990.

Wolters, Raymond. *Negroes and the Great Depression: The Problem of Economic Recovery.* Westport, Conn.: Greenwood Press, 1970.

DENTON L. WATSON (1996)
Updated bibliography

Whitehead, Colson

1969

Colson Whitehead is what many scholars would call a modern-day Renaissance man. A 1991 graduate of Harvard University, his failure to be accepted into the creative writing program brings to mind basketball player Michael Jordan's narrative of overlooked talent. Like Jordan, Whitehead would prove his doubters wrong within a decade of leaving Harvard, garnering the MacArthur Foundation's "genius" award in September 2002. His first novel, *The Intuitionist* (1998), a creative detective story framed around the black female protagonist, Lila Mae Watson, won the Whiting Writers' Award in 2000 and the Quality Paperback Book Club's New Voices Award in 1999. Whitehead was also a finalist for an Ernest Hemingway/PEN Award for First Fiction in 1999.

Whitehead's popularity stems from his ingenious approach to history, culture, and literature. Born in 1969, this Brooklyn native has written his way into the social consciousness of America's elite literary circle. Critics have located Whitehead's fiction within the tradition of mythical realism, comparing his work with that of such authors as Toni Morrison and Ishmael Reed. Whitehead himself has located his work within the tradition of the black intellectual novel, tracing his literary roots back to such writers as Jean Toomer, whose 1923 narrative *Cane* was a tour de force during the Harlem Renaissance because of its creative attention to folk culture and history. Whitehead's 2001 novel, *John Henry Days,* is inventive in the same manner as it explores the historical impact of the nineteenth-century folk hero John Henry upon a modern-day hack journalist, J. Sutter, who is sent to cover the first annual "John Henry Days" festival in Talcott, West Virginia. The ensuing narrative parallels the lives of these two black men, shaping a complex allegorical portrait of racism, history, and popular culture that explores heroism in the postmodern age. This novel likewise investigates the impact of technology on the moral and social development of American society at key moments in the nation's history.

The literary evolution of *John Henry Days* mirrors, in some respects, the real-life journey of Whitehead himself. In the summer of 1997 Whitehead found himself working at a new Internet company in San Francisco to pay off the debt he had incurred while writing *The Intuitionist.* His job—to write forty-word blurbs for upcoming Web chats in the style of *TV Guide*—allowed him the opportunity to experience not only the transcoastal worlds of the West and East Coasts with his wife; it gave him the chance to surf the Web each afternoon while completing his weekly assignment. One afternoon Whitehead stumbled across the U.S. Postal Service's press release of its John Henry stamp, which had been released in 1996 as part of its "Folk Heroes" series. Whitehead's fascination with the details surrounding not only the commercialization of folk heroes but also the life and death of John Henry—particularly his race with a steam drill engine—gave him the kernel he needed to begin his next literary project.

Whitehead's publishing career is as varied and extensive as his intellectual pursuits. His articles have appeared in the *New York Times, Salon, Vibe, Spin, Newsday,* and the *Village Voice,* where he worked as an editorial assistant and a TV critic. His third book, *The Colossus of New York: A City in 13 Parts* (2003), blends Whitehead's journalistic talents with his creative cultural voice.

See also Literature of the United States

Bibliography

Gates, Henry L. Jr., et al., eds. *The Norton Anthology of African American Literature,* 2d ed. New York: Norton, 2004.

Miller, Laura. "The Salon Interview: Going Up." An interview with Colson Whitehead. January 12, 1999. Available from <http://www.salon.com/books/int/1999/01/cov_si_12int.html>.

CAROL E. HENDERSON (2005)

Wideman, John Edgar

June 14, 1941

Born in Washington, D.C., novelist John Edgar Wideman spent much of his early life first in Homewood, Pennsylvania, and then in Shadyside, an upper-middle-class area of Pittsburgh. In 1960 he received a scholarship to the University of Pennsylvania, where he proved himself equally outstanding in his undergraduate studies and on the basketball court. He graduated Phi Beta Kappa in 1963, and his athletic achievements led to his induction into the Big Five Basketball Hall of Fame. Upon graduation, Wideman became only the second African American to be awarded a Rhodes Scholarship (Alain Locke had received one almost fifty-five years earlier), an honor that allowed him to study for three years at Oxford University in England, where he earned a degree in eighteenth-century literature.

After returning to the United States in 1966 and attending the Creative Writing Workshop at the University of Iowa as a Kent Fellow, Wideman returned to the University of Pennsylvania, where he served as an instructor (and later, professor) of English. In 1967, at the age of twenty-six, he published his first novel, *A Glance Away.* The novel was well-received by critics, and two years after its appearance Wideman published *Hurry Home* (1969), a novel that chronicled its protagonist's struggle to reconcile the past and the present. After publishing a third novel in 1973, a dense and technically complex work titled *The Lynchers,* Wideman found his name increasingly associated with a diverse set of literary forebears including James Joyce, William Faulkner, and Ralph Ellison.

During this period Wideman served as the assistant basketball coach (1968–1972) at the University of Pennsylvania, as well as director of the Afro-American Studies Program (1971–1973). In 1975 he left Philadelphia to teach at the University of Wyoming in Laramie. Six years later he ended a long literary silence with the publication of two books: a collection of stories, *Damballah,* and *Hid-*

ing Place, a novel. Both books focus on Wideman's Homewood neighborhood. And with the publication in 1983 of the third book in the trilogy, Wideman's reputation as a major literary talent was assured. *Sent for You Yesterday* won the 1984 P.E.N./Faulkner Award, winning over several more established writers.

At this point, Wideman was drawn (by circumstance rather than choice) into the world of nonfiction after his brother, Robbie, was convicted of armed robbery and sentenced to life imprisonment. At times angry, at others deeply introspective and brooding, *Brothers and Keepers* (1984) relates the paradoxical circumstances of two brothers: one a successful college professor and author, the other a drug addict struggling to establish an identity apart from his famous older brother. Nominated for the 1985 National Book Award, the memoir set the stage for what arguably might be called Wideman's "next phase."

In 1986, after seeing his son, Jake, tried and convicted for the murder of a camping companion, Wideman moved back east to teach at the University of Massachusetts at Amherst, where he was named Distinguished Professor in 2001. The following year saw the publication of his less than successful but nonetheless intriguing novel *Reuben.* Two years later, Wideman published a collection of stories, *Fever* (1989), and followed that in 1990 with a novel, *Philadelphia Fire.* Both of these works reflect Wideman's ability to interrogate his own experiences, even as his fiction takes up pertinent social issues. In the short stories and the novel, Wideman weaves fiction into the fabric of historical events (the former involves an outbreak of yellow fever in eighteenth-century Philadelphia, and the latter the aftermath of the confrontation with and subsequent bombing by Philadelphia police of the radical group MOVE). In 1992 Wideman brought out *The Stories of John Edgar Wideman* (1992), which contains ten new stories written especially for the collection, themselves titled *All Stories Are True.* What distinguishes these ten stories is their extraordinary repositioning of the reader's attention, away from the source of the stories and toward the human issues they depict. He returned to nonfiction in 1994 with *Fatheralong: A Meditation on Fathers and Sons, Race and Society* and in 2001 with the memoir *Hoop Roots: Basketball, Race, and Love.* Later works of fiction include *The Cattle Killing* (1996) and *Two Cities* (1998). As he works to make sense of his own assets and losses, one finds in Wideman's fiction a continuing engagement with the complexity of history as layered narrative and an ability to articulate the inner essence of events that often elude us.

See also Caribbean/North American Writers (Contemporary); Literature of the United States

Bibliography

Coleman, James W. "Going Back Home: The Literary Development of John Edgar Wideman." *CLA Journal* 28, no. 3 (March 1985): 326–343.

"The Novels of John Wideman." *Black World* (June 1975): 18–38.

O'Brien, John. *Interviews with Black Writers.* New York: Liveright, 1973.

HERMAN BEAVERS (1996)
Updated by publisher 2005

Wilberforce University

Wilberforce University, one of the nation's oldest historically black colleges and universities, was founded by the Methodist Episcopal Church in 1856 on the site of Tarawa Springs, a former summer resort in Greene County, Ohio. The school, which had as its purpose the education of African Americans, was named for British abolitionist William Wilberforce; its first president was Richard S. Rust. From the outset, the Methodist Episcopal Church and the African Methodist Episcopal (AME) Church maintained Wilberforce University cooperatively, despite the earlier founding of an AME school, the Union Seminary, in Columbus, Ohio.

The exigencies of the Civil War led to dwindling funds, declining enrollments, and the closing of both Union Seminary and Wilberforce University. In 1863 the AME Church purchased Wilberforce University from the Methodist Episcopal Church for $10,000, sold the property of Union Seminary, and combined the faculty of the two institutions. The prime mover of the transformation, AME Bishop Daniel Payne, served as president from 1863 to 1873, the first African-American college president in the United States; Payne continued to be involved in Wilberforce's affairs until his death in 1893. Under Payne's direction, a theology department was established in 1866 (it became the autonomous Payne Theological Seminary in 1891). Payne, concerned with establishing Wilberforce as a serious academic institution, introduced classical and science departments the following year. Among the faculty members in its first decades was the classicist William Scarborough (1856–1926), born to slavery in Georgia, who was the author of a standard textbook for Greek, translator of Aristophanes, and president of Wilberforce from 1908 to 1920. Occasional lecturers included Alexander Crummell and Paul Laurence Dunbar.

In 1887 AME Bishop Benjamin W. Arnett, who was also a successful Ohio politician, convinced the state legis-

The faculty of Wilberforce University in Ohio, 1922. *Founded in 1856, Wilberforce is one of the nation's oldest historically black universities.* GENERAL RESEARCH AND REFERENCE DIVISION, SCHOMBURG CENTER FOR RESEARCH IN BLACK CULTURE, THE NEW YORK PUBLIC LIBRARY, ASTOR, LENOX AND TILDEN FOUNDATIONS.

lature to establish a normal and industrial department at Wilberforce with its own campus, providing Wilberforce with unusual joint denominational and public supervision and sources of financial support. Shortly thereafter, from 1894 to 1896, W. E. B. Du Bois was an instructor at Wilberforce; he left in part because he was uncomfortable with the intense evangelical piety he found on the campus. Hallie Quinn Brown, a leader of the women's club movement and an 1873 graduate of Wilberforce, joined the faculty in 1893 as professor of elocution (i.e., public speaking), and remained on the faculty of the English department and the board of trustees for many years. The university library was named in her honor. In 1894 a military department was created under the leadership of Charles Young, one of the most distinguished African-American military officers.

In 1922 Wilberforce instituted a four-year degree program, and in 1939 it was formally accredited. A Wilberforce graduate, Horace Henderson, gained attention for his alma mater through a student jazz band, the Wilberforce Collegians, that he founded in the early 1920s and that went on to considerable national success. From 1942 to 1947 the historian Charles Wesley was president. In 1947 the former normal and industrial department was formally separated from Wilberforce as Wilberforce State College. Later renamed Central State University, it remains a predominantly black school, with an enrollment more than triple that of Wilberforce University.

The removal of state support for Wilberforce caused a financial crisis, a decline of enrollment, and a loss of accreditation. Under the leadership of Pembert E. Stokes, Wilberforce began to return to academic and financial health, and its accreditation was restored in 1960. In 1967 construction was begun on a new campus, a quarter mile from the old campus. In 1991 Wilberforce initiated a continuing education program for nontraditional students, Credentials for Leadership in Management and Business Education (CLIMB).

In 2002 Reverend Floyd Flake became president of the university. Financial problems continued to plague Wilberforce into the twenty-first century, and in 2003 faculty members agreed to take a pay cut and increase their workload.

See also African Methodist Episcopal Church; Bethune-Cookman College; Dillard University; Education in the United States; Fisk University; Howard University; Lincoln University; Morehouse College; Payne, Daniel Alexander; Spelman College; Tuskegee University

Bibliography

Lewis, David Levering. *W. E. B. Du Bois: Biography of the Race.* New York: Holt, 1993.

McGinnis, Frederick. *A History of an Interpretation of Wilberforce University.* Blanchester, Ohio: Brown Publishing, 1941.

Talbert, Horace. *The Sons of Allen: Together with a Sketch of the Rise and Progress of Wilberforce University.* Xenia, Ohio: Aldine Press, 1906.

VALENA RANDOLPH (1996)
JACQUELINE BROWN (1996)
Updated by publisher 2005

Wilder, Lawrence Douglas

January 17, 1931

Politician and attorney L. Douglas Wilder was born into a large, poor family in Richmond, Virginia. His grandparents had been slaves. Wilder and his six siblings grew up in a tight-knit family that had a strong work ethic. In 1947 Wilder graduated from high school and enrolled as a chemistry major at Virginia Union University, a historically black college in Richmond. After graduating, Wilder was drafted into the army and served during the Korean War (1950–53). He received a Bronze Star Medal for bravery. After returning home, Wilder worked as a chemist in the state medical examiner's office. In 1956 he enrolled in Howard University Law School in Washington, D.C. Two years later Wilder married Eunice Montgomery; they subsequently had three children.

Upon graduation from law school, Wilder returned to Richmond to practice law. His law practice brought him fame and financial prosperity. While sometimes serving low-income clients free of charge, Wilder also represented wealthy and powerful clients and in the process became a self-made millionaire. His professional success inspired him to run for the state senate in 1969.

Wilder's victory made him the first African-American state senator in Virginia since Reconstruction (1865–77). Wilder successfully promoted legislation that prohibited racially discriminatory housing and employment practices, and he helped to create a state holiday to honor Dr. Martin Luther King Jr. (1929–1968). He chaired the senate's powerful Privileges and Elections Committee, which oversaw state appointments and voting legislation. As a result, he was able to increase the hiring of African Americans to various positions in state government. In a 1985 newspaper poll, Wilder was rated as one of the five most influential members of the Virginia senate. That same year Wilder ran for the statewide office of lieutenant governor. Since African Americans constituted only 18 percent of Virginia's population, Wilder, running as a political moderate, conducted an extensive and shrewd campaign at the grassroots level to win the support of white voters. Wilder won the lieutenant governorship in November 1985. His ability to garner the support of both African American and white voters helped him to win election as chair of the National Democratic Lieutenant Governors Association.

In the 1989 Virginia gubernatorial election, which was decided by less than 2 percentage points, Wilder became the first African American elected governor of a state since Reconstruction. As governor he balanced the state's budget, created a surplus state fund during an economic recession, and increased the number of African Americans working in the state government. The *Financial World* magazine ranked Virginia as the nation's best-managed state two consecutive years during his term. Wilder also obtained legislative approval for gun-control laws, barred state agencies from investing in companies doing business with South Africa, and promoted foreign trade between Virginia and various countries, especially those of Africa.

In 1992 he made an unsuccessful bid to become president. He completed his gubernatorial tenure in January 1994, because the Virginia Constitution prohibits governors from seeking a second consecutive term. In an attempt to unseat United States Senator Charles Robb (1939–) from the United States Senate, Wilder entered the 1994 Virginia senatorial race. After Robb was renominated by the Virginia Democratic Party, Wilder ran as a political independent. Wilder withdrew from the race shortly before the election and endorsed Robb. He campaigned energetically for Robb among African Americans. The votes of African Americans were seen as providing Robb his small margin of victory.

After the election, Wilder began hosting a radio talk show, teaching courses at Virginia Commonwealth University, and speaking on a national lecture circuit. He spearheaded the effort to build the National Slavery Museum in Fredericksburg, Virginia. At the beginning of the twenty-first century, Wilder was still active in politics. In

2002, Virginia governor Mark Warner appointed Wilder to lead the Governor's Commission on Efficiency and Effectiveness. Wilder began cochairing in 2003 a drive to have Richmond's mayor elected by its citizens. The change-in-government proposal won approval by city voters and by the Virginia state legislature in 2004. In 2004 Wilder was elected mayor of Richmond, Virginia.

See also Politics in the United States

Bibliography

Baker, Donald P. *Wilder: Hold Fast to Dreams.* Cabin John, Md.: Seven Locks Press, 1989.

Edds, Margaret. *Claiming the Dream: The Victorious Campaign of Douglas Wilder of Virginia.* Chapel Hill, N.C.: Algonquin Books of Chapel Hill, 1990.

Jones, Charles E. "The Election of L. Douglas Wilder: The First Black Lieutenant Governor of Virginia." *The Western Journal of Black Studies,* Vol. 15, No. 4, 1991.

Yancey, Dwayne. *When Hell Froze Over: The Untold Story of Doug Wilder: A Black Politician's Rise to Power in the South.* Dallas, Tex.: Taylor Publishing Co., 1988.

MANLEY ELLIOTT BANKS II (1996)
Updated by author 2005

Wilkins, Roy

August 30, 1901
September 8, 1981

The civil rights leader, laborer, and journalist Roy Ottoway Wilkins was born in a first-floor flat in a black section of St. Louis, Missouri. Wilkins got his middle name from the African-American physician who delivered him, Dr. Ottoway Fields. At age four, following his mother's death, Wilkins went to St. Paul, Minnesota to live with his Aunt Elizabeth (Edmundson) and Uncle Sam Williams. The Williamses wrested legal guardianship of Roy, his brother Earl, and sister Armeda from their absentee, footloose father, William.

After graduating from the University of Minnesota in 1923, and following a stint as night editor of the college newspaper and editor of the black weekly, the *St. Paul Appeal,* Wilkins moved to Kansas City where he was editor of the *Kansas City Call* for eight years. In 1929, in Kansas City, he married Aminda Badeau. In St. Paul and Kansas City, he was active in the local National Association for the Advancement of Colored People (NAACP) chapters during a period when the NAACP was waging a full-scale attack against America's Jim Crow practices. Under Wilkins's stewardship the *Call* gave banner headline coverage to NAACP (acting) executive secretary Walter White's 1930 campaign to defeat President Herbert Hoover's nomination of Circuit Court Judge John J. Parker to the United States Supreme Court. Parker, in a race for North Carolina governor ten years earlier, had declared his antipathy toward blacks. The *Call* published Parker's photo alongside his quote during the campaign: "If I should be elected Governor . . . and find that my election was due to one Negro vote, I would immediately resign my office." The *Kansas City Call* editorialized that "for a man who would be judge, prejudice is the unpardonable sin." The NAACP's success in blocking Parker's ascension to the U.S. Supreme Court gave Walter White national prominence and a friendship was forged between White, in New York, and Wilkins, in Kansas City.

In 1931 White invited Wilkins to join the national staff of the NAACP in New York as assistant secretary. Wilkins accepted the post with great excitement and anticipation, regarding the NAACP at the time as "the most militant civil rights organization in the country." Wilkins, in his autobiography, recalled that the NAACP during the 1920s and 1930s had "pounded down the South's infamous grandfather clauses, exposed lynchings, and pushed for a federal antilynching law" and had "exposed the spread of peonage among black sharecroppers in the South, prodded the Supreme Court into throwing out verdicts reached by mob-dominated juries, and blotted out residential segregation by municipal ordinance." The NAACP was overturning the racial status quo and Wilkins wanted to be involved.

But there was also dissent within the NAACP. In 1934, following a blistering public attack on Walter White's leadership and on the NAACP's integrationist philosophy from NAACP cofounder W. E. B. Du Bois, who subsequently resigned as editor of the NAACP's penetrating and influential magazine, *The Crisis,* Wilkins succeeded Du Bois as editor of *The Crisis* while continuing in his post as assistant secretary. Wilkins was editor of *The Crisis* for fifteen years (1934–1949).

Du Bois's open flirtation with voluntary segregation did not alter the NAACP's course; throughout the 1930s, 1940s, and 1950s, the NAACP continued to attack Jim Crow laws and to work on behalf of blacks' full integration into American society. But by 1950, Walter White's leadership was on the wane; in that year Wilkins was designated NAACP administrator. White lost key support because of a divorce and his remarriage to a white woman, and his failing health made him especially vulnerable to his detractors. Upon White's death in 1955, Wilkins became executive secretary of the NAACP in the wake of its momentous victory in *Brown v. Board of Education of Topeka, Kansas* (1954), the Supreme Court case in which NAACP lawyers had successfully argued that racially separate public schools were inherently unequal.

Wilkins served as the NAACP's executive secretary and director for twenty-two years, longer than any other NAACP leader. His tenure characterized him as a pragmatist and strategist who believed that reasoned arguments, both in the courtroom and in public discourse, would sway public opinion and public officials to purposeful actions on behalf of racial equality. During the 1960s, Wilkins was widely regarded as "Mr. Civil Rights," employing the NAACP's huge nationwide membership of 400,000, and its lawyers' network, to back up the direct-action campaigns of more fiery leaders like the Reverend Dr. Martin Luther King Jr. and James Farmer. The NAACP supplied money and member support to the massive March on Washington in 1963. Always moderate in language and temperament, and lacking a charismatic personal style, Wilkins was most comfortable as a strategist and adviser. He had meetings with presidents from Franklin D. Roosevelt to Jimmy Carter, and he was a friend of President Lyndon B. Johnson. Major civil rights legislation was signed into law in Wilkins's presence, including the Civil Rights Act of 1964, the Voting Rights Act of 1965, and the Fair Housing Act of 1968.

As the standard-bearer of integration during the turbulent 1960s and throughout the 1970s, the NAACP was pilloried with criticism from black separatists and from whites who opposed school busing and affirmative action programs. Wilkins steered a steady course, however, eschewing racial quotas but insisting on effective legal remedies to purposeful and systemic racial discrimination that included race-conscious methods of desegregating schools, colleges, and the workplace. He simultaneously took to task the exponents of black nationalism. During the height of the Black Power movement, in 1966, Wilkins denounced calls for black separatism, saying Black Power "can mean in the end only black death." Although one of America's most influential and well-known leaders, Wilkins refused to arrogate to himself the plaudits due him because of his successes. He was a frugal administrator and humble individual who routinely took the subway to work.

By 1976, after forty-five years with the NAACP, Wilkins, at age seventy-five, was barely holding on to his post at the NAACP's helm. A year later, in failing health, he retired to his home in Queens, New York, where he spent his last years in the company of his wife. The winner of the NAACP's Spingarn Medal in 1964, and the recipient of many other awards, including over fifty honorary degrees, Wilkins died in September 1981. At his funeral in New York City, hundreds of mourners, black and white, remembered him as a man who refused to bend to fashion.

See also *Brown v. Board of Education of Topeka, Kansas*; *Crisis, The*; Black Power Movement; Civil Rights Movement, U.S.; Jim Crow; National Association for the Advancement of Colored People (NAACP); Voting Rights Act of 1965; White, Walter Francis

Bibliography

Wilkins, Roger. *A Man's Life.* New York: Simon and Schuster, 1982.

Wilkins, Roy, with Tom Mathews. *Standing Fast: The Autobiography of Roy Wilkins.* New York: Viking Press, 1982.

MICHAEL MEYERS (1996)

Williams, Bert

November 12, 1874?
March 4, 1922

It is likely, though unconfirmed, that Egbert Austin "Bert" Williams was born in Antigua, the West Indies, on November 12, 1874. In 1885 he moved with his parents, Fred and Julia, to Riverside, California, where his father became a railroad conductor. After high school, Bert moved to San Francisco, seeking an entertainment career. He sang in rough saloons, toured lumber camps in a small minstrel troupe, learned minstrel dialect, became a comedian, and in 1893 formed a partnership with George Walker that lasted sixteen years and brought them fame.

After years of trial and error, by 1896 they had evolved their act—the classic minstrel contrast of the "darky" and the "dandy." The large, light-skinned Williams used blackface makeup, ill-fitting clothes, heavy dialect, and a shuffle to play hapless bumblers while the smaller, darker Walker played well-dressed, cocky, nimble-footed hustlers. In 1899, they launched the first of a string of successful African-American musicals, *A Lucky Coon.* In 1903, *In Dahomey,* with exotic African elements, exciting chorus numbers, hard-luck songs and comedy for Williams, and snappy dances and a wise-guy role for Walker, brought them international acclaim, from appearances on Broadway to a command performance at Buckingham Palace in London. Their successes continued until Walker fell ill and retired in 1909.

Without Walker, Williams became a "single" in vaudeville and in 1910 was the first African American to perform in the *Ziegfeld Follies.* He was at the center of American show business, where he remained—in the *Follies* (1910–1912, 1914–1917, 1919), other top-notch revues and vaudeville (1913, 1918), and his own shows (1920–1922). A master of pantomime, pathos, understatement, and timing, he gave universal appeal to his poignant hit songs, such as "Nobody" and "I'm a Jonah Man," and his comedy sketches of sad-sack bellhops, gamblers, and porters, despite heavy dialect and caricatures. The critic Ashton Stevens in 1910 hailed Williams as "the Mark Twain of his color," whose "kindly, infectious human . . . made humans of us all."

Williams felt blackface and dialect liberated him as a comedian by letting him become "another person" onstage, but offstage this racially stereotyped minstrel mask stifled a man who longed to be accepted as a human being. "Bert Williams is the funniest man I ever saw," observed *Follies* veteran W. C. Fields, "and the saddest man I ever knew." Suffering discrimination and rejection everywhere except onstage and at home with his devoted wife, Lottie, whom he married in 1900, he became a heavy drinker plagued by depression. Despite failing health, he drove himself mercilessly onstage, where he was happiest. On February 25, 1922, weakened by pneumonia, he struggled through a matinee of his new show, *Under the Bamboo Tree.* During the performance that evening, he collapsed. He died a week later.

See also Minstrels/Minstrelsy; Musical Theater; Walker, George

Bibliography

Charters, Ann. *Nobody: The Story of Bert Williams.* New York: Macmillan, 1970.

Rowland, Mabel, ed. *Bert Williams, Son of Laughter.* Reprint. New York: Negro Universities Press, 1969.

Smith, Eric Ledell. *Bert Williams: A Biography of the Pioneer Black Comedian.* Jefferson, N.C.: McFarland, 1992.

Toll, Robert C. *On with the Show: The First Century of Show Business in America.* New York: Oxford University Press, 1976, pp. 121–133.

Williams, Bert. "The Comic Side of Trouble." *American Magazine* 85 (January 1918): 33–35, 58–61.

ROBERT C. TOLL (1996)
Updated bibliography

Williams, Billy Dee (December, William)

April 6, 1937

Born in Harlem, New York, actor Billy Dee Williams originally studied art at New York's High School of Music and Art and the National Academy of Fine Arts and Design. Although he was training as an artist, Williams also participated in the Actor's Workshop in Harlem, where he was able to study with Sidney Poitier and Paul Mann. His first appearance on the stage came at the age of seven in *The Firebrand of Florence* (1945), but Williams did not begin regularly performing in Broadway and off-Broadway productions until the late 1950s and early 1960s. His early stage credits include *Take a Giant Step* (1956), *A Taste of Honey* (1960), *The Cool World* (1961), and *The Blacks* (1962).

After his initial success on the stage, Williams traveled to the West Coast seeking roles in movies and on television. While his first movie role, as a rebellious ghetto youth in *The Last Angry Man,* came in 1959, he would not gain substantial fame for more than a decade. In 1970 he received an Emmy nomination for his portrayal of Chicago Bears football player Gale Sayers in the made-for-TV movie *Brian's Song.* He also made numerous television appearances, including guest roles in *Hawk, The Mod Squad,* as well as soap operas such as *Another World.*

Williams's early success earned him a seven-year film contract with Motown's Berry Gordy. Through vehicles such as *Lady Sings the Blues* (1972) and *Mahogany* (1975), both with Diana Ross, Williams gained a reputation as a romantic male lead. He also starred in *The Bingo Long Travelling All Stars and Motor Kings* (1976), a movie with James Earl Jones and Richard Pryor about an itinerant baseball team of African Americans during the Negro League era. In Universal's *Scott Joplin* (1978), he portrayed the famous composer.

In the 1980s Williams played leading roles in George Lucas's *The Empire Strikes Back* (1980) and *Return of the Jedi* (1983) and opposite Sylvester Stallone in *Nighthawks* (1981). His role with Diahann Carroll on the television prime-time soap opera *Dynasty* in the mid-1980s further reinforced his image as a sex symbol. In 1985 he also played in *Double Dare,* a short-lived television detective series. In the late 1980s he had roles in *Deadly Illusions* (1987) and *Batman* (1989). Other ventures were slightly more controversial; he came under harsh attack from African-American community groups in 1989 for taking part in beer commercials.

It was also in the 1980s that Williams began to receive recognition for his professional achievements. Shortly after being inducted into the Black Filmmakers Hall of Fame in 1984, Williams received a star on the Hollywood Walk of Fame in 1985. In 1988 the Black American Cinema Society awarded him its Phoenix Award.

In the early 1990s Williams continued to play parts in television movies. He also began to exhibit some of his artwork, which had become an increasingly neglected hobby as his acting career flourished. Exhibitions in galleries in New York and Washington, D.C., received favorable reviews. In 1993 the Schomburg Center for Research in Black Culture sponsored a display of Williams's work.

Since 1995 Williams has continued to be extremely active and has appeared in almost twenty TV movies, short films, and Hollywood productions. In addition to numerous guest appearances on a variety of television programs, he has also lent his voice to several projects, including a short film and at least one video game based on the Star Wars series. Since 2000 he has published (with coauthors) three works of fiction. He continues to paint; Sears chose his artwork to illustrate its 2004 Black History Month calendar. During the first half of 2004 Williams also toured with costar Robin Givens in the play *If These Hips Could Talk.*

See also Film in the United States, Contemporary

Bibliography

Bogle, Donald M., ed. *Blacks in American Films and Television: An Encyclopedia.* New York: Garland, 1988.

Mapp, Edward, ed. *Directory of Blacks in the Performing Arts,* 2d ed. Metuchen, N.J.: Scarecrow Press, 1990.

Williams, Billy Dee, and Elizabeth Atkins Bowman. *Twilight.* New York: Forge, 2002.

Williams, Billy Dee, and Rob MacGregor. *Psi/Net.* New York: Tor Books, 1999.

Williams, Billy Dee, and Rob MacGregor. *Just/In Time.* New York: Forge, 2000.

JOHN C. STONER (1996)
Updated by author 2005

WILLIAMS, ERIC

SEPTEMBER 25, 1911
MARCH 29, 1981

Eric Eustace Williams, the first prime minister of the independent Trinidad and Tobago, was born in Port of Spain, Trinidad, the eldest of twelve children of Thomas Henry Williams, a junior-level post office official, and Eliza Boissiere. He received his early education at the Tranquility Boys' School. From a tender age, his father groomed him to achieve excellence. In 1922 Williams won one of eight college "exhibition" scholarships for free tuition at Queen's Royal College (QRC) in Port of Spain. He excelled both academically and in sports, becoming captain of the school's intramural soccer team.

Williams's first goal was to win the coveted Island Scholarship, which he achieved on his third attempt, in October 1931. The following year he left for England, where he studied Latin, French, European history, and political economy at Oxford University, earning first-class honors in history in 1936. He then immediately began to read for the degree of doctor of philosophy. He received this degree in 1938 with a thesis titled "The Economic Aspect of the Abolition of the West Indian Slave Trade and Slavery."

Early Nationalist Influences

While in England, Williams attended lectures of the West Indian Association in London. There he met other prominent West Indians, including George Padmore and C. L. R. James, his former QRC teacher, who had a significant influence on his work and his early political point of view. He also socialized with future African leaders such as Jomo Kenyatta of Kenya and Kwame Nkrumah of Ghana. These men gave Williams insights into their Pan-African ideology. In London, he also met and married his first wife, a Trinidadian named Elsie Ribeiro.

Williams's failure to earn a fellowship at the prestigious All Soul's College redirected his desire to lecture at Oxford and motivated him to accept an appointment as an assistant professor at Howard University in Washington, D.C. This appointment had a major influence on his life, as it transformed him from a colonial scholar to a West Indian/Caribbean nationalist. Though Howard was (and remains) a predominantly black university, Williams was not insulated from racism while he was there. Howard University did nevertheless provide him with a sanctuary and brought him into contact with many scholars who were his academic equals, such as Abram L. Harris, Rayford Logan, E. Franklin Frazier, Sterling Brown, Charles Wesley, Alain Locke, William Hastie, and Ralph J. Bunche.

Williams was initially given a one-year appointment. In his first year he inaugurated a social-science course, "the development of civilization from primitive man to the present," for which he prepared his own text of readings (Heywood, 1998, p. 18).

Eric Williams. *The first prime minister of the independent state of Trinidad and Tobago (1962), Williams remained that nation's highest official until his death in 1981.* © BETTMANN/CORBIS.

While Williams was at Howard, he also met and befriended a number of other Trinidadians, including Ibit Mosaheb, a dental student, and Winston Mahibir, a medical student. Both Mosaheb and Mahibir were instrumental in the formation of a discussion group known as the Bacchacs, and they were original members of the People's National Movement (PNM).

Williams's years at Howard were productive. He wrote prolifically and published several articles and books, including his masterpiece, *Capitalism and Slavery* (1944). His 1940 article "The Golden Age of the Slave System in Britain," which appeared in the *Journal of Negro History,* won the first history prize at the annual meeting of the Association for the Study of Negro Life and History in New Orleans on October 29, 1939. In all his publications, Williams tried to show the contributions that Africans and their descendants made to the development of Western society. He was also establishing his own anticolonial sentiments.

Williams's Early Career

In his first year at Howard, Eric Williams received a Rosenwald Fellowship, which enabled him to travel extensively and to conduct research in Cuba, Haiti, and Puerto Rico. He also sought employment with the United States Office of Strategic Services. In 1942 Williams joined the Research and Analysis section, where he met important scholars such as Arthur Schlesinger Jr. and Herbert Marcuse. He was also recommended for a position at the U.S. War Productions Board, which was responsible for shipping in the Caribbean, but because he was not a U.S. citizen he was ineligible. In March 1943 Williams was appointed as a part-time consultant to the Anglo-American Caribbean Commission (AACC). This office stimulated his research interests, and it provided him with a larger perspective on the entire Caribbean. By the time of his appointment, Williams was well into the organization of a conference at Howard University on "The Economic Future of the Caribbean."

Williams's job as a consultant with AACC was to collate prices of essential foodstuffs and to update the laws of the Caribbean countries to achieve greater democracy. At about this time, Williams wrote a study titled "The Anglo-American Caribbean Commission: Its Problems and Prospects." The work criticized colonialism, called for a West Indian federation, expressed fears of American racism if the United States gained influence in the region, and forecast a Pan-American federation led by the United States. On March 1, 1944, a year after joining the organization, Williams was appointed secretary to the Agricultural Committee of the Caribbean Research Council, a branch of the commission. But he also continued his writings on issues that affected one or more of the European members of the commission, and the British section was unhappy with his lectures on independence for Jamaica. This brought him into open conflict with the British governor. The Americans, meanwhile, were not concerned with Williams's actions until he published "Race Relations in Puerto Rico and the Virgin Islands" in the *Journal of Foreign Affairs* in January 1945.

In May 1948 Williams left Howard University to accept full-time employment with the AACC in Trinidad and Tobago. He was appointed to a six-month term as acting deputy chairman of the Caribbean Research Council. His intellectual work, however, continued to clash with his position at the commission. He participated in a number of public events, including debates with Dom Basil Matthews, one of the leading members of the Roman Catholic clergy, on various issues dealing with philosophy, the state, and the church. The public reception of Dr. Williams at the debates indicated that the people of Trinidad were hungry for a new kind of politics. It also showed that he had successfully challenged the church's position on such issues as religious education in the schools. Williams continued to give several intellectual and informative lectures on matters of local and international politics to increasingly enthusiastic crowds. These lectures were given at Woodford Square in Port of Spain, and this venue came to be known as the "University of Woodford Square." The AACC, however, viewed his activities as having political implications that created tensions within the organization.

The People's National Movement

Williams left the AACC in 1955. On June 24, the day he left the commission, he went to Woodford Square and delivered one of his famed lectures, telling the crowd, "I will let down my bucket here with you in the West Indies" (Williams, 1981, pp. 5–10). He immediately put into action his plan for a political party, and the People's National Movement (PNM) was founded in January 1956. Later that year the PNM won the general elections and Williams became the chief minister.

Though Williams had left academic life, he continued writing during his tenure as prime minister of Trinidad and Tobago, a position he held when the nation became independent in 1962. His works did not gain the high academic acclaim of his earlier writings, however, though they played an important role in the study and documentation of local history. The most significant of these works are: *The History of the People of Trinidad and Tobago* (1962), *British Historians and the West Indies* (1964), and *From Columbus to Castro: The History of the Caribbean, 1492–1969* (1970). Their greater importance was to showcase the historian as politician.

A number of universities conferred honorary degrees on Williams during the 1960s and 1970s. The University of the West Indies was the first to award him the honorary doctor of letters, in 1963; St. Catherine's College, Oxford, followed, appointing him a fellow in 1964. He received the doctor of laws (LL.D.) from the University of New Brunswick, Canada, the same year, and Andrews University, in Michigan, gave him a similar award in 1974, the same year he was appointed as a member of the Council of the University of the United Nations.

Williams's Political Career

At the start of his political career, Williams reiterated his commitment to Trinidad and the liberation of its peoples in his famous University of Woodford Square speeches. Woodford Square was the center of mass education in politics and history—as dictated and defined by Williams. He chose the topic, set up the parameters, did the analysis, and timed and tailored his delivery to suit the packed audiences, who learned what was happening in Africa and the rest of the world through these lectures.

Williams successfully contested all national general elections held after 1956, and he remained in office until his death in 1981. Throughout this period, the PNM avoided formal ties to the trade or labor unions. Likewise, both the party and Williams had no fixed ideological tags.

Williams also played a key role in policy decisions within the PNM, and he held several ministerial positions in the party, including minister of finance, planning and development, and foreign affairs. During his twenty-five years in politics he advocated many issues, from nationalization and the "Buy Local" campaign to improved awards for calypsonians, a matter he corrected when his party came to power in 1956. Williams also introduced significant changes to recapture Trinidad and Tobago's national cultural heritage. One of the most well-known of his initiatives is the Best Village competition. In addition, he championed the decolonization of the Caribbean school curriculum, the establishment of free secondary education for all in the 1960s, socioeconomic development planning, multiracialism in politics, and anticolonialism.

Williams also had profound influence internationally. His avid support for West Indian integration was manifested in his early attempts to promote the West Indies Federation, which comprised Trinidad and Tobago and nine other British Caribbean colonies, but which only lasted from 1958 to 1962. Williams remained committed to issues of joint cooperation among the Caribbean territories, however, even though his own decision to withdraw from the federation (after Jamaica already had) may have caused some to doubt his commitment to Caribbean unity. He sought to foster amicable relationships between Venezuela and the rest of the Caribbean, and he took leading initiatives to resolve border disputes between Venezuela and Guyana. Committed to West Indian integration, Williams spearheaded numerous meetings among Commonwealth Caribbean heads of government. These served as forerunners to the establishment of the Caribbean Free Trade Area (CARIFTA) in 1968 and the Caribbean Community and Common Market (CARICOM) in 1973.

Dissension within the PNM

When Williams sought power in 1956, he proposed independence for the twin island state, promising to liberate the poor from centuries of colonial oppression. No significant attempt at reform was made, however, until the Finance Act of 1966. This caused a split within the PNM because businesses interests were opposed to the act and because it imposed a new tax system; Williams fell increasingly under the control of business interests in the party. This strengthened his accusers' assertions that no structural changes were being implemented by the government.

> **Eric Williams**
>
> "You are now a member of the Commonwealth Family in your own right, equal in status to any other of its members. You hope soon to be a member of the World Family of Nations, playing your part, however insignificant, in world affairs. You are on your own in a big world, in which you are one of many nations, some small, some medium size, some large. You are nobody's boss and nobody is your boss."
>
> INDEPENDENCE DAY ADDRESS TO TRINIDAD AND TOBAGO, AUGUST 31, 1962. REPRINTED IN SELWYN R. CUDJOE, ED. *ERIC E. WILLIAMS SPEAKS: ESSAYS ON COLONIALISM AND INDEPENDENCE*. BOSTON: CALALOUX PUBLICATIONS, 1993.

Unemployment was very high among the young, and the policy of import substitution had failed, reducing the expectation of economic growth. The disconnect between the youth of Trinidad and Tobago and the government gave rise to Williams's first real challenge, which came from the Black Power movement in February 1970, whose members felt that William's government had not made adequate changes. Williams moved to restrict the influence of the movement, and he declared a state of emergency in April. These moves helped him to survive the challenge of his adversaries in the Black Power movement. His response to the high level of unemployment was to impose an additional levy of 5 percent on all taxable incomes over $10,000.

Williams also embarked on a national localization campaign, which stressed the need for greater state participation in the economic development of the country. This move resulted in the ownership and part ownership of a considerable amount of the nation's resources by the state. As he expressed it, "We follow the pattern that is being increasingly used by developing countries where State participation is up to 51% in particular enterprises, to ensure that decision-making remains in local hands."

Later in his life, Williams concentrated his efforts on charting the economic and industrial direction of the country. He attempted to focus his efforts on increasing agricultural production and channeling the financial surplus from oil production into the industrial production of fertilizer, iron, and steel, and other energy-based industries. Petroleum would thus be used to create a large number of permanent jobs in other industries.

In 1973 Williams expressed a desire to leave politics, but in the end the party would not allow it, and he remained its leader until his death. These last years of Williams's political life were described by Ken Boodhoo as "the last difficult years." No single reason explains Williams's desire to leave office. His reforms were slow to materialize, and many members of his cabinet were opposed to any change in the status quo. Many party members did not share his vision of restructuring the society. For such an astute man, Williams must have resolved that he had failed to alter the political culture of Trinidad. On the whole, Trinidadians and Tobagonians did not seize the moment available to them, and Williams felt that he alone was carrying the burden of his vision for Trinidad and Tobago.

During his final five years in office, Williams's circle of advisers shrank significantly. At this time, Williams's physical condition, and to some extent his mental condition, deteriorated. One Cabinet official commented that Williams was spending a lot of time at home. He also spent much of these years researching and writing, as though he knew that his end was near. His last known academic endeavor was to be a project on the impact of slavery for the publisher Andre Deutsch. He also planned to compile his speeches into a book. Unfortunately, Williams died before he could complete either project.

See also Caribbean Commission; Caribbean Community and Common Market (CARICOM); International Relations of the Anglophone Caribbean; Peoples National Movement; Robinson, A. N. R.; Woodford Square

Bibliography

Boodhoo, Ken, ed. *Eric Williams: The Man and the Leader.* Lanham, Md.: University Press of America, 1986.

Boodhoo, Ken, *The Elusive Eric Williams.* Kingston, Jamaica: Ian Randle, 2002.

Cateau, Heather, and Carrington, Selwyn H. H. *Capitalism and Slavery Fifty Years Later: Eric Eustace Williams—A Reassessment of the Man and His Work.* New York: Peter Lang, 2000.

Gaspar, David Barry. "They 'Could Never Have Too Much Of My Work': Eric Williams and the *Journal of Negro History* 1940–1945." *Journal of African American History* 85, no. 3 (2003): 291–303.

Heywood, Linda. "Eric Williams: The Howard Years, 1938–1948." *Caribbean Issues* 8, no. 1 (1998): 19.

Martin, Tony. "Eric Williams and the Anglo-American Caribbean Commission: Trinidad's Future Nationalist Leader as Aspiring Imperial Bureaucrat, 1942–1944." *Journal of African American History* 88, no. 3 (2003): 274–290.

Pacquet, Sandra Pouchet, ed. "Eric Williams and the Postcolonial Caribbean" *Callaloo* 20, no. 4 (1997). Special issue devoted to Williams.

Ryan, Selwyn D. *Race and Nationalism in Trinidad and Tobago: A Study of Decolonization in a Multiracial Society.* Toronto: University of Toronto Press, 1972.

Ryan, Selwyn D. *The Politics of Succession: A Study of Parties and Politics in Trinidad and Tobago.* Saint Augustine, Trinidad and Tobago: University of the West Indies, 1978.

Ryan, Selwyn D. *The Confused Electorate: A Study of Political Attitudes and Opinions in Trinidad and Tobago.* Saint Augustine, Trinidad and Tobago: University of the West Indies, 1978.

Ryan, Selwyn D. *The Disillusioned Electorate: The Politics of Succession in Trinidad and Tobago.* Port of Spain, Trinidad and Tobago: Imprint Caribbean, 1989.

Williams, Eric E. *Forged from the Love of Liberty: Selected Speeches of Dr. Eric Williams.* Compiled by Paul K. Sutton. Port of Spain, Trinidad and Tobago: Longman Caribbean, 1981.

SELWYN H. H. CARRINGTON (2005)
FIONA ANN TAYLOR (2005)

Williams, Fannie Barrier

February 12, 1855
March 4, 1944

Fannie Barrier Williams's career in the black women's club movement of the late nineteenth and early twentieth centuries is representative of the hard work and dedication of this network of women and of their success as community organizers. Fannie Barrier was born to a free black family in Brockport, New York. After graduating from the State Normal School in her hometown, she taught school in the South and in Washington, D.C. Her experiences with racism in these contexts focused her interests on working for racial uplift.

Barrier married S. Laing Williams, a young lawyer, in 1887 and the two settled in Chicago, where they worked closely with Ida Wells-Barnett and her husband, Ferdinand Barnett. From this point Williams became involved with a wide range of organizations and activities. Along with Wells-Barnett, she pressed for the inclusion of African Americans in the World's Columbian Exposition of 1893. She worked with women's clubs, black and white, in Chicago and across the country and gained a reputation as an effective leader and lecturer.

In 1893 Williams became one of the founding members of the National League for the Protection of Colored Women, which would be among the founding organizations of the National Association of Colored Women three years later. She was also a close associate of T. Thomas Fortune and Emmett Scott, the founders of the National Negro Business League, and was elected the organization's corresponding secretary in 1902. The league was ideologically aligned with Booker T. Washington's economic and political program, and Williams's work here caused a break with the more radical Barnetts.

Williams went on to work with the National Association for the Advancement of Colored People (NAACP) and to be a strong advocate of women's suffrage. After her husband's death in 1921, she returned to her hometown, where she lived until her own death.

See also Black Women's Club Movement; National Association for the Advancement of Colored People (NAACP); National Association of Colored Women; National League for the Protection of Colored Women; Wells-Barnett, Ida B.

Bibliography

Loewenberg, Bert James, and Ruth Bogin, eds. *Black Women in Nineteenth Century American Life.* University Park: Pennsylvania State University Press, 1976.

Williams, Fannie Barrier. *The New Woman of Color: The Collected Writings of Fannie Barrier Williams, 1893–1918,* edited by Mary Jo Deegan. DeKalb: Northern Illinois University Press, 2002.

JUDITH WEISENFELD (1996)
Updated bibliography

Williams, Francis

c. 1700
1770

Francis Williams was a Jamaican poet and classical scholar. The freeborn son of John and Dorothy Williams, Francis was educated in England from the age of ten as an experiment to test the assumed intellectual inferiority of blacks. Sponsored by the Duke of Montagu, Williams studied Latin, Greek, and mathematics over a period of years.

Williams's life and work must be traced mainly from the biased account given by Edward Long in his *History of Jamaica* (1774), but a rich discussion of the significance of his achievements may be found in Michele Valerie Ronnick's valuable 1998 study. For philosophers of the Enlightenment such as David Hume, the case of this black classical scholar-poet threatened existing ideas regarding the role of race in the divine order of the cosmos. Indeed, racial justifications for slavery were to become less secure in the face of Williams's achievements.

Williams remained in England after completing his studies, during which time he wrote a popular satiric ballad, "Welcome, Welcome, Brother Debtor." Full of classical allusions, it characterizes human existence as a prison: "every island's but a prison / strongly guarded by the sea / Kings and princes for that reason / Prisonner's [sic] are as Well as We." Long casts doubt on Williams's authorship, but Jean D'Costa and Barbara Lalla present strong alternative evidence in *Voices in Exile* (1989) that Williams was indeed the author.

Williams returned to Jamaica during the governorship of Edward Trelawny (1738–1751). This was a crucial period in Jamaican history, for some eighty years of Maroon warfare had just ended with the treaty of 1739 to 1740. The island was therefore now internally safe for its English colonial overlords. In the subsequent three decades of his life, Williams witnessed the doubling of the African slave population and the economic explosion of the sugar plantations.

Intended for a position in government, Williams was rejected by Governor Trelawny. Instead, he founded a school in the capital, Spanish Town, teaching reading, writing, Latin, and mathematics with some success. Long describes a schoolmaster of fashionable dress and manner. During this period, Williams is said to have written a number of Latin odes addressed to successive governors of Jamaica. Long points to "An Ode to George Haldane" (1759) as exemplifying Williams' poetic style: a panegyric filled with classical allusions, lavishing praise on the new governor, George Haldane. Much of its forty-six lines deal with Williams's blackness and the racial abyss separating his poem's white subject (Haldane) from the poem's speaker. Here one may see the fractured Williams, living the double exile of a free black among enslaved blacks and of a cultivated mind in the intellectual wilderness of eighteenth-century Jamaican society.

See also Literature of the English-Speaking Caribbean

Bibliography

D'Costa, Jean, and Barbara Lalla, eds. *Voices in Exile: Jamaican Texts of the Eighteenth and Nineteenth Centuries*. Tuscaloosa: University of Alabama Press, 1989.

Long, Edward. *History of Jamaica*. London: Lowndes, 1774. Reprint, Montreal: McGill-Queen's University Press, 2002.

Patterson, Orlando. *The Sociology of Slavery: An Analysis of the Origins, Development, and Structure of Negro Slave Society in Jamaica*. London: MacGibbon and Kee, 1967.

Ronnick, Michele Valerie. "Francis Williams: An Eighteenth-Century Tertium Quid." *Negro History Bulletin* (April–June 1998).

JEAN D'COSTA (2005)

Williams, George Washington

October 16, 1849
August 2, 1891

Born in Bedford Springs, Pennsylvania, clergyman and legislator George Washington Williams had no formal schooling until after the Civil War. He enlisted with the Union troops in 1864, with the revolutionary forces in Mexico, and with the Tenth Cavalry in 1868. He studied briefly at Howard University and the Wayland Seminary before going to the Newton Theological Institution, where in 1874 he became the first African American to graduate. Successively he became pastor of the Twelfth Baptist Church in Boston, editor of the *Commoner* in Washington, D.C., and pastor of the Union Baptist Church in Cincinnati. There he contributed articles regularly to the *Cincinnati Commercial* under the pen name "Aristides," became the first African American to serve in the stage legislature, and manifested a lively interest in public affairs. He had a reputation as a skillful politician and a gifted orator. After studying law in the office of Judge Alfonso Taft, he passed the Ohio bar.

Meanwhile, one of Williams's greatest interests was in the study of history. He had already written a history of the Twelfth Baptist Church, as well as a historical sketch of blacks from 1776 to 1876. In 1882 he published his two-volume *History of the Negro Race in America, 1619–1880.* As the first serious work in the field, it was widely reviewed among critics, whose judgments ranged from very favorable to unenthusiastic. Williams was nevertheless an immediate success and in such great demand as a lecturer that he hired one of the major literary agents in New York to handle his engagements.

After publishing a *History of Negro Troops in the War of Rebellion* in 1887, Williams turned his interests largely to international affairs. He had received an appointment in 1885 as United States minister to Haiti, but the incoming administration of President Benjamin Harrison refused him a commission. Crushed and embittered, Williams decided to make his mark abroad. In 1889 he attended the antislavery conference in Brussels, and in the following year he journeyed to the Congo. He found conditions there so miserable that he published for circulation throughout Europe and the United States "An Open Letter to His Serene Majesty, Leopold II, King of the Belgians." He roundly condemned the king for his cruel oppression and exploitation of the people of the Congo. This first general criticism of Leopold was followed some years later by similar strictures in Europe and the United States.

Williams did not return to the United States. After traveling extensively in South Africa and East Africa, he went to England, where he died.

See also Historians and Historiography, African-American

Bibliography

Franklin, John Hope. *George Washington Williams: A Biography.* Chicago: University of Chicago Press, 1985.

JOHN HOPE FRANKLIN (1996)

Williams, Henry Sylvester

March 24, 1867
March 26, 1911

Henry Sylvester Williams was one of the ambitious, confident, outspoken, and politically conscious blacks who emerged in the British West Indies during the late nineteenth and early twentieth centuries. His parents were Barbadians who migrated to Trinidad in the second half of the nineteenth century (Williams was born in Barbados). Williams's father worked as a wheelwright on the Bon Air sugar estate in Arouca. In 1887 Williams was appointed headmaster of a primary school and simultaneously served as the Registrar of Births and Deaths in South Trinidad. His teaching career abruptly ended in 1891 when he decided to emigrate to New York City. While in the United States, he became acutely aware of the oppression of African Americans, particularly those disenfranchised in the South.

After two years, Williams left the United States and settled in the province of Nova Scotia, Canada. Between 1893 and 1894, he enrolled for a law degree at Dalhousie University in Halifax, but he never completed the course. The desire to travel led him to England in 1896. He worked as a lecturer for the Church of England Temperance Society, where he met and married a white woman named Agnes Powell. Subsequently, Williams enrolled at the University of London, and in 1897 he gained admittance to Gray's Inn, where he successfully completed his legal studies.

On September 24, 1897, Williams founded the African Association and served as its honorary secretary. The purposes of the association were "to encourage a feeling of unity and to facilitate friendly intercourse among Africans in general." It also sought "to promote and protect the interests of all subjects claiming African descent" (Mathurin, 1976, p. 41). These goals were to be achieved by appealing to the governments of local (occupied or conquered) countries or regions, as well as the governments of imperial countries (United States, Germany, France, Belgium, and Britain). Williams is credited with having coined the term *Pan-African,* and he spearheaded the organization of the first Pan-African Conference, which took place July 23 to 25, 1900, at Westminster Town Hall in London. One of the aims of the Pan-African Conference was to create a common bond or linkage among the world's blacks. Conference participants unanimously adopted an *Address to the Nations of the World*, which was circulated to the major imperial powers. This document contained an appeal for an end to racial prejudice and demanded that Britain grant "responsible government to the black colonies of Africa and the West Indies" (Mathurin, 1976, p. 71). Among the prominent blacks from the United States at the Conference were W. E. B. Du Bois, a professor at Atlanta University, and John L. Love, a teacher at a black school in Washington who served as secretary of the Pan-African Conference in 1900.

In the aftermath of this historic conference, Williams continued to take an active interest in the conditions and progress of persons of African descent. He attended the Anti-Slavery Congress in Paris from August 6 to 8, 1900. A year later, Williams attended the annual meeting of the National Afro-American Council held in Philadelphia.

Williams briefly returned to the West Indies and founded a branch of the Pan-African Association in Trinidad on June 28, 1901. During this tour, he also visited Jamaica and addressed various black groups. In October 1901 Williams began publishing a monthly journal, the *Pan-African,* but it ceased publication after less than a year. In 1903 Williams emigrated to South Africa, and he became the first black lawyer to practice in Cape Town. Between 1903 and 1908, Williams visited a number of African countries, including Liberia, Sierra Leone, and Guinea, to witness the living and working conditions of Africans.

By 1905 Williams had returned to London and become a candidate in local elections. On November 2, 1906, he was elected councilor on the St. Marylebone Council. In 1906, while in London, he was appointed vice president of the Trinidad Workingmen's Association. This was a radical working-class organization in Trinidad that campaigned for political and social reforms. In August 1908 Williams returned to Trinidad and spent his final years as a lawyer in the country's capital, Port of Spain.

Williams was a visionary West Indian and is credited with having sown the seeds of Pan-Africanism, which influenced such Caribbean personalities as Marcus Garvey, Stokely Carmichael, C. L. R. James, and George Padmore. The influence of the historic Pan-African Conference of 1900 was felt throughout the twentieth century, even serving as a catalyst for the civil rights movement, the Black Power movement, and the anticolonial struggles of the third world.

See also Pan-Africanism

Bibliography

Hooker, J. R. *Henry Sylvester Williams: Imperial Pan-Africanist.* London: Collings, 1975.

Mathurin, Owen Charles. *Henry Sylvester Williams and the Origins of the Pan-African Movement, 1869–1911.* Westport, Conn.: Greenwood, 1976.

JEROME TEELUCKSINGH (2005)

Williams, Hosea Lorenzo

January 5, 1926
November 16, 2000

Civil rights leader and politician Hosea Williams was born and raised in Attapalgus, Georgia. He served in the military from 1944 to 1946. In 1951 he graduated from Morris Brown College in Atlanta with a B.A. in chemistry, and went on to earn a master of science degree from Atlanta University. Upon graduation he worked for the U.S. Department of Agriculture as a research chemist in Savannah, Georgia. In the late 1950s and early 1960s he became active in the National Association for the Advancement of Colored People (NAACP) and participated in desegregation drives and other civil rights activities. In 1960 he became head of the Southeastern Georgia Crusade for Voters. Williams was an outspoken believer in direct action, and under his direction the crusade waged one of the most successful voter registration drives in the South.

In 1962 the crusade affiliated with the Southern Christian Leadership Conference (SCLC), and one year later Williams moved to Atlanta to join the staff of SCLC as a full-time project director. He became a top assistant to SCLC's president, Rev. Dr. Martin Luther King Jr., and organized grassroots voter registration drives. In 1965 he led the civil rights march from Selma to Montgomery, Alabama, in which marchers were brutally attacked by state troopers and local police.

After King's assassination in 1968, Williams remained active in the SCLC. From 1969 to 1971 he served as executive director of the SCLC under the leadership of Rev. Ralph Abernathy. Williams led a militant faction in the SCLC who called for "black power" and self-help and rejected integration as a movement goal. In 1971 he resigned his position and founded an SCLC chapter in Atlanta with his supporters to practice the type of grassroots activism he favored.

In 1974 Williams entered the political arena and was elected to the Georgia General Assembly as Atlanta representative. From 1977 to 1979 he returned to the position of SCLC national executive director, but he was removed from his post by members of the board of directors who were critical of his outside activities and insisted that he devote more time to his position. (In 1972 Williams had founded and served as the pastor of the Martin Luther King Jr. People's Church of Love in Atlanta; after 1976 he was proprietor of his own business, the Southeast Chemical Manufacturing and Distributing Corporation.)

Although Williams maintained his commitment to grassroots organizing and direct action, his political allegiances shifted to the Republican Party, and in 1980 he endorsed Ronald Reagan for president. He argued that African Americans should seek to make the Republican Party accountable to them and that few Democratic candidates were willing to deal with the "meat and bread" issues facing blacks and the poor. Four years later, running as a Republican, he lost the race for the Fifth District U.S. congressional seat from Atlanta, but the next year he was elected to the Atlanta city council.

Williams's consistent championing of issues that affected the poor, and his flamboyant and often contentious personal style, made him a well-known figure in Atlanta politics. In 1987 he led a march into Georgia's Forsyth County, a nearly all-white suburb, to protest residential segregation. The march attracted national attention when the participants were attacked by members of the Ku Klux Klan. In 1989 Williams made an unsuccessful bid for mayor of Atlanta on the Republican ticket. Three years later he once again led a protest march into Forsyth County.

Williams retired from the city council in 1994 and died in 2000 after a lengthy battle with prostate cancer.

See also Black Power Movement; Civil Rights Movement, U.S.; Politics in the United States

Bibliography

"Civil Rights Leader Hosea Williams Dies at 74." *Jet,* December 2000, p. 16.

Fairclough, Adam. *To Redeem the Soul of America: The Southern Christian Leadership Conference and Martin Luther King Jr.* Athens: University of Georgia Press, 1987.

Garrow, David J. *Bearing the Cross: Martin Luther King and the Southern Christian Leadership Conferences.* New York: Morrow, 1986.

STEVEN J. LESLIE (1996)
ROBYN C. SPENCER (1996)
Updated by publisher 2005

Williams, Mary Lou

May 8, 1910
May 28, 1981

Although she never led her own big band, and recorded only occasionally as a leader, the pianist Mary Lou Williams is generally acknowledged as the most significant female instrumentalist in the history of jazz. She composed and arranged works that exemplify the rhythmic drive and harmonic sophistication of the swing era. Born Mary Elfrieda Scruggs in Atlanta, Georgia, she moved to Pittsburgh, Pennsylvania, with her mother in 1914, and she performed professionally on the piano at the age of six. Using the surname of her two stepfathers, she performed as Mary Lou Burley and Mary Lou Winn at private parties in Pittsburgh and in East Liberty, Pennsylvania, before the age of ten.

At age fifteen, while a student at Pittsburgh's Lincoln High School, she played the piano on the Theater Owners Booking Association (TOBA) black vaudeville circuit. Two years later she married John Williams, a baritone saxophonist, and moved with him to Memphis. They next lived in Oklahoma City and then Kansas City, where Mary Lou Williams quickly became a prominent member of the developing swing scene. In 1929, her husband arranged for her to have an audition with the bandleader Andy Kirk. She became a full-time member of Kirk's Clouds of Joy in 1930, and she was the band's star soloist, composer, and arranger. Williams was one of the few well-known instrumentalists of the swing era.

Although Williams's early style as a soloist was influenced by Earl Hines, Jelly Roll Morton, and Fats Waller, by the late 1920s she was a well-known exponent of Kansas City swing, a somewhat lighter style of swing derived from stride influences. As one of her Kirk recordings pointed out in its title, Williams was "The Lady Who Swings the Band" (1936). She was significant as both a composer and arranger, lending harmonic sophistication and a bold sense of swing to Kirk's repertory, including "Mess-a-Stomp" (1929 and 1938), "Walkin' and Swingin' " (1936), "Froggy Bottom" (1936), "Moten Swing" (1936), "In the Groove" (1937), and "Mary's Idea" (1938).

In the mid-1930s the Clouds of Joy moved to New York, where Williams also worked as an arranger for Louis Armstrong, Earl Hines, Tommy Dorsey, and Benny Goodman, for whom she arranged the famous 1937 versions of "Roll 'Em," "Camel Hop," and "Whistle Blues." In 1940 she arranged and recorded "Baby Dear" and "Harmony Blues" as Mary Lou Williams and Her Kansas City Seven, an ensemble drawn from the Kirk band. Williams divorced her husband in the late 1930s, and she left Kirk's band in 1942, the same year she married and began performing with the trumpeter Shorty Baker. That marriage also ended in divorce. Throughout the 1940s, Williams continued to work as an arranger, again with Goodman, as well as on "Trumpets No End" (1945), an arrangement of the song "Blue Skies" done for Duke Ellington. She also continued to perform, as a solo act in the mid-to-late 1940s at both the uptown and downtown Cafe Society in New York, and with an all-female group (1945-1946). At Carnegie Hall in 1946 the New York Philharmonic performed three movements of her Zodiac Suite, a version of which she had recorded the year before.

While many giants of the swing era failed to make the transition to bebop, Williams readily assimilated into her playing the developments of Thelonious Monk (1917–1982) and Bud Powell (1924–1966), both of whom were regular guests at the informal piano salon she held at her Harlem home throughout the 1940s and 1950s. In 1952 Williams began a two-year tour of England and France. In 1954 she underwent a religious experience while performing at a Paris nightclub and walked off the bandstand in mid-set. Back home in Harlem, Williams, who had been raised a Baptist, joined a Roman Catholic church because she was allowed to pray there at any time of the day or night. She refused to play in public until 1957, when, urged on by Dizzy Gillespie (1917–1993), she performed at the Newport Jazz Festival. From the late 1950s on, she regularly toured and performed, including a concert with fellow pianists Willie "The Lion" Smith, Duke Ellington, Earl Hines, and Billy Taylor in Pittsburgh in 1965.

In the 1960s Williams, who had become a devout Roman Catholic, composed several large-scale liturgical works (*Black Christ of the Andes,* 1963; *St. Martin de Porres,* 1965), culminating in *Mary Lou's Mass* (1969), which was commissioned by the Vatican and choreographed by Alvin Ailey. In the 1970s she continued to perform and record (*Solo Recital,* 1977), particularly with the intention of educating listeners about the history of jazz. She also performed with avant-garde pianist Cecil Taylor at Carnegie Hall (*Embraced,* 1977), and in that year became an artist in residence at Duke University in Durham, North Carolina, where she died.

See also Gillespie, Dizzy; Jazz; Monk, Thelonious Sphere

Bibliography

Dahl, Linda. *Stormy Weather: The Music and Lives of a Century of Jazzwomen.* New York: Pantheon, 1984.

Dahl, Linda. *Morning Glory: A Biography of Mary Lou Williams.* New York: Pantheon, 1999.

Handy, D. Antoinette. "Conversation with Mary Lou Williams: First Lady of the Jazz Keyboard." *The Black Perspective in Music* 8 (1980): 194–214.

Kernodle, Tammy L. *Soul on Soul: The Life and Music of Mary Lou Williams.* Boston: Northeastern University Press, 2004.

D. ANTOINETTE HANDY (1996)
Updated bibliography

Williams, Patricia Joyce

August 28, 1951

Patricia Joyce Williams is a leading scholar on race, class, gender, and the law. One of the pioneers of critical race theory, she has distinguished herself as an incisive commentator and a public intellectual. Williams has stated that she is "trying to create a genre of legal writing to fill the gaps of traditional legal scholarship." She does so by using narrative, literary theory, philosophy, history, and anecdote to superb effect. She writes engagingly and uses popular events and masterful storytelling to delve into complex and important legal and social issues.

Williams began teaching at the Columbia Law School in 1991, eventually earning the position of James L. Dohr Professor of Law. Prior to entering Columbia she practiced law as a consumer advocate and deputy city attorney for Los Angeles, and as a staff attorney for the Western Center on Law and Poverty. A graduate of Wellesley College and Harvard Law School, Williams has taught at a number of institutions, including Golden Gate University, the City University of New York, the University of Wisconsin at Madison, Harvard University, and Stanford University.

In Williams's first book, *The Alchemy of Race and Rights: A Diary of a Law Professor* (1991), she discusses a range of cases, events, and personal experiences in order to unveil the politics behind abstracted legal language, and she eloquently argues on behalf of rights and redemptive measures for those traditionally marginalized in American law. For this work she received numerous distinctions, such as the National Association of Black Political Scientists Book Award. The book was named one of the twenty-five best books of 1991 by the *Village Voice Literary Supplement.*

Williams followed with two other critically acclaimed books, *The Rooster's Egg: On the Persistence of Prejudice* (1995) and *Seeing a Color-Blind Future: The Paradox of Race* (1997). In *The Rooster's Egg,* she explores the range of social forces that allow racial prejudice to persist. In *Seeing a Color-Blind Future,* a book based upon the Reith Lectures she gave at the British Broadcasting Corporation, she challenges the law's literal mandates of color-blindness for their obfuscation of the very color prejudices individuals seek to remediate.

Williams' scholarly contributions are matched by her status as a public intellectual. She is a contributing editor and columnist writing on current legal, gender, and race issues for *Nation* magazine. In addition to law review articles, she has written for publications as varied as the *New York Times Book Review,* the *Village Voice,* and *USA Today.* She has appeared on a number of television and radio shows, including *All Things Considered* and *Fresh Air* (NPR), *NewsHour with Jim Lehrer* (PBS), and the *Today Show* (NBC), as well as international radio and television programs.

While challenging the boundaries of traditional legal scholarship, Williams has made observations that are compelling to a wide spectrum of readers both within and beyond the legal profession. She is consistently one of the fifty most cited professors in law review articles. She has been the recipient of various prestigious fellowships, including a MacArthur Fellowship, and she has been awarded a number of honorary doctorates.

See also Critical Race Theory; Intellectual Life

Bibliography

Williams, Patricia. *The Alchemy of Race and Rights: A Diary of a Law Professor.* Cambridge, Mass.: Harvard University Press, 1991.

Williams, Patricia. *The Rooster's Egg: On the Persistence of Prejudice.* Cambridge, Mass.: Harvard University Press, 1995.

Williams, Patricia. *Seeing a Color-Blind Future: The Paradox of Race.* New York: Noonday Press, 1998.

IMANI PERRY (2005)

Williams, Paulette

See Shange, Ntozake

Williams, Peter, Jr.

c. 1780
October 18, 1840

Peter Williams Jr., a church founder, abolitionist, and priest, was born in New Brunswick, New Jersey, about 1780. Schooled at the New York African Free School, he was also tutored by his white pastor at the John Street Methodist Episcopal Church, the Reverend Thomas Lyell. When Lyell left the John Street Church for the Trinity Protestant Episcopal Church, Williams followed him. He was elected lay reader by the congregation in 1812.

Under his leadership, with the approval and assistance of the whites of Trinity Church, Williams organized blacks into a separate congregation in 1818. They acquired a lot and built a church that was formally consecrated as Saint Philip's African Church on July 3, 1819. Williams was licensed to preach and became rector in 1820, and after a number of years of study under Bishop John Henry Hobart, Williams was ordained as the second black Episcopalian priest in 1826.

A firm believer in equality, Williams was one of the cofounders in 1827 of the first black newspaper in the United States, *Freedom's Journal.* Dedicated to the universal welfare of mankind, unity between the races, and the elevation of all races and people, the journal included many articles on the abolition of slavery. Williams was an abolitionist who strongly opposed the ideals of the American Colonization Society. In 1830 he and other black leaders called for a national convention of African Americans. They gathered in Philadelphia and resolved to "devise ways and means for the bettering of our condition" and "to somewhat combat the lack of government recognition and equal opportunities."

Williams continued his efforts to help other blacks by establishing the Phoenix Society, a benevolent organization, in 1833. That same year, he became one of six managers of the American Anti-Slavery Society. Fueled by a rumor that Williams had performed an interracial marriage, Saint Philip's Church was looted and burned during a riot on July 4, 1934, and Williams was forced to flee for his life. Bowing to the pressure of Bishop Benjamin T. Onderdonk, Williams publicly resigned from the Board of Managers of the American Anti-Slavery Society. This action cost him severely in prestige with large sections of the black community. Although he lost his position of influence in the community, he remained at his church, where he continued to act as a mentor to promising young black men.

See also Abolition; Episcopalians; *Freedom's Journal*

Bibliography

DeCosta, B. F. *Three Score and Ten: The Story of St. Philip's Church.* New York, 1889.

Loggins, Vernon. The *Negro Author: His Development in America.* New York: Columbia University Press, 1931.

Ottley, Roi. *Black Odyssey: The Story of the Negro in America.* New York: Scribner's, 1948.

Ottley, Roi, and William J. Weatherby, eds. *The Negro in New York, an Informal Social History.* New York: New York Public Library, 1967.

Wakely, Joseph Beaumont. *Lost Chapters in the Early History of African Methodism.* New York, 1858.

DEBI BROOME (1996)

Williams, Robert Franklin

February 26, 1925
October 15, 1996

Revolutionary nationalist Robert Franklin Williams, founder of the Revolutionary Action Movement and former head of a local NAACP branch in North Carolina, was born in Monroe, North Carolina, where he attended segregated public schools. He graduated from Winchester

Street High School in 1944, was drafted into the army, and after his discharge worked briefly for the Ford Motor Company in Michigan before attending West Virginia State College in 1949. Williams enlisted in the Marine Corps in 1954 but was released when he protested being denied a position for which he was well qualified. In 1955 he returned to Monroe, and one year later he was elected president of the local branch of the National Association for the Advancement of Colored People (NAACP), an ineffective branch with only six members. Williams recruited working-class and poor people of Monroe—domestic workers and sharecroppers—to the NAACP and wrote numerous articles to local newspapers denouncing racism and segregation. Under Williams's leadership, the Monroe NAACP developed into a forthright and militant organization of over 250 members.

The group pursued several cases in the late 1950s that demonstrate Williams's growing effectiveness. In 1958 Williams worked on behalf of two young black boys, aged seven and nine, who were found guilty and sent to reform school for playing a kissing game with white children. As a result of his efforts, they were eventually released after widespread publicity and international pressure. Williams and other NAACP members also mounted protests when Louis Medlin, a white Monroe resident charged in 1959 with assault with intent to rape a black woman who was eight months pregnant, was acquitted, despite an independent eyewitness.

White vigilante violence and legal setbacks that Williams and his allies encountered in their quest for racial justice made them increasingly skeptical of the impartiality of the legal system, the ability of the federal government to protect black citizens, and the nonviolent reform agenda of mainstream civil rights groups. Williams expressed this new militant consciousness in 1959, shortly after the Medlin case was decided, when he said, "If it's necessary to stop lynching with lynching, then we must be willing to resort to that method. We must meet violence with violence." As a result of this statement, national leaders immediately expelled Williams from the NAACP.

Despite his expulsion by the national board of the NAACP, Williams was reelected president of the local branch the next year. He then continued to lead protests and pickets in Monroe, and with his wife, Mabel, started a newsletter, *Crusader*. On August 27, 1961, Williams and other Monroe residents organized a demonstration in downtown Monroe to protest the segregated white swimming pool. As a white mob gathered to challenge the protesters, tension rose and violence erupted. Later that night a white couple driving past Williams's house met a group of angry black protesters. The couple claimed Williams had kidnapped them, and a county grand jury later indicted him on two counts of kidnapping. Williams, however, asserted that he was trying to protect the couple from the angry protesters outside his house.

Fearing for their safety, Williams, his wife, and their two children escaped that night and eventually went to Cuba, where they stayed until 1966. In 1962 he published an account of his experiences in Monroe, *Negroes with Guns*. While in Cuba, Williams helped form the Revolutionary Action Movement (RAM), a Marxist organization that sought to achieve black liberation through the fundamental restructuring of the U.S. economic and political system. In 1966, the Williamses went to China for three years, finally returning to the United States in 1969. Williams lived in Michigan, where he found a job in 1971 at the Center for Chinese Studies at the University of Michigan. He fought extradition to North Carolina until the charges against him were dropped in 1976. Williams has since become a symbol of resistance for subsequent proponents of black self-defense and revolutionary nationalism.

See also National Association for the Advancement of Colored People (NAACP); Revolutionary Action Movement

Bibliography

Barksdale, Marcellus C. "Robert F. Williams and the Indigenous Civil Rights Movement in Monroe, North Carolina, 1961." *Journal of Negro History* 69 (Spring 1984): 73–89.

Forman, James. *The Making of Black Revolutionaries*. New York: Macmillan, 1972.

Tyson, Timothy B. *Radio Free Dixie: Robert F. Williams and the Roots of Black Power*. Chapel Hill: University of North Carolina Press, 2001.

Williams, Robert Franklin. *Negroes with Guns*. New York: Marzani and Munsell, 1962.

PREMILLA NADASEN (1996)
Updated bibliography

Williams, Venus and Serena

The Williams sisters, Venus and Serena, are the two most prominent African-American female tennis players since Althea Gibson (1927–2003). Participating in a sport that has traditionally been dominated by whites, they have been ranked among the top players in the world of tennis,

Venus Williams (r) consoles her younger sister Serena, after defeating Serena in a women's singles semifinal match at Centre Court, Wimbledon, 2000. PHOTOGRAPH BY ADAM BUTLER. AP/WIDE WORLD PHOTOS. REPRODUCED BY PERMISSION.

and they have introduced a style of play that combines power and grace in a way never before witnessed in professional women's tennis.

Venus Ebone Starr Williams was born in Lynwood, California, on June 17, 1980, and Serena Williams was born in Saginaw, Michigan, on September 26, 1981. Both are the daughters of Richard and Oracene Brandi Williams. Serena is the youngest of five daughters, and Venus is the second youngest. Both grew up in the suburbs of Compton, California. Their early playing careers evolved while competing on the public courts in the housing projects of Watts and Compton. Although this was an area that was full of violence, gangs, and high rates of homicides, they prevailed to become two of the elite tennis players in the world.

The family moved to Palm Beach Gardens, Florida, so that the sisters could train under coach Rick Macci, a well respected and established tennis professional. Mr. Williams looked to further his dream of both his daughters one day dominating the tennis world.

Venus Williams turned professional in October 1994, winning her first professional match against Shaun Stafford at the Bank of West Classic in Oakland. Venus participated in the event to avoid a new Women's Tennis Association (WTA) rule, to be phased in beginning in 1995, limiting the number of events in which fourteen-year-old girls could compete. As of 2005, Venus had won thirty-one WTA tour singles titles and nine doubles titles, and she had earned over fourteen million dollars in prize money.

Serena played in her first professional tournament (the Bell Challenge) in 1995. She went on to win the mixed doubles title with Max Mirnyi in July 1998. Serena officially won her first WTA tour singles championship in 1999 (the Open Gaz de France in Paris). As of 2005, Serena had won twenty-six WTA singles tournaments and eleven doubles titles. She has also won each of the four Grand Slam singles titles. As of early 2005, her career prize money totaled over fourteen million dollars.

In addition to their tennis winnings, both Venus and Serena have signed lucrative endorsement contracts. In 2003, Venus signed a five-year endorsement deal worth forty million dollars with Reebok, reported to be the richest contract ever for a female athlete. She also signed a multimillion-dollar deal with Avon Products Inc., and she has designed a collection of leather apparel sold exclusively at Wilsons Leather. In November 2003, Venus launched her own interior design business, V Starr Interiors. Serena signed an endorsement deal with the sneaker company Nike that, with performance related endorsements, could net her sixty million dollars. She also has endorsement deals with Avon Products Inc., Close-Up, McDonald's, Wilson Racquet Sports, and Wrigley/Doublemint.

When Serena met Venus in the finals of the U.S. Open in 2001, it was the first time in history that two sisters had made it to the finals of a Grand Slam tournament. They have since become the first two women in history to square off in four consecutive Grand Slam finals. (At one point Serena held all four major championships at the same time.) When Venus won Wimbledon in 2000 and Serena won the U.S. Open in 1999, it was the first time in tennis history that two sisters had each won a Grand Slam singles title.

The Williams' domination of tennis has illuminated several social and cultural aspects of the sport. Women's professional tennis has historically been predominately white. The way in which the sport of tennis had been traditionally viewed—socially, economically, and culturally—has now been challenged by the insurgence of the Williams sisters. Mainstream tennis followers have witnessed a style of tennis unlike that previously played by women, and in the process of playing tennis the Williams sisters have altered the traditional role of women in the sport. Wearing braids and beads in their hair, with stylish attire and a unique style of play, the Williams sisters brought a new energy to women's tennis. Accompanying this new and distinct style came conflict and controversy. The spectators, media, and athletes on the tour had not experienced the style of play, charisma, and flair that was on display, on as well as off the court. Suddenly, a consciousness of race and culture were infused into tennis in a scope unprecedented in the game's history.

Controversy has surfaced throughout both of the Williams' careers, and both have been subject to adverse situations during matches. In the 2003 French Open against Justine Henin Hardenne, Serena was subject to catcalls and was booed loudly by the crowd. In Indian Wells, California, in 2001, Venus was scheduled to face Serena and withdrew due to medical reasons. In the ensuing match against Kim Clijsters, Serena was loudly booed and the crowd of 16,000 was boisterous and cheered when she double faulted. Some speculated that Venus's withdrawal was done to gain or maintain both of their rankings. Serena and Venus were accused of fixing their match, while their father stated "it was the worst act of prejudice he had ever witnessed." He also claimed that ethnic slurs were directed towards Venus and him while exiting the match.

Controversy has also been directed towards the Williams' and their commitments to tennis. Several critics have expressed concerns about their involvement in fashion, movies, and other outside activities, although other players, particularly Anna Kournikova, have had similar outside activities, and Maria Sharapova, another young Russian tennis star, is also commanding large endorsement deals.

Venus and Serena Williams' presence in tennis goes beyond the sport itself. Together they have redefined the sport, not only with their athletic ability, but with the contemporary style, exposure, and infusion of African-American culture. They have had a marked effect on the media, marketing agencies, sponsorships, and young women around the world. They have also embraced the notion of social activism by meeting issues of race and culture within the world of tennis head on. The world of sport has benefited socially and culturally, and a new dimension of multiculturalism is being seen in the sport. The galleries are now filled with professional athletes, actors, and movie stars of multiple ethnicities. They have provided star power to the sport and infused it with aspects of African-American culture. In the process, they have changed the path of tennis immeasurably.

See also Ashe, Arthur; Gibson, Althea; Sports; Tennis

Bibliography

Lapchick, Richard E. "Athletes Transcending Race: How Is It Possible?" *Sports Business Journal* (June 2005).

Rossner, Scott R., and Kenneth L. Shropshire, eds. *The Business of Sport.* Sudbury, Mass.: Jones and Bartlett, 2004.

FRITZ G. POLITE (2005)

Willis, Deborah

February 5, 1948

Deborah Willis is a photographer, curator, and art and cultural historian. Born in Philadelphia, Willis developed an early interest in photography from her father's cousin, who was the proprietor of a commercial photography studio and took many photographs of her family. Willis's most vivid early memory of the impact of photography came at age seven, when she encountered Roy DeCarava's photographs in *The Sweet Flypaper of Life* (1955) at the public library. It was, she recalls, the first time she had seen a book with photographs of black people, and the impact was indelible. It inspired Willis to assemble a family photo album, trying to emulate the organization of images in DeCarava's book. She would subsequently devote her career to unearthing, promoting, and celebrating photography by artists of the African diaspora. Concurrently, she has maintained a long and successful career as an image-maker, with subject matter ranging from women bodybuilders to shotgun houses of the South, and in media ranging from photo-quilts to digital prints. Family, history, and memory are important recurring themes in her visual work.

Willis began her formal study of photography in the mid-1970s as a student at the Philadelphia College of Art in Pennsylvania, where she earned her B.F.A. degree. After receiving her M.F.A. degree from Pratt Institute in Brooklyn in 1980, Willis became curator of prints and photographs and exhibitions coordinator at the Schomburg Center for Research in Black Culture, part of the New York Public Library. For twelve years she helped not only to reorganize and develop that immense collection, she also almost single-handedly established the discipline of the history of black photographers. In her exhibitions at the Schomburg, Willis debuted the work of many now-prominent photographers, including Lorna Simpson (b. 1960) and Carrie Mae Weems (b. 1953). Willis received an M.A. in museum studies from the City College of New York in 1986.

Willis also rediscovered the forgotten careers of some of the earliest African-American photographers, including James Presley Ball (1825–1904) and James VanDerZee (1886–1983), on whom she published monographs in

1993. Her groundbreaking surveys *Black Photographers, 1840–1940: An Illustrated Bio-Bibliography* (1985) and *An Illustrated Bio-Bibliography of Black Photographers, 1940–1988* (1989) remain the most important and influential sources for information about black photographers. In 1992 Willis moved to Washington, D.C., to become curator of exhibitions at the Center for African American History and Culture, part of the Smithsonian Institution. In 2000 she published *Reflections in Black: A History of Black Photographers 1840 to the Present*, the culmination of more than twenty-five years' research and scholarship. The more than six hundred images in the book were also part of a touring exhibition organized through the Smithsonian.

As a photographic artist Willis has turned her uncompromising eye on explorations of the themes of family and history. Her series of photo quilts, made in the 1990s, incorporate the textile tradition of her grandmother and great aunt, as well as referencing her father's profession as a tailor, using vintage fabrics (including his old neckties) overlaid with photographs, some made by Willis as a teenager. In 2000 Willis became the recipient of the prestigious MacArthur Foundation "genius" grant, which allowed her to focus on personal projects, including series of photographs on beauty shops and women at work. In 2001 she became professor of photography and imaging at New York University's Tisch School for the Arts, and she completed her doctorate in cultural studies at George Mason University in Fairfax, Virginia, in 2003.

See also Art in the United States, Contemporary; Photography, U.S.

Bibliography

Hall, Stuart, and Mark Sealy, eds. *Different: A Historical Context.* London: Phaidon, 2001.

Mettner, Martina, ed. *In Their Mothers' Eyes: Women Photographers and their Children.* Zurich and New York: Edition Stemmle, 2001.

Willis-Thomas, Deborah. *Black Photographers, 1840–1940: An Illustrated Bio-Bibliography.* New York and London: Garland, 1985.

Willis-Thomas, Deborah. *An Illustrated Bio-Bibliography of Black Photographers, 1940–1988.* New York and London: Garland, 1989.

Willis, Deborah, ed. *J. P. Ball: Daguerrean and Studio Photographer.* New York and London: Garland, 1993.

Willis, Deborah, ed. *Picturing Us: African American Identity in Photography.* New York: New Press, 1994.

Willis, Deborah. *Reflections in Black: A History of Black Photographers, 1840 to the Present.* New York: Norton, 2000.

Willis, Deborah. *Family History Memory: Recording African American Life.* Irvington, N.Y.: Hylas, 2005.

Willis-Braithwaite, Deborah, and Rodger C. Birt. *VanDerZee: Photographer, 1886–1983.* New York: Harry N. Abrams, 1993.

Willis, Deborah, and Carla Williams. *The Black Female Body: A Photographic History.* Philadelphia: Temple University Press, 2002.

CARLA WILLIAMS (2005)

Wilson, August

April 27, 1945

The playwright August Wilson was born Frederick August Kittel in Pittsburgh, the fourth of six children. Growing up near the steel mills, in a neighborhood called the Hill that was populated by poor African Americans, Italians, and Jews, he had a childhood of poverty and hardship. He rarely saw his father, a German baker who visited only occasionally, and the family subsisted on public assistance and on his mother's earnings as a janitor. Wilson adopted his mother's maiden name in the 1970s as a way of disavowing his father.

Wilson's stepfather, David Bedford, moved the family to a white suburb when Wilson was a teenager. This change, however, also proved difficult. As a student at a predominantly white Catholic school in Pittsburgh, Wilson was ostracized by his white schoolmates and misjudged by his white teachers, who doubted his intelligence. He frequently found notes on his desk reading "Nigger, go home." When he was fourteen, he dropped out of school.

Wilson continued his education in the library, where he discovered the works of Ralph Ellison, Langston Hughes, Richard Wright, and other African-American writers, as well as the poetry of Dylan Thomas, which contributed to his still-evolving aesthetic. In 1965 Wilson heard recordings of the blues for the first time, and their lyrical expression of the hardships of life was to become another major influence on his work. Except for a one-year stint in the army (1967), Wilson spent the middle 1960s writing poetry at night while holding a series of menial jobs during the day.

In 1968 he returned to Pittsburgh, where he became caught up in the black arts movement. Influenced by the plays and polemical writings of Amiri Baraka, Wilson and his friend Rob Penny founded the Black Horizons on the Hill Theatre in 1968—although he had no previous theater experience. Their aim was to use theater to provoke social change. His earliest one-act plays—*Recycle* (1973), *The Homecoming* (1976), and *The Coldest Day of the Year* (1977)—were written for this theater.

In 1977 Wilson moved to Saint Paul, Minnesota, where he wrote a musical satire with a western theme: *Black Bart and the Sacred Hills*. This rambling verse narrative was staged a year later by the Inner City Cultural Center in Los Angeles. While supporting himself by writing educational dramas for the Minnesota Science Center, Wilson wrote the plays *Jitney!* and *Fullerton Street* in 1982. Both were produced that year by the Minneapolis Playwrights' Center.

It was the play *Ma Rainey's Black Bottom*, written in 1983 and first produced by the Eugene O'Neill National Playwrights Conference, that gained Wilson national attention. Produced at the Yale Repertory Theatre in 1984 under the direction of Lloyd Richards, and later that year on Broadway with the same director, the play won the New York Drama Critics Circle Award for Best Play. *Ma Rainey*, which is set in 1927 and depicts a day in the life of the famous blues singer, explores not only the exploitation of black artists of that era, but also reveals the high price such artists pay when they cut themselves off from their cultural past. Wilson's next play, *Fences* (1985), is set in 1957 and focuses on the frustrations of Troy Maxson, a Pittsburgh garbage collector who had been a star ball player in the Negro Leagues before Jackie Robinson broke baseball's color line. The play was awarded the Pulitzer Prize and the Tony Award for Best Play of the Year.

After noticing that he had fortuitously written four plays set in four separate decades, Wilson decided to continue to write a play set in each decade of the twentieth century. *Ma Rainey's Black Bottom* and *Fences* would then become part of a ten-play cycle that would chronicle the challenges that African Americans have confronted since Emancipation. In *Joe Turner's Come and Gone* (1986), set in 1911, Wilson explores the emotional and physical displacement experienced by former slaves in the early twentieth century. Produced on Broadway in 1988, it won the New York Drama Critics Circle Award for Best Play. Wilson's cycle continued with *Seven Guitars* (1994), set in the 1940s, and *Jitney* (1996), a revision of the earlier play, set in the 1970s.

The Piano Lesson (1987), set in 1936, concerns the ownership of a piano that had been built by the slave grandfather of a feuding brother and sister. The source of their contention is a 125-year-old piano that sits untouched in the living room of Berniece Charles. Her brother wants to sell it to buy land, but Berniece wants it left alone to revere. *The Piano Lesson* perhaps best expresses Wilson's view of black history as something to be neither sold nor denied, but employed to create an ongoing, nurturing cultural identity. Produced on Broadway in 1990, the play received the Drama Desk Best Play award and the New York Drama Critics Circle Award, and Wilson won his second Pulitzer Prize for the play. In 1996 it was transformed into a successful television film.

Wilson's play about the 1960s, *Two Trains Running* (1990), is also set in Pittsburgh, in 1968. It explores the allegiances and frictions among a group of friends who find themselves confronted with the era's radical social changes and by a sense that they will be swept along by large forces beyond their control. It was produced on Broadway in 1992 and won the New York Drama Critics Circle Award for Best Play.

Seven Guitars (1995), Wilson's seventh play, is the story of Floyd "School Boy" Barton, a Pittsburgh blues singer who goes to Chicago in 1948 to record two songs. After he returns to Pittsburgh to rekindle a romance, he is jailed for ninety days on a phony charge. When he gets out, he discovers that his record is getting airplay, and he is asked to come back to Chicago to make additional records. However, he is killed by the demented Hedley before he can go, and the play is told in flashback after his death.

King Hedley II (2001), set in the 1980s, revisits characters and extends the storyline introduced in *Seven Guitars*. Set in the Hill District of Pittsburgh in 1985, the play fast forwards some thirty-seven years to highlight the struggles of Ruby's now adult son, King. After serving seven years for killing the man who disfigured him, King has returned to the house where Ruby and Tonya, who is pregnant with his child, now live. Symbolized by his attempts to raise flowers out of infertile soil, King, as he is called, seeks spiritual renewal but is instead set back by the revelation that Hedley is not his biological father.

Wilson's ninth play, *Gem of the Ocean* (2004), is set in 1904 and begins the day before Aunt Ester's 287th birthday in Pittsburgh's Hill District. Citizen Barlow, who believes he's committed a mortal sin, comes to Aunt Ester to get his soul washed. Aunt Ester gives Citizen a meal, a job, and a place to stay. She later sets him on a spiritual journey that leads him on a perilous road to redemption.

In 2005, August Wilson had begun writing the tenth and final play in his history cycle. *Radio Golf*, to be set in the 1990s, concerns two golf-loving real-estate developers who plan to destroy the former home of the now familiar clairvoyant Aunt Ester (she also appears in *Two Trains Running*), who is now over three hundred years old.

See also Black Arts Movement; Drama

Bibliography

Elam, Harry. *The Past as Present in the Drama of August Wilson.* Ann Arbor: University of Michigan Press, 2004.

Elkins, Marilyn. *August Wilson: A Casebook.* New York: Garland, 1994.

Herrington, Joan. *I Ain't Sorry for Nothin' I Done: August Wilson's Process of Playwriting.* New York: Limelight, 1998.

Powers, Kim. "An Interview With August Wilson." *Theater* 16 (fall/winter, 1984): 50–55.

Shannon, Sandra G. *The Dramatic Vision of August Wilson.* Washington, D.C.: Howard University Press, 1995.

Shannon, Sandra G. *August Wilson's Fences: A Reference Guide.* Westport, Conn.: Greenwood, 2003.

Williams, Dana, and Sandra G. Shannon, eds. *August Wilson and Black Aesthetics.* New York: Palgrave-Macmillan, 2004.

Nadel, Alan, ed. *May All Your Fences Have Gates: Essays on the Drama of August Wilson.* Iowa City: University of Iowa Press, 1994.

Savran, David. "August Wilson." In *In Their Own Words: Contemporary American Playwrights.* New York: Theater Communications Group, 1988.

Wolfe, Peter. *August Wilson.* New York: Twayne, 1999.

SANDRA G. SHANNON (1996)
Updated by author 2005

Wilson, Flip

December 8, 1933
November 25, 1998

Comedian Clerow "Flip" Wilson was born in Jersey City, New Jersey. Abandoned by his mother in 1940, he was placed in foster homes from which he ran away so often that he was sent to reform school. Wilson quit school at the age of sixteen, lied about his age, and joined the U.S. Air Force. He served until 1954.

Wilson then worked as a comic in small clubs and by 1960 was working in New York. An appearance in 1966 on the *Tonight Show* was followed by many others and led to appearances on the *Ed Sullivan Show* and *Rowan and Martin's Laugh-In,* and to his own special in 1968. NBC starred him in the *Flip Wilson Show,* which ran from September 17, 1970, to June 27, 1974. The program ranked among the top ten.

Wilson was the first black entertainer to host a successful weekly variety show on network television. He was noted for his storytelling and his flamboyant impersonations of characters like the sassy waitress Geraldine.

After Wilson left the show in 1974, he went into semiretirement, appearing in specials and in movies like *Uptown Saturday Night* (1974) and *The Fish That Saved Pittsburgh* (1979). He also starred in a daytime game show and a situation comedy that were failures. In the last decade of his life, he limited his performances to occasional guest appearances on situation comedies. He died of liver cancer.

See also Comedians; Television

Bibliography

Ingram, Billy. "Flip Wilson: The Odd Disappearance of the Flip Wilson Show." Published in *TV Party.* Available from <http://www.tvparty.com/flip.html>.

Manheim, James M. "Flip Wilson." In *Contemporary Black Biography,* edited by Shirelle Phelps. Detroit, Mich.: Gale, 1999.

Watkins, Mel. "Flip Wilson, 64, Over-the-top Comic and TV Host, Dies." *New York Times,* November 26, 1998.

ROBERT L. JOHNS (2001)

Wilson, Fred

August 25, 1954

Fred Wilson was born in the Bronx, New York, and earned his B.F.A. degree from the State University of New York, College at Purchase in 1976. As a young artist he worked temporarily at the Longwoods Art Gallery, the Metropolitan Museum of Art, the Museum of Natural History, and the Just Above Midtown Gallery in New York. Since the late 1980s, Wilson has explored the intersection of race discourse and the history of museums through innovative installation art projects that emphasize archiving, collecting, and display. Unlike traditional painting and sculpture, installation art is site-specific, temporary, and designed to surround or interact with the viewer. In 1990, at White Columns Gallery in New York, the artist exhibited *The Other Museum,* a mock-ethnographic display that used African "artifacts" and innovative wall labels to highlight the historical relationship between European colonialism, slavery, and museum collecting practices.

One of Wilson's best-known exhibitions is *Mining the Museum* (1992), which was jointly supported by the Contemporary Museum in Baltimore and the Maryland Historical Society. For this work the artist studied the archives and permanent exhibitions of the Maryland Historical Society in order to reinstall the collection in new, more provocative displays. Wilson brought to light histories that had been buried in the museum's basement for decades, particularly those of African Americans and Native Americans in Maryland. One of the more powerful juxtapositions of the exhibition, *Metalwork 1793–1880*, grouped together Baltimore repoussé silver vessels with a single pair of iron slave shackles. The interdependence of slave labor and a luxury economy was made evident in the visual contrast of fine silver craftsmanship and abject ironwork. The nearly one-hundred-year time span from 1793 to 1880 also marked the gradual abolition of slavery in the Americas from the 1793 Anti-Slavery Act of Ontario, Canada, to the abolition of slavery in Cuba in 1880.

Since the early 1990s, Fred Wilson has offered critical interpretations of numerous art museums and their collections in North America, Asia, Europe, and the Middle East. He has been the recipient of major awards from the Rockefeller Foundation, the National Endowment for the Arts, the American Association of Museums, and the New York State Council on the Arts. He was given a MacArthur Foundation Fellowship in 1999. In 2003 Wilson was selected as the United States representative to the Venice Biennale, the second artist of African-American descent granted this prestigious honor. His project for the Biennale mapped the presence of Africans in the city of Venice from the time of the Moors to the present day, taking its title—*Speak of Me as I Am*—from Shakespeare's *Othello.* All of Fred Wilson's artworks offer careful critiques of representation, demonstrating how race discourse and historical relations of power circulate in museums and visual culture.

See also Art in the United States, Contemporary

Bibliography

Berger, Maurice, Fred Wilson, and Jennifer González. *Fred Wilson: Objects and Installations 1979–2000: Issues in Cultural Theory 4.* Baltimore, Md.: Center for Art and Visual Culture, University of Maryland, Baltimore County, 2001.

Corrin, Lisa G. *Mining the Museum: An Installation by Fred Wilson.* New York: New Press, 1994.

JENNIFER A. GONZÁLEZ (2005)

Wilson, Harriet E. Adams

c. 1827

c. 1863

Author Harriet E. Wilson is believed to be the pseudonymous "Our Nig," who wrote what may have been the first novel by an African American published in the United States: *Our Nig; or, Sketches from the Life of a Free Black, in a Two-Story White House, North. Showing That Slavery's Shadows Fall Even There* (1859). Some scholars also include her with Maria F. dos Reis, who in 1859 published a novel in Brazil, as the first two women of African descent to publish a novel in any language. "Our Nig's" work describes the life of Alfredo, a mulatto indentured servant, and condemns northern whites for a magnitude of racial prejudice and cruelty more commonly associated with slavery and the South. Three letters presumably written by friends of the novelist are appended to the novel, and it is because of the correspondences between the seemingly supplementary biographical information included there that the novel has been considered semi-autobiographical.

Despite these letters, however, little definite is known about Harriet Wilson's life. For instance, according to the 1850 federal census for the state of New Hampshire, a twenty-two-year-old "Black" (not "mulatto") woman originally from New Hampshire named Harriet Adams lived in the town of Milford with the family of Samuel Boyles, which in part corresponds to information included in the novel. This suggests that Wilson was born about 1827–1828. However, the 1860 federal census for the city of Boston, where Wilson moved in approximately 1855, and where she had her novel printed, lists a "Black" woman named Harriet E. Wilson born in Fredericksburg, Virginia in about 1807–1808.

The appended letters, as well as the end of *Our Nig,* provide details of the author's life between 1850 and 1860, when she lived in Massachusetts and worked as a weaver of straw hats. About 1851 Harriet Adams met Thomas Wilson, a fugitive slave from Virginia, and together they moved to Milford, New Hampshire, and married, perhaps on October 6, 1851. By the time Harriet Wilson gave birth in May or June of 1852 to their son, George Mason Wilson, Thomas Wilson had abandoned his wife and she had gone to a charity establishment in Goffstown, New Hampshire, the Hillsborough County Farm. Thomas Wilson returned and supported his wife and child for a short time, but then suddenly left them again and never returned.

Harriet Wilson, whose health had been bad since she was eighteen, was rescued by a couple who took in and cared for her and her son. When her health failed, Wilson began writing her novel in an effort to make money: "Deserted by kindred, disabled by failing health," she wrote in her preface to *Our Nig,* "I am forced to some experiment, which shall aid me in maintaining myself and child without extinguishing this feeble life." Little is known of Wilson's life after the publication of *Our Nig,* on September 5, 1859. Her son died in New Hampshire in February 1860, and Harriet Wilson died sometime between the death of her son and January 1870.

For more than a hundred years, *Our Nig* was barely noticed. In 1983, however, the critic Henry Louis Gates Jr. raised scholarly interest in Wilson and the novel by arranging to have the book republished, the text being an exact reprint of the 1859 edition.

See also Gates, Henry Louis, Jr.; Literature of the United States

Bibliography

Gates, Henry Louis, Jr. Introduction to *Our Nig; or, Sketches from the Life of a Free Black, in a Two-Story White House, North. Showing That Slavery's Shadows Fall Even There,* New York: Random House, 1983, pp. xi–lv.

Gates, Henry Louis, Jr. "Parallel Discursive Universes: Fictions of the Self in Harriet E. Wilson's *Our Nig.*" In *Figures in Black: Words, Signs, and the "Racial" Self.* New York: Oxford University Press, 1987, pp. 125–163.

PETER SCHILLING (1996)

WILSON, WILLIAM JULIUS

DECEMBER 20, 1935

Born in Derry Township, Pennsylvania, to Esco and Pauline Bracy Wilson, sociologist and educator William Wilson received degrees in sociology from Wilberforce University (B.A., 1958), Bowling Green State University (M.A., 1961), and Washington State University (Ph.D., 1966).

Wilson taught at the University of Massachusetts at Amherst (1965–1971) and the University of Chicago (1971–1976). While at Chicago he was promoted to full professor in 1975, named chair of the sociology department in 1978, and was named distinguished professor in 1994. The next year he received a rare distinction for a sociologist when he was invited to join the National Academy of Sciences. In 1993 he founded the Center for the Study of Urban Inequality, a permanent organization for poverty research located at the university. Wilson joined Harvard University in 1996, where he was appointed Lewis P. and Linda L. Gayser University Professor in the John F. Kennedy School of Government and later the Malcolm Wiener Professor of Social Policy.

Among his numerous publications, Wilson's *The Declining Significance of Race* (1978) and *The Truly Disadvantaged* (1987) are highly regarded by many, stimulating academic and popular debates on race and urban poverty. His book *When Work Disappears: The World of the New Urban Poor* (1996) furthers the discussion on poverty in inner cities and diagnoses and prescribes remedies for the ailments in these areas. Wilson's views have proved controversial, for he has supported national health and child care systems, work and training programs similar to those of the New Deal, and training programs for the poor that will allow them to gain employment.

Wilson was the recipient of the 1998 National Medal of Science, the highest scientific honor in the United States. He continues to write and edit books, including the 2002 *Youth in Cities: A Cross-National Perspective.*

See also Black Studies; Economic Condition, U.S.; Sociology

Bibliography

Newsmakers, annual edition. Detroit, Mich.: Gale, 1998.

Phelps, Shirelle, ed. *Contemporary Black Biography,* vol. 22. Detroit, Mich.: Gale, 1999.

Who's Who Among African Americans, 12th ed. Detroit, Mich.: Gale, 1999.

Wilson, Frank Harold. *Race, Class, and the Postindustrial City: William Julius Wilson and the Promise of Sociology.* Albany: State University of New York Press, 2004.

JESSIE CARNEY SMITH (1996)
Updated by publisher 2005

WINFREY, OPRAH

JANUARY 29, 1954

Born on a farm in Kosciusko, Mississippi, to Vernita Lee and Vernon Winfrey, talk-show host and actress Oprah Gail Winfrey was reared by her grandmother for the early part of her life. At age six, she was sent to live with her mother, who worked as a domestic, and two half brothers in Milwaukee. It was in Milwaukee that Winfrey began to display her oratorical gifts, reciting poetry at socials and teas. During her adolescence she began to misbehave to such a degree that she was sent to live with her father in Nashville. Under the strict disciplinary regime imposed by her father, Winfrey started to flourish, distinguishing herself in debate and oratory. At sixteen, she won an Elks Club oratorical contest that awarded her a scholarship to Tennessee State University.

While a freshman in college, Winfrey won the Miss Black Nashville and Miss Black Tennessee pageants. As a result of this exposure, she received a job offer from a local television station and in her sophomore year became a news anchor at WTVF-TV in Nashville. After graduating in 1976, Winfrey took a job with WJZ-TV in Baltimore as a reporter and co-anchor of the evening news. In 1977 she was switched to updates on local news, which appeared during the ABC national morning show *Good Morning America.* That same year she found her niche as a talk-show host, cohosting WJZ-TV's morning show, *Baltimore Is Talking.*

In 1984 Winfrey moved to Chicago to take over *A.M. Chicago,* a talk show losing in the ratings to Phil Donahue's popular morning program. Within a month Winfrey's ratings were equal to Donahue's. In three months she surpassed him. A year and a half later the show extended to an hour and was renamed *The Oprah Winfrey Show.* The show, which covers a wide range of topics from the lighthearted to the sensational or the tragic, was picked up for national syndication by King World Productions in 1986. By 1993 *The Oprah Winfrey Show* was seen in 99 percent of U.S. television markets and sixty-four countries. Since the show first became eligible in 1986, it has won Emmy awards for best talk show or best talk-show hostess each year except one. In 1998 she withdrew her name from Daytime Emmy Award consideration because that year she was given the Emmy's Lifetime Achievement Award.

In 1985 Winfrey was cast as the strong-willed Sofia in the film version of Alice Walker's novel *The Color Purple,* for which Winfrey received an Oscar nomination. The following year she formed her own production company, Harpo Productions ("Oprah" spelled backwards), to develop projects. In 1989 Winfrey produced and acted in a television miniseries based on Gloria Naylor's novel *The Women of Brewster Place*; in 1993 she starred in and produced the television drama *There Are No Children Here*; and in 1997 she produced and appeared in *Before Women Had Wings.* In 1993 *Forbes* magazine listed Winfrey as America's richest entertainer based on her 1992 and 1993 earnings of approximately $98 million; in 2003 *Forbes* listed her as the first African-American woman to become a billionaire, and by 2005 her net worth was estimated at $1.3 billion.

During the mid-1990s and beyond, Winfrey's career continued to expand. Her talk show remained the most watched daytime show, and she also produced evening interview specials, notably an exclusive interview with the reclusive singer Michael Jackson. She began a wildly successful reading club, the Oprah book club, whose books she promoted on her show. In 1998 she produced and starred in Jonathan Demme's *Beloved,* adapted from Toni Morrison's novel. In 2005 she was executive producer of *Their Eyes Were Watching God,* a television movie based on a novel with the same title written by Zora Neale Hurston. In 2000 she launched *O: The Oprah Winfrey Magazine,* which quickly developed a readership of 2.5 million.

Winfrey's wealth and influence have afforded her the opportunity to pursue numerous philanthropic ventures. In 1998 she launched Oprah's Angel Network, which in its first year provided $3.5 million in college scholarships for students with financial need. Beginning in 2000 the Angel Network donated $100,000 "Use Your Life" awards on the television show each Monday to people who used their lives to better the lives of others. She is also involved with Habitat for Humanity and A Better Chance, a Boston-based program that gives inner-city youths the opportunity to attend college preparatory schools. She has given large grants to organizations such as the United Negro College Fund. She also has made large donations and made benefit appearances for disaster relief after, for example, the terrorist attacks on the United States in 2001 and after the tsunami in the South Pacific/Southeast Asia in 2004. In 2002 she was the first recipient of the Bob Hope Humanitarian Award at the Emmy Awards.

See also Entrepreneurs and Entrepreneurship; Television

Bibliography

Garson, Helen S. *Oprah Winfrey: A Biography.* Westport, Conn.: Greenwood Press, 2004.

Harrison, Barbara Grizutti. "The Importance of Being Oprah." *New York Times Magazine* (June 11, 1989): 28–30.

Hine, Darlene Clark, ed. *Black Women in America.* New York: Carlson, 1993.

Newcomb, Peter, and Lisa Gubernick. "The Top 40." *Forbes* (September 27, 1993): 97.

KENYA DILDAY (1996)
MICHAEL O'NEAL (2005)

WINTI IN SURINAME

Winti is as old as the contacts between the Wild Coast of South Africa and Africa since the 1650s. It has been such a tabooed religious practice that it is difficult to find good studies about what it precisely is. Winti is a lifestyle in which people remain in constant exchange with Suriname. This contact does not exclusively take place in Suriname itself; it can also be in the Netherlands or elsewhere. Most important is that it connects with the place where Winti has developed and acquired its general characteristics, that is to say with Sranan, the Creole word for the language and the country of Suriname.

The word *Winti* seems to derive from the English word *wind*. A vocabulary published in 1961 in Paramaribo considers *winti* to be a Sranan word for "wind," "frenzy," "ghost," and "spirit." It is immediately followed by *winti-dansi*, or *winti-pré*, indicating the relevance of music and rhythm. The concept of Winti contains the totality of the ghosts and spirits in the Winti pantheon, with Aisa, the *gron-winti*, or the goddess of the earth, as the most important point of reference. The Christian religion has only a marginal influence, and what distinguishes Winti from other American religions is its exclusiveness; almost everything is secret and only accessible to the initiated specialists. The three poles of Winti are the *kra* (the human soul), the *wintis* or gods, as well as the *jorkas*, the ghosts of the dead. They have to be connected in order for practitioners to be able to interpret individual perceptions and human experiences in past and present. For this balance, the Winti-believer needs to consult the *lukuman*, the *bonuman* or *obiahman*, or the *wisiman*. They have knowledge of the invisible connections and can explain, heal, and cure sickness or lack of spiritual orientation. Winti is included in Sranan storytelling, understood by most of the ethnic groups in the past.

Two Surinamese, Charles Wooding and Henri Stephen, have written informative books on Winti. Wooding concentrates on the African influences, whereas Stephen shows that Winti goes through all Surinamese groups and ethnic communities. Many people are afraid of Winti because it makes use of magic. There is good and evil magic, and only the medicine man knows how to handle them properly. The importance of Winti became visible in the eighteenth century. The African-born slave Quassi (c. 1690–1787), a *lukuman* and *bonuman*, was set free and became the most important link for the white government to negotiate with slaves and Maroons. He was celebrated as a god and recognized in Europe because of his specialized knowledge of plants and herbs. Also, narratives written by contemporary Creole writers, such as Edgar Cairo, recur to the description of Winti in Surinamese reality.

See also Religion

Bibliography

Cairo, Edgard. "This Here Soul." *Callaloo* 11, no. 1 (1988): 74–79.

Stephen, Henri J. M. *Winti. Afro-Surinaamse religie en magische rituelen in Suriname en Nederland.* Amsterdam: Karnak, 1985.

Wooding, Charles J. W. *Evolving Culture: A Cross-Cultural Study of Suriname, West Africa, and the Caribbean.* Washington D.C.; University Press of America, 1981.

INEKE PHAF-RHEINBERGER (2005)

WOMAN'S ERA

Woman's Era, the first monthly newspaper published by African-American women, was a key factor in the creation of national networks of middle-class black activist women at the turn of the twentieth century. The paper was established in 1894 by Josephine St. Pierre Ruffin and her daughter, Florida Ruffin Ridley. The two had founded the Boston Woman's Era Club that same year, and Ruffin served both as the club's president and as editor of the paper until 1903. The paper dealt with issues of politics, family, health, fashion, and community. It had correspondents from around the country, many of whom were renowned activists. Victoria Earle Matthews reported from New York, Fannie Barrier Williams from Chicago, Josephine Silone-Yates from Kansas City, Mary Church Terrell from Washington, D.C., Elizabeth Ensley from Denver, and Alice Ruth Moore (later known as Alice Dunbar-Nelson) from New Orleans.

The paper was of great use in 1895 in calling a meeting to protest a letter insulting the character of black women. Using the vehicle of the *Woman's Era*, Ruffin insisted that African-American women could no longer stand idle while whites asserted that black men were natural rapists and that black women were amoral. Out of this national conference of a hundred women representing ten states came the National Federation of Afro-American Women. The federation pledged itself to deal with these attacks, among other pressing issues. The organization would become part of the larger National Association of Colored Women the following year.

Although the *Woman's Era* did not have the longevity of many other periodicals, it played a key role at a critical time for black women. Ruffin's creation of the paper as a means of linking the work of various women from around the country made possible the creation of such vitally important organizations as the National Association of Colored Women.

See also Journalism; National Association of Colored Women; National Federation of Afro-American Women; Women's Magazines

Bibliography

Neverdon-Morton, Cynthia. "The Black Woman's Struggle for Equality in the South, 1895–1925." In *The Afro-American Woman: Struggles and Images,* edited by Sharon Harley and Rosalyn Terborg-Penn, pp. 43–57. Port Washington, N.Y.: Kennikat Press, 1978.

Salem, Dorothy. *To Better Our World: Black Women in Organized Reform, 1890–1920.* Brooklyn, N.Y.: Carlson, 1990.

JUDITH WEISENFELD (1996)

WOMEN'S MAGAZINES

Though absent from most histories of American, African-American, and women's publishing, African-American women's magazines have a long history in the United States. Taken as a group, from their inception to the present, African-American women's magazines have allowed African-American women to find work as journalists, printers, writers, and editors; to define personal as well as group identities; to create a sense of unity by establishing a communication network between women in different regions; to present and comment on world and local events from an African-American female perspective; and to highlight achievements often overlooked and ignored by the white and/or African-American male press. African-American women's magazines have been and continue to be an important part of both American and African-American culture.

If African-American women's magazines are defined as those publications owned, edited, or aimed at an African-American reading public, the first magazine for African-American women was established in 1891. From 1891 to 1950 there were eight African-American women's magazines published for a variety of purposes, and from 1950 to the present another few magazines fit that definition. Some, such as *Ringwood's Journal of African American Fashion* (1891–1894), *Woman's Era* (1894–1897), and *Sepia Socialite* (1936–1938), provided a space where readers who considered themselves educated and refined could, despite geographical distance, mingle with like-minded individuals. Other publications, such as *Half-Century Magazine for the Colored Home and Homemaker* (1916–1925), *Woman's Voice* (1912–1927), and the *Home Magazine* in *Tan Confessions* (1950–1952), prepared African-American women for a place in urban social landscapes and overwhelmingly focused on the significance of consumerism for African-American women within those locales. Still others, like *Our Women and Children*, published by the Black Baptist Association from 1888 to 1891, and *Aframerican Woman's Journal* (1935–1954), attempted to speak to specific political, domestic, or religious aspirations on the part of an African-American female readership. In terms of more contemporary magazines, one of the longest-running publications to target African-American women as readers, *Essence*, initially owned by a group of four African-American men, first appeared in May 1970, and Oprah Winfrey's *O, The Oprah Magazine*, targeting women of all races, began publication in 2000.

The magazines published through the 1950s had relatively small readerships, never reaching more than forty thousand readers each month. However, the importance of those African-American women's magazines does not so much reside in their subscription numbers but rather in the fact that they ask readers to think more deeply about, or in some instances rethink, what they are sure we know about relationships between groups of African Americans during different periods of time and to listen in on intra-racial conversations from a number of historical periods. African-American women's magazines contextualized, portrayed, and communicated societal expectations to an African-American female reading audience. As a result, when taken as a group, these magazines are source material about the lives, thoughts, and political leanings of African-American women.

From the 1970s on, the import of African-American women's magazines shifted. *Essence* magazine's significance lies in its success at becoming a gateway through which mainstream advertisers are able to reach a lucrative group of African-American consumers of both sexes. In that sense, it is a profitable example of American magazine-publishing industry practices, and the magazine's founders were able to succeed at and modernize marketing strategies. Indeed, in 2001 African Americans spent $356 million on books, and *Essence* has the ability to reach upwards of 72 percent of such buyers. Within that same vein, *O* has transformed magazine publishing. Oprah Winfrey and her business partner in the venture, Hearst Publishing, with little advance marketing, were able to sell out the initial newsstand run of 1.6 million copies. In a few short months the publication signed up 1.9 million subscribers (by way of comparison, *American Vogue* has 1.1 million subscribers). Featuring an image of Winfrey, an African-American woman, on the cover of each issue, the magazine outsells more established rivals such as *In Style, Glamour, Harper's Bazaar,* and *Good Housekeeping.*

Whereas the two more contemporary magazines obviously demand more nuanced definitions of ownership and readership than did those African-American women's publications that came before, they also reveal quite a bit about a post–civil rights, post–Black Power, postintegration use and meaning of both race and gender in American and African-American magazine culture. They communicate that in many ways times have changed. They are a testament to the success of the political movements and struggles of past generations. They make clear that in some areas, such movements have paid tangible dividends. In relation to questions about ownership, marketing strategy, and an ability to firmly locate African Americans within American culture, they are at the same time substantially dependent on what came before, and a world apart.

See also *Woman's Era*; Journalism

Bibliography

Bullock, Penelope L. *The Afro-American Periodical Press, 1838–1909.* Baton Rouge: Louisiana State University Press, 1981.

Daniel, Walter. *Black Journals of the United States.* Westport, Conn.: Greenwood, 1982.

Rooks, Noliwe M. *Ladies Pages: African American Women's Magazines and the Culture That Made Them.* New Brunswick, N.J.: Rutgers University Press, 2004.

NOLIWE ROOKS (2005)

Women Traders of the Caribbean

Women's market trading activity has a long history in the Caribbean. It began in the earliest days of slavery and remains strong in the present. Anthropologists and historians conclude that this practice is a cultural inheritance from West Africa, brought to the Americas by the enslaved black population. Black women first entered the internal market as hawkers and peddlers for their owners. Eventually, they began to sell for themselves. Higglers, as they became known, sold the surplus of their provision grounds and house gardens (plots of land on which they cultivated their aliments). After emancipation, this practice became rampant with the development of a tradition of small farming, and the distribution of agricultural produce became predominantly women's work. On smaller islands in the eastern part of the region, women have dominated inter-island trade. In St. Lucia, for example, they are known as speculators. They operate on a small scale, traveling to neighboring islands to purchase both local and imported goods. They sell at different points before returning home with other consumer items.

During the late 1970s, in Jamaica, a new type of independent trader emerged as a result of shortages due to the global economic crisis, United States–supported confrontations with the International Monetary Fund (IMF), and nationally imposed trade restrictions on imports. The ruling People's National Party (PNP) sought to boost local industry and lessen the island's dependence on foreign-made products (such as shoes, bags, canned goods, and alcoholic beverages), which they referred to as "felt needs." Originally known as "suitcase traders" or "foreign higglers," these traders began as importers/exporters of these items that were absent on local shelves. They traveled throughout the Caribbean as well as North and South America where they exported Jamaican products such as music, canned goods, and arts and crafts to earn foreign exchange. Then they purchased goods (e.g., plastics, haberdashery, food items as well as clothing and other dry goods) unavailable in Jamaica, which they sold both wholesale and retail. Without spaces to conduct their activities, they squatted in front of stores, on streets of commercial areas to attract customers. Without any overhead, they sold their items more cheaply than established merchants. In many instances, they became fierce competitors with established businesses. In the early 1980s, the Jamaican government implemented a series of policies to regulate this activity. Traders were required to register with the United Vendors Association (UVA), carry identity cards, and had limited access to foreign exchange. Prior to that, they purchased dollars on the parallel market. In addition, they were officially titled Informal Commercial Importers (ICIs), which distinguished them from higglers. Lastly, special arcades were built to accommodate a significant number of them.

ICIs, like their counterparts throughout the region, abide by some guidelines and find creative ways to circumvent others. Most of their businesses are small in scale with a few employees, who are often extended family members. They use formal and informal networks to facilitate various aspects of their businesses from their buying trips abroad to the bureaucratic process of declaring goods at customs. While traditional market traders are primarily lower-classed individuals, independent importers exist across the class structure. For example, in Barbados, Dominican Republic, and Martinique, professional women—such as stewardesses, informatics agents, bank tellers, and university lecturers—also engage in this business as a sideline to supplement their income. These importers tend to travel infrequently and purchase specific goods for their customers, depending on their destinations. They sell their wares at home or other private settings, which renders them invisible to the state.

Little has changed in terms of social attitudes toward traders since their emergence during slavery. They are

Women stallholders in the marketplace at Nassau, Bahamas, 1938. HULTON ARCHIVE/GETTY IMAGES

often stereotyped as tricksters and greedy individuals who overcharge for their products. While several among them may control the market on certain items and can therefore charge what the traffic will bear, not all traders share this position. The location of their operations, how competitive the market is, and the scale of their holdings all contribute to the extent of their profit margins. What is definitive about women traders of the region is that they are capitalists who play a role in the global market at multiple levels. For that reason, in many instances, traders are tolerated. Indeed, consumers benefit from the goods they provide, though they remain a nuisance to governments, established merchants, and civil societies. The state usually regards them as a drain on local economy because they take hard currency out of the country and flood the market with imports. Social attitudes toward them tend to be negative. Also, because many import secondary products, they are viewed by the upper classes as contributors to the destruction of local taste. Initially, a notable number of traders fared extremely well and made significant profits. Rumors of their success stories still draw new recruits today. As a result, the market has become saturated, and this activity is no longer as profitable for most participants as it was during the 1980s.

While the surge in independent international trading occurred throughout the Caribbean region, it was most notable in Jamaica, Haiti, and Guyana. The numerative effect that informal traders have had on their national economies remains unclear. Without doubt, however, their impact is significant as their visibility on city streets and country roads attests. The extent of their contribution is hard to determine for multiple reasons. First, traders hardly report their full earnings to governments to avoid full taxation that disregards their periods of losses. Second, outside of regulation, they are rarely recognized by the state. They are often the backbone of nontourist-based economies as they provide employment, sustain households, and reproduce labor power. In addition, they supply goods to the poor at more affordable prices. Third, because independent traders link "formal" and "informal" sectors of the economy, the lines that demarcate legality are blurred. Hence, even existing statistics are inaccurate, due to these clandestine elements. Throughout the region informal economies contribute substantially to Gross Domestic Product (GDP). More specifically, it is estimated that in the year 1999, for example, informal economy accounted for 35 percent of Jamaica's GDP, 60 percent of Haiti's, and 10 percent of the GDP of Trinidad and Tobago.

Their impact on the global economy is more complex. On smaller islands, they are single-handedly responsible for the flow of goods that traverse the region, especially to remote areas without big businesses. Because of their import/export activities, they are directly involved in the circulation of the capital integral to globalization.

Historically, the gender of this trade is not solely a cultural phenomenon, but an economic one as well. It is most common among single-income, female-headed households. Women often turn to this profession when unemployment is high and the state fails to provide them with a social welfare net. For most of these participants, independent trading has become another low-income occupation. Women choose trading despite these shortcomings. Compared to other jobs such as free-trade-zone factory work or housekeeping, trading allows women not only to earn an income but to have considerable autonomy over their daily lives. They often emphasize that they choose this particular occupation because they want to be their own boss.

See also Caribbean Community and Common Market (CARICOM); Entrepreneurs and Entrepreneurship; Natural Resources of the Caribbean

Bibliography

Browne, Katharine E. *Creole Economics: Caribbean Cunning under the French Flag.* Austin: University of Texas Press, 2004.

Carnegie, Charles V. "Human Maneuver, Option Building, and Trade: An Essay on Caribbean Social Organization." Ph.D. diss., Johns Hopkins University, Baltimore, Md., 1981.

Freeman, Carla. *High Tech and High Heels in the Global Economy.* Durham, NC: Duke University Press, 2001.

Harrison, Faye V. "The Gendered Politics and Violence of Structural Adjustment: A View from Jamaica." In *Situated Lives: Gender and Culture in Everyday Life,* edited by L. Lamphere, H. Ragone, and P. Zavella. New York: Routledge, 1997.

Gonzalez, Victoria Durant. "Role and Status of Rural Jamaican Women: Higglering and Mothering." Ph.D. diss., University of California, Berkeley, 1976.

Katzin, Margaret. "The Country Higgler." In *Social and Economic Studies* 8 (1959): 421–440.

Mintz, Sidney, and Douglas Hall. *Caribbean Transformations.* New York: Columbia University Press, 1974.

Ulysse, Gina. "Uptown Ladies and Downtown Women: Informal Commercial Importing and the Social/Symbolic Politics of Class and Color in Jamaica." Ph.D. diss., University of Michigan, Ann Arbor, 1999.

GINA ULYSSE (2005)

Women Writers of the Caribbean

In 1831, when Mary Prince published the vivid autobiographical narrative of her experiences as a slave, *The History of Mary Prince, a West Indian Slave,* black women in the Caribbean and Latin America lived in circumstances that precluded their development as writers. The institution of slavery had been abolished in the British Caribbean in 1834, just three years after Prince's narrative—the first ever published by a black woman in England—had become a best seller with three editions in its first year. Slavery remained alive in other countries in the two regions, however, until 1888, the year it was abolished in Brazil.

The end of slavery did not put an end to the enduring power of the plantation system, nor to the social and economic oppression suffered by people of African ancestry. The lack of access to land for cultivation and restricted access to training and educational opportunities meant that as late as the early years of the twentieth century the literacy rates among former slaves in the Caribbean and Latin America remained as high as 97 percent in rural areas. With some salient exceptions, such as that of Mary Prince, most literary writing remained in the hands of the white or light-skinned upper and middle classes until well into the twentieth century. Whereas the publication of *The History of Mary Prince* played a significant role in the fostering of pro-abolition sentiment in Britain, for example, the most salient antislavery literature in the rest of the region was published by whites. *Sab* (1841), the most powerful antislavery novel in Spanish, for example, was written by Gertrudis Gómez de Avellaneda, a white upper-class Cuban woman. In the nineteenth century, for the masses of African-Caribbean women, whose lives were circumscribed by the plantation, a writing career seemed an impossibility.

It is precisely the difficulties inherent in emerging as a writer from the prevailing conditions in the Caribbean and Latin America in the nineteenth century that make the writings of individuals like Mary Prince and Mary Seacole so significant. Prince, the daughter of slaves, was born in Bermuda in 1788. Her life as a slave, which she narrates so lucidly in her autobiography, took her from field hand to the salt mines of Turk Island, where she was taught to read and write by the Moravians. The publication of her book, a remarkable tale of abuse and endurance, was promoted by the Moravians, who saw it as a powerful weapon against the institution of slavery.

Mary Seacole's *The Wonderful Adventures of Mrs. Seacole in Many Lands* (1857) is in many ways a testament to how deeply the abolition of slavery had changed conditions for urban black women in the Caribbean by the mid-nineteenth century. Seacole—born Mary Jane Grant in Jamaica in 1805—had learned nursing from her mother, who kept a boarding house for invalid soldiers in Kingston. After the death of her husband in 1844, Seacole, who had already traveled widely throughout the Caribbean and visited England, moved to Las Cruces, Panama, where she ran an inn and developed her knowledge of herbal medicine, gaining renown through her successful treatment for yellow fever. Nursing became the path to fame for Seacole. After unsuccessfully offering her services during the Crimean War (1853–1856) to Florence Nightingale, who was then assembling a contingent of nurses to follow the British Army to the Crimea, Seacole went to the war front and set up the hotel/hospital for which she became famous. *The Wonderful Adventures of Mrs. Seacole in Many Lands* was written after her return to England at the conclusion of the war. It was purportedly an attempt to reestablish her finances after her losses during the war, but it became a lively vehicle for her claim to recognition as a woman of African descent in the midst of an empire that sought to reduce her to a minor role. The text pits her against Nightingale, and she represents herself as a heroine and claims for herself equal, if not higher, status than Nightingale, since she had done better nursing with surer skills and fewer resources—though she had been turned down by Nightingale for what she hinted were racial objections. She marshaled her fame into a position as masseuse to Alexandra, the Princess of Wales, and was received by Queen Victoria.

Mary Seacole (1805–1881). *A freeborn Jamaican of Creole descent, Seacole applied for various nursing positions in Russia during the Crimean War. After several of her applications were rejected, she used her own funds to open a convalescent hospital for wounded British officers in the region. She later wrote about her experiences in the* Wonderful Adventures of Mrs. Seacole in Many Lands *(1857), a biographical account of her travels that challenged Victorian stereotypes about the proper role of women of color.* COURTESY OF THE NATIONAL LIBRARY OF JAMAICA

The success of Prince and Seacole as writers was built on the autobiographical element in their work. They did not offer their readers the creative work of their imagination, but served as witnesses who claimed the truth of testimony. As such, their work could fit into the nineteenth-century canon not as "literature," but as a "slave narrative" and the "adventures" of a colorful character that readers had come to know through newspaper reports about the Crimean War. They remained the only women of African descent writing in the Caribbean or Latin America in the nineteenth century.

The circumstances that made Prince and Seacole such rarities as writing women in the nineteenth century prevailed through the early decades of the twentieth. During this period, the writer most associated with the representation of African-Caribbean culture, Lydia Cabrera (1899–1999) was not a woman of African descent, but a *mundele* (white woman) of the Cuban upper middle class. Cabrera, a mostly self-trained ethnologist and anthropologist, is still considered a leading authority on Afro-Cuban religion, culture, and healing traditions. Having established long-lasting relationships with the black servants in her parents' house, she used the African folklore she learned from them as the basis for stories she described as "transpositions." Methodologically, she would use African folk tales as the basis of her narratives, recreating and altering elements, and fusing them with European folk narratives and tales derived from Caribbean and Latin American colonial history. Her most famous work of fiction, *Cuentos negros de Cuba* (1940), was followed in 1954 by her seminal ethnographic work, *El Monte,* which remains a basic text for the study of traditional Santería and healing practices in Cuba.

Cabrera's writings were not isolated phenomena, however. They were important texts in an exploration of the African roots of Caribbean cultures, and they would have a profound impact on the development of decolonization movements and on the process of national formation that followed independence in the 1950s and 1960s.

It was from the islands at the forefront of that decolonization movement that the first generation of twentieth-century African-Caribbean women writers emerged. In Jamaica, Una Marson (1905–1965), the Anglophone Caribbean's first major poet and a social activist who was once Haile Selassie's secretary, produced a poetry in which she mixed Calypsonian rhythms and the cadences of local speech in a conscious attempt to create a poetry true to Jamaica's Africa-derived culture. She would go on to conceive and direct the influential BBC Radio show *Caribbean Voices,* which offered a space for the dissemination of Caribbean writing in London. Among the writers for whom *Caribbean Voices* became a crucial vehicle was Jamaica's beloved poet and folklorist Louise Bennett ("Miss Lou," 1919–), an important figure in the development of a Caribbean literature in English that sought to break away from British models to become the conduit for local culture and language. Miss Lou's best-known books of poems, *Jamaica Labrish* (1966) and *Anancy and Miss Lou* (1979), use Jamaican Creole as an affirmation of what she calls "diasporic wisdom."

Francophone writers of Marson's and Bennet's generation, such as Mayotte Capécia (1928–1953), Michèle Lacrosil (1915–), and Jacqueline Manicom (1938–1976) focused instead on voicing the historical plight of the Caribbean mulatto, adrift between the black masses and the longed-for acceptance into the world of whites. The protagonists of their novels—of Capécia's *Je suis martiniquaise* (1948), Lacrosil's *Sapotille et le serin d'argile* (1960), and Manicom's *Mon examen de blanc* (1972)—are mulatto women burdened by a feeling of inferiority in society who thus seek to identify themselves with the whites, to their eventual detriment. Their quest for autonomy and racial identity is meant to mirror the African-Caribbean woman's problems of race, gender, class, and social power. Yet they fail to strike a balance between personal autonomy and acceptance as women of mixed race within their communities.

The most significant African-Caribbean writer of this generation is the Haitian novelist Marie Chauvet (1916–1973), the author of five novels. The two considered her best are *Amour, Colère, et Folie* (1968) and *Fonds-des-nègres* (1960). Chauvet, like her male contemporaries Seymour Pradel and Jacques-Stéphen Alexis, waged a frontal battle against the violence, hunger, and oppression that became the reality of life for most Haitians under the dictatorship of François (Papa Doc) Duvalier and that of his son, Jean-Claude. Her trilogy *Amour, Colère, et Folie* offers a devastating indictment of tyranny and repression in Haiti, seen primarily through the abuse and torture of the female body. Her dissection of the impact on a middle-class Port-au-Prince family of the appropriation of their lands by the Tonton Macoutes (the Duvaliers' dreaded militia) in *Colère* is the most acute and detailed indictment of the complex web of social, historical, and political forces that sustained the Duvaliers' extended dictatorship. Chauvet's blend of eroticism, social realism, and political engagement makes hers a unique voice in Caribbean writing. Her *Fonds-des-nègres* is the most nuanced and compelling literary depiction of the importance of Vodou in Haitian culture and of its powerful hold on the hearts of the Haitian people.

The generation that followed Chauvet's—that of writers born after World War II who began to write in the 1960s and 1970s—was part of a veritable explosion in Caribbean women's writing. During the 1970s, women's voices moved into the mainstream of literary activity in the region after decades of relative silence and neglect. Women of African descent moved for the first time in Caribbean literary history into the center of literary production, bringing racial oppression and African culture into the forefront. In their work, these women writers sought to articulate their gendered position in Caribbean societies through narratives that told of their search for "agency" in their personal and social lives.

The earliest texts by this generation of writers were the five great female bildungsroman (novels of development) of Anglophone Caribbean literary history: Merle Hodges's *Crick Crack Monkey* (1970), Zee Edgell's *Beka Lamb* (1982), Michelle Cliff's *Abeng* (1984), and Jamaica Kincaid's *Annie John* (1986). Hodge, born in Trinidad in 1944, writes in *Crick Crack Monkey* about the plight of a young girl, Tee, who must leave her native rural village, with its African-derived values and culture, to live with her aunt in an unfamiliar city marked by its anglicized culture. Tee's painful trajectory allows Hodges to trace the devastating psychological costs of the imposition of colonial mores and racial categories on a young black girl. The novel has become a classic of West Indian fiction, and it is often compared with Edgell's *Beka Lamb,* with which it shares many thematic elements.

Edgell, born in British Honduras in 1940, sought in *Beka Lamb*—published the year after her country became the newly independent nation of Belize—to trace her country's complex social and racial stratification through her protagonist Beka, a young black girl in a multiethnic country. Edgell's interest in portraying the political dimensions of the struggle to create new nations out of former Caribbean and Latin American colonies through her central characters is echoed by the Jamaican writer Michelle Cliff (1946–) in *Abeng* and her subsequent novels. Cliff's central concern is that of portraying the hybrid nature of identity in former colonies where racial and social categories have led women to problematic allegiances and psychological confusion. In *Abeng,* Cliff traces the need to recover and acknowledge the individual's and the nation's African past. The story is told through the struggles of the protagonist Clare—a young light-skinned girl of the impoverished middle class—to establish her identity as a Jamaican. Cliff, a fierce critic of her country's class hierarchies and dependence on color stratification, uses the form of the bildungsroman to great effect in dissecting the destructive impact of these hierarchies on the developing identities of the young.

These same concerns appear, although in more muted and less overtly political form, in Kincaid's *Annie John.* Kincaid, born in Antigua in 1949, sought in her autobiographical first novel to explore the conflict experienced by Annie when her deep affection for her mother and for her island nation (which had gained its independence in 1981) needed to give way to separation and independence. Through carefully articulated parallels between Annie's mother and British colonialism, Kincaid subtly weaves her depiction of the complexities of growing up female in a colonial environment. Kincaid would move on from *Annie John* to become one of the most widely read of Caribbean writers. She is the author of *Lucy* (1990), *A Small Place* (1988), *The Autobiography of My Mother* (1996), *My Brother* (1997), and *Mr. Potter* (2002).

Closely linked to this generation of authors of bildungsromans are two of Jamaica's most successful writers: Erna Brodber (1940–) and Olive Senior (1941–). Senior, a master storyteller, is the author of three collections of short stories: *Summer Lightning* (1986), *Arrival of the Snake-Woman* (1989), and *Discerner of Hearts* (1995). Her writing—at times autobiographical but always rooted in her experiences as a rural Jamaican—is deeply committed to exploring the Caribbean region's struggles for definition after centuries of colonial rule, which she sees as her duty as a writer. Olive, the daughter of peasant farmers, grew up with affluent relatives whose way of life and mores were quite different from those of her rural childhood. In stories like "Bright Thursdays," where she recounts the travails of a child like herself trying to adapt to the ways and notions of rich town relatives, Senior's talent for characterization and for recreating the cadences of everyday speech shine through. Her stories have been praised for their delicate exploration of the human spirit to face adversity, and for their insightful explorations of relationships across race, class, and gender differences.

Erna Brodber is the author of three novels: *Jane and Louisa Will Soon Come Home* (1980), *Myal* (1988), and *Louisiana* (1994). Her concerns as a writer were influenced by her growing up in a family of committed community activists and by contact with the Black Power and women's liberation movements while studying in the United States. A social scientist by training, her first novels were conceived as test cases to help her students understand the dangers of losing touch with community values and one's native culture. Brodber is, above all, interested in showing how characters who have strayed from their culture and community, like light-skinned Ella in *Myal,* can be healed through the combined efforts of a diverse but unified community.

While women writers in the Anglophone Caribbean have occupied center stage since the 1980s, writers from the Francophone Caribbean have struggled for a readership and international recognition, remaining in the periphery of a literature dominated by Edouard Glissant and later the members of the Creolité movement—Patrick Chamoiseau and Raphaël Confiant among them. The two names most immediately recognized are those of Maryse Condé (Guadeloupe, 1934–) and Simone Schwarz-Bart (Guadeloupe, 1938–).

Condé is a prolific and widely translated author whose novels have addressed a variety of topics, from Africa's epic past in her historical novel *Sègou* (1984–1985), through the history of witchcraft in the United States (*Moi, Tituba, sorciére noire de Salem,* 1986), to a rewriting of Emily Brontë's *Wuthering Heights* (*La migration des coeurs,* 1995). Her first novel, *Hérémakhonon,* the story of a young woman seeking her roots in Africa, appeared in 1976. Its exploration of the confrontation between a naive young woman from the diaspora seeking her identity in Africa only to come to terms with political corruption and profound disillusionment is reprised in *Une saison à Rihata* (1981). Condé's central concern as a writer is that of exploring the historical and mythical links between Africa and the nations of the diaspora through the prism of a painful history of European imperialism and the shadow of contemporary Africa as a continent of troubled and often corrupt nations.

Simone Schwarz-Bart is the author of four novels, among them *Un plat de porc aux bananes vertes* (with her husband André Schwarz-Bart, 1967), *Ti Jean l'horizon* (1979), and *Pluie et vent sur Telumée miracle* (1979). A writer concerned with the many diasporas of the twentieth century, she was encouraged to write by her husband, the author of *Le dernier des justes* (1959), which charts the history of a Jewish family since the year 1000. Together they produced *Un plat de porc aux bananes vertes* (1967), which tells the story of Mariotte, a Martiniquan woman whose search for her own identity and her alienation from French society is told from her confinement in an asylum

Maryse Condé. Born in Guadeloupe in 1934, Condé is the author of novels, historical fiction, plays, and other works generally centering on the relationship between the individual and society, particularly in the societies of Guadeloupe, other Caribbean lands, and equatorial Africa. PHOTOGRAPH BY JERRY BAUER. © JERRY BAUER. REPRODUCED BY PERMISSION.

for the aging. The novel was meant as the first of a cycle of seven novels covering the period between slavery and the present in the Antilles. Their second collaboration produced *La mulâtresse solitude* (1972). Simone Schwarz-Bart's first solo contribution to this project, *Pluie et vent sur Telumée miracle* (1972), the moving story of a young woman brought to the edge of madness by alienation and heartbreak—and of her healing through the African-derived practices and rituals of her grandmother—was praised by readers and critics for its lyrical examination of a woman's struggle to come to terms with herself and her island, as well as for the insightful rendering of the history of the Caribbean in the twentieth century through the eyes of a peasant woman. Her fourth novel, *Ti Jean l'horizon* (1979) fuses magical realism and folk myth to tell the story of a legendary Guadeloupean folk hero.

Whereas women of African descent have been able to maintain central positions in the literary histories of the Anglophone and Francophone Caribbean, the same cannot be said about writing in the Spanish-speaking Antilles, where literature by women continues to develop primarily among white or light-skinned women like Rosario Ferré, Magali García Ramis, Daína Chaviano, Zoé Valdés, and Angela Hernández. Ironically, the Cuban Revolution, despite its efforts to give a voice to the formerly oppressed masses of former cane workers, has produced only one Afro-Cuban writer of note, Nancy Morejón.

Morejón, Cuba's best known and most widely translated contemporary poet, was born in 1944. She was the first Afro-Cuban to graduate from the University of Havana. Her work—which is collected in *Mirar adentro* (2000)—addresses topics such as Cuba's Afro-Cuban identity, folklore and ethnicity, history, gender and race, and sociopolitical issues. Her poems, beginning with her most famous and most-often anthologized, "Mujer negra," incorporate the rhythm and language of Afro-Cuban speech and music while insisting that blackness is an integral part of the broader Cuban literary tradition. Working within the Afro-Antillean tradition established by Nicolás Guillén, her poems celebrate the hybrid nature of Cuban culture and explore its connections to the broader Caribbean and Latin American cultures. Critics have noted her use of humor as a vehicle for the presentation of subtle and nuanced critiques of the history of imperialism in the Caribbean, indictments of slavery and its impact on social development in the region, and the inhumane treatment of the oppressed. Her books include *Piedra pulida* (1986), *Elogio y paisaje* (1997), and *La Quinta de los Molinos* (2000).

In Puerto Rico, Ana Lydia Vega's often hilarious short stories—collected in *Encancaranublado y otros cuentos de naufragio* (1992) and *Pasión de historia y otras historias de pasión* (1987)—set the tone for Puerto Rican feminist literature in the 1980s. Vega addresses questions of race as part of her efforts at voicing the concerns of the poor and oppressed classes with which she identifies. Her stories depicting the plight of Haitians as a despised black group among lighter-skinned mulatto Antilleans are among the best of her work. The one writer to make African-Caribbean culture the very center of her work, however, has been Mayra Montero, who was born in Cuba to a white family and has been a resident of Puerto Rico most of her life. Her work bears mentioning here because of her commitment to laying bare the Haitian people's struggle against repression and poverty. This commitment was already evident in her first novel, *La trenza de la hermosa luna* (1987), a beautifully rendered tale of an exile's return to Haiti after twenty years as a wandering sailor, including the transformation that leads him from disillusionment to passionate commitment to action against the Duvalier regime. In *Del rojo de tu sombra* (1992), Montero unveils the vicious and corrupt politics and African-derived religious traditions that link the Dominican Republic and Haiti, despite the enmity that has existed between the countries for centuries. In *Tú, la oscuridad* (1995) she uncovers a new and haunting postcolonial space built upon the conflict between a scientific and an animistic worldview. This space is marked by the extinction of species due to a collapsing environment; the troubled landscape of Haiti, peopled with zombies and other frightening, other-worldly creatures; and political corruption, violence, and religious turmoil.

Of the new generation of Puerto Rican writers that followed in the wake of Rosario Ferré, Magali García Ramis, and Ana Lydia Vega, Mayra Santos-Febres (1966–), a Puerto Rican of African descent, is the most accomplished. Known as a poet—she has published a number of poetry books, including *El orden escapado* (1991), *Anamú y manigua* (1991), and *Tercer mundo* (2000)—she emerged in the first years of the twenty-first century as a gifted prose writer. The texts of Santos-Febres's short stories, collected in *Pez de vidrio* and *El cuerpo correcto,* are erotic urban vignettes about desire and its frustration as they play themselves out in contemporary Puerto Rico. Her novel *Sirena Selena vestida de pena* (2000), the story of a gay teenage boy earning a living on the streets, and of the transvestite who recognizes the crystalline sweetness of his singing voice and helps him become a famous *travestí* in the Dominican Republic, is one of the best narratives to come out of the Caribbean in many years. Santos-Febres represents the bright future of Africa Caribbean women's writing.

See also Bennett, Louise; Brodber, Erna; Condé, Maryse; Danticat, Edwidge; Kincaid, Jamaica; Literature of Haiti; Literature of the English-Speaking Caribbean; Marson, Una; Morejón, Nancy; Prince, Mary; Santos-Febres, Mayra; Seacole, Mary; Wynter, Sylvia

Bibliography

Bloom, Harold. *Caribbean Women Writers*. Philadelphia, Pa.: Chelsea House, 1997.

Dayan, Joan. "Reading Women in the Caribbean: Marie Chauvet's Love, Anger, and Madness." In *Displacements: Women, Tradition, Literatures in French,* edited by Joan DeJean and Nancy K. Miller. Baltimore, Md.: Johns Hopkins University Press, 1991.

Dayan, Joan. "Erzulie: A Women's History of Haiti." *Research in African Literatures* 25, no. 2 (1994): 5–31.

Ferly, Odile. "The Fanonian Theory of Violence in Women's Fiction from the Caribbean." In *Convergences and Interferences: Newness in Intercultural Practices/Ecritures d'une nouvelle ère/aire*, edited by Kathleen Gyssels, Isabel Hoving, and Maggie Ann Bowers. Amsterdam: Rodopi, 2001.

Garvey, Johanna X. K. "Complicating Categories: 'Race' and Sexuality in Caribbean Women's Fiction." *Journal of Commonwealth and Postcolonial Studies* 10, no. 1 (2003): 94–120.

Harris, Christine. "Caribbean Women Poets-Disarming Tradition." *Miscelánea* 22 (2000): 45–60.

Hoving, Isabel. *Caribbean Migrant Women Writers*. Stanford, Calif.: Stanford University Press, 2001.

Ippolito, Emilia. *Caribbean Women Writers: Identity and Gender*. Rochester, N.Y.: Camden House, 2000.

Kemedjio, Cilas. "Founding-Ancestors and Intertextuality in Francophone Caribbean Literature and Criticism." *Research in African Literatures* 33, no. 2 (2002): 210–29.

Mudimbe-Boyi, Elisabeth. "Breaking Silence and Borders: Women Writers from Francophone and Anglophone Africa and the Caribbean." *Callaloo* 16, no. 1 (1993): 75–76.

O'Callaghan, Evelyn. *Woman Version: Theoretical Approaches to West Indian Fiction by Women*. New York: St. Martin's Press, 1993.

Paravisini-Gebert, Lizabeth. "Decolonizing Feminism: The Home-Grown Roots of Caribbean Women's Movements." In *Daughters of Caliban: Caribbean Women in the Twentieth Century,* edited by Consuelo López Springfield. Bloomington: Indiana University Press, 1997.

Paravisini-Gebert, Lizabeth. "Women against the Grain: The Pitfalls of Theorizing Caribbean Women's Writing." In *Winds of Change: The Transforming Voices of Caribbean Women Writers and Scholars,* edited by Adele Newson and Linda Strong-Leek. New York: Peter Lang, 1998.

Wisker, Gina. *Post-Colonial and African American Women's Writing: A Critical Introduction*. New York: St. Martin's Press, 2000.

LIZABETH PARAVISINI-GEBERT (2005)

Wonder, Stevie (Morris, Stevland)

May 13, 1950

Born Stevland Morris on May 13, 1950, in Saginaw, Michigan, singer and songwriter Stevie Wonder has been blind since birth. He grew up in Detroit and by the age of nine had mastered the harmonica, drums, bongos, and piano. His early influences included rhythm-and-blues artists B. B. King and Ray Charles. Once his youthful talent as a musician and composer was discerned, Berry Gordy signed him to Hitsville, U.S.A. (later known as Motown) in 1961. He was soon dubbed "Little Stevie Wonder" and in 1963 achieved the first of many number one pop singles with "Fingertips—Pt. 2," a live recording featuring blues-flavored harmonica solos. The album of the same year, *Twelve-Year-Old Genius,* was Motown's first number one pop album. From 1964 to 1971 Wonder had several top twenty hits, including "Uptight (Everything's Alright)" (1966), "Mon Cherie Amour" (1969), and "Signed, Sealed, Delivered I'm Yours" (1970), cowritten with Syreeta Wright, to whom he was married for eighteen months.

In 1971 at the age of twenty-one, Wonder obtained a release from his Motown contract that allowed him to break free of the strict Motown production sound. With his substantial earnings he employed the latest electronic technology, the ARP and Moog synthesizers, to record original material for future use, playing most of the instruments himself. That same year he negotiated a new contract with Motown for complete artistic control over his career and production. The album *Music in My Mind* that followed was the first fruit of his new artistic freedom. In 1975 he renegotiated with Motown for an unprecedented $13 million advance for a seven-year contract.

Wonder's humanitarian interests have charged his music since the early 1970s. His material has consistently reflected an effort to incorporate contemporary musical trends (reggae and rap) and social commentary that has given a voice to the evolution of American black consciousness. This is demonstrated in "Living for the City" (1973), a ghetto-dweller's narrative; "Happy Birthday" (1980), the anthem for a nationwide appeal to honor Rev. Dr. Martin Luther King Jr.'s birthday as a national holiday; "Don't Drive Drunk" (1984); and "It's Wrong," (1985), a critique of South African apartheid. He also supported such causes as the elimination of world hunger (U.S.A. for Africa's recording "We Are the World"), AIDS research ("That's What Friends Are For" with singer Dionne Warwick and friends, 1987), and cancer research.

Wonder's popularity has been strengthened by his scores for various films, including *The Woman in Red* (1984), which won an Oscar for Best Original Song ("I Just Called to Say I Love You") and *Jungle Fever* (1991), a film about interracial relationships by Spike Lee. Wonder has been the recipient of more than eighteen Grammys, eighteen gold records, five platinum records, and five gold albums. He was inducted into the Songwriters Hall of Fame in 1982. In 1996 he won a Lifetime Achievement Award and two Grammies for his album *Conversation Peace.* In 2004 he received the Johnny Mercer Award from the National Academy of Popular Music/Songwriters Hall of Fame, he released the album *Time 2 Love,* and he won the Century Award at the *Billboard* Music Awards.

See also Rhythm and Blues

Bibliography

Hardy, Phil, and Dave Laing. *The Faber Companion to Twentieth-Century Popular Music.* London: Faber, 1990.

Horn, Martin E. *Stevie Wonder: Career of a Rock Legend.* New York: Barclay House, 1999.

"Stevie Wonder." *Current Biography.* New York: H. W. Wilson, 1975.

KYRA D. GAUNT (1996)
Updated by publisher 2005

WOODFORD SQUARE

Woodford Square, previously known as Brunswick Square, is the enclosed space that opens up across the street from the Red House, the edifice housing the government of Trinidad and Tobago. It was named after Sir Ralph Woodford, who was governor of the colony between 1813 and 1826. The square has been used by many anticolonialists to mount campaigns against the colonial establishment. Many of the country's protest leaders first hoisted their banners in Woodford Square, including Tubal Uriah "Buzz" Butler, the labor leader who in the 1930s became known as the King of Woodford Square.

A NEW KING OF WOODFORD SQUARE

In 1955, Dr. Eric Williams became the new King of Woodford Square. He was a radical, anticolonial Trinidadian scholar and the author of *Capitalism and Slavery,* the classic study of emancipation in the Anglophone Caribbean. Williams was employed by the Anglo-American Caribbean Commission, an organization sponsored and supported by the British, French, American, and Dutch governments, all of whom had colonies in the region. Williams's writings and public speeches did not sit well with the plantation elites in the region, or with the expatriate officials of the commission, who resented his radical anticolonial analyses of what colonialism meant for the peoples of the region. They were equally unhappy with his arguments about the need to West Indianize the school curriculum and the public services, and with his views on restructuring Caribbean economies to make them less mercantilist and less linked to the industrial production of Europe in general and Britain in particular—views he developed in his groundbreaking 1942 book *The Negro in the Caribbean.*

Williams's contract with the commission was not renewed when it expired in June 1955. He was instead offered a one-year extension, which meant that he was either on probation or being provoked into resignation. Williams assumed the latter and resigned, turning his energies toward politics. He had anticipated the commission's action and written to Norman Manley, the premier of Jamaica, five months earlier, telling him that "there is no doubt that throwing my hat in the ring will be a sensation. . . . Elections are to be postponed until September 1956; this will give me more time. . . . I am immersed in a vast adult education programme . . . [and] this will keep my name before the public."

Following his dismissal, Williams took his case to the people of Trinidad and Tobago in Woodford Square, delivering a speech to an audience of 10,000 that effectively launched his political career.

Addressing the question of why, if he believed the commission was an imperialist agency, he had sought to become its secretary general, he explained:

> I tolerated those conditions for over twelve years [because] I represented . . . the cause of the West Indian people. I also had more personal reasons. My connection with the Commission brought me into close contact with present problems in the territories, the study of whose history has been the principal purpose of my adult life, while my association with representatives of the metropolitan governments enabled me to understand, as I could not otherwise have understood, the mess in which the West Indies find themselves today.

Williams went on to say:

> I was born here, and I stay with the people of Trinidad and Tobago, who educated me free of charge for nine years at Queen's Royal College and for five years at Oxford, who have made me whatever I am, and who have been the victims of the very pressures which I have been fighting against for twelve years. . . . I am going to let down my bucket where I am, right here with you in the British West Indies. (*My Relations With the Caribbean Commission*)

The speech was a brilliant apologia. He had cast himself in the role of the providential messiah who had been preparing himself in the wilderness of the commission so that he might with greater effectiveness set his people free.

Educating a Generation

Following his dismissal from the commission and his resignation from Howard University, where he held the post of associate professor (from which he was on leave), Williams delivered more than a hundred lectures in Woodford Square and at other venues in the towns of San Fernando, Couva, Tunapuna, Point Fortin, Sangre Grande, Fyzabad, and Arima. The lectures dealt with a wide range of burning public issues, including the Federation of the West Indies, the need for party politics, and constitutional reform. In these lectures, Williams never patronized his audiences or simplified his presentations for the benefit of the least educated. If anything, his lectures were pitched at too high a level. Williams, however, believed that his historic mission was to raise the level of public education and bring university-type education to the public square, where it properly belonged. As he told the cheering crowd:

> The age of exclusiveness in university education is gone forever, though our West Indian University College perversely refuses to recognize this. Somebody once said that all that was needed for a university was a book and the branch of a tree; someone else went further and said that a university should be a university in overalls. With a bandstand, a microphone, a large audience in slacks and hot shirts, a topical subject for discussion, the open air and a beautiful tropical night, we have all the essentials of a university. Now that I have resigned my position at Howard University in the U.S.A., the only university in which I shall lecture in future is the University of Woodford Square and its several branches throughout the length and breadth of Trinidad and Tobago.

The University of Woodford Square

From 1955 to 1965, Williams made the people's political education the main plank in his political platform. As he said in his *History of the People of Trinidad and Tobago*:

> The PNM [People's National Movement] organised what has now become famous in many parts of the world, the University of Woodford Square with constituent colleges in most of the principal centers of population in the country. The political education dispensed to the population in those centers of political learning was of a high order and concentrated from the outset on placing Trinidad and Tobago within the current of the great international movements for democracy and self-government (1964, p. 243).

The "University of Woodford Square," the cradle of Trinidad nationalism, was closed in 1970 in the wake of the black power revolution to prevent it from being used by radical Black Power elements for their protest meetings. Although the King of Woodford Square returned to the lecture podium from time to time after 1970, the students had in effect chased Williams from the professor's chair.

Ironically, Williams had achieved his goal: He had educated a generation, and it had graduated politically, thanks to his tutelage.

See also International Relations of the Anglophone Caribbean; Williams, Eric

Bibliography

Williams, Eric. *Capitalism and Slavery.* Chapel Hill: University of North Carolina Press, 1944.

Williams, Eric. *The Case for Party Politics in Trinidad and Tobago.* Port-of-Spain, Trinidad and Tobago: Teacher's Economic and Cultural Association, Public Affairs Pamphlet, 1955.

Williams, Eric. *Constitutional Reform in Trinidad and Tobago.* Port of Spain, Trinidad and Tobago: Teacher's Economic and Cultural Association, Public Affairs Pamphlet, 1955.

Williams, Eric. *My Relations with the Caribbean Commission,* 1943–1955. Port-of-Spain, Trinidad and Tobago: B.W.I, 1955.

Williams, Eric. *History of the People of Trinidad and Tobago.* London: A. Deutsch, 1964.

SELWYN RYAN (2005)

Woodruff, Hale

August 26, 1900
September 10, 1980

Born in Cairo, Illinois, Hale Aspacio Woodruff, a painter and educator, moved with his mother to Nashville, Tennessee, where he attended public schools. In 1920 he moved to Indianapolis to study at the John Herron Art Institute while working part-time as a political cartoonist for the black newspaper the *Indiana Ledger*. In 1927 he traveled to Europe and lived in France for the next four years. He studied with the African-American painter Henry O. Tanner and at the Académie Scandinave and Académie Moderne in 1927 and 1928. Like other American artists who sought an education in the center of the art world, Woodruff spent his time recapitulating the succession of avant-garde art movements of the previous fifty years. His landscapes and figure paintings first synthesized elements of the late-nineteenth-century styles of impressionism and postimpressionism in their interest in the nonrealistic shifts of color and the manipulation of the texture of the brushstroke. His key work of the period, *The Card Players* (1930; repainted in 1978), plays on the distortions of figure and space found in the work of Paul Cézanne and the cubists Pablo Picasso and Georges Braque. This work emphasizes Woodruff's debt to African art (which had also been a source for the cubists) in the masklike nature of the faces. Woodruff had first encountered African art in Indianapolis in the early 1920s, when he saw one of the first books on the subject. As it was written in German, he could not read it, but he was intrigued by the objects. Woodruff and the African-American philosopher and teacher Dr. Alain Locke visited flea markets in Paris, where the artist bought his first works of African art.

In 1931 Woodruff returned to the United States to found the art department at Atlanta University. Through his pioneering efforts, the national African-American arts community developed the kind of cohesion that previously had been lacking. Woodruff himself taught painting, drawing, and printmaking. To teach sculpture, he recruited the artist Nancy Elizabeth Prophet. The works that came from the department's faculty and students came to be known as the "Atlanta School" because their subjects were the African-American population of that city. Fully representational with modernist nuances, they fall into the style of American regionalism practiced throughout the country at that time. The use of woodcuts and linoleum prints added a populist tone to these works, which dealt with everyday life. Besides teaching, he brought to Atlanta University exhibitions of a wide range of works, including those of historical and contemporary black artists and the Harmon Foundation exhibitions, providing a unique opportunity for the entire black Atlanta community, since the local art museum was then segregated. The year 1942 saw the initiation of the Atlanta University Annuals, a national juried exhibition for black artists that expanded opportunities for many who were frequently excluded from the American art scene. Woodruff's legacy can be seen in the remarkable list of his students—Frederick Flemister, Eugene Grigsby, Wilmer Jennings, and Hayward Oubré—and of the artists who showed in the Annuals, including Charles Alston, Lois Mailou Jones, Elizabeth Catlett, Claude Clark, Ernest Crichlow, Aaron Douglas, William H. Johnson, Norman Lewis, Hughie Lee-Smith, Jacob Lawrence, and Charles White. The exhibitions continued until 1970.

During this same period, Woodruff, as part of his efforts to present a populist art, produced a series of murals. Two of his inspirations were the murals placed in public buildings across the country by WPA artists, and the Mexican mural movement. Woodruff himself received a grant to study with Diego Rivera for six weeks in the summer of 1934, when he assisted in fresco painting. After completing two WPA murals, he painted the major work of this period, the *Amistad Murals* (1938–1939) at Talladega College (Alabama). Designed in the boldly figurative style associated with social realism, the murals depict the mutiny led by Cinqué aboard the slave ship *Amistad* in 1834 and the subsequent trial and repatriation of the Africans. Other mural projects included *The Founding of Talladega College* (1938–1939), murals at the Golden State Mutual Life Insurance Company (Los Angeles) on the contribution of blacks to the development of California (1948), and *The Art of the Negro* for Atlanta University (1950–1951).

In 1946, after receiving a two-year Julius Rosenwald Foundation Fellowship to study in New York (1943–1945), Woodruff moved to that city permanently to teach in the art education department of New York University. The move was not a rejection of the South, but came as an attempt by Woodruff to be part of the new art capital, which had shifted from Paris to New York. Woodruff changed his style from that of a figurative painter of the American scene to a practitioner of the ideas of abstract expressionism. While employing the gestural spontaneity of that style, he incorporated design elements from the African art he had studied since his student days in Indianapolis. Worked into his compositions are motifs from a variety of African cultural objects, including Asante goldweights, Dogon masks, and Yoruba Shango implements—a kind of aesthetic Pan-Africanism. This, the third major style of his career, demonstrates the adaptability of an artist always open to new currents in both the aesthetic and political worlds. He continued to be supportive of African-American artists by being one of the founders in 1963 of Spiral, a group of black New York artists (including Charles Alston, Emma Amos, Romare Bearden, Norman Lewis, and Richard Mayhew) who sought to weave the visual arts into the fabric of the civil rights struggle.

Woodruff received awards from the Harmon Foundation in 1926, 1928 and 1929, 1931, 1933, and 1935, and an Atlanta University Purchase Prize in 1955. He received a Great Teacher Award at NYU in 1966 and became professor emeritus in 1968.

See also Painting and Sculpture; Tanner, Henry Ossawa

Bibliography

Reynolds, Gary, and Beryl J. Wright. "Hale Aspacio Woodruff." In *Against the Odds: African-American Artists and the Harmon Foundation.* Newark, N.J.: The Newark Museum, 1989, pp. 275–279.

Stoelting, Winifred L. "Hale Woodruff, Artist and Teacher: Through the Atlanta Years." Ph.D. diss., Emory University, Atlanta, Ga., 1978.

Studio Museum in Harlem. *Hale Woodruff: 50 Years of His Art.* New York: Author, 1979.

Wilson, Judith. "'Go Back and Retrieve It': Hale Woodruff, Afro-American Modernist." In *Selected Essays: Art and Artists from the Harlem Renaissance to the 1980s.* Atlanta, Ga.: National Black Arts Festival, 1988.

HELEN M. SHANNON (1996)

Woods, Tiger

December 30, 1975

Eldrick "Tiger" Woods is the most acclaimed golfer of African-American ancestry to compete on the Professional Golfers' Association (PGA) tour. His enormous success is attributable to his great talent and personal appeal, especially among young people. Woods's greatest achievement thus far is his 1997 victory in the prestigious Masters Tournament by a record margin of 12 strokes. He was the youngest Masters champion in history.

Born and raised in Cypress, California, Woods became interested in golf at a young age. At two he putted against Bob Hope on the *Mike Douglas Show*. By seventeen he had won three U.S. Junior Amateur Championships (1991–1993). His come-from-behind victory at the 1996 U.S. Amateur Championship capped an impressive amateur career including the NCAA title and three successive U.S. Amateur victories.

Woods turned professional in August 1996, hoping to earn enough money in eight tournaments ($150,000) to qualify for the 1997 PGA Tour. He stunned the golf world by winning the Las Vegas Invitational and the Disney/Oldsmobile Classic, earning $790,594 and finishing twenty-fifth on the money list. He was the PGA Tour's 1996 Rookie of the Year.

Apart from his Masters victory, Woods won another four tournaments in 1997 including the Mercedes Championship, the Asian Honda Classic in Thailand, the GTE Byron Nelson Classic, the Motorola Western Open, and the Masters. He finished 1997 with a record $2,066,833—a PGA Tour record for single season earnings—and was selected 1997 Player of the Year by the PGA Tour, PGA of America, and Golf Writers Association of America. The Associated Press chose Woods as the 1997 Male Athlete of the Year.

Woods's success continued through the rest of the decade and beyond. By the end of the 1990s he had won twenty-four professional tournaments, and his total earnings approached $14 million. In 2000 he won ten tournaments, including the British Open, the U.S. Open, and the

Eldrick "Tiger" Woods. *Woods made history in 1997 as the youngest player and first African American to win the prestigious Masters Tournament.* PHOTOGRAPH BY DIEGO GIUDICE. AP/WIDE WORLD PHOTOS

PGA. In 2001 he won the Masters again, and in 2002 he repeated as Masters and U.S. Open champion. In 2003 he began to cool off a little, with five wins that year but no Grand Slam wins. In 2004 he had only one tournament win, but he seemed to be regaining his form in early 2005 with wins in the Buick Invitational and Ford Championship at Doral.

See also Sports

Bibliography

Owen, David. *The Chosen One: Tiger Woods and the Dilemma of Greatness.* New York: Simon and Schuster, 2001.

JILL LECTKA (1996)
Updated by publisher 2005

Woodson, Carter G.

December 19, 1875
April 3, 1950

The historian and educator Carter Godwin Woodson was born in New Canton, in Buckingham County, Virginia. Woodson probably descended from slaves held by Dr. John Woodson, who migrated from Devonshire, England, to Jamestown, Virginia, in 1619. He was the first and only black American of slave parents to earn a Ph.D. in history. After the Civil War, Woodson's grandfather and father, who were skilled carpenters, were forced into sharecropping. After saving for many years, the family purchased land and eked out a meager living in the late 1870s and 1880s.

Although they were poor, James Henry and Anne Eliza Woodson instilled in their son high morality and strong character through religious teachings, and they also gave him a thirst for education. One of nine children, he was the youngest boy and a frail child. As such, he purportedly was his mother's favorite and was sheltered. He belonged to that first generation of blacks whose mothers did not have to curry favor with whites to provide an education for their children. As a boy, Woodson worked on the family farm, and in his teens he was an agricultural day laborer. In the late 1880s the family moved to West Virginia, where Woodson's father worked in railroad construction and Woodson worked as a coal miner in Fayette County. In 1895, at the age of twenty, Woodson enrolled at Frederick Douglass High School. Perhaps because he was older than the rest of the students and felt that he needed to catch up, he completed four years of course work in two years and graduated in 1897. He then enrolled at Berea College in Berea, Kentucky, which had been founded by abolitionists in the 1850s for the education of ex-slaves. He briefly attended Lincoln University in Pennsylvania, but graduated from Berea College in 1903, just a year before Kentucky would pass the infamous "Day Law," which prohibited interracial education. Woodson then briefly taught at Frederick Douglass High School. Because of his belief in the uplifting power of education, and because of the opportunity to travel to another country to observe and experience its culture firsthand, he decided to accept a teaching post in the Philippines, remaining there from 1903 to 1907.

Experiences as a college student and high school teacher expanded and influenced Woodson's worldview and shaped his ideas about the ways in which education could transform society, improve race relations, and benefit the lower classes. Determined to obtain additional edu-

> *Carter G. Woodson*
>
> "If a race has no history, if it has no worthwhile tradition, it becomes a negligible factor in the thought of the world, and it stands in danger of being exterminated."

cation, he enrolled in correspondence courses at the University of Chicago. By 1907 he was enrolled there as a full-time student, earning both a bachelor's degree and a master's degree in European history. His thesis examined French diplomatic policy toward Germany in the eighteenth century. He then attended Harvard University, matriculating in 1909 and earning his Ph.D. in history in 1912. He studied with Edward Channing, Albert Bushnell Hart, and Frederick Jackson Turner, the latter of whom had moved from the University of Wisconsin to Harvard in 1910. Turner influenced the interpretation Woodson advanced in his dissertation, which was a study of the events leading to secession in West Virginia after the Civil War broke out. Unfortunately, Woodson never published the dissertation.

Woodson taught in the Washington, D.C., public schools, at Howard University, and at West Virginia Collegiate Institute. In 1915, in Chicago, he founded the Association for the Study of Negro Life and History (now the Association for the Study of African American Life and History), and began the work that sustained him for the rest of his career. Indeed, his life was given over to the pursuit of truth about the African and African-American pasts. He later founded the *Journal of Negro History* (now the *Journal of African American History*), the *Negro History Bulletin* (now the *Black History Bulletin*), and the *Associated Publishers.* In addition, he launched the annual celebration of Negro History Week in February 1926, and he had a distinguished publishing career as a scholar of African-American history.

After the publication in 1915 of *The Education of the Negro Prior to 1861,* his first book, Woodson began a scholarly career that, even if judged by output alone, very few of his contemporaries or successors could match. By 1947, when the ninth edition of his textbook *The Negro in Our History* appeared, Woodson had published four monographs, five textbooks, five edited collections of source materials, and thirteen articles, as well as five sociological studies that were collaborative efforts. With his writings covering a wide array of subjects, Woodson's scholarly productivity and range were equally broad. He was among the first scholars to study slavery from the slaves' point of view, and to give attention to the comparative study of slavery as an institution in the United States and in Latin America. His work prefigured the interpretations of contemporary scholars of slavery by several decades. Woodson also noted in his work the African cultural influences on African-American culture.

One of the major objectives of his own research and the research program he sponsored through the Association for the Study of Negro Life and History was to correct the racism promoted in works published by white scholars. Woodson and his assistants pioneered in writing the social history of black Americans, and they used new sources and methods. They moved away from interpreting blacks solely as victims of white oppression and racism. Instead, blacks were viewed as major actors in American history. In recognition of his achievements, the National Association for the Advancement of Colored People (NAACP) presented Woodson with its highest honor, the prestigious Spingarn Medal, in June 1926. In the award ceremony, John Haynes Holmes (1879–1964), the minister and interracial activist, cited Woodson's tireless labors to promote the truth "about Negro life and history."

Woodson suffered a heart attack and died in his sleep on April 3, 1950, in his Washington, D.C., home. He had dedicated his life to the exploration and study of the African-American past. In view of the enormous difficulties he faced battling white racism and in convincing whites and blacks alike that his cause was credible and worthy of support, the achievement of so much seminal work in black history seems almost miraculous. Through his own scholarship and the programs he launched, Woodson made an immeasurable contribution to the advancement of black history.

See also Associated Publishers; Association for the Study of African American Life and History; Black History Month/Negro History Week; *Journal of African American History, The*; Lincoln University; Spingarn Medal

Bibliography

Conyers, James L., Jr. *Carter G. Woodson: A Historical Reader.* New York: Garland, 1999.

Goggin, Jacqueline. *A Life in Black History*. Baton Rouge: Louisiana State University Press, 1993.

Meier, August, and Elliott Rudwick. *Black History and the Historical Profession.* Urbana: University of Illinois Press, 1986.

JACQUELINE GOGGIN (1996)
Updated bibliography

Woolridge, Anna Marie

See Lincoln, Abbey

Work, Monroe Nathan

August 15, 1866
May 2, 1945

Soon after the birth of Monroe Work, a sociologist, in rural Tredell County, North Carolina, Work's parents joined many other former slaves migrating westward and acquired a farm under the provisions of the Homestead Act. Remaining to help his aging parents, Work began secondary school when he was twenty-three. In 1903 he received his master of arts degree in sociology from the University of Chicago and accepted a teaching job at Georgia State Industrial College in Savannah, Georgia, where he met and married Florence E. Henderson.

Appalled by the plight of the city's African Americans, in 1905 he took two actions to improve conditions. He attended the conference called by W. E. B. Du Bois that established the Niagara Movement and founded the Savannah Men's Sunday Club, which combined protest, lobbying, and petitioning with the functions of a lyceum and civic club. By means of a streetcar boycott, the group attempted, but finally failed, to prevent the enactment of the city's first segregation law in 1906.

In 1908 Booker T. Washington offered Work a position at Tuskegee Institute in Macon County, Alabama. After his alliance with Du Bois, Work seemed an unlikely candidate to accept a job from Washington—the nemesis of the Niagara Movement. By 1908, however, Work was disillusioned with the power of protest and the Niagara Movement was floundering. Work reassessed his talents. Dignified instead of dynamic, he was a quiet scholar and researcher rather than a leader. Believing prejudice was rooted in ignorance, Work had long been compiling "exact knowledge concerning the Negro." The resources and audience available at Tuskegee for his research proved irresistible.

Work utilized his Department of Records and Research to compile a daily record of the African-American experience from newspaper clippings, pamphlets, reports, and replies to letters of inquiry. In 1912 he began publishing the *Negro Yearbook* and the yearly *Tuskegee Lynching Report* to enlighten black and white newspaper editors, educators, and leaders, especially in the South. In 1927 Work published *A Bibliography of the Negro in Africa and America,* the first extensive, classified bibliography of its kind. In addition, he was one of the participants invited to the conference held at Howard University on November 7, 1931, to plan the proposed (but never completed) *Encyclopedia of the Negro.*

Work also remained an activist after leaving the Niagara Movement for Tuskegee. He worked to improve black health conditions, to eradicate lynching, and to improve race relations. A pivotal figure in the establishment of National Negro Health Week in 1914, he subsequently organized it for seventeen years. He also participated in the southern antilynching movement of the Atlanta-based Commission on Interracial Cooperation and the Association of Southern Women for the Prevention of Lynching. From those contacts he became involved in other interracial groups.

By the time of his death, Work had published over seventy articles and pamphlets, including pioneering studies of Africa's contributions to and its impact on African-American culture. In 1900 he was the first African American to publish an article in the *American Journal of Sociology,* and in 1929 he presented a paper at the annual meeting of the American Historical Association.

See also Niagara Movement; Sociology; Tuskegee University

Bibliography

Guzman, Jessie P. "Monroe Nathan Work and His Contributions." *Journal of Negro History* 34 (1949): 428–461.

McMurry, Linda O. "A Black Intellectual in the New South: Monroe Nathan Work." *Phylon* 41 (1980): 333–344.

McMurry, Linda O. *Recorder of the Black Experience: A Biography of Monroe Nathan Work.* Baton Rouge: Louisiana State University Press, 1985.

LINDA O. MCMURRY (1996)

Work Projects Administration

See Great Depression and the New Deal

World War I

See Military Experience, African-American

World War II

See Military Experience, African-American

Wright, Richard

September 4, 1908
November 28, 1960

The writer Richard Wright was born near Roxie, Mississippi, the son of a sharecropper and a rural schoolteacher who supported the family when her husband deserted her. Wright's childhood, which he later described in his classic autobiography, *Black Boy* (1945), was horrific. His mother, Ella Wilson Wright, was never healthy, and she had become completely paralyzed by the time her son was ten. Wright and his family were destitute, and their lives were sharply constricted by pervasive segregation and racism. Wright and his brother Leon moved several times to the homes of relatives in Natchez and in Memphis, Tennessee, and then to their grandmother's house in Jackson. A staunch Seventh-Day Adventist, Wright's grandmother discouraged his reading, destroyed a radio he had built, and unwittingly alienated him from religious practice. Wright had already had his first story published in a local newspaper, however, by the time he completed the ninth grade, in 1925. He found employment in Memphis, where he discovered the work of H. L. Mencken. Mencken's essays spurred Wright's writing ambitions. Determined to escape the segregated South, which had plagued his childhood, Wright moved to Chicago in 1927.

Marxism

Over the next several years, during the worst of the Depression, Wright supported himself and his family, which had joined him in Chicago, through menial labor and through work at the post office, and he wrote when he could find the time. He became acquainted with contemporary literature through Mencken's essays and through friends at the post office, and in 1932 he began meeting writers and artists, mostly white, at the communist-run John Reed Club. Impressed by Marxist theory, Wright became a leader of the Chicago club and published revolutionary verse in *New Masses* and in small magazines like *Anvil, Left Front* (whose editorial board he joined), and *Partisan Review.* Recruited by communists eager to showcase African Americans in their movement, Wright became active in the party as much for literary reasons as for political ones. He wished, he later explained, to describe the real feelings of the common people and serve as the bridge between them and party theorists. Wright participated in party literary conferences, wrote poetry and stories, and gave lectures. Wright's first novel, *Lawd Today,* written during this period, was published posthumously, in 1963. In 1935, the same year he started as a journalist for *New Masses,* Wright joined the Federal Writers Project of the Works Progress Administration (WPA), helping write a guide to Illinois; he was transferred to the local Negro Theater unit of the Federal Theater Project the next year. By this time, Wright was having doubts about the Communist Party, which he believed was promoting him only because of his skin color. He insisted on freedom from the party line for his creative work, but he remained publicly committed to the party. In 1937, eager to find a publisher for his work, Wright moved to New York, where he worked as Harlem reporter for the Communist Party newspaper the *Daily Worker* and wrote the Harlem section of the WPA's *New York City Guide* (1939).

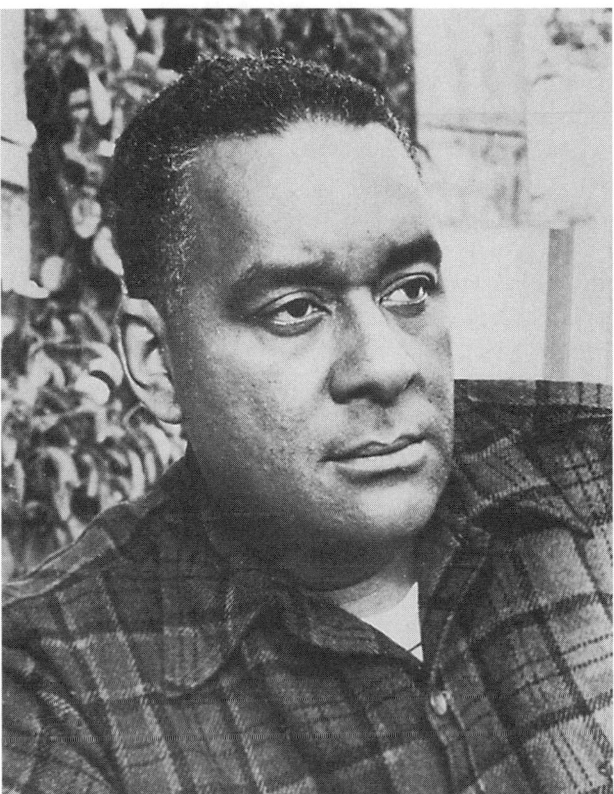

Richard Wright (1908–1960). GETTY IMAGES

In the autumn 1937 issue of the leftist magazine *Challenge,* Wright wrote his influential "Blueprint for Negro Writing," in which, within a larger Marxist perspective, he asserted and tried to encourage black nationalism among writers. Wright called on black writers to make use of folklore and oral tradition in their work, but also to pay attention to psychological and sociological data in framing their work. Wright's own short stories, whose unsparing treatment of racism and violence in the South was couched in poetic style, were winning competitions in *Story* magazine and elsewhere, and were collected under the title *Uncle Tom's Children* (1938). Although the work was a success, Wright was dissatisfied. He thought that while he had generated sympathy for victims of racism, he had not shown its effects on all of society.

Native Son (1940), Wright's first published novel, became a Book-of-the-Month Club selection and called national attention to his compelling talent, although his unrelenting depiction of racism aroused controversy. In fact, editors had already toned down some controversial material (it was not until 1992 that the unexpurgated version of the novel was published). *Native Son* is the story of a ghetto youngster, Bigger Thomas. Trapped by white racism and his own fear, Bigger accidentally murders a white woman. He tries to cover up his deed but is arrested, put on trial, and sentenced to death. Bigger's white communist lawyer argues that he is not responsible for his crimes, but Bigger feels that the murder and cover-up were his first creative acts, through which he has found a new freedom. The book's success won Wright the National Association for the Advancement of Colored People (NAACP)'s prestigious Spingarn Medal in 1941, and a dramatization by Wright and Paul Green was produced by Orson Welles. It was adapted for film twice, once as a Brazilian film, *Sangre Negra* (1950), in which Wright himself played the part of Bigger Thomas, and as *Native Son* (1986), starring Victor Love, but neither was commercially successful.

In 1941 Wright wrote a lyrical Marxist "folk history" of African Americans, *Twelve Million Black Voices.* The following year, he finally left the Communist Party. Although still a Marxist, Wright felt that the communists were unrealistic, self-serving, and not truly interested in the liberation of African Americans. During the war years, Wright worked on *Black Boy* (1945), "a record of childhood and youth," which brought him money and international fame. In *Black Boy,* Wright gives a precise, unrelenting account of how he was scarred by the poisons of poverty and racism during his early years in Mississippi. *American Hunger* (1977), a version that included Wright's Chicago years, was published posthumously.

The same year *Black Boy* appeared, Wright wrote an introduction to *Black Metropolis,* the sociological study by St. Clair Drake and Horace Cayton of African Americans in Chicago, in which Wright first expounded his major political theories. White American racism, Wright argued, was a symptom of a deeper general insecurity brought about by the dehumanizing forces of modernity and industrialization. He considered the condition of African Americans a model, and an extreme example, of the alienation of the human individual by modern life.

Exile in France

Wright was invited to France by the French government in 1945, and during the trip he found himself lionized by French intellectuals as a spokesperson for his race. Wright had married a white woman, Ellen Poplar, in 1941, and the couple had a daughter, Julia. They wished to escape America's racial discrimination. He was delighted by France's apparent freedom from racial prejudice and impressed by the central role that literature and thought enjoyed in French society. Wright decided to "choose exile," and moved to Paris permanently in 1947, although he kept his American passport.

While in France, Wright became friendly with the French existentialists, although he claimed that reading Dostoyevsky had made him an existentialist long before he met Jean-Paul Sartre and the others. Wright's thesis novel, *The Outsider* (1953), explores the contemporary condition in existentialist terms, rejecting the ideologies of communism and fascism. A posthumously published novella Wright wrote during the period, *The Man Who Lived Underground* (1971), also makes use of existential ideas. Neither *The Outsider* nor Wright's next novel, *Savage Holiday* (1954), was well received.

Wright shared the French intellectuals' suspicion of America and participated with Sartre and the existentialists in political meetings in 1948 with the idea of producing a "third way" to preserve European culture from the Cold War struggle between American industrial society and Soviet communism. Ironically, Wright was harassed for his leftist background in America, despite his repudiation of communism. The Communist Party's hostility to Wright grew after he published his essay "I Tried to Be a Communist" in the important anticommunist anthology *The God That Failed* (1950).

Wright had been an original sponsor of the review *Présence Africaine* in 1946, and he turned his primary attention to anticolonial questions during the 1950s. After visiting Africa's Gold Coast in 1954, he wrote *Black Power* (1954), "a record of reactions in a land of pathos," in which he approved of Kwame Nkrumah's Pan-Africanist policies but stressed his own estrangement from Africa. Wright's introduction to George Padmore's *Pan-*

Africanism or Communism? (1956) further disclosed his Pan-African ideas. In *The Color Curtain* (1956) he reported on the First Conference of Non-Aligned Countries held in Bandung, Indonesia, in 1955, and explored the importance of race and religion in the world of politics. The same year, he helped organize, under *Présence Africaine*'s auspices, the First Conference of Black Writers and Intellectuals. Papers from the conference, along with texts from the numerous lectures on decolonization Wright gave in Europe, were published as *White Man, Listen!* in 1959.

Final Works

Wright's last works include *Pagan Spain* (1958), a report on Franco's Spain, which included a discussion of the Catholic impact on European culture; *The Long Dream* (1959), the first novel of an unfinished trilogy dealing with the lasting effects of racism; *Eight Men* (1960), a collection of short stories; and thousands of unpublished haiku. Wright died unexpectedly in 1960 in Paris of a heart attack. He was under emotional and mental stress at the time, partly due to spying by U.S. intelligence agents on African Americans in Paris. His sudden death fostered lasting rumors that he had been poisoned by the Central Intelligence Agency (CIA) because of his persistent fight against racial oppression and colonialism.

Wright was the first African-American novelist of international stature, and his violent denunciation of American racism and the deprivation and hatred it causes was uncompromising. Wright inspired both African-American novelists such as Ralph Ellison and Chester Himes, and foreign writers such as the novelists Peter Abrahams and George Lanning and the political theorist Frantz Fanon. Wright's legendary generosity to other writers was both moral and sometimes financial, through the grants and jobs he found them. Wright also created for himself a role as expatriate writer and international social critic. His intellectual interests and earnestness, through which he melded Freudian, Marxist, and Pan-African perspectives, were matched by a deep spirituality—despite his rationalist suspicion of religion—and occasional humor and comedy in his works.

See also Communist Party of the United States; Fanon, Frantz; Literature of the United States; Padmore, George; Spingarn Medal

Bibliography

Cruse, Harold. *The Crisis of the Negro Intellectual.* New York: Morrow, 1967.

Fabre, Michel. *The Unfinished Quest of Richard Wright.* Translated by Isabel Barzun. New York: Morrow, 1973.

Fabre, Michel. *From Harlem to Paris: Black American Writers in France, 1840–1980.* Urbana: University of Illinois Press, 1991.

Gayle, Addison. *Richard Wright: The Ordeal of a Native Son.* New York: Doubleday, 1980.

Rowley, Hazel. *Richard Wright: The Life and Times.* New York: Henry Holt, 2001.

Walker, Margaret. *Richard Wright, Daemonic Genius: A Portrait of the Man, a Critical Look at his Work.* New York: Warner, 1988.

Webb, Constance. *Richard Wright: A Biography.* New York: Putnam, 1968.

MICHEL FABRE (1996)
Updated bibliography

Wright, Theodore Sedgwick

1797
March 25, 1847

Theodore Wright, a Presbyterian clergyman and abolitionist, was born in New Jersey, the son of Richard P. G. Wright, who was prominent in the early anticolonization protests and the antislavery movement. Theodore received instruction from Samuel E. Cornish (1795–1858) at New York City's African Free School. When he continued his studies at Princeton Seminary, he remained in contact with his mentor and served as an agent for Cornish's newspaper, *Freedom's Journal*. Wright shared his father's anticolonization sentiment, and he coauthored with Cornish an anticolonization pamphlet, *The Colonization Scheme Considered* (1840).

Wright succeeded Cornish as pastor of the First Colored Presbyterian Church in New York City in 1828, and he nurtured his church into the second largest African-American congregation in the city. The principles of moral reform informed his thought and activities. He created a temperance society as an auxiliary to his church. He founded the Phoenix Society, an organization dedicated to "morals, literature and the mechanical arts." He also promoted black education through his work with the Phoenix High School for Colored Youth.

Wright's commitment to abolitionism drew him to several black organizations. He participated in the New York Committee of Vigilance in the mid-1830s. A pioneer in the long, frustrating campaign to expand black suffrage in the state, he cofounded the New York Association for the Political Elevation and Improvement of the People of Color (1838) and attended the black state convention at

Albany in 1840. Occasionally, Wright revealed a streak of militancy. At the 1843 national convention in Buffalo, New York, he surprised many delegates by supporting Henry Highland Garnet's (1815–1882) call for slave violence.

Wright had a highly visible role in the organized antislavery movement. He was a founder of the American Anti-Slavery Society (AASS) and was one of the few blacks to hold a seat on the society's executive committee. He also participated in the New York State Anti-Slavery Society. Through his work in these organizations, he became aware of the subtle racism present among white reformers, and he chastised them publicly for their failure to "annihilate in their own bosom the cord of caste."

Like many black clergymen, Wright was never comfortable with the radical social doctrines of the Garrisonians. When these issues precipitated a schism in the AASS, Wright, along with several other black abolitionists, abandoned the old organization in favor of the new American and Foreign Anti-Slavery Society. Wright served on the new society's executive committee, and embraced political abolitionism as an active supporter of the Liberty Party in the early 1840s.

In his last years of public life, Wright devoted his efforts to African missions. He joined with several other black clergymen to found the Union Missionary Society in 1841; he later served as a vice president of the American Missionary Society.

See also Abolition; Cornish, Samuel E.; *Freedom's Journal*; Garnet, Henry Highland; Presbyterians

Bibliography

Swift, David E. "Black Presbyterian Attacks on Racism: Samuel Cornish, Theodore Wright and Their Contemporaries." *Journal of Presbyterian History* 51 (1973): 433–470.

MICHAEL F. HEMBREE (1996)

Writers and Writing

See Canadian Writers; Caribbean/North American Writers; Drama; Federal Writers' Project; Literature; OBAC Writers' Workshop; Poetry, U.S.; Women Writers of the Caribbean

Wynter, Sylvia

May 11, 1928

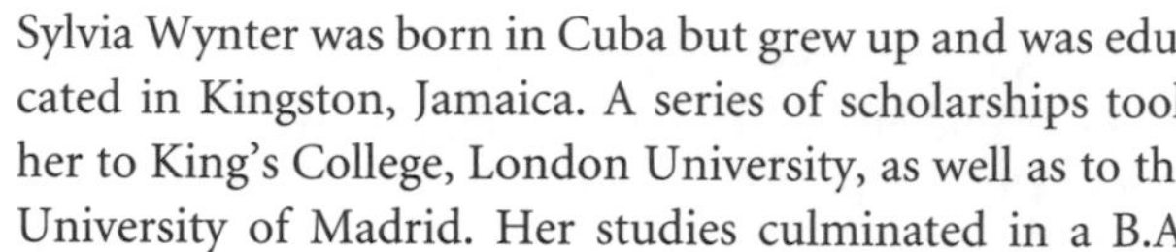

Sylvia Wynter was born in Cuba but grew up and was educated in Kingston, Jamaica. A series of scholarships took her to King's College, London University, as well as to the University of Madrid. Her studies culminated in a B.A. (with honors) in Spanish literature (with a minor in English) and an M.A. with a thesis on Golden Age Spanish drama.

Wynter spent the next decade in London as a writer. She wrote screenplays for the BBC's Third Program, as well as a novel, *The Hills of Hebron,* published in 1962. In 1963 Wynter returned to the then newly independent Jamaica and joined the faculty of the University of the West Indies (UWI). While teaching at UWI in Mona, she helped to establish *Jamaica Journal,* one of the premier Anglophone journals of Caribbean intellectual thought. During this time she also wrote several plays, including *Maskarade* and *1865: Ballad of a Rebellion,* which were directed by Lloyd Reckord. In the context of the island's postcolonial intellectual ferment, Wynter wrote "We Must Learn to Sit Down Together and Talk about a Little Culture: Reflections on West Indian Literature and Criticism," an essay that set the stage for her rethinking of the belief system of race.

Coincidentally, at the time that she began to explore the theoretical question posed by Elsa Goveia in "The Social Framework" (1970) as to the why of the premise of black inferiority and of white superiority, a parallel order of intellectual questioning had begun to emerge in the United States to accompany the civil rights movement of the late 1950s and 1960s. In the context of the call for black studies, Wynter was invited to teach at the University of California at San Diego (UCSD). At UCSD Wynter was appointed to teach and to further develop a new interdisciplinary program, Literature and Society in the Third World. Three years later, at Stanford University, Wynter was appointed chair of the Program in African and Afro-American Studies (AAAS) as well as professor in the Department of Spanish and Portuguese. She served as chair of the AAAS program until 1982 and continued to teach at Stanford until her retirement as professor emerita in June 1994.

After coming to the United States in the 1970s, Wynter authored a series of major essays in which she put forward a unified theory of culture able to explain both the fifteenth-century rise of the West and the price that the indigenous peoples of the Americas and the enslaved black population would pay for the West's global expansion and techno-scientific breakthroughs. By calling into question what she defined as our *biocentric* (as a reformulation of the feudal *theocentric*) conception of being human, Wynter opened up a path for the elaboration of a new science of the human, one able to explain, she asserts, the "puzzle of conscious experience" (Chalmers, 1995).

Wynter argued that the issue of *race*, which had become a global status-organizing principle, could be understood only within the terms of the originally Judeo-Christian religio-cultural ground out of which it emerged. In the wake of the voyages of the Portuguese into newly discovered lands in Africa and of Christopher Columbus into the Americas, together with the rise of the natural sciences in the sixteenth century, the West would become the first culture to secularize (that is, "degod," desupernaturalize) its order of knowledge. In the place of the earlier supernaturally ordained identity of the Christian, an increasingly (and by the nineteenth-century Darwinian revolution, purely) biological conception of the human, "man," was instituted. In other words, the laity/clergy issue that structured the feudal order had been transformed into that of the black/white (as well as man/native) issue. At the same time, the belief system of spiritual caste, to which the former issue had given expression, was transformed into the modern belief system of *race*, in effect, of biological caste.

Wynter hypothesized that all humans must necessarily know their social reality in adaptively advantageous terms, able to ensure the realization of their specific mode or *genre* of being human, or of *sociogeny* (Fanon, 1967), as well as of the reproduction of the specific societal order, which is each such genre's indispensable condition of existence. On the basis of Fanon's redefinition of the human as hybridly phylogeny (the evolution or development of a kind or type of animal or plant) and ontogeny (the development of an individual organism) on the one hand, and sociogeny on the other (in Western terms, a nature/culture mode of being), Wynter put forward the idea of the sociogenic principle or code as the explanatory key, both to "the puzzle of conscious experience" (Chalmers, 1995) and to the laws that govern human behaviors. She does so in the context of Aimé Césaire's 1946 proposal for a "science of the Word" (Césaire, 1982, pp. 24–25), as a science of the human able to complete what Césaire defines as the "half-starved" nature of the natural sciences, which for all their technological achievements have yet to come up with a scientific description of the reality of what it is to be human, that is, hybridly organic/meta-organic, gene *and* word.

See also Césaire, Aimé; Fanon, Frantz; Goveia, Elsa V.; Race, Scientific Theories of; Women Writers of the Caribbean

▪▪ *Bibliography*

"The Ceremony Must Be Found: After Humanism." In *On Humanism and the University: The Discourse of Humanism.* Special Issue of *Boundary II: Journal of Postmodern Literature* 12, no. 3, and 13, no. 1 (spring/fall, 1984).

Césaire, Aimé. "Poetry and Knowledge." Translated by A. James Arnold. *Sulfur* 5 (1982): 17–32.

Chalmers, David. "The Puzzles of Conscious Experience." *Scientific American* (December 1995): 80–87.

Eudell, Demetrius, and Carolyn Allen, ed. *Sylvia Wynter: A Transculturalist Rethinking Modernity.* Special Issue of *Journal of West Indian Literature* 10 (November 2001).

Fanon, Frantz. *Black Skin, White Masks.* New York: Grove Press, 1967.

Goveia, Elsa. "The Social Framework." *Savacou* 2 (September 1970): 7–15.

Wynter, Sylvia. *"Do Not Call Us Negros": How Multicultural Textbooks Perpetuate Racism.* San Francisco: Aspire, 1992.

Wynter, Sylvia. "1492: A New World View." In *Race, Discourse, and the Origin of the Americas: A New World View,* edited by Vera L. Hyatt and Rex Nettleford. Washington, D.C.: Smithsonian Institution Press, 1995.

Wynter, Sylvia. "Is 'Development' a Purely Empirical Concept or Also Teleological? A Perspective from 'We-the-Underdeveloped.'" In *The Prospects for Recovery and Sustainable Development in Africa,* edited by A. Y. Yansane, Westport, Conn.: Greenwood, 1996.

Wynter, Sylvia. "'Genital Mutilation' or 'Symbolic Birth?' Female Circumcision, Lost Origins, and the Aculturalism of Feminist/Western Thought." Colloquium—Bridging Society, Culture, and Law: The Issue of Female Circumcision. *Case Western Law Review* 47 (Winter 1997): 501–552.

Wynter, Sylvia. "Africa, the West, and the Analogy of Culture: The Cinematic Text After Man." In *Symbolic Narratives/African Cinema: Audiences, Theory and the Moving Image,* edited by June Givanni. London: British Film Institute, 2000.

Wynter, Sylvia. "Towards the Sociogenic Principle: Fanon, Identity, the Puzzle of Conscious Experience, and What It Is Like to Be 'Black.'" In *National Identities and Sociopolitical Changes in Latin America,* edited by Mercedes F. Dúran-Cogan and Antonio Gómez-Moriana. New York: Routledge, 2001.

DEMETRIUS L. EUDELL (2005)

X, Malcolm

See Malcolm X

Yerby, Frank

September 5, 1916
November 29, 1991

The son of a postal clerk, novelist Frank Garvin Yerby was born in Augusta, Georgia. He received a bachelor's degree in English from Paine College in Augusta in 1937 and a master's degree from Fisk University in Nashville, Tennessee, in 1938. He then studied education for a year at the University of Chicago while working on the Illinois Federal Writers' Project. He taught at Florida Agricultural and Mechanical College (1939), at Southern University in Baton Rouge, Louisiana (1940–1941), and then briefly at the University of Chicago, before moving to Detroit, where he worked at the Ford Motor Company's Dearborn assembly plant (1942–1944). Yerby then moved to Jamaica, New York, where he worked as the chief inspector at Ranger Aircraft until 1945.

Yerby's prolific and commercially successful literary career was launched in 1944, when he received the O. Henry Memorial Award for "Health Card," a short story about racial injustice. Some of Yerby's early stories, including "The Homecoming" (1946), also dealt with social issues, but he soon began publishing "swashbuckling" historical romance novels that won popular if not critical acclaim. Over the course of his career, Yerby was attacked by reviewers and academics for his lack of attention to racial issues, his use of primarily Anglo-Saxon protagonists, and his reliance on pulp fiction formulas, but his thirty-two novels were immensely popular with the general reading public, particularly in the 1940s and 1950s.

His first novel, *The Foxes of Harrow* (1946), focused on the white owners of an antebellum southern plantation. The book became an immediate bestseller, sold over two million copies within a few years, was translated into numerous languages, and was made into a film by Twentieth Century-Fox in 1947. Yerby then began producing melodramatic adventure novels, set in various centuries and geographical locales, at the rate of one a year. His most popular titles were *The Vixens* (1947), *The Golden Hawk* (1948), *A Woman Called Fancy* (1951), and *The Saracen Blade* (1952).

Yerby moved to France in the early 1950s, then settled in Madrid in 1955. He lived there the rest of his life and wrote such novels as *Fairoaks* (1957), *An Odor of Sanctity* (1965), and *Goat Song* (1968). Considered by many to be Yerby's masterpiece, *The Dahomean* (1971) is his only work dealing primarily with blacks; set in the nineteenth century, the novel traces the life of an African protagonist who rises to a position of great authority in Dahomean tribal culture only to be sold into American slavery by his own kinsmen. Yerby was granted an honorary doctor of letters degree by Fisk University in 1976 and a doctor of humane letters by Paine College in 1977. His last published works were *Devilseed* (1984) and *McKenzie's Hundred* (1985). He died of heart failure in Madrid in 1991.

See also Federal Writers' Project; Literature of the United States

Bibliography

Grimes, William. "Frank Yerby, Writer, 76, Is Dead; Novels of the South Sold Millions." *New York Times,* January 8, 1992, p. D-19.

Vinson, James. "Frank Yerby." In *Twentieth Century Romance and Gothic Writers.* Detroit, Mich.: Gale, 1982, pp. 731–733.

CAMERON BARDRICK (1996)

YERGAN, MAX

JULY 19, 1892
APRIL 11, 1975

Born in Raleigh, North Carolina, educator and civil rights leader Max Yergan attended Shaw University, graduating in 1914. Shortly thereafter he received an M.A. degree from Howard University. In 1915 he was hired as a traveling secretary with the student division of the Young Men's Christian Association (YMCA) in New York City. During World War I he worked in India, then was sent to Kenya to organize YMCA units among Indian and African troops in the British army. Although not an ordained minister, he was named a chaplain by the American army, and he briefly served with African-American troops in France.

In 1920 Yergan was appointed senior secretary of the International Committee of the YMCA and was stationed in South Africa, where he remained for sixteen years, working mainly with college students. He combined missionary work and improving educational facilities for black South Africans. For his efforts he received the Harmon Award in 1926 and the NAACP's Spingarn Medal in 1933. He published two sociological reports, *Christian Students and Modern South Africa* (1932), and *Gold and Poverty in South Africa* (1938), in which he described the horrible living and working conditions faced by black African gold miners.

In 1936, claiming he had done all he could for Africans within the YMCA framework, Yergan returned to New York. City College hired him as a professor in history, one of the first African-American professors at an integrated college. Among the courses he taught was Negro History, the first such course taught outside black colleges. In 1937, with the support of Paul Robeson and others, he founded the Council on African Affairs (CAA)—then the International Committee on African Affairs—which promoted interest in Africa and lobbied against colonialism, and became its executive director.

While in New York, Yergan grew active in Harlem communist political circles. Together with Rev. Adam Clayton Powell Jr., at the time an ally of the communists, he published a newspaper, *The People's Voice.* He also became active in the communist-dominated National Negro Congress (NNC). In 1940, after A. Philip Randolph resigned as executive director, Yergan was named to lead the organization. He led the NNC in its opposition to military preparedness programs and its support of Powell's successful mass transit boycott in New York City during 1940–1941. In 1941 the Communist Party promoted Yergan as a candidate for the New York City Council, but Powell convinced him to drop out of the race.

After 1941 Yergan supported the war effort but spoke out in favor of decolonization and African self-determination and against discrimination in the army. During the war years the CAA grew in size and power, and Yergan devoted more time to it. In 1946, at a CAA meeting in New York City, Yergan accused the Truman administration of opposing African freedom. In 1946 he led a delegation of the NNC to the United Nations to present a petition against "political, economic and social discrimination against Negroes in the United States," and lobbied against poll taxes in southern states.

Sometime in 1947, however, Yergan underwent a dramatic shift in his political views and turned away from his former associates. In October of that year he resigned from the NNC, by then largely inactive, claiming that "Communists sought to sabotage the decisions of the board." In December, after the U.S. government charged that the CAA was a subversive organization, Yergan affirmed its noncommunist character. In 1948 the CAA board, led by Robeson, opposed the statement. Yergan claimed that a communist-led minority had seized control of the CAA in order to attack American foreign policy. Yergan attempted to seize the organization's property and brought suit against Robeson's procommunist faction. He was expelled from the board and resigned in October.

In later years Yergan became an increasingly strident anticommunist. In 1948 he testified on communist involvement in civil rights efforts before a subcommittee of the House Committee on Un-American Activities. During the 1950s and 1960s he lectured and wrote articles for conservative magazines and was a leading consultant on Africa to the U.S. State Department. He was also rumored to be an FBI informer. In 1962 he organized and chaired the Free Katanga Committee, which worked against UN involvement in the former Belgian Congo and supported the Belgian-backed Katanga secessionist movement of Moise Tshombe. In 1964, while speaking in South Africa, Yergan praised the country's apartheid policy as a "realistic policy" in a "unique situation," which gave Africans "dignity and self-respect." During the 1970s he spoke in support of Ian Smith's white minority government in Rhodesia. These actions prompted widespread criticism that Yergan had "sold out," and that his earlier activism had been self-serving and insecure. Yergan died near his home in Ossining, New York, in 1975.

See also Civil Rights Movement, U.S.; Council on African Affairs; National Negro Congress; Robeson, Paul

Bibliography

Duberman, Martin B. *Paul Robeson.* New York: Knopf, 1988.

Lynch, Hollis R. *Black American Radicals and the Liberation of Africa: The Council on African Affairs, 1937–1955.* Ithaca, N.Y.: Cornell University Press, 1978.

Naison, Mark. *The Communists in Harlem During the Depression.* New York: Grove Press, 1983.

GREG ROBINSON (1996)

Yoruba Religion and Culture in the Americas

The Yoruba presence in the Americas is evident in Cuban Santería, Brazilian Candomblé and Xangô, and the Orisha and Shango religions of Trinidad and Grenada. Less well known are the St. Lucian Kele, or Shango cult, and Jamaican Kumina. These diasporic religions are testimony to the memory and determination of those Africans and their descendants who retained their sacred traditions, often in the face of attempts to marginalize or eliminate them. Some returned to Africa to renew their knowledge. Brazilian Candomblé has been nourished by ongoing contact with its sources of origin. In recent years, Nigerian traditional religious leaders have visited Cuba, Brazil, and Trinidad.

Many features of diasporic Orisha worship remain close to their origins, including myths, elements of ritual, language, material culture, and the names of deities. Yet changes have also occurred. These reflect the challenges of transmission, societal constraints on practice, and encounters with other cultures. Today, people of all colors can assume a Yoruba identity through initiation into the religion. Religious teachings formerly handed down solely by word of mouth are now available in written form. Equivalents for the plants and herbs used for healing and ritual work have been sought out among the American flora.

This capacity to successfully translate an African culture to a new environment—while at the same time absorbing outside influences—was not simply a product of enslavement, as some scholars have suggested. An openness to other cultural traditions was already a feature of Yoruba society. Recent studies of Orisha cults show how their decentralized nature made them suitable for transmission. However, it must be noted that their vitality in the diaspora contrasts with West Africa, where the cults have largely lost ground to Christianity and Islam.

Religious Syncretism

Many accounts of African-derived religions focus on the syncretism with Roman Catholicism. Devotees identified similarities among the religions and sometimes concealed their gods behind the mask of Catholic saints. For example, Ogun, the *orisha* (deity) of metalworking and war, is matched with the sword-carrying Saint George in Rio de Janeiro. In Bahia, his counterpart is Saint Antony, the soldier; in Cuba he is linked with Saint Peter, who holds an iron key; and in Trinidad and Grenada, he is linked with Saint Michael the Archangel.

Orisha worshippers in the Americas commonly display images of the Catholic saints among their ritual objects, but the *orishas* are represented by the sacred stones and other items that embody their *ashe* or spiritual power. These are kept hidden from public view. In some cases, practices that originated out of the need for concealment became enshrined in tradition. In Cuban Santería and Recife Xangô, the annual celebrations in honor of the *orishas* are held on the feast days of their Catholic saint counterparts. Some devotees attend church on these days, though the main rituals are celebrated in the cult houses. The

Bahian traditional Candomblés differ in that the annual cycle of Orisha festivals is determined by divination. Catholic baptism is often a prerequisite for initiation into Cuban Santería and Brazilian Candomblé. Similarly, in Trinidad, some Shango priests insist that novices be baptized by the Baptists before initiation. This lack of religious exclusivity is found in West Africa, where some Yoruba celebrate birth, marriage, and burial with ceremonies from more than one religious tradition.

Yet external elements were not always incorporated for reasons of secrecy. Yorubas and their descendants drew not only upon Christianity, but also on Kardecan spiritism and religious practices from other parts of Africa and from Asia. Brazilian Candomblé incorporated elements from the Congo-Angola, Aja-Ewe-Fon, and other African groups. Trinidad Orisha shows Hindu influences, including the use of prayer flags, brought to the island with East Indian indentured laborers. A Cuban avatar of Changó, Sanfancón (San Fan Kung), demonstrates the incorporation of Chinese cultural elements. Yoruba deities and ceremonial structures also appear in practices originating among other African nations.

The Merging of Separate Cults

Focusing on syncretism with Catholicism sometimes leads scholars to overlook other important adaptations. In Africa, each Orisha cult is self-contained as far as devotees are concerned. In the Americas, while devotees of Santería and Candomblé are only initiated into the cult of one *orisha*, they worship others. Priests and priestesses of separate Orisha cults had to exchange religious knowledge because of the difficulties of reconstituting the cults under slavery. Similarly, declining numbers of worshippers and priests sometimes leads to integration and exchange between cult groups in West Africa.

Each Orisha cult has a dedicated priesthood and a public temple or shrine in Africa. The practice became more secretive and compressed in the Americas. In Cuba, the sacred objects of a number of *orishas* are housed in the *ilé ocha* or *casa de santo,* usually the home of the *iyalocha* or *babalocha*. They are kept in covered china soup tureens, called *soperas*, which are often placed in a *canastillero*—a type of sideboard that may have doors for further concealment. In Trinidadian temples, or *palais,* the ritual objects or emblems of all *orishas*, or "powers," are stored in a room called the *chapelle*. In Grenada they are kept in the home of the priestess. Bahian Candomblé has remained more public and spacious. A *terreiro* may consist of several buildings. The sacred items of indoor deities such as Oxala or Shango are kept in small shrines called *peji*. Outdoor gods such as Exu, Omolu, Ossâim, and Oxóssi reside in a garden where plants used in rituals and for healing are cultivated.

There are an indefinite number of *orishas* in Africa—mythical figures are sometimes given, such as 401 or 1,444. However, surveys of specific towns show that a finite number of cults are important for inhabitants. Between twenty and twenty-five *orishas* are worshipped in Cuba, with perhaps fifteen being the most popular. In Bahia, around twelve *orishas* find devotees in nearly all *terreiros*.

Societal conditions and a new geography made certain *orishas* less relevant. Obatala, the creator of humankind, remains important everywhere, as does Eshu-Elegbara, the guardian of social order and the messenger of the gods who is invoked at all ceremonies. The most widely revered *orishas,* both in Africa and the diaspora, are those connected with aspects of daily life, such as motherhood, love, wealth, health, and sex. Sometimes their functions are modified: in Cuba and Brazil, Yemayá/Yemanja, the goddess of the River Niger, is associated with the sea. Hence, in Cuba, the cult of the African sea god Olokun has gradually been subsumed into that of Yemayá. This tendency to fuse *orishas,* or, conversely, for an *orisha* to split off into different avatars, ensures the flexibility and adaptability of the system of worship. In Cuba these avatars are known as *caminos* and in Brazil as *firmas*. Obatala, an *orisha* with numerous regional manifestations in West Africa, has a profusion of *caminos,* each having different characteristics and syncretized with different Catholic saints. Another example of this flexibility is the way in which the myths of the *orishas* retain their African historical references and fields of experience while acquiring others relevant to their new environment.

The prominence of one *orisha*, Shango, whose cult plays a central role in the installation of kings of Oyo, is a feature of diaspora worship. In Cuban Santería, rituals and items specific to Changó's cult, such as the kingly crown, the mortar, and batá drums, appear in the rituals of all *orishas*. In Brazil, *orisha* worship is called Xangô in Alagôas and Pernambuco, and in Trinidad and Grenada, Shango. St. Lucian Kele is named after the *ikele* beads of Shango worshippers. There are historical reasons for this. Following the collapse of the Oyo empire, the Shango cult spread throughout Yorubaland with the dispersal of refugees. A larger proportion of slaves from that region were transported to the Americas late in the slave trade.

Yet the traditions of other Yoruba subgroups are also apparent. Some Bahian Candomblé houses are identified as Ketu or Ijexá (Ijesha). In Recife Xangô there were formerly Ijesha and Egba cult groups, though today the differences between them survive only in music and songs. In the Cuban province of Matanzas, there are cult groups

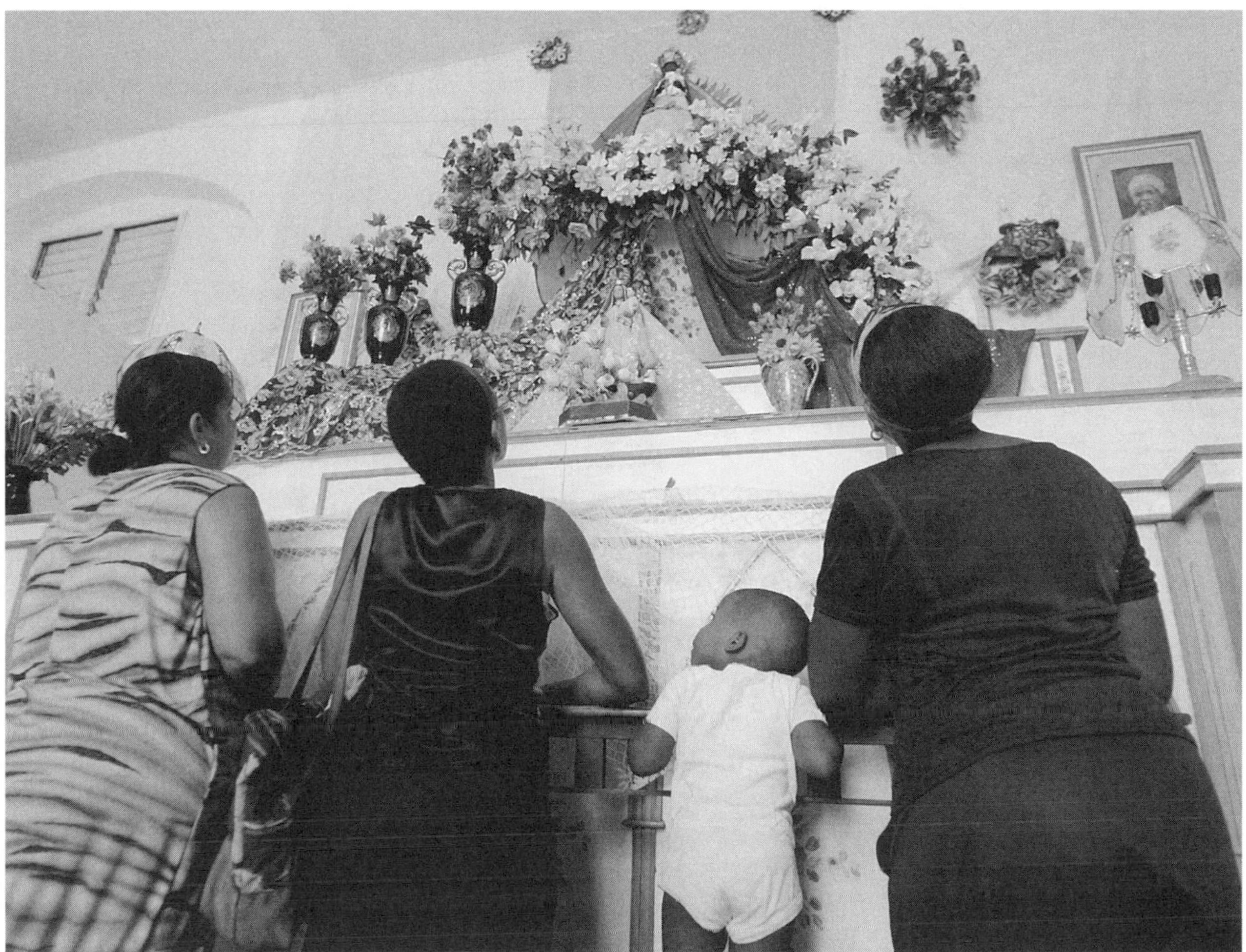

A Santeria shrine to the Virgin of Regla, Havana, Cuba, 2004. *The image of a black virgin holding a white child is venerated as Yemaya, goddess of the sea, in the Afro-Cuban religion of Santeria, whose deities were worshipped by Yoruba slaves brought to Cuba centuries earlier.* © CLAUDIA DAUT/REUTERS/CORBIS

called *iyesá* (Ijesha) and *egguado* (Egbado). Differences between this and Havana Santería are found in the ritual use of plants, ritual language, dances, and musical instruments.

Ritual

In West Africa, devotees petition *orishas* for children, wealth, health, and long life. In the Americas, worshippers rarely petition the gods for fertility, perhaps because in the past enslaved women were reluctant to bear children. Ceremonies are performed to offer praise or thanks or when specified by divination. As in Africa, they involve blood sacrifice, drumming, and possession trance, which offer devotees a direct experience of the divine. Spiritual power, or *aché/axé,* is received during these ritual encounters.

The merging of Orisha cults is apparent in that, even in ceremonies to honor one *orisha*, all the gods are praised in turn. Each deity is distinguished by particular drum rhythms, dance steps, symbols, colors, sacrificial animals, and offerings. The prayers and songs are generally in a form of the Yoruba language.

A Trinidad drum dance starts and ends with Catholic prayers. Eshu is sent away by means of a song. Then Ogun is summoned, followed by the other *orishas.* In Grenada, the ceremony begins with invocations to the deities in French patois interspersed with African words. At a Cuban *tambor* or *toque de santo,* the liturgy, called *oro,* begins with prayers in Lucumí—the Cuban form of Yoruba—to pay homage to Olofin and the ancestors. Then the *orishas* are called down one by one, beginning with Elegguá, as befits his role as opener of paths, followed by Ogun and the rest. At a Bahian *obrigação,* the annual public ceremony to honor an *orisha*, the liturgy to call down the *orisha* is called *xiré.* Percussion is an important feature of ceremonies, though drums are sometimes replaced with gourds or box drums, recalling past laws restricting the use of African instruments.

In Yoruba society, seniority is important. People will curtsy, bow, or prostrate themselves before their elders and betters as a mark of respect. Orisha worshipers in the Americas also physically express their deference to the gods and those with religious seniority. Respect for the ancestors is also important. However, the *egungun* masquerades, which offer communication with the ancestors, are generally no longer found in the Americas, though there is evidence of their former existence in Cuba. This may be because, unlike the Orisha cults, they were dependent on kinship systems destroyed by the Middle Passage and slavery. However, in Bahia there is a secret society of *egún*, which has a special priesthood, and Recife Xangô cult houses have a *balé*, or house of the dead. In Cuban Santería, Kardecan spiritism offers cultic possibilities for dealing with the dead, which are called *eguns*. Many santeros have a little altar to the spirits called a *bóveda espiritual* (spiritual vault).

Priesthood

In Africa, membership in an Orisha cult is normally determined by birth. One consequence of enslavement was the disruption of family lineages, and thus of the inheritance of ritual responsibilities. Today, with a few exceptions, to become the devotee of a particular *orisha* one must become initiated into the cult. In Cuban Santería this is a staged process. Receiving bead necklaces called *elekes* or *collares* is the minimum requirement for becoming a member of an *ilé ocha*. The next stage is to receive the *guerreros* (warriors), a Cuban innovation, so called because Elegguá, Oggún, Ochosi, and Osun are regarded as *orishas* who will "fight" to protect their owner.

Some devotees are recommended to enter into a deeper relationship with one *orisha*. During this initiation, which takes a similar form in Africa and the Americas, an *orisha*, determined or confirmed by divination, is said to be "seated" in the initiate's head. In Cuba, a number of other *orishas* are also received as part of this initiation. This contrasts with both African and Brazilian practice. For a period after the initiation, the *omo oricha* (child of the *orisha*) is required to sit on a mat and eat using the hands. This obliges them to recreate an African experience and identity.

Whereas both men and women head Cuban *ilé ocha*, priestesses are excluded from some of the higher ritual roles. In traditional Bahian Candomblé houses, the salient role of women marks a departure from Yoruba tradition. Male Candomblé members, called *ogan*, do not become initiated. In Trinidad, although many temples are headed by male priests, the majority of cult leaders are women. In Grenada, "Queens of Shango" usually come from families in which the cult is popular in the female line.

Divination

Divination is an important feature of worship. It enables devotees to shed light on a problem or to determine their destiny. *Obí* (kola nut) and *owó merindinlogun* (sixteen-cowry) divination are found everywhere. In Cuba, *obí* divination is commonly called *los cocos*, because pieces of coconut have replaced kola nuts. These and other liturgical items continued to be imported from Yorubaland to Brazil after the ending of the slave trade. Another Cuban modification, which reflects the merging of Orisha cults, is that a varying number of *orishas* speak through the *diloggún* oracle, including Orunmila. In African *owó merindinlogun*, only the presiding deity of the particular cult will speak, and Orunmila only ever speaks in Ifá divination. In Brazilian sixteen-cowry divination, called *jogo de búzios*, only Exu speaks.

Another Cuban modification is that shells are sometimes cast to obtain double figures *(mejis)* or combinations of *odu*. This makes *diloggún* more complex, thus resembling Ifá divination, which is performed by male priests of the cult of Orunmila called *babalawo*. Yet Cuba is unique in the Americas in having preserved its own version of Ifá with a huge corpus of divination verses. In Recife and Bahia, the *babalawo* has largely been replaced by *babalorixá*, who perform sixteen-cowry divination, though elements of the Ifá corpus have survived as part of the knowledge of the *mãe* or *pai de santo*.

See also Africanisms; Candomblé; Orisha; Santería

Bibliography

Apter, Andrew. *Black Critics and Kings: The Hermeneutics of Power in Yoruba Society*. Chicago: University of Chicago Press, 1992.

Barber, Karin. "Oríki, Women, and the Proliferation and Merging of Òrìsà." *Africa* 60, no. 3 (1990): 313–337.

Barnes, Sandra T., ed. *Africa's Ogun: Old World and New*, 2d ed. Bloomington: Indiana University Press, 1997.

Bascom, William. "Two Forms of Afro-Cuban Divination." In *Acculturation in the Americas*, edited by Sol Tax (1952). Reprint, New York, Cooper Square, 1967.

Bascom, William. *Shango in the New World*. Austin: University of Texas, 1972.

Bascom, William. *Sixteen Cowries: Yoruba Divination from Africa to the New World*. Bloomington: Indiana University Press, 1980.

Bastide, Roger *The African Religions of Brazil: Toward a Sociology of the Interpenetration of Civilizations*. Baltimore, Md.: Johns Hopkins University Press, 1978.

Brandon, George. *Santería from Africa to the New World: The Dead Sell Memories.* Bloomington: Indiana University Press, 1993.

Cohen, Peter F. "Orisha Journeys: The Role of Travel in the Birth of Yoruba-Atlantic Religions." *Archives de Sciences Sociales des Religions* 117 (2002): 17–36.

Herskovits, Melville J. "African Gods and Catholic Saints in New World Negro Belief." *American Anthropologist* 39 (1937): 635–643.

Matory, James Lorand. *Sex and the Empire That Is No More: Gender and the Politics of Metaphor in Oyo Yoruba Religion.* Minneapolis: University of Minnesota Press, 1994.

Murphy, Joseph M. *Working the Spirit: Ceremonies of the African Diaspora.* Boston: Beacon, 1994.

Peel, J. D. Y. "Syncretism and Religious Change." *Comparative Studies in Society and History* 10, no. 2 (1968): 121–141.

Pollak-Eltz, Angelina. "The Shango Cult and other African Rituals in Trinidad, Grenada, and Carriacou and their Possible Influences on the Spiritual Baptist Faith." *Caribbean Quarterly* 39, nos. 3–4 (1993): 12–26.

Thompson, Robert Farris. *Flash of the Spirit: African and Afro-American Art and Philosophy.* New York: Vintage, 1984.

Voeks, Robert A. *Sacred Leaves of Candomblé: African Magic, Medicine and Religion in Brazil.* Austin: University of Texas Press, 1997.

CHRISTINE AYORINDE (2005)

Young, Andrew

October 23, 1932

Civil rights activist and politician Andrew Jackson Young Jr. was born in New Orleans. His father was an affluent, prominent dentist, and Young was raised in a middle-class black family in a racially mixed neighborhood. He attended Howard University in Washington, D.C., and graduated in 1951. Young pursued his growing commitment to religion at Hartford Theological Seminary in Connecticut and was awarded a bachelor of divinity degree in 1955. He was ordained a Congregational minister, and from 1955 to 1959 he preached in churches in Georgia and Alabama. In the course of this work, Young experienced firsthand the wrenching poverty that shaped the lives of African Americans in the rural South. He became active in challenging racial inequality, joined the local civil rights movement, and helped organize a voter-registration drive in Thomasville, Georgia, one of the first of its kind in southern Georgia.

In 1959 Young went to New York to become an assistant director of the National Council of Churches and help channel New York City philanthropic money into southern civil rights activities. Two years later he returned to Georgia and joined the Southern Christian Leadership Conference (SCLC), a civil rights organization headed by the Rev. Dr. Martin Luther King Jr. Young became an active participant in the SCLC, building a reputation for coolness and rationality and often providing a moderating influence within the movement. From 1961 to 1964 he served as funding coordinator and administrator of the SCLC's Citizenship Education Program—a program aimed at increasing black voter registration among African Americans in the South.

Young grew to be one of King's most trusted aides. In 1964 he was named executive director of the SCLC and three years later took on additional responsibility as executive vice president. During his tenure, he focused on creating social and economic programs for African Americans to broaden the scope of SCLC's activism. In 1970 Young relinquished his executive positions. However, he continued his affiliation with SCLC, serving on the board of directors, until 1972.

In 1972 Young turned his energies to the political arena and launched a successful campaign to become the first African American elected to the House of Representatives from Georgia since 1870. In Congress he served on the House Banking Committee and became familiar with the national and international business markets. In 1976 he vigorously supported the candidacy of fellow Georgian Jimmy Carter for president and vouched for Carter's commitment to black civil rights to many who were skeptical of supporting a white Democrat from the Deep South. Upon Carter's election, Young resigned his congressional seat to accept an appointment as the U.S. ambassador to the United Nations.

As ambassador Young focused on strengthening the ties between the United States and the third world. In 1979 he was forced to resign his position when it was revealed that he had engaged in secret negotiations with representatives of the Palestine Liberation Organization (PLO) in violation of U.S. policy. Young's supporters argued that Young was merely doing the job of a diplomat by speaking to all interested parties in sensitive negotiations. Many Jews and other supporters of Israel, however, believed that Young's actions gave the PLO unwarranted legitimacy. The furor that surrounded his actions forced him to submit his resignation.

In 1982 Young mounted a successful campaign for mayor of Atlanta. During his administration he faced the same urban problems that plagued other big-city mayors, including a shrinking tax base, rising unemployment, and rising costs—all of which required difficult decisions in fund allocation. Despite these constraints, he was able to increase business investment in Georgia. He successfully ran for reelection in 1986, despite growing criticism from some African Americans who argued that black Atlantans had been hurt by his economic development programs. In 1990, after he ran unsuccessfully for the Democratic gubernatorial nomination, Young reentered private life. He served as chair of Law International, Inc., until 1993, when he was appointed vice chair of its parent company, Law Companies Group, an internationally respected engineering and environmental consulting company based in Atlanta.

During the course of his career, Young has received many awards, including the Presidential Medal of Freedom—America's highest civilian award—and more than thirty honorary degrees from universities such as Yale, Morehouse, and Emory. In 1994, his spiritual memoir, *A Way Out of No Way*, was published. Young lobbied successfully to bring the 1996 Summer Olympics to Atlanta and served as cochair of the Atlanta Committee for the Olympic Games.

Young's papers are housed at the Atlanta-Fulton Public Library. In 2004 Young participated in a DNA test that helped determine that his ancestors originated in Sierra Leone and the Sudan in Africa.

See also Civil Rights Movement, U.S.; Mayors; Politics in the United States; Southern Christian Leadership Conference (SCLC)

Bibliography

Clement, Lee, ed. *Andrew Young at the United Nations*. Salisbury, N.C.: Documentary Publications, 1978.

Gardner, Carl. *Andrew Young, A Biography*. New York: Drake, 1980.

Powledge, Fred. *Free at Last? The Civil Rights Movement and the People Who Made It*. Boston: Little, Brown, 1991.

Young, Andrew. *A Way Out of No Way*. Nashville, Tenn.: Nelson, 1994.

CHRISTINE A. LUNARDINI (1996)
Updated by publisher 2005

Young, Coleman

May 18, 1919
November 29, 1997

Coleman Alexander Young, a politician, was born in Tuscaloosa, Alabama. He moved to Detroit at the age of five and grew up in an integrated eastside Detroit neighborhood called Black Bottom. After graduating from high school in 1936, he went to work for the Ford Motor Company. At the Ford plant Young became an organizer for the United Auto Workers, fighting in the auto industry's nascent labor movement. The draft interrupted his labor career. During World War II, he was given a commission in the army and joined the Army Air Corps's elite all-black flying unit, the Tuskegee Airmen. After he returned from the service, he rose through the ranks to become the first paid African-American union staff officer in the city. Young, who had previously been the executive secretary of the National Negro Council's Detroit branch, was a founder and executive director of the National Negro Labor Council (NNCL).

In 1951 Young was called before the House Committee on Un-American Activities to answer charges that the NNCL was a subversive organization. He refused to provide the committee with the membership list of the organization and publicly rebuked committee members for questioning his patriotism. Rather than responding to its questions, he chided the panel for its members' positions on racial issues. The exchange angered top labor leaders, who promptly blackballed him. During the 1950s Young found it difficult to find steady employment and operated a short-lived cleaning business, among other occupations.

The next decade marked a change in Young's fortunes. He found steady work as a salesman, then reentered public life. In 1960 he was elected a delegate to the Michigan Constitutional Convention. In 1962 he lost a race for the state assembly, but in 1964 he was elected to the state senate and became a Democratic Party floor leader. In 1968 he was the first African American elected to the Democratic National Committee.

Young wanted to run for the office of mayor of Detroit in 1969 but was stopped by a state law that prevented sitting state legislators from running for city office. The law was later changed, and in 1973 Young launched an improbable mayoral campaign. He promised to curb police brutality and made disbanding of the police special "decoy squad" his defining campaign issue. Blessed with rhetorical skills and the support of black trade unionists, he finished a strong second in the primaries. In the general election, he received few white votes, but he carried 92 percent of the black vote and narrowly defeated Detroit police chief John Nichols. In January 1974 he took office as Detroit's first black mayor.

Young eased the formerly troubled relations between the city's residents and police, but the search for ways to revitalize the depressed local economy occupied much of the mayor's time. Among the developments and projects associated with Young's administration were the Joe Louis

Arena, the General Motors Poletown plant, the Renaissance Center (a hotel, office, and retail complex), and the Detroit People Mover (an elevated rail system around the central business district).

Although his aggressive style and personality aroused opposition, Young's popularity among his core constituency of black working-class voters, plus the support of the Detroit business community, won him an unprecedented five terms as mayor. In 1993, however, he announced that he would not seek a sixth term. Following his retirement, Young wrote an autobiography, *Hard Stuff* (1995).

See also Mayors; National Negro Labor Council; Politics in the United States

Bibliography

Rich, Wilbur C. "Coleman Young and Detroit Politics: 1973–1986." In *The New Black Power*, pp. 200–221. New York, 1987.

Rich, Wilbur C. *Coleman Young and Detroit Politics: From Social Activist to Power Broker*. Detroit: Wayne State University Press, 1989.

Rich, Wilbur C. "Detroit: From Motor City to Service Hub." In *Big City Politics in Transition*, edited by H. V. Savitch and John Clayton Thomas, pp. 64–85. Newbury Park, Calif.: Sage Publications, 1991.

WILBUR C. RICH (1996)
Updated by publisher 2005

Whitney M. Young Jr. (1921–1971). *Young, a skilled negotiator, served as executive director of the National Urban League during the turbulent civil rights era of the 1960s, greatly expanding its programs and its funding.* NATIONAL URBAN LEAGUE. REPRODUCED BY PERMISSION.

Young, Whitney M., Jr.

July 31, 1921
March 11, 1971

The civil rights leader Whitney Moore Young Jr. was born and raised in rural Lincoln Ridge, Kentucky, the son of Whitney and Laura Ray Young. He grew up on the campus of Lincoln Institute, a vocational high school for black students where his father taught and later served as president. In this setting, Young, who attended the institute from 1933 to 1937, was relatively isolated from external racism. At the same time, he was surrounded by black people who held positions of authority and were treated with respect. In September 1937, Young enrolled at Kentucky State Industrial College in Frankfort; he graduated in June 1941. In college he met Margaret Buckner, whom he married in January 1944; the couple later had two daughters.

In the spring of 1946, after serving in World War II, Young entered a master's program in social work at the University of Minnesota, which included a field placement with the Minneapolis chapter of the National Urban League (NUL). He graduated in 1947 and, in September of that year, became industrial relations secretary of the St. Paul Urban League, where he encouraged employers to hire black workers. Two years later he was appointed to serve as executive secretary with the NUL's affiliate in Omaha, Nebraska.

During his tenure in Omaha, Young dramatically increased both the chapter's membership base and its operating budget. He fared less well, however, in his attempts to gain increased employment opportunities for African Americans; victories in this area continued to be largely symbolic, resulting primarily from subtle behind-the-scenes pressure exerted by Young himself. Through his Urban League experience, Young became adept at cultivating relationships with powerful white corporate and political leaders.

In early 1954 Young became dean of the Atlanta University School of Social Work. He doubled the school's budget, raised teaching salaries and called for enhanced professional development. With the 1954 *Brown v. Board of Education* decision and the unfolding of civil rights activism, his activities became increasingly political. He served on the board of the National Association for the Advancement of Colored People (NAACP) in Atlanta and played a leadership role in several other organizations committed to challenging the racial status quo, including the Greater Atlanta Council on Human Relations and the Atlanta Committee for Cooperative Action. Unlike some other black community leaders, Young supported and even advised students who engaged in sit-in demonstrations in 1960. Yet Young personally opted for a low-key approach characterized by technical support for the civil rights movement rather than activism.

Young retained close ties with NUL, and in 1960 he emerged as a top candidate for executive director of the New York–based organization. Although by far the youngest of the contenders for the position, and the least experienced in NUL work, Young was selected to fill the national post effective October 1961. Since its founding in 1910, NUL had been more concerned with social services than social change, and its successes had long depended on alliance with influential white corporate and political figures. However, by the early 1960s it was clear that unless it took on a more active and visible role in civil rights, the organization risked losing credibility with the black community. It was Whitney Young who, in more ways than one, would lead NUL into that turbulent decade.

For years, local Urban League activists had lobbied for a more aggressive posture on racial issues. At Young's urging, NUL's leadership reluctantly resolved to participate in the civil rights movement—but as a voice of "respectability" and restraint. In January 1962, Young declared that, while NUL would not engage actively in protests, it would not condemn others' efforts if they were carried out "under responsible leadership using legally acceptable methods." By helping to plan the 1963 March on Washington, Young simultaneously hoped to confirm NUL's new commitment and ensure that the march would pose no overt challenge to those in authority. Young also furthered NUL's moderate agenda by participating in the Council for United Civil Rights Leadership (CUCRL), a consortium founded in June 1963 to facilitate fundraising and information sharing. (CUCRL was initiated by wealthy white philanthropists concerned with minimizing competition among civil rights organizations and tempering the movement's more militant elements.)

As "Black Power" gained currency within the movement, new tensions surfaced inside NUL itself. Students and other Urban League workers disrupted the organization's yearly conferences on several occasions, demanding the adoption of a more action-oriented strategy. Young continued to insist on the primacy of social-service provision. But in June 1968, in an address at the Congress of Racial Equality's (CORE) annual meeting, he spoke favorably of self-sufficiency and community control. The NUL initiated a "New Thrust" program intended to strengthen its base in black neighborhoods and to support community organizing.

During his ten-year tenure, Young made his mark on NUL in other significant ways. He guided the development of innovative new programs meant to facilitate job training and placement, and he vastly increased corporate and foundation support for the organization. In the early and mid-1960s, as corporations (especially government contractors) came under fire for failing to provide equal employment opportunities, business leaders turned to the NUL and its affiliates for help in hiring black workers. At the same time, by aiding NUL financially, they hoped to demonstrate convincingly a commitment to nondiscriminatory policies.

Of the three U.S. presidents in office during Young's tenure with the league, Lyndon B. Johnson proved to be the closest ally; he drew on Young's ideas and expertise in formulating antipoverty programs, tried to bring Young into the administration, and awarded him the Medal of Freedom in 1969. Although the relationship with Johnson was important for accomplishing NUL's goals, at times it constrained Young's own political positions. In mid-1966, Young clashed with the Reverend Dr. Martin Luther King Jr. and other civil rights leaders who opposed the Vietnam War—Young insisted that communism must be stopped in Southeast Asia, and he disagreed that the military effort would divert resources away from urgent problems facing African Americans at home. A year later he was no longer so sure, however. Nonetheless, at Johnson's request, he traveled to South Vietnam with an official U.S. delegation. Young did not speak publicly against the war until late 1969, when Richard M. Nixon was president.

In addition to overseeing NUL's "entry" into civil rights, Young heightened the organization's visibility to a popular audience. He wrote a regular column, "To Be Equal," for the *Amsterdam News*, which was syndicated through newspapers and radio stations nationwide. He published several books, including *To Be Equal* (1964), and *Beyond Racism* (1969). At the same time, Young continued to maneuver in the highest echelons of the corporate world; among other activities, he served on the boards of the Federal Reserve Bank of New York, the Massachusetts Institute of Technology, and the Rockefeller Foundation. He also remained a prominent figure in the social-work profession, serving as president of the National Conference on Social Welfare in 1967 and acting as president of the National Association of Social Workers from June 1969 until his death.

In March 1971, Young traveled to Lagos, Nigeria, with a delegation of African Americans, in order to participate in a dialogue with African leaders. He died there while swimming, either from drowning or from a brain hemorrhage.

See also *Brown v. Board of Education of Topeka, Kansas*; Civil Rights Movement, U.S.; Congress of Racial Equality (CORE); King, Martin Luther, Jr.; National Association for the Advancement of Colored People (NAACP); National Urban League

Bibliography

Johnson, Thomas A. "Whitney Young Jr. Dies on Visit to Lagos." *New York Times,* March 12, 1971, p. 1; *NASW News* 13, no. 4 (August 1968): 1.

Parris, Guichard, and Lester Brooks. *Blacks in the City: A History of the National Urban League.* Boston: Little, Brown, 1971.

Weiss, Nancy J. *Whitney M. Young, Jr. and the Struggle for Civil Rights.* Princeton, N.J.: Princeton University Press, 1989.

TAMI J. FRIEDMAN (1996)

Zydeco

Zydeco is a style of popular dance music played by African Americans of Francophone descent in the Gulf Coast region, particularly in the bayou country of southwestern Louisiana. Despite its frenetic tempos, often led by a buoyant singer doubling on accordion, the term *zydeco* derives from the old Louisiana song "Les Haricots Sont Pas Salés," literally translated as "the green beans aren't salted," but commonly having the meaning "times aren't good."

The origins of zydeco go back to the popular dance tunes of French settlers, or Acadians, who were expelled from Nova Scotia by the British and arrived in Louisiana in the eighteenth century. They intermarried with African Americans and Native Americans of French and Spanish descent, and their European-derived string music absorbed Afro-Caribbean rhythmic elements. The first zydeco recordings, difficult to distinguish from other forms of Cajun music, are 1934 field recordings, including "Cajun Negro Fais Dos-Dos Tune," by Ellis Evans and Jimmy Lewis, and "Les Haricots Sont Pas Salés," by Austin Coleman and Joe Washington. Accordionist Amadé Ardoin was an important early zydeco musician whose "Les Blues de la Prison" (1934) shows a strong blues influence.

After World War II, rhythm and blues began to influence zydeco, a development clearly heard on Clarence Garlow's "Bon Ton Roula" (1950), which translates as "Let the Good Times Roll." During this time, the accordionist Clifton Chenier (1925–1988), perhaps the greatest of all zydeco musicians, came to prominence. Born in Opelousas, Louisiana, in 1925, he made his first recordings in the 1950s. Chenier pioneered the use of the piano accordion (an accordion with a keyboard) in zydeco music. Among the many popular and important records, noted for their heavy dance rhythms, that Chenier made before his death from diabetes in 1987 are "Black Gal" (1965), "Jambalaya" (1975), and *Country Boy Now* (1984).

In Louisiana, zydeco is invariably performed for dancers, often at nightclubs, dance halls, churches, picnics, and house parties known as "fais-do-do." Zydeco bands are typically led by a singer; with lead accompaniment by fiddle, button or piano accordion, or guitar; and with backing by a rhythm section of bass, piano, and drums. The harmonica, washboard, "frottoir" (a metal rubbing board played with household implements), and the "bas trang" (triangle), were often used earlier in the century, but today are often replaced by electric instruments. Zydeco is sung in the patois of Creole Louisiana, with lyrics ranging from narrative tales, love songs, and laments to simple invocations of dancing and good times.

Although zydeco has been, along with jazz and blues, a mainstay of the secular music scene among the Creole-descended population along the Gulf Coast from Louisiana to Texas, it has also achieved international popularity, and its greatest exponents have become celebrities with prolific touring and recording schedules. In addition to Chenier, other important zydeco musicians include accordionist Boozoo Chavis ("Paper In My Shoe," 1984), singer Queen Ida (*Cookin' With Queen Ida,* 1989), Rockin' Sidney ("My Toot Toot," 1984), and Lawrence "Black" Ardoin ("Bayou Two Step," 1984). Important ensembles include the Lawrence Ardoin Band, Terrence Semiens and the Mallet Playboys, and Buckwheat Zydeco's Ils Sont Partis Band.

Although zydeco and Cajun music share many musical elements and have common sociocultural origins in the late nineteenth-century contact between Creoles and Acadians, they are distinct forms, representing two aspects of the complex, multiracial culture that also produced jazz. Zydeco tends toward faster tempos, a syncopated rhythmic structure, and a de-emphasis of the melodic line. Cajun's rhythms are often more rigid two-step dances or waltzes emphasizing melody. Zydeco has been documented in such films as *Zydeco: Creole Music and Culture in*

Rural Louisiana (1984), and *J'ai Eté au Bal* (1991). Zydeco continues to be popular. In some cases, as with musicians such as Buckwheat Zydeco, who studied with Clifton Chenier, zydeco traditions have been mixed with influences of other forms of music.

See also Music; Rhythm and Blues

Bibliography

Ancelet, Barry Jean, and E. Morgan. *The Makers of Cajun Music.* Austin: University of Texas Press, 1984.

Broven, John. *South to Louisiana: The Music of the Cajun Bayous.* Gretna, La.: Pelican Publishing Co., 1983.

Spitzer, Nicholas. "Zydeco and Mardi Gras: Creole Identity and Performance Genres in Rural French Louisiana." Ph.D. diss., University of Texas at Austin, 1986.

JONATHAN GILL (1996)
Updated by publisher 2005